FOURTH EDITION

Principles and Practice of
SPORT MANAGEMENT

Edited by

Lisa P. Masteralexis, JD
Department Head and Associate Professor
Mark H. McCormack Department of Sport Management
Isenberg School of Management
University of Massachusetts, Amherst
Amherst, Massachusetts

Carol A. Barr, PhD
Associate Dean for Undergraduate Programs
Isenberg School of Management
University of Massachusetts, Amherst
Amherst, Massachusetts

Mary A. Hums, PhD
Professor
Department of Health and Sport Science
University of Louisville
Louisville, Kentucky

JONES & BARTLETT
LEARNING

World Headquarters

Jones & Bartlett Learning
40 Tall Pine Drive
Sudbury, MA 01776
978-443-5000
info@jblearning.com
www.jblearning.com

Jones & Bartlett Learning
Canada
6339 Ormindale Way
Mississauga, Ontario L5V 1J2
Canada

Jones & Bartlett Learning
International
Barb House, Barb Mews
London W6 7PA
United Kingdom

Jones & Bartlett Learning books and products are available through most bookstores and online booksellers. To contact Jones & Bartlett Learning directly, call 800-832-0034, fax 978-443-8000, or visit our website, www.jblearning.com.

Substantial discounts on bulk quantities of Jones & Bartlett Learning publications are available to corporations, professional associations, and other qualified organizations. For details and specific discount information, contact the special sales department at Jones & Bartlett Learning via the above contact information or send an email to specialsales@jblearning.com.

This publication is designed to provide accurate and authoritative information in regard to the Subject Matter covered. It is sold with the understanding that the publisher is not engaged in rendering legal, accounting, or other professional service. If legal advice or other expert assistance is required, the service of a competent professional person should be sought.

Production Credits

Publisher, Higher Education: Cathleen Sether
Senior Acquisitions Editor: Shoshanna Goldberg
Senior Associate Editor: Amy L. Bloom
Editorial Assistant: Prima Bartlett
Production Manager: Julie Champagne Bolduc
Production Editor: Jessica Steele Newfell
Production Assistant: Sean Coombs
Associate Marketing Manager: Jody Sullivan

V.P., Manufacturing and Inventory Control: Therese Connell
Composition: Publishers' Design and Production Services
Cover Design: Scott Moden
Rights and Permissions Supervisor: Christine Myaskovsky
Photo and Permissions Associate: Emily O'Neill
Cover Image: © Zsolt Nyulaszi/ShutterStock, Inc.
Printing and Binding: Malloy, Inc.
Cover Printing: Malloy, Inc.

Library of Congress Cataloging-in-Publication Data

Principles and practice of sport management / edited by Lisa P. Masteralexis, JD Carol A. Barr, PhD, Mary A. Hums, PhD. -- 4th ed.
  p. cm.
Includes bibliographical references and index.
ISBN 978-0-7637-9607-5 (pbk.)
1. Sports--Management. 2. Sports administration. I. Masteralexis, Lisa Pike. II. Barr, Carol A. III. Hums, Mary A.
GV713.P75 2012
796.06'9--dc22
                                                                    2011010488

ISBN-13: 978-0-7637-9607-5
ISBN-10: 0-7637-9607-7

6048
Printed in the United States of America
15 14 13 12 11   10 9 8 7 6 5 4 3 2

Brief Contents

Contents

Preface

As the sport industry evolves at a dramatic rate, the goal of providing a comprehensive, current, and concise introductory textbook on sport management becomes a challenging task. Yet, we have attempted to do just that, in providing our readers (students, professors, and practitioners alike) with this *Fourth Edition* of *Principles and Practice of Sport Management*.

This is a textbook intended for use in introductory sport management courses. The focus of these courses, and this textbook, is to provide an overview of the sport industry and cover basic fundamental knowledge and skill sets of the sport manager, as well as to provide information on sport industry segments for potential job employment and career choices.

Directed toward undergraduate students, the textbook has three distinct sections. The first six chapters provide an overview of basic knowledge areas for the successful sport manager, presenting fundamental principles and key skills as well as information on current issues. Chapters 7 through 21 present overviews of major sport industry segments in which a sport manager could work, followed by case studies intended to spark debate and discussion. The last chapter, Chapter 22, provides the reader with the basics of breaking into the highly competitive sport management industry. Where appropriate, we have included an international perspective to give readers a broad view of sport management in the global context, which they will need as the world grows increasingly "smaller" in the decades to come.

We would like to draw special attention to Chapter 9, which focuses on sport in the international setting. Chapter 9, International Sport, guides the reader through the global "sportscape" by examining the burgeoning sport industry around the world. In this chapter, the reader should pay particular attention to use of the word "football" instead of the word "soccer," to which most Americans are accustomed. This terminology is used purposefully, to remind the reader that in the majority of the world "football" in fact does not mean American football as played by the National Football League (NFL), but rather the traditional sport played at the much-anticipated and celebrated World Cup. The chapter also makes the point that the reader should not confuse "globalization" of sport with the "Americanization" of global sport.

This textbook offers a mix of contributions from scholars and practitioners. The second half of the text tends to have a somewhat different tone from the first half, as these chapters are written by practitioners. In addition, many of the scholars who contributed to the book returned to the classroom after years of working in the industry, so their thoughts offer a unique blend of information from both academic and industry perspectives.

This *Fourth Edition* is full of current data and information. Based on feedback from faculty using the text, each chapter has undergone review and revision, and chapter authors have been attentive to providing new material and updated information. New case studies have been added throughout the text. Specific updates include a new section on women in sport management and a sport management timeline in Chapter 1. Chapter 4, on financial principles, now includes information on the economic principles applied to sport management. The "Sport for All" movement and sport diffusion are discussed in Chapter 9. This chapter also has an updated discussion on doping and offers more coverage of sport tourism and sport in international markets. Chapter 10 provides a new case study focused on the conduct challenges facing the NFL. Chapter 11 provides a new discussion of the evolution of sport agencies and a look toward the future challenges in this industry. New chapters on sport and new media and the club sport industry, heavily focused toward golf, are great additions to the text intended to introduce students to new areas of career focus for sport management students. Chapter 22 offers practical advice on how virtual communities and social networking Web sites like Facebook and MySpace can affect the job search process.

Overall, this textbook allows the reader to learn both the foundations and the principles on which sport management operates and offers an opportunity to apply those foundations and principles to the sport industry. This textbook offers historical perspectives as well as thoughts about current and future industry issues and trends. For all these reasons, this textbook will prove a valuable resource to those seeking employment in this field, as well as to those whose role it is to educate future sport managers.

Acknowledgments

We would like to acknowledge the efforts of some individuals without whom this text would not be possible. First and foremost, we express our deep appreciation to our contributing authors. Each author contributed his or her valuable expertise and experience to create a work that provides a wealth of knowledge to the sport management student. Through the editorial process, we have gained from them a greater understanding of the sport industry and our introductory sport management curriculum.

We have made some changes to the chapters and contributing authors since the last edition of this book. You should note that we have left some chapter contributors' names from the previous editions to note the significance of the material carried over from those editions to this *Fourth Edition*. We would like to thank those authors who did not participate in this edition, but whose original work remained a part of this book.

We also thank those faculty members who have adopted *Principles and Practice of Sport Management* for their classes and whose feedback we have incorporated into this edition. Specifically, we thank the reviewers of the *Third Edition*:

Paul Downing, MSS, ATC, Loras College
Bonnie Everhart, PhD, Casenovia College
Matt Garrett, PhD, Loras College
Doak Geiger, University of Wisconsin, Milwaukee
Geoffry Alan Haines, PhD, ATC, LAT, Delta State University
Jordan I. Kobritz, JD, Eastern New Mexico University
Kurt A. Stahura, PhD, University of Nevada, Las Vegas

We also thank everyone at Jones & Bartlett Learning for their efforts in seeing this project through. Their enthusiasm for the text was a wonderful motivation for tackling the *Fourth Edition*. The competent efforts of Shoshanna Goldberg, Senior Acquisitions Editor; Amy Bloom, Senior Associate Editor; Julie Bolduc, Production Manager; and Jody Sullivan, Associate Marketing Manager, also lessened the burden of pulling this edition together because all were so patient on this journey.

Finally, we thank graduate students Michael McCarthy and Tara Mahoney from the Universities of Massachusetts and Louisville who provided great help through the editorial process.

Contributors

Editors

Lisa P. Masteralexis, JD
Department Head and Associate Professor
Mark H. McCormack Department of Sport
  Management
Isenberg School of Management
University of Massachusetts, Amherst
Amherst, Massachusetts

Carol A. Barr, PhD
Associate Dean for Undergraduate Programs
Isenberg School of Management
University of Massachusetts, Amherst
Amherst, Massachusetts

Mary A. Hums, PhD
Professor
Department of Health and Sport Science
University of Louisville
Louisville, Kentucky

Chapter Authors

Gregory Bouris
Director of Communications
Major League Baseball Players Association
New York, New York

Dan Covell, PhD
Associate Professor
School of Business
Western New England College
Springfield, Massachusetts

Todd W. Crosset, PhD
Associate Professor
Mark H. McCormack Department of Sport
  Management
Isenberg School of Management
University of Massachusetts, Amherst
Amherst, Massachusetts

Sheranne Fairley, PhD
Assistant Professor
Mark H. McCormack Department of Sport
  Management
Isenberg School of Management
University of Massachusetts, Amherst
Amherst, Massachusetts

Kevin Filo, PhD
Research Fellow
Centre for Tourism, Sport, and Service
  Innovation
Griffith University
Australia

Troy Flynn
Vice President of Operations
Prudential Center
Newark, NJ

Betsy Goff, JD
Lawyer and Consultant

Virginia R. Goldsbury, MEd
Assistant Director for Career Planning
  (Retired)
Career Services
University of Massachusetts, Amherst
Amherst, Massachusetts

Laurie Gullion, MS
Clinical Assistant Professor
The Outdoor Education Program
New Hampshire Hall
University of New Hampshire
Durham, New Hampshire

Neil Longley, PhD
Professor
Mark H. McCormack Department of Sport
  Management
Isenberg School of Management

University of Massachusetts, Amherst
Amherst, Massachusetts

Stephen M. McKelvey, JD
Associate Professor
Mark H. McCormack Department of Sport
   Management
Isenberg School of Management
University of Massachusetts, Amherst
Amherst, Massachusetts

Tracy Schoenadel, MS
Director and Lecturer
McCormack Center for Sport Research and
   Education
Mark H. McCormack Department of Sport
   Management
Isenberg School of Management
University of Massachusetts, Amherst
Amherst, Massachusetts

Rodney Warnick, PhD
Professor
Department of Hospitality and Tourism
Isenberg School of Management
University of Massachusetts, Amherst
Amherst, Massachusetts

Glenn M. Wong, JD
Professor
Mark H. McCormack Department of Sport
   Management
Isenberg School of Management
University of Massachusetts, Amherst
Amherst, Massachusetts

Foundations of Sport Management

History of Sport Management

Todd W. Crosset and Mary A. Hums

■ INTRODUCTION

The contemporary sport industry is complex and has unique legal, business, and management practices. As a result, many of the ways we organize this industry are unique, too. The organization of sport developed over the past 150 or so years and continues to evolve. Most recently, for example, sport managers have been tinkering with structures such as conference alignments, drafts, and playoff systems.

This chapter explores the roots of our modern **sport management structures**. The management structures of sport reviewed in this chapter are **clubs**, **leagues**, and **professional tournaments**. These structures help managers organize sport and are the basic building blocks of many of our sports today. The chapter also addresses the development of the sport management academic discipline, which came along as

the need for trained sport management professionals became apparent.

The primary theme of this chapter is that sport management structures are conceived and evolve in response to broad social changes or to address specific issues within a segment of the sport industry, or both. The evolution of these structures illustrates that sport managers need to be creative in the ways they run their sport organizations. One particular management structure won't work in all situations. History suggests that sport managers who are flexible and adapt to broader changes in society and who have a keen sense of their sport are the most successful. This chapter gives a few examples of innovative and successful sport managers.

Many events have shaped the world of sport and the sport industry. While it is nearly impossible to create a time line that hits all the highlights, we have placed one at the end of this chapter for your reference. The time line includes the founding dates of many sport organizations as well as a number of "firsts" in the sport industry in terms of events. Try thinking about events or people you would add to this time line—it is a good conversation starter!

Two secondary themes run throughout this brief examination of the history of sport management structures: honesty and inclusion. The legitimacy of modern sport demands honest play, or at least the appearance of honest play. Nothing in sport is more reviled than the athlete who does not try. An athlete who does not put out an honest effort is a spoilsport. Players who throw games are sellouts. So critical is the perception of an honest effort that sport managers will kick people out of a sport for life if they tarnish the game by the mere possibility they bet on their team to lose (e.g., Pete Rose).

The appearance of an honest effort is one of the most important precepts organizing modern sport. It is more important, for example, than fair play or equality of competition. Although there are structures leveling the playing field (e.g., drafts, salary caps), disparities among teams remain, giving some teams advantages over others. The public is much more tolerant of players breaking the rules when trying to win than it is of players throwing games. The public's notion of what ensures an honest effort changes over time. One issue addressed throughout this chapter is how sport managers have changed or adapted sport to ensure the appearance of honesty as broader structures have changed.

Another issue this chapter explores is the tension between democratic inclusiveness and the regulation of participation. The desire to create a meritocracy is implicit in modern sport—if you are good enough, you should play. But, by necessity, in any form of organized sport, there are rules limiting who is allowed to participate. For example, most contemporary sports leagues or teams have age and gender requirements.

International governing bodies as well as local leagues have citizenship and residency requirements. Athletes who have just moved to a new nation or town are sometimes excluded from participating in sports.

Answering the questions "Who gets to play?", "Who is encouraged to watch?", and "Who is left out?" requires both an understanding of sport-specific issues and broader social issues. When it comes to who gets to play, what seems "fair" at a particular juncture in history often reflects broader social beliefs. For example, not long ago it would have been unthinkable for women to compete against men on the Professional Golfers' Association (PGA) tour. Although it is still unusual, women have competed in PGA tournaments. Michelle Wie has played against men in 14 tournaments, including eight PGA Tour events. Both Wie and Si Re Pak have made the cuts in Asian men's competitions as well.

Historically, the groups with the most power have often defined the limits of participation, usually to their benefit. Sport in the first half of the twentieth century, for example, developed along with the eugenics movement, legal racial segregation, and an ideology of white racial superiority in the United States and South Africa. For many generations, mainstream sport structures in the United States and South Africa either excluded or limited participation by people of color. These structures reflected and promoted an ideology of white racial superiority.

Notions of what makes for honest play and who should be allowed to play or watch sport change over time. Sport managers have adapted sport to reflect changes in the broader society.

■ THE CLUB SYSTEM: SPORTS AND COMMUNITY

England is the birthplace of modern sport and sport management (Mandell, 1984). The roots of most Western sports, including track and field, all the variations of football, and stick-and-ball games such as baseball, field hockey, and cricket, can be traced to England. The broad influence of England's sporting culture is the result of the British Empire's imperial power in the eighteenth and nineteenth centuries. Britain had colonies all over the world and took her sports to all of them.

The continuing influence of the British sports tradition after the empire's demise has as much to do with how the English organized sport as it does with England's political and cultural domination. Even sports that originated outside England, such as basketball, gymnastics, and golf, initially adopted English sport organizational structures.

In the eighteenth century, the English aristocracy, made up of nobles and the landed gentry, began to develop sports clubs. Membership in these clubs was limited to the politically and economically powerful of English society. The earliest clubs simply organized one-time events or annual competitions and brought members together for social events. By the nineteenth century, clubs standardized rules, settled disputes between clubs, and organized seasons of competitions.

Thoroughbred racing was one of the first sports transformed by the club management system. Other English sports, such as cricket, rugby union, and soccer, also adopted a similar club management structure. The focus here is on thoroughbred racing simply because it is the earliest example of club management.

Thoroughbred Racing

Early races were local events, often associated with holidays or horse sales. By the mid-eighteenth century, thoroughbred racing and breeding had established a broad following among the English aristocracy. Local groups of breeders organized races. Horse owners arranged the events, put up purses, and invited participants to show off their best horses and demonstrate their prestige.

At this time horse racing was managed on a local level. The organization was essentially a volunteer system of management, controlled by the same wealthy men who owned the horses and estates. Despite the extreme stratification of eighteenth-century English society, horse races drew a broad and diverse audience. All levels of society attended races. The owners, the elite of the community, in keeping with tradition and meeting their social obligation to entertain the masses, did not charge admission.

Even though horse races were important for demonstrating prestige, they were rarely the primary business interest of the horse owners who controlled the sport. Consequently, seventeenth-century horse racing and sport remained largely separate from the growing capitalist economy. Horse racing existed primarily for the entertainment of wealthy club members and did not have to be an independent, self-supporting financial entity. This system gave horse racing the appearance of honesty. The public believed that the aristocracy—men of breeding, culture, and wealth—would not be tempted by bribes, influenced by petty feuds, or swayed to make unfair decisions.

The local club system governed the sport successfully as long as racing remained local. Soon, however, two factors combined to create a need for more systematic management: (a) the desire of owners to breed and train the fastest horses in England and (b) the increasing complexity of gambling.

As the elite gained prestige for owning the fastest horses, horses were bred for no other purpose than to win races. Speed was appreciated for its own sake, distinct from its religious, military, or economic purpose—a uniquely modern phenomenon (Mandell, 1984). Races usually consisted of a series of four-mile heats. The ideal horse combined speed with endurance.

By the 1830s rail transportation enabled owners to compete nationally. Local-level management governing area breeders, owners, and jockeys had worked well because of the familiarity among all involved, but national competition meant race organizers now managed participants they did not know very well, if at all. Thus, managing thoroughbred racing needed to become more systematic.

Gambling on thoroughbred horse races was common among all classes. Much as speed became appreciated for its own merits, betting on thoroughbred races began to be appreciated for its own value. Gambling not only provided exciting entertainment but also provided bettors with tangible evidence of their knowledge of horses and ability to predict who would win (Mandell, 1984).

Gambling also ensured honest competition. The crowd policed the jockeys. At that time, horse racing was a head-to-head competition. Races were a series of four-mile runs. The winning horse had to win two out of three races. If the crowd suspected a jockey had allowed the other contestant to win, the crowd would punish that jockey, often physically.

By the eighteenth century, innovations to the sport designed to draw larger audiences and enhance the ways spectators could wager also made the gambling system more complex. The English created handicapping, tip sheets, and sweepstakes; used the stopwatch to time races; standardized race distances; and added weights to horses. All of these innovations enhanced the public's interest in the sport. As the influence and importance of gambling grew and the systems of weights and handicapping leveled the playing field, the opportunity for a "fixed" race to go undetected also increased. All the enhancements and innovations made it difficult for the audience to detect when and how races were fixed. As a result, conventional methods could not be counted on to police the sport (Henriches, 1991).

The Jockey Club: The Birth of Club Governance

The roots of the management system in thoroughbred racing can be traced to around 1750, when a group of noble patrons in Newmarket established the **Jockey Club**. This group's responsibility was to settle disputes, establish rules, determine eligibility, designate officials, regulate breeding, and punish unscrupulous participants. The club organized, sponsored, and promoted local events (Vamplew, 1989). Like other local clubs, members of the Newmarket Jockey Club put up the purse money and restricted entries to thoroughbreds owned by club members.

The effective organization and management of thoroughbred racing in Newmarket made it a national hub for the sport. Local champions faced challenges from owners outside their region. The Jockey Club sponsored prestigious races that attracted horse owners from across England. As the need grew for a strong national governing body to establish rules and standards and to create a mechanism for resolving disputes, the Jockey Club from Newmarket emerged to serve those functions (Henriches, 1991).

Some of the lasting contributions the Jockey Club made to racing included sponsoring a stud book listing the lineage of thoroughbreds, helping ensure the purity of the breed; promoting a series of race schedules; announcing, regulating, and reporting on horse sales; and restricting the people involved with thoroughbred breeding and racing to the English elite. The Jockey Club served as a model for wider sport management practices in England.

Cricket, boxing, and other English sports adopted the management and organizational structures developed in thoroughbred horse racing. In each case, one club emerged as the coordinating and controlling body of the sport, not out of a formal process but by collective prominence. The Marylebone Cricket Club, for example, revised the rules of cricket in 1788 and became the international governing club for the entire sport (Williams, 1989). In 1814, the Pugilist Society was formed by a group of gentlemen to regulate bare-knuckle boxing and guarantee purses. Even sports such as association football (soccer) and rugby, which were organized much later, adopted the club organizational structure (Henriches, 1991).

Club structure depended on the appearance of fairness, loyal support, and volunteer management for its success. The aristocrats who managed and sponsored sport were presumed to be honest and disinterested, giving spectators the sense that competition was fair. Fairness was cultivated through the reputation of sport organizers and their nonprofit motives. Loyalty to specific clubs was cultivated through membership.

The Modern Olympic Games: An International Club Event

The club structure is also the foundation for the **modern Olympic Games**. Indeed, the early games can be viewed as an international club event. Created at the peak of the club system, the modern Olympic Games resemble international club events much more than they do the ancient Games for which they are named. The ancient Games, at least initially, were part of a larger religious ceremony and were initially only for male Greek citizens. These Games ex-

isted for 1,169 years and over time became an international gathering of athletes. The Games were discontinued in AD 393, although they were held in some form until AD 521 (Ministry of Culture–General Secretariat for Sports, 1998). Almost 15 centuries would pass before an international Olympic Games would be revived in another form.

Although 1896 marked the first official staging of the modern Olympic Games, Olympic-like festivals and revivals had been organized on a local level in England much earlier. The most important in the revival of the Games was the annual festival at Much Wenlock, Shropshire, started in 1850 by Dr. William Penny Brookes. As a logical extension to his annual games, Brookes organized the Shropshire Olympian Association in 1861, which led to the founding of the National Olympian Association four years later (Young, 1996).

The current International Olympic Committee's founding conference for the modern Olympic Games was held in 1894. **Pierre de Coubertin**, a young French physical educator who was influenced by Brookes' vision of an International Olympic Games, Professor William Sloane of Princeton University, and Charles Herbert, Secretary of the (British) Amateur Athletics Association, were the initiating forces behind this meeting, which they dubbed an "international athletic congress." More than 70 attendees representing 37 amateur athletic clubs and associations from at least a dozen

different nations came to the congress. The primary focus of the congress was the meaning and application of the concept of amateurism. De Coubertin, inspired by the English Olympic revivals, the Victorian notion of character development through sport, and an international peace movement, argued for an Olympic festival at the meeting. These Games, he suggested, would be held every four years, in rotating sites, and participants would be amateur athletes. He proposed that the first Games be held in Paris in 1900. So receptive were the attendees that they voted to convene the Olympic Games in 1896 in Athens, Greece.

The first modern Olympic Games were a nine-day event and drew 311 athletes from 13 nations. The participants were exclusively amateurs. Most entrants were college students or athletic club members, because the concept of national teams had not yet emerged. Clubs such as the Boston Athletic Association, the Amateur Athletic Association, and the German Gymnastics Society sent the largest delegations. Spectators filled the newly built Panathinaiko Stadium to watch the Games, which featured nine sports: cycling, fencing, gymnastics, lawn tennis, shooting, swimming, track and field, weight lifting, and wrestling (Ministry of Culture–General Secretariat for Sports, 1998). For several Olympic Games following (Paris, St. Louis), the event floundered and did not hit solid footing until, not surprisingly, London hosted the Olympic Games in 1908. The Olympic Games are discussed in more detail in the chapter on international sport.

The Club Structure Today

Many contemporary sports and events have organizational roots in the club sport system. These include U.S. collegiate athletics and European football. Although the club system for the organization of elite sports is fading in some

places, it is still a popular way to organize sport and recreation.

Some clubs remain committed to serving their broad membership and managing an elite sports enterprise. Many European football clubs and the Augusta National Golf Club, host of the Masters Golf Tournament, are examples of contemporary club governance. Larger clubs such as Olympiakos or Panathinaikos in Athens, Greece, provide recreation for members in addition to managing their high-profile teams or events. Clubs often organize youth teams and academies, adult recreational leagues, and social events such as dinners and dances for their members. Some club sports, like association football in Europe, have large built-in memberships and loyal fan bases and consequently rarely have a problem attracting crowds for their matches.

These organizations are characterized by their nonprofit status and exclusive membership. Challenges to the exclusive male-only membership policies of the Augusta National Golf Club, for example, have made headlines and have been met with stiff resistance from the leadership of the club itself.

Once the dominant management structure of elite sport, the club system is slowly being replaced by other sport management structures. Clearly, the Olympic Games have changed dramatically from the early days and now resemble the tournament structure discussed later in this chapter. Even European football, once the prime example of the club system, is changing. Elite European club teams such as Manchester United, Real Madrid, and Olympiakos are increasingly controlled by wealthy individuals and run like entertainment businesses (King, 1997).

Clubs are also no longer local in nature. Today's large clubs feature players from all over the world. For example, in the 2010 World Cup, players on the French soccer team played on clubs in a number of different countries, not just clubs in France. A look at the roster of the Real Madrid team lists players from not only Spain but also Brazil, Germany, and Argentina.

The emerging European sport management system has its roots in the U.S. professional sport league system that appeared in the nineteenth century. The league system in the United States developed when the English club system proved poorly suited to the economic and cultural atmosphere of the nineteenth-century United States.

Sport Structures in the United States: Sport Clubs Adapt to a Different Culture

In the early 1800s, upper-class sports enthusiasts in the United States attempted to develop sports along the lines of the English club system but found limited success. The wealthy elite formed clubs throughout the nineteenth century, complete with volunteer management, but these clubs were not able to establish a place in U.S. culture the way clubs had done in England and throughout Europe.

Whereas European clubs emphasized sport to attract large and broad memberships, the most prestigious clubs in the United States were primarily social clubs that did not sponsor sporting events. Athletic clubs, such as the New York Athletic Club, did not gain prestige until late in the century when the profit-oriented league system had already established a foothold on the cultural landscape in the United States (Gorn & Goldstein, 1993).

Nineteenth-century thoroughbred horse racing in the United States, although occasionally wildly popular, repeatedly fell on hard times. One obstacle to the club system in the United States was the country's lack of the aristocratic tradition that had given the club system both its means of support and its legitimacy in Europe. Another was the political power of religious

fundamentalism, which periodically limited or prohibited gambling.

Out of the shadow of the struggling thoroughbred horse racing scene, a uniquely American sport developed: harness racing. The league structure, which dominates sport in the United States, grew out of the success and failure of harness racing in the 1830s and 1840s. As such, it is worthwhile understanding this transition between clubs and leagues.

Harness Racing: The First National Pastime and Professional Sport

Nineteenth-century harness racing was the sport of the common person, an early precursor of stock car racing. In the 1820s, the horse and buggy was not only commonplace, it was the preferred mode of transportation of a growing middle class. Many early harness races took place on hard-packed city streets, and anyone with a horse and buggy could participate. The sport was more inclusive than thoroughbred horse racing. The horses pulling the buggies were of no particular breeding. It was relatively inexpensive to own and maintain a horse, and

horses that worked and pulled wagons by day raced in the evening (Adelman, 1986).

As the popularity of informal harness races grew, enterprising racing enthusiasts staged races on the oval tracks built for thoroughbred racing. Track owners—whose business was suffering—were eager to rent their tracks to harness racers. Promoters began to offer participants purse money raised through modest entry fees and paid track owners rent by charging admission (Adelman, 1986).

The nineteenth-century middle class in the United States, including artisans, shopkeepers, dockworkers, clerks, and the like, was far more likely to participate in this sport than were wealthy merchants. Because harness racing lacked the elitist tradition of horse racing, the public believed the sport was its own and was more willing to pay admission to subsidize the events. Promoters counted on spectator interest, and participation grew. By the 1830s, harness racing surpassed thoroughbred racing as the most popular sport in the United States (Adelman, 1986).

Although harness racing was not always as dramatic as thoroughbred racing, it was a better spectator sport. A traditional horse racing event was a four-mile race. The races were so grueling that horses raced only once or twice a year. Consequently, it was difficult for individual horses to develop a reputation or following among fans. In contrast, harness racing was a sprint. Horses recovered quickly and could compete almost daily. Promoters offered spectators as many as a dozen races in an afternoon. Horses of any breed could race, ensuring a large field of competitors. These dynamics gave the public more races, excitement, and opportunities to gamble (Adelman, 1986).

The management structure of harness racing was also distinct from thoroughbred racing. Track owners and race promoters managed the sport. Unlike members of Jockey Clubs, these entrepreneurs' livelihood depended on gate revenues, and therefore they catered to spectators. Ideally, promoters tried to match the best horses against each other to build spectator interest.

This desire for intense competition, however, created problems for harness racing promoters. Potential contestants often tried to increase their chances of victory by avoiding races with other highly touted trotters. To ensure a high level of competition and "big name" competitors, innovative promoters began to offer the owners of the best and most famous trotters a percentage of the gate (Adelman, 1986).

Unfortunately, this arrangement led some participants and promoters to fix races in an effort to promote and create demand for future races. Highly regarded trotters traded victories so as to maintain spectator interest. Harness races were sometimes choreographed dramas. This practice violated the notion of honesty critical to a sport's success. Once the word got out that some races were fixed, harness racing lost its appeal with the public. Unlike members of the Jockey Club, harness racing promoters and participants lacked the reputation to convince the public that their races were legitimate. Ultimately, spectators lost faith in the integrity of the sport, and the race promoters, no matter how honest, lacked the legitimacy to convince the public otherwise. By the start of the Civil War, harness racing had lost its appeal and its audience (Adelman, 1986).

■ LEAGUES

Harness racing's popularity and commercial promise led sports enthusiasts and managers to further refine and develop a sport management system that would work in the United States. The result was the profit-oriented league, which baseball organizers pioneered in the 1870s. Baseball was the first sport to successfully employ the league structure.

William Hulbert's National League

At first, baseball was organized according to the club system. Club leaders organized practices, rented field time, and invited other clubs to meet and play. Loosely organized leagues formed, encouraged parity of competition, and regulated competition between social equals. For example, the Knickerbockers played their games in Hoboken, New Jersey, to ensure that they competed only against upper-class teams who could afford the ferry ride over and back from New York.

Only the best teams, such as the Cincinnati Red Stockings of 1869–1870, were able to sustain fan interest. This Cincinnati team was the first openly all-professional team. The Red Stockings' road trips to play eastern teams drew thousands of fans and earned enough to pay the team's travel expenses and player salaries. Then after two seasons of flawless play, the team lost three games at the end of the 1870 season. Despite the Red Stockings' impressive record, they were no longer considered champions, and their popularity fell along with revenue. The team disbanded prior to the next season (Seymour, 1960).

In the late 1860s and early 1870s a rift developed along social/class lines. Teams that paid their players a salary conflicted with teams that did not. The business elite in local communities managed both types of clubs, but there were subtle and growing class and ethnic differences among the participants.

In 1871, a group of professional baseball teams formed the **National Association of Professional Baseball Players** and split off from the amateur club system. Any club that was willing to pay its elite players could join. The league, like other club sports, still depended on the patronage of its well-off members and consequently lacked stability. Members managed and participated in sporting activities haphazardly, and the break-even financial interests of individual clubs carried more authority than any association of clubs. It was common for teams to form, fall apart, and re-form within a season (Adelman, 1986; Leifer, 1995; Seymour, 1960).

In 1876, **William Hulbert** took over management of the National Association and renamed the body the **National League of Professional Baseball Players**. Hulbert became known as the "Czar of Baseball" for his strong leadership of the game and his role as a major figure in the development of sport management in the United States. He believed baseball teams would become stable only if they were owned and run like businesses. Teams, like other firms, should compete against one another and not collude (secretly work together), as was the case in harness racing. Hulbert called the owners of the best baseball clubs in the National Association to a meeting in New York City. When they emerged from the meeting, the groundwork had been laid for the new National League of Professional Baseball Players. The initial members of the league were from Boston, Chicago, Cincinnati, Hartford, Louisville, New York, Philadelphia, and St. Louis (Abrams, 1998).

Hulbert also understood that unless there were strict rules to ensure honest competition, baseball team owners would be tempted by collusion. For the National League to succeed, authority needed to rest with the league, not with a loose association of teams. Hulbert revamped the management of baseball to center on a league structure and created strong rules to enforce teams' allegiance (Leifer, 1995; Seymour, 1960).

Learning from earlier experiences of owners and supporters abandoning a team or season when it began to lose money, Hulbert structured the National League to force team owners to take a financial risk. Previously, teams had simply stopped playing when they began to lose money, much like a Broadway show. Hulbert understood how ending a season early to decrease short-term costs eroded the long-term faith of the public. In Hulbert's league, teams were expected to complete their schedules regardless of profit or loss.

Tying owners to a schedule resulted in costs from fielding bad teams and benefits from having a competitive team. Hulbert understood fans would see that teams were in earnest competition with one another. The public would have faith that owners needing to win to increase their profits would put forth an honest effort.

Hulbert established the league's credibility by strictly enforcing these rules. In the first year of National League play, two struggling teams, Philadelphia and New York, did not play their final series. Even though the games would not have had an impact on league standings, Hulbert banned the two teams from the league (Leifer, 1995; Seymour, 1960; Vincent, 1994). The message was clear: The integrity of the league would not be compromised for the short-term financial interests of owners.

Hulbert also understood that the integrity of baseball was suspect as long as the players' honesty was questionable. Baseball became popular at the height of the Victorian period in the United States. Large segments of Middle America followed strict cultural conventions. Many followed religious regimes prohibiting gaming and drinking—staples of the sporting subculture. Hulbert needed to create a cultural product that did not offend the sensibilities of the middle and upper classes. To appeal to this large market segment, Hulbert prohibited betting at National League ballparks. He also prohibited playing games on Sunday and selling beer at ballparks. The Cincinnati club objected to the no-liquor rule and was ultimately expelled from the National League (Hickok Sports, n.d.). Hulbert tried to clean up the atmosphere at ballparks further by banning "unwholesome groups" and activities from the game. He raised ticket

prices to decrease the number of working-class patrons and make the games more appealing to the "better" classes (Abrams, 1998).

The credibility of the players, many of them working-class immigrants, benefited from the widely held Victorian notion that a strong athletic body was a sign of strong moral character. The National League owners imposed curfews on the players to maintain their clean image. Hulbert policed the sport with a vengeance. Players caught gambling were banned from the league for life (Leifer, 1995; Seymour, 1960; Vincent, 1994), a rule emphasizing the importance of the appearance of honest effort.

Central to the organization of American Victorian culture were notions of biological distinctions among ethnic and racial groups. The National League, not surprisingly, prohibited African Americans from participating. Although other major and minor leagues had blacks on their rosters in the mid- to late-1880s, by 1888 the ban would extend to all white baseball leagues.

Once the league established a solid structure and the appearance of honest play, Hulbert still needed to create a market for the game. It was relatively easy to attract spectators to championships and other big games between rival clubs, but team owners needed to find a way to attract audiences to regular-season games. Hulbert's dilemma was complicated by the fact that many of the independent clubs (not affiliated with his league) fielded superior teams. In the late 1870s, National League teams lost more often than they won in non-League play (Leifer, 1995).

Hulbert's solution was to create the pennant race, a revolutionary idea in 1876. The success of the National League depended on spectators viewing baseball as a series of games and not a single event. A genuine pennant race requires fairly even competition. In other words, for the league to be a successful business, even the best teams had to lose a substantial portion of their games (Leifer, 1995).

League rules were designed to cultivate pennant fever. Hulbert kept his league small by limiting it to eight teams. A team was either in the league or not. Although local rivalries had been important in the past, Hulbert's league limited membership. As such, the National League was small enough to ensure that no team was so far out of first place that winning the pennant seemed impossible.

Other innovations that Hulbert brought to the sport significantly influenced the history and development of sport management. For example, to protect their teams from being raided by other National League teams during the season, owners agreed to respect each other's contracts with players for one year. Other leagues could pay the National League a fee to participate in this "reservation" system and protect themselves from raids by National League teams. The practice not only helped distribute talent more evenly but also kept player salaries down. This practice eventually developed into the "reserve system," which included a "reserve clause" in player contracts and a "reserve list" of protected players on each team roster. These rules also limited the movement of players, enhancing the sense of a local team and, thus, fan loyalty.

The league structure enjoyed a significant boost from newspapers, another rapidly expanding U.S. institution. Although the initial response to the National League by the media was generally unfavorable (Vincent, 1994), newspapers with teams in the League warmed to the idea of a pennant race. In the 1870s, most major cities supported a dozen or more newspapers. One effective way to attract readers was to cover local sporting events. Newspapers played up the concept of the hometown team in a pennant race to hold the attention of sports fans between games. Reports on injuries, other teams' records, players' attitudes, and coaching

strategies were given considerable coverage before and after games. Presenting baseball in terms of an ongoing pennant race sold newspapers and underscored Hulbert's desire to promote continuing attention to and attendance at regular-season games (White, 1996).

The National League also appealed to fans' loyalty and pride in their towns and cities. League rules prohibited placing more than one National League team in or near any current National League city and prohibited teams from playing non-League teams within the same territory as a National League team (Seymour, 1960). The prohibition required discipline on the part of team owners because non-League games, especially against local non-League rivals, generated strong short-term profits. By avoiding "independent" clubs in National League cities, the League promoted the notion that National League teams represented the community exclusively. Independent teams, languishing from this National League prohibition, moved on to non-League cities, and spectators increasingly identified the National League teams with their cities (Leifer, 1995). The notion of a team's "territory" persists in the management of major and minor league baseball as well as in all other league sports (e.g., NBA, NFL, NHL).

National League teams had an early form of revenue sharing. Home teams were required to share their gate revenues with the visiting team. This practice allowed even the least talented teams to draw revenue when they played away from home. Gate sharing redistributed wealth around the National League, enabling teams to compete financially for players (Leifer, 1995).

Leagues Today

The National League's successful strategy seems fairly straightforward when compared with the business strategies used by today's professional sports leagues that take into account naming rights, licensing agreements, and league-wide television deals. But successful contemporary commercial sports leagues still depend on consolidated league play with strong centralized control and regulation. League play is in large part designed to encourage the fans' faith that teams operate on an equal footing, both on the field and off, and that owners, managers, and players are putting forth an honest effort.

The audience has changed over time, however. The need to see teams as independent firms has faded. Recent start-up leagues such as the WNBA and MLS have experimented with a single-entity structure, in which each team is owned and operated by the league, although the WNBA has since moved away from this model. The public's perception of locus of honest effort resides more with the players than it does with the ownership structure.

Not all professional sports are organized in the league structure. Sports such as golf or tennis developed and continue to operate today using a different organizational structure. Sometimes referred to as professional tournament sports, their development is chronicled in the next section.

■ PROFESSIONAL TOURNAMENT SPORTS: MIXING BUSINESS AND CHARITY

Professional tournament sports such as tennis and golf have their roots in the club system. Early tournaments were usually sponsored by private clubs for the benefit of their membership. By the turn of the century, professionals—usually club employees who taught club members the game—were often excluded from club tournaments. Without support from wealthy patrons to sponsor tournaments, professional athletes in some sports needed other alternatives if they were going to compete. This was the case with golf.

Professional Golf

Many early golf professionals were European men brought to the United States by country clubs to help design, build, and care for golf courses and teach the finer points of the game to club members. By its very nature, golf was an exclusive game, one that catered to upper-class white males. Although these golfers were technically professionals, they were much different from the tournament professionals of the contemporary Ladies Professional Golf Association (LPGA) and Professional Golfers' Association (PGA). The early golf professionals were club instructors and caddies. They made extra money by giving exhibitions. Golf manufacturers hired the best-known professionals as representatives to help publicize the game and their brands of clubs at exhibitions and clinics.

Numerous attempts were made to organize golf leagues prior to the 1930s, but professional leagues failed to capture public interest or attract golf professionals. Professionals shunned these risky tournaments in favor of the stability of exhibitions and clinics, and when they competed they vied for prize money they had put up themselves. Professional tournaments did not stabilize until the professionals found someone else—in the form of community and corporate sponsors—to put up the prize money.

One entrepreneurial type of tournament, which ultimately failed, was an attempt to generate a profit from gate revenues for country club owners. In the first half of the twentieth century, spectator attendance was the primary revenue stream for most sports. Following the proven approach of boxing promoters and baseball owners, individual country club owners produced golf events themselves, selling tickets to the events and operating concessions.

The failure of the privately owned tournaments to catch on had less to do with the energy and creativity that owners put into the events or with broader social issues than it did with the nature of the sport. Individually owned golf courses were rare, and even if there were a consortium of course owners, as was the case in baseball, players operated independently. The players did not need teams, managers, or promoters, and therefore were difficult to control.

Corcoran's Tournaments

Fred Corcoran, the architect of the professional golf tournament, understood the unique qualities of golf. Golf, he wrote, "operates upside down" in comparison to other sports. "The players have to pay to tee off, and they use facilities constructed for the use of the amateur owners who, occasionally, agree to open the gates" to professionals (Corcoran, 1965, p. 246).

To manage this "upside down" sport, Corcoran took his lead from Hollywood and advertising executives. Corcoran used athletes and golf tournaments the same way newspapers used news—to sell advertising space to the public. Corcoran never promoted golf strictly as entertainment. The golf tournament, for Corcoran, was the medium through which a celebrity, a local politician, a manufacturer, a charity, a town, or a product gained exposure. He sold the event. As a result, the contemporary professional tournament, unlike other sports operating 50 years ago, was less dependent on ticket sales and more dependent on sponsorship from community groups and corporations.

In 1937, a consortium of golf manufacturers hired Fred Corcoran as tournament director for the men's PGA circuit. He served in that capacity for more than a decade, making arrangements with public and private clubs to host professional tournaments. Then, in 1949, the golf equipment manufacturers hired him again to organize the women's tour (Corcoran, 1965; Hicks, 1956). Corcoran organized the players into associations with rules governing play and eligibility. In essence, the players governed themselves.

One of Corcoran's first contributions to the professional golf tour was the creation of the financially self-sufficient tournament. Prior to 1937, the PGA, through entry fees, had guaranteed to pay the players' purse to entice communities to sponsor tournaments. Corcoran, who had spent a decade organizing amateur tournaments in Massachusetts, understood the potential revenue a tournament produced for a community. Corcoran was able to convince communities to take responsibility for providing the purse by demonstrating how the revenue generated by 70 professional golfers eating in restaurants and sleeping in hotels would be three times greater than the minimum $3,000 purse (Corcoran, 1965).

Corcoran enhanced the tremendous growth in competitive golf by sharing status with celebrities like Bing Crosby. In addition to being a famous movie star and singer, Crosby was a sports entrepreneur associated with horse racing and golf. In 1934, Crosby orchestrated the first celebrity professional and amateur (pro-am) tournament preceding a men's golf tournament to raise money for charity. The combination of a celebrity and a pro playing together on a team in a mock tournament was extremely successful. Amateur golfers, celebrities, and community leaders paid exorbitant fees to participate. Although these funds were directed toward charity, there were also spin-off professional golf benefits. The appearance of celebrities not only enhanced the athletes' status but also increased attendance, thereby increasing the proceeds for charity and the exposure for professional golf. The celebrity pro-am has been the financial core around which most professional golf tournaments have been built (Graffis, 1975).

The financial power of this type of charity event became clear during World War II. During the war, golf was used to raise money for the Red Cross. Using a celebrity pro-am format, Bing Crosby teamed up with movie costar Bob Hope, professional golfers, and various other celebrities, including Fred Corcoran, to raise millions of dollars for the war effort and the Red Cross (Graffis, 1975). At the end of the war, Corcoran kept the pro-am tournament format and used civic pride and charities such as hospitals and youth programs to draw crowds.

Tying professional golf to charity was good business in addition to being good for the community. Donations to charitable organizations were fully tax deductible. Local businesspeople not likely to benefit directly from a golf tournament were more easily persuaded to contribute to the tournaments with tax deductions as incentives. In addition, a good charity attracted the hundreds of volunteers and essential in-kind donations needed to run a tournament. Further, a charity with broad reach and many volunteers acted as a promotional vehicle for the tournament. Thus, Corcoran transformed a potentially costly, labor-intensive event into a no-cost operation. By appealing to the altruism of a community to host a tournament, Corcoran obtained a tournament site, capital, and event management for no cost.

A consortium of golf equipment manufacturers paid Corcoran's salary to organize the golfers into an association and to help arrange tournaments. Golf manufacturers understood that the costs of retaining player representatives would be reduced with a solid tournament circuit in place. Manufacturers could retain player representatives at a fraction of the cost and increase players' values as marketing tools. The better players earned their salaries through prize money. The cost of sponsoring a player to play on tour was far less than hiring a player full-time as a representative and paying expenses.

It was clear to Corcoran that if manufacturers could use their association with tournaments to sell golf products, then celebrities could use it to add to their status, and local community groups could use it to raise funds or gain political influence. Tournaments could also be sold as an advertising medium for non-golf-related merchandise. As tournament director of the PGA and the LPGA, Corcoran orchestrated the first non-golf-related corporate sponsorship of professional golf tournaments. Corcoran arranged for Palm Beach Clothing to sponsor men's tournaments. A few years later he orchestrated a transcontinental series of women's tournaments sponsored by Weathervane Ladies Sports Apparel (Corcoran, 1965).

Corcoran's adaptation of Crosby's celebrity tournaments to tournaments funded by advertising for clothing foreshadowed the immense corporate involvement in contemporary professional tournaments. Still, professional golf was not able to take full advantage of corporate interest in athletes until the late 1950s. Until that time, the major media wire services, Associated Press and United Press International, followed a policy of using the name of the city or town to distinguish a tournament. They argued that using the name of the corporate sponsor was a cheap way to avoid paying for newspaper advertising. In the late 1950s, the newspaper industry reversed its policy and agreed to call tournaments by the name of their corporate sponsors. By sponsoring a national sporting event, a corporation now gained tax-free exposure to a target market in the name of charity (Graffis, 1975). In the end, professional golf, charities, and corporations all benefited from this arrangement.

Tournaments Today

Variations of the tournament structure just described can be found today in golf, tennis, track and field, and in multisport events like the Olympic and Paralympic Games. Like Corcoran, today's tour promoters do not sell the event solely as entertainment. Instead, they promote tournaments as a medium through which a person, community, or corporation can buy exposure. Gallery seats, pro-am tournaments, and the pre- and post-tournament festivities are the foci of interaction, access to which can be sold. Although communities, politicians, and radio and movie personalities have found tournaments a worthwhile investment, the corporate community has benefited the most handsomely. The golf tournament has evolved into a corporate celebration of itself and its products (Crosset, 1995).

Associations such as the PGA have been viewed as private groups. They set the rules of eligibility. However, challenges to that idea, as seen with Casey Martin's successful attempt to have the PGA accommodate his disability, suggest that these associations cannot be as exclusive as private clubs. In Casey Martin's case, he used the fact that Qualifying School (Q-School) was open to the public as a means of applying the Americans with Disabilities Act public accommodation provisions to force the PGA to allow him to compete using a cart.

In another trend that is pushing tournament management away from nonprofit private associations, today's tournaments are just as likely to be created by marketing agencies or broadcast media as by player associations. For example, the X-Games and the Alli Dew Tour are the products of corporations. The X-Games are owned by ESPN, which is a subsidiary of the Disney Corporation. The Alli Dew Tour is owned in a partnership between NBC Sports and MTV. It is not yet clear how corporate-owned tournaments will affect older associations or if "made-for-TV" tournaments will be able to sustain their legitimacy with the public. However, a decade into the X-Games and Dew Tour type tours, the public seems to be willing to follow them.

The first section of this chapter has focused mainly on the historical aspects of professional sports, particularly teams and leagues. Most certainly the sport industry includes many more segments other than these two. This fact becomes obvious simply by looking at the broad range of chapters in this introductory textbook. Many of the basic tenets covered in this chapter are applicable across other segments as well. To learn more about the historical developments in segments such as intercollegiate athletics, high school and youth sport, recreational sport, and many more areas, the reader can turn to the chapters designed to cover those specific industry segments in-depth. Each chapter has a section devoted to the important historical events for that industry segment.

■ WOMEN IN SPORT MANAGEMENT

A book like this one serves to bring together information across different sport industry segments so that the reader is exposed to as broad a landscape of the industry as possible. However, as is the case with many disciplines, parts of the history and the names of some important contributors are sometimes overlooked.

Female sport managers have contributed to the growth of the sport industry as a whole, yet all too often their contributions as sport leaders are not formally recognized (Hums & Yiamouyiannis, 2007). This section introduces the reader to a selection of these women and their contributions.

Perhaps the first female sport managers lived in the time of the ancient Olympic Games. While we know women were not allowed to participate in those early Games, because participation was limited to free Greek male citizens, this does not mean no competitions for women existed. As a matter of fact, around the same time period of the ancient Olympic Games, a competition was held for women known as the Heraea Games. These Games, which also took place at the grounds of Olympia but not at the same time as the Olympic Games, consisted of footraces for unmarried girls. The event was organized by a group known as the Sixteen Women. These women, who were considered respected elders of their communities, gathered from nearby locations every four years to administer the Games (Hums, 2010). After the Heraea Games were discontinued, centuries would pass before we would see more women organizing such events.

A woman who could be recognized as the first significant modern female sport manager was Effa Manley (O'Connor-McDonogh, 2007). As co-owner of the Newark Eagles in the Negro Baseball League, Manley was responsible for the day-to-day operations of the ballclub and was active in league management (Berlage, 1994). For her contributions to professional baseball, in 2006 Manley became the first woman elected to the Baseball Hall of Fame in Cooperstown, New York (MacNeil Lehrer Productions, 2010). She most certainly paved the way for women such as Kim Ng, Assistant General Manager for the Los Angeles Dodgers and the only woman to have interviewed for a General Manager (GM)

position with a Major League Baseball (MLB) team. Ng is paving the way for others. Prior to working for the Dodgers, Ng was Assistant General Manager with the New York Yankees; she was succeeded by Jean Afterman, a former player agent who is now the Yankees' Assistant General Manager.

Today other women hold high executive positions in North American professional leagues, including Heidi Ueberroth, the president of international business operations for the NBA; Rita Benson LeBlanc, owner/executive vice president of the New Orleans Saints; and Jeanie Buss, executive vice president of business operations for the Los Angeles Lakers. As with many men in the sports business, lineage or marriage often plays a role in getting to the top. Five of *Forbes'* top ten women in sports business were in the business through heritage or marriage (Van Riper, 2009). It is a point not lost on Jeanie Buss in her comments about Ng's chances of becoming the first female GM in MLB:

"I'm lucky," she said, "because I have a certain power base because of who my dad is. I'm also a realist. I want to see in my time frame a successful female GM in one of the major leagues. It's going to be tough. She's going to get one chance, and it has to have all the pieces in place. I don't know Kim personally, but from what I know, she really does things the right way. She knows her job; she's done the work. She deserves an opportunity. But like I said, she's going to get one shot, and then people would love to say the experiment is over if it's not a success" (Brown, 2008, p. 44).

No writing on women in sport would be complete without including the contributions made by women's tennis superstar Billie Jean King. While perhaps best remembered for her victory over Bobby Riggs in the 1973 "Battle of the Sexes," King also established the Women's Tennis Association and was a founder of *WomenSports* magazine, World Team Tennis, and the Women's Sports Foundation, which has done a great deal of work to promote leadership and management opportunities for women in sport (Lough, 2007; Women's Sports Foundation, 2008).

A number of women played important roles in the development of intercollegiate athletics, especially Christine Grant and Judy Sweet. Grant, former Women's Athletic Director at the University of Iowa and former President of the Association for Intercollegiate Athletics for Women (AIAW), championed Title IX and gender equity efforts for female athletes. Sweet was one of the first women to serve as athletics director of a combined men's and women's intercollegiate athletics program in the United States (at University of California–San Diego) and was the first female President of the NCAA (Hums & Yiamouyiannis, 2007).

In terms of recreational sport, three women attended the founding meeting of the National Intramural Association (NIA), with Annette Akins being named Vice President. This organization was the forerunner of the National Intramural and Recreational Sport Association (NIRSA), the primary sport organization in campus recreation. Since then, three other women have served as NIRSA presidents, including Mary Daniels from Ohio State University and Juliette Moore from the University of Arizona. Moore was the first African-American woman to hold that post (Bower, 2007). Vicki Highstreet, from the University of Nebraska–Lincoln, served as NIRSA's President in 2009.

Finally, a number of women have contributed to the modern history of the sport industry in terms of their contributions in sport-related businesses. Some of these women are Lesa France Kennedy, CEO of International Speedway Corporation; Stephanie Tolleson, Former Senior Corporate Vice President at International Management Group (IMG); Buffy Filipell, founder of TeamWork Online; and Becky Heidesch and Mary Lou Youngblood of Women's Sports Services, which operates two online career placement services accessed by WomenSportsJobs.com and WSSExecutiveSearch.com (Lough, 2007).

The list of names of women who contributed to the modern history of sport management is certainly much longer than this abbreviated introduction suggests. What is important to note is that these businesswomen, and many others whose names are not listed here, have influenced the sport industry as we know it today.

■ THE BIRTH OF SPORT MANAGEMENT AS AN ACADEMIC FIELD

It is clear that as the sport industry evolved, it increasingly took on business characteristics of other industries. The early sport managers discussed in this chapter came to their sport management positions with some background in sport or some background in business. Very few brought the combination of the two to the workplace. However, to be a successful sport manager in today's industry, preparation in both sport and business is becoming a necessity. Because of this need, the academic field of sport management began to develop, and you are majoring in sport management today! How did this field come into existence, and what makes it unique?

Sport clubs, leagues, and tournaments are three of the more prevalent structures currently used to manage and organize sport. Management systems, including amateur bodies such as the National Collegiate Athletic Association and the United States Track and

Field Association or professional organizations such as the World Boxing Association and the National Basketball Association, employ some variation of these structures to produce sporting events. But contemporary sport management is far more complex than its historical antecedents. Furthermore, the growing popularity of newer sports such as mountain biking, snowboarding, and rock climbing and the increasing power of global media are encouraging the evolution of new management structures.

The continuing growth of the sport industry and its importance to numerous sponsors and institutions created demand for the systematic study of sport management practices. Since the late 1960s, the academic field of sport management has focused on the unique and special issues facing the people who conduct the business of sport.

As the sport management profession began to grow and prosper, it became apparent that although similarities existed between running a general business and running a sport organization, there were also intricacies peculiar to the sport industry. Early on, sport managers learned from hands-on experiences gained in the industry. However, as the sport industry became more complex, the need to train sport managers in a more formal fashion became a necessity. The formal study of sport management emerged from this need.

The concept of a sport management curriculum is generally credited to two people: **James G. Mason**, a physical educator at the University of Miami–Florida, and **Walter O'Malley** of the Brooklyn (now Los Angeles) Dodgers, who discussed the idea in 1957 (Mason, Higgins, & Owen, 1981). The first master's program in sport management was established at **Ohio University** in 1966 and was based on Mason's and O'Malley's ideas (Parkhouse & Pitts, 2001). Shortly after the Ohio University graduate program began, Biscayne College (now St. Thomas

University) and St. John's University founded undergraduate sport management programs (Parkhouse & Pitts, 2001). The University of Massachusetts–Amherst started the second master's program in 1971.

The number of colleges and universities in the United States offering sport management majors grew rapidly. By 1985 the National Association for Sport and Physical Education (NASPE) indicated there were more than 40 undergraduate programs, 32 graduate programs, and 11 at both levels offering sport management degrees. Today, the total number of sport management programs is just over 300 (North American Society for Sport Management, 2010c). Approximately a dozen Canadian universities offer programs as well. The growth of sport management as an academic field was prompted by the sport industry's need for well-trained managers, but it also was pushed by universities' and colleges' need to attract students. Some schools wishing to increase enrollments in a highly competitive market added sport management programs to their curricula in the 1980s.

Given the rapid growth of the academic field, concern developed among sport management educators over what constituted a solid sport management curriculum capable of producing students qualified to work as managers in the sport industry. The first group of scholars to examine this issue formed an organization called the Sport Management Arts and Science Society (SMARTS), which was initiated by the faculty at the University of Massachusetts–Amherst. This group laid the groundwork for the present scholarly organization, the **North American Society for Sport Management (NASSM)** (Parkhouse & Pitts, 2001).

The purpose of NASSM is to promote, stimulate, and encourage study, research, scholarly writing, and professional development in the area of sport management, both in the theoretical and applied aspects (North American Society for Sport Management, 2010a). NASSM and NASPE monitor sport management curricula. Currently, the NASSM/NASPE guidelines for approved sport management programs include content areas such as sport marketing, legal aspects of sport, management and leadership in sport, ethics in sport management, budget and finance in sport, communication in sport, and the sociocultural context of sport (Parkhouse & Pitts, 2001). Currently the movement to program accreditation is the topic of debate. NASSM is holding discussions about moving to this level of program evaluation via the Commission on Sport Management Accreditation (COSMA).

Sport management professional organizations also exist in a number of nations outside North America. Two of these organizations are the Sport Management Association of Australia and New Zealand (SMAANZ) and the European Association of Sport Management (EASM). In addition, 2010 marked the establishment of the African Sport Management Association, with great hopes for collaborations among these various international organizations. As sport management becomes more global in nature, universities implementing successful country-specific curricula outside North America are producing successful sport managers as well. Universities in Belgium, England, Germany, Greece, Ireland, Spain, and the Netherlands, for example, are preparing future sport managers (North American Society for Sport Management, 2010b). Programs are also thriving in Japan. As the sport industry evolves, sport management curricula will continue to change to meet the needs of this global industry.

■ SUMMARY

It is impossible in one chapter to cover the complex history of sport thoroughly. This chapter discussed the historical origins of three basic sport management structures: clubs, leagues, and tournaments. Sport management structures that developed over the past 150 or so years organized sporting events in different ways to meet the particular needs of participants, spectators, and sponsors at particular points in history. The club structure, the league structure, and the tournament structure each arose in response to changes in broad social structures and addressed specific issues within a segment of the sport industry. The evolution of each of these three management structures illustrates that managers need to be creative in the ways they manage sports.

Throughout this text you will see mentions of some of the innovators and contributors to the management of sport. Keep an eye open for historic figures such as John Montgomery Ward, Albert Spalding, Judge Kennesaw Mountain Landis, and Marvin Miller in baseball. Other notable sport managers include Peter Ueberoff in the Olympic Games, David Stern in basketball, Pete Rozelle and Paul Tagliabue in football, Gary Bettman in hockey, Roone Arledge in sport broadcasting, and agents C. C. Pyle and Mark McCormack. These people, along with many others, have contributed to making sport one of the most popular forms of entertainment.

In contemporary sport, we can still see the three basic management structures (clubs, leagues, and tournaments) operating. But the management structures operate within highly complex organizational systems. As a result, the sport industry demands well-trained managers. Sport management developed as an academic field to meet this demand. To maintain quality control in this fast-emerging field of study, the NASSM/NASPE, and now COSMA, curriculum guidelines have been established. As the sport industry continues to evolve globally, the academic field of sport management will evolve as well in order to produce the future leaders in the industry.

■ KEY TERMS

clubs, Fred Corcoran, Pierre de Coubertin, William Hulbert, Jockey Club, leagues, James G. Mason, modern Olympic Games, National Association of Professional Baseball Players, North American Society for Sport Management (NASSM), National League of Professional Baseball Players, Ohio University, Walter O'Malley, professional tournaments, sport management structures

■ REFERENCES

Abrams, R. (1998). *Legal bases: Baseball and the law.* Philadelphia: Temple University Press.

Adelman, M. (1986). *A sporting time: New York City and the rise of modern athletics, 1820–70.* Urbana, IL: University of Illinois Press.

Berlage, G.I. (1994). *Women in baseball: The forgotten history.* Westport, CT: Praeger.

Bower, G.G. (2007). Campus recreation. In M.A. Hums, G.G. Bower, & H. Grappendorf (Eds.), *Women as leaders in sport: Impact and influence* (pp. 115–136). Reston, VA: NAGWS.

Brown, T. (2008). Can Kim Ng break the gender barrier? Yahoo sports. Retrieved September 29, 2010, from http://sports.yahoo.com/mlb/news?slug=ti-femalegm070308

Corcoran, F. (1965). *Unplayable lies.* New York: Meredith Press.

Crosset, T.W. (1995). *Outsiders in the clubhouse: The world of women's professional golf.* Albany, NY: SUNY Press.

Gorn, E., & Goldstein, W. (1993). *A brief history of American sport.* New York: Wang and Hill.

Graffis, H. (1975). *The PGA: The official history of the Professional Golfers' Association of America.* New York: Crowell.

Henriches, T. (1991). *Disputed pleasures: Sport and society in preindustrial England.* New York: Greenwood Press.

Hickok Sports. (n.d.). The first major league (1875–1889). Retrieved September 29, 2010, from http://www.hickoksports.com/history/baseba04.shtml

Hicks, B. (1956). Personal correspondence, LPGA Archives.

Hums, M.A. (2010). Women's leadership in the Olympic Movement. In K. O'Connor (Ed.), *Gender and women's leadership* (pp. 842–850). Thousand Oaks, CA: Sage Publishing.

Hums, M.A., & Yiamouyiannis, A. (2007). Women in sport careers and leadership positions. In M.A. Hums, G.G. Bower, & H. Grappendorf (Eds.), *Women as leaders in sport: Impact and influence* (pp. 1–23). Reston, VA: NAGWS.

King, A. (1997). New directors, customers and fans: The transformation of English football in the 1990s. *Sociology of Sport Journal, 14,* 224–240.

Leifer, E.M. (1995). *Making the majors: The transformation of team sports in America.* Cambridge, MA: Harvard University Press.

Lough, N. (2007). Women in sport related business. In M.A. Hums, G.G. Bower, & H. Grappendorf (Eds.), *Women as leaders in sport: Impact and influence* (pp. 191–206). Reston, VA: NAGWS.

MacNeil Lehrer Productions. (2006). First woman in the Hall of Fame. Retrieved September 28, 2010, from http://www.pbs.org/newshour/bb/entertainment/jan-june06/baseball_2-28.html

Mandell, R. (1984). *Sport: A cultural history.* New York: Columbia University Press.

Mason, J.G., Higgins, C., & Owen, J. (1981, January). Sport administration education 15 years later. *Athletic Purchasing and Facilities,* 44–45.

Ministry of Culture–General Secretariat for Sports. (1998). *Greek athletics: A historical overview.* Athens, Greece: Author.

North American Society for Sport Management. (2010a). NASSM home. Retrieved November 10, 2010, from http://www.nassm.org

North American Society for Sport Management. (2010b). Sport management programs. Retrieved November 10, 2010, from http://www.nassm.com/InfoAbout/SportMgmtPrograms

North American Society for Sport Management. (2010c). Sport management programs: United States. Retrieved November 10, 2010, from http://www.nassm.com/InfoAbout/SportMgmtPrograms/United_States

O'Connor-McDonogh, M. (2007). Professional sport. In M.A. Hums, G.G. Bower, & H. Grappendorf

(Eds.), *Women as leaders in sport: Impact and influence* (pp. 233–250). Reston, VA: NAGWS.

Parkhouse, B.L., & Pitts, B.G. (2001). Definition, evolution, and curriculum. In B.L. Parkhouse (Ed.), *The management of sport: Its foundation and application* (3rd ed.) (pp. 2–14). New York: McGraw-Hill.

Seymour, H. (1960). *Baseball: The early years*. Oxford, UK: Oxford University Press.

Vamplew, W. (1989). *Pay up and play the game: Professional sport in Britain, 1875–1914*. Cambridge, UK: Cambridge University Press.

Van Riper, T. (2009 October 14). The most powerful women in sports. *Forbes.com*. Retrieved September 29, 2010, from http://www.forbes.com/2009/10/14/nascar-wwe-football-business-sports-women.html

Vincent, T. (1994). *The rise and fall of American sport*. Lincoln, NE: Nebraska University Press.

White, G.E. (1996). *Creating the national pastime: Baseball transforms itself, 1903–1953*. Princeton, NJ: Princeton University Press.

Williams, J. (1989) Cricket. In T. Mason (Ed.), *Sport in Britain: A social history*. Cambridge, UK: Cambridge University Press.

Women's Sports Foundation. (2008). Billie Jean King: Founder, leader, legend. Retrieved November 10, 2010, from http://www.womenssportsfoundation.org/cgi-bin/iowa/about/article.html?record=86

Young, D. (1996). *The Modern Olympics: A struggle for revival*. Baltimore, MD: Johns Hopkins University Press.

SPORT MANAGEMENT TIMELINE

BC 776	First ancient Olympic Games
AD 393	Last ancient Olympic Games
1750	Establishment of Jockey Club in Newmarket
1851	First America's Cup (sailing)
1869	Cincinnati Red Stockings become first professional baseball club
1871	National Association of Professional Baseball Players founded
1875	First running of Kentucky Derby (horse racing)
1876	National League of Professional Baseball Players established
1892	Basketball invented
1894	International Olympic Committee founded
1896	First modern Olympic Games in Athens, Greece
1900	Women first compete in Olympic Games
1903	First Tour de France
1904	Fédération Internationale de Football Association (FIFA) founded
1906	Intercollegiate Athletic Association of the United States issues first constitution/bylaws
1910	Intercollegiate Athletic Association of the United States changes name to National Collegiate Athletic Association (NCAA)
1911	First Indianapolis 500
1912	International Association of Athletics Federation (IAAF) began

SPORT MANAGEMENT TIMELINE *(Continued)*

1916	First PGA Championship
1917	National Hockey League (NHL) established
1920	National Football League (NFL) began/National Federation of State High School Association (NFSHSA) founded
1924	First Winter Olympic Games in Chamonix, France/International Association of Assembly Managers (IAAM) established
1930	First FIFA World Cup (soccer) in Uruguay/First Commonwealth Games
1933	First NFL Championship
1939	First NCAA basketball tournament/Baseball Hall of Fame inducts first class
1943	First women's professional baseball league (All-American Girls Professional Baseball League)
1946	National Basketball Association (NBA) (originally known as Basketball Association of America) established
1947	Jackie Robinson integrates Major League Baseball
1950	First Formula One Championship (F1)/Ladies Professional Golf Association (LPGA) founded/National Intramural-Recreational Sports Association (NIRSA) began
1951	First Asian Games/Bill Veeck sent Eddie Gaedel up to bat
1959	First Daytona 500
1960	First Paralympic Games in Rome, Italy/Arnold Palmer signed as IMG's first client
1961	International Olympic Academy officially inaugurated in Olympia, Greece
1966	Marvin Miller appointed Executive Director of Major League Baseball Players Association (MLBPA)
1967	First Super Bowl
1971	Nike Swoosh designed by Carolyn Davidson
1972	Title IX passed
1974	Women's Sports Foundation founded by Billie Jean King
1975	Arbitrator declares MLB players Andy Messersmith and Dave McNally free agents
1976	First Winter Paralympic Games
1978	First Ironman Triathlon
1982	First NCAA women's basketball tournament
1985	North American Society for Sport Management (NASSM) established/First Air Jordan shoes debut at retail/The Olympic Partner (TOP) Program created
1990	Americans with Disabilities Act signed into law

SPORT MANAGEMENT TIMELINE *(Continued)*

1991	First FIFA Women's World Cup (soccer)
1992	NBA players first played in the Summer Olympic Games
1994	NFL salary cap came into effect
1996	Women's National Basketball Association (WNBA) founded
1998	NHL players first competed in the Winter Olympic Games/first BCS games played
1999	World Anti-Doping Agency established
2001	Beijing, China awarded Olympic and Paralympic Games for 2008/U.S. Supreme Court ruled golfer Casey Martin allowed to use a cart in PGA events
2003	Nike acquires Converse
2004	William Perez succeeds Phil Knight as President and CEO of Nike/ATHOC (Athens Organizing Committee) becomes first Organizing Committee for the Olympic Games to jointly manage both Summer Olympic and Paralympic Games/Nextel takes over sponsorship of NASCAR's Winston Cup
2005	Adidas acquires Reebok/NHL labor problems cause first postponement of an entire major professional league season/NHL suspends operations for 2004–2005 season/MLB Players Association and owners announce new drug testing agreement including suspensions and release of player names/United Nations designates 2005 as the International Year of Sport and Physical Education
2006	Germany hosts successful World Cup, featuring a "Say No to Racism" campaign
2007	Barry Bonds becomes new MLB home run king amid steroid allegations
2008	Beijing, China hosts the Summer Olympic Games/Arena Football League announces cancellation of 2009 season/Final year for Yankee Stadium
2009	Rio de Janeiro, Brazil awarded 2016 Summer Olympic Games, marking the first time the Games will be held in South America/Members of Sri Lanka national cricket attacked by gunman in Pakistan, resulting in cancellation of remainder of tour
2010	NCAA conference realignment: Big 10, Big 12, and Pac-10/South Africa hosts first World Cup on African continent

CHAPTER

Management Principles Applied to Sport Management

Carol A. Barr and Mary A. Hums

■ INTRODUCTION

It has been said that sport today is too much of a game to be a business and too much of a business to be a game. The sport industry in the United States is growing at an incredible rate. Current estimates by *Forbes* magazine of the value of individual professional team sport franchises list the average National Football League (NFL) team's value at $1.02 billion (Badenhausen et al., 2010a), the average National Basketball Association (NBA) franchise at $367 million (Badenhausen et al., 2009a), the average Major League Baseball (MLB) franchise at $491 million (Badenhausen et al., 2010b), and the average National Hockey League (NHL) franchise at $223 million (Badenhausen, 2009b). Total annual licensed-product sales for major

sport properties were as follows: NHL, $1 billion; NFL, $3.25 billion; MLB, $3.3 billion; NBA, $2.15 billion; National Association of Stock Car Auto Racing (NASCAR), $1.2 billion, and colleges and universities, $3.1 billion (Dvorchak, 2008). In 2010, the National Collegiate Athletic Association (NCAA) reached a 14-year, nearly $11 billion agreement with CBS and Turner Sports for television rights to the 68-team NCAA men's basketball tournament (an increase of 3 teams from the previous year's 65-team tournament) (Wieberg & Hiestand, 2010). In 2007, the NBA signed a new eight-year, $7.4 billion national television deal with ABC, ESPN, and Turner Sports (Chmielewski & Johnson, 2007). The U.S. health and sports club industry reported a 2008 total annual dollar volume of $19.1 billion (International Health, Racquet and Sportsclub

Association, 2010). As the sport industry has grown, there has been a shift in focus toward a more profit-oriented approach to doing business (Hums, Barr, & Gullion, 1999).

While keeping the financial scope of the sport industry in mind, it is important to note that in whatever segment of the sport industry they work, sport managers need to be able to organize and work with the most important asset in their organization: people. This chapter on management will help the future sport manager recognize how essential utilization of this most important asset is to the success of a sport organization. Every sport manager needs to understand the basics of being a manager in the twenty-first century. A manager in a sport organization can go by many different titles: athletic director, general manager, director of sales, coach, health club manager, ski resort operator, and so on. The purpose of this chapter is to introduce the reader to basic management knowledge areas and skills that sport managers can apply in any segment of the industry.

■ DEFINITION AND HISTORY OF MANAGEMENT PRINCIPLES

Management has been defined in a number of different ways, but common elements of these various definitions include (a) goals/objectives to be achieved (b) with limited resources and (c) with and through people (Chelladurai, 2009). The goal of managerial work and the role the manager plays within an organization is to get the workers to do what the manager wants them to do in an efficient and cost-effective manner. The management process is performed using knowledge areas such as planning, organizing, leading, and evaluating. These knowledge areas are discussed in the next section of this chapter.

The development of management theory has gone through a number of distinct phases. Two of the earlier phases were scientific management and the human relations movement. Frederick Taylor was one of the first true pioneers of management theory. The publication of Taylor's 1911 book, *The Principles of Scientific Management*, laid the foundation for the **scientific management** movement (sometimes referred to today as "Taylorism") in the early 1900s (Frederick Winslow Taylor, 2002). Taylor worked as an industrial engineer at a steel company and was concerned with the way workers performed their jobs. Taylor believed that through scientific study of the specific motions making up a total job, a more rational and efficient method of performing that job could be developed. In other words, workers should not be doing the same job in different ways, but instead there existed "one best way" to perform a job the most efficiently. In Taylor's view, the manager could get workers to perform the job this "best way" by enticing them with economic rewards.

The second major phase in management theory is known as the **human relations movement**. From 1927 to 1932, Elton Mayo was part of the team conducting the Hawthorne studies at Western Electric's Chicago plant. In the Hawthorne studies, the workers' motivations were studied by examining how changes in working conditions affected output. Mayo found that social factors in the workplace were important, and job satisfaction and output depended more on cooperation and a feeling of worth than on physical working conditions (Elton Mayo, 2002). The human relations movement was also popularized by the work and writings of Mary Parker Follett. Follett was a pioneer as a female management consultant in the male-dominated industrial world of the 1920s. Follett saw workers as complex combinations of attitudes, beliefs, and needs. Follett believed that effective motivational management existed in partnership and cooperation, and that the ability to persuade people was far more beneficial to everyone than hierarchical control and competition (Mary Parker Follett, 2002). The human

relations movement was significant in that it changed management thinking to focus on the behavior of people and the human components in the workplace rather than on the scientific approach to performing a task.

Today, it is common to view the study of human behavior within organizations as a combination of the scientific management and human relations approaches. **Organizational behavior** (OB) characterizes the modern approach to management. The field of organizational behavior is involved with the study and application of the human side of management and organizations (Luthans, 2005). Organizations have undergone numerous changes over the past decades, including downsizing, globalization, installation and usage of information technology, and an increasingly diverse workforce. Managers have been preoccupied with restructuring their organizations to improve productivity and meet the competitive challenges created by organizational changes. Through all the organizational changes and evolution of management thought and practices, one thing remains clear: The lasting competitive advantage within organizations comes through human resources and how they are managed (Luthans, 2005). Current management theory stresses the concepts of employee involvement, employee empowerment, and managers' concern with the human component of employees. Topics explored within organizational behavior research include communication, decision making, leadership, and motivation, among others. However, the essence of organizations is productivity, and thus managers need to be concerned with getting the job done.

In looking at the study of management theory, we can see how the approaches to management have moved from the simple to the complex, from a job orientation to a people (worker) orientation, from the manager as a dictator and giver of orders to the manager as a facilitator and team member. Human beings, though, are complex and sometimes illogical, and therefore no one method of management can guarantee success. The role of managers can be challenging as they try to assess the needs of their employees and utilize appropriate skills to meet the needs of the employees, all while also getting the job done.

■ FUNCTIONAL AREAS

Sport managers must perform in a number of functional areas and execute various activities in fulfilling the demands of their jobs. Some of the functional areas used to describe what managers do include planning, organizing, leading, and evaluating (Chelladurai, 2009). Although these functional areas may be helpful in providing a general idea as to what a manager does, these terms and their descriptions do not provide a comprehensive list. Organizations are constantly evolving, as are managers and the activities they perform. The functional areas used here describe an overall picture of what a manager does, but keep in mind it is impossible to reduce a manager's activities to the level of a robot following a set pattern of activities.

Planning

The **planning** function includes defining organizational goals and determining the appropriate means by which to achieve these desired goals (Gibson, 2006). Planning involves setting a course of action for the sport organization (VanderZwaag, 1998). Based on VanderZwaag's (1984) model, Hums and MacLean (2008) define the planning process as establishing organizational mission statements, goals, objectives, tactics, roles, and evaluation. It is important to keep in mind that the planning process is continuous. Organizational plans should change and evolve—they should not be viewed as set in stone. In case of problems or if situations arise causing the goals of the organization to change, the sport manager must be ready to adjust or change the organizational plan to make it more appropriate to what the organization is trying to accomplish.

The planning process consists of both short- and long-term planning. Short-term planning involves goals the organization wants to accomplish soon, say within the next couple of months to a year. For example, an athletic shoe company may want to order enough inventory of a particular type of shoe so its sales representatives can stock the vendors with enough shoes to meet consumer demands for the upcoming year. Long-term planning involves goals the organization may want to try to reach over a longer period of time, perhaps five to ten years into the future. That same shoe company may have long-term goals of becoming the number one athletic shoe company in the nation within five years, so the company's long-term planning will include activities the company will participate in to try to reach that goal. Managers must participate in both short- and long-term planning.

The planning process also includes ongoing and unique plans. An example of an ongoing plan would be a parking lot plan for parking at every university home football game. A unique plan might involve use of that same parking lot as a staging area for emergency vehicles if the city were hit by an unexpected natural disaster such as a flood or tornado.

Organizing

After planning, the sport manager next undertakes the **organizing** function. The organizing function is all about putting plans into action. As part of the organizing function, the manager determines what types of jobs need to be performed and who will be responsible for doing these jobs.

When determining what types of jobs need to be performed, an organizational chart is developed (**Figure 2-1**). An organizational chart shows the various positions within an organization as well as the reporting schemes for these positions. In addition, an organizational chart may contain information about the people filling the various positions. After an organizational chart has been put together, the next step is to develop position descriptions for the various positions within the organizational chart. These position descriptions are important in defining the tasks and responsibilities for each position. The position descriptions define responsibilities and indicate the authority accompanying each position. For example, the position description of the Assistant Athletic Director for Marketing may include soliciting corporate sponsors, promoting teams or special events, and selling stadium signage. Finally, position qualifications must be developed. Position qualifications define what is needed in the person filling a particular position. Position qualifications will depend on the organizational chart, the responsibilities of a particular position, and the authority given to a particular position. Thus, the position qualifications for the Assistant Athletic Director for Marketing may include a master's degree, three to five years' athletic department experience, and good written and oral communication skills.

The need for a well-developed and well-communicated organizational chart cannot be overemphasized. On numerous occasions organizations may find problems starting to occur because one person does not know what another person in the organization is doing. The organizational chart can be extremely beneficial in showing employees the various positions within the organization, who fills those positions, the responsibilities of each position, and who reports to whom. Once the organizational chart has been developed and the position qualifications established, staffing can take place.

Staffing determines who will be responsible for the jobs in the organizational chart. Staffing involves the effective recruitment and selection

of people to fill the positions within an organization. The position qualifications developed during the organizing function come into play here. Recruiting and selecting an employee means finding the right person, with the appropriate qualifications, to get the job done. To find that person, managers must do their homework and go through the proper steps to really get to know and understand the people they interview. These steps include appropriate advertising of the position, reviewing completed applications, choosing qualified people for the interview process, checking references, and selecting the "best fit" person for the job.

In addition to the selection process, staffing includes the orientation, training, and professional development of staff members (Quarterman & Li, 1998; VanderZwaag, 1984). Orientation introduces the new person to the

FIGURE 2-1 Athletic Department Organizational Chart

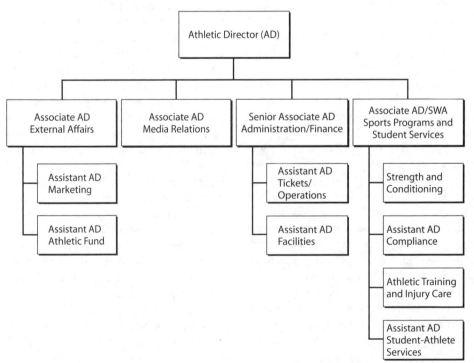

nature of the organization, to organizational goals and policies, and to his or her fellow employees. Training focuses on the actual job and teaching the employee how to do the job. For example, new ushers may be involved in a half-day training seminar to learn seating arrangements, locations of first aid stations and uniformed security, and procedures for checking in and out of work. Professional development involves a commitment to improving the employees' knowledge, skills, and attitudes, allowing them the opportunity to grow and become better employees. For example, sending athletic department employees to a week-long seminar on new technology used in the workplace is one way development can occur. Unfortunately, many sport organizations are so busy trying to do the day-to-day work that they ignore the development of their employees. Professional development can help lead to more efficient and productive workers.

Leading

The **leading** function has often been referred to as the "action" part of the management process. This is where it all happens. The sport manager is involved in directing the activities of employees as he or she attempts to accomplish organizational goals. In carrying out the leading function, the manager participates in a variety of activities, including delegating, managing conflict, managing change, and motivating employees. In carrying out these activities, the manager utilizes numerous skills, which are discussed in the next section of this chapter.

The leading function begins with the process of **delegation**, which involves assigning responsibility and accountability for results to employees. Effective communication is critical to the delegation process. Employees need to know what they are being asked to do and need to be assigned the appropriate authority to get the job done. The importance of delegation cannot

be overstated, yet it is one of the most difficult skills for new managers to acquire. One's first inclination is simply to "do it myself" so that a task will get accomplished the way the individual manager wants. Realistically, it is impossible for one person to do everything. Could you imagine if the general manager of a Major League Baseball team tried to do everything? In addition to making personnel decisions and negotiating contracts, the person would be broadcasting the game, pulling the tarp, and selling beer! Also, delegation plays an important part in new employees learning to be sport managers. Just as a coach allows substitutes to slowly learn the game plan until they are ready to be starters, so too do sport managers allow their subordinates to hone their managerial skills via delegation.

The leading function also requires the manager to take on a leadership role and manage any differences or changes that may take place within the organization. Ultimately, the manager is responsible for the employees and how they perform their duties. The manager must handle any types of conflicts, work problems, or communication difficulties so that the employees can achieve their goals. The manager also must be ready to stimulate creativity and motivate the employees if needed. Thus, the manager takes on a very active role in the operations of the organization when performing the leading function.

Evaluating

The manager performs the **evaluating** function by measuring and ensuring progress toward organizational objectives. This progress is accomplished by the employees effectively carrying out their duties. The manager evaluates the workers by establishing reporting systems, developing performance standards, comparing employee performance to set standards, and designing reward systems to acknowledge successful work on the part of the employees. Position descriptions, discussed earlier in this chapter, are important in the evaluating function as well, for they establish the criteria by which employee performance is measured.

The reporting system involves the collection of data and information regarding how a job is being performed. For example, the director of corporate sponsorship for an event would collect information on how many sponsorship packages the local corporate sponsorship representative has sold. This information would be reported to the event director. Developing performance standards sets the conditions or expectations for the employee. In the previous example, the local corporate sponsorship representative, in conjunction with the director, would determine how many local sponsorship packages should be sold. Employee performance can then be evaluated based on how well (or poorly) the employee did in meeting these performance standards. Finally, a reward system should be put in place so employees believe their work is noticed and appreciated. Recognition for good performance and accomplishments helps motivate employees to reach their job expectations. Employees will not be motivated to reach the performance standard placed before them if they believe they will not be rewarded or recognized in some way. There will also be times, however, when employees do not meet the levels of performance expected of them. Managers must deal with these situations, which may be quite unpleasant. It is necessary to have a plan in place to help employees adjust their work efforts in order to be successful, and a plan in place to deal with employees who may need to be asked to leave the organization.

As mentioned previously, managerial functions involve a manager performing a number of activities requiring various skills. The next section discusses the skills managers use when fulfilling their job responsibilities.

■ KEY SKILLS

People Skills

As mentioned earlier, the most important resources in any sport organization are the human resources—the people. The sport management industry is a "people-intensive" industry. Sport managers deal with all kinds of people every day. For example, on a given morning a ticket manager for a minor league baseball team may have the task of meeting with chief executive officers or chief financial officers of local businesses to arrange the sale of stadium luxury boxes. That afternoon, he or she may be talking with the local Girl Scouts, arranging a special promotion night. The next morning may bring a meeting with the general manager of the team's Major League Baseball affiliate to discuss ticket sales. Before a game, a season ticket holder may call to complain about his or her seats.

Managers in professional sport interact with unique clientele. On the one hand, they deal with athletes making millions of dollars. On the other hand, they deal with the maintenance crew, who may merely be paid minimum wage. The sport manager must be able to respond appropriately to each of these different constituencies and keep everyone in the organization working as a team. Using interpersonal skills and promoting teamwork are two valuable ways sport managers utilize their people skills (Bower, 2009). Without proper **people skills**, the sport manager is destined to fail. Learning to treat all people fairly, ethically, and with respect is essential for the sport manager's success.

Communication Skills: Oral and Written

The importance of mastering both oral and written **communication skills** cannot be overstated (Bower, 2009). Sport managers deal with all kinds of people on a daily basis, and knowing how to say something to a person is equally as important as knowing what to say to that person. Communication may take place one-on-one with employees or customers, or in a large group setting. When questions arise, people will call wanting help, such as a person with a disability who has questions about parking and stadium access. Sometimes people just need general information, such as when the next home event takes place. To sport managers, sometimes these types of questions begin to seem mundane and repetitive. However, the sport manager must remember that for the person asking the question, this may be the first time he or she asked it, and this instance also may be his or her first personal contact with anyone in the organization. Answering each question professionally and courteously wins a lifelong fan. Being rude or uncooperative only ensures an empty seat in your arena or stadium. Remember: People who have had bad experiences talk to others, which may result in the loss of other existing or potential fans.

Being representatives of their sport organizations, sport managers are often asked to give speeches to community groups, schools, and business leaders. Sport managers need to learn how to give a proper oral presentation to a group. What are some basic tips to remember before giving a presentation? To assess one's readiness to give a presentation, one should consider the following (Hartley & Bruckman, 2002, p. 304):

1. Do you have clear objectives?
2. Do you know your audience?
3. Do you have a clear structure?
4. Is your style of expression right?
5. Can you operate effectively in the setting?

After thinking about those questions, you need to have a plan for your presentation. To help to organize yourself for a presentation, Gallagher, McLelland, and Swales (1998) offer the following suggestions:

- Set your objective.
- Analyze the audience.
- Analyze the setting.
- Write down the central theme.
- Write your outline.
- Develop your visual aids.
- Prepare your delivery notes.
- Deliver the presentation.

No doubt in your sport management classes you will have numerous opportunities to practice and perfect your oral presentation skills!

In addition to oral communication skills, successful sport managers need excellent written communication skills. Sport managers must be able to write in many different styles. For example, a sports information director needs to know how to write press releases, media guides, season ticket information brochures, interoffice memos, and business letters to other professionals, as well as lengthy reports that may be requested by the athletic director or

university faculty. Coaches need to be able to write solid practice plans, letters to parents or athletes, and year-end reports on a team's status. A marketing researcher for a footwear company has to write extensive reports on sales, consumer preferences, and product awareness. Remember: Professional writing is *not* the same as writing text messages. Always write using complete sentences and never include texting abbreviations! Usage of e-mail for business communication purposes needs to follow a succinct, professional approach. Knowing how to communicate facts and information in an organized, readable fashion is truly an art, one a sport manager must master to be successful.

Managing Diversity

Diversity is a fact of life in today's sport workplace and there is a need to include more women, people of color, and people with disabilities at the managerial level in the sport industry. "Diversity—often mistakenly confused with old-style equal opportunities—refers to any differences between individuals, including age, race, gender, sexual orientation, disability, education, and social background. Such differences can affect how people perform and interact with each other in the workplace, hence the need for a diversity management programme" ("Remember Five Things," 2003, p. 31). More recently, Cunningham (2007, p. 6) defined diversity as "the presence of differences among members of a social unit that lead to perceptions of such differences and that impact work outcomes. This definition highlights (a) the presence of differences, (b) the dyadic or group nature of diversity, (c) the manner in which actual differences can influence perceptions of such heterogeneity, and (d) the impact diversity has on subsequent outcomes."

The face of the U.S. workforce is changing rapidly. In 2008, minorities accounted for approximately 34.4% of the workforce (U.S. Equal Employment Opportunity Commission, 2008). Women hold approximately 50.8% of managerial positions in the workforce (U.S. Department of Labor, 2008). Information from the National Organization of Disability indicates that approximately 18% of all Americans (54 million people) have a disability (National Organization of Disability, 2010).

As a part of the greater business community, the sport industry must keep pace with this diversification in the workplace and encourage the inclusion of people of diverse cultures into the management of sport. However, there has been increasing discussion about how well the sport industry is doing in that regard (Lepovsky, 2009). The latest data in the 2009 Racial and Gender Report Card (Lapchick, 2009) revealed that 89.2% of all NCAA Division I head coaches of men's sports were white males, and only 7.2% were African-American males. In 2009, white athletic directors held 90.0% of the NCAA Division I positions, with African Americans holding 7.2%. Women increased slightly in representation among Division I athletic directors from 7.3% in 2004 to 7.8% in 2009.

At the senior administration level, 17% of Major League Baseball employees were people of color, while women occupied 18% of these positions. In the NBA during 2008–2009, there were five African-American CEO/presidents and one additional African-American president of basketball operations. The NBA also maintained the percentage of women with 18% of total team vice president positions.

The Rooney Rule has helped the NFL to double the number of African-American head coaches in recent years, from three in 2003 to six in 2009. As of July 2009, the NFL reached a record high of five African-American general managers. The history of NFL teams regarding the hiring of women is poor. The percentage of women did increase slightly in the team vice presidents category but dropped in professional administration. In Major League Soccer (MLS), there were three women and two persons of color among the 42 vice presidents for MLS teams in 2009.

These representative statistics illustrate how women and minorities are still underrepresented in managerial positions in the sport industry (Lapchick, 2009). Concerns over the lack of women, minorities, and people with disabilities in management positions in sport has also been well documented in several other areas of sport, including the sporting goods and retail industry (Alleyne, 2005), facility management (*Street & Smith's SportsBusiness Journal*, 1999), campus recreation (Bower & Hums, 2003), sport for people with disabilities (Hums, Moorman, & Wolff, 2003), the Olympic Movement and Paralympic Movement (Döll-Tepper, 2010; Hums, 2010a; Women's Sports Foundation, 2009), and athlete representation (Hong, 2005; Shropshire & Davis, 2003). Additional research is definitely needed in these industry segments to track progress in diversifying the workforce. The underrepresentation of women, minorities, and people with disabilities in the sport industry is an important issue for sport managers who value diversity in the workplace.

The employment process, from hiring through retention through the exiting of employees from an organization, has become a much more complex process than in the past. Given the low number of women, minorities, and people with disabilities in leadership positions in the sport industry, steps must be taken to increase opportunities for access to the industry. When undertaking to follow ethical considerations for including all qualified individuals in the employment process, each phase of the employment process should be examined. These stages include recruitment, screening, selection, retention, promotion, and ending employment. The following suggestions offer concrete steps that sport managers can take to successfully manage diversity in the sport industry (Hums, 1996):

- Be knowledgeable about existing labor laws related to discriminatory work practices.
- Be knowledgeable about existing affirmative action guidelines for the employment process.
- Increase knowledge and awareness of multiculturalism.
- Be knowledgeable and supportive of issues of importance to all groups in the workplace.
- Write statements about valuing diversity into the organization's code of ethics.
- Expand personal and professional networks to include those of different races, genders, physical abilities, and social classes.
- Act as a mentor to people of diverse cultures in one's sport organization.
- Be courageous enough to "buck the system" if necessary. This is indeed a personal challenge and choice. A sport manager who perceives discrimination or discriminatory practices within a sport organization should speak out against these practices.

The North American workforce is rapidly changing and diversifying. Sport leaders must be aware of how this trend will affect their sport organizations. By being proactive and inclusive, sport leaders can ensure that all qualified individuals have an opportunity to work in the sport industry, allowing for the free exchange of new and diverse ideas and viewpoints, resulting in organizational growth and success. Sport leaders advocating this proactive approach will have organizations that are responsive to modern North American society and will be the leaders of the sport industry.

Managing Technology

Technology is evolving more and more rapidly every day, and **managing technology**—that is, being familiar with technology and using it to one's advantage—is something every manager should strive for. Managers need to be aware of technological advances in two ways. The first is the usage of technology in the sport industry. This includes customer data collection and advanced ticketing systems. Second, managers must be current and proficient with technological skills for usage in the workplace, such as video conferencing and multimedia presentations.

The Internet and the World Wide Web have become pivotal sources of information on a variety of subjects. Computerized ticketing systems such as Paciolan and Prologue are used on a daily basis by professional sport teams, major college athletic departments, theme parks, and museums. According to CBS Interactive,

> *Founded in 1980, Paciolan is a leading ticketing enabler, providing ticketing, fundraising and marketing technology solutions for top venues across North America. Collectively, Paciolan clients sell over 100 million tickets annually representing approximately 25 percent of all live event tickets sold in the U.S. (CBS Interactive, 2005, para. 7).*

The latest development in ticketing is M-ticketing, which is a bar-coded ticket bought over the phone or online that can be sent to a customer's mobile phone for scanning through the turnstiles at a stadium entrance (Bisson, 2010). Also, computerized ticketing systems are encouraging digital marketing and promotions, such as Paciolan's "PACMail," which provide real-time reporting and analyses that measure the performance of client e-mail marketing campaigns. By incorporating marketing and promoting online ticket sales, season renewals, subscriptions, and last-minute incentives, professional organizations and collegiate athletics departments are able to maximize ticket sales (Paciolan, 2010).

Online surveys are being used for data collection by sport teams and organizations, providing information on such things as fan demographics, purchasing decisions, and brand identity. Numerous sport teams have kiosks in their stadiums or arenas where fans can fill out in-game surveys, providing valuable information about those attending the game. Baseball has invested in programs called the MLB Media Tracker and Fan Tracker, a collection of demographic information distributed to executives involved in the game (Miller, 2003).

In addition, sport managers use technology to access these data via their laptops and transform them into analyzed information for presentation to sponsors. Students will also need to be aware of how sport organizations are using social networking sites such as Facebook and Twitter to promote their athletes, teams, and products (Hambrick et al., 2010). With the explosion of the Internet and other multimedia interactive technologies, sport managers and sport management educators are now facing new challenges: how to analyze and benefit from the effects of ever-expanding technologies on the sport industry and how to educate future sport managers who are entering into this exciting high-tech world.

Decision Making

People make decisions every day, ranging from simple to complex. Any decision we make consists of two basic steps: gathering information and then analyzing that information. For example, when you got up this morning, why did you choose the clothes you have on? Because they matched? Because they were clean? Because they were on the top of the clothes pile? Because of the weather? Because you had a presentation to give in class? Although this is a relatively simple decision (for most people), other decisions are more complex. Think about choosing a college major: What made you decide to major in sport management as opposed to management or accounting or theater management? A decision like that involves **decision making** on a much deeper level.

Sport managers have to make decisions on how to pursue opportunities or solve problems every day. Sport managers, therefore, need to have a comprehensive understanding of the opportunity or problem and engage in a decision-making process that will lead to an effective decision. The classic model of decision making has four steps (Chelladurai, 2009):

1. *Problem statement/framing the problem.* This first step involves defining the goal to be achieved or the problem that needs to be solved.
2. *Generating alternatives.* The next step involves determining as many courses of action or solutions as possible.
3. *Evaluate alternatives.* The evaluation of each alternative identified takes place in this step. This evaluation may involve cost determination, risk identification, and the effects the alternative will have on employees.
4. *Select the best alternative.* The manager makes and implements the final decision here. Following an organized decision-making process helps ensure consistent decision making throughout the sport organization and assures that no piece of important information is overlooked.

There is one other consideration for sport managers when making decisions: When is it necessary to include group input and feedback in the decision-making process? **Participative decision making** involves employees or members of the organization in the actual decision-making process. There are benefits as well as drawbacks to using the participative decision-making process within an organization. According to Chalip (2001), groups can be used in a number of decision-making situations, including planning, idea generation, problem solving, agenda setting, governance, and policy making. He suggests that group decision making should be used when more ideas need to be generated, there is a great deal of information to share, alternative perspectives are needed, and the fairness of the decision is highly valued. Another consideration is the effect on others' jobs. The more an individual's job may be affected by the decision, the more outside input the decision maker should seek before making the decision.

Organizational Politics

What is meant by the term **organizational politics**? Gray and Starke (1988) note that political behavior occurs when people use power or some other resource outside of the formal definition of their jobs to get a preferred outcome. Although it is somewhat intangible and hard to measure, politics pervades all sport organizations (Slack & Parent, 2006). Organizational politics and political behavior are met with mixed results. Some people believe that political behavior is demeaning and possibly destructive to an organization. Others view politics as a way of accomplishing goals and objectives. Whatever their beliefs on the subject, sport managers must be aware of the presence of politics within their organization and the different types of political tactics people may use. Four generally accepted types of political tactics used in organizations are as follows (Slack & Parent, 2006):

1. Building coalitions with others so as to increase a person's political power
2. Using outside experts to support or legitimize a person's position
3. Building links or creating a network of contacts with people inside and outside the organization
4. Controlling information, thereby influencing decisions and the outcomes of decisions within the organization

What is most important for future sport managers is that they learn to be aware of the political environment around them. Who is truly the most "powerful" person in a sport organization? Sport organizations, like all organizations, have two different types of leaders: formal and informal. The formal leader is a leader because of title, such as athletic director, director of community relations, or store manager. The formal leader may indeed be the person who holds the most power in an organization and is able to influence employees in achieving organizational goals. Informal leaders, by contrast, are leaders because of the power they possess from knowledge, association, or length of time with an organization. Informal leaders may be very influential in terms of what takes place within an organization. For example, if the coaches in an athletic department are trying to convince the athletic director to make some sort of change, the coaches may ask the coach who has been there for many years, knows the ins and outs of the organization, and knows how to persuade the athletic director to speak on their collective behalf. Alternatively, the coaches may ask the coach of the team with the largest budget or one of the higher-profile coaches to talk to the athletic director about making this change. Identifying the informal leaders in an organization can help new sport managers understand the politics of a sport organization.

Managing Change

Sport organizations change on a daily basis. New general managers are hired, teams move into new facilities, league policies and rules change, health clubs purchase new fitness equipment, and environmental use laws affect state or national park recreation areas. Change can be internally driven, such as a professional sport team implementing a new ticket distribution system, or externally driven, such as changes dictated by new government regulations or changes in consumer demand. Just as life is all about adapting to change, so, too, the sport industry is all about adapting to change.

Although most change happens without major resistance, sport managers have to be aware that people tend to resist change for a number of reasons, including: fear of failure, creatures of habit, no obvious need for change, loss of control, concern about support system, closed minded, unwillingness to learn, fear that the new way may not be better, fear of the unknown, and fear of personal impact (Peter Barron Stark Companies, 2010). For example, a sales representative for a sporting goods company who is assigned to a new geographic area may resist because he or she is scared about getting a new territory (fear of the unknown), may be concerned that the potential for sales and commissions is lower in the new territory (the new way may not be better), may have had friends in the old territory (concern about support system), may now have a territory not as highly regarded in the company (fear of personal impact), may wonder if he or she will be able to establish new contacts (unwillingness to learn), or may just see the change as another hassle (no obvious need for change). Although not all of these reasons may be present, sport managers need to be aware of what employees may be thinking.

How, then, should sport managers effectively implement change in the workplace? When **managing change**, managers should do the following ("Implementing an Effective Change Program," 2002, pp. 504–505):

1. Appreciate the depth of employees' resistance to change. Plan for resistance and provide additional training and communications.
2. Select priorities for change instead of attempting to address everything at once.

3. Plan to deliver early tangible results and publicize successes to build momentum and support.
4. Involve employees at every stage of designing and implementing change.
5. Make sure top management and sponsors are fully committed to the agreed implementation.

Sport managers need to be keenly tuned into how employees are responding to change so that any resistance can be dealt with fairly and honestly.

Motivation

The ability to motivate employees to strive to achieve organizational goals and objectives as well as their personal goals and objectives is an art form. For example, both a head coach and a player for an NBA team want their team to win. However, the player also knows that his personal game statistics will determine his salary. As a head coach, how do you motivate a player to be a "team player" (organizational goal) while still allowing him to maximize his personal statistics (personal goal)?

Theories of **motivation** abound, with works including Maslow's hierarchy of needs, Herzberg's two factor ideas, Vroom's expectancy theory, and Adam's equity theory (Luthans, 2005). After reviewing these and other theories, Katzell and Thompson (1990) point out seven practices that can raise the level of employee motivation:

- Ensure that workers' motives and values are appropriate for the jobs in which they are placed.
- Make jobs attractive to and consistent with workers' motives and values.
- Define work goals that are clear, challenging, attractive, and attainable.

- Provide workers with the personal and material resources that will facilitate their effectiveness.
- Create supportive social environments.
- Reinforce performance.
- Harmonize all of these elements into a consistent socio-technical system.

Motivating employees on a daily basis is a constant challenge to any sport manager. For any sport organization to be successful, it is critical for everyone to be on the same page when it comes to working to accomplish organizational goals and objectives.

Taking Initiative

"What else needs to be done?" Sport managers should be ready to ask this important question at any time. When evaluating employees, one of the characteristics an employer in the sport industry looks for is **initiative** (Robinson et al., 2001). No doubt, speaker after speaker from the sport industry has or will come into your classroom and talk about the importance of taking initiative in his or her sport organization. This will be especially true when you do your internship. When you have the opportunity to help out with an additional task, take advantage of that opportunity. First, it may enable you to learn about a different aspect of the sport organization with which you are working, and learning is a valuable skill in and of itself (Bower, 2009). Second, it may allow you to meet and interact with people outside of the office you work in, thus increasing your network. Finally, it shows your employer your commitment to working in the industry. Working in the sport industry is not always easy. The hours are long, the pay is low, and the work is seemingly endless. People in the organization recognize when someone is willing to do what is necessary to make sure an event happens as it should. Remember, "First impressions last," so leave the impression at your workplace that you are willing to work hard and take initiative.

■ CURRENT ISSUES

Diversity in the Workforce

As mentioned in the previous section, the demographics of the North American workforce are ever-changing. Sport management professionals need to stay abreast of these changes. Women, racial/ethnic minorities, people with disabilities, people from different nations, and people with various religious backgrounds all contribute to the sport industry. Sport organizations embracing diversity will be seen as the leaders in the twenty-first century. Sport managers need to stay on top of the latest legislation and managerial theories in their efforts to help their organizations become truly multicultural. In addition to staying knowledgeable about the current status of diversity in the sport management workforce, it is important for sport managers to be proactive. One suggestion is for sport managers to perform a self-study of their organization to evaluate their effectiveness in terms of recruiting and employing women, racial/ethnic minorities, people with disabilities, and people from different nations and religious backgrounds. The development and implementation of strategies involving recruitment and employment methods can then take place to encourage diversity in the workplace.

Managing Technology

As mentioned earlier, the technology that sport managers work with is changing every day. Sport managers need to be aware of how these changes affect the segment of the sport industry in which they work and how new technology can be incorporated into the workplace. It is imperative for sport managers to understand how expanding technology will improve customer relations and service. Internet sites such as Universal Sports, ParalympicSport.TV, and ESPN3 are changing how fans consume sport media. Social networks now heavily influence sport organizations, and many sport consumers are Facebook and Twitter users. Just as the computer replaced the typewriter and e-mail and text messaging are replacing phone correspondence, the next wave of technology will affect how sport managers run their daily business operations.

International Sport Management

Sport management is not unique to North America. Sport, and with it the field of sport management, continues to grow in popularity throughout the world. For example, Europe has a number of successful major professional soccer and basketball leagues as well as motor sports events. The Olympic Games, the Paralympic Games, the World Cup, and other multinational events are important elements of the sport industry.

In addition, U.S. professional sports leagues are increasingly exporting their products around the world. The NBA has 16 offices around the world, and is organized 442 events in 191 cities in 30 countries in 2009 (Stack, 2010). The NFL has broadcast packages for international TV viewers (ESPN MediaZone, 2010). An NFL regular season game is held at London's Wembley Stadium (NFL London, 2009). MLB focuses on worldwide growth and international activities through Major League Baseball International (MLBI) (MLB International, 2010). Opening Day series were played in Japan for the past three years, and 2010 saw exhibition games between the Dodgers and Padres in China (Major League Baseball, 2010). The World Baseball Classic continues to create excitement among fans from many nations. Sport managers from North America working abroad must be aware that they cannot unilaterally impose domestic models of sport governance on other cultures. Differences exist in terms of language, culture, etiquette, management, and communication styles. Sport managers need to learn, understand, and respect these differences when working in the international sport marketplace.

New Management Theories

Management theory and approaches to management are constantly changing, with new thoughts and ideas taking hold on a regular basis. Two of the more recent approaches to management are empowerment and emotional intelligence. **Empowerment** refers to the encouragement of employees to use their initiative and make decisions within their area of operations (Luthans, 2005). Workers within the organization are provided with appropriate information and resources in making these decisions. As such, empowerment encourages innovation and accountability on the part of the employee (Luthans, 2005). The idea behind empowerment is that the employee will feel more a part of the organization, be more motivated, and therefore perform more effectively. In his book *Good to Great* (2001), Jim Collins conducted research on those companies that achieved long-term success and superiority. His findings support the empowerment approach to management and identify a culture of discipline common among "great" companies. Collins found that good-to-great companies build a consistent system with clear constraints, but they also give people freedom and responsibility within the framework of that system. They hire self-disciplined people who don't need to be managed, and then manage the system, not the people (Collins, 2001).

Emotional intelligence** was first defined in the 1980s by John D. Mayer and Peter Salovey but has received more attention with the studies of Daniel Goleman (Goleman, 1997).

People at work may experience a variety of different emotions, both positive and negative. These emotions can be detrimental to the work process and organizational work environment. Emotional intelligence refers to the ability of workers to identify and acknowledge these emotions when they occur, and instead of having an immediate emotional response, to take a step back, allowing rational thought to influence their actions (Goleman, 1997).

■ BEYOND THE BOTTOM LINE

As we move through the twenty-first century, sport managers are more accountable than ever for looking at how their organizations can act in a socially responsible manner (Babiak & Wolfe, 2009; Bradish & Cronin, 2009). Sport managers now need to think about how their organizations will contribute to society in relation to issues such as sport and the environment, sport and human rights, and sport for development and peace (Hums, 2010b). These are new skill sets and knowledge areas for managers in the sport industry, but they are becoming more and more essential in the international sport marketplace.

■ SUMMARY

Sport managers today face ever-changing environments. One constant, however, is the necessity to successfully manage the sport organization's most valuable resource: its people. The workforce of the twenty-first century will be vastly different from the workforce of even the recent past. The influence of people of different cultures, rapidly changing technology, and the globalization of the marketplace all make it necessary for tomorrow's sport managers to adapt. The measures of a good sport manager are flexibility and the ability to move with changes so that the sport organization and, more importantly, the people within that sport organization continue to grow and move forward successfully into the future.

Functional areas of management have been used to explain and prepare managers for the various activities they get involved in as a result of their management role. These functional areas include planning, organizing, leading, and evaluating. In fulfilling these functional activities of management, managers employ a variety of skills essential to success as a manager. The skills discussed within this chapter included people skills, communication skills (oral and written), diversity management skills, managing technology management, decision-making skills, organizational politics awareness, managing change, motivating employees, and initiative.

Sport managers in today's sport organizations need to be aware of ever-changing management thought and ideas, to learn from these theories, and to incorporate what works best within their organizations. Sport managers also need to think of their organizations in terms of being good corporate citizens. Management is all about finding the best way to work with the employees to get the job done. The fact that there is no one best way to manage underscores the excitement and challenge facing managers today.

■ KEY TERMS

communication skills, decision making, delegation, diversity, emotional intelligence, empowerment, evaluating, human relations movement, initiative, leading, managing change, managing technology, motivation, organizational behavior, organizational politics, organizing, participative decision making, people skills, planning, scientific management

■ REFERENCES

Alleyne, S. (2005 June). Count on this: New report on the number of blacks on corporate boards. *Black Enterprise*. Retrieved October 5, 2010, from http://findarticles.com/p/articles/mi_m1365/is_11_35/ai_n13798755/

Babiak, K., & Wolfe, R. (2009). Determinants of corporate social responsibility in professional sport: Internal and external factors. *Journal of Sport Management, 23*(6), 717–742.

Badenhausen, K., Ozanian, M.K., & Settimi, C. (2010a August 25). The most valuable NFL teams. *Forbes.com*. Retrieved November 10, 2010, from http://www.forbes.com/2010/08/25/most-valuable-nfl-teams-business-sports-football-valuations-10-intro.html

Badenhausen, K., Ozanian, M.K., & Settimi, C. (2010b, April 7). The business of baseball. Forbes.com. Retrieved November 10, 2010, from http://www.forbes.com/2010/04/07/most-valuable-baseball-teams-business-sportsmoney-baseball-valuations-10_land.html

Badenhausen, K., Ozanian, M.K., & Settimi, C. (2009a, December 9). The business of basketball. Forbes.com. Retrieved November 10, 2010, from http://www.forbes.com/2009/12/09/nba-basketball-valuations-business-sports-basketball-values-09-intro.html

Badenhausen, K., Ozanian, M.K., & Settimi, C. (2009b, November 11). The business of hockey. Forbes.com. Retrieved November 10, 2010, from http://www.forbes.com/2009/11/11/nhl-team-values-business-sports-hockey-values-09-intro.html

Bisson, M. (2010 October 15). Arriva's m-ticketing gets smart. Retrieved November 10, 2010, from http://www.arrivabus.co.uk/content.aspx?id=10705

Bower, G.G. (2009). *A guide to field experiences and careers in sport and physical activity*. Deer Park, NY: Linus Publications.

Bower, G.G., & Hums, M.A. (2003). Career considerations of women working in the administration of campus recreation. *Recreational Sport Journal, 27*(2), 21–36.

Bradish, C., & Cronin, J.J. (2009). Corporate social responsibility in sport. *Journal of Sport Management, 23*(6), 691–697.

CBS Interactive. (2005, November 4). USC partners with PACIOLAN on ticketing system. Retrieved October 5, 2010, from http://gamecocksonline.cstv.com/genrel/110405aaa.html

Chalip, L. (2001). Group decision making and problem solving. In B. Parkhouse (Ed.), *The management of sport* (3rd ed.). New York: McGraw-Hill.

Chelladurai, P. (2009). *Managing organizations for sport and physical activity: A systems perspective* (3d ed.). Scottsdale, AZ: Holcomb Hathaway.

Chmielewski, D.C., & Johnson, G. (2007 June 28). NBA contract takes digital leap forward. *Los Angeles Times.* Retrieved October 5, 2010, from http://articles.latimes.com/2007/jun/28/business/fi-espn28

Collins, J. (2001). *Good to great.* New York: HarperCollins Publishers Inc.

Cunningham, G.B. (2007). *Diversity in sport organizations.* Scottsdale, AZ: Holcomb Hathaway Publishers.

Döll-Tepper, G. (2010). Winning women! Towards increasing the number of women in leadership positions. Retrieved October 5, 2010, from https://congress.cc.jyu.fi/wsfa2010/schedule/proceedings/pdf/1252.pdf

Dvorchack, R. (2008 November 10). Vintage Penguins jerseys selling up a blue streak. *Pittsburgh Post-Gazette.* Retrieved October 5, 2010, from http://www.post-gazette.com/pg/08315/926805-61.stm

Elton Mayo. (2002). In *Business: The ultimate resource* (pp. 1020–1021). Cambridge, MA: Perseus Publishing.

ESPN MediaZone. (2010 April 1). ESPN America and NFL extend partnership with four-year agreement. *ESPN MediaZone.* Retrieved October 5, 2010, from http://www.espnmediazone3.com/us/2010/04/espn-america-and-nfl-extend-partnership-with-four-year-agreement-2

Frederick Winslow Taylor. (2002). In *Business: The ultimate resource* (pp. 1054–1055). Cambridge, MA: Perseus Publishing.

Gallagher, K., McLelland, B., & Swales, C. (1998). *Business skills: An active learning approach.* Oxford: Blackwell.

Gibson, J.L. (2006). *Organizations: Behavior, structure, processes* (12th ed.). Chicago: Richard D. Irwin.

Goleman, D. (1997). *Emotional intelligence.* New York: Bantam Books.

Gray, J.J., & Starke, F.A. (1988). *Organizational behavior: Concepts and applications* (4th ed.). Columbus, OH: Merrill Publishing Company.

Hambrick, M.E., Simmons, J.M., Greenhalgh, G.P., & Greenwell, T.C. (2010 May). Examining the use of Twitter in sport: A content analysis of professional athlete tweets. Presented at the annual North American Society for Sport Management, Tampa, FL.

Hartley, P., & Bruckman, C.G. (2002). *Business communication.* London: Routledge.

Hong, E. (2005 June 12). Female agents a rarity in team sports. *ESPN.com: SportsBusiness.* Retrieved October 5, 2010, from http://sports.espn.go.com/espn/sportsbusiness/news/story?id=2079652

Hums, M.A. (1996). Increasing employment opportunities for people with disabilities through sports and adapted physical activity. In *Proceedings from the Second European Conference on Adapted Physical Activity and Sports: Health, well-being and employment.* Leuven, Belgium: ACCO.

Hums, M.A. (2010a). Women in the Olympic movement. In K. O'Connor (Ed.), *Gender and women's leadership. A reference handbook.* Thousand Oaks, CA: Sage Publishing.

Hums, M.A. (2010b). The conscience and commerce of sport management: One teacher's perspective. Earle F. Zeigler Lecture. *Journal of Sport Management, 24*(1), 1–9.

Hums, M.A., Barr, C.A., & Gullion, L. (1999). The ethical issues confronting managers in the sport industry. *Journal of Business Ethics, 20,* 51–66.

Hums, M.A., & MacLean, J.C. (2008). *Governance and policy in sport organizations* (2d ed.). Scottsdale, AZ: Holcomb Hathaway.

Hums, M.A., Moorman, A.M., & Wolff, E.A. (2003). The inclusion of the Paralympics in the Olympic and Amateur Sports Act: Legal and policy implications for the integration of athletes with disabilities into the United States Olympic Committee and national governing bodies. *Journal of Sport and Social Issues, 23*(3), 261–275.

Implementing an effective change program. (2002). In *Business: The ultimate resource* (pp. 504–505). Cambridge, MA: Perseus Publishing.

International Health, Racquet and Sportsclub Association. (2010). About the Industry. Retrieved October 5, 2010, from http://cms.ihrsa.org/index.cfm?fuseaction=page.viewpage&pageId=18735

Katzell, R.A., & Thompson, D.E. (1990). Work motivation: Theory and practice. *American Psychologist, 45,* 144–153.

Lapchick, R. (2009). 2009 racial and gender report card. Orlando, FL: University of Central Florida, Institute for Diversity and Ethics in Sport. Retrieved October 5, 2010, from http://www.tidesport.org/racialgenderreportcard.html

Lepovsky, L. (2009 November). The White House Project report: Benchmarking women's leadership. Retrieved October 5, 2010, from http://www.thewhitehouseproject.org/documents/Report.pdf

Luthans, F. (2005). *Organizational behavior* (10th ed.). Boston: McGraw-Hill.

Mary Parker Follett. (2002). In *Business: The ultimate resource* (pp. 988–989). Cambridge, MA: Perseus Publishing.

Major League Baseball. (2010). News and features. Retrieved October 5, 2010, from http://mlb.mlb.com/mlb/international

Miller, S. (2003 June 16). Major investment in research part of playing the demographics game. *Street & Smith's SportsBusiness Journal, 22.*

MLB International. (2010). Overview. Retrieved November 10, 2010, from http://mlb.mlb.com/mlb/international/sections.jsp?feature=mlbi

National Organization on Disability. (2010). About us. Retrieved October 5, 2010, from http://www.nod.org/about_us

NFL London. (2009, October 5). NFL London 2010. Retrieved October 5, 2010, from http://www.nfllondon.net

Paciolan. (2010). Retrieved November 10, 2010, from http://paciolan.com/solutions/marketing

Peter Barron Stark Companies. (2010 January 12). Why employees resist change. Retrieved November 10, 2010, from http://www.peterstark.com/why-employees-resist-change

Quarterman, J., & Li, M. (1998). Managing sport organizations. In J.B. Parks, B.R.K. Zanger, & J. Quarterman (Eds.), *Contemporary sport management* (pp. 103–118). Champaign, IL: Human Kinetics.

Remember five things. (2003). *Personnel Today,* 31.

Robinson, M., Hums, M. A., Crow, B., & Phillips, D. (2001). *Profiles of sport management professionals: The people who make the games happen.* Gaithersburg, MD: Aspen Publishers.

Shropshire, K.L., & Davis, T. (2003). *The business of sports agents.* Philadelphia: University of Pennsylvania Press.

Slack, T., & Parent, M. (2006). *Understanding sport organizations* (2nd ed.). Champaign, IL: Human Kinetics.

Stack, K. (2010 May 3). The NBA's global plan. Retrieved October 5, 2010, from http://www.slamonline.com/online/nba/2010/05/the-nbas-global-plan

Street & Smith's SportsBusiness Journal. (1999 November 8). Support industry. *Street & Smith's SportsBusiness Journal,* 25.

U.S. Department of Labor. (2008). Household data annual averages. Retrieved October 5, 2010, from http://www.bls.gov/cps/cpsaat9.pdf

U.S. Equal Employment Opportunity Commission. (2008). 2008 EEO-1 national aggregate report, United States, 2008. Washington, DC: Author.

VanderZwaag, H.J. (1984). *Sport management in schools and colleges.* New York: John Wiley & Sons.

VanderZwaag, H.J. (1998). *Policy development in sport management* (2nd ed.). Westport, CT: Praeger.

Wieberg, S., & Hiestand, M. (2010, April 22). NCAA reaches 14-year deal with CBS/Turner for men's basketball tournament, which expands to 68 teams for now. *USAToday.com.* Retrieved October 5, 2010, from http://content.usatoday.com/communities/campusrivalry/post/2010/04/ncaa-reaches-14-year-deal-with-cbsturner/1

Women's Sports Foundation. (2009). Women in the 2000, 2004, and 2008 Olympic and Paralympic Games: An analysis of participation, leadership, and media opportunities. Retrieved October 5, 2010, from http://womenssportsfoundation.org/~/media/Files/Research%20Reports/2008Olympicreport%202010.pdf

CHAPTER 3

Marketing Principles Applied to Sport Management

Sheranne Fairley, Tracy Schoenadel, James M. Gladden, and William A. Sutton

■ INTRODUCTION: WHAT IS SPORT MARKETING?

How does Major League Baseball (MLB) reverse the trend of waning interest among youth? How can the Seattle Storm of the Women's National Basketball Association (WNBA) sell more tickets? How does your local health club increase memberships? What events, athletes, or teams should Mountain Dew sponsor? How can Major League Soccer (MLS) increase its television ratings? How will conference realignment change the college landscape? How can Australian Rules Football penetrate the American sportscape? These questions and many others fall under the purview of sport marketing.

As defined by Kotler (2003, p. 5), "Marketing is typically seen as the task of creating,

promoting, and delivering goods and services to consumers and businesses." Functions such as product development, advertising, public relations, sales promotion, and designing point-of-sale materials are all covered within this definition. However, Kotler ultimately boils the marketer's job down to one action: creating demand (2003). If the marketer can cause a consumer to want a product, then that marketer has been successful. To do this, marketing entails identifying customer wants and needs, and then identifying ways to satisfy them. According to Ries and Trout (1993, p. 106), "Brilliant marketers have the ability to think like a prospect thinks. They put themselves in the shoes of the consumer." Demand for a product will continue only as long as consumers see a value to it in their lives. As such, one of the marketer's greatest challenges is to obtain the best possible understanding of what consumers want.

Sport marketing, therefore, consists of all activities designed to meet the needs and wants of sport consumers. According to this definition, sport marketing includes the marketing of (a) products, such as equipment, apparel, and footwear; (b) services and experiences, such as attendance at a sporting match or participation in sport; (c) entities, such as leagues, teams, or individuals; and (d) the recruitment and retention of volunteers as a **relationship marketing** exercise. Further, the sport marketer must think outside of their home stadium and consider providing an experience to attend away games, events, or tournaments through the development of sport tourism product. Much of this chapter focuses on the marketing of leagues, teams, and individuals. This chapter also focuses on the use of sport promotion to market consumer and industrial products through **sponsorships**, partnerships, and or/endorsements.

HISTORICAL DEVELOPMENT OF SPORT MARKETING

Given the multifaceted nature of the definition of sport marketing, there are a variety of significant historical developments relating to key sport marketing concepts. These developments arose to more effectively communicate with **target markets**, the group of consumers to whom a product is marketed. In some cases these concepts were utilized as the result of experimentation, in other cases because of the intuitive nature of the sport marketer, and in still other cases because they were found to be successful in mainstream business marketing. It is widely viewed that Mark McCormack and his agency, International Management Group (IMG), invented sport marketing in the late 1960s. What started as a one man show, McCormack and IMG created their niche in sport

marketing from athlete representation to sponsorship rights fees to television broadcasts. IMG's influence in sports can be felt in over 26 major countries. In a 1990 *Sports Illustrated* article, McCormack predicted that Southeast Asia was going to be the center of future sports growth, followed by South America and Africa (Swift, 1990). With the 2008 Olympics in Beijing, the World Cup (2014) and Olympics (2016) being awarded to Brazil, and the 2010 World Cup located in South Africa, his predictions were correct. The legacy of McCormack, along with the reach, scope, and vertical integration of IMG, continues to impact the industry. For more on McCormack, IMG, and sports agencies generally, see Chapter 11.

This section examines a number of these key concepts, along with the innovators responsible for these developments. We have separated these developments into four categories: the evolution of sport broadcasting, the growth of sponsorship, the development of promotional strategies, and the birth of research in sport marketing.

The Evolution of Sport Broadcasting

Beyond the actual broadcasting of sporting events, first on the radio, then on television, and now on the Internet and handheld wireless devices (as detailed in Chapters 16, 17, and 18), one of the most dynamic changes in sport marketing was the evolution of sport broadcasting from pure, factual reporting aimed at sports fans to sport entertainment aimed at the masses. This was achieved most notably through the efforts of ABC's Monday Night Football television program and an ABC executive named Roone Arledge. Arledge was the first person to recognize that sports televised in prime time had to be more than sport—it also had to be entertainment. He incorporated that philosophy into Monday Night Football through the use of three broadcast personalities: initially sports journalist Howard Cosell; the voice of college football, Keith Jackson (who would be replaced the next year by Frank Gifford); and former National Football League (NFL) star Don Meredith. In doing so, Arledge "was the first executive who refused to let sports owners or leagues approve the announcers" (Bednarski, 2002, p. 41). Arledge also instituted more cameras and more varied camera angles, video highlights of the preceding day's games, commentary, criticism, humor, and wit. From these beginnings, Monday Night Football has become a sports institution.

When asked about his approach and view that sport was entertainment, Arledge responded that his job was "taking the fan to the game, not taking the game to the fan" (Roberts & Olson, 1989, p. 113). Arledge wanted the viewer sitting in his or her living room to see, hear, and experience the game as if he or she were actually in the stadium:

What we set out to do in our programming (College Football, Monday Night Football, Wide World of Sports, and the Superstars to name a few) was to get the audience involved emotionally. If they didn't give a damn about the game, they might still enjoy the program (Roberts & Olson, 1989, p. 113).

Arledge's innovations—most notably instant replay, multiple cameras, crowd mikes, and sideline interviewers—added to the enjoyment of the program.

The manner in which Monday Night Football (and other Arledge creations, such as the Wide World of Sports—a 1970s and 1980s favorite) married sport and entertainment paved the way for the success of other sports in prime time, and today represents the norm. Think about it: When was the last time you saw a National Basketball Association (NBA) Finals game, or MLB World Series game on during the daytime? This confluence of sport and entertainment is

now visible 24 hours a day through ESPN. From the zany nicknames and commentary offered by Chris ("Boomer" or "Swami" depending on the persona) Berman, to the Top Ten List and Did You Know? features on SportsCenter, ESPN has expanded into a global multimedia brand with seven U.S. networks (ESPN, ESPN2, ESPN3D, ESPN Classic, ESPNU, ESPN News, Spanish-language ESPN Desportes) and 46 international networks reaching all seven continents, ESPN radio and ESPNDeportes Radio (syndicated in 11 countries), restaurants, games and shopping (ESPN Zone), and popular Web sites (ESPN .com, ESPNDeportes.com, and market-specific sites) (ESPN, 2010). Today, we have seen additional growth in sport-dedicated networks such as the Big Ten Network, Mountain West Network, Versus, and Spike TV. Further, the televised experience has changed substantially in recent times with the introduction of High Definition Television (HDTV) and Three Dimensional Television (3DTV). The evolution of broadcasting is also international in scope. Viewers can now follow almost any team, sport, or event live from anywhere in the world through an array of international broadcasting options. Internationally, the World Cup has been televised since 1954. However, the 1970 World Cup broadcast from Mexico in color is largely credited with the growth of international sports television as a whole. During this early time, the growth of international television was also sparked by Olympic and Track and Field content.

The Acceptance and Growth of Sport Sponsorship

Sponsorship, or "the acquisition of rights to affiliate or directly associate with a product or event for the purpose of deriving benefits related to that affiliation" (Mullin, Hardy, & Sutton, 2000, p. 254), is not a recent phenomenon. The very first collegiate athletic event, an 1852 rowing contest between Harvard and Yale, was held in New Hampshire and sponsored by a railroad company. Coca-Cola has been a sponsor of the Olympic Games since 1928 (Coca-Cola Company, 2006). Sugar (1978) has documented the early roles of such companies as Coca-Cola, Bull Durham Tobacco, Curtiss Candy Company, Chalmers Motor Car Company, Purity Oats, American Tobacco Company, and Gillette in exploiting the country's interest in sport through sport promotions, contests, advertising, and the use of sport personalities as endorsers. A picture of a professional baseball stadium from the early 1900s shows many signs on the outfield wall. Although the money involved may seem insignificant by today's standards, these early activities set the tone for what is perceived to be acceptable and advantageous in today's marketplace.

There have been, and continue to be, many pioneers in sport sponsorship and corporate involvement related to sport. One of the earliest pioneers was Albert G. Spalding, a former professional baseball player who parlayed his fame into what at one time was one of the largest sporting goods manufacturing companies in the world. Spalding was the first marketer to capitalize on the term official as it relates to a sport product, when his baseball became the "official baseball" of the National League in 1880 (Levine, 1985). Having secured the "official" status, Spalding then marketed his baseball as the best because it had been adopted for use in the National League, the highest level of play at that particular time. In the consumer's mind, this translated to the following: "Why choose anything but Spalding? If it is good enough for the National League, it must be superior to any other product in the market." Spalding carried over this theme when he began producing baseball uniforms for the National League in 1882. Such a practice is still prevalent today. Think for a moment—what company makes the highest-quality football or basketball? Why is that your perception?

Whereas Spalding had the most profound impact on sport sponsorship in the latter part of the nineteenth century, two forces had a tremendous impact on sport sponsorship in the latter half of the twentieth century. The first was Mark McCormack, who built the sport marketing agency IMG from a handshake with legendary golfer Arnold Palmer in 1960 (Bounds & Garrahan, 2003). At the time, Palmer was the most popular professional golfer. McCormack capitalized on this popularity by securing endorsement contracts for Palmer, helping companies promote and sell their products. As a result, Palmer's earnings skyrocketed and paved the way for McCormack to sign other popular golfers, such as Jack Nicklaus and Gary Player. Today, IMG represents thousands of athletes worldwide, including Tiger Woods.

Nike was the second significant force affecting sponsorship in the second half of the twentieth century. From its beginning as Blue Ribbon Sports in 1964 (an American offshoot of the Onitsuka Tiger brand), to its emergence as a brand in 1972, to its dominant role in the industry today, Nike has faced numerous challenges and emerged victorious on every front. One of the key elements in the history of Nike and its role in the world today was the packaging of the Nike brand, product, advertising, and athlete into one personality. This was achieved when Nike and Michael Jordan created "Air Jordan" (Strasser & Becklund, 1991). Understanding the impact of an athlete on footwear sales, and having experienced disloyalty among some of its past endorsers, Nike sought to create a win–win situation by involving the athlete—in this case, Jordan—in the fortunes of the product. Nike looked at the long term and created a package that provided royalties for Jordan not only for shoes but for apparel and accessories as well. It was Nike's opinion that if a player had an incentive to promote the product, he or she became a member of the "team." The result of this strategy was the most successful athlete endorsement in history, with more than $100 million of Air Jordan products being sold in a single year (Strasser & Becklund, 1991). More recently, Nike has continued to partner with not only premier athletes but also premier athletes with unique identities. From its successful endorsement of one-of-a-kind golfer Tiger Woods to its 2003 endorsement of the highly promoted basketball phenomenon LeBron James, Nike regularly strives to identify with athletes who personify the best.

Beyond athlete endorsements, Nike has been extremely influential in other aspects of sponsorship. In an attempt to associate with the best college athletic programs, Nike initiated and signed university-wide athletic sponsorship agreements with major athletic programs such as the University of Michigan (now with adidas) and the University of North Carolina (still with Nike). This has been a trend followed by Nike competitors Reebok and adidas. Throughout the 1990s, Nike was also known for how it increased business while not paying to be "an official sponsor." Perhaps most visibly at the Atlanta Summer Olympic Games in 1996, Nike was very adept at **ambush marketing**—capitalizing on the goodwill associated with an event without becoming an official sponsor. Even though Nike was not an International Olympic Committee (the governing body overseeing the Olympics) sponsor, many people thought it was. To create this impression, Nike employed a variety of strategies. Among them, Nike turned a parking garage in close proximity to the Olympic Village into a "mini-Niketown" experience that included autograph sessions and appearances from Nike athletes such as track star Michael Johnson. Ambush marketing and sponsorship in general are discussed in more depth in Chapter 15, Sport Sponsorship.

Sponsorship has expanded its look and feel over the past 10 years. Whether they are larger events such as the Olympics and World Cup or a local soccer club, the dynamics of the sponsorship have penetrated far beyond field signage and television mentions. The digital era is evolving sponsorship into mobile phones applications. Further, some of the sanctities of sponsorship in the United States are slowly diminishing. For example, naming rights of teams, and sponsor logos on team uniforms are no longer off limits as companies such as Red Bull are branding teams in their image with the creation of the New York Red Bulls.

Emphasis on Product Extensions and Development of Promotional Strategies

The emphasis on product extensions and the development of team sport promotional strategies can be attributed to the late Bill Veeck (1914–1986), a sport marketing pioneer in professional baseball for almost 40 years. At various times from the 1940s through the 1970s, Veeck was the owner of the Cleveland Indians, the St. Louis Browns, and the Chicago White Sox (on two different occasions). Prior to Veeck, sporting events were not staged for the masses but rather for the enjoyment of sports fans. Veeck recognized that to operate a successful

and profitable franchise, one could not totally depend upon the success of the team to generate capacity crowds. In other words, Veeck believed that a team must provide reasons other than the game itself for people to attend and support the franchise.

Several philosophies guided much of Veeck's efforts and left a lasting legacy on how sport is promoted. First, Veeck was firm in his belief that fans came to the ballpark to be entertained (Holtzman, 1986). Veeck's promotional philosophy embraced the goal of "creating the greatest enjoyment for the greatest number of people . . . not by detracting from the game, but by adding a few moments of fairly simple pleasure" (Veeck & Linn, 1962, p. 119). Promotions and innovations attributed to Veeck include giveaway days like Bat Day, exploding scoreboards, outfield walls that went up and down, fireworks, and the organizing of special theme nights for students, Scouts, and church groups (Veeck & Linn, 1962).

Second, Veeck recognized that to build a loyal fan base, the attending experience had to be pleasurable: "In baseball, you are surprisingly dependent upon repeat business. The average customer comes to the park no more than two or three times a year. If you can put on a good-enough show to get him to come five or six times, he has become a source of pride and a source of revenue" (Veeck & Linn, 1965, p. 20). In addition to being entertaining, part of creating loyal customers entailed ensuring the best possible attending atmosphere. As such, Veeck focused on providing a clean facility and a hospitable environment. He carried out this philosophy by enlarging bathrooms, adding daycare facilities, greeting his "guests," and standing at the exits to thank them for coming.

Finally, Veeck suggested:

It isn't enough for a promotion to be entertaining or even amusing; it must create conversation. When the fan goes home and talks about what he has seen, he is getting an additional kick out of being able to say he was there. Do not deny him that simple pleasure, especially since he is giving you valuable word-of-mouth advertising to add to the newspaper reports (Veeck & Linn, 1965, p. 13).

In an effort to have people talk about their experience, Veeck devised unique and unorthodox promotions such as "Grandstand Managers" night, in which a section of the audience voted on what a manager should do in a particular situation. While Veeck was often criticized for his practices (and they were quite radical), his legacy is still visible today throughout sport events.

The Birth of Research in Sport Marketing to Improve Performance and Acceptance

Although some early pioneers like Veeck communicated well with their customers through informal contacts, letters, and speaking engagements, Matt Levine is the individual most often credited with formalizing customer research in the sport industry. Like Veeck, Levine was well aware that there were marketing variables other than winning and losing. Employed as a consultant by the Golden State Warriors in 1974 and given the goal of increasing attendance, Levine developed what he termed an "audience audit" to capture **demographic** and **psychographic** information about fans attending games (Hardy, 1996). Levine was also a pioneer in using intercepts (one-on-one on-site interviews) and focus groups (discussion groups involving 8 to 12 individuals with similar characteristics discussing a predetermined agenda) to gather marketing information for professional sport franchises.

The purposes of Levine's research and, for that matter, most research in sport marketing, are as follows:

- To profile the sport consumer demographically, geographically, or psychographically
- To categorize attendance behavior and segment attendance by user groups related to potential ticket packages
- To analyze purchasing behavior as it relates to product extensions such as merchandise, concessions, and so on
- To evaluate operational aspects of the sport product such as parking, customer service, entertainment aspects, and employee courtesy and efficiency
- To measure interest in new concepts that may be under consideration
- To document viewing and listening behavior
- To understand the consumer's information network so as to determine efficient methods of future communication to that consumer and like consumers
- To offer two-way communication with the target market

One of the most successful applications of Levine's market research techniques involved the National Hockey League's (NHL's) San Jose Sharks. Levine used a series of what he calls **"pass-by interviews"** or **intercept interviews**. Pass-by interviews are on-site interviews in heavy-traffic areas such as malls. These interviews utilize one or more visual aids and assess the interviewee's reaction to the visual aid. The visual aid is usually a sample or interpretation of a product (style, color, or logo) under consideration. Levine's pass-by interviews were used to determine the reaction of people who had submitted ticket deposits for the expansion San Jose Sharks to a series of proposed logo and uniform designs. The results of Levine's research efforts? The color scheme under consideration was eliminated and the graphic logo of the shark was changed. In 1992, the new logo and colors resulted in estimated retail sales of Sharks' merchandise in the United States and Europe of $125 million (Hardy, 1996). As a result of Levine's approach and success with his clients and their acceptance of his methods and findings, market research in the sport industry is increasingly becoming a common practice rather than the exception. Although consumer research continues to be very popular, today's research tends to focus more on sponsorship evaluation such as brand fit, commitment and loyalty, media exposure, digital impact, and one of the toughest concepts, Return on Investment (ROI), or Return on Objectives (ROO).

■ KEY SPORT MARKETING CONCEPTS

The Sport Marketing Mix

As defined by McCarthy and Perreault (1988), the **marketing mix** refers to the controllable variables the company puts together to satisfy a target group. The marketing mix, then, is the recipe for creating a successful marketing campaign. The elements of the marketing mix most commonly associated with sport are often referred to as the "four Ps": product, price, place, and promotion (Kotler, 2003). In sport marketing, we often refer to the "five Ps" with the inclusion of public relations as its own P (instead of being included as part of promotion), given the significant role it plays in sport marketing. In comparison with the marketing of a laundry detergent, soup, car, or stereo, there are some unique aspects of marketing the sport product that must be accounted for when discussing the marketing mix. Some of the most important differences are presented in **Table 3-1**. These differences and their relevance to sport marketers will be discussed throughout the rest of this chapter.

■ PRODUCT

Whereas marketing sporting goods is similar to marketing mainstream products because

TABLE 3-1 Some Key Differences Between Traditional Marketing and Sport Marketing	
Traditional Marketing	**Sport Marketing**
• The success of any entity may depend on defeating and eliminating the competition.	• In many cases, sport organizations must simultaneously compete and cooperate.
• Very few consumers consider themselves experts and instead rely on trained professionals for information and assistance.	• Due to the preponderance of information and the likelihood of personal experience and strong personal identification, sport consumers often consider themselves experts.
• Customer demand is more predictable because the product is always the same.	• Consumer demand tends to fluctuate widely.
• When a customer purchases a sweater, it is tangible and can be seen and felt and used on more than one occasion.	• The sport product is invariably intangible, subjective, and heavily experiential.
• Mainstream products have an inventory and a shelf life, and supplies can be replenished.	• The sport product (the game) is simultaneously produced and consumed; there is no inventory.
• Although other people can enjoy the purchase of a car, the enjoyment or satisfaction of the purchaser does not depend upon it.	• Sport is generally publicly consumed, and consumer satisfaction is invariably affected by social facilitation.
• Inconsistency and unpredictability are considered unacceptable—for example, if a particular car occasionally went backward when the gear indicated forward, consumers would be up in arms.	• The sport product is inconsistent and unpredictable.
• The mainstream marketer works with research and design to create the perceived perfect product.	• The sport marketer has little or no control over the core product and often has limited control over the product extensions.
• Only religion and politics, which in and of themselves are not viewed as products or services but rather as beliefs, are as widespread as sport.	• Sport has an almost universal appeal and pervades all elements of life.

tangible benefits can be provided, marketing a sporting event (such as a minor league baseball game), a sport service (such as a health club), or even an athlete is different. There has been some debate as to what constitutes the "core" product in sport marketing. For example, some posit that the core product is the actual event. On the other hand, if we applied a mainstream marketing definition, the "core" product is the *benefit* that consumers seek from a product, service, or experience, therefore taking the

focus off the actual event. Thus, for an Ladies Professional Golf Association (LPGA) event, one side would view the core product as the golfers on the course, whereas the counterargument would name the core product as the benefits that consumers received from attending the event that may or may not be related to what actually happens on the course. Spectators at the event and television viewers cannot touch or taste the product—they merely experience it. Further, spectators and viewers have no idea who is going to win the event. Such unpredict-ability is both an advantage and a disadvantage for sport marketers. In one sense, it allows the sport marketer to promote the fact that fans don't want to miss out on a chance to see something spectacular. However, from another perspective, the sport marketer cannot entice people to attend by promising success for a par-ticular athlete or team. In fact, in nearly all cases relating to spectator sport, the sport marketer has little control over the core product. Again, however, this depends on what one views as the core product. The vice president of marketing for the LPGA cannot orchestrate who will win the LPGA championship. The chief marketing officer (CMO) for the Dallas Mavericks of the NBA cannot do anything to enhance the chances that the Mavericks will win.

The sport marketer must account for these unique differences relating to the sport product. For example, because the sport marketer has little control over what happens on the playing surface, he or she must focus on the extensions surrounding the game that can be managed. This is where the works of Veeck, who employed a variety of tactics to enhance the attending experience beyond what happened on the field, are important lessons. For example, if you were to attend almost any NBA game today, you would be entertained during every time-out with on-court performances and the extensive use of video boards to provide an interactive with fans as they are able to text messages and often view themselves on the big screen.

■ PRICE

Like any other product, most sport products have a price associated with them. A variety of products within the sport industry must be priced: tickets, health club memberships, satel-lite television packages, special access areas on sport Web sites, and so on. When attending an event, there is usually more than one price.

For example, beyond the cost of a ticket, the attendee may have to pay to park or to purchase concessions or a souvenir.

Increasingly, the cost of a ticket is separated into the actual ticket price and an additional charge per ticket for access to premium services such as restaurants or waiter/waitress service. Because the sport product is often intangible and experiential, the price of the sport product often depends on the value (or perceived value) provided by the sport product or experience. Consumers can perceive a higher price to mean higher quality. However, the sport marketer needs to be careful to balance perceived value versus perceived quality. Using concessions at a new MLB stadium as an example, just because a Coca-Cola costs $5 does not mean that the consumer will perceive it to be a good value because it is of high quality. Further, in a time when both ticket prices associated with profes-sional sport and the costs of ancillary items such as concessions have risen dramatically, sport marketers are challenged to provide at-tendees with more value than ever. A consumer attending an event considers the entire cost of attending when determining the value of the event. This cost includes both the monetary costs (such as the ticket price, concessions, and parking) and the personal cost of attending (which includes the time it takes to travel to a stadium or arena).

■ PLACE

The typical mainstream product is made at a manufacturing site and then transferred to a location where it is available for customers to purchase. Further, most products have a shelf life; that is, if they are not bought today, they can still be sold tomorrow. Neither condition is true when examining team sports and events. The place where the product is produced (the stadium or arena) is also the place where the product is consumed. Further, once a game is over, the tickets for that game cannot be sold. What would happen if someone offered to sell you tickets to one of your favorite team's games that had already happened? You would laugh, right? Because of these unique nuances associated with the place at which the sport product is distributed, sport marketers must aggressively pre-sell sporting events.

Although there are some unique differences associated with place in sport marketing, there are also some similarities to mainstream marketing. Location can be very important. People talk about going to Wrigley Field in Chicago for a variety of reasons, including the history and tradition of the facility as well as its location in a popular North Chicago neighborhood. Similarly, the location of a health club can be vitally important to its success. Referring back to Veeck again, facility aesthetics also play an important role. Veeck believed in a clean facility. From 1990 to present, MLB experienced a surge in new ballparks with "retro" features that reminded fans of baseball parks from the early 1900s. Further, the amenities available in new stadiums or health clubs can be a very important part of the place a sport product is sold. Because the sport consumption experience is a social one, most new stadiums and arenas have significant space dedicated to upscale restaurants and bars. One of the newest and most fan-friendly stadiums is Cowboys Stadium. Opened in 2009, it is 3 million square feet and seats 80,000 spectators, but it can comfortably accommodate 100,000 thanks to fan-friendly, standing-room-only spaces among the facility. There are 2,900 television screens (not to mention the largest center video board) throughout the facility, making it virtually impossible to miss a play on the field no matter where a fan may be seated. Traditions and the atmosphere of facilities are a vital part of the fan experience. Vuvuzela horns at the 2010 Fédération Internationale de Football Association (FIFA) World Cup in South Africa, the Pagoda at Indianapolis Motor Speedway, or the Green Monster at Fenway Park are fixtures in their fans experience. As facilities expand, renovate and/or begin new construction, the fan experience is invoked by the facility. Today, it is difficult to go to a major sporting facility that does not offer a tour for interested fans.

■ PROMOTION

Promotion typically refers to a variety of functions, including advertising (paid messages conveyed through the media), personal selling (face-to-face presentation in which a seller attempts to persuade a buyer), publicity (media exposure not paid for by the beneficiary), and sales promotion (special activities undertaken to increase sales of a product) (Mullin, Hardy, & Sutton, 2000). In undertaking sport promotion, the unique aspects of sport marketing are important to understand. Sport entities often both compete and cooperate. For example, the Chicago White Sox will probably heavily promote the fact that the New York Yankees are visiting in an effort to increase attendance for the Yankees series, even though they are competing with the Yankees on the field. In fact, in many cases, a sport team's competition may help it draw fans.

In promoting sport, the sport marketer must also take into account the unpredictable and experiential nature of the product. The Seattle Storm of the WNBA would probably promote the chance to have a good time while watching a Storm game instead of promising a Storm win. Staying with the experiential nature of sport, promotion can help offer a tangible aspect through the use of souvenir sales or giveaways. A fan who receives a LeBron James bobblehead doll after attending a Miami Heat game is likely to remember that attending experience.

Sponsorships typically try to take advantage of all of the elements of promotion. Consider the MasterCard "Priceless" ad campaign as an example. Sponsorship plays a very large role in portraying priceless moments. Because Master-Card is a sponsor of MLB, it is able to create advertising featuring priceless moments associated with following professional baseball. In addition, it creates publicity by holding promotions such as selecting the 50 greatest baseball players of all time. Further, MasterCard's sponsorship allows the company to create promotions that will increase card acceptance and utilization. Finally, these sponsorships create hospitality opportunities at events such as the MLB's All-Star Game, where MasterCard can host personnel from banks that either offer a MasterCard or could offer a MasterCard as a means of increasing its business from these banks.

Segmentation

As opposed to mass marketing, where an organization markets its products to every possible consumer in the marketplace, **segmentation** entails identifying subgroups of the overall marketplace based on a variety of factors, including age, income level, ethnicity, geography, and lifestyle tendencies. Although the sport product has nearly universal appeal, it would still be foolish of sport marketers to market their product to the entire population. A target market is a segment of the overall market that has certain desirable traits or characteristics and is coveted by the marketer. These traits or characteristics can be (a) demographic, such as age, income, gender, or educational background; (b) geographic, such as a region or a postal code; (c) psychographic, lifestyles, activities, or habits; or (d) product usage, such as type of beer they drink, car they drive or credit card they use most often. Using a women's college basketball program as an example, target markets could include girls aged 8 to 18 (age segmentation) who play organized basketball (psychographic segmentation) within 30 miles of the university campus (geographic segmentation).

Two increasingly popular bases of segmentation are ethnic marketing and generational marketing. As of 2009, 15.8% of the U.S. population was Hispanic (U.S. Census Bureau, 2009). Recognizing the fact that the Hispanic population is a fast-growing and large segment of the U.S. population, sport teams now attempt to market directly to Hispanics through such strategies as producing radio broadcasts and Web sites in Spanish. For example, ESPN has created ESPN Deportes, a United States–based Spanish-language network targeted to Hispanics (Liberman, 2003). The MLS in particular pays particular attention to the Hispanic market. Almost half of the MLS' league office staff is Latino, it has more Spanish-speaking TV partners than any other U.S. league, and the league hosts SuperLiga, InterLiga, and Mexican national team appearances in the United States.

Sport marketers also are expending significant energies to reach Generation Y (people born between 1977 and 1996). This segment is unlike others in that—in addition to mainstream sports such as football, basketball, and baseball—Generation Y consumers are very interested in "action" sports such as skateboarding and motocross. For sports such as MLB, this presents a challenge as it relates to creating future generations of fans.

Another base of segmentation receiving increased attention is product usage segmentation as it relates to attendance at sporting events. This tactic assumes that the consumption of people who attend a few games per year can be increased. Teams naturally have information about all people who purchased single-game tickets during a given season. Using these data, the sales force for a given team will call someone after that person has attended a game and inquire about the experience. If the fan had an enjoyable time at the game, then the salesperson will attempt to sell the fan additional games or a partial season ticket package of five or eight games. This strategy is commonly adopted by teams that have excess seats to sell.

Fan Identification

Fan identification is defined as the sense of oneness with or belongingness to an organization (Bhattarcharya, Rao, & Glynn, 1995). In theory, the more a fan identifies with a team or organization, the greater the likelihood the fan will develop a broad and long-term relationship with that team and attach his or her loyalty to the organization. Sport is unique in the significant fan identification it engenders among its consumers. Think about it: Are you more emotionally connected to your toothpaste or your favorite sports team? Manifestations of fan identification are everywhere. Message boards, painting one's face, and wearing logo apparel are all ways in which sports fans demonstrate their connection to a team. When you talk about your favorite team's games, do you refer to your favorite team as "we" or "they"? Many people refer to their team as "we" (especially after a team wins) although they have no direct impact on the team's performance. This is an example of high fan identification. Beyond teams, recent research suggests that fans may also identify with an array of elements including coaches, individual players, smaller subgroups of fans, or with sports in general.

Fan identification also is very important for sponsors of sporting events. Ideally, a sponsor will be able to tap into some of the strong emotional connection between a fan and his or her sport team through a sponsorship. For example, it is often thought that sponsors of National Association of Stock Car Auto Racing (NASCAR) drivers earn the business of the drivers' fans through association with the race team. Similarly, it could be argued that a sponsorship with the Dallas Cowboys or New York Yankees, each of which has a large group of vocal and loyal supporters, could result in increased business, at least in part due to the ability to capitalize on the strong identification that exists with each of these teams.

Relationship Marketing

If marketers adopt relationship marketing strategies, they can help foster identification with sport teams. According to Kotler (2003, p. 13), "relationship marketing has the aim of building mutually satisfying long-term relations with key parties—customers, suppliers, distributors—in order to earn and retain their business." Rather than looking at consumers as transactions, relationship marketing suggests that organizations seek to build long-term relationships with their customers, ultimately converting them to or maintaining them as loyal product users (Berry, 1995). Relationship marketing begins with the customer and in essence encourages the organization to integrate the customer into the company; to build a relationship with the customer based upon communication, satisfaction, and service; and to work to continue to expand and broaden the involvement of the customer with the organization. In effect, this integration, communication, service, and satisfaction combine to create a relationship between the consumer and the organization (McKenna, 1991). The implementation of relationship marketing practices is often called **customer relationship management**.

In addition to sport organizations seeking to develop and sustain a lasting relationship with sport fans, relationship marketing is also key in the recruitment and retention of a volunteer workforce. Many sport organizations and events rely on the ongoing contributions of volunteers to run and sustain their operations. Therefore, it is key to develop relationships with these volunteers who provide an ongoing commitment and service to the organization.

▪ KEY SKILLS

Because marketing is a form of communication, the key skills involved in sport marketing are communication based and are in many ways similar to the key skills outlined in Chapter 2, Management Principles Applied to Sport Management.

1. *Oral communication:* The ability to speak in public, speak to large groups, and make persuasive presentations demonstrating knowledge about the product and its potential benefit to the consumer.
2. *Written communication:* The competence to prepare sales presentations, reports, analyses, and general correspondence in a concise and insightful manner.
3. *Data analysis skills:* The use of data to inform the decision-making process. Whether it be projecting the return on investment for a sponsorship program or analyzing a customer database to identify the organization's best customers, quantitative skills are increasingly in demand in sport organizations.
4. *Computer capabilities:* Beyond basic word processing skills, expertise in all types of software, including databases, spreadsheets, desktop publishing, ticketing systems, Web page design and utilization, and social media tools. In particular, in-depth knowledge of presentation software (such as Microsoft's PowerPoint) is important to the preparation of professional presentations.
5. *Personnel management:* The skills to develop, motivate, and manage a diverse group of people to achieve organizational goals and objectives.
6. *Sales:* The ability to recognize an opportunity in the marketplace and convince potential consumers of the value and benefits of that opportunity. Part of identifying opportunities is understanding the wants and needs of consumers. Therefore, listening is a very important, yet often overlooked, skill for anyone in a sales capacity.
7. *Education:* A minimum of a bachelor's degree in sport management or a bachelor's

degree in business with an internship in a sport setting. A master's degree in sport management or a master of business administration (MBA) degree, although not essential in some positions, is desirable for advancement and promotion.

Finally, the successful marketer must also understand the sport product. It is not essential for the marketer to be a dedicated follower of the sport; however, the marketer must comprehend the sport product, know its unique differences, and know how these differences assist and hinder the marketing of the sport product.

■ CURRENT ISSUES

Because the development of trained sport management professionals is a relatively new occurrence (over the past 40 years or so), innovation in sport marketing practices has traditionally lagged behind innovation in other service indus-

tries, in mainstream marketing, and in business in general. However, in recent years, certain approaches and philosophies have begun to be accepted and have become widespread in the sport industry. Yet, as sport moves forward in the twenty-first century, it faces a variety of challenges that will require an increased focus on marketing innovation and sophistication. Some of these challenges, as well as practices being developed to adapt to them, are discussed in this section.

The Rising Cost of Attending a Sporting Event

Table 3-2 depicts the drastic increase in the overall cost of attending an MLB, NBA, or NFL game from 1991 to 2009. In an era when owners have become more focused on bottom-line performance (in some cases due to the assumption of millions of dollars of debt associated with new stadiums), ticket prices and the overall cost of attending a major professional event in North America have increased dramatically.

TABLE 3-2 Comparison of the Average Ticket Prices and Cost of Attending an MLB, NBA, NFL, and NHL Game in 1991 and 2009

	1991		2009			
League	Average Ticket Price	Average Cost of Attending	Average Ticket Price	Average Cost of Attending	Increase in Ticket Price	Increase in Cost of Attending
MLB	$9.14	$79.41	$26.74	$197.17	193%	148%
NBA	$22.52	$141.91	$49.47	$291.93	120%	106%
NFL	$25.21	$151.33	$72.20	$396.36	186%	162%
NHL	n/a	n/a	$49.66	$288.23	n/a	n/a

Sources: Brown, M. (2009 April 2). Average ticket price up 5.4 percent in MLB. Yankees/Mets skew total. The Biz of Baseball. Retrieved October 6, 2010, from http://www.bizofbaseball.com/index.php?option=com_content&view=article&id=3147:average-ticket-price-up-54-percent-in-mlb-yankeesmets-skew-total&catid=56:ticket-watch&Itemid=136; Greenberg, J. (2008 October 28). 2008–09 NBA fan cost index. Team Marketing Report. Retrieved October 6, 2010 from http://www.teammarketing.com/blog/index.html?article_id=41; Team Marketing Report, Inc. (2009 September). TMR's fan cost index. Retrieved October 6, 2010, from http://teammarketing.com.ismmedia.com/ISM3/std-content/repos/Top/News/nfl%20fci%202009.pdf

However, there is increasing evidence that sport fans are not able to pay such prices. For example, a 2000 *Sports Illustrated* article reported the results from a research study conducted by the Peter Harris Research Group. One of the findings was that 57% of sport fans cited the total cost of attending as a reason that they are less likely to attend a sporting event (Swift, 2000). Based on these facts, it can be suggested that fans either do not have the wherewithal to attend or do not see the value in attending major professional sporting events. Additionally, such information suggests that major professional sport teams are increasingly challenged in their efforts to undertake relationship marketing with their fans. In fact, sport fans appear to be more skeptical of the motivations of team owners than ever before. In the same Harris Research Group study, "85% of fans believe owners are more interested in making money than in making it possible for Joe Fan to attend games" (Swift, 2000, p. 78).

This circumstance presents a significant challenge for sport marketers. During the time period in which prices and the cost of attending increased so dramatically, a large number of new stadiums and arenas were built and renovated. In many cases, owners of professional teams were responsible for financing at least part of these building projects. So, owners today also have to worry about paying off debt associated with stadium development. Increasing ticket prices has clearly been one way that owners have sought to generate revenue. Unfortunately, the aforementioned statistics suggest that sport fans may not be willing to pay much more to attend a sporting event. Some teams, sensing this trend and attempting to repair damaged relationships, have actually decreased ticket prices. But if owners cannot increase ticket prices substantially, they must find additional ways to generate revenue. As such, one of the key challenges for anyone in team sport marketing will be increasing revenues for sport teams.

One way that teams and other sport entities are attempting to enhance relationships while at the same time increasing revenue is through database marketing. Database marketing involves creating a database, usually consisting of names, addresses, and other demographic information related to consumers, and then managing that database. Managing the database usually involves developing and delivering integrated marketing programs, including promotions and sales offers, to the database universe or to appropriate segments or target markets of that database. For example, if the Texas Rangers knew that a season ticket holder purchased extra tickets the last time the Seattle Mariners visited Texas, the Rangers could contact that season ticket holder with a special offer for the Mariners' next visit. In one sense, this would communicate to the season ticket holder that the Rangers cared about serving his or her needs. In another sense, it might help sell several tickets that might have gone unused for a particular game. Database marketing is often an integral factor in a company's decision to sponsor an event. For example, corporate sponsors often create promotions at events where they offer to give away something special, such as a trip or a valuable product such as a golf driver, if people attending the event will provide their name, address, and other relevant information. The next time you attend an event and a credit card company offers you a T-shirt or floppy hat for your personal information, realize you have just been engaged in database marketing.

The Cluttered Marketplace

Competition is fierce for sport organizations and corporations marketing their products through sport. As never before, there are numerous and greatly varied entertainment options available to a consumer with leisure time. Of particular concern to sport marketers is the next generation of sport fans—children and young adults. Think of the technology options available to a young person today: instant messaging, text messaging, social networking sites, cell phones, digital video disc (DVD) players, video games, the Internet, and so on. There are even new sports that have entered the marketplace with success. Action sports—sports such as skateboarding and motocross—have captured the interest of young kids today. Consider these facts:

- In 2004, 8.4 million people skateboarded and 6.2 million snowboarded (SBRnet, 2009).
- The 2008 Dew Tour drew more than 272,009 people to its five events (*Street & Smith's SportsBusiness Daily*, 2008).
- Skateboarding legend Tony Hawk's video games have generated $1.1 billion in sales (Hyman, 2006).

With their leisure time absorbed by multiple technology entertainment options and following action sports, do young people have the additional time and resources to participate in other mainstream sports? Creative strategies will attempt to answer that question as marketers focus on youths in the future. For this reason, there will be a heightened focus on marketing to youth in the future.

A cluttered marketplace is also an issue for sponsors of sporting events and endorsers of athletes. Two factors have contributed to create a sponsorship marketplace that is extremely cluttered:

1. The rise in the sheer number of events and athletes to sponsor. For example, there are now a variety of action sports events, such as the X-Games, Dew Tour, and Vans Triple Crown of Surfing. Similarly, a corporation could sponsor an NFL star or a women's professional basketball star.
2. The increased focus by sport managers on increasing revenue by identifying as much

saleable inventory as possible. Watch the next NASCAR race. Count how many places that sponsor logos appear.

Because the sponsorship marketplace is cluttered, it may be increasingly difficult for sponsors to be recognized as sponsors and thus achieve the benefits of sponsorship. In response, sponsors are asking sport teams and events to provide more benefits and are increasing the degree of sophistication with which they measure sponsorship effectiveness (see "Evaluating Sport Sponsorships" in Chapter 15). Thus, sporting events in the future will increasingly be challenged to demonstrate how a sponsor will benefit from a sponsorship if they are to attract and retain sponsors.

Image Matters

The development and cultivation of a positive image is becoming increasingly important in sport marketing. This is true for several reasons. First, the cluttered marketplace just discussed makes it imperative that corporations identify sports, events, or athletes who have unique images. Second, since the turn of the twenty-first century, corporate ethical scandals, highlighted by the collapse of energy giant Enron, have decreased the amount of trust that consumers have in large companies. Coupled with this perception, reports of athlete arrests may have served to decrease the overall image of professional athletes and professional sports.

For these reasons, corporations are more discerning in how they spend their sponsorship and endorsement dollars. One outcome is that corporations are investing more money to sponsor nonprofit organizations (Tatum, 2003). In fact, the International Events Group suggested that $1.1 billion would be spent on nonprofit sponsorships in 2006, an increase of 20.5% from 2005 (Scott, 2006). A corporation may choose to sponsor the activities of a nonprofit organization in an effort to capitalize on the positive image associated with that organization or event.

Image also is important when it comes to athlete endorsements. Although there are still a handful of very large endorsement contracts, such as LeBron James's $90 million deal with Nike ("Nike Foots Bill," 2003), companies are increasingly careful about whom they choose as an endorser. Media accounts of athletes running afoul of the law or breaking the rules of their specific sport are commonplace, even for some athletes who have very positive images. For example, baseball slugger and one-time popular endorser Sammy Sosa was found to be using a corked bat in 2003. Following the dismissal of the sexual assault charges against him, it took NBA star Kobe Bryant time to win back companies hiring him as an endorser. Recently, Ben Roethlisberger and Tiger Woods have had problems keeping their sponsors based on their off-the-field issues.

One athlete with widespread global appeal is soccer player David Beckham. He has been successful at crafting an image of someone who is fashionable, tolerant, and family oriented (Hale, 2003). Such an image makes him very attractive to corporations as an endorser, and as a result he makes at least $14 million a year from endorsement agreements with such companies as Vodafone (a cellular phone service), Adidas, and Armani (Hale, 2003; Rossingh, 2010).

Athletes are besieged with issues associated with steroids, arrests, and infidelity. Today's superstar could be tomorrow's headlines. The increase in social improprieties over the past decade is impacting the sport marketing efforts of leagues, teams, and sponsors. An athlete is recognized not only for his or her on-field performance, but also off it. Therefore, many leagues, teams, and sponsors are protecting their brand by strategically placing moral clauses in their rules and contracts. To protect the NFL brand, Commissioner Roger Goodell has clamped down on off-field indiscretions by players and other

employees by strengthening the Personal Conduct Policy and handing out stiffer penalties to offenders (Associated Press, 2007). For more information on the NFL's conduct policy, see the case study in Chapter 10.

■ SUMMARY

The marketing of sport includes unique advantages and disadvantages when compared with the marketing of more traditional products and services. Sport benefits from the immense media coverage afforded the industry, often at no cost, while simultaneously it can suffer from the scrutiny imposed by the same media. Besides sport, there is probably no other industry in which the majority of the consumers consider themselves experts. Finally, the sport marketer's control over the core product offered to the consumer is often significantly less than that of his or her counterparts in other industries.

Sport marketers must not only understand the unique aspects of their own product, but they also must be well informed and knowledgeable about marketing innovations and practices in more traditional business industries and be able to adapt or modify these practices to fit the situations they encounter in sport. In particular, the application of such concepts as the marketing mix, segmentation, fan identification, and relationship marketing is central to the success of a sport marketer. Similarly, recognizing and adapting to current issues such as the rising cost of attending an event, the cluttered nature of the marketplace, and the importance of building a positive image are central to most sport marketers' work. Beyond an understanding and appreciation for these factors and practices, a sport marketer must have strong interpersonal skills, computer skills, and in many cases the ability to sell a product or concept if he or she is to be successful.

■ KEY TERMS

ambush marketing, customer relationship management, demographic, fan identification, intercept interviews, marketing mix, pass-by interviews, psychographic, relationship marketing, segmentation, sponsorships, target markets

■ REFERENCES

Associated Press. (2007 April 10). Goodell unveils new conduct policy. *ESPN.com*. Retrieved October 6, 2010, from http://sports.espn.go.com/nfl/news/story?id=2832098

Bhattarcharya, C.B., Rao, H., & Glynn, M.A. (1995). Understanding the bond of identification: An investigation of its correlates among art museum members. *The Journal of Marketing, 59*(4), 46–57.

Bednarski, P.J. (2002 December 9). Applauding Arledge: He invented fresh ways to report sports and news on TV. *Broadcasting & Cable*, 41.

Berry, L.L. (1995). Relationship marketing of services—Growing interest, emerging perspectives. *Journal of the Academy of Marketing Sciences, 23*(4), 236–245.

Bounds, A., & Garrahan, M. (2003 June 26). A question of sport and image: Mark McCormack, the sports marketing pioneer, died in May. *Financial Times*, p. 12.

Brown, M. (2009 April 2). Average ticket price up 5.4 percent in MLB. Yankees/Mets skew total. The Biz of Baseball. Retrieved October 6, 2010, from http://www.bizofbaseball.com/index.php?option=com_content&view=article&id=3147:average-ticket-price-up-54-percent-in-mlb-yankeesmets-skew-total&catid=56:ticket-watch&Itemid=136

Coca-Cola Company. (2006). The Olympic Games. Retrieved November 10, 2010, from http://www.thecoca-colacompany.com/heritage/olympicgames.html

ESPN. (2010 January 10). ESPN Fact Sheet. Retrieved October 6, 2010, from http://espnmediazone3.com/wpmu

Greenberg, J. (2008 October 28). 2008–09 NBA fan cost index. Team Marketing Report. Retrieved October 6, 2010, from http://www.teammarketing.com/blog/index.html?article_id=41

Hale, E. (2003 May 9). He's the most famous athlete in the world (except in the USA). *USA Today*, p. 1A.

Hardy, S. (1996). Matt Levine: The "father" of modern sport marketing. *Sport Marketing Quarterly, 5*, 5–7.

Holtzman, J. (1986 January 3). Barnum of baseball made sure fans were entertained. *Chicago Tribune*, pp. D1, D3.

Hyman, M. (2006 November 13). How Tony Hawk stays aloft. *Business Week*, p. 84.

Kotler, P. (2003). *Marketing management.* Upper Saddle River, NJ: Prentice Hall.

Levine, P. (1985). A.G. *Spalding and the rise of baseball.* New York: Oxford University Press.

Liberman, N. (2003 June 16). Defining Hispanic market challenges teams. *Street & Smith's Sports Business Journal*, 20.

McCarthy, E.J., & Perreault, W.D. (1988). *Essentials of marketing.* Homewood, IL: Richard D. Irwin.

McKenna, R. (1991). *Relationship marketing.* Reading, MA: Addison-Wesley Publishers.

Mullin, B., Hardy, S., & Sutton, W.A. (2000). *Sport marketing*. Champaign, IL: Human Kinetics.

Nike foots bill for James at $90M. (2003 May 23). *The Washington Post*, p. D2.

Ries, A., & Trout, J. (1993). *The 22 immutable laws of marketing*. New York: Harper Business.

Roberts, R., & Olson, J. (1989). *Winning is the only thing: Sports in American society since 1945*. Baltimore: Johns Hopkins University Press.

Rossingh, D. (2010). David Beckham's 2009 income from endorsements company fell 9 percent. Retrieved November 10, 2010, from http://www.bloomberg.com/news/2010-10-07/david-beckhams-2009-income-from-endorsements-company-fell-9-percent.html

SBRnet. (2009). Skateboarding participation. Retrieved November 10, 2010, from http://www.sbrnet.com.silk.library.umass.edu:2048/research.asp?subRID=370

Scott, A. (2006 April 1). Goal tending promo. Retrieved October 6, 2010, from http://promomagazine.com/mag/marketing-goal-tending

Street & Smith's SportsBusiness Daily. (2008 October 30). AST Dew Tour ratings up, attendance down from 2007. Retrieved November 10, 2010, from http://www.sportsbusinessdaily.com/article/125119

Strasser, J.B., & Becklund, L. (1991). *Swoosh: The unauthorized story of Nike and the men who played there*. New York: Harcourt Brace Jovanovich.

Sugar, B. (1978). *Hit the sign and win a free suit of clothes from Harry Finklestein*. Chicago: Contemporary Books.

Swift, E.M. (1990 May 21). The most powerful man in sports: Mark McCormack, founder and CEO of International Management Group, rules his empire as both agent and impresario. Retrieved October 6, 2010, from http://sportsillustrated.cnn.com/vault/article/magazine/MAG1136857/index.htm

Swift, E.M. (2000 May 15). Sit on it! The high cost of attending games is fattening owners' wallets while it drives average fans from arenas, and it may be cooling America's passion for pro sports. *Sports Illustrated*, pp. 71–85.

Tatum, C. (2003 August 8). Companies more hesitant to sponsor splashy sports events. *Denver Post*.

Team Marketing Report, Inc. (2009 September). TMR's fan cost index. Retrieved October 6, 2010, from http://teammarketing.com.ismmedia.com/ISM3/std-content/repos/Top/News/nfl%20fci%202009.pdf

U.S. Census Bureau. (2009). Annual estimates of the population by sex, race, and Hispanic origin for the United States: April 1, 2000 to July 1, 2009. Retrieved November 10, 2010, from http://www.census.gov/popest/national/asrh/NC-EST2009-srh.html

Veeck, B., & Linn, E. (1962). *Veeck—As in wreck*. New York: G.P. Putnam's Sons.

Veeck, B., & Linn, E. (1965). The hustler's handbook. New York: G.P. Putnam's Sons.

Financial and Economic Principles Applied to Sport Management

Neil Longley

■ INTRODUCTION

The media are constantly drawing our attention to the financial aspects of the sport world. Some of the numbers that we read and hear can seem staggering to the average person. To get a sense of the magnitude of the dollar values being generated by the industry, consider these numbers:

- The average player salary in the National Basketball Association (NBA) is currently $5.765 million per season (Coon, 2010).
- The ten-year contract that star baseball player Alex Rodriguez signed in 2008 pays an average salary of $27.5 million per year (Associated Press, 2007).
- The cost of the new stadium that the National Football League's (NFL's) Arizona Cardinals opened in 2006 was $455 million, and the naming rights to the stadium were sold to the University of Phoenix for approximately $7.7 million per season for the next 20 seasons (University of Phoenix, 2010).
- The NFL's current television contract calls for the league to be paid more than $3 billion per year, or about $100 million per team per year (SportsBusiness Daily, 2007).
- The estimated market value of the NFL's Washington Redskins is $1.55 billion, making it the second-most valuable franchise in North America and third in the world (behind Manchester United and Dallas Cowboys), despite the fact that the Redskins' on-field performance in recent years has been less than stellar (Van Riper, 2010).

In college sports, the pattern is the same: Participants in college football's Bowl Championship Series (BCS) championship game receive payouts of more than $17 million per team; the National Collegiate Athletic Association's (NCAA's) 14-year contract with CBS and Turner Sports, signed in 2010, to televise the NCAA Mens' Basketball Tournament every March will pay the NCAA about $11 billion over the life of the contract; the budget of the athletic department at Ohio State was about $120 million in 2008–2009 (Turner, 2009). The list could go on and on, but one thing is clear—sport is very big business.

Actually, the examples given here are from only one segment of the sport industry—the spectator sport segment. The sport industry is much broader than just the spectator side. It includes not only a wide range of service businesses related to participatory recreational activities (such as fitness centers, ski resorts, and golf courses) but also the entire sporting goods and related apparel industry.

The sport industry is definitely a major force in North American business, although it is difficult to get an accurate, reliable measure of its true financial magnitude. According to Plunkett Research (2010), the entire U.S. sport industry in 2010 accounted for $414 billion in total spending. Of that, $27.3 billion is sports advertising. The U.S. sporting goods industry in 2009 accounted for $71.8 billion in spending (Plunkett Research, 2010). *SportsBusiness Journal* estimates that total spending in the industry amounted to approximately $214 billion in 2006, up from $196 billion three years earlier. In contrast, the U.S. Department of Commerce estimated the combined gross economic output of the sport, recreation, entertainment, and arts categories in the United States combined to be about $221 billion in 2008.

Part of the practical problem in measuring the exact size of this industry is deciding

what to include. For example, the gambling sector, while not part of the sport sector per se, derives much of its business from betting on spectator sports. So, should gambling be included? Perhaps more importantly, different studies may be measuring different variables. For example, if a golf club manufacturer sold a set of golf clubs to a retailer for $1,000, which in turn sold the clubs to a customer for $1,500, one could naively (and incorrectly) add the two together and say the total output of the industry is $2,500. While this might seem like an obvious error—the $1,000 is double-counted, and the true value of the transactions is $1,500—it is surprising how often errors such as these are made by those conducting impact studies. The point is that unless you know how someone is calculating the magnitude of the industry, you should exercise extreme caution before you have too much faith in the result.

This raises a related issue. There is a difference between an industry's sales and its value-added. For example, the golf club manufacturer mentioned earlier may have bought raw materials (e.g., graphite, titanium, rubber) from its suppliers for $300, used these materials to manufacture the clubs, and then sold the clubs to the retailer for $1,000. Although the manufacturer's sale totals $1,000, its value-added is only $700 because $300 of the $1,000 sale prices was attributable to those outside the industry. When one adjusts for the concept of value-added, the numbers change considerably. For example, while the Department of Commerce estimates total output for the sport industry in 2008 to be $221 billion, it estimates the value-added to be only $195 billion. This $195 billion represents about 0.9% of the U.S. gross domestic product (GDP). The concept of value-added is probably the best single measure of an industry's impact.

Despite these practical complexities with actually measuring the size of the industry and the caution one must always take when interpreting the numbers, one thing is certain: Regardless of how one specifically measures it, the sport industry is both significant and growing. Inside sport organizations (whether they be professional or college spectator sports), the recreational service sector, or the sporting goods industry, many managers are now responsible for multimillion-dollar budgets. This financial boom has created a great need in the industry for people with training in finance. Even where the sport organization operates on a more modest scale than the examples given earlier—whether it be a locally owned fitness center, a minor league baseball team, or a Division III athletic department in college sports—the need for sound financial management practices is no less urgent.

This chapter provides an introduction to the field of finance within a sport context. It examines what finance is and what it is not. It discusses how money flows into and out of a sport organization, and it examines the types of management decisions that must be made to maximize the financial success of the organization. It also discusses some of the current issues facing various sectors of the industry.

■ KEY CONCEPTS

What Is Finance?

The term *finance* often has quite different meanings to different people. For some individuals not specifically trained in finance, the term is often used very broadly to describe anything to do with dollars, or money, or numbers. This definition implies that almost everything that occurs in an organization falls under the broad umbrella of "finance," given that almost everything that occurs in an organization has monetary implications.

In fact, those trained in finance tend to define the field somewhat more narrowly. Part of the purpose of this chapter is to illustrate what finance actually is and, just as importantly, what it is not. Because the finance discipline tends to intersect with other managerial disciplines—for example, marketing—it sometimes might be unclear to some as to where the marketing function ends and where the finance function begins.

Perhaps the best way to make this distinction is to consider that what defines finance is not as much the subject matter—it could be ticket sales, merchandise sales, the signing of a free agent, or the construction of a new stadium—but rather the concepts and techniques used to solve problems and make decisions about these issues.

For example, the act of a college athletic department selling a corporate sponsorship has clear financial implications: Sponsorship salespeople must be paid for their services, and the sponsorships they ultimately sell will generate **revenues** for the department. The act in itself is not about finance, however, but rather is about sales.

Of course, finance issues could still be embedded within this process. For example, there might be a question as to how many salespeople should be allocated to the sponsorship sales department. Might some of the sales staff be more effectively employed in selling season ticket packages instead of selling sponsorships? This question, while not necessarily straightforward, is crucial, and is an example of a financial allocation decision that a sport organization must make. Allocation decisions such as these tend to occur in the course of the **budgeting** process.

The basic financial "answer" to this question is that the organization should allocate its sales staff based on the magnitude of the financial payoff that each department (tickets and sponsorships) can return for a given salesperson. In essence, the question is this: Would shifting one salesperson from sponsorship sales to ticket sales increase or decrease the overall revenue that flows into the department? In other words, finance isn't as much about simply identifying where and how money flows into the organization, but about how organizations make allocation decisions to ensure the net inflow is maximized.

In summary, the managerial discipline of finance refers to something much more specific than simply anything to do with money or dollars. While there is no single, universally agreed-upon definition of finance, *finance* generally refers to two primary activities of an organization: how an organization *generates* the funds that flow into an organization, and how these funds get *allocated* and spent once they are in the organization.

Some Basics: Financial Flows in Sport Organizations

In many ways, the finance function in a sport organization is no different than the finance function in any other organization. The context may be different, but the underlying concepts and principles remain the same. Like any other field, finance is an area that has its own terminology. Being familiar with this terminology is a

necessary prerequisite to better understanding the finance function.

This terminology is best introduced by thinking about the process by which funds (i.e., dollars) flow through a sport organization. Let's start with how funds flow into an organization.

For organizations in the spectator sport sector, their primary business is to provide entertainment through the staging of athletic contests. The selling of these events is the primary way in which sport teams raise funds. These funds are called **revenues**. Revenues may come from a variety of sources: from ticket sales, from concession and merchandise sales, from media contracts, or from sponsorship revenues, to name only a few. With sponsorships, other companies try to use the broad appeal of the sports industry to market their own products. For college athletic programs, funds may also come from nonrevenue sources, such as budgetary allocations from the university to the athletic department.

In the nonspectator sport sector, revenues come from the sale of the organization's primary goods and/or service. For example, in a golf country club, revenues might come from a variety of sources, such as yearly memberships, green fees, golf lessons, equipment sales in the pro shop, and food and drink sales at the clubhouse restaurant.

Obviously, money doesn't just flow into sport organizations; some also flows out. In other words, **expenses** must be incurred to generate revenues. For the golf country club, expenses might include such items as staff salaries, water to irrigate the fairways, electricity to light the clubhouse, and food and beverage items to prepare meals at the clubhouse restaurant. In the spectator sport sector—whether it be college or pro—teams must buy uniforms and equipment (e.g., bats, balls, hockey sticks) for the players; they must pay for player travel, including transportation and hotel accommodation; and so on. Facility-related costs are also incurred: The facility must be staffed on game day with ticket takers, ushers, and concession workers; electricity is used to provide lighting and to run equipment; the facility must be cleaned after an event; and the playing surface must be maintained. For major professional teams, these types of costs are all secondary to the single biggest expenditure item: player salaries.

In a basic sense, the financial success of an organization is ultimately dependent on the difference between revenues and expenses. This difference is called **profits** (sometimes referred to as **income**). Profits can be increased by increasing revenues, by decreasing costs, or both. An organization's revenues, expenses, and profits over a given time period (for example, a year) are usually summarized on a financial statement called an **income statement**.

Another important financial concept is **assets**. Broadly speaking, assets are anything that an organization owns that can be used to generate future revenues. For example, a fitness center's primary assets are its building and exercise equipment; a golf club maker's primary assets are the manufacturing equipment at its production facility. With spectator sports, a team's stadium is an important asset because it provides the team with a venue at which to stage games, which in turn allows the team to earn various types of revenue. As we will see later in the chapter, new stadiums tend to have dramatic and immediate effects on a franchise's revenue stream.

For major professional sports franchises, one of the most important assets they possess is their membership in the league to which they belong. For example, the NFL's popularity as a league is so high that prospective franchise owners will pay large sums of money simply to join the league. The owners of the NFL's most recent expansion franchise, the Houston Texans, paid the NFL an expansion fee of $700 million (*SportsBusiness Journal*, 2006). This fee was paid just to "join the club" and to enjoy all the future financial benefits that such membership in the NFL may bring; it did not include money for such large-scale expenditures as stadium construction and player salaries.

In essence, all sport organizations, like any other businesses, must spend money up-front to generate what they hope will be even greater inflows later on. For example, fitness centers can't sell memberships until they first buy or lease a building and then stock that building with exercise equipment; golf club manufacturers can't make and sell any golf clubs until they first purchase the necessary production equipment. In financial terms, any business must make an initial investment in assets to generate future revenues.

One further element can be added to the mix. Assets have to be bought, so where do the dollars come from that are invested in these assets? A new stadium, for example, may cost hundreds of millions of dollars to construct.

For some assets, such as stadiums, professional teams have been very successful in convincing local governments to pay for all or part of the costs of the facility. Since the year 2000, it is estimated that about two-thirds of all stadium construction costs have come from government (i.e., taxpayer) sources. (Leeds and von Allmen, 2008).

This issue aside, professional teams can fund or "finance" assets in a number of ways. First, **owners' equity** (sometimes simply referred to as "equity") can be used to finance assets. Owners' equity is essentially the amount of their own money that owners have invested in the firm. Much of this investment of funds typically occurs when the owners initially purchase (or start up) the firm, but the amount can also increase if the owners reinvest any profits back in the firm, rather than removing these profits and paying themselves dividends.

In major pro sports, most franchise owners (i.e., the equity holders) tend to be either a sole individual or a small group of individuals. Sometimes, existing owners will sell part of their ownership stake in a team (i.e., sell part of their equity) as a means to inject more cash into the team. For example, in 2004, owner John McCaw infused much-needed cash into his Vancouver Canucks franchise by selling 50% of his ownership stake in the club (Ozanian & Badenhausen, 2006). A few franchises have been owned by corporate conglomerates: Cablevision owns the New York Rangers and Knicks, Comcast-Spectacor owns the Philadelphia Flyers and 76ers, The Tribune Company owned the Chicago Cubs until 2007, and Disney owned Major League Baseball's (MLB's) Angels and the National Hockey League's (NHL's) Ducks until the mid-2000s. In a somewhat more unusual situation, the Ontario Teachers' Pension Fund— a depository for pension contributions of the teachers of the province of Ontario, Canada—is majority owner of both the Toronto Maple Leafs and Toronto Raptors.

There have even been a few occasions where a franchise's shares have been publicly traded on a stock exchange. In these cases, there are literally thousands of owners of a team, most of whom own only a small portion of the franchise. At one time or another in the past 20 years, teams such as the Boston Celtics, Cleveland Indians, Vancouver Canucks, and Toronto Maple Leafs have had publicly traded shares.

In the nonspectator sector, publicly traded shares are much more common than in the spectator sector. **Table 4-1** shows some of the sport organizations whose shares are publicly traded. Publicly traded shares give firms a much wider access to investment capital, which potentially allows them to expand more quickly than they otherwise would be able to do.

Besides owners' equity, the other major way that sport organizations raise money to finance their assets is to borrow money. The amount of money that an organization borrows is referred to as its **debt** (also referred to as **liabilities**).

When organizations borrow, they are legally obligated to pay back the original amount they borrowed (the **principal**), plus **interest**. Money might be borrowed from banks, or it might be borrowed from other lenders in financial markets, through, for example, instruments such as **bonds**. Bonds are financial instruments that allow the borrower to both borrow large dollar amounts and to borrow this money for a relatively long period of time (usually 20 or more years). Bonds are normally issued only by relatively large corporate entities and by governments. There is usually a secondary market for bonds, meaning the original buyer (i.e., the lender) can sell the bonds to another buyer any time prior to the bonds "maturing." Bonds are normally purchased by institutional investors,

TABLE 4-1	Examples of Publicly Traded Sport Companies	
Name	**Type of Business**	**Stock Exchange**
Callaway Golf	Golf products	NYSE
Churchill Downs	Thoroughbred racing	NASDAQ
Electronic Arts	Video games	NASDAQ
Nike	Shoes	NYSE
Vail Resorts	Skiing	NYSE

Abbreviations: NYSE = New York Stock Exchange; NASDAQ = National Association of Securities Dealers Automated Quotations.

Source: Fried, G., Shapiro, S., & DeSchriver, T. (2008). *Sport finance.* Champaign, IL: Human Kinetics.

such as mutual funds, insurance companies, and pension funds.

In spectator sports, stadium construction projects are often financed with bonds. Notre Dame, for example, financed the expansion of its football stadium during the mid-1990s with a $53 million bond issue (University of Notre Dame, 2006); at the University of Iowa, renovations to Kinnick Stadium were financed with a $100 million bond issue (University of Iowa, 2005). While most bond issues in spectator sports are used to finance stadium construction, bonds are occasionally used for other purposes. In 2000, for example, the YankeeNets organization issued $200 million worth of bonds to the market, ostensibly to finance its planned takeover of the New Jersey Devils hockey team (Fried, Shapiro, & DeSchriver, 2008).

The interest rate at which any money is borrowed depends on the lender's perception of the borrower's ability to repay. In turn, this ability to repay depends on a variety of factors: the popularity of the organization's goods or services, the magnitude and stability of the organization's revenue streams, the future prospects for revenue growth, the degree to which costs are controlled and contained, the amount of debt the organization is already carrying, and so forth.

Leagues such as the NFL, NBA, and MLB all maintain "credit facilities," sometimes called loan pools, and borrow extensively in financial markets to fund these facilities. Individual teams in the league can then borrow from the credit facilities, rather than borrowing directly in financial markets. Leagues can borrow less expensively than can individual teams, simply because league loans are backed by the collective revenues of all teams in the league, whereas loans to teams are backed only by that individual team's revenues. Companies such as Fitch and Moody's "rate" this debt of major professional leagues (and teams). Generally, the NFL's debt receives the highest credit rating

in sports, indicating that the League has the lowest credit risk, which allows it to borrow at the lowest possible interest rate. For example, Fitch has rated recent debt issues of the NFL as A+ (Business Wire, 2010); MLB received an A– rating (News Blaze, 2009).

An organization's assets, liabilities, and owners' equity at any given point are shown on a financial statement called a **balance sheet**.

College athletic programs are nonprofit organizations and can have quite different sources of funds. In college athletics, there are no real equity holders—no one "owns" these programs. Typically, outside sources of funds flow into the athletic department through budgetary transfers from the university itself. However, some athletic programs are finding very innovative ways to raise capital. For example, a venture capital fund recently started whose goal is to donate funds to Duke University basketball. This particular fund, like other venture capital funds, uses the dollars of wealthy individuals (many of whom are Duke alumni) to invest in various start-up companies. The idea is that the fund's earnings from these investments would then be ultimately donated to Duke. The hope is that the fund will eventually earn up to $75 million—an amount that would permanently endow the men's basketball team (Karmin, 2006).

Some Typical Financial Decisions

With these basic concepts in mind, let's look at some examples of financial decisions that sport organizations may face. Many of the financial decisions in a sport organization ultimately revolve around the management of assets. For example, in any given season, there may be a variety of investment expenditures that a golf country club could make to increase the value of its assets. Because investment dollars are likely limited, however, choices have to be made as to which options will be the most rewarding.

One option might be for the country club to expand its golf facilities by adding another 18-hole course. Another option might be to expand its clubhouse and restaurant. Still another choice might be to upgrade the quality of the existing course by adding a state-of-the-art irrigation system. All of these options will have different initial investment costs, and all will have different revenue potentials.

In the spectator segment, a baseball team might face similar choices. For example, one option might be for the team to go into the free agent market and sign a star player. This move would presumably increase the team's performance on the field, which in turn might lead to more tickets being sold and/or higher TV ratings. Alternatively, the team could take the money that it would have used to sign the free agent and instead upgrade the luxury suites in the stadium. By making these upgrades, the team could then charge a higher price to its corporate clients to lease the suites. Another option might be to install a state-of-the-art scoreboard in the stadium. This novelty might increase the overall fan experience, making people more likely to attend games. Furthermore, it may provide increased sponsorship and advertising opportunities for the team. Or perhaps the team might want to replace its existing natural grass field with an artificial surface. This change might reduce player injuries, perhaps increasing team performance, and hence ticket revenues, and might also reduce future expenses, in that fewer players will appear on a roster during the season, as fewer replacement players will be needed to take over for injured players. A new artificial surface may also increase revenues in other ways by making the venue usable for a wider range of events.

It is these types of decisions that lie at the heart of finance. Finance-trained people approach these kinds of problems by applying certain concepts and techniques. In this case, one approach is to calculate each alternative's

return on investment (ROI). The concept of ROI is very common in finance: It shows the expected dollar-value return on each alternative investment, stated as a percentage of the original cost of each investment. For example, an ROI of 9% indicates the team would recover all of its initial investment, plus an additional 9%.

To calculate ROI, the financial analyst would need to estimate two basic things. The first task is to calculate the initial cost of each investment: What will it cost to sign the free agent, or what will the new turf or scoreboard cost? The second, somewhat more difficult task is to estimate the magnitude of the revenues that each alternative will generate. For example, with the free agent, the player's on-field performance should ultimately affect (positively, one hopes) the team's winning percentage, which should in turn affect attendance and media revenues.

An interesting case study has arisen in recent years that pertains to the ROI of player personnel decisions. The somewhat-famous book *Moneyball* (Lewis, 2003) chronicles the processes that Oakland A's general manager (GM) Billy Beane uses to make player selection decisions. Beane contends that many teams in baseball often make systematic players selection errors—"overvaluing" some players while "undervalu-

ing" others. As the GM of a small-market team, one of Beane's strategies to more effectively compete with large-market teams is to identify and acquire these undervalued players. In essence, an investment in an undervalued player produces a higher ROI than a comparable investment in an overvalued player; undervalued players create more wins per dollar of payroll than do overvalued players, and hence make a greater contribution to team profits.

When examining free agents, a player's off-field performance must also be evaluated. That is, would he increase merchandise sales? Would she increase the overall visibility of the team?

This raises another key issue. Investments such as these require managers to think about the future. The future is often notoriously difficult to predict accurately. For example, no one can know for certain the magnitude of the increased revenues that would result from a golf course expanding in size from 18 holes to 36 holes. Many uncertainties exist: Will golf's popularity, relative to other activities, continue to grow at rates seen in the past two decades? Will overall economic conditions improve from their recessionary levels of the late 2000s, ensuring consumers continue to have the disposable income necessary to engage in leisure activities like golf? Will other competing golf courses enter the market, thereby reducing market share for the existing course?

Similarly, in the baseball example, no one can say for certain what value the free agent will actually add to revenues. The player might not perform as expected; adding the player may affect team chemistry in ways not foreseen; the player might be plagued by injuries; and so on.

These difficulties in making accurate predictions about the future relate to the concept of **risk**. Risk is one of the most important concepts in finance. It refers to the fact that the future is uncertain, so that the future benefits of any investment made today cannot ever be known with certainty at the time the investment is made. Of course, some investments inherently carry more risk than others. Financial managers need to take into account these different levels of risk when they evaluate investment projects. For example, investing in upgraded luxury suites may be less risky than investing in a free agent, in the sense that the future revenue payoffs from the former move are more predictable than they are for the latter investment.

Making decisions about which assets to invest in is not the only place where the concept of risk arises in sport finance. As we have seen, there is a whole other class of decisions, called financing decisions, where risk is a crucial factor. These financing decisions revolve around the degree to which financing will occur with equity versus debt. In other words, owners must decide how much of the assets of the franchise they will finance with their own money versus how much they will finance with borrowed money. There are always tradeoffs. Generally, financing with borrowed money is less expensive than equity, but it carries more risk. It is less expensive because lenders do not have any ownership stake in the organization, and thus are only entitled to repayment of their original loan, with interest. If the organization's financial performance is better than expected, none of this upside has to be shared with lenders, so it can be retained by the current equity holders.

However, debt carries more risk because the organization is legally obligated to repay the borrowed money, with interest, at a prespecified date. If the borrower is unable to do so—perhaps because revenues are lower than expected—then the borrower is said to be in **default** on the debt. If a default occurs, the lenders may force the organization into bankruptcy. Such a scenario is not merely hypothetical: It has occurred four times in the NHL in the past few seasons, involving the Ottawa Senators, Buffalo Sabres, Pittsburgh Penguins, and, most recently (in 2009), Phoenix Coyotes (Harris & Watters, 2009).

Similar situations have occurred in the non-spectator sport sector. For example, when the shoe manufacturer Converse filed for bankruptcy in 2001, its spokesperson at the time said, "It's not a lack of business, but our debt structure that made it difficult for the company to survive" (Fried et al., 2008).

The Economics of Sport

What we have discussed up to now falls within the realm of sport finance. It looks at how managers make decisions about where to raise funds and where to spend those funds. A related area, called sports economics, is also relevant to anyone interested in the financial aspects of sport.

The general field of (micro) economics examines, among many other issues, how an industry organizes itself, and how this industry structure affects competition and profits among firms in the industry. In recent years, an entire subfield of economics has developed that examines the peculiar aspects of the spectator sport industry. The focus has been on the spectator sport industry because it is organized so differently from the nonspectator industry and, for that matter, from the rest of American business. In most industries, firms directly compete with each other for market share: General Motors competes with Ford and Toyota, Coca-Cola competes with Pepsi, Sony competes with Toshiba, New Balance competes with Nike, Ping competes with Callaway. There are little or no common interests among the competitors. For example, every set of golf clubs that Ping sells is a set that Callaway didn't sell. In fact, all else equal, Callaway would be better off if Ping didn't exist, and vice versa.

In the spectator sport industry (whether college or pro), the issue is very different. While teams may compete against each other on the field, they must cooperate off the field. For example, the Boston Red Sox baseball franchise would be less valuable if the New York Yankees didn't exist. Thus the Red Sox and the Yankees are not competitors in the same way that Ping and Callaway are; in a business sense, the Red Sox and Yankees are more like partners. They are both members of the American League, and the existence of one franchise benefits the other franchise.

The other significant feature that differentiates major professional sports leagues from the non-spectator sport sector, and from the rest of American business, is that these sports leagues are considered monopolies. That is, these leagues face no direct competition for the products and services they produce. For example, the NBA is currently the only seller of elite-level professional basketball in North America. Fans who enjoy watching the highest caliber of professional basketball must watch the NBA's version of the product because no other league supplies a comparable product. Again, compare this situation to the golf club industry, where a consumer shopping for a new set of clubs has a wide range of manufacturers from which to choose.

Businesses that are a **monopoly**, by definition, face no direct competition. This gives them greater bargaining power when dealing with stakeholders, and allows the monopoly to potentially charge a higher price for its product than would be the case if it faced competitors. Thus fans pay higher prices for tickets, media companies pay higher fees for broadcast rights, corporations pay higher amounts to lease luxury suites, and taxpayers pay a large share of stadium construction costs. In short, the monopoly status of sports leagues allows them to earn much higher profits than would otherwise be the case.

North American sports leagues have not always had the luxury of this monopoly status. Until about 25 years ago, many leagues regularly faced competitors. The league that has faced the most competitors over the years is, perhaps somewhat surprisingly, the NFL. Since World War II, the NFL has faced serious competition from the All American Football Conference (AAFC) during the late 1940s, the American Football League (AFL) during the 1960s, the World Football League (WFL) during the mid-1970s, and the United States Football League (USFL) in the mid-1980s. In basketball, the NBA was actually formed in the late 1940s from the merger of two competing leagues—the National Basketball League (NBL) and the Basketball Association of America (BAA)—and then faced competition from the rival American Basketball Association (ABA) from 1967 to 1976. In hockey, the NHL faced competition from the rival World Hockey Association (WHA) during the 1972 to 1979 time span. Only in baseball has there not been a competitor league emerge since World War II.

The presence of these leagues rapidly and dramatically bid up player salaries. In some cases, they also forced a merger with the established league. The AFL was the most successful of all **rival leagues**, gaining a complete merger in 1966, with all eight AFL teams at the time being accepted into the NFL. The ABA and the WHA were also successful in gaining at least partial mergers, with four ABA teams entering the NBA in 1976, and four WHA teams entering the NHL in 1979.

Why have no new rival leagues emerged in more than 25 years? Rival leagues need two elements to be successful. First, they need players, at least some of whom are talented enough to be able to play in the established league, but who have chosen to play in the rival league. Many great players are alumni of rival leagues—Joe Namath and Herschel Walker in football, Julius Erving and Moses Malone in basketball, and Wayne Gretzky and Mark Messier in hockey, to name only a few. Before the emergence of strong players associations, and before the emergence

of free agency, players often were "underpaid," with players generally earning only 20% to 25% of league revenues, compared to the situation today where 55% to 60% is the norm. Thus players today have much less incentive to jump to a rival league.

In addition to having quality players, a second factor that rival leagues need to be successful is viable cities and markets in which to play. Over the past three decades, the major professional leagues have undergone successive rounds of expansion, to the point where all four currently have 30 or more franchises. This larger geographic footprint forces potential rival leagues either to place franchises in more mid-size, and probably less viable, markets, or to challenge the established league in head-to-head competition in the markets where the established league is already located.

While the examination of rival leagues can make for an interesting history lesson, what relevance does it have to business and finance in today's sport world? It turns out that the monopoly status of sports leagues has a great impact on financial issues. With no real threat of outside competition ever occurring, at least for the foreseeable future, the established sports leagues have large degrees of market power. This, in turn, allows them to have greater bargaining power with players, with broadcasters, with corporate sponsors, and with local governments regarding stadium funding issues. All else equal, it makes the major professional sports leagues much more profitable than they otherwise would be. It also allows them to enact financial policies—such as salary caps and revenue sharing—that would simply not be possible if a league faced direct competition from a rival league.

This level of monopoly power is almost unheard of in any other American business or industry. In fact, some economists argue that major professional sports leagues and their member teams are the only legal monopolies in the United States today. Some economists (Quirk & Fort, 1999) have even called for the federal government to break up the monopoly leagues, similar to the forced breakup of AT&T in 1984. For example, one possibility is that the NFL could be broken into two different leagues, with each league acting completely independent of the other, thus introducing a measure of competition back into the industry not seen in decades. This competition would benefit—at least theoretically—fans, the media, taxpayers, and players by reducing the bargaining power of the leagues. While this forced breakup is unlikely to occur (the industry simply has too much political power), the industry will no doubt have to continue to occasionally publicly defend its monopoly status from challenges by economists or by certain members of Congress.

Of course, this monopoly position of leagues and teams does not guarantee financial success, nor does it guarantee that every team in every league will enjoy equal financial success. Leagues and teams must still produce a quality product, and they must display sound and innovative business management practices to achieve maximum success. While the monopoly position of the major professional leagues ensures no direct competition in the same sport, teams must still compete for the broader entertainment dollar of consumers. Consumers in many cities have a wide variety of entertainment options, including major professional sports, minor professional sports, college sports, the theater, the symphony, and theme parks.

For example, even though the NFL and the NHL are both monopolies, the former is obviously a much stronger, much more successful business entity. Even within a league, management quality still matters. In the NFL, the New England Patriots went from the lowest-valued franchise in 1991 to the second-highest-valued franchise in 2006 (they have since dropped to third place by 2009), largely, according to some, due to the Kraft family's purchase of the team

in 1994, and the subsequent innovative management approaches that were adopted.

■ KEY SKILLS

The future will continue to provide many growth opportunities for sport organizations, but will also present challenges. As sport organizations continue to increase their managerial sophistication, the need for well-trained individuals in finance will become even greater. The specific issues will likely change: The key financial issues facing the industry in 15 years may be quite different than the ones facing the industry today. Thus there is a need for managers to understand underlying financial principles and techniques, rather than just simply being familiar with current issues and facts. The issues will change, but the underlying analytical tools to analyze the issues will not.

No matter what type of sport organization is involved, the finance function is crucial. It is important to remember that finance isn't defined as much by the subject matter being analyzed—it could be decisions related to ticket or sponsorship sales, team marketing, stadium operations, or player personnel—but rather by how the issue is analyzed. Finance is a "way of thinking" about problems that makes use of specific principles, concepts, and techniques to help managers make better decisions. Academic and practical training in finance helps people to "think like a finance person" and to evaluate problems using the fundamental concepts of financial analyses. Specifically, it forces managers to examine problems in terms of the age-old finance concepts of risk and return, and to effectively use tools such as ROI to better analyze problems.

While finance people do need some comfort in "working with numbers," this is far from the only skill needed. In addition to formal training in corporate finance, those interested in a career in the area should have a solid grounding in managerial and financial accounting, and in the advanced use of spreadsheets (e.g., Microsoft Excel). For those with aspirations of working in the spectator sport industry, a familiarity with sports economics is also very beneficial.

The specific issues may differ depending on the setting. For example, the issues facing the vice president of finance of a major golf club manufacturer will be different than those faced by an athletic director at a Division III college program, which in turn will be different than those faced by a chief financial officer of a major professional team. However, the common link is that financial decision making in each of these settings should be grounded in the same basic set of principles, techniques, and thought processes.

■ CURRENT ISSUES

Can Growth Continue?

In the nonspectator sport sector, a key issue is the extent to which the recreation and leisure market will continue to grow. Much of this sector—from golf to fitness to skiing—is driven by demographics, affluence, and societal values. Over the past 30 years, the U.S. population has aged, our overall affluence has increased, and our societal concerns over health-related issues have grown. The effects have been an explosion in spending on recreational and fitness activities. This large growth in the market has, in turn, propelled the industry to financial heights not seen before.

For individual segments of the nonspectator sport industry, predicting consumer trends also becomes a factor in their growth. For example, will golf remain as "hot" as it has been for the past two decades? Will a new recreational activity emerge that will provide enormous financial potential? These are crucial financial questions because capital investments (e.g., new golf courses, new ski resorts) are made now,

but the payoff from these investments doesn't occur until later. Thus, if our assumptions about the future growth in the industry are incorrect, our ROI calculations will also be incorrect. For example, if golf's popularity begins to wane over the next decade, the ROI on any new golf course construction will be lower than it has been in the recent past, and it may even be low enough to cause the investor to not undertake the new project.

Broadly similar questions exist for the spectator side of the sport industry; in particular, can the financial successes of the past continue at their same level into the future? Both the major professional leagues and the major revenue-generating college sports (Division I football and men's basketball) have seen tremendous revenue growth in the past 15 years. **Table 4-2** shows how franchise values in the major professional leagues have changed over this time period. Franchise values capture the future expected profitability (revenues minus expenses) of the franchise and represent the current market price of the franchise. All four leagues have shown significant growth in franchise values over the time period, largely because revenues have risen faster than expenses.

Revenues have also risen in the major revenue-generating college sports. **Table 4-3** compares revenues in 1989 with 2008 revenues for football, men's basketball, and women's basketball. All three show healthy yearly revenue growth. Of the three, women's basketball grew the most, showing an 11.69% increase per year over the time period, although this must be tempered with the fact that women's basketball started with by far the lowest base revenue (in 1989) of the three. In absolute terms, football continues to lead the revenue parade, with the average Division I–Football Bowl Subdivision program now earning almost $15 million per year in revenues. While not shown in Table 4-3, the NCAA reports that the highest-revenue college football program in 2008–2009 earned almost $87.5 million in revenues (McMurphy, 2010).

TABLE 4-2   Average Franchise Values: 1991 and 2009 (in millions of dollars)

	2009	1991	Average Annual Growth Rate
NFL	1,040	132	12.15 %
MLB	491	121	8.09 %
NBA	367	70	9.64 %
NHL	223	44	9.44 %

Sources: Ozanian, M., & Badenhausen, K. (2006 November 9). NHL on the rebound. Retrieved October 7, 2010, from http://www.forbes.com/business/2006/11/09/nhl-teams-owners-biz_06nhl_cz_mo_kb_1109nhlintro.html; Ozanian, M., & Badenhausen, K. (2009, April 22). Baseball's most valuable teams. Retrieved November 10, 2010, from http://www.forbes.com/2009/04/22/yankees-mets-baseball-values-09-business-sports-land.html; Ozanian, M., Beadenhausen, K., & Bigman, R. (2009, September 2). The business of football. Retrieved October 7, 2010, from http://nfl-pro-football-business-sportsmoney-football-values-09-nfl_land.html; Badenhausen K., Ozanian, M., & Settimi, C. (2009b November 11). The business of hockey. Retrieved October 28, 2010, from http://www.forbes.com/2009/11/11/nhl-team-values-business-sports-hockey-values-09-nhl_land.html; Badenhausen K., Ozanian, M., & Settimi, C. (2009a December 9). The business of basketball. Retrieved October 7, 2010, from http://www.forbes.com/2009/12/09/nba-team-valuations-business-sports-basketball-values-09-nba_lander.html; and Quirk, J., & Fort, R. (1997). *Pay dirt: The business of professional team sports.* Princeton, NJ: Princeton University Press.

This increased revenue in spectator sports has come from a number of specific areas: gate receipts, broadcast contracts, sponsorship sales, stadium naming rights, and so on. As for gate receipts, ticket prices have increased considerably in all leagues. These increased prices reflect the growing popularity of sport, the increased ability to pay of sport consumers, and the scarcity of tickets in some locations. For example, at the University of Tennessee, some premium club (football) seats require a $25,000 donation, payable over five years, plus $4,000 per year for the seats (Adams, 2006).

In fact, The *Wall Street Journal* reports that the prices of premium tickets for some college football programs are now higher than the prices of tickets for NFL teams in the same market (Adams, 2006).

Gate receipts have certainly been enhanced by the preponderance of new (or refurbished) stadiums that now exist. The revenue-generating ability of a stadium depends not only on the quantity of seats, but also on the quality. Teams prefer luxury seating and club seating because these premium seats have much greater revenue potential than the ordinary regular

TABLE 4-3   NCAA Division I (Football Bowl Subdivision) Programs Median Revenues per School, by Sport: 1989 and 2008 (in thousands of dollars)

	2008	1989	Average Annual Growth Rate
Football	14,841	4,300	6.74 %
Men's Basketball	4,758	1,600	5.90 %
Women's Basketball	490	60	11.69 %

Source: Fulks, D. (2008). 2004–08 NCAA revenues and expenses of Division I intercollegiate athletics programs report. Retrieved October 7, 2010, from http://www.ncaapublications.com/p-4135-revenues-expenses-2004-08-ncaa-revenues-and-expenses-of-division-i-intercollegiate-athletics-programs-report.aspx

seating. These premium seats allow teams to better target high-income individuals and/or corporate clientele, and they allow teams to capture the increased ability and willingness to pay of these groups. Older stadiums simply do not have configurations that allow for this type of premium seating. In essence, new stadiums give sport consumers many more ways to spend their money. Many new stadiums have been able to generate even more revenues by selling the naming rights to the stadium. For example, Citigroup purchased the naming rights to the New York Mets new stadium that opened in 2009 for a record $20 million per year (Buxbaum, 2009).

In addition to these "new" assets, the sport industry has been able to more effectively leverage its popularity and brand through newer media technologies such as the Internet, satellite TV, "on-demand" television, smartphones, and handheld wireless devices. The industry has also been able to better leverage its assets by adopting more sophisticated and professional management techniques, particularly in the areas of marketing and finance.

Media revenues have also continued to grow strongly. For example, a seven-year deal (which began in 1991) between the NCAA and CBS to televise the men's basketball tournament paid the NCAA an average of about $140 million per season. In contrast, the new 14-year agreement signed in 2010 will pay almost $800 million per year. In football, ESPN will pay about $125 million per year to televise the BCS games from 2011 to 2014. These large contracts mean, in turn, lucrative payouts for the teams that reach a BCS game. For example, in 2009 the Fiesta Bowl paid out more than $17 million to each of the two participating teams. Contrast this with the payouts in 1991, when each participating team received only about $2 million.

In professional sports, all four leagues have substantially increased their total TV revenues over the past 20 years. For sports such as baseball and hockey, the growth has been particularly at the local—as opposed to national—level. In the NFL, where almost all TV money is through national contracts, the growth has been the most dramatic. The NFL's current contracts with Fox, CBS, NBC, and ESPN, signed in 2005, collectively pay each NFL team about $100 million per year in revenues, compared to approximately $30 million per team in 1991 (*SportsBusiness Daily*, 2007).

Challenges

While revenues have certainly increased over the past 15 years, the cost of doing business has also gone up. In the nonspectator sport sector, increasingly large capital investments are needed to be able to continue to generate revenues. With technological advances and more sophisticated consumer tastes, fitness and recreation businesses are forced to spend ever more dollars on their capital assets. For example, many consumers of fitness centers want the newest and most advanced exercise equipment; golfers want to play on challenging, well-maintained courses; skiers want to stay at resorts that offer the latest amenities. Thus, if

businesses are to remain competitive, they must always be evaluating the quality of their capital assets, and must always be prepared to upgrade these assets to counter the competition's moves. As we learned earlier in the chapter, revenues flow from assets. If a firm's assets decline in quality, then its revenues will be negatively affected. Similar ideas exist in the spectator sport industry, where much of the revenue growth is attributable to teams playing in new or refurbished stadiums.

The financial challenge arises because these assets cost money. For example, new stadiums cost hundreds of millions of dollars. While the scale of investment may not be as great for a local fitness club investing in new exercise equipment, it is proportionately no less significant. Usually, these large-scale investments are financed, at least in part, by borrowed money (i.e., debt). However, debt is risky, in that interest and a proportion of the principal must be paid back to the lender at regular, prespecified intervals, regardless of whether the business meets its revenue expectations. Failure to meet these loan payments could ultimately result in the firm's bankruptcy. This issue is even more critical when one considers that unpredictable events like the severe recession that started in 2008 can make future revenue flows much lower than originally expected.

These debt issues have certainly been prominent in the major pro leagues, as teams have often borrowed heavily to finance their portion of stadium costs. Many new team owners have also borrowed heavily to finance the purchase price of the team. In fact, MLB has been concerned with the high debt levels of some of its teams, and it negotiated a provision into the 2002 collective bargaining agreement (CBA) that placed new limits on the amount of debt that a team could carry.

College sports have faced some unique challenges. The high-profile financial successes of the major revenue-generating sports often

TABLE 4-4 Average Surplus (Deficit) per School, Excluding Institutional Support: 1993 and 2003 (in thousands of dollars)

Division	1993	2003
I-A	200	600
I-AA	1,420	3,690
II (with football)	810	1,640
II (without football)	500	1,270

Source: Fulks, D. (2005). 2002–2003 NCAA Revenues and Expenses of Division I and II Athletic Programs. Retrieved October 7, 2010, from http://www.ncaapublications.com/p-3830-2002-03-ncaa-revenues-expenses-of-division-iii-intercollegiate-athletics-programs-report.aspx

overshadow the rest of the college athletics spectrum. In fact, college athletics, taken as a whole, continue to be unprofitable. **Table 4-4** shows the breakdown of profits (revenues minus expenses) by division. As the table shows, even Division I schools are, on average, in significant deficit positions with their athletic programs. The revenue-generating abilities of football and men's basketball are insufficient to compensate for the deficits that occur in the other sports. The numbers indicate that Division I-AA schools seem to be in the worst financial position: They are unable to generate the revenue of the Division I-A schools, but still incur many of the same costs as I-A, and certainly incur much higher costs than their Division II or III counterparts.

There is another issue that relates to the financial differences between programs. Even if one focuses on just Division I-A programs, there is a very unequal distribution of revenues across programs. For example, the formula used by the NCAA to pay out revenues to conferences from the men's basketball tournament is based, in part, on the success of conference teams in the tournament. Thus conferences that are traditional powers tend to get the highest payouts, which can help to perpetuate their success while inhibiting the ability of other conferences to increase their success. In football, similar issues exist. For example, payouts from the BCS bowls tend to heavily favor the six BCS conferences, leaving relatively small amounts for other conferences. Schools and conferences that receive greater payouts correspondingly increase their chances of future success: More revenue means schools can hire better coaches, can build better practice facilities, can do more upgrades to their stadium, and so forth.

This issue of revenue disparities across schools and conferences is part of a larger issue that economists have recently begun to study— namely, the **competitive balance** problem. The competitive balance issue is rooted in the notion that consumers of a spectator sport seek to be entertained by the game itself. Research by economists reveals that this entertainment value is connected to a concept of "uncertainty of outcome": The greater the uncertainty of outcome, the greater the entertainment value for fans. This concept of uncertainty of outcome can be defined for an individual game, for a season, or over a number of seasons.

For an individual game, while local fans may prefer the home team to win, they also value competitiveness. Games that are expected to be a mismatch, where the outcome is largely predetermined, will reduce fan interest. Similarly, if one looks at an entire season rather than an individual game, fans tend to prefer situations where teams in the league are relatively closely bunched in the standings, as opposed to situations where there is a high level of disparity among the teams. In this latter situation, games played later in the season will become much less meaningful if large gaps separate the teams in the standings. Furthermore, one can look at this concept of uncertainty of outcome across seasons. Are the same teams successful year in and year out, or is there considerable change in the standings from year to year? For example,

the order of finish in the American League East Division of baseball was exactly the same (New York Yankees, Boston, Toronto, Baltimore, Tampa Bay) for six consecutive seasons, from 1998 to 2003 (and again in 2005). Again, the suspicion is that fan interest will be reduced if fans enter each season believing that their favorite team's place in the standings is largely predetermined.

While the concern over competitive balance certainly is relevant to college sports, given the highly differential payouts that tend to favor the already dominant conferences, this issue has received the most attention in professional sports, particularly with baseball. Those who argue that MLB has a competitive balance problem point to the fact that large-market teams are still more likely to make the playoffs over the past decade than small-market teams. For example, since baseball went to the wild card system in 1995, the New York Yankees have made the playoffs in all 14 of the 15 seasons since then, through the 2009 season. The Boston Red Sox, another large-market team, have made the playoff in nine of those seasons. Contrast this with small-market teams such as those in Kansas City and Pittsburgh, neither of which has made the playoffs since 1995.

This example highlights the economic roots of the competitive balance problem: All else equal, large-market teams have greater revenue potential than small-market teams, and thus will find it more beneficial (in a revenue-generation sense) than small-market teams to employ higher-quality players than will small-market teams. To the extent that this higher level of talent ultimately translates into better on-field team performance, large-market teams should, over the long run, be able to field consistently better teams than their small-market counterparts.

Leagues have long had policies that have attempted to improve the on-field fortunes of poor-performing teams. All leagues use some form of a "reverse-order" draft, whereby those teams with the poorest records during the previous season have the top draft choices for the following season. The NFL also has used the scheduling system to foster competitive balance, by giving teams with poorer records during the previous season "easier" schedules in the following season.

These two mechanisms could be termed "nonfinancial" ways to alter competitive balance. However, neither directly addresses the root of the problem: the fact that differences in market sizes across franchises cause differences in revenue potential, which cause differences in the ability to pay players, which cause differences in team payroll, which cause differences in on-field performance.

In an attempt to better deal with these underlying causal factors, professional leagues have introduced a number of "financial" mechanisms to alter competitive balance. One of these mechanisms is a **salary cap**. Both the NFL and the NHL have "hard" caps, while the NBA has a "soft" cap. With the hard cap, the team payroll limit is an absolute, and cannot be violated. A hard cap has been used in the NFL since 1994 and in the NHL since 2005. These hard caps have been the result of negotiations between the leagues and their players' associations. The hard cap limit is typically set as a percentage of league revenues, usually between 55% and 60%. The philosophy behind the hard cap is that it will constrain all franchises to spend about the same amount on payroll (hard caps usually include a minimum payroll as well), presumably ensuring that franchises are fielding relatively equally balanced teams on the field. In essence, a hard cap prevents large-market teams from using their natural financial advantage to buy the best teams.

With a soft cap, a payroll limit is still set, but teams can exceed this limit through various types of "exclusions." For example, one type of exclusion is for situations in which teams sign their own free agents, as opposed to another team's free agents. Given this fairly wide array of exclusions, there is generally a much wider disparity in payrolls across teams with a soft cap than there is with a hard cap. The NBA has had a soft cap since 1984, and made history that year when it was the first league in the modern era of professional sports to implement any type of salary cap.

Revenue sharing is another financial mechanism intended to foster greater competitive balance. With revenue sharing, teams in the league agree to share certain types of revenues among themselves. For example, all four major professional leagues share national television revenues equally. However, the relative significance of this sharing of national television revenues differs across leagues, with the NFL being the only league where national television revenues account for a large portion of total league revenues. In the other three leagues, "local" revenues (such as gate receipts and local television) are much more crucial. These local revenues can vary widely across teams, as mentioned previously, and are directly related to the market size in which the teams play. Thus, unless leagues also have a mechanism to share these revenues, large disparities in total revenues will persist across teams. Historically, there has been little or no sharing of these local revenues, but this has changed significantly in recent years. For example, under the current 2007–2011 CBA, MLB teams share 31% of their net local revenues, a slight decrease from the 34% figure under the 2002–2006 CBA. In the NHL, the 2005 CBA created the first-ever revenue-sharing plan for that league.

Most economists have suggested that revenue sharing, in and of itself, will do little to improve competitive balance. The reason is that teams receiving revenue-sharing transfers may have little incentive to use the money to increase payroll, but instead may be motivated to simply retain the transfer as added profit. In other words, if it were beneficial (in an ROI sense) for small-market teams to increase their payroll, they would have already done so, even without the revenue-sharing transfers. This criticism of revenue sharing has frequently been leveled at baseball's revenue-sharing plan, where some small-market teams that received significant revenue transfers in recent years do not seem to be noticeably improving their on-field performance (but do seem to be improving their profitability). This is particularly a problem in baseball, because there is no payroll floor to which teams must adhere.

Where revenue sharing may be effective as a tool to improve competitive balance is when it is used in conjunction with a hard salary cap. Hard caps, in addition to having a payroll ceiling, have a payroll floor. For some small-market teams, revenues may not be sufficient to meet this floor without revenue-sharing dollars. Thus the hard cap essentially requires small-market teams to use all or part of their revenue-sharing transfers on payroll.

Finally, a **luxury tax** has been used as a mechanism to influence competitive balance. Both the NBA and MLB have a form of a luxury tax. With a luxury tax, a payroll threshold is set prior to a season. Teams that exceed this threshold pay a tax on the excess amount. In baseball, for example, team payroll thresholds under the existing CBA are $170 million in 2010 and $178 million in 2011 (the last year of the CBA). Teams are taxed at a rate of 22.5% for a first violation of the threshold, 30% for a second violation, and 40% for a third violation. The luxury tax works somewhat differently than salary caps or revenue sharing, in that the luxury tax is focused solely on changing the behavior of high-payroll teams, such as the New York Yankees. The Yankees have been the only team to exceed the threshold every season since the tax was introduced in 2003. In 2009, for example, the team paid a luxury tax of almost $26 million, and have cumulatively paid $174 million since 2003, with the other 29 clubs combined paying only $16 million over that time period (Brown, 2009).

■ SUMMARY

While the recession that started in 2008 has temporarily dampened economic growth across all industries, including sport, if one takes a broader perspective, there is no question that the past two decades have proven especially lucrative for all facets of the sport industry. An aging population and growth in the amount of disposable income available to be spent on recreation and entertainment have resulted in skyrocketing revenues in many sectors of the industry.

This financial boom has created a great need in the industry for people with training in finance. The future will continue to provide many growth opportunities for sport organizations but will also present challenges. As sport organizations continue to increase their managerial sophistication, the need for well-trained individuals in finance will become even greater.

The specific issues will likely change: The important financial issues facing the industry in the future may be quite different than the ones facing the industry today. Thus there is a need for managers to understand underlying financial and economic principles and techniques, rather than just simply being familiar with current issues and facts. The issues will change, but the underlying analytical tools to analyze the issues will not.

■ KEY TERMS

assets, balance sheet, bonds, budgeting, competitive balance, debt, default, expenses, income, income statement, interest, liabilities, luxury tax, monopoly, owners' equity, principal, profits, return on investment (ROI), revenues, revenue sharing, risk, rival leagues, salary cap

■ REFERENCES

Adams, R. (2006 August 12). Deep in the pocket. *Wall Street Journal.* Retrieved October 7, 2010, from http://online.wsj.com/article/SB115533449289433679.html

Associated Press. (2007 December 13). Rodriguez finalizes $275 million deal with Yankees. Retrieved November 10, 2010, from http://sports.espn.go.com/mlb/news/story?id=3153171

Badenhausen, K., Ozanian, M., & Settimi, C. (2009a December 9). The business of basketball. Retrieved October 7, 2010, from http://www.forbes.com/2009/12/09/nba-team-valuations-business-sports-basketball-values-09-nba_lander.html

Badenhausen, K., Ozanian, M., & Settimi, C. (2009b November 11). The business of hockey. Retrieved October 7, 2010 from http://www.forbes.com/2009/11/11/nhl-team-values-business-sports-hockey-values-09-nhl_land.html

Brown, M. (2009 December 21). Yankees hit with luxury tax bill of nearly $26 million. Retrieved November 10, 2010, from http://www.bizofbaseball.com/index.php?option=com_content&view=article&id=3860:yankees-hit-with-luxury-tax-bill-of-nearly-26-million&catid=30:mlb-news&Itemid=42

Business Wire. (2010). Fitch closely monitoring National Football League negotiations. Retrieved November 10, 2010, from http://www.businesswire.com/portal/site/home/permalink/?ndmViewId=news_view&newsId=20100308006134&newsLang=en

Buxbaum, E. (2009 April 13). Mets and the Citi: $400 million for stadium-naming rights irks some. Retrieved November 10, 2010, from http://articles.cnn.com/2009-04-13/us/mets.ballpark_1_citi-field-mets-home-stadium-naming?_s=PM:US

Coon, L. (2010). Larry Coon's NBA salary cap FAQ. Retrieved November 10, 2010, from http://members.cox.net/lmcoon/salarycap.htm#Q25

Fried, G., Shapiro, S., & DeSchriver, T. (2008). *Sport finance.* Champaign, IL: Human Kinetics.

Fulks, D. (2008). 2004–08 NCAA revenues and expenses of Division I intercollegiate athletics programs report. Retrieved October 7, 2010, from http://www.ncaapublications.com/p-4135-revenues-expenses-2004-08-ncaa-revenues-and-expenses-of-division-i-intercollegiate-athletics-programs-report.aspx

Fulks, D. (2005). 2002–2003 NCAA Revenues and Expenses of Division I and II Athletic Programs. Retrieved October 7, 2010, from http://www.ncaapublications.com/p-3830-2002-03-ncaa-revenues-expenses-of-division-iii-intercollegiate-athletics-programs-report.aspx

Harris, C., & Watters, C. (2009 May 6). Now bankrupt, Coyotes could end up in Canada. Retrieved November 10, 2010, from http://www.azcentral.com/business/articles/2009/05/05/20090505biz-coyotes0506.html

Karmin, C. (2006 March 13). Going for the big score for college basketball. *Wall Street Journal.* Retrieved September 1, 2007, from http://online.wsj.com/article/SB114193106453693897.html

Leeds M., & von Allmen P. (2008) *The economics of sport.* Boston: Pearson Addison Wesley.

Lewis, M. (2003). *Moneyball: The art of winning an unfair game.* New York: W.W. Norton.

McMurphy, B. (2010 June 30). For Longhorns money grows on football program instead of trees. Retrieved November 10, 2010, from http://ncaafootball.fanhouse.com/2010/06/30/for-longhorns-money-grows-on-football-program-instead-of-trees

News Blaze. (2009). Fitch downgrades MLB club trust securitization to "A–"; Outlook stable. Retrieved November 10, 2010, from http://newsblaze.com/story/2009101915161100001.bw/topstory.html

Ozanian, M., & Badenhausen K. (2009 April 22) Baseball's most valuable teams. Retrieved November 10, 2010, from http://www.forbes.com/2009/04/22/yankees-mets-baseball-values-09-business-sports-land.html

Ozanian, M., & Badenhausen, K. (2006 November 9). NHL on the rebound. Retrieved October 7, 2010, from http://www.forbes.com/business/2006/11/09/nhl-teams-owners-biz_06nhl_cz_mo_kb_1109nhlintro.html

Plunkett Research. (2010). Sports industry overview. Retrieved November 8, 2010, from http://

www.plunkettresearch.com/Industries/Sports/SportsStatistics/tabid/273/Default.aspx

Quirk, J., & Fort, R. (1997). *Pay dirt: The business of professional team sports*. Princeton, NJ: Princeton University Press.

Quirk, J., & Fort, R. (1999). *Hard ball: The abuse of power in pro team sports*. Princeton, NJ: Princeton University Press.

SportsBusiness Daily. (2007 September 6). NFL media rights deals for '07 season. Retrieved November 10, 2010, from http://www.sportsbusinessdaily.com/article/114714

SportsBusiness Journal. (2006 July 31). Tagliabue's tenure: The NFL during Paul Tagliabue's reign as commissioner, p. 32.

Turner, J. (2009 August 29). With a few budget cuts here and there, Ohio State athletics nearly breaks even in 2008–09. Retrieved October 7, 2010, from http://www.cleveland.com/osu/index.ssf/2009/08/with_a_few_budget_cuts_here_an.html

University of Iowa. (2005). Financial plan. Retrieved November 10, 2010, from http://www.hawkeyesports.com/kinnick-renovation/financial-plan.html

University of Notre Dame. (2006). Notre Dame Stadium. Retrieved October 7, 2010, from http://und.cstv.com/trads/nd-m-fb-stad.html

University of Phoenix. (2010). University of Phoenix Stadium statistics. Retrieved November 10, 2010, from http://www.universityofphoenixstadium.com/index.php?page=stadium_facts&section=statistics

Van Riper, T. (2010 January 12). The most valuable teams in sports. Retrieved November 10, 2010, from http://www.forbes.com/2010/01/12/manchester-united-yankees-cowboys-business-sports-valuable-teams.html?boxes=Homepagetopspecialreports

CHAPTER

Legal Principles Applied to Sport Management

Lisa P. Masteralexis and Glenn M. Wong

■ INTRODUCTION

Sport law is the application of laws to sport and recreation. This application to the industry segments signifies the body of law, rather than the creation of a new area of law. However, in a few instances new **statutes** (laws) have been enacted to regulate the sport industry. The following federal laws are examples: the Sports Agent Responsibility and Trust Act of 2004 (regulates agents); the Sports Broadcasting Act of 1961 (sport broadcasting antitrust exemption); Title IX and the Civil Rights Restoration Act (regulates discrimination in education, including athletics); and the Amateur Sports Act and Ted Stevens Olympic and Amateur Sports Act (regulates Olympic and other amateur sports). At the state level, 38 U.S. states and two U.S. territories have adopted the 2001 Uniform Athlete Agent Act and another three have their own laws regulating agents.

Sport governing bodies operate much like federal and state administrative bodies. **Administrative law** describes the body of law created by rules, regulations, orders, and decisions of administrative bodies. Governance documents of sport organizations resemble state or federal laws, rules, and regulations. For instance, the recommended guidelines for National Football League (NFL) training camps closely mirror traditional state tort law principles. Another example lies in the National Collegiate Athletic Association (NCAA) manual that contains all the NCAA rules and regulations and reads like a statute book. As a result, when a dispute arises over the interpretation of a rule or regulation, sport lawyers often represent both the governing body and the participant(s) to resolve the dispute through the administrative process established by the sport organization. One reason for the involvement of sport lawyers is that many sport organizations hire lawyers to draft their rules and regulations. Thus, when a dispute arises, lawyers can best interpret, challenge, or defend the rules and regulations.

Over the past 50 years the sport industry has evolved into a complex multibillion-dollar global entity. With such growth, much is often at stake for those involved in the business and the participation segments of the industry. When decisions cause disputes, those in sport rely heavily on the legal system for a resolution. Thus, sport managers must have a basic understanding of legal principles to manage risk in their daily activities and to know when to seek legal assistance.

■ HISTORY

Early sport and recreation cases were tort law cases involving participation in sport and games dating from the early evolution of tort law in the United States and Great Britain. For instance, a treatise published in 1635 in Britain and a landmark 1800s tort case, *Vosburg v. Putney*, both discuss tort liability for participation in games and horseplay (Yasser et al., 1999).

Many of the earliest U.S. lawsuits in the sport industry involve the business of baseball. Professional baseball has the greatest amount of litigation of all professional sports, due in part to the fact that it is the oldest organized professional league, but also due to its arduous labor history. Early cases in professional sport involved baseball players challenging the reserve system adopted by owners to prevent players from achieving any form of free agency (*Metropolitan Exhibition Co. v. Ewing*, 1890; *Metropolitan Exhibition Co. v. Ward*, 1890). Interestingly, a player involved in one of these case, John Montgomery Ward, led the first union efforts in baseball in the late 1800s and went on to become a lawyer (Staudohar, 1996). Throughout the early to mid-twentieth century, most cases in the sport industry were based

in contract, antitrust, and labor law applied to professional sport.

At the time of these early cases there was no formally recognized specialty called "sport law." Sport law was first documented in 1972 when Boston College Law School's Professor Robert Berry offered a course focused on legal issues in the professional sport industry titled, Regulation of the Professional Sport Industry (Wong & Masteralexis, 1996). Numerous law schools and sport management programs now include sport law courses in their curricula.

There are many reasons for the considerable growth in the field over the past four decades. The legal profession as a whole has moved toward a greater degree of specialization. The amount of litigation and the diversity of cases in the sport industry have increased as people rely on the courts to resolve disputes. Many athletic associations have adopted their own governance systems with rules, regulations, and procedures that are based on the U.S. legal system. Lawyers have developed specialties in the sport industry to address the challenges to governing bodies. Lawyers now specialize in representing schools and athletes in investigations by and hearings before the NCAA (Haworth, 1996).

There are four professional associations devoted to sport law in North America, and one each in Europe, Australia, and New Zealand. The North American associations are the American Bar Association Forum Committee on Sport and Entertainment Law, the Sports Lawyers Association, the Marquette University Law School's National Sports Law Institute, and the Sport and Recreation Law Association (SRLA; formerly the Society for the Study of the Legal Aspects of Sport and Physical Activity). All four associations publish journals and newsletters.

While possessing a law degree is not a necessity for a sport manager, the skills a legal education provide are beneficial to many positions in the industry. Legal education teaches written and oral communication, analytical reasoning, critical thinking, problem solving, and negotiating skills. Many in the sport industry possess law degrees but work in sport management rather than practicing law. For instance, in professional sport, the current commissioners of the National Hockey League (NHL; Gary Bettman), and the National Basketball Association (NBA; David Stern) are lawyers, as were some previous commissioners in Major League Baseball (MLB; Fay Vincent, Bowie Kuhn, Kennesaw Mountain Landis) and the NFL (Paul Tagliabue). Plus, many of the commissioners' staff, professional team general managers, players association executive directors and staff, NCAA officials, college conference commissioners and staff, athletic directors and compliance staff, International and U.S. Olympic Committee members and staff, national governing body members and staff, player representatives, and facility managers possess law degrees but do not practice law in the traditional sense. Their knowledge of law guides their decision making and may save organizations the expense of hiring counsel. For example, a facility manager may need to understand local ordinances and codes, tort law, contract law, labor and employment laws, and the Americans with Disabilities Act, just to name a few. A facility manager also may be responsible for negotiating many contracts, including leases with teams, event contracts, concessionaire contracts, sponsorship agreements, employment contracts, collective bargaining agreements with labor unions, and pourage rights for the beverages sold in the facility.

■ KEY CONCEPTS

Legal disputes occur more frequently in the sport industry today than they did years ago, as more people turn to the legal system to resolve disputes. One reason is the rising financial interests involved in high school, col-

legiate, Olympic, and professional sport. On the high school and intercollegiate side, gender discrimination, constitutional rights violations, recruiting violations, use of ineligible players, and rule violations by athletes, coaches, and educational institutions are all sources of litigation (Wong, 2010). On the professional side, labor disputes, broken contracts, misconduct by athletes and owners, and the enforcement of and challenges to rules are the primary sources of litigation. Personal injury and product liability cases filed by recreational sport participants have increased. To make legally sound decisions, it is important for sport managers to have a basic understanding of legal principles.

Risk Management

Risk management is an important lesson a sport manager can learn from sport law. Managing risk requires developing a management strategy to maintain greater control over the legal uncertainties that may wreak havoc on a sport business. Whatever the type of sport business, risk management plans contain the same goals: prevention and intervention. Prevention involves keeping problems from arising, whereas intervention involves having a plan of action to follow when problems do occur. Risk management strategy encourages sport managers to develop a plan to prevent legal disputes from occurring and a plan for intervening when a legal problem does arise. Through such risk management, sport managers may limit their losses by avoiding becoming defendants in court actions. (Note that a **plaintiff** is the person or organization who initiates a lawsuit, and a **defendant** is the person or organization against whom the lawsuit is brought.)

The D.I.M. Process is one method used to establish a risk management program. The D.I.M. Process consists of three steps: (a) *developing* the risk management plan, (b) *implementing* the risk management plan, and (c) *managing* the risk management plan (Ammon & Robinson, 2007). It is important that sport managers use these steps to create a risk management program specifically tailored to their organizations. The risk management plan should address all potential legal liability. Many people think of risk management plans only for addressing the potential for tort liability—in particular, negligence. Instead the plan should include the many areas of law discussed throughout this chapter. For example, a risk management philosophy may also keep a sport manager from losing an employment discrimination suit, an arbitration proceeding, or a challenge to an athletic association's rule. A key to a successful risk management strategy is to have all the organization's employees involved in the three stages of the process. This way, employees will have "ownership" in the plan (Ammon & Robinson, 2007). They will know why the plan is in existence and what its goals are, and thus be more likely to follow it.

Judicial Review

Athletic administrators make decisions regarding athletic rules and regulations daily, about areas such as eligibility or recruiting. As decision makers, athletic administrators must realize they do not possess complete control over athletes and coaches. Courts may review their decisions. **Judicial review** occurs when a plaintiff challenges a rule and the court evaluates it to determine whether it should apply. Historically, courts have declined to overturn rules of voluntary athletic organizations, except where the rule or regulation meets one of the following conditions (Masteralexis, 2007a):

1. The rule violates public policy because it is fraudulent or unreasonable.
2. The rule exceeds the scope of the athletic association's authority.

3. The athletic association breaks one of its own rules.
4. The rule is applied in an arbitrary or capricious manner.
5. The rule violates an individual's constitutional rights.
6. The rule challenged by the plaintiff violates an existing law, such as the Sherman Antitrust Act or the Americans with Disabilities Act.

A court will not review the merits of a rule, but will simply grant a remedy if one of these conditions exists. Judicial review is not limited to high school and college athletics, but is used more frequently there than in professional sport. In professional sport, owners or players generally use judicial review to challenge a rule or decision made by a commissioner or ownership committee.

When a plaintiff seeks judicial review, he or she will also request an **injunction**, that is, an order from the court to do or not do a particular action. Courts have the power to grant two types of remedies: monetary damages and injunctive relief. Monetary damages compensate a plaintiff or punish a defendant. Money, however, is not always the best remedy. A student ruled ineligible for a tournament simply wants to play. In cases involving a challenge to an athletic association's rule, the plaintiff's interest may be to keep the rule from applying or to force the athletic association to apply it differently. Injunctive relief is a better remedy because it provides a court order with the power to do exactly that, which often is to maintain the status quo until there is a full trial on the matter. Injunctions prevent current and future wrongs and can only be used to prevent an irreparable injury. An injury is considered irreparable when it involves the risk of physical harm or death, the loss of a special opportunity, or the deprivation of unique, irreplaceable property (Wong, 2010).

Money does not provide adequate compensation for an irreparable injury such as being barred from participation in sport. For example, assume a high school provided a boys' soccer team but no girls' soccer team. A girl tried out and made the boys' team. Her play impressed the coach, and he gave her a starting position after the first game of the season. Her team went undefeated in the regular season. The night before the first playoff game, the league commissioner called the coach to tell him that the other coaches in the league had launched a complaint against the team for having a girl on its roster when they were competing in a boys' league. The commissioner also stated that if the girl showed up to play in the tournament, the team would have to forfeit those games. In this situation, the coach and the female student-athlete might seek an injunction to compete in the tournament. They are not interested in money. Besides, there is no way to determine how much participating in the soccer game is worth. The girl will argue that she will face irreparable harm by the fact that she is being kept from the opportunity to play with her teammates. She may never have

the opportunity to participate in this type of tournament again, and even if she were to have another opportunity, it would not be the same because she has worked hard with this team. Further, the other coaches had all season to complain and they waited until the playoffs in an attempt to damage an undefeated team. No amount of money can compensate her for this opportunity. Besides seeking injunction, the plaintiff here would file suit against the league for gender discrimination.

Tort Liability

A **tort** is an injury or wrong suffered due to another's improper conduct. The goals of tort law are to provide monetary damages to compensate an injured person (plaintiff) and to deter defendants and others in society from engaging in similar conduct in the future. The sport industry is susceptible to tort claims because people participating in sport may hurt themselves or others and tort law allows people to assess loss and allocate blame.

The intent of the defendant while committing the tort aids the court in determining what tort the defendant committed and in assessing damages owed to the plaintiff. Intentional torts allow for additional damages, called punitive damages, to punish the defendant. Intentional torts occur when one person purposely causes harm to another or engages in an activity that is substantially certain to cause harm. Assault, battery, defamation, intentional infliction of emotional distress, intentional interference with contractual relations, and invasion of privacy are all intentional torts.

Gross negligence falls between negligence (discussed below) and an intentional tort. **Gross negligence** occurs when a defendant acts recklessly. Recklessness exists when a person knows that the act is harmful, but fails to realize it will produce the extreme harm that results (*Hackbart v. Cincinnati Bengals, Inc.*, 1979). This theory is applied routinely in participant versus participant cases, except in Arizona, Nevada, and Wisconsin (*Mark v. Moser*, 2001).

Negligence is an unintentional tort and is the most common tort that sport managers encounter. Therefore, the focus in this introductory chapter is on negligence and not intentional torts.

Sport managers are negligent when they commit an act or omission that causes injury to a person to whom they owe a duty to act with care. To determine whether a sport manager has been negligent, a court will focus on the relationship between the plaintiff (injured) and the defendant (sport manager). Before a sport manager is liable for negligence, the plaintiff must show that the sport manager owed the plaintiff a **duty of care**. A legal duty of care is more than simply one's moral obligation. According to Van der Smissen (2003), a legal duty arises from one of three origins: (a) from a relationship inherent in a particular situation, (b) from a voluntary assumption of the duty of care, or (c) from a duty mandated by a law.

For example, assume a college track-and-field coach was conducting a private training session with her top athlete. After running 500 meters, the athlete collapsed. Because of her special relationship with the runner, the coach has a duty to provide the athlete with prompt medical assistance. Assume further that a citizen of the community who has no connection to the team is exercising at the facility. The citizen may be under a moral obligation to help the athlete, but the citizen has no relationship to the athlete, and thus no legal duty to render assistance. However, if the citizen ran over to the collapsed athlete to help the coach administer cardiopulmonary resuscitation (CPR), the citizen would then voluntarily assume a duty of care toward the athlete. Finally, the law may impose a duty of care on certain individuals due to their special training or skills. Assume further that the citizen is an off-duty emergency medi-

cal technician (EMT) and that the state where the incident occurs requires all certified EMTs to respond to emergencies. Such a law would create a relationship between the collapsed athlete and the EMT who is exercising there. In such a case, if the EMT did not respond, the athlete could argue that the EMT was negligent. To be negligent, a defendant must also be the actual cause of the injury and the injury must be a reasonable, foreseeable consequence of the defendant's action.

Negligence imposes a duty to refrain from careless acts. A good risk management plan, then, can help a sport manager avoid lawsuits based on negligence. Risk management involves developing a plan to avoid liability. To develop the plan, sport managers must brainstorm about the potential problems the business may face and contemplate what is reasonable and foreseeable. If the sport manager then implements a plan to avoid reasonable and foreseeable injuries, the risk manager is working to establish an environment free from negligence (see "Current Issues" at the end of this chapter). This way, the sport manager will also reduce the risk of a successful tort claim.

An issue that arises often is the liability of teams and facilities to spectators injured while attending games. Some courts have adopted a "no duty" or "limited duty rule to limit negligence cases, particularly in baseball. For example, in *Thurmond v. Prince William Baseball Club, Inc.* (2003), the court held that when an adult spectator of ordinary intelligence and a familiarity with the sport attends a game, he assumes the normal risks of watching a baseball game, such as being hit by a ball when sitting in an unscreened area. Similarly, in *Turner v. Mandalay Sports Entertainment* (2008), a minor league baseball team did not provide a protective screen around its concession area. A patron who was sitting in the concession area was hit in the face with a ball hit from the field of play. The court found that the baseball team had a "limited duty" to the plaintiff and that the plaintiff had been unable to demonstrate that the area in which she was seated constituted an "unduly high risk of injury."

However, in *Crespin v. Albuquerque Baseball Club* (2009), a New Mexico appellate court declined to adopt the limited duty rule holding that the team and city owed a general duty of reasonable care to all spectators, and whether they breach the duty should depend on the facts and circumstances of each case. The court found no compelling reason to adopt the baseball rule due to the state's comparative negligence statute, under which juries could evaluate risks that spectators accept while attending games. Applying traditional tort law principles, the court found the trial court's granting of summary judgment (due to the limited duty rule) inappropriate, emphasizing that a jury should determine whether the team and city breached their duty to the spectator by failing to screen the picnic area or warn that batting practice was underway. In dismissing the claims against the Houston Astros and minor leaguer Dave Matranga, the court noted that Matranga was merely practicing to perform in a manner consistent with the rules of the game, under which his team would be rewarded for home runs.

Contact sports also pose an interesting question for the court to consider, which generally provides immunity from liability for amateurs engaging in that sport. In *Noffke ex. rel Swenson v. Bakke* (2009), the court found that cheerleading should be considered a contact sport and that a male cheerleader's inability to prevent the plaintiff's fall was not an act of negligence. (As noted above, most courts adopt a gross negligence standard of liability for co-participant torts.)

Agency Law

The law of **agency** affects all businesses, including those in sport. The term *agency* describes

"the fiduciary relation which results from the manifestation of consent by one person to another that the other shall act on his behalf and subject to his control and consent," (*Black's Law Dictionary*, 1979, p. 58) One purpose of agency law is to establish the duties that the **principal** and the **agent** owe each other. Although the principal and the agent often have an underlying **contract** to establish the relationship's parameters, agency law is not concerned with promises established by contract (such promises are subject to contract law). **Fiduciary duties** are inherent in the principal–agent relationship and are imposed on the parties in accordance with agency law, regardless of what a contract between the parties specifies. The term *fiduciary* comes from Roman law and means a person holding the character of a trustee. A fiduciary duty obligates a fiduciary to act with trust that one will be loyal and hones and act in the best interest of the other (*Black's*, 1979). A second purpose of agency law is to hold the principal responsible to others for the actions of the agent, provided the agent is acting under the authority granted to the agent by the principal.

Under agency law, the principal owes the agent three duties:

1. To comply with a contract if one exists
2. To compensate the agent for his or her services
3. To reimburse the agent for any expenses incurred while acting on the principal's behalf

The agent owes the principal five fiduciary duties (Howell, Allison, & Henley, 1987):

1. To obey
2. To remain loyal
3. To exercise reasonable care
4. To notify
5. To account (for information and finances on a reasonable basis)

This list of fiduciary duties is fairly self-explanatory. However, the second duty, to remain loyal by avoiding conflicts of interest, may need some clarification. Because conflicts of interest arise so frequently, an agent can continue representing a principal when a conflict of interest is present, provided the agent fully discloses the conflict to the principal and gives the principal the option to work with a neutral party in place of the agent. For example, assume a player representative has two clients who are all-star catchers and free agents. Both have similar defensive skills and are power hitters. Assume the Atlanta Braves are in need of a top-shelf catcher. The player representative may be in a position of favoring the interest of one free agent over another, as the Braves will need just one of the players. The agent and catchers need not end their relationship. The agent should disclose the conflict to the catchers and give one the option of finding another negotiator for that contract negotiation.

Another example that occurs quite frequently in the sports industry is when a sport management agency, such as Creative Artists Agency (CAA) Sports, International Management Group (IMG), or Octagon, represents both an athlete and the event in which the athlete is competing. For a major event, the athlete may receive an appearance fee that is negotiated by one division of the agency and the agent of the athlete, both of whom work for the same parent company. (Further information on conflicts of interest is in Chapter 11, Sports Agency).

Under agency law, a principal will be liable for any torts committed by an agent, provided the agent was acting within the scope of employment. The discussion of vicarious liability in the next section addresses this issue in greater detail. A principal is also liable for any contracts an agent has entered into on the principal's behalf, provided the principal gave the agent authority to enter into contracts.

Agency law is an important component to the sports representation industry. Among other reasons, athletes and coaches hire sports agents to gain a level of parity in negotiations with more experienced negotiators, such as club management or university representatives (Shropshire & Davis, 2003). A player representative works as an agent for an athlete who acts as a principal. These relationships are often based in contract law, but are also governed by the law of agency and its imposition of fiduciary duties. When lawsuits do occur, they may involve claims under contract (*Total Economic Athletic Management of America v. Pickens*, 1995; *Williams v. CWI, Inc.*, 1991; *Zinn v. Parrish*, 1981), tort (*Vick v. Wong*, 2009; *In re Ekuban*, 2004; *Brown v. Woolf*, 1983), and/or agency law (*Hillard v. Black*, 2000; *Buse v. Vanguard Group*, 1996; *Jones v. Childers*, 1994; *Detroit Lions, Inc. and Sims v. Argovitz*, 1984). NCAA Bylaws permit student athletes to retain the service of an attorney or an outside consultant provided that this personal representative does not consult with professional teams. In *Oliver v. NCAA* (2009), pitcher Andy Oliver was ruled ineligible by the NCAA for a violation of this Bylaw. The Ohio state district court upheld Oliver's argument that the NCAA's ruling was against public policy and affected an attorney-client relationship with the court adding that the Bylaw was "capricious . . . [and] . . . arbitrary." Oliver settled with the NCAA prior to appeal, thus limiting the precedential value of this case. In a similar case, the Kentucky Court of Appeals upheld a decision by the Fayette County Circuit Court to deny an injunction to allow star University of Kentucky pitcher James Paxton to be eligible to play pending an investigation as to whether he violated the no agent rule by having Scott Boras as his advisor (Kobritz, 2010). The NCAA asked to question Paxton about allegations in a news report that Boras had negotiated with the Toronto Blue Jays, the team that drafted Paxton, prior to Paxton's decision to return to Kentucky. Paxton felt he risked his eligibility in answering the questions and thus, he sought the injunction on the grounds that the Student-Athlete Code of Conduct at Kentucky ensured him due process protections. In hindsight, it has been suggested that Paxton should have participated in the interview, been declared ineligible, and then followed Oliver's lead of challenging the NCAA Bylaw (Kobritz, 2010). Representation of athletes and coaches is explored in greater detail in Chapter 11, Sports Agency.

Vicarious Liability

Vicarious liability provides a plaintiff with a cause of action to sue a superior for the negligent acts of a subordinate. Often lawsuits arise when an employee commits a tort and a plaintiff seeks to hold the employer, who has money and a greater ability to pay damages, liable. Under vicarious liability the employer need not be negligent to be liable. The employer is legally responsible provided the employee is in fact an employee and the employee committed a tort while acting in the scope of employment. If the employer is also negligent for hiring an unqualified individual or not providing proper training, the employer's negligence may provide an additional legal claim.

Three defenses are available to an employer faced with a vicarious liability claim. First, if the employee was not negligent, the employer cannot be held liable. Second, the employer may argue that the employee was not acting within the scope of employment, as is the case when an employee acts on his or her own. Third, the employer may argue that the employee is an **independent contractor**. An independent contractor is an employee who is not under the employer's supervision and control. Examples of employees who may be independent contractors include freelance sportswriters or photographers, sport officials, part-time instructors or personal trainers at health and fitness centers, and team physicians or athletic trainers.

Contract Law

A **contract** is a written or verbal agreement between two or more parties that creates a legal obligation to fulfill the promises made by the agreement. Every aspect of the sport industry uses contracts. Sport managers use contracts for employing players, officials, and other staff; television and radio broadcasting deals; licensed properties; merchandise sales; facility leases; sponsorship deals; concession arrangements; ticket sales; membership arrangements; scholarships; purchasing equipment, uniforms, and other goods and services; and scheduling games, events, and appearances. Many sport managers negotiate and enter into contracts regularly with or without help from a lawyer. It is essential that sport managers have a basic understanding of contract law to limit their liability. Sound contract drafting and analysis should be part of a sport manager's risk management plan.

A valid contract must have an offer by one party and an acceptance by another. A contract also requires both parties to give **consideration**. Consideration is something of value, such as money, property, or something intangible. For example, if Big State University (BSU)

FIGURE 5-1 Contract Formation

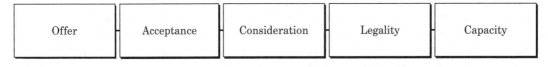

hires a football coach for four years at a salary of $500,000 per year, BSU's consideration is $500,000 plus any fringe benefits offered to BSU employees. BSU's consideration might also include perks received by the coach due to his contract (*Rodgers v. Georgia Tech Athletic Assoc.*, 1983). The coach's consideration is his skill, talent, time, effort, and the promise not to coach anywhere else for four years.

People entering into contracts must have the **capacity** to understand the nature and effects of their actions. Generally, individuals older than the age of 18 possess capacity. Under contract law, minors and mentally incompetent individuals may enter contracts, but may **disaffirm** (opt out of) them at any time. Thus, sport managers agreeing to appearances or endorsements with athletes younger than age 18 should enter into those contracts at their own risk, knowing that minors may disaffirm the contracts provided they return anything of value that was not earned. The subject matter of a contract must be legal which means it cannot violate laws or public policy. This concept is known as **legality**. **Figure 5-1** depicts the formation of a contract.

Once a contract is made, if a promise is broken it is considered a **breach**. A full breach occurs when the contract is entirely broken, and a partial breach occurs when one or more, but not all, of the provisions in the contract are broken. The remedy for a breach is usually monetary damages to compensate the injured party, for money will usually enable an individual to fulfill his or her expectations elsewhere. In rare cases an injunction is a remedy to force a party to

comply with a contract. Most often this remedy is available only when the subject matter of the contract is so rare that no amount of money will provide an adequate remedy. For example, if a sports memorabilia collector entered into a contract to purchase the only mint-condition Honus Wagner rookie baseball card in existence and the seller backed out of the deal after the contract was made, then the collector may go to court to obtain a court order to force the seller to comply with the contract.

Waivers and **releases of liability** are contracts that may form an important component of one's risk management plan. Through waivers, parties agree contractually to give up their right to sue for negligence. Waivers cannot be used to waive a right to sue for gross negligence or intentional torts. A *waiver* is signed before one participates in the activity for which one is waiving the right to sue. A *release of liability* is similar to a waiver, but is a contract that a party signs after an injury occurs by which the injured party gives up the right to sue later, usually in exchange for a financial settlement.

Jurisdictions vary as to whether a waiver will be upheld against a plaintiff. When using a waiver, a sport manager should be concerned with drafting it carefully so that it will be enforceable. Many courts will invalidate a waiver if there is a flaw in the waiver's language. Flawed language may lead a court to conclude that the individual signing the waiver did not knowingly and voluntarily agree to waive his or her right to sue. A waiver should be drafted with clear, unambiguous, and precise language that is easily understood by non-lawyers. Waivers should also be printed in large, readable print, preferably 10- or 12-point type.

Regardless of the fairness of the waiver contract, some courts have on principle ruled waivers invalid as a matter of **public policy**. Generally, a waiver violates public policy if (a) it pertains to a service important to the public, (b) the parties are not of equal bargaining power, (c) there is an employer–employee relationship between the parties entering into the waiver contract, or (d) it attempts to preclude liability for extreme forms of conduct such as gross negligence or intentional acts (Cotten, 2007). At least one case has also invalidated the mandatory use of waivers to bar negligence claims by high school athletes on public policy grounds (*Wagenblast v. Odessa School District*, 1988). Using waivers for minors produces another important challenge. Because waivers are contracts and minors may disaffirm contracts, it is advisable to have parents of a minor also sign

a waiver involving a minor. Three state courts have indicated that under some circumstances, waivers signed by parents for children or signed by both parents and children will withstand judicial scrutiny (Cotten, 2007).

Constitutional Law

Constitutional law is developed from precedents established by courts applying the language of the U.S. Constitution and state constitutions to the actions and policies of governmental entities. State constitutions vary. Some are models of the U.S. Constitution, whereas others grant greater rights to their citizens. Although many rights are guaranteed by the U.S. Constitution, four challenges tend to arise in the sport industry more frequently: due process, equal protection, the right to be free from unreasonable searches and seizures, and invasion of privacy. Occasionally there are challenges regarding the First Amendment freedoms of religion, speech, and the right to assemble peaceably.

■ STATE ACTION

As a rule, the U.S. Constitution and state constitutions do not apply to private entities such as professional teams, athletic associations, private high schools or colleges, or private golf or health and fitness clubs. However, in some cases it can be argued that the private entity is so enmeshed with the public entity that the two are dependent upon one another. When a private entity meets this standard, it is called a **state actor** and the court may apply the Constitution to that private entity. One example is *Brentwood Academy v. Tennessee Secondary School Athletic Association (TSSAA)* (2001), in which the U.S. Supreme Court found state action in the TSSAA's regulatory activity due to the pervasive entwinement of state school officials in the TSSAA's structure. The plaintiff, Brentwood Academy, is a private parochial high school member of the TSSAA.

The TSSAA found that Brentwood violated a rule prohibiting "undue influence" in recruiting athletes when it wrote to incoming students and their parents about spring football practice. The TSSAA placed Brentwood's athletic program on probation for four years, declared its football and boys' basketball teams ineligible to compete in playoffs for two years, and imposed a $3,000 fine. When the penalties were imposed, all the voting members of the board of control and legislative council were public school administrators. In *Brentwood Academy*, the Court found that the TSSAA's private character was overshadowed by the pervasive entwinement of public institutions and public officials in its structure and activities. Factually, 84% of the TSSAA's members were public schools whose officials acted in their official capacity to provide interscholastic athletics to their students. Thus, without the public school officials, who overwhelmingly determine and perform all but the TSSAA's purely ministerial acts, the TSSAA could not function. Further, the TSSAA's staff is eligible to participate in the state retirement system. To complement the entwinement from the bottom up, the state has provided entwinement from the top down: State board members sit *ex officio* on the TSSAA's governing bodies and association. As a result, the Court found it not unfair to apply constitutional standards to the TSSAA.

In *NCAA v. Tarkanian* (1988), the Court refused to find state action when the NCAA ordered the University of Nevada to suspend its basketball coach, Jerry Tarkanian. The difference between the two cases is that the NCAA's policies were shaped not by the University of Nevada alone, but by several hundred member institutions, many of them private and most of them having no connection with Nevada. In *Tarkanian*, the Court did, however, predict in dictum that state action could be found where there is public entwinement in the management or control of an entity whose member

public schools are located in a single state (*Id.* at 193).

■ DUE PROCESS

Athletic associations adopt many rules and regulations that they enforce through their own administrative processes. If the athletic association is a state actor, then its administrative process must also provide procedural **due process**. Procedural due process is the right to notice and a hearing before life, liberty, or property may be taken away. Obviously, no athletic association makes decisions to take away a life. Some decisions, however, do affect liberty and property interests protected by the due process clauses in the Fifth and Fourteenth Amendments. Examples of liberty interests include the right to be free from stigma, to be free from damage to one's reputation, and to pursue one's livelihood. Property interests involve the taking away of anything of value. The U.S. Supreme Court has found property interests arise from explicit understandings that can support a claim of entitlement (*Perry v. Sindermann*, 1972). College scholarships have long been held to be property interests (*Gulf South Conference v. Boyd*, 1979), as have tenured positions of employment (*Perry v. Sindermann*, 1972).

■ EQUAL PROTECTION

The **equal protection** clause of the Fourteenth Amendment guarantees that no person shall be discriminated against unless a constitutionally permissible reason for the discrimination exists. *Discrimination* occurs when two similarly situated individuals are treated differently on the basis of a status or classification. The equal protection clause often applies in sport when there are allegations of discrimination on the basis of race, gender, or alienage in eligibility or employment decisions. The court employs different standards of review depending upon the status or classification of the party alleging discrimination to decide whether a rule or regulation in sport discriminates. The first standard of review, **strict scrutiny**, applies where one discriminates on the basis of race, religion, or national origin. To withstand a constitutional challenge, a defendant must convince the court it has a compelling need to violate a fundamental right or discriminate. This standard is the most challenging to meet, so defendants usually lose.

The second standard of review applies to discrimination on the basis of gender. A defendant may discriminate on the basis of gender only if a **legitimate interest** for doing so exists. In high school and college athletics, courts have found two legitimate reasons for upholding the use of separate-gender teams. The first reason is to protect the health and safety of the athletes, such as when a girl is attempting to participate on a boys' football or ice hockey team in which a high degree of contact and injuries are prevalent. The second reason for which the court has found separate-gender teams necessary is to avoid existing discrimination or make up for past discrimination. Typically, such a case arises when a boy is seeking to participate on a girls' team in a sport not offered for boys, such as field hockey or volleyball.

However, a legitimate reason may not exist to have separate-gender practices in the management side of sports. For instance, in 1975, MLB Commissioner Bowie Kuhn enacted a rule that banned female reporters from baseball clubhouses. Despite the contrary wishes of Yankee players, Kuhn insisted that Melissa Ludtke, a female *Sports Illustrated* sportswriter covering the 1977 World Series, be banned from the Yankees' clubhouse (*Ludtke and Time, Inc. v. Kuhn*, 1978). Ludtke challenged the rule because it discriminated against her on the basis of her gender and kept her from pursuing her profession, a liberty protected by the Fourteenth Amendment's equal protection and due process clauses. The court found that MLB's expressed legitimate reason of protecting the privacy of the players and the family image of the game could not withstand judicial scrutiny when it allowed television cameras in clubhouses at the game's end to obtain interviews from scantily clad players.

The third standard of review applies to discrimination based on any other status or classification. Discriminatory actions have been challenged on the basis of economic or social background, sexual orientation, physical or mental disability, or athletic team membership. The court will allow the defendant's actions if it convinces the court there is a **rational basis** for the discriminatory rule. Rational basis standard cases are the easiest for defendants to win. For instance, in *Letendre v. Missouri State High School Activities Association (MSHSAA)* (2002), the plaintiff was a swimmer who continued to practice in a private club while participating on her high school team, despite knowing the high school athletic association rule prohibited such conduct. When the rule was enforced against her, Letendre responded with a lawsuit seeking injunctive relief claiming the rule violated her equal protection rights. The court reviewed the equal protection claim using the rational basis test and found that the rule was reasonably related to the MSHSAA's goals. The MSHSAA's stated goals included preventing interference with school academic programs, preventing interference with athletic programs by organized nonschool athletics, promoting competitive equity, avoiding conflicts in coaching philosophies, avoiding scheduling problems, and encouraging students not to overemphasize athletic competition.

■ UNREASONABLE SEARCH AND SEIZURE

The Fourth Amendment provides that people have the right "to be secure in their persons, houses, papers and effects against **unreasonable searches and seizures**." Applying this to a drug testing program, the act of taking the athlete's urine or blood may constitute a seizure and the testing may constitute a search within the meaning of the Fourth Amendment. Such a search may be considered reasonable by a court if the defendant can show a compelling need for the search. The U.S. Supreme Court has upheld drug testing of high school athletes on the grounds that the school has a compelling interest in deterring drug use by children to ensure their health and safety and in keeping the school environment free from the disciplinary problems created by drug use (*Vernonia School District 47J v. Acton*, 1995). In 2002, the U.S. Supreme Court (in a narrow 5–4 decision) upheld the constitutionality of a random, mandatory suspicionless test of all students engaged in all competitive extracurricular activities because it was a reasonably effective means of addressing the school district's legitimate concerns in preventing, deterring, and detecting drug use (*Board of Education v. Earls*, 2002). The competitive extracurricular activities included the band, choir, academic teams, Future Farmers of America, and cheerleading. Because the only disciplinary consequence of a positive test for illegal drugs was to limit participation in those activities, the Court allowed the school board to use the testing as a method of deterrence without waiting for a crisis to develop before imposing a testing policy. More recently, the Supreme Court of Washington ruled that a similar random and suspicionless drug testing policy for student athletes contravened the State of Washington's Constitution and upheld the parents' appeal (*York v. Wahkiakum School Dist. No. 200*, 2008). The Court agreed with the appellant parents' contention that such a policy violated Washington's State Constitution which provides "[n]o person shall be disturbed in his private affairs, or his home invaded without authority of law" (*Id.*). On the state level, several courts have also held that the NCAA drug testing program does not violate

state constitutional rights (*Brennan v. Board of Trustees*, 1997; *Hill v. National Collegiate Athletic Association*, 1994).

Invasion of Privacy

The U.S. Constitution does not specifically state that there is a fundamental right to be free from an **invasion of privacy**; however, the U.S. Supreme Court has implied one from the constitutional amendments. To bring an action for invasion of privacy, a plaintiff must establish that the invasion is substantial and is in an area for which there is an expectation of privacy. In the sport industry, these cases most often arise as challenges to drug testing programs. In *Vernonia School District 47J v. Acton* (1995), James Acton challenged Vernonia School District's drug testing program as an invasion of privacy. The Supreme Court found that school children had a reduced expectation of privacy when they entered school. The Court reasoned that athletes had an even lesser expectation of privacy, because athletics subjected one to a locker room environment, physical examinations, and the need for medical attention. Therefore, the Supreme Court held that the drug testing of high school athletes was not an invasion of privacy.

It is uncertain if the *Vernonia* ruling applies to collegiate athletes. In the *Vernonia* opinion, Justice Scalia went to great lengths to state that the high school students had a lower expectation of privacy due to the fact they were minors who were under the school's care while away from their parents, and in such a situation the teachers had to have discipline in the school (*Vernonia School District 47J v. Acton*, 1995). Collegiate athletes are adults under considerably less supervision from the administration of their colleges and universities. Additionally, just over a year before the *Vernonia* decision, the U.S. Supreme Court refused to hear an appeal of the Supreme Court of Colorado's decision that found that drug testing of football players at the University of Colorado was an invasion of privacy (*University of Colorado v. Derdeyn*, 1993). In *Derdeyn*, the Supreme Court of Colorado held that despite the University of Colorado's interest in protecting the health and welfare of student-athletes and although student-athletes do consent to restrictions on their private lives by participating in collegiate athletics, it is not enough to justify the intrusion on privacy interests of the nature and extent involved in the random, suspicionless testing for drugs.

No constitutional challenge to drug testing in professional sport has been successful. In 1994, the federal district court for the Western District of Pennsylvania ruled the NFL's drug testing program was not subject to a constitutional challenge because there was no state action (*Long v. National Football League*, 1994). The court found that neither the business relationship between the City of Pittsburgh and the Steelers nor the city's acquiescence to testing by the NFL was enough to establish the interdependent relationship necessary for the NFL to be a state actor.

Drug testing challenges in professional sport are most effectively made through the administrative or arbitration process set up under each league's rules or **collective bargaining agreement** (CBA). (The CBA is the contract agreed to by the players association and the owners for all provisions related to hours, wages, and terms and conditions of employment. It is discussed in greater detail in Chapter 10, Professional Sport.) Under federal law, arbitration decisions as a result of collective bargaining agreements are accorded great deference, preempting state law claims. That said, Minnesota Vikings players Pat and Kevin Williams are waging claims in state and federal courts against the NFL over their use of the diuretic StarCaps that challenge that principle. The Williams challenged their suspensions based on positive drug tests on the grounds that the test violated the Minnesota

Drug and Alcohol Testing in the Workplace Act. The Eighth Circuit Court of Appeals held that the players' challenge to their suspension was based on Minnesota state law, not the NFL policy or the CBA, and as a result their claims were not preempted by federal law (*Williams v. National Football League*, 2009).

Title IX of the Educational Amendments of 1972

Title IX is a comprehensive statute aimed at eliminating gender discrimination in educational institutions that receive federal funding. Thus, Title IX cases only involve interscholastic and intercollegiate athletics (employment discrimination and participation opportunities). When applying Title IX to employment discrimination, courts rely on the standards set forth in Title VII, discussed later in this chapter in the Labor and Employment Laws section (*Perdue v. City University of New York*, 1998; *Pitts v. University of Oklahoma*, 1994; *Stanley v. University of Southern California*, 1994).

The U.S. Department of Education's Office of Civil Rights (OCR) establishes policies for applying Title IX to athletic participation. To decide whether a school or college is in compliance, the OCR focuses on three areas. First, the OCR assesses whether an institution's athletic scholarships are awarded on a substantially proportionate basis (male versus female). Second, the OCR assesses the degree to which a school or college has given equal treatment, benefits, and opportunities in specific athletic program areas. The OCR examines areas such as the provision of publicity, promotions, facilities, equipment, and supplies; the opportunity to benefit from quality coaching and support staff; and the scheduling of games and practices. Third, the OCR assesses the degree to which a school or college has equally and effectively accommodated the interests and abilities of male and female students. Most cases have been brought under this third factor, but recently the OCR

and potential plaintiffs are placing some attention on examining the treatment of athletes. It has been an area of growing litigation since the U.S. Supreme Court ruled that Title IX did not preclude a plaintiff from receiving compensatory damages and attorneys' fees (*Franklin v. Gwinnett County Public Schools*, 1992). As a result, athletes and attorneys can better afford the cost of pursuing Title IX lawsuits.

The Secretary of Education's Commission on Opportunities in Athletics, appointed by President George W. Bush in June 2002, was charged with collecting information, analyzing issues, and obtaining broad public input to improve the application of federal standards for measuring equal athletic opportunities for men and women under Title IX. In February 2003, the Commission issued a final report to the Department of Education that contained over 25 recommended policy changes that could have dramatically altered current Title IX standards. In June 2003, the U.S. District Court for the District of Columbia granted a motion to dismiss a lawsuit brought against the U.S. Department of Education by the National Wrestling Coaches Association that sought to challenge the regulations that enforce Title IX (*National Wrestling Coaches Association v. United States Department*

of Education, 2003). The court ruled that the plaintiffs did not have standing and did not show that their injury—a reduction in men's sport teams—would be redressed even if the court found in the plaintiff's favor. At issue in the case was whether the enforcement of Title IX has caused college athletic programs to cut their men's teams to achieve compliance through the proportionality test (the proportion of male to female athletes must reflect the proportion of male to female undergraduate students). Then, in July 2003, the Department of Education reported there would be no changes to the law or regulations.

Some other recent decisions highlight the various applications of Title IX. After cutting seven men's and three women's sports at James Madison University (JMU) in 2006 in an attempt to comply with Title IX requirements, an action group (Equity in Athletics, Inc.) was formed by athletes, coaches and fans to oppose the move. In *Equity in Athletics, Inc. v. The United States Department of Education* (2008), the plaintiff argued that the defendant university was discriminating against male athletes and thus violating Title IX. The court took a "balance of hardship" approach to its analysis and noted that students were unfettered in being able to transfer to other schools and would still keep their scholarship entitlements, while JMU would be significantly disadvantaged if it was forced to reconvene any or all sports. The court also denied the plaintiff's argument that equal opportunity should be determined by "expressed interest" rather than "actual participation."

The court applied the triple-pronged test of compliance in *Miller v. University of Cincinnati* (2008), in which the women's rowing team contended that the program was inadequately facilitated in terms of resources and later eliminated in favor of women's lacrosse. The court found that the University was in compliance, with 47.5% of the student population being female and 48.9% of student-athletes being female.

The latest Title IX lawsuit, *Biediger v. Quinnipiac University* (2010), was brought as a class action by Quinnipiac University women's volleyball players and their coach (Robin Sparks). In April 2009, Quinnipiac University announced that it would be eliminating its women's volleyball program. The plaintiffs requested an injunction to prevent Quinnipiac University from dropping the volleyball program and Judge Underhill granted the injunction (*Biedinger v. Quinnipiac University*, 2009). He later accepted a motion allowing the case to proceed as a class action lawsuit. Quinnipiac's plan was to eliminate volleyball and add competitive cheerleading. The plaintiffs argued that Quinnipiac was not in compliance with Title IX because the proportion of male to female students was 38.13% male and 61.87% female. The composition of male to female athletes was 37.73% male to 62.27% female according to the University. However, because Judge Underhill found competitive cheerleading was not a recognized NCAA sport, he found Quinnipiac out of compliance. While Quinnipiac lost the case, Judge Underhill's decision is instructive. The reasons the cheer team was not considered a competitive sport were varied: there was no off-campus recruiting, the season was inconsistent in terms of rules governing competition and the types and quality of opponents, the university did not treat it as a varsity team, and finally, the postseason did not follow the structure of a competitive team. Judge Underhill did acknowledge that in no way did he mean to belittle the athletic endeavor of the athletes on the cheer team, but that the at this point the sport is too disorganized and unstructured to be considered a competitive sport for purposes of Quinnipiac's compliance with Title IX (*Biedinger v. Quinnipiac*, 2010).

Antitrust Laws

A capitalist economy depends on competition (economic rivalry) between businesses, such that they are engaged in a contest for customers (Howell et al., 1987). To promote competition in the free market, Congress enacted the Sherman Antitrust Act of 1890 (the **antitrust law**). The Sherman Act's goal was to break up business trusts and monopolies and prohibit anticompetitive activity by businesses. There are two types of antitrust violations: Section 1 prohibiting contracts, combinations, or conspiracies that restrain trade and Section 2 prohibiting monopolies. Both carry a penalty of tripling the damage award. Because professional teams are worth hundreds of millions of dollars and athletes' salaries total millions of dollars, an anticompetitive practice that injures a competitor league, a team owner, or a player's ability to make use of a free market may create a crippling damage award. However, we rarely see damage awards in sports antitrust cases because most result in settlements.

■ ANTITRUST AND PROFESSIONAL SPORT

The application of antitrust laws to leagues has left an indelible mark on their structure and the nature of labor–management relations. Antitrust challenges have primarily occurred in professional sport, in which monopolization of the player, product, and geographic markets and restrictive policies are common. Plus, with only one viable major professional league for each sport, their domination of the market for each sport has been challenged by competitors in violation of the Sherman Act (*United States Football League v. National Football League*, 1986; *Philadelphia World Hockey, Inc. v. Philadelphia Hockey Club, Inc.*, 1972; *American Football League v. National Football League*, 1963; *Federal Baseball Club of Baltimore v. National League of Professional Baseball Clubs*, 1922). Restrictive policies are inherent to the operation of professional sports as they strive to maintain competitive balance. Over time, many cases have been brought by players, owners, competitor leagues, prospective cities, and prospective owners challenging the restraints imposed upon them through league rules and policies.

Two recent cases highlight the antitrust issues being litigated as this text goes to press. In *American Needle v. National Football League* (2010), the U.S. Supreme Court reversed the Seventh Circuit Court of Appeals and ruled that the NFL Properties was a not a **single entity** when promoting NFL football by licensing the teams' intellectual property. Relying on Copperweld Corp. v. Independence Tube Corp., 467 U.S. 752, 773, n. 21, the Court reiterated that "'substance, not form, should determine whether a[n] . . . entity is capable of conspiring under section 1.' . . . The key is whether the alleged 'contract, combination, . . . or, conspiracy' is concerted action—that is whether it joins together separate decision makers." The Court found that each of the teams is a substantial, independently owned, and independently managed business and their objectives are not common. More specifically, the Court noted that NFL teams "compete with one another, not only on the playing field, but to attract fans, for gate receipts, and for contracts with managerial and playing personnel" (*Id.* at 9). The Court further explained that NFL teams do compete in the market for intellectual property, a fact directly relevant to the question of whether NFL Properties is a single entity. The Supreme Court remanded American Needle back to the district court for a trial consistent with its finding that the NFL Properties was not a single entity. After this case, it is not likely that a traditionally created sport league will be considered a single entity, and thus, immune from Section 1 of the Sherman Antitrust Act.

However, a recent Third Circuit Court of Appeals case upheld the jury's decision in *Deutscher Tennis Bund v. ATP Tour, Inc.* (2010), that the Association of Tennis Professionals (ATP) Tour was not in breach of antitrust law when it stripped the annual Hamburg event of its Masters series designation and demoted the tournament to "second-tier" status. The Third Circuit also upheld the jury's finding that the ATP Tour was a single entity, immune from Section 1 liability.

■ ANTITRUST EXEMPTIONS

Curt Flood Act of 1998

All professional sport organizations except MLB are subject to antitrust laws. In 1922, the U.S. Supreme Court found that baseball was not subject to the Sherman Act (*Federal Baseball Club of Baltimore v. National League of Professional Baseball Clubs*, 1922). MLB's antitrust exemption survived two further Supreme Court challenges, and much of it remained intact despite the adoption of the **Curt Flood Act** of 1998 (*Flood v. Kuhn*, 1972; *Toolson v. New York Yankees*, 1953). The Curt Flood Act granted MLB players, but not minor leaguers, the legal right to sue their employers under the Sherman Act. It also confirmed that the exemption still applies to business areas, including: the minor leagues; the minor league player reserve clause; the amateur draft; franchise expansion, location, or relocation; franchise ownership issues; marketing and sales of the entertainment product of baseball; and licensed properties. This protection from antitrust liability sets MLB apart from the other professional sports organizations, whose rules and practices are subject to antitrust scrutiny. In *Los Angeles Memorial Coliseum Commission v. National Football League* (1984), the Ninth Circuit Court of Appeals upheld a jury decision that the NFL's application of its franchise relocation rule was an unreasonable restraint of trade. The threat of prolonged litigation and the threat of a potentially large damage award have allowed for unprecedented franchise movement in the NFL and NHL.

Labor Exemption

Although at first blush it appears the Curt Flood Act opens MLB to increased antitrust litigation, it does not. All unionized professional sports leagues are shielded from antitrust liability by the **labor exemption**, and a strong labor union, the Major League Baseball Players Association, negotiates collectively with MLB. The U.S. Supreme Court has well established that during the term of a collective bargaining agreement, terms negotiated in that agreement are exempt from antitrust scrutiny. Provided the defendant proves the plaintiff is, was, or will be a party to the collective bargaining agreement; that the subject being challenged on antitrust grounds is a mandatory subject for bargaining (hours, wages, and other terms and conditions of employment); and that the collective bargaining agreement was achieved through bona fide arm's-length bargaining (bargaining that occurs freely, without one party having excessive power or control over the other); the defendant's actions will be exempt from antitrust (*Wood v. National Basketball Association*, 1987; *McCourt v. California Sports, Inc.*, 1979; *Reynolds v. National Football League*, 1978).

Courts have ruled that the labor exemption continues to protect parties from antitrust scrutiny after a collective bargaining agreement has expired (*Brown v. Pro Football, Inc.*, 1996; *National Basketball Association v. Williams*, 1995; *Powell v. National Football League*, 1989; *Bridgeman v. National Basketball Association*, 1987). In *Brown v. Pro Football*, the U.S. Supreme Court noted that when a bargaining relationship exists between a league and players association, labor policy favors limiting antitrust liability. Thus, provided that the league is engaged in lawful collective bargaining activities, the labor exemption will continue to insulate the employer from antitrust liability. The Court clarified, however, that it did not intend its holding to "insulate from antitrust liability every joint imposition of terms by employers, for an agreement among employers could be sufficiently distant in time and circumstances from the collective bargaining process that a rule permitting antitrust intervention would not significantly interfere with that process" (*Id.* at 250). The Court did not, however, give an example of such time and circumstance.

Brown affects professional sports collective bargaining by removing the players association's threat of antitrust litigation from the negotiation process. To maintain the negotiating leverage of the antitrust threat, the ruling in *Brown* encourages players to forgo union movements or to decertify their bargaining units, thereby eliminating their bargaining relationship with management. NFL players found success challenging the "Plan B" free agency system unilaterally imposed by the owners after the players and owners had reached an impasse in their negotiations and the players decertified the NFL Players Association as their union (*McNeil v. National Football League*, 1992).

Sports Broadcasting Act of 1961

In 1961 Congress passed the Sport Broadcasting Act of 1961 to exempt sports leagues' national television deals from antitrust liability (15 U.S.C. §§ 1291–1294). This statute grants professional teams the right to pool their television rights as a league and increase their bargaining power when negotiating league-wide television packages without the threat of antitrust challenges. It also restricts leagues from defining geographical areas into which the pooled telecasts are broadcast and limits Friday and Saturday telecasts within a 75-mile radius of college and high school football.

■ ANTITRUST AND COLLEGE ATHLETICS

In the past, the NCAA and other athletic associations have been free from antitrust scrutiny.

Member institutions, coaches, athletes, and alumni have challenged NCAA rules on antitrust grounds (*Adidas America, Inc. v. National Collegiate Athletic Association*, 1999). Before subjecting association rules and regulations to antitrust scrutiny, the court will decide if the rule regulates a commercial or noncommercial activity. Courts have ruled that eligibility rules are noncommercial (*Banks v. National Collegiate Athletic Association*, 1992; *McCormack v. National Collegiate Athletic Association*, 1988), but rules restricting coaches' earnings (*Law v. National Collegiate Athletic Association*, 1995) and limitations on NCAA members' television contracts (*National Collegiate Athletic Association v. Board of Regents of the University of Oklahoma and the University of Georgia Athletic Association*, 1982) are commercial and subject to antitrust laws.

As college and high school athletics continue to increase in prominence and in their capability to bring in money, organizations such as the NCAA have increasingly become targets of antitrust scrutiny. Two legal actions involving the NCAA are evidence of this antitrust scrutiny. The first involved a suit by the Metropolitan Intercollegiate Basketball Association (MIBA), the five-university venture that operated the National Invitation Tournament (NIT). In its suit, MIBA alleged that the NCAA's bundle of post-season rules unreasonably limited Division I teams to participation only in the NCAA tournament and thereby effectively eliminated the NIT as a viable competitive post-season basketball event (*Metropolitan Intercollegiate Basketball Association v. NCAA*, 2004). In 2005, while the suit was in the midst of trial, the NCAA agreed to purchase the preseason and postseason NIT from MIBA for $40.5 million and settled with the schools for an additional $16 million. The second case involves the 2006 class action antitrust suit by three former student-athletes (*White v. NCAA*, 2008) who alleged that NCAA by-laws unlawfully capped the amount of financial aid a student-athlete may receive under NCAA rules. The plaintiffs argued that if schools could compete without the cap, they could potentially offer higher amounts of financial aid than the grant-in-aid limits that involve tuition, fees, room and board, and required books. The plaintiffs alleged and NCAA itself admitted that the grant-in-aid limit is less than the cost of admission as a student; the two just differ on how much less. The suit settled with the NCAA agreeing to an expansion of the Special Assistance and Academic Enhancement Fund, plus an additional $10 million allocated to fund career development and educational reimbursements for former student-athletes.

Labor and Employment Laws

The sport industry is people intensive, so sport managers must have a working knowledge of how the law affects human resource management, particularly a basic knowledge of labor and employment laws. There are both state and federal labor and employment laws. Because state laws vary by jurisdiction, this chapter focuses on the following federal laws: the National Labor Relations Act, the Equal Pay Act of 1963, Title VII of the Civil Rights Act of 1964, the Age Discrimination in Employment Act, and the Americans with Disabilities Act.

■ THE NATIONAL LABOR RELATIONS ACT

Enacted in 1935, the **National Labor Relations Act** (NLRA) applies to private employers. This law establishes the procedures for union certification and decertification and sets forth the rights and obligations of union and management once a union is in place. The law also created the National Labor Relations Board (NLRB) as the federal agency administering labor laws in the United States. The primary areas of the sport industry in which the NLRA applies are facility management, interscholastic athletics, and professional sports. Facility managers may employ various unionized employees, all with different collective bargaining agreements. In some cases, interscholastic coaches may be members of a teachers union. In collegiate athletics, staff members are often unionized, but coaches are not (except in the Pennsylvania state college system). Currently, the four major professional sport leagues (MLB, NBA, NFL, NHL), Major League Soccer (MLS), the Women's National Basketball Association (WNBA), Arena Football League (AFL), the National Lacrosse League (NLL), and minor league hockey players in the ECHL (formerly the East Coast Hockey League), American Hockey League (AHL), and the International Hockey League (IHL) are unionized.

Labor relations in professional sports are unique for many reasons, notably the individual bargaining power professional athletes derive from their unique talent. This bargaining power creates leverage for players in the major leagues. As a result, professional leagues have adopted restrictive practices for the efficient management of their players (Masteralexis, 2007b). Restrictive practices are those that limit a player's ability to make money or to move throughout the free market and include such practices as the draft, salary cap or luxury tax, and restrictions on free agency that may violate antitrust laws (*Smith v. Pro Football, Inc.*, 1978; *Mackey v. National Football League*, 1976). However, under labor laws, practices that normally violate players' antitrust rights that are agreed to through the collective bargaining process may be free from antitrust liability by the labor exemption (*Zimmerman v. National Football League*, 1986; *McCourt v. California Sports, Inc.*, 1979). Therefore, it is in the leagues' best interests to have unions and to negotiate restrictive practices through the collective bargaining process. This approach is unique to sports, because most management groups either prefer not to deal with unions or simply tolerate them. Generally, management in other industries tends to perceive that unions take power and control from them. A good example of the irony of the professional sport situation arose in 1996 when some star NBA players sought an election to decertify their players association and NBA Commissioner David Stern publicly supported the players who favored keeping the players association. Another example occurred in 2000, when the National Labor Relations Board moved to have the Arena Football League's then-union, the AFL Players Organizing Committee (AFL-POC), decertified after certain NLRB officials claimed that owners coerced players into joining the union (IBL, 2000).

Players associations differ from unions in other industries. For one thing, job security is limited. The turnover rate for sport union members is much higher than for other union members because athletes' careers are far shorter than those of employees in other industries. This forces players associations to constantly spread their message to new members. In spreading the message, the players associations also face the logistical challenges of being a bargaining unit with employees on different teams throughout the United States and Canada, not to mention employees from many different countries and cultures. Further, there is a great disparity between players' talent and thus their need for the union. A player such as LeBron James does not need the services of the union as much as a late-round draft pick or a recently released free agent trying to make his way back onto an NBA roster. When negotiating for the collective interests of the players, unions must struggle to keep the superstars and the players on the bench equally satisfied. Without the solidarity of all players, a players association loses its strength (Masteralexis, 2007b).

■ THE EQUAL PAY ACT

Enacted in 1963, the **Equal Pay Act** (EPA) prohibits an employer from paying one employee less than another on the basis of gender when the two are performing jobs of equal skill, effort, and responsibility and are working under similar conditions. EPA only applies to sex-based discrimination on the basis of compensation. To qualify, the plaintiff and comparable employee must be of opposite genders. For instance, the statute would not apply if a man coached a women's team and argued under the EPA that he should be paid a sum equal to the male coach of the men's team. Trivial differences between two jobs will not prevent them from being considered equal in terms of the EPA. Comparable worth is not an issue under the EPA.

Female coaches whose salaries are not equal to those of their male counterparts have filed EPA lawsuits. *Stanley v. University of Southern California* (1999) involved the complaint by the University of Southern California's women's basketball coach, Marianne Stanley, that she was not paid equally to the male basketball coach, George Raveling. In finding that their jobs were not equal, the court focused on the additional pressure to raise revenue and the responsibility it said Raveling had due to the fact that the men's team had a larger season ticket base and a greater national presence. The court found that such responsibility created more media pressure and a greater time investment in dealing with fans and the media (*Stanley v. University of Southern California*, 1999). Interestingly, the court never considered whether Stanley actually could have had more responsibilities and pressure than Raveling because she constantly labored to get a larger season ticket base and more media attention for her team and herself. The court also focused attention on a comparison of Stanley's and Raveling's skills, qualifications, and work experience. Stanley had 17 years of coaching experience, whereas Raveling had 31. Raveling had a background and prior work experience in marketing that Stanley did not have. Raveling had also worked in the public eye as a television

commentator, author, and actor. However, Stanley had done speaking engagements and had won four national championships while also traveling to three other NCAA tournaments. Raveling had coached teams to the NCAA tournaments but had never won a national championship. Despite this last comparative, the court found Raveling's skills and qualifications outpaced Stanley's and justified the pay difference.

If an employee proves the elements of an EPA violation, the four defenses available to the employer are that the disparity in pay is due to the presence of (a) a seniority system, (b) a merit system that is being followed in good faith, (c) a system measuring pay on the basis of quality or quantity of production, or (d) a factor other than gender.

■ TITLE VII OF THE CIVIL RIGHTS ACT OF 1964

The Civil Rights Act of 1964 is a federal law prohibiting discrimination in many settings, including housing, education, and public accommodations. **Title VII** covers employers with 15 or more employees. Title VII, however, excludes Native American tribes and "bona fide membership clubs" (such as country clubs) from its definition of an employer. Title VII specifically prohibits any employment decision, practice, or policy that treats individuals unequally due to race, color, national origin, gender, or religion (*Wallace v. Texas Tech University*, 1996).

Although much of the U.S. civil rights movement focused on discrimination against African Americans, Title VII's definition of race is not that limited. It protects all classes of people from dissimilar treatment, including, but not limited to, Hispanics, Native Americans, and Asian Americans. The focus for color under Title VII is on skin pigment or the physical characteristics of one's race. Regarding national origin, the court focuses on one's ancestry. Title VII does not prohibit employment discrimination solely based on a lack of U.S. citizenship;

however, the lack of U.S. citizenship may not be used to disguise discrimination that is actually based on race or national origin. In other words, an employer may follow a policy of employing only U.S. citizens but may not give unequal treatment to different noncitizens based on their country of origin. In addition, rules that require communication in "English only" are allowed only if the employer can prove the rule is a business necessity. As for gender, Title VII is self-explanatory, but it also includes sexual harassment (*Ortiz-Del Valle v. National Basketball Association*, 1999; *Faragher v. Boca Raton*, 1998). Title VII does not provide for remedies against discrimination on the basis of sexual orientation (*Rene v. MGM Grand Hotel*, 2002), although several states, including California, Connecticut, Hawaii, Massachusetts, New York, New Jersey, Vermont, and Wisconsin, prohibit such discrimination under state law. Title VII prohibits religious discrimination against all well-recognized faiths, and also those considered unorthodox, provided the court is convinced that the belief is sincere and genuinely held and not simply adopted for an ulterior motive. Employers must make reasonable accommodations to religious practices and observances, unless they would place an undue hardship on the employers.

It is not illegal to discriminate based on religion, gender, or national origin if the classification is a **bona fide occupational qualification** (BFOQ). Race and color are never BFOQs. The BFOQ must be reasonably necessary to the normal operation of the business. The BFOQ defense requires the employer to prove that members of the excluded class could not safely and effectively perform essential job duties, and the employer must present a factual basis for this belief. An example of a BFOQ might be as follows: An all-male boarding school makes it a requirement that resident directors in the school's dormitories also be male, justifying the requirement with such reasons as the comfort and security of the male students living in all-male dormitories and the school's desire to establish male role models in the school's social settings.

Affirmative action policies involve giving preference to those underrepresented in the workplace. These policies often contain goals and timetables for increasing the percentage of the underrepresented classes to rectify past discrimination. The affirmative action policy may be voluntary, or it may be court ordered due to a discrimination suit. Affirmative action policies may result in discrimination against the overrepresented classes; this is termed *reverse discrimination*.

An interesting extension of Title VII can be seen in *Holcomb v. Iona College* (2008). The plaintiff, who was a white male, made allegations that he was dismissed from his role as an assistant men's basketball coach by virtue of his marriage to an African-American woman. This case was dismissed at the District Court level as being outside the contemplation of Title VII. The Second Circuit Court of Appeals, however, vacated the district court's decision and directed the district court to examine the facts in light of its finding that being associated with a person of another race can be read into Title VII as a protected class.

■ THE AGE DISCRIMINATION IN EMPLOYMENT ACT

Enacted in 1967, the **Age Discrimination in Employment Act** (ADEA) prohibits employment discrimination on the basis of age. Currently there is no age limit to protection, but the ADEA exempts several classes of workers, such as public safety personnel and certain top-level managers. It applies to employers who engage in commerce and hire over 20 workers for 20 or more calendar weeks, as well as labor unions and state and federal governments. Proving discrimination under the ADEA is very similar to doing so under Title VII. The ADEA also contains a BFOQ exception that is almost identical to Title VII's. An employer can defend a claim by proving the decision was made due to reasonable factors other than age.

An example of how courts have applied the ADEA to age discrimination cases is *Moore v. University of Notre Dame* (1998). The plaintiff, Joseph Moore, the offensive line coach for Notre Dame, sued the school, alleging age discrimination. In ruling against Notre Dame, a jury found that the school did fire Moore because of his age, a violation of the ADEA. In choosing a suitable remedy, the district court refused to grant Moore's request for reinstatement to his former coaching position because it was not an appropriate remedy in this case as it would cause significant friction as well as disruption of the current football program because someone else was currently occupying Moore's position. Although reinstatement is the preferred remedy in ADEA cases, the court granted Moore front pay, which represents the difference between earnings an employee would have received in his old employment and the earnings he can be expected to receive in his present and future employment (Wong, 2010).

■ THE AMERICANS WITH DISABILITIES ACT

Enacted in 1990, the **Americans with Disabilities Act** (ADA) protects employees with disabilities from discrimination at all stages of the employment relationship. An applicant or employee who is disabled must be able to perform all the essential functions of a position in order to challenge discrimination in employment on the basis of disability. Therefore, an employer must assess the responsibilities required for a position and assess the individual's ability to perform the responsibilities. When interviewing, an employer cannot question an applicant about the specific nature of his or her disability or

require medical records or exams as part of the screening process. An employer may, however, prepare a list of essential functions and ask if the applicant can perform those tasks. Although the ADA promotes the removal of barriers, it does not relieve employees with disabilities from carrying out the same job responsibilities as their able-bodied coworkers. If the individual can perform the job with or without a reasonable accommodation, the employer cannot refuse the employee based on disability. An employer must attempt to reasonably accommodate employees with disabilities unless doing so would cause undue hardship to the employer.

The most important ADA court decision related to sport management is *PGA Tour Inc. v. Martin* (2001). The case was initially brought in Oregon federal district court when Martin, a disabled golfer suffering from Klippel-Trénaunay-Weber syndrome, a condition making it very painful and potentially dangerous to walk for long distances, sued the Professional Golfers Association (PGA) Tour, alleging that the failure to make a golf cart available to him and the failure to make its golf tournaments accessible to disabled individuals, violated Title III of the ADA. In defense, the PGA Tour argued that its walking-only rule was an essential element of professional golf on the PGA and Nike tours, and that waiving the rule would fundamentally alter the nature of the sport. The U.S. Supreme Court affirmed the Oregon District Court and Ninth Circuit Court of Appeals decision for Martin, rejecting the PGA's argument that allowing Martin to use a golf cart would fundamentally alter the sport and finding that PGA golfers are not a protected class under Title III. Within days of ruling in Martin, the U.S. Supreme Court ordered the Seventh Circuit Court of Appeals to reconsider a contradictory ruling in *Olinger v. United States Golf Association* (2000). The Martin ruling has clarified the application of the ADA to sports participation issues and has led to an expansion in ADA sports-related cases being filed (*Kuketz v. MDC Fitness Corp.*, 2001).

The ADA reaches beyond employment law to ensure that people with disabilities have access to places of public accommodation. Thus, the ADA requires public assembly facilities, stadiums, theaters, and health and fitness centers to be barrier-free. Sport managers working in facilities that are open to the public must be sure their facilities comply with the ADA regulations for such areas as entrances and exits, seating, walkways, parking, and locker room and bathroom facilities (*Access Now, Inc. v. South Florida Stadium Corp.*, 2001). The ADA should continue to have a positive impact on the ability of those with disabilities to be sport spectators and participants. This aspect of the ADA is discussed in greater detail in Chapter 12, Facility Management, and Chapter 21, Recreational Sport.

Intellectual Property Law

Intellectual property refers to creations of the mind. Intellectual property law governs the rights to protect one's inventions, literary and artistic works, and symbols, names, images, and designs used in commerce (World Intellectual Property Organization, 2010). A **trademark** is a word, name, or symbol used by a manufacturer or merchant to identify and distinguish its goods from those manufactured and sold by others (Reed, 1989). The trademark performs the following functions:

- It designates the source of origin of a product or service.
- It denotes a particular standard of quality that the customer comes to expect from the owner.
- It symbolizes the goodwill of its owner.
- It represents a substantial advertising investment.

- It protects the public from confusion and deception.
- It enables courts to fashion a standard of acceptable business conduct from mark holders.

Trademarks can be strong, entitled to a wide scope of protection, or weak, entitled to limited protection in only a narrow field (Reed, 1989). Strong trademarks are those that are completely distinguishable, such as Exxon, Polaroid, and Kleenex. Gus Macker (outdoor 3-on-3 basketball tournament), and Rucker Park Street Ball are good examples of fanciful, distinguishable event names. On the other end of the spectrum are the weak names, like Musicfest, Food Fest, and Art Expo, which use common words in their ordinary meanings and would be difficult, although not impossible, to protect (Reed, 1989). Such names may be protected if they possess "**secondary meaning**." Secondary meaning exists if the public distinguishes one product or event from another by the trademark. Reed (1989) uses *World's Fair* as an example. Although the words are common and used in their ordinary meaning, the trademark is descriptive due to the amount of advertising and public exposure it receives. Because there is only one World's Fair, use of this trademark by others without permission may lead consumers to confuse the secondary use with the original trademark.

The **Lanham Act**, which governs trademarks and service marks, gives protection to the owner of a name or logo, keeps others from selling goods as the goods of the original source, and helps to protect against consumer confusion (Wilde, 2003). A **service mark** differs from a trademark in that a service mark is used to identify the source of an intangible service. Professional sports franchises' marks are registered as service marks that identify and represent the entertainment value of sports events (Wilde, 2003). The Lanham Act is a federal law that does not preempt state laws. State laws are useful for businesses not engaged in interstate commerce, such as an organization operating a purely local event (Reed, 1989). The Lanham Act has become increasingly important for sport managers involved with licensed products, sports events, and exhibitions. As colleges, professional teams, and the Olympic Movement seek to maximize revenues from names, logos, and goodwill, the Lanham Act is the source of protection of their property. The law in this area is somewhat complex, and those sport managers involved with licensed products should rely on attorneys who are experts in trademark law to handle registering trademarks and pursuing claims against those who misappropriate them.

Some case examples may help to illustrate the diversity of intellectual property issues. The University of South Carolina attempted to trademark the letters "S" and "C" that appeared in an interlocked design for use mainly on its baseball team's caps. The University of Southern California formally opposed this trademark application and in 2008, the United States Patent and Trademark office did in fact find a likelihood of confusion would occur if the mark was allowed and subsequently denied the application. In *Board of Supervisors for La. State Univ. v. Smack Apparel Co.* (2008), the plaintiff's argument that its university color scheme, when used in concert with specific information pertaining to the school on a t-shirt, even without the University's logo or other marks being present, infringed upon the trademark rights of the school, was upheld. Finally, in *Callaway Golf Company v. Acushnet Company* (2008), Callaway filed suit against the parent company of Titleist alleging that the Pro VI golf ball, the most popular golf ball on the PGA Tour at that time, infringed upon preexisting Callaway patents. The court's reasoning focused on a person of "ordinary skill" in the golf ball manufacturing industry and whether he or she would have created the Pro VI without Callaway's already patented material. Ultimately the court found

that this would not have been the case and found in favor of Callaway. The preceding discussion of legal concepts is not all-inclusive. It should, however, serve as a place for a future sport manager to begin to build a legal knowledge base to manage risk and limit liability.

■ KEY SKILLS

Rather than focusing on those skills necessary for becoming a practicing sport lawyer, this section examines the skills that studying law will bring to a sport manager. The study of law involves a great deal of problem solving. By practicing problem solving, sport managers can improve their logical and analytical reasoning skills. Such skills will make it more likely that a sport manager facing a crisis will resolve it in a logical, thoughtful manner.

For most people, analysis of case and statutory law will lead to more persuasive and clear written and oral communication. The study of law involves studying the language used in cases and statutes and making arguments to apply it to various situations. Practice in this area will aid the student in developing clearly stated written policies and procedures. Such clearly stated rules and regulations are an important part of a sound risk management plan. Excellent communication also is a key to good leadership and good relations with staff, peer and superior administrators, the public, and clients. Verbal communication skills can also enhance negotiating skills, and sport managers negotiate on a daily basis, even if they do not realize it. Managers negotiate for everything they need, whether it is in a formal setting, such as negotiating with a television network to broadcast games, or on a more informal scale, such as negotiating with a staff member to cover a shift for someone who has called in sick. The study of law, particularly in areas such as negotiation and client interviewing, also focuses on good listening skills. A successful sport manager should be prepared to invest time listening to staff and clients. A good listener will be a better judge of people and will know what it takes to motivate staff and to keep staff and clients satisfied.

Law and ethics are entwined. In setting parameters for acceptable conduct, the law establishes codes of ethical conduct. Studying law may not change a sport manager's behavior, for values may already be instilled, but it may help sport managers to better establish codes of ethical conduct in their workplaces. Sport law also may guide sport managers in how to best resolve disputes and violations of ethical codes without violating individual rights.

Putting Skills to Practice

The challenge for sport managers is to know and understand potential legal problems, to manage legal problems, and to reduce the likelihood of legal problems arising. A sport manager can effectively manage legal problems by knowing and understanding law and sport law. By knowing legal pitfalls, managers can avoid, prevent, or reduce many kinds of problems. A well-written and well-administered risk management plan can help a sport manager avoid legal liability.

For example, a health and fitness club manager may be faced with the option of adding wall-climbing equipment at his or her club. The manager must make this decision based on consumer interest and also financial benefits, costs, and potential legal liability. When considering legal liability, a club manager should consider all of the potential problems that may arise with the wall-climbing equipment. This analysis should involve creating a list of issues to consider, such as the following:

- Who should be allowed to use this equipment?
- Should training be required before use?
- Who is qualified to train users? What additional training will staff need?

- Should participants be required to provide medical approval?
- Should participants be required to sign a waiver of liability?
- Should minors (and their parents) be required to sign a waiver of liability?
- What if someone refuses to sign a waiver of liability?
- If used, how should a waiver of liability be drafted? Is it likely to hold up in court?
- What type of signs or warnings should be posted on or near the equipment?
- What if a physically challenged member wants to participate in the activity?
- What emergency procedures and services are in place if a participant is injured while using equipment?
- Should an individual who became injured while using the equipment be allowed to participate again? When?

Although this list was compiled for a club manager, similar lists can be created for other programmatic and policy decisions made by sport managers in other segments of the industry.

A second example reflects decisions to be made by sport managers at an association, institution, or organization considering the implementation of a drug testing program. The following list of important issues should be considered (Wong, 2010):

- Is the drug testing policy clearly defined and in writing?
- Does the organization's drug testing policy conform to conference and association rules and regulations?
- Who will conduct the tests?
- Who will pay for the tests?
- Will the tests be random and mandatory, or only for probable cause or reasonable suspicion?
- What constitutes probable cause or reasonable suspicion?
- How much notice should be given before testing begins?

- What types of drugs (recreational, performance enhancing) will be tested for?
- How frequently will athletes be tested?
- What actions should be taken when an athlete tests positive?
- Will there be an appeal process for a positive test result?
- Is there a method for retesting positive results?
- What confidentiality and constitutional law issues does drug testing raise?
- Do the sanctions to be imposed adhere to federal and/or state constitutional law and statutes?

Sport managers considering drug testing professional athletes must ask many of the same questions, but they must also be cognizant of player rights outlined in the collective bargaining agreement. Even if no drug testing policy has been negotiated in the collective bargaining agreement, it is still likely that issues involving player rights, such as discipline and arbitration, may affect the creation of the policy.

The job of a general manager of a professional sport team once primarily consisted of evaluating talent, drafting amateur players, and making trades. Today a general manager has many other responsibilities, often arising from provisions negotiated in the league's collective bargaining agreement or individual players' contracts. As such, the general manager may find a law degree helpful in doing his or her job. As a result of the more complex nature of their jobs, here are some other factors general managers must consider when making decisions:

1. Factors affecting the cost of acquiring a new player
   - For an MLB or NHL player: What impact will signing a player who is eligible for salary arbitration have on the team's budget?
   - For an MLB player: How will his salary affect the team's luxury tax?

- For an NBA or NFL player: How will his salary affect the salary cap?
2. Factors affecting the ability to keep a player
   - When will the player become a free agent?
   - Are there any rights of first refusal?
   - Is there any compensation due to the club in the event the free agent signs with another club?
   - Is the player one who is highly sought after by other clubs?
3. Insurance issues
   - Can the club reduce its risk when agreeing to a long-term guaranteed contract by purchasing temporary or permanent disability insurance to pay the club in the event the player is seriously injured?

The challenge for sport managers is to understand the legal implications, if any, of their decisions. Sport managers must know, or know how to obtain, the answers to these questions, either alone or with the advice of in-house or outside counsel.

Sport managers who can anticipate potential problems can then reduce risk. For example, the health club manager who allows only trained and healthy adults who have signed waivers of liability to participate in an activity has established parameters that reduce the club's risk. People who meet the conditions can then participate in a carefully and adequately supervised activity, with medical procedures in place. (Note that the sport manager has already eliminated some risk by not allowing minors to participate.)

A professional team's general manager may decide against acquiring a particular player because the potential salary of the player, either through salary arbitration or through leverage from free agency, will be too expensive. Or the general manager may take the approach of reducing the risk of this expense by signing a multiyear contract. In the NFL, the general manager can negotiate a "salary cap friendly" contract. For instance, the contract can be negotiated so that the salary cap impact is spread evenly over the years, or it can be structured so that the impact can be made in the early or late years of the contract. Thus, a general manager whose team currently has room under the salary cap can structure the contract so that the salary cap impact is in the early years. This reduces the salary cap cost of the player in later years and gives the club more money and freedom to sign other players.

■ CURRENT ISSUES

The impact of the law on sport organizations is more likely to increase rather than decrease in the future. Sport business is becoming ever more complex. For instance, the NFL collective bargaining agreement is a detailed 267-page document accompanied by several ancillary documents. The NCAA manual also is very detailed and complex. Due to restructuring in 1997–1998, the NCAA now publishes three manuals (one for each division). The 2009–2010 NCAA Division I manual is now 431 pages; Division II is 357 pages; and Division III is 322 pages. Each manual has numerous provisions, rules, and regulations that require interpretations, resulting in more legal considerations for sport managers.

Olympic Games

In the Olympic sport industry, there are a growing number of challenges over rules and regulations imposed on participants. Sport managers working in the Olympic arena are facing legal challenges resulting from **ambush marketing**, the rights of individual athletes to market themselves, and the imposition of codes of conduct for athletes. Ambush marketing occurs when an organization misappropriates the trademarks,

logos, and goodwill of an event or organization (Reed, 1989). An ambush marketing campaign often takes place around an event but does not involve payment of a sponsorship fee to the event (Ambush marketing, 2010). For most events of any significance, one brand will pay to become the exclusive and official sponsor of the event in a particular category or categories, and this exclusivity creates a problem for one or more other brands. Those other brands then find ways to promote themselves in connection with the same event, without paying the sponsorship fee and without breaking any laws.

For example, a company that has not paid to be a sponsor but confuses the public into thinking it is a sponsor by indirectly associating itself with the events or organizations by buying commercial airtime during broadcasts or sponsoring individual athletes or teams at a fraction of the cost is engaging in ambush marketing (Ambush marketing . . . , 1988).

Ambush marketing has been especially prevalent at other Olympic events. In early 2010, the U.S. Olympic Committee (USOC) accused Subway of ambush marketing ahead of the Winter Olympic Games in Vancouver. Subway aired a commercial depicting Michael Phelps swimming toward Vancouver. The USOC said that by using Phelps, an Olympic gold medalist, and the words "Vancouver" and "winter" in its commercial, Subway was trying to falsely promote itself as a sponsor of the 2010 Winter Games (Mickle, 2010). In anticipation of the London Olympics of 2012, the United Kingdom has take the proactive approach of promulgating specific legislation aimed at preventing ambush marketing (Lowen, 2006). The legislation, The London Olympic Games and Paralympic Games Act of 2006, includes the creation of a right known as the "London Olympics association right," which is designed to prevent false representations of sponsorships (London Olympic Games and Paralympic Games Act, 2006). This prevents the use of a combination of a list of words, including "games," "2012," "twenty-twelve," "two thousand and twelve" "gold," "silver," "bronze," "medals," "sponsor" and "summer." Ambush marketing is discussed in Chapter 3, Marketing Principles Applied to Sport Management.

■ COLLEGIATE

On the collegiate level, challenges are arising regarding NCAA amateurism rules and the conflict with the commercialism so predominant in Division I football and basketball. This comes at a time when many Division I football and basketball players are questioning NCAA rules that prohibit them from earning revenue from their playing talent and public image while they have remaining eligibility. Thus, problems will continue to arise regarding restrictions on athletes' involvement with sport agents and restrictions on athletes' abilities to market themselves, particularly in men's college basketball, where first- and second-year college players face an opportunity cost in the millions of dollars if they wish to stay in college and graduate with their respective class. Moreover, the pending cases of Ed O'Bannon and Sam Keller illustrate the Court's willingness to address the issue of the use of image and likeness of former college players by the NCAA. Both have sued the NCAA, Collegiate Licensing Company, and Electronic Arts (EA) Sports over the use of their names and likenesses in video games. While preventing student-athletes access to the yearly profits it generates from merchandise such as commemorative DVDs and video games, the NCAA claims that the blurring of professionalism and amateurism forms the root of its actions. Despite this, the rights signed away by former student-athletes in aid of the amateur virtue, the basic proprietary rights to their own image and likeness, may be too great to stand up to legal reason (*Keller v. EA Sports*, 2009; *O'Bannon v. NCAA*, 2009).

Gender equity continues to present legal and financial challenges for athletic administrators on the high school and collegiate levels. In addition to participation rate issues, administrators need to be cognizant of how female coaches and administrators are treated in the athletic departments. As an example of the costly litigation when this form of risk is not managed, the California State University system in 2008 and 2009 settled gender discrimination lawsuits totaling over $17.5 million on behalf of Fresno State and San Diego State Universities' Athletics Departments (Hostetter, 2008; Schrotenboer, 2009).

Professional Sport

For years, the legal issues in professional team sport have focused on whether leagues could maintain labor peace. Professional sport leagues are about to enter a period of significant labor instability, with all four of the major professional sport leagues in the midst of collective bargaining agreements that are set to expire in 2011. The NFL is about to enter a season in which it will not have a salary cap due to league ownership opting out of the existing league collective bargaining agreement.

Legal issues likely to arise in individual professional sports include the implementation and administration of drug testing policies. For instance, the PGA Tour now has a drug testing policy. Men's and women's tennis and cyclists' tours do have testing, but challenges are waged regularly over their test procedures and test results. Another emerging area is the potential for unionization efforts among individual athletes (e.g., WTA and ATP Tours, boxers, cyclists, action sports, NASCAR team members) who seek to improve their working conditions. Jockeys are currently unionized in the Jockey's Guild, but the organization has faced serious problems stemming from mismanagement, misconduct of principals, and corruption.

Governmental Scrutiny

There has been a steady increase in governmental scrutiny and regulation of the sport industry. Following governmental scrutiny of performance-enhancing drug use resulting from the BALCO (Bay Area Laboratory Co-Operative) scandal, Congress has called for increased bans on such substances and increased testing of athletes. Congressional hearings have already spurred changes in amateur and professional leagues' drug testing policies, such as in professional baseball where the testing has been a subject of collective bargaining. Other pending Congressional actions include rethinking the unrelated business income tax's application to college athletics, commercialization of college athletics, and whether the BCS structure violates antitrust laws. State and federal regulation of player agents has increased over the past decade as well.

Conduct Issues and Contracts

In 2009–2010, there were several high profile cases in professional and college sports dealing with conduct issues and the potential impact on the contracts between the parties. The most notable professional sports case involved Tiger Woods and whether his extramarital scandals would impact his endorsement contracts with various sponsors. While some sponsors (e.g., Nike, EA Sports) continued their endorsement contracts with Tiger, others (e.g., Gatorade, Gillette, AT&T, Accenture) ended their contracts with him (Tiger Woods . . . , 2009). Nike reportedly restructured its contract with Tiger to reduce the amount of guaranteed money, opting for sales and performance bonuses (Nike reportedly . . . , 2010). While none of the contract details have been made public, it has been widely assumed that they contained morality clauses that allowed the companies to restructure or terminate the contracts (Belson & Sandomir, 2010).

Other professional sports cases involving conduct included workplace related misconduct and outside the workplace misconduct. Gilbert Arenas of the Washington Wizards, who brought guns into the locker room, is an example of a work-related misconduct situation. After an earlier argument, on December 21, 2009, Arenas left several handguns in teammate Javaris Crittenton's locker with a note telling him to "PICK 1." Arenas faced criminal charges in the District of Columbia because carrying handguns outside the home is illegal in Washington, DC. Arenas also violated the NBA's collective bargaining agreement by possessing a weapon in the NBA workplace. Arenas was sentenced to 400 hours of community service, a $5,000 fine, and one month in a halfway house (Duggan, 2010). It was ultimately determined by David Stern, Commissioner of the National Basketball Association, that Arenas would also be suspended on January 6, 2010 for the balance of the 2009–2010 season without pay. This meant that Arenas was suspended for 50 games and reportedly lost $7,400,000 of his $16,100,000 salary (Arenas suspended . . . , 2010).

There are several examples of professional team sports athletes who have been penalized by the leagues (by the Commissioner) for outside the workplace misconduct. The National Football League and its commissioner, Roger Goodell, have been involved in a number of these since the NFL and Goodell implemented a NFL Player Conduct Policy in 2007 (NFL Personal Conduct Policy, 2007). The strengthened policy, implemented in the wake of multiple off-field incidents involving NFL players, applies to all NFL employees and holds teams responsible for the actions of their employees (Goodell strengthens . . . , 2007). The first players suspended as a result of the strengthened policy were Adam "Pacman" Jones of the Tennessee Titans and Chris Henry of the Cincinnati Bengals (Goodell suspends . . . , 2007). Jones was suspended for the 2007 season for several off-field incidents that resulted in police interviews, although he was never convicted of any crime. He was suspended again in 2008 for another incident of misconduct outside of the workplace (Pacman suspended . . . , 2008). Henry was suspended because he violated the policy with his four arrests in a 14 month period. The suspension of Michael Vick of the Atlanta Falcons was also in response to violations of the policy (NFL suspends . . . , 2007). In 2010, Ben Roethlisberger of the Pittsburgh Steelers was suspended after he was accused of sexual assault, although he was never arrested or charged with a crime (Roethlisberger suspended . . . , 2010). His suspension is exemplary of Goodell's intention for the policy to be stricter than standards outside of the NFL.

In college sports, three football coaches were involved in cases of alleged physical and/or mental abuse of players. In all three cases, the employers relied upon contract language governing conduct in dealing with the coaches. In the Mark Mangino and University of Kansas litigation, the sides settled the case with Mangino's resignation (after a law firm was hired and completed an investigation into the allegations of physical and mental abuse) (Kansas . . . , 2009) and a reported payment of $3,000,000, far less than the reported balance of $11,000,000 remaining on his contract (Confidential . . . , 2009). The other two cases are still in litigation at this writing. The first involves Mike Leach, a football coach and Texas Tech University. Leach was suspended indefinitely on December 28, 2009, after player Adam James's family filed a complaint about James's treatment after an injury. James alleged that Leach forced the player to stand in a dark equipment closet for more than three hours. Leach was fired on December 31, 2009, for his misconduct and also on grounds of insubordination (Judge says . . . , 2010). On January 7, 2010, Leach filed a lawsuit seeking damages for breach of contract, fraudulent inducement, defamation, and depravation of due process, as well as seeking of waiver of Texas Tech's sovereign immunity (*Leach v. Texas Tech University*, 2010). The second case involves Jim Leavitt, a football coach, and the University of South Florida. Leavitt allegedly struck a player in the locker room during a November 21, 2009, home game against the University of Louisville. Leavitt claims that he "was merely trying to console the player and never struck him." Leavitt was fired for cause on January 8, 2010, and given one month's base salary ($66,667). On January 13, 2010, Leavitt met with the provost of the University of South Florida and petitioned for reinstatement. It was denied (Bennett, 2010). Leavitt subsequently filed a lawsuit against the University of South Florida in state court on March 15, 2010, alleging a breach of contract (*Leavitt v. University of South Florida Board of Trustees and University of South Florida Foundation, Inc.*). Leavitt is seeking to recover the remaining $7,000,000 left on his contract.

■ SUMMARY

As the sport industry has evolved into a complex multibillion-dollar global entity, law has played a dominant role in carrying out management functions in sport organizations. When sport managers make decisions and disagreements arise, those working and participating in sport are relying more heavily on the legal system for resolutions. Thus, knowledge of key aspects of sport law has become increasingly important to the sport manager's ability to manage risk and to know when to seek legal assistance to aid in decision making and dispute resolution.

■ KEY TERMS

administrative law, Age Discrimination in Employment Act, agency, agent, Americans with Disabilities Act, ambush marketing, antitrust law, bona fide occupational qualification, breach, capacity, collective bargaining agreement, consideration, constitutional law, contract, Curt Flood Act, defendant, disaffirm, due process, duty of care, Equal Pay Act, equal protection, fiduciary duties, gross negligence, independent contractor, injunction, intellectual property, invasion of privacy, judicial review, labor exemption, Lanham Act, legality, legitimate interest, National Labor Relations Act, negligence, plaintiff, principal, public policy, rational basis, release of liability, risk management, secondary meaning, service mark, single entity, sport law, state actor, statutes, strict scrutiny, Title VII, Title IX, tort, trademark, unreasonable searches and seizures, vicarious liability, waivers

■ REFERENCES

Access Now, Inc. v. South Florida Stadium Corp., 161 F. Supp. 2d 1357 (S.D. Fla. 2001).

Adidas America, Inc. v. National Collegiate Athletic Association, 64 F. Supp. 2d 1097 (D. Kan. 1999).

Age Discrimination in Employment Act of 1990, 29 U.S.C. §§ 621–634 (West 1990).

Ambush marketing. (2010). Retrieved November 10, 2010, from http://www.glossaryofmarketing.com/definition/ambush-marketing.html

Ambush marketing is becoming a popular event at Olympic games. (1988 February 8). *The Wall Street Journal*, p. A25.

American Football League v. National Football League, 323 F.2d 124 (4th Cir. 1963).

American Needle v. National Football League, 130 S. Ct. 2201 (2010).

Americans with Disabilities Act of 1990, 42 U.S.C. §§ 151–169 (West 1990).

Ammon, R., & Robinson, M.T. (2007). Risk management process. In D.J. Cotten & J.T. Wolohan (Eds.), *Law for recreation and sport managers* (4th ed.) (pp. 288–300). Dubuque, IA: Kendall/Hunt Publishers.

Arenas suspended indefinitely. (2010 January 7). ESPN. Retrieved October 11, 2010, from http://sports.espn.go.com/nba/news/story?id=4802267

Banks v. National Collegiate Athletic Association, 977 F.2d 1081 (7th Cir. 1992).

Belson, K. & Sandomir, R. (2010 January 31). Insuring endorsements against athletes' scandals. *New York Times*. Retrieved October 11, 2010, from http://www.nytimes.com/2010/02/01/sports/01insurance.html

Bennett, B. (2010 March 15). Fired Leavitt files suit, seeks millions. ESPN. Retrieved October 11, 2010, from http://sports.espn.go.com/ncf/news/story?id=4996720

Biediger v. Quinnipiac University, 616 F. Supp. 2d 277 (D. Conn 2009).

Biediger v. Quinnipiac University, No. 3:09cv621 (SRU) (D. Ct. 2010). Retrieved October 11, 2010, from http://courtweb.pamd.uscourts.gov/courtweb-search/ctxc/KX330R32.pdf

Black's Law Dictionary, (5th ed.). (1979).

Board of Education v. Earls, 536 U.S. 822 (2002).

Board of Supervisors for La. State Univ. v. Smack Apparel Co., 550 F.3d 465 (5th Cir. 2008).

Brennan v. Board of Trustees for University of Louisiana Systems, 691 So.2d 324 (La. Ct. App. 1st Cir. 1997).

Brentwood Academy v. Tennessee Secondary School Athletic Association, 535 U.S. 971 (2001).

Bridgeman v. National Basketball Association, 675 F. Supp. 960 (D.N.J. 1987).

Brown v. Pro Football, Inc., 518 U.S. 231 (1996).

Brown v. Woolf, 554 F. Supp. 1206 (S.D. Ind. 1983).

Buse v. Vanguard Group of Investment Cos., No. 91-3560, 1996 U.S. Dist. LEXIS 19033 (E.D. Pa. 1996).

Callaway Golf Company v. Acushnet Company, 585 F. Supp. 2d 600 (D. Del. 2008).

Confidential settlement agreement and release between Mark Mangino, the University of Kansas, and Kansas Athletics, Inc. (2009). *USA Today*. Retrieved October 11, 2010, from http://i.usatoday.net/sports/college/football/2009-12-16-mangino-settlement.pdf

Copperweld Corp. v. Independence Tube Corp., 467 U.S. 752, 773, n. 21.

Cotten, D.J. (2007). Waivers and releases. In D.J. Cotten & J.T. Wolohan (Eds.), *Law for recreation and sport managers* (4th ed.) (pp. 85–94). Dubuque, IA: Kendall/Hunt Publishers.

Crespin v. Albuquerque Baseball Club, LLC, 216 P.3d 827 (N.M. Ct. App. 2009).

Curt Flood Act, 15 U.S.C. § 27 (1998).

Detroit Lions, Inc. and Sims v. Argovitz, 580 F. Supp. 542 (E.D. Mich. 1984).

Deutscher Tennis Bund et al. v. ATP Tour, Inc., 2010 WL 2541172 (C.A.3 (Del.).

Duggan, P. (2010 March 27). Wizards star Gilbert Arenas avoids jail time in gun incident. *The Washington Post*. Retrieved October 11, 2010, from http://www.washingtonpost.com/wp-dyn/content/article/2010/03/26/AR2010032603887.html

In re Ekuban, 2004 WL 1088340 (Bkrtcy. N.D.Tex., April 16, 2004).

Equal Pay Act of 1963, 29 U.S.C. § 206 (d)(1) (West 1990).

Equity in Athletics, Inc. v. The United States Department of Education, 291 Fed. Appx. 517 (2008).

Faragher v. Boca Raton, 524 U.S. 775 (1998).

Federal Baseball Club of Baltimore v. National League of Professional Baseball Clubs, et al., 259 U.S. 200 (1922).

Flood v. Kuhn, 407 U.S. 258 (1972).

Franklin v. Gwinnett County Public Schools, 112 S. Ct. 1028 (1992).

Goodell strengthens NFL personal conduct policy. (2007 April 11). *USA Today*. Retrieved October 11, 2010, from http://www.usatoday.com/sports/football/nfl/2007-04-10-new-conduct-policy_N.htm?csp=34

Goodell suspends Pacman, Henry for multiple arrests. (2007 May 17). ESPN. Retrieved October 11, 2010, from http://sports.espn.go.com/nfl/news/story?id=2832015

Gulf South Conference v. Boyd, 369 So.2d 553 (Sup. Ct. Ala. 1979).

Hackbart v. Cincinnati Bengals, Inc., 601 F. 2d 516 (10th Cir. 1979).

Haworth, K. (1996 December 20). A cottage industry helps sports programs in trouble. *Chronicle of Higher Education*, A35.

Hill v. National Collegiate Athletic Association, 865 P.2d 633 (Cal. 1994).

Hillard v. Black, 125 F. Supp. 2d 1071 (N.D. Fla. 2000).

Holcomb v. Iona College, 521 F.3d 130 (2nd Cir. 2008).

Hostetter, G. (2008 July 15) Fresno state settles with softball coach for $605,000. *The Fresno Bee*. Retrieved October 11, 2010, from http://www.fresnobee.com/2008/07/11/726448/fresno-state-settles-with-softball.html

Howell, R.A., Allison, J.R., & Henley, N.T. (1987). *The legal environment of business* (2nd ed.). New York: Dryden Press.

IBL, *Class Action Reporter*. (2000 September 19). Retrieved October 11, 2010, from http://bankrupt.com/CAR_Public/000919.MBX

Jones v. Childers, 18 F.3d 1899 (11th Cir. 1994).

Judge says Leach's Lawsuit vs. Texas Tech can move forward. (2010 June 1). *USA Today*. Retrieved October 11, 2010, from http://www.usatoday.com/sports/college/football/big12/2010-06-01-mike-leach-lawsuit-texas-tech_N.htm

Kansas, Mangino reach settlement. (2009 December 17). ESPN. Retrieved October 11, 2010, from http://sports.espn.go.com/ncf/news/story?id=4749169

Keller v. EA Sports, No. C 09-1967 CW (N.D. Calif. 2009). Order re: Motion to Dismiss. Scribd. Retrieved October 11, 2010, from http://www.scribd.com/doc/26624013/Keller-v-NCAA-Order-re-Motion-to-Dismiss

Kobritz, J. (2010 April 23). Presumption of guilt prevents athlete from competing in college sports. Sports Litigation Alert. Retrieved October 11, 2010, from http://www.hackneypublications.com/sla/archive/001036.php

Kuketz v. MDC Fitness Corp., 2001 WL 993565 (Mass. Super. Ct. 2001).

Law v. National Collegiate Athletic Association, 902 F. Supp. 1394 (D. Kan. 1995).

Leach v. Texas Tech University, No. 2009-550,359. (2010 January 7).

Leavitt v. University of South Florida Board of Trustees and University of South Florida Foundation, Inc., No. 10005807. (Fla. March 15).

Letendre v. Missouri State High School Activities Association, 86 S.W.2d 63 (Mo C. App. 2002).

London Olympic Games and Paralympic Games Act 2006. (United Kingdom), s. 33. Retrieved October 11, 2010, from http://www.opsi.gov.uk/acts/acts2006/pdf/ukpga_20060012_en.pdf

Long v. National Football League, 870 F. Supp. 101 (W.D. Pa. 1994).

Los Angeles Memorial Coliseum Commission v. National Football League, 726 F.2d 1381 (1984).

Lowen, D. (2006 March 3). The London Olympic Games and Paralympic Games Act. Retrieved October 11, 2010, from http://www.couchman-sllp.com/documents/news_press/London%20 Olympics%20Act.pdf

Ludtke and Time, Inc. v. Kuhn, 461 F. Supp. 86 (S.D.N.Y. 1978).

Mackey v. National Football League, 543 F.2d 606 (8th Cir. 1976).

Mark v. Moser, 746 N.E.2d 410 (Ind. App. 2001).

Masteralexis, L.P. (2007a). Judicial review. In D.J. Cotton & J.T. Wolohan (Eds.), *Law for recreation and sport managers* (4th ed.) (pp. 420–428). Dubuque, IA: Kendall/Hunt Publishers.

Masteralexis, L.P. (2007b). Labor law: Professional sport applications. In D.J. Cotton & J.T. Wolohan (Eds.), *Law for recreation and sport managers* (4th ed.) (pp. 655–665). Dubuque, IA: Kendall/Hunt Publishers.

McCormack v. National Collegiate Athletic Association, 845 F.2d 1338 (5th Cir. 1988).

McCourt v. California Sports, Inc., 600 F.2d 1193 (6th Cir. 1979).

McNeil v. National Football League, 790 F. Supp. 871 (D. Minn. 1992).

Metropolitan Exhibition Co. v. Ewing, 42 F. 1989 (S.D.N.Y. 1890).

Metropolitan Exhibition Co. v. Ward, 9 N.Y.S. 779 (Sup. Ct. 1890).

Metropolitan Intercollegiate Basketball Association v. NCAA, 339 F. Supp. 2d 545 (S.D.N.Y. 2004).

Mickle, T. (2010 February 11). Subway campaign 'Crossed the line,' USOC's Baird says. *Street and Smith's SportsBusiness Daily.* Retrieved October 11, 2010, from http://www.sportsbusinessdaily .com/wintergames/entries

Miller v. University of Cincinnati, 2007 WL 2783674 (S.D. Ohio 2008).

Moore v. University of Notre Dame, 22 F. Supp. 2d 896 (N.D. Ind. 1998).

National Basketball Association v. Williams, 43 F.3d 684 (2nd Cir. 1995).

National Collegiate Athletic Association v. Board of Regents of the University of Oklahoma and the University of Georgia Athletic Association, 468 U.S. 85 (1982).

National Collegiate Athletic Association v. Tarkanian, 488 U.S. 179, 193 (1988).

National Labor Relations Act, 29 U.S.C. §§ 151–69 (West 1990).

National Wrestling Coaches Association v. United States Department of Education, 263 F. Supp. 2d 82 (D.D.C. 2003).

NFL Personal Conduct Policy. (2007). ESPN. Retrieved October 11, 2010, from http://sports.espn.go.com/ nfl/news/story?id=2798214

NFL suspends Vick indefinitely. (2007 August 24). CNN. Retrieved October 11, 2010, from http:// www.cnn.com/2007/US/law/08/24/michael .vick/index.html

Nike reportedly restructures contract Tiger Woods signed in '06. (2010 April 4). *Street and Smith's SportsBusiness Daily.* Retrieved November 10, 2010, from http://www.sportsbusinessdaily.com/ index.cfm?fuseaction=tdi.ClosingBell&tdidate= 2010%2D04%2D09

Noffke ex. rel Swenson v. Bakke, 760 N.W.2d 156 (Wis. 2009).

O'Bannon v. NCAA, No. C 09-1967 CW (N.D. Calif. 2009). Order re: Motion to Dismiss. Scribd. Retrieved October 11, 2010, from http://www .scribd.com/doc/26623903/O-Bannon-v-NCAA-Order-re-Motion-to-Dismiss

Olinger v. United States Golf Association, 205 F.3d 1001 (7th Cir. 2000).

Oliver v. NCAA, 2009 Ohio 6587 (2009).

Ortiz-Del Valle v. National Basketball Association, 42 F. Supp. 2d 334 (S.D.N.Y. 1999).

Pacman suspended at least 4 games for violating conduct policy. (2008 October 15). ESPN. Retrieved October 11, 2010, from http://sports.espn.go.com/ nfl/news/story?id=3643240

Perdue v. City University of New York, 13 F. Supp. 2d 326 (E.D.N.Y. 1998).

Perry v. Sindermann, 408 U.S. 593 (1972).

PGA Tour Inc. v. Martin, 532 U.S. 661 (2001).

Philadelphia World Hockey, Inc. v. Philadelphia Hockey Club, Inc., 351 F. Supp. 462 (1972).

Pitts v. University of Oklahoma, No. Civ. 93-1341-A (W.D. Okla. 1994).

Powell v. National Football League, 930 F.2d 1293 (8th Cir. 1989).

Reed, M. H. (1989). *IEG legal guide to sponsorship.* Chicago: International Events Group.

Rene v. MGM Grand Hotel, Inc., No. 98-16924 (9th Cir. Sept. 24, 2002).

Reynolds v. National Football League, 584 F.2d 280 (8th Cir. 1978).

Rodgers v. Georgia Tech Athletic Association, 303 S.E.2d 467 (Ga. Ct. App. 1983).

Roethlisberger suspended NFL. (2010 April 22). ESPN. Retrieved October 11, 2010, from http://sports .espn.go.com/nfl/news/story?id=5121614

Schrotenboer, B. (2009 October 2). SDSU settles equal pay lawsuit brought by coach. *Sign On San Diego*. Retrieved October 11, 2010, from http://www.signonsandiego.com/news/2009/ oct/02/sdsu-settles-equal-pay-lawsuit-brought-coach/?sports

Shropshire, K.L., & Davis, T. (2003). *The business of sports agents*. Philadelphia: University of Pennsylvania Press.

Smith v. Pro Football, Inc., 593 F.2d 1173 (D.C. Cir. 1978).

Sport Broadcasting Act, 15 U.S.C. §§ 1291–1294 (1961).

Stanley v. University of Southern California, 13 F.3d 1313 (1994).

Stanley v. University of Southern California, 178 F. 3d 1069 (9th Cir. 1999).

Staudohar, P.D. (1996). *Playing for dollars: Labor relations and the sports business*. Ithaca, NY: Cornell University Press.

Thurmond v. Prince William Professional Baseball Club, Inc., 574 S.E.2d 246 (Va. 2003).

Tiger Woods in new sponsorship loss as AT&T drops deal. (2009 December 31). *BBC News*. Retrieved October 11, 2010, from http://news.bbc.co.uk/2/ hi/business/8436514.stm

Title VII of the Civil Rights Act of 1964, 42 U.S.C. § 2002 (a)(1)(2) (West 1990).

Title IX of the Educational Amendments of 1972, 20 U.S.C. §§ 1681–88 (West 1990).

Toolson v. New York Yankees, 346 U.S. 356 (1953).

Total Economic Athletic Management of America, Inc. v. Pickens, 898 S.W.2d 98 (Mo. App. 1995).

Turner v. Mandalay Sports Entertainment, LLC. 180 P.3d 1172 (Nev. 2008).

United States Football League v. National Football League, 634 F. Supp. 1155 (S.D.N.Y. 1986).

University of Colorado v. Derdeyn, 863 P.2d 929 (1993).

Van der Smissen, B. (2003). Elements of negligence. In D.J. Cotten & T.J. Wilde (Eds.), *Law for recreation and sport managers* (3rd ed.). Dubuque, IA: Kendall/Hunt Publishers.

Vernonia School District 47J v. Acton, 115 S. Ct. 2386 (1995).

Vick v. Wong et al., 263 F.R.D. 325 (U.S. Dist. 2009).

Wagenblast v. Odessa School District, 758 P.2d 968 (Wash. Sup. Ct. 1988).

Wallace v. Texas Tech University, 80 F.3d 1042 (5th Cir. 1996).

White v. NCAA, C.D. Cal. Case No. CV 06 0999 VBF.

Wilde, T.J. (2003). Principles in trademark law. In D.J. Cotten & T.J. Wilde (Eds.), *Law for recreation and sport managers* (3rd ed.). Dubuque, IA: Kendall/Hunt Publishers.

Williams v. CWI, Inc., 777 F. Supp. 1006 (D.D.C. 1991).

Williams v. National Football League, 582 F. 3d 863 (8th Cir. 2009).

Wong, G.M. (2010). *Essentials of sports law* (4th ed.). Westport, CT: Praeger Publishers.

Wong, G.M., & Masteralexis, L.P. (1996). Legal aspects of sport administration. In F.J. Bridges & L. L. Roquemore (Eds.), *Management for athletic/sport administration: Theory and practice* (2nd ed.) (pp. 85–132). Decatur, GA: ESM Books.

Wood v. National Basketball Association, 809 F.2d 954 (2nd Cir. 1987).

World Intellectual Property Organization (WIPO). (2010). What is intellectual property? Retrieved October 11, 2010, from http://www.wipo.int/ about-ip/en

Yasser, R., McCurdy, J., Goplerud, P., & Weston, M. (1999). *Sports law* (4th ed.). Cincinnati, OH: Anderson Publishing.

York v. Wahkiakum School Dist. No. 200, 163 Wash.2d 297 (Wash. 2008).

Zimmerman v. National Football League, 632 F. Supp. 398 (D.D.C. 1986).

Zinn v. Parrish, 644 F.2d 360 (7th Cir. 1981).

CHAPTER

Ethical Principles Applied to Sport Management

Todd W. Crosset and Mary A. Hums

■ INTRODUCTION

Sport managers make tough decisions. Imagine for a moment you had to decide if and when to play a football game after the terrorist attack on the World Trade Center in New York on September 11, 2001. Managers across the country were faced with conflicting and equally compelling desires to mourn those who died and to get back to normal. How would you go about making that decision? What would be your approach? Although this is an extreme example, sport managers frequently face decisions involving ethical dilemmas. What can help guide them in their decision making in complex situations?

Ethics is the systematic study of the values guiding our decision making. The process

of making a correct and fair decision is called **ethical reasoning**. Ethical reasoning depends on our values or the values of the organizations for which we work and reflects how we believe people should behave and how we want our world to operate. This chapter provides a framework to help future sport managers think critically and systematically about ethical issues. It discusses two types of ethical issues: ethical dilemmas and morality.

An **ethical dilemma** is a practical conflict involving more or less equally compelling values or social obligations (Solomon, 1992). When to resume play after a community or national tragedy is an example of an ethical dilemma. Ethical dilemmas are solved when we articulate which commonly held values we admire most.

However, ethical values should not be confused with personal preferences. **Ethical decision making** affects other people in a way that personal preferences do not. Ethical dilemmas have social implications. As such, ethics requires decision makers to consider how their actions will affect different groups of people and individuals.

Morality, like ethics, is concerned with values guiding behavior. However, morality deals with a specific type of ethical issue. **Morals** are the fundamental baseline values dictating appropriate behavior within a society (Solomon, 1992). The beliefs that stealing and murder are wrong, for example, are moral values in most societies. Morality is sometimes summarized as a list of those actions people ought to do or refrain from doing. The concept of morality is discussed in further detail later in this chapter.

■ ETHICAL CONSIDERATIONS

The world of sport has certainly seen its share of scandals of late. Congressional hearings dealing with steroid use in Major League Baseball revealed the extensive use of performance enhancing drugs in that sport. Other sport organizations were hit with drug-related scandals as well, including 2006 Tour de France winner Floyd Landis failing a drug test and the 2007 event experiencing several doping controversies resulting in two teams and three racers leaving or being removed from the race (Wyatt, 2007). Officials disqualified Landis. After years of denial Landis owned up to his doping and went on to accuse cycling icon Lance Armstrong of doping. Tiger Woods' extreme infidelity tainted his image and caused corporate sponsors to rethink their association with Woods. Soccer fans in numerous European cities have subjected black players to racial insults and taunts. Back in 2005 news broke that Reggie Bush, a star running back for the University of Southern

California (USC) had taken gifts from would-be agents in exchange for allowing them to represent him when he turned professional. In June 2010, the National Collegiate Athletic Association (NCAA) slapped USC with a two-year ban on postseason play and a reduction of 30 scholarships for turning a blind eye to Reggie Bush's dealings with these unscrupulous agents. Bush ultimately decided to return his Heisman Trophy, the first player in its 75 year history to do so (Pennington, 2010). Whenever events like this occur, sport managers need to respond in an ethical manner, making decisions that are guided by strong ethical principles. It is not always easy to do so, as situations are complex and demanding, but sport managers need to answer these challenges with positive responses.

Sport managers face ethical dilemmas on a daily basis. Consider the following, for example:

- Changing the start time of a contest to accommodate television programming at the expense of class time for college athletes
- Encouraging the use of painkillers by injured athletes to enable them to play hurt
- Helping an athlete with a drug, alcohol, marital, or criminal problem
- Using a team's limited resources to make stadiums accessible for people with disabilities
- Relocating a professional team from a profitable site to another city promising even more revenue
- Deciding between cutting less visible, successful nonrevenue sport teams or a highly visible football program when facing a budget crisis in an NCAA Division I collegiate athletic program

Few areas of sport management present managers more difficulty than ethical dilemmas. Sport managers' decision making is complicated because the outcomes of their decisions affect diverse groups of people (e.g., athletes, fans, the community, businesses, the media) whose interests are often in conflict. Plus, sport managers' decisions about ethical dilemmas tend to fall under greater public scrutiny than decisions made by managers in other industries without high-profile employees (professional athletes) or without great media interest. At the same moment that managers are weighing decisions regarding the right thing to do, they are also considering financial costs, the effect on a team's and league's reputation, the law, and the impact on winning games. If a sport manager does not approach ethical dilemmas systematically, the complexity of issues and interests involved can easily overwhelm his or her judgment—especially when conflicting options seem to make equally good sense and are being argued emotionally by opposing parties.

How does a sport manager know when he or she is facing such a dilemma? Zinn (1993) suggests managers ask the following questions to ascertain if they are facing an ethical dilemma:

- When talking about the matter at hand, do people use words or expressions such as right or wrong, black or white, bottom line, conflict, or values?
- Will anyone be harmed because of my action/inaction or decision?
- Am I concerned about my decision being equally fair to all parties?
- Do I feel a conflict between my personal values and my professional interest?
- Is there controversy or strong opposition regarding this decision?
- Do I have a feeling something is "just not right" about the situation?
- Will I be hesitant to reveal my decision to others?

If a sport manager answers "yes" to any of these questions, he or she is most likely facing an ethical dilemma.

To solve an ethical dilemma, decision makers try to make a rational argument. They weigh the pros and cons of two or more seemingly valid choices that reflect equally cherished values. In recreational softball leagues, for example, teams are faced with the decision of whether to play only their best players or to play everyone. The decision is based on the relative value team members place on winning versus the value they place on participation. The argument could be made that the primary purpose of a recreational softball league is for participants to play and have fun. Recreational leagues provide camaraderie and emphasize team spirit that grows out of cheering for each other, playing, and going out together after games. However, an equally compelling argument could be made for competition and winning, which are central to the enjoyment of sport—even on the recreational level. Therefore, teams should field their best players so competition and victory are more intense and more satisfying. Both outlooks make sense; hence, an ethical dilemma exists. In the softball league example, the decision makers have to put themselves in the shoes of both the bench warmers and the starters and consider how both will be affected. They also have to think about what type of values they want to emphasize through their teams.

When sport managers are faced with ethical dilemmas, their decisions are difficult. Ethical decision making is not a random process in which the sport manager just reacts from his or her "gut" feeling. Ethical analysis involves a systematic process of reasoning. It is not a haphazard procedure where one guesses at the best solution (Cooke, 1991). Ethical decision making is similar to the regular decision-making process in business situations in that there is a given structure to follow when making an ethical decision. A model suggested by Zinn (1993) and adapted by Hums and MacLean (2008) outlines the following steps in the ethical decision-making process:

1. Identify the correct problem to be solved.
2. Gather all the pertinent information.
3. Explore codes of conduct relevant to your profession or to this particular dilemma.
4. Examine your own personal values and beliefs.
5. Consult with your peers or other individuals in the industry who may have experience in similar situations.
6. List your options.
7. Look for a "win-win" situation if at all possible.
8. Ask yourself this question: "How would my family feel if my decision and how I arrived at my decision were printed in the newspaper tomorrow?"
9. Sleep on it. Do not rush to a decision.
10. Make your best decision, knowing it may not be perfect.
11. Evaluate your decision.

Although this may seem like a complicated process, remember that ethical decisions and ethical dilemmas involve complicated problems, and that often, reasonable people will disagree over what is the "right decision." It is essential for sport managers to fully think through any ethical decisions they must make.

Consider the following case. The 2010 NCAA Men's National Swimming and Diving Championships were scheduled for Thursday through Saturday, March 24–27. On Tuesday, 18 members of the Arizona, Texas, and Stanford teams fell ill. (About 1/3 of each squad became sick.) All three teams had traveled on the same flight into Columbus and had picked up a viral infection resulting in nausea, vomiting, and diarrhea. On Wednesday, the day prior to the start of the meet, the athletes were being treated at a local hospital. The teams affected were some of the best in the country and each had a chance to win a team trophy. The coaches of these teams are very powerful within the world of swimming. Their athletes, weakened by the stomach bug

would not perform at their best until they could recover. An emergency coaches' meeting was called to discuss the situation. Should the meet proceed as scheduled or be delayed?

The NCAA Crisis Management Team led the effort to resolve the dilemma. Health experts from the Centers for Disease Control and Prevention (CDC) and from Ohio State University were consulted. Officials quickly realized that the first issue at hand was the health and safety of all athletes and spectators. The initial decision made by the NCAA Crisis Management Team was to have event managers go all out to keep the pool area sanitized as athletes (even the sick ones) were trying to prepare for the meet. Coaches of affected teams were asked to keep their athletes separated from other teams. Whatever the illness was they didn't want it spreading. But what to do about the competition?

The NCAA Crisis Management Team prioritized health and safety and then considered the fairest option in light of health priority. Officials didn't want sick athletes on the deck or the pool with other athletes until they were sure they the athletes were no longer contagious. Health experts recommended that the sick athletes not compete on Thursday. That meant either barring them from competition for one day or delaying the entire meet for one day.

Three options were considered. Start on the meet Thursday as scheduled and leave it up to the medical experts, coaches, and athletes to decide on a case-by-case basis which of the sick athletes could compete. Some coaches thought this was the right thing to do. They argued they had their athletes ready to go for Thursday. Delaying the meet was to their disadvantage. Stick to the original plan, they argued. Athletes get injured all the time. Let's swim and let the chips fall where they may. If there was a health risk, this argument goes, affected athletes should not compete (similar to the rule that a player may not participate in a sport if he or she is bleeding). Healthy athletes should not be affected by the sick athletes. Delaying the meet is an unfair burden for the healthy teams to bear. Further, these coaches argued, if a smaller number of athletes from weaker teams got sick the emergency meeting would never have been called. The fair thing to do was to treat every situation in a similar fashion. Many of the coaches who made this argument also knew they would gain a competitive advantage by starting the meet on time.

Another suggestion was to start the meet on Friday. This would ensure that the bug did not spread, but it also would enable affected athletes one more day to recover. Having a one day delay enabled those athletes 24 more hours to recover, which no doubt was the primary concern of the Texas, Stanford, and Arizona teams. People who made this argument appealed to the notion of least harm. A one day delay wouldn't harm healthy athletes and teams as much as asking sick athletes not to compete or to compete in their weakened state on the first day.

Delaying the meet led to another dilemma: how to run the event starting the meet one day later. One suggestion was to run the Thursday and Friday events as timed finals on Friday, compressing the meet into two days. This choice ended the meet on Saturday and had the benefit of not disrupting team travel schedules. Another option was to push the entire meet back one day and run it as intended, over three days, Friday through Sunday.

Most coaches thought running two thirds of the meet as timed finals on Friday was too great of a modification and quickly rejected the idea of compressing the meet into two days. That left two options for the NCAA Crisis Management Team: start the meet on Thursday and make medical decisions on a case-by-case basis, or delay the meet by one day. In the end the NCAA Crisis Management team decided the "fairest" way to proceed was to run the meet in full, beginning on Friday.

That decision seemed the most fair because it allowed all athletes who qualified to compete as intended and had the least disruptive impact on the outcome. Because such a large percentage of top athletes took ill, running the meet without them, even for one day, would dramatically change the outcome of the Championships. It was not clear if the athletes would still be contagious on Thursday. Barring the affected athletes put some teams at a disadvantage for a medical precaution that might not be necessary. However, allowing them to compete in a weakened state might cause medical problems and many of these athletes would not perform up to their capabilities. Pushing the meet back one day, the NCAA Crisis Management Team reasoned, was medically prudent and had the least adverse impact on the performances of the greatest number of athletes. While not a perfect solution, the outcome of the meet would be decided by the athletes and not administrative choices of coaches, officials, and medical staff.

Making ethical decisions is challenging. Managers in any industry need guidelines to help them make decisions and principles to help them assess themselves and their personal values. The Josephson Institute of Ethics (2006) provides an interesting framework for managers to use when making ethical decisions, by offering what it calls the Six Pillars of Character. **Table 6-1** illustrates these Six Pillars and some of the subsets within each.

Codes of Conduct

The third recommendation from the ethical decision-making model just described is to consult an organization's **codes of conduct** (also called **codes of ethics**). The recent rash of corporate scandals in the United States illustrates the need for establishing solid ethical climates within corporations. According to Sims (1992), an organization's ethical climate establishes the

TABLE 6-1   Josephson's Six Pillars of Character℠

Pillar 1	Trustworthiness
	Includes honesty, integrity, reliability, and loyalty
Pillar 2	Respect
	Includes civility, courtesy, and decency; dignity and autonomy; and tolerance and acceptance
Pillar 3	Responsibility
	Includes accountability, pursuit of excellence, and self-restraint
Pillar 4	Fairness
	Includes process, impartiality, and equity
Pillar 5	Caring
	The "heart" of ethics
Pillar 6	Citizenship
	Includes civic virtues and duties

Source: © 2007 Reprinted with permission of Josephson Institute. www.charactercounts.org

shared set of understandings that determine correct behavior and the manner in which ethical issues will be handled. One way to establish this climate is through codes of conduct or codes of ethics. Codes of conduct are probably the most visible statements of a company, business, or organizational ethical philosophy and set of beliefs (DeSensi & Rosenberg, 1996). These codes of conduct explicitly outline and explain the principles under which an organization or profession operates. Implicit in any code of conduct are the institutional/organizational values that should help managers and employees resolve ethical dilemmas. Codes of conduct provide employees with guidelines for their behavior.

Codes of conduct and codes of ethics are not twentieth-century inventions. In fact, they are as old as the earliest religious oral traditions and writings, such as the Torah and the Koran. Although the development of modern codes in the United States was initiated in the medical, accounting, and legal professions, these are not the only professional areas to have codes of ethics. The need to address ethical questions and encourage correct actions has led many professions to establish codes of conduct (Jordan et al.,

2004). Codes of conduct are found in virtually every type of organization and corporation in the United States. Within the last decade many corporations have hired ethics officers or created ethics boards to address ethical issues within organizations.

In the sport world, codes have been adopted or are being considered by a number of sport organizations. The U.S. Olympic Committee, the International Olympic Committee, the National Intramural and Recreational Sports Association, the American Camping Association, and USA Hockey are just a few examples of sport organizations with codes of conduct. Numerous youth sport programs, including the Indiana Youth Soccer Association, the U.S. Lacrosse Youth Council, and the National Association for Sport and Physical Education, have adopted codes of conduct as well, often having separate codes for participants, coaches, and parents. The state of New Jersey passed a code of conduct law that established athletic codes of conduct for players, coaches, officials, and parents (Youth Sports Research Council, 2002).

Codes of conduct are not unique to the sport industry in the United States. The Geelong

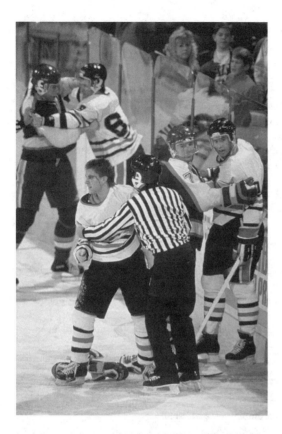

Cricket Association of Australia has a series of codes for junior cricket players, spectators, and coaches (Geelong Cricket Association, 2002). The Australia Sports Commission has a series of codes of behaviors written for administrators, players, coaches, spectators, officials, parents, and even teachers and the media (Australia Sports Commission, n.d.). England Basketball has an extensive set of codes for administrators, players, coaches, spectators, referees, and parents (England Basketball, 2002). Speed Skating Canada has a code (Speed Skating Canada, 2001), as does British Columbia Athletics (BC Athletics, n.d.).

Periodically, managers are asked to review or create codes of conduct. According to a 2000 Ethics Officer Association survey, 96% of ethics officers had created or rewritten codes of con-

duct over a five-year period (Petry, 2001). Codes of conduct should be clear and straightforward, and need not be long or complex. They should encourage employees to understand the goals they are trying to accomplish instead of just outlining rules and punishments.

If done well, codes of conduct can help create an ethical climate in an organization. According to Mahony, Geist, Jordan, Greenwell, and Pastore (1999), a number of factors are necessary for a sport organization to possess an effective code of conduct:

- Codes need to avoid being too vague (De-Sensi & Rosenberg, 1996).
- Codes should be based on a few overriding principles that can be used to deal with a variety of ethical dilemmas faced by members of the organization (Fraliegh, 1993).
- Codes should clearly state to whom they apply. If codes are to be influential, leadership and membership within the organization must accept and be willing to adhere to the prescribed standards.
- Codes should contain consequences for violations (DeSensi & Rosenberg, 1996).

An example of a code of conduct for a sport organization is given in **Figure 6-1**, which reproduces the National Intramural Recreational Sports Association members' code of ethics (2010). The organization also has a code of ethics for student members.

Codes of conduct are not the be-all and end-all of organizational ethics. If codes of conduct are too long or complex to easily understand, if they try to intimidate employees into acting morally, or if the organization does not demonstrate a commitment to them, codes of conduct may be counterproductive. Further, if codes of ethics are too detailed, they can actually discourage moral reasoning. The NCAA "has become so rule dependent, so comprehensive and so situation specific," sport ethicist Russell Gough argues,

FIGURE 6-1   National Intramural and Recreational Sports Association (NIRSA) Member Code of Ethics

PREAMBLE

An outstanding characteristic of a profession is that its members are continually striving to improve the quality of life for the population they serve. In making the choice to affiliate with a professional association, individuals assume the responsibility to conduct themselves in accordance with the ideals and standards set by the organization. For NIRSA members, this means they will strive to uphold the Bylaws in a manner illustrated in the Code of Ethics.

Article I

The NIRSA member in fulfilling professional obligations shall:

1. Seek to extend public awareness of the profession and its achievements.
2. Be true in writing, reporting and duplicating information and give proper credit to the contributions of the others.
3. Encourage integrity by avoiding involvement or condoning activities that may degrade the Association, its members or any affiliate agency.
4. Perform dutifully the responsibilities of professional membership and of any offices or assignments to which appointed or elected.
5. Encourage cooperation with other professional associations, educational institutions and agencies.
6. Practice nondiscrimination on the basis of diversity related to age, disability, ethnicity, gender, national origin, race, religion, and sexual orientation.

Article II

The NIRSA member in relations with employers and employees staff shall:

1. Promote and implement the concept of equal opportunity and fairness in employment practices and program administration.
2. Refrain from exploiting individuals, institutions or agencies for personal or professional gain.
3. Secure the trust of employees by maintaining, in confidence, privileged information until properly released.
4. Support the contributions of fellow employees by properly crediting their achievements.
5. Assist and encourage the education of employees in the area of professional development.

Article III

The NIRSA member in providing programs and services shall:

1. Endeavor to offer the safest and highest quality program achievable with available resources.
2. Take responsibility for employing qualified individuals in positions that require special credentials and/or experience.
3. Strive to keep abreast of current skills and knowledge and encourage innovation in programming and administration.
4. Promote integrity by accepting gratuities for service of no more than nominal value.
5. Encourage promotion of the ideals of Recreational Sports by incorporating such values as sportsmanship, fair play, participation, and an atmosphere that promotes equitable opportunity for all.

Source: National Intramural-Recreational Sports Association, 2010.

"that athletic administrators, coaches and support staff are increasingly not required to make ethical judgments. A myopic emphasis on rule conformity has displaced a more circumspect emphasis on personal integrity and considered ethical judgment" (Gough, 1994, p. 5).

Morality

Not all ethical issues are dilemmas among equally compelling values. Some ethical dilemmas are about choosing between right and wrong, two opposing choices. When the issue is about doing what is right, we are usually dealing with a moral issue. People tend to use the terms morals and ethics interchangeably; however, morality relates to a specific type of ethical issue. As defined earlier, morals are the fundamental baseline values dictating appropriate behavior within a society (Solomon, 1992). A distinctive feature of moral values is their grounding in the practical affairs of social life, whereas other ethical decisions are based on broader abstract principles (DeSensi & Rosenberg, 1996).

In sport, an example of a moral principle is that all athletes give an honest effort whenever they compete. If athletes stopped trying to win, the essence of sport would be threatened. If you ask someone: "Why aren't athletes allowed to throw games (lose on purpose) in exchange for a nice pay check from the highest bidder?", they are likely to say, "Because it is wrong." Pushed further they might say, "Because it would ruin sport."

Similarly, in business, everyone needs to be able to trust that other parties will be honest and deliver the agreed-to goods and services. Bernie Madoff, the disgraced financier, played on people's trust to pull off his $50 billion ponzi scheme. To cultivate and maintain trust, Madoff lied to clients, created fraudulent documents of trades and—on paper—produced consistent profits. But it was, as he put it, "A big lie." He was simply paying off old clients with new clients' money. When the stock market turned bearish in 2008, and his clients wanted to cash out, he ran out of money. The gig was up and the largest fraud in U.S. history exposed. Madoff wasn't just being unethical, his actions were immoral.

Our social practices depend on people upholding certain baseline values. When people act morally—according to generally acceptable standards of behavior—they contribute to the maintenance and smooth functioning of society. Shared morality cultivates trust between strangers and enables individuals to function in a society.

Moral values are generally accepted so broadly within a community that they are considered self-evident and largely go unquestioned. Because people perceive moral values as basic and inalienable, it is often assumed these values derive from a "higher order" or from common sense. If, for example, an athlete is asked why he or she strives to win, a common response would be "Because that's what sports are about." Managers will know if they are dealing with a moral issue as opposed to an ethical dilemma if people justify their position with a simple, "Because it is the right thing to do." If pushed, they might refer to a higher principle based in their religious convictions or their sense of good sporting conduct. Ethical decisions (e.g., the decision of whether to play everyone or only the best players) may be difficult to make and have serious implications for others, but they do not inherently ruin the game.

Morality Versus the Law

Many moral values in a society are codified in laws. For example, theft is not only immoral but also against the law. Occasionally, someone may justify distasteful behavior by saying, "It's not against the law, is it?" In sport, doping is one area where this happens. At times performance enhancing substances are developed or discovered that are not yet against the rules. Taking these drugs may not be against the rules, but doing so constitutes an immoral act because they artificially enhance an athlete's performance, violating the principle of fair play. The "It is not against the rules" argument does not justify the behavior. Laws and morality are not the same.

Laws are created and enforced to maintain order and to help society function smoothly. Even so, at times immoral laws are instituted. For much of the twentieth century in the United States, laws in some states prohibited interracial competitive sports. Teams with both white and black players complied with these laws and at times left their black players at home (Adelson, 1999). The long history of legal segregation in this country was clearly immoral, and yet it was protected by law.

Likewise, moral behavior cannot always be legislated, and people cannot be forced to act morally. For example, it is generally accepted that people should try to help others in need or distress, but laws cannot and do not require people to do so. If we see someone who is injured or the victim of a crime, our moral sensibility directs us to come to his or her aid, but in most cases laws do not punish us for failing to do so. Our moral sensibility creates a stronger obligation than the law. There may be cases where some individuals decide that the right thing to do is to break the law (i.e., civil disobedience).

Sometimes people are able to comply with the letter of the law without achieving its spirit or its stated goals. For example, sport teams and events are increasingly adopting charity nonprofit status to gain tax advantages and beneficial bond ratings. They claim the team or event is a fundraiser for a group in need, or that the new stadium will foster economic development. Meanwhile they hire a private firm, often comprising the same people who created the nonprofit, to manage the event. Any

substantial revenue generation is eaten up by the private management firm and does not go to the group in need. This practice is legal, but certainly immoral.

Morality in the Workplace

Sound moral reasoning is the basis of a healthy sport organization. Some **moral principles** are universal and esteemed in all aspects of life. Such principles include cooperation, courage, perseverance, foresight, and wisdom. Virtues such as these are esteemed across the board. Other moral principles are tied to particular situations. For example, a moral value like competition is esteemed in business but not in family relations. Honesty is essential in scientific research, but in sport "faking out" an opponent is seen as an acceptable strategy and a way to gain advantage. These moral principles are tied to a specific social situation.

Academic discussions of morality often start with a discussion of **absolutism** versus **relativism**. Absolutism argues that moral precepts are universal; that is, applicable to all circumstances. Relativism argues that what is moral depends on the situation. Making moral decisions in the practical world of work falls somewhere in between these two extremes. We like to use the expression *situational absolutes* to describe this hybrid approach.

Moral rules prescribing "correct" behavior in one situation can generally be applied to similar situations within similar specific social contexts. For example, people believe it is always wrong for an elite athlete not to give his or her honest effort. It is also wrong for a recreational athlete not to give an honest effort. In the workplace, regardless how large or small the monetary value of a contract, it is always wrong to violate a business agreement made voluntarily in good faith.

According to Jacobs (1992), work life consists of two types of work, commercial and noncommercial. The moral rules guiding each type of work are distinct from each other. Commercial moral rules have their roots in the rules of the marketplace and guide activities such as sales and marketing. Honesty is a linchpin of commercial trading. Honesty ensures fair trading practices and allows individuals to trust that they will receive agreed-upon goods or services. In commercial occupations, insider trading and deceiving customers are forms of dishonesty and are condemned.

Noncommercial moral values guide other kinds of occupations, including accountants, police, and building inspectors. In sport, officials, league commissioners, athletes, and coaches most likely operate according to noncommercial principles. The most important value in noncommercial endeavors is loyalty. These occupations demand loyalty to an oath of office or professional standards to guard against "selling out." Here loyalty trumps honesty. In these professions it is sometimes all right to withhold information from others for

the sake of the overall task (e.g., undercover police work, general managers' discussions of player personnel). Whereas innovation is admired in the commercial realm, tradition is admired in the noncommercial realm. If people holding these noncommercial positions violate moral precepts associated with loyalty, they will be accused of treason, selling out, or failure to uphold an oath.

Jacobs (1992) argues that our moral reasoning gets muddled when we do not understand which moral principles our job requires. Take, for example, the role of athlete. The moral order in which athletes operate is generally noncommercial. The expectation is that athletes should be loyal to their team, be obedient to and disciplined by the coach, and never compromise the integrity of the game. Within limits imposed by the rules of the game, athletes are expected to try to win by any means available to them. Many sport strategies depend on forms of deception. Feints and setting up opponents to believe you intend to do one thing when you plan to

do another are fundamental sport strategies. Athletes are trusted not to cheat, gamble, or "sell out" the game. Conversely, if an equipment manager does not send purchase orders out in the marketplace for competitive bid but instead purchases from a loyal friend, he or she could create unnecessary departmental expenses and would be violating the principles of honesty and open competition in the commercial sphere.

■ MORALITY AND MULTIPLE ROLES

Moral decisions are complicated by the fact that moral principles are often applied and valued differently in different social contexts. Decision making is made more difficult given the variety of roles each of us fills. One collection of moral rules does not necessarily apply to all situations even within the same job.

Some jobs in sport do not actually reside completely within either the commercial or the noncommercial sphere. Look at the position of director of media relations for a college athletic department, for example. To complete the tasks of this job, the director of media relations operates in both moral systems. At one point in the day, this person may be required to be absolutely honest (producing statistics for coaches and reporters) and at another time may exude loyalty to the point of stretching the truth (creating recruiting materials for a team). Professional athletes who demonstrate team loyalty throughout the season become commercially minded when renegotiating their contracts. Finally, recall the equipment manager. He or she has a job that is primarily driven by noncommercial precepts that include loyalty to the team, upholder of traditions, etc. But periodically—such as when purchasing new equipment—he or she enters the commercial sphere. At that point noncommercial values are set aside and the manager embraces values that are admired within the commercial sphere. Although jobs fall more or less into one moral order or the other (commercial or noncommercial), it is unrealistic to suggest that any occupation is completely commercial or completely noncommercial.

Consequently, the process of making a moral choice, of deciding what is right and wrong, involves understanding the parameters of acceptable behavior within the context of one's multiple roles within society. However, this does not mean people can arbitrarily choose which values will guide their behavior. Specific situations and roles in our society demand specific moral values.

■ MORALITY AND CORRUPTION

One of the biggest distinctions between moral decision making and other ethical decisions is the extensive ramification of immoral choices. An immoral decision (e.g., to shave points) can ruin a whole enterprise. One of the most infamous immoral acts in sport occurred at the 1980 Boston Marathon when Rosie Ruiz fooled the world—momentarily at least. Ruiz was crowned the women's champion but actually had jumped out of the crowd and had ran the last half mile to cross the finish line first. Later it was revealed that her qualifying time from the New York City marathon was a fraud, too. She broke from the race to ride the subway to the finish line. To this day, "pulling a Rosie Ruiz" means skipping out on part of an event only to show up at the end to garner undeserved accolades.

Immoral behavior, such as cheating in sports, violates our basic assumptions of right and wrong. There are clear cut examples of immoral practices in sport like Rosie Ruiz' subway run or the Black Sox scandal of 1919 when players cooperated with organized gamblers to lose games in the World Series. Immoral practices can also become institutionalized, which leads corruption. Corruption may start small, when just a few people act immorally, but can ultimately become a standard operating procedure.

In the world of work, corruption usually occurs when people hop from one set of moral precepts to another when it is inappropriate to do so. For example, the job of stock analysts requires honestly reporting the facts. When a stock analyst works for a large financial firm there is supposed to be a "Chinese Wall" (a reference to the Great Wall of China) between the analysts and the business side of the firm. But during the boom years of the late 1990s, some companies that received poor reports from stock analysts would sometime threaten to pull business from investment banks. The wall broke down. Stock analysts employed by investment banks felt pressured to give hyper-positive reports about certain companies in order to help drive up stock prices. In these cases, the analysts became team players, stretching the truth a wee bit to help their employer, who hoped to gain brokerage fees from investment deals. Actually, they were helping their firm compete by setting aside their core job responsibility, which was the duty to provide clients a fair assessment of a company.

Corruption might start when an employee takes a precept common to his or her profession and applies it in the wrong place. For example, accountants take an oath to be loyal to their profession. They are guardians of business. Morally they have more in common with the medical profession than they do sales and marketing. However, when an in-house accountant is convinced he or she needs to be loyal to the company and must do so by employing "aggressive accounting" techniques rather than staying loyal to the accounting profession and fulfilling his or her fiduciary duties, it leads to immoral behavior. In a nutshell this is what happened in the infamous Enron accounting scandal of 2001. In this case, Enron obscured its finances with a complex web of partnerships and questionable accounting practices that fooled debt-rating agencies, Wall Street analysts, and investors. In this case, the accountants took

their tendency to be loyal (to the accounting profession) and extended it to the company they were supposed to be regulating. In both of these examples, the little lies of the accountants and analysts became standard operating procedure or systemic. When immoral behavior is systemic we call it *corruption.*

When an organization's immoral actions become standard practice, moral reasoning becomes muddled and the rationale for moral behavior unclear. People justify immoral behavior by suggesting that this is how things are done here or that others are doing the same thing and they, too, must act this way to maintain their competitiveness. Consider, for example, the recent doping scandals in Major League Baseball and cycling. In both cases the incidents and extent of performance enhancing drug (PED) use may have been sporadic, but when regulators and officials turned a blind eye to the drug use, the use of steroids and human growth hormone spread. Early adopters of these drugs justified their use in a variety of ways: to recover from injury, to be able to stay in the game, to help them recover from long workouts. Eventually some baseball players and cyclists were using PEDs just to keep up with the competition. Little by little PED use spread, and when cheating became the norm it didn't seem so wrong.

Consider the representation/agency business. Agents now pursue younger and younger athletes. Even though some agents may be hesitant to do this, many come to believe they have to follow suit to win clients. This same sort of muddled moral thinking can push college coaches to act immorally when recruiting athletes. When one coach offers certain inducements to a recruit to accept a scholarship, other coaches may feel compelled to offer similar inducements for fear of losing a potential star recruit.

Corruption spreads little by little through an organization or a sport. Once it does, there is usually no way to fix the problem, at least not without some serious consequences. These consequences usually extend far beyond the people who initiated the immoral behavior. When their house of cards finally collapsed in 2001, Enron was forced to file for bankruptcy. Once the seventh-largest company in the United States, its bankruptcy caused huge losses for investors and Enron employees, many of whose company 401(k) retirement accounts became nearly worthless. The bankruptcy extended beyond Enron's walls. In the wake of the bankruptcy, Arthur Andersen, Enron's former accounting firm, was convicted in June 2002 of obstructing justice for destroying documents related to Enron. The once "Big Five" accounting firm collapsed later that year as a result of this scandal and others. The scandal is tied to sport, too, because Enron had purchased the naming rights to the Houston Astros' ballpark in a 30-year, $100 million deal. When Enron collapsed, the Astros no longer wanted to be associated with the company. The Astros paid Enron over $2 million to remove its name from the stadium, and later resold the rights to Coca-Cola. The stadium is now known as Minute Maid Park (Reuters, 2002). The Bernie Madoff investment scandal, discussed earlier, impacted thousands of investors, including many nonprofit foundations. Major League Baseball's doping scandal resulted in Congressional hearings and tainted some of baseball's biggest stars of the 1990s.

■ MORAL REASONING AND THE CHANGING NATURE OF WORK

Contemporary society is characterized by innovation, which continually presents new ethical dilemmas. Consider, for example, how computer technology forces us to think about privacy and intellectual property in new ways. It was once thought unsportsmanlike for coaches to send in plays from the sideline in football (quarterbacks called the plays). Now coaches call in plays from booths high above the playing field,

utilizing technological advances. This changes ideas about the role of the coach.

What we consider to be right or wrong, ethical or unethical, changes as society progresses or changes. Technology, for example, has made it much easier to spy on other teams. Teams have always tried to steal signs. In the past, coaches might have tried to steal signs with the naked eye and notation. Knowing this, teams did just enough to change up their signs to throw other teams off. In 2007, Bill Belichick, head coach of the New England Patriots, was fined half a million dollars for stealing the New York Jets' defensive signals with a video camera. In addition, the team was ordered to pay $250,000 and had to give up one draft pick. This may seem to be a stiff penalty for doing more efficiently what coaches have been trying to do for decades. Belichick's intent was to review the video tape to learn defensive signs or patterns of signs to decode the Jets' system and to use the knowledge in the next game. The use of technology to steal signs pushed what some might argue is unethical behavior into an immoral act. National Football League (NFL) Commissioner Roger Goodell called Belichick's scheme a "calculated and deliberate attempt to avoid long-standing rules designed to encourage fair play and promote honest competition on the playing field" (Associated Press, 2007, para. 4). Goodell's severe punishment reflects his understanding that new technologies employed to steal signs could ruin the game.

As society changes, we periodically need to assess whether our current practices are in keeping with the values that underlie a just society or fair sports. Moral and ethical principles evolve over time. To make moral decisions in the sport industry, managers are required to understand the responsibilities and duties of their jobs. People never hold only one position in society and therefore cannot simply adopt one set of moral guidelines. Managers have to assess their responsibilities and choose virtues to help them complete their work fairly and morally.

KEY SKILLS

Although sport organizations tend to operate as a whole, sport managers must remember that all sport organizations are made up of individuals who have certain duties to perform. Each person brings something unique to the workplace and each person's job requires certain moral behaviors. Each and every individual in a sport organization has the ability to make a difference within that sport organization. People sometimes ask, "What difference does it make if I act ethically or not?" It makes a significant difference, because each individual can and does influence her or his sport organization. How, then, can sport managers attempt to establish a moral work climate?

Ensuring Morality in the Workplace

The complexity of competing interests in sport makes moral and ethical dilemmas especially difficult to resolve. Sometimes athletes are simple participants in an athletic competition, whereas at other times they are businesspeople who have to reconcile endorsements or salaries relative to the game and their willingness to play. Rules designed to protect the integrity of sport operate uncomfortably alongside the business structure underwriting it. Increasingly, managers, athletes, and coaches have to operate under commercial and noncommercial principles simultaneously, and it is easy for distinctions between the two to become blurred.

This complexity makes decision making more difficult—and more critical—for sport managers. However, there are ways to simplify the decision-making process and ensure decisions are made as intelligently and conscientiously as possible. Organizations can help individuals make moral choices promoting and supporting moral reasoning in four ways:

1. Establish clear standards of moral behavior (such as codes of conduct) and publicize them within the organization.
2. Encourage employees to periodically examine and review their individual moral judgments through self-examinations.
3. Provide support structures through which employees can consult each other during and after the decision-making process.
4. Make clear that violations of the code will not be tolerated, and publicize a process for enforcing codes within the organization.

SELF-EXAMINATIONS

One way to promote moral reasoning is to ask employees to think about hypothetical ethical dilemmas. This strategy assumes most people want to make the correct and moral decision. More people will do the right thing if they think about ethical behavior prior to making important decisions or if they think people in their organization care about their behavior. Self-examinations are effective tools to remind people of ethical actions and express institutional concern for ethical issues.

Self-examinations do not have to be reviewed by management to be effective, nor is it necessary to take severe punitive measures against those who do poorly. The NCAA, for example, requires all coaches involved in recruiting to take and pass a test (National Collegiate Athletic Association, 2002). The exercise tests the coaches' knowledge of recruiting rules. It is not a difficult test, and most coaches pass it with little trouble. Coaches who fail the test can retake it until they pass. The test is not designed to keep immoral coaches from recruiting but to remind coaches of "right" actions. The simple

act of reviewing the rules reminds coaches of the rules and reinforces the view that abiding by these rules matters. Despite this, both the number of major violations and the severity of those violations are continually increasing (Mahony, Fink, & Pastore, 1999). It appears self-examination may not be enough to make college coaches do the right thing, as they are constantly pressured to engage in questionable recruiting practices to remain competitive.

Self-examinations can be performed on the organizational level as well. The NCAA instituted an accreditation process mandating that athletic departments review their organizational practices (National Collegiate Athletic Association, 2002). A review committee made up of outside experts reviews the athletic department and makes recommendations as to how the department might better fulfill the mission of the NCAA. The real benefit of the accreditation program is the process of preparing for the review. The accreditation process forces department administrators to examine their day-to-day practices in light of institutional goals. Such reflection might not happen otherwise, given the demands placed on most sport management professionals working in athletic programs.

■ FORUM FOR MORAL DISCOURSE

Isolation contributes greatly to immoral behavior. Because morality is tied to social situations, communication is critical in decreasing corruption and resolving ethical dilemmas. Employees should be encouraged to get together to discuss where and how they face specific problems. By doing so, employees understand they are not alone in making difficult choices and that their colleagues can provide significant insight, perspective, and help. The process takes the pressure off individuals and clarifies the issues at stake. It also brings employees together to resolve problems. Discussions of ethical or moral behavior can be incorporated into normal management systems, such as staff meetings or sales meetings. Decisions should not be reviewed only after they have been made. Employees should be encouraged to consult with one another and with their supervisors during the decision-making process. This helps employees avoid making wrong choices, leaving out important parts of the decision, or being overwhelmed by the weight and complexity of issues.

Forums for discussion should not be confined to individual organizations. This is especially true for managers. Because management is often the smallest branch of an organization, there may not be an effective forum for the exchange of ideas. Annual conventions, executive education, or management training may be employed as forums for ethical discourse. Informal settings such as lunches among friends, confidential calls to colleagues with similar responsibilities, or casual conversations at a golf outing also contribute to keeping the discussions alive.

■ CONSEQUENCES

Finally, employees need to know there are consequences for immoral behavior. Even in the best organizations, some people will be motivated solely by self-interest. However, if people understand that corruption comes with certain risks, they are less likely to engage in immoral acts. Simply making consequences clearly understood can eliminate much poor judgment. People need to understand they will lose their jobs, customers, or eligibility if caught violating rules. By making the consequences of immoral acts clear, organizations help promote ethical actions.

To be effective, discipline must meet two criteria: It must be meaningful and it must be enforceable. One complaint about rules imposing fines on professional athletes or professional team owners is that some of these individuals earn so much money fines of even thousands of dollars are of little consequence to them. Sometimes an athlete's team will pay a fine imposed on the athlete. Thus, fines have limited impact on behavior and are not meaningful in some cases. All the rules in the world will be ineffective if they are not enforceable, which is the second criterion of discipline. For example, prior to the 1980s schools and coaches had little fear they would be punished by the NCAA because the NCAA enforcement staff was woefully inadequate to investigate charges of corruption (Mitchell, Crosset, & Barr, 1999).

■ SUMMARY

Sport managers need to be aware of the importance of morality and ethics in the sport workplace. The decisions sport managers make on a daily basis affect large numbers of people, ranging from athletes to team owners to fans. Therefore, sport managers need to understand the far-reaching effects of their decisions and how management structures and personal values shape those decisions. Incorporating codes

of ethics, self-examinations, forums for moral disclosure, and statements of consequences for ethical violations into organizational documents helps ensure that sport managers and employees make the "right" decisions.

■ KEY TERMS

absolutism, codes of conduct, codes of ethics, ethical decision making, ethical dilemma, ethical reasoning, ethics, morality, moral principles, morals, relativism

■ REFERENCES

Australia Sports Commission. (n.d.). Official's code of ethics. Retrieved November 11, 2010, from http://www.officiatingaus.org/ethics.htm

Adelson, B. (1999). *Brushing back Jim Crow: The integration of minor league baseball in the American South.* Charlottesville, VA: University of Virginia Press.

Associated Press. (2007). NFL fines Belicheck, strips Patriots of draft pick. Retrieved October 14, 2010, from http://www.nfl.com/news/story?id=09000d5 d80251b7e&template=with-video&confirm=true

BC Athletics. (n.d.). BC Athletics codes of conduct. Retrieved October 14, 2010, from http://www .bcathletics.org/main/codesofconduct.htm

Cooke, R.A. (1991). Danger signs of unethical behavior: How to determine if your firm is at ethical risk. *Journal of Business Ethics, 10,* 249–253.

DeSensi, J.T., & Rosenberg, D. (1996). *Ethics in sport management.* Morgantown, WV: Fitness Information Technology.

England Basketball. (2002). Codes of conduct. Retrieved October 14, 2010, from http://www .copleybasketball.co.uk/Conduct.pdf

Fraleigh, W.P. (1993). Codes of ethics: Functions, form and structures, problems and possibilities. *Quest, 45,* 13–21.

Geelong Cricket Association. (2002). Codes of conduct. Retrieved November 11, 2010, from http://gca .cricketvictoria.com.au/codesofconduct.html

Gough, R. (1994). NCAA policy's strangling effect on ethics. *For the Record*, 3–5.

Hums, M.A., & MacLean, J.C. (2008). *Governance and policy in sport organizations*. (2d ed.). Scottsdale, AZ: Holcomb-Hathaway Publishing.

Jacobs, J. (1992). *Systems of survival: A dialogue on the moral foundations of commerce and politics*. New York: Random House.

Jordan, J.S., Greenwell, T.C., Geist, A.L., Pastore, D., & Mahony, D. (2004). Coaches' perceptions of conference codes of ethics. *Physical Educator, 61*(3), 131–145.

Josephson Institute of Ethics. (2006). The six pillars of character. Retrieved October 14, 2010, from http://www.josephsoninstitute.org/MED/MED-2sixpillars.htm

Mahony, D., Fink, J., & Pastore, D. (1999). Ethics in intercollegiate athletics: An examination of NCAA violations and penalties, 1952–1997. *Professional Ethics, 7*(2), 53–74.

Mahony, D., Geist, A., Jordon, J., Greenwell, T.C., & Pastore, D. (1999). Codes of ethics used by sport governing bodies: Problems in intercollegiate athletics. *Proceedings of the Congress of the European Association for Sport Management, 7*, 206–208.

Mitchell, R., Crosset, T., & Barr, C. (1999). Encouraging compliance without real power: Sport associations regulating teams. *Journal of Sport Management, 13*, 216–236.

National Collegiate Athletic Association. (2002). *2002–2003 NCAA Division I manual*. Indianapolis, IN: Author.

National Intramural and Recreational Sports Association. (2010). Professional member code of ethics. Retrieved November 11, 2010, from http://www.nirsa.org/Content/NavigationMenu/AboutUs/GoverningDocuments/CodeofEthics/Code_of_Ethics.htm

Pennington, B. (2010 September 14). Reggie Bush, ineligible for '05, returns Heisman. *New York Times*. Retrieved November 11, 2010, from http://www.nytimes.com/2010/09/15/sports/ncaafootball/15heisman.html

Petry, E. (2001). EOA survey: Companies seeking to integrate ethics through the whole organization. *Ethikos, 15*(1), 1–3, 16.

Reuters. (2002 June 6). Baseball: Astros' park is Minute Maid. *New York Times*. Retrieved from http://www.nytimes.com/2002/06/06/sports/baseball-astros-park-is-minute-maid.html

Sims, R.R. (1992). The challenge of ethical behavior in organizations. *Journal of Business Ethics, 11*, 505–513.

Solomon, R.C. (1992). *Above the bottom line: An introduction to business ethics*. Fort Worth, TX: Harcourt, Brace.

Speed Skating Canada. (2001). Ethics and code of conduct policy. Retrieved October 14, 2010, from http://www.speedskating.ca/client/cmsUploads/speed_skating/File/policies/en/INT100-EthicsandCodeofConductPolicy.pdf

Wyatt, E. (2007 July 26). Tour in tatters: Team ousts the race leader. *New York Times*. Retrieved October 14, 2010, from http://www.nytimes.com/2007/07/26/sports/sportsspecial1/26tour.html?ex=1190260800&en=675dded2491fi56f&ei=5070

Youth Sports Research Council. (2002). Code of conduct law, 74 New Jersey Stat. Ann. C.5:17-1, et. seq. Retrieved October 14, 2010, from http://youthsports.rutgers.edu/resources/legal/new-jerseys-code-of-conduct-law

Zinn, L.M. (1993). Do the right thing: Ethical decision making in professional and business practice. *Adult Learning, 5*, 7–8, 27.

Amateur Sport Industry

CHAPTER 7

High School and Youth Sports

Dan Covell

■ INTRODUCTION

Consider the following statistics as reported in 2010:

- More than 650,000 boys and girls ages 7 through 18 participated on more than 50,000 teams sanctioned by the American Youth Soccer Organization (AYSO) ("History of AYSO," 2009).
- Pop Warner Little Scholars, Inc. sponsors more than 5,000 teams in eight weight/age classifications for 240,000 football players, along with programs for 160,000 cheer and dance team members ages 5 through 16 (Pop Warner Little Scholars, Inc., 2009).
- Nearly four and a half million young men and more than three million young women participated in high school athletics during the 2008–2009 school year ("2008–09 High School Athletes," 2009).

- More than 2 million coaches have been certified by the National Alliance for Youth Sports (NAYS), more than 65,000 families have gone through the NAYS's parents' program, and more than 2,000 administrators have earned their certification credentials through NAYS's Academy for Youth Sports Administrators (National Alliance for Youth Sports, 2010).

Tables 7-1 and **7-2** show the most popular high school sports by participant, as compiled by the **National Federation of State High School Associations (NFHS)** (see the "Governing Bodies" section of this chapter) in 2009 and participation totals over the previous three decades.

In addition, the following studies indicate that athletics provide positive influences in the lives of adolescents at a crucial juncture of their lives:

TABLE 7-1 Top 5 Boys' and Girls' High School Sports by Participants, 2008–2009

Boys' Sport (Number of Participants)	Girls' Sport (Number of Participants)
Football–11 man (1,113,062)	Basketball (444,809)
Basketball (545,145)	Outdoor Track and Field (457,732)
Outdoor Track and Field (558,007)	Volleyball (404,243)
Baseball (473,184)	Softball–Fast pitch (368,921)
Soccer (383,824)	Soccer (344,534)

Source: 2008–09 High School Athletics Participation Survey, 2009.

TABLE 7-2 Total Participants in High School Sports in 1971, 1986, 2002, 2009

Year	Total Male Participants	Total Female Participants
1971	3,666,917	294,015
1986	3,344,275	1,807,121
2002	3,960,517	2,806,998
2009	4,466,224	3,114,091

Source: Participation in high school sports increases again: Conforms NFHS commitment to stronger leadership. (2006). National Federation of State High School Associations. Retrieved on October 24, 2006, from http://www.nfhs. org/web/2006/09.participation.aspx; 2008-09 High School Athletics Participation Survey, (2009).

- Students who spend no time in extracurricular activities are 49% more likely to use drugs and 37% more likely to become teen parents than those who spend one to four hours per week in extracurricular activities.
- A 2006 research project published by the Center for Information & Research on Civic Learning & Engagement (CIRCLE) found that 18- to 25-year-olds who participate in sports activities while in high school were more likely than nonparticipants to engage in volunteering, regular volunteering, registering to vote, voting in the 2000 election, feeling comfortable speaking in a public setting, and watching news (especially sport news) more closely than nonparticipants (Lopez & More, 2006).
- According the College Entrance Examination Board, music students scored about 11% higher than nonmusic students on the 2001 SAT. Students with coursework/ experience in music performance and music appreciation scored higher on the SAT than students with no arts participation. Students in music performance scored 57 points higher in the verbal area and 41 points higher in math, and students in music appreciation scored 63 points higher on verbal and 44 points higher on math (National Federation of State High School Associations, 2008).

So what do all these facts and figures mean? The conclusion is that school and youth sports are arguably the most influential sport programs in the United States today and directly reflect the importance people in the United States place on involving youth in sport activities. While professionals working in school and youth league sports do not garner the limelight and national prominence as do sport management professionals, to work in this industry segment means significant and important challenges and substantial personal rewards. A coach, official, or administrator at this level never lacks for responsibilities, and every day brings a fresh set of issues to tackle to ensure that the educative framework of youth athletics is maintained. To work in this segment is to make a difference in the lives of youth in North America.

■ HISTORY

The recognition of the positive educational and developmental aspects of athletic participation is not a recent phenomenon. The history of youth athletic participation predates the signing of the Constitution and the formation of the United States. Native Americans played a game that French Jesuit priests called "lacrosse," because players used a stick that resembled a bishop's cross-shaped crosier. European settlers brought tennis, cricket, and several early versions of what would become baseball, and Africans brought to the United States as slaves threw the javelin, boxed, and wrestled. Despite all this, formally organized athletic participation, particularly those programs run under the auspices of secondary educational institutions, did not emerge until the mid-nineteenth century (Swanson & Spears, 1995).

School Athletics in the Nineteenth Century

In 1838, educator Horace Mann noted that in an increasingly urbanized United States, outdoor recreation space was becoming scarce and children were at risk of physical deterioration. Urban populations were doubling every decade due to steady country-to-city migration as well as immigration from Europe. In response to the common popular appeal of baseball in the nineteenth century, schools and other agencies began to promote the sport to aid in solving broad social problems such as ill health and juvenile delinquency (Seymour, 1990).

Private schools in the United States were the first to provide athletic participation opportunities. At many schools, activities were informal and organized by students with little oversight from faculty or administrators. The Round Hill School in Northampton, Massachusetts, was the first institution known to have promoted the physical well-being of its students as part of its formal mission and curriculum. The school's founders appointed a German, Charles Beck, as their instructor of gymnastics, making him the first known physical education instructor in the United States. Many other early U.S. private schools followed the model of elite English boarding schools such as Eton, Harrow, and Rugby, where athletic programs were more formalized (although still managed by students) but intended to promote the ideal of "muscular Christianity," creating gentlemen who were morally and physically able to go out and take on the challenges of modern life. Campus-based club teams focused on intramural-type play, which formed the early models of competition in the United States. In 1859 the Gunnery School in Washington, Connecticut, became the first school to feature games against outside competition in athletic programs actively encouraged and promoted by an administrator, school founder Frederick Gunn. Students who attended the school at the time noted that students were required to play baseball, and that Gunn "encouraged and almost compelled every kind of rational exercise as part of his scheme of character-building" (Bundgaard, 2005, p. 74). In 1878, St. Paul's School in Concord, New Hampshire, hired the first full-time faculty member specifically to coach team sports, and in 1895, Phillips Exeter Academy, also in New Hampshire, appointed the first permanent faculty member as Director of Athletics (Bundgaard, 2005).

Educators at established **public schools** were slow to embrace the value of exercise and play, whereas private schools recognized it much earlier. As at the collegiate level, students organized the games. Interscholastic athletics, much as with the collegiate system after which they were patterned, were seen by students as not only an outlet for physical activity but as a vehicle for developing communal ties with classmates and alumni.

The acceptance of University of Chicago educator John Dewey's theories encouraging games helped to hasten the incorporation of athletics into school curricula. The State of New York required every public school to include an adjacent playground; citywide school baseball tournaments were held in the 1890s in Boston and in Cook County, Illinois; and students from several Boston area public and private schools formed the Interscholastic Football Association in 1888 (Hardy, 2003; Wilson, 1994). Concurrently, statewide high school athletic associations in Illinois and Wisconsin were formed to coordinate interscholastic competition.

School Athletics in the Twentieth Century

During the first two decades of the last century, youth athletics were popular vehicles through which newly formed secular government organizations sought to combat the proliferating ills of urban life. The social and political efforts of

educators aligned with the **Progressive Movement**, touting athletics as a tool to prepare for the rigors of modern life and democracy and to assimilate immigrants into American culture. They promoted child welfare by advocating for increased playground space, such as the development of year-round play spaces in Los Angeles in 1904 and in Chicago's congested South Side in 1905. Progressives also promoted formalized public school athletics as an antidote to regimented physical education curricula based on the German tradition of body-building through repetitive exercise (Dyreson, 1989).

Emerging city, state, and parochial school athletic associations coordinated competitions in baseball, track, and rifle shooting and emphasized sportsmanship and academic integrity. As a result of the movement promoting athletics as a critical part of the educational experience, government-funded educational institutions eventually assumed the administration and provision of the vast majority of athletic participation opportunities for youth in the United States (Vincent, 1994).

In the period during and immediately after World War I (1914–1918), school sports for males were promoted as a source of physical training for the armed forces without directly encouraging militarism. Sports were also seen as a means to develop social skills such as cooperation and discipline, which were valued by an increasingly ethnically diverse and industrial

High School Football and Girls' Basketball Teams

society. Sports also boosted student retention and graduation rates—important considerations, because in 1918 only one-third of grade school students entered high school, and only one in nine graduated (O'Hanlon, 1982).

During this period athletics became entrenched in schools, and educators took control of athletics from students. But concerns from educators about their ability to administer and teach in an athletic capacity had been voiced since the 1890s. Individuals such as Dr. Dudley Sargent, James Naismith, and Amos Alonzo Stagg made significant contributions toward meeting the burgeoning instructional and curricular development needs. While students initially organized most teams, by 1924 state associations managed high school athletics in all but three states.

Nonschool Youth Sport Organizations

Athletics promoted by **nonschool agencies** emerged in various locations in the United States nearly simultaneously. The most prominent private agency to promote youth athletics was the Young Men's Christian Association (YMCA). Protestant clergyman George Williams founded the YMCA in England in 1844, and the organization established itself in the United States in 1851 to attract urban youth to Christianity through athletics. By 1900, the YMCA had grown to include 250,000 members (this number would double by 1915) at 1,400 branches, with a national athletic league under the direction of Dr. Luther H. Gulick (Putney, 1993). The Young Women's Christian Association (YWCA), established concurrently with the YMCA, began offering calisthenics in its Boston branch in 1877 and opened a new gym there in 1884. By 1916, 65,000 women nationwide attended gym classes and 32,000 attended swimming classes sponsored by the YWCA (Cahn, 1994).

From the 1930s through the 1950s, YMCA branches were opened in suburban areas that allowed female members to join as determined by local policies. Family memberships were made available in an effort to retain and attract members. In the 1960s, the organization's leadership faced the issue of whether to reestablish its Christian evangelical elements and drift away from promoting its athletic programs, even as the exercise-seeking membership grew to over 5.5 million in 1969. The YMCA chose to emphasize individual values and growth which dovetailed nicely with individual personal fitness goals (Putney, 1993).

The financial calamities of the Great Depression of the 1930s launched unprecedented governmental involvement in recreation. Private companies and businesses cut back on the athletic participation opportunities they had sponsored before the economic downturn, and government agencies were asked to fill the void. The Works Progress Administration (WPA)

MEEKER-HIGH-SCHOOL-BASKET-BALL-TEAM. MEEKER-HIGH-SCHOOL-FOOT-BALL-TEAM.

provided funds ($500 million by 1937) and labor for field and playground construction, and city recreation departments provided "schools" for athletic skill instruction and league coordination (Seymour, 1990).

Local government fostered participation as well. In 1931, 107 teams entered Cincinnati's boys' baseball tournament, and in 1935, 75 teams of boys under age 16 played in a municipal baseball league in Oakland, California (Seymour, 1990). Many significant private and parochial youth sport organizations were also initiated during this period, including American Legion Junior Baseball in 1925, Pop Warner Football in 1929, the Catholic Youth Organization (basketball, boxing, and softball) in 1930, the Amateur Softball Association in 1933, and Little League Baseball in 1939.

■ GOVERNANCE

The administration of school and youth sports is primarily a local affair, with most policy and procedural decisions made at the district, school, or youth league level. However, the existence

of local, state, and national **governing bodies** ensures the running of championships, coordination of athlete eligibility, dissemination of instructional information, and implementation of certain coaching and administrative certification programs. Governing bodies also create and maintain stated rules and guidelines and apply them to all affiliated athletic programs equitably and consistently.

The National Federation of State High School Associations

The National Federation of State High School Associations (NFHS), a nonprofit organization headquartered in Indianapolis, Indiana, serves as the national coordinator for high school sports as well as activities such as music, debate, theater, and student council. NFHS encompasses all 50 individual state high school athletics and activity associations as well as the District of Columbia and a number of affiliate members. NFHS represents more than 11 million participants in more than 19,000 high schools, as well as coaches, officials, and judges through the individual state, provincial, and territorial organizations. In addition to compiling national records in sports and national sport participation rates, NFHS coordinates officials' certification; issues playing rules for 17 boys' and girls' sports; prints eight million publications annually, including officials' manuals and case books, magazines, supplemental books, and teaching aids; holds national conferences and competitions; and acts as an advocate and lobbying agent for school-based youth sports. NFHS also maintains a high school Hall of Fame (National Federation of State High School Associations, 2010).

Three facets comprise the organizational structure of the NFHS. The legislative body, the National Council, is made up of one representative from each member state, provincial, or territorial association. Each council member has one vote, and the council meets to conduct business twice each year. The administrative responsibilities are handled by the 12-member board of directors, elected by the National Council from professional staffs of member associations. Eight board members are elected to represent one of eight geographic regions, with the remaining four chosen on an at-large basis. The board of directors approves the annual budget, appoints an executive director, and establishes committees for conducting association business. NFHS has a paid administrative and professional staff of 50, including the current executive director, Bob Gardner, named to the post in 2010 (National Federation of State High School Associations, 2010).

Other professional organizations and services offered by or affiliated with the NFHS include:

- The National Interscholastic Athletic Administrators Association (NIAAA), made up of 5,000 individuals responsible for the administration of high school athletics
- The NFHS Coaches Association, comprised of 30,000 member high school coaches
- The NFHS Officials Association, which includes 130,000 member officials who benefit from liability insurance and skills instruction
- The NFHS Spirit Association, formed in 1988 to assist members and coaches of cheerleading, pompom, and spirit groups (Little League Baseball, Inc., n.d., 2010)

State Associations

The NFHS model is typically replicated at the state level by **state associations**. State associations, which are also nonprofit, have a direct role in organizing state championships and competitions in athletics and activities and are the final authority in determining athlete eligibility. The scope of activities, size of full-time administrative and support staff, and number of schools represented vary from state to state and are proportionally related to that state's population.

The legislative business of state associations is administered in much the same manner as the NFHS, with several general meetings each year attended by one voting representative from each member institution. While championships and competitions are administered by the associations, committees consisting of coaches and administrators perform most of the actual duties associated with the events, including determining criteria for selection of event participants, event management, and the general rules pertaining to regular season competition.

National Youth League Organizations

National youth league organizations focus administrative efforts on promoting participation in a particular sport among children. The activities and duties of these organizations are illustrated by examining one such association, Little League Baseball, the best-known youth athletic organization in the United States. Factory worker Carl Stotz founded Little League Baseball in 1939 as a three-team league in Williamsport, Pennsylvania. The organization, initially for boys ages 9 through 12 (girls were admitted in 1974), grew to 867 teams in 12 states over the next decade. By 1963, Little League boasted 30,000 teams in 6,000 leagues on four continents. In 2002, 2.8 million children ages 5 to 18 in 105 countries participated in t-ball, baseball, and softball at four age-group levels and for children with mental and physical disabilities. Little League requires strict adherence to administrative guidelines, including standardized field size and use of uniforms, formalizes rosters composed via the draft system, and promotes its ability to provide adult supervision and safe play (Little League Baseball, Inc., 2010; Little League Baseball, Inc., n.d.).

Little League governance structure is organized on four levels: local, district, region, and international. Each league program is organized within a community that establishes its own boundaries (with total population not to exceed 20,000) from which it may register players. A board of directors guides each local league and is responsible for the league's day-to-day operations. Ten to twenty teams in a given area usually comprise a district. The District Administrator organizes district tournaments. The District Administrator reports to the Regional Director, of which there are five in the United States, and four internationally. All Little League operations are led by the president and Chief Executive Officer (CEO; Stephen Keener), who reports to a Board of Directors comprised of eight District Administrators elected to rotating terms by their colleagues at the periodic International Congress. There are 110 full-time league employees and a million volunteers worldwide (Little League Baseball, Inc., 2010).

■ CAREER OPPORTUNITIES

There are many similarities in the employment opportunities in school and youth league sports.

What follows is a brief listing of the roles critical to the operation of school and youth league sports, including major job functions and responsibilities.

School Athletic Director/League Director

Supervising a school athletic program or youth league includes responsibilities such as hiring, supervising, and evaluating coaches; coordinating nearly all facets of contest management, including the hiring and paying of officials and event staff; setting departmental/league training and disciplinary policies; determining departmental/league budgets; overseeing all associated fund-raising; determining and verifying game scheduling and athlete eligibility; transmitting relevant publicity; and handling public relations. In addition, most school athletic directors do not have the luxury of devoting their whole working day to this job. Most must also coach, teach, perform other administrative roles, or do some combination of all three.

Youth league directors must sometimes perform their duties on a completely voluntary basis, without compensation or work release time. Compared to coaches, **school athletic directors** have less direct involvement with athletes and perform their duties less publicly, but these administrators by no means have a less important role in successfully managing an athletic program. Some of their major responsibilities and concerns are risk management, insurance, employment issues, sexual harassment, gender equity, and fund-raising.

The job description for a school or youth league coach is indeed demanding. **Coaches** face complex human resource management issues, deal with constant and extreme pressure to perform successfully, and work long and irregular hours for low (or no) pay. Significant knowledge of injuries and physical training, equipment, and bus-driving skills are also highly recommended. High school coaches in most states are also required to pass certain certification requirements, many of which are delivered through the NFSH. For example, coaches in Kansas must pass a coaching education certification course (waived for coaches who are also certified classroom teachers) and a sport first aid course within one year of hiring (National Federation of State High School Associations, 2008).

Because injuries inevitably occur in athletic activities, **trainers** and **physical therapists** are critical for school and youth sport operation. Most school districts and state associations require medical personnel and emergency medical transportation to be present at football games or other high-risk contact sports, while the dictates of youth leagues vary. Most schools and leagues do not have the personnel or financial resources to provide trainers or medical personnel (paramedics, certified athletic trainers, emergency medical technicians, physicians) for all contests, and such personnel are infrequently provided for practices. Providing adequate medical treatment for injured athletes significantly reduces the risk of litigation against coaches, schools; and leagues and can reduce injury rates by 41%. However, because 62% of injuries occur during practices and training (PRWeb, 2010), some schools are looking to contract trainers or medical personnel to be present at all times and to set up year-round training and fitness programs.

Schools and leagues can contract trainers from a local hospital, physical therapy center, or fitness club. The position can also be linked to internal jobs such as a classroom or physical education teacher, school doctor or nurse, or athletic administrator. Such programs benefit the school athletic program and can provide a student-trainer with an educational opportunity. Salaries for this position vary widely, depending on the employment status (part-time or full-time) and the other job responsibilities linked to the post.

Officials and Judges

Officials and **judges** are vital to the proper administration of school and youth athletics, and they share much of the public scrutiny associated with coaches and administrators. Officials are employed by schools and leagues but are considered independent contractors because the school or league exhibits no supervisory capacity over officials. Depending on the locale, officials may require certification from national, state, and local sanctioning organizations to gain approval to work in interscholastic events. Most youth leagues rely on volunteers with such accreditation to officiate contests. While this aids in the logistical operations, the use of such unprofessionalized personnel can leave a league liable for litigation for the actions of these individuals. Officials possess a significant amount of control over game administration and supervision. In game situations, officials usually have the responsibility and authority to postpone and cancel games due to inclement and dangerous weather situations, and they are responsible for controlling rough and violent play. At this level, officials work on a part-time basis as compensation is not sufficient to cover full-time employment. Officials are also responsible for submitting their income figures to the IRS for tax purposes.

■ APPLICATION OF KEY PRINCIPLES

Management

■ PROGRAMMATIC GOALS

Critics of highly organized youth athletics often cite that such activities create increased pressure to win and rob children of the opportunity to create and initiate their own play and competition. Professional physical educators and organizations such as the American Alliance for Health, Physical Education, Recreation and Dance (AAHPERD) decried the "win at all costs" approach as early as the 1930s (Berryman, 1978). Today, these concerns continue with many examples, some of which impact the health and safety of participants. Consider the case of linemen on the football team at Brockton (Massachusetts) High School, a perennial power in that state. In 1972, the team won a regional championship, and the average height and weight of the offensive line was 6´, 210 pounds. Twelve years later, another championship squad offensive line averaged 5´11˝, 199 pounds (and these numbers were probably high, as longtime Brockton head coach Armond Colombo confessed he often inflated the size of his linemen for listing in game programs. In 1984, Colombo's center was 5´6˝, 170, and he stated, "Therefore he went to 200. And that's the truth" [O'Brien, 2008, p. A4]). But in 1996, the same group on another championship team averaged 6´2˝, 268, and in 2008, 6´3˝, 262. While it is true that football players, especially linemen, have always been large, a recent study published by the American Medical Association and the *Journal of Pediatrics* found that children who play football are overweight and obese at rates far exceeding those who do not play. Another study of nearly 3,700 high school football linemen in Iowa found that 45% were overweight and nine percent would be classified with severe adult obesity. A second study of 650 Michigan players aged 9 to 14 found that weight problems began before players reached high school, and that 40% of the study group were obese (O'Brien, 2008).

So what is the cause of this "growing" trend? One coach put it succinctly: "[These players] are just obese. It's not that their hugely muscular . . . They're overweight for the same reason that 80 percent of the rest of the country is overweight. Their diets have been horrible their whole lives. They eat French fries and McDonald's food" (O'Brien, 2008, p. A8). Other studies have shown that overweight and obese players suffer injuries at a higher rate than slimmer teammates, especially in terms of ankle injuries. From the players' perspective, they need to get bigger to be successful and for the possibility to play in college and earn an athletically related aid award. Brockton's aptly named Khaldun Brickhouse (6´7˝, 300 pounds, down 30 pounds from the summer before his senior year) wanted to play "for any school that will take me. I want to go NCAA Division I, though" (O'Brien, 2008, p. A8). Andrew Knowlton, a player at St. John's Prep in Danvers, Massachusetts, felt pressure from peers: "All the older guys tell you, 'You've got to lift. Got to eat. Eat right, but eat a lot.' So there's pressure from everyone" (O'Brien, 2008, p. A1). In response, Knowlton bulked up from 200 to 293 pounds by his senior year, lifting weights six days a week and eating five or six times a day. The mother of another Brockton player, who weighed 265 as a sophomore, said, "He tells me to pray about (gaining weight) all the time. He really, really wants to go to college and play football, and I want him to do that, too" (O'Brien, 2008, p. A4).

Concerns do arise about participants who train and play too much and the injuries that can result from this hyper-intensive focus. Studies of U.S. high school athletes indicate boys suffer more injuries than girls, but that is in part explained by football and the fact that boys still outnumber girls in participation percentages. Studies also show, however, that girls are more likely to suffer chronic knee pain, stress fractures, hip and back pain, and concussions (Sokolove, 2008)

The injuries that stand out in the comparison between boys and girls are anterior cruciate ligament (ACL) tears, which occur five times more often in girls and young women. The injury is problematic because of the short-term and long-term effects on athletic careers. As described by writer Michael Sokolove:

The ACL is a small, rubber band–like fiber, no bigger than a little finger, that attaches to the femur in the upper leg and the tibia in the lower leg and stabilizes the knee . . . An ACL doesn't tear so much as it explodes, often during routine athletic maneuvers . . . After an ACL pulls off the femur, it turns into a viscous liquid. The ligament cannot be repaired; it has to be replaced with a graft, which the surgeon usually forms by taking a slice of the patellar tendon below the kneecap or from a hamstring tendon. One reason for the long rehabilitation is that the procedure is really two operations—one at the site of the injury and the other at the donor site, where the tendon is cut . . . The mystery is why a knee works properly for many years—through game after game, practice after practice, long season after long season, for tens of thousands of repetitions— and then, without warning, a tiny but crucial component suddenly malfunctions . . . If you are the parent of an athletic girl and live in a community that bustles with girls playing sports—especially the so-called jumping and cutting sports like soccer, basketball, volleyball and lacrosse—it may seem that every couple of weeks you see or hear about some unfortunate young woman hobbling off the field and into the operating room (2008, pp. 56, 59).

Sokolove goes on speculate that, based on the statistics and studies, the average high school girls' soccer team will experience four ACL injuries over the course of four years. Part of the explanation of this phenomenon is physiological: estrogen makes women more flexible but ligaments more lax, and higher fat levels in females force them to train longer to get stronger (high levels testosterone in males allows them to add muscle much easier). Wider hips also make more women knock-kneed, which contributes to the ACL stress. One researcher commented, "The big concern for me is the girl down the street who wants to play soccer on the rec team or the travel team. They're ripping their knees up . . . and we're really on the up curve of this, because it's still relatively recent that girls played sports in these large numbers . . . So if you think we have a problem now, 10 years from now we'll have a much bigger problem" (Sokolove, 2008, p. 60).

This epidemic is also explained by social and individual factors. Janelle Pierson, a soccer player at St. Thomas Aquinas High School in Fort Lauderdale, Florida, who sustained ACL injuries to both knees before her senior year (and would injure her left knee again later), had to wear a heavy brace on her right knee after her second year, but played in a first-round playoff game against the wishes of her parents. "You have to learn to deal with pain, because if you don't you'll never get to play," she said. "This is my last year, and I want to win the state championship" (the school had previously won 10 such titles) (Sokolove, 2008, p. 56). Others are playing in pursuit of opportunities to play in college, like the football linemen discussed previously. Those athletes specialize in soccer at an early age, play year-round, and participate in regional club tournaments, where teams play a dozen or more matches over the course of several weeks in multiple locations. Anson Dorrance, longtime and successful head soccer coach at the University of North Carolina–Chapel Hill, described the issue this way: "Now everybody's got a tournament . . . So now girls are going somewhere every two or three months and playing these inordinate number of matches . . . The were overplayed and never rested" (Sokolove, 2008, p. 76). According to Sokolove, much of the involvement in girls' sports has less to do with the stereotypical hard-driving parents, and more to the choices of the girls. As Janelle Pierson's father noted,

"We've raised these girls to be headstrong and independent . . . We had no idea what we were getting into. She started playing with a local team, just once or twice a week, then began playing with a travel team, and after that it just builds up. It's where all your leisure time goes. It becomes your social set" (Sokolove, 2008, p. 76). Sport psychologist Colleen Hacker puts responsibility back on the parents. "I don't think anybody's saying, 'Honey, how do we screw (our kids) up tomorrow?' But the attention, judgment and objectivity that parents bring to their work lives and other spheres of importance, they don't bring to their kids sports" (Sokolove, 2008, p. 76).

■ PERFORMANCE EVALUATION AND SUPERVISION

Coaches are the principal supervisors of the athletic activities of their teams and it is their responsibility to provide and ensure a reasonably safe environment for all participants. A coach's performance will be assessed through issuing proper equipment, maintaining issued equipment, ensuring all participants have had physical examinations and been found fit to participate, and maintaining the various necessary forms of documentation (confirmation of physical status, confirmation of eligibility, proof of insurance, parent permission to participate). In terms of the actual play of participants, coaches are responsible for organizing drills, ensuring physical mismatches are minimized, maintaining safe practice and playing grounds, suspending practice or play during dangerous weather conditions, and monitoring locker rooms during the time preceding and following activities. In play situations, coaches must monitor activities to be sure student-athletes are not performing in an improper and dangerous manner that might harm themselves and/or other participants.

■ EVALUATING COACHES

Each given all the focus of performance evaluations outlined above, schools often fail to follow even the most basic of procedures. This occurred in 2010, when Wally Covell, head baseball coach at Lawrence High School in Fairfield, Maine, had to endure a session of criticism in an open public meeting without being present to address the concerns. Several weeks before the 2010 season, Covell, a high school and college coach in Maine for 55 years and a member of the state's Baseball Hall of Fame, had coordinated with the program's booster club to order personalized uniforms for the upcoming season (school budgetary policies dictated that virtually all equipment and uniforms were paid for by team booster clubs and not the school). Returning players were contacted by team captains and money was collected for payment. The parent of a junior varsity player, however, chose to interpret the actions as a determination that the 2010 roster had already been determined, and complained to the school's athletic director Bill McManus, principal Pam Swett, and Superintendant Dean Baker. Several meetings were held between the administrators and Covell, and the money collected was returned to address the concern of the parent.

However, at a meeting of the school's board of control a week before preseason practice was scheduled to begin, where the contracts of all spring sports coaches were to be voted on by the board members, the parent appeared at the open meeting and publicly denounced Covell and his coaching techniques, calling the 75-year-old's methods "old and outdated." Covell, who had been named conference coach of the year two seasons previous, was not alerted of this beforehand, but several team members had caught wind of the action ahead of time and attended the meeting and spoke on his behalf. No evidence of Covell's job performance could be provided by the athletic director (AD), because Covell had never had any form of performance review during his six years of employment at the school. The school board ultimately voted to approve the entire slate of spring coaches on a vote of 6–3 with one abstention. As a result, Covell was charged with creating a formal player evaluation sheet that he and his assistant would complete for each prospect during preseason practice. The player whose parent complained about the process was never evaluated, however, because he decided to try out for the school's tennis team instead.

Covell was unable to complete the season when another parent (the president of the booster club) complained to the AD of Covell's disciplining of his son after the player's inattentiveness during a postgame meeting after a loss to Cony High School of Augusta. Athletic Director McManus told Covell he would be suspended two games for his actions, but Covell opted to resign instead (Covell made a public statement that the resignation was due to the health of his wife, who would die of congestive heart failure several weeks later) effectively ending his coaching career at Lawrence, still without a formal performance review from his AD.

Financial Concerns

While school and youth sport organizations are not-for-profit enterprises, this does not mean that associated programs are not concerned with controlling costs and maintaining balanced budgets. This issue has been particularly problematic since 2008, as the global economic recession has meant that many school and youth programs across the United States have severely curtailed athletic offerings in light of reduced funding from local and state sources. For example, in 2009, the South-Western City Schools district, which serves part of Columbus, Ohio, and nearby towns (and is the state's sixth largest school district), cancelled all athletic activities. The move saved the district, which had been facing budget shortfalls for years (a total of $22 million in reductions with 330 positions reduced since 2006), a total of $2.5 million. The action was forced after a proposed tax increase was rejected for the third time by local voters in an August 2009 referendum. The district expects its better athletes at Grove City High School to transfer to other schools (Garcia, 2009).

Other schools facing cuts have resorted to finding other resources for the funding necessary to operate programs. At Dixon (California) High School (located 20 miles southwest of Sacramento, described by one student as, "There's a Wal-Mart and that's about it" [Ortiz, 2009, p. 2A]), the school system decided in February 2009 to cut all sports for the upcoming school year, a move that impacted 600 of the school's 1,243 students. However, the district school board reconsidered the move in May 2009, and provided $110,000 (down from $280,000 the previous year) for basic funding after parents, booster groups, and community members worked to close the budget gap (Ortiz, 2009). Through fundraisers, the provision of student transportation by parents, and reduced playing schedules, Dixon High kept all 17 of its existing programs, and even added boys' and girls' water polo. However, coaching stipends were not reinstated, forcing many coaches to leave their positions, while those who remained did so without pay. Of the transportation element, a district official commented, "It's a challenge in lots of ways. If you have a team of 40, that's a lot more organizational work. It creates greater liability. There are a series of forms the kids have to fill out, the drivers have to fill out. There's proof of insurance needed, medical consent forms for kids for treatment in case of accidents. It's a lot of management" (Ortiz, 2009, p. 2A).

Other schools facing similar cuts, such as Brighton (Michigan) High School, have instituted pay-to-play fees. The school fields 98 teams in 32 sports—a high total—but receives only enough funding from its district to cover 38% of the $1.5 million necessary to operate its programs. School AD John Thompson notes that the remaining $930,000 is covered by fundraising and activities fees. Student-athletes pay $175 per sport, with the fee for a third sport waived, and also pay a transportation fee ranging from $30 to $75. Fees are waived for those who demonstrate financial hardship. Of the system, Thompson says, "Unfortunately, one day sports will be out there for people who have money. We can say we'll take care of those without money, but I can tell you it will be the kids with talent. The average kid is going to be left behind" (Garcia, 2009, p. 2A).

State associations have also made adjustments to their sponsored activities to control costs. For the 2009–2010 academic year, the New Mexico Activities Association (NMAA) changed its state championship format in five sports. For example, the girls' volleyball (the NMAA does not sponsor boys' volleyball) and softball tournaments have gone from double-elimination to single-elimination, saving a night in hotel costs for some teams. Boys' and girls' soccer tournaments have dropped pool play for tournament seedings, saving a week's worth of travel and hotel costs. Baseball and boys' and girls' tennis tournaments have also been curtailed by a week. NMAA assistant executive director Robert Zayas said that the precise amount saved by the moves is difficult to calculate due to varying roster sizes and travel distances. "Eliminating even just one night is significant when you consider the costs of meals, bus drivers, gas, hotels, and other expenses" (Ruibal, 2009, p. 2A). The NMAA is also looking to hold down its expenses (on a budget of $3 million raised from dues, championship gate receipts, and sponsorships—each accounting for about a third of the total), cutting back on professional expenses such as travel to the annual meeting of the NFHS (Ruibal, 2009, p. 2A).

Marketing

■ CORPORATIONS PROFITING FROM SCHOOL AND YOUTH SPORTS PARTICIPATION

Most of you are well aware of the impact of ESPN on the national and international sports landscapes and are probably also aware that ESPN's parent company is the Disney Corporation. Disney is also impacting the school and youth sports world through its Wide World of Sports Complex in Lake Buena Vista, Florida. In 1997, Disney Sports Enterprises created a $100 million sports facility to lure athletes and coaches and to steer more tourists to its Orlando-area theme parks. Today, the complex encompasses two field houses, eight outdoor fields, four baseball diamonds, six softball diamonds, a track-and-field venue, a cross-country course, ten tennis courts, and a 100-lane bowling center on 220 acres, and it hosts more than 180 events year-round in 50 different sports. In 2008, 15,000 boys and girls aged 9 to 18 from more than 900 teams from across the United States and around the world played at the facility in the Amateur Athletic Union (AAU) national championships in baseball and basketball. Disney has a formal alliance with AAU, which hosts 70 of its 250 championships at the site. The complex has also become a training facility for many high school teams during spring break vacations, as 670 teams with 12,000 athletes travelled there during a ten-week period in 2008 (Smith, 2008).

In all, more than 2 million young athletes— an average of 250,000 a year—have competed at the complex. Disney officials claim they do not know the percentage of competitors and their families who buy theme park passes, but they do cite the fact that 85% of participants would not otherwise visited the Disney parks. As for the associated revenue, AAU president Bobby Dodd says three AAU teams stayed for nearly two weeks at a cost of $4,500. The parent company Walt Disney Co. reported total revenues from parks and resorts to be $2.7 billion in 2008 (Smith, 2008).

■ EXPANDING PARTICIPATION OPPORTUNITIES

In an effort to reach more students, some state associations have been exploring whether to add new activities for high school students. Such has been the case recently in Illinois, where the Illinois High School Association (ISHA) investigated adding competitive bass fishing to its sanctioned sports and championships. According to ISHA director Marty Hickman, "We think interscholastic participation is good for kids, and we think with bass fishing we'll possibly reach some kids who haven't been participating in IHSA activities in the past" (Temkin, 2007, sect. 3 p. 10). When the ISHA authorized the possibility of adding the sport, schools from across the state expressed interest, as did several companies seeking to become sponsors. Such sponsor support is vital because the ISHA would need that revenue to sustain any state-wide competitions. Terry Brown, a writer for the Web site BassFan.com, a daily media service covering the sport, noted that sponsor interest is "about turning a 16-year-old into a die-hard who buys equipment or a boat." Mike Mulligan, an avid fisherman and biology teacher at Taft High School in Chicago who attended Gordon Tech (another Chicago high school), is more focused on the potential educational benefits of the sport. "I think it's something the kids need," he said. "Especially in the city . . . I noticed it when you take kids to (local forested areas), and you see the expressions of their faces . . . That's what we are doing as instructors in the life sciences, getting them to

appreciate the outdoors and become stewards themselves" (Temkin, 2007, p. 10).

Ethics

■ USE OF PERFORMANCE ENHANCING SUBSTANCES

Roger Clemens. Barry Bonds. Lance Armstrong. These names are familiar to many of us because of the recent attention focused on the alleged use of performance enhancing substances and techniques at the professional sport level, both in the United States and in international events such as the Olympic Games and cycling. While obtaining these substances is often illegal, there are ethical considerations associated with their use, namely, the health risks and the unfair advantage gained by those who use over those who are clean.

These issues have impacted school and youth sports, as seen in 2008 when Bobby J. Guidroz, sheriff of rural St. Landry Parish, Louisiana, announced an undercover investigation of area gyms that produced the area's largest ever anabolic steroid drug bust. Ten arrests were made, including two former high school football players. One unconfirmed tip indicated two coaches in the area encouraged players to use steroids. Of the arrests, Guidroz said, "I think there's more steroid use, after talking to my investigators, in sports activities, than originally thought" (Longman, 2008, p. B10).

Across the country, efforts are being made to test for and detect the use of such substances, but testing efforts are, in the words of *New York Times* reporter Jere Longman, "expensive, scattered, and full of loopholes," and "experts question methods frequently used to inform athletes about the health hazards and ethical considerations of doping" (Longman, 2008, p. B10). Law enforcement personnel across the country also cite the fact that some parents allow or encourage the use of these substances to improve player performance. Some reports indicate substance use is declining, but many experts dispute this, claiming that use is being significantly underreported. Charles Yesalis, a former Penn State University professor and expert on performance enhancing drugs, stated: "We could well be past the point that—unless something dramatic happens, like 20 kids dying—of doing anything about this. I'm not sure people want to take care of this problem . . . The few states that have instituted testing systems have set them up to fail. It's mainly to make coaches and parents feel good" (Longman, 2008, pp. B10, B13). Illinois, New Jersey (which only tests postseason competition participants), and Texas (random unannounced testing, but none during the summer) have mandatory testing of high school participants. New Jersey reported two positives out of 1,000 athletes tested between 2006 and 2008, and Texas reported only two out of 10,000 in 2007, in a program that cost $3 million. Because of the loopholes, many call these protocols not drug testing but IQ testing, meaning that anyone seeking to beat the tests could figure out when to stop doping to avoid detection (Longman, 2008).

Many cite cost as the biggest factor in testing. Florida ended its program in 2008 after state budget cuts. Individual tests can cost as much as $300. In St. Landry Parish, the six public high schools can test 10% of their athletes three times a year for recreational drugs, and one of those tests can be focused on detecting performance enhancing substances. Parish AD Donnie Perron favors enhanced education because of the cost of testing (Longman, 2008).

Studies also show that even with testing, high school athletes were not deterred from using these substances, because teenagers often feel impervious to risk and enjoy challenging authority, coupled with the fact that so few athletes were tested with little frequency. The co-author of the study, Dr. Linn Goldberg, also recommends increased education to deal with these ethical challenges and said that $15 million has been earmarked for such programs under the 2004 federal Anabolic Steroid Control Act, but that none of the dollars in funding have yet been made available (Longman, 2008).

■ GENDER EQUITY

Most sex discrimination challenges in high school athletics have been based on state or U.S. Constitution equal protection clauses, state equal rights amendments, Title IX of the Education Amendments of 1972, or a combination thereof. Gender equity is a flashpoint of controversy for schools but is less so for youth leagues, unless they depend on municipal funding or utilize public facilities. Administrators are responsible

for ensuring that athletic programs treat boys and girls equally. The NFHS states as one of its legal foundations for the administration of high school athletics that interscholastic athletic programs must demonstrate equity or substantive and continuous progress toward equity in all facets of girls' and boys' athletics.

However, even though Title IX is the law of the land, certain factors influence how girls play. A recent study indicated that in suburban locations, girls play sports at essentially the same rate as boys, but in urban areas only 36% of girls surveyed describe themselves as moderately involved athletes. Some of this difference can be attributed to money, as schools struggle with resources to sustain basic programs. Another factor is that many urban families, often recent immigrants and lower-income, see the benefits of participation for their sons but not for their daughters, and that girls have more responsibilities in the areas of family care, such as babysitting. The work schedules of players' parents also means that often no one gets to games to see their children play (Thomas, 2009).

All of these factors have come into play for the girls' basketball team at Middle School 61 (MS 61), a public school in the Crown Heights section of the New York City borough of Brooklyn. For one road game against Public School 161 in the Bronx, head coach Bryan Mariner had to borrow his nephew's car to drive his team through snarled city traffic to the game—with only five players—and paid the cousin of his best player $2 to cover her babysitting responsibilities for the afternoon. He also had to stop during the trip and convince the father of one player that it was safe to travel to the Bronx after the parent caught up to the car in traffic and wanted to pull his daughter off the trip. Once they made it to the school, they found out the game had to be cancelled because the other team didn't have enough players (Thomas, 2009).

There are also very real financial disparities between suburban and city girls' programs. At

MS 61, Mariner asks his players to contribute $80 for uniforms, transportation, and other expenses. Only half could pay in full, with most paying $1 or $2 at a time. Most nearby suburban middle schools on Long Island have a full complement of programs and children can play at no cost. Participants are so plentiful that many schools field separate teams for seventh and eighth graders, with some schools playing extended games so that all participants can get into games. Coaches are paid as much as $5,000 a season. Mariner's salary was $2,500 (Thomas, 2009).

These differences mean that the level of play at MS 61 is somewhat ragged. Girls sometimes dribble the wrong way and often miss layups. Some are good enough to play in high school, such as Olivia Colbert, who competed in a city-wide girls' tournament at Hunter College. When Olivia later gained acceptance to a local private parochial high school, there was concern over whether her mother, a single mother working as a school crossing guard, could afford the $5,600 tuition (Thomas, 2009).

Legal

■ ENFORCING PARTICIPATION RULES AND CODES OF CONDUCT

In April 2010, officials from the Yarmouth (Maine) School District sought to discipline a 16-year-old female lacrosse student-athlete who had violated the school's honor code by appearing on her Facebook page along with four other students holding a can of Coors Lite beer. When school officials obtained a copy of the image, each of the five students was questioned by Yarmouth High School assistant principal Amy Bongard, and the female lacrosse player admitted to drinking the beer, a violation of the school's honor code, a four-page document that students must sign to participate in all school co-curricular activities. The code demands that

CASE STUDY: Cardinal Ruhle Academy: National Champions?

In 2002, after 14 years as athletic director (AD) at Green Valley District High School, Derron Damone had taken a job at Cardinal Ruhle Academy (CRA), a private Catholic high school of 350 boys, located in Akropolis, a fading industrial city of 75,000 people. CRA was just a few miles from Green Valley, but light years apart in every other way. It had a strict dress code, a traditional curriculum focusing on math and science (along with religious education), a 70-year-old building that had seen better days, and a mix of students, many of whom were first generation immigrants from Central America, Russia, and Somalia, and some of whom traveled more than two hours on the city's transportation system to attend. Sixty-five percent of the school's students were ethnic minorities.

When he took the job, Damone had been charged by CRA's head, Monsignor Gennaro (Jimmy) DiNapoli, to improve the school's profile and enrollment (which had been falling due to concerns about the school's dangerous surroundings and fallout from the clergy sex-abuse scandals that had rocked the U.S. Catholic church) through expanding its athletic programs, specifically boys' basketball. At that point, he learned the school was about to undertake a significant fundraising campaign (with a goal to raise $40 million) to refurbish its crumbling facilities. The creation of a nationally ranked boys' basketball team was going to be part of the public relations campaign to generate interest amongst alumni and prospective students. The move to create a nationally prominent program had gone well. CRA had sent several players to top National Collegiate Athletic Association (NCAA) Division I men's basketball programs, and even had one player currently in the NBA, DeRay Higgins, who played collegiate one year and then entered the NBA draft. Higgins, unfortunately, had brought some unwanted attention as well. In the last few years, "high school" institutions have sprouted up across the United States: Lutheran Christian Academy and Rise Academy in Philadelphia; Boys to Men Academy in Chicago; God's Academy in Irving, Texas; One Christian Academy in Mendenhall, Mississippi; and Stoneridge Prep in Simi Valley, California, among others. Some of these "schools," none of which has been accredited by the appropriate state education oversight organizations, have actual classes, although often for only two hours a day, but their students in most cases are all African-American male basketball players looking to become eligible to play in college. At least 200 players have been deemed academically eligible by the NCAA in the last decade by enrolling in such "schools" (Thamel, 2006b; Thamel & Wilson, 2005).

In the summer of 2006, the NCAA released a list of 16 schools from which it would not accept graduated students as academically eligible, and another 22 that would be subject to ongoing review. Lutheran Christian, along with several others mentioned above and other well-known boys' prep hoop powers such as Fork Union Military Academy and Oak Hill Academy in Virginia, and Bridgton Academy in Maine, were among the schools identified (Thamel, 2006a). In 2008, the Association's High School Review Committee denied approval for Charis Prep, located in Wilson, North Carolina, after reviewing the school's curriculum and visiting the site. The committee cited concerns over a lack of quality control or organized curriculum structure. The ruling meant that Charis graduates could not use core courses earned at the school, grades, or completion of its course of study to meet initial eligibility requirements (Associated Press, 2008).

While CRA had never been one of these fly-by-night operations, whispers about its academics had gotten louder with each player who transferred to the school and played his way to a Division I grant-in-aid. Also, the hoped-for fundraising boost that the ascendant program would bring had yet to materialize. The long-serving and much-beloved DiNapoli had died in 2006, and his replacement, the much-younger and less-charismatic Walter MacMullen who, while well-meaning, has not been able to connect with the alumni and other potential donors to meet the lofty $40 million goal.

On a gray January morning in 2010, as he waited in the drive-through line for his morning coffee, Damone's phone buzzed. It was an e-mail message that the state activities association was considering a vote at its next meeting on a measure to participate in a newly established national championship in boys' basketball for the 2010–2011 school year. Damone knew that the National High School Coaches Association in Pennsylvania had opted to partner with the sport marketing company International Management Group (IMG) to create a series of such championships at the company's training academy in Bradenton, Florida, and had read that more than half of other state associations had indicated support of the initiative. The e-mail read that the NFSH was also set to consider sanctioning the events at its upcoming meeting.

Damone knew why IMG was doing this: the sale of television rights, charging fees for teams to participate, and the possibility of having participants jump from teams to enroll at its academy. He was less sure about how it made sense for his school. This wasn't like the NCAA tournaments, he thought, which had a national appeal and all associated costs picked up by the NCAA. True, the state championship meant something to CRA and its community members, but what about the increased travel time and cost and missed class time another level of play would require? Would there be additional academic scrutiny because of this? And would all this really help further the school's fundraising initiatives?

The e-mail asked Damone to send back an initial response on how CRA would vote on such a measure. If the initial responses were positive, the association would put it to a formal vote by all school principals and ADs the next month. Damone put the phone down and drove ahead to pick up his large French vanilla coffee with cream and two sugars. He then pulled ahead to a parking spot, picked up his phone, and texted his response.

Questions for Discussion

1. How does the issue of potential national championship involvement reflect a change in program goals and focus for CRA?
2. Is the phenomenon of national championships consistent with marketing trends impacting school and youth sports?
3. With which governing bodies will Damone need to interact to determine how involvement with such national championships might impact CRA's athletic programs?
4. With whom, if anyone, should Damone confer to determine his action on this issue?

Note: Information used in this case, as well as sources cited, is from Wieberg, 2010.

students refrain from using alcohol or tobacco, participating in activities that can be construed as hazing, or taking part in any activities that might embarrass the school, be it on or off school property, regardless of whether the participant is in or out of season. As a result, the student was suspended from games for three weeks and was not permitted to go on an out-of-region team trip during the school's April vacation. The student was also required to have six substance abuse counseling sessions before she could return to playing (Menendez, 2010).

However, at a later date the family chose to sue the school in federal court for imposing the penalties, claiming that the school was reaching beyond its authority when the parents are the appropriate authority. The student also claimed she was not allowed to call her mother before she was questioned, and that she felt intimidated and forced into confessing. The school district responded, saying it had "the authority and the obligation to discipline its students who violate its substance abuse policy," citing case law decisions noting that the courts should not interfere in the daily operations of school systems and that students do not have a constitutional right to participate in interscholastic athletics. Both the student and her mother had signed the code and were aware of the penalties for violation. The school also claimed that Assistant Principal Bongard did not "badger, intimidate or interrogate . . . she simply asked (the student) what had happened and in response to her question (the student) frankly admitted that she was holding a beer" (Hench, 2010, pp. C1, C11).

Three days after the suit was filed, a hearing was held to determine whether the court would grant a temporary injunction in favor of the plaintiffs and allow her to continue to play while the case was being decided. U.S. District Court Judge D. Brock Hornby denied the request, ruling that the plaintiff's lawyer was unable to demonstrate a likelihood of success in a future trial, and that the school's need for an enforceable honor code trumps the student's need for relief from school punishment. In the hearing before the judge, the school district's lawyer, Melissa Hewey, stated, "This is a matter that should not be in federal court. This is a code permitted by state statutes. It is important to point out that what we're talking about here is illegal conduct" (Menendez, 2010, p. 2). The family was still considering continuing the lawsuit immediately after the hearing, but to date no action has been taken.

■ SUMMARY

School and youth sport has evolved from its modest beginning in New England private schools in the early 1800s to incorporate boys and girls of all ages in a multitude of sports and activities. These participation opportunities have expanded as administrators, coaches, and other associated personnel have developed the skills and expertise to deal with the challenges and issues that have accompanied this booming expansion. Although some contemporary issues complicate today's high school and youth sport landscape, the need and demand for well-run sport programs has never been greater. As long as there are boys and girls, the need for play and competition will exist, as will the need for well-trained professionals to ensure these needs will be met.

■ RESOURCES

American Alliance for Health, Physical Education, Recreation and Dance (AAHPERD)
  1900 Association Drive
  Reston, VA 20191-1598
  1-800-213-7193
  http://www.aahperd.org

American Sport Education Program (ASEP)
  Box 5076
  Champaign, IL 61825-5076
  800-747-5698; Fax: 217-351-2674
  http://www.asep.com

American Youth Soccer Organization
  12501 South Isis
  Hawthorne, CA 90205
  800-USA-AYSO
  http://www.soccer.org

Little League Baseball International
  P.O. Box 3485
  Williamsport, PA 17701
  570-326-1921; Fax: 570-322-4526
  http://www.littleleague.org

National Federation of State High School Associations

> P.O. Box 690
> Indianapolis, IN 46206
> 317-972-6900; Fax: 317-822-5700
> http://www.nhfs.org
> *Each state, Canadian province, and U.S.*
>   *territory also has a high school athletic*
>   *and activity association.*

Pop Warner Little Scholars, Inc.

> 586 Middletown Blvd., Suite C-100
> Langhorne, PA 19047
> 215-752-2691; Fax: 215-752-2879
> http://www.popwarner.com

YMCA of the USA

> 101 N. Wacker Drive
> Chicago, IL 60606
> 312-977-0031
> http://www.ymca.net

■ KEY TERMS

coaches, governing bodies, judges, National Federation of State High School Associations (NFHS), national youth league organizations, nonschool agencies, officials, physical therapists, private schools, Progressive Movement, public schools, school athletic directors, trainers, state associations, youth league directors

■ REFERENCES

2008–09 high school athletics participation survey. (2009). National Federation of State High School Associations. Retrieved February 23, 2011, from http://www.nfhs.org/content.aspx?id=3282&link identifier=id&itemid=3282

Associated Press (2008, September 15). NCAA rules against Wilson's Charis prep. Retrieved November 10, 2010, from http://www.highschoolot.com/content/story/3551220/

Berryman, J. W. (1978). From the cradle to the playing field: America's emphasis on highly organized competitive sports for preadolescent boys. *Journal of Sports History, 5*(1), 31–32.

Bundgaard, A. (2005). *Muscle and manliness: The rise of sport in American boarding schools.* Syracuse, NY: Syracuse University Press.

Cahn, S.K. (1994). *Coming on strong: Gender and sexuality in twentieth century women's sport.* New York: The Free Press.

Dyreson, M. (1989). The emergence of consumer culture and the transformation of physical culture: American sport in the 1920s. *Journal of Sport History, 16*(5), 3.

Garcia, M. (2009, September 2). At some schools, budget cuts shut down sports. *USA Today,* pp. 1A–2A.

Hardy, S. (2003). *How Boston played: Sport, recreation, and community, 1865–1915.* Knoxville, TN: The University of Tennessee Press.

Hench, D. (2010, April 11). Yarmouth schools: Discipline suit flimsy. *Portland (Maine) Press Herald,* pp. C1, C11.

History of AYSO (2009). American Youth Soccer Organization (AYSO). Retrieved October 18, 2010, from http://soccer.org/AboutAYSO/history.aspx

Little League Baseball, Inc. (n.d.) Little League chronology. Retrieved October 18, 2010, from http://www.littleleague.org/learn/about/historyandmission/chronology.htm

Little League Baseball, Inc. (2010). Structure of Little League Baseball and Softball, Inc. Retrieved October 18, 2010, from http://www.littleleague.org/learn/about/structure.htm

Longman, J. (2008, November 28). High schools fight doping with little consensus. *New York Times,* pp. B10, B13.

Lopez, M.H., & Moore, K. (2006). Participation in sports and civic engagement. Retrieved November 10, 2010, from http://www.civicyouth.org/PopUps/FactSheets/FS_06_Sports_and_Civic_Engagement.pdf

Menendez, J. (2010, April 14). Judge: No putting off honor code punishment. *Portland (Maine) Press Herald.* Retrieved October 18, 2010, from: http://www.pressherald.com/news/judge-no-putting-off-honor-code-punishment_2010-04-14.html

National Alliance for Youth Sports. (2010). Frequently asked questions. (2010). Retrieved October 18, 2010, from http://www.nays.org/Who_We_Are/frequently_asked_questions.cfm#1

National Federation of State High School Associations. (2008). The case for high school activities. Retrieved February 23, 2011, from http://www.nfhs.org/WorkArea/DownloadAsset.aspx?id=3288

National Federation of State High School Associations. (2010, February 9). Bob Gardner named NFSH executive director. Retrieved October 18, 2010, from http://www.nfhs.org/content.aspx?id=3831

O'Brien, K. (2008, October 5). Tipping the competitive scales. *Boston Sunday Globe*, pp. A1, A4.

O'Hanlon, T.P. (1982). School sports as social training: The case of athletics and the crisis of World War I. *Journal of Sport History, 9*(1), 5.

Ortiz, J.L. (2009, September 2). In California, a community rallies to save school sports. *USA Today*, p. 2A

Pop Warner Little Scholars, Inc. (2009). About Pop Warner. Retrieved October 18, 2010, from http://www.popwarner.com/aboutus/pop.asp

PRWeb. (2010). Playing through the pain is not OK. Young athletes should play it safe to avoid injury. Retrieved November 10, 2010, from http://www.prweb.com/releases/2010/08/prweb4438484.htm

Putney, C.W. (1993). Going upscale: The YMCA and postwar America, 1950–1990. *Journal of Sport History, 20*(2), 151–166.

Ruibal, S. (2009, September 2). New Mexico trims its state tournaments to save money. *USA Today*, p. 2A.

Seymour, H. (1990). *Baseball: The people's game.* New York: Oxford University Press.

Smith, D. (2008, September 10). And they will come. *USA Today*, pp. 1C–2C.

Sokolove, M. (2008, May 11). Warrior girls. *New York Times Magazine*, pp. 54–61, 76, 81.

Swanson, R.A., & Spears, B. (1995). *Sport and physical education in the United States* (4th ed.). Dubuque, IA: Brown & Benchmark.

Temkin, B. (2007, October 21). ISHA angles for fishing. *Chicago Tribune*, pp. 3–10.

Thamel, P. (2006a, July 6). Oak Hill officials upset with N.C.A.A. listing. *New York Times*, p. C18.

Thamel, P. (2006b, February 26). Schools, with few classes, build hoop dreams. *New York Times*, pp. A1, B18–B19.

Thamel, P., & Wilson, D. (2005, November 27). Poor grades aside, top athletes get to college on $399 diploma. *New York Times*, pp. A1, A9.

Thomas, K. (2009, June 14). A city team's struggle shows disparity in girls' sports. *New York Times*, pp. 1, 23.

Vincent, T. (1994). *The rise of American sport: Mudville's revenge.* Lincoln, NE: University of Nebraska Press.

Wieberg, S. (2010, January 25). Prep national title events on the horizon. *USA Today*, p. 1C.

Wilson, J. (1994). *Playing by the rules: Sport, society, and the state.* Detroit, MI: Wayne State University Press.

CHAPTER

Collegiate Sport

Carol A. Barr

◼ INTRODUCTION

Intercollegiate athletics is a major segment of the sport industry. It garners increasingly more television air time as network and cable companies increase coverage of sporting events and athletic conferences create their own networks (e.g., Big Ten Network), it receives substantial coverage within the sports sections of local and national newspapers, and it attracts attention from corporations seeking potential sponsorship opportunities. Television rights fees have increased dramatically. Sport sponsorship opportunities and coaches' compensation figures have escalated as well. The business aspect of collegiate athletics has grown immensely as administrators and coaches at all levels have become more involved in budgeting, finding revenue sources, controlling expense items, and participating in fund development activities. The administrative aspects of collegiate athletics have also changed. With more rules and regulations to be followed, there is more paperwork in such areas as recruiting and academics. These changes have led to an increase in the number of personnel and the specialization of positions in collegiate athletic departments. Although the number of athletic administrative jobs has increased across all divisions, jobs can still be hard to come by because the popularity of working in this segment of the sport industry continues to be high.

The international aspect of this sport industry segment has grown tremendously through the participation of student-athletes who are nonresident aliens (a term used by the National Collegiate Athletic Association for foreign student-athletes). Coaches are more aware of international talent when recruiting. The number of nonresident alien student-athletes competing on U.S. college sports teams has grown from an average of 1.8% of the male student-athletes in all divisions in 1999–2000 to 4.0% in 2008–2009. The male sports with the most nonresident alien representation are ice hockey (29.8% of all male ice hockey student-athletes), tennis (25.9%), and squash (22.0%) (National Collegiate Athletic Association [NCAA], 2010b). On female sport teams, a similar increase in the number of nonresident alien participation has occurred. In 1999–2000, 1.5% of all female student-athletes were nonresident aliens, a percentage that increased to 4.4% in 2008–2009. The sports showing the largest representation on the women's side include the same sports of ice hockey (29.3%), tennis (20.8%), and squash (20.6%) (NCAA, 2010b). Athletic teams are taking overseas trips for practice and competitions at increasing rates. College athletic games are being shown internationally, and licensed merchandise can be found around the world. It is not unusual to stroll down a street in Munich, Germany, or Montpellier, France, and see a Duke basketball jersey or a Notre Dame football jersey.

■ HISTORY

On August 3, 1852, on Lake Winnepesaukee in New Hampshire, a crew race between Harvard and Yale was the very first intercollegiate athletic event in the United States (Dealy, 1990).

What was unusual about this contest was that Harvard University is located in Cambridge, Massachusetts, and Yale University is located in New Haven, Connecticut, yet the crew race took place on a lake north of these two cities, in New Hampshire. Why? Because the first intercollegiate athletic contest was sponsored by the Boston, Concord & Montreal Railroad Company, which wanted to host the race in New Hampshire so that both teams, their fans, and other spectators would have to ride the railroad to get to the event (Dealy, 1990). Thus, the first intercollegiate athletic contest involved sponsorship by a company external to sports that used the competition to enhance the company's business.

The next sport to hold intercollegiate competitions was baseball. The first collegiate baseball contest was held in 1859 between Amherst and Williams (Davenport, 1985), two of today's more athletically successful Division III institutions. In this game, Amherst defeated Williams by the lopsided score of 73–32 (Rader, 1990). On November 6, 1869, the first intercollegiate football game was held between Rutgers and Princeton (Davenport, 1985). This "football" contest was far from the game of football known today. The competitors were allowed to kick and dribble the ball, similar to soccer, with Rutgers "outdribbling" its opponents and winning the game six goals to four (Rader, 1990).

The initial collegiate athletic contests taking place during the 1800s were student-run events. Students organized the practices and corresponded with their peers at other institutions to arrange competitions. There were no coaches or athletic administrators assisting them. The Ivy League schools became the "power" schools in athletic competition, and football became the premier sport. Fierce rivalries developed, attracting numerous spectators. Thus, collegiate athletics evolved from games being played for student enjoyment and participation in fierce competitions involving bragging rights for individual institutions.

Colleges and universities soon realized that these intercollegiate competitions had grown in popularity and prestige and thus could bring increased publicity, student applications, and alumni donations. As the pressure to win increased, the students began to realize they needed external help. Thus, the first "coach" was hired in 1864 by the Yale crew team to help it win, especially against its rival, Harvard University. This coach, William Wood, a physical therapist by trade, introduced a rigorous training program as well as a training table (Dealy, 1990). College and university administrators also began to take a closer look at intercollegiate athletics competitions. The predominant theme at the time was still nonacceptance of these competitive athletic activities within the educational sphere of the institution. With no governing organization and virtually nonexistent playing and eligibility rules, mayhem often resulted. Once again the students took charge, especially in football, forming the **Intercollegiate Football Association** in 1876. This association was made up of students from Harvard, Yale, Princeton, and Columbia who agreed on consistent playing and eligibility rules (Dealy, 1990).

The dangerous nature of football pushed faculty and administrators to get involved in governing intercollegiate athletics. In 1881, Princeton University became the first college to form a faculty athletics committee to review football (Dealy, 1990). The committee's choices were to either make football safer to play or ban the sport all together. In 1887, Harvard's Board of Overseers instructed the Harvard Faculty Athletics Committee to ban football. However, aided by many influential alumni, the Faculty Athletics Committee chose to keep the game intact (Dealy, 1990). In 1895, the **Intercollegiate Conference of Faculty Representatives**, better known as the **Big Ten Conference**, was formed to create student eligibility rules (Davenport, 1985). By the early 1900s, football on college campuses had become immensely popular, receiving a tremendous amount of attention from the stu-

dents, alumni, and collegiate administrators. Nevertheless, the number of injuries and deaths occurring in football continued to increase, and it was evident that more legislative action was needed.

In 1905 during a football game involving Union College and New York University, Harold Moore, a halfback for Union College, died of a cerebral hemorrhage after being crushed on a play. Moore was just one of 18 football players who died that year. An additional 149 serious injuries occurred (Yaeger, 1991). The chancellor of New York University, Henry Mitchell MacCracken, witnessed this incident and took it upon himself to do something about it. MacCracken sent a letter of invitation to presidents of other schools to join him for a meeting to discuss the reform or abolition of football. In December 1905, 13 presidents met and declared their intent to reform the game of football. When this group met three weeks later, 62 colleges and universities sent representatives. This group formed the **Intercollegiate Athletic Association of the United States (IAAUS)** to formulate rules making football safer and more exciting to play. Seven years later, in 1912, this group took the name **National Collegiate Athletic Association (NCAA)** (Yaeger, 1991).

In the 1920s, college and university administrators began recognizing intercollegiate athletics as a part of higher education and placed athletics under the purview of the physical education department (Davenport, 1985). Coaches were given academic appointments within the physical education department, and schools began to provide institutional funding for athletics.

The **Carnegie Reports of 1929** painted a bleak picture of intercollegiate athletics, identifying many academic abuses, recruiting abuses, payments to student-athletes, and commercialization of athletics. The Carnegie Foundation visited 112 colleges and universities. One of the disturbing findings from this study was that although the NCAA "recommended against" both recruiting and subsidization of student-athletes, these practices were widespread among colleges and universities (Lawrence, 1987). The Carnegie Reports stated that the responsibility for control over collegiate athletics rested with the president of the college or university and with the faculty (Savage, 1929). The NCAA was pressured to change from an organization responsible for developing playing rules used in competitions to an organization that would oversee academic standards for student-athletes, monitor recruiting activities of coaches and administrators, and establish principles governing amateurism, thus alleviating the paying of student-athletes by alumni and booster groups (Lawrence, 1987).

Intercollegiate athletics experienced a number of peaks and valleys over the next 60 or so years as budgetary constraints during certain periods, such as the Great Depression and World War II, limited expenditures and growth among athletic departments and sport programs. In looking at the history of intercollegiate athletics, though, the major trends during these years

were increased spectator appeal, commercialism, media coverage, alumni involvement, and funding. As these changes occurred, the majority of intercollegiate athletic departments moved from a unit within the physical education department to a recognized, funded department on campus.

Increased commercialism and the potential for monetary gain in collegiate athletics led to increased pressure on coaches to win. As a result, collegiate athletics experienced various problems with rule violations and academic abuses involving student-athletes. As these abuses increased, the public began to perceive that the integrity of higher education was being threatened. In 1989, pollster Louis Harris found that 78% of Americans thought collegiate athletics were out of hand. This same poll found that nearly two-thirds of Americans believed that state or federal legislation was needed to control college sports (Knight Foundation, 1993). In response, on October 19, 1989, the Trustees of the Knight Foundation created the **Knight Commission**, directing it to propose a reform agenda for intercollegiate athletics (Knight Foundation, 1991). The Knight Commission was composed of university presidents, corporate executive officers (CEOs) and presidents of corporations, and a congressional representative. The reform agenda recommended by the Knight Commission played a major role in supporting legislation to alleviate improper activities and emphasized institutional control in an attempt to restore the integrity of collegiate sports. The Knight Commission's work and recommendations prompted the NCAA membership to pass numerous rules and regulations regarding recruiting activities, academic standards, and financial practices.

Whether improvements have occurred within college athletics as a result of the Knight Commission reform movement and increased presidential involvement has been debated among various constituencies over the years. Proponents of the NCAA and college athletics cite the skill development, increased health benefits, and positive social elements that participation in college athletics brings. In addition, the entertainment value of games and the improved graduation rates of college athletes (although men's basketball and football rates are still a focus of concern) in comparison with the student body overall are referenced. Those critical of college athletics, though, cite the continual recruiting violations, academic abuses, and behavioral problems of athletes and coaches. These critics are concerned with the commercialization and exploitation of student-athletes as well. The "Current Issues" section of this chapter discusses some of the more recent controversial issues and events taking place in college athletics.

Women in Intercollegiate Athletics

Initially, intercollegiate sport competitions were run by men for men. Sports were viewed as male-oriented activities, and women's sport participation was relegated to physical education classes. Prevailing social attitudes mandated that women should not perspire and should not be physically active so as not to injure themselves. Women also had dress codes that limited the type of activities in which they could physically participate. Senda Berenson of Smith College introduced basketball to collegiate women in 1892, but she first made sure that appropriate modifications were made to the game developed by James Naismith to make it more suitable for women (Paul, 1993). According to Berenson, "the selfish display of a star by dribbling and playing the entire court, and roughhousing by snatching the ball could not be tolerated" (Hult, 1994, p. 86). The first women's intercollegiate sport contest was a basketball game between the University of California–Berkeley and Stanford University in 1896 (Hult, 1994).

The predominant theme of women's involvement in athletics was participation. Women physical educators, who controlled women's athletics from the 1890s to 1920s, believed that all girls and women, and not just a few outstanding athletes, should experience the joy of sport. Playdays, or sportsdays, were the norm from the 1920s until the 1960s (Hult, 1994). By 1960, more positive attitudes toward women's competition in sport were set in motion. No governance organization for women similar to the NCAA's all-encompassing control over the men existed until the creation of the **Commission on Intercollegiate Athletics for Women (CIAW)** in 1966, the forerunner of the **Association for Intercollegiate Athletics for Women (AIAW)**, which was established in 1971 (Acosta & Carpenter, 1985).

The AIAW endorsed an alternative athletic model for women, emphasizing the educational needs of students and rejecting the commercialized men's model (Hult, 1994). The AIAW and NCAA soon became engaged in a power struggle over the governance of women's collegiate athletics. In 1981, the NCAA membership voted to add championships for women in Division I. By passing this legislation, the NCAA took its first step toward controlling women's collegiate athletics. The NCAA convinced women's athletic programs to vote to join the NCAA by offering to do the following (Hult, 1994):

- Subsidize team expenses for national championships
- Not charge additional membership dues for the women's program
- Allow women to use the same financial aid, eligibility, and recruitment rules as men
- Provide more television coverage of women's championships

Colleges and universities, provided with these incentives from the NCAA, began to switch from AIAW membership for their women's teams to full NCAA membership. The AIAW immediately experienced a 20% decrease in membership, a

32% drop in championship participation in all divisions, and a 48% drop in Division I championship participation.

In the fall of 1981, NBC notified the AIAW that it would not televise any AIAW championships and would not pay the monies due under its contract (a substantial percentage of the AIAW budget). Consequently, in 1982, the AIAW executive board voted to dissolve the association (Morrison, 1993). The AIAW filed a lawsuit against the NCAA (*Association for Intercollegiate Athletics for Women v. National Collegiate Athletic Association*, 1983), claiming that the NCAA had interfered with its commercial relationship with NBC and exhibited monopolistic practices in violation of antitrust laws. The court found that the AIAW could not support its monopoly claim, effectively ending the AIAW's existence.

Much has changed within women's college athletics since Title IX took effect in 1972. Since 1981, women's participation in collegiate athletics has increased from 74,239 to 182,503 student-athletes in 2008–2009 (NCAA, 2010a). The 2010 NCAA Division I women's basketball championship involving the University of Connecticut against Stanford drew an average of 3.5 million viewers, up 32% from the 2009 championship game (Jenkins, 2010). The popularity and importance of successful women's basketball programs is also reflected in the coaching salaries being provided. In 2010, Geno Auriemma at the University of Connecticut possessed the highest salary, receiving $1.6 million per year in base and other compensation incentives. Pat Summitt at the University of Tennessee earns $1.3 million per year, with Gail Goestenkors of Texas and Kim Mulkey at Baylor also members of the $1 million or more per year women's basketball coaching salary club ("Top paid," 2010). The growth in women's sports provides evidence that college athletics today is both a men's and a women's game and has come far from its birth in 1852.

■ ORGANIZATIONAL STRUCTURE AND GOVERNANCE

The NCAA

The primary rule-making body for college athletics in the United States is the NCAA. Other college athletic organizations include the **National Association of Intercollegiate Athletics (NAIA)**, founded in 1940 for small colleges and universities and having close to 300 member institutions (National Association of Intercollegiate Athletics, 2010), and the **National Junior College Athletic Association (NJCAA)**, founded in 1937 to promote and supervise a national program of junior college sports and activities and currently having approximately 525 member institutions (National Junior College Athletic Association, 2010).

The NCAA is a voluntary association with more than 1,200 institutions, conferences, organizations, and individual members. NCAA **Division I** consists of 335 member institutions (120 in the Football Bowl Subdivision, 118 in the Football Championship Subdivision, and 97 in Division I sponsoring no football program), **Division II** comprises 288 member schools, and there are 432 active institutions within **Division III** (these NCAA division classifications are defined later in this chapter) (NCAA, 2010d). All collegiate athletics teams, conferences, coaches, administrators, and athletes participating in NCAA-sponsored sports must abide by the association's rules.

The basic purpose of the NCAA as dictated in its constitution is to "maintain intercollegiate athletics as an integral part of the educational program and the athlete as an integral part of the student body and, by so doing, retain a clear line of demarcation between intercollegiate athletics and professional sports" (NCAA, 2009a, p. 1). Important to this basic purpose are the cornerstones of the NCAA's philosophy: namely, that college athletics are amateur competitions and that athletics are an important component of the institution's educational mission.

The NCAA has undergone organizational changes throughout its history in an attempt to improve the efficiency of its service to member institutions. In 1956, the NCAA split its membership into a University Division, for larger schools, and a College Division, for smaller schools, in an effort to address competitive inequities. In 1973, the current three-division system, made up of Division I, Division II, and Division III, was created to increase the flexibility of the NCAA in addressing the needs and interests of schools of varying size ("Study: Typical I-A Program," 1996). This NCAA organizational structure involved all member schools and conferences voting on legislation once every year at the NCAA annual convention. Every member school and conference had one vote, assigned to the institution's president or CEO, a structure called **one-school/one-vote**.

In 1995, the NCAA recognized that Divisions I, II, and III still faced "issues and needs unique to its member institutions," leading the NCAA to pass Proposal 7, "Restructuring," at the 1996 NCAA convention (Crowley, 1995). The restructuring plan, which took effect in August 1997, gave the NCAA divisions more responsibility for conduct within their division, gave more control to the presidents of member colleges and universities, and eliminated the one-school/one-vote structure. The NCAA annual convention of all member schools still takes place, but the divisions also hold division-specific miniconventions or meetings. In addition, each division has a governing body called either the Board of Directors (Division I) or Presidents Council (Division II and III), as well as a Leadership Council (Division I) or Management Council (Division II and III) made up of presidents, chancellors, and athletic administrators and faculty athletics representatives from member schools who meet and dictate policy and legislation within that division (**Figure 8-1**). The NCAA Executive Committee, consisting of representatives from each division as well as the NCAA President and chairs of each divisional Leadership or Management Council, oversees the Presidential boards and Leadership or Management Councils for each division.

Under the unique governance structure of the NCAA, the member schools oversee legislation regarding the conduct of intercollegiate athletics. Member institutions and conferences vote on proposed legislation, thus dictating the rules they need to follow. The **NCAA National Office**, located in Indianapolis, Indiana, enforces the rules the membership passes. The NCAA National Office is organized into departments, including administration, business, championships, communications, compliance, enforcement, educational resources, publishing, legislative services, and visitors center/special projects.

Two of the more prominent areas within the NCAA administrative structure are **legislation and governance** and **academics**. These two areas are pivotal because they deal with interpreting new NCAA legislation and enforcing these rules and regulations, while also providing information and guidance about the educational environment, including how student-athletes stay eligible to compete. In August 2002, the Legislative Services Database for the Internet (LSDBi) was launched through NCAA Online (http://www.ncaa.org). The LSDBi provides NCAA members immediate access to NCAA manuals, rule interpretations, administrative-review cases, eligibility issues, and cases of major and secondary infractions. This database is updated whenever legislation is adopted, providing all three divisions with timely access to NCAA legislation (Legislative Services Database, 2010).

The **enforcement** area of the NCAA was created in 1952 when the membership decided that such a mechanism was needed to enforce the association's legislation. The process con-

FIGURE 8-1 NCAA Governance Structure

ASSOCIATION-WIDE COMMITTEES

A. Committee on Competitive Safeguards and Medical Aspects of Sports.
B. Honors Committee.
C. Minority Opportunities and Interests Committee.
D. Olympic Sports Liaison Committee.
E. Postgraduate Scholarship Committee.
F. Research Committee.
G. Committee on Sportsmanship and Ethical Conduct.
H. Walter Byers Scholarship Committee.
I. Committee on Women's Athletics.
J. International Student Records (Divisions I and II).
K. NCAA Committees that have playing rules responsibilities.

EXECUTIVE COMMITTEE

Responsibilities

A. Approval/oversight of budget.
B. Appointment/evaluation of Association's president.
C. Strategic planning for Association.
D. Identification of Association's core issues.
E. To resolve issues/litigation.
F. To convene joint meeting of the three presidential bodies.
G. To convene same-site meeting of Division I Legislative Council and Division II and Division III Management Councils.
H. Authority to call for constitutional votes.
I. Authority to call for vote of entire membership when division actions is contrary to Association's basic principles.
J. Authority to call special/annual Conventions.

Members

A. Eight FBS members from Division I Board of Directors.
B. Two FBS members from Division I Board of Directors.
C. Two Division I members from Division I Board of Directors.
D. Two members from Division II Presidents Couicl.
E. Two members from Division II Presidents Couicl.
F. Ex officio/nonvoting—President.1
G. Ex officio/nonvoting—Chairs of Division I Leadership Coucil and Division II and Division III Management Coucils.

1May vote in case of tie.

DIVISION I
BOARD OF DIRECTORS

Responsibilities

A. Set policy and direction of division.
B. Consider Legislation at its discretion.
C. Delegate responsibilities to Leadership and Legislative Council.

Members

A. Institutional Presidents or Chancellors.

DIVISION I
LEADERSHIP COUNCIL

Responsibilities

A. Recommendations to primary governing body.
B. Handle responsibilities delegated by primary governing body.

Members

A. Athletics administrators.
B. Faculty athletics representatives.

DIVISION I
LEGISLATIVE COUNCIL

Responsibilities

A. Recommendations to primary governing body.
B. Handle responsibilities delegated by primary governing body.

Members

A. Athletics administrators.
B. Faculty athletics representatives.

DIVISION II
PRESIDENTS COUNCIL

Responsibilities

A. Set policy and direction of division.
B. Delegate responsibilities to Management Council.

Members

A. Institutional Presidents or Chancellors.

DIVISION II
MANAGEMENT COUNCIL

Responsibilities

A. Recommendations to primary governing body.
B. Handle responsibilities delegated by primary governing body.

Members

A. Athletics administrators.
B. Faculty athletics representatives.

DIVISION III
PRESIDENTS COUNCIL

Responsibilities

A. Set policy and direction of division.
B. Delegate responsibilities to Management Council.

Members

A. Institutional Presidents or Chancellors.

DIVISION III
MANAGEMENT COUNCIL

Responsibilities

A. Recommendations to primary governing body.
B. Handle responsibilities delegated by primary governing body.

Members

A. Institutional CEOs.
B. Athletics administrators.
C. Faculty athletics representatives.
D. Student-athletes.

Source: National Collegiate Athletic Association. (2010). 2010–2011 NCAA Division I manual. Indianapolis, IN: Author, 29. © National Collegiate Athletic Association. 2010.

sists of allegations of rules violations being referred to the association's investigative staff. The NCAA enforcement staff determines if a potential violation has occurred, with the institution being notified of such finding and the enforcement staff submitting its findings to the Committee on Infractions (NCAA, 2010e). The institution may also conduct its own investigation, reporting its findings to the Committee on Infractions.

If a violation is found, it may be classified as a secondary or a major violation. A secondary violation is defined as "a violation that is isolated or inadvertent in nature, provides or is intended to provide only a minimal recruiting, competitive or other advantage and does not include any significant recruiting inducement or extra benefit" (NCAA, 2009g, p. 289). A major violation is defined as "[A]ll violations other than secondary violations . . . , specifically those that provide an extensive recruiting or competitive advantage" (NCAA, 2009g, p. 290).

It is important to note that although the NCAA National Office staff members collect information and conduct investigations on possible rule violations, the matter still goes before the Committee on Infractions, a committee of peers (representatives of member institutions), which determines responsibility and assesses penalties. Penalties for secondary violations may include, among others, an athlete sitting out for a period of time, forfeiture of games, an institutional fine, or suspension of a coach for one or more competitions. Major violations carry more severe penalties to an institution, including, among others, bans from postseason play, an institutional fine, scholarship reductions, and recruiting restrictions.

The NCAA also has in place committees at the various divisional levels to oversee sports rules and conduct championships. There are also Association-wide groups, such as the Committee on Women's Athletics and the Minority Opportunities and Interests Committee, which examine issues specific to certain segments of the NCAA

membership as well as the Student-Athlete Advisory Committee that provides student-athletes at each divisional level representation in the NCAA's governance structure (NCAA, 2010f).

Divisions I, II, and III

The latest NCAA organizational restructuring, which became effective in 1997, called for divisions to take more responsibility and control over their activities. This was due to the recognition of substantial differences among the divisions, both in terms of their philosophies as well as the way they do business. A few of the more prominent differences among divisions are highlighted in this section. The sport management student interested in pursuing a career in intercollegiate coaching or athletic administration should be knowledgeable about the differences in legislation and philosophies among the divisions so as to choose a career within the division most suited to his or her interests. Students should be aware that each institution has its own philosophy regarding the structure and governance of its athletic department. In addition, generalizations regarding divisions are not applicable to all institutions within that division. For example, some Division III institutions, although not offering any athletic scholarships, can be described as following a nationally competitive, revenue-producing philosophy that is more in line with a Division I philosophy. The student should thoroughly research an athletic department to determine the philosophy that the school and administration embraces.

Division I member institutions, in general, support the philosophy of competitiveness, generating revenue through athletics, and national success. This philosophy is reflected in the following principles taken from the Division I Philosophy Statement (NCAA, 2009h):

- Strives in its athletics program for regional and national excellence and prominence

- Recognizes the dual objective in its athletics program of serving both the university or college community (participants, student body, faculty/staff, alumni) and the general public (community, area, state, nation)
- Sponsors at the highest feasible level of intercollegiate competition one or both of the traditional spectator-oriented, income-producing sports of football and basketball

Division I athletic departments are usually larger in terms of the number of sport programs sponsored, the number of coaches, and the number of administrators. Division I member institutions have to sponsor at least seven sports of all-male or mixed-gender teams and seven all-female teams, or six sports of all-male or mixed-gender teams and eight all-female teams (NCAA, 2009i). Division I athletic departments also have larger budgets due to the number of athletic scholarships allowed, the operational budgets needed for the larger number of sport programs sponsored, and the salary costs associated with the larger number of coaches and administrators.

Division I schools that have football are further divided into two subdivisions: **Football Bowl Subdivision (FBS)** is the category for the somewhat larger football-playing schools in Division I and was formerly called Division I-A, and the **Football Championship Subdivision (FCS)** is the category for institutions playing football at the next level and was formerly called Division I-AA. FBS institutions must meet minimum attendance requirements for football as well as higher standards for sports sponsorship (16 teams rather than the minimum of 14 teams required of Division I members), whereas FCS institutions are not held to any attendance requirements. Division I institutions that do not sponsor a football team do not have a FBS or FCS classification (NCAA 2009j).

Division II institutions usually attract student-athletes from the local or in-state area who may receive some athletic scholarship money

but usually not a full ride. Division II athletics programs must offer at least 10 sports (at least four to five for men and five to six for women) and sponsor at least two team sports for each gender (NCAA, 2010d).

Division III institutions do not allow athletic scholarships and encourage participation by maximizing the number and variety of athletics opportunities available to students. Division III institutions also emphasize the participant's experience, rather than the experience of the spectator, and place primary emphasis on regional in-season and conference competition (NCAA, 2010d).

Conferences

The organizational structure of intercollegiate athletics also involves **member conferences** of the NCAA. Member conferences must have a minimum of six member institutions within a single division to be recognized as a voting member conference of the NCAA (NCAA, 2009b). Conferences provide many benefits and services to their member institutions. For example, conferences have their own compliance director and run seminars regarding NCAA rules and regulations in an effort to better educate member schools' coaches and administrators. Conferences also have legislative power over their member institutions in the running of championship events and the formulation of conference rules and regulations. Conferences sponsor championships in sports sponsored by the member institutions within the conference. The conference member institutions vote on the conference guidelines to determine the organization of these conference championships. Conferences may also provide a revenue-sharing program to their member institutions in which revenue realized by the conference through NCAA distributions, TV contracts, or participation in football bowl games is shared among all member institutions. The increase in TV contracts with conferences over the years has contributed substantially to the revenue sharing plans within conferences, but of even greater significance was the emergence of conferences owning their own television networks. The Big Ten Conference distributed $22 million per institution in 2009 as a result of revenue received from the Big Ten Network (Kalafa, 2010).

Conferences have their own **conference rules**. Member institutions of a particular conference must adhere to conference rules in addition to NCAA rules. It is important to note, though, that although a conference rule can never be less restrictive than an NCAA rule, many conferences maintain additional rules that hold member institutions to stricter standards. For example, the Ivy League is a Division I NCAA member conference, but it prohibits its member institutions from providing athletic scholarships to student-athletes. Therefore, the Ivy League schools, although competing against other Division I schools that allow athletic scholarships, do not allow their athletic departments to award athletic scholarships.

Conference realignment is an issue that has occurred periodically affecting the landscape of college athletics. Some of the reasons for a school's wanting to join a conference or change conference affiliation are (1) exposure from television contracts with existing conferences, (2) potential for more revenue from television and corporate sponsorships through conference revenue sharing, (3) the difficulty independent schools experience in scheduling games and generating revenue, and (4) the ability of a conference to hold a championship game in football, which can generate millions of dollars in revenue for the conference schools if the conference possesses at least 12 member institutions. The most recent conference realignment taking place in 2010 speaks to the revenue sharing gain that can be experienced, as Nebraska will benefit greatly from joining the Big Ten Conference due to the Big Ten Network monies that each Big Ten institution receives ("Nebraska approved by Big Ten," 2010).

One of the biggest conference realignments involved the demise of the 80-year-old Southwest Conference. In 1990, the Southwest Conference (SWC) comprised nine member schools (Mott, 1994). In August 1990, the University of Arkansas accepted a bid to leave the Southwest Conference and join the Southeast Conference (SEC). The university stated that the SEC gave it bigger crowds in revenue-producing sports and more national exposure ("Broyles Hopes," 1990). In 1994, four Southwest Conference schools—Texas, Texas A&M, Baylor, and Texas Tech—announced they were leaving to join the Big Eight Conference (Mott, 1994). In April 1994, three other SWC schools—Rice, Texas Christian University, and Southern Methodist University—joined the Western Athletic Conference (WAC) ("Western Athletic," 1994). Thus, the Southwest Conference had lost all of its member schools except Houston. This led to the demise of the Southwest Conference because it dropped below the six-member school minimum required by the NCAA for recognition as a member conference. Houston, the sole remaining SWC school, joined Conference USA in 1995.

The demise of the Southwest Conference due to conference realignment was rivaled by the 2003–2004 realignment that affected six Division I-A (now called FBS) conferences. This realignment was initiated by the movement of the University of Miami, Virginia Tech, and Boston College from the Big East Conference to the Atlantic Coast Conference. With three of its eight football-playing schools leaving for the ACC, the Big East invited five schools from Conference USA (Cincinnati, Louisville, South Florida, Marquette, and DePaul) to join it (Lee, 2003). Conference USA also lost two schools (St. Louis and University of North Carolina–Charlotte) to the Atlantic 10 Conference. Conference USA subsequently went looking for schools for its conference, with Marshall and Central Florida from the Mid-American Conference, and Southern Methodist University, Tulsa, Texas–El Paso, and Rice from the Western Athletic

Conference accepting the invitation (C-USA Milestones, 2010). The Western Athletic Conference added New Mexico State and Utah State from the Sun Belt Conference (Lee, 2003). More recently, in 2010 there were four institutions changing conferences (Nebraska from the Big 12 to the Big Ten, Colorado from the Big 12 to the Pac 10, Utah from the Mountain West to the Pac 10, and Boise State departing the Western Athletic Conference and joining the Mountain West Conference). There is sure to be more conference shuffling among NCAA member institutions as the conferences seek stability and individual institutions seek potential revenue gains from conference affiliation.

■ CAREER OPPORTUNITIES

For many decades, the traditional route followed for a career in collegiate athletics was to be an athlete, then a coach, and then an athletic administrator. It was a very closed system, with college athletic administrators selecting from among their own who would coach teams and then move into administrative positions. A 1992 study of Division I and Division III athletic directors found that 86% of the athletic directors in both divisions had been athletes at the col-

legiate level, while 78% in Division I and 90% in Division III had collegiate coaching experience (Barr, 1992). Yet, when asked whether more emphasis in the hiring process was placed on the athletic participation and coaching experience or the educational background of the applicant, the athletic directors in both Division I and Division III emphasized the importance of educational background over athletic participation and coaching experience (Barr, 1992). Much has changed since the original apprentice system used in college athletics, though, with athletic administrators being able to understand the financial and legal complexities that are a part of college athletics today.

Coaches and Athletic Directors

Differences exist among the divisions in terms of coaching and administrative duties and responsibilities. When moving from the smaller Division III institutions to the larger Division I institutions, the responsibilities and profiles of coaches within these athletic departments change. At the smaller Division III institutions, the coaches are usually part-time, or if full-time, they serve as coach to numerous sport programs. These coaches may also hold an academic appointment within a department or teach activities classes. The Division III coach's budget on average is smaller than that of a Division I coach because most competition is regional and recruiting is not as extensive. There are no athletic scholarships allowed in Division III. Division III athletic directors may sometimes also coach or hold an academic appointment. Depending on the size of the athletic department, the Division III athletic director may wear many hats, acting as manager of the athletic department and coaches, business manager of the athletic department budget, media relations staff person, fundraiser, and compliance officer. Some Division III athletic directors (ADs), due to the size of the athletic department, have a staff of assistant or associate athletic directors providing administrative help in these various areas.

Athletic department budgets at the Division I, and especially FBS, level are in the tens of millions of dollars. It is common at this level to find coaches and assistant coaches employed full-time coaching one sport program. Athletic scholarships are allowed, increasing the importance of recruiting, travel, and other activities geared toward signing blue-chip athletes. Individual sport program budgets are larger, providing more resources for recruiting and competitive travel opportunities. Division I athletic departments usually employ a large number of associate and assistant athletic directors with specialized responsibilities. The athletic director usually attends public relations and fund-raising events, participates in negotiating television contracts, and looks out for the interests of the athletic department in the development of institutional policies and financial affairs.

As college athletics has become more complex and business-like, colleges and universities have looked to the corporate world for CEOs or administrators with business backgrounds to run their athletics department. University of Florida President Bernard Machen, in talking about Florida AD Jeremy Foley, states, "The athletic director is more like a CEO of a corporation than a guy who hires coaches. Jeremy oversees everything from the sale of bonds for capital construction to tickets and sponsorships, and he manages more than 500 employees" (Eichelberger, 2009). To assist in the hiring process and identify key corporate world candidates to take over as athletic director, these schools are using search firms. Chuck Neinas, founder of Neinas Sports Services in Boulder, Colorado, and a former Big Eight Conference Commissioner, has helped place athletic directors at the University of Kansas, University of Missouri, and the University of Oklahoma among others. Neinas states that the days of

hiring the retired football coach to run the athletic department are long gone. Today's athletic directors need years of practical experience and contacts, and need skills in budgeting, hiring coaches, sports marketing, and fundraising as well (Eichelberger, 2009). Similar to the stock options and performance-based bonuses used in the business world, college athletic directors also are negotiating bonus clauses in their contract based on performance in areas such as wins and postseason appearances for high-profile teams, fiscal management within the athletic department, graduation rate of student-athletes, and lack of NCAA violations and probation of teams, to name a few (Bennett, 2003).

Assistant or Associate Athletic Director Areas of Responsibility

Reporting to the athletic director are assistant and associate athletic director positions functioning in specialized areas, such as business manager, media relations director, ticket sales manager, fund development coordinator, director of marketing, sport programs administrator, facilities and events coordinator, academic affairs director, or compliance coordinator. Depending on the student's interest, various educational coursework will be helpful in preparing for a position in these areas. For example, business courses will prepare the student for positions working within the business aspect of an athletic department, communications courses will prepare the student for a position working with public relations and the media, educational counseling coursework is beneficial for positions within academic affairs, and a legal background will be helpful to administrators overseeing the compliance area.

Areas of growth where increased attention is being directed within collegiate athletic departments are **student-athlete services**, **fund development**, and **compliance**. Student-athlete services addresses the academic concerns and welfare of student-athletes, overseeing such areas as academic advising, tutoring, and counseling. Fund development has increased in importance as athletic departments seek new ways to increase revenues. Fund development coordinators oversee alumni donations to the athletic department and also oversee fund-raising events. Compliance is the term used to describe adherence to NCAA and conference rules and regulations. The compliance coordinator works closely with the coaches to make sure they are knowledgeable about NCAA and conference rules. The compliance coordinator also oversees the initial and continuing eligibility of the student-athletes as well as being directly involved in preventing or investigating any violations that take place within the athletic department.

Two other positions important to the collegiate athletic department are the **senior women's administrator (SWA)** and the **faculty athletics representative (FAR)**. The senior women's administrator is the highest-ranking female administrator involved with the conduct of an NCAA member institution's intercollegiate athletics program (NCAA, 2009d). The faculty athletics representative is a member of an institution's faculty or administrative staff who is designated to represent the institution and its faculty in the institution's relationships with the NCAA and its conference (NCAA, 2009c).

Conference/NCAA or Other Association Opportunities

Opportunities for students interested in a career in college athletics exist within the NCAA member conferences as well as in the NCAA itself. With the specialization of positions and increased activities taking place within the athletic department, conference administration and management activities have followed a similar path. The size of athletic conference staffs has increased over the years, with conference administrators being hired to oversee growth areas such as conference championships, television negotiations, marketing activities, and compliance services offered to member schools.

The NCAA, as well as other college athletic associations such as the NJCAA and NAIA involved in the governance of college athletics, employs numerous staff members. Students may be interested in pursuing a career in college athletics at the NCAA, NJCAA, or NAIA National Office level.

At whatever level or area in which the student is interested, one thing must be kept in mind: A job in college athletics is hard to come by because many people are trying to break into this segment of the sport industry. Therefore, students should set themselves apart from all the other applicants for the position to get noticed and hired. The way to do this is to prepare yourself academically by taking appropriate coursework and excelling in the classroom, to volunteer or help out in any way possible with the athletic department at your institution to gain valuable experience that you can include on your resume, to network and get to know people working in the industry because it is an industry that relies on who you know and word-of-mouth during the hiring process, and to pursue fulfilling an internship. Even if unpaid, the internship gives you a valuable first step into the industry, where you then have the ability to prove yourself so that you can be hired into that first job.

■ CURRENT ISSUES

Current issues affecting collegiate athletics abound and are constantly changing. Coaches and athletic administrators must be aware of the financial, legal, managerial, and ethical impact of these issues.

Title IX/Gender Equity

Perhaps no greater issue has affected collegiate athletic departments over the past couple of decades than **Title IX** or gender equity. As discussed in Chapter 5, Legal Principles Applied to Sport Management, Title IX is a federal law passed in 1972 that prohibits sex discrimination in any educational activity or program receiving federal financial assistance. Early in its history, there was much confusion as to whether Title IX applied to college athletic departments. Title IX gained its enforcement power among college athletic departments with the passage of the 1988 Civil Rights Restoration Act. In 1991, the NCAA released the results of a gender-equity study that found that although the undergraduate enrollment on college campuses was roughly 50% male and 50% female, collegiate athletic departments on average were made up of 70% male and 30% female student-athletes. In addition, this NCAA study found that the male student-athletes were receiving 70% of the athletic scholarship money, 77% of the operational budget, and 83% of the recruiting dollars available (NCAA Gender Equity Task Force, 1991). In response to such statistics, an increase in the number of sex discrimination lawsuits took place, with the courts often ruling in favor of the female student-athletes.

Collegiate athletic administrators started to realize that Title IX would be enforced by the Office for Civil Rights (OCR) and the courts, and as athletic administrators they would be required to provide equity within their athletic departments. The struggle athletic administrators are faced with is how to comply with Title IX given institutional financial limitations, knowing that lack of funding is not an excuse for not complying with Title IX. To bring male and female participation numbers closer to the percentage of undergraduate students by sex at the institution, numerous institutions are choosing to eliminate sport programs for men, thereby reducing the participation and funding on the men's side. Another method selected by some institutions is capping roster sizes for men's teams, known as **roster management**, thus keeping the men's numbers in check while try-

ing to increase women's participation. A third, and most appropriate, option under Title IX is increasing participation and funding opportunities for female student-athletes. Of course, in selecting this option, the athletic administrator must be able to raise the funds necessary to add sport programs, hire new coaches, and provide uniforms for the new sport programs.

The debate surrounding Title IX continues, with numerous organizations (e.g., the National Women's Law Center, Women's Sports Foundation, and National Organization for Women), as well as advocates within the college athletic setting, arguing the merits of Title IX and that the appropriate enforcement methods are being used. In contrast, though, organizations such as USA Gymnastics and the National Wrestling Coaches Association are concerned about the effects Title IX has had on their sport (men's teams) and in particular are questioning the appropriateness of certain Title IX compliance standards. About 400 men's college teams were eliminated during the 1990s, with the sport of men's wrestling being hit particularly hard. The National Wrestling Coaches Association filed a lawsuit against the Department of Education arguing that the male student-athletes were being discriminated against as a result of the Title IX enforcement standards directly causing a reduction in men's sports. This lawsuit was dismissed in May 2004, with an appeals court panel ruling that the parties lacked standing to file the lawsuit, which instead should be litigated against individual colleges that eliminated men's sports ("Appeals Court," 2004). To date, these types of lawsuits have not been effective for male student-athletes. In May 2004, Myles Brand, former president of the NCAA, endorsed Title IX while speaking at a meeting of the National Wrestling Coaches Association, stating that it should not be used as an excuse or a cause for elimination of sport programs. Instead, these are institutional decisions reflected in the statistic that although the number of men's wrestling and gymnastics teams, among others, has declined over the past two decades (from 363 to 222), the number of football teams over the same time period has increased (from 497 to 619) ("Brand Defends Title IX," 2004).

The most recent issue involving Title IX compliance involves the definition of what constitutes a qualified sport program for women. In July 2010, a federal judge ruled that Quinnipiac University was violating Title IX by failing to provide equal athletic opportunities to female students. In March 2009 Quinnipiac University in Hamden, Connecticut announced the school was cutting three sport teams: women's volleyball, men's golf, and men's outdoor track. The school also stated that it was establishing varsity cheerleading beginning in the 2009–2010 season. Five female student volleyball players and the coach of the volleyball team filed suit claiming that Quinnipiac was violating Title IX (Mahony, 2010). In his ruling, U.S. District Judge Stefan Underhill stated that the competitive cheerleading team does not qualify as a varsity sport for the purposes of Title IX and, therefore, its members may not be counted as athletic participants under the statute (*Biediger et al v. Quinnipiac University*, 2010) (For further information on this case and gender equity, see Chapter 5, Legal Principles).

Hiring Practices for Minorities and Women

Minority hiring has long been an issue of concern and debate within collegiate athletics. In 1993–1994, the NCAA's Minority Opportunity and Interests Committee found that African Americans accounted for fewer than 10% of athletic directors and 8% of head coaches, and when predominantly African-American institutions were eliminated from the study, the results dropped to 4% representation in both categories (Wieberg, 1994). The more recent 2008–2009 NCAA data do not show much improvement, with only about 4% of all athletic directors being black (Brown, 2010). Modest improvements have been made in the coaching profession as representation for minority head coaches for both men's and women's teams has increased approximately 3% since 1995–1996 (Brown, 2010).

The Black Coaches and Administrators Association (BCA; formally called the Black Coaches Association) in October 2003 announced the establishment of a "hiring report card" to monitor football hiring practices at major institutions. Grades are based on contact with the BCA during the hiring process, efforts to interview candidates of color, the number of minorities involved in the hiring process, the time frame for each search, and adherence to institutional affirmative action hiring policies (Dufresne, 2003). In Fall 2009, Randi Shannon at the University of Miami was the only black head coach at one of the six major conferences that make up the Bowl Championship Series (BCS). In Fall 2010, Shannon was joined by the new hires of Charlie Strong at Louisville, Turner Gill at Kansas, and Mike London at Virginia. There were a total of 13 head coaches of color at FBS schools during the Fall 2010 season after seven got jobs since the end of the 2009 season (Strange, 2010).

Women have also lacked appropriate representation among administrators at the collegiate level. In 1996, women represented 17 (5.6%) of the 305 Division I athletic director positions, with only 6 of these 17 female athletic directors at Division I-A (now FBS) institutions (Blauvelt, 1996). In Division II, 36 (14.6%) of the 246 athletic directors were female, and in Division III 84 (23.9%) of the 351 athletic directors were female (Blauvelt, 1996). More recent statistics (2008–2009) show a slight improvement, with women accounting for 9.4% of Division I athletic director positions (32 out of 341), 16.8% in Division II (49 out of 291), and 27.5% in Division III (124 out of 451) (NCAA, 2010c). This issue continues to demand—appropriately so—the attention of college athletic directors, in the hiring of coaches, and of institutional presidents, in the hiring of athletic directors.

Academic Reform

Since the early 1990s and the publication of the Knight Commission reports that criticized the NCAA's academic legislation and academic preparation of student-athletes, the NCAA has been involved in numerous **academic reform** measures. The Knight Commission noted that although Proposition 48 was in place (to be eligible to play his or her first year in college, the student-athlete was required to possess a 2.0 minimum grade-point average [GPA] in 11 high school core curriculum courses while also meeting a minimum 700 SAT requirement [equates to an 820 score under the "revised" SAT]), student-athlete graduation rates were low. Student-athletes could maintain eligibility to compete in athletics while not adequately progressing toward a degree (Knight Foundation, 1991). Satisfactory progress requirements were added, requiring student-athletes to possess a minimum GPA while taking an appropriate percentage of degree-required courses each year.

In response to concern that the SAT may be biased and in an attempt to increase the graduation rates of student-athletes, Proposition 16 went into effect in 1996–1997. This initial eligibility academic legislation required student-athletes to possess a minimum GPA in 13 core courses, with a corresponding SAT score along a sliding scale. If the student-athlete had a minimum GPA of 2.0, he or she needed a minimum SAT score of 1010. The student-athlete would then need to possess a corresponding GPA and SAT score along a scale to the minimum SAT of 820, which corresponded with a 2.5 GPA requirement. This legislation was changed through Bylaw 14.3, which became effective for all student-athletes entering a collegiate institution on or after August 1, 2005. Bylaw 14.3 requires student-athletes to meet a minimum GPA standard in 14 core courses, with a corresponding SAT score, but the sliding scale was changed to range from a 2.0 GPA with a 1010 SAT minimum to a 3.55 GPA with a minimum 400 SAT (NCAA, 2009f). In addition, satisfactory progress requirements were made more stringent to push student-athletes toward graduating within six years.

The NCAA initiated the latest academic reform proposal, the **Academic Progress Rate (APR)** in the fall of 2004. The APR collects data on a team's academic results based on eligibility and retention of student-athletes each academic year. The APR is calculated by awarding up to two points per student-athlete per semester or quarter (one point for being enrolled and one point for being on track to graduate or eligibility). The total points earned are divided by the total possible points with a benchmark of 925. An APR score of 925 predicts an approximately 50 percent Graduation Success Rate (GSR). The sport's APR is then based on the past four years' performance. Teams scoring below 925 can face penalties, such as scholarship losses and restrictions on practice and competition ("Most Division I," 2010).

Academic progress, academic preparations, and the graduation rate of student-athletes will continue to be issues of importance as college athletics and the educational mission of colleges and universities continue to coexist.

Agents, Gambling and Amateurism (AGA)

Over the past ten years the NCAA has placed additional emphasis in the areas of agents and gambling to assist student-athletes with these issues and how they may impact their amateur status. On June 20, 2010, the NCAA handed down sanctions on the University of Southern California (USC) football team as a result of improper benefits Heisman Trophy running back Reggie Bush received from his involvement with agents while still competing as a student-athlete at USC. The penalties include the loss of 30 football scholarships over three years, vacating 14 victories in which Bush played, and a two-year post-season bowl ban for the football team (Beachem, 2010). According to NCAA Bylaw 12.3: "An individual shall be ineligible for participation in an intercollegiate sport if he or she ever has agreed (orally or in writing) to be represented by an agent for the purpose of marketing his or her athletics ability or reputation in that sport (NCAA, 2009e, p. 69)." This bylaw also spells out how the student-athlete will be deemed ineligible if they accept or receive benefits from a prospective agent. Many states have passed laws that criminalize behaviors by agents that jeopardize the amateur status of collegiate student-athletes. The NCAA, through the **Agents, Gambling and Amateurism (AGA)** area, is also working to not only investigate alleged violations of involvement by student-athletes with agents, but also to inform and educate student-athletes and agents themselves surrounding acceptable and unacceptable practices.

According to the NCAA's 2008 gambling survey, about 30% of male student-athletes and 7% of female student-athletes reported wagering on sporting events within the past year (*Results from the 2008 NCAA study on collegiate wagering*, 2009). With the proliferation of the Internet, sports gambling has become easier to access with virtual anonymity by anyone, including student-athletes. As well, student-athletes within revenue-producing sports may be viewed as easy targets by organized crime or gambling units. In addition to NCAA legislation that prohibits sports wagering activities, the NCAA tries to proactively educate student-athletes and coaches on the dangers of sports wagering by producing information materials, holding information sessions, creating an interactive educational Web site among other activities (College sports betting, 2010). The NCAA also conducts background checks of officials and umpires in select, high-profile sport competitions (College sports betting, 2010).

New Technologies

As with many industries and disciplines today, college athletics has been impacted both negatively and positively by the explosion of new technologies and their usage. With the development of technological advances in communication methods and the widespread availability of various electronic communication devices, the use of such technology in the recruiting process has increased exponentially. The NCAA has since needed to revise and update its policies to keep up with new technologies and social media sites, in particular in regards to recruitment activities. NCAA rules do not allow comments or photos about possible recruits on an institution's social media page or a page belonging to someone affiliated with the institution. In addition, messages cannot be sent to recruits using these social media technologies other than through their e-mail function ("Social media and recruiting," 2010). Text messaging is not permissible, but a prospect (high school student-athlete being recruited) may elect to receive direct messages as text messages on a mobile device. Twitter has also become a popular recruiting tool and is permissible as long as coaches are not using it to contact individual prospective student-athletes ("Social media and recruiting," 2010).

Beyond the usage of technology for recruiting purposes, the World Wide Web has infiltrated the college athletic ranks through such sites as Facebook.com, MySpace.com, and Badjocks.com. In 2006, pictures of University of South Florida football players as well as members of the baseball and volleyball teams engaged in underage drinking were posted to Facebook ("Athletes' online pics causing concern," 2006). Photographs of hazing found on Badjocks.com resulted in the May 2006 suspension of the Northwestern University women's soccer team (Sandomir, 2006). Blogs, personal Web sites, and social networking sites, such as Facebook and MySpace, have made policing improper contact between fans and athletes all but impossible, while forcing athletic departments to take disciplinary action against the growing number of student-athletes found through these Web sites to be engaged in improper behavior.

These new technologies can be used in positive ways, for example: to help market various sports and college athletic department activities, sell tickets to college sporting events, help in the promotion of a student-athlete for the Heisman or some other athletic award, and help garner additional revenues to the athletic department via video streaming or the selling of Internet media rights. The key for athletic administrators will be in providing appropriate oversight and establishing social media policies for athletes, coaches, and the athletic department staff so that these new technologies can be used in positive ways.

■ SUMMARY

Sport management students and future athletic department employees need to be aware that intercollegiate athletics, as a major segment of the sport industry, is experiencing numerous organizational, managerial, financial, and legal issues. The NCAA, first organized in 1905, has undergone organizational changes throughout its history to accommodate the needs of its member institutions. Knowing the NCAA organizational structure is important because it provides information about the power and communication structures within the organization.

It is also important for students to know the differences that exist among the various divisions within the NCAA membership structure. These differences involve the allowance of athletic scholarships, budget and funding opportunities, and competitive philosophies. Distinct differences exist among divisions and even among schools within a particular division. Students, future collegiate athletic administrators, and coaches must become informed of these differences if they hope to select the career within a school or NCAA membership division that best fits their interests and philosophies.

In pursuing an administrative job within collegiate athletics, the sport management student should be aware of and work on developing skills that current athletic directors have identified as important. These skills include marketing expertise, strong public speaking and writing skills, creative and problem-solving abilities, the ability to manage complex financial issues, and the ability to manage and work with parents, students, faculty, alumni, booster groups, and sponsors. Appropriate coursework and preparation in these areas can better prepare the student interested in a career in collegiate athletic administration.

Probably the most important quality a coach or administrator needs to possess is being informed and knowledgeable about issues currently affecting this sport industry segment. Perhaps the most prominent issue currently affecting collegiate athletic departments is Title IX and gender equity. Coaches and administrators must educate themselves in understanding what the law requires and how to comply with it. Another issue foremost in collegiate athletic administrators' minds is finances. Today, millions of dollars go into athletic department budgets, and television contracts play a large role in the operation and scheduling of intercollegiate athletic competitions. Staying on top of these and other issues affecting college athletics is important for all coaches, administrators, and people involved in the governance and operation of this sport industry segment.

CASE STUDY: The Role of an Athletic Director

Rebecca Jones has thoroughly enjoyed her job as athletic director at a Division FCS institution. She has always enjoyed the day-to-day activities of managing a $25 million athletic budget, overseeing 25 sport programs (well beyond the minimum 14 needed for NCAA Division I membership), and interacting with the 15 assistant and associate athletic directors. But when she came into work one spring Monday morning, she knew some very difficult days were ahead of her that would test her managerial, financial, and communication skills. At the lacrosse game on Saturday, the chancellor cornered Rebecca to let her know of an emergency meeting the state legislators had the previous day. The governor was forwarding, with the legislators' endorsement, a budget that called for a 10% reduction to the university's budget starting July 1. The chancellor, in turn, told Rebecca that she would need to reduce the $25 million athletic budget by 10% (or $2.5 million). Word spread quickly of this impending budget cut, and there in her office early on this spring morning were three head coaches (men's soccer, men's swimming, and women's volleyball). Rebecca has always employed an open-door philosophy encouraging any coach, student-athlete, student, or faculty member at the university to stop by and talk to her whenever he or she had a question or concern. Rebecca could tell by the faces of these three coaches that they were worried that their sport programs, and their jobs, would be eliminated as part of the budget reduction.

Rebecca invited the coaches into her office and began to listen to what they had to say. The men's soccer coach was concerned that his was a low-profile sport and therefore was easily expendable. The men's swimming coach was concerned that even though he had been modestly successful over the years, the pool was in drastic need of repair—an expense the university could not afford—and therefore he felt it made the men's swimming program a target for elimination. The women's volleyball coach was concerned because of the high cost of volleyball (a fully funded sport at the university), with a huge potential savings possible by cutting just this one sport program. Also, volleyball wasn't as popular in the region and therefore wasn't drawing a lot of fan support.

As Rebecca was talking to the coaches, her administrative assistant interrupted to tell her that the local newspapers had been calling for a comment, and a local television station was camped outside the basketball arena interviewing coaches as they came to work. The administrative assistant overheard one of the questions being asked by the reporter: "Whether the Division FCS football program, that had been running a deficit of between $1.3 million and $2.2 million per year over the past couple of years, should be dropped completely or go non-scholarship?" Rebecca knew she had two initial concerns: one of an immediate nature, dealing with the media, and the second of a communication nature, regarding the coaches and administrators within the department. The chancellor asked her to submit a preliminary report in two weeks, so she had a little bit of time to address the bigger issue: What to do?

Questions for Discussion

1. Put yourself in Rebecca's position. What is the first thing that you should do with the media and with the coaches and other athletic department administrators?
2. What types of information and data does Rebecca need to collect to make a decision on how to handle cutting $2.5 million from the athletic department's budget?
3. If you were Rebecca, would you involve anyone in the decision-making process or make the decision by yourself? If involving other people, who would they be and why would they be an important part of the process?
4. What types of communication need to take place, and how would you go about communicating this information?
5. What are some potential solutions in terms of budget reduction? What are the possible ramifications surrounding these solutions?
6. If you choose to eliminate sport programs, what criteria would you use to determine which teams are eliminated?

■ RESOURCES

National Association for Intercollegiate Athletics (NAIA)
> 1200 Grand Blvd.
> Kansas City, MO 64106
> 816-595-8000
> http://naia.cstv.com

National Association of Collegiate Directors of Athletics (NACDA)
> 24651 Detroit Road
> Westlake, OH 44145
> 440-892-4000
> http://www.nacda.com

National Association of Collegiate Women's Athletic Administrators (NACWAA)
> 2000 Baltimore, Ste. 100
> Kansas City, MO 64108
> 816-389-8200
> http://www.nacwaa.org

National Collegiate Athletic Association (NCAA)
> 700 W. Washington Street
> P.O. Box 6222
> Indianapolis, IN 46206-6222
> 317-917-6222
> http://www.ncaa.org

The NCAA, through its member login function on the Web site, provides a number of resources helpful to collegiate athletic administrators and coaches, including the NCAA Manual, links for Legislation and Governance as well as Academics and Athletes, and News/Updates items.

National Junior College Athletic Association (NJCAA)
> 1755 Telstar Drive, Suite 103
> Colorado Springs, CO 80920
> 719-590-9788
> http://www.njcaa.org

National Women's Law Center
> 11 Dupont Circle NW, Suite 800
> Washington, DC 20036
> 202-588-5180
> http://www.nwlc.org

Women's Sports Foundation
> Eisenhower Park
> 1899 Hempstead Turnpike, Suite 400
> East Meadow, NY 11554
> 516-542-4700
> http://www.womenssportsfoundation.org

■ KEY TERMS

Academic Progress Rate (APR), academic reform, academics, Agents, Gambling and Amateurism (AGA), Association for Intercollegiate Athletics for Women (AIAW), Big Ten Conference, Carnegie Reports of 1929, Commission on Intercollegiate Athletics for Women (CIAW), compliance, conference realignment, conference rules, Division I, Division II, Division III, enforcement, faculty athletics representative (FAR), Football Bowl Subdivision (FBS), Football Championship Subdivision (FCS), fund development, Intercollegiate Athletic Association of the United States (IAAUS), Intercollegiate Conference of Faculty Representatives, Intercollegiate Football Association, Knight Commission, legislation and governance, member conferences, National Association of Intercollegiate Athletics (NAIA), National Collegiate Athletic Association (NCAA), National Junior College Athletic Association (NJCAA), NCAA National Office, one-school/one-vote, roster management, senior women's administrator (SWA), student-athlete services, Title IX.

■ REFERENCES

Acosta, R. V., & Carpenter, L. J. (1985). Women in sport. In D. Chu, J. O. Segrave, & B. J. Becker (Eds.), *Sport and higher education* (pp. 313–325). Champaign, IL: Human Kinetics.

Appeals court: Individual colleges to blame for cuts. (2004, May 14). *ESPN.com.* Retrieved October 19, 2010, from http://sports.espn.go.com/espn/news/story?id=1801717

Association for Intercollegiate Athletics for Women v. National Collegiate Athletic Association. 558 F. Supp. 487 (D.D.C. 1983).

Athletes' online pics causing concern. (2006, April 27). The Oracle. Retrieved November 22, 2010, from http://www.usforacle.com/2.5741/athletes-online-pics-causing-concern-1.623293

Barr, C. A. (1992). A comparative study of Division I and Division III athletic directors: Their profiles and the necessary qualifications they deem as essential in their positions. Unpublished master's thesis, University of Massachusetts, Amherst.

Beachem, G. (2010, June 10). NCAA drops the hammer on USC football. Retrieved October 19, 2010, from http://nbcsports.msnbc.com/id/37621070/ns/sports-college_football/

Bennett, B. (2003, July 13). Athletic directors: In the money; bonus clauses pay for wins, good grades, bottom line. *The Courier-Journal,* p. C11.

Biediger et al v. Quinnipiac University. Case No. 3:09cv621 (SRU), (U.S. Dist. Ct., 2010).

Blauvelt, H. (1996, October 2). Women slowly crack athletic director ranks. *USA Today,* p. 1C.

Brand defends Title IX. (2004, May 21). LubbockOnline.com. Retrieved October 19, 2010, from http://lubbockonline.com/stories/052104/col_0521040012.shtml

Brown, G. (2010, May 19). NCAA study shows slow progress with women and minority hiring. *The NCAA News.* Retrieved October 19, 2010, from http://www.ncaa.org/wps/wcm/connect//ncaa/ncaa/ncaa+news/ncaa+news+online/2010/association-wide/ncaa+study+shows+slow+progress+with+women+and+minority+hiring_05_19_10_ncaa_news

Broyles hopes a move won't end Arkansas' SWC rivalries. (1990, August 1). *The NCAA News,* p. 20.

College sports betting–NCAA official statement (2010). Retrieved October 19, 2010, from http://www.ncaa.org/wps/portal/ncaahome?WCM_GLOBAL_CONTEXT=/ncaa/ncaa/media+and+events/press+room/current+issues/sports+wagering

Crowley, J. N. (1995, December 18). History demonstrates that change is good. *The NCAA News,* p. 4.

C-USA Milestones (2010). C-USA. Retrieved November 22, 2010, from http://conferenceusa.cstv.com/ot/c-usa-milestones.html

Davenport, J. (1985). From crew to commercialism—the paradox of sport in higher education. In D. Chu, J. O. Segrave, & B. J. Becker (Eds.), *Sport and higher education* (pp. 5–16). Champaign, IL: Human Kinetics.

Dealy, F. X. (1990). *Win at any cost.* New York: Carol Publishing Group.

Dufresne, C. (2003, October 22). BCA to grade hiring efforts. *Los Angeles Times*. Retrieved October 19, 2010, from http://articles.latimes.com/2003/oct/22/sports/sp-bca22

Eichelberger, C. (2009, January 6). Florida enters BCS title game with top-paid athletic director. Retrieved October 19, 2010, from http://www.bloomberg.com/apps/news?pid=newsarchive&sid=aYYY_mDwYMkY

Hult, J. S. (1994). The story of women's athletics: Manipulating a dream 1890–1985. In D. M. Costa & S. R. Guthrie (Eds.), *Women and sport: Interdisciplinary perspectives* (pp. 83–106). Champaign, IL: Human Kinetics.

Jenkins, S. (2010, June 4). On television, highlights of women's sports are running low. *The Washington Post*. Retrieved October 19, 2010, from http://www.washingtonpost.com/wp-dyn/content/article/2010/06/03/AR2010060302030.html

Kalafa, J. (2010, February 28). Big Ten revenue sharing: Are Michigan & Ohio State getting fair shares? *Bleacher Report*. Retrieved October 19, 2010, from http://bleacherreport.com/articles/353856-big-ten-revenue-sharing-are-michigan-ohio-st-getting-fair-share

Knight Foundation Commission on Intercollegiate Athletics. (1991, March). *Keeping faith with the student-athlete*. Charlotte, NC: Knight Foundation.

Knight Foundation Commission on Intercollegiate Athletics. (1993, March). *A new beginning for a new century*. Charlotte, NC: Knight Foundation.

Lawrence, P. R. (1987). *Unsportsmanlike conduct*. New York: Praeger Publishers.

Lee, J. (2003, December 8–14). Who pays, who profits in realignment? *SportsBusiness Journal*, 25–33.

Legislative Services Database (LDSB*i*). (2010). NCAA. Retrieved November 22, 2010, from https://web1.ncaa.org/LSDBi/exec/homepage

Mahony, E.H. (2010, July 21). Judge says Quinnipiac discriminates against female student athletes. Retrieved October 19, 2010, from http://articles.courant.com/2010-07-21/sports/hc-quinnipiac-decision-0721-20100721_1_title-ix-athletic-participation-opportunities-female-student-athletes

Morrison, L. L. (1993). The AIAW: Governance by women for women. In G. L. Cohen (Ed.), *Women in sport: Issues and controversies* (pp. 59–66). Newbury Park, CA: Sage Publications.

Most Division I teams post top grades (2010, June 9). NCAA News Release. Retrieved October 19, 2010, from http://www.ncaa.org/wps/portal/ncaahome?WCM_GLOBAL_CONTEXT=/ncaa/ncaa/media+and+events/press+room/news+release+archive/2010/academic+reform/20100609+apr+release

Mott, R. D. (1994, March 2). Big Eight growth brings a new look to Division I-A. *The NCAA News*, p. 1.

National Association of Intercollegiate Athletics (NAIA). (2010). Member institutions. Retrieved October 19, 2010, from http://naia.cstv.com/member-services/about/members.htm

National Collegiate Athletic Association. (2009a). Article 1.3.1: Basic purpose. In *2009–10 NCAA Division I manual*. Indianapolis, IN: Author.

National Collegiate Athletic Association. (2009b). Article 3.3.2.2.2.1: Full voting privileges. In *2009–10 NCAA Division I manual*. Indianapolis, IN: Author.

National Collegiate Athletic Association. (2009c). Article 4.02.2: Faculty athletics representative. In *2009–10 NCAA Division I manual*. Indianapolis, IN: Author.

National Collegiate Athletic Association. (2009d). Article 4.02.4.1: Senior woman administrator. In *2009–10 NCAA Division I manual*. Indianapolis, IN: Author.

National Collegiate Athletic Association. (2009e). Article 12.3: Use of agents. In *2009–10 NCAA Division I manual*, Indianapolis, IN: Author.

National Collegiate Athletic Association. (2009f). Article 14.3: Freshman academic requirements. In *2009–10 NCAA Division I manual*. Indianapolis, IN: Author.

National Collegiate Athletic Association. (2009g). Article 19.02.2: Types of violations. In *2009–10 NCAA Division I manual*. Indianapolis, IN: Author.

National Collegiate Athletic Association. (2009h). Article 20.9: Division I philosophy statement. In *2009–10 NCAA Division I manual*. Indianapolis, IN: Author.

National Collegiate Athletic Association. (2009i). Article 20.9.4: Sports sponsorship. In *2009–10 NCAA Division I manual*. Indianapolis, IN: Author.

National Collegiate Athletic Association. (2009j). Article 20.9.7: Football bowl subdivision requirements. In *2009–10 NCAA Division I manual*. Indianapolis, IN: Author.

National Collegiate Athletic Association. (2010a). *1981–82–2008–09 NCAA sports sponsorship and participation rates report*. Retrieved October 19, 2010, from http://www.ncaapublications.com/productdownloads/PR2010.pdf

National Collegiate Athletic Association. (2010b). *1999–2000–2008–09 NCAA student-athlete race/ethnicity report*. Retrieved October 19, 2010, from http://www.ncaapublications.com/productdownloads/SAEREP10.pdf

National Collegiate Athletic Association. (2010c). *2008–09 race and gender demographics*. Retrieved October 19, 2010, from http://www.ncaapublications.com/productdownloads/RGDMEMB10.pdf

National Collegiate Athletic Association. (2010d). Differences among the three divisions. Retrieved October 19, 2010, from http://www.ncaa.org/wps/wcm/connect/public/NCAA/About+the+NCAA/Who+We+Are/Differences+Among+the+Divisions/

National Collegiate Athletic Association. (2010e). Enforcement process. Retrieved October 19, 2010, from http://www.ncaa.org/wps/wcm/connect/public/NCAA/Issues/Enforcement/The+Enforcement+Process

National Collegiate Athletic Association (2010f). Student-Athlete Advisory Committee (SAAC). Retrieved November 22, 2010, from http://www.ncaa.org/wps/portal/ncaahome?WCM_GLOBAL_CONTEXT=ncaa/NCAA/Academics+and+Athletes/SAAC/index+-+SAAC

National Junior College Athletic Association. (2010). *Today's NJCAA*. *History*. Retrieved October 19, 2010, from http://www.njcaa.org/todaysNJCAA_History.cfm?category=History

NCAA Gender Equity Task Force. (1991). *NCAA gender equity report*. Overland Park, KS: National Collegiate Athletic Association.

Nebraska approved by Big Ten. (2010, June 12). *ESPN.com*. Retrieved November 20, 2010, from http://sports.espn.go.com/ncaa/news/story?id5276551

Paul, J. (1993). Heroines: Paving the way. In G. L. Cohen (Ed.), *Women in sport: Issues and controversies* (pp. 27–37). Newbury Park, CA: Sage Publications.

Rader, B. G. (1990). *American sports* (2nd ed.). Englewood Cliffs, NJ: Prentice Hall.

Results from the 2008 NCAA study on collegiate wagering. (2009, November 13). NCAA Research. Retrieved October 19, 2010, from http://www.ncaa.org/wps/wcm/connect/5a30d30040962f3190739a7e5b626114/Results_2008_NCAA_Study_Collegiate_Wagering.pdf?MOD=AJPERES&CACHEID=5a30d30040962f3190739a7e5b626114

Sandomir, R. (2006, May 18). On the web, college athletes acting badly. *The New York Times*. Retrieved October 19, 2010, from http://www.nytimes.com/2006/05/18/sports/18hazing.html

Savage, H. J. (1929). *American college athletics*. New York: The Carnegie Foundation.

Social media and recruiting (2010). *NCAA*. Retrieved October 19, 2010, from http://www.ncaa.org/wps/wcm/connect/public/NCAA/Issues/Recruiting/Social+Media+and+Recruiting

Strange, M. (2010, February 19). Black coaches finally getting call to take over major college football programs. *Knoxnews.com*. Retrieved October 19, 2010, from http://www.knoxnews.com/news/2010/feb/19/making-head-way

Study: Typical I-A program is $1.2 million in the black. (1996, November 18). *The NCAA News*, p. 1.

Top paid college basketball coaches (2010, May 7). *The Hartford Courant*. Retrieved October 18, 2010, from http://articles.courant.com/2010-05-07/sports/hc-college-basketball-coaches-salaries_1_michigan-state-average-yearly-salaries-basketball-coaches

Western Athletic Conference to become biggest in I-A. (1994, April 27). *The NCAA News*, p. 3.

Wieberg, S. (1994, August 18). Study faults colleges on minority hiring. *USA Today*, p. 1C.

Yaeger, D. (1991). *Undue process: The NCAA's injustice for all*. Champaign, IL: Sagamore Publishing.

International Sport

Sheranne Fairley and Mireia Lizandra

Editor's Note: Most of the world refers to soccer as "football," so throughout this international chapter we will do the same. When referring to football played in the National Football League (NFL), Canadian Football League (CFL), and NFL Europe, we will use the phrase "American football."

■ INTRODUCTION

While sport has been played on an international level as early as the ancient Olympic Games in 776 BC, sport continues to see an increasing degree of interaction and expansion across national borders. The increasing reach of broadcast media, improvements in communication, relaxation of trade barriers, and increased ease of international travel have helped sport further diffuse through the boundaries of countries and continents. Many sport events or competitions are now telecast live in multiple countries around the world, allowing fans to watch their favorite teams' performance as it happens. Additionally, live scores and statistics are generally available globally on the Internet, with fans having access to live televised coverage of sporting contests. As a result, people throughout the world can more easily access major sport leagues and events. It is now easier than ever to stay up-to-date with the latest sport, team, or player information regardless of where you are in the world—provided the technology and communication are there.

Oftentimes when talking about international sport, we view the internationalization and globalization of sport as the influence of contemporary superpowers on spectator sports, with special attention given to those sports that are widely disseminated in the popular media (Lai, 1999). This view has contributed to the use of the term *globalization* being treated synonymously with *Americanization*. In other words, the process of globalization is often thought of in terms of how spectator sport in the United States is communicated to, received by, and adopted by other parts of the world. In truth, the scope of international sport is much wider. The internationalization of sport can be seen on many different levels, which include, but are not limited to:

- The continual introduction of sport into new countries where the sport has not traditionally been played
- Countries competing against one another in international competition
- The international broadcasting of sport competition and events
- International coverage of sport events and competition through various forms of news and print media
- Travel to sport events in different countries as a spectator, participant, official, or volunteer
- The expansion of "national" leagues to include teams based in different countries
- Teams touring foreign countries to generate interest and awareness of their sport or league
- Individuals competing alongside players from different countries in organized leagues
- The availability of licensed merchandise outside of the country of the team or player
- Global companies sponsoring international sport events
- The use of sport as a social and political tool

As a result of the increasingly global nature of sport, abundant career opportunities exist for sport management students. Further, today's sport managers should have a general knowledge of the global platform in which sport is performed and consumed, as challenges for sport

managers inevitably accompany the industry's continual expansion.

This chapter first examines the historical development of sport in the international marketplace. It then looks at the factors behind the global expansion of sport, addressing the growth of sport-related corporate activities, professional sport, sport tourism, grassroots sport, and the diffusion of sport into new cultural settings. The chapter next focuses on the growth of sport tourism. It then examines the Olympic Movement, including its organization and primary responsibilities. Finally, because the international emphasis on sport will continue to grow, resulting in an increased number of job opportunities in international sport, this chapter concludes by addressing the variety of potential employment opportunities in international sport. While many of the examples in this chapter involve American sports or leagues, this trend is not meant to suggest that international sport is in any way limited to the United States. The examples are included for illustrative purposes only.

Additionally, it is useful to know that the organization of sport in the United States is not typical of the organization of sport throughout the world. Unlike the school-based (high school or college) sport system in the United States, the club system form of sport organization is more common throughout the rest of the world. The club-based system is separate and distinct from the education system (i.e., one does not have to attend college to play at the elite level). The primary purpose of the club sport system is to fulfill social and fitness functions, rather than to promote superior athletes. The club system allows anyone to participate and take advantage of good facilities that are often maintained by local or state government. Given the social and fitness benefits the club-based system provides, the government contributes substantially to the sport system. Thus, the funding structure for sport for many countries outside the United

States entails much more government involvement, with some countries even having their own federal minister for sport (e.g., Canada and Australia).

■ HISTORY

Sport first spread across international borders through imperialistic efforts. As nations such as Great Britain colonized various areas throughout the world, sport was used to impose the conquerors' culture on the colonized land. For example, the British introduced cricket, rugby union, and rugby league to Australia when they colonized that continent. Today, cricket, rugby union, and rugby league are immensely popular in Australia, and an intense rivalry exists between Australia and Great Britain. In this way, sport has fueled a feeling of pride in one's country, also known as **nationalism**. Nationalistic sentiments have also assisted in the growth of international sport today. In some instances, a win on an international level has led to increased interest and participation in a particular sport. The United States' victory over the Soviet Union's ice hockey team in 1980, for example, increased nationalistic pride as well as the interest in hockey toward the end of the Cold War.

Similarly, Australia's advancement to the 2006 Fédération Internationale de Football Association (FIFA) World Cup for the first time in 32 years produced an increased interest in football in that country. In other cases, embarrassment at an international level has served as the catalyst for the further development of sport. For example, the Australian Institute of Sport (AIS), a center designed to train and develop elite athletes and teams, was established in 1981 as a result of Australia's disappointing performance at the 1976 Montreal Olympic Games. It is reported that Nigerian President Goodluck Jonathon suspended the Nigerian Football Team from international competition for two years after the side produced a disappointing performance, finishing at the bottom of Group B in the 2010 FIFA World Cup.

Given the international exposure and media attention that sport attracts, sport is often used as a platform for political and social protests and boycotts. Various human rights groups have staged protests and disruptions of international sport events to bring international attention to their causes (Hums & Wolff, 2008). To protest against the practice of apartheid, the Stop the Seventy Tour Committee (STST) was established in 1970 to stage mass demonstrations and disruptions when the white South African cricket and rugby union teams toured the United Kingdom. The protest was not about sport, but

rather used sport as a platform to showcase that apartheid was unacceptable.

Athletes have also used their positions to protest various issues. During the medal ceremony for the 200-meter track event at the 1968 Mexico Olympic Games, Tommie Smith and John Carlos staged a silent protest against racial discrimination of black people in the United States. During the victory ceremony, Smith and Carlos stood with their heads bowed, no shoes, black scarves around their necks, and black-gloved fists raised during the U.S. national anthem—an image that earned international recognition for the fight against racial discrimination.

Sport has also provided a platform through which different cultures can come together and celebrate a common goal. Much of the world shares in the excitement of popular sporting events. Many sport events provide what Turner (1977) refers to as *liminoid space*, where traditional status barriers are transcended and individuals momentarily neglect differences in order to share in a common experience of sport.

Concurrent with the growth of the Olympic Games, professional sport leagues and corporations have seized the opportunity to sell

their products in international markets. Of the North American professional sport leagues, Major League Baseball (MLB) has the longest history of attempting to export its product. In 1888, driven by Albert Spalding's desire to sell more sporting goods, a group of professional baseball players traveled overseas to play exhibition games and introduce the sport of baseball through clinics. Such practices continued following the turn of the century as Babe Ruth and other stars of the time regularly toured Canada, Latin America, and Japan (Field, 1997).

The major North American leagues now play actual league games overseas. In 1986, the NFL became the first North American professional sport league to export an exhibition between two teams. Exhibition games by North American league clubs now occur regularly overseas, primarily in Europe and Asia. In 2008, MLB played its first Opening Day series in Japan, and the NFL hosted a regular-season game in England in 2007; both leagues have continued this practice. Other leagues now have teams positioned in different countries and continents. For example, the Investec Bank Super 14s Rugby Union competition has teams placed in Australia, New Zealand, and South Africa.

While each of the four major North American professional sport leagues aggressively attacks the international marketplace, the world's most popular sport is still football (soccer). In fact, just as American football, basketball, baseball, and hockey leagues are attempting to spread the popularity of their sport overseas, so, too, is football attempting to spread its popularity. However, in the case of football, recent efforts have focused on increasing the interest and participation in the United States. Even though football has been played in the United States since before the turn of the twentieth century, its popularity has been limited to the last 30 years. Professional football garnered widespread interest and popularity in the late 1970s and early 1980s with the North American

Soccer League (NASL). The presence of foreign talent, such as all-time great Pelé, made outdoor football an attractive entertainment option for many people in the United States. However, due to financial mismanagement and a talent pool devoid of any top North American players, the league folded in 1985.

As the 1990s dawned, the hope for outdoor professional football rested with FIFA, the international federation for football. FIFA awarded the 1994 World Cup to the United States with the hope of reenergizing interest and participation in football in that country. As part of the agreement to host the World Cup, USA Soccer, the national governing body for football, was to spearhead the efforts to start another professional outdoor football league. The 1994 World Cup was immensely successful, generating sellout crowds and larger-than-expected TV audiences, and ultimately producing a revenue surplus of $60 million (Gilbert, 1995). As a result, in 1996 Major League Soccer (MLS), the first Division I professional football league on U.S. soil in 12 years, was launched. Ten teams and nearly 3.1 million fans in its first season made the league a big success. Its rapid development helped lead the United States to the quarterfinals of the World Cup Korea/Japan in 2002.

Besides targeting women, MLS markets itself to and attracts much interest from the Latino population (Langdon, 1997b). With such significant interest from minority groups, football attracts a more diverse following than the other four U.S. professional sports. Its broad range of participants also makes football more appealing to sponsors, which are attempting to reach diverse audiences with their sponsorship programs. Accordingly, many large companies have signed on as MLS sponsors, including adidas, Pepsi, Visa, and Anheuser-Busch. MLS executives have also attempted to increase league popularity by focusing on increasing the amount of licensed merchandise in the marketplace.

They have been so aggressive in this area that they even sold a license to a company to produce action figures (Langdon, 1997a).

The popularity of football in the United States increased during the brief period in which David Beckham, arguably the world's most marketable football player (and former English captain) played for the Los Angeles Galaxy, a feat that was enabled by the MLS relaxing its salary cap. Recently, French star Thierry Henry joined Red Bull New York. Similarly, Australia is seeing an increased interest in football as an outcome of the rebranding of the national league (now called the Hyundai A-League) coupled with the recent success of the Australian national team reaching the round of 16 after qualifying for the World Cup for the first time in 32 years.

■ THE GLOBALIZATION OF SPORT

To capitalize on the global marketplace, corporations have begun to adopt a **global strategy** for selling their products. The premise for a global strategy is basic: create products with the same appeal and which generate the same demand in all corners of the world. Early proponents of this strategy were Coca-Cola, Levi's, and Disney (with theme parks in Tokyo and Paris). However, even these large companies found that in order to create demand, the product or advertising message must be adapted to account for differences in local culture and laws (Miller, 1996). Hundreds of different languages and dialects are spoken throughout the world. For example, the term *footy*, a word commonly used in Australia to describe the sport of football (rugby league, rugby union, and Australian Rules Football), has little to no meaning in the North American sport context. In addition, customs and traditions in one country may be disrespectful in another country. For example, a recent Kentucky Fried Chicken (KFC) commercial shown in Australia showcased a group of West Indian cricket supporters (another member of the cricket fraternity) eating KFC chicken while cheering on their cricket team. In Australia and the West Indies, there is no race-related connotation associated with the commercial. However, while not shown in the United States and not targeted at the U.S. market, this commercial saw cries of racist outrage in the United States, and subsequently it was taken off air. Cricket supporters in Australia and the West Indies could not understand how or why this commercial would cause such outrage. When selling products overseas, some degree of adaptation to the local or regional culture is necessary. This example illustrates that the global reach of Internet and communication technologies can spark controversy in places where the commercial is not even placed.

To maximize profits, corporations have realized they must look outside their boundaries to sell their products. Technological advances and increased accessibility to technology worldwide have been major factors driving the globalization of sport. The presence of satellite and digital technology as well as the popularity of the Internet has made the transmission of visual images worldwide simple and virtually simultaneous. Globalization of sport is largely influenced by the contemporary superpowers which dominate these media. As a result, high-profile spectator sports in those countries with media dominance receive greater media exposure and, therefore, are the sports typically associated with globalization. While spectator sports that attract greater media attention have an advantage in reaching global markets, globalization and diffusion are not dependent on media alone. This makes sense given the fact that only about 310 million of the world's 6.86 billion people live in the Continental United States (U.S. Census Bureau, 2010). Clearly, to sell more products corporations must sell their products globally. This presents a challenge not just to mainstream businesses but also to sport organizations.

Increasingly, sport organizations are eyeing a global strategy. Why does a Nike commercial for the Air Jordan running shoe have no spoken or printed words? Why does it include only visual images followed by Nike's trademark symbol, the Swoosh, at the end of the commercial? The answer to these questions is simple. These ads are created to be shown to a global audience. People in the United States will see the same ad as people in Japan. Further, the ad will have the same impact on American and Japanese consumers. Unfortunately, exporting the sport product is not always this easy. As with mainstream consumer products, adaptations based on cultural preferences often must be made. For example, the style of basketball played in the National Basketball Association (NBA) is not in adherence with Fédération Internationale de Basketball (FIBA) rules and is not indicative of how the way the sport is played in the rest of the world and at international competitions. Efforts at globalizing the sport product can be seen on numerous fronts: corporations are attempting to utilize the sport theme and sport products to enter the international marketplace; professional sport leagues are attempting to spread the popularity of their leagues and associated products (e.g., televised games, licensed products) overseas; event and destination marketers are leveraging events as sport tourism opportunities; and sport is being used on a global scale as a medium that can aid in health and social issues.

Corporate Involvement with International Sport

People attend and watch sporting events expecting a good experience. With advances in technology, particularly satellite technology, audiences worldwide now have access to the top sporting events. Realizing that such access exists, corporations are increasingly using sport to sell their products to consumers on other continents. Generally, such activities can be grouped into two categories: (a) efforts by manufacturers of sport-related products, such as athletic shoes, athletic equipment, and sport drinks; and (b) efforts by non–sport-related companies, which sponsor international sporting events, teams, and athletes to gain name recognition and thus sell their products in new global markets.

■ INTERNATIONAL EFFORTS OF SPORT PRODUCT MANUFACTURERS

Similar to many corporations throughout the world, manufacturers of sporting goods and sport-related products are increasingly attempting to capitalize on potential overseas sales. The reason for such efforts is very simple: North American markets are becoming saturated. Today, many companies compete for the North American sporting enthusiasts' dollars because North Americans are sport oriented and have money to spend on sport products. However, the average consumer will purchase only a certain amount of sport products and merchandise in a given year.

In the United States today, sporting goods manufacturers are reaching a point where they can no longer drastically increase sales to consumers. Yet the need to continually grow and expand product sales is the corporate mission. As a result, sport corporations are attempting to broaden their product distribution. For example, since 2000 Nike has sold more products overseas than in the United States. To do so, Nike not only focused on its most popular product lines, such as running and basketball shoes, but also looked to other products such as golf shoes and apparel, hockey equipment, and football cleats and apparel. Because more people play and watch football than any other sport in the world, it was logical for Nike to expand its operations and focus on increasing its share of the football market. To meet this goal, Nike has signed with

great teams like the Brazilian national football team, Manchester United, Juventus, and F.C. Barcelona. It is also sponsoring the world's best football players, such as Ronaldo.

Some equipment manufacturers and distributors are looking beyond simply selling their products to the existing global markets. These companies now play a direct role in developing and diffusing sports into new markets in an attempt to create new markets for their products. The globalization of sport is aided by capitalist enterprise (Martin & Schumann, 1996). For example, floorball, the second largest sport in Sweden and Finland, made its way into Australia due in no small part to the sales aspirations of an equipment manufacturer and distributor (Lai, 1999). Floorball is an indoor team sport that can be best visualized as a combination of football and ice hockey (without the skates), where the aim is to put a light plastic ball into the opponent's goal. The equipment manufacturer implemented an active development program in Australian schools. The development program included distributing catalogs of floorball equipment, providing videotapes explaining the sport of floorball, and offering to run free clinics in schools in an attempt to create a new market for floorball equipment. Floorball was positioned as a safe alternative to field hockey for school-age children, as it is played with a lightweight plastic ball and lightweight stick with a plastic vented blade. Thus, administrators and teachers were open to trying out floorball as an activity to be played in schools, which in turn grew the market for the manufacturer of floorball equipment.

■ INTERNATIONAL DEVELOPMENT VIA SPONSORSHIP OF SPORTING EVENTS

Non–sport-related corporations are also attempting to use sport to sell products internationally. Primarily, this is done through the sponsorship of international athletes and teams. Generally, such efforts are geared toward increasing awareness and sales overseas. By sponsoring prominent international sport efforts, corporations hope to benefit from the increased interest in sport. Coca-Cola is another large U.S. corporation that attempts to increase its popularity worldwide through international event sponsorship. Coca-Cola sponsored some of the NBA's international events in an effort to increase sales and distribution of Sprite overseas. In conjunction with exhibition games played in Mexico City, Coca-Cola produced more than 1 million cans of Sprite with the NBA logo in an attempt to increase sales in Mexico (National Basketball Association, 1997).

Professional Sport Leagues' International Focus

Today, most professional sport leagues are aggressively seeking to increase the popularity and consumption of their respective products overseas. International travelers who see people in other countries wearing Chicago Bulls T-shirts or New York Yankees hats are witnessing the potential impact of new distribution channels for the major professional sport leagues.

North American professional leagues are aggressively attempting to spread the popularity of their leagues internationally. Organizationally, each of the leagues has created an international division to guide such efforts. Within each of these divisions, each league maintains offices in cities throughout the world. For example, Major League Baseball International Partners has an office in Sydney, Australia, focusing on improving the popularity of baseball through merchandise sales, game telecasts, and grassroots programs. It has also opened an office in Tokyo so it will be able to help clients put together programs that drive their business while promoting the league and its players.

These divisions and international offices have focused on increasing the popularity of North American professional sport by utilizing several common techniques and strategies: (a) broadcasting, (b) licensing and merchandising, (c) playing exhibition and regular season games, (d) cultivating participation in sport throughout each country (grassroots efforts), and (e) placing teams in international markets. In addition to increasing the popularity of the sport and the league on an international level, the leagues hope to increase participation in the sport. This increased participation should eventually increase the talent pool from which they can then recruit for the professional ranks.

■ BROADCASTING

Many people around the world are introduced to sport from outside their home countries through television broadcasts of games and highlights. Visual images are easily exportable commodities. It is much easier for a professional sport league to reach international markets by first exporting its product through visual images. This strategy is aided by the fact that access to television sets and the Internet is increasing at a rapid rate.

Mergers in the mass media industry have also spurred growth. Major corporations now own major media outlets in numerous countries throughout the world. Perhaps the most notable conglomerate is the series of networks owned by Rupert Murdoch. Murdoch owns media outlets throughout Australia, Asia, Europe, and North America. In this case, MLB games televised by Murdoch's Fox Sports in the United States can also be packaged for overseas viewers on other Murdoch-owned stations such as BSkyB and Star-TV. ESPN, which is not part of Murdoch's holdings, has an international division that beams games out in Mandarin Chinese to the Pacific Rim and in Spanish to Latin America. Similarly, the English Premier League is broadcast around the globe primarily on networks owned and/or controlled by NewsCorp.

Professional sport leagues have seized on the opportunity to capitalize on such trends. Many professional sport leagues around the world are aggressively seeking to increase the popularity and consumption of their respective products overseas. The NFL's Super Bowl XLII was televised in 230 countries and territories in 33 languages. During the 2006–2007 season, the NBA was telecast in 215 countries around the world and translated into 41 languages. In an effort to introduce their sports into other countries, leagues not only rely on actual game broadcasts but also offer highlight show formats. For example, the NBA produces and distributes a half-hour weekly show called NBA Jam to more than 15 countries throughout the world. The format of the show incorporates highlights in a music video format, giving would-be fans a behind-the-scenes look at the NBA. Highlights are used rather than extended action clips in an attempt to attract young people to the sport's excitement.

Another tool for the NBA is NBA TV, a 24-hour television network that offers NBA news and information, live games, and behind-the-scenes specials that fans can access 365 days a year through their local cable company or satellite provider. NBA TV is distributed to 80 countries (NBA Media Ventures, 2011).

The Internet has also played a major role in spreading leagues' messages to new fans. All of the professional leagues have elaborate Web sites offering up-to-the-minute information on their respective leagues that are accessible to everyone with a computer.

While the four major North American professional sporting leagues crown their champions as "world champions" and refer to their playoff series with names such as the "World Series," this may not be an accurate description. These titles have garnered some criticism from international markets given that these competitions are limited to teams from North America.

■ LICENSING AND MERCHANDISING

Another tactic typically used to expand a sport to international markets is to sell **licensed merchandise**. Team-logoed merchandise provides people with a means to identify and associate with their favorite teams. However, sales of team-logoed items traditionally were isolated to the country in which the sport team competed. Increasingly, though, sport leagues are utilizing the sales of logoed merchandise as a means to increase league popularity overseas. The increase in popularity of online shopping has also increased the sales of team-related merchandise. Further, the sale of licensed merchandise serves as a promotional vehicle for teams or leagues. People purchasing and wearing Houston Rockets T-shirts and hats in Beijing serve to increase the awareness of both the NBA and the Houston Rockets in China. When David Beckham chose to wear the number 23 on his shirt (the same number made famous by Michael Jordan), he had an eye on the U.S. market ("New Balance," 2003).

■ EXHIBITION AND REGULAR-SEASON GAMES

The most obvious step a professional sport league can take in exporting its product is to actually hold matches or games on foreign soil. In this way, people in different countries have the opportunity to witness the sport in person. The NFL has played exhibition games outside the United States since 1986 and is now committed to playing at least one regular-season game on foreign soil each year. Other North American professional sport leagues have also undertaken significant efforts to export their product in game format. In August 1996, the San Diego Padres and New York Mets played a three-game regular season series in Monterrey, Mexico.

Major League Baseball now features an Opening Day series in Japan, a practice that started in 2008. The NBA began playing exhibition games in 1988, when the Atlanta Hawks traveled to the former Soviet Union. Since then, NBA exhibition games have been played in Spain, the Bahamas, Mexico, France, Germany, the United Kingdom, and Japan. In 1996, the NBA went one step further, having the New Jersey Nets and the Orlando Magic play two regular-season games in Tokyo. More than 70,000 tickets were sold for the two games in less than five hours, a testament to the popularity of basketball in Japan. In 2006, the Denver Nuggets and Golden State Warriors faced off in a high-scoring exhibition game in Monterrey, Mexico, which created excitement among the Mexican fans.

■ MARKETING FOREIGN ATHLETES

As trade barriers between countries have diminished, so too have barriers preventing the top players in the world from playing in various professional sport leagues. The presence of foreign players has enabled these professional leagues to increase their popularity overseas. Specifically, by marketing these players in their homelands, professional leagues are able to increase the popularity of both the players and their respective sports overseas. The 2008–2009 NBA season set a record, with teams having a total of 77 international players from 32 countries and territories. At least one international player is signed to 28 of the 30 NBA teams. In MLB, 28% of players on 2006 opening day rosters were born outside the United States, representing 15 different countries and territories. Further, 47.8% of minor league baseball players under contract in 2009 were born outside the United States.

The rise of satellite television has aided this diversification. Improving technology allows worldwide audiences to see Emanuel (Manu) Ginobili play for the San Antonio Spurs, An-

drew Bogut play for the Milwaukee Bucks, and Yao Ming play for the Houston Rockets, which in turn increases the popularity of basketball throughout Argentina, Australia, and China, respectively. Increasingly, exhibition games featuring some of these foreign stars are being held in foreign countries.

■ PLACING TEAMS IN INTERNATIONAL MARKETS AND THE CREATION OF INTERNATIONAL LEAGUES

Throughout the world, some national leagues are aggressively seeking to expand into new markets—not just by showcasing their existing teams to overseas markets, but also by placing teams in foreign countries and continents. For example, the National Basketball League (NBL) of Australia has teams in two countries: Australia and New Zealand. The league sought to grow its international audience by aggressively placing a team in the Asian market, the Singapore Slingers. However, after one season, that team was removed from the league.

Other national governing bodies are working together to create international leagues. For example, governing bodies for rugby unions in South Africa, New Zealand, and Australia created a joint union known as SANZAR to administer an annual provincial competition and the Tri-Nations Test Series. The provincial series, now known as the Investec Super 14s, hosts four teams from Australia, five teams from New Zealand, and five teams from South Africa. Each team plays 13 games during the regular season. SANZAR signed a new international media deal with NewsCorp worth $437 million in April 2010.

■ SPORT TOURISM

An element of international sport involves travel to different countries to participate in, watch, or volunteer at various sport events or competitions, or to view sport halls of fame, stadia, or museums. While participation in sport tourism is not a recent phenomenon, the increased ease and convenience of international travel have brought an increase in international sport tourism. Sport-related travel in the United Kingdom is now estimated to account for 5.9% of the total expenditure on sport (Collins & Trenberth, 2005).

Three types of sport tourism are commonly identified: travel to participate in a sport activity; travel to view a sport activity; and travel to visit a sport hall of fame, sport facility, or museum. Additionally, recent research has noted that individuals do, in fact, travel internationally to volunteer at sport events, including the Olympic and Paralympic Games. For example, the 2004 Athens Olympic and Paralympic Games received more than one-third of its applications of interest to volunteer at the Games from outside Greece, indicating that many individuals were willing to travel internationally to volunteer for the event.

The increasing linkage between sport and tourism is the result of an increasing convergence between the governance and policy of sport and tourism (Chalip, 2001; Weed, 2003). Factors that have driven this blending of sport and tourism include economic gain for the host destination, social benefits to the host community, tourism generation through hosting mega-sport events, and holidays as catalysts for involvement in sport. Along with some of the positives comes the potential for scandals, boycotts, and crowding at the host destination. Tourism also has potential benefits for sport. First, highlighting the potential tourism benefits from hosting an event can justify money being spent on sporting facilities and infrastructure improvements. Second, hosting a successful sport event can enhance the sporting profile of a region (Weed & Bull, 1997). It is now common to see many countries and destinations compete fiercely to host international sport events such as the Olympic and Paralympic Games owing

to the economic benefits these events are said to contribute to the host economy.

While international sport contests have always evoked nationalism and a support for one's country, recent years have seen an emergence of semi-structured sport tourism opportunities for fans to support an international team or nation at various sporting events. These groups act in a manner akin to a travel agency, providing travel and accommodation options along with tickets (often in a special section) to cheer on the country's sport teams. Three of these groups include the Barmy Army (England), the Fanatics (Australia), and the Beige Brigade (New Zealand). The Barmy Army supports English cricket through its use of songs and chants, which combine both irony and wit (England's Barmy Army, 2010). An estimated 40,000 Britons traveled to Australia for the 2007 Ashes Cricket Series, thus injecting millions of dollars into the economy. The Fanatics, an Australian fan group, originated as a means for supporting Australian tennis players at international events (e.g., the Davis Cup) and has since expanded to support many Australian sport teams and individuals all over the world. The Fanatics now have more than 62,000 members and have organized travel for over 28,000 individuals while working closely with the national governing bodies for the respective sports.

Smaller-scale events such as regular-season games benefit the host community given that the marginal cost of provision is small because the events are hosted within existing infrastructure (Higham, 1999). Therefore, for leagues that host teams in different countries and, by extension, regular-season games abroad, international sport tourism becomes a regular component of the league.

■ GRASSROOTS PROGRAMS

Grassroots efforts are programs and activities undertaken to increase sport participation and interest in a particular international region. Each professional sport league undertakes significant grassroots efforts, thus providing many potential employment opportunities for future sport managers. These efforts are primarily focused in two areas: (a) increasing participation in and (b) educating people about the specifics of a particular sport. The theory behind grassroots efforts is that long-term popularity and interest will be achieved only when both a knowledgeable fan base exists and a significant portion of the population participates in the sport.

MLB implements several grassroots programs in its effort to spread the popularity of baseball. The Pitch, Hit, and Run program has reached more than three million schoolchildren in Australia, Germany, Japan, Italy, Korea, Mexico, Puerto Rico, South Africa, Taiwan, and the United Kingdom (MLB International, 2010). The program helps teach baseball fundamentals to school children over a six- to ten-week period, culminating with a competition of throwing, hitting, and base running. In an effort to help individual schools teach the fundamentals, MLB provides each school with baseball equipment, instructional videos, and manuals (MLB International, 2010).

■ SPORT FOR ALL

The Sport for All movement is an international movement that seeks to promote mass participation in sport without discrimination. The movement began in Europe in the 1960s and has since expanded globally. Unlike most forms of elite and professional sport, the purpose of Sport for All is not competition, but rather participation for participation's sake, as sport is viewed as both a human right and a key component of a healthy lifestyle. Specifically, the Sport for All movement seeks to involve all sectors of the population in physical activity regardless of age, gender, social or economic distinction, or physical or mental ability. The movement is, therefore, seen as a proponent of social integration. One of the goals of Sport for All is to make sport affordable and available to all communities, including underserved populations (e.g., children and youth, girls and women, the elderly, and people with disabilities). Many organizations working with these populations implement social marketing campaigns to increase levels of participation.

Regional, national, and international Sport for All organizations have been created to provide individuals with opportunities to participate in sport. Trim and Fitness International Sport for All (TAFISA) was formed in 1991 in Bordeaux, France, and now has members from 153 organizations in more than 100 countries. The organizational members include national government and nongovernmental organizations such as National Sport Federations, **National Olympic Committees**, Ministries, and Councils for Sport, all of which are involved in Sport for All initiatives in their respective countries. The movement has been relatively successful in Europe, Australia, some parts of Latin America, and Africa, but has had limited impact in the United States.

The IOC Sport for All Commission was created in 1985 to integrate grassroots sport into the goals of the Olympic Movement and to globally disseminate sport as a basic human right. The Eleventh World Sport for All Congress was held in Havana, Cuba, in 2006; the theme of the conference was "Physical Activity: Benefits and Challenges." The conference was sponsored by the IOC and had the support of the World Health Organization (WHO) and the General Association of International Sport Federations (AGFIS). The 2010 Congress was held in Jyväskylä, Finland and featured the theme, "Promoting Sport for All as a Strategy for a Better 21st Century Society."

The United Nations (UN) is also an advocate of sport as a basic human right and has established an Office for Sport for Development and Peace. According to the UN, the principles of sport—"respect for opponents, and for rules, teamwork and fair play"—are congruent with the principles of the United Nations Charter (United Nations, 2007, p. 1).

While not the intention of the Sport for All programs, sport participation has several other benefits. Sport:

- enlarges the sport market by growing the pool of potential elite athletes,
- increases the demand for sporting equipment,
- increases the demand for sport facilities, and
- generates further interest in sport, which could lead to increased spectatorship.

■ SPORT DIFFUSION

We often hear that sport has become universal. Indeed, sport can be seen all around the world in some form. Sport, in practice, is easily introduced to other countries because it is governed by standardized rules of play. However, while the practice of sport is the same across many different countries, the meaning of sport is not universal. While many Western cultures

measure success in terms of winning the actual competition itself, other cultures place higher value on participation and cooperation.

When introducing sport to a new cultural setting, Thoma and Chalip (1996) suggest three strategies: (a) adapt the sport practice to the values of the new cultural setting, (b) foster the interest of elites, and (c) foster community interest. The sport can be tailored to the local culture by adapting the style of play, coaching, and even administration. For example, Trobriand Islanders were exposed to the game of cricket by Christian missionaries. Instead of playing the game in the traditional British way, the game was adapted to Trobriand culture by increasing the number of participants to allow whole tribes to participate, introducing ritualistic dances, using chants to communicate many traditional practices of the Trobriand people (relating primarily to tribal war), and modifying the equipment (bat and ball).

■ THE OLYMPIC MOVEMENT

The Olympic Games have played an important role in the development of international sport. Modern **Olympism** was conceived by Baron Pierre de Coubertin, on whose initiative the International Athletic Congress of Paris was held on June 23, 1894. There the **International Olympic Committee (IOC)** was constituted as the supreme authority of the Olympic Movement. Beginning with the inaugural modern Olympic Games in 1896 in Athens, Greece, the IOC has been entrusted with the control and development of the modern Olympic Games. In this capacity, the IOC has been quite successful. The Olympic Games are the largest international sporting event today. In 2004, the Summer Olympic Games returned to Athens, Greece, the birthplace of the modern Summer Games. The Games attracted athletes from 201 nations and involved competition in 301 events. In addition, television coverage reached 3.9 billion viewers, up from the 3.6 billion viewers who had access to the coverage of the Sydney 2000 Olympic Games (IOC, 2007b).

While familiarity with the Olympic Games as a sport event is global, the key philosophy behind the Games, termed *Olympism*, is less well known. The Olympic Charter States that Olympism is:

> *a philosophy of life, exalting and combining in a balanced whole the qualities of body, will, and mind. Blending sport with culture and education, Olympism seeks to create a way of life based on the joy found in effort, the educational value of good example and respect for universal fundamental ethical principles (IOC, 2010, p. 11).*

The Olympic Games extend well beyond the actual sport competition, corporate sponsorships, media broadcasts, and commercialism. The Olympic Games provide a space where countries from around the world can unite through a shared interest in festival and sport, a space where traditional status barriers are commonly transcended. While the description of Olympism makes no mention as to whether the athletes competing should be amateurs or professionals, prior to the 1980s, a major mission of the Olympic Movement was to ensure that only amateurs competed. However, as the Games grew, the cost of financing the Games increased, and thus Games organizers were forced to rely more heavily on commercial enterprises.

The 1984 Summer Olympic Games in Los Angeles marked the turning point for commercial involvement with the Olympic Games, generating a profit of more than $200 million largely due to corporate involvement (Graham, Goldblatt, & Delpy, 1995). However, as they committed significant sums of money, corporations also saw the athletes and individual Olympic teams as opportunities through which to market their products. As such, it became very difficult to maintain amateurism as a standard for Olympic competition. All pretenses of amateurism were dropped in 1992, when professional basketball players from the NBA and other professional leagues around the world competed for their home nations on "Dream Teams" at the 1992 Summer Olympic Games in Barcelona.

In 2000, the IOC started the "Celebrate Humanity" campaign, which sought to highlight that the Olympic ideals are universal and extend far beyond sport. The 2004 campaign consisted of a variety of television announcements and print media, which were translated into six different languages. The IOC sought to create further interest in the Olympic Games by stressing that the Games are more than just a sport event. The television announcements included internationally recognized spokespeople such as Nelson Mandela (human rights leader), Kofi Anan (Secretary-General of the United Nations), Andrea Bocelli (maestro and Italian tenor), Christopher Reeve (actor, director, and activist), and Avril Lavigne (Canadian singer and songwriter)—none of whom had any direct link to the Olympic Movement—to portray the Olympic ideals. The television announcements utilized imagery of sport competition; however, the narration emphasized the Olympic values of hope, friendship, fair play, dreams and inspiration, and joy in effort, emphasizing that sport can be used as a means to an end, rather than being an end in itself.

For a better understanding of the Olympic structure, see **Figure 9-1.** At the top is the International Olympic Committee (IOC), which is responsible for overseeing the Olympic Movement throughout the world. Beneath the IOC, the Olympic structure splits into two arms. On one side are the National Olympic Committees (NOCs), the organizations responsible for the development and protection of the Olympic

Movement in their respective countries. The NOCs promote the fundamental principles of Olympism at a national level within the framework of sports. On the other side of the Olympic structure are the **international federations (IFs)**, the organizations responsible for the administration of individual sport competitions throughout the world. For example, the International Amateur Athletics Federation (IAAF) oversees the World Track and Field Championships.

Related to both arms are the national federations (NFs) or **national governing bodies (NGBs)** and the **organizing committees for the Olympic Games (OCOGs)**. The NGBs operate within the guidelines set forth by their respective IFs to administer a specific sport in a given country. USA Track and Field is the NGB or NF in the United States that selects athletes to compete in the World Track and Field Championships. The OCOGs are the organizations primarily responsible for the operational aspects of the Olympic Games. The OCOGs have to converse with the NOC of the country hosting the Games as well as with the IFs. Each of these organizational entities is explored in depth in the following discussion.

The International Olympic Committee

The defined role of the IOC is to promote Olympism in accordance with the Olympic Charter. The IOC is a nongovernmental, nonprofit organization based in Lausanne, Switzerland. The Olympic Charter is the codification of the fundamental principles, rules, and by-laws adopted by the International Olympic Committee. The Charter governs the organization and operation of the Olympic Movement and stipulates the conditions for the celebration of the Olympic Games. As such, the IOC has a key role because it is the final authority on all questions concerning the Olympic Games and the Olympic Movement.

FIGURE 9-1 Organizational Structure of the Olympic Movement

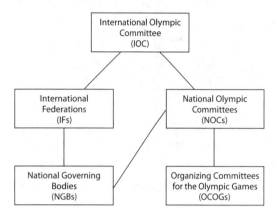

Source: J. M. Gladden.

The IOC owns exclusive rights to the Olympic Games, the Olympic symbol (the five rings used alone, in one or in several colors), the Olympic flag (white background with the Olympic symbol in its five colors located in the center), the Olympic anthem, the Olympic motto ("Citius, Altius, Fortius," meaning "swifter, higher, stronger"), the Olympic flame, and the Olympic torch. Corporations wanting to use any of these marks must first pay the IOC a rights fee.

The IOC is governed by its members, who are self-selected (i.e., there is no outside vote on who is an IOC member). IOC members are its representatives in their respective countries and not delegates of their countries within the IOC. IOC members must speak at least one of the languages used at the IOC sessions (French, English, German, Arabic, Spanish, and Russian). There cannot be more than one member elected per country, except in the case of countries that have hosted an Olympic Games. In this case, countries are allowed two members. The IOC initially consisted of 14 members, with Demetrius Vikelas (of Greece) as its president. Today it has 106 members, 22 honorary members, and 1 honor member. The

late Juan Antonio Samaranch was an Honorary President for Life.

The IOC is governed by three bodies: the Session, the Executive Board, and the president. The IOC Session, the general meeting of IOC members, is held at least once a year and is the supreme operating entity of the IOC. However, the president can call an extraordinary session if necessary. In these general sessions, the IOC members elect one president, four vice-presidents, and 10 additional members to form the executive board. The main function of the Session is to adopt, modify, and interpret the Olympic Charter. Its decisions are final.

The Executive Board meets several times a year outside the Session to fulfill the duties assigned to it by the Olympic Charter. The Executive Board manages the affairs of the IOC, including approval of the IOC internal organization, management of the IOC's finances and preparation of the annual budget, presentation of a report to the Session on any proposed change of rules or by-laws, submission to the IOC Session of the names of persons it recommends for IOC membership, supervision of the procedure for acceptance and selection of candidatures for the organization of the Olympic Games, and performance of all other duties assigned to it by the Session.

The president heads the International Olympic Committee and is elected by IOC members by secret ballot for an initial term of eight years, renewable once for four additional years. The president presides over all activities of the IOC, acting as its permanent representative. In addition, the president can nominate special commissions to study certain specific subjects and submit recommendations to the Executive Board. Some of these special commissions are joint, comprising members of the IOC, representatives of the IFs and NOCs, technicians, consultants, and specialists. Examples of these commissions include the IOC Radio and Television Commission, Press Commission, Finance Commission, Medical Commission, and Athletes Commission.

National Olympic Committees

The NOCs are responsible for developing and protecting the Olympic Movement in their respective countries, in accordance with the Olympic Charter. Specifically, NOCs are responsible for the following:

- Supporting the fundamental principles of Olympism in their countries
- Ensuring the observance of the Olympic Charter in their countries
- Encouraging the development of high-performance sport as well as sport for all within their respective countries
- Assisting in the training of both athletes and sport administrators
- Representing their respective countries at the Olympic Games and at regional, continental, and world multi-sport competitions patronized by the IOC.

In addition, NOCs have the authority to designate cities that may bid to host Olympic Games in their respective countries.

The NOCs are organized regionally. The umbrella organization is the Association of National Olympic Committees (ANOC). Underneath ANOC, the NOCs are organized into five regional NOC organizations: the Association of National Olympic Committees of Africa (ANOCA), the Olympic Council of Asia (OCA), the Pan American Sports Organization (PASO), the European Olympic Committees (EOC), and the Oceania National Olympic Committees (ONOC). There are currently 203 NOCs spanning five continents.

Before existing as an NOC, an organization must be recognized by the IOC. Recognition can be granted only to an NOC whose jurisdiction coincides with the limits of the country in which it is established and has its headquarters.

The United States Olympic Committee

The NOC for the United States is the United States Olympic Committee (USOC). The USOC is the organization mandated by Congress under the Amateur Sports Act of 1978 (as amended by the Stevens Amendment of 1998) to govern activities in the United States related to the Olympic Games, Paralympic Games, and Pan American Games. The USOC represents Olympic, Paralympic, and Pan American sport athletes, coaches, administrators, and the American people who support the Olympic Movement. Most important, the USOC is responsible for sending the U.S. Olympic teams to the Olympic Games, Paralympic Games, and Pan American Games. USOC affiliated organizations include four categories: Olympic and Paralympic Training sites, Community Olympic Development Programs, community partners, and multi-sport organizations.

The organizational structure of the USOC includes an executive committee and a board of directors. The executive committee meets as often as needed and is responsible for supervising the conduct of the business affairs of the USOC, according to the policy guidelines

prescribed by the board of directors. The board of directors carries out the purposes and objectives of the USOC. It meets twice a year, unless otherwise decided by the constituency.

Organizing Committees for the Olympic Games

The honor of hosting the Olympic and Paralympic Games is entrusted by the IOC to the city designated as the host city of the Olympic and Paralympic Games. This honor is given to a city after it has gone through the bidding process. The bidding process has become increasingly complex due to the enhanced interest in hosting the Games.

The corruption crisis in 1998 in Salt Lake City brought many changes at the IOC. The crisis revealed that the IOC faced serious problems regarding its composition, organization, and role as well as some of its procedures—in particular the selection of host cities for the Olympic and Paralympic Games. Criticism came when Salt Lake City admitted having influenced the votes of critical IOC members in its pursuit of hosting the Olympic and Paralympic Games.

The crisis brought a positive side because it allowed the formation of a commission (IOC, 2002) that studied the crisis and brought solutions to the table. As a result of its work, a new procedure was adopted by the 110th IOC Session in December 1999 for the selection of the host city.

Once a city has been awarded the Games, it forms an organizing committee for the Olympic Games (OCOG). At this time, the IOC enters into a written agreement with the host city and the NOC. From that moment, the OCOG is responsible for planning, implementing, and staging the Games. The responsibilities of the OCOG are enormous. The OCOG is ultimately responsible for the construction of all the venues, accommodations for the athletes and coaches, accreditation, logistics, host broadcasting, security, medical services, technology, tickets, transportation, communications, finances, risk management, government relations, protocol, volunteer services, operations, and sports competition, among other duties. It must also establish a marketing program and sign sponsorship agreements separate from those implemented by the IOC. The OCOG is also responsible for staging the Paralympic Games.

International Federations

IFs are the international governing bodies for one or several sports throughout the world. They are nongovernmental organizations recognized by the International Olympic Committee to administer one or more sports at the world level and encompass organizations administering such sports at the national level. IFs must petition for formal recognition by the IOC. To be recognized, these organizations must apply the Olympic Movement Anti-Doping Code and conduct effective out-of-competition tests in accordance with the established rules. The IOC then grants two years (or any other period fixed by the Executive Board) of provisional recognition during which the IOC observes the federation to determine whether it deserves official recognition. At the end of such a period, the

recognition automatically lapses in the absence of definitive confirmation given in writing by the IOC.

After each Olympic Games, the IOC reviews the Olympic Programme and determines whether new sports or new events should be added. At this time, IFs recognized by the IOC but not included on the Olympic Programme can petition to be included. For a sport to be included on the Summer Olympic Programme, it must be practiced by men in at least 75 countries on four continents and by women in at least 40 countries on three continents. To be included on the Winter Olympic Programme, a sport must be practiced in at least 25 countries on three continents.

The IFs can be classified under different categories:

- All the recognized international federations whose sports are not part of the Olympic Programme form the Association of IOC Recognized International Sports Federations (ARISF).
- All the recognized international federations whose sports appear on the Olympic Programme are known as International Olympic Federations. The ones whose sports appear on the Summer Olympic Programme are grouped under the Association of Summer Olympic International Federations (ASOIF). The ones whose sports appear on the Winter Olympic Programme are grouped under the Association of International Winter Sports Federations (AIWF).
- All the federations are grouped under the General Association of International Sports Federations (GAISF).

International Federations are run as international organizations, with their staffs determined by financial resources and objectives. **Table 9-1** presents a listing of the IFs. **Table 9-2** presents their Web site addresses. Sports

TABLE 9-1	International Sport Federations (Recognized Olympic Sports)	
Sport	**International Federation**	**Abbreviation**
Aquatics	Fédération Internationale de Natation	FINA
Archery	International Archery Federations	FITA
Athletics	International Association of Athletics Federation	IAAF
Badminton	Badminton World Federation	BWF
Baseball	International Baseball Federation	IBAF
Basketball	Fédération Internationale de Basketball	FIBA
Biathlon	International Biathlon Union	IBU
Bobsleigh	International Bobsleigh & Tobogganing Federation	FIBT
Boxing	International Boxing Association	AIBA
Canoe/kayak	International Canoe Federation	ICF
Curling	World Curling Federation	WCF
Cycling	Union Cycliste Internationale	UCI
Equestrian	Fédération Équestre Internationale	FEI
Fencing	Fédération Internationale d'Escrime	FIE
Football	Fédération Internationale de Football Association	FIFA
Golf	International Golf Federation	IGF
Gymnastics	International Gymnastics Federation	FIG
Handball	International Handball Federation	IHF
Hockey	International Hockey Federation	FIH
Ice hockey	International Ice Hockey Federation	IIHF
Judo	International Judo Federation	IJF
Luge	International Luge Federation	FIL
Modern pentathlon	Union Internationale de Pentathlon Moderne	UIPM
Rowing	International Federation of Rowing Associations	FISA
Rugby	International Rugby Board	IRB
Sailing	International Sailing Federation	ISAF
Shooting	International Shooting Sport Federation	ISSF
Skating	International Skating Union	ISU
Skiing	International Ski Federation	FIS
Softball	International Softball Federation	ISF
Table tennis	The International Table Tennis Federation	ITTF
Taekwondo	World Taekwondo Federation	WTF
Tennis	International Tennis Federation	ITF
Triathlon	International Triathlon Union	ITU
Volleyball	Fédération Internationale de Volleyball	FIVB
Weightlifting	International Weightlifting Federation	IWF
Wrestling	International Federation of Associated Wrestling Styles	FILA

Source: Gathered from http://www.olympic.org/uk/sports/index_uk.asp (2007), http://www.internationalgolffederation. org/ (2010), and http://www.irb.com/ (2010).

TABLE 9-2	Web Addresses for International Federations of Olympic Sports	

Federation	Sport	Web Address
Fédération Internationale de Natation (FINA)	Aquatics	http://www.fina.org
Fédération Internationale de Tir à l'Arc (FITA)	Archery	http://www.archery.org
Badminton World Federation (BWF)	Badminton	http://www.bwfbadminton.org
International Biathlon Union (IBU)	Biathlon	http://www.biathlonworld.com
Fédération Internationale de Bobsleigh et de Tobogganing (FIBT)	Bobsleigh and Skeleton Sports	http://www.fibt.com
Association Internationale de Boxe Amateur (AIBA)	Boxing	http://www.aiba.org
International Canoe Federation (ICF)	Canoe/kayak	http://www.canoeicf.com
World Curling Federation (WCF)	Curling	http://www.worldcurling.org
Fédération Equestre Internationale (FEI)	Equestrian	http://www.horsesport.org
Fédération Internationale d'Escrime (FIE)	Fencing	http://www.fie.ch
Fédération Internationale de Gymnastique (FIG)	Gymnastics	http://www.fig-gymnastics.com
International Handball Federation (IHF)	Handball	http://www.ihf.info
International Judo Federation (IJF)	Judo	http://www.ijf.org
Fédération Internationale de Luge de Course (FIL)	Luge	http://www.fil-luge.org
Fédération Internationale des Sociétés d'Aviron (FISA)	Rowing	http://www.worldrowing.com
International Rugby Board (IRB)	Rugby	http://www.irb.com
International Sailing Federation (ISAF)	Sailing	http://www.sailing.org
International Shooting Sport Federation (ISSF)	Shooting	http://www.issf-sports.org
International Table Tennis Federation (ITTF)	Table tennis	http://www.ittf.com
World Taekwondo Federation (WTF)	Taekwondo	http://www.wtf.org/wtf_eng/ main/main_eng.html
International Weightlifting Federation (IWF)	Weight lifting	http://www.iwf.net
Fédération Internationale des Luttes Associées (FILA)	Wrestling	http://www.fila-wrestling.com

Source: http://www.olympic.org/sports/index_uk.asp, 2007.

such as basketball and football have large international federations, sometimes employing more than 25 people. In contrast, IFs for sports such as field hockey and team handball have very few employees.

In addition to actual Olympic competitions, each IF sanctions international competitions and establishes its own eligibility rules. An IF can have one set of eligibility rules for the Olympic Games, which must be approved by the IOC, and another set of rules for all other international competitions. For example, the International Ice Hockey Federation (IIHF) could decide to use different eligibility standards during the World Cup of Hockey than during the Olympic Games.

National Governing Bodies

National governing bodies (NGBs), or national sports federations (NFs), are the organizations governing a specific sport within each country. Each IF recognizes a single NGB in each country participating in the sport. For example, in the United States, USA Basketball is the NGB for basketball recognized by Fédération Internationale de Basketball (FIBA), the international federation for basketball. An NGB's membership must be open to all national organizations concerned with promoting the sport. Each NGB is responsible for approving and sanctioning competitions open to all athletes in its country (United States Olympic Committee, 2010). For example, USA Track and Field is responsible for the coordination and administration of the United States Track and Field Championships. In addition, NGBs set national policies and eligibility standards for participation in their respective sports. Finally, NGBs are responsible for the training, development, and selection of the Olympic teams in their respective sports. USA Track and Field uses the United States Track and Field Trials to select the Olympic team for every Summer Olympic Games.

The Paralympic Games

The Paralympic Games, where the world's best athletes with physical disabilities compete, also represent one of the world's largest sporting extravaganzas. In 2004, 3,806 athletes from 136 countries competed at the Athens Paralympic Games (IOC, 2010). The Beijing Paralympic Games hosted 3,951 athletes from 146 countries (International Paralympic Committee, 2010a). A wide variety of athletes compete in the Paralympic Games, including amputees, wheelchair athletes, the visually impaired, dwarfs, athletes with cerebral palsy, and athletes with spinal cord injuries. Introduced in Rome in 1960, the Summer Paralympic Games have been held every Olympic year since. The Winter Paralympic competition began in 1976 in Sweden (Hums & MacLean, 2008). The 2006 Torino Paralympic Games had 474 athletes from 39 nations (International Paralympic Committee, 2010b) and the Vancouver Paralympic Games featured 502 athletes from 44 countries (International Paralympic Committee, 2010c). Starting in 1988 in Seoul, South Korea, the Paralympic Games immediately followed the competition dates of the Olympic Games and shared common facilities.

Organizers of the Paralympic Games face the same major challenge as organizers of the Olympic Games: raising money to cover operating costs. With the Paralympic Games increasing in size and scope, the Games must generate revenues from corporate sponsorships, licensing agreements, and ticket sales. For example, in 2003 the International Paralympic Committee (IPC) signed an exclusive partnership agreement with VISA. VISA has extended its sponsorship of the Olympic and Paralympic Games through 2012 and has become a Worldwide Partner as evidence that Paralympic sponsorship has grown. The International Paralympic Committee also added three other Worldwide Partners—Otto Bock Healthcare, Samsung, and Atos Origin— and created a second level of sponsorship called *Patrons* and a third known as *Ambassadors*. Two Gold Patrons are Allianz and Deutsche Telekom. The Paralympic Games face an added challenge in that they are not governed by the IOC and thus do not share in the millions generated by the Olympic Movement. Instead, the Paralympic Games are governed by the International Paralympic Committee (IPC). The Paralympic Games have an organizational structure similar to that of the Olympic Games. The IPC oversees national Paralympic committees (NPCs). Since the 2004 Athens Games, the management of the Olympic and Paralympic Games has been overseen by the Organizing Committee for the Olympic Games (OCOG). For example, in 2010, the Vancouver Organizing Committee (VANOC) was responsible for staging both the Olympic and Paralympic Winter Games. In May 2001, U.S. Paralympics became a division of the USOC. This structure is not the case in other countries, which usually have an independently operating NPC.

■ CAREER OPPORTUNITIES

This chapter examines a wide variety of settings in which sport crosses international boundaries.

It is evident that significant growth is occurring in each of these settings. As a result of such development, a wide variety of career opportunities are potentially available to future sport managers. Before discussing the areas in which job opportunities may exist, it is important to note two unique competencies required of most international sport managers. First, with the many different languages spoken throughout the world, working in the sport industry in other countries requires that sport managers be multilingual. Therefore, the future sport manager should take every opportunity to learn a second language. Second, different countries have different customs. Sport managers must not only make themselves aware of these customs but also must appreciate and accept the differences that exist.

Corporate Sport

With corporations throughout the world expanding the markets for their products through sport, increased opportunities will open up for experts in international sport management. Regardless of whether a corporation is sponsoring the Olympic Games or a 3-on-3 basketball tournament in Paris, sport management experts are needed to ensure that a corporation's association with the sporting event is maximized. Corporations (both sport- and non–sport-related) may have job openings specifically in international sport.

Professional Sport Leagues

Professional sport leagues are aggressively attempting to expand the popularity of their leagues in markets throughout the world. Trained sport managers are needed to help the leagues increase their visibility through broadcasting agreements, licensing agreements, exhibition games, marketing athletes, and grassroots programs. In fact, professional sport leagues have international divisions within league offices and also place a number of employees in overseas offices. For example, the Sydney, Australia, and Tokyo, Japan, offices of MLB employ people who focus on increasing the distribution and promotion of MLB in Australia and Japan, respectively. In Australia, these efforts include working with local retailers to sell MLB-logoed hats and T-shirts, as well as working with Australian television stations to secure broadcast coverage of MLB in Australia.

Sport Marketing Companies

As highlighted in Chapter 11, Sports Agency, and Chapter 13, Event Management, behind nearly every major event is a sport marketing company. This is also true with respect to international sport. Corporations, Olympic organizations, and professional sport leagues regularly hire sport marketing agencies to coordinate their international efforts. For example, even though the NBA and Nike sponsor the NBA 3-on-3 basketball tour throughout Europe, these street basketball events are organized, marketed, and administered by Streetball Partners, a Dallas-based company specializing in grassroots tournaments. To coordinate the various tournaments held throughout Europe, a number of Streetball Partners employees travel throughout Europe organizing and managing these tournaments. International Management Group (IMG), the largest sport marketing agency, has over 2,600 employees in more than 60 offices in 30 countries (IMG, 2007).

Numerous sport marketing companies work integrally with the Olympic Games. Several years ago the IOC started working with Meridian as the marketing agency for the IOC and **The Olympic Partner (TOP)** program. Meridian, founded in January 1996, has its headquarters in Lausanne, Switzerland, and a U.S. office in Atlanta. Octagon and IMG have Olympic clients,

mainly Olympic sponsors and Olympic athletes. To support their clients, both of these agencies have offices around the world.

International Olympic Committee

The IOC is an international organization, and most of its staff has international experience. Language skills are mandatory to work for the IOC, and most IOC employees are fluent in either French or English. A sport manager interested in working for the IOC should identify his or her area of interest and contact the appropriate department within the IOC. Some departments offer internship programs. If a sport management student is interested in pursuing this approach, it is important to consider the time and distance factors and start the application process well in advance.

Organizing Committees for the Olympic Games

Jobs become available with the organizing committees for the Olympic Games from the time the committee is formed (about six years prior to the Games). However, the last three years before the Games are a crucial time for recruiting the right staff to work the Olympic and Paralympic Games. The available jobs can be related to any of the aspects needed to organize the Games, including administration, hospitality, international relations, logistics, protocol, technology, transportation, and ticketing. Usually jobs with OCOGs are temporary, lasting until the Games are over. However, some people work for one organizing committee after another because they have become experts in a specific area and enjoy living in a variety of different settings. The most appealing part of working for an organizing committee is receiving a unique experience. The drawback is that it is temporary and usually there is not much opportunity to grow inside the organization. Most of the time, an employee is hired to perform a specific task, and there is not much room for advancement.

National Olympic Committees

Different job opportunities exist within a National Olympic Committee. Depending on its size, an NOC can have anywhere from zero to 100 or more employees. In the United States, the USOC is a large organization, employing approximately 100 people. This number can increase with temporary jobs during Olympic/Paralympic years. In the case of the USOC, many employees are hired via internships. The USOC offers a formal internship program, soliciting applications and conducting interviews prior to hiring interns. Job opportunities at the USOC vary, but include positions in athlete development, broadcasting, coaching, corporate sponsorship, fundraising, government relations, grants, human resources, international games preparation, international relations and protocol, legal aspects, licensing, management information systems, marketing, national events and conferences, public information and media relations, sports medicine, sports science, sports for people with disabilities, and training centers. In addition, the NOC may be helpful in securing a position with one of the many NGBs within each country's sport movement. Again, the number of opportunities will vary greatly from country to country and from sport to sport.

International Paralympic Committee

The IPC is headquartered in Bonn, Germany. Similar to the IOC, the IPC offers employment opportunities for sport managers, including interns. Sport managers interested in working for the IPC should contact its office directly for additional information. Just as with the IOC, language fluency is necessary.

■ CURRENT ISSUES

Cultural Awareness and Sensitivity

Individuals and organizations conducting business in different cultures need to appreciate differences in the world and understand how the same sport can be interpreted differently from country to country, and from culture to culture. Similarly, the advertising message must be adapted to account for differences in local culture and laws (Miller, 1996). People speak hundreds of different languages, and myriad dialects of those languages are spoken throughout the world. In addition, customs and traditions in one country may be perceived as disrespectful in another country. Therefore, when selling products overseas, some degree of adaptation to the local or regional culture is necessary.

In undertaking any international sport management effort, the sport manager must always be sensitive to **cultural differences**. Nike tailors the presentation of its product to the markets it serves. For example, Nike has always portrayed an anti-establishment image, allying with athletes who were prone to challenge conventional wisdom or accepted traditions. However, as Nike attempts to expand into the global marketplace, it has found that such a brash stance is frowned upon in many countries throughout the world (Thurow, 1997). Rather than attempting to buck established tradition, Nike must instead focus on respecting the cultures of other countries. Thus, in its initial efforts to sell more shoes in Europe, Nike featured a number of popular professional athletes in opera-themed ads. Incorporating one of Europe's most popular traditions, the opera, into its advertising enabled Nike to sell products to Europeans.

Foreign Student-Athletes in U.S. Colleges and Universities

In addition to the presence of international players in U.S. professional sport leagues, U.S. colleges and universities have seen an increase in the number of foreign student-athletes competing in intercollegiate athletics (Popp, Hums, & Greenwell, 2009). Foreign student-athletes have been participating in intercollegiate athletics since the early 1900s. In the late 1950s and early 1960s, college coaches began recruiting older foreign student-athletes who had several years of experience with international teams from their respective countries. In an effort to curb this practice, the National Collegiate Athletic Association (NCAA) ultimately implemented a rule whereby a student-athlete loses a year of eligibility for every year any student-athlete competes after his or her twentieth birthday (Barr, 1996). The implementation of this rule has not had a dramatic effect on the recruitment of foreign student-athletes. In fact, participation by foreign student-athletes is on the rise (see Chapter 8, Collegiate Sport). Although some people argue that there are too many foreign student-athletes, others suggest the presence of foreign student-athletes improves the caliber of play in U.S. colleges and universities.

Marketing the Olympic Games

Today, all levels of the Olympic Movement rely heavily on revenues from broadcasting and sponsorship agreements.

■ BROADCASTING RIGHTS

Broadcasting rights fees are significant for the IOC, since they account for 50% of all Olympic revenue (International Olympic Committee, n.d.). The IOC delegates the responsibility for a broad portfolio of marketing opportunities, including the development and implementation of the Olympic broadcast rights and marketing strategy, to the IOC Television & Marketing Services SA. This includes negotiating Olympic broadcast rights and TOP sponsor contracts, and managing and servicing the TOP Programme and Olympic brand management. The IOC Television & Marketing Services SA has offices in Lausanne, Switzerland, and Atlanta, Georgia.

Figure 9-2 depicts the growth of global broadcast revenues. The primary funding source for the Olympic Games in the 1980s was U.S. broadcasting revenue. Recently, Olympic broadcast rights outside of the United States have grown dramatically, thereby reducing the Olympic Movement's dependency on U.S. broadcast revenue. The additional broadcasting revenue has supported the Olympic Organizing Committees, the World Anti-Doping Agency, and international federations (International Olympic Committee, n.d.).

The IOC's long-term broadcasting strategy is to increase revenue and secure a consistent sum for the Olympic Movement and future host cities while avoiding market fluctuations. Establishing long-term rights fees contracts with profit-sharing arrangements and commitments to provide additional Olympic programs and guaranteed improved global coverage are related goals. Finally, a specific marketing strategy is to forge stronger links among sponsors, broadcasters, and the Olympic family to promote an agenda that goes beyond the Games to support the entire Olympic Movement.

Deals have been signed with broadcasters having prior experience in televising the Olympic Games, thus ensuring the broadest coverage and best possible production quality for viewers. The IOC has often declined higher offers for broadcast on a pay-per-view basis or when a broadcaster could reach only a limited part of the population, as this is against Olympic Broadcast Policy. This fundamental IOC policy, which is set forth in the Olympic Charter, ensures the

FIGURE 9-2 Global Broadcast Revenue for Olympic Games

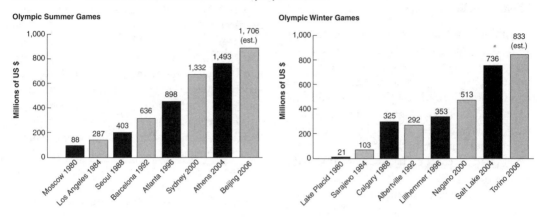

Source: IOC. (2001 July). *Marketing Matters.* © International Olympic Committee. Reprinted with permission.

maximum presentation of the Olympic Games by broadcasters around the world to everyone who has access to television. Rights are sold only to broadcasters that can guarantee the broadest coverage throughout their respective countries free of charge ("Olympic Broadcasting," 2007).

■ SPONSORSHIP SALES

All levels of the Olympic Movement (IOC, NOCs, OCOGs, IFs, and NGBs) rely on sponsorship sales to finance their operations. Following the IOC principles established in the Olympic Charter, there are three levels of sponsorship for the Olympic Games: The Olympic Partner Program, NOC sponsorship program, and OCOG sponsorship programs.

The Olympic Partner Program

As touched on previously, the Olympic sponsorships sold by the IOC and its selected agencies are referred to as The Olympic Partner Program (TOP). Based on the success of the

1984 Los Angeles Olympic Games, in 1985 the IOC established TOP, under which corporations pay millions of dollars for status as an official Olympic sponsor for a four-year period (quadrennium). Some current TOP members include McDonalds, Coca-Cola, Samsung, and VISA, among others.

NOC Sponsorship Programs

NOCs have their own sponsorship programs as well. The NOCs usually use these programs to target domestic companies in an effort to generate funds for the development and travel of their Olympic teams. The TOP sponsors are encouraged to sign agreements with each of the NOCs. A preference in each category will be given to the TOP sponsor before the NOC signs with another company to protect its rights.

OCOG Sponsorship Programs

An OCOG also identifies and targets its own sponsors. However, it needs approval from both the IOC and the host country NOC.

Doping

Doping allegations have dominated the media coverage of several international sports, such as Olympic events, the Tour de France, World Cups, and many others. Doping is "the deliberate or inadvertent (accidental) use by athletes of banned substances or methods that may enhance performance" (Sports Medicine Australia, 2006, p. 44). Many athletes in competitive sports have turned to doping as a means of gaining an advantage. Famous cases, such as the East German swim team of the 1970s and the cycling bust on the eve of the 2006 Tour de France, may lead some to believe that doping is problematic only in certain sports and in certain countries, but this is not the case. In recent years, cases of doping have arisen across a variety of sports and in numerous countries.

After a drug scandal in cycling in 1998, the IOC recognized the severity of the doping issue and convened a World Conference on Anti-Doping. In 1999, the World Anti-Doping Agency (WADA) was established with the goal of coordinating and promoting the fight against doping on an international scale. WADA was set up as an independent international agency funded by the world's governments and sport programs, and remains universally accepted as the authority in anti-doping efforts. Guidelines and principles developed by WADA (the Code) have been adopted by the IOC, the IPC, all Olympic and Paralympic sports, national Olympic and Paralympic committees, athletes, national anti-doping organizations, and international agencies (World Anti-Doping Agency, n.d.).

WADA works with both athletes and organizations to protect athletes from the potentially harmful effects of performance-enhancing drugs and strives to create an equal playing field for athletic competition. In addition, WADA coordinates anti-doping programs at the international and national levels (World Anti-Doping Agency,

2003). International cooperation among countries allows a worldwide standard of definitions and procedures to be put in place, in a system that replaces the isolated and disjointed efforts by individual governing bodies.

One of WADA's most visible functions is as a testing agency. It conducts "out-of-competition," or "year-round," testing for athletes. It also provides independent observers to monitor procedures at events such as the Olympic Games, Paralympic Games, FIBA World Championships (basketball), and Commonwealth Games. In addition to testing, the agency provides education, funds research, and conducts athlete outreach to connect one on one with athletes worldwide.

The IOC has stated that the fight against doping is its top priority. As a consequence, the IOC is adopting a zero-tolerance policy at Olympic events. Through a concerted effort among governments, WADA, and the world of sport, the IOC strives to educate athletes about the detrimental effects doping can have on health, the credibility of sport, and the athlete's career.

■ SUMMARY

Today, more than ever, corporations, sport leagues, and sport governing bodies are attempting to increase their popularity and revenues in international markets. Technology, particularly with respect to the transmission of visual images, greatly enhances the ease with which sport managers can introduce their products to foreign markets. In effect, the world is becoming smaller. Corporations are attempting to capitalize on this trend by sponsoring international sporting events in an effort to increase the distribution channels for their products. Major professional sports worldwide are attempting to utilize the shrinking marketplace to increase exposure for their respective leagues and sports in an effort to expand their revenue bases. This

CASE STUDY: Growing Australian Rules Football in the United States

Australian Rules Football (Aussie Rules) is the number one spectator sport in Australia, but only recently has been seen on an international scale. In 1997, the United States Australian Football League (USAFL) was founded with the mission of growing Aussie Rules in the United States. In particular, the USAFL's stated mission is to develop Australian Rules Football through "promoting awareness and knowledge of the Australian culture, by promoting a sense of community among USAFL clubs and club members, and by fostering women's and junior programs across the United States" (United States Australian Football League, 2010).

In April 2007, when the USAFL Board met in Louisville, Kentucky, it was noted that in ten years the league had expanded to the point where it had more than 35 teams, located in nearly every major market in the United States, with over 2,000 players. At the meeting the Board discussed the goals of the league for the next ten years. It agreed on three primary goals for the next decade: (1) to grow the league to more than 10,000 participants, (2) to have 1% of the U.S. population become aware of and interested in Aussie Rules, and (3) to secure four new league sponsors.

A. J. Hudson, Director of Development, was put in charge of devising a plan to create and foster awareness and increase participation in Australian Rules Football. Hudson walked away from the meeting and started asking himself, "How will I generate interest in a game that only a limited number of people have heard of? How will I convince Americans to participate in a sport that is relatively new to the country? How will I position Aussie Rules to compete against baseball, American football, basketball, and hockey? Which community stakeholders could I get involved to help me with this project?"

Hudson knew that his budget was limited, because the USAFL is a nonprofit organization. He had to find a way to spread the word about the USAFL with a very limited budget.

Questions for Discussion

1. How could Hudson create awareness and interest in Aussie Rules?
2. What could Hudson do to inform the public of the league?
3. How should Hudson position Aussie Rules so that it is seen as an attractive alternative to American football, baseball, basketball, and hockey?
4. Which community groups could Hudson target to become involved with Aussie Rules?
5. Toward which target markets should Hudson focus his marketing campaign?
6. Which stakeholders (or sponsors) could Hudson approach to help to reach the USAFL's goals?

is true for both the popular North American professional sports as well as for the world's most popular sport, football. Ultimately, both corporations and professional sport leagues are attempting to improve the global appeal of their products, and to do so they must hire people with experience in international sport management.

The Olympic Movement also offers career opportunities for sport managers. Whether at the top with the IOC, or with an NOC, NGB, or OCOG, the opportunities within the Olympic and Paralympic Movements continue to increase as the size, proportion, and number of competitions continues to grow.

Such growth creates an increased need for revenues. Such financing, most often in the form of sponsorships, is heavily reliant on the corporate sector. Thus, sport managers are needed to sell sponsorships and assist the corporations in implementing their sponsorship programs.

There is clearly a diversity of opportunities for the sport manager interested in international sport. Further, because technology will continue to improve and trade barriers between countries will continue to diminish, the volume of opportunities in international sport will increase. However, to capitalize on these opportunities, the sport management student must become knowledgeable about and sensitive to the cultures of other countries. The prospective international sport manager should also be prepared to learn new languages because multilingual capabilities are necessary at the highest levels of international sport.

■ RESOURCES

Beijing Organizing Committee for the Games of the XXIX Olympiad (BOCOG)
Beijing Olympic Tower
267 Beishuanzhonglu
Hajdan, Beijing
P.R. China
100083
(86010) 66 69 9185; fax: (86010) 66 69 9229
http://www.beijing2008.com

IMG International Headquarters
McCormack House
Hogarth Business Park
Burlington Lane
Chiswick London W4 2TH
(44) 208-233-5300; fax: (44) 208-233-5301

International Olympic Committee
Chateau de Vidy
Lausanne CH 1009
Switzerland
41-21-612-6111
http://www.olympic.org

London 2012
One Churchill Place
Canary Wharf
London E14 5LN
United Kingdom
0203-2012-000

Major League Baseball International Partners
350 Park Avenue, 22nd Floor
New York, NY 10022
212-350-8304
http://www.mlb.com

Major League Soccer/Soccer United Marketing
110 E. 42nd Street, Suite 1000
New York, NY 10017
212-687-1400
http://www.mls.com
http://www.sumworld.com/

National Basketball Association International
645 Fifth Avenue
New York, NY 10022
212-407-8000; fax: 212-832-3861
http://www.nba.com

Octagon
The Grace Building
1114 Avenue of the Americas, 18th floor
New York, NY 10036
212-597-8170
http://www.octagon.com

United States Olympic Committee
One Olympic Plaza
Colorado Springs, CO 80909
719-578-4654
http://www.olympic-usa.org

VANOC
3585 Gravely Street #400
Vancouver, BC V5K 5J5
Canada
778-328-2010
778-328-2011
http://www.vancouver2010.com

World Anti-Doping Agency (WADA)
Stock Exchange Tower
800 Place Victoria, Suite 1700
P.O. Box 120
Montreal, Quebec H4Z 1B7
Canada
514-904-9232
514-904-8650
http://www.wada-ama.org

■ KEY TERMS

cultural differences, global strategy,
grassroots efforts, international federations
(IFs), International Olympic Committee (IOC),
licensed merchandise, national governing
bodies (NGBs), nationalism, National Olympic
Committees (NOCs), Olympism, organizing
committees for the Olympic Games (OCOGs),
The Olympic Partner Program (TOP)

■ REFERENCES

Barr, C. A. (1996). Multiculturalism within United States collegiate sport: Recruitment of international student-athletes. *Proceedings from the Fourth European Congress on Sport Management*, Montpellier, France, 465–473.

Chalip L. (2001). Sport and tourism: Capitalising on the linkage. In D. Kluka & G. Schilling (Eds.),

The business of sport (pp. 77–89). Oxford, UK: Meyer & Meyer.

Collins, C., & Trenberth, L. (2005). *Sport business management in Aotearoa/New Zealand*. South Melbourne, Australia: Cengage Learning Australia.

England's Barmy Army. (2010) Our history. Retrieved October 22, 2010, from http://barmyarmy.com/about/index.php?m=history

Field, R. (1997). Play ball: Just whose pastime is it anyway? *Play Ball*, 109–117.

Gilbert, N. (1995, February 14). Kickoff time for soccer: Can U.S. pro soccer turn from bush league to big league? *Financial World*, 79–85.

Graham, S., Goldblatt, J. J., & Delpy, L. (1995). *The ultimate guide to sport event management and marketing*. Chicago: Irwin Publishing.

Higham, J. (1999). Commentary: Sport as an avenue of tourism development: An analysis of the positive and negative impacts of sport tourism. *Current Issues in Tourism, 2*(1), 82–90.

Hums, M.A., & MacLean, J.C. (2008). *Governance and policy development in sport organizations* (2nd ed.). Scottsdale, AZ: Holcomb Hathaway Publishers.

Hums, M.A., & Wolff, E.A. (2008). Sport and human rights. In J. Borms (Ed.) *Directory of sport science* (5th ed.), pp. 467–487. Berlin, Germany: International Council on Sport Science and Physical Education.

IMG. (2007). Company facts: Locations. Retrieved October 22, 2010, from http://www.imgworld.com/about/company_facts.sps

International Olympic Committee. (n.d.). Final report: Administration. Retrieved March 12, 2011, from http://multimedia.olympic.org/pdf/en_report_969.pdf

International Olympic Committee. (2002). *Report by the IOC 2000 Commission to the 110th IOC session*. Lausanne, Switzerland: Author.

International Olympic Committee. (2007). Athens 2004: Games of the XXVIII Olympiad. Retrieved October 22, 2010, from http://www.olympic.org/en/content/Olympic-Games/All-Past-Olympic-Games/Summer/Athens-2004-summer-olympics/

International Olympic Committee. (2010). *Olympic charter: Fundamental principles of Olympism*. Lausanne, Switzerland: Author.

International Olympic Committee. (2010). Official site of the Olympic Movement. Retrieved October 22, 2010, from http://www.olympic.org

International Paralympic Committee. (2010a). Beijing 2008. Retrieved October 22, 2010, from http://www.paralympic.org/Paralympic_Games/Past_Games/Beijing_2008/index.html

International Paralympic Committee. (2010b). Retrieved October 22, 2010, from http://www.paralympic.org/Paralympic_Games/Past_Games/Torino_2006/index.html

International Paralympic Committee. (2010c). Paralympic Games Vancouver 2010. Retrieved October 22, 2010, from http://www.paralympic.org/Paralympic_Games/Past_Games/Vancouver_2010/index.html

Lai, F. Y. (1999). Floorball's penetration of Australia: Rethinking the nexus of globalisation and marketing. *Sport Management Review, 2,* 133–149.

Langdon, J. (1997a, January 9). MLS devises strategy to help fans get hands on merchandise. *USA Today,* p. 10C.

Langdon, J. (1997b, January 17). Survey: Pro game attracts young, families. *USA Today,* p. 11C.

Martin, H., & Schumann, H. (1996). *The global trap: Globalization and the assault on prosperity and democracy.* Leichhardt, NSW: Pluto Press.

Miller, C. (1996, December 2). Chasing a global dream. *Marketing News,* 1–2.

Major League Baseball (MLB) International. (2010). PitchHit&Run. Retrieved October 22, 2010, from http://www.mlb.com/phr

National Basketball Association (NBA). (1997). Global. Retrieved October 22, 2010, from http://www.nba.com/global/

NBA Media Ventures. (2011). 2007–2008 season offers broadest global TV distribution in league history. http://www.nba.com/global/0708_global_tv_071109.html

New Balance liking strategy more and more. (2003). *SportsBusinessDaily.com.* Retrieved October 22, 2010, from http://www.sportsbusinessdaily.com/article/77620

Popp, N., Hums, M. A., & Greenwell, T. C. (2009). Do international student-athletes view the purpose of sport differently than United States student-athletes at NCAA Division I universities? *Journal of Issues in Intercollegiate Athletics, 2,* 93–110.

Sports Medicine Australia. (2006). *Sport medicine for sport trainers.* Australia: Author.

Thoma, J. E., & Chalip, L. (1996). *Sport governance in the global community.* Morgantown, WV: Fitness Information Technology, Inc.

Thurow, R. (1997, May 5). In global drive, Nike finds its brash ways don't always pay off. *The Wall Street Journal,* pp. A1, A10.

Turner, V. (1977). Variations on a theme of liminality. In S. F. Moore & B.G. Myerhoff, (Eds), *Secular ritual* (pp 36–52). Assen, Netherlands: Van Gorcum.

United Nations. (2007). Sport for Development and Peace. Our mandate: What does sport have to do with the UN? Retrieved October 22, 2010, from http://www.un.org/themes/sport/intro.htm

United States Australian Football League (USAFL). (2010). About the USAFL. Retrieved October 22, 2010, from http://www.usafl.com

United States Olympic Committee. (2010). The United States Olympic Committee history. Retrieved October 22, 2010, from http://www.teamusa.org/about-usoc/usoc-general-information/history

U.S. Census Bureau. (2010). Home page. Retrieved October 22, 2010, from http://www.census.gov/

Weed, M. (2003). Why the two won't tango! Explaining the lack of integrated policies for sport and tourism in the UK. *Journal of Sport Management, 17*(3), 258–283.

Weed, M., & Bull, C. J. (1997). Integrating sport and tourism: A review of regional policies in England. *Progress in Tourism and Hospitality Research, 4,* 129–148.

World Anti-Doping Agency. (n.d.). *Play true.* Montreal: Author.

World Anti-Doping Agency. (2003). *World anti-doping code.* Montreal: Author.

Professional Sport Industry

CHAPTER

Professional Sport

Lisa P. Masteralexis

■ INTRODUCTION

The professional sport industry creates events and exhibitions in which athletes compete individually or on teams and are paid for their performance. The events and exhibitions are live, include a paying audience, and are sponsored by a professional league or professional tour. The professional sport industry is a major international business grossing billions of dollars each year (see Chapter 4, Financial and Economic Principles Applied to Sport Management). Although leagues and events derive revenue from **gate receipts** (ticket sales) and **premium seating** (personal seat licenses, luxury suites, club seating) sales, they obtain the bulk of their revenue from the sale of media rights to their events or exhibitions. The drafting of more international players by North American sport leagues has catapulted professional sport into new markets. Professional sport globalization has come with improved access to the Internet combined with increased demand for cable sports programming. The international sale of professional sport teams' licensed products (apparel, videos, books, memorabilia) and the worldwide availability of online services further characterize the industry's international growth (see Chapter 9, International Sport).

North America is home to five preeminent professional leagues: Major League Baseball (MLB), the National Basketball Association (NBA), the National Football League (NFL), the National Hockey League (NHL), and Major League Soccer (MLS). As of 2010, those five leagues included 138 franchises. Each year new leagues such as the Arena Football League (AFL), Major League Lacrosse and the National Lacrosse League (NLL), the Women's NBA (WNBA), National Pro Fastpitch (softball) (NPF), and the Women's Professional Soccer (WPS) emerge—some survive, and others do not. The minor leagues in baseball, basketball, soccer, hockey, and football are far too numerous to list here. Table 10-1 gives a breakdown of the number of major and minor league professional sport franchises operating in the North American professional sport industry as of April 2010.

TABLE 10-1 Numbers of Professional Sport Teams in North America (2010)

Baseball	
Major league (MLB)	30
Minor league affiliates (includes AZ Fall, Venezuelan Summer League, and Gulf Coast League)	240
Minor league independents	72
Basketball	
Men's basketball	
Major league (NBA)	30
Minor leagues	160
Women's basketball	
Major league (WNBA)	12
Minor leagues	4
Football	
Men's football	
Major league (NFL)	32
Minor leagues (outdoor)	34
Minor leagues (indoor)	114
Women's football	87
Hockey	
Men's ice hockey	
Major league (NHL)	30
Minor leagues	97
Roller hockey	35
Soccer	
Major league outdoor (MLS)	13
Minor league outdoor	42
Minor league indoor	8
Other	
Men's lacrosse	
Outdoor	6
Indoor	13
Team tennis	12
NASCAR teams	39

Numerous professional leagues also operate throughout South America, Europe, the Middle East, Asia, Australia, and Africa in the sports of rugby and rugby union, cricket, baseball, basketball, Australian Rules and American football, soccer, hockey, and volleyball. Athletes in leagues are salaried employees whose bargaining power and ability to negotiate salaries vary. In some cases athletes are unionized, enabling them to negotiate collectively for better wages, benefits, and conditions of employment. In the (MLB-affiliated) minor leagues, unless the player has prior major league experience, the player has little leverage to negotiate. In minor league baseball, salaries are relatively uniform across the league and for many players fall below what would be considered a living wage. For example, in baseball's minor leagues, players' salaries start at $1,100 per month during the season only plus a small amount of per diem money for meals incurred when on the road ($25/day). (Players with some level of major league experience earn higher monthly wages). Assuming that in an average week half of the team's games are home and half away, a player works (travel, practice, games, and community/fan relations) approximately 60 hours. At the lower levels of baseball, this is hardly a living wage. Players generally have one to two days off per month. A good comparison is to look to minor league hockey players in the American Hockey League (AHL) and ECHL (formerly the East Coast Hockey League), where conditions are far more favorable because the league is subject to antitrust laws and the players are unionized and have negotiated collective bargaining agreements. The minimum salary in the AHL for 2009–2010 was $36,500 U.S. or $39,000 Canadian ($28,000 U.S. for players on loan to the AHL from lesser leagues) with $63/day per diem (PHPA, 2010a). The ECHL has a minimum weekly salary due to player movement. The 2010–2011 weekly minimum falls between $370 and $410 U.S. (depending on player's experience level) and daily per diem is $36/day (PHPA, 2010b).

Countless professional sports events are also staged around the world in individual sports, including action sports, boxing, fencing, figure skating, golf, tennis, racquetball, running, and track and field. Individual sports are often organized around a tour, such as the National Association of Sports Car Auto Racing (NASCAR) Sprint Cup Series, the Professional Golfers' Association of America (PGA), or Ladies Professional Golf Association of America (LPGA) tours. An athlete on a professional tour earns prize money, and a top (seeded) player considered a "draw" might earn an appearance fee. Athletes on some tours are also required to play in pro-ams the day before the tournament. For some tours, like the LPGA, the pro-ams are the lifeblood of the sport, as they are a place where players cater to their sponsors, and players are disqualified for failing to participate or showing up late (Crouse, 2010). Sponsorship provides income and the products necessary for individual athletes to compete (e.g., golf clubs, tennis racquets, and shoes). The value of sponsorship to athletes is easily apparent with just a quick look at a NASCAR vehicle or the apparel worn by a tennis player such as Serena Williams. A tour stops at various sites for events and exhibitions that are usually sponsored by one named corporation (the title sponsor) and a number of other sponsors. Some tours have broadcast television, radio, and/or cable contracts.

Tours or exhibitions have also been created for athletes by sport agencies, in sports such as tennis, golf, and figure skating. These events serve many purposes such as generating revenue for the athletes and their agencies as well as satisfying fan interest. For instance, the 2010 "Smucker's Stars on Ice" annual tour began within a month of the Vancouver Olympic Games and featured many medalists and competitors capitalizing on their Olympic achievements and name recognition. Television and cable networks have also created exhibitions for programming purposes in action sports (ESPN's X-Games and NBC and MTV's Alli Dew Tour), golf (ABC's Skins Game), and other sports (ESPN's Outdoor Games). These tours and exhibitions generate income for athletes, sport management firms, and the broadcasting industry primarily from sponsorship, media, and ticket sales. Occasionally, some of the income generated from these events is donated to charity (see Chapter 10, Professional Sports, Chapter 11, Sports Agency, and Chapter 13, Event Management, for more information on agency firms).

■ HISTORY

Professional Sport Leagues

In 1869 the first professional team, the Cincinnati Red Stockings, paid players to barnstorm the United States (Jennings, 1989). The ten-player team's payroll totaled $9,300. At the time, the average annual salary in the United States was $170, so the average player's salary of $930 shows that as early as 1869 a professional athlete's income exceeded an average worker's wages (Jennings, 1989).

In 1876 North America's first professional sport league, the National League, was organized (Jennings, 1989). Among the principles from the National League's Constitution and By-Laws that continue as models for professional sports today are limits on franchise movement, club territorial rights, and a mechanism for expulsion of a club. Interestingly, these rules also allowed a player to contract with a club for his future services (Berry, Gould, & Staudohar, 1986). It did not take long—just three years—for owners to change that rule.

Following the National League's lead, other professional leagues have organized themselves into a system of **self-governance**, as opposed to a **corporate governance model** (Lentze,

1995). Under a corporate governance model, owners act as the board of directors, and the commissioner acts as the chief executive officer (CEO). Although it may appear that leagues have adopted a corporate governance model, Lentze (1995) argues that the commissioner's power over the owners does not place the commissioner under the direct supervision and control of the owners in the same manner that a CEO is under the direct supervision and control of a corporate board. This distinction is made because the commissioner in professional sport possesses decision-making power, disciplinary power, and dispute resolution authority (Lentze, 1995). The commissioner's role is discussed in greater detail later in this chapter.

Learning from the fiscal challenges facing a new sport league, MLS was structured as a limited liability company with owners initially investing $50 million in the league as a single entity to avoid financial and antitrust liability (Garber, 2004). Other leagues, namely the Women's National Basketball Association (WNBA), Arena Football League, Major League Lacrosse, National Lacrosse League, to name a few, have followed this trend to establish themselves as single entities to avoid antitrust liability and to create centralized fiscal control. The legal definition of a single entity is governed by substance, not form. In other words, to determine if a league operates as a single entity and thus, is not subject to Section 1 Sherman Antitrust Act liability, one must evaluate whether the league joins together separate economic actors that would be actual or potential competitors (*American Needle v. NFL*, 2010).

Soon after the MLS was established, the **single entity structure** was scrutinized in a lawsuit. The structure withstood an antitrust challenge from MLS players who argued that it was a sham created for the purpose of restraining competition and depressing player salaries (*Fraser v. MLS*, 2002). Although the First Circuit Court of Appeals disagreed with the players'

allegations, it did not conclusively find that the MLS was a single entity, instead construing it as a hybrid that settled somewhere between a traditional sports league and a single company (*Fraser v. MLS*, 2002). As a strategy, the MLS players chose not to unionize because doing so and negotiating a collective bargaining agreement would allow the league access to the labor exemption defense in an antitrust suit. After losing the lawsuit, the players established the Major League Soccer Players Union (MLSPU). Interestingly, the WNBA players chose to unionize rather than pursue an antitrust challenge. Shortly after the union negotiated its second collective bargaining agreement with the league, the WNBA abandoned the single-entity league structure in favor of a traditional team ownership model. The U.S. Supreme Court recently ruled that traditionally structured leagues with separate owners having individual control of their teams are not single entities for antitrust purposes (*American Needle v. NFL*, 2010).

Franchise Ownership

Historically, sport team ownership was a hobby for the wealthy. Many teams were family owned and were operated as "Mom and Pop" businesses. This is no longer true because team ownership has become a revenue-driven proposition. The owners of NFL clubs are listed in Table 10-2. Note that the teams are almost exclusively family or individually owned. For these owners, the investment is not simply a hobby, but a profitable business venture. In the NFL, family or individual ownership is still the norm, but the focus of these owners is on running the team like a business rather than a hobby.

Family or individual ownership is successful in the NFL because it engages in far more revenue sharing than do the other professional leagues. That system, however, has been under fire as more of the newer owners who have paid hundreds of millions of dollars for their teams

TABLE 10-2 NFL Ownership	
NFL Team	**Ownership**
Arizona Cardinals	Bidwell family
Atlanta Falcons	Arthur Blank
Baltimore Ravens	Steven Bisciotti, Jr.
Buffalo Bills	Ralph Wilson
Carolina Panthers	Jerry Richardson*
Chicago Bears	McCaskey (Halas) family*
Cincinnati Bengals	Brown family*
Cleveland Browns	Randolph Lerner*
Dallas Cowboys	Jerry Jones
Denver Broncos	Pat Bowlen
Detroit Lions	William Clay Ford
Green Bay Packers	Publicly owned
Houston Texans	Bob McNair*
Indianapolis Colts	James Irsay
Jacksonville Jaguars	Wayne Weaver*
Kansas City Chiefs	Clark Hunt
Miami Dolphins	Steven Ross
Minnesota Vikings	Wilf family, David Mandelbaum, Alan Landis, and Reggie Fowler
New England Patriots	Bob Kraft/Kraft Family
New Orleans Saints	Tom Benson
New York Giants	Mara* and Tisch families
New York Jets	Woody Johnson
Oakland Raiders	Al Davis
Philadelphia Eagles	Jeffrey Lurie
Pittsburgh Steelers	Rooney family*
San Diego Chargers	Spanos family
San Francisco 49ers	Denise DeBartolo and John York
Seattle Seahawks	Paul Allen
St. Louis Rams	Chip Rosenbloom
Tampa Bay Buccaneers	Glazer family
Tennessee Titans	Bud Adams
Washington Redskins	Daniel Snyder

*Denotes original owner or descendant of original owner
Sources: Data compiled from http://www.nfl.com and team Web sites

are seeking to maximize their local revenue to make a return on their investments (Foldesy, 2004). Jerry Jones, who paid $140 million for the Dallas Cowboys, began the challenge to this system by entering into marketing deals through his stadium, some of which ambushed the league's exclusive deals and led to a legal battle with the NFL (*National Football League Properties, Inc. v. Dallas Cowboys Football Club, Ltd.*, 1996). The chasm lies in the fact that some owners have paid as much as $600 million (Steve Bisciotti, Baltimore Ravens), $700 million (Bob McNair, Houston Texans), and $800 million (Daniel Snyder, Washington Redskins), whereas others have inherited their franchises and have no acquisition costs to recover (Brown family, Cincinnati Bengals; Halas-McCaskey family, Chicago Bears; Mara family, New York Giants; Rooney family, Pittsburgh Steelers). Although a vote in 2004 extended for 15 years the NFL's Trust, which owns all team logos and trademarks, oversees and administers the league properties rights, and distributes revenue for those rights to each club, there is a growing number of owners clamoring for more local control over the potential marketing revenues from using team logos, trademarks, and sponsorships. While not the sole factor in determining that the NFL was not a single entity for purposes of licensing, the battle for local control of licensing revenues certainly undermined the NFL's argument in *American Needle v. NFL* (2010).

Ownership Rules

Not just anyone can become a sports franchise owner. It takes a great deal of capital, but even having the financial capacity and the desire to purchase a team does not guarantee eventual ownership of a team. Permission to own a sports franchise must be granted by the ownership committee of the league in which one seeks team ownership. Each league imposes restrictions on ownership, including a limit on the number of **franchise rights** granted and restrictions on franchise location. Franchise rights, the privileges afforded to owners, are granted with ownership. These include such rights as **territorial rights**, which limit a competitor franchise from moving into another team's territory without league permission and providing compensation to the rights holder; and **revenue sharing**, which gives a team a portion of various league-wide revenues (expansion fees, national television revenue, gate receipts, and licensing revenues). Owners also receive the right to serve on ownership committees. Ownership committees exist for such areas as rules (competition/rules of play), franchise ownership, finance, labor relations/negotiations, television, and expansion. Ownership committees make decisions and set policies for implementation by the commissioner's office.

Leagues may also impose eligibility criteria for franchise ownership. For instance, MLB has no formal ownership criteria, but it does have key characteristics it looks for when granting ownership rights (Friedman & Much, 1997). Key considerations include substantial financial resources, a commitment to the local area where the franchise is located, a commitment to baseball, local government support, and an ownership structure that does not conflict with MLB's interests (Friedman & Much, 1997).

The NFL has the most strict ownership rules. It is the only league to prohibit **corporate ownership** of its franchises, which it has done since 1970. The NFL has made one exception to its rule for the San Francisco 49ers. In 1986, then-owner Eddie DeBartolo, Jr., transferred ownership of the team to the Edward J. DeBartolo Co., a shopping mall development corporation. Although the NFL fined DeBartolo $500,000 in 1990, it let the corporate ownership remain (Friedman & Much, 1997). The team is currently operated by DeBartolo's sister and brother-in-law. The NFL also bans **public ownership**, but here it also has made

one exception—in this case for the Green Bay Packers—which were publicly owned prior to the creation of the 1970 rule and thus were exempted from it.

Until March 1997, the NFL strictly banned **cross-ownership**, that is, ownership of more than one sport franchise (Friedman & Much, 1997). The NFL softened, but reaffirmed, its rule on cross-ownership to allow Wayne Huizenga, then-majority owner of MLB's Florida Marlins and the NHL's Florida Panthers, to purchase the Miami Dolphins, and Paul Allen, majority owner of the NBA's Portland Trailblazers, to purchase the Seattle Seahawks. The new rule allows an NFL owner to own other sports franchises in the same market or own an NFL franchise in one market and another franchise in another market, provided that market has no NFL team (Friedman & Much, 1997). This change also paved the way for the Kansas City Chief's Lamar Hunt, the New England Patriots' Robert Kraft, and the Seattle Seahawks Paul Allen to become key investor-operators of the MLS's Kansas City Wizards, Dallas Burn, and Columbus Crew, and the New England Revolution, the now defunct San Jose Earthquakes, and the Seattle Sounders, respectively. Although clubs are in NFL markets, soccer club ownership does not violate the rule because investors in MLS invest in the league as a single entity, not in individual teams. The investors then operate the club locally and retain a percentage of local revenue.

The Commissioner

The role of the **commissioner** in professional sport leagues has evolved over time. Until 1921 a three-member board, the National Commission, governed baseball. In September 1920 an indictment was issued charging eight Chicago White Sox players with attempting to fix World Series games, an incident commonly known as the Black Sox scandal (*Finley v. Kuhn*, 1978). To squelch public discontent, baseball owners appointed Judge Kennesaw Mountain Landis the first professional sport league commissioner in November 1920. Landis was signed to a seven-year contract and received an annual salary of $50,000 (Graffis, 1975). Landis agreed to take the position on the condition that he was granted exclusive authority to act in the best interests of baseball; then, in his first act, he issued lifetime bans to the eight "Black Sox" players for their involvement in the scandal. In his first decade in office he banned 11 additional players, suspended Babe Ruth, and said no to any attempts to change the game by introducing marketing strategies or opening baseball to black players (Helyar, 1994).

In North American professional sport leagues, the league constitution and by-laws set forth commissioner powers. Players associations have used collective bargaining to limit the commissioner's powers by negotiating for grievance arbitration provisions that invoke a neutral arbitrator and for procedures to govern disputes between the league or club and a player. Players view the commissioner as an employee of the owners and believe that he or she will usually rule in the owners' favor for fear of damaging his or her standing with them. For example, many people cite former MLB Commissioner Fay Vincent's intervention in the lockout of 1990—which he did because of his belief that it was in the best interest of baseball and the best interest of the fans—as the beginning of the end of his term as commissioner.

Team owners have tried court challenges to limit the power of the commissioner. Three cases have upheld the baseball commissioner's right to act within the best interests of the game, provided that the commissioner follows league rules and policies when levying sanctions. In *Milwaukee American Association v. Landis* (1931), Commissioner Landis's disapproval of an assignment of a player contract from the major league St. Louis Browns to a minor league Milwaukee team was upheld. In *Atlanta National League Baseball Club, Inc. v. Kuhn* (1977) the

court upheld Commissioner Kuhn's suspension of owner Ted Turner for tampering with player contracts, but found that the commissioner's removal of the Braves' first-round draft choice exceeded his authority because the MLB rules did not allow for such a penalty. In *Finley v. Kuhn* (1978), the court upheld Commissioner Kuhn's disapproval of the Oakland A's sale of Vida Blue to the New York Yankees and of Rollie Fingers and Joe Rudi to the Boston Red Sox for $1.5 and $2 million, respectively, as being against the best interests of baseball. *Finley v. Kuhn* (1978) is particularly interesting when viewed against some recent moves made by team management to liquidate talent that have gone unchecked by the current commissioner. Following Fay Vincent's departure, MLB operated without a permanent commissioner. Its current commissioner, Bud Selig, has been accused of operating with a conflict of interest due to his former ownership of the Milwaukee Brewers.

To this day commissioners maintain some of the original authority granted by baseball, particularly the authority to investigate and impose penalties when individuals involved with the sport are suspected of acting against the best interests of the game. The commissioner generally relies on this clause to penalize players or owners who gamble, use drugs, or engage in behavior that might tarnish the league's image. Typically, the commissioner no longer has the power to hear disputes regarding player compensation. Except in the MLS, where compensation is determined at the league level by the commissioner's staff. Because the MLS is a single entity, compensation and personnel decisions are made centrally. Commissioners continue to possess discretionary powers in the following areas:

- Approval of player contracts
- Resolution of disputes between players and clubs
- Resolution of disputes between clubs
- Resolution of disputes between player or club and the league

- Disciplinary matters involving owners, clubs, players, and other personnel
- Rule-making authority (Yasser, McCurdy, Goplerud, & Weston, 2003, p. 381)

Commissioners in other professional sports were modeled after baseball's commissioner; however, not all embraced the role of disciplinarian as did Landis. Modern sport commissioners are as concerned with marketing as they are with discipline. For example, in the 1960s, Pete Rozelle took the NFL to new levels of stability with his revenue-sharing plans. Rozelle introduced NFL Properties, an NFL division that markets property rights for the entire NFL instead of allowing each team to market its own property rights. This idea was consistent with the **"league think"** philosophy he introduced to the NFL (Helyar, 1994). With league think, Rozelle preached that owners needed to think about what was best for the NFL as a whole, as opposed to what was best for their individual franchises (Helyar, 1994).

Labor Relations

John Montgomery Ward, a Hall of Fame infielder/pitcher and lawyer, established the Brotherhood of Professional Base Ball Players as the first players association in 1885 (Staudohar, 1996). Although the Brotherhood had chapters on all teams (Staudohar, 1996), it became the first of four failed labor-organizing attempts. Ward fought the reserve system, salary caps of between $1,500 and $2,500 per team (depending on the team's classification), and the practice of selling players without the players' receiving a share of the profits (Jennings, 1989). Under the reserve system, players were bound perpetually to their teams, so owners could retain player rights and depress players' salaries. (The reserve system is also discussed in Chapter 11, Sports Agency.)

When owners ignored Ward's attempts to negotiate, about 200 players organized a revolt, which led to the organization of the Players League, a rival league that attracted investors and was run like a corporation, with players sharing in the profits. The Players League attracted players by offering three-year contracts under which the salary could be increased but not decreased. The Players League folded after its first year, but only after the National League spent nearly $4 million to bankrupt it and after the media turned on the Brotherhood. Most players returned to their National League teams, and collective player actions were nonexistent for about ten years (Jennings, 1989).

In the six decades following the Players League, three organizing attempts were unsuccessful largely due to the owners' ability to defeat the labor movement or the players' own sense that they did not belong to a union. Players were somewhat naive in their thinking and they viewed their associations more as fraternal organizations than trade unions (Cruise & Griffiths, 1991). Cruise and Griffiths noted that NHL players started the organizations to acquire information and improve some working conditions, but feared that if they positioned themselves as a trade union their relationship with the owners would automatically be adversarial and would damage their sport.

Formed in 1952, the Major League Baseball Players Association (MLBPA) was initially dominated by management, and its negotiations were limited to pensions and insurance (Staudohar, 1996). However, in 1966, things changed when Marvin Miller, an executive director with a trade union background, took over. Miller's great success is attributed to, among other things, organizing players by convincing all players that each of them (regardless of star status) was essential to game revenues and by bargaining for provisions that affected most players (minimum salary, per diem, pensions, insurance, salary and grievance arbitration, etc.) (Miller, 1991).

Miller also convinced the players to develop a group promotional campaign in order to raise funds for the players association. The players authorized the association to enter into a group licensing program with Coca-Cola in 1966, which provided $60,000 in licensing fees. Miller also encouraged the players to hold out with Topps Trading Card Company. By holding out, the players association doubled the fees for trading cards from $125 to $250 per player and contributed a percentage of royalties to the union (8% on sales up to $4 million and 10% thereafter). Twenty-five years after these agreements were made, the players association brought in approximately $57 million in licensing fees and $50 million in trading card royalties from five card companies (Miller, 1991).

The National Basketball Players Association was established soon after in 1954, but it took 10 years for the NBA to recognize it as the players' exclusive labor union. In 1964, the average annual salary was $8,000, there was no minimum salary, pension, per diem, or healthcare benefits. The 1964 All-Star team, led by union leaders and future hall of famers Bob Cousy, Tommy Heinsohn, and Oscar Robertson threatened not to play in the NBA's first televised all-star game, resulting in a players victory (NBPA, 2010).

National Hockey League players attempted to unionize in 1957 when Ted Lindsay, Doug Harvey, Bill Gadsby, Fernie Flaman, Gus Mortson, and Jimmy Thomson sought to protect the average hockey player and establish a strong pension plan. They received authorization from every NHL player but one. After the owners publicly humiliated players, fed false salary information to the press, and traded or demoted players (including Lindsay) in retaliation for their involvement with the union, the NHL finally broke the players association. Many average players feared for what would happen to them, because the NHL owners seemed to have no problem humiliating, threatening, trading, and/or releasing superstars such as Lindsay

for their involvement in the players association (Cruise & Griffiths, 1991).

Among the minor leagues, the Professional Hockey Players Association, established in 1967, is the oldest union. It has represented minor league hockey players in the AHL and ECHL. More recently, newer leagues' unions were created as divisions of more established unions. For example, the Women's National Basketball Players Association became part of the National Basketball Players Association in 1998 and the Arena Football League Players Association became part of the National Football League Players Association in 2001.

Thus, labor relations did not play a major role in professional sports until the late 1960s but have become a dominant force in recent times. By the early 1970s the professional sport industry had begun its transformation to a more traditional business model. Growing fan interest and increased revenues from television and sponsorship transformed leagues into lucrative business enterprises that lured additional wealthy business owners looking for tax shelters and ego boosters. New leagues and expansion provided more playing opportunities and, thus, more bargaining power to the players. The increased bargaining power and financial rewards led players to turn increasingly to agents and players associations (Staudohar, 1996). Players associations, once "weak or nonexistent, became a countervailing power to the owners' exclusive interests" (Staudohar, 1996, p. 4).

Currently players are unionized in the following leagues: Arena Football, NLL, AHL, ECHL, MLB, MLS, NBA, NFL, NHL, and WNBA. Under labor law, once players have unionized, professional sport league management cannot make unilateral changes to hours, wages, or terms and conditions of employment. These items are mandatory subjects for bargaining and must be negotiated between the league and the players association. The contract that results from these negotiations is called a **collective bargaining** agreement (CBA). Collective bargaining in professional sports is far messier than in other industries. Players are impatient in negotiating provisions in the CBA. They have short careers and need to earn as much as possible in a short period of time, thus shifting their priorities to the wage provisions; therefore, more is financially at stake for both sides. In effect, it is a negotiation of millionaires against billionaires. The owners are seeking cost containment in the form of salary caps and other wage restrictions, whereas players do not like controls over the free market.

Strikes and lockouts are also far more disruptive in professional sports than in other industries, because players possess unique talents and cannot be replaced. Thus, a strike or lockout effectively shuts the business down. A good example of the difference can be seen in the nationwide United Parcel Service (UPS) strike of 1997. Although the strike severely disrupted UPS's service, it did not completely shut down business because managers could deliver packages and hire replacement workers. In contrast, it would be very difficult to find a replacement for a Derek Jeter, Kobe Bryant, Peyton Manning, or Sidney Crosby. Fans will not pay to see unknown players on the field, and television networks and sponsors would pull their financial support from the league. In the 1995 baseball strike, the owners' attempt to use replacement players failed. The one time that replacement players did make an impact was during the NFL strike of 1987 shortly after the United States Football League (USFL) disbanded. The owners were able to break the strike by using replacement players from the available labor pool of marquee, unemployed, talented USFL players.

When the collective bargaining process reaches an **impasse** (a breakdown in negotiations), the players can opt to strike or the owners can opt to "lock out" the players in order to spur movement in the process. Over the three-decade history of labor relations in professional sports, there have been numerous strikes (involving MLB, NFL, and NHL) and lockouts (involving MLB, NBA, and NHL). It is unique to sport that often prior to negotiating to impasse, owners will announce an inevitable lockout or players will announce a strike. In other industries, the lockout or strike is an economic weapon of last resort after bargaining to impasse. In sports, the lockout or strike is threatened as leverage before the sides even get into the same room to negotiate.

Another aspect unique to professional sport is the leagues' interest in players unionizing. Universally, in other industries, management prefers their workplaces to be free from unions. However, in professional sports, with a union in place the league can negotiate with the players associations for acceptance of restrictive practices through the collective bargaining process. Under antitrust law, any restrictive practices that primarily injure union members and that are negotiated in a collective bargaining agreement are exempt from antitrust laws. All of the restrictive practices in professional sport included in the collective bargaining agreement—the draft, salary cap, restrictions on free agency, and the like—are thereby immune from antitrust lawsuits, saving the owners millions of dollars in potential damages.

Individual Professional Sports

Individual professional sports generally exist around a professional tour of events, meets, or matches. This chapter discusses the history of just one professional tour, the PGA Tour, as an example of the different challenges facing these professional organizations.

The first U.S. Open was held in 1895, but the PGA was not born until January 1916, when a New York department store magnate called together area golf professionals and amateur golfers to create a national organization to promote the game of golf and to improve the golf professional's vocation ("History of the PGA Tour," 1997). Its constitution, by-laws, and rules were modeled after those of the British PGA and were completed in April 1916 (Graffis, 1975). The PGA's objectives were as follows:

1. To promote interest in the game of golf
2. To elevate the standards of the golf professional's vocation
3. To protect the mutual interest of PGA members
4. To hold meetings and tournaments for the benefit of members
5. To establish a Benevolent Relief Fund for PGA members
6. To accomplish any other objective determined by the PGA ("History of the American PGA," 1997)

During the PGA's formative years (1916–1930), much of its energy was focused on developing rules of play, establishing policies, cleaning up jurisdictional problems with manufacturers and the U.S. Golf Association, standardizing golf equipment, and learning its own administrative needs. In 1921, the PGA hired an administrative assistant and began a search for a commissioner. Unlike MLB, the PGA was not looking for a disciplinarian, but rather for an individual with strong administrative capabilities to conduct its daily operations. Nine years later, the PGA hired Chicago lawyer and four-time president of the Western Golf Association Albert R. Gates as commissioner for a salary of $20,000. Gates's guiding principle in making decisions was to ask the question, "What good will it do golf?" (Graffis, 1975).

The practice of charging spectators began at fund-raisers by top male and female golfers to benefit the Red Cross during World War I. The PGA later adopted the practice for its tournaments to raise money for the PGA's Benevolent

Fund. Soon golfer Walter Hagen began to charge for his performances (Graffis, 1975).

When the PGA was founded there was no distinction between club and touring professionals. Tournaments were small and manageable until television began paying for golf programming. The influence of television made golf more of a business than a game. In the early to mid-1960s a number of factors created a growing tension between the PGA tournament professionals and country club professionals, as the two groups' interests clashed. Questions were raised concerning the mission of the PGA. Was it to operate PGA Business Schools for local club professionals, primarily given the task

of promoting interest in golf and golf-related products locally? Or was it to work with professionals coming through the Qualifying School (Q-School) for the PGA tour circuit?

At annual meetings held from 1961 to 1966, the PGA became a house divided over control and power. Tour professionals claimed they had the support of a majority of golf's sponsors and threatened to leave the PGA to form a new association and tour. At the 1966 meeting, the PGA identified two different constituencies in professional golf: first, the club professionals who served the amateur players; and second, the showcase professionals who provided the entertainment for golf's spectators (Graffis, 1975). Two years later, the PGA tournament players broke away to form a Tournament Players Division, which in 1975 was renamed the PGA TOUR ("History of the American PGA," 1997). The PGA TOUR, headquartered in Ponte Verde, Florida, operates three tours: the PGA Tour, the Champions (Senior) Tour, and the Nationwide Tour (PGA TOUR, 2010). Television revenues and corporate sponsorship have increased the purses for players on the PGA Tour ("History of the PGA Tour," 1997). The PGA Tour now runs year round, and tournament purses range from $800,000 to $9.5 million (PGA TOUR, 2010b).

In golf, players must qualify annually for the PGA Tour. "There are two ways to avoid the hell of qualifying: winning and earning" (Feinstein, 1996, p. 69). Winning a PGA tournament exempts a player from qualifying for two years, with each additional win adding another year (up to five). Winning one of the four majors (Masters, U.S. Open, British Open, and PGA Championship), the FedEx Cup, or the Players Championship exempts a player for five years, and winning the Tour Championship exempts a player for three years (PGA TOUR, 2010a). Players who do not make the PGA Tour usually compete on the Nationwide Tour for a smaller percentage of revenue than they would make on the PGA Tour.

Tours in the various individual sports have their own rules and regulations. In tennis, the 50 top-ranked players are required to submit their tournament schedules for the following year to their respective governing bodies by the conclusion of the U.S. Open "so decisions can be made on designations and fields can be balanced to meet the commitments the WTA and ATP have made to their tournaments" (Feinstein, 1992, p. 392). Throughout Wimbledon and the U.S. Open, players' agents and tournament directors negotiate appearance fees and set schedules for the top-ranked players' upcoming seasons, while the other players are left to make decisions about whether to return to the tour the following year.

For information on the management of tour events, see Chapter 13, Event Management.

■ KEY CONCEPTS

League Revenues

Leagues derive revenue from national television and radio contracts, league-wide licensing, and league-wide sponsorship programs. Leagues do not derive revenue from local broadcasting, gate receipts, preferred seating sales, or any of the stadium revenues. All those forms of revenue go to the teams and as a result have caused competitive balance problems among teams, as discussed in the previous section. For detailed information on league revenues see Chapter 4, Financial and Economic Principles Applied to Sport Management, and for information on broadcasting revenues, see Chapter 17, Sport Broadcasting.

Franchise Values and Revenue Generation

In all leagues but the NFL, today's franchise costs make family or single ownership a challenge. Most franchise owners need to diversify investments to protect against the financial risk of franchise ownership. Many owners purchase teams as a primary business investment, whereas others purchase teams as an ancillary business to their primary business. Still others are fulfilling a dream with a number of co-owners. Due to rising franchise fees, expansion fees, player salaries, and the leveling off of or decrease in television revenues, there is too much at risk for one owner if that person does not have diverse pools of money to cover a team's operating costs. For instance, when the Boston Red Sox and New England Sports Network (NESN) were sold for $660 million, more than 20 individuals made up the ownership group led by John Henry (Bodley, 2002).

Currently, franchise values for major league clubs are in the hundreds of millions of dollars. Much and Gotto (1997) note that the two most important factors in determining a franchise's value are the degree of revenue sharing and the stability of the league's labor situation. Revenue sharing is a factor in creating competitive balance among the teams in the league. The NFL shares virtually all national revenues but does not share stadium revenue. In an effort to generate greater revenues, teams have used their leverage to negotiate favorable lease agreements that provide the teams with revenue from luxury boxes, personal seat licenses, club seating, and other revenues generated by the facility, including facility sponsorship (signage and naming rights), concessions, and parking. As a result of the race for these revenues, a strategy called **franchise free agency** emerged in the 1990s. Under this strategy, team owners threaten to move their teams if their demands for new stadiums, renovations to existing stadiums, or better lease agreements are not met. Because the business of baseball is exempt from antitrust law, we have not seen many baseball teams relocate. Without antitrust liability, owners do not have the leverage to threaten a treble damage antitrust suit in response to a no vote on moving to a new territory. At the

same time, this exemption from antitrust has allowed MLB teams leverage over their home cities to demand stadium renovations at their current sites (knowing the cities cannot sue on antitrust grounds either).

Like never before, sport managers are at work to maximize revenue streams. An excellent example lies in the strategy of the Boston Red Sox to maximize the revenue potential in every inch of Fenway Park while adding to the fans' Fenway experience. Since taking over the Red Sox in 2002, the management team has turned Yawkey Way into a fan-friendly concourse to market the club and sell more concessions and licensed products. Because demand exceeds supply for tickets, the club has built additional seating in box seats near the dugout, on top of the Green Monster section of the park, and on the rooftop and in front of the grandstand. Since adding the seats, the Red Sox have discovered "dead space" used for media parking and laundry. They moved those uses off-site to create more concourse space for revenue-generating opportunities, plus an improved fan experience as there is less congestion around the concourse and restrooms (Migala Report, 2004).

Outside of Fenway Park, the Red Sox have created other innovations intended to maximize revenues. One marketing innovation is to show games live at stadium-style movie theaters in select locations throughout New England. The movie theater experience comes complete with vendors. The team has worked to stretch its market by hosting "state" days at Fenway Park and taking the Sox players and World Series Trophies on tour throughout New England.

Another marketing innovation involves the Fenway Sports Group (FSG) that works from the built-in Red Sox Nation fan base. FSG is a venture of New England Sports Ventures (NESV), the holding company that also owns and operates the Red Sox, Fenway Park, and NESN (Fenway Sports Group, 2010a). FSG is a sports agency created with the goals of diversifying

way Racing (NASCAR) (Fenway Sports Group, 2010c). In maximizing revenue, FSG has a goal of leveraging the audience of 12 million Red Sox fans for cross-over marketing, while reaching beyond that with new properties, new ventures, and ultimately new revenue streams.

A second issue affecting franchise values is particular to MLB: the large-market to small-market dichotomy created by the disparity in local broadcast revenues. MLB does not share local broadcast revenues. This means that a large-media-market team, such as the New York Yankees, derives far more revenues than does a small-market team, such as the Kansas City Royals. This disparity results in an unfair advantage for a large-market team in terms of operating revenue and franchise valuation. Due to this disparity, small-market teams, such as the Pittsburgh Pirates, are constantly building from their farm systems and often losing franchise players to the free market, because they lack sufficient revenue to meet players' salary demands. In fact, disparity led Commissioner Selig to call for contraction of two teams at the end of 2001, a plan that subsequently was put on hold through collective bargaining with the MLBPA.

interests of the parent company and to drive more revenue into the venture. Its pioneers were Red Sox staff moonlighting at FSG (Donnelly & Leccese, 2007). In addition to working with the Red Sox, FSG represents sports properties such as Boston College, MLB Advanced Media, Fulham Football Club, Athletes Performance, and the Deutsche Bank Championship (golf). Additionally, it engages in corporate consulting and event business for clients such as Stop and Shop, Dunkin Donuts, Cumberland Farms, and Gulf Oil (Fenway Sports Group, 2010b). It also is entrepreneurial, operating FSG sports-related properties such as the Salem (VA) Red Sox (minor league baseball team), Fanfoto (a fan-centric sports photography business), Red Sox Destinations (travel agency), and Roush Fen-

To meet the challenge of competitively operating a small-market club, teams like the Oakland A's, under the leadership of General Manager Billy Beane, are focusing on efficiency and a new value system now termed *moneyball* after the book by that name. In a nutshell, the concept is to win games with a small budget. Put simply, it is a system that involves focusing on less commonly used statistics, drafting wisely, and drafting players who are "signable" in an effort to take away some of the uncertainty of drafting and developing players. According to Lewis (2003), Beane did not create the theories but effectively used the ideas of the baseball statistical wizard Bill James and those of some of today's best baseball writers and Web sites, and put them all together. Despite much vocal opposition from the establishment in the baseball fraternity (long-time general managers, scouts, and baseball writers), General Managers of the Toronto Blue Jays, Texas Rangers, and Boston Red Sox have adopted many of these theories in building their teams. In fact, James is a consultant to the Boston Red Sox and has led the team to the use of more quantitative analysis of player performance and evaluation alongside its traditional qualitative observations of players (Neyer, 2002). Despite the very vocal resistance by the baseball establishment to the strategies recounted in the book *Moneyball*, these strategies have had an immediate impact on the baseball draft, with more teams drafting college players. Only time will tell if these theories to create greater certainty in cost containment and player development will pan out. However, the book has inspired employees and fans alike in other professional sports to try to rely on new statistical theories. In this way it has brought more innovative management to all professional sport organizations and in the process created a few new jobs for individuals focused on using statistics to bolster decisions on player development, investment, and acquisition.

The other piece of the franchise value equation is labor stability. The NFL has had unprecedented labor peace with a collective bargaining agreement that was ratified in 1993 and has been extended through 2010. This CBA has created cost stability for teams. The combination of strong leadership from commissioners, shared revenue, and cost stability has enabled NFL teams to market what is arguably the strongest brand in North American professional sports. A quality product and the knowledge of long-term labor peace (and thus a lack of interruption in games) translates to media revenues in the billions. This stability may soon face a major challenge. In 2008, NFL ownership voted unanimously to opt out of this CBA at the end of the 2010 season, which will require negotiation of a new one. As this text goes to print,

both sides are gearing up for a fight by building war chests of funds in the event of a strike or lockout. Additionally, both sides are warring in the media and on their own Web sites.

Legal Issues

Almost all areas of law are relevant to the professional sport industry, but those most prevalent are contracts, antitrust, labor, and intellectual property (trademark and licensing). Historically, many high-profile cases have developed either when players and owners (current and prospective) have challenged league rules or when rival leagues have tried to compete against the dominant established league that possesses market power.

Over time many contract issues have been resolved, and all team-sport athletes now sign a standard player contract particular to each league. This does not mean that contract disputes are eliminated. Occasionally there will be cases if the commissioner refuses to approve a player's contract if he or she believes it violates a league rule or policy. For instance, sometimes player contracts contain provisions that the commissioner finds will circumvent the salary cap. The team and player may either renegotiate the contract or challenge the commissioner's finding. A good example is the recent rejection of the New Jersey Devils' 17-year contract with star left winger Ilya Kovalchuk. The NHL rejected the 17-year, $102 million deal, which would have been the longest in its history. The NHL's rejection of the contract was upheld by an arbitrator who found many problems with the contract, particularly the significant frontloading of salary and the length, which would have had Kovalchuck playing until he was 44. Only one player has played past age 43 and only 6 of 3,400 players in the past 20 years have played at age 42, making it unrealistic that Kovalchuk would still be an active contributing player on the roster at 44 (National Hockey League and

National Hockey League Players Association, 2010). The Devils and Kovalchuk did submit a new 15-year, $100 million contract that the NHL did approve. However, the NHL allegedly in the process issued the NHLPA an ultimatum on long-term deals, conditioning them on changing the salary cap hit for contracts that end with the player over 40 years of age and a new formula that counts the five highest years of salary in long term (over 5 year) deals carrying additional weight in the cap calculation (Brooks, 2010). Such a change in the salary cap during the term of the CBA is unusual and shows the depth of the commitment by the NHL to the cap and actions they perceive will harm competitive balance.

In a global market, contract disputes also arise over which team retains the rights to a particular player who is attempting to move from one league to another. Such disputes may lead to legal battles between teams and players of different countries. To avoid these types of disputes, North American leagues and those abroad are continually evaluating their player transfer agreements.

Antitrust law is a second area where disputes arise. Antitrust laws regulate anti-competitive business practices. MLB is exempt from antitrust laws (see Chapter 5, Legal Principles Applied to Sport Management). All professional sport leagues adopt restrictive practices to provide financial stability and competitive balance between their teams. The game would not be appealing to fans if the same teams dominated the league year after year because they had the money to consistently purchase the best players. Similarly, fans and front office staff would not like to see their teams change player personnel year after year. It is the nature of sport that teams must be built and that players and coaches must develop strong working relationships. However, restrictive practices such as drafts, reserve systems, salary caps, free agent restrictions, and free agent compensation developed for competitive balance may have another effect, such as depressing salaries or keeping competitor leagues from signing marquee players. Therefore, players and rival leagues have used antitrust laws to challenge such practices as anticompetitive, arguing that they restrain trade or monopolize the market for professional team sports. Additionally, in the past decade, owners have sued their own leagues on antitrust grounds to challenge restrictive practices (see Chapter 5). Antitrust laws carry with them a treble damage provision, so if a league loses an antitrust case and the court triples the amount of damages, the league could effectively pay millions or billions in damages.

Race and Gender in the Professional Sport Industry

Critics have argued that since there is great racial diversity among athletes on the field, more people of color should be represented in management positions. By the year 2004, the four major leagues had marked their fiftieth anniversaries of integration. In 2003, the NBA and MLB achieved major milestones by welcoming minority owners African-American Bob Johnson and Mexican-American Arte Moreno to the Charlotte Bobcats and Los Angeles Angels, respectively. Lapchick and colleagues (2009) reported that for the first time in the 20-year history of publishing his Racial and Gender Report Card, each of the five major leagues received a grade of "A" for hiring people of color. All leagues also showed increases for women in management positions, so it appears some positive movement forward is occurring. Tables 10-3 and 10-4 contain a full breakdown of racial and gender representation by league.

In his book *In Black and White: Race and Sport in America*, Shropshire (1996) stresses pointedly that integration of more diverse employees into management positions will not happen without a concerted effort by owners,

TABLE 10-3 Racial Diversity in Professional Sports (Percentage)

Segment	NBA	NFL	MLB	MLS	WNBA
Player	78	69	40	40	66
League office	32	NA	34	8	35
Head coach	37	19	27	27	15
Assistant coach	38	34	33	23	35
CEO	12	0	0	0	10
Principal	23	13	3	0	27
Vice-president	13	10	11	14	9
Senior administrator	20	14	17	34	20
Professional administrator	26	11	14	42	30

Source: Lapchick, R., Bartter, J., Diaz-Calderon, A., Hanson, J., Harless, C., Johnson, W., Kamke, C., Lopresti, C., McMechan, D., Reshard, N. & Turner, A. (2009). 2009 racial and gender report card. Retrieved on October 27, 2010, from http://web.bus.ucf.edu/documents/sport/2009_RGRC.pdf

TABLE 10-4 Gender Diversity in Professional Sports (Percentage)

Segment	NBA	NFL	MLB	MLS	WNBA
Player	0	0	0	0	100
League office	41	NA	40	24	70
Head coach	0	0	0	0	38
Assistant coach	0	0	0	0	65
CEO	3	2	7	0	10
Principal	0	0	0	0	67
Vice-president	18	8	17	8	27
Senior administrator	23	16	18	21	37
Professional administrator	42	32	29	28	50

Source: Lapchick, R., Bartter, J., Diaz-Calderon, A., Hanson, J., Harless, C., Johnson, W., Kamke, C., Lopresti, C., McMechan, D., Reshard, N. & Turner, A. (2009). 2009 Racial and gender report card. Retrieved October 27, 2010, from http://web.bus.ucf.edu/documents/sport/2009_RGRC.pdf

commissioners, and those in positions of power. He suggests that to combat racism in professional sport there must be recognition of what "both America and sport in reality look and act like" as well as what both "should look and act like in that ideal moment in the future [when racism is eliminated]" (Shropshire, 1996, p. 144). Between these two phases is an intermediate period of transition, and during that transition a number of steps must be taken. First, the black community's youth must alter its focus away from athletic success as being a substitute for other forms of success. Second, athletes must take a stronger united stand against racism. Third, league-wide action evidencing a commitment to address diversity is needed. The final step is a combination of continued civil rights political action coupled with legal action to combat racism through lawsuits and government intervention by such organizations as the Department of Justice and the Equal Employment Opportunity Commission. Further information on managing diversity is in Chapter 2, Management Principles Applied to Sport Management.

CAREER OPPORTUNITIES

Commissioner

The role and responsibilities of a league commissioner are detailed earlier in this chapter. A wide variety of skills are required to be an effective commissioner. They include: an understanding of the sport and the various league documents (league constitution, by-laws, rules and regulations, standard player contract, and collective bargaining agreement); negotiating skills; diplomacy; the ability to work well with a variety of people; an ability to delegate; a good public image; an ability to handle pressure, crises, and the media; an ability to make sound decisions; and in general, a vision for the league. These are not skills that are easily taught. For the most part, they evolve over time through a combination of education and life experience.

Other League Office Personnel

Each league has an office staff working in a wide variety of positions (Figure 10-1). Although the number of positions varies in league offices, there are literally hundreds of employees in a range of areas, from the commissioner's staff to the legal department to properties and marketing divisions to entertainment to communications to research and development. For instance, departments in the NBA's Commissioner's Office include administration, broadcasting, corporate affairs, editorial, finance, legal, operations, player programs, public relations, security, and

special events (**Figure 10-1**). Departments in the NBA Properties Division include business development, finance, international offices, legal, licensing, marketing, media and sponsor programs, and team services. Departments in NBA Entertainment include administration, accounting, legal, licensing, operations, photography, production, and programming. Thus, a wide variety of opportunities in league offices are available for individuals with degrees in sport management and business and for those who couple their initial degrees with a graduate degree in fields such as law, sport management, or business administration. Skills necessary for working in a league office vary with the position, yet a few universal skills include having a working knowledge of the sport, the teams in the league, and the professional sport industry in general; good customer relations skills; and a willingness to work long hours (especially during the season and postseason).

Team General Manager

A team general manager is in charge of all player personnel decisions. These include overseeing the scouting and drafting of players, signing free agents, trading players, and negotiating contracts with players and their agents. The general manager must understand the sport and be able to assess talent. He or she must also possess a working knowledge of all league documents (constitution, by-laws, rules and regulations, collective bargaining agreement, standard player contract). A career path for a general manager has traditionally been to move into the position from the playing or coaching ranks. As the position has become more complex, individuals with graduate degrees in sport management, business administration, law, or a combination of these have become desirable employees. Some teams will continue to have a general manager who has risen from the playing or coaching ranks, but will hire one or

FIGURE 10-1   NBA League Office/Team Front Office Flowcharts

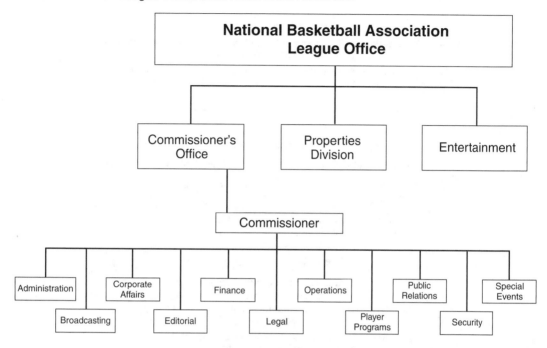

more assistant general managers to deal with complex contract negotiations and to decipher league rules and policies, such as salary caps as well as interpret and develop statistical models that have become commonplace in the moneyball era.

Other Team Front Office Personnel

Like league office staffs, team front offices offer a wide variety of positions. In the past decade the number of positions and specialization of jobs has increased greatly. When the first edition of this text was published, the Miami Heat front office staff provided a glimpse of the variety of positions available. At that time the team possessed 40 full-time employees, four partners, and four limited partners (Miami Heat, 1993–1994). Compare that to a current Miami Heat directory (**Figure 10-2**) and the Philadelphia 76ers, whose Web site lists 100 front office employees in 2010. The employees include the following positions: a chairman (owner); a president/chief operating officer; two executive vice-presidents; three senior vice-presidents; two vice-presidents; a director of player personnel; a sales staff of 17 (including director and managers); a customer service staff of 6 (including directors and managers); a marketing and promotions staff of 3; a game operations staff of 6; a communications staff of 6 (includes community relations and public relations); and numerous other employees such as coaches, scouts, broadcasters, accountants, and administrative assistants throughout the basketball and business operations (NBA, 2010c). It is noteworthy that the basketball operations staff is considerably smaller than the business operations side. The business side drives the revenue into the operation and, therefore, there tend to be more opportunities for employment on that side of the "house."

FIGURE 10-2   Miami Heat Front Office Directory

Executive Office

**Managing General Partner President of Basketball Operations General Manager
President of Business Operations**

Executive Vice Presidents: Chief Marketing Officer, HEAT Group
Enterprises, Sales, General Manager, Chief Financial Officer, General Council

Vice Presidents

Senior VP of Basketball Operation Senior VP/Chief Information Officer

Vice Presidents: Sports Media Relations, Arena Bookings and
Marketing, Marketing Division, Operations, Assistant General
Manager, Finance, Corporate Partnerships, Ticket Operations
and Services, Human Resources, Player Personnel

Basketball Operations

Senior Director of Team Security

Directors: Sports Media Relations, College/International
Scouting, Team Services, Team Security, Pro/Minor League
Scouting

Other: NBA Scout, Scout, Assistant Director of Sport
Media Relations, Sport Media Relations Assistant,
Business Media Relations Assistant, Scouting and
Information Coordinator

Source: http://www.nba.com/heat/contact/directory_list.html (December, 2006).

Front office entry-level positions tend to be in the sales, marketing, community relations, and media/public relations departments. Salaries tend to be low, because many people would love to work for a professional team and therefore supply always exceeds demand. Often in the sales departments, salaries are higher because employees earn a base plus commissions for ticket, corporate, or group sales productivity. (Further information on careers in sales and sponsorship are in Chapter 14, Sport Sales, and Chapter 15, Sport Sponsorship.) As with league office positions, skills necessary for working in a front office are knowledge of the sport and the professional sport industry, good customer relations abilities, and a willingness to work long hours (particularly during the season and postseason). As for educational requirements, a sport management degree and, depending on the position, possibly an advanced degree such as a law degree or an MBA are appropriate for someone looking to break into a front office position.

Tour Personnel

Tours such as the PGA Tour and the Association of Tennis Professionals (ATP) Tour employ many sport managers. The Dew Tour, which debuted in June 2005, consists of five major multi-sport events with a cumulative points system, a $2.5 million competitive purse (the largest in action sports), and an additional $1 million bonus pool based on participants' year-end standings (according to allisports.com). As with league sports, the positions vary from commissioner to marketer to special events coordinator.

For example, in 2009 the ATP Tour held 65 tournaments in 32 countries and was organized into three main offices: Player Council, Board of Directors, and Tournament Council. Each office is led by an executive and has a number of staff positions available. The ATP has offices located in several countries, including Monaco, Australia, London, and the United States (Florida). An executive organizational chart is shown in **Figure 10-3**.

As with league sports, the positions vary from commissioner to marketer to special events coordinator. Much of the event man-

agement work for the actual site operations for the tour is, however, often left to an outside sports agency. Tours and sites contract with event marketing and management agencies such as Game Day Management to take care of all of the details of putting on the event at a particular country club. (Details on these kinds of positions are in Chapter 13, Event Management.)

Agents

Almost all team and individual athletes in the professional sport industry have sports agents representing them and coordinating their business and financial affairs. In addition, a growing number of professional coaches rely on sports agents. (For more details on the skills and responsibilities of this career choice, see Chapter 11, Sports Agency.)

FIGURE 10-3 ATP Executive Organizational Chart

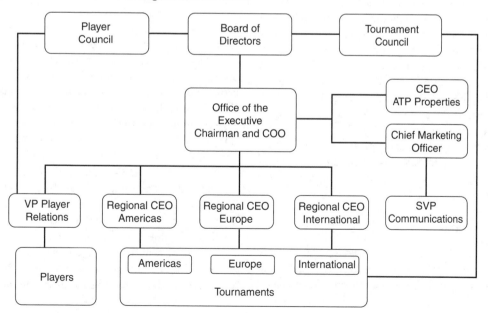

■ CURRENT ISSUES

Salary Caps

In an effort to contain player personnel costs, salary caps continue to be the rage in professional sport. They are used in the AFL, NBA, NFL, NHL, MLS, WNBA, ECHL, and NLL. Salary caps are intended to create parity among teams by capping how much a team can spend on its players' salaries. Salary caps are adjusted annually for changes in revenue.

To impose a salary cap in a league in which a union exists, owners must negotiate with the players (because the cap impacts wages). In the negotiation process, the union will inevitably negotiate for some exceptions to the salary cap. These exceptions have in reality created loopholes for creative general managers and agents representing players. For instance, in the NFL, signing bonuses are applied to the cap by prorating them across the life of the contract. Another problem with the caps is that they routinely force teams to cut established players or renegotiate their contracts to make room under the cap to sign another player. A third problem is that the caps provide a team with spending minimums, so low-revenue teams are prevented from cutting their payrolls to stay competitive (Fatsis, 1997). In the WNBA, the combination of a tight salary cap and a minimum salaries scale is negatively impacts veterans, whose minimum salaries are higher based upon years of service. Thus, in the case of a talented veteran competing for a spot against an equally talented rookie, the club may choose the rookie because she takes up less room under the cap (Bergen, 2004).

Globalization

All major leagues are drafting and signing players from other nations and moving into those countries with marketing efforts. Major League Baseball has an office in Tokyo to oversee its efforts in Japan, Taiwan, and China, plus the league has been playing one game to open the season in Japan for the past few years. The NFL no longer operates NFL Europe, but has begun playing a marquee regular season game in Europe, and the NBA has expanded throughout the globe with probably the most international movement of all the North American leagues. Currently the NBA hosts 14 international NBA Web sites in addition to its main North American site (NBA, 2010a). Following the NFL and MLB, the NBA has moved away from an exhibition game in Europe and has a regular season game scheduled there for the 2010–2011 season (NBA, 2010b).

A great case study exists in examining NBA China and NBA India. NBA International is following its game plan in China to move into the Indian market. For China, the NBA spent two decades building courts, teaching youth the game, and hosting promotions. Now over 300 million people in China play basketball. The league notes 89% of Chinese aged 15 to 54 are aware of the NBA brand and NBA.com/China averages 2 million unique users a month. Games are shown in China on 51 outlets, drawing 1.6 billion viewers in 2008–2009 (34% more than in 2006–2007). China is now the NBA's biggest foreign market for its branded merchandise. Outside investors—including Disney/ESPN, Bank of China Group, Legend Holdings, China Merchant Group, and the Li Ka-shing Foundation—bought 11% of NBA China in January 2008 for $2.3 billion with a goal of launching a professional league (Van Riper & Karmali, 2009). NBA China has already had a setback, as the Anschutz Entertainment Group Facilities pulled out of its plan to build and/or operate NBA arenas in Beijing, Shanghai, and Guangzhou.

NBA International began bringing NBA stars to India in 2006. Since November 2008, the NBA has been staging youth tournaments in Mumbai, New Delhi, and Bangalore. NBA games on ESPN in India reach 120 million homes, nearly a third of the country. That said, becoming the second most popular sport in India (behind cricket), will be a challenging goal because India has not fielded an Olympic team since 1980 (Van Riper & Karmali, 2009).

Journalists credit the global interest in the NBA to the 1992 Dream Team (Crowe, 2004), but it must also be a product of the NBA's strategy of integrating international stars into their teams. To continue its global expansion, many NBA teams have drafted and signed players from other nations. NBA official rosters in the 2009–2010 season included 83 players from 36 different countries or territories, such as Puerto Rico and the Virgin Islands. Fans of these players open new revenue sources for the NBA. Foreign markets generate as much as 20% of the $900 million the NBA earns in television revenue, and they provide about 20% of merchandise sales (Crowe, 2004). In 2010 the NBA Finals were broadcast in 215 countries and in 41 languages (NBA, 2010a).

The growth into a global market influenced the 2006 NBA draft, for which 36 international players had declared themselves eligible. The 2006 NBA draft contained the third largest number of international players, topped only by the two prior years' drafts of 39 (2005) and 38 (2004) players. Players hailed from Australia, Belgium, Bosnia-Herzegovina, Brazil, Canada, Croatia, Dominican Republic, France, Germany, Greece, Italy, Latvia, Lithuania, Martinique, Nigeria, Poland, Puerto Rico (considered international), Russia, Serbia-Montenegro, Slovenia, Spain, Sudan, and Turkey. The interest may also be stemming from overtures made by David Stern indicating that the NBA is looking to move into Europe. These overtures have encouraged the Anschutz Entertainment Group to build NBA-style arenas in London and Berlin (McCosky, 2002). Stern noted the opening up

the arenas in London and Berlin allowed the NBA to consider many options from exhibitions to games to permanent homes for franchises (McCosky, 2002). As mentioned earlier in this section, the NBA will hold its first regular season game in Europe during 2010–2011 season (NBA, 2010b).

■ SUMMARY

The professional sport industry involves the sale of the entertainment value of sport events and exhibitions. Revenue is generated primarily through media rights fees, licensed product sales, gate receipts, and stadium revenues. The leagues and tours face a number of challenges, including keeping fans satisfied in light of their perceptions regarding the "highly paid athlete." Directly related to this is finding a means for achieving labor stability in the leagues while developing methods of keeping a fan base that is representative of society as ticket prices continue to skyrocket. The dominant major professional leagues (MLB, MLS, NBA, NFL, and NHL) also face a challenge in market share from the new upstart leagues (e.g., arena football), women's sports, expansion in the minor leagues, and the growing professionalization and commercialization of collegiate sport.

The professional sport industry is entering an exciting period. Innovations in technology are making professional sport more global, particularly as leagues look for unsaturated markets and new revenue streams. This exciting environment, coupled with the perception of the glamour of working for a team or league, attracts many job seekers to professional sports. Therefore, landing an entry-level position is competitive, and salaries tend to be lower than in other segments of the industry. Those who are persistent, are willing to intern in the in-

CASE STUDY: Is the NFL Conduct Policy Working?

In response to the murder charges levied against Baltimore Ravens linebacker Ray Lewis, the NFL owners established a Personal Conduct Policy in 2000. Former Commissioner Paul Tagliabue used it to issue short suspensions. In 2007, the NFL invoked the integrity of the game powers to lengthen the suspensions a commissioner could levy and even allowed for indefinite ones, if the player's actions involved violent or criminal behavior that undermines the NFL's integrity, erodes public confidence, or results in tragic consequences to perpetrator and/or victim (Maravent, 2010).

From January 2006 through April 2007, more than 50 players were arrested (Bell, 2007a). Two—Tennessee Titans cornerback Adam "Pacman" Jones and Cincinnati Bengals wide receiver Chris Henry—were among the worst offenders. Jones had been arrested five times and questioned an additional five times since he had been drafted in 2005. Jones' arrests involved felony and misdemeanor charges involving fights and incidents that included one in which a security guard was left paralyzed after being shot by someone in Jones' party. Over a 14-month period, Henry had been arrested four times in three different states for charges involving firearms use and concealment, as well as driving recklessly, DUI, and providing alcohol to minors. After seven months on the job, NFL Commissioner Roger Goodell held hearings with Jones and Henry to determine their fate. (Bell, 2007a).

> "Moments after announcing a one-year suspension of Jones and an eight-game ban of Henry, NFL commissioner Roger Goodell released his strengthened conduct policy … 'It is important that the NFL be represented consistently by outstanding people as well as great football players, coaches, and staff,' Goodell said. 'We hold ourselves to higher standards of responsible conduct because of what it means to be part of the National Football League. We have long had policies and programs designed to encourage responsible behavior, and this policy is a further step in ensuring that everyone who is part of the NFL meets that standard'" (Associated Press, 2007, par. 4).

The policy resulted from the NFL officials' frustration with the players' behavior. As owner, Bob McNair of the Houston Texans remarked, "[f]ines are such a small part of a player's total compensation. They don't pay attention to it," … "A $50,000 fine, (it's like), 'I spent that last night when I got arrested. That's what I gave *one* girl.'" (Bell, 2007b, par. 10). Many NFL players were equally frustrated, according to Gene Upshaw, then-Director of the NFL Players Association who supported the approach by Goodell. "The conduct of some players is what got us to this point," Upshaw says. "But I think the insistence of a lot of players also drives the need for a stronger policy. This is a grass-roots movement." (Bell, 2007b, par. 34). "The NFL Players Association and the Player Advisory Council have been discussing this issue for several months," Upshaw said. "We believe that these are steps that the commissioner needs to take and we support the policy. It is important that players in violation of the policy will have the opportunity and the support to change their conduct and earn their way back" (Associated Press, 2007, par. 14). Goodell called former players for input and put together a six-player advisory panel on conduct issues (Bell, 2007b).

The conduct policy Goodell introduced applies to all NFL employees. The definition of NFL employees is broad, including players under contract plus those drafted and undrafted players about to commence negotiations with teams. It also includes coaches, officials, owners, front-office, and league personnel (NFLPA, 2008).

In 2010, three years into the policy, the NFL continues to battle its image problem. In response to sexual assault allegations being raised against Pittsburgh Steelers quarterback Ben Roethlisberger, in March 2010, Commissioner Goodell re-confirmed how seriously he takes the conduct policy. The memo he sent to all NFL teams, stated:

"The Policy makes clear that NFL and club personnel must do more than simply avoid criminal behavior. We must conduct ourselves in a way that 'is responsible, that promotes the values upon which the league is based, and is lawful.' This standard reflects the recognition that the conduct and behavior of our players and other league and team employees is critically important. Whether it involves your team or another, these incidents affect us all—every investigation, arrest, or other allegation of improper conduct undermines the respect for our league by our fans, lessens the confidence of our business partners and threatens the continued success of our brand" (La Canfora, 2010, par 5).

Questions for Discussion

1. Once a players association (union) is in existence, any changes in the workplace that involve mandatory subjects for bargaining may not be unilaterally implemented by the league (management) but must be negotiated with the players. Mandatory subjects for bargaining are hours, wages, and terms and conditions of employment. Should this new conduct policy have been negotiated with the players association through collective bargaining?
2. Commissioners have long held power to make decisions to maintain the integrity of the game. Historically, the integrity of the game decisions have involved gambling, drug use, on-field bad behavior, and bad behavior toward fans. Does this conduct policy fit within the integrity of the game provision? Does regulating off-field behavior go too far? Because the commissioner can act simply when someone in the organization is arrested, how do we reconcile it with the concept of innocent until proven guilty?
3. What will be some of the challenges in enforcing the policy? How will the league impose fairness?
4. As a manager, what strategies would you adopt to keep from having this policy invoked against members of your team (players and staff)?
5. What suggestions do you have for Commissioner Goodell and the NFL Players Association about player conduct and discipline issues when they sit down to negotiate their next collective bargaining agreement?
6. Using Google, examine the news over a two to three year period to determine if the NFL policy is working. Does it apply to team and league management and coaches as well as players? What is your assessment as a fan? Does the behavior of players on and off the field influence your decision to follow the NFL? Do you think it would affect the decisions of sponsors to be associated with the NFL? Individual teams? Individual players?

dustry, and are committed to keeping abreast of this fast-paced industry will be rewarded. Professional sports are constantly changing and are often addressing challenges. The sport manager who can adapt to change and resolve problems and who possesses a vision for the professional sport industry in the twenty-first century will find success in this field.

■ RESOURCES

Professional Sport Leagues

American Hockey League (AHL)
One Monarch Place
Springfield, MA 01069
413-781-2030; fax: 413-733-4767
http://www.theahl.com

ECHL
116 Village Boulevard, Suite 304
Princeton, NJ 08540
609-452-0770; fax: 609-452-7147
http://www.echl.com

Major League Baseball (MLB)
350 Park Avenue
New York, NY 10022
212-339-7800; fax: 212-355-0007
http://www.mlb.com

Major League Soccer (MLS)
110 East 42nd Street
New York, NY 10017
212-450-1200; fax: 212-450-1300
http://www.mlsnet.com

Minor League Baseball (MLB)
201 Bayshore Drive, S.E.
St. Petersburg, FL 33701
727-822-6937; fax: 727-821-5819
http://www.milb.com

National Basketball Association (NBA)
645 Fifth Avenue
New York, NY 10022
212-407-8000; fax: 212-832-3861
http://www.nba.com

National Professional Fastpitch (NPF)
4610 S. Ulster Drive, Suite 150
Denver, CO 80237
303-290-7494; 303-415-2073
http://profastpitch.com

National Football League (NFL)
410 Park Avenue, 6th Floor
New York, NY 10022
212-758-1500; fax: 212-872-7464
http://www.nfl.com

National Hockey League (NHL)
1251 Avenue of the Americas
New York, NY 10020-1198
212-789-2000; fax: 212-789-2020
http://www.nhl.com

Women's National Basketball Association (WNBA)
645 Fifth Avenue
New York, NY 10022
212-688-9622; fax: 212-750-9622
http://www.wnba.com

Professional Sport Tours

Association of Tennis Professionals (ATP) Tour
200 ATP Boulevard
Ponte Vedra Beach, FL 32082
904-285-8000; fax: 904-285-5966
http://www.atptennis.com/

Dew Tour
Alli (Alliance of Action Sports)
150 Harvester Dr., Suite 140
Burr Ridge, IL 60527
630-908-6300
http://www.allisports.com/

Indy Racing League (IRL)
4565 W. 16th Street
Indianapolis, IN 46222
317-492-6526
http://www.indycar.com

Ladies Professional Golf Association (LPGA)
100 International Golf Drive
Daytona Beach, FL 32124
386-274-6200; fax: 386-274-1099
http://www.lpga.com

National Association for Stock Car Auto Racing Inc. (NASCAR)
1801 W. International Speedway Boulevard
Daytona Beach, FL 32114
386-253-0611
http://www.nascar.com

Professional Golfers' Association (PGA) Tour
Nationwide Tour
Champions Tour
> 112 PGA Tour Boulevard, Sawgrass
> Ponte Vedra, FL 32082
> 904-285-3700; fax: 904-285-7913
> http://www.pgatour.com

Women's Tennis Association (WTA) Tour
> One Progress Plaza, Suite 1500
> St. Petersburg, FL 33701
> 727-895-5000; fax: 727-894-1982
> http://www.sonyericssonwtatour.com

XGames/EXPN
> ESPN Events
> ESPN Plaza
> Bristol, CT 06010
> http://www.sports.espn.go.com

Players Associations

Canadian Football League Players' Association (CFLPA)
> 603 Argus Road
> Oakville, Ontario, Canada L6JG60
> 306-525-2158; fax: 306-525-3008
> http://www.cflpa.com

Major League Baseball Players Association (MLBPA)
> 12 E. 49th Street, 24th Floor
> New York, NY 10017
> 212-826-0808; fax: 212-752-3649
> http://www.mlbplayers.mlb.com

National Basketball Players Association (NBPA)
> 1775 Broadway, Suite 2401
> New York, NY
> 212-463-7510; fax: 212-956-5687
> http://www.nbpa.com

National Football League Players Association (NFLPA)/Arena Football League Players Association (AFLPA)
> 2021 L Street, N.W.
> Washington, DC 20036
> 202-436-2200; fax: 202-857-0380
> http://www.nflpa.org;
>> http://www.aflplayers.org

National Hockey League Players Association (NHLPA)
> 20 Bay Street, Suite 1700
> Toronto, Ontario, Canada M5J 2N8
> 416-408-4040; fax: 416-408-3685
> http://www.nhlpa.com

Professional Hockey Players' Association (PHPA)
> One St. Paul Street, Suite 701
> St. Catherines, Ontario, Canada L2R 7L2
> 905-682-4800; fax: 905-682-4822
> http://www.phpa.com

Womens' National Basketball Players Association (WNBPA)
> 2 Penn Plaza, Suite 2430
> New York, NY 10121
> (212) 655-0880; fax (212) 655-0881
> http://www.wnbpa.org

■ KEY TERMS

collective bargaining agreement, commissioner, corporate governance model, corporate ownership, cross-ownership, franchise free agency, franchise rights, gate receipts, impasse, "league think," premium seating, public ownership, revenue sharing, self-governance, single entity structure, territorial rights

■ REFERENCES

American Needle v. NFL, 130 S.Ct. 2201 (2010).

Associated Press. (2007, April 10). Goodell unveils new conduct policy. *ESPN*. Retrieved October 26, 2010, from http://sports.espn.go.com/nfl/news/story?id=2832098

Atlanta National League Baseball Club, Inc. v. Kuhn, 432 F. Supp. 1213 (N.D. Ga. 1977).

Bell, J. (2007a, April 11). Conduct unbecoming: NFL sets new standards with suspensions. *USA Today*. Retrieved October 26, 2010, from http://www.usatoday.com/sports/football/nfl/2007-04-10-pacman-henry-suspensions_N.htm

Bell, J. (2007b, April 10). NFL will confront discipline issue, unveil new policy within days. *USA Today.* Retrieved October 26, 2010, from http://www .usatoday.com/sports/football/nfl/2007-04-09-conduct-policy_N.htm

Bergen, M. (2004, May 7). Salary issues scuttle WNBA veterans' chances. *Seattle Post-Intelligencer.* Retrieved October 26, 2010, from http://www .seattlepi.com/wnba/172352_storm07.html

Berry, R. C., Gould, W. B., & Staudohar, P. D. (1986). *Labor relations in professional sports.* Dover, MA: Auburn House Publishing.

Bodley, H. (2002, January 16). Baseball owners approve sale of Red Sox to Henry. *USA Today.* Retrieved October 26, 2010, from http://www .usatoday.com/sports/baseball/redsox/2002-01-16-sale-ag.htm

Brooks, L. (2010, Sept. 2). NHL gives union ultimatum on Kovalchuk, Luongo, Hossa. *New York Post.* Retrieved October 26, 2010, from http://www .nypost.com/p/sports/devils/nhl_gives_players_assn_ultimatum_UEbYgwfB6I4E4y7xGbE1OP

Crouse, K. (2010, April 1). Absences worsen L.P.G.A.'s headache. Retrieved October 26, 2010, from http://www.nytimes.com/2010/04/02/sports/golf/02wgolf.html

Crowe, J. (2004, June 15). Outside influence. *Los Angeles Times.* Retrieved October 26, 2010, from http://articles.latimes.com/2004/jun/15/sports/sp-nba15

Cruise, D., & Griffiths, A. (1991). *Net worth.* Toronto: Viking Penguin Group.

Donnelly, G., & Leccese, M. (2007, April 23). Q&A: Dee leads Red Sox parent's drive to diversify. Retrieved October 26, 2010, from http://boston.bizjournals.com/boston/stories/2007/04/23/story9.html

Fatsis, S. (1997, June 25). Is battle looming over salary caps? *The Wall Street Journal,* p. B9.

Feinstein, J. (1996). *A Good Walk Spoiled.* Boston: Little, Brown & Company.

Feinstein, J. (1992). *Hard courts.* New York: Villard Books.

Fenway Sports Group. (2010a). About us: Who we are. Retrieved October 26, 2010, from http://www.fenwaysportsgroup.com/

Fenway Sports Group. (2010b). Clients. Retrieved October 26, 2010, from www.fenwaysportsgroup .com/

Fenway Sports Group. (2010c) Ventures. Retrieved October 26, 2010, from www.fenwaysportsgroup .com/

Finley v. Kuhn, 569 F.2d 527 (7th Cir. 1978).

Foldesy, J. (2004, June 17). NFL owners fear death of golden goose. *Washington Times.* Retrieved October 26, 2010, from http://www.washingtontimes .com/sports/20040617-120824-5896r.htm

Fraser v. Major League Soccer, 284 F.3d 47 (1st Cir. 2002).

Friedman, A., & Much, P. J. (1997). *1997 Inside the ownership of professional sports teams.* Chicago: Team Marketing Report.

Garber, D. (2004). Major League Soccer: Establishing the world's sport in a new America. In *Inside the minds: The business of sports.* (pp. 109–129). Boston, MA: Aspatore Books.

Graffis, H. B. (1975). *The PGA: The official history of the Professional Golfers' Association of America.* New York: Crowell.

Helyar, J. (1994). *Lords of the realm.* New York: Villard Books.

History of the American PGA. (1997). *WorldGolf.com.* Retrieved October 26, 2010, from http://worldgolf .com/wglibrary/history/ampgahis.html

History of the PGA Tour. (1997). *WorldGolf.com.* Retrieved October 26, 2010, from http://www .worldgolf.com/wglibrary/history/tourhist.html

Jennings, K. (1989). *Balls and strikes: The money game in professional baseball.* Greenwich, CT: Praeger Publishing.

La Canfora, J. (2010, April 15). Goodell issues memo highlighting NFL's personal conduct policy. *NFL .com.* Retrieved October 26, 2010, at http://www.nfl.com/news/story/09000d5d8178bb24/article/goodell-issues-memo-highlighting-nfls-personalconduct-policy

Lapchick, R., Bartter, J., Diaz-Calderon, A., et al. (2009). *2009 Racial and gender report card.* Retrieved October 26, 2010, from http://web.bus.ucf.edu/documents/sport/2009_RGRC.pdf

Lentze, G. (1995). The legal concept of professional sports leagues: The commissioner and an alternative approach from a corporate perspective. *Marquette Sports Law Journal, 6,* 65–94.

Lewis, M. (2003). *Moneyball: The art of winning an unfair game*. New York: W.W. Norton.

Maravent, B. (2010, July 27). Big Ben and the conduct policy. *The Biz of football*. Retrieved October 26, 2010, from http://bizoffootball.com/index.php?option=com_content&view=article&id=474:big-ben-and-the-nfl-conduct-policy&catid=44:articles-and-opinion&Itemid=61

McCosky, C. (2002). Overseas markets interested in NBA. *Detroit News Online*. Retrieved from http://www.detnews.com/2002/pistons/0206/10/f06-511202.htm

Miami Heat. (1993–1994). *Miami Heat media guide*. Miami, FL: Author.

Migala Report. (2004, May). Trading spaces: How to examine new revenue opportunities that exist within your facility. Retrieved October 26, 2010, from http://www.migalareport.com/may04_story2.cfm

Miller, M. (1991). *A whole different ballgame*. New York: Birch Lane Publishing.

Milwaukee American Association v. Landis, 49 F.2d 298 (D.C. Ill. 1931).

Much, P. J., & Gotto, R. M. (1997). Franchise valuation overview. In A. Friedman & P. J. Much, *1997 Inside the ownership of professional sports teams* (pp. 6–7). Chicago: Team Marketing Report.

National Football League Properties, Inc. v. Dallas Cowboys Football Club, Ltd., 922 F. Supp. 849 (S.D.N.Y. 1996).

National Hockey League and National Hockey League Players Association (2010). The full document: Richard Bloch's ruling in the Ilya Kovalchuk arbitration case. Retrieved October 26, 2010, from http://www.sbnation.com/2010/8/10/1614815/arbitration-ruling-ilya-kovalchuk-full-document

NBA. (2010a). *NBA.com*. Global sites. Retrieved October 27, 2010, from http://www.nba.com/global/

NBA (2010b). *NBA.com*. NBA to stage first-ever regular season games in Europe. Retrieved October 27, 2010, from http://www.nba.com/global/europe_games_100809.html

NBA. (2010c). *NBA.com*. Philadelphia 76ers. Front office directory. (n.d.). Retrieved October 27, 2010, from http://www.nba.com/sixers/front_office/index.html

NBPA. (2010). About the NBPA. Retrieved October 27, 2010, from http://www.nbpa.org/about-us

Neyer, R. (2002, November 5). Red Sox hire James in advisory capacity. ESPN.com. Retrieved from http://espn.go.com/mlb/s/2002/1105/1456563.html

NFLPA. (2008). NFLPA 2008 player conduct policy. Retrieved October 27, 2010, from http://images.nflplayers.com/mediaResources/images/oldImages/fck/NFL%20Personal%20Conduct%20Policy%202008.pdf

PGA TOUR, Inc. (2010a). Tournament schedules. Retrieved October 27, 2010, from http://www.pgatour.com/tournaments

PGA TOUR, Inc. (2010b). 2010 PGA Tour schedule. Retrieved October 27, 2010, from http://www.pgatour.com/2009/r/11/02/2010_schedule/index.html

PGA TOUR, Inc. (2010c). All-exempt tour priority ratings. Retrieved October 27, 2010, from http://www.pgatour.com/players/pgatour-exempt

PHPA. (2010a). AHL-PHPA collective bargaining agreement summary. Retrieved October 27, 2010, from http://www.phpa.com/en/content/home/about/ahl-collective-bargaining-agreement

PHPA. (2010b). ECHL-PHPA collective bargaining agreement summary. Retrieved October 27, 2010, from http://www.phpa.com/en/content/home/about/echl-collective-bargaining-agreement

Shropshire, K. (1996). *In black and white: Race and sports in America*. New York: New York University Press.

Staudohar, P. M. (1996). *Playing for dollars: Labor relations and the sports business*. Ithaca, NY: ILR Press.

Van Riper, T., & Karmali, N. (2009, June 22). The NBA's next frontier. Retrieved October 27, 2010, from http://www.forbes.com/global/2009/0622/china-india-adidas-nba-next-frontier.html

Yasser, R., McCurdy, J., Goplerud, P., & Weston, M. A. (2003). *Sports law: Cases and materials* (5th ed.). Cincinnati, OH: Anderson Publishing.

CHAPTER

Sports Agency

Lisa P. Masteralexis

■ INTRODUCTION

This chapter focuses on the field of sports agency, examining how athlete management and marketing firms operate. Many sports agency firms started by representing athletes, evolved to also include sports marketing and event management segments, and continue today to evolve as the sports agency business responds to competition.

A quick examination of International Marketing Group (IMG), one of the very first sports agencies, shows the evolution. IMG began in 1960 when its founder and sports agency industry innovator **Mark McCormack** began representing golfer Arnold Palmer; he soon added Gary Player and Jack Nicklaus to his list of clients before moving into tennis with Rod Laver in 1968 (IMG, 2004a). In more than 40 years leading IMG, McCormack transformed the company into the leader in managing golfers

as well as "running tournaments all over the world in both golf and tennis, even controlling the computer that assigns worldwide rankings to golfers" (Feinstein, 1992, p. 131). "The business of representing people—whether models, opera singers or rugby players—is the essence of IMG's business" (Christy, 2002). Beyond representing talent, IMG owns and runs events for their talent, plus then produces, distributes, and markets television programming of those events as well as others. In 2003, IMG's Web site described the company as follows:

The world's largest athlete representation firm [that], through its broadcast division, TWI, is both the world's largest independent producer of televised sports programming and distributor of sports television rights. IMG also promotes, manages, and owns hundreds of sporting events and classical music events throughout the world. The company is one of the world's largest sports marketing consultants to major corporations, owns the world's top sports academy, and is a pioneer in interactive media. IMG's multifaceted sports and lifestyle businesses also include the number one modeling agency in the world, the world's largest independent licensing agency, a prominent literary agency, an agency that manages and presents world-renowned classical music artists, and a division specializing in the development of golf courses and other recreational amenities for world-class destination resorts (Johnston & Kain, 2004).

Excluding TWI, prior to its $750 million sale to Ted Forstmann in 2004, IMG listed 26 areas of business on its Web site (IMG, 2004b). Compare the 2003 self-description with the 2010 description, which has evolved through Forstmann's streamlining:

> *IMG is the world's premier and most diversified sports, entertainment, and media company. We partner with the world's leading marketers and media networks to help them grow their businesses through our event properties, media production and distribution, talent brands, sponsorship consulting, brand licensing, sponsorship sales, and other services. From emerging leadership in areas like digital media, licensing, and entertainment programming, to our long-standing strength in sports, fashion, and traditional media, IMG is committed to providing business-building solutions. Our partners include many of the world's most famous brands, media outlets, sports governing bodies, national and local governments, athletes, entertainers, models, and fashion designers.*
> *IMG is the global leader in event management and talent representation across golf, tennis, and fashion and has a significant presence in many other sports, cultural, and lifestyle categories. Our media division is one of the world's top independent producers of sports and entertainment television across multiple genres and is an emerging leader in video and interactive content creation for broadband and mobile platforms* (IMG, 2010).

Forstmann's description lists seven areas of expertise:

1. Media production and distribution
2. Event creation, management, and sponsorship sales
3. Client representation and brand management
4. Sponsorship and media consulting
5. Global sponsorship and media sales
6. Consumer products licensing
7. Athlete training

That description takes advantage of its synergies in two areas: (1) sports and entertainment and (2) media. Forstmann reinvigorated IMG by streamlining the organization and its cost structure by letting go that which was not vertically integrated throughout the company, such as its team-sport athlete and celebrity representation. Also, as you'll learn later in the chapter, team-sport athlete representation has more costs for fewer financial rewards. Forstmann has expanded IMG's focus to a more global one, acquiring only new companies that complement the strengths of IMG. These moves again position IMG as the innovator in the field. IMG has a staff of 2,800 employees in 60 offices in 30 countries (IMG, 2010).

How does a smaller agency compete with such a behemoth? It is a logical question to ask at a time when many agency firms are operating in an environment of mergers and acquisitions. In the past decade, the sports agency business has seen SFX Sports come and go; built through the acquisition of more than

20 different sports and entertainment firms, it was later sold to Clear Channel and spun off with Live Nation. Many of the original agents whose firms were bought by SFX (such as Arn Tellem, the Hendricks brothers, and David Falk) bought back their firms to make a fresh start as SFX Sports became lost within the entertainment giant Live Nation. Others who sought vertical integration in the sports and entertainment media and marketing businesses, such as Octagon, have outlasted SFX. Octagon is the sports arm of Interpublic Group, a large advertising and marketing communications agency developed through similar acquisitions of established sports agencies. Octagon boasts over 800 employees in 51 offices across 22 countries (Octagon, 2010). Octagon works with over 500 companies worldwide while managing over 3,200 events. It also represents more than 800 professional athletes and celebrities in music and entertainment (Octagon, 2007a; 2007b). Still others—namely, Creative Artists Agency (CAA) and Wasserman Media Group (WMG)— are continuing to move into the industry segment created by IMG. The concept of developing a sports agency business through such acquisitions will be discussed in greater detail later in this chapter. This chapter primarily focuses on representatives of athletes and coaches. The sports event management and marketing side of the industry is discussed in greater detail in Chapter 13, Event Management.

A **sports agent** is difficult to define. As Ruxin (2004) points out, the term *sports agent* covers a broad range of relationships with an athlete, including friend, lawyer, teacher, or coach. In some aspects, a sports agent is similar to a talent agent in the entertainment industry in that both serve as personal managers who find the best outlet for the client's talent (Ruxin, 2004). When an agent acts as a representative of an athlete or coach, the law of agency imposes certain fiduciary duties on the agent. Chapter 5, Legal Principles Applied to Sport Management, discusses the fiduciary duties that establish the parameters within which the agent must operate.

Many people hold themselves out as sports agents. The exact number is hard to pinpoint, but there are far more people claiming to be agents than there are potential clients, because the client pool is limited. There are over 4,300 professional athletes in the four major leagues. There are between 1,600 and 1,800 agents registered or certified with the respective players associations. This number includes 350 to 400 agents representing at least one of the 1,200 players on a 40-man roster in Major League Baseball (MLB) (Rivera 2007), 155 agents in the National Hockey League (NHL) (NHLPA, 2010), 350 agents in the National Basketball Association (NBA), and 800 to 1000 agents in the National Football League (NFL) (Martino, 2009). Shropshire and Davis (2003) estimate that fewer than 100 NBA agents have clients, and only 50% of agents represent a client in the NFL (Levin, 2007). Many agents either have no clients or are doing agency work part-time while supplementing their incomes through other professions such as law, marketing, accounting, or financial planning. The fact that some athletes have more than one person representing their interests may contribute slightly to the high number of agents. For instance, one agent may be retained for contract negotiations; another employed for marketing, public relations, and media work; and yet another for financial advising. In any case, the number of sports agents clearly exceeds the number of potential clients, creating an environment ripe for unscrupulous conduct by sports agents recruiting clients. Ironically, often those who resort to unethical conduct during the recruiting process do not end up with the clients they were pursuing. This chapter discusses in detail the field's challenges to entry and clarifies the role of the sports agent and agency firms in the sport industry and in the lives of the athletes they represent.

Due to the competition in the industry, potential agents look for other areas to do business. The representation of coaches and management personnel in professional sports and big-time Division I college programs is one such emerging area. The reasons for this growth will be explored in greater detail later in the chapter. Another area in the United States is in soccer due to the growth in its popularity and the Major League Soccer (MLS). The MLS relies on Fédération Internationale de Football Association (FIFA) regulations. FIFA has not certified agents since 2001. Instead, member associations do, by relying on FIFA regulations. Currently there are 5,513 soccer agents registered in the world, including 77 in the United States and 20 in Canada (FIFA, 2010). The Canadian Football League (CFL) is yet another

market explored by agents and their players. For this reason, the CFL Players Association (CFLPA) currently lists 164 registered agents on its site, many of whom also are registered with the National Football League Players Association (NFLPA) (Canadian Football League Players Associaton, 2010).

■ HISTORY

Theater promoter C. C. "Cash and Carry" Pyle is often called the first sports agent. In 1925 Pyle negotiated a deal with George Halas's Chicago Bears for Red Grange to earn $3,000 per game and an additional $300,000 in endorsement and movie rights (Berry, Gould, & Staudohar, 1986). A few years later, New York Yankee

Red Grange signs movie contract (left to right: W.E. Shallon Bergger, H.G. Kustah, Grange, C.C. Pyle).

Courtesy of the Harold E. "Red" Grange Collection, Wheaton College (IL)

George Herman "Babe" Ruth allegedly consulted sports cartoonist Christy Walsh to serve as his financial advisor through the Great Depression (Neff, 1987). Until the 1970s it was extremely rare for a player to have a sports agent because teams generally refused to deal with agents. Some players even found that having an agent turned out to be a detriment to their contract negotiations. One often-told story involves a Green Bay Packers player, Jim Ringo, who, in 1964, brought his financial advisor to help him negotiate his contract with legendary coach and general manager Vince Lombardi. Lombardi immediately excused himself for a minute. When Lombardi returned he told the agent he was negotiating with the wrong team, for he had just traded Ringo to Philadelphia (Hofmann & Greenberg, 1989).

This type of treatment and the inability to negotiate on what the players believed was a level playing field led the Dodgers' star pitchers Sandy Koufax and Don Drysdale to hire Hollywood agent Bill Hayes to represent them in 1965. Hayes orchestrated Koufax's and Drysdale's joint holdout in which they each demanded a three-year, $1 million contract, up from the $85,000 and $80,000 the Dodgers had paid them the season before (Helyar, 1994). The idea of a joint holdout, the amount of money the two demanded, and the prospect of other players trying the tactic outraged the Dodgers, and Hayes lined up an exhibition tour for Koufax and Drysdale in Japan and threatened to get Drysdale a movie contract. Although the two had immense talent, they had little bargaining power because the rules in MLB did not allow them to negotiate with other major league teams. As a result, Koufax and Drysdale ended up settling for $125,000 and $115,000, respectively (Helyar, 1994). It was a great deal less than they sought, but more than they would have received had they bargained individually and without an agent.

Few players in team sports had agents until the late 1960s. In that era, even those who had agents used them more as advisors than as agents. In 1967 Bob Woolf counseled Detroit Tigers pitcher Earl Wilson (Woolf, 1976). Wilson went to the front office of the Tigers alone while Woolf stayed in Wilson's apartment; whenever Wilson had a question he excused himself from the room and called Woolf for more advice (Woolf, 1976). Despite the fact that the door to representation in team sports began to open in 1970 when the Major League Baseball Players Association negotiated for a player's right to be represented by an agent, it did not fully open until free agency was won in 1976 through the Messersmith–McNally arbitration decision.

Players in individual sports such as golf and tennis have relied on agents for a longer time. C. C. Pyle also made his mark in professional tennis when, in 1926, he guaranteed French tennis star Suzanne Lenglen $50,000 to tour the United States (Berry, Gould, & Staudohar, 1986). At the time people were startled by the sum, but by the end of the tour, Pyle had helped popularize professional tennis, and all involved earned a handsome share of the revenue it generated (Berry, Gould, & Staudohar, 1986). Mark McCormack, founder of IMG and one of the first agents to represent individual athletes, was known as the pioneer of the sports marketing industry. He revolutionized the sport industry by "establishing athlete representation as a distinct business discipline" (IMG, 2003). A college golfer at William & Mary, McCormack became "famous for launching the modern sports-marketing business when he packaged and marketed Arnold Palmer, endorsement king of the pre-Michael Jordan era" (Katz, 1994, p. 231). To develop new opportunities for revenue streams for individual athletes, McCormack branched off into marketing and managing events in which they could participate. From there he developed TWI, a broadcast division that is currently the largest independent producer of televised sports programming and distributor of sports television rights (IMG, 2003).

Growth of the Sports Agency Business

By the late 1970s most segments of the sport industry had acknowledged the role that agents play in professional sports. According to Sobel (1990), five factors account for the growth of the sports agency business: the evolution of players associations, the reserve system, players' need for financial advice, the development of competing leagues, and rising product endorsement opportunities.

▪ EVOLUTION OF PLAYERS ASSOCIATIONS

Expounding on Sobel's factors, we first examine the evolution of the players associations in the late 1960s and early 1970s that opened the door of the team front offices for sports agents. The Major League Baseball Players Association (MLBPA) led the move through its negotiation of the second collective bargaining agreement. In the negotiations, the players received a written guarantee of the right to use an agent in their contract negotiations with management (Lowenfish, 1991). In its negotiations with Major League Baseball's Management Council, the MLBPA also achieved the right to labor grievance arbitration. Labor grievance arbitration is a system that allows both players and management to settle work-related conflicts in a hearing before a neutral arbitrator. Players achieved free agency through such an arbitration award in 1975.

Achieving free agency opened the door for sports agents to negotiate better contracts for the players. Players associations opened the door for the agents to have more power, and they often monitor and work with agents through negotiations and arbitrations because both represent the players' interests. The difference between the two is that the union represents the collective interests of all players, whereas an agent represents the individual interests of a particular player. As such, the union negotiates a contract for all players in the league, called the collective bargaining agreement, and the agent negotiates a contract for the player he or she represents, called the **standard or uniform player contract**. Through collective bargaining the players associations establish salary and benefit minimums, and agents negotiate for salaries and benefits above and beyond the minimums in their individual contracts. This is unique to sport and entertainment, since in most labor relationships the union represents all employees. Players associations support agents by sharing a great deal of salary and contract data and information to support contract negotiations and by providing invaluable guidance in salary and labor arbitrations.

▪ THE RESERVE SYSTEM

Until the mid-1970s, players in MLB were bound perpetually to their teams by the **reserve system**. Each league used a restrictive system to limit a free and open market so that the owners could retain the rights to players and depress salaries. Baseball's reserve system was the first and serves as a great example. The system consisted of two parts: the reserve clause and the reserve list. The **reserve clause** in the players' standard contracts gave teams the option to renew players for the following season. Each contract contained a reserve clause, and thus a player could be renewed season after season at the team's option. The **reserve list** was a list sent to each team in the league. League rules entitled each team to place its reserved players on a list, and the teams had a "gentlemen's agreement" not to offer contracts to any other teams' players reserved on the list. This two-part system kept players bound to their teams, depressing their salaries and bargaining leverage.

Sports agency grew when free agency emerged in 1976 by the Messersmith–McNally arbitration that successfully challenged baseball's reserve system. Once free agency descended on baseball, agents such as Jerry Kapstein (who represented 60 baseball players) elevated salaries by holding auctions for talented players (Helyar, 1994). Kapstein played to the owners' lust for talent by driving them into bidding wars for his free agents (Schwarz, 1996). As salaries increased, so too did the players' demand for agents.

■ ATHLETES' NEED FOR FINANCIAL PLANNING

As athletes' salaries increased, tax planning (Sobel, 1990), financial planning (Grossman, 2002), and other forms of business advice became vital to a player's financial success. Agents help athletes negotiate more favorable contract clauses for increased income, tax breaks, and post career income. According to Shropshire (1990), an agent also provides a level of parity between the athlete and the team, event, or sponsor with which he or she is negotiating. Sports team or event management people have had a great deal of experience negotiating many contracts each year, whereas an athlete may have just one opportunity to negotiate and thus should hire an agent with comparable negotiating experience to level the playing field (Shropshire, 1990). This is particularly important when complex systems such as salary caps are involved. It is highly likely that most athletes have not seen a player's contract before, let alone a collective bargaining agreement. Without an agent's help, an athlete might be at a severe disadvantage.

Agents also allow athletes to focus their attention on performing in their sport while the agent acts as a shield to outside distrac-

tions. The shield is the transparent bubble that agents build around their clients to protect them from such distractions as tax and insurance forms, payment of bills, travel arrangements, the media, and the emotional challenges of being a professional athlete (Schwarz, 1996). Further, according to Grossman (2002), an athlete's long-term financial success requires the conversion of current income into longer-term financial resources. The dynamics are such that an athlete's career earnings debut at a rate far exceeding those of his or her peers in other industries. Often an athlete may be transformed from relative poverty to wealth almost overnight but be without the wisdom and maturity to control his or her spending and save for the future. Grossman (2002) suggests that an athlete's financial team should consist of an accountant or tax advisor, business attorney, banker, investment advisor, insurance professional, and estate attorney. These individuals are separate from the agent representing the athlete's interest in contract negotiations or marketing.

■ DEVELOPMENT OF COMPETING LEAGUES

The development of competing leagues from the 1960s through the 1980s furthered the growth of the sports agency business (Sobel, 1990). Competing leagues such as the American Football League (1960–1966), the American Basketball Association (1967–1976), the World Hockey Association (1972–1978), and the United States Football League (1982–1986) offered higher salaries to induce marquee players to join the leagues, and these offers provided leverage during contract negotiations. As players jumped to competing leagues their salaries increased, and correspondingly the salaries of players that owners were trying to keep in the dominant leagues increased. Agents often played a crucial role in locating interested teams in the new leagues, sifting through players' offers, and negotiating contracts. This concept can be taken one step further as sport has become more of a global phenomenon over the past two decades. With more athletes moving into a worldwide market for team sport, agents with an understanding of leagues and teams on a global scale and with international contacts are critical to athletes moving into playing opportunities in other nations.

■ GROWTH OF PRODUCT ENDORSEMENT OPPORTUNITIES

As professional sport grew into a nationally televised business and its entertainment value increased, so too did opportunities for athletes to increase their income through product endorsements (Sobel, 1990). Martin Blackman pioneered the negotiation of endorsement contracts for athletes with his deals for retired athletes to star in Miller Lite's television commercial series (Shropshire, 1990). Now, many athletes hire sports marketing experts to help them create images, market their images and services, and negotiate endorsement deals.

Beyond product endorsement, agents for athletes are involved in parlaying their images into entertainment and celebrity. Some athletes, such as Mike Tyson, Dwayne Johnson ("The Rock"), Reggie Jackson, Michael Jordan, and Shaquille O'Neal, have starred in movies, whereas others, including Michael Strahan, Tiki Barber, Rocco Mediate, Peyton Manning, Derek Jeter, and Serena Williams, have appeared on television shows. Professional athletes have also moved into the popular reality television genre. Former NFL stars Emmitt Smith and Jerry Rice, former NBA star Clyde Drexler, boxers Laila Ali and Evander Holyfield, auto racer Helio Castroneves, and Olympians Apolo Anton Ohno and Kristi Yamaguchi have participated on "Dancing with the Stars." Shaquille O'Neal hosts his own show called, "ShaQ vs." in which he challenges other star athletes and entertainers to competitions in their expertise, following

in the footsteps of popular shows from the late 1970s, such as ABC's Wide World of Sports Superstars and Battle of the Network Stars where athletes and entertainers compete. The latter two were joint productions between IMG's television production arm and ABC Sports, once again demonstrating the branding of the athlete as celebrity and the integration of sports and entertainment. NFLers Chad Ochocinco ("The Ultimate Catch"), Terrell Owens ("The T.O. Show"), and even the New York Jets ("Hard Knocks") have reality shows. Bernie Williams, Shaquille O'Neal, and Tony Parker record music. The sports agent often obtains the opportunities for athletes to be involved in entertainment and then navigates the public relations needs for their celebrity status.

Still other athletes get into entrepreneurial ventures such as product development, theme restaurants, sports bars, and music clubs. The sports agent often performs a crucial role carrying out business transactions to establish these ventures.

■ EVOLUTION OF SPORT AGENCIES

The name of the game in the sports agency world in the late 1990s was to create "uberagencies." This trend was spawned by SFX founder Robert F.X. Sillerman's attempted corporate aquisition revolution in 1998. At the time Sillerman's two companies, the Marquee Group and SFX Entertainment, were international leaders in marketing, concert promotion, and live entertainment production. He moved into the sporting world by buying up sports agencies, spending $150 million in just 18 months. As lines between sports and entertainment blurred, Sillerman believed SFX Sports Group could provide athletes with one-stop shopping for marketing and negotiation. SFX Sports could use its resources to achieve vertical integration (Wertheim, 2001). Octagon jumped into the fray, pursuing multiple acquisitions of smaller agencies to keep up with SFX Group and IMG, already the model of vertical integration that Sillerman sought to achieve.

SFX was brought down by internal strife. What Sillerman did not effectively plan for is the idea that these agencies that were fiercely competitive would now have to work in a cooperative manner. What ensued were numerous power struggles and a sale of SFX in August 2000 to Clear Channel that made Sillerman $4.4 billion. However, the move weakened SFX, because sports accounted for less than 10% of SFX's business and SFX was less than 10% of Clear Channel's core business (Weirtheim, 2001). As SFX Sports disintegrated and many began to think that the age of agency mergers and acquisitions was over, along came Wasserman Media Group (WMG)[1] and CAA Sports.[2]

WMG grabbed Arn Tellem's agency, which he had recently bought back from SFX (WMG, 2006a); Touring Pro, an events firm (WMG, 2006b); soccer representation firm SportsNet, SFX's European soccer division (WMG, 2006c, 2006d); Reich and Katz's baseball agency (Mullen, 2007b); sport and entertainment marketing agency OnSport (WMG, 2007a); and two agents from Octagon and one agent from IMG who represent athletes in the areas of women's sports, action sports, and golf (Mullen, 2007b). Meanwhile, CAA Sports acquired IMG's baseball, football, and hockey divisions, along with SFX's football division, and Leon Rose's basketball division, which represents LeBron James (Mullen, 2006, 2007a). More recently, CAA has picked off some of IMG's executives and their clients followed (Futterman, 2010; Mullen, 2010a, 2010b). IMG settled its lawsuit against former coaches' agent Matthew Baldwin over his defection to CAA and an alleged attempt to steal its coaching representation business (Futterman, 2010; Mullen, 2010c). Incidentally, CAA dismissed Baldwin prior to his settlement with IMG (Futterman, 2010b).

These aggressive moves to merge and acquire agencies caught many observers by surprise, because this approach seemed to fail in the SFX experiment. However, according to Randy Vataha, president of Boston-based Game Plan, "If it was a complete failure the first time, it wouldn't be happening now . . . The agent world is extremely entrepreneurial." Companies such as the old SFX Entertainment

---

[1] According to its Web site, Wasserman Media Group, LLC, is a leading sports and entertainment management, marketing, and content company. WMG's complementary divisions of management, marketing, media, and investments collectively represent some of the industries' most recognized athletes and brands. WMG Marketing secures naming rights for popular sports and entertainment destinations, generates corporate sponsorships, and develops marketing programs for leading consumer brands. Through long-term relationships with the organizations and people who influence today's youth market culture and consumer, WMG Consulting specializes in developing customized marketing programs that leverage campaigns and fuse brands with the power, emotion, and affinity of sports and entertainment. WMG was a holding company for the Los Angeles Avengers of the Arena Football League. WMG has offices in Los Angeles, New York, North Carolina, San Diego, and London (WMG, 2007b).

[2] CAA Sports represents more than 350 of the world's best athletes in team sports such as baseball, football, hockey, and soccer, in addition to icons in individual sports, on-air broadcasters, and other sports personalities. Beyond traditional athlete representation, CAA Sports provides unique opportunities for clients off the field, in areas including licensing, endorsements, speakers, philanthropy, and video games. CAA Sports also helps develop sports programming opportunities and sports marketing strategies for its clients. CAA Sports is a division of Creative Artists Agency (CAA), a talent and literary agency that represents the most creative and successful artists working in film, television, music, theater, and video games, and provides a range of strategic marketing services to corporate clients.

and the former Assante Corporation, which also bought a number of top sports agencies about a decade ago, only to dissolve the business a few years later, saw a big opportunity initially. "But once the dust cleared, they had to manage all these mavericks," Vataha said. "I think the people doing this now think they have learned from the mistakes of the earlier deals" (Mullen, 2006). Some industry experts, including agents and others who have talked to CAA President Richard Lovett, who is leading the sports agency acquisition charge, note that that company may be able to avoid some of the pitfalls of the past because, after all, talent representation is CAA's core business (CAA represents such entertainment stars as Tom Cruise, George Clooney, and Steven Spielberg).

Tellem, who was one of the agents acquired by the old SFX Entertainment and is now the head of athlete management for WMG, knows about the mistakes of the past firsthand. "Our plan is not to do a roll-up of sports agencies. I have been there and that is a recipe for disaster," said Tellem. SFX's aggregation of sports

agencies "was done as a way of building up a company of critical mass and then selling it," Tellem said. Tellem added that he decided to join WMG because the company's owner, Casey Wasserman, is committed to building something that lasts and because the company's core business is sports. CAA Sports and WMG were the top two sports agencies in brokering player salaries in the four major team sports according to a list published in the summer of 2008 by *SportsBusiness Journal* (Table 11-1) (Mullen and Broughton, 2008). Only time will tell if WMG and CAA Sports are leading the next wave of firms to have the lasting impact of an IMG, but it appears they are not going the way of SFX. A further challenge that faced SFX was an issue noted by Donald Dell, sports agency pioneer and founder of Pro Serv, "[w]e had 15 companies bought in 2-1/2 years," . . . [so, w]e had 15 egomaniacs, all strutting around telling everyone what to do, and nothing happened" (Mullen and Broughton, 2008). Finally, AEG president and CEO Tim Leiweke notes another difference between the SFX example and CAA

TABLE 11-1	Top Athlete Representation Firms	
Agency	**Number of Athletes Represented**	**Notable Clients**
IMG	Many	Roger Federer, Maria Sharapova, Tiger Woods, Evan Lysacek, Joe Mauer, Lindsay Vonn
Octagon	>800	NFL, NBA, NHL, and MLB first-round draft picks in 2006, 15% of NHL players, 20% of NBA players, Michael Phelps, 16 other Olympic gold medalists
Wasserman Media Group (WMG)	>200	Dave Mirra, Ryan Nyquist, Travis Pastrana, Jason Giambi, Hideki Matsui, Jermaine O'Neil, Tracy McGrady
CAA Sports	>300	David Beckham, Tony Hawk, Oscar de la Hoya, Derek Jeter, Sidney Crosby, LeBron James
Scott Boras Corporation	>60	Alex Rodriguez, Carlos Beltran, Magglio Ordonez, Greg Maddux, Barry Zito

Sources: Mullen, L. (2006, October 16–22). New players emerge in athlete rep business: Ranking the agencies. *Street & Smith's SportsBusiness Journal*, p. 26; plus client information taken from agency Web sites.

Sports and WMG: "SFX was in live entertainment, motor sports, management, sponsorship and other areas and seemed to be all over the place. CAA is an agency, period. WMG is very focused on this business and will be for a very long time" (Mullen and Broughton, 2008).

Representing Individual Athletes

Representing the individual athlete differs significantly from representing the team-sport athlete. Much of what the individual athlete earns is dependent on consistent performance in events, appearance fees from events, and the ability to promote and market his or her image. Therefore, an agent representing an individual athlete often travels with the athlete, tending to daily distractions so the athlete can stay focused on winning. For instance, as Ivan Lendl's agent for seven years, Jerry Solomon of ProServ spent nearly 24 hours a day for seven days a week traveling and representing Lendl. This takes a toll on one's social and personal life, but often is necessary to retain a client. When Solomon eventually pulled away from this relationship with Lendl, Lendl resented it and moved from ProServ to IMG (Feinstein, 1992). An agent of an individual-sport athlete is often more involved in managing the individual player's career, much like business managers hired by entertainers.

Management tasks include booking exhibitions and special competitions to supplement the athlete's winnings from regular tour or circuit events as well as managing training, travel, lodging, and the athlete's personal life. For the team-sport athlete, the professional team takes care of many of these details. However, this may be changing a bit, because competition in acquiring and retaining clients is causing agents to offer more services. Some agents are taking a more active role in their athletes' training regimens by providing access to trainers and coaches (Helyar, 1997), or even signing an alliance with

a sports medicine and performance institute to help athletes get drafted to a higher position or signed onto a team. Some may be doing this to compete with large competitor IMG, which owns a multi-sport training academy in Florida. As the agency business has evolved, many athletes have begun to expect that agents will pick up much of the cost of training for them. For instance, one football agent suggested that the NFL Combine preparation runs about $1,000 per week for training, plus the athletes will need housing, a stipend, a car, and food; thus, an agent is investing close to $20,000 on preparing one player for the Combine (Kuliga, 2007). Creating alliances or partnerships with training facilities and car dealerships is one method of limiting the costs or even deriving some revenues from the relationships for sports agencies.

A key difference between firms that represent individual athletes and those that primarily represent team-sport athletes is that the firms doing individual representation are intimately involved in all aspects of the sport, from running the sports' tournaments to televising them. Such involvement can create a conflict of interest. As Brennan (1996) points out, athletes often decide that the conflict created when their agent becomes their employer is not as trying as the conflict created when their training and traveling bills come due and they have generated no income from their sport.

As the Olympic Movement has moved away from its rigid rules on amateurism, top-level Olympic athletes have increasingly found that they, too, have a greater need for sport agents. In figure skating, for example, new revenues from television rights increased the athletes' earning opportunities. Senior manager/agent Michael Rosenburg, two-time Olympic medalist and ice skating commentator Dick Button, and the management firm IMG had worked to develop professional skating careers for athletes such as Dorothy Hamill, Janet Lynn, and doubles partners Tai Babilonia and Randy Gardner after their Olympic appearances (Brennan, 1996). As figure skating's popularity has increased, so has the amount of money flowing into the sport, legitimately creating an increased need for agents. Like other national governing bodies, the U.S. Figure Skating Association expects stars to be out participating in promotions, interviews, tours, and various competitions, and as a result these young athletes are now hiring agents to promote them and to protect them from the "blastfurnace media" (Brennan, 1996, p. 126). In previous years a family struggled financially to enable a daughter or son to pursue the Olympic dream, but now with the help of an agent, an Olympic athlete may earn money to help pay some of his or her training and traveling expenses (Brennan, 1996).

Marketing is similar for agents of individual- and team-sport athletes. Marketing is critical for individual-sport athletes who are dependent on sponsorship contracts to provide product and earn income for travel and training costs. Although not a recent development, today there is greater emphasis on branding all athletes. While branding is not exclusive to individual athletes, the opportunities for branding are greater due to the individual nature of their performances. Although branding is the current buzzword, innovative sport marketing agencies such as IMG have been doing it for years. For instance, in a 2004 interview with the Associate Editor of *BusinessWeek*, Arnold Palmer's response about his relationship with IMG shows that even in the 1960s IMG was thinking about the development of the Arnold Palmer brand:

Q: At this point in your career, what are you looking for from IMG?

A: Of course, I'm cutting back quite a lot at my age. I'll tell you what I'm looking for. I remember an [IMG agent] named Jules Rosenthal back in the 1960s. I remember being in the midst of a very heavy commercial shoot, where we were doing stills

and stuff. I said, "You know. This is all well and good, but what are you going to do when I get old?" This was a question to him and to IMG. And his answer was, "We will have established you as a business, and you personally will not be so important" (Brady, 2004).

According to Brian Dubin, head of WMA's East Coast commercial division and brand expert for skateboarder Tony Hawk, "Building a brand out of a client is not necessarily suitable for every client, . . . The key is finding those clients who do have an interest in building a brand out of their name or out of an image that they represent. . . . Your client . . . has intangible assets: a name, a reputation, a credibility, and an image. All of those attributes may be combined into something that could be made into a brand. When they are turned into a product or a service, then they become tangible assets" (Towle, 2003).

However, there are challenges in athlete branding. For instance, if the advertisements and products are not a fit with the athlete's personality or do not work to raise an athlete's image, it can work against the athlete. A good example of this dilemma is Yao Ming, whose branding has been criticized for not maintaining better control of his image outside of China. He has done advertisements that further cultural stereotypes (VISA check cards) and position him as freakishly tall (Apple Computer), rather than as a premier athlete. By doing advertisements that pander to his height or foreignness, he moves away from his image in China—that of a premier basketball superstar—an image that should be the linchpin of his branding in the United States and beyond (Sauer, 2003). To change this perception, some marketers, such as branding expert Wendy Newman, advocate an approach called *person-centered branding,* in which an authentic brand is created based on who the person is, focusing on the person's identity to establish an enduring brand as opposed to capitalizing for the short term on an athlete's game or performance and contriving an image to fit a product or brand. The first strategy promises to last a lifetime, whereas the second will likely fade away with the end of the athlete's playing career (Newman, 2007).

Another challenge that arises from athlete branding "is that, while it trades on the allure of a personality, it is vulnerable to the public's acceptance of that personality. Some observers argue that, in sports, where celebrity branding originated, a backlash already has occurred. 'In the sports world, you see corporations backing away from exclusive athlete endorsements and licensing,' Jim Andrews, [Editorial Director at *IEG Sponsorship Report*] says. 'When you involve yourself with one individual, you are putting all your eggs in one basket: If that individual gets involved in criminal activity or has a professional slump, you've attached your company's reputation to a product that's no longer in favor with the public'" (Towle, 2003). For more information on branding, see Chapter 3, Sport Marketing.

Representing Coaches and Management Professionals

There are a handful of sports agents who represent professional and collegiate coaches. Not all coaches have sports agents, but the number who have representation is growing. The growing income of coaches is one reason. For instance, the average salary of coaches in the NFL in 2009 exceeded $3 million, with the leaders in the $5 to $5.5 million range, and in the NBA in 2009 coaches' salaries exceeded $4 million, with the Lakers' Phil Jackson in the top spot with a $10.3 million contract (Van Riper, 2009). The compensation (excluding benefits, incentives, perks, and endorsements) of the top college basketball coaches whose programs make it to the NCAA March Madness tournament average $1.3 million. In the top programs the average is $1.9 million, with some such as John Calipari of Kentucky, Rick Pitino of Louisville, and Mike Krzyzewski of Duke exceeding $4 million annually (Van Riper, 2009; Upton, Gillum and Berkowitz, 2010). Coach Mack Brown at the University of Texas leads the pack for college football coaches, earning $5.1 million annually to exceed $35 million in a seven-year deal, not counting outside compensation from endorsement opportunities (Berkowitz, 2009). During the period 2006–2009, college football coaches' salaries increased an average of 46% (Upton, Gillum, & Berkowitz, 2010).

A second reason may be the increased job movement and added pressures on coaches to succeed (Greenberg, 1993). The increased complexities of the position of head or top assistant coach may make having an agent to rely on for advice and counsel almost a necessity. One agent credited with growing the salaries of NFL coaches, Bob LaMonte, views the modern-day coach as a CEO; he therefore prepares the coach to be a CEO while at the same time negotiating CEO-like pay from club owners (Wertheim, 2004). For these same reasons, management professionals, such as general managers in professional sports, are also turning to sports agents and attorneys to assist in their contract negotiations with clubs. The "Career Opportunities" section later in this chapter discusses specific details regarding coaching contract negotiations.

■ SPORTS AGENCY FIRMS

There is no blueprint for how a sports agency firm should operate. In smaller firms, an agent works alone or with a small group of employees, and often work may be outsourced to other professionals. In larger firms, the agent may be part of an international conglomerate representing many athletes in a broad range of sports and working on many aspects of an athlete's career. Often these divisions will have a big-name agent as the head of the division, with a number of subordinate agents working to make the operation run smoothly.

In a presentation before the American Bar Association's Forum Committee on the Entertainment and Sports Industries, law professor Robert A. Berry stated that there are three models for the sports agency business (Berry, 1990). The first and most popular model is the **freestanding sport management firm**. It is established as a full-service firm providing a wide range of services to the athlete. Although each sport management firm may not perform all the services discussed in the "Career Opportunities" section, it is likely that a firm performs several, including contract negotiations, marketing, and some financial planning. These freestanding sport management firms may be further divided into two categories: (1) those that represent athletes only, such as the Scott Boras Corporation (baseball) and Newport Sports Management (hockey); and (2) those that combine athlete representation, event management, and industry consulting, such as IMG, Octagon, CAA Sports, and WMG, all of which have many divisions across many sports and events (Berry, 1990).

According to Shropshire (1990), a freestanding sport management firm's benefits are as follows: (1) The athlete is presumably able to receive the best service without having to shop around for many experts, and (2) the agent retains all aspects of the athlete's business. The firm benefits because the athlete usually pays fees for any services provided beyond the contract negotiation. Fees will be discussed in greater detail later in this chapter.

Berry (1990) identifies a second type of firm as a **law practice only**. In this type of firm, "lawyer sports representatives often participate as principals in a sports management firm, but opt to include this as just one aspect of their law practice" (Berry, 1990, p. 4). In this practice, the lawyer performs many legal tasks for the athlete, such as contract negotiation, legal representation in arbitration or other proceedings, legal counseling, dispute resolution, and the preparation of tax forms. Often the lawyers do not undertake financial management, marketing, or investing of the athlete's money; the sports lawyer may, however, oversee the retention of other needed professionals to advise the athlete and protect him or her from incompetent service (Berry, 1990). Lon Babby, a partner at the Washington, D.C., law firm of Williams & Connolly, was known for charging clients an hourly rate and represented such basketball players as NBA stars Grant Hill and Tim Duncan as well as WNBA stars Alana Beard and Tamika Catchings. This practice was first popularized by Babby before he became the President of Basketball Operations for the Phoenix Suns. Babby had also introduced the hourly rate to baseball representation. Williams & Connolly partner James Tanner, Jr. will continue the practice of hourly representation on behalf of the firm.

The third type of firm identified by Berry (1990) is the **sport management firm affiliated with a law firm**. Many sports lawyers who represent athletes originally developed a law practice, and as their businesses grew they recognized the advantages of expanding the services they offered the athlete beyond legal services. Some have abolished their law practices in favor of a freestanding sport management firm, but others have retained a law practice and created a sport management subsidiary within the practice to provide those services not traditionally offered by lawyers. A trend in the past twenty years has been for law firms to create an affiliate relationship whereby the law firm remains its own entity, but creates a working relationship with a freestanding sport management firm, each filling the void by providing the services the other does not offer (Berry, 1990).

Small firms find greater success representing athletes in one sport and focusing on one or two services for the athletes or coaches. The work outsourced to other professionals by smaller firms is generally tax planning and preparation, financial investing, public relations, and, more recently, physical and psychological career preparation. Large firms employ professionals from many disciplines to provide services ranging from negotiating contracts to marketing the athlete's image to financial planning and developing outside business interests (Ruxin, 2004). Most agents fall somewhere in between, although the large multifaceted firm with offices worldwide is becoming an increasingly dominant force in the athlete representation market (Ruxin, 2004).

It is important to realize that the different types of firms are market driven. Some athletes prefer association with a large firm, whereas others prefer the individual attention of a small firm. Those who choose the large firms often do so for the following reasons: (1) A large firm provides one-stop shopping by employing many skilled professionals to take care of all services; (2) a large firm may have a more established history, reputation, and industry contacts; (3) many athletes prefer representation by firms representing other star players (it's similar to being on the same team); and (4) some athletes believe that being with an agent who represents many players helps their own bargaining position. For instance, some athletes choose an agency such as Octagon on the assumption that the sheer number of athletes it represents (over 800) must translate into contacts with a large number of general managers or events and a larger number of marketing opportunities. Still others may choose to go with an agent due to the perceived or real influence that person has on the industry. For example, over the past 25 years **Scott Boras** has built an agency in baseball that some have argued influences the

entire baseball industry. He has revolutionized the approach to player–team negotiations by relying on a deep understanding of the game and the business of baseball that enables him to wield baseball statistics, tough negotiating tactics, knowledge of the rules, and a free market philosophy to change the market for players (Anderson, 2007; Pierce, 2007). In fact, it has been argued that Boras' player signings and deals with the owner of the team (to the chagrin of the club's general manager) influenced the ability of the Detroit Tigers to make it into the 2006 World Series (Kepner, 2006). Athletes have been known to choose Boras on the basis of this reputation (Pierce, 2007), as they are very aware that they have limited opportunities to get their value in the market. Other athletes might prefer to be one of the few individuals represented by a person with whom they build a bond or whom they trust rather than becoming one of a number of clients at a large firm (Steadman, 2004).

Athletes who choose small firms often do so because of the attention they receive from such a firm. At large firms, the attention of the more established agents will often go to their superstar clients. Those professional athletes on the bottom of the priority list may be assigned an assistant to deal with or may have trouble getting telephone calls returned. Even established athletes may have difficulty with the large firms. For example, golfers Greg Norman and Nick Price moved away from the large IMG and formed their own management companies to focus solely on their own needs because they found that calls to IMG often took a couple of days to be answered—not because IMG was irresponsible but because it had so many clients to service. Both golfers also thought it more cost-effective to hire their own staff than to pay IMG's 20% to 25% commissions on business deals (Feinstein, 1995). Interestingly, Greg Norman returned to IMG as a client and has since switched to CAA Sports.

Fees Charged by Sports Agents

Fees charged by agents vary because fees are market driven and depend on whether the players association limits the fees. Fees are usually based on one of four methods: the flat fee, the percentage of compensation, an hourly rate, or a combination of an hourly rate with a percentage of compensation cap (McAleenan, 2002). The first method, the flat fee arrangement, requires an athlete to pay the agent an amount of money agreed upon before the agent acts for the athlete (McAleenan, 2002).

The second method, the percentage of compensation, is by far the most popular arrangement. Although it is criticized as being inflated, agent Leigh Steinberg defends it. Steinberg "dismisses those who bill by the hour as 'egg-timer agents' and argues that such a fee structure militates against an important aspect of the agenting: developing a personal relationship with clients" (Neff, 1987, p. 83). The fee often covers not just the negotiation, but all of the work related to the provisions of the contract over its term.

There is a drawback to the percentage formula, though. There may be no guarantee that the agent receives his or her expected percentage, in that the agent is paid as the athlete earns the money. For instance, the National Football League Players Association (NFLPA) limits the agent's fee to 3% of the contract, and in the NFL there is no such thing as a guaranteed contract. An agent may negotiate a contract and then the athlete may be cut during training camp, with the team owing nothing more than a signing or reporting bonus (if that was in the contract). Thus, despite the time invested, the agent may never see the full 3% of the contract he or she negotiated. Another example is in baseball, where the agent regulations limit an agent from earning any income from an athlete in the minor leagues. An agent may charge a fee for negotiating a signing bonus when a player is drafted, but the regulations prohibit an agent from receiving a percentage fee until the athlete has exceeded the league minimum salary (usually in the player's second season in the majors). While representing players in the minor leagues, an agent incurs a number of expenses, among them equipment, travel, and telephone expenses, and costs associated with negotiating trading card and in-kind product deals. In fact, because of the way the sporting goods industry has evolved, the agent actually supplies the products (e.g., gloves, cleats, bats, apparel) a minor leaguer needs to succeed out of his or her own budget. Thus, until an agent makes it by landing a top-round client, the agent is often left paying dues and investing a great deal of time, energy, and money into clients who may not provide a financial return. To make matters worse, some established agents make it their practice to market themselves to players only once those players are legitimate prospects or once the players are called up to the major leagues. As a result, players may leave their agent from the minors for a more established one once they reach the majors, never having paid a cent to the agent who invested in him in the minors. There are also numerous examples of agents in the NFL losing clients between the time of the draft and the actual signing of the contract. The recruiting by competitors does not stop simply because someone is drafted. In such a case, though, if there was a signed representation contract, the agent has the ability to pursue an arbitration case against the athlete for services rendered and maybe a lawsuit against the other agent for tortuous interference with a contractual or advantageous business relationship.

The third method, the hourly rate, is often not used for the reasons stated previously by Leigh Steinberg. For a high-round draft pick or a superstar free agent, however, McAleenan (2002) suggests that an hourly rate will provide the lowest fee. For example, assume the agent charges $150 per hour and works 40 hours negotiating a three-year $1 million compensation package. Working on a 4% fee structure, the agent would receive $40,000, but working the hourly rate the agent would receive only $18,000 (McAleenan, 2002). What this example fails to recognize, though, are the numerous hours spent on the telephone with the athlete in career counseling or working out details of the contract with the team or athlete, which does not usually occur with, for example, a corporate client. The relationship between athlete and agent is such that for most athletes it would probably sour the relationship to turn on the clock every time an athlete called to ask his or her agent a question or tell them about the previous night's game. The relationship between the athlete and agent is as much a personal one as a business one.

The fourth method, the hourly rate with a compensation cap, addresses the athlete's concern that the agent may pad the billable hours and inflate the fee. This option provides an hourly rate, the total of which will not exceed a certain percentage of the athlete's compensation, called the percentage cap (McAleenan, 2002).

A key component of the MLBPA, the NFLPA, the National Hockey League Players Association (NHLPA), and the National Basketball Players Association (NBPA) regulations governing agents is the limitation on agent fees. Players associations have set ceilings for agents' fees at between 3% and 6%. The fierce competition for clients has driven the average fees down closer to 2% to 3%, although well-established agents still charge the maximum percentages (Burwell, 1996). The NFLPA and NBPA have set maximum fees. The NBPA's regulation sets the maximum fee an agent can charge for negotiating a minimum salary at $2,000, or 4% for those contracts above the minimum. The NFLPA has a similar measure that limits an agent's fee to between 1% and 3% of the player's compensation based on the player's contract and status/designation (i.e., free agent, franchise, transition player). The MLBPA and NHLPA do not limit the fee charged by an agent. However, the MLBPA does not allow an agent to charge a fee that would put the player in the position of receiving less than the minimum salary annually. For example, if an agent negotiated a contract in 2010 of $420,000 and had a 5% fee arrangement with the player, he or she would generate a fee of $21,000. However, after paying the fee the athlete would be earning only $399,000. Because the fee would bring the athlete's salary below the minimum salary of $400,000 under the MLBPA guidelines, the agent could charge the athlete just $20,000. Other aspects of player association regulations are discussed later in the chapter.

The fee limitations, though, exist only for the fees the agents can charge for negotiating the athlete's contract. In an attempt to undercut competition, occasionally some agents will charge the same fee percentage for negotiating the athlete's marketing deals as for negotiating the player's contract. That is definitely not the norm, as marketing fees charged by agents generally range between 15% and 33%. Although this is much higher than the team contract negotiation compensation, a great deal of investment goes into creating an image for an athlete in the media and selling that image to marketers at companies that create a positive fit for the athlete and product. Imagine being the agent responsible for marketing athletes in the midst of scandals, such as Tiger Woods or Roger Clemens, or the numerous NFL stars engaged in improper off-field conduct and alleged illegal activities, such as Adam "Pacman" Jones, Chad Johnson, and Michael Vick. These high-profile scandals force agents to put a great deal of time and energy into crisis management at the time of the incident and then into resurrecting images and convincing corporations to invest in endorsement opportunities with athletes whose images come with some baggage. Beyond the marketing fees, agents may also charge for other services rendered, such as tax planning, financial planning, and investment advising.

For athletes in other sports and for coaches, there are no regulations regarding fees, so the fees tend to be higher. The athlete or coach and the agent negotiate these fees individually, so the fee will depend on market factors and bargaining power. In tennis, for example, the standard fee players pay agents when they first become professionals is 10% of their prize money and 20% to 25% of all other revenue, whereas superstars usually will have their prize money fee waived and off-court fees cut to 10% or less (Feinstein, 1992). For example, when Ivan Lendl was a ProServ client, his contract provided for a flat fee of $25,000 and 7.5% of all earnings (Greenberg, 1993).

■ CAREER OPPORTUNITIES

A sports agency is a business and, as with any other business, there are a range of opportunities available to potential employees. As many sports agencies have evolved, they have hired employees similar to those in mainstream consulting businesses. These employees include individuals with expertise in marketing, management, finance, accounting, operations, and the like. They may be working to keep the agency business afloat or they may be working as consultants to the agency's clients. A quick look at job listings for one of the larger agencies on its Web site postings includes openings for accountants, a finance executive, account executives (sales/marketing), production assistants (broadcasting), communications specialists, event specialists, and more.

Sports Event Manager

Some sport management firms also control the rights to sporting events and hire **sports event managers** to run these events. Event managers

generally have no involvement with the representation of professional athletes. Chapter 13, Event Management, provides information on careers in event management and the skills necessary for success.

Sports Marketing Representative

The **sports marketing representative** coordinates all of the marketing and sponsorship activities for sports properties. Sports properties include sporting events run by the agency firm and the athletes the agency represents. A sports marketing representative's responsibilities may include conducting market research, selling sponsorships for an event, promoting an event and the athletes participating in it, or making calls to find endorsement opportunities for athletes who are clients of the firm. As sports agencies face greater competition in the market, more firms are focusing energies on marketing activities and even consulting in marketing because marketing activities generate significant new revenue streams and there are no restrictions to fees charged for them. To learn more about careers in sports marketing and the skills necessary for success, refer to Chapter 3, Marketing Principles Applied to Sport Management.

Sports Agent

Sports agents often refer to themselves as athlete representatives or sports lawyers. To some, the term *sports agent* has a negative connotation. However, many sports agents are not lawyers and need not be lawyers, but are now required by player's associations to hold a minimum qualification of a graduate degree.

The functions of sports agents vary more widely than do the types of firms. Keep in mind that some agents perform just one function and others may have a number of employees performing these functions for clients. The ability to offer a broad range of services depends on an agent's education, skills, and training, and the amount of time he or she can devote to these tasks. The amount of time spent per athlete is also dependent on the number of athletes the agent represents and their needs at the time. The number of agents or employees in the firm and the variety of skills each has to offer will influence the ability to offer many services. The eight essential functions performed by sports agents are as follows:

1. Negotiating and administering the athlete's or coach's contract
2. Marketing
3. Negotiating the athlete's or coach's marketing and endorsement contracts
4. Financial planning
5. Career and post-career planning
6. Dispute resolution
7. Legal counseling
8. Personal care

These eight functions are discussed individually in the following sections.

◼ NEGOTIATING AND ADMINISTERING THE CONTRACT

The Athlete's Contract

Contract negotiation varies depending on whether the agent is negotiating a contract for an individual athlete to participate in an exhibition or event or negotiating a team-sport contract. When negotiating a contract for an individual athlete, the agent must be familiar with the sport and the rules, regulations, and common practices of its governing body. When negotiating a contract for a team-sport athlete, the agent must understand the value of the player's service, be knowledgeable about the sport, and know the collective bargaining agreement, the standard or uniform player contract, and the league's constitution.

Some examples of negotiable terms for team-sport athletes include the following:

- Bonuses: signing, reporting (to training camp), attendance, incentives
- Deferred income (income paid after the player has retired from the sport)
- Guaranteed income (income guaranteed to be paid to the player even if he or she has retired)
- A college scholarship plan (available for MLB players leaving college early)
- Roster spots (generally not available, but positions on the 40-man roster in baseball are negotiable)

While it appears that with standard player contracts and many contractual limitations, such as restrictions on rookie contracts, anyone can negotiate an athlete's contract, such a thought loses sight of all that is involved in contract negotiations. For instance, a player's value should drive the negotiating process and a great deal of preparation goes into knowing and maximizing the player's value. Understanding how that value and the team's needs create leverage on one side or another is also a key to preparation. It will be important to assess the role that salary caps will play in the contract negotiation. There are also differences in negotiating depending on where an athlete falls career-wise, as there are differences in rookie versus veteran contract negotiations. Such a discussion exceeds the scope of this chapter, but please do give the differences in the types and context of negotiations some thought.

After negotiating the contract, the agent's work continues. Agents must administer the contract. This involves ensuring that the parties comply with their contract promises. If promises are not kept, the agent may be involved in conversations, negotiations, and ultimately dispute resolution between the player and the club. The agent may have to resolve unanticipated situations through informal channels, such as partial or full contract renegotiation, or through formal ones, such as alternative dispute resolution systems or courts. As the representative of the player and the negotiator of the contract, when problems arise, it is the agent's responsibility to represent the athlete's interests.

The Coach's Contract

Due to the lack of job security for coaches in the Division I college and professional ranks, it has become increasingly important for coaches to have well-drafted contracts and a representative available to administer the deal (Greenberg, 1993). When negotiating a contract for a college coach, an agent must be familiar with the sport, the NCAA and conference rules, any applicable state open records laws, and common concerns of collegiate athletic directors and university presidents (Greenberg, 1993). It has also become standard that coaches' contracts contain a clause restricting coaches from seeking endorsements outside of university apparel contracts without consent from the university.

When negotiating a contract for a professional coach, an agent must understand the league's constitution and by-laws, as well as the coaching and management environment of a particular team or league. There is no uniform coaching contract, so there may be more flexibility in negotiable terms.

Examples of negotiable terms in coaches' contracts include the following (Greenberg, 1993):

- Duties and responsibilities
- Term of employment and tenure
- Compensation clauses (guaranteed, outside/ supplemental, endorsement, and deferred income; bonuses; moving expenses; retirement; and fringe benefits)
- Termination clause
- Buyout/release of contractual obligations by either side

- Support of the team by athletic program or ownership
- Support staff (assistant coaches, other personnel)
- Confidentiality (to the extent allowable under law, the promise to keep terms confidential)
- Arbitration of disputes

In the past decade, representing coaches has become far more lucrative for agents, particularly for those representing Division I college football and basketball coaches and NBA coaches. The trend in the NBA is for coaches' salaries and terms to be higher and longer than those of the athletes on their teams (Boeck, 1997). Agents have also played an important role in negotiating for coaches to serve in dual roles as general managers or team presidents. Such clauses give the coach more power in player personnel decisions and presumably more control over the athletes and the direction in which the team is headed in achieving its goals. This trend is a direct reaction to athletes' apparent loss of respect for their coaches and the athletes' temptation to remove the coach due to athletes' leverage and financial clout with the team (Boeck, 1997). It is also a reaction to the coaches having to take the brunt of the blame for a losing season. The long-term multimillion-dollar deals for coaches may well change the dynamics in the locker rooms and on the basketball courts (Boeck, 1997).

Coaches' agents, such as Lonnie Cooper, President and CEO of Career Sports and Entertainment, who represents eight head NBA coaches, numerous assistant NBA coaches, and 14 Division I college coaches, are also the beneficiaries of these deals. Another example is Bob LaMonte, who operates the boutique firm Professional Sports Representation, Inc. (PSR) with his wife and has cornered the market on head football coaches, including among his clients Mike Holmgren, Brad Childress, John Fox,

Mike Nolan, Charlie Weiss, and Andy Reid's numerous NFL assistant coaches, coordinators, and front office staff. During his career, he has negotiated well over $250 million in coaching contracts (Farmer, 1999). LaMonte notes that in the mid-1980s salaries for NFL head coaches ranged from $100 to $15,000 (CBS News, 2004), whereas by the end of 2009 the average salary was $3,226,565 (Top NFL News, 2010). The higher salaries reflect the greater importance placed on the role of head coach as leader. The game is far more complicated and strategic than in years past owing to the greater reliance on statistics, video, scouting, and the like (CBS News, 2004). Further, the head coach must manage a fluid team whose roster changes frequently due to salary caps, free agency, and the occasional disciplinary problem.

Marketing the Athlete

The sports agent should develop a plan in which each endorsement creates an image consistent with the athlete or coach's ambitions and long-range goals (Lester, 2002). At the same time, the agent must keep in mind that the client's career and public persona may be short-lived, and thus "every opportunity should be assessed according to its potential to maximize the [client's] earnings and exposure during and after his or her active playing [or coaching] career" (Lester, 2002, p. 27-2). The sports agent must also be familiar with restrictions that may limit an athlete or coach's marketing opportunities. Restrictions include limitations on compensation set by the NCAA, national governing bodies, professional sports regulations, group licensing programs, and rules prohibiting the endorsement of alcohol or tobacco products (Lester, 2002).

Group licensing programs are very popular among professional sports unions, where often a major share of the players association's funding comes from trading card deals or marketing arms, such as the NFLPA's Player's, Inc. Under these group licensing programs, the players pool their bargaining power and licensing resources in exchange for a prorated (proportionate) share of any surplus income. It allows licensees one-stop shopping for multiplayer promotions. The definition of a group varies by league.[3] Most athletes agree to participate in these programs, the recent exceptions being Michael Jordan (NBA), Barry Bonds (MLB), and LaVar Arrington (NFL). Keeping in mind that agents do not receive compensation from group licensing programs, the movement away from group licensing by superstars may provide additional revenues for agents. It is also likely to damage the unions' revenue generation.

Agents usually seek product endorsements (goods necessary for the athlete to play the sport) before non-product endorsements because they are easier to obtain (Lester, 2002). Before targeting potential endorsements, the agent should assess the athlete's marketability. The assessment should be realistic and include the following (Lester, 2002):

- An assessment of the athlete's past and present endorsements, including the athlete's desire for endorsements, willingness to make appearances, likes/dislikes of products, and his or her strengths and weaknesses
- Consideration paid to intangible factors of an athlete's marketability, including his or her image, reputation, geographic appeal, achievements on and off the field, unique skills, personality, public speaking ability, and physical appearance

---

[3] The numbers of players necessary in group licensing programs are as follows: at least six for the NFLPA, at least three for MLBPA, at least six for NBPA, and five to ten for the NHLPA (Lester, 2002).

- Creating and maintaining an image can enhance a determination of factors listed in the last item (Lester, 2002).

The agent should also conduct a market assessment. Some agents have a well-developed network of contacts with sports product and non-product endorsement companies. For those who do not, the following four steps are useful (Lester, 2002):

1. Choose a product category and determine which manufacturers market those products.
2. Compile an exhaustive list of manufacturers of those products.
3. Determine which companies spend money on athlete endorsers.
4. Learn about potential target companies.

Marketing an athlete or coach may include creating or polishing a public image for that person. To assist with image building, some agents are beginning to hire "sports-media coaches" to train athletes or coaches for meeting the press and public. Sports-media coaches offer training sessions that mix lectures, mock interviews, a question-and-answer session, and videotapes of other athletes or coaches to critique (Dunkel, 1997). For instance, Jerry Stackhouse's media coach, Andrea Kirby, began his session with an exercise in which he wrote down a list of his personal positive qualities (Thurow, 1996). Stackhouse's list included "friendly, caring, talkative, athletic, well-dressed . . . good son, good family person, a leader, warm, respectful, generous" (Thurow, 1996, p. A4). Kirby copied the list and told Stackhouse to carry it with him and review it every time he faced fans, the media, or commercial cameras so that he would consistently portray the image he had of himself. Beyond the media coaching, Stackhouse's training also included taking a couple of college drama courses, practicing speaking with

a smoother cadence, and shaving his mustache (Thurow, 1996). This image building supports the standard sport marketing practice for athletes, brand building. As branding for athletes becomes more sophisticated, sport marketers are taking new approaches to it. For instance, Wendy Newman is a personal branding coach and has created Person-Centered Branding that she claims endures because it is not contrived or based on temporary factors, but rather authenticates who the athlete is as a person. Newman's system has been embraced by the LPGA, who hired her to work with elite golfers to develop personal narratives and individual brands (Dell, 2007). Table 11-2 sets forth the differences in her system versus traditional branding.

Another solution to the challenge is being championed by the firm Sports Identity and is called BrandMatch. The goal with BrandMatch is

TABLE 11-2   Traditional versus Person-Centered Branding

Traditional Branding	Person-Centered Branding
Outside-in	Inside-out
Brand with shelf life; burns out	Brand built for endurance
Strategy dictates image	Identity dictates strategy
Short-term revenues; fad	Long-term revenues; consumer/brand loyalty
Starts with athlete's performance	Starts with athlete's life
Only as good as the last win	Sustains image regardless of performance
Starts with desired image of who/what athlete is being told to be	Starts with the identity of who athlete is
Revenues first; then happiness	Happiness and fulfillment first; then revenues and fulfillment
Brands athlete	Brands person
Athlete trying to be something	Being who athlete is
Contrived	Authentic
Endurance = sport, tenure, performance	Endurance = sustainable brand personality
Temporary	Permanent

Source: Courtesy of Wendy Newman, MA, Founder Developer, Person-Centered Branding®

to create a profile of the athlete to find out who he or she is, then to use that unique image to strategically market the athlete based on where he or she is professionally and personally. Once that task is accomplished, the sports marketers at Sports Identity match the athlete with brands that will create opportunities and experiences for both the athlete and the company that are meaningful promotional experiences. This practice differs from that of some sport marketers who will just "dial for dollars," calling any and every company just to deliver an endorsement opportunity for the athlete, with no thought being paid to the long-term value or relationship between the athlete and the company. Sports Identity has also created a BrandMatch process for businesses, but that goes beyond the scope of this chapter (Sports Identity, 2007).

Finally, the agent should determine the athlete's market value. Many factors influence an athlete's market value, including the athlete's skill/success in sport, individual characteristics (image, charisma, physical appearance, and personality), how badly the organization wants the athlete, and any negative factors (crimes, drug use, public scandal) (Lester, 2002).

■ NEGOTIATING THE ATHLETE'S OR COACH'S MARKETING AND ENDORSEMENT CONTRACTS

Due to salary caps and rookie wage scales, an agent's ability to supplement a team salary with lucrative endorsement contracts has gained greater importance in athlete representation (Thurow, 1996). Economically, agents fare far better in the amounts of compensation they can command from marketing work. As far as the specifics of marketing deals go, the agent must first know any limitations the sport places on an athlete's abilities to endorse products. For instance, all major professional sport leagues prohibit the use of team names and logos in endorsements, and most professional sport leagues ban the endorsement of alcoholic beverages and tobacco products (Lester, 2002). Agents representing athletes in individual sports, such as golf, tennis, racquetball, figure skating, and auto racing, should examine the rules and regulations of the sport. Restrictions vary from the simple requirement of the PGA Tour that endorsements be "in good taste" to the specific limitations in tennis and racquetball that limit the number and size of patches displayed on players' clothing and equipment bags (Lester, 2002).

Negotiation of endorsement deals has been a lucrative supplement to Division I coaches' income. University athletic departments, however, have begun to examine the coaches' outside endorsement deals and to negotiate contracts with athletic shoe, apparel, and equipment companies that benefit the entire athletic department. NCAA rules also require that the university's chancellor or president approve coaches' endorsement deals. Table 11-3 shows the highest amounts of nonsalaried income for the top ten NCAA Football coaches in the United States.

When negotiating an endorsement contract, an agent should be certain to maintain the client's exclusive rights and control over his or her image and other endorsements. The agent must also be familiar with the following terms typically negotiable in athlete endorsement contracts (Lester, 2002):

- Endorsed products
- Contract territory
- Term (length)
- Annual base compensation
- Bonus compensation
- In-kind compensation
- Signature products
- Promotional efforts to be made by company
- Personal appearances
- Athlete's approval of company advertising
- Athlete to use/wear product
- Company protection of athlete endorsement

TABLE 11-3 Top Ten College Football Coaches (2009) Nonsalary Income*		
Name	**University**	**Nonsalary Income**
Urban Meyer	Florida	$3,750,000
Nick Saban	Alabama	$3,675,000
Les Miles	Louisiana State	$3,451,000
Bob Stoops	Oklahoma	$2,953,000
Jim Tressel	Ohio State	$2,657,000
Houston Nutt	Mississippi	$2,309,000
Mark Richt	Georgia	$2,287,236
Mack Brown	Texas	$2,000,000
Paul Johnson	Georgia Tech	$1,975,000
Gary Pinkel	Missouri	$1,950,000

*Nonsalary income** defined as income from contract provisions other than those related to salary or from other agreements (e.g., shoe and/or apparel contracts; consideration for appearing on TV, radio or other media shows; making speeches or other public appearances; camps). Universities generally guarantee most—but not all—of this income; some might come from outside sources.

Sources: Haurwitz, R.K.M. (2009, Dec. 14). Mack Brown's salary deemed "unseemly." *American-Statesman.* Retrieved October 28, 2010, from http://www.statesman.com/news/texas/mack-browns-salary-deemed-unseemly-121287.html

USA Today. (2009, November 10). 2009 NCAA football coaches contracts. Retrieved October 28, 2010, from http://www.usatoday.com/sports/college/football/2009-coaches-contracts-database.htm

- Rights of termination by athlete or company
- Indemnity and insurance
- Approval of assignment

■ FINANCIAL PLANNING

Financial planning covers a wide range of activities, such as banking and cash flow management, tax planning, investment advising, estate planning, and risk management (Grossman, 2002). Many lawsuits concerning sports agents' incompetence, fraud, and breaches of fiduciary duties involve financial planning and investing. These cases have exclusively involved athletes, so financial planning for athletes will be the focus in this section. Many sports agents have made mistakes because of the complex nature of the financial affairs of athletes. Sports agents often attempt to take on this function without proper skills and training; this can lead to allegations of incompetence and negligence. Also enticing to a less scrupulous agent is access to the athlete's money. There are many allegations of agents "double dipping" into athletes' funds, investing money into businesses from which the agent derives benefit, and outright embezzlement of an athlete's money. This behavior is discussed in greater detail later in the chapter.

An athlete earning a multimillion-dollar salary should adopt a budget (Willette & Waggoner, 1996). Without a budget, athletes who earn sudden wealth face risks (Waggoner, 1996), one of which is rushing into an investment. Athletes often receive many unsolicited prospectuses and requests for investments, and many have lost money in failed business ventures. Thus, planners often advise athletes to see a written business plan and have the plan analyzed by a professional before investing—and even if an investment seems to be worthy, planners advise an athlete to commit no more than 5% to 20% of the athlete's portfolio to it (Willette & Waggoner, 1996). The second risk is making a radical lifestyle change. NBA agent Curtis Polk shares this example: For a client earning $10 million per year, he gives the athlete a budget of $1 million per year and invests $4 million, leaving the remaining $5 million for local, state, and federal taxes (Willette & Waggoner, 1996). The third risk is guilt, which often leads athletes to make bad loans to family and friends or to hire them as an entourage; to overcome guilt, advisors suggest that athletes raise money for charities (Waggoner, 1996).

Athletes should be aware of the recent surge of companies reaching out to athletes with predraft lines of credit. One such company, Datatex Sports Management, a division of Huntleigh Securities in St. Louis, uses its own in-house football analysts to calculate predraft lines of credit for potential draft picks. Those projected to go in the first round qualify for $100,000, and those in the seventh qualify for $1,500. Obviously, problems arise for athletes who do not end up drafted. Southern Mississippi offensive lineman Torrin Tucker and New York City high school guard Lenny Cooke were given predraft lines of credit and neither was drafted. For Cooke, taking the line of credit also eliminated his ability to play for the University of Louisville because it violated NCAA rules for two reasons: He arranged it through a sports agency firm, Immortal Sports, and the line of credit through CSI Capital Management was based on Cooke's future earnings potential. Some, such as Louisville's head basketball coach Rick Pitino, fault the agents and banks for acting irresponsibly, but others, such as CSI Capital Management's Chairman Leland Faust and a runner for agents, Ernest Downing, Jr., argue that lines of credit are now so common that athletes request them before hiring the agent (Farry, 2003).

Finally, insurance plays a key role in an athlete's financial planning. Star athletes in the major professional team sports usually invest in disability insurance plans to protect themselves

during and after his or her playing career. Simultaneously, the agent must protect against overexposure of the athlete's image. The agent must balance the need to maximize exposure with doing what is best personally and professionally for the athlete. For instance, in Inside Edge, Olympic silver medalist Paul Wylie criticized the handling of Nancy Kerrigan after the 1994 Olympics, in which she won a silver medal but failed miserably in the poll of public opinion (Brennan, 1996). According to Wylie,

> "After seven weeks of pressure, [Kerrigan] needed to go to an island, be deprogrammed, debriefed. What happened was she wasn't allowed to come down off that . . . to normalize . . . to feel good about herself . . . In fact she was under more and more pressure. Saturday Night Live, Disney, missing closing ceremonies, all of a sudden her image had spun out of control because CBS had used a bad quote [Kerrigan criticizing Oksana Baiul]. . . . At that point . . . Jerry Solomon . . . should take care of his client more for the long term as opposed to feeling that they have to [pursue and say yes to every opportunity]. They said 'have to' way too much. She's too big a star to 'have to,' at that point" (Brennan, 1996, p. 122).

from career-ending injuries. In contract negotiations with a professional team, the agent may negotiate for the team to cover the cost of this policy. Athletes in individual sports also insure against these types of injuries. Many insurance companies, though, will only insure an athlete after that athlete is likely to achieve a certain level of income.

■ CAREER AND POSTCAREER PLANNING

An agent must help an athlete with the transition to a professional career and again with the transition into retirement from the sport. The average career length varies by sport, but generally it is under five years. Thus, the agent must maximize the athlete's earning potential

Career planning may also involve the agent investing time, energy, and money into a player's career while the player is training in the minor leagues or training toward events, exhibitions, or the Olympics. While in the minor leagues or while trying to make it into the professional ranks, more and more athletes have come to expect that agents will cover costs of products, some training and coaching costs, and even travel. This has evolved due to a number of factors, among them athletes who have come to expect a certain level of treatment and a competitive industry in which those trying to recruit clients will throw many inducements their way. Further, the product companies have taken note of this, and until a player makes it into the major leagues, in lieu of giving products in-kind, the manufacturers and suppliers have created agent accounts to purchase products for athletes. Often this investment is required when the agent is also trying to break into the business, and it creates a financial barrier to entry. The agent may reap little financial benefit from this investment if the athletes do not make it or if they are wooed away by a bigger-name agent who has made no investment in that athlete's career.

Another aspect of career planning the agent may take on is the establishment of sports camps or charitable organizations under the athlete's name. Running sports camps and charitable organizations does many positive things for the athlete. Camps provide additional income, but beyond that camps and charities create goodwill for the athlete's name and image; give the athlete contact with his or her community; give something back to children, communities, or a worthy cause; provide a useful outlet for the athlete's energy and time in the off-season; and may provide a hefty tax break. The camps and charitable organizations are also activities the athlete can stay involved with after his or her playing career is finished.

During the career transition out of sport, the agent must address the potential for a financial crisis (Grossman, 2002). Proper financial planning that includes income investment, insurance coverage, and contracting for deferred income can avert a disaster. Beyond the financial aspect, the athlete needs a sense of purpose. Participation in sport has defined many athletes' lives and self-images, and agents can be helpful in preparing athletes for the psychological difficulties that may accompany retirement. By exploring career and business opportunities for the athlete inside and outside the sport industry, such as in broadcasting, the agent can help the athlete make a more successful transition.

■ DISPUTE RESOLUTION

It is the sports agent's responsibility to resolve disputes the athlete or coach may have with his or her league, team, teammates, fans, referees or umpires, press, endorsement companies, and the like. Baseball agent Dennis Gilbert likens the role of the agent to a "shield," stating that it is the agent's task to protect the athlete from the headaches that go along with resolving disputes (Schwarz, 1996). The shield allows the athlete to focus solely on playing or coaching to the best of his or her ability without distractions. To resolve disputes, the sports agent may find himself or herself in a labor or commercial arbitration forum, or occasionally in court.

■ LEGAL COUNSELING

If the sports agent is a lawyer, the agent may provide legal counseling. Legal counseling may include contract negotiation, legal representation in court, arbitration or sport-related administrative proceedings, estate planning, and the preparation of tax and insurance forms. However, the nature of the legal work may dictate that a lawyer specializing in a particular area is better suited for providing the actual legal services. For instance, a given sports agent may be very confident in providing negotiation and contract advice on any matter in his or her client's life, yet that same agent will not likely be the best lawyer to handle the client's divorce proceedings. For such a dispute, the best advice an agent can give is to encourage the client to find an attorney experienced in high-profile, high-income divorce proceedings.

■ PERSONAL CARE

The tasks required under this function are personal in nature. They include such responsibilities as assisting when an athlete is traded, arranging transportation, finding and furnishing a house or apartment for the season or training camps, purchasing cars, and helping the athlete's family and friends.

Key Skills Required of Sports Agents

There are no established educational standards or degree requirements necessary to become a sports agent. Many sports agents do, however, possess professional degrees and credentials. Some are lawyers, some are certified public accountants, and others are investment advisors or financial planners. With the various services demanded of agents by athletes and in light of competition in the field, a professional degree is practically a necessity.

Primarily, the sports agent must have a good working knowledge of the sport industry, particularly the specific sector of the industry in which he or she practices. This knowledge should include an understanding of the economic picture of the sport industry, insight into the inner workings of the industry, the sport the athlete plays, the documents used in the industry (e.g., contracts, policies, rules and regulations, constitutions and by-laws, and collective bargaining agreements), and a great network of contacts in the industry. Although the skills needed by sports agents vary depending on the services provided, all agents must possess good listening and counseling skills. The agent works for the athlete and must invest time in getting to know the athlete on a personal level. This builds trust and a stronger relationship between the two. Agents must make decisions according to the athlete's desires and goals. The agent should act only after consulting the athlete and must always act in the athlete's best interest.

Excellent oral and written communication skills are also essential, because the agent represents the athlete in many forums. Many of the agent's functions require polished negotiation skills. An agent must also be loyal to the athlete and be strong enough to shield the athlete from the media and even from his or

her own front office staff. Professional athletes, like entertainers, find their lives scrutinized by the press, and the agent must help the athlete adjust to the pressure that accompanies fame and counsel the athlete to properly deal with the media. When the athlete has to negotiate a contract or go into arbitration against his or her team, the relationship is adversarial. This is not always the best situation for professional athletes, for whom psychology plays a key role in their on-field success. The agent must shelter the athlete from the derogatory statements made about him or her in those forums, because often those statements can damage the athlete's confidence.

■ CURRENT ISSUES

Unethical Behavior

In the five decades that the sports agency field has been active, there has been a great deal of criticism and a public perception that the behavior of those in the profession is excessively unethical. There are, in fact, many ethical agents who run their businesses professionally; however, there have been many high-profile cases of unethical and illegal behavior reported, tainting the image of the profession. In addition, sports agency is a field in which outsiders perceive there is quick, easy money to be made and a field in which clients are scarce. These two factors combine to bring an element of corruption to the profession.

According to Sobel (1990), there are five key problems in the profession: (1) income mismanagement, (2) incompetence, (3) conflicts of interest, (4) charging of excessive fees, and (5) overly aggressive client recruitment. Of the five, **income mismanagement** is probably the most devastating to the athlete. Because the agent is often dealing with the income of a multimillion-dollar athlete, the losses can be great, and it is unlikely the athlete will be able to reclaim the money from the agent or earn back the amount lost. Although many reported cases stem from incompetence, others begin with incompetence and further deteriorate to fraud or embezzlement (Sobel, 1990). A good example is the case of agent Tank Black, who was sentenced to five years in prison for swindling millions of dollars out of the NFL players he represented and also sentenced to more than six years in jail for laundering $1.1 million for a drug ring in Detroit. In abusing his clients' trust, Black stole in excess of $12 million from them by encouraging them to invest in bogus investments and pyramid schemes (Fish, 2002a). The Tank Black saga has made the NFLPA more vigilant in its efforts to regulate agents. As a result, in 2003 the NFLPA created the first certification system for financial advisors who work with NFL players.

Agents have also been accused of performing their responsibilities negligently because of sheer *incompetence*. As the industry has become more complex, some agents have run into problems because they are incapable of figuring out their clients' worth, working with the complex documents necessary to effectively negotiate, or carrying out the tasks they promise athletes they will do. It is likely this problem has been compounded by the competition in the industry. Agents may make promises they cannot keep for fear of losing a client or may exaggerate when trying to land a client. If they are not, for example, trained as lawyers or are without experience in arbitration, they may be more likely to settle a case to avoid having to proceed to the actual arbitration. Due to fear of losing a client to a competitor, many are afraid to outsource a labor or salary arbitration case.

Conflicts of interest raise serious questions about the fiduciary duty of loyalty required of all agents under agency law (see Chapter 5, Legal Principles Applied to Sport Management). A conflict of interest occurs if there is a situation in which the agent's own interest may be furthered over that of the athlete's (principal's) interest. Keep in mind that an agent works for an athlete and possesses a fiduciary duty to put the athlete's interest first. It is clear, though, that in business settings there are bound to be conflicts of interest. If the agent fully discloses the conflict and allows the athlete to direct the agent, or in some cases suggests that the athlete hire a neutral party to see the athlete through the conflict, the agent will not have breached his or her fiduciary duties.

There are many examples of conflicts of interest in the sports agency business. Earlier in the chapter, conflicts that arise for agency firms that also run events were mentioned. Those firms have a fiduciary duty to fully reveal the extent of the conflict of interest and to allow the athlete to bring in a neutral negotiator to negotiate with that particular event. Some, such as Jerry Solomon, however, argue that these companies operate as diverse entities (athlete representation versus event management) and that as a result the two groups have built invisible walls between them that prevent such a conflict from arising (Feinstein, 1992; Solomon, 1995). Another conflict may arise when an agent is representing two players on the same team or two players who may be vying for the same position on a team. Clearly, in these situations there may be a tendency for the agent to give greater attention to the athlete who will better serve the agent's own interest. Another example is dual representation. It occurs when an agent represents both a coach and a player or represents a player and is also the head of the union. The NBAPA and NHLPA prohibit representation of both a coach and player, but it is allowed in the NFL and MLB. The days of representation by an agent who also leads the union in the major leagues are past, but the potential for it to exist again in the future with emerging sports is real.

The complaint of *charging excessive fees* occurs when agents charge fees that do not fairly represent their time, effort, and skills. To an extent, this complaint has been addressed by players association regulations mentioned earlier and also by competition in the market. Competition for clients has forced some agents in the market to reduce their fees to entice clients. However, although the fees have dropped for the negotiation of team-sport contracts, many agents continue to charge what may be considered excessive fees in the marketing area. Another recent complaint is charging the athlete for every service the agent performs, when the athlete may believe that all services are provided in the fee charged for the contract negotiation. Such confusion may arise because some agents do not use written representation agreements. This problem is also being overcome as the players associations are insisting that players use standard-form representation agreements that clearly establish fees and contractual promises; however, in individual sports or emerging leagues there are no such requirements.

Overly aggressive client recruitment is a problem that has plagued the amateurism requirement of collegiate athletics. First, it can wreak havoc with NCAA rules because an athlete loses his or her eligibility if he or she signs with a sports agent or accepts anything of value from a sports agent. In fact, in 2008 collegiate pitcher Andy Oliver was ruled ineligible for simply engaging advisors who contacted a Major League team on his behalf after being drafted in 2006. In the competition for clients, many agents have resorted to underhanded tactics such as paying athletes to encourage them to sign with agents early. The difficulty in becoming an agent or obtaining clients has led some to offer inducements. For example, World Sports Entertainment (WSE), an athlete representation firm operated by entertainment agent Norby Walters and partner Lloyd Bloom, spent approximately $800,000 to induce athletes to sign representation agreements with them before their NCAA eligibility expired. Walters argued that what he did broke no laws (just NCAA rules) and was a common practice in the music industry, where entertainers often received financial advances from their agents (Mortensen, 1991). The athletes, too, are to blame, because some encourage this type of activity from the agent, believing that their skills and talent should enable them to make this money for signing. For instance, when football player Ron Harmon signed with WSE as a junior at the University of Iowa, the FBI investigation discovered he ran up expenses of over $54,000 in cash, plane, concert tickets, and other entertainment. Clearly, Harmon was taking advantage of the situation for his own entertainment and was not using the money, as other athletes did, for bills and family expenses (Mortensen, 1991). Notorious agent Tank Black was accused of paying athletes up to $15,000 while in college to sign with him when they became professionals (Fish, 2002b).

Second, it has created a very ugly side to the sports agency industry. Most agents can tell stories about the dirty recruiting that goes on in the industry as competitors vie for clients. The behavior mirrors the recruiting scandals prevalent in big-time college athletics. Many veteran agents claim the unethical recruiting has reached epidemic proportions that will have a lasting negative effect on the industry (Mullen, 2004). In addition to the promises of prohibited inducement, among the noted lasting negative impacts from unethical recruiting are the following: (1) Representatives are spending more time on retaining clients, so it cuts back on their time to develop new business opportunities for current clients; (2) recruiters are targeting teenagers in the sports of basketball, baseball, and hockey, making promises that may not come to fruition; and (3) in an effort to compete with the large conglomerates, smaller agencies are promising late-round picks marketing guarantees in the six-figure range that will be difficult to achieve (Mullen, 2004).

It has gotten so intense that the MLBPA and its Executive Board (made up of active players) examined how to curb the behavior. As a result the MLBPA put new agent regulations into effect on October 1, 2010. The 48 pages of regulations are so sweeping in their changes that all certified agents will have to re-apply for certification and those who are operating as recruiters or handlers for the players must also apply for certification. That requirement signals the union is going to more seriously monitor contact between players and competitor agents. According to Clifton and Toppel (2010), "a second major change will affect the way agents 'recruit' prospects who are currently represented by other certified agents. While agents traditionally have had free rein to speak with and encourage players to switch representation at any time without informing the Association, the new regulations require all communications between an agent and a player not represented by that agent to be disclosed to the Players Association."

The regulations also limit the players' freedom to switch agents at whim because any player facing salary arbitration or free agency must consult with the union before switching agents during those critical periods of the player's career (Clifton & Toppel, 2010). The final two areas of significant change in the regulations involve the areas of restrictive covenants and the use of arbitration to settle disputes among the Association's player-agent group. Historically, the union's position has been focused on the player's choice of agent being a priority over supporting an agency firm's restrictive covenant against allowing a player agent who has left the firm and taken the player. These new regulations permit employers to utilize "reasonable" restrictive covenants in agent employment agreements. The determination of the reasonableness of each covenant will be made on a case-by-case analysis. Lastly, the union is requiring all disputes involving agents to be resolved in arbitration rather than litigation (Clifton & Toppel, 2010).

The NFLPA has been the most active in disciplining agents and through its Committee on Agent Regulations and Discipline has imposed discipline on 130 agents between 1993 and 2008 (Golka, 2008). One of the challenges faced by the players associations in going after agents is that it is difficult to find proof unless athletes are willing to testify against agents. In addition, pursuing these cases takes a great deal of energy and personnel away from the main mission of the union. Still, the NFLPA is continuing to take the lead in this area, as in 2004 it announced that all registered agents must also list their runners with the NFLPA so it may keep better tabs on the individuals who recruit clients for agents. This step is another first in the regulation of the agency industry and it will be interesting to see if the other unions follow the NFLPA's lead.

Another step some regulatory groups are taking is the requirement of professional liability insurance, which is now required by the NFLPA and FIFA and is under consideration by CFLPA.

Regulation of Sports Agents

In the words of Lionel Sobel (2002), "sports agents today must maneuver through a maze of conduct governing regulations" set forth by college governing bodies and university athletic departments, players associations, state ethics boards, state legislatures, and the federal government.

Of these forms of regulation, the NCAA or other college and university regulations carry the least weight with agents. Because agents are not NCAA members, the NCAA cannot enforce its rules against them. Instead, NCAA agent regulations are intended for the athletes and member institutions to stop athletes from having contact with agents.

Agents representing athletes in MLB, the NFL, the NBA, the NHL, and the CFL are regulated by players associations. The MLS has adopted the FIFA agent regulations, but neither MLS or MLSPA regulate agents. Instead MLS and MLSPA defer to FIFA's certification program.

Application fees to become registered or certified by the players associations are as follows:

MLBPA	$500 application fee
NBPA	$1500 annually, plus $100 application fee
NFLPA	$1200 annually if representing 10 or fewer players; $1700 for more than 10 players
NHLPA	$1500 annually

Players must annually submit to the union uniform athlete-agent representation agreements that set forth the terms of the relationship and contain clauses mandating the arbitration of disputes between players and their agents. The uniform agreement is renewable annually by the player, but the player is free to abolish it at any time to go to another agent. This puts the players associations on notice about who is representing the athlete and also allows the agent access to union assistance with salary information, dispute resolution, and the like.

Currently, 44 states have some form of athlete-agent regulation. The National Conference of Commissioners, with prodding and backing from the NCAA and the Sports Lawyers Association, created a uniform agent registration law, called the Uniform Athlete Agent Act (UAAA), that can be adopted by all states. Thirty-eight states, plus the District of Columbia and the Virgin Islands, have adopted this legislation. As of April 2010, adoption of the UAAA was pending in three states. In addition, three states have their own statutes on athlete-agents that predate the UAAA.

After many years of attempts at federal legislation, in September 2004 President George W. Bush signed the Sports Agent Responsibility and Trust Act (SPARTA), Public Law No. 108-304. The Act seeks to "designate certain conduct by sports agents relating to the signing of contracts with student athletes as unfair and deceptive acts or practices to be regulated by the Federal Trade Commission (FTC)" (SPARTA, 2004). SPARTA prohibits athlete agents from directly or indirectly recruiting or soliciting a student to enter into an agency contract by providing false or misleading information, making false promises, or providing anything of value to amateur athletes or their families. It also prohibits agents from entering into an oral or written agency contract with a student without providing a required disclosure document both to the student-athlete and to the athlete's academic institution. Finally, SPARTA prohibits the act of predating or postdating an agency contract (SPARTA, Sec. 3, 2004). Each violation of SPARTA is deemed an unfair or deceptive act or practice under the Federal Trade Commission Act, FTCA (SPARTA, Sec. 4, 2004). Further, SPARTA authorizes civil actions by the Federal Trade Commission, state attorneys general, and educational institutions against violators. It supplements, but does not preclude, other actions against agents taken under other federal or state laws (SPARTA, Sec. 5, 2004).

With the enactment of this law, the maze of legislation regulating sports agents grows deeper. The goal of the law is to protect student-athletes from deceptive practices and keep the athletes eligible to play NCAA sports. Senator John McCain noted that SPARTA serves as federal backstop for the ongoing effort by the NCAA, college coaches, university presidents, and athletic directors to support state level legislation developed by the National Conference of Commissioners on Uniform State Laws that had by September of 2004 been adopted in 29 states. (Associated Press, 2004). The UAAA legislation requires that sports agents be registered with the states in which they operate and provide uniform state laws addressing their conduct and practices.

One challenge for agents is that the law is one-sided; only the agents are regulated and the athletes are perceived as playing no role in the practice of inducements being given to athletes to sign with agents. In fact, stories abound of athletes and families of athletes literally "selling" their services to the highest bidder among the myriad of agents competing to sign a high-round pick to an agency agreement. If little or no penalty is assessed against the athlete, it will be interesting to see if the federal law actually addresses the unethical recruitment of athletes.

Legal action under UAAA and SPARTA is scarce. However, it appears that with the NCAA responding to the scandals at the University of Southern California involving Reggie Bush and O.J. Mayo, as well as its recent investigation started at the South East Conference (SEC; Universities of Alabama, Georgia, and South Carolina) and Atlantic Coast Conference (ACC; North Carolina) schools, we may see a changing tide. For instance, shortly after news broke of the NCAA's investigation of North Carolina football, the North Carolina Secretary of State launched an investigation in accordance with its own state statute (Editorial staff, 2010).

Finally, athletes and others abused by agents can seek recourse under tort, criminal, agency, and consumer protection laws. More agents are resorting to the courts, filing 12 lawsuits for unfair competition, tortuous interference with contract, libel, and slander in the past couple of years (Mullen, 2004). The willingness to resort to the courts may be a result of the large amount of money involved and the fact that in a legal proceeding, witnesses can be subpoenaed and thus witness testimony may be more easily obtainable than in a complaint filed with a players association.

CASE STUDY: King Sport Management

King Sport Management (KSM) is a sports agency firm based in Chicago that has been in business for five years. KSM is owned and operated by law school graduate Jake King. KSM has suddenly arrived on the sports business radar screen as the company having one of the largest stables of clients in baseball behind the Scott Boras Corporation, WMG, and ACES, which have been in business for many more years. As the owner of Baseball Talent, Inc., an agency in business for just over a decade, Nate Baxter was bewildered about how an agency with so little experience in the industry grew so quickly. Soon that would change. Nate's Baseball Talent represented 30 players, 25 of whom were in the minors and five on major league rosters. Two of the players on the 40-man roster were still in the minor leagues at the AAA level.

One day Nate received a call from Mark Hartman, a top prospect of his in AA, telling him that he had just met with an agent from KSM. The agent told Hartman that he could get him a Topps trading card deal worth $10,000 and that if his current agent couldn't deliver that kind of money, then he must not know what he was doing in the trading card business. Nate knows that Topps is the exclusive baseball card licensee of Minor League baseball ('MiLB') and that the MiLB license provides Topps the right to include every player who playing in the Minors. Minor League players are not compensated for inclusion in these products, so Nate told Mark that he doubted KSM could arrange such a deal. Nate told the client to ask KSM to show him a trading card contract with those figures on it. The client said, "I really don't care where the money comes from because at this point I could really use the $10,000. If you can't find a similar deal, I may have to leave. Besides, KSM has been to visit my dad and the KSM representative and my dad wait for me after every game with a KSM contract to sign. I think they have given my father some money to cover some of his bills and I can't let my own father down." Two weeks later, Nate received a standard form letter terminating their business relationship postmarked from Chicago even though the prospect was playing for a team on the West Coast.

The next day Nate called one of his clients, Terrence Sharpe, to talk about the client's outing the day before. Sharpe was an all-star high school athlete in Florida and a top pitching prospect for the Tampa Bay Devil Rays. Sharpe struggled the first two years in baseball, but had suddenly begun winning and had just been moved from A-ball to AA. When Nate reached Sharpe, he was on the golf course with his roommate Mike Hanson and some agents. Sharpe told Nate about the brand-new golf clubs he had just purchased at the club's pro shop. Sharpe told Nate that he really didn't feel like talking about yesterday's outing and, because he had just purchased a laptop computer, Nate should e-mail him at IMSharpe@gmail.com so he could get back to his golf game. Nate hung up the phone and thought, "Where would Terrence get the money for golf clubs and a laptop?" Nate knew that Terrence barely had enough money to get by because he came from a poor background and had given his signing bonus to his grandmother, who had raised him. Nate had a terrible feeling that he was going to lose Terrence to KSM. Nate sent a few e-mails to Terrence, but received no response. A week later, Nate received the same form letter in the mail from Terrence that he had received from Mark. It, too, was postmarked from Chicago.

Two months later Nate was visiting Josh Bartley, a catcher and a 40-man roster player for the Atlanta Braves. Josh told Nate that he knew he was great defensively and if he could just hit more homeruns, he was told he'd make the major league roster the next year. Josh felt that if he could use steroids and bulk up, then he'd make that goal. Josh asked Nate to help him get steroids. Nate told Josh that there were many reasons he should not use steroids, top among them being his own health and the violation of baseball's rules. Nate assured Josh that the best way to better his hitting ability was to work with a hitting coach. Nate suggested that Josh work more closely with his club's hitting coach, and Nate told Josh that he'd happily invest in a hitting coach and nutritionist for Josh to work with in the off-season. Nate also suggested some books for Josh to read on hitting. Josh said that he was convinced steroids were the answer to his hitting problems. Nate ended the evening worried about Josh. Three days later Nate received a call from Josh's dad that began, "So I understand you won't help my son bulk up . . ."

Shocked, Nate took a moment to respond. "Excuse me, is this Ken Bartley, Josh's dad?"

"Yes, Nate, you know it's me. I thought you were on our side. Here to help Josh make it to the 'bigs,' and now you won't get him steroids."

Nate said, "Ken, you are aware of the health risks to your son and the fact that baseball conducts tests for steroid use . . ."

Ken said, "Sure, I know, I know. But Josh just needs it to get to the majors, then he'll stop. Short-term use should not be that big a deal. I don't understand your reasoning. I thought you were here to help us. Isn't that what you said when you recruited Josh as a client?"

Nate said, "I did say that. However, none of us know the real risks of steroid use. Besides, using steroids violates the rules of baseball. And steroids are illegal substances. As a lawyer, I'm not going to lose my license trying to acquire steroids for your son—end of story! I told Josh I'd happily invest in a hitting coach for him in the off-season. In my professional judgment, that is his best way to the majors."

At that point, Ken ended the conversation by saying, "Nate, we like your service, but you're making a big mistake. If you want to compete with the big dogs, sometimes you have to bend the rules."

Nate immediately called Josh. Josh told him that if Nate wouldn't find him steroids, he'd find an agent who would. A month later, Nate received a letter from Josh postmarked from Chicago terminating their contractual relationship.

As the baseball season was nearing an end, Nate couldn't help but worry about his business. He had lost three of his top prospects to KSM, and two of his better clients were off to the Arizona Fall League, long known as a place where clients are ripe for the picking by unscrupulous agents. One of his clients, Chad Kramer, was like a son to Nate, and Nate had a heart-to-heart with him before he left about the types of inducements Chad should expect to receive while in Arizona. Chad left by saying, "Nate, you should know by now, you have nothing to worry about."

A few weeks later Nate flew to Arizona to see Chad. With a smile on his face, Chad said, "Have I got a story for you!" Chad went on to explain that he had relented about going to dinner with a KSM runner only after the runner had asked him to dinner numerous times. Chad figured that after that much badgering he deserved a free steak! At dinner the runner offered him money to leave Nate for KSM. Chad said, "I have all the money I need." Then the runner offered a car. Chad said, "I have a nice car and don't need another." Then the runner coyly offered a prostitute. Chad said, "I'm engaged and am not interested." The runner said, "Then why are we having dinner?" Chad said, "You tell me—you're the one who made the invitation." So the runner went on to tell Chad that at the beginning of the year KSM hired ten runners under a one-year contract and gave them a list of prospects to recruit. The two runners who recruited the most clients from that prospect list at the end of the year would then be hired into full-time positions. Nate thought he had heard it all.

As he arrived home from the trip, he opened up his *SportsBusiness Journal* to see a special edition on sports agents. There staring up at him was a picture of Jake King with the headline, "KSM Principal Lobbies for New Ethical Standards to Govern Agents." Nate angrily thought, "Sure, now that he's broken the rules and built his business by stealing our clients, he wants to clean up the industry."

Questions for Discussion

1. Should Nate contact the Major League Baseball Players Association to pursue a claim against KSM? What about the state of Illinois (which has an agent regulation statute)? What about the Illinois bar association?

2. Should Nate engage in legal action against KSM for unfair competition or tortuous interference with contractual or advantageous business relations? Should Nate consider legal action against the players who have left him for KSM?

3. Should Nate contact the police, the Chicago U.S. attorney's office, or the state or federal legislators about the steroid allegation against KSM?

4. Do you think the actions taken by Jake King to build KSM are the norm in the industry? What would be your response if Jake King were to tell you that to compete in this industry you must give the athletes what they want or someone else will?

5. What do you think about the athletes and their decisions? What is their role and responsibility in the sports agency business?

■ SUMMARY

The field of sports agency can be exciting. Landing a first-round draft pick and negotiating a playing contract or creating an image and negotiating major marketing deals for a Wimbledon champion can bring an incredible thrill for an agent. Servicing clients' needs expose agents to the world of these elite athletes; as a result, it is a highly competitive business. Those seeking an entry-level position face an uphill battle, for there are tremendous barriers to entry, among which is fierce competition for a scarce number of potential clients. Recruiting a client is just part of the struggle because keeping the client in this competitive market is an equally competitive battle. Furthermore, it is estimated that more than 80% of athletes are represented by approximately 20% of agents, so many agents work part-time supplementing their income through other professions such as law, marketing, or financial planning. Nevertheless, there are a handful of large, dominant multiservice firms engaged in athlete representation and event management that may provide a good launching point to break into the field. On the representation side, few entry-level positions at these firms are in client recruitment. In reality, employment exists if the entry-level agent can deliver a client. With the trend toward mergers and acquisitions, many entry-level positions seem to be limited to those who have a few clients already in hand. This competitive environment may lead new agents to act in an overly aggressive manner while recruiting clients.

■ RESOURCES

Professional Associations

American Bar Association Forum Committee on the Entertainment & Sport Industries
321 North Clark Street
Chicago, IL 60610

312-988-5000
http://www.abanet.org/forums/entsports/home.html

Sports Lawyers Association
12100 Sunset Hills Road, Suite 130
Reston, VA 20190
703-437-4377; fax: 703-435-4390
http://www.sportslaw.org

Agency Firms

BDA Sports
822 Ashley Lane, Suite A
Walnut Creek, CA 94597
925-279-1040; fax: 925-279-1060
http://www.bdasports.com

Beverly Hills Sports Council
131 S. Rodeo Drive
Beverly Hills, CA 90212
310-858-1872

Career Sports and Entertainment
600 Galleria Parkway, Suite 1900
Atlanta, GA 30339
770-955-1300; fax: 770-952-5691
http://www.careersports.com

CAA Sports
2000 Avenue of the Stars
Los Angeles, CA 90067
424-288-2000; fax: 424-288-2900
http://www.sports.caa.com

Gaylord Sports Management
13845 North Northsight Boulevard, Suite 200
Scottsdale, AZ 85260
http://www.gaylordsports.com

IMG
U.S. Headquarters
767 5th Avenue
New York, NY 10153
212-355-5656; fax: 212-759-9059
International Headquarters
McCormack House
Hogarth Business Park
Burlington Lane
Chiswick London W4 2TH

(44) 208-233-5300; fax: (44) 208-233-5301
http://www.imgworld.com

Newport Sports Management, Inc.
Suite 400
201 City Centre Drive
Mississauga, ON L5B 2T4
905-275-2800; fax 905-275-4025
http://www.thehockeyagency.com

Octagon Worldwide
1751 Pinnacle Drive
Suite 1500
McLean, VA 22102
703-905-3300
http://www.octagon.com

Priority Sports and Entertainment
325 N. LaSalle, Suite 650
Chicago, IL 60610
312-664-7700; fax: 312-664-5172
http://www.prioritybasketball.biz

PSR, Inc.
2425 Manzanita Lane
Reno, NV 89509
775-828-1864; fax: 775-828-1865
http://www.psr-inc.net/index.php?click=main

The Scott Boras Corporation
2100 Main St. #300
Irvine, CA 92614
949-833-1818; fax: 949-833-1816
http://www.borascorp.com

Wasserman Media Group (WMG)
12100 W. Olympic Boulevard
Los Angeles, CA 90064
310-407-0200
http://wmgllc.com

To find a more definitive list of sports agencies go to: http://www.sportsagentblog.com/agencies/agencies-by-alphabetical-order/

■ KEY TERMS

conflicts of interest, freestanding sport management firm, income mismanagement, law practice only, Mark McCormack, overly aggressive client recruitment, reserve clause, reserve list, reserve system, Scott Boras, sports agent, sports event managers, sport management firm affiliated with a law firm, sports marketing representative, standard or uniform player contract

■ REFERENCES

Anderson, J. (2007, May 22). The Boras factor. *LA Weekly*. Retrieved October 28, 2010, from http://www.laweekly.com/2007-05-24/news/the-boras-factor/

Associated Press. (2004, September 10). Legislation aims to protect student athletes. Retrieved November 13, 2010, from http://sports.espn.go.com/espn/news/story?id=1878699

Berkowitz, S. (2009, December 10). Texas' Mack Brown becomes highest paid football coach. *USA Today*. Retrieved October 28, 2010, from http://www.usatoday.com/sports/college/football/big12/2009-12-09-mack-brown-salary_N.htm

Berry, R. C. (1990). Representation of the professional athlete. In American Bar Association Forum on the Entertainment and Sports Industries (Ed.), *The law of sports: Doing business in the sports industries* (pp. 1–6). Chicago: ABA Publishing.

Berry, R. C., Gould, W. B., & Staudohar, P. D. (1986). *Labor relations in professional sports*. Dover, MA: Auburn House Publishing.

Boeck, G. (1997, September 25). Cooper cashes in for NBA coaches: Agent snags rewarding deals. *USA Today*, pp. C1–C2.

Brady, D. (2004, July 12). Arnold Palmer: With IMG from the start. *BusinessWeek Online*. Retrieved October 28, 2010, from http://www.businessweek.com/magazine/content/04_28/b3891131.htm

Brennan, C. (1996). *Inside edge: A revealing journey into the secret world of figure skating*. New York: Doubleday.

Burwell, B. (1996, June 28). David Falk: The most powerful man in the NBA? *USA Today*, pp. C1–C2.

Canadian Football League Players Association (2010). Players agents. Retrieved October 28, 2010, from http://www.cflpa.com/players-agents.html

CBS News. (2004, December 26). The secret of their NFL success. Retrieved October 28, 2010, from http://www.cbsnews.com/stories/2004/09/16/60minutes/main643894.shtml

Christy, J.H. (2002, July 8). The alchemy of relationships. *Forbes Magazine*. Retrieved October 28, 2010, from http://www.forbes.com/global/2002/0708/026_print.html

Clifton, G., & Toppel, J. (2010, September 24). MLBPA issues new sweeping regulations governing agents. Retrieved November 13, 2010, from http://www.hackneypublications.com/sla/archive/001133.php

Dell, K. (2007, Apr. 26). New driver at the LPGA. *Time*. Retrieved October 28, 2010, from http://www.time.com/time/magazine/article/0,9171,1615197-1,00.html

Dunkel, T. (1997, March). Out of the mouths of jocks. *Sky*, 97–103.

Editorial staff (2010, July 24). Editorial: policing sports agents. *Greensboro News & Record*. Retrieved October 28, 2010, from http://www.news-record.com/content/2010/07/23/article/editorial_policing_sports_agents

Farmer, S. (1999, September 29). Teacher has history of being good sports agent. *The Holland Sentinel*. Retrieved from http://www.thehollandsentinel.net/stories/092999/spo_teacher.html

Farry, T. (2003, August 28). Bank(rupting) on the future. *ESPN.com*. Retrieved from http://sports.espn.go.com/espn/ print?id=1605207&type=story

Feinstein, J. (1992). *Hard courts*. New York: Villard Books.

Feinstein, J. (1995). *A good walk spoiled: Days and nights on the PGA tour*. Boston: Little, Brown and Co.

FIFA.com. (2010). About FIFA: Player agents list. Retrieved October 28, 2010, from http://www.fifa.com/aboutfifa/federation/administration/playersagents/list.html

Fish, M. (2002a, May 7). A black eye: Headed to prison, Black should be a lesson to agents. Retrieved November 11, 2010, from http://sportsillustrated.cnn.com/inside_game/mike_fish/news/2002/05/07/tank_black/

Fish, M. (2002b, May 7). Q&A with Tank Black. Retrieved November 11, 2010, from http://sportsillustrated.cnn.com/football/college/news/2002/05/07/black_qa/

Futterman, M. (2010a, May 7). Talent agencies cry fowl, lawsuits fly. *Wall Street Journal*. Retrieved October 28, 2010, from http://online.wsj.com/article/NA_WSJ_PUB:SB10001424052748703686304575228314238507620.html#articleTabs%3Darticle

Futterman, M. (2010b, May 28). CAA dismisses talent agent hired from rival firm. *Wall Street Journal*. Retrieved December 28, 2010, from http://online.wsj.com/article/SB1000142405274870363300575270912343901640.html

Greenberg, M. J. (1993). *Sports law practice*. Charlottesville, VA: The Michie Co.

Golka, J. (2008). Golka's athlete regulation blog. NFLPA—Basics of agent certification. Retrieved October 28, 2010, from http://www.gaarb.com/2008/06/nflpa-basics-of-agent-certification.html

Grossman, J. W. (2002). Financial planning for the professional athlete. In G. A. Uberstine (Ed.), *Law of professional and amateur sports* (pp. 3-4–11). St. Paul, MN: West Group.

Helyar, J. (1994). *Lords of the realm*. New York: Villard Books.

Helyar, J. (1997, June 25). Net gains? A Providence guard leaves college early, hoping for NBA gold. *The Wall Street Journal*, pp. A1, A8.

Hofmann, D., & Greenberg, M. J. (1989). *Sport$ biz*. Champaign, IL: Leisure Press.

IMG. (2003). IMG chairman's letter. Retrieved December 29, 2003, from http://www.imgworld.com/chairmansletter/default.htm

IMG. (2004a). IMG history. Retrieved May 30, 2004 from http://www.imgworld.com/history/

IMG. (2004b). IMG home. Retrieved May 30, 2004 from http://www.imgworld.com/

IMG. (2010). IMG home. Retrieved October 28, 2010, from http://www.imgworld.com/home/default.sps

Johnston, A. J., & Kain, R. D. (2004). CEO message. Retrieved May 30, 2004, from http://www.imgworld.com/message/

Katz, D. (1994). *Just do it: The Nike spirit in the corporate world*. New York: Random House.

Kepner, T. (2006, October 21). Baseball; The Boras bunch. *New York Times*. Retrieved October 28, 2010, from http://select.nytimes.com/search/restricted/article?res=F20815F93D5B0C728EDDA90994DE404482

Kuliga, K. (2007, April 4). Interview as part of the "Someone to be Proud of Series." University of Massachusetts Club, Boston, MA.

Lester, P. (2002). Marketing the athlete; endorsement contracts. In G. A. Uberstine (Ed.), *Law of professional and amateur sports* (pp. 27-2–27-39). St. Paul, MN: West Group.

Levin, M. (2007, February 12). Telephone conversation with Director of Salary Cap and Agent Administration of NFLPA.

Lowenfish, L. (1991). *The imperfect diamond* (rev. ed.). New York: Da Capo Press.

Martino, R.J. (2009, Nov. 22). Sports agents: Changing the compensation method. Retrieved October 28, 2010, from http://www.scribd.com/doc/22951011/Sports-Agents-Changing-the-Compensation-Method

McAleenan, G. (2002). Agent-player representation agreements. In G. A. Uberstine (Ed.), *Law of professional and amateur sports* (pp. 2-10–2-12). St. Paul, MN: West Group.

Mortensen, C. (1991). *Playing for keeps: How one man kept the mob from sinking its hooks into pro football*. New York: Simon & Schuster.

Mullen, L. (2004, April 19–25). Dirty dealings spark debate. *Street & Smith's SportsBusiness Journal*, 23–27.

Mullen, L. (2006, October 16–22). New players emerge in athlete rep business: Ranking the agencies. *Street & Smith's SportsBusiness Journal*, p. 26.

Mullen, L. (2007a, January 15). LeBron's agent close to CAA deal. *Street & Smith's SportsBusiness Journal*, p. 1.

Mullen, L. (2007b, January 8). Two agents exit Octagon for WMG. *Street & Smith's SportsBusiness Journal*, p. 5.

Mullen, L. (2010a, May 17) Lawsuits may affect big-name sports agencies. *Street & Smith's SportsBusiness Journal*, p. 1.

Mullen, L. (2010b, May 17) Bear with them: CAA Sports signs to represent Jack Nicklaus. *Street & Smith's SportsBusiness Journal*, p. 14.

Mullen, L. (2010c, September 16) IMG, Matthew Baldwin both claim victory in lawsuit settlement. Retrieved March 1, 2011, from http://www.sportsbusinessdaily.com/Daily/Issues/2010/09/Issue-4/Sports-Industrialists/IMG-Matthew-Baldwin-Both-Claim-Victory-In-Lawsuit-Settlement.aspx

Mullen, L. and Broughton, D. (2008, August 25). Survey puts CAA tops in player salaries. *Street & Smith's SportsBusiness Journal*, p. 1.

National Hockey League Players Association (NHLPA). (2010). Certified agents. Retrieved October 28, 2010, from http://www.nhlpa.com/About-Us/Certified-Agents/

Neff, C. (1987, October 19). Den of vipers. *Sports Illustrated*, 74–104.

Newman, W. (2007). Person-centered branding: Coaching to create an authentic brand. Retrieved October 28, 2010, from http://www.personcenteredbranding.com

Octagon. (2007a). Worldwide offices. Retrieved October 28, 2010, from http://www.octagon.com/GlobalNetwork

Octagon. (2007b). About us. Retrieved October 28, 2010, from http://www.octagon.com/AboutUs/42

Octagon. (2010). Join our team. Retrieved October 28, 2010, from http://www.octagon.com/aboutus/44

Pierce, C. (2007, April 1). Why Scott Boras is the best (and worst) thing to happen to baseball. Retrieved October 28, 2010, from http://www.boston.com/news/globe/magazine/articles/2007/04/01/why_scott_boras_is_the_best_and_worst_thing_to_happen_to_baseball/

Rivera, R. (2007, February 12). Telephone conversation with representative of MLBPA.

Ruxin, R. (2004). *An athlete's guide to agents* (4th ed.). Sudbury, MA: Jones & Bartlett Publishers.

Sauer, A. D. (2003, March 17). Yao Ming falls short. *brandchannel.com*. Retrieved October 28, 2010, from http://www.brandchannel.com/features_profile.asp?pr_id=116

Schwarz, A. (1996, March 4–17). Agents: What's the deal? *Baseball America*, 14–19.

Shropshire, K. (1990). *Agents of opportunity*. Philadelphia: University of Pennsylvania Press.

Shropshire, K. L., & Davis, T. (2003). *The business of sports agents*. Philadelphia: University of Pennsylvania Press.

Sobel, L. (1990). The regulation of player agents and lawyers. In G. A. Uberstine (Ed.), *Law of professional and amateur sports* (pp. 1-1–1-107). Deerfield, IL: Clark, Boardman, and Callaghan.

Sobel, L. (2002). The regulation of player agents and lawyers. In G. A. Uberstine (Ed.), *The law of professional and amateur sports* (pp. 1-1–1-6). St. Paul, MN: West Group.

Solomon, J. (1995, April 26). Guest lecture: Professional sports and the law class. University of Massachusetts, Amherst.

Sports Agent Responsibility and Trust Act, Pub. L. No. 108-304, (2004) (enacted).

Sports Identity. (2007). BrandMatch® for athletes. Retrieved October 28, 2010, from http://sportsidentity.com/bm_athletes.php

Steadman, T. (2004). Owens faithful to his agent in Triad. *News and Record*. Retrieved from http://www.news,record.com/ cgi,bin/print_it.pl

Thurow, R. (1996, February 9). The 76ers are lowly, but Jerry Stackhouse scores big in marketing. *The Wall Street Journal*, pp. A1, A4.

Top NFL News (2010). 2009 NFL salaries of coaches. Retrieved November 13, 2010, from http://www.topnflnews.com/2009-nfl-salaries-of-coaches/01/2010/

Towle, A. P. (2003, November 18). Celebrity branding: Making the brand. *Hollywood Reporter*. Retrieved from http://www.hollywoodreporter.com/hr/search/article_display.jsp?vnu_content_id=2030984

Upton, J. Gillum J. and Berkowitz, S. (2010, April 12). Rising salaries of coaches force colleges to seek budget patch. *USA Today*. Retrieved October 28, 2010, from http://www.usatoday.com/sports/college/mensbasketball/2010-04-01-coaches-salaries-cover_N.htm?csp=34

Van Riper, T. (2009, May 14). Highest paid coaches. *Forbes.com*. Retrieved October 28, 2010, from http://www.forbes.com/2009/05/13/highest-paid-coaches-business-sports-nba.html

Waggoner, J. (1996, July 12). Walk, don't run, after a windfall. *USA Today*, p. 5B.

Wertheim, L.J. (2001, November 5). Sfx needs an rx. *Sports Illustrated*. Retrieved October 28, 2010, from http://sportsillustrated.cnn.com/vault/article/magazine/MAG1024185/index.htm

Wertheim, L.J. (2004, May 3). The matchmaker: Agent Bob LaMonte represents NFL coaches on the rise. Retrieved November 13, 2010, from http://sportsillustrated.cnn.com/vault/article/magazine/MAG1031945/index.htm

Willette, A., & Waggoner, J. (1996, July 12). Rich can't afford to dismiss budget: Even superstars need financial coaching. *USA Today*, p. 5B.

WMG. (2006a, January 27). Wasserman Media Group acquires Arn Tellem's prominent baseball and basketball athlete representation business. Retrieved October 28, 2010, from http://www.thefreelibrary.com/Wasserman+Media+Group+Acquires+Arn+Tellem's+Prominent+Baseball+and...-a0141346234

WMG. (2006b, May 11). Wasserman Media Group forms WMG Events via acquisition of Touring Pro. Retrieved from http://wmgllc.com/news/wmgevents.html

WMG. (2006c, June 5). Wasserman Media Group acquires SportsNet, the nation's premier soccer management business. Retrieved from http://wmgllc.com/news/sportsnet.html

WMG. (2006d, November 9). Wasserman Media Group becomes market leader in soccer—acquires SFX Sports Group European soccer practices. Retrieved from http://wmgllc.com/news/soccerleader-11_09_06.html

WMG. (2007a, June 25). Wasserman Media Group acquires sport and entertainment marketing leader, OnSport. Retrieved from http://wmgllc.com/news/onsport.html

WMG. (2007b). WMG marketing: Consulting. Retrieved from http://wmgllc.com/marketing/consulting.html

Woolf, B. (1976). *Behind closed doors*. New York: New American Library.

Sport Industry Support Segments

CHAPTER 12

Facility Management

Troy Flynn, Nancy Beauchamp, Robert Newman, Michael J. Graney, and Kevin Barrett

■ INTRODUCTION

People congregate in large groups for a number of reasons. Public assembly facilities must be large enough to accommodate the large numbers of people who want to be entertained at a sport or entertainment event or who meet together for social or business purposes. The facilities that are designed and built to accommodate these large groups of people include arenas, stadiums, convention centers, theaters (or performing arts facilities), racetracks, and amphitheaters. Arenas and stadiums are the primary venues for professional and amateur **sports events**. Although convention centers and theaters are not designed primarily to host sports events, they are utilized and marketed for this function. The growth in popularity of sports such as volleyball, wrestling, and even fencing has created a new market for these venues because

their availability of large, unobstructed space is vital for successful functions. Additionally, convention centers host sports-related conventions such as sporting goods expositions, sports card shows, and league meetings. Management principles are similar for all types of these facilities, and their managers are eligible for membership in the **International Association of Auditorium Managers (IAAM)**, the professional trade association for this field. In this chapter, the discussion of public assembly facilities considers arenas, stadiums, convention centers, and theaters. The facility managers provide the public with a safe, enjoyable experience while providing a cost effective and efficient means for the venue owner. This chapter focuses on significant areas in facility management to identify the structure and reasons why facilities are managed in certain ways.

■ HISTORY

Public assembly facilities have existed since ancient times. In fact, the word **stadium** is derived from the ancient Greek *stade,* a site for early Olympic-style athletic competition. Many of today's famous facilities bear the names of ancient and medieval facilities (Forum, Coliseum, Globe Theater). Throughout recorded history, people have gathered to witness sporting competitions and live theater at their era's version of public assembly facilities. From a sport management perspective, today's version of public assembly facilities evolved during the late nineteenth and early twentieth centuries in America, coinciding with the development of professional and intercollegiate athletics.

Stadiums

As professional baseball and intercollegiate football began to gain widespread popularity, open fields and parks became inadequate to handle the number of spectators who wanted to watch the contests. Baseball team owners and universities began to construct stadiums to accommodate fans. The constraints of urban space limitations dictated the irregular sizes and shapes of the older ballparks (Danielson, 1997). Some of these facilities still exist and are much beloved. Many authors, poets, journalists, and ordinary fans have waxed poetic about Fenway Park and Wrigley Field (Quirk & Fort, 1992). The question of their financial viability in today's sports market will be addressed later, but their status as cultural sports icons is unquestioned.

In the early twentieth century, baseball was the national pastime. Team owners built stadium facilities for themselves, so teams stayed in the home cities for years. The era of team movement and expansion did not begin until the late 1950s and 1960s. The National Football League (NFL) was founded in 1923 and slowly grew into the sport marketing powerhouse we know today. As the league gained popularity, its need for larger stadiums grew. Early on, NFL teams typically played in the major league baseball stadiums in their cities. These stadiums were designed and built for baseball, resulting in occasional quirks, such as end zones that were a yard short and generally poor sightlines for football. It was not until the public stadium construction boom in the 1960s and early 1970s that sightlines for both sports were taken into consideration.

Arenas

In the early twentieth century, indoor team professional sports were in their infancy. The National Hockey League (NHL) started in 1927 but was limited for the first 40 years to teams in four American and two Canadian cities (Boston, New York, Detroit, Chicago, Toronto, and Montreal). Hockey owners followed the lead of baseball owners and built arenas to host their teams. The hockey season then was roughly one-third the length of the baseball season (50 games compared with 154), so hockey owners had more empty nights to fill their arenas with events. Boxing filled some empty nights in both stadiums and arenas. It may surprise boxing aficionados who came of age in the 1980s and 1990s that championship fights were not always held in casinos. New York and Madison Square Garden were to boxing for most of this century what Las Vegas is today. Still, the occasional fight did not by itself satisfy the hockey barons' need for more activity in their facilities, so they pursued other events.

NHL arena owners along with some of their minor league counterparts founded the Ice Capades, the first large-scale annual touring ice show, so they could fill a week or two of their arena schedule with skating fans, creating an additional revenue stream for themselves. The Ice Capades was very successful and lasted for over 50 years as a skating variety show.

(It was put out of business by a number of more specialized figure skating shows, such as Disney on Ice, the Tour of Olympic and World Figure Skating Champions, and Stars on Ice.) However, even profitable week-long runs of the Ice Capades did not have a significant enough impact on arena profits. Arena owners needed another major sport to limit the number of dark days. Basketball filled this need.

Basketball is the youngest of the four major North American professional sports and the only one with a verifiable birth date and place: December 22, 1891, in Springfield, Massachusetts. Professional basketball prior to the National Basketball Association (NBA) was primarily a touring, barnstorming event. Good teams would travel from city to city playing the best the locals had to offer. The NBA and its forerunner, the Basketball Association of America, changed that and established a league structure similar to those already established in Major League Baseball (MLB), the NFL, and the NHL.

The original arena owners, though, initially capitalized on college basketball. Colleges and universities built field houses for their basketball teams, but as the sport's popularity grew, it became necessary to host big games and tournaments in the big city arenas. College basketball doubleheaders became a staple of major arena event calendars, particularly at Madison Square Garden, which was as much a mecca for college basketball as it was for boxing. The National Invitation Tournament (NIT), the nation's oldest collegiate basketball tournament founded by the Metropolitan Basketball Writers and held in Madison Square Garden since 1938, when the inventor of basketball, Dr. James Naismith, presented the first NIT trophy to the undefeated Blackbirds of Long Island University. Although the NIT is now owned by the National Collegiate Athletic Association (NCAA), the NIT and the "World's Most Famous Arena" continue their relationship over seventy years later (NCAA, 2010).

Arena owners then earned revenue from two tenants (hockey and basketball). Given the popularity and marketing scope of the NHL and the NBA today, the historical truth that basketball owners paid rent to hockey owners may be hard to believe. However, that relationship still exists in some cities, such as Boston, where the Boston Celtics rent from the Delaware North Companies, Inc., owners of the Boston Bruins and the TD Banknorth Garden.

The Modern Era of Stadium and Arena Construction

Basketball and hockey, as tenants of one arena, are much more compatible in terms of building design and sightlines than are baseball and football. Stadium quirks and fan annoyance factors were never as critical in developing arenas capable of hosting both indoor sports as they were in stadiums attempting to host both outdoor sports. Still, it is clearly advantageous for sports facility owners (whether indoor or outdoor) to have two prime sport tenants. Baseball-only stadiums that had served their owners and fans for more than 40 years were becoming obsolete during the 1960s. Some were too small, and most lacked modern amenities such as wide seats, leg room, easy access to concession stands, and artificial turf. Several new stadiums were built during the 1960s and 1970s, but not by the team owners.

Team owners at that time were beginning to learn a lesson they would use to their advantage in the future: they could save a great deal of money by having their host city build their stadium rather than building it themselves. Cities, driven by the civic pride that "big league" status endows, built shiny new facilities to keep their teams as enthusiastic about their hometowns as were the civic leaders. It made sense for the cities to build facilities with both their football and baseball tenants in mind because more activity justified the public investment. The result was the so-called "cookie-cutter stadiums" like Veterans Stadium in Philadelphia, Three Rivers Stadium in Pittsburgh, and Riverfront Stadium in Cincinnati. They were new, they were modern, they had artificial turf (so field maintenance was easy), and they all looked alike. Arena construction boomed during this era, too. Civic centers and civic arenas sprang up in a number of major and secondary markets as cities competed for major and minor league sport teams by building suitable facilities. This time also marked the dawn of the touring concert industry, and concerts became an extremely lucrative addition to a facility's schedule. City leaders generally believed that a publicly built stadium with both baseball and football tenants or a publicly built arena with both basketball and hockey tenants, along with the concert and family show tours, was a good investment. Such facilities contributed to the city's quality of life by providing sports and entertainment for the citizens and spin-off benefits for the local economy.

Eventually, team owners, and many of their fans, decided that multipurpose facilities were not quite good enough. Stadiums designed to be acceptable for both baseball and football ended up being desirable for neither. The trend over the past two decades favors single-purpose stadiums. This specialization has extended to facilities built solely for soccer teams, called **soccer-specific stadiums** (SSS). SSS have become the legacy of soccer investor, Lamar Hunt, owner of the Columbus Crew, whose soccer specific stadium in Columbus, Ohio, was the first venue of its size to be built in the United States and has fueled SSS growth. The Crew Stadium opened 1999 and has become a model for all Major League Soccer (MLS) franchises. Now, twelve soccer-specific stadia operate in the MLS with clubs in San Jose, Vancouver, and Washington D.C. attempting to put stadium plans into action. **Table 12-1** details the SSS growth in MLS.

Financing these facilities has become an interesting dilemma, particularly given team owners' desire to use facility revenues to compete for free-agent players and to boost their own profits. Some cities have constructed (or promised to construct) facilities that will provide team owners the design and revenue streams they need to be successful. Team owners are now seeking lucrative stadium leases that provide revenue from four sources: preferred seating (luxury suites, club seating, and personal seat licenses), parking, concessions, and stadium sponsorship (signage and naming rights) (Greenberg & Gray, 1993). As a result, franchise free agency has developed. Team owners flee their traditional locations for greener pastures not because of market size and growth but because of more profitable facility deals. In fact, the facility in which a professional sport team plays has the most significant impact on its profitability and is often its primary consideration in choosing to remain or move to a new location. For more information see Chapter 4, Financial and Economic Principles Applied to Sport Management, and Chapter 10, Professional Sport.

■ TYPES OF PUBLIC ASSEMBLY FACILITIES

Arenas

Arenas are indoor facilities that host sporting and entertainment events. They are usually built to accommodate one (or more) prime sports tenant(s) or to lure a prime tenant to the facility. Colleges and universities typically build an arena for their basketball teams and occasionally their hockey teams. These arenas may also be used for volleyball and gymnastics as well as concerts and other touring shows. Intercollegiate facilities are financed by private donations, endowments, student fees, fund-raising campaigns, and, in

TABLE 12-1 Soccer Specific Stadiums in Major League Soccer

Stadium	MLS Team	Location	Capacity	Open	Cost
Columbus Crew Stadium	Columbus Crew	Columbus, OH	22,500	1999	$28.5 million
Home Depot Center	Los Angeles Galaxy	Carson, CA	27,000	2003	$150 million
Pizza Hut Park	FC Dallas	Frisco, TX	21,000	2005	$80 million
Toyota Park	Chicago Fire	Bridgeview, IL	20,000	2006	$98 million
Dick's Sporting Goods Park	Colorado Rapids	Commerce City, CO	18,500	2007	$130 million
BMO Field	Toronto FC	Toronto, Ontario	20,000	2007	$62 million
Rio Tinto Stadium	Real Salt Lake	Sandy, UT	20,000	2008	$110 million
Red Bull Park	New York Red Bulls	Harrison, NJ	25,000	2009	$100 million
PPL Park	Philadelphia Union	Chester, PA	18,500	2010	$120 million
PGE Park	Portland Timbers	Portland, OR	17,000 (up to 22,000)	2011	$31 million (renovation)
Houston Dynamo Stadium	Houston Dynamo	Houston, TX	22,000	2012	$60 million

the case of public institutions, public grants or capital bonds.

Some NBA and NHL teams have built their own arenas. In other cases, municipalities, state governments, or public authorities have built them. Sometimes the public owner manages its facility and sometimes it contracts out for private management. The public or private manager then negotiates a lease with the prime sports tenant. If the arena is privately built, commercial lenders issue loans to the team, which pledges facility revenue streams as collateral. Public financing typically involves issuing bonds that can be tied to direct or indirect facility revenue but more often are a general obligation of the governmental entity

(see Chapter 4, Financial and Economic Principles Applied to Sport).

Basketball and hockey teams can generally peacefully coexist in the same arena without either being forced into unacceptable compromises. Arenas also host indoor soccer leagues, arena football, concerts, ice shows, family shows, graduations, other civic events, and some types of conventions. Recent trends in facility construction include adjacent practice facilities for the primary tenants. The Nationwide Arena, home of the Columbus, Ohio, Blue Jackets, which opened in September 2000, was the first NHL venue to have an attached NHL-regulation practice rink. The Amway Center in Orlando, Florida has just completed an attached practice facility for the NBA's Orlando Magic. This allows the facility to further achieve its goal of increasing event bookings and, just as importantly, maximizing revenues. With the growth of new leagues such as the National Lacrosse League (NLL) and the Arena Football League, the availability of the main arena is critical to achieving an effective programming mix.

Stadiums

Stadiums are similar to arenas, but they are outdoor or domed facilities. Stadiums provide sites for baseball, football, and outdoor soccer teams. The ownership, financing, and management issues discussed in the arena section also apply to stadiums. Like their arena counterparts, stadium managers try to maximize bookings, but it is more difficult. First, baseball and football teams do not coexist as easily as basketball and hockey teams. Second, there are far fewer non-sport events that can play stadiums, primarily because stadiums are significantly larger than other venues and most other events cannot attract stadium-sized crowds. The main non-sport events for stadiums are outdoor concerts given by performers who have the drawing power to

fill a stadium. Stadium managers have become increasingly effective in creating events for their venues that take advantage of all available spaces. For example, the Kraft Sports Group, owner of the Patriots, Revolution and Gillette Stadium, has hosted concerts, collegiate lacrosse and football games/championships, and private events (such as weddings and proms). The large parking facilities that are adjacent to most stadiums have long been utilized for pre-game tailgating. However, now on non-game days they are being utilized and marketed to fairs, festivals, circuses, carnivals, outdoor marketplaces, and drive-and-buy car shows.

Convention Centers

Convention centers are almost always built and owned by a public entity. Convention centers are built to lure conventions and business meetings to a particular municipality. They are publicly financed because the rents and fees they charge do not always cover costs. However, the municipality they serve benefits in other ways, namely, through the economic impact the convention or business meeting has on the municipality. The International Association of Convention and Visitors Bureau has standard multipliers that are effective in calculating the economic impact of various events. Consideration is given to visitor or "delegate" spending that includes hotel, meal, entertainment, and related expenditures.

Convention centers are typically located near the downtown districts of large cities. The convention business is extremely competitive, and municipalities (and states) offer significant financial inducements to convention and meeting planners for the opportunity to host visitors. The conventioneers and meeting attendees stay in local hotels, eat in local restaurants, shop in local stores, and patronize local tourist attractions, all of which supports business and employment in the region. Conventioneers are also typically taxed, so the state and municipality receive indirect revenue from the events. The increased business, employment opportunities, and indirect fiscal revenue justify the public entity's construction and continued subsidy of convention centers.

In addition to the nontraditional sporting events previously discussed, convention centers host a wide variety of events. These include conventions and trade shows attended by a specific industry member; public "flat" shows such as car, boat, and home shows; corporate meetings; banquets; and similar functions.

Theaters

Theaters are public assembly facilities that are primarily utilized for the presentation of live artistic entertainment. Universities, public entities, and private (usually not-for-profit) groups construct them. Like stadiums and arenas, theaters often house prime tenants such as symphony orchestras, opera and dance companies, and resident theater groups. Theaters attract an active touring market of popular and classical concerts, Broadway musicals and plays, dance troupes, lecture series, and children's and family theater. Theater managers base their schedules around the needs of their prime tenant(s) and then try to book as many touring events as possible.

The arts are heavily subsidized by governmental and corporate entities. Revenue earned by most arts organizations does not cover their costs. Public or private nonprofit theater owners typically subsidize their arts tenants' rents and try to generate revenue from touring shows. Profits are rare, but the spin-off business from theater attractions (hotel stays for touring artists and restaurant business from theater patrons) again justifies public subsidy. Theater performances also provide culture and entertainment for a community, enhancing its quality of life in a similar way to its sport teams.

Other Types of Venues

■ UNIVERSITY VENUES

University venues consist of stadiums, arenas, and theaters that have different economic factors under which they operate. The market for university and college venues is generally dictated by the student population. Universities and colleges have different geographic locations, but the general intent when selling tickets is to market to the student population and, therefore, certain types of events will play better than others. Universities tend to provide the venue with tenant teams as well as a certain amount of content through the university. Providing the university with the content that may be routing through the area can sometimes prove to be difficult based on the occupied dates scheduled for university programs.

■ METROPOLITAN FACILITIES

Metropolitan facilities are venues located in large cities such as Madison Square Garden in New York, The Wells Fargo complex in Philadelphia, and the Staples Center in Los Angeles. Venues like these are generally referred to as a *must play* based on the size of the potential audience. The three venues listed previously can present as many as 400 events a year if the scheduling allows for it. They often have multiple tenant teams including NHL, American Hockey League (AHL), NBA, Women's National Basketball Association (WNBA), NLL, and arena football leagues. Typically the staffs operating these venues are larger based on the event load, where as a smaller venue will generally run a more streamlined staff. A must play venue is popular with promoters for several different reasons. Promoters with established routing have a variety of local staff, making tour travel less expensive and more efficient. Metropolitan venues often have larger capacities allowing for a greater number of tickets to be sold. Skilled labor in metropolitan venues is almost always unionized. In smaller venues specific labor may be mandated to be contracted to the unions, but there is often a component that can be non-union. The venues located within city limits utilize skilled labor from the union, but their expertise often costs more than hiring a private contractor. Venue managers are often required to use union labor because of contracts negotiated before the venue opened that were based on funding and economic impact studies.

Local/Civic Venues

Local/civic venues may have a smaller capacity and are located in towns or small cities. The Sun National Bank Center in Trenton, New Jersey, and The Sovereign Center in Reading, Pennsylvania, are examples of a local or civic venue. They have a smaller surrounding population and seating capacity. The venues themselves are able to host large scale events and concerts but tend to host smaller capacity events due to artist costs. The venue manager needs to identify what works for venues in the 5,000 to 10,000 seat range. An NBA or NHL minor league affiliate will be the tenant team for the venue, but it is essential to have the additional events to fill the calendar. Facility operating teams have been successfully hosting events that play to local groups like cheerleading, political conventions, and church conferences. The civic venue has a niche that is based in the surrounding community and the support the venue receives is critical to the success of the facility.

Types of Events

Several types of events exist today. They are as mainstream as Disney On Ice or somewhat nontraditional, like the X-Games or Dew Tour. Venue managers should know a wide variety of genres and need to be able to quickly access the type of event that would have the biggest impact on the community and the venue. When looking at event types, the promoter and facility director must consider the market in order to assure the success of an event. Certain family shows like The Harlem Globetrotters are a well known act that encompasses comedy, athleticism, and pop culture. They are routed throughout the world and are well received in every venue they play. Other family events like a traveling circus may not do as well because of some groups that believe the animals involved in the program are being unethically treated. Venue managers and promoters need to take market concerns like this into consideration prior to booking a routing event. The facility manager also has to be aware of the specifics of his or her market in order to provide the public with the desired event at the best time of the year to avoid undue competition with other events that may be occurring simultaneously. Listed below are some event genres and how they operate.

■ SPORT EVENTS

Sports have seasons that allow events to be scheduled approximately eight months out. Several venues will have tenant teams that play the home schedule and require certain dates contractually. Facility managers walk a fine line when budgeting shows around team games because of playoffs. Should the tenant team make playoffs they will require that home days be available. A close eye needs to be kept on the booking calendar to make sure conflicts or double bookings do not occur. Non-tenant sports are constantly touring and can play based on availability. Tennis tours featuring former stars rout annually and do well with tennis fans. Traveling basketball groups are often seen booking in urban locations. The groups set up and invite the neighborhood out for clinics and competitions before the show.

■ FAMILY EVENTS

Family events are products geared toward the toddler and through the "tween" markets. Often these are acts produced from television or movie programs that are run on mainstream television or theaters. Sesame Street, Nickelodeon, and Disney are among the top names in the family genre. They produce the artists that children identify with such as Miley Cyrus from the television show Hannah Montana. When the acts and artist play a venue, the show normally has a multiple day run and generates large demands for food and beverage as well as merchandise sales. Booking can be challenging based on the amount of preparation the venue will need and the run of play. Ice programs will need ice specifically tailored to the artists and the performance. Preparation for changes to an ice sheet from hockey usage to ice show usage can take time and commitment from the operations team. Should the schedule be tight and a quick turnaround necessary, the venue manager may need to look at the event and try to find alternate dates that work.

■ CONCERTS

Concerts are booked on average six months before the play date. Tours and routings are established and the dates are promoted after an agreement is reached. When booking concerts it is important to look at the potential ticket sales and the intended market. Timing is critical and is illustrated well by looking at the university dynamic. Students have breaks throughout the year that generally include a fall, winter, and spring break. Some schools are more of a commuter type and don't have a central location where students are housed in large numbers. These are all critical factors when looking at booking a venue with a show geared towards a student body. The student body must be present and able to go to the program. If promoter or facility manager books an event during the university's spring break, the show may not do as well as anticipated.

■ TRADE SHOWS

Trade shows are mostly multiple day events held annually in the same location. Trade shows work best in convention centers because hotel and exhibition space are specifically intended for that usage, but they can also play in stadiums and arenas that can convert to accommodate the event. An example is the Phoenix Convention Center in Arizona that hosts an annual expo for outdoor enthusiasts and fans of recreational vehicles. This venue utilizes its retractable roof and stadium field in order to fill dates, which gives the promoter the ability to expand the show into a larger, more unique space.

■ RELIGIOUS EVENTS

Religious events encompass mass worship. These events are generally booked as a rental with expenses guaranteed. The rental structure is preferred because religious organizations generally doesn't charge for tickets. Some groups like the Jehovah Witnesses can provide a good opportunity to utilize a venue when bookings for the facility are slow. Arenas have been able to schedule religious events in the summer to fill dates that would otherwise go vacant. Concerts and tours tend to play outdoor facilities in the summer, so religious events present a nice opportunity to make a small profit on days that would otherwise not be utilized.

■ CONVOCATIONS

Convocations, graduations, and speaking engagements are great ways to get community involvement and interaction with the venue. Venue managers generally approach these types of events with the understanding that graduations happen in the spring and weather conditions may present certain challenges to hosting them outside. Another plus is the capacity of the venue and the graduates' ability to have additional tickets for friends and family. Graduation can be a busy time of year depending on the amount of local schools hosting at the facility and the size of the class.

SEASONAL EVENTS

Seasonal events are defined as events that take place during a specific time frame. Summer tours are a perfect example of a seasonal event. In the past large summer tours were held mostly at outdoor theaters, but more recently stadiums are hosting large country music festivals and touring programs. One event that seems to mark the beginning of the summer for many concert goers is Jimmy Buffet. Jimmy Buffet and his Margaritaville culture are some of the most heavily attended summer touring events in recent history. These shows are generally held at outdoor facilities so the fans can experience the music in an outdoor and relaxed fashion. Other types of seasonal programming that the facility manager may consider are seasonal programs directed at holidays, such as the Radio City Music Hall Rockettes touring holiday program, or the TranSiberian orchestra. Both programs tour around the November–December holiday season and attract good attendance from families looking to get into the holiday spirit.

■ FACILITY FINANCING

Facility financing starts with the federal government, which allows state and local governments to issue tax-exempt **bonds** to help finance sports facilities. Tax exemption lowers interest on debt, thereby reducing the amount that cities and teams must pay for a stadium. In addition, there are a variety of ways to finance public assembly facilities, but the specific financing decision is always preceded by a single fundamental question: Will the facility be financed publicly or privately? The answer depends on a number of factors, including the type of facility being constructed. Convention centers are almost always financed publicly because they are not intended to make money. Convention centers do not book events to make a profit for themselves; rather, they book events that maximize the impact on the local economy, particularly the hospitality industry. Because of their "public" focus, the public sector pays for them, often by initiating or raising taxes on the state or local hospitality industry (e.g., hotel room taxes, restaurant meal taxes, and rental car fees).

Arena and stadium financing is not as clear-cut, particularly when a major league professional sport team is a prime tenant. Professional sport teams are in business to make money—sometimes enormous amounts of money. There are those who argue that any for-profit enterprise should build its own facility where it conducts its business. At the same time, some studies show that sports facilities provide significant economic benefits to their host communities, and teams are undeniable sources of civic pride and community spirit. Attracting a sport team can provide a public relations boost to a city, too, particularly one attempting to prove it is "major league."

Stadium/arena financing has fluctuated between public and private methods over the years. In the early years of the current major professional sport leagues, team owners generally built their own facilities. A public building boom, generally of multipurpose facilities, ensued during the 1960s and 1970s as the original facilities were approaching obsolescence. Over the past 20 years, as free agency has increased player salaries, team owners have had to look for additional revenue to compete for, and pay, their players while maintaining profitability.

Controlling stadium revenue streams such as concessions, advertising, sponsorship, premium seating and suites, and seat licenses has become the primary means to the owners' ends. Single-purpose facilities designed to the specifications of a particular sport with one team as primary tenant are desirable to team owners because revenue streams do not have to be shared.

For the cities, states, stadium authorities, and other representatives of the public sector, these issues became increasingly problematic. The public benefits justifying stadium construction remained, but the costs were going up, particularly if two teams were each looking for their own stadium or arena. Cities in particular faced hard choices because most had stable or declining tax revenue and increasing municipal government costs. Building public assembly facilities meant other services had to be neglected. In many locations the question of publicly financing a stadium was put to a vote.

In the early 1980s, Joe Robbie, owner of the NFL Miami Dolphins, became disenchanted with the Orange Bowl, a facility the Dolphins shared with the University of Miami. He proposed a new stadium, but the voters in south Florida did not approve public funding. Robbie then proposed a novel solution. He pledged stadium revenues from suites and specialty seating, secured by multiple-year contracts from their users, as collateral to his bankers and privately financed his stadium. The NBA Detroit Pistons followed suit and privately constructed the Palace of Auburn Hills, ushering in a new era of private facility construction financed by anticipated stadium or arena revenue.

Still, this was not a perfect world for a team owner. Pledging facility revenue streams to pay for debt service or mortgage expenses takes income away from profits. If a team owner could find a city or state willing to build a new facility and let the team control the stadium revenue streams, the owner could maximize revenue without heavy debt service expenses.

Two interesting case studies are Baltimore and Cleveland. Both cities decided to construct new facilities in their downtowns to maintain or attract sport teams while simultaneously revitalizing decaying sections of their cities. Their strategies have proven successful. Baltimore, through the Maryland Stadium Authority, agreed to build a new baseball stadium, Oriole Park at Camden Yards, for the Orioles and a football stadium for an NFL expansion team or any existing team willing to move there. Baltimore had previously lost its football team, the Colts, to a better stadium deal in Indianapolis. Cleveland built a new baseball stadium, Jacobs Field, for the Indians and a new arena, Gund Arena, for the NBA Cavaliers. The new stadiums fostered tremendous spin-off economic benefit in both cities, and a host of new businesses have started up in the vicinity of the facilities. All of the facilities received excellent marks for design and for their ability to mesh into the urban fabric while providing great ballpark ambience. Camden Yards and Jacobs Field, in particular, were enthusiastically supported by baseball fans, as each has the charm of Fenway Park or Wrigley Field combined with the modern fan comforts and revenue opportunities of Dolphin Stadium or the Palace.

The Orioles and Indians took advantage of their new facilities, rocketing from the middle of the pack to close to the top of MLB in attendance and revenue. Each team used its newfound financial strength to sign free agent players and to keep its own stars, guaranteeing winning teams that keep fans coming and provide more revenue. MLB teams from around the country are trying to emulate Baltimore and Cleveland by convincing public officials and voters to build new stadiums like Camden Yards and Jacobs Field. If they get turned down, team owners threaten to move to cities that will build the facilities they want.

In today's revenue-hungry major league sports, huge markets and loyal fans pale in comparison o the profitability of new stadiums and arena Not one but two NFL teams have vacated I Angeles, the second-largest media market the United States, because of more lucrati tadium offers. Oakland, which lost its Raide o Los Angeles a decade earlier, enticed then ck by upgrading their former home, the Co um, and guaranteeing stadium revenue ns. St. Louis, which had lost the Cardinals st rizona, built a new facility, the Trans World me, now named the Edward Jones Dome, to tice a new team and convinced the Rams to orsake Los Angeles, too. In Cincinnati, Ohio, the Cincinnati Bengals were successful in having a new stadium, which was primarily publicly financed, built for their team. The Bengals claimed that the new stadium was necessary for them to maintain a competitive team. The team's poor win–loss record in the first two years in the new stadium prompted one county commissioner to call for lease concessions from the Bengals franchise. For further information, see the discussion of franchise free agency in Chapter 10, Professional Sport.

Facility Financing Mechanisms

Facility construction and renovation are expensive undertakings. For a construction project to begin, funding must be sought from different sources, both public and private. This section provides a brief overview of the different types of financing available for facility construction or renovation.

■ BONDS

The money to build facilities is usually obtained by issuing bonds. According to Howard and Crompton (1995), "Bonds are formally defined as a promise by the borrower (bond issuer) to pay back the lender (bond holder) a specified amount of money, with interest, within a specified period of time" (p. 98). Bonds may be issued by local authorities (cities, counties, or states) to underwrite the cost of sport facility construction. Bonds usually fall into one of two categories: general obligation bonds or revenue bonds. *General obligation bonds*, backed by the local government's ability to raise taxes to pay off the debt, are considered relatively safe investments. *Revenue bonds*, backed specifically by the facility's ability to generate revenues, are somewhat riskier because the facility has to generate sufficient funds to meet both the annual operating costs of the arena and the annual debt payments (Howard & Crompton, 1995). If the facility has a down year financially, there may not be enough money left after covering the annual operating costs to make the debt payments.

■ TAXES

A number of different taxes can be used to generate money to fund sports facilities, each of which has advantages and disadvantages. The first of these taxes is property taxes. These taxes are paid by homeowners, who are often long-term residents of a city. It makes sense to tax these people, because they live in the location where the facility is being constructed and would be most likely to receive its full benefit. However, for a property tax to be imposed, people must be given the chance to vote. In terms of facility financing, this is an especially problematic aspect because long-term residents, who most likely are property owners whose taxes will go up, tend to vote regularly and are not inclined to vote to raise their own taxes. A second option is an occupational tax, which taxes anyone who works in the community, regardless of whether that person actually resides in the community. This tax must also be voted on, but in many instances it has been more likely to pass than a property tax (Mahony, 1997).

All of these taxes are imposed on local residents, but there are other taxes that pass the burden onto out-of-town visitors instead. Most notable among these is a hospitality tax, such as the one used in Atlanta to help build the Georgia Dome and the one used in Chicago to construct the new Comiskey Park. This tax forces visitors to pay directly for the facility, but a locality must be careful not to make the tax so high that it becomes a barrier to people visiting the location or to organizations deciding to hold business meetings or conventions there. Rental car taxes meet this same description. Local residents often prefer these types of taxes, since the local residents receive the benefit of the facility without shouldering so much of the construction costs (Mahony, 1997).

Some tax plans affect both local residents and visitors. The first of these is the general sales tax, which is imposed on nearly all transactions, although sales of food for at-home consumption and prescription drugs are typically exempted (Howard & Crompton, 1995). A sales tax was used to help fund the Fargo Dome. The "sin tax," which taxes only alcohol and tobacco products, was used in the construction of the MetroDome in Minneapolis. Other options include a meals tax placed on people who dine out or a transportation tax on bus and taxi travel (Mahony, 1997).

The 2008 $500 million retractable-roof Lucas Oil Stadium and Indianapolis Convention Center expansion project for the Indianapolis Colts was partially funded by tax increases that include a 1% tax increase on all prepared food in the nine counties that surround Indianapolis, a 1% increase on the tax already charged to Marion County (Indianapolis) residents for the RCA Dome, and an increase in the Marion County hotel tax and rental car tax. Additional revenue sources included the sale of Colts vanity license plates and future lottery tickets earmarked for the project (Tully, Fritze, & Corcoran, 2007).

■ CORPORATE INVESTMENT

In addition to public sources of funding, there are a number of private sources a sport facility could tap to cover construction costs. One source is corporate sponsorship. As mentioned in Chapter 14, Sport Sales, and Chapter 15, Sport Sponsorship, the sale of naming rights for stadiums and arenas is a current trend. Facilities such as CitiField in Queens and Barclays Arena in Brooklyn, New York, Coors Field in Denver, Miller Field in Milwaukee, the Edward Jones Dome in St. Louis, the United Center in Chicago, the Wachovia Center in Philadelphia, University of Phoenix Stadium in Glendale, Arizona (home of the Arizona Cardinals), and the Papa John's Cardinal Stadium at the University of Louisville all received millions of dollars from naming rights. Soft drink companies, such as Coca-Cola or Pepsi, and beer companies, such as Anheuser-Busch or Miller, will also pay considerable sums for *facility pouring rights*, which means the company would be the facility's exclusive soft drink or beer distributor. In addition, corporations may make outright donations to defray costs in exchange for the publicity and public relations benefits that may result from such a donation (Mahony, 1997).

Facility Revenues

Finally, money for construction may come directly from facility revenues. As mentioned in Chapter 4, Financial and Economic Principles Applied to Sport Management, and Chapter 14, Sport Sales, the sale of personal seat licenses (PSLs) as well as luxury suites and club seating make up a considerable source of revenue for stadium construction. This money, which is paid up front, can be used to offset facility costs. A ticket tax may also be imposed on the sale of tickets to events at existing facilities. An organization may also use other facility revenues, such as rent from tenants, concessions, and parking, to pay for the cost of the facility. As mentioned earlier, depending on these revenue sources is riskier because they are not earmarked specifically for the facility and are not guaranteed in any way (Mahony, 1997).

■ WHY CITIES SUBSIDIZE SPORTS FACILITIES

The economic rationale for cities' willingness to subsidize sports facilities comes from the thought that sports facilities will improve the local economy in four ways. First, building a facility creates construction jobs. Second, people who attend games or work for the team generate new spending in the community, expanding local employment. Third, a team attracts tourists and companies to the host city, further increasing local spending and jobs. Finally, all this new spending has a "multiplier effect" as increased local income causes still more new spending and job creation (Noll & Zimbalist, 1997a). Advocates argue that new stadiums spur so much economic growth that they are self-financing: Subsidies are offset by revenues from ticket taxes, sales taxes on concessions and other spending outside the stadium, and property tax increases arising from the stadium's economic impact.

Unfortunately, these arguments contain bad economic reasoning that leads to overstatement of the benefits of stadiums. Economic growth takes place when a community's resources—people, capital investments—and natural resources like land become more productive. Building a stadium is good for the local economy only if a stadium is the most productive way to make capital investments and use an area's workers (Noll & Zimbalist, 1997a). A new sports facility has an extremely small (perhaps even negative) effect on overall economic activity and employment (Baade & Sanderson, 1997). No recent facility appears to have earned anything approaching a reasonable return on investment.

No recent facility has been self-financing in terms of its impact on net tax revenues (Noll & Zimbalist, 1997a).

Sports facilities attract neither tourists nor new industry. Probably the most successful export facility is Oriole Park, where about a third of the crowd at every game comes from outside the Baltimore area. (Baltimore's baseball exports are enhanced because it is 40 miles from the nation's capital, which up until 2004, with the move by the Montreal Expos [now Washington Nationals] to Washington, D.C., had no major league baseball team.) Even so, the net gain to Baltimore's economy in terms of new jobs and incremental tax revenues is only about $3 million per year, which is not much of a return on a $200 million investment (Hamilton & Kahn, 1997).

Another rationale for subsidized stadiums is that stadiums generate more local consumer satisfaction than alternative investments. Professional sports teams are very small businesses, comparable to large department or grocery stores. They capture public attention far out of proportion to their economic significance. A professional sports team, therefore, creates a "public good" or "externality," a benefit enjoyed by consumers who follow sports regardless of whether they help pay for it. As a result, sports fans are likely to accept higher taxes or reduced public services to attract or keep a team (Noll & Zimbalist, 1997b). These fans constitute the base of political support for subsidized sports facilities.

Prospects for cutting sports subsidies are not good. Although citizen opposition has had some success, without more effective intercity organizing or more active federal antitrust policy, cities will continue to compete against each other to attract or keep artificially scarce sports franchises. Given the profound penetration and popularity of sports in American culture, it is hard to see an end to rising public subsidies of sports facilities. A great example of this is the relationship of the city of New York to its professional sports teams. Despite the current economic challenges, the city helped to subsidize the building of new stadiums for the Yankees and Mets. Current Mayor Michael Bloomberg nixed the plan of his predecessor Rudy Giuliani to spend $800 million in city funds due to the recession. However, three years later, Bloomberg's own plan, while calling on the two teams to pay for the construction of their stadiums, provided for the city to build parks, parking garages, and transit stations near the stadiums at a cost of $485 million to the city and another $201 million to the state. These totals do not also include an estimated $480 million in tax breaks to the teams; while the teams are also receiving use of city-owned land tax free (Bagli, 2008).

Facility Ownership and Management Staff

The relationship between the owner of a facility and management is critical, with efficiency and profitability determined by the purpose of the building (Farmer, Mulrooney, & Ammon, 1996). Facility ownership generally falls into three categories: community or state, which may have a "plethora of regulations and procedures in place"; colleges, where "funding is based on continued student growth, gifts, and institutional subsidies"; and private facilities, whose motive is solely for profit (Farmer, Mulrooney, & Ammon, 1996).

Responsibilities of the management staff include serving tenants' needs and providing a clean, safe, and comfortable environment for patrons. Various functions performed by the management team include security, cleanup, marketing and sales, scheduling and booking, operations, event promotions, and finance and box office operations.

Private Management Options

The growth of private management in the operation of public assembly facilities in the past decade is indicative of the pressure to achieve maximum operating results by municipal and private ownership entities. Private management offers expertise and resources not usually available to individual venue managers. Most private management companies have a network of facilities that create leverage in cultivating key event relationships, and in-turn event bookings. Additionally, these companies have dedicated corporate personnel who are available to provide oversight and assistance, which otherwise would most likely have to come from other municipal departments. Other examples of the benefits of private management include increased operating efficiencies, purchasing leverage for supplies and maintenance items, and labor negotiation resources. Some of the larger private facility management companies include Spectacor Management Group (SMG); Global Spectrum, a subsidiary of Comcast-Spectacor; Ogden Entertainment; and AEG. SMG, previously co-owned by Aramark and Hyatt Corporation, was acquired in June 2007 by American Capital, a publicly traded asset management company (Muret, 2007a).

Private management companies have also added many career options for individuals entering the venue management field. With a network of facilities, these companies may offer growth and advancement opportunities to their employees across a wide geographic area.

■ FACILITY MARKETING

Marketing

Identifying the market and the specifics of the venue are critical to successfully marketing the facility and its events. The facility manager needs to account for the location of the venue, the types of events that best fit the community and culture of the facility, and how those events will be produced. Routing shows and artists are key elements to making a new or existing venue a sustainable option for the community and owners of the facility. Concerts generally confirm dates several months out, whereas family programs like Disney On Ice, Sesame Street, Ringling Brothers, and Barnum and Bailey's Circus book annual dates. There are several reasons these two types of events book in the manner that they do. Annual events generally have a several day run and provide groups such as schools, churches, Boy and Girl Scouts, and or clubs the ability to budget for the program. Concerts many times rotate of off the release of an album, or an event that sparks public interest.

Being able to react to the market and the needs of the promoters to assist their efforts with programs coming through the area is a primary goal that can only be accomplished by conceptualizing the strengths and weaknesses of the area the venue is located in. Facility managers should take an honest and direct approach to the market identifying any limitations that may inhibit the success of the program.

The information culture that has developed as a result of the Internet explosion gives the facility manager the ability to access information much more quickly than in the past. This critical advance in technology also increases the demand for the manager to utilize his or her facility's calendar and team in the most efficient and effective manner. By using online tools such as eventbooking.com to access event calendars and dates, the manager can quickly react to inquiries for available dates and can establish a routing for a program or show by using a cell phone.

The geographic location of a facility is a critical factor in the routing of artists and acts. *Saturated markets* are markets with several venues in a close proximity to one another. When booking programs, some acts may have radius clauses preventing the same act to play a venue that may be less than 50 miles away. These types of clauses are very difficult when defining a geographic market, because state lines are often crossed and in certain circumstances communities will not travel across state lines to see a program. Markets tend to define themselves but the venues can define the market and how and what type of programs play at the venue.

Finally, the local economy will be the driving force of ticket sales and ticket price points. Promoters will need to earn a base amount to cover the artist guarantees and venue expenses depending on the way the deal is negotiated.

Promoting

Shows and events can be promoted in several different ways. The facility manager may have a series of rules or guidelines to use when negotiating a contract for an event or program for the facility. His or her task is to keep financial risks low and profit margins high. Deal structures can be negotiated between promoters and venue managers to share revenue streams and risk certain profits such as rent, facility fee, or parking. A deal structure where risk and revenue are shared is generally defined as a *co-promotional model*. Should the venue management be prohibited from taking risk in holding events, most likely he or she will operate under a rental agreement that guarantees a specified rental amount and external costs are to be covered by the promoter. Co-promotional agreements can provide a greater profit, but they also carry the risk of loss should ticket sales not be favorable. The rental is a fixed cost for the venue but relies on ancillary revenue to help increase the profit margin.

Some venues have groups associated with them that will assist with booking for the venue by helping promote in-house. University and college venues often have student-run groups that have school-allocated funds to promote in-house shows for the student body.

Generally, the majority of shows are brought to venues by professional promoters. Live nation, AEG LIVE, and Feld Entertainment are three of the largest promoters in the world. Large promoters like Feld own their products and tour them internationally or regionally. Feld's most recognizable program is Disney On Ice. The long running ice program features children's themed stories acted out by figure skaters. This successful series of entertainment allowed Feld to expand and purchase more family-oriented entertainments to tour. Feld motor sports, a division of the Feld Entertainment group, tours Monster trucks and Motocross events.

Promoters like Live Nation and AEG LIVE Events have adjusted their business model similarly. Historically the promoters have contracted with artists or agents of artists when a tour was being planned. Stars like Madonna, Jay Z, Lars Ulrich of Metallica, and Hank Williams, Jr. have signed agreements to play for promoters for a guaranteed amount. These are all-inclusive deals where merchandise, branding, and tour dates are given to the promoter for an agreed upon fee.

Non-university venues often rely on the local center for visitors bureau (CVB) to help push certain types of events. The CVB has better synergies with convention centers, but is able to work with most public facilities in order to promote the town and help create commerce.

Facility Revenues

Ticket sales offer the lion's share of revenues when promoting events. Venues can have ticket deals with ticketing agents and artists and promoters can have deals that can be tied into the facility's contract with those artists and promoters.

Strategies to provide ticketing are developing quickly and new profit centers are being realized daily. The most common of the profit center is the **ticket rebate**. The rebate is part of the surcharge that the consumer must pay

when they purchase a ticket to an event. This is an additional fee that is structured based on the ticket price and returned to the facility or venue as a result of the sale. Most ticketing contracts are awarded based on the size of the rebates and the ability or amount of points of sale available to the consumer. Ticketing to the public is more convenient now than it has ever been. Internet tickets or print-at-home tickets are frequently used, which comprise the majority of purchases.

Ticketing and event promotion can make or break a program. The promoter and the venue manager need to work together to ensure that tickets are priced reasonably. If the artist has packages for fan clubs or the venue holds a number of tickets for sponsors, these need to be accounted for prior to any tickets going on sale to the public. Certain groups mandate that fan club members get the first opportunity to buy tickets to the program. These groups are contacted by band representatives and are given codes to access a *pre-sale* prior to the ticket sale to the general public. The code grants the buyer access to different seats in the facility and price points for the tickets. When the tickets go on sale to the general public, it is possible that the capacity of the program is less than initially estimated based on the size of the fan group in that area.

When promoters are establishing ticket prices, they look at the guarantee from the artist, the venue expenses, and the capacity of the venue to find a price point for the program. Should one of these numbers be too little or too great, the promoter will need to decide how or if it makes sense to host a particular show or artist at a venue. This type of market knowledge makes the difference between venues that host successful programs and those that do not. An additional factor is the demographic that the show is playing to. As previously discussed, the audience for a family program is not necessarily same as the audience for a rock show. Ticket prices for the rock concert can be higher and the audience will have different event behavior that would affect how a facility would prepare for the show. Family events geared towards children will have lower ticket process and security costs because of the nature of the events and the manner of the event culture.

Ancillary revenue occurs from the sale of food and beverage, merchandise, parking charges, ticket fees, and sponsorships. These fees are useful to the venues not only for their obvious income, but their profit margins allow venue managers to get creative with promoters when developing their deal structures.

Markets are becoming more and more saturated with venues hosting large scale events. Facility managers are forced to constantly re-evaluate the model they are using to fill the venue. One plan of action is to allow the promoters to share in profits from the ancillary revenues. Depending on the deal structure, all or only certain revenues can be included in the mix. Promoters are incentivized to bring larger acts to an area based on the potential revenue they will earn. Ticket sales are the first attempt at making a show profitable, but promoters have realized that opportunities exist beyond the standard ticket price. The bond fee or facility fee can be increased and rebated back to the promoter, or there can be a ticket rebate to the promoter based on the venue contract deal. Companies like Ticketmaster, New Era, Eventim, and Ticket Pro all return a percentage based on the ticket price back to the facility as part of the program. Venues are incentivized to sell tickets because of the added fees that will return to the bottom line.

In the case of in-house promotion, some of the catering companies have joined forces with the venues to set aside a marketing fund. This **marketing fund** is a pool of money that is set aside from the profits of other shows. The concessionaire and the venue director each agree to

a certain share of the percentage of sold goods, and they use the pool to help invest in future programs. The investment by both parties allows each to earn more money in the future.

One of the largest revenue drivers in venues today is the sale of alcohol. Alcohol sales are effective drivers of sponsorship dollars as well as being very popular at sporting and entertainment events. Alcohol sales have brought about changes in the venue's structure, which include sponsored areas such as suites as well as renovations for sports themed bars and pubs. Alcohol and the culture that goes with selling it do open more liability to the concessionaire, but experienced and trained venue operators should be well aware of the dangers that present themselves as well as prepare for the artists and acts that may be more high risk oriented.

Sponsorship is also an important part of the equation. The application of trade for services is always a bonus, but cash is always the preferred medium. Sponsorship needs to be approved by the promoter and act prior to its sale, but is a sure-fired means of revenue and event generation. When applied correctly, the revenue can be the deciding factor between a break even and a loss.

When looking at a calendar, a facility manager should always be trying to fill nonevent days with some type of function. Events that break even are still good events to hold.

■ CAREER OPPORTUNITIES

College graduates seeking career opportunities in the facility management industry will be pleasantly surprised at the wide variety of options available in arenas, convention centers, stadiums, and performing arts centers. The career opportunity areas in facility management are shown in **Table 12–2** and discussed in the sections that follow.

TABLE 12-2 Career Opportunity Areas in Facility Management
Marketing
Public relations/Communications
Event management
Booking
Operations
Advertising, signage, and sponsorship sales
Group ticket sales
Box office

Marketing Director

Being the **marketing director** for an arena, performing arts center, or other venue is one of the more exciting careers in facility management. It is a fast-paced, highly stressful, enormously challenging career track that can lead a successful individual all the way to the executive suite.

Facility marketing directors act primarily as in-house advertising agents for the various events booked into facilities. Buying media (e.g., TV, radio, print, billboards), coordinating promotions, and designing marketing materials (e.g., TV commercials, brochures, flyers, newspaper advertisements) are some of a marketing director's primary responsibilities. A typical day in the life of a facility marketing director may include creating a marketing plan and ad budget for Sesame Street Live, meeting with radio and TV sales staff to discuss cross promotions with McDonald's for the Harlem Globetrotters, and designing a print ad for Sunday's newspaper.

The more successful marketing directors are multiskilled performers who possess excellent people skills, sales ability, and written and oral communication skills. Most important, a successful marketing director possesses an almost uncanny ability to consistently earn profits for facilities or promoters. The quickest way to become a facility general manager or executive director is to showcase the talents and skills it takes to improve the bottom line. Moneymakers are few and far between, so proven producers will get noticed—and promoted.

Public Relations/Communications Director

A good **public relations (PR) or communications director** is essential for facilities as they deal with the media on a wide variety of issues. A talented PR or communications director can "spin" the news, good or bad, and position a facility in the best possible light. This is a very important skill to have when the media are banging on the door wanting to know why the arena's $2 million scoreboard just came crashing down on the ice, why attendance is down 20%, or why the box office is missing $25,000 and the director has just left for a long trip to Mexico.

One of the primary goals for a facility's PR department is to forge solid working relationships with TV and radio news directors, newspaper editors, and reporters so that when bad news hits, the media report a balanced story. Good rapport with local media helps a great deal when seeking publicity for positive stories, and at times it can mean the difference between receiving front-page coverage or being buried next to the obituaries.

A typical day in the life of a facility PR director may include coordinating a live TV broadcast from the arena with the local sports anchor to publicize that evening's basketball game, writing a press release announcing that tickets are going on sale that weekend for a Keith Urban concert, and arranging a publicity stunt for Bert and Ernie to visit the local children's hospital while they are in town for an upcoming Sesame Street Live tour. The most important attributes of a good PR director are a strong writing ability, a creative mind, and an ability to respond rationally while under pressure. Excellent training grounds for facility

PR people are college and daily newspapers, TV stations, and internships in corporate PR departments.

Event Director

Events are the lifeblood for all types of facilities. Hundreds of events may be booked at a facility in the course of a year. With thousands of people in the venue at any given time, it is imperative that there be excellent crowd control and exceptional customer service provided at all times. The **event director** acts as the point person for the facility during each show. Supervising a full staff of ushers, police officers, firefighters, emergency medical technicians, and private concert security forces, the event director manages the show from start to finish.

The event director must be able to think and react quickly to any problems arising during the event and must be able to deal with show promoters, angry customers, lost children, intoxicated patrons, and other situations calmly but forcefully. He or she must handle all this pressure while thousands of guests are in their seats enjoying the show. Being in charge of the safety and satisfaction of so many people is an immense responsibility, and for this reason the event director's position is not for everyone.

A typical day in the life of an event director might begin as early as 8:00 AM, with six tractor-trailer trucks pulling up to the facility to begin the load-in for a major concert. The event director supervises and schedules traffic, parking, and security personnel to help ensure that the concert load-in runs as smoothly as possible. Later that day, he or she meets with the band road manager and reviews all security requirements for that evening's show. As the concert time draws near, the event director will meet with all ushers, police, and private security staff, giving instructions on how to handle that evening's event. During the concert, he or she will likely deal with customers, emergency situations, intoxicated patrons, and perhaps an altercation or two. By the end of the night, he or she will have been at the facility for 18 long hours.

Booking Director

Events in smaller facilities are booked by the general manager or executive director. In larger venues, however, there is usually a separate position devoted to booking events. This person works in tandem with the general manager or executive director to land as many events as possible. This is an exciting career path involving much time spent talking on the telephone to agents and promoters and attending conventions to solicit events.

A facility **booking director** can land events in several different ways. Most concerts and Broadway shows are booked by dealing directly with agents who represent the acts or by negotiating with promoters who rent the facility and deal directly with agents on their own. The booking director may choose to rent the facility to a promoter, to co-promote an event, or to purchase the show directly from an agent. There are advantages and disadvantages associated with all three methods. Renting the facility to a promoter is a risk-free way to increase the number of events; however, it limits the amount of income a building may receive from an event. For some events with limited income potential or risky track records (e.g., conventions, trade shows), this method is the smartest way to do business. For potentially highly lucrative events (e.g., concerts, family shows, Broadway shows), partnering with a promoter in a share of the profits or purchasing the event directly from an agent may be the more profitable strategy— albeit also the one with the greatest risk to lose money if the show is not successful.

A typical day in the life of a booking director might begin at 8:00 AM with telephone calls to local radio program directors gauging the current popularity of a specific concert act. At 10:00 AM the constant phone calls back and forth with Broadway agents in New York begin as the booking director tries to fill up next year's Broadway lineup for the performing arts center. Lunch with a local concert promoter cutting a rental deal for an upcoming show will be followed by telephone tag the rest of the day with other agents and promoters. Negotiating contracts and getting them out in the mail completes a typical facility booking director's day.

Operations Director

Facility operations departments are the heart and soul of this industry. The **operations director** supervises facility preparation for all types of events. He or she typically spends the lion's share of a facility's annual expense budget on labor, maintaining and repairing all equipment, and purchasing all necessary supplies (e.g., toilet paper, cleaning materials) that the events require on a weekly basis.

Perhaps the most important part of an operations director's job is coordinating, scheduling, and supervising the numerous change-overs that take place each year as one show moves in and another moves out. An operations director faces logistical problems daily because the facil-

ity may change over from hockey to basketball, then to a concert, and then to a Broadway show, all in one week. The job requires a mechanical knowledge of a facility's inner workings. A good operations director must be an expert on heating, ventilation, and air conditioning equipment, ice making, and structural issues such as how many pounds of pressure can be rigged to the roof without it collapsing. An operations director must also possess superior people skills, because he or she is directly in charge of the majority of the facility's staff, including foremen, mechanics, laborers, stagehands, and the 50 to 200 part-time workers required to set up events and clean up after them.

A typical day in the life of an operations director likely begins early in the morning with a check of the previous night's changeover from basketball to hockey. Inspecting the overnight cleanup and the temperature and condition of the ice surface and discussing any problems with assistants will keep the operations director busy most of the morning. Then it will be time to plan ahead for next week when the circus rolls into town with 30 elephants, 14 tigers, and other assorted animals and equipment. The circus will take over the entire facility and two square blocks in the downtown business district for six days. Meetings with circus managers and city officials to plan for the event, as well as scheduling, will complete the day for the person with his or her hand constantly on the pulse of the facility operation.

Advertising, Sponsorship, and Signage Salesperson

Advertising and sponsorship revenue represent a significant total of a facility's annual revenue. Most facilities, depending on size, designate a staff person or an entire department to sell signage and event sponsorships to corporations. College graduates who perform well in high-pressure sales environments can make a substantial amount of money selling signage and sponsorships. This area offers good entry-level positions. Most facilities hire sales staff on a commission-only basis. Commissions can range from 5% to 20% depending on the size of the deal.

Salespeople must possess excellent interpersonal and presentation skills. They also must be able to handle plenty of rejection on a daily basis. For every 100 telephone calls a salesperson makes to corporations, an average of only 5 or 10 will result in actual business. Sales are a numbers game, and only strong, thick-skinned personalities are successful in such an environment. Successful salespeople generate money for themselves and the facility—and that will be noticed at the executive level. It is common for good salespeople to ultimately end up in the general manager's or executive director's chair.

A typical day in the life of an aggressive signage and sponsorship salesperson will include at least 25 cold calls to corporate decision-makers, two to four face-to-face sales presentations, and plenty of writing. A good salesperson must have strong writing skills because he or she must create outstanding sales proposals, follow up meetings with thank you letters, and draft contracts once deals have been finalized.

Group Ticket Salesperson

Many college graduates begin their facility management careers in the group sales department. Entry-level opportunities are numerous because there is a fairly high turnover rate. Group salespeople are primarily responsible for selling large blocks of tickets for various events to corporations, charity organizations, schools, Boy Scout and Girl Scout troops, and other parties. Group sales for certain types of shows (e.g., Sesame Street Live, Disney On Ice, the Ringling Brothers and Barnum & Bailey Circus, the Harlem Globetrotters, professional sport teams) contribute significantly to an event's success. Similar

to the successful signage and sponsorship staff person, a good group salesperson is tenacious and excels on the telephone and in face-to-face presentations. Usually paid on a commission basis (typically 10% to 15%), group sales is also a numbers game. However, renewal business is usually strong, and solid personal relationships with key decision-makers at area corporations and other organizations can result in excellent sales year after year. A good group salesperson is an important asset to a facility.

Box Office Director

This facility position is responsible for the sale of all tickets to events as well as the collection of all ticket revenue. The facility box office is typically the first impression patrons have of the venue, making good customer service critical. The **box office director** must be a patient, understanding individual with a great mind for numbers. He or she must also have good supervisory skills. Within most venues the box office is usually the second largest department, after operations. Made up of a combination of full- and part-time help, the box office personnel must be completely trustworthy because millions of dollars and thousands of credit card numbers flow through the department each year.

A typical day for a box office director begins at 9:00 AM. On any given day, event tickets may be going on sale, and the telephones and lobby windows are generally extremely busy. Meetings with promoters to set up scaling of shows and filling ticket orders for advertisers and very important persons (VIPs) takes up a good portion of the day. Scheduling staff for all of the shows and daytime hours is also a time-consuming job. The box office director will be in his or her office for most of the day, but the real work begins when the event starts.

Dealing with customers who have lost their tickets, are unhappy with their seats, or have other concerns will occupy the box office director's time during the event. The box office will usually close halfway through the event so the staff can begin their paperwork. Counting all the money, preparing settlement documents for the promoter's review, and other tasks take up the rest of the evening. By the time all is said and done, the box office director will have worked 12 to 18 hours.

■ CURRENT ISSUES

Security

The area of security was propelled to the highest level of importance of facility management after the terrorist attacks of September 11, 2001. Bag checks, pat downs, and metal detectors are now used as normal, regular functions in day-to-day operations. Large arenas and stadiums have placed barricades, posts, and fencing around the perimeters of facilities to create a "moat" effect to keep potential threats and terrorist activities away from crowds and buildings. Special attention is being given to the U.S. Homeland Security system of rating possible threats and to facility managers implementing procedures to safeguard both patrons during events and the facility itself. Facility managers must evaluate every event for its security risk, taking into account its performer and crowd attendance profiles as well as its anticipated media coverage. Recently, the National Center for Spectator Sports Safety and Security has put forth a tripartite approach to stadium and arena security. The formula involves video security surveillance combined with personnel training and implementing processes that balance safety with creating a positive experience for fans. This strategic stadium security plan protects stadiums and arenas from attack while providing a fan-friendly experience (Titch, 2010).

The best management tool for crowd management is a **crowd management plan**. This plan encompasses categorizing the type of event; knowing the surrounding facilities and environment, team or school rivalries, threats of violence, and the crowd size and seating configuration; using security personnel and ushers; and having an emergency plan.

In November 2004, an on-court fight during a Detroit Pistons–Indianapolis Pacers NBA game ended up spilling into the stands, involving members of the attending crowd as well. In response, NBA Commissioner David Stern stated that the NBA would set new security guidelines for its arenas, an area previously left to individual teams to control ("League to set," 2004). Shortly thereafter, the NBA issued to all teams Arena Guidelines that included policies dealing with the deployment of security personnel, alcohol sales, and a new Fan Code of Conduct (NBA, 2005). The NCAA has also gotten involved with this issue by publishing a Crowd Control Global Check List/Tool Kit that institutions can use when they plan for and put in place crowd control policies (National Collegiate Athletic Association, 2006). Despite the NCAA's tool kit, worries abound as to whether colleges and universities are prepared in the event of an attack at one of its facilities. Because more than 48 million spectators attend NCAA football in a given season, the issue is one that needs to be addressed to create risk management plans, training, and emergency services (Associated Press, 2007).

Sustainability

Public facilities, such as convention centers, stadiums, and arenas, consume more energy per square foot than any other retail industry (Jackson, 2008). As a result, the facility management industry is working to build green buildings, create "green management teams," reduce waste, cut energy usage and pollution, and implement recycling program (Jenkins, 2007; Jackson, 2008). For facilities, it not only makes good environmental sense, it also makes good business sense. In the words of Scott Jenkins, Vice President of Ballpark Operations at SAFECO Field, the Seattle Mariners stadium, "[g]oing green makes good financial sense in that it reduces operating expenses and builds a socially responsible brand. Besides, consumers and government are starting to demand that we operate in environmentally responsible ways" (Jenkins, 2007). Further, Jenkins shared the savings of $250,000 by reducing the stadium's natural gas bill by 36% and electric bill by 18% simply through paying attention to how the ballpark was operated and the investment of water controls—a $6,200 cost (Jenkins, 2007).

Americans with Disabilities Act

On July 26, 1990, President George H. W. Bush signed into law the **Americans with Disabilities Act (ADA)**. The intent of the ADA is to prevent discrimination against qualified people with disabilities in employment, public services, transportation, public accommodations, and telecommunications services. The ADA defines an "individual with a disability" as a person who has a physical or mental impairment that substantially limits one or more major life activities, who has a record of such an impairment, or who is regarded as having such an impairment. The ADA law requires new facilities to be accessible to people with disabilities so they can enjoy equal access to entertainment and leisure (Department of Justice, 1997).

A common misconception regarding the ADA and renovations is that if a facility renovates, the whole facility must be brought into compliance (Huggins, 1997). However, the ADA only requires that when a facility is renovated, the renovations must comply with the Act. In addition, if a primary function area is renovated, 20% of the total cost must be spent to improve access for those with disabilities

(Huggins, 1997). Finally, for facilities not being renovated, the ADA guidelines encourage the facilities to implement "readily achievable barrier removal," such as lowering paper towel dispensers, replacing steps with curb cuts or ramps, and installing grab bars in the restrooms (Huggins, 1997).

A key accessibility requirement is seating. Under the ADA, at least 1% of seating must be wheelchair accessible, a companion seat must be provided next to each wheelchair seat, and whenever more than 300 seats are provided, wheelchair seating must be dispersed throughout all seating areas and price ranges (Department of Justice, 1997). In addition, wheelchair seating must be on an accessible route from parking areas to public areas (e.g., restrooms, concessions) and to stage, performing, and playing areas.

Finally, wheelchair seating locations must provide sightlines comparable to those provided to spectators without disabilities (Department of Justice, 1997). In October 1996, the Justice Department filed a lawsuit against Ellerbe Becket, a facility architectural firm, charging that it had designed several well-known sport stadiums and arenas improperly. These facilities did not provide wheelchair users with lines of sight over standing spectators. In 1998, this lawsuit was settled, with Ellerbe Becket agreeing to provide all wheelchair users with comparable lines of sight including lines of sight over standing spectators (Department of Justice, 1998).

Other accessible features include concession areas, public telephones, restrooms, parking areas, drop-off and pick-up areas, entrances and exits, water coolers, visual alarms, and signs. Assisted listening systems must also be provided when audible communications are integral to the use of the facility.

The law requires that a facility adapt, but only to the extent that the reasonable accommodation does not cause an undue burden on the facility. A good example of this was the case of *Cortez v. NBA*, in which a group of disabled fans sought to have the San Antonio Spurs provide live-time captioning at games. To provide live-time captioning, the Spurs would have had to provide a court reporter typing all that was announced in the arena onto the scoreboard. Because the Spurs' scoreboard did not provide the technology for such captioning, providing an interpreter for fans was selected as a fair alternative (Department of Justice, 1997).

Cutting-Edge Facilities

A Marquette National Sports Law Institute study estimates that $4 billion was spent in 2009 and it predicts that it is not likely to approach that level in the near future (National

CASE STUDY: The Booking Process in a University Venue

The Mullins center is a 10,000 seat multipurpose facility with an attached ice rink located on the campus of the University of Massachusetts in Amherst, Massachusetts. The Mullins Center is managed for the University of Massachusetts by Global Spectrum. As part of the management contract, the general manager for the Mullins Center is responsible for the booking of the main facility and the attached practice rink. The Mullins Center has three tenant teams: the university's men's hockey, women's basketball, and men's basketball.

The campus and surrounding five college area have up to 30,000 students from September to May. During that time frame the Mullins Center is busy hosting athletic events and entertainment programs. In order to be successful, the general manager utilizes several different setups and capacities in order to provide the university and the community with entertaining programs. Concert seating capacities are set at a 7,200, 8,500, or 9,000 seat capacity. Comedy or theater programs are set at a 1,700, to 3,500 seat capacity. Basketball events are set at a 9,400 seat capacity. Hockey or ice show events are 8,400 seat capacity. Using this information and topics discussed in the chapter, please answer the following questions.

Questions for Discussion

1. Acting as the general manager of the Mullins center, please identify a specific genre of entertainment you believe would do well in the venue, taking into account the demographic, time frame, and seating capacity in the various setups.
2. Identify a group, act, team, or entertainer that will be touring with available dates to play the Mullins Center and specify who will be acting as the promoter for the event.
3. Concerning the event promotion, assume that the act will cost $75,000.00 and the venue will be rented for an all inclusive package of $35,000.00. Provide ticket prices that will appeal to the target demographic market in a spreadsheet that reflects the total costs and the balance according to estimated ticket sales.
4. Explain the impact of ancillary revenue on the event, including the potential role food and beverage, ticket fees, and parking play when negotiating a deal with a promoter.
5. Provide an event recap with reasoning why or why not you booked this event at the Mullins Center and why it was successful or unsuccessful.

Sports Law Institute, 2009). Much of this new and renovation construction has been fueled by efforts to explore and provide new revenue sources for facilities as well as modernize the facility. The University of Phoenix Stadium in Glendale, Arizona, opened in 2006 with features including a retractable roof, the first full-retractable natural-grass playing surface, and an Alltel Wireless antenna built into the structure providing wireless network access from every seat (University of Phoenix Stadium, n.d.). The new Yankee Stadium, opened for the 2009 season, has 60 luxury suites, including three outdoor suites and eight party suites, and also has many restaurants and entertainment areas (The New York Yankees, 2007). As evidence of today's environmentally conscious society, the D.C. Sport and Entertainment Commission received a grant of $101,670 from the Chesapeake Bay Foundation, an environmental nonprofit organization, to cover the cost to plant grass and other plant life on top of a waterproof surface above a concession stand in left field of the new Washington Nationals' ballpark (Muret, 2007b).

■ SUMMARY

Public assembly facilities provide a site for people to congregate for entertainment, social, and business purposes. The many types of facilities range from stadiums and arenas to convention centers and theaters. The key challenges facing facilities involve financing new facilities or renovations, retaining the revenue generated by the facility, preparing fully integrated security programs, retaining tenants, and addressing the ADA. Facility management provides a career field that is fast-paced and exciting, though filled with long hours and, at times, pressure and stress.

■ RESOURCES

AEG Corporate Headquarters
800 West Olympic Blvd.
Suite 400
Los Angeles, CA 90015
213-742-7100
http://www.aegworldwide.com

ARAMARK Corporation
1101 Market Street
Philadelphia, PA 19107
215-238-3000
http://www.aramark.com

European Association of Event Centers (EVVC)
Ludwigstrasse 3
D-61348 Bad Homburg v.d.H.
Germany
49(0)61-72-27-96-900
http://www.evvc.org

Global Spectrum
3601 S. Broad Street
Philadelphia, PA 19148
215-389-9587
http://www.global-spectrum.com

International Association of Assembly Managers (IAAM)
635 Fritz Drive
Suite 100
Coppell, Texas 75019
972-906-7441
http://www.iaam.org

International Association of Congress Centres (AIPC)
55 Rue de l'Amazone
1060 Brussels, Belgium
[32](496) 235327
http://www.aipc.org

SMG
300 Conshohocken State Rd Ste 770
West Conshohocken, PA 19428
(610) 729-7900
http://www.smgworld.com

Stadium Managers Association
525 SW 5th Street, Suite A
Des Moines, IA 50309-4501
515-282-8192
sma@assoc-mgmt.com

Venue Management Association Limited
P.O. Box 1871
Toowong Queensland 4066
Australia
61-0-7-3870-4777
http://www.vma.org.au

■ KEY TERMS

Americans with Disabilities Act (ADA), ancillary revenue, arenas, bonds, booking director, box office director, concerts, convention centers, convocations, crowd management plan, event director, family events, International Association of Auditorium Managers (IAAM), local/civic venues, marketing director, marketing fund, metropolitan facilities, operations director, public relations (PR) or communications director, religious events, seasonal events, soccer-specific stadium, sports events, stadium, theaters, ticket rebate, trade shows, university venues

■ REFERENCES

Associated Press. (2007, December 26). Stadium security a concern at colleges. *New York Times.* Retrieved November 1, 2010, from http://www.nytimes.com/2007/12/26/sports/ncaafootball/26stadiums.html

Baade, R. B., & Sanderson, A. R. (1997). The employment effect of teams and sports facilities. In R. G. Noll and A. Zimbalist (Eds.), *Sports, jobs, and taxes: The economic impact of sports teams and stadiums* (pp. 92–118). Washington, DC: Brookings Institution Press.

Bagli, C. (2008, November 4). As stadiums rise, so do costs to taxpayers. New *York Times.* Retrieved November 1, 2010, from http://www.nytimes.com/2008/11/05/nyregion/05stadiums.html?_r=1

Danielson, M.N. (1997). *Home team: Professional sports and the American metropolis.* Princeton, NJ: Princeton University Press.

Department of Justice, Civil Rights Division, Disability Rights Section. (1997). Accessible stadiums. Retrieved November 1, 2010, from http://www.ada.gov/stadium.txt

Department of Justice. (1998, April 27). Justice Department reaches settlement with architect of new sports arenas. Retrieved November 1, 2010, from http://www.usdoj.gov/opa/pr/1998/April/200.htm.html

Farmer, P., Mulrooney, A., & Ammon, R. Jr. (1996). *Sport facility planning and management.* Morgantown, WV: Fitness Information Technology.

Greenberg, M. J., & Gray, J. T. (1993, April/May). The stadium game. *For the Record,* 2–3.

Hamilton, B. W., & Kahn, P. (1997). Baltimore's Camden Yards ballparks. In R. G. Noll and A. Zimbalist (Eds.), *Sports, jobs, and taxes: The economic impact of sports teams and stadiums* (pp. 245–281). Washington, DC: Brookings Institution Press.

Howard, D. R., & Crompton, J. L. (1995). *Financing sport.* Morgantown, WV: Fitness Information Technology.

Huggins, S. (1997, Spring). Sports facilities and the Americans with Disabilities Act. *The Sports Lawyer, 2,* 9–11.

Jackson, A. (2008, February-March). Sustainability baby steps. *Facility manager.* Retrieved November 1, 2010, from https://www.iaam.org/Facility_manager/Pages/2008_Feb_Mar/BusinessFinance.htm

Jenkins, S. (2007, December-January). Going green makes good business. *Facility manager.* Retrieved November 1, 2010, from https://www.iaam.org/Facility_manager/Pages/2007_Dec_Jan/Stadiums.HTM

League to set new security guidelines. (2004, December 1). *Indystar.com.* Retrieved from http://www2.indystar.com/articles/3/198833-9753-245.html

Mahony, D. (1997). Facility funding. Reading packet provided to SPAD 390, Current Trends and Issues in Sport Administration, undergraduate course, The University of Louisville KY.

Muret, D. (2007a, May 28). Reports: American Capital buys SMG. *Street & Smith's SportsBusiness Journal*, p. 3.

Muret, D. (2007b, June 25). Green design taking root in the roof at Nationals ballpark. *Street & Smith's SportsBusiness Journal*, p. 14.

National Collegiate Athletic Association. (2006, June 8). Crowd control global check list/tool kit. Retrieved from http://www.ncaa.org/sportsmanship/crowd_control_checklist.pdf

National Sports Law Institute (2009). An analysis of sports facility costs and development from 1989–2009. Retrieved November 22, 2010, from http://law.marquette.edu/s3/site/images/sports/v10-sports-facility-costs.pdf

NBA. (2005, February 17). NBA establishes revised arena guidelines for all NBA arenas. Retrieved November 1, 2010, from http://www.nba.com/news/arena_guidelines_050217.html

NCAA (2010). NIT history. Retrieved November 1, 2010, from http://www.ncaa.com/sports/m-baskbl/champpage/inc/div1/m-baskbl-nit-history.html

Noll, R. G., & Zimbalist, A. (1997a). "Build the stadium—Create the jobs!" In R. G. Noll and A. Zimbalist (Eds.), *Sports, jobs, and taxes: The economic impact of sports teams and stadiums* (pp. 1–54). Washington, DC: Brookings Institution Press.

Noll, R. G., & Zimbalist, A. (1997b). The economic impact of sports teams and facilities. In R. G. Noll and A. Zimbalist (Eds.), *Sports, jobs, and taxes: The economic impact of sports teams and stadiums* (pp. 55–91). Washington, DC: Brookings Institution Press.

Quirk, J., & Fort, R. D. (1992). *Pay dirt*. Princeton, NJ: Princeton University Press.

The New York Yankees. The New Yankee Stadium. (2007). Retrieved November 1, 2010, from http://newyork.yankees.mlb.com/nyy/ballpark/new_stadium.jsp

Titch, S. (2010, October 8). Convergence adds new dimension to stadium security. *Security squared*. Retrieved November 1, 2010, from http://www.experteditorial.net/securitysquared/2010/10/convergence-adds-new-dimension-to-stadium-security.html

Tully, M., Fritze, J., and Corcoran, K. (2004, December 20). Indy, Colts agree on $500 million stadium. *Indystar.com*. Retrieved November 1, 2010, from http://www2.indystar.com/articles/5/203557-4955-196.html

University of Phoenix Stadium. (n.d.). Retrieved November 1, 2010, from http://www.universityofphoenixstadium.com/index.php?page=stadium_facts&section=history

CHAPTER 13

Event Management

James M. Gladden, Mark A. McDonald, and Carol A. Barr

■ INTRODUCTION

A local Young Men's Christian Association (YMCA) basketball game, the State Junior Golf Championship, and the Super Bowl are all examples of events that are managed. They all also share one common element: the need for educated and trained managers and marketers to ensure success. Further, the critical event management functions are quite similar, whether the event is small (i.e., a local 5K road race) or large (Major League Baseball's All-Star Game). For the purposes of this chapter, we define sport event management as all functions related to the planning, implementation, and evaluation of a sport event.

This chapter presents an overview of the event management segment of the sport industry. First, the historical evolution of event management is discussed. Then, because many large and small events are managed and marketed

by sport management/marketing agencies, the types and roles played by these unique sport organizations are explored. Successful event management requires the appropriate application of all the management functions, so this chapter reviews finance/budgeting, risk management, tournament operations, registration, volunteer management, and event marketing within the context of event management. The next-to-last section explores career opportunities in event management, including information on educational backgrounds appropriate for those in sport event management. Finally, current issues surrounding the management of events are discussed.

■ HISTORY

Although there was probably a need for management involved with the earliest documented sport event, it was not until the late 1800s that the focus turned to the professional aspects of managing sport events. A desire to increase profits was the catalyst for such an emphasis. Following his retirement as a professional baseball player in the 1870s, Albert Spalding organized tours throughout North America to promote baseball to create a larger market for his products. Spalding's tours were an early example of what were called **barnstorming tours**. The touring of star athletes and teams to promote the popularity of a particular sport soon became exercises in event management. George Halas, longtime owner of the Chicago Bears, used his star player, Red Grange, to increase the popularity of professional football in the early 1900s (Schaaf, 1995). Professional boxing also provided a platform for professional event management. With the stakes of boxing events reaching more than $1 million by the turn of the twentieth century, boxing event promoters were forced to attend to the business aspects of managing such events.

Just as the need for a business focus prompted the creation of the sport management discipline, so too profit motives spurred the creation of professional event managers in the 1960s and 1970s. The growth of sport event management led to the emergence of multifaceted companies called **sport management/marketing agencies**. A sport management/marketing agency is defined as a business that acts on behalf of a sport property. A **sport property** can be a person, company, event, team, or place. Sport management/marketing agencies were initially established to represent the legal and marketing interests of athletes. International Management Group (now known as IMG), for example, was founded in 1960 by Mark McCormack to locate endorsement opportunities for professional golfer Arnold Palmer (for more information on the athlete representation side to these sport management/marketing agencies please see Chapter 11, Sports Agency). As the sport

industry evolved, agencies expanded to incorporate a myriad of functions beyond representing athletes. For example, as IMG signed more athletes as clients, its business soon expanded to include managing and promoting events in which its athletes competed. Agencies capitalized on the concurrent growth of and public's interest in televised sporting events to rapidly increase the revenues generated through events of all sizes. Agencies also started to create their own made-for-TV events (content creation) that they both owned and managed. Today, there are hundreds of sport management/marketing agencies, which are intricately involved with the creation and promotion of most events. A number of these agencies have also expanded beyond sporting events to other entertainment or charitable types of events, such as IMG has done with its entertainment division. The sport event management industry has also evolved with its very own industry conference. The 5th International Sports Event Management Conference took place in London, United Kingdom, bringing together sport industry professionals, international and national federations, and representatives of local and national governments who are involved in the planning and delivery of sports events (5th International Sports Event Management Conference, 2010). A list of sports agencies identified by the various services these agencies perform can be found in **Table 13-1**.

■ SPORT MANAGEMENT/MARKETING AGENCY FUNCTIONS

Table 13-2 provides a list of the various roles sport management/marketing agencies play. It should be noted that although some agencies perform all of the functions on this list, many of these sport agencies may specialize in only one or a few of these functions. The first function listed in Table 13-2, client representation, refers to acting on behalf of a client in contract negotia-

TABLE 13-1	Sport Management/Marketing Agencies		
Corporate Consulting, Marketing, and Client Services	**Sports Event Marketing Firms**	**Talent Representation and Management**	**Property Consulting, Sales, and Client Services**
Genesco Sports Enterprises	BeCore Promotions	IMG	IMG
GMR Marketing	SportsMark	Octagon	Leverage Agency
IMG	Vivid Marketing	Wasserman Media Group	Premier Partnerships
Momentum Worldwide			Van Wagner Sports & Entertainment
Octagon			Wasserman Media Group

Source: Sports Business Awards. (2010, May 17–23). *Street & Smith's SportsBusiness Journal*, pp. 3A–38A.

tions. Contract negotiations can take place with any type of sport property, such as a franchise, an event, the media, or a licensee. Detailed information regarding this agency function is included in Chapter 11, Sports Agency. The function of client marketing is closely related to client representation. Marketing includes locating appropriate endorsement opportunities, booking personal appearances, and developing entertainment extensions. For example, Michael Jordan earned $90 million in total salary dur-

TABLE 13-2 Sport Management/Marketing Agencies' Roles

Client representation
Client marketing
Event development
Event management
Television production
Sponsorship solicitation
Hospitality services
Grassroots programs
Market research
Financial planning

ing his National Basketball Association (NBA) career with the Chicago Bulls and Washington Wizards, but in comparison he brought in $750 million from sponsorship endorsement deals. Current golfer Tiger Woods pulls in more than $70 million annually from off-the-course endorsements, appearance fees and his golf course design business (Badenhausen, 2010).

In addition to representing the interests of individuals, agencies are involved in event development and management. Given the increased number of outlets for events, such as satellite and digital television and the Internet, a variety of events have been created to provide programming. The X Games (summer and winter), for example, are a direct result of the growth in sports television. ESPN created the X Games to provide programming and elects to manage the two X Games in-house. (The term *in-house* refers to producing a product or service within the organization.) Alliance of Action Sports (Alli) is an organization that "brings together the best sports properties, athletes, and brands globally for the fans of action sports" and is involved in properties including the Dew Tour, the Winter Dew Tour, the China Invitational, the Maloof

Money Cup, AMA Motocross, The King of Wake, and the Free Flow Tour (Alli, 2010).

While one result of the growth in televised sports has been the creation of new events, another impact has been increasing demand for television production and development work. Potential revenue streams from television have led to the creation of television production divisions within some of the larger agencies. For example, IMG Media is the world's largest independent producer and distributor of sports programming (IMG, 2010a). IMG distributes more than 300 events and thousands of hours of live and finished programming each year including among its many clients the All England Lawn Tennis Club (Wimbledon), The European

Tour, The English Premier League, and The Royal and Ancient Golf Club of St. Andrews (IMG, 2010b).

Soliciting corporate sponsorships is a role the majority of sport agencies play. With corporations spending $16.51 billion in 2009 (IEG, 2010), a viable market has been created for organizations skilled in identifying and acquiring sponsors. Likewise, corporations often hire sport management/marketing agencies to locate and negotiate sponsorship agreements with teams and events whose fans match their target markets. In each of these cases, the sport agency is paid a set percentage of the sponsorship fee. It should be noted, though, that the economic recession caused the dollar amount being spent on sponsorship to decrease in 2009 for the first time (more information on the impact of the economic recession on sport sponsorship activities can be found in the Current Issues section of this chapter). To facilitate matching corporations with sport properties, Team Marketing Report annually publishes the *Sports Sponsor FactBook*. This publication lists and provides detailed information on the activities of sport sponsors, advertisers, facility naming rights, and promotional sponsors (Team Marketing Report, 2010).

Another function of sport management/ marketing agencies is to develop and market **grassroots programs**. These programs are created by organizations attempting to target individuals at the most basic level of involvement, sport participation. A number of professional sport leagues are involved in grassroots programming including the National Football League (NFL) Punt, Pass, & Kick national skills competition; the NFL Flag Football league (NFL, 2010); the Urban Youth Academy program of Major League Baseball (MLB) (MLB, 2010); the NHL endorsement of the North American Roller Hockey Championships (NARCh) (NARCh, 2010); and NBA youth basketball programs through the

NBA Fit initiative such as the Dribble, Dish & Swish competition (NBA, 2010).

One of the most successful grassroots sport event management companies is Team Championships International (TCI), which supports participatory sports tours in cities across the country. TCI manages events in 60 different markets across the country through its Kick-It 3v3 Soccer Shootout, Hoop It Up 3on3 Basketball tour, Let It Fly 4on4 Flag Football tour, and Rock the Shoot 5v5 National Lacrosse Tour (Team Championships International, 2010).

Sport organizations require market research to evaluate the success of events and initiatives. By implementing mail surveys, focus groups, on-site surveys, and sponsorship/economic impact surveys, sport management/marketing agencies assist sport properties in documenting the relative success or failure of programs and pinpointing areas needing improvement. Market research is particularly crucial for corporations wanting to know the impact of their sponsorship activities. This function is usually handled by sport marketing agencies that specialize in market research. For example, IFM Sports Marketing Surveys provides sport market research to clients including sponsorship evaluations, economic impact studies, return on investment modeling, retail and consumer behavior, and attitude surveys among others (Sports Marketing Surveys, 2010).

■ TYPES OF SPORT MANAGEMENT/ MARKETING AGENCIES

Sport management/marketing agencies vary widely in terms of numbers of employees, revenue generation, scope of services provided, and types of target clients. Sport agencies can be categorized as full-service agencies, specialized agencies, or in-house agencies. These types of agencies are briefly described in this section.

(For more detailed information, see Chapter 11, Sports Agency.)

Full-Service Agencies

Full-service agencies perform the complete set of agency functions discussed in the previous section. Although a number of firms fall into this category, the largest are IMG and Octagon. IMG, for example, has 60 offices with nearly 3,000 employees in 30 countries throughout the world (IMG, 2010a). With operating divisions for athlete management services, event management services, licensing, broadcasting (both production and negotiation), Internet consulting, and marketing and consulting services, this

firm covers the entire gamut of sport event and athlete functions. IMG's clients include athletes such as Maria Sharapova (tennis), Tiger Woods (golf), and Danica Patrick (motorsports). Octagon, by contrast, has more than 800 employees globally, works with more than 800 athletes and personality clients, and manages more than 5,000 events per year (Octagon, 2010).

Specialized Agencies

Specialized agencies limit either the scope of services performed or the type of clients serviced. For example, Redmandarin is a London-based sport marketing agency that focuses exclusively on advising corporations on how to maximize their involvement with sponsorship opportunities. Redmandarin takes pride in the fact that it helps companies align sponsorship strategy with corporate objectives focusing on the delivery of a clear return on investment (ROI) (Redmandarin, 2010).

In-House Agencies

A trend to be discussed later is the formation within major corporations of separate departments or divisions dealing with event management, typically called **in-house agencies**. For example, MasterCard International has a department solely dedicated to identifying sponsorship opportunities, creating activation programs, and overseeing the implementation of the sponsorship. These in-house agencies exist to coordinate the sponsorship function across the various divisions of the company.

■ CRITICAL EVENT MANAGEMENT FUNCTIONS

Regardless of the size of the event or the responsible agency, nearly all events must attend to a variety of critical functions. These functions include the following:

- Finance/budgeting
- Risk management
- Tournament operations
- Registration
- Volunteer management
- Event marketing

The remainder of this section examines these six functions in depth.

Finance/Budgeting

The complexity of managing events, coupled with the need to constantly monitor financial conditions, places the functions of budgeting and finance at the forefront of successful sport event management. **Budgeting** is the process of developing a written plan of revenues and expenses for a particular accounting cycle. For events, an *accounting cycle* is usually the time period necessary to plan, organize, and operate the upcoming event. This cycle can be as short as a month or, in the case of an organization such as the United States Olympic Committee (USOC), budgeting can attempt to predict revenues and expenses for the following four years of activity.

Although there are a number of different types of budgets and budgeting processes, two that are particularly important for events are zero-base budgeting and cash-flow budgeting. **Zero-base budgeting** requires a review of all activities and related costs of an event as if it were the first time. Previous budgets and actual revenues and expenses are ignored. All projected revenues and expenses have to be justified prior to becoming part of the overall budget. This type of budget process forces managers to view their event from a fresh perspective, never taking elements for granted and always searching for ways to become more efficient and effective. **Cash-flow budgeting** refers to accounting for the receipt and timing of all sources and expenditures of cash. Cash-flow budgeting informs the manager of the cash amount needed to pay expenses at predetermined times throughout the accounting cycle. Events often expend sizable amounts of cash during the planning and organizing phases, while only receiving cash just prior to the actual execution of the event; therefore, planning carefully to avoid cash shortfalls is critical.

Risk Management

According to Prairie and Garfield (2004), **risk management** is defined as "the function or process by which [an organization] identifies and manages the risks of liability that rise from its activities" (p. 13). Usually this refers to personal injury risk management, although the sport event manager should broaden this definition to also include financial loss, equipment or property damage, loss of goodwill (customers becoming unhappy based on their experience), and loss of market share, to name a few.

Thus, risk management is broader than just protecting one's organization from a lawsuit. It essentially encompasses protecting the organization from anything that could possibly go wrong and lead to a loss of revenue or customers.

A common tool used by events to reduce the potential for a lawsuit from a participant or volunteer is the *waiver and release of liability*. This is a form signed by participants and volunteers that releases the venue and event organizers from a negligence action in case of accident or injury. If the participant is a minor, the signature of a parent is suggested. The validity of a waiver is determined by the law in each state; therefore, the best practice for event organizers to follow is to consult with an attorney to determine whether waivers are recognized in a particular state and, if so, what important phrases and description of activities need to be included within the waiver. Event organizers must remember that a waiver or release of liability does not exonerate them from all responsibility and liability regarding the event.

Waivers and releases of liability can only be used to waive or release a defendant from negligence claims. Event organizers are still responsible for running an event in a responsible, safe manner or they may be found liable for any injuries or problems that may occur.

Another approach necessary when handling risk factors associated with an event is to purchase insurance. Insurance can be purchased not only to cover safety concerns, but also to provide security to an event regarding potential financial losses. For example, an outdoor event that collects sponsorship dollars and registration fees from participants in advance may need to refund a portion, if not all, of this revenue if the event is cancelled due to inclement weather. The event organizers, though, still incurred expenses in getting ready to host the event. Purchasing cancellation insurance can help to offset some of these expenses. Most venues require that the promoter, sponsor, or organizer of the event maintain a minimum level of insurance. The premiums for these types of insurance are based on the level of risk.

A variety of insurance policies can be purchased, including the following (Sharp, Moorman, & Clausen, 2007):

- *Property insurance:* Covers buildings, structures, or contents when vandalism, theft, or certain natural disasters occur
- *Business interruption insurance:* Provides protection against cancellation of the event (due to weather) or closing of a business
- *Liquor liability insurance:* if alcohol is served
- *General liability insurance:* Provides protection against bodily injury or property losses to a third party

Risk management and insurance are of primary importance to event organizers and should never be overlooked when running an event. Appropriate advance planning in these areas can help alleviate problems when the event actually takes place. In addition, event organizers should realize the importance of addressing risk management and insurance concerns surrounding an event to limit the legal liability of the event.

Tournament Operations

Tournament operations can be described as the nuts and bolts of an event. The tournament operations staff stage the event, meet facility and equipment needs, and provide any operational items for the event. Tournament operations can be divided into pre-event, actual event, and post-event activities.

Pre-event tournament operations require appropriate planning and information collection

to ensure that all aspects and details surrounding the actual event are identified. Depending on the size and scope of the event, pre-event tournament operations planning may start four months prior to an event, as is common for local events such as bike races or basketball tournaments, or eight to ten years prior to an event, as is common with large events such as the Olympic Games. During the pre-event planning stages, it is important for the tournament operations staff to be clear as to the type of event being planned and the event's goals. This information is critical in determining how the tournament will be organized and run—components central to the responsibilities and concerns of the tournament operations staff.

Items that should be addressed in the pre-event planning stages include the following:

- Venue plan and layout
- Equipment and facility needs
- Schedule of activities
- Sponsorship needs
- Signage commitments and locations
- Food and beverages
- Merchandise sales
- Media concerns
- Promotional activities and needs
- Transportation concerns
- Housing of athletes
- Staff communication
- Personnel responsibilities
- Lines of authority
- Security issues
- Americans with Disabilities Act requirements
- Policies to address other legal concerns such as alcohol use
- Crowd control

This list is not all-inclusive, because the items handled by the tournament operations staff will vary depending on the type, goals, size, and scope of the event.

During the actual event, the tournament operations staff are responsible for ensuring that the event takes place as planned. This includes attending to the activities and needs relating to participants, sponsors, and spectators. To help in this area, many events utilize a script of activities. The **script** is a specific, detailed, minute-by-minute (or even second-by-second) schedule of activities throughout the day, including information on the tournament operations responsibilities for each activity. This script provides information relative to (1) the time of day and what is taking place, (2) the operational needs (equipment and setup) surrounding each activity, and (3) the event person(s) in charge of the various activities. During the actual event, the tournament operations staff implement the tournament script while also troubleshooting as needed. Advance preparation and planning can certainly assist in running an event, but the tournament operations staff must also be prepared to troubleshoot and to be flexible and adaptable to change when an unforeseen problem arises.

The post-event stage consists of the activities surrounding the completion of an event. Areas covered during the post-event stage include the following:

- Tear-down of the venue
- Storage of equipment and supplies
- Trash pickup and disposal
- Return of borrowed equipment, sponsorship signage, and other items
- Final financial accounting regarding expenses relative to the operations portion of the event
- Thank-you notes sent to appropriate constituencies who assisted in the tournament operations area

It is important for the tournament operations staff to realize that the completion of the actual event does not signal the end of their responsibilities. Numerous items such as those just listed still need to be addressed before the event is wrapped up.

Registration

Registering participants for an event is of the utmost importance because this is the first time event staff members come into contact with participants. An efficient **registration system** is crucial for making a good first impression on the event's clientele. Appropriate advance planning and attention to information needed from participants guide the development of a registration system that is appropriate for the event and convenient for participants.

In developing a registration system, event managers must consider the following:

- Number of participants who will be registering
- Information that needs to be collected from or disseminated to the participants (e.g., waiver forms, codes for sportsmanship conduct, inclement weather policy, event schedule)
- Registration fees that must be collected
- Whether identification is needed (e.g., regarding age limitations)
- Whether information will be collected manually or via a computer system
- Whether the event involves minors, who require the signature of a parent or guardian on a waiver form

This list is not all-inclusive, because the event will dictate the items that need to be covered during the registration process.

Different systems can be used to accommodate the participants and alleviate congestion during the registration process while still collecting or disseminating appropriate information. Examples of such registration systems include using a staggered schedule that provides times when certain divisions of participants for an event should register or using different registration sites for different categories of participation. Note that it is important to create or establish security measures if registration fees are being collected.

The registration process for numerous sporting events has evolved to incorporate online registration processes. Also, an increasing number of sporting events are choosing to outsource their registration process instead of developing and servicing an online platform themselves. One of the more successful online registration and database management companies is The Active Network, which hosts Active.com, an online event search and registration Web site, and eteamz.com, an online community and registration portal for teams, leagues, camps, and tournaments in more than 100 sports (The Active Network, 2010).

Volunteer Management

The importance of volunteers to an event cannot be emphasized enough. Most events cannot be successfully executed without volunteers. This is a good opportunity for sport management students looking to gain experience. You should always be able to find an event in your area that is in need of a volunteer. Events from the smallest local bike race to those as large and complex as the Olympic Games rely on volunteer help.

Volunteer management staff supervise the volunteers involved with an event. Volunteer management can be divided into two areas: (1) working with event organizers and staff to determine the areas in which volunteers are needed and the quantity needed and (2) soliciting, training, and managing the volunteers. Once again, advance planning and preparation are critical in determining how many volunteers are needed and in what capacities they will serve. The volunteer management staff must communicate with every division or area within an event to determine its volunteer needs. Information must include the number of volunteers a particular area may need, qualifications of volunteers, and the type of work to be performed. This information is important when scheduling volunteers because the volunteer management staff would not want to assign a volunteer to work moving heavy equipment, for example, if the volunteer were not physically capable.

Once the volunteer management staff have calculated or estimated the number of and areas of work where volunteers are needed, the staff can make sure that recruitment efforts are appropriate to solicit that number of volunteers. Volunteer recruitment should begin well in advance of the event to ensure that the appropriate number of volunteers are recruited. In addition, the volunteer management staff should be aware of the method in which volunteers are being recruited. (For example, if adult volunteers are needed, the recruitment efforts obviously should not be aimed at area middle schools.)

After the recruitment of volunteers takes place, appropriate training sessions must be held. Training sessions typically include several components, starting with a general information session and progressing to more specialized direction on how to manage the specific responsibilities in each of the individual event departments. Items covered in the basic educational component training session may include how the volunteers should dress or obtain their volunteer uniforms, how they can obtain food and beverages during the event, and how the communication system will be used so they know whom to contact in case of a problem; in addition, all volunteers should be trained concerning risk management and the procedures they should follow in case of an injury or accident. Specific department training may include a description of volunteer duties, how to carry out these duties, when and where volunteers should check in, the name of their direct supervisor, and any other information specific to the volunteer work they will be performing. For example, for a professional golf tournament, people working in the box office would be trained in the printing of passes and the handling of money, while people working at each of the holes would be trained on how to create space for the golfers and how to quiet the crowds when the golfers are ready to take their shots.

Event organizers must also understand the importance of volunteers to the continual operation and success of an event. It is important for the volunteer management staff and event organizers to make sure certain things are done to keep the volunteers happy so they will keep coming back year after year. First, volunteers should not be scheduled into too many time slots so they do not become tired. The schedule should also include appropriate food and bathroom breaks. Second, volunteers need to be recognizable to participants and spectators. Uniforms can help the volunteers be more recognizable while increasing the professional perception of the event. Additionally, uniforms help build goodwill with volunteers in that they are the only ones able to wear the special volunteer uniform. Finally, volunteers need to be recognized for their assistance and contribution to the event. This can be done in a number of different ways, including constant recognition during the event, holding a volunteer party after the event is over, and running volunteer raffles in which the volunteers have a chance to win prizes or receive some benefits in exchange for volunteering.

Event Marketing

Sport and special events cannot be successful without carefully planned **event marketing** programs. There are nine areas on which event marketers must focus:

- Sales of corporate sponsorship
- Advertising efforts
- Public relations activities
- Hospitality
- Ticket sales
- Broadcasting
- Web site development and management
- Licensing/merchandising
- Fundraising

These nine areas are intricately linked. Efforts toward soliciting corporate sponsors will affect advertising strategies, and broadcasting agreements will influence ticket sales. Because these areas are so interrelated, the event marketer must employ an integrated marketing approach. **Integrated marketing** entails long-term strategic planning to manage functions in a consistent manner. For example, ticket sales strategies should be formulated considering the potential sales promotion efforts of sponsors. Similarly, tickets and/or registration should be possible on the Web site. With this in mind, each of the nine event marketing areas will now be explored.

■ CORPORATE SPONSORSHIP

As already discussed in this chapter, the number of events has grown significantly in recent years. With this growth, the competition for sponsors (and other marketing revenues such as ticket sales) has increased. At the same time, events have become increasingly reliant on sponsorship. This is true of small events as well as large events as is evident in the cancellation of the 2009 Arena Football League due to financial difficulties. Estimated sponsorship fees for selected events are presented in **Table 13-3**.

Typically, corporate sponsorships are either sold by the event (in-house) or by an outside sport marketing agency. Sport marketing agencies are hired by a sport property because the property does not have sufficient personnel or

TABLE 13-3	Top Sports Ad Spending Companies	
Company	**2009 Sports Ad Spending**	**Sponsorships (sample)**
Anheuser-Busch InBev	$309.2 million	2010 FIFA World Cup, PGA Championship, NASCAR Daytona 500
AT&T	$226.7 million	AT&T Cotton Bowl Classic, Champions Tour AT&T Championship, PGA Tour AT&T Pebble Beach National Pro-Am
Ford	$197.3 million	Sprint Cup Daytona 500, Little Caesars Pizza Bowl, ASP World Tour of Surfing
McDonald's	$155.4 million	2012 London Olympics, three NBA D-League teams, McDonald's All American High School Basketball Games
UPS	$48.8 million	Breeders' Cup, ING New York City Marathon and Marine Corps Marathon

Source: Top 25 sports spenders, their ad spending, key executives, agencies and sponsorships. (2010, May 10–16). *Street & Smith's SportsBusiness Journal*, pp. 21-23.

expertise in selling sponsorships. In the early 1980s, the International Olympic Committee (IOC) decided the Games were becoming too reliant on broadcasting fees for funding. In response, it decided to sell worldwide sponsorships for the Olympic Games. However, it did not have the expertise or personnel to approach global companies asking for multimillion-dollar sponsorship commitments. Therefore, in 1983 the IOC turned to ISL Marketing, which raised $100 million for the 1988 Olympic Games (Simson & Jennings, 1992). In an effort to generate more revenue and garner more control over sponsorship sales, the IOC partnered with Chris Welton and Laurent Scharapan to form the sport marketing agency Meridian in 1997 (Woodward, 2003). Meridian was responsible for finding and servicing IOC sponsors. In 2003, the IOC brought its sponsorship effort completely in-house when it purchased the Meridian Agency. This move allows the IOC to earn more money from its sponsorship sales because it no longer has to pay fees to an outside agency (Woodward, 2003).

■ ADVERTISING

Many events operate on very tight budgets. As a result, such events are not able to allocate significant expenditures for advertising through the traditional forms of media. Most often advertising expenditures are a very minor portion of an event's expenses. However, this does not mean that events do not expend energy devising alternative means for mass media advertising. Events typically seek advertising through one of two means: (1) media sponsors or (2) attachment to corporate sponsor advertisements.

In addition to selling corporate sponsorships, nearly all successful events sell sponsorships to media outlets. Such sponsorships are often referred to as in-kind sponsorships. **In-kind sponsorships** rarely involve a cash exchange. Instead, an event provides the typical sponsorship benefits to a newspaper, magazine, radio station, or television station in exchange for a specified number of free advertising spots or space. Event promoters will also work with sponsors to promote their events through traditional forms of mass media. Most often, such advertising is geared toward promotions. For example, a shoe company might purchase a newspaper ad to inform potential customers that it will be selling shoes at an upcoming 3-on-3 basketball tournament. In this case, the advertising would serve to promote the basketball tournament as well.

■ PUBLIC RELATIONS

Because events are so constrained in their advertising efforts, generating free publicity is extremely important. Most important to attaining publicity is developing a good working relationship with the members of the media. Hospitality efforts can greatly assist in this endeavor and will be discussed later in this section. In addition, regular communication with media outlets helps enhance the publicity an event receives. However, because members of the media seek stories of interest to the masses, the event must be creative.

■ HOSPITALITY

Hospitality refers to providing a satisfying experience for all stakeholders of the event. This includes participants, spectators, media, and sponsors. Most events occur on a regular basis, and providing good hospitality is one way of improving event loyalty. The sport manager should take strides to ensure that prominent event participants receive private housing, meals, changing areas, and warm-up space. If the participants are also celebrities, the sport manager must ensure that extra security is available to shield them from the public. If hospitality is not successfully implemented, the participants are less likely to return to the event. With respect to spectators, hospitality entails attempting to ensure that people attending the event have an enjoyable time. This includes clear signage directing participants to their

seats, to restrooms, and to concession stands. In addition, training all support staff personnel is imperative so that interpersonal interactions with event staff are always positive.

The event manager will often expend the most energy providing hospitality to members of the media, to corporate sponsors, and to other very important persons (VIPs). Because the event manager is seeking positive publicity from the media, there should always be a separate, prime seating location for the media. In addition, members of the media are accustomed to having private meals and accessibility to a private room where they can complete their work. Increased spending on corporate sponsorships has led to growing awareness and interest in hospitality services. Sport sponsors utilize hospitality for a variety of reasons, including the following:

- To reward and build relationships with current customers
- To generate business from new customers
- To reward employees for good performance
- To reward suppliers for excellent sales

For these reasons, hospitality has become one of the ten most common functions of a sport management/marketing agency (as presented in Table 13-2). Most sponsors will seek some sort of entertainment area where they can host selected guests. For example, as part of the 2010 Fédération Internationale de Football Association (FIFA) World Cup, SportsMark was the exclusive agent in the U.S. of match hospitality for the sale of the Official Hospitality Programme of the 2010 FIFA World Cup South Africa. This package included the best tickets and 3-, 4-, and 5-star hotels with secure match day transportation ("Africa and the beautiful game," 2009).

■ TICKET SALES

Sporting events rely on ticket sales to varying degrees. For larger events, such as college football games in stadiums, for example, the University of Michigan that has a seating capacity of over 109,000, ticket sales are a very important revenue stream. However, for medium-sized and smaller events, ticket sales are a less effective way to generate revenues. Much of the ability to charge admission for these events is dependent on where the event occurs and how easily the event manager can control entry to the event. For example, many professional golf tournaments experience difficulty generating revenues through ticket sales because it is hard to control entry to the course and because so many tickets are given away to corporate sponsors. In these cases, the event is more reliant on sponsorship or broadcasting revenues. However, event managers have discovered creative ways to increase revenues tied to ticket sales. In exchange for a higher monetary outlay, golf tournaments have begun offering preferred viewing lanes whereby spectators receive premium seating in front of the typical gallery areas.

Advancements in technology have had an impact in the ticket sales area. A number of professional sport franchises have recently adopted usage of Flash Seats, a paperless ticketing system in which spectators gain entrance to a sporting event via an encrypted code that can be placed on a driver's license, credit card or other form of identification (Sutton, 2010). This technology has aided in eliminating fraud and duplicate tickets, and has declined the no-show rates of spectators (Sutton, 2010).

■ BROADCASTING

Radio and television broadcasts of an event add credibility to the event and provide increased exposure benefits to sponsors. There are a wide variety of broadcast outlets for sporting events:

- National television networks (e.g., ABC, NBC, CBS, Fox)
- National sports networks (e.g., ESPN, ESPN2, Fox Sports Net)
- National cable outlets (e.g., TNT, TBS, TNN, The Golf Channel)
- Local television stations
- Regional sports networks (e.g., Big Ten Network, New England Sports Network)
- National radio (e.g., CBS, ESPN, XM/Sirius)
- Local radio stations
- Web sites (e.g., mlb.com coverage of baseball games)

Although the increased number of sport outlets has accelerated the demand for sport event programming, a sport property must still meet certain criteria to interest a radio or television broadcast outlet. In fact, only the most valuable sport properties, such as the Super Bowl, the Olympic Games, Wimbledon, the Masters, professional sports, and Division I college athletics, are able to secure direct rights fee payments from broadcasting affiliates. It is important to remember that television and radio stations are funded by advertising sales. Advertisers purchase advertising time during programs that will attract large viewing or listening audiences. Therefore, if a broadcast outlet does not believe an event will be attractive to a large audience, which limits the ability to sell advertising time, then the outlet will not be willing to pay a rights fee to televise or broadcast an event.

Sport organizations and governing bodies have also pursued access to consumers through broadcasting of games and highlights via popular video-sharing sites such as YouTube and social-networking sites such as Facebook, MySpace, and Second Life. The NBA Channel, which shows game and user-generated highlights, debuted on YouTube in February 2007. The National Hockey League (NHL) struck a similar deal with YouTube in November 2006 (Lombardo, 2007).

WEB SITE DEVELOPMENT AND MANAGEMENT

Because access to the Internet is now widespread and the connection speeds associated with such access are no longer an issue, people are becoming more reliant on Web sites for information. For this reason, it is imperative that every event, no matter the size, has a Web site to promote important information about the event. Ideally, the Web site's uniform resource locator (URL) will be the name of the event or something that is very close to the name of the event. In terms of content, the Web site can include a wide variety of information. At the very least, it should include the basic details of when and where the event is occurring and how tickets can be purchased. If the event charges admission, it is sometimes easier for customers to purchase tickets through a Web site than by phone or at the event. The Web site can also be a source for the most up-to-date information about the event. For example, it can include news releases about the event or can provide real-time updates of event results. In the event of inclement weather during an outdoor event, the Web site can serve to inform participants and spectators about whether the event is actually occurring.

LICENSING/MERCHANDISING

The sale of **licensed merchandise**—that is, items that display an event's name or logo— is beneficial in a number of ways, including advertising and brand recognition of the event as well as a potential revenue source through sales generated. For popular events such as the Olympic Games and the Super Bowl, there will be significant demand for licensed merchandise. However, for smaller, less recognizable events, such as a high school football game or a 10K road race, the effort and expense needed to sell merchandise may be higher than the revenue generated from such sales. To cover the costs of inventory, staffing, and space allocation,

significant sales must be achieved for the event to make a profit. Typically, selling tens or even hundreds of pieces of merchandise will not allow the event promoter to record a profit from merchandise sales.

FUNDRAISING

When an event is classified as **not-for-profit**, another marketing tool is fundraising. Fundraising differs from sponsorship in that it does not offer advertising benefits associated with a donation. Most often, not-for-profit events center around raising money for some charitable enterprise, such as the Susan G. Komen Race for the Cure, which generates money for breast cancer research. The Komen Race for the Cure is the largest series of 5K runs/fitness walks in the world, with well over 1 million participants since 2005 (Susan G. Komen for the Cure, 2010a).

Cause-related marketing efforts by corporations are another instance in which fundraising may be appropriate. For example, the CVS Caremark Charity Classic is a men's professional golf tournament sponsored by CVS, a drugstore chain, for the purpose of generating money for charity. Since its inaugural event in 1999, the CVS Caremark Charity Classic has raised more than $13 million for charities around the Rhode Island region (Charity, 2010). Similarly, since 1993, the V Foundation has raised more than $100 million and awarded cancer research grants in 38 states and the District of Columbia with events such as the Jimmy V Basketball Classic and the ESPY Awards (The V Foundation, 2010). Sport teams and leagues are engaged in their own charitable type of activities. The NHL currently endorses the Ace Bailey Children's Foundation Got Skills Challenge for pee wee–aged youth hockey players (ages 11–12). Tournaments take place in local rinks across the United States. Perhaps one of the more well known, internationally recognized charitable organizations related to sports is the Lance Armstrong Foundation, the umbrella organization to LIVESTRONG. One of the more recognizable symbols representing the work of this charitable foundation is the yellow LIVESTRONG wristband seen around the world. Since its inception in 1997, the Lance Armstrong Foundation has raised more than $325 million to support people affected by cancer, providing financial resources to more than 550 organizations that conduct cancer survivorship research or offer services to people affected by cancer (LIVESTRONG, 2010).

■ CAREER OPPORTUNITIES

Event management offers a diverse array of career possibilities. Any event, from the local 3-on-3 basketball tournament to the Olympic Games, requires event management expertise. As a result, the event management field offers one of the most fertile areas for career opportunities. However, to successfully run a sporting event, the event manager's day often begins before dawn and concludes late at night. In addition, because events are usually held on weekends, employment in event management often requires extensive travel and work over weekends. Thus, to be successful in event management, one must be prepared to work long and typically inconvenient hours. Career opportunities in event management center on working with one of three types of organizations: sport management/marketing agencies, events, and charities.

Sport Management/Marketing Agencies

Because of the wide range of tasks carried out by these agencies, job responsibilities within such agencies vary. Typically, an entry-level position with a sport marketing agency will require a person to implement programs on behalf of corporate clients. These programs can include any combination of the key event management functions already discussed. Although an entry-level person is usually not responsible for recruiting corporate clients, he or she is required to successfully manage events and programs created for specific sponsors. For example, an account manager might be responsible for supervising hospitality at an event or for ensuring that a corporation's signs are properly placed throughout an event site. To move beyond an entry-level position within an agency, a person is usually required to accept more business development responsibilities. For example, most vice presidents of sport management/marketing agencies are responsible for attracting new clients for the agency. This function is typically called **business development**.

Events

Although sport management/marketing agencies are typically involved with any sport event, many events have their own offices of full-time employees. This is most often true for events to which a corporation or sport management/marketing agency does not own the rights. Instead, the rights to the event may be owned locally. In this case, the management team for the event would not be from an agency or corporation. However, because most events are seasonal in nature, the full-time year-round staffs for such events are not very large; in other cases, the full-time staff for an event may be only one person.

Charities

Many charities view events as a way to increase revenues. To raise money and manage the events, staff is needed. For example, the Komen Foundation is led by more than 100,000 survivors and activities in nearly 200 countries

(Susan G. Komen for the Cure, 2010b). The Tiger Woods Foundation lists a total of 25 staff members on its Web site who are dedicated to running the various events and programs of the Foundation (Tiger Woods Foundation, 2010).

Key Skills

As this chapter illustrates, an event manager assumes a variety of responsibilities. To successfully execute these responsibilities, the sport manager must have the necessary skills and experience. First, the sport manager must possess the proper educational background. Therefore, students interested in event management should seek a sport management program or business school that will provide them with coursework in areas such as sport marketing, event management, sport management, business, and finance. Many events are created by one person and begin as a small business, so classes in entrepreneurship and accounting are also appropriate for the prospective event manager.

In terms of experience, an internship is almost always required prior to being hired for an entry-level position in event management. In many cases, sport management/marketing agencies will turn to their most effective interns when seeking to fill full-time entry-level positions. Because agencies are charged with supporting corporate clients, new accounts often mean that agencies will need to hire additional personnel. Therefore, students must put themselves in a position to be hired when new accounts are acquired. In addition, it is never too early to begin working for events. A number of volunteer and paid opportunities exist in any university community: the athletic department, intramural department, community recreation programs, charity events, and so on. Nearly all of these activities can help improve a student's background in event management, making him or her more knowledgeable and marketable.

■ CURRENT ISSUES

Niche Sports

Horse jumping, sailing, Le Mans road racing, and action sports such as skateboarding and snowboarding are considered by many to be niche sports. **Niche sports** are unique and appealing to a distinct segment of the market, whether that is defined by age demographics, such as the Millennial Generation or Generation Y (the teenagers and 20-somethings of today), or socio-economic class, as is seen with sailing and polo's appeal to a higher income level. These niche sports can be very valuable to an organization from a sponsorship perspective. Alltech, a worldwide leader in animal nutrition, health, and performance, paid $10 million to be title sponsor for the 2010 World Equestrian Games (Show, 2009a). These events can also provide a luxury brand connection to its target market. The Rolex Kentucky Three Day Event, an equestrian event, drew 103,000 fans last year and offered a full-service hospitality area for $460 (Show, 2009a).

New events have spawned from the appealing nature of these sports to their respective demographic groups. The Dew Tour was established in 2005 and has grown to include five stops from June through October with TV coverage on NBC Universal and the USA Network (Dew Tour, 2010). The Dew Tour has also expanded to the winter with the 2010–2011 three-tour events comprising the third season of Dew Tour Winter (Dew Tour Winter, 2010). Unlike the growth in popularity and exposure of the action sports market, many of these niche sports suffer from a lack of exposure and corporate support beyond their small demographic cohort. The 2009 World Croquet Championships were held in the United States for the first time, yet organizers did not need to spend much time at all worrying about crowd control as they were fearful that attendance would be quite small even with offering free admission (Show, 2009a). The growth and popularity of niche sporting events targeting specific demographic cohorts will continue. What will be interesting to follow, though, is which sports are able to secure the needed sponsorship, spectator interest, and network coverage in order to make it.

Consolidation of Sport Management/ Marketing Agencies

The benefits of vertical integration created significant consolidation among sport management/marketing agencies in the late 1990s. **Vertical integration** refers to the efforts of a sport management/marketing agency to control all aspects of an event, including the agency representing the athlete who competes in an event owned by the agency who is also selling sponsorship of the event and controlling the television coverage. Larger, more diversified sport and entertainment companies purchased sport management/marketing agencies. For example, SFX Entertainment, a large entertainment conglomerate, created the SFX Sports Group in 1999 (Bernstein, 2002). SFX struggled to compete with IMG in the event management and marketing industry. Ultimately, SFX Sports started selling off its properties in 2006, including its baseball, football, golf, tennis, and events businesses ("Best of the rest," 2006).

We have seen partnerships, joint ventures, and acquisitions within the sport management/ marketing agency field in an effort to gain a competitive advantage. In 2007, IMG acquired HOST Communications and formed IMG College to expand their presence within the college sports marketplace. In addition to a 30-year relationship with the National Collegiate Athletic Association (NCAA), HOST provided sport marketing services to a number of college universities and conferences (IMG to acquire, 2007). IMG College quickly established itself by signing Ohio State University to a $110 million over 10

years marketing and media rights deal in 2009 (Smith, 2009). In 2007, BDR Marketing Group LLC, the parent company of Miami Marketing Group, and Peter Jacobsen Sports launched Style Villa Sports (BDR Marketing, 2007). Style Villa Sports brings an entertainment marketing approach to sporting events and has hosted separate events around the 2009 U.S. Opens in golf and tennis (Show, 2009b). More recently, in 2010 Velocity Sports & Entertainment joined forces with Vivid Marketing and two other agencies owned by marketing communications holding company Aegis Group, Sri and a portion of the digital shop Isobar, to form a single sports and entertainment agency operating under the name Team Epic (Lefton, 2010). This partnership combines various expertise from the different organizations involved into one comprehensive company.

The Economic Recession

The worldwide economic recession has changed the approach of sponsorships in sport. First, financial institutions and the auto industry have been among the biggest spenders in the sport sponsorship area, yet both of these industry segments experienced tremendous loss, even resulting in bankruptcy for such institutions as Lehman Brothers. In addition, the landscape changed, moving institutions from evaluating the value of a sport sponsorship from beyond awareness to more pressure being placed on properties to deliver to corporate clients in the areas of purchase consideration, purchase intent, purchase and use ("Changes made," 2009).

The 2009 IEG Sponsorship Report found that sponsorship spending fell by $100 million from that spent in 2008. This represented for the first time less money was spent on sponsorship by North American companies than in the previous year (IEG, 2010). As industry brands reevaluate their sport spending practices, sport

CASE STUDY: Planning for a New Event

David Tompkins sat in his third-floor office contemplating the new challenge dropped in his lap by his employer, Excellent Events, Inc. David has been working for Excellent Events as Northeast Regional Director of 3-on-3 Basketball Operations for the past four years. David's job responsibilities involve overseeing all operational details and sponsorship properties of the 3-on-3 basketball tournaments run by Excellent Events. This morning at a meeting with the chief executive officer (CEO) of the company, David had been presented with a new challenge. Excellent Events is looking to expand into the soccer market, hosting soccer tournaments throughout the Northeast region. Excellent Events has been in the 3-on-3 basketball tournament business for over ten years. The company has seen participation in these tournaments start to fall in recent years, so it is looking to introduce a new sporting event. After researching various potential events, such as beach volleyball and lacrosse, the company decided to go with soccer. It was up to David Tompkins to organize and run these soccer tournaments in his territory.

Raised in Minnesota, David had never played organized soccer while growing up. But while working in the Northeast over the past four years he had realized that soccer was a popular sport in the area. Just how popular, though, he wasn't sure, and he made a note on the pad in front of him to find out. David also wasn't familiar with the rules of soccer, the equipment that would be needed, different formats that soccer tournaments follow, age classifications that are used for playing divisions, risk management or liability concerns surrounding the sport of soccer, or even the types of youth soccer leagues and organizations that might already exist in the area. Again, the pen was busy scratching down ideas and thoughts on the pad of paper in front of him.

David was also well aware of the financial goals of Excellent Events. He realized that the financial success of the soccer events was contingent on a combination of team registration fees and corporate sponsorships. But he also knew that the demographics for soccer participants might differ from what he knew regarding participants and spectators for the 3-on-3 basketball tournaments. David also wanted to explore the possibility of the event giving back to the community, perhaps through a connection with a local charitable organization. Once again David made note of these thoughts.

David had never felt so challenged in his life. Although he considered himself a great event manager, he was not sure how much of his success at running 3-on-3 basketball tournaments would transfer to this new venture. However, one thing he had learned in his four years as an event manager was that attention to details sprinkled with creativity could carry an event manager far.

Questions for Discussion

1. David decided the first thing he needed to do was to research the sport of soccer in his area. What types of information would you suggest that David should research and collect?
2. Although David is well aware of the equipment and supplies necessary to run a 3-on-3 basketball tournament, he lacks familiarity with the sport of soccer. And depending on the age divisions of the participants, the equipment might vary (for example, a smaller soccer ball and goal size might be used for younger age divisions that play on a smaller field). Provide a comprehensive list of all equipment required to successfully operate a soccer event.
3. Given the demographics and psychographics (see Chapter 3, Marketing Principles Applied to Sport Management) of soccer participants and spectators, what type of corporations should be targeted by David for sponsorship solicitation?
4. What suggestions would you have for David in terms of a marketing strategy? How should David market these new tournaments?

properties will be reevaluating their business plans. With the economy as a driving force we have witnessed that sports are not recession-proof. The question remains as to how and to what extent the sport property and sponsorship landscape will change.

SUMMARY

By virtue of the continued increase in sporting events, sport event management offers a wide variety of career opportunities for young sport managers. Most of these opportunities exist within sport management/marketing agencies, the entities that most often organize, manage, and market sport events. Due to the variety of event management functions, it is possible for multiple agencies to work together on a sporting event. For example, a professional golf tournament may have one sport agency responsible for the operational aspects of the event and another agency responsible for the sponsorship sales, public relations, and hospitality of sponsors and VIPs. Yet another agency could be financially and legally responsible for the event and thus be in charge of implementing budgeting and risk management practices. In some cases, one large agency will handle all of these aspects and perhaps even produce a television broadcast of the event. Regardless of how these functions are delegated, each one is crucial to the sporting event's success. With the proliferation of made-for-TV events, opportunities for sport managers in event management will continue to grow. To enter the event management field, however, a student must have a strong background in sport management, marketing, entrepreneurship, finance, and accounting. The good news is that the student can begin immediately by seeking both volunteer and paid opportunities with sporting events on campus and in the local community.

RESOURCES

16W Marketing, LLC
75 Union Avenue, 2nd Floor
Rutherford, NJ 07070
201-635-8000
http://www.16wmktg.com

Alli (Alliance of Action Sports)
http://www.allisports.com

Bronskill & Co.
55 Fieldway Road
Toronto, Ontario M8Z 3L4
Canada
416-703-8689
http://www.bronskill.com

Fuse Integrated Marketing, Inc.
P.O. Box 4509
Burlington, VT 05406
802-864-7123
http://www.fusemarketing.com

Genesco Sports Enterprises
1845 Woodall Rodgers Freeway, Suite 1250
Dallas, TX 75201
214-303-1728
http://www.genescosports.com

GMR Marketing
5000 South Towne Drive
New Berlin, WI 53151
262-786-5600
http://www.gmrmarketing.com

IMG
U.S. Headquarters
767 5th Avenue
New York, NY 10153
212-355-5656
http://www.imgworld.com

IEG, Inc.
640 North LaSalle, Suite 450
Chicago, IL 60654-3186
800-834-4850
http://www.sponsorship.com

IFM Sports Marketing Surveys
The Courtyard

Wisley, Surrey
United Kingdom GU23 6QL
http://www.sportsmarketingsurveys.com

Millsport, LLC
1999 Bryan Street, Suite 1800
Dallas, TX 75201
214-259-3200
http://www.millsport.com

Octagon Marketing
800 Connecticut Avenue
Norwalk, CT 06854
203-354-7400
http://www.octagon.com

Redmandarin
Clerkenwell Workshops
31 Clerkenwell Close
London, England
EC1R 0AT
http://www.Redmandarin.com

Team Championships International
10497 Centennial Road
Littleton, CO 80127
303-948-7108
http://www.teamchampionships.com

Velocity Sports and Entertainment
230 East Avenue
Norwalk, CT 06855
203-831-2000
http://www.teamvelocity.com

■ KEY TERMS

barnstorming tours, budgeting, business
development, cash-flow budgeting, cause-
related marketing efforts, event marketing,
full-service agencies, grassroots programs,
hospitality, in-house agencies, in-kind
sponsorships, integrated marketing, licensed
merchandise, niche sports, not-for-profit,
registration system, risk management, script,
specialized agencies, sport management/
marketing agencies, sport property,

tournament operations, vertical integration,
volunteer management, zero-base budgeting

■ REFERENCES

5th International Sports Event Management Conference (2010). Retrieved on November 5, 2010, from
http://www.iirme.com/isem/home

Africa and the beautiful game (2009, September
28–October 4). *Street & Smith's SportsBusiness
Journal*, p. 21.

Alli (2010). Alli homepage. Newest jobs. Retrieved
March 2, 2011, from http://alli.teamworkonline.
com/teamwork/jobs/default.cfm

Badenhausen, K. (2010, September 23). America's rich-
est athletes. *Forbes*. Retrieved November 5, 2010,
from http://blogs.forbes.com/kurtbadenhausen/
2010/09/23/americas-richest-athletes/

BDR Marketing, Peter Jacobsen Sports launch Style
Villa Sports (2007, November 16). *Worldgolf.
com*. Retrieved from http://www.worldgolf.com/
newswire/browse/11767-BDR-Marketing–Peter-
Jacobsen-Sports-launch-Style-Villa-Sports

Bernstein, A. (2002, December 2). Spotlight on SFX:
Triumph or tragedy. *Street & Smith's Sports-
Business Journal, 1*, pp. 42–43.

Best of the rest. (2006, October 16). *Street & Smith's
SportsBusiness Journal*, p. 24.

Changes made, changes to come. (2009, September
28–October 4). *Street & Smith's SportsBusiness
Journal*, pp. 19–23.

Charity. (2010). CVS Caremark Charity Classic.
Retrieved November 5, 2010, from http://www
.cvscaremarkcharityclassic.com/content/charity

Dew Tour (2010). Dew Tour. Retrieved November 5,
2010, from http://www.allisports.com/dew-tour

Dew Tour Winter (2010). Dew Tour Winter. Retrieved
November 5, 2010, from http://www.allisports.com/
winter-dew-tour

IEG. (2010). IEG insights article. Retrieved March
1, 2011, from http://www.sponsorship.com/IEG-
Insights/Content/IEG-Isights-Article.aspx?
id=6&redirect=/IEG-Insights/Sponsorship-
Spending-Recedes-For-First-Time;-Bette.aspx

IMG. (2010a). About IMG. Retrieved November 5, 2010, from http://www.imgworld.com/about/default.sps

IMG. (2010b). Content distribution & rights. Retrieved November 5, 2010, from http://www.imgworld.com/media/rights_distribution/default.sps

IMG to acquire HOST Communications (2007, November 12). IMG Press Room. Retrieved November 5, 2010, from http://www.imgworld.com/press_room/fullstory.sps?iType=13708&iNewsid=505499&iCategoryID=12543

Lefton, T. (2010, June 7). Velocity, Vivid team in new agency. *Street & Smith's SportsBusiness Journal*, p. 3.

LIVESTRONG (2010). Financial information. Retrieved November 5, 2010, from http://www.livestrong.org/Who-We-Are/Our-Strength/Financial-Information

Lombardo, J. (2007, February 27). NBA giving YouTube a tryout. *Street & Smith's SportsBusiness Journal*, p. 36.

MLB (2010). Urban youth academy. Retrieved November 5, 2010, from http://mlb.mlb.com/mlb/official_info/community/urban_youth.jsp

NARCh (2010). North American Roller Hockey Championships. Retrieved November 5, 2010, from http://www.narch.com

NBA (2010). NBA Fit. Retrieved from http://www.nba.com/nbafit/kids/home.html

NFL (2010). NFL youth football. Retrieved March 1, 2011, from http://www.nflyouthfootball.com

Octagon (2010). About us. Retrieved from http://www.octagon.com/AboutUs/42

Prairie, M., & Garfield, T. (2004). *Preventive law for schools and colleges.* San Diego, CA: School & College Law Press.

Redmandarin. (2010). Strategy creation and development. Retrieved from http://www.redmandarin.com/what-we-do/strategy-creation-and-developoment

Schaaf, P. (1995). *Sports marketing: It's not just a game anymore.* New York: Prometheus Books.

Sharp, L.A., Moorman, A.M., & Claussen, C.L. (2007). *Sport law: A managerial approach.* Scottsdale, AZ: Holcomb Hathaway, Publishers, Inc.

Show, J. (2009a, April 13). Top-shelf sports. *Street & Smith's SportsBusiness Journal*, p. 15.

Show, J. (2009b, May 11). Style Villa to link U.S. Open golf, tennis events. *Street & Smith's SportsBusiness Journal*, p. 7.

Simson, V., & Jennings, A. (1992). *Dishonored games: Corruption, money and greed at the Olympics.* New York: S.P.I. Books.

Smith, M. (2009, March 30). Ohio State lands $110M deal. *Street & Smith's SportsBusiness Journal*, p. 1.

Sports Business Awards (2010, May 17–23). *Street & Smith's SportsBusiness Journal*, pp. 3A–38A.

Sports Marketing Surveys (2010). About us. Retrieved March 1, 2011, from http://www.sportsmarketingsurveys.com/about-us

Susan G. Komen for the Cure. (2010a). Susan G. Komen Race for the Cure. Retrieved March 1, 2011, from http://ww5.komen.org/findarace.aspx

Susan G. Komen for the Cure (2010b). Our people. Retrieved March 1, 2011, from http://ww5.komen.org/AboutUs/OurPeople.html

Sutton, B. (2010, May 10–16). Using technology to build ticket database can boost bottom line. *Street & Smith's SportsBusiness Journal*, p. 11.

Team Championships International. (2010). Retrieved March 1, 2011, from http://www.teamchampionships.com

Team Marketing Report (TMR). (2010). *Sports Sponsor FactBook.* Retrieved November 5, 2010, from http://www.teammarketing.com/fact/

The Active Network. (2010). Corporate overview. Retrieved November 5, 2010, from http://www.activenetwork.com/about/corporate-overview.htm

The V Foundation. (2010). Our story. Retrieved November 8, 2010, from http://www.jimmyv.org/about-us.html

Tiger Woods Foundation. (2010). About the foundation. Retrieved November 8, 2010, from http://web.tigerwoodsfoundation.org/aboutTWF/staff

Top 25 sports spenders, their ad spending, key executives, agencies and sponsorships. (2010, May 10–16). *Street & Smith's SportsBusiness Journal*, pp. 21–23.

Woodward, S. (2003, May 26). IOC does a 180, buys Meridian agency in move to take marketing in-house. *Street & Smith's SportsBusiness Journal*, p. 5.

CHAPTER

14

Sport Sales

Stephen McKelvey

■ INTRODUCTION

Perhaps no avenue within the sport industry holds more job opportunities, particularly at the entry level, than sales. Chances are, many of you reading this now are already sufficiently discouraged: Sales?! However, as you read on within this chapter, you will begin to realize three important things about sales. First, sales is the lifeblood of any sport organization. Whether it be tickets, outfield signage, advertising spots on the team's local radio station, print advertisements in the game-day magazines, luxury suites, or multiyear sponsorship deals, the sales function accounts for the vast majority of revenues for any sport organization. Those who can learn to master the art of selling become invaluable and often irreplaceable assets to their organizations.

Second, sales can be fun! Successful salespeople are not born but can be made through training, experience, and enthusiasm. Sales involves interacting and communicating with other people—typically people who are predisposed to like and even admire your product or service. The sales process entails conversing, learning, and negotiating, ideally with a touch of humor. The successful salesperson wakes up each morning not bemoaning sales as a drudgery, but enthusiastic about the opportunity to help meet the wants and needs of his or her potential customers.

Third, regardless of your job in the industry, it will entail some element of sales. Baseball executive Mike Veeck, the son of the legendary founder of sport promotion, Bill Veeck, provides a quote that he attributes to "17,325 failed potential major-minor league executives": "Oh, I love marketing. But you won't catch me selling. It's just not something I do" (Irwin, Sutton, & McCarthy, 2002, p. ix). The point of Veeck's quote is that whether you are employed in the marketing department, the public relations department, or the operations department, you will always be selling: selling yourself and selling your ideas!

Regardless of the sport, organizations—from the major professional leagues to the lowest rungs of the minors—are being challenged daily to better utilize traditional sales methodologies, employ innovative sales tactics, create new inventory, and discover new ways of packaging their sales inventory to provide not only new revenues to the organization but also longer-term value to their customers. In today's world, consumers have more and more options for spending their entertainment dollars and companies have more and more options for investing their advertising and sponsorship dollars. In this competitive environment, how then do sport organizations use the sales process to attract and retain consumers? What do sport organizations have to sell? Which methodologies do they use to sell it? What does it take to be a successful salesperson in sport? In exploring the evolving world of sport sales, this chapter provides an introduction to the range of sales approaches and methodologies that sport organizations are embracing in the increasingly competitive sport marketplace. Among them is a shift in emphasis from product-oriented to consumer-oriented sales, and recognition of the importance of building long-term relationships with customers. But first, it is important to understand how we arrived at this point.

■ HISTORY

As sport management as a discipline has become more sophisticated, so too has the sales process within sport. What was once viewed as a form of "hucksterism"—one-size-fits-all ticket packages and short-term gimmicks to "put fannies in seats"—has evolved into a dynamic discipline. Historically, sport sales consisted of simple tactics like handing out season ticket brochures or mailing out simple two-page proposals listing a range of advertising and sponsorship options that could be purchased by companies. As noted by Mullin, Hardy, and Sutton (2000), sport marketing, including the sales function, has historically fallen victim to an array of "marketing myopias," defined as "a lack of foresight in marketing ventures" (p. 9). The following illustrate some of the myopias that slowed the growth of the sport marketing profession, particularly as they relate to sport sales (Mullin, Hardy, & Sutton, 2000):

- The belief that winning absolved all other sins. In other words, by fielding a winning team, sales would take care of themselves.
- An emphasis on selling the sport organization's goods and services instead of identifying and satisfying consumers' wants and needs.
- A short-sighted focus on quick returns like selling sponsorships and in-stadium giveaway days, rather than developing long-term relationships with consumers and corporate partners.
- A lack of collection and use of customer research data. In the past, sport organizations would conduct sweepstakes or take ticket orders and not even save the names and addresses of these customers.
- A reliance on the misguided notion of filling seats by mass dissemination of free tickets to attract fans, without thought being given to the message the sport organization was sending about the perceived quality of the product: *If it's free, it must not be worth all that much.*
- Poor sales techniques and a lack of investment in sales training. Historically, sport organizations hired interns and entry-level personnel to sell their product or service. These organizations provided little if any pre-sales training to sales personnel. Additionally there was little coordination and management of the sales process. The prevailing methodology was: "Here's the phone

book . . . start dialing." Little consideration was given to the fact that sales personnel, such as those manning the phones, the ticket windows, and the front desks, are usually the first line of communication and interaction between the sport organization and its potential customers, and that first impressions mean everything. Major League Soccer (MLS) stepped to the forefront of this issue in May 2010 when it announced the launch of the first-ever league-wide ticket sales training center in Minnesota (Mickle, 2010). The MLS National Sales Center provides a 45-day curriculum teaching beginners the basics of sales in preparation for them to join an MLS team.

The ever-increasing competition for the consumer's entertainment dollar, the influx of professionally trained sport marketers, and the continued evolution of sport management and marketing as a scientific discipline has gradually eradicated these marketing myopias. This has resulted in a much higher level of sophistication and understanding of the sales process and its importance to the overall success of any sport organization. As you read on, you will hear more about how sport organizations are changing their attitudes toward sales as well as enhancing their ability to succeed in selling in an increasingly competitive environment through the use of new technologies and creative innovation.

■ SALES IN THE SPORT SETTING

Sales is the revenue-producing arm of a sport organization. It has been defined as "the process of moving goods and services from the hands of those who produce them into the hands of those who will benefit most from their use" (Mullin, Hardy, & Sutton, 2000, pp. 223–224). Any discussion of sport sales might best begin with Mark McCormack, the industry-proclaimed

"founder of sport marketing" who built IMG (formerly International Management Group) into one of the world's premier sport management conglomerates. McCormack explained that selling consists of four ingredients: (1) the process of identifying customers, (2) getting through to them, (3) increasing their awareness and interest in your product or service, and (4) persuading them to act on that interest (McCormack, 1996).

As suggested by Honebein (1997), sales can also be viewed as "customer performance: When a customer purchases your product, he or she performs the act of buying" (p. 25). As Mullin, Hardy, and Sutton (2000) further elaborate, there are four main factors that cause sport consumers to purchase (or not purchase) a sport organization's product or service:

1. *Quality:* Teams' win–loss records are one obvious example of identifying the quality of the product or service and influencing consumers' purchase-behavior decisions.
2. *Quantity:* An individual might purchase a mini-plan from an NBA team rather than a full season ticket package, so the numbers (the units) in which the product is sold can become an influencing factor.
3. *Time:* Family obligations, work schedules, and everyday life can dictate whether the consumer has the time to consume the product. For instance, to make a season ticket purchase worthwhile, the individual must have the time available to attend the majority, if not all, of the team's home games.
4. *Cost:* Each year, *Team Marketing Report* (*TMR*), one of the leading industry trade publications, publishes a Fan Cost Index (FCI). The FCI measures the cost of taking a family of four to a game for each of the major professional sport leagues and includes not only the cost of tickets but also the other costs that consumers likely incur, including the purchase of parking,

concessions, and souvenirs. Although the average cost of tickets for a family of four to attend a Major League Baseball (MLB) game in 2010 was $107 (by far the lowest of the three major professional sport leagues), the overall cost of attending the game, factoring in the other elements, was $194.98 for the 2010 season (Team Marketing Report, 2010). Thus, the price of game tickets is just part of the equation that influences consumers' purchase decisions. In addition to direct out-of-pocket expenses, the concept of cost also relates to such aspects as payment options and value received for the purchase price.

One element that distinguishes sport sales from the selling of other traditional consumer products or services like cereal or telecommunications services is the presence of emotion (Mullin, Hardy, & Sutton, 2000). The emotion inherent in sport adds a special excitement to the sales process. Think about it: Would you rather work the phones calling Boston residents to sell them a new credit card or to sell them Red Sox tickets? Of course, again unique to sport, the presence of emotion can cut both ways. In the early part of the 2000s, the Detroit Pistons were a powerful sales proposition, featuring a World Championship–caliber team with charismatic stars like Chauncy Billups and Ben Wallace. A few years later, the Pistons were a tough sell. This example illustrates the need for professional sales methodologies that transcend the annual roller-coaster of win–loss records and negative media coverage.

■ SALES STRATEGIES AND METHODS

Innovation in the sales process and methodologies within the sport industry have often lagged behind those in other service industries, due in part to the myopias described earlier in this chapter. However, in recent years, certain innovative sales methodologies have begun to be more widely utilized throughout the sport industry. Historically, sport organizations communicated with customers once it was time to "renew the order." With the increased competition for the loyalties of the sport consumer, organizations have recognized the need to expand and enrich their relationships with current and potential customers. This section provides an overview of the methodologies and terminology that have become the linchpins of the sales process in the sport industry today.

Database marketing involves the creation of a database, usually consisting of names, addresses, phone numbers, and ideally other demographic information relating to current and potential customers, and then managing that database. Depending on the level of the sport organization, databases can range in sophistication from a file of index cards to high-tech software packages with the ability to cross-reference and segment consumers by a broad range of demographic characteristics. Through this marketing information system (MIS), a sport organization with a well-updated and managed database could identify all those families with two or more children who live within one hour of the stadium and who have purchased at least four tickets within the past two years. The ability to access, understand, and utilize such information can be extremely valuable to the maximization of the sport organization's sales efforts. Teams typically obtain much of their database information from customers' credit cards used for the purchase of tickets and merchandise, through surveys and contests through which customers provide personal information, and from letters and e-mails sent by consumers to sport organizations requesting information or voicing concerns. Teams may also occasionally purchase subscription lists, such as all the *Sports Illustrated* subscribers within their local market areas, to add to their databases of information as sources for generating sales leads.

As with any industry, new technologies are continually emerging to enhance efficiency and effectiveness. Sport organizations, their sales managers, and their sales staff need to be constantly aware of new technologies that can drive incremental sales revenue to the bottom line. Two new technologies are having a dramatic effect on the ability of sport organizations to build, manage and maximize their sales databases. The first is Flash Seats by Veritix, a paperless ticketing system in which customers enter the stadium or arena via an encrypted code that can be placed on a driver's license, credit card, or other form of identification. "What I have loved about this product . . . is the data-capture ability that enables the venue or the team to know the identity of every person in the building on any given night," said Bill Sutton, one of the sport industry's leading sales gurus. "The value of the data for future marketing and sales efforts along with cross-promotional opportunities is a significant revenue opportunity" (Sutton, 2010, p. 11).

The second new technology is a product called Prospector, developed and owned by Turnkey Sports (Sutton, 2010). Prospector is a program that analyzes and "scores" sales leads, thus increasing the efficiencies of selling tickets in a variety of ways. For instance, the program can prioritize leads based upon customer segments and also allows the sales manager to better understand who is best at selling different types of inventory (i.e., season tickets, partial plans, premium seating) by measuring the revenue generated in direct correlation to the leads the sales person is assigned. The Prospector program also increases accountability in terms of assigned leads and the revenue produced by those leads, and it allows the sales manager to rotate assigned leads equally or to create a system whereby the best leads (those with five stars) can be assigned to those salespeople who meet their sales goals the previous week (Sutton, 2010). "[Prospector] is all about improving

the efficiency of the sales staff and trying to move from a 1 percent success rate of outbound calling to a rate of 3 or 4 percent or perhaps higher," said Turnkey Sports executive Haynes Hendrickson (Sutton, 2010, p. 11).

Sport organizations utilize their databases to generate sales through three primary methods: direct mail, telemarketing, and personal sales. **Direct mail** solicitations are widely used in the sport industry. As suggested by Mullin, Hardy, and Sutton (2000), the major advantage of using direct mail campaigns is that they reach only those people the organization wants to reach, thus minimizing the expense of circulating a sales offer to individuals who would have little interest in the offer. Organizations often promote season tickets, partial season ticket plans, and single-game tickets through direct mail campaigns. Through the wonders of computers, the information stored in the database can be merged to create letters that are personalized for each individual. Furthermore, because you can easily measure the effectiveness of direct mail, organizations can devise accurate head-to-head tests, formats, pieces, terms, or so forth, to better ensure the success of future direct mail initiatives. Of course, one potential drawback of the direct mail approach is that, unlike the telemarketing and personal selling methodologies discussed next, direct mail solicitations do not provide an opportunity to verbally explain the sales offer, counteract objections, nor answer questions. Thus, the organization must clearly communicate the sales offer so that it is easily understood by the recipient.

Telemarketing is also widely used within the sport industry. Whereas in the past, sport organizations literally handed their sales interns a phone book ("dialing for dollars," as it was often called), the advent of database marketing has brought a greater degree of sophistication and training to the sales process. Telemarketing utilizes telecommunications technology as a part of a well-planned, organized, and managed sales effort that features the use of non-face-to-face contact (Mullin, Hardy, & Sutton, 2000). Telemarketing can be one-dimensional, such as handling inbound calls from consumers in response to a promotional offer through the use of a toll-free number. The Red Sox, for example, have implemented a telemarketing system that can handle up to 90,000 incoming orders in one hour, operates 24 hours per day seven days a week, and generates a database that can also be used to conduct surveys (Team Marketing Report, 1998). The other approach is two-dimensional, whereby salespeople use the phone to prospect for customers, follow up leads, or solicit existing customers for repeat

or expanded business. Telemarketing involves training the sales personnel to "follow a script," become effective listeners, and complete the sales process by countering any objections and best meeting the specific needs of the customer. More and more teams, however, are realizing that telemarketing is just the start of the sales process. For instance, the Arizona Diamondbacks are training their sales representatives to use the phone only as a starting point to gather information about a prospect. To close the sale, they are meeting in person with the prospect or, better yet, inviting the prospect for a tour of the stadium (King, 2010). "People aren't going to make purchases over the phone anymore," predicts Diamondbacks CEO Derrick Hall. "They're not going to commit. We've got to get them here [to the stadium for a tour] and then we have success" (King, 2010, p. 1).

Personal selling describes face-to-face, in-person selling and again usually incorporates the use of the sport organization's database. Although personal selling is often more costly than direct mail or telemarketing, personal selling can be more precise by enabling marketers to more closely target the most promising sales prospects. Personal selling is often necessary, and more effective, for successfully selling higher-priced inventory such as luxury suites and sponsorship packages because these items involve a greater financial investment by the prospective customer. It is rare indeed that a company would ever purchase a team sponsorship package over the phone!

As the race to obtain—and retain—the business and the loyalties of both consumers and corporations has intensified over the past decade, successful sport organizations have also adopted proactive sales approaches, or philosophies, that are premised on the concept of relationship marketing that was discussed in Chapter 3, Marketing Principles Applied to Sport Management. These include benefit selling, aftermarketing, up-selling, and eduselling. Each of these concepts is introduced in the following section.

Benefit Selling

What should a sport organization do when the product or service package it is selling doesn't meet the specific wants or needs of a consumer? One approach, called **benefit selling**, "involves the promotion and creation of new benefits or the promotion and enhancement of existing benefits to offset existing perceptions or assumed negatives related to the sport product or service" (Irwin, Sutton, & McCarthy, 2008, p. 107). The first step in benefit selling is to understand what objections customers have to your product or service, and why. This can be achieved through customer surveys and focus groups. Once benefits have been identified, they must be publicized and must be judged by the consumer to have worth or value.

The concept of the *Flex book* is one example of benefit selling in action (Irwin, Sutton, & McCarthy, 2008). This concept arose in response to the frequent objection by potential customers, when being pitched partial season ticket plans, that they were not able to commit to a certain number of games on specific dates well in advance of the season. Flex books (sometimes also called Fan Flex plans) contain undated coupons for a specified number of games that can be redeemed for any games of the customers' choosing (subject to seating availability). It is an example of creating a new benefit to offset existing perceptions or assumed negatives related to the sport product or service. Another increasingly popular example is *open houses*, in which teams allow potential consumers into their venues to get a feel for the "experience" and the benefits associated with it.

Aftermarketing

Direct selling, telemarketing, and personal selling are the most widely used methodologies for prospecting and achieving initial sales. As competition for customers intensifies and the emphasis shifts from acquiring customers to retaining customers, the ability to provide consistent high-quality service is a source of competitive advantage for sport organizations (McDonald, 1996). **Aftermarketing**, defined by Vavra as "the process of providing continued satisfaction and reinforcement to individuals or organizations who are past or current customers" (1992, p. 22), is a critical consideration because of the significant competition for the sport consumer's entertainment dollars. No market better illustrates this competition than the sport landscape of the New York metropolitan area. In this specific marketplace, the consumer is provided the opportunity to purchase tickets for the following professional sport franchises: New York Liberty (Women's National Basketball Association, WNBA), New York Knicks (National Basketball Association, NBA), New Jersey Nets (NBA), New York/New Jersey Red Bulls (MLS), New York Yankees (MLB), New York Mets (MLB), New York Giants (National Football League, NFL), New York Jets (NFL), New York Rangers (National Hockey League, NHL), New York Islanders (NHL), and New Jersey Devils (NHL). These 11 professional league teams do not even include the minor league teams or the collegiate sport programs operating in the area that also vie for the sport consumer's dollar and loyalties (Mullin, Hardy, & Sutton, 2000). Thus, it has become critical for sport organizations to have an aggressive plan for retaining their market share of fans. From a practical business standpoint, aftermarketing serves to encourage an organization to view a season ticket holder not as a one-time $3,000 customer but, based on a potential span of ten years, as a $30,000 client. Through this lens, every single season ticket holder becomes much more worthy of cherishing! "It's all about relationships," said Mullin. "If you didn't build the relationship with a sponsor or season-ticket holder or fan back when things were good, it's very hard to all of a sudden do it now" (King, 2010, p. 1).

An organization-wide commitment to quality service has become the trademark of successful sport organizations, as exemplified by the Minnesota Wild of the NHL. The Wild maintain a customer service philosophy that is proactive, responsive, and focused on fans first at all times, based on its mission statement: "Building winning relationships and experience through Passion, Caring, Teamwork and Excellence" (Minnesota Wild, 2002–2003). Customer service permeates the Wild's sales and service team, and each member of the team is able to make decisions and take actions that will provide fans with a positive experience and relationship with the organization through every contact they have with the team. The Wild's aftermarketing program includes the following elements (Minnesota Wild, 2002–2003):

- Personal calls by sales account reps to 50 season ticket holders per week
- E-mails to 50 season ticket holders per week
- Personal notes to 25 season ticket holders per week
- Direct-dial phone numbers and e-mail addresses given to each season ticket holder for contacting his or her personal service representative
- In-seat visits by sales account reps during home games
- Maintenance of a customer sales and service booth in the arena that is staffed by sales and service team members
- Invitations to attend "Fan Forums" with the team's general manager and team president

- A *Hockey Operations Handbook* sent to season ticket holders describing the goals and values of the team's on-ice product
- A complimentary *Rinkside* magazine sent to season ticket holders and fans on the season ticket holder waiting list
- Advance sale opportunities for season ticket holders for concerts held at the team's arena, the Xcel Energy Center
- An *Xpress Newsletter* highlighting the team and other events at the Xcel Energy Center for fans who choose to receive e-mail notification
- Skating parties for season ticket holders
- Automated phone calls (called "Perfect Calls") from players, coaches, and general manager to fans identified in the team's database
- A holiday card from the team with a redemption coupon for a gift, such as a team yearbook or team media guide

As a follow-up to these benefits—all designed to "aftermarket" the Wild to its *raving fans*—the Wild accesses feedback on customer satisfaction through regular independent marketing surveys, online polls, and monitoring of chat rooms. All comments and feedback are logged on individual accounts to allow the Wild sales staff to track patterns and uncover opportunities to improve service to specific individuals and overall.

Up-Selling

Successful sport organizations are never satisfied with simply renewing a customer at his or her current level of involvement. By effectively managing and maintaining their database and by embracing the sales philosophies of relationship marketing and aftermarketing, sales personnel should be well positioned to up-sell current customers. When it comes to tickets, the idea of **up-selling** corresponds to the "escalator concept," whereby sport organizations are continually striving to move customers up the escalator from purchasing single-game tickets to purchasing mini-ticket plans, and then to full season ticket packages (Mullin, Hardy, & Sutton, 2000). For those involved in sponsorship sales, the goal should always be to increase, over time, the company's involvement with the sport organization. Relationship marketing and aftermarketing put the salesperson in an advantageous position when it comes time to renew and up-sell a client.

Eduselling

At this point, one thing should be clear to you, the reader and future sales executive: *The customer rules!* Product- or service-focused sales activities that emphasize the product (its benefits, quality, features, and reputation) or the sport organization itself have been replaced by the mantra of customer-focused selling that stresses the needs and requirements of the customer (Irwin, Sutton, & McCarthy, 2008). A salesperson engaged in customer-focused selling views himself or herself as a consultant to the prospective customers, helping to provide them with a *solution*, rather than simply trying to convince them to purchase a product or service they may not want or need. Irwin, Sutton, and McCarthy (2008) specifically describe the importance of **eduselling** in the context of selling corporate sponsorships; they define *eduselling* as "an instructive process that continually and systematically supplies information and assistance to the prospective sponsorship decision maker in order to enhance product knowledge, facilitate understanding of product benefits, and establish a sense of partnership between rights holder and buyer" (p. 175). Eduselling is more than just educating a customer before the sale, or providing short-term service after the sale (such as a consumer warranty). Eduselling is a

continual process which involves the sales staff monitoring consumer utilization and satisfaction through regular communication. Through this monitoring process the sales staff is able to ensure the product or service is being utilized properly. By ensuring the product is being utilized properly and to its fullest extent, the sales staff is able to maximize customer satisfaction and ultimately the lifetime value of the client.

One way a salesperson engages in eduselling is by proactively assisting customers in developing ways to better utilize and leverage their investment with the organization. For instance, more and more teams are providing corporate season ticket holders with something as simple as a chart that allows the company to more easily keep track of who has use of which tickets for which games. Other teams are providing a means for season ticket holders to forward unused tickets to worthy local charities, through which the company can derive some goodwill. Tactics such as these are aimed at helping to make sure that the season tickets don't end up buried in a desk drawer, unused—a scenario that would make the season ticket renewal process quite difficult. Furthermore, sport organizations committed to eduselling will themselves develop promotional ideas showing how their sponsors can utilize the team's game tickets and other merchandise to help generate new business opportunities and sales. Remaining in constant communication with customers, and displaying a vested interest in achieving customers' business goals, helps ensure that both parties, if they live up to their commitments, will benefit from the relationship in both the short and the long term.

■ KEY SKILLS: WHAT MAKES A GOOD SALESPERSON?

It is the rare breed of person who is "born to sell." It takes a certain degree of confidence to pick up the phone and cold call strangers to interest them in purchasing season tickets or an outfield sign. If you are engaged in personal selling, it takes a certain degree of courage to knock on a company door, ask yourself in, and pitch a group sales or sponsorship package. More often than not, successful salespeople develop their skills through training, trial and error, and experience.

Mark McCormack, a salesman who mastered his craft by selling clients such as Arnold Palmer, Jack Nicklaus, and Tiger Woods to corporate America, has stated that "Effective selling is directly tied to timing, patience, and persistence—and to sensitivity to the situation and the person with whom you are dealing. An awareness of when you are imposing can be the most important asset a salesman can have. It also helps to believe in your product. When I feel that what I am selling is really right for someone, that it simply makes sense for this particular customer, I never feel I am imposing. I think that I am doing him a favor" (McCormack, 1984, p. 92).

The following is a "Top Ten Rules for Successful Selling" list that incorporates McCormack's sage advice (McCormack, 1996) in addition to experience gleaned by this author during 15 years in the sport sales business:

1. *Laugh.* It never hurts to have a sense of humor. Remember, sports is entertainment!
2. *Use a common-sense fit.* Make sure that what you are selling makes sense for your prospective customer. Never try to shoehorn inventory down a prospect's throat.
3. *Wear Teflon.* The most successful salespeople believe that being told "no" is the start of the sales process; they don't take rejection personally, and they accept it as a challenge. (Beware, however, of rule 2!)
4. *Know the prospect.* There's an old adage: Knowledge is power. Undertake to know as much as you can about the sales prospect. If you're calling on an individual,

does your database show that he or she has attended games in the past? If you're pitching a local company for sponsorship, do you know if that company is currently sponsoring other sports properties? Is the person you're going to meet with a sports fan? Find out in advance (ask his or her assistant!). Knowing that, alone, can make the sales process easier.

5. *Pump up the volume.* Sales is a numbers business. As a rule of thumb, ten phone calls to solicit a meeting may result in one actual sales call. For every ten meetings, you might get one sales nibble. Sales is about volume—making a lot of calls and seeing a lot of people (see rule 3).
6. *Knock on old doors.* Don't abandon potential customers just because they turned you down the first time. Individual consumers' interests and financial circumstances change, as do companies' business strategies and personnel, and when they do you don't want to be a stranger. Be polite, but persistent.
7. *Consult, don't sell.* Successful salespeople seek to learn potential customers' wants and needs, and then work with them to find solutions that are mutually beneficial. They let the sale come to them.
8. *Listen!* Perhaps the best skill a salesperson can develop is the art of listening. If you ask, prospective customers will always provide clues that open avenues toward an agreement, if not today, then somewhere down the road (see rule 6). Good listeners pick up on these clues.
9. *Have two kinds of belief.* Successful salespeople have an unwavering belief in what they are selling and in themselves.
10. *Ask for the order.* This sounds self-explanatory, but closing the sale is one of the toughest steps to successful selling. You will never know if a potential customer wants to buy your product until you ask!

Chad Estis cut his teeth in an entry level sales position with the then down-trodden Cleveland Cavaliers and eventually worked his way up through a series of sport sales positions to become the vice president of sales and marketing for the Dallas Cowboys. He sums up well what it takes for team success in ticket sales:

> To me, there's no silver bullet in ticket sales. Ticket sales is a grind-it-out business. No matter if you're in a stadium like the one I'm in [the new state-of-the-art Cowboys Stadium] or working for a team at the bottom of the . . . league, the tactics and the success factors are the same. You have to have a focused, dedicated, skilled, well-trained, highly professional sales team approaching the market in a strategic way, working out of a database that has been well thought out, representing your organization in a very professional way and building relationships, and making sales that if you didn't do all those things right would not be made. That's what's going to make or break your business, not a half-price promotion or a free dog and a Coke (King, 2010, p. 1).

■ SALES INVENTORY

Because sales is the lifeblood of a sport organization, for many a position in sales is often the first step into the industry. **Sales inventory** is "the products available to the sales staff to market, promote and sell through a range of sales methodologies" discussed earlier (Mullin, Hardy, & Sutton, 2000, p. 227). Sport organizations have a broad range of sales inventories, each of which entails different sales methodologies as well as levels of sales experience. The typical front office of a team sport organization includes the following staff positions reporting to the vice-president of sales and marketing: manager (or director) of season ticket sales, manager

of group sales, manager of advertising sales, manager of sponsorship (or corporate) sales, manager of luxury suite sales, and manager of broadcast sales. It is important to note, as we review the sales inventory of a typical sport organization in this section, that many of the inventory items discussed are often packaged together when being presented to a company (Mullin, Hardy, & Sutton, 2000).

Tickets and Hospitality Inventory

People traditionally get their start in the industry in the ticket sales department, first staffing the ticket booth and then advancing up the sales ladder to group sales and partial- or full-season ticket plans. Mullin, Hardy, and Sutton (2000) describe the game ticket inventory as a "club sandwich" (p. 245) consisting, from the bottom up, of community promotional tickets, tickets bought through day-of-game "walk-up" sales, advance sales, group tickets, and partial plans, and topped off by full-season tickets. The authors suggest the following "recipe" for a good-tasting and profitable "club sandwich" through which to maximize ticket sales revenue (Mullin, Hardy, & Sutton, 2000, p. 244):

Ingredient	Percentage of Customers
Season ticket equivalencies (full and partial plans)	50
Advance ticket sales	25
Group sales	20
Day-of-game/walk-up sales	5

While historically the "sizzle" in sport sales was in selling sponsorships and advertising, sport organizations have come to realize that the "steak" is in ticket sales. As the lifeblood of most franchises, sales from tickets and club seats make up more than half of a typical franchise's local revenue in all the four major sport leagues, ranging as high as 80% for some teams (King, 2010). Bernie Mullin, former CEO of the Atlanta Hawks and Thrashers and senior vice president of team marketing for the NBA, summed it up:

> *You look at most teams' locally generated revenue, it's at least three dollars in ticket sales for every dollar in sponsorships. Yet the resources were pumped into people selling and servicing sponsorships, and ticket sales people were in cubicles in the bowels of the stadium and the back of the ticket office. Now, however, the economics, coupled with technology that allows teams to do a better job of mining ticket buyers and getting those who buy to buy even more, have turned ticket sales into a sophisticated endeavor at most franchises (King, 2010, p. 1)*

Sport organizations' continued emphasis on customer accommodation and hospitality has expanded the sales inventory over the past decade to include club seats (with personal waiter service), luxury suites complete with catered food service, private seat licenses (PSLs), and very important person (VIP) parking, among others.

Advertising Inventory

Advertising inventory includes both electronic and print inventory. Electronic advertising inventory includes television, radio, and team Web sites. Although most sport organizations still sell their local broadcast rights to media outlets (called *rightsholders*) in exchange for an annual rights fee, some teams have brought their television or radio rights or both in-house. Although in this latter situation the team bears the production costs of its broadcasts, it also has the opportunity to retain all of the advertising sales. The New York Yankees provide an example of a team willing to bear this risk, having taken control of their television broadcasts through

the creation of the YES Network and the hiring of their own in-house sales staff to sell the advertising inventory. Print inventory includes advertising in game programs, media guides, and newsletters as well as on ticket backs, ticket envelopes, scorecards/roster sheets, and team faxes, among others.

Signage Inventory

Signage inventory has traditionally been limited to dasherboards, scoreboards, outfield signs, and concourses. However, the quest for new revenue streams has expanded the signage sales opportunities to include the playing surface itself, the turnstiles, and the marquees outside the venue, among others.

Naming Rights

Naming rights provide a sport organization the opportunity to sell entitlement of its arena or stadium, practice facility, or the team itself. The corporate naming of stadiums and arenas has resulted in a significant new revenue stream for sport organizations. In some instances, naming rights agreements have also caused issues for the sport organizations that sold the rights and/

or the companies that have purchased the rights. Consider the embarrassment and financial hardship sport organizations endured during the 1990s as a result of entering into naming rights deals with companies such as Enron, PSINet, TWA, and Pro Player that eventually went bankrupt. On the heels of this string of bankruptcy filings, one industry expert commented: "When the naming rights craze started . . . there was such excitement that a lot of discipline hadn't been put into the deals. In hindsight, there probably wasn't as much due diligence" (Radcliffe, 2002, p. 26). Today, facility naming rights deals often include clauses designed to ensure that sport organizations get back, for free, their ability to sell their facility's name if the signing company becomes insolvent. On the other side of the arrangement, some companies that have bought naming rights from sport organizations have also experienced major issues. Soon after the financial meltdown in late 2008 (and subsequent government bank bailout) many U.S. Congressional Representatives criticized CitiBank's naming of Citi Field in New York City. Congress questioned how CitiBank could afford a $20 million annual naming rights agreement with the Mets yet required a government bailout to continue day-to-day operations. These are just a few of the issues that must be considered when selling naming rights. The top 10 most valuable sport facility naming rights agreements can be found in **Table 14-1**.

Online Inventory

Web sites hosted by sport leagues and teams represent attractive platforms for sponsors to advertise as the products and (or) services they sell. Banner ads, blogs, instant messaging applications, and pop-up-ads are all common online inventory sport organizations can sell. The high traffic sport Web sites attract makes this online inventory both valuable and important for a sport organization's bottom line. Often online inventory (e.g., banner ads, company links) is included as an important value add in a larger sponsorship deal.

Promotions Inventory

Promotions inventory ranges from premium giveaway items and on-floor/on-field promotions to DiamondVision scoreboard promotions and

TABLE 14-1 Ten Most Valuable Sport Facility Naming Rights Agreements

Venue	City, State	Years	Annual Value (Millions)	Expiration Year
Barclays Center	Brooklyn, NY	20	$20.0	2029
Citi Field	Queens, NY	20	$20.0	2028
Reliant Stadium	Houston, TX	31	$10.0	2032
FedEx Field	Landover, MD	27	$7.59	2025
American Airlines Center	Dallas, TX	30	$6.5	2030
Philips Arena	Atlanta, GA	20	$9.25	2019
Minute Maid Park	Houston, TX	28	$6.36	2029
University of Phoenix Stadium	Glendale AZ	20	$7.72	2025
Bank of America Stadium	Charlotte, NC	20	$7.0	2023
Lincoln Financial Field	Philadelphia, PA	20	$6.98	2022

Source: Marta, S. (2008, March 31). Dallas Cowboys stadium naming rights may top record deal. *Dallas Morning News.* Retrieved November 3, 2010, from http://www.dallasnews.com/sharedcontent/dws/spt/football/cowboys/stories/033008dnbusnamingrights.2b2caec.html

pre- or postgame entertainment. Popular examples include sponsored "T-shirts blasts," in which team-logoed T-shirts are shot up into the stands by a specially designed, hand-held cannon, and the fan-favorite sponsored "Dot Races" that appear between innings on the DiamondVision scoreboard. Many sport organizations also sell the rights to local companies to "present" postgame entertainment such as the ever-popular fireworks displays.

Community Programs

Community programs offer a wealth of inventory for sport organizations to sell to local organizations, including but not limited to school assemblies, camps and clinics, awards and banquets, kick-off luncheons, and golf tournaments.

Miscellaneous Inventory

Miscellaneous inventory is often up to the ingenuity and resourcefulness of the sport organization. Miscellaneous inventory can include fantasy camps, off-season cruises with players, locker room tours, and road trips. Sport organizations have gotten increasingly creative in developing new inventory and thus generating new revenue streams by selling companies the opportunity to associate with their sanctioned events. For instance, many teams now conduct off-season "fanfests" involving interactive games and exhibits, which provide an entirely new source of sponsorship and advertising inventory.

Several professional sport teams have been successful in selling companies the entitlement to their individual playoff games. For example, Cub Cadet, a manufacturer of lawn mowers, served as the presenting sponsor of the Cleveland Cavaliers' 2010 Playoff run. As a result of the sponsorship, Cub Cadet received a number of banner ads on the Cavaliers' Web site, and the designation "Cleveland Cavaliers

Playoffs Presented by Cub Cadet" was used on all local radio broadcasts. The New Jersey Nets broke new ground in this regard following the 2009–2010 season, selling a local auto insurance company the presenting sponsorship of the team's *off-season*! The sponsorship included brand exposure in all Nets' off-season communications, including press releases, e-mail campaigns, advertising on the team's Web site, and sponsorship of a sweepstakes tied to the NBA draft (Brennan, 2010).

Sponsorships

Of all the inventory that a sport organization has available to sell, sponsorships, discussed in detail in Chapter 15, Sport Sponsorship, are often the most involved and time-consuming. Before even presenting a sponsorship proposal, the property must do extensive homework on the targeted company. Who is the decision maker? Who are its competitors? What have the company and its competitors done in the past in the area of sport sponsorship? Based on your research, who are the company's primary customers and how does your property or event deliver this audience? Is the company on solid financial ground? (After all, you don't want to sign a sponsor that either can't afford to properly leverage its sponsorship or that may be out of business in a year!) What are some top-line promotional ideas that you might suggest that can reinforce the company's marketing objectives or its company slogan? Why do you believe the targeted company would be a good fit for your organization, and why would the company believe this?

Sponsorship packages typically incorporate some, if not all, of the various inventory described previously. The sponsorship sales process requires a great deal of up-front research, creativity, sales acumen, and patience. First, sponsorship packages often entail a much larger emotional and financial commitment on the part of the potential customer. Second, because of the

CASE STUDY: The Outsourcing of College Ticket Sales Operations

For decades, colleges and universities have relied upon the expertise of consulting companies to handle the development and management of its various marketing assets. For instance, industry leading firms such as Collegiate Licensing Corporation (now a division within IMG College) and Licensing Resource Group have been representing the licensing interests of colleges and universities since the 1970s. The former Host Communications (also now a division of IMG College) was on the forefront of representing colleges and universities for their broadcasting rights. These and other industry players, including Learfield, CBS College Sports, and ISP, have also been retained by collegiate institutions to develop, manage, and sell their sponsorship programs. In some cases, one outside firm may handle all three areas of assets for the college or university.

These consulting arrangements typically provide the collegiate institution with a guaranteed annual cash rights fee payment (and in some cases a percentage of revenues above a certain monetary threshold) in exchange for allowing the outside company with the rights to reap the potential monetary benefits from the sales of the collegiate institution's broadcast advertising, sponsorship packages, and licensed products. It has historically been viewed as a win–win relationship for both parties. The focus of colleges and universities is typically on the educational mission and, hence, many athletic departments lack the sales personnel and resources that one would typically find within a professional sport organization.

In the spring of 2009, Georgia Tech announced the hiring of an upstart sports marketing firm, The Aspire Group, to handle ticket sales for football and men's basketball (Lombardo and Smith, 2009). Although it was not the first such arrangement involving the outsourcing of ticket sales, the publicity attendant to the announcement suggested the ushering in of a new trend in the collegiate marketplace.

"Major universities are already outsourcing licensing and broadcasting rights so this is a natural progression to do it with ticket sales," said Bernie Mullin, founder of The Aspire Group. "It will be a more integrated and sophisticated approach. The first opportunity will be doing a better job of data collection" (Lombardo and Smith, 2009, p. 1)

The arrangement calls for The Aspire Group to handle full and partial season-ticket sales in exchange for a flat management fee and a percentage of any increase in ticket sales. Georgia Tech's athletic department maintains control of ticket prices and season ticket plans as well as ticket sales of premium seating and suites. After signing the agreement with Georgia Tech, The Aspire Group set up a full time sales staff of around 15 people who work on Georgia Tech's Atlanta campus.

"It boils down to cost containment and efficiency," said Mullin. "Traditionally, schools have a smaller number of year-round sales staff, but we can put more staff and resources behind the sales efforts. The school is providing the infrastructure and we are providing the management, systems, and procedures" (Lombardo and Smith, 2009, p. 1). Added Georgia Tech's Athletic Director Dan Radakovich: "We look at this as the next frontier for what we need to do to sell tickets" (Lombardo and Smith, 2009, p. 1).

The outsourcing of college ticket sales is by no means a new concept. Following a lengthy career in ticket sales for leagues such as the NFL, Chris Hutson founded New Jersey-based Turnstyles Ticketing in the late 1990s. One of his first clients was the University of Miami, challenged with re-building their football season ticket base as the Hurricanes were coming off of serious NCAA sanctions. "There are a lot of hard costs involved in the ticketing function," said Hutson. "The ticket sales business has evolved to the point where it makes more sense for a lot of schools to outsource, as opposed to investing in such things as the latest ticketing software packages, hardware, sales personnel, and telephone calling charges" (Personal communication, June 11, 2010).

Given his two decades of hands-on experience in the sport ticket sales business, Hutson has strong feelings about the value that outside sales firms can bring to collegiate institutions: "They tend to depend too much on gimmicks. Marketing plans are nice, but by themselves they are not going to move the needle. What we offer is a staff of people who are not only trained in ticket sales, but who also have years of ticket sales experience" (Personal communication, June 11, 2010).

To Outsource or Not to Outsource? That Is the Question

Between the 2005 and 2008 Georgia Tech football seasons, attendance at the 55,000 seat Bobby Dodd stadium declined from an average of 51,607 per game to an average of 47,489 (a nearly 8% decline in attendance). In the season in which Georgia Tech outsourced its ticket sales to The Aspire Group, attendance increased by over 12% to a per game average of 51,584 (**Table 14-2**). Additionally, during the first four months of 2010 The Aspire Group had sold more than 770 new season-ticket packages, representing over $240,000 in additional revenue (Roberson, 2010).

Revenue generated from football and men's basketball ticket sales is the lifeblood of collegiate athletic department. Consider that during the 2006 fiscal year, ticket sales accounted for nearly 30% of the revenue generated by members of the NCAA's Football Bowl Subdivision, the single largest source of revenue (Fulks, 2008). Research has indicated that a number of factors influence consumer demand for collegiate sport (Groza, 2010). While a number of these factors are outside of the control of the sales department, the ticket sales department must nonetheless strive to promote and ultimately sell tickets by highlighting the value to the customer. For high demand games (i.e., the home team is having a successful season and/or is playing a quality opponent), creating a value proposition for the customer is not difficult. However, selling tickets to low demand games (i.e., the home team is having an unsuccessful season and/or is playing an undesirable opponent) represents a much more challenging task for the ticket sales department.

The art of selling is becoming increasingly scientific and technology-driven. Today, advanced analytics such as consumer demand modeling and customer relationship management (CRM) systems allow sales managers to intelligently predict demand and sales personnel to better understand the individual customer.

TABLE 14-2 Georgia Tech Football Attendance

Year	Average Attendance	Percent of Capacity	Change from Previous Season
2009	51,584	93.78	+12.43%
2008	47,489	86.34	−5.55%
2007	50,280	91.42	−0.67%
2006	50,617	92.03	−1.92%
2005	51,607	93.83	+10.23%

Source: National Collegiate Athletic Association. (n.d.). Retrieved from http://www.ncaa.org/stats

The goal of implementing systems such as these is ultimately to increase sales revenue. However, procuring and implementing advanced analytic programs is often quite expensive, requires dedicated staff, and intense training. Not all colleges and universities have the financial wherewithal, or the sales acumen, to invest in new sales systems and technologies. "In our experience," said Hutson, "there are often layers of bureaucracy within colleges and universities, and especially state universities, that require bid processes that can hinder progress on even simple things like adding phone lines to improve the sales department. This is another potential advantage of outsourcing, since companies like ours can absorb that cost and responsibility" (Personal communication, June 11, 2010).

Although The Aspire Group hired and managed 15 sales people who were physically located within the Georgia Tech athletic facility, the more prevalent model to date has been for outside firms such as Turnstyles Ticketing to handle all ticket sales from their corporate headquarters in New Jersey. "This enables us to achieve economies of scale in terms of selling for multiple collegiate institutions, without adding overhead and costs for setting up a sales center at each and every institution," added Hutson (Personal communication, June 11, 2010).

Questions for Discussion

1. The outsourcing of licensing, media, and sponsorship rights is a business-to-business (so-called B2B) operation. Outside firms like IMG College and Learfield endeavor to find local, regional, and national businesses to buy advertising, sponsorships, and the like. Conversely, selling tickets is primarily a business-to-consumer (so-called B2C) endeavor. Assume you are the Athletic Director for a mid-sized Division I university. What would you see as some fundamental differences in these two sales approaches?

2. Assuming the same situation, what concerns might you have about an outside firm selling tickets for your university from a sales call center in another location, perhaps even another state?

3. Assume you are the Athletic Director for a major Division I football powerhouse. Would you recommend that your athletic department outsource its ticket operations? Why or why not? What factors would influence your decision?

many inventory elements typically included in sponsorship packages, they often require input, review, and sign-off by a number of departments within the company, including advertising, sales, promotions, and public relations. Third, because the company will want to fully utilize and effectively leverage its sponsorship, the process of selling sponsorship packages must allow the company sufficient lead time, particularly if the company needs to plan retail promotions.

For instance, if a company were interested in sponsoring its local NFL team, which begins play in September, the deal would ideally have to be completed by the prior April to allow the company sufficient lead time to develop and begin to implement its sales promotion and advertising campaign by the start of the season. In short, it is much easier for an individual to decide to purchase a ticket package than for a corporation to decide to invest in a sponsorship package.

In selling sponsorship packages, Mullin, Hardy, and Sutton (2000) have suggested the following sales process:

1. Schedule a meeting with the sponsorship decision-maker. Remember, don't accept a "no" from someone who is not empowered to say "yes."
2. At the first meeting, listen 80% of the time and sell only when you have to. You are there to observe and learn. Where does the potential sponsor spend its marketing dollars right now? What is working? What isn't working? What other sport organizations or events does the company sponsor or support? What does the company like or dislike about these relationships?
3. Arrange a follow-up meeting for the presentation of your proposal before leaving this initial meeting (ideally, within one week).
4. Create a marketing partnership proposal. Give the potential sponsor a promotional program that can be proprietary to that company. Act more like a marketing partner than a salesperson.
5. Present the proposal as a "draft" that you will gladly modify to meet the company's needs. Custom-tailored proposals are much more likely to succeed than generic proposals.
6. Negotiate the final deal and get a signed agreement. Close the deal when you have the opportunity—ask for the order! Be sure

that the final signed deal has agreed-upon deliverables, payment terms, and mutually agreed-upon timetables.

■ SUMMARY

The steadily increasing competition for customers—both individuals and corporate—has sparked an evolution in sales methodologies within the sport industry. Today, smart sport organizations build and manage well-trained sales staffs that are committed to the philosophy of customer-focused relationship building. If you choose to begin your sport management career with a team sport organization, as so many do, chances are you will find yourself situated somewhere within the organization's sales department. There is no better place to begin! Sales are the lifeblood of any sport organization, and regardless of your career path—from ticket sales to suite sales to sponsorship sales and perhaps into other disciplines within a sport organization—you will always be selling. The tools and experience garnered from responsibilities as unromantic as telemarketing—a sport industry form of "paying one's dues"—will pay big dividends as you move up in your career.

■ KEY TERMS

aftermarketing, benefit selling, database marketing, direct mail, eduselling, personal selling, sales inventory, telemarketing, up-selling

■ REFERENCES

Brennan, J. (2010, June 9). Insurer the "cure" for Nets' sponsorship needs in off-season. *Bergen (NJ) Record*. Retrieved November 3, 2010, from http://www.northjersey.com/news/bergen/95932319_Nets_a_good_investment__CURE_says.html

Fulks D.L. (2008). *2004–06 NCAA Revenue and Expenses of Division Intercollegiate Athletics Programs Report*. National Collegiate Athletic Association: Indianapolis, IN.

Groza M.D. (2010) ."NCAA conference realignment and football game day attendance" *Managerial and Decision Economics* (in press). Abstract retrieved on November 3, 2010, from http://onlinelibrary .wiley.com/doi/10.1002/mde.1506/abstract

Honebein, P. (1997). *Strategies for effective customer education*. Lincolnwood, IL: NTC Business Books.

Irwin, R., Sutton, W.A., & McCarthy, L. (2002). *Sport promotion and sales management*. Champaign, IL: Human Kinetics.

Irwin, R., Sutton, W.A., & McCarthy, L. (2008). *Sport promotion and sales management* (2nd edition). Champaign, IL: Human Kinetics.

King, B. (2010, March 15). Always be closing. *Street & Smith's SportsBusiness Journal*, p. 1.

Lombardo J. & Smith M. (2009, May 25). Ga. Tech hands ticket sales to Aspire Group. *Street & Smith's SportsBusiness Journal*, p. 1.

Marta, S. (2008, March 31). Dallas Cowboys stadium naming rights may top record deal. *Dallas Morning News*. Retrieved November 3, 2010, from http://www.dallasnews.com/sharedcontent/dws/ spt/football/cowboys/stories/033008dnbusnami ngrights.2b2caec.html

McCormack, M. (1984). *What they don't teach you at Harvard Business School*. New York: Bantam.

McCormack, M. (1996). *On selling*. West Hollywood, CA: Dove Books.

McDonald, M.A. (1996). Service quality and customer lifetime value in professional sport franchises.

Unpublished doctoral dissertation, University of Massachusetts, Amherst.

Mickle, T. (2010, May 24). MLS will be first league to run extensive ticket sales training. *Street & Smith's SportsBusiness Journal*, p. 5.

Minnesota Wild. (2002–2003). Customer Service program. Unpublished information from application for PRISM Award.

Mullin, B., Hardy, S., & Sutton, W.A. (2000). *Sport marketing* (2nd ed.). Champaign, IL: Human Kinetics.

National Collegiate Athletic Association. (n.d.) Retrieved March 1, 2011, from http://www.ncaa.org/stats

Radcliffe, J. (2002, April 29–May 5). Name game gets more complicated for teams. *Street & Smith's SportsBusiness Journal*, p. 26.

Roberson, D. (2010, April 28). Tech season-ticket sales improving. *Atlanta Journal Constitution*. Retrieved November 3, 2010, from http://blogs .ajc.com/georgia-tech-sports/2010/04/28/tech-season-ticket-sales-improving

Sutton, B. (2010, May 10). Using technology to build ticket database can boost bottom line. *Street & Smith's SportsBusiness Journal*, p. 11.

Team Marketing Report. (1998, February 8). *Red Sox telephone ticket systems dials up immediate sales results*. Chicago: Author.

Team Marketing Report. (2010). *Fan cost index*. Retrieved on June 1, 2010, from http:// teammarketing.com.ismmedia.com/ISM3/std-content/repos/Tpo/Fan%20Cost%20Index/MLB/ MLB_FCI_2010.pdf

Vavra, T.G. (1992). *Aftermarketing: How to keep customers for life through relationship marketing*. New York: Irwin.

15

Sport Sponsorship

Stephen McKelvey

■ INTRODUCTION

When the Dayton Dragons of minor league baseball's Class A Midwest League first opened the gates of newly minted Fifth Third Field in April 2000, a standing-room-only crowd was greeted by what the team dubbed the "world's largest outdoor billboard." Instead of continuing the age-old minor league baseball tradition of plastering the outfield walls with upwards of 50 hand-painted sponsor signs—the epitome, some might argue, of advertising "clutter"—the Dragons had constructed one outfield sign (240 feet long by 6 feet high) to cover the entire outfield wall. The sign is backlit and rotates every half-inning with a wall-to-wall advertisement from one of the team's major sponsors. Thus, at any time during the game, only one company is promoted to the entire crowd.

This innovative strategy for selling their outfield wall signage was meant to create and deliver, as the Dragons call it, a "dominant identity" for their sponsors. The Dragons carried the concept of "dominant identity" even further by limiting the total number of team sponsors to just 30. This approach to sponsorship represents a dramatic shift in strategy from the traditional minor league team that boasts anywhere from 75 to 300 sponsors. The Dragons' approach to sponsorship—sell fewer sponsorships and give those sponsors incrementally more benefits, exposure, and "identity" to consumers—illustrates just one type of approach, or philosophy, that sport organizations can take with respect to corporate sponsorship. This chapter provides an introduction to sponsorship within the sport industry. What is sport sponsorship all about? What benefits can sport organizations provide to sponsors? What are the key elements of a sponsorship package? How do companies use sport sponsorship to achieve their marketing objectives, such as generating increased brand awareness and incremental sales of their products and services?

As you proceed, one common theme will run throughout this chapter. The Dayton Dragons' example illustrates the growing need and desire for sport organizations to think outside the box in terms of attracting corporate sponsors in a sport marketplace that continues to be increasingly competitive. The continuing influx of new sport leagues, teams, and events has created more and more options for companies large and small to engage in sport sponsorship. Ultimately, sport organizations that can best meet the needs and objectives of companies, and deliver on their promises, will be the ones that are most successful in attracting and retaining sponsorship partners.

Sponsorship is one of the most prolific forms of sport marketing. It has been defined as "a cash and/or in-kind fee paid to a property . . . in return for access to the exploitable commercial potential associated with that property" (Ukman, 1995, p. 1). For the major professional sport leagues and associations, sponsorship fees often exceed $10 million per year per sponsor and are often structured as multiyear deals. Sponsorship provides a company with the right to associate with a sport property. A sponsorship agreement also gives the company the opportunity to leverage its affiliation with the sport property to achieve marketing objectives that range from generating incremental sales to entertaining key customers to generating positive awareness for the company and its products or services. Sponsorship is more integrated than other promotion activities and contains a variety of marketing-mix elements designed to send messages to a targeted audience. These elements include but are not limited to advertising, sales promotion, grassroots event programs, public relations and publicity, cause marketing, and hospitality.

■ A BRIEF HISTORY OF SPORT SPONSORSHIP

Although we can trace some semblance of sport sponsorship back to the ancient Greek Olympics—local businesses paid charioteers to wear their colors—the increasing commercialization of sport has led to a tremendous growth in the area of sport sponsorship. Whereas $300 million was spent on sport sponsorship in 1980 (Mullin, Hardy, & Sutton, 2000), that number had grown to $11.28 billion by 2009 (IEG, 2010). One of the fastest-growing industry segments is action sports, as more companies seek to reach the youth market. North American–based companies were projected to spend an estimated $120 million in 2006 to sponsor skateboarding, snowboarding, freestyle motocross, and other action sports properties (IEG, 2006). **Table 15-1** lists the top 25 sport advertisers in 2009.

Industry pundits have identified the 1984 Los Angeles Olympic Games as a watershed event in the evolution of sport sponsorship. The Los Angeles Olympic Organizing Committee, under the direction of its president, Peter Ueberroth, brought a new commercial mind-set to the L.A. Games in its effort to make its Games the first Olympic Games to ever turn a profit for the host city. Employing a "less is more" sales strategy, Ueberroth and his marketing team signed a limited number of companies (30) to exclusive official sponsorship contracts ranging in fees from $4 million to $15 million per company. AT&T alone paid $5 million to sponsor the first-ever cross-country Olympic torch relay. Fuji Photo Film USA paid $9 million to outbid goliath Kodak for the official sponsorship rights in the film and camera category in an effort to firmly entrench itself in America as a major player (Dentzer, 1984). By effectively leveraging its Olympic sponsorship, Fuji was able to grab tremendous increased market share in southern California that it has

TABLE 15-1	2009 Top U.S. Sport Advertising Spenders				
Rank	Company	Sport Ad Spending (millions)	Total Ad Spending (millions)	Pct. of Ad Spending Dedicated to Sports	Change in Sports Spending (2009 vs. 2007)
1	Anheuser-Busch	$309.2	$408.0	75.8	15.5
2	Verizon Communications	228.2	1,131.2	20.2	5.0
3	Sprint Nextel	205.0	569.4	36.0	15.9
4	Ford	197.3	599.4	32.9	-1.2
5	AT&T Wireless	180.9	757.9	23.9	0.1
6	Geico Direct	171.3	431.4	39.7	105.7
7	Toyota Motor Sales USA	166.8	509.3	32.7	-18.3
8	DirecTV	166.7	383.0	43.5	65.7
9	Chevrolet Motor Division	160.3	450.9	35.6	-24.6
10	McDonald's	155.4	724.5	21.5	24.6
11	Pfizer Pharmaceuticals	129.2	648.4	19.9	216.4
12	Southwest Airlines	126.5	196.8	64.3	11.0
13	State Farm	117.1	268.2	43.7	37.8
14	MillerCoors	116.8	173.1	67.5	10.0
15	Coors Brewing	115.2	143.2	80.5	1.3
16	Taco Bell	112.2	226.7	49.5	28.1
17	Warner Bros. Entertainment	111.1	459.2	24.2	93.9
18	Subway	98.6	377.2	26.2	28.2
19	Apple	97.1	384.5	25.2	8.7
20	Microsoft	94.9	358.8	26.5	287.3
21	GMC Truck Division	89.8	190.8	47.1	9.2
22	Dodge Car-Truck Division	87.0	275.9	31.5	-23.7
23	Coca-Cola	79.8	159.0	50.2	-4.3
24	Lexus	78.7	177.0	44.4	22.9
25	Lilly Icos Pharmaceuticals	78.1	144.0	54.2	27.5

Source: Broughton, D. (2010b, April 19). A-B again leads list of top sports advertisers. *Street & Smith's SportsBusiness Journal*, p. 11.

never relinquished. The publicity surrounding this highly successful commercial venture not only resulted in Ueberroth being named *Time* magazine's "Man of the Year" but also ushered in a new era of sport sponsorship by demonstrating that companies could gain tremendous benefits from sponsorships.

On the heels of his commercial success with the L.A. Olympics, Ueberroth became commissioner of Major League Baseball (MLB) and quickly raised the sponsorship bar for the major professional sport leagues as well. Utilizing his proven "less is more" strategy, in 1985 Ueberroth and his MLB marketing team created

MLB's first-ever league-wide program that again signaled to corporate America and the business media that a new age was dawning in the world of corporate sponsorship. The innovative corporate sponsorship program, dubbed the "2-2-1 Plan," required that companies annually commit a minimum of $2 million in advertising to support and promote MLB, a minimum of $2 million in promotional spending allocated equally to every MLB team (to prevent sponsors from cherry-picking the most popular MLB teams for promotional involvements), and $1 million in a cash and/or in-kind rights fee. MLB rigidly held to its "2-2-1" standard, frequently turning away companies that could not or would not commit to this sponsorship formula, and also rigidly required all sponsors to commit to MLB for no less than three years. Although companies such as Gillette, a decades-old sponsor of MLB's annual All-Star Balloting program, balked at a financial commitment that represented in the neighborhood of a 20-fold increase, MLB had within three years built, literally from scratch, a stable of national sponsors that included such blue-chip companies as Chevrolet, Coca-Cola, Equitable, Fuji Photo Film USA, Kellogg's, Leaf Candies, MasterCard, and *USA Today*. In many respects due to Ueberroth's high-profile stature, MLB's national sponsorship program became a model for the other major professional sport leagues, and sped the emergence of sponsorship as a viable marketing platform.

In addition to the commercial success of the 1984 Los Angeles Olympics, there are several other reasons for the tremendous growth in sport sponsorship over the past two and half decades. One influence is the increased media interest in sport, which has provided companies with a built-in mechanism for promoting their sponsorship involvements. This has assured sponsors a better opportunity that their sponsorship will be publicized. Concurrently, sponsorship began to be viewed as a way for companies to break through the clutter of traditional adver-

tising. Through sponsorship, companies are able to derive numerous in-venue, in-broadcast, and online promotion and publicity benefits that go far beyond the impact of a 30-second commercial spot in connecting with consumers.

Further, companies began to realize the impact that sponsorship could have in reaching their target consumers through their lifestyles (Mullin, Hardy, & Sutton, 2000). Corporate marketing executives have found that linking their messages to leisure pursuits conveys their messages immediately, credibly, and to a captive audience. Targeted sponsorships also enable corporate marketers to reach specific segments, such as heavy users, shareholders, and investors, or specific groups that have similar demographics, psychographics, or geographic commonalities. For instance, the director of marketing for Golden Flake Snack Foods, a regional snack food company, remarked in discussing his company's sponsorship of Southeastern Conference (SEC) football: "College football is a religion in the Southeast. Sponsorship lets us tap into the emotions people have for these events and be part of something they value. Because we try to maintain long-term relationships, people recognize and appreciate that we're not a fly-by-night sponsor, but have a commitment to [the SEC]" (IEG, 2003b, p. 6). Another example of using sport sponsorship to target a specific geographic market is Glidden Professional's sponsorship of the Big South Athletic Conference (Smith, 2010). Glidden Professional, an Ohio based paint company, sought to enhance awareness of their brand in the South by sponsoring a sport property based in that region. Through its agreement with the Big South Conference, Glidden is designated the conference's "official paint supplier" and will have access to all 10 of the league's schools throughout South Carolina, North Carolina and Virginia (Smith, 2010). PepsiCo has long used sponsorship to reach specific target markets. Take for example, PepsiCo's title sponsorship of NBC's action sports series "The Dew Tour." Through this sponsorship PepsiCo is able to reach a demographic that they have assessed as the typical Mountain Dew consumer: young, active, and daring (Mickle, 2010).

Last but not least, the discipline of sport sponsorship emerged as the decision-making process was gradually transferred from the company's corporate executive officer (CEO) to the company's team of marketing professionals. Historically, companies delved into a sponsorship program because the CEO wanted to; the CEO liked to golf, so he made sure his company became a sponsor of the Professional Golf Association (PGA). However, today sport sponsorship has become a discipline involving serious research, large investments, and strategic planning (Mullin, Hardy, & Sutton, 2000). Buying decisions have become much more sophisticated, requiring sellers to provide compelling business reasons to the prospective sponsor (e.g., demographic information demonstrating that his or her property will deliver the right target audience for the company) and requiring potential buyers to demonstrate to their CEO that a sponsorship program will meet the company's specific marketing and sales objectives in some measurable way. This is commonly referred to as **return on investment (ROI)**, a topic that will be more fully discussed in the section entitled "Evaluating Sport Sponsorships."

The increased competition for the loyalties of sport consumers has also changed the priorities of sport properties in terms of the companies with which they choose to partner. Today, sport properties prefer not to partner with companies that simply purchase the sponsorship rights (thereby blocking out their category from their competitors) and then do little or nothing to utilize, or leverage, their sponsorship to the benefit of both the sponsor and the sport property itself. Thus, more and more sponsorship contracts today require that the sponsor commit financial resources in support of its sponsorship through promotion and advertising that thematically includes the sport property's imagery. This is a concept known as sponsorship **activation**. The oft-cited rule of thumb for activating a sponsorship is 3 to 1 ($3 in advertising/promotion support for every $1 spent in rights fees). Research has shown, however, that this ratio is rarely met. In fact, a 2001 survey of sport sponsors found the average ratio of activation dollars to rights fees to be 1.2 to 1. While the average ratio had grown to 1.9 to 1 by 2007, it still is far less than the suggested 3 to 1 ratio (Weeks, Cornwell, & Drennan, 2008).

Concurrently, given the increased competition for corporate sponsorship dollars, prospective sponsors have gained leverage in negotiations. It's the age-old question: Who needs whom more? Thus, companies have become more demanding of sport properties in terms of the marketing rights and benefits they are provided. "Sponsors are pushing harder," noted the vice-president of PepsiCo's Sports Marketing Division, "and leagues are working harder to add value and measurable results" (Solomon, 2002, p. 1). The National Hockey League (NHL), for example, allowed Pepsi to conduct a promotion in which the grand prize winner would have the Stanley Cup delivered to his or her house by Mark Messier, the NHL's second-leading all time scorer. It is now routine for leagues to allow their official sponsors to conduct sweepstakes that reward winners with the chance to throw out first pitches at the World Series and drop the ceremonial puck at Stanley Cup Games.

From beverage companies and fruit growers' associations to gambling casinos and airlines, the range of companies engaging in sport sponsorship continues to expand. If your organization or property can deliver the audience that companies are seeking to target, there is a sponsorship possibility for those with creative minds and strong sales skills.

SALES PROMOTION IN SPORT SPONSORSHIP

Sponsorship programs are often built upon some type of promotional activity, generally referred to as sales promotion. **Sales promotion** is defined as "a variety of short-term, promotional activities that are designed to stimulate immediate product demand" (Shank, 2009, p. 312). Although aimed primarily at driving sales in the short term, typically over the course of a month or two, sponsors' sales promotion efforts may also be aimed at increasing brand awareness, broadening the sales distribution channels for their product or service, and getting new consumers to sample their product or service. A typical example of a sport-themed sales promotion is when a sponsoring company provides all fans with a free item featuring the company's logo (also known as a *premium item*) as they enter the arena. In addition to such in-venue activities, sales promotions are often implemented at the retail level (known as *in-store promotions*), such as an offer of a free game ticket when fans redeem a soft drink can at the box office. This section first discusses the implementation and benefits of in-venue promotions, then discusses in-store promotion tactics.

In-Venue Promotions

No other sport has utilized in-stadium promotion as widely as baseball. One major reason for this is that "putting fannies in seats" has traditionally been more of a priority in baseball than in the other major sports: Major League Baseball teams have 81 home dates with thousands of seats to fill each game. At the opposite extreme, National Football League (NFL) teams have historically had little need to attract additional fans with "freebies" and giveaways because the majority sell out their stadiums for all home games. The trend across all sports, however, has

been to increase the amount of "value-added" benefits that teams provide their paying customers, which has resulted in a growth in in-stadium promotions across the sport industry. In-stadium promotions run the gamut from traditional giveaway days, in which the sponsor underwrites the cost of a premium item in exchange for its logo on the item and advertising support that promotes the event, to themed-event days such as nostalgia-driven "Turn Back the Clock Days" popular in Major League Baseball. Many teams have also created what are known as *continuity promotions*; these require fans to attend multiple games to obtain, for instance, each player card in a limited-edition trading card set (and thus build attendance frequency).

Sport organizations are constantly on the prowl for the hottest fad in giveaway items. For instance, back in the late 1980s and early 1990s, baseball teams gorged on the collectible trading card craze. Fans would line up hours before games to ensure that they received the hottest new trading card–themed giveaway item, ranging from the Surf detergent–sponsored Topps Baseball Card books to the Smokey the Bear–themed collectors sets and the Upper Deck Heroes of Baseball card sheets. Beanie Babies emerged as the hot items in the late 1990s, and the bobblehead doll craze followed shortly thereafter. **Table 15-2** lists Major League Baseball's most successful giveaways during the 2009 season.

The success of an in-venue promotion varies widely based on a number of factors, including time of season (and teams' current win–loss records), the day of promotion (weeknight versus weekend), opponent, and perceived quality of the giveaway item or themed promotion event day. Contrary to what one might expect, teams generally build their promotional calendars to feature their most attractive giveaways or events on their more attractive dates (in terms of opponents and game times) because of the popu-

TABLE 15-2	2009 MLB In-Stadium Giveaways		
Givaway	Number of Dates	Attendance Per Date	Percent Increase in Attendance From Average
Webkinz toy	17	39,857	31.60
Blanket	11	36,742	21.20
Banner/pennant	10	35,054	15.60
Magnetic schedule	41	34,438	13.70
Bobblehead	75	34,074	12.70
Figurine	29	33,006	8.90
Cap	85	32,379	7.00
Backpack/bag	48	31,720	4.60
Jersey	34	31,486	3.80
Lunch box/school supplies	25	29,740	−2.00
Calendar	23	29,580	−2.60
Poster	33	28,157	−7.30
Helmet/gloves	14	27,788	−8.50
Shirt	67	26,920	−11.60
Baseball cards	11	20,175	−33.50

Sources: How goes the gate? Giveaways and other promotions and their effect on attendance. (2009, October 19). *Street & Smith's SportsBusiness Journal.* Retrieved November 4, 2010, from http://www.sportsbusinessjournal.com/Journal/Issues/2009/10/20091019/SBJ-In-Depth/How-Goes-The-Gate-Giveaways-And-Other-Promotions-And-Their-Effect-On-Attendance.aspx

lar notion that a strong promotional giveaway or event typically attracts a larger *incremental* audience. For example, the Chicago White Sox staging a fan appreciation day against an unattractive opponent on a midweek night might attract an incremental 1,000 fans. That same promotion versus the Yankees on a Saturday afternoon might draw an incremental 10,000 fans. **Table 15-3** shows a ranking of the most effective in-stadium promotions for MLB teams during the 2009 season, based upon the percentage increase in turnstile attendance.

In-Store Promotions

One of the primary reasons that companies secure sponsorships is to drive sales of their product or service. Hence, not surprisingly, companies often leverage their sponsorships at the retail level: in stores where their product is sold, or within their own retail stores. In-store promotion encompasses a wide variety of tactics to incentivize consumers and to communicate offers, including the following:

- **Premiums** can be described as "merchandise offered free or at a reduced price as an inducement to buy a different item or items" (Block & Robinson, 1994, p. 876). One of the most popular tactics is offering premiums to consumers who redeem a certain number of proof-of-purchase seals (also known as UPCs) that are printed on the product itself. Premiums can also be delivered to consumers in-pack or on-pack. For example, a cereal company can activate its National Association of Stock Car Auto Racing (NASCAR) sponsorship by offering

| | | | Percent Change in |
| | Number | Attendance | Attendance (from average |
Promotion	of Dates	Per Date	game with no promotion)

TABLE 15-3 MLB In-Stadium Promotions

Promotion	Number of Dates	Attendance Per Date	Percent Change in Attendance (from average game with no promotion)
Team history tribute	19	34,488	13.8
Autographs	48	33,294	9.9
Fan appreciation day	29	33,113	9.2
Concert	36	33,020	8.9
Fireworks	195	32,743	8.6
Run the bases	53	32,511	7.3
Cultural celebration	61	31,811	4.9
Military day	28	30,195	-0.6
Concessions discount	122	29,063	-4.5
Health awareness day	26	28,491	-6.2
Kids day	60	28,148	-7.4
Family day	41	26,853	-11.7
Pet day	15	26,287	-13.5
Little League day	26	26,180	-13.9
College night	22	24,176	-20.5

Sources: How goes the gate? Giveaways and other promotions and their effect on attendance. (2009, October 19). *Street & Smith's SportsBusiness Journal.* Retrieved November 4, 2010 from http://www.sportsbusinessjournal.com/Journal/Issues/2009/10/20091019/SBJ-In-Depth/How-Goes-The-Gate-Giveaways-And-Other-Promotions-And-Their-Effect-On-Attendance.aspx

consumers a free mini-race car inside specially marked boxes.

- **Contests** and **sweepstakes** are other popular sales tools used in sales promotion. Contests are competitions that award prizes based on contestants' skills and ability, whereas sweepstakes are games of chance or luck. A sport team or company may require a purchase as a condition of consumers being entered into the contest (e.g., requiring contestants in a football accuracy throwing contest to enter by submitting proofs-of-purchase); however, contests typically appeal to a much smaller universe of potential customers than sweepstakes (where everyone has a *chance* to win). Companies and sport teams conducting sweepstakes may not require the purchase

of the product or service for consumers to become eligible to win prizes (thus, the "No Purchase Necessary" notice that precedes all sweepstakes rules).

Sweepstakes typically offer trips to special sporting events, the opportunity for the winner to meet a celebrity athlete, or some other "aspirational" prize that would be difficult (if not impossible) for the winner to otherwise obtain. For example, Pepperidge Farms Goldfish Baked Crackers signed National Basketball Association (NBA) star Dwayne Wade for a sweepstakes in which customers could sign up online to win prizes including an all-expenses paid trip for four to the NBA All-Star game. Staples has leveraged its role as the NFL's "official office supply retailer" with a sweepstakes called the "Staples Score NFL Season Tickets Sweepstakes," offering one of 32 lucky winners season tickets to the team of his or her choice. Consumers entered by filling out a sweepstakes entry form at their local Staples store that also requested valuable demographic and purchase-decision information that surely went into Staples' customer database for use in future direct mail campaigns. Sport teams and companies have also increasingly turned to an online sweepstakes entry process as a means of driving traffic to their Web sites. After all, it is easier to post a sweepstakes entry form on one's own Web site than to hope that the sweepstakes entry forms get posted and displayed in stores.

- **Sampling** is one of the most effective sales promotion tools to induce consumers to try a product; it is most often used in the introduction of a new product. Companies typically use sampling to leverage their sport sponsorship by gaining access to a major sporting event, such as the MLB All-Star FanFest or a college bowl game, at which they can hand out product samples to the captive and targeted audience that attends such events. Sampling is not without its hard costs. Although the product samples may be free to consumers, bear in mind when planning a sampling campaign that it still costs money for the company to produce the samples and hire individuals (usually a professional sampling firm) to distribute them to the 70,000 consumers attending, for instance, MLB's All-Star FanFest.
- **Point-of-sale** or **point-of-purchase marketing**, interchangeably referred to in industry lingo as POS or POP, is used by marketers to attract consumers' attention to their product or service and their promotional campaign at the retail level. POS display materials can include end-aisle units

(large cardboard displays that sit on the floor and are featured at the end of retail store aisles), "shelf-talkers" (cardboard displays that hang on aisle shelves), and banners that are designed to attract potential customers. The life-sized cardboard cut-outs of star athletes that you see in grocery and footwear stores are examples of POS materials. Typically these display pieces hold brochures, coupons, or sweepstakes entry forms.

- **Coupons**, certificates that generally offer reductions in price for a product or service, are another popular sales promotion tool. They most often appear in print advertisements such as **freestanding inserts (FSIs)**, which are the coupon sections that appear each week in Sunday newspapers. Coupons may also be delivered to consumers on the product package itself, inserted into the product itself, or mailed to consumers. In-store promotions are also typically supported by coupons that appear in the participating retailers' circular (the coupon magazines available in-store). Although coupons have been found to induce short-term sales, one disadvantage is that the continual use of coupons can detract from the product's image in the mind of consumers. In addition, studies have shown that most coupon redemption is done by consumers who already use the product, thereby limiting the effectiveness of coupons to attract new customers (Shank, 2009).

Putting It All Together: Kraft's "Taste of Victory" Promotion

Kraft Foods is one of the world's largest sport sponsorship spenders. Kraft's "taste of victory" promotion, a multifaceted corporate-wide engagement, perfectly illustrates the implementation of the various sales promotion tactics discussed previously. The promotion, thematically tied to Kraft's celebration of its 100 years in business, leveraged the company's sponsorship of Dale Earnhardt's NASCAR race team and was supported by a multitude of Kraft brands, including Country Time Lemonade, Miracle Whip, A1 Steak Sauce, and Grey Poupon mustard. Entitled "Get a Taste of Victory," the promotion was communicated via in-store POS end-aisle displays, advertisements and coupons in retailers' circulars, and a full-page FSI in the nation's Sunday newspapers. The FSI included a mail-in form enticing consumers to mail in two proofs-of-purchase from any featured Kraft products (plus $4.00 shipping and handling) to receive a "free" premium: a Kraft 100th anniversary die-cast race car (miniature die-cast cars being one of the hottest collectibles in the auto-racing industry). The FSI also encouraged consumers to visit Kraftfoods.com to enter a sweepstakes to win the grand prize: a "street-legal" version of Kraft's 100th anniversary race car valued at $31,000. The POS displays served as a means to attract consumers to Kraft products in-store, the premium offer of the die-cast racing car served as a means of driving incremental sales (particularly among the extremely loyal race car fans), and the online sweepstakes served as a vehicle for collecting the names and addresses of Kraft customers (for future direct mailings). Finally, Kraft's purchase of advertisements and coupons in retailers' circular magazines served to ensure the retailers' in-store support of the promotion, in the form of providing Kraft with the most valuable "real estate" in any store: the end of aisles, where the bulk of impulse purchases take place. If this sounds like a creative form of blackmail, well, it is! It is how the game is played at the retail level.

The Emergence of Cross-Promotion

As companies tackle the need to break through the clutter, drive sales, and better leverage their sport sponsorship investments, they have

sought to expand the scope of their sponsorships through **cross-promotion** with other companies or with other business units within the same company. This joining together of two or more companies to capitalize on a sponsorship is becoming increasingly popular and effective. Cross-promotion is viable in today's marketplace for a number of reasons, as suggested by Irwin, Sutton, and McCarthy (2008). Cross-promotions:

- Allow companies to share the total cost of the sponsorship, and/or the promotional execution.
- Allow promotion of several product lines within the same company, often drawing from separate budgets, as illustrated in Kraft's "Taste of Victory" promotion.
- Enable companies to utilize existing business relationships.
- Enable a weaker company to "piggyback" on the strength and position of a bigger company to gain an advantage over its competitors.
- Allow testing of a relationship when future opportunities are under consideration.

• Create a pass-through opportunity, typically involving grocery chains that agree to a sponsorship and pass some or all of the costs (and benefits) to product vendors in their stores. For example, Kroger sponsors a NASCAR team but then passes most of the sponsorship rights fees on to vendors such as Pepsi and Nabisco. In exchange, Kroger then agrees to feature Pepsi and Nabisco products in-store.

Sponsors team with other sponsors to create more bang for their buck under the premise that two sponsors working together can generate more interest and awareness among the targeted sport consumers. "Got Milk's" leveraging of its NASCAR sponsorship through a cross-promotion with Kellogg's illustrates the growing amount of sponsorship activation involving what has been dubbed "peanut butter and jelly" (PB&J) partners (IEG, 2003a). These PB&J partners illustrate cross-promotions by discrete brands that go together but can also stand alone.

Another increasingly popular cross-promotion tactic involves *co-dependent partners*, companies whose products or services are integral to each other, such as computer software and hardware manufacturers, teaming up to leverage a sport sponsorship (IEG, 2003a). For example, IBM, as a sponsor of the NBA, might offer a free NBA video game with the purchase of a new laptop. Finally, cross-promotions can be staged between *customer-partners*, two discrete brands that stand alone but do so much business with each other that they are almost siblings (IEG, 2003a). For example, to better leverage its sponsorship of MLB, Pepsi incorporated one of its biggest national customers, Subway restaurants, as a partner in an official All-Star Game balloting promotion. Such involvement between customer-partners not only greatly broadened the impact and awareness of MLB's All-Star balloting program nationwide but also enabled Pepsi to pass through an invaluable marketing asset to one of its largest national customers, thereby strengthening its business relationship with Subway.

As a sport marketer, whether on the property side or the corporate side, it has become increasingly important to think outside the box as to how sponsors can be joined together to increase the overall effectiveness of their sponsorship investments. Many of the official sponsors of the major professional sport leagues are hard at work looking for creative ways to cross-promote their companies. **Tables 15-4 through 15-7** provide either a list or a sampling of the official sponsors for several of the major North American professional sport leagues; **Table 15-8** provides a list of the International Olympic Committees' TOP (The Olympic Partner) Program sponsors. Here's a challenge: See if you can develop a few effective cross-promotion opportunities for them! Would you classify them as PB&J promotions, co-dependent partner promotions, or customer-partner promotions?

■ SPONSORSHIP PACKAGES

In 2010 Bridgestone Tire signed a five-year sponsorship deal with the National Hockey League. Bridgestone's sponsorship of the NHL provides a good illustration of the benefits typically included in a league or team sponsorship package as well as the types of commitments the sponsoring company makes to the sport organization. Benefits typically include the following:

• *Exclusivity* in one's product or service category (e.g., Bridgestone became the only company the NHL could sign as a national sponsor in the tire category).
• *"Official" designations:* Leagues and teams offer multiple designations tied to the sport and to the sponsor's product or service category. For instance, Bridgestone became the "official tire of the NHL," "official tire

of the NHLPA," and the "official tire of the Hockey Hall of Fame." (Many sport organizations, embracing a relationship marketing mentality, today prefer the use of "official partner" designations.)

- *Rights* to utilize the sport organization's intellectual property in advertising and

TABLE 15-4   NHL Corporate Marketing Partners (as of 2010)

Sponsor	Category	Since
Kraft	Cracker, cookie, snack mix	1989
McDonalds	Fast-Food restaurant	1993
Bud Light	Beer	1994
Verizon Wireless	U.S. Wireless telecom service	2000
Sirius XM Satellite Radio	Satellite radio	2003
Reebok	Apparel	2004
Gatorade	Sports & energy drinks	2006
Pepsi (Max)	Soft drink	2006
Bridgestone	Tire	2007
Scotiabank	Bank	2007
Ticketmaster	Secondary tickets	2007
Cisco	Technology solutions provider	2008
Honda	Automobile	2008
Visa	Credit card	2008
Compuware	Software applications	2009
Energizer	Battery	2009
U.S. Army	Government	2009
Bell	Canadian mobile phones	2010
Enterprise	Rental car	2010
Geico	Car insurance	2010
Starwood	Hotel	2010

Source: NHL Marketing Partners (2010). *NHL.com.* Retrieved November 4, 2010, from http://www.nhl.com/ice/page.htm?id=26370

TABLE 15-5   NBA Corporate Marketing Partners (as of 2010)

Sponsor	Category	Since
Gatorade	Sports & energy drinks	1984
Coca-Cola	Soft drinks, juice, and flavored drinks	1986
Nike	Footwear	1992
Anheuser-Busch	Beer (alcoholic and non-alcoholic malt beverages)	1998
adidas	Apparel/footwear	2002
Southwest Airlines	Airline	2003
FedEx	Overnight delivery services	2004
Electronic Arts	Video game software	2005
Sirius/XM Radio	Satellite radio	2005
Spalding	Basketballs	2005
T-Mobile	Wireless service provider & handset	2005
AutoTrader.com	Online auto retailer	2006
Haier America	High definition TVs & consumer appliances	2006
Cisco	Information technology & networking solutions	2007
HP	Personal computers, printers & IT services	2008
Kia Motors	Automotive	2008
Right Guard	Antiperspirant, deodorant & body wash	2008
Taco Bell	Quick service restaurant	2009
Bacardi	Rum	2010
State Farm	Insurance (all kinds)	2010

Source: "Spons-o-Meter: NBA boasts list of 20 marketing partners" (2010). Sports Business Daily.com. Retrieved from http://www.sportsbusinessdaily.com/article/138724. Courtesy of Sports Business Daily.

TABLE 15-6   NFL Corporate Marketing Partners (as of 2010)

Sponsor	Category	Since
News America	Super Bowl FSI	1979
Gatorade	Isotonic beverage	1983
Canon USA	Cameras and equipment, binoculars/field glasses, photo printers, camcorders	1984
Visa	Payment systems services	1995
Campbell Soup Company	Soup, canned pasta, tomato food sauces, salsa, chili	1998
Motorola	Wireless telecommunications equipment	1999
FedEx	Worldwide package delivery service	2000
Frito-Lay	Salted snacks, popcorn, peanuts/peanut products, salsa	2000
General Motors	Passenger cars and passenger trucks	2001
Coors Light	Beer	2002*
Mars Snackfood	Chocolate and non-chocolate candy products	2002
Pepsi	Soft drinks	2002
Tropicana	Juice	2002
National Dairy Council	Milk products	2003
IBM	Computer hardware and software, IT services	2003
Samsung	Televisions, stereo and speaker components of home audio entertainment systems, DVD players and recorders	2005
Sprint	Wireless telecommunications services	2005
Bank of America	Team identified credit cards, official banking of the NFL/NFL affinity credit cards	2007
Bridgestone	Automotive tires	2007
Ticketmaster	Online ticket exchange provider	2008
Monster.com	Career services	2008
Procter & Gamble	Over-the-counter heartburn medication, locker room products	2005** 2009
National Guard	Presenting sponsor of NFL High School Player Development	2009

* Bud Light will become the official beer of the NFL in the 2011 season

** Procter & Gamble first signed as an NFL sponsor in 2005 and extended their NFL presence in 2009

Source: "Spons-o-Meter: NFL lines up 23 partners to start '09 season" (2009). Sports Business Daily.com. Retrieved from http://www.sportsbusinessdaily.com/article/133218. Courtesy of Sports Business Daily.

promotion campaigns. For Bridgestone this includes the rights to use the NHL logo in promotional activities. (Typically, the major professional sport league sponsorship departments do not have the authority, via their agreement with their member teams, to grant national sponsors the right to uti- lize team logos on an individual team basis; such rights must be obtained directly from the desired team or teams.)

- *Title naming rights* for the "Bridgestone NHL Winter Classic," an annual regular sea- son outdoor hockey game typically played on or near New Years Day.

TABLE 15-7 MLB Corporate Marketing Partners (as of 2010)

Sponsor	Category	Since
Gillette	Grooming products and household batteries	1939
Anheuser-Busch	Alcoholic and non-alcoholic malt beverages	1980
Gatorade	Isotonic beverage/energy bar	1990
Pepsi-Cola	Soft drinks	1997
MasterCard Worldwide	Credit card	1998
Nike	Athletic footwear and eyewear	1998
Frito Lay	Salty snack provider	2002
Bank of America	Retail banking	2004
FIA Card Service, NA	Card	2004
Sirius XM	Satellite radio network	2004
Taco Bell	Quick-service restaurant	2004
General Motors (Chevy)	Vehicle	2005
InterContinental Hotels	Hotel	2006
KPMG	Accounting firm	2007
State Farm	Insurance	2007
Bayer (One a Day)	Multivitamin	2008
Firestone	Tire	2010
Scotts	Lawn care	2010

Source: Official sponsors of MLB.com. (2010). *MLB.com.* Retrieved November 4, 2010, from http://mlb.mlb.com/mlb/official_info/official_sponsors.jsp

TABLE 15-8 Top Olympic Sponsors (Vancouver 2010 and London 2012)

Company	Category	Headquarters
Acer	Technology manufacturer/IT support services	Taipei (Taiwan)
Atos Origin	IT service provider	Paris (France)
Coca Cola	Soft drinks	Atlanta, GA (USA)
General Electric	Diversified–energy	Fairfield, CT (USA)
McDonalds	Quick-service restaurant	Oak Brook, IL (USA)
Omega	Watch manufacturer	Bienne (Switzerland)
Panasonic	Consumer electronics	Kadoma (Japan)
Samsung	Consumer electronics	Seoul (South Korea)
Visa	Financial services	San Francisco, CA (USA)

Source: Sponsorship. (2010). *Olympic.org.* Retrieved November 4, 2010, from http://www.olympic.org/en/content/The-IOC/Sponsoring/Sponsorship/

- *In-stadium signage and promotional announcements* during NHL-controlled events such as the All-Star Game and the Stanley Cup Playoffs, often in the form of 30-second commercials and sponsor "thank you" messages via scoreboards, matrix boards, and public address (PA) announcements.
- *Access to tickets* for NHL-controlled events, including the All-Star Game, and the Stanley Cup Playoffs.
- *Access to the use of* NHL Player rights and images.

In exchange for these benefits, Bridgestone, again illustrative of most sport sponsorship contracts, made the following contractual commitments to the NHL:

- *A rights fee* in the form of a cash payment (typically spread out in periodic payments throughout the season)
- *Multiyear commitment* (most established sport properties insist on multiyear sponsorship deals to ensure stability for the league and a longer-term commitment by the sponsor; Bridgestone entered into a 5 year agreement with the NHL)
- *Advertising commitment* to spend a predetermined dollar amount on NHL-controlled media and/or with NHL's broadcast partners (i.e., NBC, CBC, and RDS)

Companies engaged in sport sponsorship use a wide variety of marketing elements, often collectively, to achieve their marketing objectives. The next section considers some possible sport sponsorship platforms.

■ SPORT SPONSORSHIP PLATFORMS

There are a broad range of platforms upon which a company can become involved in sport sponsorship. As suggested by Irwin, Sutton, and McCarthy (2008), these platforms are often integrated to expand the depth and breadth of the sponsorship.

Governing Body Sponsorship

A governing body sponsorship entails securing the "official sponsor" status with a national or international sport league or governing association. Companies that play upon this platform tend to be larger, international companies due to the size of the financial investment required. Governing bodies range from the International Olympic Committee (IOC), which grants companies the right to be an "official worldwide partner" of the Olympic Games, to the major professional sport leagues (e.g., MLB, NFL), to organizations such as the National Collegiate Athletic Association (NCAA) and Little League Baseball. Most of these sponsorships, while providing "official sponsor" status across the entire organization, do not necessarily grant "official sponsor" status to the individual teams within the organization. These rights must be secured separately from the individual teams.

Team Sponsorship

Team sponsorship is often a more appropriate platform for local or regional companies or companies with smaller marketing budgets. Such sponsorships typically include the right to be the "official sponsor" of the team, the opportunity to conduct in-venue promotions, and access to team tickets and hospitality. Most governing bodies allow for competitors of their sponsorship partners to sign sponsorship deals with the local teams. For instance, although Bank of America is the "Official Bank of the NFL," many NFL teams have sponsorship deals with local banks.

This loophole has served as an avenue for ambush marketing for some companies. Take for example the 2010 Fédération Internationale de Football Association (FIFA) World Cup: Although adidas was the "Official Licensee and Supplier of the FIFA World Cup," Nike was a sponsor (and jersey provider) of many national teams including the USA, Brazil, and The Netherlands.

Athlete Sponsorship

Athlete sponsorship serves as a platform for companies to develop a sponsorship based on support of an individual athlete (versus a team or a league). Such arrangements typically involve some type of endorsement of the sponsor's product or service. Athletes in individual sports, such as tennis and golf, tend to attract more sponsor interest because they are able to generate a greater number of visible, well-focused sponsor impressions on television. Perhaps the most prolific example of athlete sponsorship is Michael Jordan, who in his prime earned over $50 million annually through deals with Nike, Rayovac batteries, and Ballpark Franks, among others.

One of the services that companies use to help determine which athletes to sponsor is QScores, compiled by New York City–based Marketing Evaluations/TvQ (http://www.qscores .com), a research firm that has been measuring the notoriety of athletes, actors, and entertainers for over 40 years. QScores use a scale to measure celebrities' familiarity and appeal among the general public. The top twelve ranking of sports celebrities in 2009 was as follows: Michael Jordan, Tiger Woods, John Madden, Nolan Ryan, Joe Montana, Cal Ripken Jr., Payton Manning, Jerry Rice, Julius Erving, Michael Phelps, and Wayne Gretzky (Lefton, 2009a).

There is, however, increased risk in sponsoring an individual athlete as opposed to sponsoring a league or team. Sport celebrities garner a great deal of attention and interest from the public and thus the media is quick to report on any news involving the athlete. Unfortunately for sponsors, this news typically involves the sport celebrity getting into some sort of trouble. Take for example the personal issues golf great Tiger Woods experienced in late 2009. While Woods was ranked as having the second highest QScore among sport celebrities in 2009, that ranking had dropped to 25 twelve months later (Lefton, 2010). Companies must carefully evaluate the risk associated with sponsoring an individual athlete prior to entering into any agreement. The problem is the true risk is difficult (if not impossible) to accurately calculate.

Media Sponsorship

Media sponsorship occurs most often in the form of broadcast sponsors, companies that purchase advertising or programming during sport-related broadcasts. For several years, Home Depot has been the presenting sponsor of ESPN's *College GameDay* show, positioned as "College GameDay Built by the Home Depot" (a clever way to further entrench Home Depot's brand message into the minds of consumers). This media sponsorship includes commercial spots, on-site signage, and game tickets for hospitality and entertainment purposes. The sponsorship "helps Home Depot fortify its base of active, male, do-it-yourself customers," said a Home Depot marketing executive. "College football and home improvement projects are two things that people associate with the weekend, particularly Saturdays. This sponsorship allows Home Depot to strengthen that connection with our consumers" (Wilbert, 2003, p. 1D).

Often broadcast sponsors have no affiliation or entitlement to the team or league being broadcast, a situation that can result in ambush marketing whereby the broadcast sponsor seeks to convey to consumers some "official" relationship that does not in fact exist. Although not illegal, one classic example was Wendy's advertising as an "official broadcast sponsor" of the Olympics, although McDonald's was the official sponsor of the Olympics in the fast food category. Many sport organizations now either require their official sponsors to purchase advertising within their event broadcasts or, alternatively, provide them a "right of first refusal" to purchase broadcast advertising time, with the intent of eliminating or curtailing such ambush marketing activity.

Facility Sponsorship

Facility sponsorship is one of the fastest-growing sponsorship platforms, most notably in the form of naming rights agreements. Over the past ten years, almost every professional sport facility (and many collegiate athletic stadiums and arenas) has sold naming rights to companies (Table 14-1 in Chapter 14, Sport Sales, provides a sampling of these deals). For example, Citizens Bank signed a 25-year, $95 million naming rights deal that put its name on the Philadelphia Phillies' ballpark. As an example of platform integration, Citizens Bank was already an official sponsor of the team, and its naming rights deal also included a commitment to media sponsorship (i.e., advertising within Phillies television and radio broadcasts). Another example of platform integration is Red Bull's sponsorship of both the New York Red Bulls (an MLS team) and Red Bull Arena (the facility where the team plays). Essentially, facility sponsors typically sponsor the sport properties that play in the facility in some other capacity.

Event Sponsorship

Event sponsorship enables companies to tie directly into the event atmosphere. Examples include sponsorship of triathlons and marathons, college football bowl games, and professional golf tournaments, typically events that are locally based and annual.

Sport-Specific Sponsorship

Sport-specific sponsorship enables a company to direct its sponsorship efforts to a specific sport that best appeals to the company and its targeted consumers and provides a strong fit for generating brand identity. For instance, ING Group, a Dutch financial services company, identified sponsorship of marathons as a perfect platform to launch "Globe Runner," one of ING's worldwide financial services products. As part of this sponsorship strategy, ING Group purchased the first-ever title sponsorship of the New York City Marathon (a three-year, $5 million deal), in addition to entitlement of other high-profile marathons in Brussels, Amsterdam, Taipei, and Ottawa (Lefton, 2003a). Given the current economic uncertainty and potential change in ING's marketing strategy, ING's continued involvement in the breadth of marathon sponsorship activity is less than certain (Lefton, 2009b). Such sport-specific sponsorships are often most effectively leveraged and enhanced through the additional use of governing body, athlete, and/ or media channel sponsorships.

■ EVALUATING SPORT SPONSORSHIPS

With the growing financial commitments necessary to sponsor and effectively activate sport sponsorship programs, the evaluation of sponsorships has become of vital concern to sport marketers. Measuring ROI from sport sponsorships, however, poses several challenges for sponsors. First, there is no one exact formula for measuring ROI, thus leaving companies to establish their own internal criteria. Companies use a wide range of criteria to help determine whether their sport sponsorship is a valuable asset in achieving their marketing objectives. These include internal feedback, sales/ promotion bounceback measures, print media exposure, television media exposure, primary consumer research, dealer/trade response, and syndicated consumer research. Second, it is difficult to precisely determine how much incremental sales are directly attributable to a specific sponsorship program, or how a sponsorship has directly affected consumers' awareness of the sponsoring company or brand.

Consumer surveys are often deployed as a first step in measuring sponsorship ROI. For example, a survey administered following the 2010 Winter Olympics found that over 45% of respondents identified Visa, a long-time Olympic sponsor, as an official partner of Team USA (Broughton, 2010a). The same survey showed that only about 4% of surveyed consumers identified Hilton Hotels as an official partner of Team USA. Surveys such as the one just described provide sponsors a general understanding of the level of awareness consumers have of the sponsorship alliance. It is difficult, however, to use this type of survey research to conclude Visa's sponsorship of Team USA is ten times more valuable than Hilton's sponsorship of Team USA. Thus, a more scientific approach to sponsorship evaluation is necessary to more accurately measure ROI.

Sponsorship evaluation has become a burgeoning business and today many companies specialize in measuring sponsorship ROI. Research companies such as Performance Research, Nielsen Sports Marketing Service, Repucom, and Sponsorship Research International (SRi) have emerged to provide professional services for evaluating, through quantitative and qualitative research instruments, various aspects of a sponsor's involvement with a sport property. Some key questions in evaluating sponsorships include the following: Do consumers understand your sponsorship? Has the sponsorship made a connection with your target audience? How many media impressions has your sponsorship generated? Has your sponsorship resulted in new business opportunities?

Sport properties often hire professional research firms to perform evaluation research that examines the value the property provides to their sponsors. This is done to increase sponsor satisfaction and maximize potential sponsorship revenues. The NBA, for example, has worked with SRi to measure the effectiveness of basketball-themed promotions of commercials versus ones that are not themed around the sport (Show, 2009). The study indicated that the NBA does in fact provide a significant lift in promotions. The PGA Tour has also worked with research companies to show the value the Tour can provide sponsors. The PGA Tour working with Repucom evaluated the value in terms of international television exposure a title sponsor receives (Show, 2009). Repucom estimated the television exposure of a title sponsor of one PGA Tour event at over $20 million.

Students with an aptitude for and interest in the research process may find career opportunities with market research companies that specialize in sport marketing and sponsorship, such as those listed in the "Resources" section at the end of this chapter.

■ SPONSORSHIP AGENCIES

As we already know, there is much that makes the sport product, sport consumers, and thus sport marketing unique. Hence, many companies engaged in sport sponsorship outsource the negotiation and/or implementation of their sponsorship programs and leave the nuances of sport marketing to the experts. You would not believe the number of corporate marketers, experts in marketing their own products and services, who don't know that the World Series is not played in the same location every year, or that you cannot just stick the Super Bowl logo in your advertisements without first obtaining the NFL's approval, or that using

Babe Ruth in a commercial shoot may not be possible ("Uh, Babe Ruth is no longer with us"). These are all true tales from the front lines of sport sponsorship agency work that serve to reinforce the fact that sport marketing is a different animal and is sometimes better left to the experts! Many companies therefore rely on agencies because they do not possess the expertise, the experience, or the resources to negotiate and implement sponsorship programs on their own. Thus, often those charged with selling sport property sponsorships will deal directly with sport marketing and promotion agencies in pitching their sponsorship opportunities. Therefore, career opportunities exist for trained sport marketers to apply their skills on the agency side. A list of the major sport marketing and promotion agencies that specialize in the negotiation and implementation of sport sponsorships on behalf of their clients (the sponsoring companies) is provided in the "Resources" section of this chapter.

■ CURRENT ISSUES

Ethnic Marketing through Sport Sponsorship

The expanding market of ethnic consumers, coupled with the increasing globalization of sport, is compelling more and more corporations to direct a portion of their sport sponsorship spending to **ethnic marketing**. Likewise, sport organizations have begun to adopt strategies to more effectively target ethnic groups, particularly Hispanics and African Americans, who historically have represented only a small percentage of the sport spectator base in the United States. The Hispanic market, in particular, is the fastest-growing ethnic population in the United States. Fans with roots in Latino nations make up 13% of MLB attendance, and the number of Hispanics that watch or listen to MLB baseball on the radio is up over 15%

over the last decade (Hyman, 2006). The influx of Asian athletes into major U.S. professional sport leagues (particularly soccer, basketball, and baseball) has also fueled the interest of companies in using sport sponsorship to target Asian communities.

Many of the companies that sponsor MLS, such as Sierra Mist, Kraft, and Budweiser, have identified an interest in reaching the largely Hispanic audience that attends these games. The arrival of Yao Ming to the NBA in 2002 serves to illustrate the impact that athletes and their fans are having on the corporations' ethnic marketing initiatives. Shortly after Ming signed with the Houston Rockets, Harbrew Imports of New York, marketers of Yanjing Beer, signed a multiyear sponsorship deal with Ming's team (shortly thereafter, the company also signed a sponsorship deal with the Los Angeles Clippers after that team signed Chinese player Wang Zhizhi). The ability for Ming to resonate with Chinese consumers both in the United States and China quickly resulted in athlete sponsorship deals between Ming and companies that included Pepsi, Gatorade, Apple Computers, and Visa. Although companies entering sponsorship arrangements with Ming hope to capitalize on his marketing impact in the United States, "the real marketing value of the 7-foot-6 center is in using him to sell goods and services in the biggest consumer market in the world, his native China" (Lefton, 2003b, p. 22).

Companies have also recognized the ability of sport sponsorship to reach the African-American market. Nike, for example, has through its sponsorship of high-profile African-American athletes "demonstrated an understanding of how to effectively employ a culturally based approach to communicating with black consumers. Its promotional messages contain content that is tasteful and culturally appropriate for black consumers, yet also appealing to the mainstream market" (Armstrong, 1998). Russell Athletic (through its association with the

Black Coaches and Administrators Association) and footwear marketer Converse (through its grassroots inner-city basketball tours "Converse Open Gym") are other examples of companies effectively utilizing sport sponsorship platforms to target the African-American market.

Sport marketers, however, must be cognizant of key cultural differences among and between ethnic groups in terms of how sponsorship and its various tactics are communicated to and perceived by targeted ethnic groups (Cordova, 2009). For example, ethnic marketing cannot be, or be perceived as, a token effort by the company to reach out to a particular ethnic market. Sport marketers must also understand the difference between marketing to first-generation immigrants and those who, although identified as part of an ethnic group, are in fact well indoctrinated into American culture. Armstrong (1998) has identified a number of strategies that sport organizations and corporations should employ when marketing to black consumers, including involving the black media, demonstrating concern and respect for the black community and causes salient to it through socially responsible cause-related marketing, and patronizing black vendors. There remains, however, much research and work to be done in effectively reaching ethnic markets through sport sponsorship.

Overcommercialization of Sport Sponsorship

The potential overcommercialization of sport is raising a critical question for sport marketers: When is enough . . . enough? Sport marketers have built a world in which consumers visit a stadium called Comerica Park and pass through a turnstile featuring Chevrolet ads to watch a team sponsored by Bank One in a game sponsored by Sprint, during which he or she passes a luxury suite section sponsored by Papa John's Pizza, to witness a first pitch sponsored by ReMax, followed by an inning sponsored by Joe's Trucking. Add to this a plethora of sponsored scoreboard messages and between-innings promotions, and one begins to see the potential magnitude of the issue.

Even the most sacred of venues have not escaped sport marketers' quest for new revenue streams. For instance, beginning in 2002 corporate advertisements were placed on Fenway Park's famed outfield wall, the Green Monster. A similar signage issue arose at a 2003 Chicago Cubs game in ivy-covered Wrigley Field, when television rights holders Fox and ESPN lobbied MLB for the opportunity to place an electronic messageboard on the brick wall behind home plate that for the first time exposed Cubs fans and viewers at home to ads from Budweiser, Subway, and a number of other sponsors during a *Saturday Game of the Week* telecast. In 2010 a permanent 16-by-22 foot Toyota backlit sign was placed above the left center-field bleachers at Wrigley Field. In addressing fans' concerns one Cubs executive stated, "We can't do something like 67 signs around the ballpark. We have to be much more careful and respect the character of the ballpark (Fisher, 2010)." Sport marketers must carefully balance the traditions of the game and (or) stadium with the need to increase revenues.

The potential overcommercialization of sport teams and events raises interesting questions as to whether sport consumers may have an emotional threshold or tolerance level for accepting a constant bombardment of corporate names, logos, and messages. Is there, as well, a point at which companies' sponsorship investments become so mired in clutter that they lose all effectiveness? As sport marketers continue to push the envelope in search of new revenue streams, one is left to wonder if, and when, sport sponsorship may reach a law of diminishing returns. Thus, sport marketers must always be careful and cognizant of how innovative sponsorship deals will be perceived by consumers and the media and, at the very least, take steps to proactively position such ground-breaking sponsorships in as positive a light as possible.

The Marriage of Gambling, Hard Liquor, and Other Vices with Sport Sponsorship

Sport organizations have historically shunned affiliations with legalized gambling establishments (LGEs), fearing negative public perceptions and threats to the on-field integrity of the games. Gambling has, however, taken a strong hold in the United States over the past decade, as the number of LGEs (e.g., tribal casinos, state lotteries, riverboat casinos) has grown exponentially. One industry trade publication estimates that the number of casinos in the United States increased 25% in four years, from 405 in 1999 to 508 in 2003, spanning 27 states (IEG, 2003c). In Massachusetts alone, there are no less than 35 different scratch-and-win lottery games operating at any one time. With increased government endorsement and public acceptance of gambling, sport organizations have embraced LGEs as a growing source of sponsorship revenue. For example, over the past several years, the relationship between LGEs and sport organizations has grown to include the following:

- The NBA and NHL have licensed their team logos to state lotteries for use in scratch-and-win games whose prizes include cash, trips to their championship games, and league-licensed merchandise. Both leagues also allow their teams to sell or distribute lottery cards as in-arena premiums.
- The Sycuan Indian tribe, which operates one of the largest casinos in California, bought sponsorship of the San Diego Padres season that included in-stadium PA announcements and broadcast opening that referred to the "2003 Padres season,

presented by Sycuan." Even the Padres' telephone welcome greeting invited consumers to purchase tickets to the "2003 Padres season, presented by Sycuan."
- Par-A-Dice Hotel & Casino served as the title sponsor of the East Coast Hockey League's 2004 All-Star Game, which included the right to serve as the "official hotel" for the event.
- The WNBA Connecticut Suns are owned by the Mohegan Sun Resort and Casino. The team plays its games in the Mohegan Sun Arena, situated a short walk from the slot machines and card tables (Butler, 2003, p. 85).

LGEs are engaging in sport sponsorship for much the same reasons as other traditional sport sponsors. One primary objective is to drive traffic to casinos. For example, Mohegan Sun activated a sponsorship of the Boston Red Sox by sending "brand ambassadors" throughout the city with a book in which fans could write good luck messages to the team. Each person penning a note received a scratch-and-win game piece that could be brought to the casino for the chance to win $1 million as well as various Red Sox–related prizes (IEG, 2003c). Another objective is the desire of gaming establishments to retain and reward their premium players (the high rollers). Based on one study that showed that 5% of customers account for 40% of the casinos' gross gaming win, gaming establishments have turned to sports to provide an attractive lure. For instance, the best customers of Foxwoods Resort Casino in Connecticut are invited to private dinners with Boston Celtics stars (IEG, 2003c). Casinos are also turning to sport sponsorship as a means of fighting negative perceptions of gambling and to position themselves as concerned corporate citizens through community relations tie-ins. "When we put up a sign at Fenway Park, we are trying to

CASE STUDY: Introducing . . . The FedEx, I mean, the Discover Orange Bowl!

For more than two decades, FedEx was the title sponsor of the Orange Bowl, one of college football's most prestigious holiday season bowl games and one of the four Bowl games included in the Bowl Championship Series (BCS). Through this entitlement sponsorship, the FedEx name became synonymous with the Orange Bowl, and the game became FedEx's biggest hospitality platform. Each year, the company hosted hundreds of key customers and rewarded top employees with a four-day party built around the Orange Bowl game in Miami.

However, in May 2010, after a 21-year run, FedEx publicly announced its decision to not renew its title sponsorship of the Orange Bowl, the longest-running title sponsorship of any of the BCS games that include the Tostitos Fiesta Bowl, Allstate Sugar Bowl, and the Rose Bowl presented by Citi (the bank). Why would FedEx, after two decades of building tremendous sponsorship equity in the FedEx Orange Bowl, suddenly decide to drop its sponsorship?

For one thing, the dynamics of the Orange Bowl entitlement deal had changed. After years of being televised by FOX and ABC, ESPN had recently acquired the rights to air all of the BCS games beginning with the 2010 season. In addition to the broadcast rights, however, ESPN had also secured the rights to sell all sponsorship and advertising inventory. Upon securing the rights to the BCS games, ESPN significantly increased the entitlement sponsor price-tag over what BCS title sponsors had previously been paying FOX (ESPN was reportedly seeking $20 million annually over four years for any new BCS game entitlement deal). Furthermore, ESPN was requiring that the entitlement sponsor purchase a lengthy and more expensive college football advertising package that would start in September and would run throughout the entire college football season. While the Orange Bowl game itself was important to FedEx, the company decided that it was not interested in committing to a larger college football platform.

The Orange Bowl had also lost some of its prestige in recent years because of lackluster match-ups that had led to a steady decline in television ratings (**Table 15-9**). For instance, the 2009 game between Virginia Tech and Cincinnati drew a 5.4 rating and 9.3 million viewers, the lowest numbers ever for a BCS game. Although the FedEx Orange Bowl match-up between Iowa-Georgia Tech game on January 5, 2010 generated a 6.8 rating and 10.9 million viewers, it still ranked as the smallest audience of the four BCS games in 2010.

Declining television ratings, coupled with a higher financial commitment as required by ESPN, were important factors in FedEx's decision to relinquish its title sponsorship of the Orange Bowl after 21 years. Furthermore, as a shipping company, FedEx had been especially hit hard by the recession and had to make tough decisions to cut back on sports marketing expenditures that were once routine, including its television advertisement that had appeared in 12 straight Super Bowls until 2009. It had also become increasingly expensive to host elaborate parties for hundreds of customers and employees at the Orange Bowl.

Despite having relinquished its Orange Bowl entitlement deal, FedEx still holds league deals with the NFL and NBA and has several other sports sponsorships, including naming rights for FedEx Field in suburban Washington, D.C., and FedEx Forum in Memphis. It also has several sponsorship positions with NFL, MLB, and NBA teams, including the Dallas Cowboys, Florida Marlins, and Detroit Pistons as well as sponsorship on the No. 11 NASCAR Sprint Cup Series car at Joe Gibbs Racing.

TABLE 15-9	Orange Bowl Ratings in the Bowl Championship Series Era			
Year	Network	Matchup	Rating	Viewers
2010	Fox	Iowa–Georgia Tech	6.8	10,879
2009	Fox	Virginia Tech–Cincinnati	5.4	9,319
2008	Fox	Kansas–Virginia Tech	7.4	11,958
2007	Fox	Louisville–Wake Forest	7	10,655
2006	ABC	Penn State–Florida State	12.3	18,557
2005*	ABC	USC–Oklahoma	13.7	NA
2004	ABC	Miami–Florida State	9.1	NA
2003	ABC	USC–Iowa	9.7	NA
2002	ABC	Florida–Maryland	9.5	NA
2001*	ABC	Oklahoma–Florida State	17.8	NA
2000	ABC	Michigan–Alabama	11.4	NA
1999	ABC	Florida–Syracuse	8.4	NA

NA: not available

* BCS National Championship Game

Source: Ourand, J., Smith, M., & Lefton, T. (2010, May 3). FedEx name will come off Orange Bowl. Street & Smith's SportsBusiness Journal, p. 1. Courtesy of Sports Business Journal.

The Orange Bowl 'Discovers' a New Title Sponsor

The Orange Bowl was not without an entitlement sponsor for very long. On the heels of FedEx's decision to end its long-running association with the game, ESPN announced the Orange Bowl's new entitlement sponsor: Discover Card, the credit card and financial services company.

The entitlement sponsorship of the Orange Bowl was viewed by Discover Financial Services, issuer of the Discover Card, as a way to enter the sports sponsorship landscape in a major way. The new entitlement deal was reported to be a four-year contract worth just under $20 million a year. In addition to entitlement of the Orange Bowl ("The Discover Orange Bowl"), other marketing benefits include commercials within ESPN's Saturday afternoon college football telecasts, sponsorship of the "Discover Play of the Day" feature every Saturday afternoon of college football season, over 100 on-air announcements promoting the "Discover Orange Bowl" leading up to the game, rights to use ESPN college football analyst Lee Corso in point-of-sale promotional materials, and 500 tickets to the Orange Bowl.

A marketing platform that stretches from the start of college football season in late August through the BCS games after New Year's Day provides Discover with a four-month-plus platform, in addition to the game's entitlement rights. With the entitlement sponsorship package, Discover will put its brand on the rotating national championship game at least once during the four-year deal (next to be held at the Orange Bowl in 2013).

Entitlement sponsorship of the Orange Bowl was deemed by Discover's marketing team as a way to significantly expand Discover's position in sport sponsorship landscape. In the extremely competitive market of credit card services, competitors such as market leaders Visa and Master Card have long established portfolios of sport sponsorships. Visa, for example, sponsors the National Football League, the Olympic Games, the FIFA World Cup, NASCAR, and the Kentucky Derby. Master Card has been a long time sponsor of Major League Baseball and is an active sponsor on the PGA Tour. These companies have been able to successfully leverage their sport sponsorships by issuing affinity cards (credit cards which allow customers to earn points that can be used to purchase tickets and officially licensed merchandise) and offering give-a-ways in which credit card users are entered into a drawing to win tickets to various sporting events. Discover hopes to capitalize on their new sponsorship by leveraging their association with the Orange Bowl as effectively as possible.

Questions for Discussion

1. Assume you are the Director of Sport Sponsorship for FedEx. What other factors, beyond those stated above, would help inform your decision to continue with or relinquish your 21-year entitlement of the Orange Bowl? If it was your decision, would you also decide to relinquish it? Why or why not?
2. Now assume you were the Director of Sport Sponsorship for Discover, presented with this new entitlement sponsorship opportunity. Would you recommend Discover invest in entitlement sponsorship of the Orange Bowl? Why or why not?
3. The association of Discover's orange logo (the O in Discover is always presented as an orange figure) with the Orange Bowl is a very obvious and logical fit. However, other than this fit, what are some of the challenges you, as the Director of Sport Sponsorship for Discover, can expect to face in trying to leverage your new sponsorship?
4. FedEx leveraged their Orange Bowl sponsorship primarily as a B2B opportunity, by using the event as a platform to entertain key corporate customers. As the Director of Sport Sponsorship for Discover, what are some of the promotional tactics you would recommend using to leverage your entitlement of the Discover Orange Bowl to build your business?

tell people we're part of the crowd," said Mitchell Etess, executive vice-president of marketing for Mohegan Sun (IEG, 2003c, p. 8).

The sponsorship of sport properties by hard liquor companies has also gained popularity in the last few years. In 2005 both NASCAR and the PGA Tour began permitting events and teams (or players) to sign sponsorship deals with hard spirit alcoholic beverage brands. By 2010, Diageo's Ketel One vodka was the PGA Tour's official distilled spirit and Crown Royal was the primary sponsor of the popular

NASCAR driver Matt Kenseth's #17 race car. In 2009, the NBA followed the trend when the league loosened its alcohol marketing regulations. Soon after the league signed a sponsorship deal with Bacardi Gold rum in 2010 (Lefton & Lombardo, 2010). Just as gambling sponsorships gained acceptance in the late 1990s and early 2000, hard liquor sponsorships are now becoming more acceptable amongst sport marketers.

One of the key concerns for sport organizations entering sponsorship agreements with

gaming establishments and hard liquor manufacturers is the possible negative perceptions
fans may have toward these sport organizations.
Another is the possible longer-term effects that
such associations may have on impressionable
youngsters through the tacit condoning or encouragement of gambling and drinking. One
commentator has noted that the marriage of
sport organizations and vices such as gambling "is the beginning of a slippery slope.
As the search for revenues in sports becomes
more acute, the intellectual distinction between
negatives of gambling and the purism of sports
becomes blurry, if not obliterated" (Heistand,
2003, p. C1). Only time will tell.

■ SUMMARY

Over the past two decades, sport sponsorship
has evolved into a billion-dollar industry that has
grown increasingly competitive. The increase in
the sheer number of sport organizations pursuing corporations' sponsorship dollars and the
never-ending expansion of inventory—including
everything from venue naming rights to turnstile signage to championship parades—has
sparked a heightened degree of sophistication
in the sales, implementation, and servicing of
sport sponsorships. At the same time, there
has been a tremendous increase in the market
of companies and industry trade associations
eager to engage in sport sponsorship. These
companies, while today much more attuned to
the benefits of sport sponsorship, continue to
put increasing emphasis on the evaluation and
measurement of their sport sponsorship involvements to ensure a return on their investment.
Thus, there is a broad range of opportunities
for individuals seeking careers in the area of
sport sponsorship, including the sport organization side, the corporate side, and the agency/
sponsorship evaluation side.

■ RESOURCES

Sport Research Firms

Performance Research
25 Mill Street
Newport, RI 02840
401-848-0111
http://www.performanceresearch.com

Sponsorship Research International
230 East Avenue
Norwalk, CT 06855
203-831-2060
http://www.teamsri.com

Turnkey Sports & Entertainment
9 Tanner Street, Suite 8
Haddonfield, NJ 08033
856-685-1450
http://www.turnkeyse.com

Sports Marketing and Promotion Agencies

16W Marketing
75 Union Avenue
Rutherford, NJ 07070
201-635-8000
http://www.16wmarketing.com

ARC Worldwide
35 West Wacker Drive
15th Floor
Chicago, IL 60601
312-220-5959
http://www.arcww.com/

Championship Group, Inc.
1954 Airport Road
Suite 2000
Atlanta, GA 30341
770-457-5777
http://www.championshipgroup.com

**Edelman Worldwide Event and Sponsorship
Marketing**
250 Hudson Street
16th Floor
New York, NY 10013
212-704-0128
http://www.edelman.com

Fuse Integrated Sports Marketing
P.O. Box 4509
Burlington, VT 05406
802-864-7123
http://www.fusemarketing.com

GMR Marketing
5000 South Towne Drive
New Berlin, WI 53151
262-786-5600
http://www.gmrmarketing.com

Hill & Knowlton, Inc.
825 3rd Avenue
New York, NY 10027
212-885-0300
http://www.hillandknowlton.com

IEG, LLC
640 N. LaSalle
Suite 450
Chicago, IL 60654
800-834-4850
http://www.sponsorship.com

IMG
IMG Center
1360 E. Ninth Street, Suite #100
Cleveland, OH 44114
216-522-1200
http://www.imgworld.com

Ion Marketing
10 E. 38th Street
New York, NY 10016
646-827-3300
http://www.ionmktg.com

Momentum, Inc.
250 Hudson Street
New York, NY 10013
646-638-5400
http://www.momentumww.com

Octagon
800 Connecticut Avenue, 2nd Floor
Norwalk, CT 06854
203-354-7400
http://www.octagonNA.com

Strategic Sports Group
209 East 31st Street
New York, NY 10016
212-869-3003
http://www.strategicsportsgroup.com

Velocity Sports & Entertainment
230 East Avenue
Norwalk, CT 06855
203-831-2000
http://www.teamvelocity.com

■ KEY TERMS

activation, contests, coupons, cross-promotion, freestanding inserts (FSIs), ethnic marketing, premiums, return on investment (ROI), sales promotion, sampling, point-of-sale/point-of-purchase marketing, sweepstakes

■ REFERENCES

Armstrong, K. (1998). Ten strategies to employ when marketing sport to black consumers. *Sport Marketing Quarterly, 7*(3), 11–18.

Block, T., & Robinson, W. (Eds.). (1994). *Dartnell sales promotion handbook*. Chicago, IL: Author.

Broughton, D. (2010a, March 15). Visa's visibility recognized by Olympics fans. *Street & Smith's SportsBusiness Journal*, p. 12.

Broughton, D. (2010b, April 19). A-B again leads list of top sports advertisers. *Street & Smith's SportsBusiness Journal*, p. 11.

Butler, J. (2003, March 6). Sun plays in shadow of casino: Is WNBA team taking gamble in Connecticut? *New York Newsday*, p. 85.

Cordova, T. (2009, April 27). Success begins with understanding the demo. *Street & Smith's SportsBusiness Journal*, p. 17.

Dentzer, S. (1984, August 20). What price prestige. *Newsweek*, p. 28.

Durand, J., Smith, M., & Lefton, T. (2010, May 3). FedEx name will come off Orange Bowl. *Street & Smith's SportsBusiness Journal*, p. 1.

Fisher, E. (2010, March 29). Sponsorship growth a slippery slope at historic ballpark. *Street & Smith's SportsBusiness Journal*, p. 15.

Heistand, M. (2003, June 19). As casino lures customers with NBA team, alliance creates concern about purity of sports. *USA Today*, p. C1.

"How goes the gate? Giveaways and other promotions and their effect on attendance." (2009, October 19). *Street & Smith's SportsBusiness Journal*. Retrieved November 4, 2010, from http://www.sportsbusinessjournal.com/article/63847

Hyman, M. (2006, October 2). The racial gap in the grandstands. *Bloomberg Businessweek*. Retrieved November 4, 2010, from http://www.businessweek.com/magazine/content/06_40/b4003093.htm

IEG, Inc. (2003a, February 10). Assertions. *IEG Sponsorship Report*. Retrieved from http://www.sponsorship.com/iegsr.aspx

IEG, Inc. (2003b, February 10). Sponsorship is key ingredient for venerable Southern snack brand. *IEG Sponsorship Report*.

IEG, Inc. (2003c, May 26). Casinos place their bets on sponsorship. *IEG Sponsorship Report*.

IEG, Inc. (2006, September 11). Spending on action sports to total $120 million in '06. *IEG Sponsorship Report*.

IEG, Inc. (2010, January 26). Sponsorship spending receded for the first time in 2009. *IEG Sponsorship Report*.

Irwin, R., Sutton, W.A., & McCarthy, L. (2008). *Sport promotion and sales management* (2nd ed.). Champaign, IL: Human Kinetics.

Lefton, T. (2003a, April 21). ING Group nears deal to title NYC marathon. *Street & Smith's SportsBusiness Journal*, p. 1.

Lefton, T. (2003b, May 19). China brawl: Coke and Pepsi fight over Yao. *Street & Smith's SportsBusiness Journal*, p. 22.

Lefton, T. (2009a, June 29). Some of the interest in new Sports Q scores isn't at the top. *Street & Smith's SportsBusiness Journal*, p. 8.

Lefton, T. (2009b, October 26). ING to shift strategy for marathons? *Street & Smith's SportsBusiness Journal*, p. 1. Retrieved December 29, 2010, from http://www.sportsbusinessjournal.com/article/63871

Lefton, T. (2010, June 7). Penalty drop: Tiger Woods plummets on Sports Q Scores list. *Street & Smith's SportsBusiness Journal*, p. 10.

Lefton, T., & Lombardo, J. (2010, April 5). NBA strikes sponsor gold with Bacardi. *Street & Smith's SportsBusiness Journal*, p. 1.

Mickle, T. (2010, January 25). Dew keeps tour name through '11. *Street & Smith's SportsBusiness Journal*. Retrieved November 4, 2010, from http://www.sportsbusinessjournal.com/article/64648

Mullin, B., Hardy, S., & Sutton, W.A. (2000). *Sport marketing* (2nd ed.). Champaign, IL: Human Kinetics.

NHL Marketing Partners. (2010). *NHL.com*. Retrieved November 4, 2010, from http://www.nhl.com/ice/page.htm?id=26370

Official sponsors of MLB.com. (2010). *MLB.com*. Retrieved November 4, 2010, from http://mlb.mlb.com/mlb/official_info/official_sponsors.jsp

Shank, M. (2009). *Sports marketing* (4th ed.). Upper Saddle River, NJ: Prentice Hall.

Show, J. (2009, February 23). Properties try to show dollars well spent. *Street & Smith's SportsBusiness Journal*, p. 21.

Smith, M. (2010, May 24–30). Glidden hopes to make inroads in southern markets with Big South paint sponsorship. *Street & Smith's SportsBusiness Journal*, p. 8.

Solomon, J. (2002, April 21). The sports market is looking soggy. *New York Times*, p. 1.

"Spons-o-Meter: NFL lines up 23 partners to start '09 season." (2009). *Sports Business Daily.com*. Retrieved November 4, 2010, from http://www.sportsbusinessdaily.com/article/133218

"Spons-o-Meter: NBA boasts list of 20 marketing partners." (2010). *Sports Business Daily.com*. Retrieved November 4, 2010, from http://www.sportsbusinessdaily.com/article/138724

Sponsorship. (2010). *Olympic.org*. Retrieved November 4, 2010, from http://www.olympic.org/en/content/The-IOC/Sponsoring/Sponsorship/

Ukman, L. (1995). *The IEG's complete guide to sponsorship: Everything you need to know about sports, arts, events, entertainment and cause marketing*. Chicago, IL: International Events Group, Inc.

Weeks, C., Cornwell, T., & Drennan, J. (2008). Leveraging sponsorships on the Internet: Activation, congruence, and articulation. *Psychology & Marketing, 25*(7), 637–654.

Wilbert, T. (2003, June 24). Home Depot to sponsor ESPN college pregame show. *Atlanta Constitution*, p. 1D.

16

Sport Communications

Andrew McGowan and Gregory Bouris

■ INTRODUCTION

According to Don Middleberg (2001), author of *Winning PR in the Wired World*, "public relations isn't just about 'ink' anymore. It's about a brilliant idea, creatively communicated by traditional and new media, in new ways" (p. xi). Like public relations, sport public relations has come a long way. With the ever-increasing growth of sport as big business, coupled with the Internet and other emerging technologies, the sport industry's need for highly skilled communications professionals has never been greater.

Because advances in technology have made the world much smaller as sport has moved onto the global stage, the sport industry has seen a dramatic shift in its communications needs and demands. The business has evolved from implementing passive methods of communicating with its fans, such as advertising a sports event, to more aggressive and proactive forms

of communications that strive to build strong relationships through one-to-one communications. Sport organizations have found that more aggressive and strategic communication plans are vital to their overall success. This change in philosophy has resulted in positive media impressions, stronger relationships with core stakeholders—the fans, sponsors, media rights-holders, and alumni—and, in the case of professional team sports, stronger franchise values.

Today, the financial success of the sport organization and the media are inextricably linked. According to Nichols, Moynahan, Hall, and Taylor (2002), media sources "provide sport organizations with substantial revenue, as well as opportunities for increased public exposure" (p. 4). In fact, sport teams have attracted attention and investment from several media conglomerates, such as Cablevision, owner of the New York Rangers, Knicks, Liberty, Hartford

Wolfpack, and Madison Square Garden; Time Warner, former owner of the Atlanta Braves and *Sports Illustrated*; and the Walt Disney Corporation, owner of ESPN and the former owner of the Mighty Ducks and Anaheim Angels.

Sports and media have become so intertwined that leagues, professional teams, and college conferences have launched cable networks of their own such as the National Football League (NFL) Network and the Big Ten Network. Despite steep costs involved in launching a cable network, these entities are leveraging their popularity and access to programming to tap into the local and national subscriber fees available to successful cable networks. In addition to game broadcasts, these networks serve as lucrative branding and messaging vehicles to their legions of hard-core supporters. Major League Baseball (MLB) launched its MLB Network to the largest audience in cable TV history, when it debuted in January 2009. The National Hockey League (NHL), New York Yankees, and New York Mets are examples of others entering the media side of the sports industry.

Despite all the evolutionary changes the sport industry has experienced, one area or discipline that has remained part of the professional and amateur sport organizational chart since the beginning is public relations or, in today's sports vernacular, communications. For the purposes of this chapter, **communications** will be defined as all methods used by a sport organization to proactively deliver its key messages to a diverse universe of constituencies. In the past, communications was limited to contact with a select number of mostly print media representatives. However, today's sport organizations employ communications professionals to help deliver key messages to a greater number of stakeholders. **Stakeholders** are groups and individuals that have a direct or indirect interest in an organization. Newsom, Turk, and Kruckeberg (2004) state that stakeholders have "evolved to encompass employees, customers,

government and investors" (p. 89). In sports, additional stakeholders include season ticket holders, sponsors, licensees, alumni, peer organizations (e.g., league offices), and the general public.

As in the past, the media continue to play an important role in how sport organizations deliver their messages. However, sport organizations have learned that in the changing media world, it is better to communicate directly with a desired target than rely upon the media to deliver (and run the risk of inaccurately retelling) their key messages. Additionally, economic pressures and generational changes in how people consume their news have impacted the newspaper industry. As they attempt to re-invent themselves in the Internet age, newspapers have cut back on their budgets. The sports departments of newspapers in major cities have been hit particularly hard. In certain cases, newspapers only assign writers to cover home games and opt for wire service coverage for away games. This trend should be watched closely by today's sports communications professional. Because of this, sport organizations now use an integrated marketing communications approach that includes advertising, direct marketing, and public relations to deliver messages directly to their stakeholders. Some organizations, such as the NHL's LA Kings, have taken this a step further by hiring writers away from their local newspapers to provide in-depth and constant coverage on team Web sites.

Not all communications activities are proactive. Gone are the days of once-daily news reports. The Internet has brought with it the 24/7 news cycle, and a constant thirst by Web-based media outlets to constantly post "breaking" new reports. The lines are beginning to blur between hard news and information posted on **blogs**, which are diary-type entries (coined from the term "web logs") regularly posted on the Internet. This adds further to the demands on sports communications professionals. They must stay up to date on emerging Internet-based news outlets while also assigning someone to monitor known sites from time to time to ensure accuracy and control their organization's branding efforts. The demand of the public, and subsequently the media, to know everything possible about a sport organization helps feed this 24/7 news engine, placing enormous pressure on an organization to protect its image. Therefore, today's sport communications professional needs to have a well-rounded understanding of the role communications plays in the successful operation of the twenty-first century sport organization, as well as a complete understanding of the role the Internet plays in the information and news cycles.

History

Sport coverage in the United States dates back to 1773. The first outlet to cover a sporting event was the *Boston Gazette*, when it sent a reporter to London to cover a boxing match. Joseph Pulitzer is credited with introducing the first sports section in the *New York Herald* in 1896 (Nichols et al., 2002).

As a result of the continued growth in the sport industry, the variety of business activities practiced by professional and amateur sport organizations began to grow dramatically in the 1980s. This growth was brought on by the expansion of cable television and its need to use sports programming to lure subscribers, which substantially increased the rights fees organizations received for their game broadcasts. Prior to the 1980s, a professional sport team's organizational chart consisted of an owner, president, general manager, coach(es), public relations director, ticket manager, and accounting staff. Noticeably absent, when compared with modern-day organizations, were disciplines such as marketing, game operations, sponsorships and group sales staff, customer services, Web site staff, and community relations. Of

these areas or disciplines, public relations has played, and continues to play, a major role in the structure and operation of every amateur and professional sport organization.

How the Media and Communications Have Changed

Sport communications has seen dramatic changes in terms of the number of stakeholders as well as the methods used to communicate. Times have changed. The media have changed. News coverage and the news cycle have changed, and the corporate world has taken notice of sports. Franchises are no longer run as secondary businesses, managed neatly on a game-to-game basis. Cable television introduced the concept of 24-hour news and later 24-hour sports programming and news. Sports radio became one of the top formats on the radio dial. Thus, teams began cashing in on their strong local brand awareness, and leagues began cashing in on the national as well as international popularity of their sport. In the past, team public relations staffs worked almost exclusively on a seasonal basis with the newspaper reporters assigned to cover their respective teams. Today sport communications professionals work with, and communicate to, a larger audience 12 months a year.

On the college level, the sport communications area has evolved from a one-person staff position known as a **sports information director (SID)** to a full media relations staff. Larger Division I athletic departments may have a media relations department with anywhere from five to ten full-time staff members. Smaller athletic departments may have an assistant athletic director for media relations or even a coach with a dual appointment who also oversees media relations for the entire athletic department. A college athletics media relations department oversees game-day operations, including running the press box at football games or overseeing press row at basketball games. Other duties may include fielding calls from the media, coordinating press conferences, working with the athletic director on press releases about athletic department announcements, designing and writing media guides for sport teams, and developing and writing athletic department publications for print or the Internet. A community relations staff position does not exist in the collegiate athletic department, although the athletic department does community relations projects. In a large Division I program, these community service–based activities may be carried out by coordination of the coaching staff, marketing, student-athlete services, and media relations departments.

Today's sport communications professional should possess a well-rounded knowledge of communications, including media relations, public relations, government relations, internal communications, advertising, and direct marketing. In addition, today's public relations professional must keep abreast of all the communications opportunities available to him or her through emerging technologies. Related coursework includes journalism, public relations, public speaking, Internet-related courses such as hypertext markup language (HTML) writing, and audio/video production classes.

Current and future generations of professionals are entering the workforce with personally gained hands-on experience in social media and the ability to upload and download media to the Internet. These skills are useful when advising and assisting, for lack of better terms, the aging workforce.

■ KEY TOPICS

Media Relations

Most sport organizations are blessed with so much mass appeal that media organizations are compelled to cover these entities on a regular basis. This popularity creates a "pull" from the media, whereas most other industries have to "push" their information to the media and hope to receive publicity for their efforts. In other words, it is highly unlikely that the local company has someone from the local newspaper showing up every day needing to fill a number of column inches in the paper. Most media outlets, especially newspapers, turn the public's insatiable desire to know all they can about their favorite team and players into revenue dollars by selling more papers and advertising to increase their own profits.

The media can be broken into categories such as print, television, radio, and the Internet, a category that didn't even exist just a few years ago. **Table 16-1** contains a working media list. Given the free publicity received, most sport organizations have developed strong working relationships with the media. It is a priority to determine the key media members (or reporters) as well as their individual needs. They are not all the same.

Print editions of daily newspapers have deadlines in the evening that must be met to guarantee coverage in the following day's paper. A writer working on a story with an approaching deadline must be given priority over a writer working for a weekly or longer-lead publication, such as *ESPN the Magazine* or *Sports Illustrated*. Most, if not all, sportswriters of major daily newspapers also have blogs on their paper's Web site that are maintained and updated throughout the day.

Wire service reporters may not be very well known by name, but their stories have the potential to reach a large audience through a distribution network consisting of hundreds of newspaper, radio, television, and Internet outlets. Wire services should be given priority treatment because they have the potential to reach the widest audience. The main wire service is the Associated Press. Other wire services include Reuters and Bloomberg News.

TABLE 16-1	Working Media List

Print Media

Local daily newspapers

Wire services (e.g., Associated Press, Reuters, Scripps Howard)

National daily newspapers (e.g., *USA Today*, *Wall Street Journal*)

Weekly newspapers (business journals, local town weeklies)

National sport magazines (e.g., *Sports Illustrated*, *ESPN the Magazine*, *Sporting News*)

Local magazines (city magazines, such as *Washingtonian*, *Bostonian*)

Specialty pulp papers (e.g., *USA Today Sports Weekly*, *The Hockey News*)

Trade publications (e.g., *SportsBusiness Journal*, *Team Marketing Report*)

Television Media

Local over-the-air network affiliates (ABC, CBS, Fox, NBC)

National over-the-air networks

Regional sports networks (e.g., Madison Square Garden Network)

National cable sports networks (e.g., ESPN)

Local cable programs

National cable programs (e.g., Nickelodeon's G.A.S.)

National cable networks (e.g., CNN, MSNBC, CNBC)

On-demand programming

Radio Media

Local all-sports stations

Local radio, nonsports

National sports radio networks (e.g., ESPN Radio, Fox Sports Radio, Sporting News Radio Network)

Nationally syndicated sports programs (e.g., Westwood One, Premier Radio Network, Jim Rome Show)

Satellite radio (e.g., XM and Sirius)

Internet Media

ESPN.com

SI.com

Yahoo! (yahoo.com)

CBS SportsLine (cbssportsline.com)

League sites (e.g., nfl.com, mlb.com, nba.com)

Team sites (e.g., atlanta.braves.mlb.com, newyorkjets.com)

Blogs (e.g., fanblogs.com, yankeefan.blogspot.com)

Communicating directly with the news media occurs in many ways. For example, the most common way for professional and major college sport teams to communicate is daily contact with the **beat reporter** assigned by the local media outlet to cover an organization, its games, and its practices. In most cases, this person is from the local newspaper and is known as the **beat writer**. According to Nichols and colleagues (2002), in the 1920s and 1930s newspapers assigned beat writers to baseball and these beat writers "traveled with their respective Major League Baseball team to cover them" (p. 5). Today, it is common for five or more beat reporters to be assigned to a particular professional or major collegiate sport team by the numerous local media outlets. This makes for a very competitive group all aiming to get a unique angle and story.

■ PRESS RELEASES

The main way a sport organization gets its news out is with a **press release** (also called a news release). Seitel (2001) states that press releases serve as "the basic interpretive mechanism to let people know what an organization is doing and are sent out to editors and reporters in hopes of stimulating favorable stories about their organizations" (p. 328).

News releases are written in the standard **inverted pyramid** style of writing. The inverted pyramid style presents the most important facts in the lead paragraph. The remaining paragraphs are arranged in descending order of importance. News releases should be written in a matter-of-fact fashion.

■ PRESS CONFERENCES

For more important announcements, a press release may not be sufficient to get your message out. In that case, then the **press conference**, where the media are invited to a specific location, would be the chosen method of communicating. Seitel (2001, p. 345) suggests the following guidelines in preparation of a press conference:

1. Notify the media well in advance.
2. Don't play favorites.
3. Hold a news conference in an appropriate location.
4. Follow up early and often.
5. Keep the speaker(s) away from the media before the conference.
6. Remember TV.

In the ever-changing world of sports, advance notice might be as little as two hours. This usually is the case when a coach is fired, a major trade occurs, or it may be the case when something negative happens and you must act quickly to get your message out.

Regardless of where a press conference is held, accommodating the needs of the attending media is a top priority. There must be proper lighting, sound, enough electrical outlets, a backdrop with a logo, a raised platform in front of the room with a podium, a raised platform in the rear of the room for TV cameras, and a **multibox** device to allow multiple camera operators and radio reporters to plug into the audio feed without having to place an unwieldy number of microphones on the podium. A number of questions need to be answered just in planning the news conference, before the real questions are even asked. A brief outline of a press conference can be found in **Figure 16-1**.

■ MEDIA GUIDES

It is routine to distribute packages of notes and other related pieces of information to the media. **Media notes** packages contain all the statistical information and biographical information about the two teams competing in a game, from individual athletes or coaches, as well as the team perspective.

Annual team **media guide** publications must be created and distributed to the media before the season begins. The media guide serves an invaluable role for all of a team's beat reporters and television and radio announcers, as well as for media members who are not as familiar with an organization. This publication contains all the information a reporter will need to know

FIGURE 16-1   Press Conference Outline

The following is a brief outline for a press conference to announce the hiring of a new coach:

1. PR (or media relations [MR]) director welcomes media and announces any ground rules to be followed.
2. PR or MR director introduces general manager (GM) or athletic director (AD).
3. GM or AD announces and introduces new coach.
4. Coach greets media, makes comments.
5. PR or MR director conducts questions and answers (Q&A) between GM or AD, coach, and media.
6. PR or MR director thanks media for attending and announces procedure for one-on-one or small group interviews with coach and/or GM or AD.

about the organization, including staff directories; biographies of all coaches, players, owners, and front office staff; and team and individual records. When a fan listening at home hears a sportscaster recite some interesting facts or figures, it's a safe bet that the information was pulled together from the media guide or media notes package provided to him or her by the home team's media relations department.

Another example of how technology has influenced the area of sports communications is the migration from print publications (i.e., media guides) to electronic, or digital, editions. For example, for the 2010 Major League Baseball season, the league's communications department distributed its array of annual publications such as the media information directory, and the Red and Green Books on flash drives. The popular Red and Green books (in-depth guides to the American and National Leagues, respectively), published annually for decades, are no longer produced in print form. They are distributed exclusively in a digital format. Additionally, the National Basketball Association (NBA) has granted its teams permission to distribute their media guides exclusively in a digital format.

■ PHOTOGRAPHY

Photography is another key area for a sport communications professional. It is imperative to hire a capable photographer, preferably one who can attend press conferences, games, selected practices, community relations events, and other team functions requiring some level of photo capturing. Today, a team photographer must have the capability to shoot digitally. Digital images afford communications professionals an easier way to file, retrieve, and distribute photos than prints, slides, and negatives. Today, digital images can be taken, edited, and uploaded to Internet sites, newspapers, and magazines for almost instantaneous usage.

■ VIDEOGRAPHY

Other forms of communicating with the media include the use of video. In the digital age, video has quickly become the public's chosen media. With the potential to reach millions of fans and potential fans through Web sites such as YouTube, not to mention an organization's own Web site, access to a professional videographer and/or video production house has become paramount. A written press release is most beneficial to the print and radio media. However, the Internet and television media live in a world of moving images and sound. It is becoming more common to see organizations offering their own video of special events and activities to the news media via Internet downloading. This helps get their message out while also easing the burden placed on the staff and financial resources of news organizations. That is why a **video news release (VNR)** is sometimes worth the price of production and distribution. A VNR is not produced for every announcement. However, a VNR with strong imagery will help your message get picked up by television outlets. A VNR is a pre-produced piece that includes a written story summary or press release that is edited

for broadcast, making it more attractive for a TV producer to air.

A cousin of the VNR is **b-roll**, a tape of raw footage, not a finished segment, that accompanies a written news release. The footage, which the organization selects, arms a news producer with proper video to support a written announcement. Keep in mind that anytime the use of video and video distribution is considered, there are costs involved that may serve as a deterrent. In addition to the costs of hiring a video crew to shoot the material, which will run about $1,500 for a full-day shoot, the editing costs could run as high as $250 per hour, and the copying/tape-dubbing costs could be as high as $50 per Beta format tape (the preferred format of producers). There are additional charges to digitize the footage for uploading and downloading purposes. It is imperative that all video material be digitized for wider distribution and more efficient in-house archiving purposes.

■ CONFERENCE CALLS

In this day and age of high-tech gadgetry, one of the most successful ways of communicating with the media is to use the telephone. Now that virtually everyone has 24-hour, seven-day-a-week access to a phone, telephone **conference calls** have become a very common and extremely convenient method of communication. A conference call can be organized by one of a number of service providers (e.g., AT&T, Sprint, or MCI) in a matter of minutes and scheduled for as early as 30 minutes after setting it up. Some organizations go so far as to have their own teleconference phone number that doesn't change. This allows the media relations department to organize a call in the time it takes to get the word out to the media. The media then dials in and participates in the call, and the organization is billed for the service just as it would be for any other phone usage. Many teams

use this method when they have traded players late in the day or are on the road.

Some features to consider when setting up a conference call include having an operator record a list of call participants with their affiliations, having the callers in a listen-only mode (this reduces background noise and cell phone static), and using a question and answer (Q&A) moderator who introduces the media member before he or she asks a question. Conference calls can also be recorded and played back on a toll-free number for a predetermined amount of time following the call. This allows media unable to participate in the call a chance to hear the call in its entirety. Recordings from the calls are also available in electronic or digital formats, which allow for easy electronic mail (e-mail) distribution, uploading to Web sites, and archiving. Full typed transcripts of the calls can be provided for accurate record keeping, archival purposes, and posting a print version on a team's Internet site.

In the near future one can imagine a day when the Web conference replaces the conference call. The Internet has the ability to provide the same audio quality capability as the telephone, but provides all parties involved with the ability to enhance their communications with shared access to important documents and video. Many companies (e.g., WebEx, Skype, GoToMeeting.com) are gaining market share and penetration daily.

Legal Issues

Sport communications professionals must be conscious of the laws affecting their work. For instance, defamation (libel and slander) may come into play if the sport communication professional provides information to the media that may be accurate. Professionals working with intercollegiate athletics need to be aware of the Family Educational Rights and Privacy Act (FERPA), also known as the Buckley Amendment. FERPA sets the parameters for providing personal academic and medical information to the media. For years FERPA has required that student-athletes at universities receiving federal funding consent to release academic and medical information to non-university personnel, such as college conferences and the media. The new Health Insurance Portability and Accountability Act (HIPAA) sets limits on providing medical information to others, and has caused some confusion in college athletic departments about what sort of medical information can be released to the press. However, HIPAA addresses this point by excluding from the definition of "protected health information" a student's college or university education records. Thus, those records continue to be subject to FERPA (NCAA, 2003).

Public and Community Relations

There was a time in sports when public relations covered media relations, **community relations**, and public relations. Today, the role of the sport communications professional has become more specific and defined. For the purposes of this section, public relations is defined as all non-media-related communications efforts aimed at delivering a direct message to the fans.

Many public relations activities generate some media exposure and, it is hoped, portray an organization in a positive manner. However, most public relations activities are undertaken to have a positive impact on the community. They are not undertaken for the sole purpose of gaining publicity.

One of the most visible and common public relations practices is community relations. Community relations activities and departments are extensions of an organization's public relations department and, prior to the mid- to late 1980s, were generally handled by the public relations department. In the era of specialization in

the front offices of sport organizations, more emphasis was given to the effort of improving an organization's image through community involvement, such that it required the efforts of a full-time staff member.

Community relations objectives include developing substantive programs to benefit charitable causes as well as educational and outreach programs in an organization's local business area. These programs can include creating a 501(c)(3) nonprofit foundation to raise funds and distribute financial contributions to worthy causes or to serve as a link to a community's charitable organizations.

Community relations programs allow organizations and their athletes a chance to give back to the communities in which they live and work. These programs can also result in positive public relations and media coverage for both the players involved and their team.

Community relations departments also make in-kind contributions of licensed merchandise, game tickets, and autographed memorabilia to help a cause raise funds through auctions, special events, and raffles. Given the demands on the time of today's professional and amateur athletes, in-kind contributions tend to be the most popular method of supporting local charities. Charities auction or raffle these items to help raise incremental funds.

In most cases, this type of support is not intended to generate any substantial publicity but rather to create a benevolent reputation for the organization in the eyes of its fans and community leaders. These relationships also offer organizations a chance to reach out to the general public and try to increase their recognition among people who may not be avid or even casual sports fans. Bear in mind that if a strong community relations program is allowed to mature, over time the program will likely generate media exposure to further enhance an organization's image within its community.

New Media and the Internet

The **new media industry** "combines elements of computing, technology, telecommunications, and content to create products and services which can be used by consumers and business users" (Thornton, 1999, Biomedical section, ¶2). Most people think of new media as a **Web site** and the use of e-mail, but it is much more.

In terms of communications, Web sites are one of an organization's most valued public relations outlets. The time it has taken the Internet to grow from a fad to a mainstream media outlet has been astounding. Recent numbers put the wired world in North America at over 266 million home users, or 77% of the population (Internet World Stats, 2010). In terms of sports, Nielsen//NetRatings reported that sports Internet sites reached 35% of the active online population (Nielsen//NetRatings, 2004). That's 49 million unique visitors looking at sports sites from home and work. European numbers are also strong, as 36% of European Internet users visit sport sites (Netimperative, 2007). In November 2006, 78% of active home Web users connected to the Internet via broadband, up 13 percentage points from November 2005. Broadband users spend an average of 34 hours and 50 minutes online in a month, compared to an average 26 hours and 13 minutes for narrowband users (Nielsen//NetRatings, 2006b).

Special sporting events such as the Olympic Games and the Super Bowl can drive new daily traffic to Web sites. For instance, during the National Collegiate Athletic Association (NCAA) college basketball tournament known as March Madness, NCAA-related sports Web sites enjoyed a daily increase of 21% (9.7 million) in unique visitors from March 15–16, 2006. CBSSportsline.com, which streamed games live onto the Internet, saw an 84% increase (3.6 million) in unique visitors, followed by AOL Sports with an increase of 31% (1 million) in

new users. Traffic on Fox Sports on MSN grew 29% to almost 2 million new visitors (**Table 16-2**) (Nielsen//NetRatings, 2006a). In addition, traffic on the NCAA, CBS, and CSTV (College Sports TV) sites showed growth in the two weeks prior to March Madness (**Table 16-3**).

With those facts in mind, Internet sites are clearly a key tool for sport communications professionals to get their messages out and to interact one-to-one with stakeholders. Also, an organization's Web site allows a sport organization's message to be published in the way the organization wants it to be presented and not filtered by the media. To that end, it has become common for teams to make important announcements on their own sites before or at the same time as the information is distributed to the media.

The sport communications professional should do all he or she can to develop a trusted and resourceful Web site. Stakeholders should be able to go to an organization's Web site for all the latest information, including updated scores, ticket information, feature stories, photographs, audio and video clips, and merchandise. Today's sports Internet sites "more than any other medium [have] the ability to feed the insatiable appetite of sports fans" (McGowan, 2001, p. 33). By building a trusted site, an organization reduces its need to rely upon the outside media to deliver its messages to its most valued customers.

Web sites also provide organizations with the ability to distribute their message and product to a worldwide audience. Given the nearly boundless nature of the Internet, organizations can develop one-to-one relationships with fans from every corner of the globe. No other tool presently exists that allows a sport organization the opportunity to reach out and interact directly with its stakeholders as well as receive instant feedback. Though many of these relationships may be impossible to turn into ticket sales, they can most certainly generate

TABLE 16-2 Daily Web Traffic Increase During Initial Dates of March Madness 2006

Web Site	Wednesday, March 15	Thursday, March 16	Friday, March 17	Wednesday–Friday Growth
CBSSportsline.com Network*	1,958	3,603	3,135	84%
AOL Sports	761	999	1,006	31%
FOX Sports on MSN	1,510	1,953	2,237	29%
Yahoo! Sports	2,121	2,601	2,377	23%
SI.com	724[†]	819[†]	773[†]	13%[†]
ESPN	3,074	3,312	2,914	8%
Total unduplicated	8,005	9,659	9,573	21%

* Traffic to CBSSportsline.com Network includes CBSSportsline.com, CSTV Networks, NCAASports.com, PGA Tour, and TennisDirect.com, and does not include traffic to NFL Internet Network.

[†] These estimates are calculated on smaller sample sizes and are subject to increased statistical variability as a result.

Source: Nielsen//NetRatings. (2006a, March 26). March Madness spurs nearly 10 million sports fans to jump online the first day of the NCAA tournament for news and live video, according the Nielsen//NetRatings. Press release. Retrieved November 9, 2010, from http://www.nielsen-online.com/pr/pr_060321.pdf

TABLE 16-3 Weekly Web Traffic Increase Prior to March Madness 2006

Web Site	Week Ending March 5, 2006	Week Ending March 12, 2006	Week-to-Week Percentage Change
NCAASports.com	391*	1,178	201%
CSTV.com Network	2,261	3,296	46%
CBS Sportsline.com	1,869	2,398	28%

* These estimates are calculated on smaller sample sizes and are subject to increased statistical variability as a result.

Source: Nielsen//NetRatings. (2006a, March 26). March Madness spurs nearly 10 million sports fans to jump online the first day of the NCAA tournament for news and live video, according the Nielsen//NetRatings. Press release. Retrieved November 9, 2010, from http://www.nielsen-online.com/pr/pr_060321.pdf

incremental revenue through the sale of licensed products such as hats, T-shirts, pennants, and posters. For example, consider that the number of Internet users in Asia (825 million) and Europe (475 million) represents only 21% and 58% of their populations respectively. This should explain why a number of North American sports leagues are eager to take their games abroad (Internet World Stats, 2010). Additionally, a Web site has the ability to increase brand awareness as well as provide unique insights into the organization to the Web site user.

The Internet and Web sites have also changed how sport communications professionals prepare and utilize publications, including printed newsletters, media guides, and annual yearbooks. The printed newsletter is rapidly becoming an endangered species as organizations move to utilize e-mail as a more personal and effective way to communicate with their publics. **Electronic newsletters** sent via e-mail are generally less costly, easier to produce, and more timely than printed newsletters and can include additional links to other Web-based information and various multimedia features such as audio and video.

The delivery of these publications has changed as well. Printing and mailing costs have almost been eliminated with the creation of the electronic newsletter. Many organizations have produced media guides and yearbooks on CD-ROMs or in electronic PDF files delivered on flash drives, thereby decreasing the number of copies printed.

E-mail has changed how sport organizations communicate with their numerous stakeholders, such as the media. News releases, previously mailed and faxed, can now be distributed almost instantly. Further, media members can be targeted by creating specific **media lists**, such as beat writers, editors, columnists, and news directors. E-mail has also enabled the sport organization to communicate directly with its key stakeholder—the fan—on a one-to-one basis.

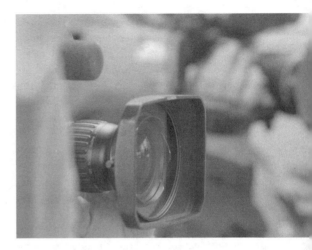

■ PREPARING FOR THE INTERVIEW

Sport communications professionals spend a great amount of time trying to generate publicity for their respective organizations. This is accomplished through interviews between the media and members of the organization, such as the president, general manager, athletic director, coaches, or athletes. An interview is a question-and-answer session employed by the media to gather information and present it to an audience. The interview provides insights into a sporting contest, event, or other announcement. The media members are looking to gain answers to the basic news questions of who, what, where, when, why, and how.

Nichols and colleagues (2002, p. 122) offer several common characteristics of an interview:

- An interview is an interchange of information between two or more parties. In the sport setting, it may involve an interaction between two parties, such as a one-on-one interview.
- An interview has a specific purpose or goal. The primary purpose of a newspaper story, radio interview, or television interview is to inform and/or entertain.
- Both parties in an interview exchange information by asking and answering questions.

To prepare the interviewee, the first item is for the sport communications professional to prepare **key messages** the organization wants to convey to the media during the interview. Two or three key messages are critical to being effective in an interview setting. These messages are what should be included in response to the questions the media ask during the interview.

In addition to the key messages, the sport communications professional should create a list of potential questions, including suggested responses. The sport communications professional needs to think like the media and anticipate what questions the media are likely to ask. What follow-up questions will flow from likely answers? How should answers be crafted to reinforce the key messages? In addition, the interviewee could be asked questions unrelated to the interview. These questions could refer to current events or events that happened in other places. The interviewee should be prepared for these types of questions as well. Lastly, the sport communications professional should meet in advance with the interviewee to review the probable questions and answers.

It is easy to take this aspect of the communications process for granted. Most senior-level front office people generally deal with the media on a regular basis and may feel they can handle themselves without help. However, even the most media-savvy individual will do these preparatory exercises in their heads, if not by jotting down some thoughts on a piece of scrap paper or a napkin.

Crisis Management

For the most part, the day-to-day contact between the sport communications professional and the media focuses on the game, rivalries, the players' performances, player transactions, and the business of sport. However, crises in sport have become almost regular occurrences. Just follow the newspapers, radio, or television and it won't take long to find one. Some examples include Tiger Woods' extramarital affairs, the BALCO drug inquiry leading to allegations of steroid use by professional and Olympic athletes, Michael Vick's involvement with a dog-fighting ring, and the NCAA violations-plagued University of Southern California's football program.

A crisis is any nonroutine event that could be disruptive to your organization. It can also be an unusual short-term incident that has a real or perceived negative impact on the general welfare of the organization or its stakeholders. A crisis situation for a sport organization, individual athlete, or coach can create a very stressful time. It can also cause irreparable damage to an individual involved, a team, or a college athletic

department. The damage can include damage to one's reputation and brand equity, which could erode endorsement and marketing opportunities and ticket and sponsorship sales. To combat these serious incidents, sport organizations should create a **crisis plan** in advance. The amount of reaction time saved when time is at a premium will pay off in the long run when a crisis occurs. Barton (2001) states that "because so many incidents have become mismanaged, new demands have emerged for corporations . . . to have a crisis plan in place" (p. 62).

In preparing for a potential crisis, identifying crises that may affect the organization, identifying the probability of their occurrence in advance, and creating a plan of action are the starting points to better management. A list of potential sport crisis areas appear in **Table 16-4**.

The most common mistake made during a crisis is overreaction. When a crisis occurs, it is important to not panic by simply reacting to the situation. Take a step back and gather as many of the facts as quickly as possible. Once the facts have been gathered, prepare a plan of action, not one of reaction. It should be done swiftly, but not before as much information as possible has been gathered. When preparing an action plan, be sure to deal with the issue head-on, promptly, and with honesty. Then use the heightened level of media attention to get the message out.

Seitel (2001, p. 214) offers ten general principles for communicating in a crisis:

1. Speak early and often.
2. Don't speculate.
3. Go off the record at your own peril.
4. Stay with the facts.
5. Be open and concerned, not defensive.
6. Make your own point and repeat it.
7. Don't war with the media.
8. Establish yourself as the most authoritative source.

9. Stay calm, and be truthful and cooperative.
10. Never lie.

In addition to identifying potential crises and creating a crisis plan, a prepared sport organization should create a **crisis team**. The crisis plan should identify roles and responsibilities for members of the organization. Additionally, it should include a system to notify key members of the organization as soon as possible should a crisis arise. A crisis team is a group of key organizational individuals who will be responsible for managing the crisis effectively. A crisis team should include some of the following executives: president, general manager/athletic director, director of communications, director of marketing, director of finance, facilities manager, legal counsel, and other key technical experts of the organization.

Early on in a crisis, it is important for the organization to speak with one voice. That one voice should be communicated by the organization's spokesperson. The spokesperson should be a senior management person and be the only person to speak publicly on the crisis issue.

In a crisis situation, there are always at least two sides to a story. At times, the media look to create an environment that pits the sides against each other—tune into any cable news network and you will see ongoing examples. With that said, sometimes the best way to deal with a crisis is to tell your side of the story up-front, ensure it is easily understood, and refuse to take the bait to extend the story. Crises sell newspapers, drive radio listenership, and increase television viewership. Contributing or responding to every claim made by the other side merely prolongs the coverage of the issue, which may not be in the organization's best interest. As long as the story has been told accurately, no one owes it to the media to sustain the story.

When dealing directly with the media, it is always helpful to keep in mind that the media

TABLE 16-4 Potential Crises in Sports
Accident (crash of plane, train, bus, car)
Arena disaster (building collapse, object falls, power outage)
Criminal activity (DUI, drugs, domestic violence, gambling, weapons)
Customer relations (problems with ticket service)
Death of executive, coach, player
Employee/management misconduct (sexual harassment, sexual misconduct, sexual abuse, bribery, kickbacks, discrimination)
Employee problem (inappropriate comments or behavior by ownership, department staff, coaches, athletes)
Gambling
Hiring/firing
Investor relations (going public, IPO, merger, acquisition)
Labor relations (strike, lockout, contract negotiations, holdouts)
Lawsuits (ticket holders)
Natural disaster (earthquake, fire, tornado)
Product liability (jersey, hat)
Protestors at site of arena, stadium, team or athletic department offices
Rule violations
Social controversies/issues (hazing, drugs, alcohol, AIDS, diversity, domestic violence)
Terrorism
Ticket price increase

This list is meant as a starting point in assessing potential crises and crisis planning. Abbreviations: DUI = driving under the influence; IPO = initial public offering; AIDS = acquired immunodeficiency syndrome.

are always looking for a "crisis" or hot-button issue to cover. Therefore, it is imperative to learn how to avoid falling into some traps regularly practiced by members of the media such as **speculation** and asking for off-the-record comments.

■ SPECULATION

The media will often ask questions that include the words "what if" or "suppose." These questions are highly speculative in nature, and it is seldom in anyone's best interest to speculate or offer a guess to a question. Politely respond by stating that you prefer not to answer a speculative or hypothetical question.

■ OFF-THE-RECORD COMMENTS

Going **off the record** with the media is a very dangerous practice. If the information is very compelling or newsworthy, a reporter may use the information regardless of an off-the-record agreement. The level of trust with a media member has to be very high for a sport communications professional to engage in this practice.

■ AWARENESS

Whenever the media are around, a sport communications professional should be mindful of what is said and done. Words can be picked up by a turned-on tape recorder, a nearby television camera can record sound and actions, and so too can most cell phones and other hand-held devices. It is the media's responsibility to report a story, and in many major markets members of the media, especially print journalists, are under extreme pressure to break exclusive stories. The more time that is dedicated to learning the needs and wants of the media covering an organization, including individual reporting styles, the easier it will be to do the job effectively.

■ MEDIA TRAINING

Several companies offer **media training** tips for communications professionals and for anyone likely to be dealing with the media. Several sport organizations have used these companies to provide players, coaches, athletic directors, and senior executives with tips on proper interviewing techniques, handling hostile interviewers, and shaping messages into sound bites. Many of these companies provide videotape analysis to compare the before and after performances. An experienced sport communications professional should be able to provide similar services or support to his or her organization's key personnel or should locate a company that can provide this service to the organization.

Internal Communications

One of the most overlooked forms of communications is **internal communications**. Organizations are often so involved with generating positive news, posting information on their Web sites, creating printed publications, and so on that communicating to the organization's staff is overlooked. This seemingly small issue can become a major problem for an organization, resulting in poor morale and lower productivity. According to Barton (2001), employees are key stakeholders who can be especially valuable to the organization in a time of crisis.

The solution to this potential problem is rather simple and can be achieved in a number of ways. The president or general manager can distribute a daily or weekly e-mail that includes a status report on any existing projects, new hiring, new partnership agreements, ticket sales updates, employee of the month award, and anything else that engages the employees. Another common practice is a weekly or monthly breakfast where the staff can gather in an informal environment with senior staff and discuss organizational happenings. Always keep in mind the old adage that says your most important customers are your employees. If the employees don't feel strongly about the organization, how can they be expected to positively represent the organization in their day-to-day business relationships?

Integrated Marketing Communications

Demands placed on the sport communications professional continue to change. The new buzzword is **integrated marketing communications (IMC)**, which, according to Seitel (2001), is the symbiosis of advertising, marketing, and public relations. Today's sport communications professionals need to be knowledgeable in these areas because they will be called upon to participate in campaigns utilizing these areas to promote their organizations.

■ ADVERTISING

Advertising often does not fall under the job responsibilities of the sport communications specialist, but is an area of communications that must be fully understood. Cutlip, Center, and Broom (2000) define advertising as "information placed in the media by an identified sponsor that pays for the time or space. It is a controlled method of placing messages in the media" (p. 11). Public relations relies upon news outlets to convey its message. Although less expensive than advertising, public relations efforts are subject to whatever editing the media decides upon. There is no guarantee a press release will generate any publicity at all. In contrast, advertising guarantees the message will gain the space and coverage purchased. Although advertising promises to get the message out there, it does not ensure that message will be trusted or believed.

Perhaps the most significant difference between the two is that advertising is more costly to produce and place than media relations activities. For example, a successfully placed news item published by *Sports Illustrated* will get the item in front of more than 3 million avid sports fans at virtually no cost other than staff time. To place a full-page ad in *Sports Illustrated* to reach the magazine's subscriber base would cost more than $352,800 (color) and $229,300 (black and white), not including the costs involved in creating the ad (*Sports Illustrated*, 2010).

There are, generally speaking, two types of ads: **image ads** and **call-to-action ads**. Image ads are created to reinforce an organization's brand imagery in the minds of consumers. These ads tend to highlight the quality of a service. Call-to-action ads aim to encourage consumers to do something, such as buy tickets.

■ MEDIA PLANNING

Choosing the correct medium in which to place advertising requires a thorough examination of each potential outlet's ability to reach the most people fitting a target audience's demographic profile. This is known as **media planning**. Because advertising can be costly, it is imperative to make the effort to ensure that the advertising will be successful. Once the total advertising budget has been decided, it must be determined how the ad dollars will be effectively spent in the media of TV, radio, print (newspapers and magazines), and the Internet. A trained **media buyer**, who purchases advertising for clients, can provide the information required to make the right decision for each particular circumstance. Always keep in mind that the goal is to reach the greatest possible number of people who fit the targeted customer profile, not just the greatest number of people. A benefit to advertising on the Internet is the medium's ability to allow for cost-effective and near instantaneous monitoring of an ad's success. Checking a Web ad's click-through rate allows a marketer to alter the ad to generate an increase in clicks. Text copy, background colors, and everything in between can be tweaked and measured for success. When the winning formula is found, the ad, in theory, should wind up being more successful. Try doing that with traditional mediums of print, radio, and TV! It's too costly and time consuming to even try.

■ DIRECT MARKETING

As previously discussed, reaching a targeted audience through advertising is not an easy process. With this in mind, another form of communications is **direct marketing**. As consumers, we have come to refer to this widely used practice as junk mail. However, thousands of very successful companies use this method of communication exclusively to sell their products or services, and the sport industry is just beginning to fully understand the powers of successful direct marketing campaigns.

Before beginning a direct marketing campaign, it is important to fully understand your key customers by creating a customer profile. Once the customer profile is developed, the proper message and the creative look or design that are likely to appeal to the audience for your direct marketing piece must also be developed. After the creative material has been carefully crafted so that it is visually appealing to the target audience, the next step is to acquire an appropriate mailing list of the people fitting the customer profile. In most cases, the names and addresses of people living within certain ZIP codes can be purchased from a list provider. In turn, the direct marketing material will be sent to these people and, if done properly, will capture their interest. The success rates of a direct marketing campaign vary widely, but successful campaigns return a positive response from approximately 2% of individuals targeted.

Direct marketing is now being utilized via the Internet. Similar to obtaining a mailing list, electronic mailing lists of qualified e-mail addresses can be purchased or created internally and utilized to send targeted messages and/or offerings. E-mail is a much more cost-effective method, can be sent instantaneously, and generates a faster and higher response rate.

■ CAREER OPPORTUNITIES

Over the past 25 years, sport organizations have enjoyed tremendous growth in popularity thanks to expanded media coverage (cable television, magazines, 24-hour sports radio, and the Internet) as well as corporate support. This popularity has resulted in an explosion of sorts in the number of sports-related organizations, including professional sports leagues and teams, sport marketing and public relations firms, and the number of corporations employing sports-specific personnel.

This growth has been a boon to the area of sport communications. On the professional sports side, 25 years ago there were far fewer teams with fewer communications professionals. As this text went to print, there were 144 teams at the North American major league level (MLB, NBA, NFL, NHL, and Major League Soccer [MLS]) with hundreds of communications-related positions (media relations, public relations, community relations, and publications in print and online). This expansion on the professional level has also changed the structure of the department responsible for communications. Twenty-five years ago, a one- or two-person public relations staff handled a team, but today staffs consist of six to ten individuals with titles ranging from the vice-president level to directors, assistant directors, and other support staff.

Additionally, auto racing (e.g., National Association of Stock Car Auto Racing [NASCAR], Indy Racing League [IRL]) and minor league sports (e.g., Minor League Baseball, NBA Development League [NBDL], National Association of Professional Baseball Leagues [NAPBL], American Hockey League [AHL], East Coast

Hockey League [ECHL]) have enjoyed tremendous growth over the same period of time. New professional sports leagues (e.g., Arena Football, AFL2, Major League Lacrosse), women's leagues (e.g., Women's National Basketball Association [WNBA]), and nontraditional sports (i.e., X-Games) have burst onto the scene in recent years, resulting in an increase in opportunities available to those interested in pursuing a career in sport communications. On the amateur level, sport communications professionals work in college athletic departments, college athletic conferences, Olympic committees, and other governing bodies. Finally, many sports facilities also have a communications professional working for the venue.

Even though opportunities in the area of sport communications have experienced tremendous growth over the past 30 years, obtaining one of these coveted positions is as difficult as ever. Because these jobs do not generally get listed in the local Help Wanted section of the newspaper, coursework and related work experience are required to obtain an internship, let alone a full-time position.

Not all job candidates possess sport management degrees. As a matter of fact, many sport communications professionals possess degrees in communications, public relations, or journalism. It is important to accumulate coursework or volunteer or paid work experience to help you understand the fundamentals of public relations, communications, marketing, advertising, and journalism. Public speaking skills, writing skills, and knowledge of TV/video production and computer technology (Internet uploading, downloading, text posting, etc.) are a must for all future sport communications professionals. Therefore, coursework rich in these areas will help prepare students for their internships.

There used to be a time when an internship offered students a chance to learn on the job. However, the competition for the most coveted internships is so intense that when an internship is available several applicants will have already amassed relative experience. Some will have written for their school or local newspaper. Some will have created their own Web sites and blogs. Many willhave volunteered in their school's sports information department or served as public relations staffers for not-for-profit organizations. It is no longer acceptable to enter the sports communications field, even as an intern, without some practical, first-hand experience.

The internship remains invaluable to starting a career in sport communications. It is important to choose an internship offering real opportunities to contribute to the communications activities of an organization. This does not mean that interns should be expected to make day-to-day strategic decisions. What this does mean is that internships should offer candidates

a chance to get first-hand experience through actual tactical responsibilities. Interns should look for opportunities that promise more than "gofer" responsibilities. Interns should look for opportunities offering hands-on experience, but they should also choose an environment offering a complete learning experience, including a chance to work closely with proven professionals. Because most internships do not lead to full-time job offers, the internship will serve as the launching pad for your career. However, landing that desired entry-level position is a very difficult process. It will be a matter of timing, experience, and, to a large extent, who you know, and who knows you.

Make no mistake: the relationships and networks built during an internship will prove instrumental in gaining that first real job.

Despite the fact that men seem to dominate most sport organizations, women have an equal opportunity to gain internships and full-time opportunities in the area of sport communications. In fact, in 2010, women held no fewer than 43 positions in the public/media relations departments of the 30 MLB teams. This number does not even count the areas of sales, marketing, and community relations, which offer additional opportunities for women. Of all areas of the front office, public relations, media relations, and community relations are perhaps the most diverse (Major League Baseball, 2004).

Sport communications staffers at the professional and collegiate team levels get as close to the field of play as anyone outside of players and coaches. This makes for a professional career full of memorable moments. If one wants to advance within the ranks of the organization's hierarchy, the ability to quickly establish oneself as a trustworthy employee who understands that what is heard and seen can often never be repeated is a necessity. Breaching this implied level of trust and confidentiality is sure to tarnish a reputation and result in a short-lived professional career.

Those fortunate enough to earn one of these coveted positions will soon learn that long hours, low starting pay, and slow-moving advancement come with this unique territory. Most senior sport communications professionals, such as professional team public relations (PR) directors, have to attend every home game, most, if not all, road games, and most of the team's practices. This means that time for family and friends is extremely limited during the season, which can put a strain on most personal relationships.

Perhaps because most sport communications professionals share a lot in common, they are a close-knit group and communicate regularly with one another, formally, informally, inter-sport, and intra-sport. It is common for a PR director from a team in one league to contact a peer in another league to ask for a favor or get an opinion on a writer, among other things. Although there are no real peer associations to speak of in professional sports, college sports offers its communications professionals a great opportunity for peer interaction through a professional association known as the College Sports Information Directors of America (CoSIDA). CoSIDA is entering its 60th year and has more than 2400 members. The group holds an annual meeting with workshops. It also publishes monthly digests, newsletters, has an e-directory, sponsors scholarships, and boasts a well-developed Web site with useful professional information and a career center (College Sports Information Directors of America, 2010). Other organizations can serve as resources as well as networking opportunities, such as the Public Relations Society of America (PRSA) and the International Association of Business Communicators (IABC). The PRSA has a Public Relations Student Society of America (PRSSA) to help students explore the field and enter the profession. In its 40th year, PRSSA has more than 10,000 members at 303 colleges and universities in the United States and abroad. Its

Web site boasts useful career information plus scholarship listings. The group also hosts an annual conference (Public Relations Student Society of America, 2010). In addition, the Association of Women in Sports Media (AWSM) serves as "a support network and advocacy group for women who work in sports writing, editing, broadcast and production, and public and media relations" (Association of Women in Sports Media, 2010).

◼ CURRENT ISSUES

Technology

As technology continues to have perhaps its greatest impact on the way we communicate with one another, expect Internet-based communications efforts to only increase. For example, social media Web sites such as Facebook and MySpace offer organizations additional means to communicate directly with their current and future core fans in a space and time(less) way. These Web sites also pose challenges, as they require constant monitoring and updating. In 2010, one MLB club hired a senior director of social media.

"Push" technologies, such as Twitter, allow individuals and organizations to communicate with their loyal or interested followers in real-time. In some respects, today's technology has rendered a sport's organization's dependency on the media to get its message out obsolete. However, traditional mediums still reach more of the masses and provide organizations with an implicit third-party endorsement that organizations willing to bypass traditional media relations do at their own peril.

Web conferencing, as mentioned earlier, should become increasingly popular in the world of sport communications. Already popular with public companies and their investor relations activities with stock analysts, shareholders, and other important constituencies who may be dispersed throughout the world, Web conferencing allows for real-time exchange of audio, video, and text-based messaging. WiFi, or wireless Internet connection, is also gaining in popularity. Virtually all major sports league press boxes and press areas have WiFi access. As WiFi expands its reach, it is easy to imagine real-time communications between teams and their fans from the moment they enter the stadium to the moment they leave. With third-party service providers such as Skype, video Web conferencing is likely to enjoy continued growth in popularity and use.

Outside Agencies

A growing trend, especially at the league and association level, is hiring an outside public relations firm to help develop and administer public relations programs or special events. These agencies allow the staffs of the leagues and associations to concentrate on their day-to-day responsibilities, most of which are reactive in nature, and shift the implementation of these public relations programs to someone else. These agencies, in essence, act as extensions of the hiring organization, allowing the organization to have greater impact in the area of public relations without being limited by its staff resources. These agencies can range from moderate or large companies with offices around the world to smaller agencies run by just an individual or two. The agencies can be hired on a **retainer** basis, where they are paid monthly to be of service to the organization, or they can be hired on a project-by-project basis.

Government Relations

One of the most recent trends in public relations activities focuses on government relations. **Government relations** or lobbying is used by all major sports leagues and unions, the NCAA, and in some cases by individual teams. Most organizations hire outside firms with legislative and other government contacts as well as more experience in this delicate area to represent their interests. Leagues, unions, and NCAA have had lobbyists at the federal level for years. On the state level, the increased need to improve government relations has been influenced by the increase in new stadium and arena construction. Needing to finance such costly projects, sport

CASE STUDY: Communications Strategies for the Cricket League

Congratulations! You just graduated with a degree in sport management and landed a job in professional sports. An overseas professional cricket league hired you as its director of international communications. The premise behind your hire is that the United States is populated with numerous expatriates from several cricket-playing countries, and this cricket league wants to tap into that market. League officials want to host matches on U.S. soil and use the Internet to engage current cricket fans in their league and nurture new fans.

The cricket league is relying on you to help choose the three markets in the United States that should host matches, and they want you to generate local publicity to help sell tickets to these events. They are also counting on you to generate national buzz in the United States for the purpose of increasing exposure for the remainder of the cricket season.

You must now develop and implement several strategies and tactics that incorporate traditional media and the Internet to generate publicity for the league.

Questions for Discussion

1. Determine the three cities in the United States to host the matches during the cricket tour. What can be done in each market to engage local sports fans? How would you locate and communicate with fans from cricket-playing countries living in these markets? Would there be a benefit to engaging in a community-minded project while in each market? If so, what types of projects would you pursue and why? How would you go about gathering information from cricket fans in each local market for future communications purposes?

2. In order to make a national "splash," your bosses want you plan a press conference in New York City upon the cricket team's arrival. Where would you plan the press conference? League officials and the players are unfamiliar with the U.S. sports press. Prepare a background sheet with brief information on some national outlets likely to attend the press conference. What key messages will you craft and share with league officials and players? What kinds of questions will the media likely ask the officials and players? What other national media opportunities might you pursue while the teams are in New York?

3. Upon the conclusion of the series, you must sustain your superb efforts by creating and implementing an ongoing communications program during the cricket season. Relying heavily on the Internet as the main medium of communications, what types of communications elements will your plan include? Consider your main goals to promote merchandise sales, keep fans up to date on scores, player features, standings, and live and on-demand Web viewing of matches and highlights.

organizations have turned to their local legislators to help them gain access to federal, state, and local funds, as well as contributions from existing or specially created tax funds.

SUMMARY

As indicated by the breadth of information covered in this chapter, today's sport communications professional serves one of the organization's most vital roles. This role has direct contact with local, national, and international media, the general public, the coaching staff, management staff, and the players, so it is imperative to know virtually all there is to know about an organization. Communications professionals must know all about an organization's ticket packages, sponsorship rates, history, rules of the game, community activities, players' interests and backgrounds, and on and on.

Communication professionals serve in the most vibrant area of the organization. In many cases, they travel to away games, may sit in on trade discussion meetings, often offer input into how the team or athletic department will be marketed and promoted, and are the first to respond in a time of crisis. They will be quoted in the newspaper, conduct television and radio interviews, and are the first people to whom others in the organization turn for information of all sorts. This is what makes sport communications an extremely challenging and exciting career choice. To be successful, sport communications professionals must remain cool, calm, and collected at all times. They need to be trustworthy, resourceful, and display common sense. If they don't know the answer to a question or a request, they need to know where to find it (and quickly). They must be good listeners, friendly, and approachable. Professional opportunities are numerous and growing, and an exciting future awaits those who choose this as a career path.

Lastly, today's sports communications professional must be technologically savvy. Rapidly advancing communications technologies provide the sports communications professional with ample opportunities to take matters into his or her own hands when developing and implementing organizational communications strategies and tactics.

RESOURCES

College Sports Information Directors of America (CoSIDA)
http://www.cosida.com

International Association of Business Communicators
One Hallidie Plaza, Suite 600
San Francisco, CA 94102
415-544-4700
http://www.iabc.com

Public Relations Society of America
Public Relations Student Society of America
33 Maiden Lane, 11th Floor
New York, NY 10038
212-460-1400 (PRSA)
212-460-1474 (PRSSA)
http://www.prsa.org
http://www.prssa.org

KEY TERMS

b-roll, beat reporter, beat writer, blogs, call-to-action ads, communications, community relations, conference calls, crisis plan, crisis team, direct marketing, electronic newsletters, government relations, image ads, integrated marketing communications (IMC), internal communications, inverted pyramid, key messages, media buyer, media guide, media lists, media notes, media planning, media training, multi-box, new media industry, news release, off the record, press conference, press release, retainer, speculation, stakeholders, video news release (VNR), Web conferencing, Web site

■ REFERENCES

Association of Women in Sports Media. (2010). About. Retrieved December 2, 2010, from http://awsmonline.org/about/

Barton, L. (2001). *Crisis organizations II*. Cincinnati, OH: South Western College Publishing.

College Sports Information Directors of America. (2010). General information. Retrieved November 9, 2010, from http://www.cosida.com/about/general.aspx

Cutlip, S.M., Center, A.H., & Broom, G.M. (2000). *Effective public relations* (8th ed.). Upper Saddle River, NJ: Prentice Hall.

Internet World Stats. (2006). Internet world statistics. Retrieved November 9, 2010, from http://www.internetworldstats.com/am/us.htm

Major League Baseball. (2004). *Major League Baseball media information directory*. New York: Major League Baseball Public Relations.

McGowan, A. (2001). Don't wait for a crisis to write a crisis plan. *Street & Smith's SportsBusiness Journal, 4*(23), p. 33.

Middleburg, D. (2001). *Winning PR in the wired world*. New York: McGraw-Hill.

NCAA. (2003, March 3). Privacy rules affect exchange of student-athlete medical records. *NCAA News*. Retrieved December 2, 2010, from http://fs.ncaa.org/Docs/NCAANewsArchive/2003/Association-wide/privacy+rules+affect+exchange+of+student-athlete+medical+records+-+3-3-03.html

Netimperative. (2007). Sports fans amongst Internet's biggest users. Retrieved December 2, 2010, from http://www.netimperative.com/news/2008/june/2/sports-fans-amongst-internet2019s-biggest-users

Newsom, D., Turk, J., & Kruckeberg, D. (2004). *This is PR: The realities of public relations* (8th ed.). Belmont, CA: Wadsworth/Thompson Learning.

Nichols, W., Moynahan, P., Hall, A., & Taylor, J. (2002). *Media relations in sport*. Morgantown, WV: Fitness Information Technology.

Nielsen//NetRatings. (2004, January 8). Fifty million users connect via broadband. Retrieved from http://www.nielsen-netratings.com/pr/pr_040108.pdf

Nielsen//NetRatings. (2006a, March 26). March Madness spurs nearly 10 million sports fans to jump online the first day of the NCAA tournament for news and live video, according the Nielsen//NetRatings. Press release. Retrieved November 9, 2010, from http://www.nielsen-online.com/pr/pr_060321.pdf

Nielsen//NetRatings. (2006b, December 12). Over three-fourths of US active Internet users connect via broadband at home in November, according to Nielsen//NetRatings. Retrieved November 9, 2010, from http://www.nielsen-netratings.com/pr/pr_061212.pdf

Public Relations Student Society of America (2010). What is PRSSA? Retrieved November 9, 2010, from http://www.prssa.org/about/

Seitel, F. (2001). *The practice of public relations* (8th ed.). Upper Saddle River, NJ: Prentice Hall.

Sports Illustrated. (2010). *Sports Illustrated* rate card #68. Retrieved from http://www.simediakit.com/media/property/download/ratecard/Sports%20Illustrated%202010%20Rate%20Card.pdf

Thornton, T.V. (1999). Illinois has developed into the world's high tech hub. *Illinois Labor Market Review*. Retrieved November 9, 2010, from http://lmi.ides.state.il.us/lmr/hightech.htm

CHAPTER

17

Sport Broadcasting

Betsy Goff and Tim Ashwell

■ INTRODUCTION

The electronic media—television, radio, and digital computer technology—have utterly transformed the sport industry and its relationship with the public. Until the development of radio broadcasting in the 1920s and television broadcasting in the 1930s, the only people who could witness a game as it was being played were the fans who paid their way into the ballpark. If the event was important enough—say, a heavyweight championship boxing match or the baseball World Series—the most eager nonattending fans gathered outside newspaper offices or in hotel ballrooms to monitor the Western Union telegraph circuit for the latest bulletins from the stadium. The rest of the public waited for the story in the morning paper to find out who won and what happened.

Today, sports fans can watch events unfold around the world as they happen, no matter

where, no matter when. Images and sounds of every major event—and many not so major ones—flash into our homes at the speed of light, and we have come to expect the instant replays, dazzling computerized graphics, and expert commentary that accompany the games. When Lance Armstrong crossed the finish line in Paris to claim his seventh Tour de France victory, viewers in the United States saw it as it happened. So, too, did vast audiences watching in Africa, Europe, Asia, and the Americas. Thanks to advanced video technology, fans not only saw the race and Armstrong's triumphant victory lap in lifelike color, but also saw it replayed in slow motion, from several different camera angles, and in extreme close-up. The view at home was, in fact, far superior to that of any fan in the stands. Most of the fans in attendance watched the race replayed on television, too, on giant video screens showing the details they could not see in real life. Ironically, for that reason,

rights holders of sports events feared the coming of age of television as they had previously feared radio: viewers could watch sports events in the comfort of their own homes, with their own (reasonably priced) snacks, and the benefit of instant replays, often in slow motion, expert analysis and dazzling new technologies. What, then would happen to the live gate? It has increased exponentially. As we have learned in previous chapters, nothing can replace the emotional and social experience of actually attending a game, and radio and television have allowed fans to stay current with any team in any sport, in most cases in anticipation of one's next in-stadium or in-arena experience.

If broadcasting has changed the way fans experience sport, it has also profoundly altered the business of sport. Television and radio organizations around the world pay billions of dollars for the **broadcast rights** to sporting events, and sport organizations gain priceless exposure, publicity, and status by being showcased by the electronic media. The term *broadcast rights* as used in this context is intended to include cable, often called narrowcast rights, and rights in all other developing distribution media. A more appropriate term, therefore, would be **telecast rights**, which would include broad- and narrowcast rights, but as in all other walks of life, old habits in the television industry die hard. *Live streaming, webcasting,* and other sophisticated online viewing opportunities are discussed in Chapter 18, Sport and New Media, and Chapter 16, Sport Communications. Broadcast revenues have fueled the explosive growth of spectator sports since World War II, and the search for new audiences and new revenues has spurred professional league expansion, college conference realignment, and the era of franchise relocation. Major League Baseball's fractious battle between large- and small-market clubs is largely due to differences in local television revenue paid to teams in major metropolitan areas and those in smaller cities. The financial

success of the National Football League (NFL) can be traced to the league's decision to pool and divide equally its network television revenue, ensuring the financial stability of teams in cities as huge as New York and as small as Green Bay, Wisconsin. It must be noted, however, that NFL teams play 16 regular season games, all of which are televised, often on a regional basis, but under national **rights agreements**. This schedule and media coverage lend themselves much more readily to revenue sharing than a league such as Major League Baseball (MLB), whose teams play 162 games in each season. As we shall see, the MLB, National Basketball Association (NBA), and National Hockey League (NHL) have rights' agreements with various national over-the-air networks and cable networks for specified national or regional telecasts, and each major league team is permitted to have rights' agreements with local broadcasters for games not covered under a national or regional contract. NFL teams, however, are constrained to the agreements entered into by the League itself and are not at liberty to make local telecast arrangements.

The sport industry and the broadcasting business are closely allied in a **symbiotic relationship**. While sport organizations rely on broadcasters for revenue and publicity, the electronic media know that sporting events are a sure-fire means of attracting the audiences that advertisers will pay to reach. Popular sporting events also lend prestige to the radio and television organizations associated with them. The Fox television network used its contract with the NFL to prove to advertisers, station operators, and the public that it was a major network. In small towns across the country, local radio stations air hometown college and high school games to prove they care about their communities. It was, in fact, through the marketing and promotional efforts associated with its first NFL television rights agreement that Fox established itself as not only a viable television entity, but as the fourth over-the-air network, fully competitive with ABC, CBS, and NBC, which had existed for close to fifty years before Fox broadcast its first signal. Ironically, Rupert Murdoch (majority owner and corporate executive officer [CEO] of NewsCorp, which in turn owns of Fox Television), realizing the value of telecasting one of the four major United States sports, first approached MLB to bid on television rights to a series of games, but MLB turned him down. Possibly fearing a perceived diminution of the value of MLB games, the Commissioner's office apparently thought that Fox's relatively small average audience was not in the best interest of the game. The NFL's Commissioner's office apparently thought the risk was one worth taking, and it has reaped the enormous financial benefits of that risk ever since.

Broadcasters also know sports programming is a proven way to convince consumers to invest in new technology or purchase additional services from existing media. For more than 75 years, promoters of new communications systems, from radio in the 1920s to direct satellite television broadcasting and the Internet today, have understood that the lure of sport, the opportunity to get more information faster about more games and events, could convince hundreds of millions of consumers to spend tens of billions of dollars on new equipment.

The Electronic Media

All electronic media—radio, television, and computer data transmitted on the Internet—function in fundamentally the same manner (Head, Sterling, & Schofield, 1994). Sound and images are captured by electronic devices (microphones and cameras) and electronically encoded. The information is then transmitted at the speed of light via land lines such as fiber-optic and coaxial cable or through the air by broadcast transmitters or satellites to a receiver, where

it is decoded and transformed back to sound and images that can be heard through speakers or seen on a video screen. In short, television is broadcast via radio waves in native analog form or digitally compressed. By virtue of standardized "codes" such as MPEG (acronym for Moving Picture Experts Group or audio/visual file format), or streaming media players, digital distribution uses the radio spectrum apportioned for broadcast transmission far more efficiently. A local radio broadcast of a high school football game might involve a single announcer speaking into one microphone linked by telephone lines to equipment at the radio station and then transmitted to receivers within range of the station. A Super Bowl telecast involves dozens of cameras and microphones augmented by videotape recorders, computerized graphics, and special effects units operated by hundreds of skilled engineers and technicians. The signal is then flashed from the game site to a communications satellite orbiting nearly 23,000 miles over the earth and relayed to network headquarters in New York or California. The game broadcast, augmented by commercials, promotional announcements, and material presented live in studios at network headquarters, is then distributed via satellite to local stations across the country, which add their own commercial announcements and transmit the complete program to viewers in their area. If people subscribe to cable television, the local station's signal is received by the cable company—which may add its own local commercials to the mix—and transmitted to their homes through a network of wires. The entire process takes less than a second. You can Google "how television works," "how cable works," or "how satellite television works" for a deeper, yet very understandable analysis of those media.

All that electronic information can also be recorded for use at a later time. Electromagnetic impulses depicting the sound and images of a sporting event can be embedded on audio- and videotape or transformed into computer language of bits and bytes and preserved on varying and ever growing forms of computer memory. This allows broadcasters to replay highlights or entire games at any time in the future. It also allows fans to search the Internet and summon recordings of crucial plays or postgame interviews. Computer programs also allow the images to be manipulated in countless ways. Images created by computer can be inserted to allow Michael Jordan to play basketball with Bugs Bunny the cartoon character, as in the 1996 movie *Space Jam*. Electronic media technology has advanced to the point that if someone can imagine a sound or sight he or she would like to hear or see, it can be created.

■ HISTORY

Electronic communications began with the telegraph and the telephone. In 1844 Samuel F. B. Morse opened the first operational telegraph, a 40-mile circuit between Washington, D.C., and Baltimore (Head, Sterling, & Schofield, 1994). Morse sent messages along a wire by opening and closing an electrical circuit in a series of dots and dashes representing letters and numbers. In 1876, Alexander Graham Bell demonstrated his telephone, using a simple microphone to transmit sound along wires (Head, Sterling, & Schofield, 1994). Both inventions relied on electricity and conductive wires, and since scientists knew that electricity could also travel through the atmosphere without wires, many inventors around the world set to work to develop wireless communications. In 1888, German physicist Heinrich Hertz published the results of an experiment proving that radio waves could be generated, transmitted, and detected. Although Hertz failed to understand the implications of his work, many others did not. Within a decade, several wireless transmission systems had been devised, the most famous by Guglielmo Marconi, who patented his device in 1896 (Head, Sterling, & Schofield, 1994).

By World War I the *wireless* (radio) was a well-established fact of life, a standard method of communication for business and government as well as a valuable military asset. Thanks to the new invention, messages could be sent across the ocean and over inaccessible terrain beyond the reach of telephone or telegraph wires. Major corporations, including General Electric and American Telephone & Telegraph, as well as American Marconi, a subsidiary of Marconi's British company, developed improved transmitters and receivers, and soon messages were flashing around the world at the speed of light. Unfortunately, the corporations agreed, there was one problem with the wireless: Once a message was transmitted, anyone within range who had a receiver tuned to the proper frequency could hear the message. It seemed to be an insurmountable problem. Why would anyone want to send a message through the air that thousands, perhaps millions, of people could listen to?

A few visionaries understood that the perceived weakness of the wireless would prove to be its greatest virtue (Douglas, 1987). One was a Westinghouse Electric Company executive named Harry Davis, whose company had a warehouse full of World War I surplus radio receivers. Perhaps, he reasoned, if a wireless station broadcast entertainment and news programs every day on a fixed schedule, people would buy his receivers and listen. On November 2, 1920, the evening of the presidential election, radio station KDKA signed on from studios at the Westinghouse plant in Pittsburgh to broadcast the returns as well as some musical entertainment, and the radio boom of the 1920s began (Barnouw, 1966–1970). Radio broadcasting took the United States, and much of the rest of the world, by storm. For the first time, listeners could hear events as they happened, and some of the most important early broadcasts involved sporting events. KDKA first broadcast a baseball game on August 5, 1921, an 8–5 Pirates victory over the Philadelphia Phillies at Forbes Field in Pittsburgh. WJZ in Newark, New Jersey, broadcast the heavyweight title fight between Jack Dempsey and George Carpentier and the Yankees–Giants World Series later that same year. By the end of the 1920s, local broadcasts or those done nationally on networks of radio stations throughout the country linked by telephone lines covered virtually every major baseball and football game and boxing match plus dozens of other lesser events. Network radio—or *chain broadcasting* as it was called in the early days—allowed many local stations across the country to broadcast the same event. This had the obvious advantage of allowing listeners across the country to hear a game or news event, but it also allowed advertisers to reach an audience far greater than any single station could reach.

Broadcasters understood that sports sold radios. One industry analyst estimated that $14 million was spent on radio receivers across the country in the days leading up to the second Dempsey–Gene Tunney heavyweight title fight in 1927. "The broadcast of a heavyweight title fight is the biggest boon that the industry can have,"

the Boston Globe reported following the fight. "In second place . . . the World Series baseball championship, then the more important football games, and then events of national importance such as national political conventions . . . and Presidential speeches" ("Fight Booms," 1927, p. 19). Sports were also among the first radio programs to attract sponsors willing to pay handsomely to have their products promoted in connection with the event. The Royal Typewriter Company paid a reported $30,000 to sponsor the first Dempsey–Tunney fight on a national network in 1926 (Burton, 1999).

At first, few teams profited directly from radio coverage. Gradually, however, sport managers began to understand the value of their product. Dempsey's promoter, Tex Rickard, was among the first to demand payments in exchange for the right to broadcast fights, but others quickly followed. By the 1930s, many colleges sold exclusive rights to their football games to a sponsor, which in turn purchased radio time from broadcasters to air the games. As mentioned above, some baseball teams (as well as other sport organizers) worried that radio broadcasts of home games would hurt attendance, but most agreed that radio games increased fan support and were a valuable publicity and promotional tool. Additionally, in the Depression era, cash payments from sponsors were always welcome. In 1938, the Pittsburgh Pirates sued a local radio station for broadcasting the team's games without permission and won (*Pittsburgh Athletic Co. v. KQV Broadcasting Co.*, 1938). It was a landmark case, establishing the right of sport organizations to control the broadcast rights to their events The case made clear that the person, group, or entity that takes the effort to establish a team; train and pay the players, rent (or own) a venue; provide security, access, egress, amenities, and safety to spectators; and engage in such other activities as are required to conduct a sports competition is the *rights' holder*, the person or entity who owns all rights to that competition, including the right to permit a broadcaster to distribute an audiovisual account of the competition to the viewing or listening audience.

When television arrived on the scene following World War II, the pattern was similar. Broadcasters used sports to convince men to purchase televisions, which in turn created the male audiences advertisers desired (Rader, 1984). Set manufacturers supplied free televisions to bars, and retailers left televisions on in store windows to show consumers that they could now both hear and see their heroes in action. Advertisers such as Gillette, with its long-running series of Friday night boxing matches, and the leading automakers and breweries quickly jumped on board the sports television bandwagon.

Three men dominated the growth of sport broadcasting in the 1960s and beyond: NFL commissioner **Alvin "Pete" Rozelle**, ABC executive **Roone Arledge**, and the man generally credited with creating sport marketing, IMG (International Management Group) founder Mark McCormack. Rozelle was only 33 years old when he became NFL commissioner in 1959; Arledge was 29 years old when he joined ABC in 1960. Each played a vital role in shaping the sport broadcasting industry.

Rozelle had been a publicist for the Los Angeles Rams prior to becoming commissioner. He knew both the broadcasting and advertising industries and sensed that the NFL was on the brink of cashing in on a coming sport broadcasting boom. Because he understood that television was driven by ratings and demographics, he knew the appeal of football. He also understood that large-market teams such as the New York Giants and Chicago Bears would soon be rolling in television revenues that teams in small cities such as the Green Bay Packers could never match. This, he feared, would create a competitive imbalance and might destroy the League. Throughout the 1950s, NFL teams had signed individual contracts with broadcasters, with each team keeping the revenue it earned. Soon after taking office, Rozelle proposed a new idea: The NFL would pool its regular season and playoff television rights and sell them to the highest bidder. The revenue would then be divided equally among the teams. The first pooled network contract was signed in 1960 and promptly ruled in violation of antitrust laws by a federal judge. Rozelle was unfazed. Calling on his contacts in the television business as well as mobilizing the nation's professional sport teams and their fans, he pushed Congress to pass the Sports Broadcasting Act of 1961. The act explicitly granted professional football, baseball, hockey, and basketball immunity from antitrust actions regarding the pooled sale of broadcast rights. The NFL immediately re-signed its contract with CBS, and today, thanks to the immunity granted by the 1961 law, NFL teams share annual television revenues of more than $1 billion. And the small-market New Orleans Saints, who receive a share equal to the major-market teams, won the 2010 Super Bowl.

Arledge was an award-winning producer of children's programs at NBC when he jumped to ABC. His new network was by far the weakest of the three national chains, but Arledge wanted to produce sports and ABC gave him the opportunity. Television technology was evolving rapidly. Innovations such as color broadcasting and videotape recording as well as better cameras and more sensitive microphones were opening the door to new ideas, and Arledge had one. "Television has done a remarkable job of bringing the game to the viewer," he wrote in a famous memo to his new employers in 1960. "Now, we are going to take the viewer to the game" (Gunther, 1994, p. 17). Arledge proposed using television technology to capture the experience of sports: the color, the excitement, "the thrill of victory and the agony of defeat." Instead of simply showing the game, ABC cameras would show the fans in the stands, the exhausted players on the bench, the cheerleaders, and the mascots. The idea, he explained, was to bring the viewer "up close and personal," to involve them emotionally with the contest. "In short," Arledge explained, "we are going to add show business to sports!" (Gunther, 1994, p. 18). Arledge understood that sports television could reach new heights if it broadened its appeal beyond the hard-core fan to the casual viewer. To reach that new audience, sports would have to feature drama, humor, character development, emotion, and, always, state-of-the-art production values. Sports, in other words, should be entertainment for those who might not care for the game but would enjoy the show.

Together, Rozelle and Arledge created one of the enduring hits of sports television: *ABC Monday Night Football*. When it debuted in 1970, *Monday Night Football* was a revolutionary concept. Pro football belonged on Sunday afternoons. Monday nights were for entertainment programs. Rozelle, however, saw an opportunity. CBS and NBC were already broadcasting NFL games on Sundays. Monday games would give the league an opportunity to forge a new broadcast partnership and open a new revenue channel. Arledge saw the chance to prove that football, in his hands, could be successful mass entertainment, and he was eager to break the CBS/NBC stranglehold on what was rapidly becoming the nation's favorite sport. Arledge turned *Monday Night Football* into a television extravaganza, using more cameras, more videotape machines, and more announcers than ever before. In an inspired decision, he chose to use a three-man team: the traditional play-by-play announcer, an expert analyst, and a color commentator. The unlikely trio of Don Meredith, the laid-back former Dallas Cowboy quarterback from Mount Vernon, Texas; Howard Cosell, the abrasive and opinionated lawyer-turned-broadcaster from New York City; and old reliable Keith Jackson, the original play-by-play announcer, was an immediate sensation,

and *Monday Night Football* rocketed into the Nielsen Top Ten, where it remains today, the second longest-running hit show on television. Similarly, it was under Arledge's watch that the Olympics were not only telecast in prime time (weeknight hours between 8 and 11 PM), but also beat the competition for viewership.

The huge ratings garnered by popular sport programming such as *Monday Night Football* and the Olympic Games led broadcasters to pursue the rights to additional sporting events. Many sport managers assumed rights fees would continue to spiral upward and eagerly sought television contracts. From the 1950s until the 1970s, the National Collegiate Athletic Association (NCAA) operated a television cartel, tightly controlling the broadcast rights to every game played by member schools. College games were rationed as the NCAA limited the number of times any one university could appear on television and distributed television revenue among its members. The Saturday game of the week, however, was a smash hit. People who were college football fans watched the game. It might not always be the game they wanted to watch, but it was the only game in town.

By 1982, the NCAA football contract was worth $280 million, and major college football powers, realizing they were the principal attraction and hoping they could make that much or more themselves, sued the NCAA on antitrust grounds for the right to sell their broadcast rights themselves and keep all the money. The case went all the way to the U.S. Supreme Court, and the colleges won their freedom (*National Collegiate Athletic Association v. Board of Regents of the University of Oklahoma*, 1983). The NCAA television contract was dissolved, and colleges and conferences from coast to coast rushed to make their own deals. Today, instead of a single game of the week, college fans can choose from literally dozens of broadcasts every Saturday. That is good news for fans, but the news for many colleges has been bad. Notre

Dame, the most popular college football team of them all, was a big winner, signing a five-year, $75 million deal with NBC. Major conferences such as the Big Ten and Southeastern Conference also fared well, signing lucrative network pacts for broadcast rights to their games. Many smaller schools, however, found the brave new world of free market competition a harsh and unprofitable place. Teams from the Mid-American Conference and the Ivy League, for example, had been guaranteed occasional network appearances under the NCAA contract, but now they were on their own. As the number of games on television climbed, the football audience fragmented. Smaller audiences for each game meant less advertising revenue and lower rights fees for many colleges. By the 1990s, member schools of the Eastern Collegiate Athletic Conference were forced to pay $10,000 per week in production subsidies to televise a game of the week on a regional cable channel.

The NCAA's reign over basketball is quite a different story. Whereas college football championship games are conducted under the auspices of the individual conferences, the NCAA is the organizer and television rights holder for "March Madness," the college basketball championships. Immediately following the 2010 Championship Game, the NCAA announced it has reached a 14-year, nearly $11 billion agreement with CBS and Turner Sports for the TV rights to a 68-team tournament—up three teams from the current 65. Negotiations with CBS/Turner, ESPN, and Fox Sports initially had targeted a 96-team bracket. (*USA Today*, 2010) In a formula not made public, the bulk of the revenue is distributed to conferences according to how well their schools do in the tournament, and directly to schools based on the number of sports sponsored by the NCAA and the number of grants and amount of financial aid awarded.

The now famous 1960 handshake between Mark McCormack and Arnold Palmer started an entirely new media and commercial platform of sport marketing, merchandising, and licensing. McCormack, an amateur golfer and budding young attorney, struck up a friendship with golf icon Palmer. Realizing their complementary skill sets, McCormack suggested that Palmer should take care of golf and McCormack would take care of business. Since that time, Palmer has become one of the most financially successful athletes through his tournament play, product endorsements, golf course design, speaking engagements, and a myriad of other endeavors choreographed by IMG. IMG has become the world's premiere sport marketing, athlete representative, and sport event creator and management agency. Endemic commercial entities such as equipment and apparel manufacturers as well as those unrelated to the sport such as financial institutions, automotive, and food and beverage purveyors, have enjoyed fantastic growth in sales with the phenomenon of athlete endorsements owing in no small part to the television exposure guaranteed by the endorsing athlete. McCormack not only represented athletes and created made-for-television sports events, he also served as a sales and business consultant to many non-sport–related corporations. How did he serve those clients? By recommending (and implementing) association with sports and sports figures, of course, capitalizing on the vast popularity of America's idols. Title sponsors and presenting sponsors (see below) were a natural outgrowth. Perusing and, indeed, studying, any of the IMG Web sites is a valuable a way to spend time as there is for anyone truly interested in the *business* of sport.

■ THE BUSINESS OF BROADCASTING

Technological wizardry makes sport broadcasting possible, but it is the economics of broadcasting that make sport broadcasting a reality. Broadcasting in the United States, and increasingly in countries around the world, is a business, and each party has quite specific responsibilities. The competition or *event* as it is usually called, must be distinguished from the television *program*, which encompasses the event as well as all elements provided by the broadcaster such as commentary, music, graphics, interviews, feature pieces, promotional announcements, and of course advertising (and more, depending on how elaborate the **production** is), all of which is the responsibility of the broadcaster. The rights holder is responsible for putting the event on the field: all arrangements with the teams and athletes, all arrangements with the site where the event is being held, and all preparations necessary both to attract and to accommodate spectators.

To date, advertising on cable has cost considerably less than advertising on broadcast television for two reasons: (1) The *cable universe* (homes with cable) has always been smaller than the *over-the-air* (free, broadcast television) universe (discussed later) though the gap is shrinking every year, and (2) cable programming is generally much more specific, appealing to many fewer people than network programming, and because of fewer viewers, appealing proportionately less to advertisers. The financial gap between cable and over-the-air television is closed to varying degrees by the additional revenue cable networks realize from the **subscriber fees** we all pay to receive cable television in our homes. **Content providers**, such as ESPN, Fox SportsNet, Versus, and so many more, buy the rights to televise sporting events from the rights' holders, such as the NFL, MLB, colleges and universities, and all others including the relatively obscure ones such as the Professional Rodeo Cowboys Association and the Association of Volleyball Professionals for negotiated rights fees. The content providers then sell that content—programming—to **delivery systems** such as Comcast, Cablevision, Cox, Liberty Media, Time Warner, and

so on for a negotiated amount *per* **subscriber** to that system. The amount is a function of the desirability of the content provided: ESPN can charge far more than, say, Versus because its overall program lineup offers more of what consumers want to see. Subscriber fees (again, the amount delivery systems such as Comcast pay content providers such as ESPN) can range from as little a 10¢ to nearly $3.00 per month. We, the consumers, are the subscribers who pay a monthly fee to our cable systems and those numbers are almost incomprehensible. Subscribers who opt for the most basic cable system available pay a minimum of $25 per month (Charter Communications, 2010), which means in a roughly 90+ million cable household universe, the delivery systems generate no less than a combined $2,250,000,000 *a month* in subscriber fees. And that is the absolute minimum, as some pay more than $50 per month for much more inclusive cable packages.

Before a television network—cable or over-the-air—can telecast a certain event or a season of events, it must obtain the rights from the rights' holder through a bidding process or *rights' negotiations*. If several networks are interested, a bidding war can drive up the rights fee. Exclusive rights to events also drives the rights fee higher; however, certain television programming, such as NFL games, can command enormous rights fees from multiple networks. Currently, three American over-the-air (also called *terrestrial*) television networks—CBS ($3.73 billion), NBC ($3.6 billion), and Fox ($4.27 billion), as well as cable television's ESPN ($8.8 billion)—are paying a combined total of $20.4 billion to broadcast NFL games through the 2011 season for CBS, Fox, and NBC, and through 2013 for ESPN. However, the League imposes several strict television policies to ensure that stadiums are filled and sold out, to maximize TV ratings, and to help leverage content on these networks. League-owned NFL Network, on cable television, broadcasts eight games per season nationally. It is likely that by the time this book is published, the terrestrial networks will have new agreements with the NFL. One now wonders if ABC will be back in the mix. After airing 555 *Monday Night Football* games from 1970 to 2005, the NFL ended its contract with ABC and moved *Monday Night Football* to ESPN, ABC's sister network. *Monday Night Football* is the second longest-running prime-time television show, behind CBS's *60 Minutes*. NBC Sports returned as a NFL partner after an eight-year absence, taking over the Sunday evening games that had previously aired on ESPN ("Monday Night Football," 2005). Since 2006, ABC has been the only network not to air NFL games. In addition, the NFL launched its own television network, the NFL Network, on November 4, 2003. The NFL Network features more than 2,000 hours of original programming 24 hours a day, 7 days a week, 365 days a year (About the NFL Network, 2010). Note that this means that the NFL can sell an "exclusive" over-the-air package of AFC games, an "exclusive" over-the-air package of National Football Conference (NFC) games, an "exclusive" over-the-air package of weeknight, prime-time games, and an "exclusive" cable package. John Lazarus, when he was head of sales for ABC Sports, coined the term *shared exclusivity* for this arrangement, and, oxymoron though it is, the term has stuck. As of this writing, it is more lucrative for the NFL to sell telecast rights to its games to the highest bidding networks and to place additional games on the NFL Network. Speculation, of course, is that as the business model of sports on television evolves, the NFL may find it more to its liking to keep the rights to considerably more games to itself and license only enough games to supplement its coverage. Time will tell.

There are three typical rights arrangements. In a **rights and production** deal, the network pays the rights holder a rights fee, is responsible for all costs and expenses as-

sociated with producing the game(s) or event for television, sells all of the advertising time itself, and retains all the revenue. Rights and production deals have all the risk but provide all the reward. In the early days of sports television, this was the predominant type of rights agreement, but as the number of distribution channels (how many cable stations telecast sports and only sports 24/7?) has exploded, the risk that the network or cable channel will sell sufficient advertising to pay for both rights and production has become entirely too high, and alternative methods have become more prevalent. In a **rights-only** agreement, the network pays a rights fee, and the organizer is responsible for production that must meet network standards of quality. The network is thus relieved of the vagaries of production costs by shifting some of the risk. Quite frequently, rights-only deals generally include some barter, which is an arrangement whereby the rights holder is entitled to sell a certain number of the network's commercial spots and keep all of the proceeds to help defray production costs. (In barter arrangements, the network and the rights holder decide in advance which product category each will pursue to avoid trying to sell the same time to the same advertisers.) Finally, in a **time buy**, the organizer actually buys the time (e.g., one-hour or two-hour blocks) on the network and, subject to the network's quality control, is responsible for production and sales. The network has no upside from a successful sales effort, but there is also no financial risk. An outgrowth of the networks' aversion to financial risk has been sponsored or underwritten programs. *Title sponsors*, particularly prevalent in golf tournaments and telecasts, are commercial entities that pay premiums to organizers to have their names associated with a sporting event, such as FedEx sponsoring the FedEx Cup for the PGA Tour. In addition to the television exposure of having a commercial name directly tied to the event (The Dew Tour, as another example), varying amounts of the fee for the title sponsorship are allocated to commercial units within the program of the event. As a *title sponsor*, an event becomes identified by a company's name and a combined event/company logo. A less expensive but quite effective sponsorship relationship is that of *presenting sponsorship*, where the company is not mentioned in every reference to the event, but it still garners far more exposure than a traditional commercial unit. By way of example only, consider The Shell Houston Classic presented by Titleist.

Broadcasters, whether they are national television networks such as NBC or local radio stations with signals covering a single city, survive by attracting audiences and selling time to advertisers that want to sell those listeners and viewers—us—their wares. The bigger the audience, the more valuable the commercial time. The Super Bowl, which nets the largest television audience of the year, also features the most expensive advertising time: CBS charged between $2,500,000 and $2,800,000 for a single 30-second announcement, or "spot," to advertise in the 2010 game, down from the staggering $3,00,000 NBC charged for thirty seconds of advertising time during the 2009 Super Bowl telecast (Associated Press, 2010). A 30-second commercial on a local radio station in a small town might retail for $500 or less. That local radio station might have as few as 2500 listeners at one time; according to the Nielsen Company, the 2010 Super Bowl had an estimated 106 million viewers (ESPN.com News Service, 2010).

One of the critical goals of advertising is to attract the attention of the largest possible number of consumers or potential customers in a particular *target market*, introduced in Chapter 14, Sport Sales, and Chapter 15, Sport Sponsorship. Advertising efficiency is measured by calculating an advertisement's **cost per thousand (CPM)** ("M", of course, is the Roman numeral for 1,000). This allows advertisers to gauge the relative efficiency of a high-cost advertisement that reaches a large audience and a less expensive spot that reaches a smaller audience. If an advertisement on a local television station costs $100 and reaches 10,000 viewers, the CPM is $10. A $250,000 spot on a network program reaching 25 million viewers also has a CPM of $10. Although the size of the audience is vital, the demographic make-up of the audience is even more important. An advertiser that sells products to older women would not want to pay to advertise on a program that attracts an audience made up of young men. Every advertiser strives to deliver the right message to the right audience at the right time for the best price. And broadcasters do their best to provide the programming that produces the audiences advertisers crave.

Because the broadcasting business is so closely tied to the advertising industry, **audience research** plays a vital role in deciding what sports get on the air. The leading broadcast media research firm in the United States today is the A. C. Nielsen Company (Nielsen Media Research, 2010). Founded in 1923, Nielsen first began measuring nationwide radio audiences in 1942 by attaching a device called an Audimeter to radio sets in a sample of 800 homes across the country. The Audimeter, developed in the 1930s by researchers at the Massachusetts Institute of Technology, mechanically recorded when the radio was turned on and off and noted where the dial was set. Today, Nielsen monitors television sets in approximately 5,000 homes across the country chosen to represent a statistical model of the nation with a computer-age version of the Audimeter called the People Meter. The People Meter monitors which channel the set is tuned to, but it also measures who is watching. Each member of every "Nielsen family" is assigned a code number to punch into the meter when he or she is watching television. Early every morning, the data collected by each People Meter are downloaded via telephone lines to computers at

Nielsen's research center in Dunedin, Florida. By mid-morning, broadcast executives and advertising agencies that subscribe to Nielsen's service receive detailed breakdowns of who watched what the night before.

Nielsen divides the nation's 115,900,000 (representing 294,650,000 viewers) television households into 210 discrete units called **designated market areas (DMAs)**. The largest, New York City, encompasses very nearly 7.5 million; the smallest, Glendive, Montana, includes just 3,940 homes in rural eastern Montana (Nielsen Wire, 2010a). Nielsen defines each DMA by determining which local stations residents most often watch, a system that reflects the technical limitations of television. Because television signals, like FM radio signals, travel in a straight line, the coverage area of a station can be calculated by factoring its channel number or frequency, power, and the height of its transmitting tower above average terrain with topography and the curvature of the earth. The most powerful television stations—very high frequency (VHF) channels 2 through 6—can be seen about 65 miles from their transmitter. Stations at the upper end of the ultra high frequency (UHF) band—channels 41 through 69—can reach only about 30 miles.

The Federal Communication Commission (FCC), established as an independent agency by the Communications Act of 1934, regulates the communications industry. In addition to 1,784 full-power broadcast television stations, it licenses 14,503 AM, FM, and FM Educational radio stations and regulates other communications media, including both wired and cellular telephone service (Federal Communications Commission, 2010). The FCC replaced the Federal Radio Commission (FRC), which had been established by the Radio Act of 1927. The FRC was created after both the radio industry and the listening public complained that the radio dial was being choked with static and interference as new stations went on the air

and interfered with existing broadcast signals. The commission's role was likened to that of a traffic officer. Today, television and radio stations are licensed to avoid interference with one another's signals and to create a mosaic of clear broadcast signals for viewers and listeners across the country.

Nielsen uses its People Meter data supplemented by viewer diaries and other research tools to measure national audiences as well as audiences in each DMA. Audience size is most often discussed in terms of ratings and shares. A program's **rating** represents the percentage of television households in the survey universe—whether the entire nation, a particular DMA, or a selection of DMAs—that are tuned into the program. A program with a national 22 rating, therefore, was watched by 22% of the nation's television homes. Each rating point represents 1% of the nation's television households, about 1,115,000, homes. Thus, a 22 rating means the program was viewed in 24.53 million homes. A program's **share** represents the percentage of the television households watching television at the time that are tuned in to the program. Obviously, not every television is on all the time. Viewing peaks during the prime-time evening hours and is significantly lower during the day. The number of viewers, a rating point, and a share point are all quite fluid and will certainly have changed between the writing and publication of this book. The lesson, though, is unchanged: millions of people watch television every minute of every day. The current business model is advertising-supported over-the-air stations and subscription plus advertising supported cable systems. Advertisers pay telecasters to reach not only specified quantities of viewers, but also a targeted quality of viewer, distinguished by demography, geography, and psychography. Identifying that quality of sports television audiences is reliable and consistent.

Although ratings and shares are the most often discussed audience measurements, Nielsen data also allow broadcasters to calculate their cumulative audience over time, a figure usually referred to as the **cume**. This is an important number in sport broadcasting. A single telecast of a baseball game, for instance, may garner a small audience because only the most devoted fans watch every game. When the cumulative audience over the course of the season is calculated, however, the total numbers can be impressive. In radio, the weekly cume, the total number of people who tune in during a week, is the standard audience measurement.

In addition to providing national and local audience counts, Nielsen and similar market research firms conduct surveys, focus groups, and other studies to further break down audiences by **demographic segments** along age, gender, and ethnic lines, as well as according to income, purchasing habits, and other lifestyle factors.

If audience research is a science, the interpretation of data produced by Nielsen and other market research firms is an art. Broadcasters and advertising agencies constantly spar with Nielsen over the accuracy of its information and comb through the data to find the most positive information. Sport broadcasting has been an important programming feature of broadcasting largely because audience research confirms a widely held stereotype: Men love sports. Whereas the audience for prime-time television entertainment shows is typically 60% female, sports broadcasts routinely attract audiences that are 60% or 70% male. The sports audience is on average wealthier, better educated, and older than the typical television audience. Although sports audiences in general do tend to be older, game broadcasts attract a disproportionate number of younger men in the important 18-to-34 age group, a group that is notoriously difficult to reach through most mass media. Sports audiences are also intensely loyal and predictable. If an NFL game is on, pro football fans will watch it. The audience for

sports such as basketball, soccer, and football also includes a far higher percentage of young African-American and Hispanic males than virtually anything else on television. Tennis provides the most balanced male–female audience. According to *Ad Age*, the Tennis Channel has a unique audience of televised sports programming, marked by women comprising about half of its viewers and 67% in the 25-to-54 age range (*Ad Age*, 2009). The 2009 Mendelsohn Affluent Survey reports that the average annual household income of the tennis viewing audience is $233,000 (Ipsos Mendelsohn, 2009). While that audience is relatively small—5.7 million viewers for the 2009 Wimbledon Championship—the significant average income makes that small audience extremely valuable to advertisers. For advertisers in search of those key demographics, sports broadcasts are just the ticket.

The economics of the sport broadcasting industry are based on advertising. The value of a program, whether it is a football game or a situation comedy, is determined by the size and composition of the audience it attracts because that determines the amount of advertising revenue that can be generated. One formula broadcasters use to calculate how much revenue must be generated is as follows: cost of rights plus cost of production (which includes personnel and all equipment and facilities needed to produce the program, as well as the cost of lighting, electricity, satellite delivery, and all other costs associated with getting the sporting event to the camera and ultimately to the viewer) plus allocable overhead (the broadcaster's or the event's share [depending on the accounting system in use for the calculation] of its parent company's total overhead) plus the ideal profit for its efforts. If the sales people think the number is attainable, the deal is made; if the sales people are not so optimistic, there are alternatives. The first option, of course, is not to proceed. Another choice is to see if the rights holder will reduce its anticipated rights fee while the broadcaster reduces its profit expectation and tries to trim production costs. Or, the sales team always has the option to explore a barter deal with the rights holder to share some of the financial risk. Finally, the broadcaster may determine that the total return (see the next paragraph) is sufficient, so that the formula need not be a perfect monetary equation.

Sport managers must determine what broadcast rights to their games are worth in the marketplace to gain top dollar for those rights. Although both broadcasters and sport managers are in business to make a profit, in the competitive environment of the two industries, profit is not always easily defined. Both broadcasters and sport managers must look beyond the bottom line. Each side should consider benefits that do not immediately appear on the balance sheet. Klatell and Marcus (1996) describe these benefits as **total return**. For broadcasters, this could include gaining a competitive edge over a rival station or network, generating goodwill and favorable public relations, or building good relations with a team, league, or conference to gain the inside track when additional, more profitable events are up for bid. At a time when ABC, CBS, and NBC were the only true broadcast networks in the United States, Rupert Murdock and his multinational communications conglomerate, NewsCorp, understood the full potential of total return. Although NewsCorp's Fox Television Network reportedly lost more than $1 billion on its first television rights agreement with the NFL, Fox is now unequivocally identified as the fourth United States network, and that status is universally agreed to be a direct result of its association with football.

For sports producers, total return from broadcast exposure might include promotional opportunities to stimulate additional ticket or licensed merchandise sales or favorable publicity to introduce a new team or sport to a market. College athletic directors should consider how broadcasts of a school's games might generate new applications from high school students or raise the spirit of alumni who might be inspired to make donations. Televised games also provide a significant recruiting edge. Many star high school athletes want to play on television and would never consider signing with a school that is not on ESPN. From the beginning of the electronics age, both broadcasters and sports producers have sought to maximize total return.

■ INTERNATIONAL SPORTS

Technological advances such as satellite television, including pay-per-view opportunities, have not only created huge audiences, previously untapped, to international sports, they have also created "massive commercial systems . . . [whose] spheres of influence include the process of globalization, the flow of trade and the ways in which nations seek status on the international stage" (Nicholson, 2007, p. 36). Soccer ("football" to the rest of the world) is generally considered the most popular spectator sport in the world, but until quite recently garnered very little traction in the United States. The previously unfamiliar rules of the game, and most particularly the nonstop play format yielding little opportunity for commercial interruption made soccer quite unfriendly to American television executives and hence to the viewing audiences. In fact, not until 2006 did The Disney Company (parent of ABC and ESPN) agree to pay a rights fee to MLS, $8,000,000 a year for eight years (SportsBusiness Daily, 2006). While not even on the radar screen for the Big Four, this is a rather considerable sum for soccer in the United States. World Cup soccer telecasts clearly generate the largest audiences on a world scale and, even before the semifinal matches of the 2010 World Cup, matches aired on all English and

Spanish language U.S. networks reached an estimated 112 million U.S. TV viewers, according to statistics released by The Nielsen Company (Nielsen Wire, 2010b).

Cricket also relies on technology for exposure in the United States. Although still an embryonic sport in the USA, cricket is the second most popular sport in the world, only behind football (soccer). With approximately 15 million cricket fans living in the United States, the goal of the strategic partnership between New Zealand Cricket and USA Cricket is to generate awareness and establish a fan base and appetite for the sport (USACA Media Release, 2010). ESPN3.com, a broadband network, began making cricket available in the United States with the 2010 season. Financial terms are not available.

The National Association for Stock Car Auto Racing (NASCAR) is one of the most viewed professional sports in terms of television ratings in the United States, and was one of the only two (golf being the other) sports to enjoy rising, rather than flat, television ratings during most of the first decade of this century. In fact, professional football is the only sport in the United States to hold more viewers than NASCAR (Ourand and Mickle, 2010). Internationally, NASCAR races are broadcast in over 150 countries (Christley, 2008). Similarly, Formula 1 Racing is one of the most popular television sports in the world, in part because it travels to a significant number of countries (Nicholson, 2007) much like soccer, but unlike American football, baseball, and basketball.

As all-sports-all-the-time networks such as ESPN, MLB Network, NFL Network, Fox Sports, and so many more have dominated U.S. television viewing, channels like ESPN Deportes, BSkyB, Eurosport, and so many others have done the same on a worldwide basis, demonstrating yet again the pervasive influence sport has on society and the world.

■ CAREER OPPORTUNITIES

As sport organizations become increasingly involved in producing their own game broadcasts, as delivery systems expand, as writing blogs for the Internet increases and as other ancillary activities present themselves, career opportunities in sport organizations multiply. The Internet is fast becoming the world's most successful employment agency. Visit any Web site for any sport—major or minor, United States or foreign based—and you will inevitably find a link to "employment opportunities" or something similar. If you find your passion, you do yourself an injustice by not exploring every avenue to get there. Most major colleges, conference offices, and professional teams now employ associate athletic directors, associate commissioners, or vice-presidents in charge of broadcasting who serve as the liaison with the team's telecast partners. Many sport organizations also sell television advertising as part of their overall corporate sponsorship and marketing strategy, so knowledge of the broadcasting industry and its operation is an important qualification for anyone interested in a sales and marketing career. The number of televised sports events

and niche distribution outlets is growing exponentially, while the number of advertising and sponsorship dollars is barely keeping pace. The sport manager who can create innovative revenue streams, significantly reduce the cost of broadcasting sports events, or transform the current business model to accommodate this ever-increasing imbalance will be the next icon of the television industry. It is the opinion of some (this author included) that the enormous growth of viewing outlets will have a significant impact on the current advertiser/subscription-based business model for televising everything, and particularly sports events. Will you be that icon?

A growing number of colleges and minor league professional teams produce their own game broadcasts and utilize employees—frequently former players or coaches now employed in public relations or development—as announcers. In most cases, the actual nuts-and-bolts production of the broadcast is handled by employees of the flagship radio or television station or by a professional production firm that supplies the necessary equipment and personnel on a contract basis. By producing its own games, however, a sport organization maintains total control of the broadcast and its content and can present its product in the most favorable light. But remember, it also bears all of the financial risk.

The men and women who appear on camera to broadcast major sporting events are usually employed by the broadcaster, although it is common for a club or organization to include the right to approve the announcers as a condition of the contract. On-the-air performers in the radio and television industries are often referred to as the *talent*, but because sport broadcasting is fundamentally show business, success in the crowded field requires not only talent but also hard work and plenty of good luck. Veteran football announcer Pat Summerall was the placekicker for the New York Giants

when he got his first broadcasting job in the 1950s. As Summerall tells the story, a New York radio station wanted to hire Giants' quarterback Charley Connerly, Summerall's roommate at the time, but Connerly was taking a shower when the station manager called. Summerall answered the phone, and by the time Connerly got out of the shower, Summerall had the job. Baseball announcers Joe Buck and Skip Carey are the sons of established announcers and literally grew up in the business. Chip Carey became the third generation of the family to break into the business when he became the voice of the Orlando Magic. Carey has been a baseball play-by-play announcer for the Atlanta Braves since 2005. Most play-by-play announcers, however, got their jobs the old-fashioned way: They started out in college radio or as part-time announcers for local events and gradually worked their way up the ladder. Bob Costas, for example, was the basketball play-by-play announcer during his college years at Syracuse.

Students pursuing a career on the air should explore courses in radio and television production and performance as well as communications and journalism courses, which will provide them with necessary reporting skills. Courses in public speaking and theater are also valuable. Experience, however, is the best teacher. College radio and campus television stations provide excellent opportunities to develop on-air techniques, and many radio and television stations offer internship opportunities. Entry-level sport broadcasting positions frequently require budding announcers to wear several hats. In addition to broadcasting the local high school or college's games, for example, an announcer might be expected to sell advertising time, cover local news, or be responsible for administrative duties behind the scenes. Color commentators, hired to add their insights and personality to the broadcast, are often former players or coaches chosen because they are recognizable to the audience. The best way to become the next Terry Bradshaw or Phil Simms is to quarterback a winning team in the Super Bowl. Anyone who truly wants to be a play-by-play announcer should practice all the time: do the research on players, watch as many games in the sport of one's choice as possible, turn the volume off, and "call" the game into a recording device. It is surprising how much more skilled one becomes by doing whatever the chore, and that will be the difference should the opportunity for an audition arise.

■ CURRENT ISSUES

The sport broadcasting industry today is still coming to terms with trends that began to develop soon after the debut of *Monday Night Football*. In 1970, most Americans with television sets chose from among five or six stations. Cable television, with its vast array of choices, was still in the future. Only 7% of the nation's homes subscribed to cable at this time, most of them in rural areas where small systems picked distant network stations off the air and sent the re-amplified signal to their customers. In 1975, Time Incorporated announced it would distribute Home Box Office, its new premium entertainment channel, to cable systems around the country. Soon, more programmers realized they could distribute television programming coast-to-coast via satellite, and cable operators realized that once they provided unique programming that was not available over the air, they could move into the densely populated suburban and urban areas.

Not surprisingly, sports again played a key role. On September 7, 1979, a new cable service was launched: **ESPN**, the world's first all-sports channel. ESPN's satellite signal was delivered to cable systems across the country, providing sports coverage beyond anything available over the air. The all-sports channel had the time to cover at length events ranging from the Amer-

ica's Cup yacht races to the NFL player draft. The audience was small but intensely loyal, and because viewers could watch ESPN only if they subscribed to cable, the new service helped promote the new medium. In 1980, only 18% of television homes subscribed to cable, but by 1985 the statistic had soared to 43%. By 1990, nearly 60% were hooked up, and today more than 90% are subscribers: 60+% are wired for cable and nearly 30% for satellite (TVB, 2010). In short order, the ESPN service—once thought preposterous—expanded to include ESPN2, ESPNews, ESPN Classic, and no fewer than 25 owned or co-owned networks throughout the world. ESPN and similar specialty services—HBO, CNN, MTV, CMT, and dozens more—gave television viewers a reason to buy cable television and thus changed the broadcast industry radically.

Although cable TV service continues to lose market share to satellite TV, penetration of digital cable has increased 20 percentage points, according to TVB over the period from 2004–2010 (TVB, 2010). CAB, the cable television industry's customer-facing trade association, notes that ad-supported cable has 58.4% of the television viewing audience, versus 39.4% of the broadcast viewing audience (CAB, 2010).

As the television dial has grown more diverse, the television audience has divided into ever-smaller chunks. Audience fragmentation has changed the economics of the industry and created a new programming philosophy. While the networks continue to vie for the mass audience, hoping to appeal to all of the people some of the time, ESPN and other specialty services pursue niche programming, hoping to reach some of the people all of the time. CNN pursues news addicts around the clock and around the world. For those who want to track the hurricane swirling in the Atlantic, The Weather Channel offers constant updates. Care for some country music? The Country Music Television network is there. ESPN and its competitors offer wall-to wall sports and take direct aim at the sports audience. ESPN offers a variety of specialty programming options with its own networks: ESPN, ESPN2, ESPNU, ESPNClassic, and ESPNNews. ESPN's competitors? The Golf Channel, the Tennis Channel, the Outdoor Channel, Versus, Speed Channel, CSTV, NBA TV, the YES Network, the NFL Network, Fox Sports Net, New England Sports Network (NESN), and counting. Not only is cable's audience growing at a significant pace, but its viewers are also spending more time with the medium. Viewers of all ages are devoting an average of 7.7 hours weekly watching ad-supported cable in prime time versus only 5.3 hours for the broadcast Big Four (CAB, 2010). A 2010 article in *The Hollywood Reporter* suggests that the ratio of cable to Big Four network viewing is roughly 60/40, making the fall of the Big Four even more pronounced (Szalai, 2010).

One challenge facing exclusive rights broadcasters is the impact that exclusive deals with limited availability has on fans. Take, for example, the NFL Network, which holds exclusive rights to certain NFL and college bowl games. If the dominant cable operators do not opt to purchase the NFL Network as part of the package available to fans, then access becomes a challenge. The NFL Network is demanding a monthly subscription price of 70 cents. Time Warner, Charter, and Cablevision have said that rate is too expensive; thus, in some markets, NFL games are not available. In 2006, the NFL was reportedly offered $450 million annually by Comcast to carry eight games on its Versus channel (which the chief operations officer [COO] of NFL Network said is an erroneous number, but did not elucidate), which has 70 million subscribers, but the NFL declined and now just shows those games to its 41 million NFL Network subscribers (Sandomir, 2006). As of 2007, the NFL Network was in 70 million homes (About NFL Network, 2010).

Major League Baseball's created an exclusive rights deal with DirecTV, worth $700 million over seven years for the Extra Innings package of out-of-market MLB games. Initially, MLB refused to extend this opportunity to 200,000 cable subscribers who had previously been purchasing this same package through their cable companies. Enraged by losing the package, a group called In Demand, owned by affiliates of the Time Warner, Comcast, and Cox cable systems, demanded that MLB give them a chance to match the offer. MLB did and initially rejected their offer. However, soon after, due to pressure from disgruntled fans and Congress, MLB reached a seven-year deal with iN DEMAND that includes a clause requiring the cable stations to carry the Baseball Channel. MLB was forced to restructure the exclusive deal with DirecTV, but since DirecTV owns 20% of The Baseball Channel, DirecTV was not injured by the accommodation, despite its preference for exclusivity (Cross, 2007).

DirecTV has also entered into a multiyear extension with CBS under which DirecTV will continue showing out-of-market games during CBS Sports' broadcast of the NCAA Division I men's basketball tournament on an exclusive basis. DirecTV's "NCAA Mega March Madness" package will offer up to 37 out-of-market games, including those in HD, from the event's first three rounds. The deal also moves to subscribers of a different DirecTV package, thereby increasing viewership from 2 million to 8 million homes (CBSSports.com, n.d.).

Cable television, the simultaneous growth of FM radio stations in the 1970s and 1980s, the introduction of videocassette recorders, and, in the 1990s, the increasing popularity of the Internet have turned the electronic mass media into something entirely new. Thanks to digital technology, people around the world can listen to or watch a game, concert, or other event simply by logging on to their computers, telephones, or other handheld devices. No longer do consumers all watch or listen to the same broadcasts. Thanks to the choices offered by new technology, today each member of the audience can choose to watch or listen to any program he or she desires at his or her convenience. It is interesting to note that sporting events are far less vulnerable to the technologies allowing viewers to record now and watch later because of the immediacy of sports: it's happening live, now; when the outcome is known, the thrill is dramatically decreased. The economic rules of the media, however, remain the same, at least in the short term: Financial success depends on creating an audience that is either large enough to attract advertisers that will pay the bills or eager enough to purchase information and entertainment in numbers great enough to cover the cost of production. The threat to traditional economic expectations, however, is that although Internet technology is sophisticated enough to deliver relatively clear digital images in an interactive format to limitless numbers of computers throughout the world, it is sometimes difficult to assure rights owners that those images will be delivered only to authorized users. A new technology called *digital rights management (DRM)* may eventually help protect rights holders. DRM is a flexible platform that makes it possible to protect and securely deliver content

by subscription or individual request for playback on a computer, portable device, or network device. For example, NHL.com uses Windows Media DRM, which works by encrypting a given digital media file, locking it with a "key" and bundling additional information from NHL.com. This results in a packaged file that can be played only by the person who has obtained a license to it. Windows Media Rights Manager can also act as the license clearinghouse, authenticating the consumer's request for a license and issuing the license to the user. While DRM technology has become more sophisticated, however, there are still ways to circumvent the program and obtain unauthorized media files (Windows Media, n.d.). The notion of "walled gardens" or secure environments where only authorized users can gain access to certain content is ambitious but as yet imperfect. Sport managers and financial analysts in this field must ponder the future of–and perhaps alternatives to–the exclusive television broadcast rights agreement.

■ WHERE DO WE GO FROM HERE?

For sport managers, the new electronic environment presents both opportunities and challenges. Major sports such as the NFL and NBA will continue to prosper because they offer broadcasters readily identifiable entertainment with a proven track record. Their loyal fans will seek out the games and watch. There is only one Super Bowl and only one NBA Finals. These events will continue to dominate the ratings because they stand out from the crowd, and the major networks will continue to pay dearly for the right to broadcast the games. Critics fear, though, that the financially beneficial and symbiotic relationship between television and sports may eventually kill the golden goose. Prime-time television hours command the highest advertising dollars; hence, almost all of the marquee events are shown in prime-time hours. If a championship game starts at 9:00 p.m. on the East Coast and does not end until after midnight, future generations, too young to stay up so late, may not have the same enthusiasm for these now-precious telecasts. Nevertheless, the new environment also offers bright opportunities to less well-known sports. Action sports have benefited greatly from their use in providing sports programming to ESPN, ESPN2, and ABC (X-Games) or NBC (Gravity Games/Dew Tour). These action sports tours have provided access to the teen demographic, as 95% of teens identify themselves as action sports fans and/or participants, representing 14% of the U.S. population (Fuse, 2009). All four terrestrial networks provide some coverage of action sports, as do ESPN, Versus, FoxSports Net, and other cable carriers. On July 1, 2003, FoxCable Networks launched Fuel TV, currently available in over 30 million homes and growing, dedicated exclusively to action sports (Fuel TV, 2010). While a unit of advertising or a title or presenting sponsorship may be relatively inexpensive because it reaches relatively few viewers, its impact is formidable because of the almost perfectly identified demographic of the audience. In 2008, The X Games and the Dew Tour enjoyed 342.5 hours of original and often live television coverage (Fuse, 2009).

Women's sports have benefited greatly from the multichannel television environment. A generation of women has grown up since the passage of Title IX in 1972, and they are now adult consumers and mothers whose daughters are playing organized sports. Broadcasters and advertisers are hopeful that women's sports will be a way to reach "soccer moms," the archetypical upper-middle-income working women and mothers who market researchers believe determine how a large portion of the nation's consumer dollars is spent. Televised women's sport, once limited to Olympic events such as figure skating and gymnastics, and major women's golf and tennis tournaments, now includes team sports such as college and professional basketball and volleyball.

The launch of the Women's National Basketball Association (WNBA), both as a new league and as a television property, in the summer of 1997 sought to capitalize on the potential that women, like traditional male sports viewers, will watch games they once played themselves or watched as youngsters. With girls' basketball a staple in high school athletic programs across the country, programmers, sponsors, and advertisers are gambling that the audience for the professional and college versions of the game will expand. But the stakes are high, indeed. Despite a mostly female live audience—WNBA's live audience is 80% female—International Basketball Association's (FIBA's) research has shown that the audience for the WNBA on television is closer to a 50:50 male-to-female ratio (FIBA, 2006). Scarborough Sports Marketing surveys indicate that only 6% of men have an interest in the WNBA and 8% in the Ladies Professional Golf Association (LPGA); when the Women's United Soccer Association (WUSA) was operational, only 4% of men said they followed women's soccer even casually.

There are doubters who say women's sports are simply not as exciting as men's sports and will never find a permanent home on television. ESPN has experimented with *appointment television* (an identifiable place and time to find a particular genre of programming) for women's sports, but for the most part the results have been disappointing. Lifetime and A&E, cable channels targeting women, air little to no women's sports. Oxygen TV, together with Oxygen .com, an all-women/all-platform effort, hired a knowledgeable, experienced, predominantly female staff of programmers and producers specifically to create women's sports programming, but Oxygen TV is carried by so few cable systems that the future of the network, and with it its sports department, is worrisome. Similarly, many in the industry believe that the original

WNBA television deals with NBC and ESPN were not the result of arm's-length negotiations based on careful financial and audience research analysis, but rather the result of the commissioner of the NBA, David Stern, using his considerable leverage with NBA sponsors and with the broadcasters to make the deals happen.

The combination of a potentially valuable audience and available broadcast time may also offer an opportunity for international sports such as soccer, rugby, and cricket. Soccer, despite the best efforts of its promoters, has yet to attract a significant television audience in the United States, but the game remains a passion for European and Latin and South American immigrants. Broadcast stations and cable services serving the immigrant community, such as the Spanish-language networks Telemundo and Univision, have found soccer a successful means of reaching ethnic communities. Rugby, a major spectator sport in Europe and Australia, has also begun to appear on U.S. cable systems. Cricket is rarely seen, but the sport is avidly followed in India, Pakistan, and Sri Lanka, and edited highlights of international matches could prove an effective means of reaching those communities.

Because specific audiences are smaller than in the past, however, advertising revenue is less and the cash rewards for playing on television have diminished. Many broadcasters are eager to air sport programs that will associate them with local franchises and college teams and set them apart from their competition, or to find new types of sport, not previously seen on television, with the hope of attracting new viewers and hence expanding the total audience. They may be unwilling, however, to guarantee significant rights fees in advance. This has led to revenue sharing. (This *revenue sharing* refers to an agreed-upon allocation between the network and the rights holder of the revenue realized from advertising sales. It should not be confused with the revenue sharing that refers to all teams in a particular league receiving equal shares of monies generated by the league through the sale of broadcast rights.) This financial arrangement spreads the risk between the broadcaster and the rights holder, creating more of a partnership than the more familiar rights and production agreement.

For example, NBC Sports and the Arena Football League (AFL) entered into an agreement in 2002 in which all advertising revenue for all broadcasts is pooled; all expenses for staging and producing games for broadcast are paid from that pool first, and the remaining money is distributed between the league and NBC in accordance with an elaborate formula agreed upon in advance. Such a formula provides for future income to absorb previous losses and creates an inextricable bond between NBC and the league. The obvious benefit to the broadcaster in a revenue-sharing arrangement is that if ad sales are disappointing, the network has not already committed to a sometimes staggering rights fee. While the so-called broadcast partner or event organizer must share some of the risk that there will be an audience for its product, it also stands to enjoy a significant upside—ideally considerably more than the rights fee would have been—if ad sales exceed expectations. Patience is the most important virtue for both sides of this equation, particularly with new television sports like arena football, because fan bases and loyal audiences take time to build. Unfortunately for the AFL, its agreement with NBC expired in 2006 and was not renewed. NFL Network currently televises one AFL game per week at undisclosed terms.

Revenue sharing in this context has been successful with sports having only national telecasts with no third-party local broadcaster. Among Major League Baseball teams, for example, a few successful franchises in the largest markets can command rich guaranteed contracts in their local markets, provided that the MLB network contract takes priority in scheduling games for national broadcasts. The New York Yankees signed a 12-year television deal in 1989 that paid the team an average of $42 million per year. Although the local carrier, Madison Square Garden cable television (MSG), was prepared to extend the agreement for many years after the 2000 season at even greater annual rights fees, the YankeeNets organization, parent of the Yankees, the New York Nets basketball franchise, and the New York Devils NHL team, opted to start its own 24-hour cable channel called the YES Network. MSG sued the Yankees on a provision in the expiring agreement that MSG interpreted as prohibiting the Yankees from proceeding with its own network. After much legal parrying and many exorbitant legal fees, a settlement was reached and the YES network launched for the 2002 season. Based on its very early rather grim financial news, YES network appeared to have won the battle but lost the war for the Yankees, but eight years later, the YES Network has news, feature, and game programming 24/7. The majority of small-market clubs, however, do not command large rights fees, but they retain the rights to their own games, sell advertising time, and then buy time on local stations to air the broadcasts.

Revenue sharing, broadcasters say, is a favorable development both because it frees them from financial burdens and because it forces teams and leagues to become active partners with a vested interest in marketing and promoting the games. Sport organizations and broadcasters have always been partners, each with a serious stake in the success of the other. No team wants its games broadcast in a less-than-professional manner. A haphazard broadcast reflects on the team and alienates the audience, resulting in less advertising revenue and lower rights fees. Broadcasters, for their part, know that even the most creative and entertaining broadcast can only partially offset a lackluster game. A winning, exciting team

will attract more viewers and more advertising revenue. Ultimately, broadcast contracts are like any other business agreement: Both sides must benefit if the partnership is to survive and prosper. So far, survive and prosper they have. According to Kagan World Media, the highly regarded communications research firm, the NFL's television revenues are approximately $3 billion annually (SportsBusiness Daily, 2007), and the NBA's television revenues are $930 million annually (Cohen, 2007).

Sport managers must understand how the media works and keep in mind the total return principle. Television and radio rights fees can become an important source of revenue, but sport managers must be able to fairly assess the value of their product in the marketplace. If a team has not established a record of commercial success in the broadcast marketplace, revenue sharing may be a possible solution. Teams can also package radio and television advertising with live-streaming webcasts, stadium signage, program advertisements, and other promotional opportunities when recruiting corporate sponsors. Many colleges help ease the financial burden of their broadcast partners by underwriting production costs or travel expenses. Many colleges and professional teams also produce their own game broadcasts, purchasing or renting the necessary equipment, hiring the personnel, and selling advertising. Complete game broadcasts are then placed on local stations or cable systems, sometimes with advertising time left available for the station to sell, sometimes with the team paying the station to carry the broadcast. Most radio and many television stations will accept a time to buy and sell blocks of airtime to organizations seeking exposure. Ideally, advertising sales will offset the costs of productions, but sport managers must consider the promotional and marketing benefits of having their games on the air.

Broadcasting games may not always net a cash windfall, but broadcasting remains an important part of establishing a team's status and promoting its goals. The cost of producing a game broadcast is difficult to estimate because it involves many variables such as location, transmission costs, and the cost of assembling equipment and crews. A two-hour basketball game telecast, however, could be professionally produced and delivered complete to a local broadcasting station for as little as $10,000. The same game with special effects, an allocation of the sportscasters' salaries and all of television's technological enhancements could easily run past $250,000. A college athletic department could cut costs further by utilizing teleproduction equipment owned by the campus audiovisual or distance learning department and relying on salaried employees and student volunteers. Ideally, advertising sales would offset the cost, but should a broadcast fail to make money, is that actually a loss? Two hours of television time can provide important promotional and marketing opportunities for an athletic program and the campus at large. How much is the opportunity to spread the good news about the college worth? Will it result in increased ticket sales, alumni donations, or freshman applications? Major colleges today routinely spend tens of thousands of dollars to publish and distribute promotional literature. A two-hour telecast with six or eight minutes of commercial time devoted to selling team-related products and a halftime feature devoted to praising the college's new science center could be considered an investment well worth several thousand dollars.

Many teams and most colleges today have home pages on the Internet. Few directly profit from them, but a presence on the Internet is deemed a worthy promotional tool. In the future, perhaps, fans will routinely buy their tickets and T-shirts simply by clicking a computer mouse and charging the cost to a credit card or debit account. That day has not yet arrived, but the relatively modest cost of a Web page can be justified as increasing the team or college's total return on its media investment.

■ SUMMARY

Electronic media are changing at the speed of light. New technology emerges nearly every month, and the future becomes more exciting and uncertain every day. The landscape continues to change: As more and more consumers have computers and access to the Internet, and as technology advances in compressing images (whether text, audio, or visual) and in widening the pipes (known as broadband) through which those images travel, **interactivity** is becoming important. Sports fans can now watch a sporting event on television and, at the same time, request and receive customized information on their computers about that event. New technology has become available that allows sports fans to purchase tickets directly from a team's Web site and print them at home. For example, New York Yankees Ticketing Technology allows you to purchase and print single-game and season tickets, pay your account online, and electronically forward your tickets to others up to two hours before the start of the game (New York Yankees Ticketing Technology, n.d.). And of course, there are always opportunities to purchase relevant products such as team jerseys or sporting goods on those computers. Innovative sales managers have developed integrated sales and marketing campaigns through which advertisers are offered opportunities both to advertise within the television coverage of the event and on related Web sites and to create promotional announcements incorporating their support of both. It is predicted that in very short order, the space-age concept of "convergence of technologies," in which telephone, television, and computer equipment and software technologies merge, will be commonplace. The notion of viewing a sports event on a telephone was science fiction when the first edition of this book was published.

The fundamentals, however, hold. Electronic media remain powerful tools for getting the

CASE STUDY: The Impact of New Media on Television Negotiations

Negotiations for exclusive telecast rights in the United States and its territories for a significant annual international golf event, the World Cup of Golf (World Cup), which takes place in Europe, were substantially under way. The agent conducting the negotiations, Sport Ventures International (SVI), has represented the rights holder, the World Cup Organizing Committee (WCOC), in all aspects, such as selling television rights, selling sponsorships, and dealing with new and evolving electronic media, for as long as the event has commanded international attention. A U.S. television network, QRS Sports, broadcast the event exclusively in the United States long before cable television was developed. Currently, both QRS Sports and the cable network SportViz have been identified as the carriers of the World Cup, and most of the material deal points—term of the contract, rights fees, decisions about which of the various rounds of the World Cup will be broadcast by QRS Sports and which by SportViz, production specifications, contingency plans for inclement weather, and so on—have been agreed upon. The open issue is the extent to which WCOC, QRS Sports, and SportViz will each be entitled to show video images of the event on their own respective Web sites. It must be noted that an affiliated company of SVI, which we will call SVI Interactive, created the WCOC's Web site and is a financial partner in any revenues generated by that Web site.

The World Cup is world renowned and has been televised nationally and internationally for more than 30 years, but has always generated only modest television ratings in the United States. There is, however, a small and fiercely loyal audience as well as a much larger and far more casual viewership, and the fan base is growing. Contributing to the ratings problem in the United States is a timing issue: The World Cup takes place during daytime hours only, several hours ahead of any time zone in the United States, so that scheduling the World Cup for live telecast would require early morning viewing; the alternative is taped replays in the evening or prime-time hours. Daytime programming of news, talk shows, and soap operas generates much more money for QRS Television, the parent company of QRS Sports, than this particular golf event does, but SportViz is much more amenable to preempting its daytime schedule.

WCOC has granted exclusive television rights, on a country-by-country basis throughout the world, requiring each broadcaster to take all necessary steps to contain its broadcast within its borders, thus respecting the exclusivity granted its neighbors. In some locations such as Windsor, Ontario, and Detroit, Michigan, overlapping signals cannot be prevented, and both U.S. and Canadian broadcasters have learned to live with that anomaly.

It is well-settled law that news stories are not "owned" by anyone. However, although the results of significant sporting events are certainly considered news, any visual depictions ("clips") of those events are not news and are owned by the rights holder or television entity to which the rights have been granted. Although there are exceptions, networks and cable companies generally have sharing arrangements whereby each may air news clips of others' exclusively owned events under certain guidelines (e.g., clips are limited in length, shown a limited number of times during the 24-hour period immediately following the conclusion of the event, only during regularly scheduled news or sportscasts, or only after the specific event is off the air, and the "borrowing" network or cable company must include a credit for the "owning" network or cable company). Until the advent of the Internet, this was a very workable solution in the realm of exclusive television rights.

WCOC, through SVI, has indicated its intention to use the Internet as follows: In addition to seeing constantly updated scores, visitors to WorldCup.org could find endless facts about the World Cup, the athletes, and WCOC; read commentary about the World Cup; see interviews with players; play online fantasy games; and see real-time, streamed video of highlights of a day's activity. Further, for a fee, users could see actual live play of certain competitions within the World Cup on their computer screens. WCOC points out that this very specific "network" would be available only on a fee basis and would show a comparatively small portion of the actual World Cup. Besides, it argues, this is not television as we know it, and the organization has granted exclusive television and exclusive cable rights, not all media rights. In their negotiations, the talks break down as follows.

WCOC's Position as Articulated by SVI

The Internet is not television. Remember how upset you were, QRS Sports, 20 years ago when you were "forced" to share the exclusive broadcast of this World Cup with cable television, only to discover that any effect on ratings was positive and we got greater exposure for the World Cup, which, as you know, is a significant part of our goal. We will charge a fee to see limited competitions from the World Cup, which will attract only hard-core fans who will watch as much coverage as there is available. The imperfect, choppy images of streamed video on the Internet are no real substitute for the perfect resolution of television. Viewers will have an opportunity to see portions of the World Cup at work or when no part of the World Cup is on television, and that will whet their appetites for evening and weekend viewing.

The Position of QRS Sports and Sport Viz

What will be shown on your Web site are television images, which may be very unclear but certainly are close enough to television to violate our exclusive rights. For the rights fee we're paying, which is already disproportionate to the advertising revenues we are likely to generate, we consider any visual depiction to be within our exclusive domain. Your Web site will contain advertising banners that may conflict with our television advertisers. There is a finite appetite for this sport, and fans who get their fill on their computers at work will be less likely to watch at home. What if your secure network isn't so secure after all, and even viewers who don't pay a fee will be able to watch visual images? Isn't this just another step toward cutting deeper into our already weakened exclusive rights?

Questions for Discussion

1. As a staff member for WCOC, how do you balance the desire to maximize worldwide exposure of the World Cup with the need to maintain harmony with your broadcast partners throughout the world?
2. As a representative of QRS Sports or SportViz, do you raise the issue that SVI Interactive may be encouraging WCOC to support its own endeavors at the expense of harmonious relationships with QRS Sports and SportViz? Defend your reasoning.
3. As an observer of the Internet, do you believe QRS Sports' and SportViz's concerns about their exclusivity are realistic or emotional? Defend your reasoning.
4. As an employee of SVI, devise a plan for a "co-branded Web site," such as WorldCup.QRS.com or WorldCup.SportViz.com, where all entities enjoy some degree of Internet exposure without

jeopardizing the telecasts. What is the impact on broadcasters in other parts of the world who have also bought exclusive rights?

5. Do you think the fact that QRS Sports and SportViz pay higher rights fees than any other international broadcaster imposes on WCOC a higher degree of care for them than its other broadcast partners?

6. As an employee of QRS Sports or SportViz, is there some concession you want from WCOC before you agree to streamed video on the Internet?

7. Looking five years ahead, do you think the problem will grow or subside? What about in ten years?

word out about sport. A team that is featured on radio, television, and the Internet can appeal to fans both old and new who in the future will buy tickets and merchandise. The economics of broadcasting also remain the same: Sport managers must either assemble an audience valuable enough to attract advertisers or else provide a service that individual fans are willing to pay to receive. Thanks to the proven loyalty of sports fans, sport managers are in a position to cash in on the dynamics of the emerging media environment. It must be noted that although the economics may stay the same, the Internet, the complexity of contracts, nonrecoupable rights fees, and the growing number of media outlets have all helped usher in a sea of change in how media business is conducted. Sport managers must keep up with new technical and competitive developments in the field. They must also be able to honestly assess the comparative value of their games or events in the eyes of broadcasters and advertisers. Although broadcast rights fees can provide an important revenue stream for sport organizations, sport managers must keep the idea of total return in mind. Promotional opportunities, favorable publicity, the status of having an organization's games broadcast to fans in the widest possible area, and other nonmonetary factors are important and have long-lasting implications for the success of any sport organization.

There is a place in the electronic media for virtually every sport organization. Those with a national audience can command lucrative network contracts. Local organizations may find homes on local radio or television outlets or local cable television. Although local contracts may require a sport organization to share the cost of production or produce the games itself, sport managers may still discover that the total return factors of exposing their products to the public through the electronic media are well worth the time, effort, and expense.

■ RESOURCES

Because the sport broadcasting industry changes so rapidly, it is important for sport managers to keep abreast of the latest news of the industry. Although many of the details of the broadcasting business are in theory confidential, the trade press has cultivated sources in the broadcasting, production, and advertising businesses that are often glad to share the news about the latest contracts, advertising packages, and demographic trends. The best single source of industry news is *Broadcasting & Cable* magazine, published weekly in Washington, D.C., and available in many college and larger municipal libraries as well as on the Web. Other trade journals, including *MediaWeek*, *AdWeek*, and *Advertising Age,* are also valuable. The annual *Broadcasting & Cable Yearbook* includes listings for every radio and television station in the country, hundreds of broadcast service companies, and trade organizations. Web sites such as http://www.Nielsen.com, http://www .SNL Kagan.com, and http://www.espn.com are just the smallest fraction of available resources on the Internet.

The major television broadcast organizations maintain Web sites that contain useful information. For a listing, check http://www .ultimatetv.com. Often the most up-to-date information on the industry can be obtained from local television and radio stations and cable systems throughout the country.

Network and cable public relations offices are often helpful if contacted directly:

ABC Sports
    47 W. 66th Street, 13th Floor
    New York, NY 10023
    212-456-7777
    http://www.abcsports.com

CBS Sports
    51 W. 52nd Street
    New York, NY 10019
    212-975-5230
    http://cbs.sportsline.com

CSTV Networks, Inc.
    85 10th Avenue, 3rd Floor
    New York, NY 10011
    212-342-8700; fax: 212-342-8899
    http://www.cstv.com

ESPN
    ESPN Plaza
    935 Middle Street
    Bristol, CT 06010
    860-766-2000
    http://www.espn.go.com

Fox Sports/Fox Sports Television Group
    10210 West Pico Boulevard
    Los Angeles, CA 90035
    310-369-6000

Fox Sports Net
    1211 Avenue of the Americas, 2nd Floor
    New York, NY 10019
    212-556-2400
    http://www.foxsports.com

The Golf Channel
    7580 Commerce Center Drive
    Orlando, FL 32819-8947
    407-355-4653
    http://www.thegolfchannel.com

MLB Network
    40 Hartz Way, Suite 10
    Secaucus, NJ 07094
    201-520-6400
    http://mlbnetwork.mlb.com

NBC Sports Division
    30 Rockefeller Plaza
    New York, NY 10112
    212-664-3930
    http://www.nbcsports.com

The Tennis Channel
    2850 Ocean Park Boulevard, Suite 150
    Santa Monica, CA 90405
    310-314-9400
    http://www.thetennischannel.com

VersusComcast Center
    One Comcast Center
    Philadelphia, PA 19103
    1-877-VERSUS-ON
    http://www.versus.com

Yankees Entertainment and Sports Network (YES Network)
    The Chrysler Building
    405 Lexington Avenue, 36th Floor
    New York, NY 10174-3699
    646-487-3600; fax: 646-487-3612
    http://www.yesnetwork.com

■ KEY TERMS

Alvin "Pete" Rozelle, audience research, broadcast rights, content providers, cost per thousand (CPM), cume, delivery systems, demographic segments, designated market areas (DMAs), ESPN, interactivity, production, rating, rights agreement, rights and production, rights holder, rights-only, Roone Arledge, share, subscriber, subscriber fees, symbiotic relationship, telecast rights, time buy, total return

■ REFERENCES

About the NFL Network. (2010). Retrieved November 15, 2010, from http://www.nfl.com/nflnetwork/fastfact

Ad Age. (2009). Cable guide: Tennis channel. Retrieved November 15, 2010, from http://brandedcontent.adage.com/cableguide09/network.php?id=25

Associated Press. (2010, January 11). Super bowl ad prices dip, but still pricey. CBSNews.com. Retrieved November 15, 2010, from http://www.cbsnews.com/stories/2010/01/11/sportsline/main6082591.shtml

Barnouw, E. (1966–1970). *A history of broadcasting in the United States* (Vols. 1–3). New York: Oxford University Press.

Burton, R. (1999, December 19). From Hearst to Stern: The shaping of an industry over a century. *New York Times*, p. 11.

CAB. (2010, June).Why ad-supported cable? Retrieved December 5, 2010, from http://www.thecab.tv/main/bm~doc/why-cable-june-2010.pdf

CBSSports.com. (n.d.). CBS Corporation and DirecTV reach expansive sports programming agreement. Retrieved December 7, 2010, from http://www.cbssports.com/cbssports/story/9949810

Charter Communications. (2010). Price guarantee. Retrieved December 1, 2010, from http://connect.charter.com/landing/cpg/PriceGuarantee_bbBF.html

Christley, J. (2008, December 26,). NASCAR Camping World Series East 2009 schedule announced. Retrieved December 4, 2010, from http://www.doverspeedway.com/track/press/article.php?dir=200812&id=2468

Cohen, R. (2007, June 27). NBA extends TV deals with ESPN/ABC, TNT. Retrieved December 7, 2010, from http://www.usatoday.com/sports/basketball/2007-06-27-3096131424_x.htm

Cross, S. (2007, April 5). MLB Extra Innings makes deal with iN DEMAND. Retrieved December 6, 2010, from http://www.associatedcontent.com/article/204540/mlb_extra_innings_makes_deal_with_in.html?cat=14

Douglas, S. (1987). *Inventing American broadcasting: 1899–1922*. Baltimore: Johns Hopkins University Press.

ESPN.com news service. (2010, February 9). Game sets viewer, advertising marks. Retrieved December 5, 2010, from http://sports.espn.go.com/nfl/playoffs/2009/news/story?id=4897094

Federal Communications Commission (FCC). (2010, June). Broadcast Station Totals (Index) 1990–Present. Retrieved November 15, 2010, from http://www.fcc.gov/mb/audio/BroadcastStationTotals.html

FIBA. (2006). The past and the future of the WNBA. *FIBA Assist Magazine* 20, 36. Retrieved November 15, 2010, from http://www.fiba.com/asp_includes/download.asp?file_id=728

Fight booms sales of radio equipment. (1927, September 23). *Boston Globe*, p. 19.

Fuel TV. (2010). Fuel TV is . . . Fuel.tv.com. Retrieved November 15, 2010, from http://www.fuel.tv/about/

Fuse. (2009, October). Action sports diligence report. Burlington, VT: Author.

Gunther, M. (1994). *The house that Roone built: The inside story of ABC news*. Boston: Little, Brown and Co.

Head, S., Sterling, C., & Schofield, L. (1994). *Broadcasting in America* (7th ed.). Boston: Houghton Mifflin.

Ipsos Mendelsohn. (2009, December 2). The Mendelsohn affluent survey. American Association of Advertising Agencies. Retrieved November 15, 2010, from http://www.aaaa.org/news/bulletins/Documents/2009Mendelsohn.pdf

Klatell, D., & Marcus, N. (1996). *Inside big time sports: Television, money and the fans*. New York: MasterMedia.

Monday Night Football changes the channel. (2005, April 19). Washingtonpost.com. Retrieved November 15, 2010, from http://www.washingtonpost.com/wp-dyn/articles/A63538-2005Apr18.html

National Collegiate Athletic Association v. Board of Regents of the University of Oklahoma, 104 S. Ct. 1 (1983).

New York Yankees Ticketing Technology. (n.d.). Retrieved November 15, 2010, from http://newyork .yankees.mlb.com/NASApp/mlb/nyy/ticketing/ ticket_tech.jsp

Nicholson, M. (2007). *Sport and the media: managing the nexus.* Boston: Elsevier.

Nielsen Media Research. (2010). Nielsen media research. Retrieved December 5, 2010, from http:// www.nielsen.de/pages/english.aspx

Nielsen Wire (2010a). Number of U.S. TV households climbs by one million for 2010-11 TV season. Retrieved November 15, 2010, from http://blog .nielsen.com/nielsenwire/media_entertainment/ number-of-u-s-tv-households-climbs-by-one-million- for-2010-11-tv-season/

Nielson Wire. (2010b). 2010 World Cup reaches nearly 112 million U.S. viewers. Retrieved December 5, 2010, from http://blog.nielsen.com/nielsenwire/ media_entertainment/2010-world-cup-reaches- nearly-112-million-u-s-viewers/

Ourand, J., & Mickle, T. (2010, November 29). NASCAR's slide on TV continues. Retrieved December 4, 2010, from http://www.sportsbusiness journal.com/article/67435

Pittsburgh Athletic Co. v. KQV Broadcasting Co., 24 F. Supp. 490 (W.D. Pa. 1938).

Rader, B. (1984). *In its own image: How television has transformed sports.* New York: Free Press.

Sandomir, R. (2006, December 27). TV Sports: For N.F.L. fans, the cable picture isn't any clearer. *New York Times.* Retrieved November 15, 2010, from http://select.nytimes.com/search/restricted/ article?res=F30B13F635550C748EDDAB0994 DE404482

SportsBusiness Daily. (2006, August 7). ESPN, MLS reach eight-year TV deal that includes rights fees. Retrieved December 7, 2010, from http://www.sports businessdaily.com/index.cfm?fuseaction=sbd .main&storyID=SBD2006080705

SportsBusiness Daily. (2007, September 6). NFL media rights deals for '07 season. Retrieved December 7, 2010, from http://www.sportsbusinessdaily.com/ article/114714

Super Bowl XL's ad rates flat. (2006, January 12). About.com: Advertising. Retrieved November 15, 2010, from http://advertising.about.com/b/a/ 232373.htm

Szalai G. (2010, April 21). Cable, TV edge 60%–40% share stasis. *The Hollywood Reporter*, p. 4.

TVB. (2010, October). TV basics. Retrieved on December 2, 2010, from http://www.doverspeedway.com/ track/press/article.php?dir=200812&id=2468

USA Today. (2010, April 10). NCAA reaches 14-year deal with CBS/Turner for men's basketball tournament, which expands to 68 teams. Retrieved November 15, 2010, from http://content.usatoday .com/communities/campusrivalry/post/2010/04/ ncaa-reaches-14-year-deal-with-cbsturner/1

USACA Media Release. (2010). USA to host an International T20 series between New Zealand and Sri Lanka in May 2010. Retrieved December 5, 2010, from http://community.dreamcricket.com/ community/blogs/usa_cricketer/archive/2010/ 02/12/usa-to-host-an-international-t20-series- between-new-zealand-and-sri-lanka-in-may-2010 .aspx

Windows Media. (n.d.). DRM FAQ. Retrieved November 15, 2010, from http://www.microsoft.com/ windows/windowsmedia/forpros/drm/faq.aspx# drmfaq_1_4

CHAPTER

18

Sport and New Media

Kevin Filo

■ INTRODUCTION

New media can be defined as the emergence of digital, computerized, or networked information and communication technologies in the later part of the twentieth century. Examples of these technologies include destination Web sites and social media, blogs, podcasts, online video streaming, and mobile technology (Flew, 2008). Each of these technologies have become critical elements within the sport industry. New media is distinguished by a number of unique characteristics including geographic distance, volume of communication, speed of communication, interactivity, and interconnection and overlap among communication (Croteau & Hoynes, 2003). These characteristics relate directly to sport management and each characteristic has markedly impacted the sport landscape.

New media transcends geographic boundaries and can eliminate geographic distance.

Sport fans can now follow their favorite teams or players from anywhere in the world through new media technologies. Scores, updates, and additional information for all sports are now available via the **Internet**. News, scores, and in-game updates can be sent to fans via text message. Also, audio or video feeds of games can be streamed on an individual's personal computer or mobile phone. Furthermore, individuals can interact with fans of the same team, athlete, or sport around the world through a variety of new media-based mechanisms within social media. In addition, sport managers can introduce and market their products to fans around the globe via new media technologies. For instance, the popularity of English Premier League soccer in the United States has increased significantly due to the emergence of new media technologies providing information, real-time scoring, and highlights, along with live streaming of games online.

The volume of communication speaks to the sheer number of mechanisms by which fans can connect with sport organizations, along with the vast array of connections shared among sport fans and organizations. Social media technologies, including platforms such as Twitter, YouTube, and Facebook, connect fans from around the globe. Meanwhile, blogs, podcasts, and discussion forums allow organizations to provide information, while allowing fans to share opinions. The volume of communication inherent to new media technologies offers sport fans a number of different ways to express their fandom and connect with teams, athletes, and other followers.

The speed of communication is exemplified through sport being able to obtain scores, statistics, and game features both during and immediately following games. The days of being forced to wait until the arrival of the next morning's newspaper to acquire news, analysis, and statistics concerning the previous night's games have passed. Highlight-based shows such as ESPN SportsCenter once developed narratives and content to introduce highlights for games based on the premise that the show represented the first time the final score and the clips from the game would be available to those who did not attend or watch the games. This practice is no longer in place as the outcome is available online as soon as the game is decided.

The interactive component of new media is a by-product of the impacts of geography, volume of communication, and speed of communication. Sport fans can communicate with fans across the globe through a variety of channels in immediate real-time. In addition, a number of mechanisms, such as online polls and contests, and user comments within blogs and news features, facilitate direct interaction among sport fans as well as between fans and sport organizations. Finally, the interconnection and overlap among communication is a reflection of each of these components. The connections sport fans share, along with their expression of these connections, are linked together in a number of ways. For example, an individual can follow an athlete via Twitter. This can then connect him or her with other fans who follow this athlete, while also directing the fan to other online resources such as an official Web site or Facebook fan page, or perhaps the individual player's personal blog. These online destinations can then link the fan to the latest stories on the team, player, and league as well as news concerning different teams or sports. Collectively, these distinguishing features of new media provide sport fans with a wide variety of opportunities to connect with sport organizations and other fans in a convenient and efficient manner. Likewise, new media allows sport organizations to bolster these connections and promote the sport product. The emergence of the Internet served as a precursor to new media technologies. A brief history of the Internet follows below.

■ HISTORY

The term *Internet* derives from the word *inter-network*, which relates to the connection shared between two or more computer networks. The Internet can be defined as an interconnected network of thousands of networks and millions of computers that, in turn, connect businesses, institutions, government, universities, and individual consumers. The Internet has evolved in three distinct phases: innovation, institutionalization, and commercialization. During the innovation phase (1961–1974) the first steps towards creating the Internet were taken with the goal of connecting large mainframe computers across college campuses. Next, the institutionalization phase (1975–1995) built upon these developments through funding provided from the Department of Defense and the National Science Foundation. The Department of Defense funding focused on utilizing the

Internet to enhance military communication, while the funding from the National Science Foundation addressed civilian communication via the Internet. The current phase, commercialization (1995–present) has seen the government encourage corporations to expand the Internet beyond college campuses and the military (Laudon & Guercio Traver, 2009). A distinguishing characteristic of the Internet is that no single organization is in control, nor does a governing body own the Internet.

As of 2010, there were more than 1.9 billion Internet users worldwide (Internet World Stats, 2010). That number is expected to exceed 2 billion by 2012. The pervasiveness of mobile wireless Internet access is a major contributor to the growth in Internet usage. Further, Internet access from mobile phones has had additional impact on the expansion of Internet usage. The accessibility of the Internet, along with the corresponding growth in usage, has contributed to a number of developments that have had a pronounced effect on the online environment and the world of sport. These developments can be collectively referred to as *new media*. This chapter describes these new media developments, while outlining their impact on sport management. The chapter also discusses several mechanisms by which sport fans and organizations can engage via new media, specifically, destination Web sites, social media, blogs, podcasts, online video, and mobile technology. Destination Web sites represent a traditional new media mechanism sport organizations use to connect with fans.

■ KEY CONCEPTS

Destination Web Sites

Within the context of this book, a **destination Web site** is an official site on the Internet employed by a sport organization for communication and commerce. Destination Web sites initially emerged as effective tools for the marketing communication of sport organizations due to the low costs associated with their development and simultaneous emergence of the Internet as a critical resource for gathering information. Destination Web sites can achieve a number of objectives including providing information concerning a business, products, and services; purchasing or reserving products; and facilitating transactions and physical delivery of products (Van den Poel & Leunis, 1999).

Established professional sport leagues such as the National Basketball Association (NBA) and Major League Baseball (MLB) employ a stock template for teams to adhere to within their destination Web sites. These content guidelines can decrease variability in the content and information provided across team Web sites, ensuring specific product features are communicated effectively on each team's official Web site. Newly established sport leagues may employ less strict standards for Web site design. This underlies the importance of investment in destination Web site development to differentiate the product, raise awareness, and attract fans. The stringency and standardization of destination Web site content guidelines could vary based upon the stage of the product lifecycle, and how successful a sport organization has become.

A destination Web site is critical for sport organizations. Initially, providing information concerning marketing mix variables (i.e., product, price, promotion, place, public relations) represented the primary objective of a sport organization's destination Web site. Increasingly, importance has been placed on allowing consumer-based interest features to shape **Internet marketing communication** and content (Beech, Chadwick, & Tapp, 2000). This shift, along with the development of additional new media technologies, has led to the advancement of user-generated content, in which users are increasingly engaged, while creating and distributing their own content. **Social media** reflects a critical platform for engaging consumers and allowing for user-generated content.

Introduction to Social Media

An online **social network** can be defined as an online area in which people who share common ties can engage and interact with one another. Online social networks are unique in that individual members may or may not meet in person but can still share opinions and attitudes with one another through an online medium, or what can be referred to as social media. In 2010, social networking via social media technologies—including Facebook, Twitter, and MySpace—represented the second most popular online activity, ranking ahead of e-mail and software manufacturers, while behind online searching via sites such as Google or Bing. The amount of time consumers spend engaged with social media accounts for almost 10% of all time spent online (Nielsen, 2009). In terms of unique visitors, by 2008, social networking sites such as MySpace and Flikr had 120 million and 64 million members, respectively. In that same year, Facebook, the most popular social media platform, had over 200 million members (TechCrunch, 2008), and the site reached 500 million unique users in 2010. To put these statistics into historical perspective, radio took 38 years to reach 50 million unique users, while television took 13 years to reach 50 million unique users. Facebook has added 100 million users at a time in the course of nine-month spans (Qualman, 2009).

Research has demonstrated that individuals engage with social media technologies for personal, social-based reasons. Keeping in touch with friends and family is the most frequently cited motivation for joining, followed by fun as well as being invited by a colleague. Professional motivations such as job search, business development, and recruiting are less influential, and cited far less frequently. Once an individual has joined, a variety of motivations direct continued usage, including fostering new relations, correspondence with existing friends, information gathering and debate, and time-killing (Nielsen, 2009). Two of the most influential social media platforms in the realm of sport management are Facebook and Twitter.

■ FACEBOOK

Over 100 million users log-on to Facebook on the average day. Half of these users are ages 18 to 34, but Facebook use continues to grow throughout a number of age brackets, and the site is experiencing its fastest growth among adults over the age of 35. While the average Facebook user spends 14 minutes per day on the site, overall time spent on Facebook exceeds time spent on Google, Yahoo!, YouTube, Wikipedia, and Amazon combined.

Facebook has gained popularity for a number of reasons. First, its design is simple, consistent, and user-friendly. Second, Facebook enjoys a broad appeal. While the social media platform was originally designed for use by college students, Facebook is now used by individuals across all demographics. Third, the focus on activity inherent to Facebook allows for user engagement, along with the distribution of information, while bolstering the emotional attachment users share with the site and their content. Finally, Facebook has benefited considerably from a great deal of media exposure. References in news, television, music, and film have made Facebook a staple of popular culture, while contributing to the immense popularity enjoyed by the site.

Sport managers have utilized Facebook primarily through two different means: group pages and fan pages. *Group pages* are discussion-focused pages created to facilitate smaller scale interaction. Group pages are most effective in rallying support for a cause, or for raising awareness and promoting a one-time event. *Fan pages* can involve a team, individual players, or members of a coaching staff. Fan pages are developed by sport brands as a mechanism to interact directly with fans and customers. The most effective Facebook fan pages include a distinct and branded landing page, one of the few components of Facebook that can be customized. In addition, successful fan pages highlight promotions and deals surrounding the sport brand, while incorporating interactivity through fan polls, voting, and discussion. A successful fan page can serve as a 'mini-Web site' for a sport organization and can be used to distribute team, player and competition information, integrate sponsors, solicit fan contributions, and drive traffic to the official Web site. Examples of quality Facebook fan pages in sport include the New England Patriots Fan Zone and the National Hockey League (NHL) on Facebook.

Facebook allows sport managers to connect with and engage a large and diverse audience of users; however, a number of content issues must be addressed in order to effectively manage this new media technology. Sport organizations have been continually confronted with issues concerning Facebook content. Two Louisiana State University swimmers lost their spot on the swim team due to content on their Facebook pages that was interpreted as disparaging to their head coach (Brady & Libit, 2006). The University of Southern California football team found itself mired in controversy after a player created a group page that included off-color content and inappropriate images (Reynolds, 2007). A stadium operations employee for the Philadelphia Eagles lost his job due to a post on his personal Facebook account questioning a personnel move made by the organization (Stamm, 2009). These examples underscore the importance of sport organizations developing social media policies to ensure that the technology is used appropriately and effectively. Sport organizations must make an effort to harness

the power and audience of both Facebook and Twitter.

■ TWITTER

Twitter is a free social networking and microblogging platform that allows users to send and read short messages, referred to as *tweets*. These tweets are 140 characters or fewer that are communicated to a user's followers, the individuals connected to the user's account. In 2009, Twitter boasted 75 million active accounts, with older adults (ages 35+) the most frequent users (Gaudin, 2010).

Sport managers can use Twitter to announce promotions and break news (Hambrick, Simmons, Greenhalgh, & Greenwell, 2010). For example, sport organizations are increasingly using their Twitter feed to first announce transactions and draft picks to their followers. In addition, Twitter can facilitate improved customer service as crisis situations can be addressed quickly, while the platform can be used to ask questions and solicit feedback from fans. Many sport organizations have used Twitter to hold virtual focus groups with followers. Similar to Facebook, sport managers can also use Twitter to build community through interaction with fans, integration of sponsors, and driving traffic to the organization's official Web site.

To date, sport managers have utilized Twitter to humanize their brand. This can be accomplished through instant access to new photos, videos, and updates as well as direct interaction with athletes and coaches. Also, Twitter has allowed sport organizations to reach beyond their current fan base through the extensive reach provided by the platform. The most successful Twitter accounts place a focus on authenticity and credibility, while communicating to followers in a less structured manner. Examples of high quality and prolific Twitter accounts in sport include teams such as the Chicago Bulls, San Diego Chargers, and Portland Trail Blazers; along with individual athletes such as Lance Armstrong and Shaquille O'Neal. Twitter has been particularly effective for niche sports and leagues. As an example, the Women's United Soccer Association (WUSA) attracted headlines for encouraging players to actively tweet during matches. Overall, Twitter represents a critical means to bolster the connection between sport organizations and fans in the realm of social media.

Select sport organizations have taken an extreme approach and banned Facebook and Twitter use by employees to ensure their players do not get into trouble due to content. During the 2010 Fédération Internationale de Football Association (FIFA) World Cup, players from Spain, Brazil, Mexico, Holland, Germany, Argentina, and England were forbidden from using Twitter. The head coach for Chile's national team banned any social networking altogether. In 2009, Texas Tech head football coach Mike Leach implemented a ban on Twitter use among his players in response to a number of tweets from players expressing disappointment with team activities. However, these hard-line responses seem overzealous and can eliminate the potential positive outcomes of a presence on Facebook or Twitter. Beyond simply developing policy, sport managers need to ensure that the guidelines are clear to avoid confusion among athletes. During the 2010 Vancouver Winter Olympic Games, athletes such as Lindsey Vonn and Nick Pearson reached out to their social media followers at the outset of the Games to let them know they would not be posting any updates via Facebook and Twitter. This was a response to the IOC Blogging Guidelines for the 2010 Games. However, Bob Condron, Director of Media Services for the United States Olympic Committee, contended that athletes could utilize social media, yet restrictions regarding use of first person, and references to advertisers and sponsors further confounded the policy (McClusky, 2010). Sport managers should work closely with their athletes and other employees

to determine the most effective use of platforms such as Facebook and Twitter, along with all social media.

Other Social Media

Beyond Facebook and Twitter, a holistic understanding of social media by sport organizations is imperative. This is not only because of the popularity and sheer number of users but also because the conversations about sports, teams, and athletes are occurring via social media regardless, and sport managers simply cannot ignore these online interactions. The consumer base in sport is unique because of the passion, emotion, and collectivism inherent to sport fans. Sport consumers share their passion, emotions, and opinions with other fans, and this sharing is now taking place across social media.

Contrasting approaches to managing social media in sport can be found through the policies of two National Collegiate Athletic Association (NCAA) Division I Athletics conferences: The Big Ten and The Southeast Conference (SEC). According to Kruse (2009), in August 2009 the SEC released a new media policy that read, in part:

> *Ticketed fans can't produce or disseminate (or aid in producing or disseminating) any material of information about the Event, including, but not limited to, any account, description, picture, video, audio, reproduction or other information concerning the Event.*

In other words, this policy stated that event attendees were no longer allowed to use Twitter, Facebook, YouTube, TwitPic (Twitter's photo sharing component), or any other service that could in any way compete with authorized media coverage of the event. The SEC implemented this policy as a proactive means to protect the network, CBS, which owned the authorized media coverage rights of SEC football for an estimated $3 billion over 15 years. The Conference organizers foresaw the day when fans' mobile devices could record live events and stream online in real-time at high quality, and did not want this user engagement to undercut their high dollar traditional media partner.

While arguably well-intentioned, this policy was criticized by fans and media alike. These criticisms were based upon the alleged unfairness of the policy to fans (It's not the fans' fault that technology is developing at this pace.); questions concerning the enforceability of the policy (Were they going to confiscate cameras and mobile phones as fans walked into stadiums?); and opinions that the policy was counterproductive because it would discourage people from talking about events and the SEC conference overall (The conversations would take place anyway.). Shortly after the backlash, the SEC amended its policy to state that:

> *Personal messages and updates of scores or other brief descriptions of the competition throughout the Event are acceptable.*

The Conference organizers felt this amended policy still protected the broadcasting rights of CBS, while allowing for casual, not-for-profit social media use by fans (Kruse, 2009).

In contrast, The Big Ten Conference actively promotes the use of social media among both fans and other media. This Conference shares content online through a variety of different formats to allow fans to redistribute and utilize. The official Big Ten Conference Web site allows users to embed their videos so that independent bloggers can post these videos to their blogs. The Web site also lists all of the Big Ten team Twitter and Facebook accounts, while encouraging fans to submit additional information and resources. In addition, the Conference has its own active Twitter account employed to continually promote all Big Ten-related activities. Instead of viewing social media as a threat to traditional media, The Big Ten views embracing social media

as a means towards free advertising. The word-of-mouth fostered via social media may lead to viewership, this viewership can then lead to increased advertising dollars, and advertising dollars equate to increased revenue (Athletic Business, 2009).

When leveraged properly, social media can allow sport organizations to build fan participation and interaction, drive traffic to their official Web site, and develop sponsor programs to increase revenue. Effective employment of social media requires four important steps: find, listen, engage, and lead (Hessert, 2009). First, sport managers must find out where the online conversations are taking place. This can be accomplished through a Really Simple Syndication (RSS) feed or by simply searching sites such as Facebook and Twitter. In addition, blog searches such as Google Blog Search and Technorati can be effective in tracking down online discussion. Second, sport managers should listen to these conversations and perform content analyses in order to gauge who is participating, what participants are talking about, and what participants are looking for from their organizations. Different social media communities have different nuances and characteristics that the organization must learn and understand prior to participation. Next, once sport managers have listened and determined objectives based upon fans' perspectives, these organizations can then engage in social media with a focus on building relationships with fans. Here it is imperative to focus on relationship-building and bolstering connections, rather than simply revenue generation. Finally, sport organizations can then take the lead by providing compelling and unique content, keeping this content up to date and consistent, and driving traffic to the organizations' websites.

Engagement via social media presents a tremendous opportunity for sport organizations to bolster relationships with, and among, fans. Social media allows sport fans to connect with other fans through a variety of different rapidly growing and increasingly layered mechanisms. In addition, sport organizations can interact with these fans like never before. The challenge for sport managers is developing a sound and consistent social media policy that allows for effective employment of these technologies. From there, sport managers must locate all of the different conversations that are occurring via social media. Once these conversations have been uncovered, sport managers must listen to and learn from what users are discussing, before becoming involved in the conversation. This involvement should include the provision of compelling content that adds value to the ongoing conversations. Collectively, these steps allow sport organizations to participate in and facilitate the online discourse concerning their product. As noted above, blogs represent an environment in which a number of these conversations take place.

Blogs

A **blog** can be defined as a personal Web site featuring a series of chronological entries by an author. These posts are presented in order from newest to oldest, and postings often contain links to related Web sites or content. A number of additional features differentiate blogs from traditional news and content. First, a *blogroll* is a collection of links to other related blogs featured alongside entries. Second, *trackbacks* are a list of entries in other blog postings that refer to a post on the first blog. Third and most distinguishing, blogs include a comments section below entries, in which readers can post comments that the author, along with additional readers, can respond to in order to facilitate interaction concerning select posts.

While readership and the overall scope and scale of blogs are difficult to gauge due to the expansiveness of the Internet, 133 million blogs were estimated to exist in 2009. Across these

blogs, an estimated 1.6 million blog postings are made each day. Overall, an estimated 21 million U.S. adults have created a blog, while 67 million U.S. adults indicate they read a blog regularly. Globally, an estimated 346 million people read blogs (Technorati, 2009). From a demographic standpoint, bloggers are young, Internet savvy, wealthy, and educated. This profile demonstrates an alignment with the demographic characteristics of sport fans. Blogs can be categorized in a number of ways. Personal blogs reflect an individual's ongoing commentary, musings, or online diary. These represent the most common category of blogs, but very few rise to fame. Corporate blogs are professional blogs that an organization utilizes for communication. These blogs are often employed by sport organizations for marketing, branding, and public relations purposes. In addition, blogs can be categorized by genre (e.g., political, travel, music, art, fashion) or media type (e.g., video, links, photos).

Blogs have made an impact on the sport industry in a number of ways. They give a voice and platform to the everyday fan as blogs can be created relatively easily and affordably by individuals. The blog can then be used as an avenue to express the individuals' opinions concerning his or her favorite sport, team, or player. Also new sources utilize blogs to complement their mainstream reporting. Sport news outlets such as ESPN, Yahoo!, Sports Illustrated, and Fanhouse supplement their traditional news content with insights and postings from bloggers on staff. Furthermore, blogs, along with micro-blogging technologies such as Twitter, have strengthened athlete connections with fans through open dialogue between the athlete and his or her readers, or followers. Similar to corporate blogs utilized by organizations to reach out to consumers, athletes use blogs to communicate directly to fans. The everyday activities of various athletes, from training regimens and post-game reactions to what music the athlete currently listens to, can now be made available to fans via blogs

(Hambrick, Simmons, Greenhalgh, & Green-well, 2010). Finally, a variety of sport-based blogs, such as Deadspin.com, have emerged and gained popularity as media watchdogs. These blogs monitor the established and traditional sport news entities, often providing dissent and criticism, or alternative viewpoints.

A number of examples demonstrate the influence blogs have had on the sport landscape. In June 2007, a *Louisville Courier-Journal* sports reporter had his media credential revoked and was forced to leave the press box during an NCAA baseball super-regional because the NCAA alleged the reporter was violating media policy by providing live updates online via the *Louisville Courier Journal's* blog during the game (i.e., *live blogging*). The *Louisville Courier Journal*, in turn, asserted that the reporter was deprived of the right to report from a public facility as protected within the First Amendment of the Constitution. The organization maintained further that this coverage was part of the evolution of presenting news to readers, and that once a home run is hit in a game, it represents a fact the NCAA cannot copyright (Bozich, 2007). Live blogging is now a common component of the coverage of sport and entertainment events. A variety of software programs have been developed to facilitate and ease live blogging.

Negative consequences of blogging among athletes and sports figures are also pervasive. Dallas Mavericks owner Mark Cuban launched his own personal blog for the initial purpose of responding to how the traditional media was treating him. Within his blog, Cuban would share his business ideas and musings. In the process of sharing these thoughts via his blog, Cuban often posted content critical of different business practices of the NBA. Cuban criticized the NBA regular season opening date within a blog post in November 2004 and was quickly fined by the NBA. Cuban was also fined by the NBA for a blog post that dissected and ultimately

questioned the selection process of referees for the NBA playoffs.

NBA player Gilbert Arenas emerged as the first 'blog superstar' in sports, but eventually retired from blogging amidst concerns that his prolific (and often notorious) blogging served as a distraction from his job as a professional basketball player. Furthermore, professional basketball players Rod Benson and Paul Shirley have expressed belief that their blogging is a 'red flag' for NBA teams that do not want to sign a player who may create controversy or distractions via blog content. Just as traditional employees must be wary of blog posts and discussion of their employer, athletes and sport figures must be cognizant of the insight they provide, along with how they represent themselves via their blog.

The examples highlighted above demonstrate the emergence of blogs as a platform for communication. In addition, these examples also underscore the relationship that exists between blogs and sport. These relationships uncover a variety of challenges that sport managers must confront with regard to blogs. The challenges sport managers need to tackle with regard to the presence of blogs include addressing rumors spread via blogs; over-reaction or firestorms on the part of fans and media via blogs; granting access to bloggers versus traditional media without compromising existing media relations; and using blogs as an effective platform for marketing communication among the organization·or members of the organization as well as how much liberty to give them in using this platform. Similar to blogs, podcasts also provide sport managers with a number of opportunities and challenges.

Podcasts

Podcasts are a series of digital audio files that can be downloaded through online syndication. These files are program and content driven, as each file often represents an individual episode. Podcasts are downloaded through the Internet, and can then be played on media players or computers. Examples of the categories of podcasts include radio shows, discussion forums, or personal audio presentations. As podcasts have gained popularity, the format has emerged as an effective distribution channel for professional news and talk-based content. Successful podcasts should include consistent delivery of episodes, highlighted by interesting content, humor, music and a specific topic of conversation.

In 2008, 18% of the U.S. population reported listening to a podcast. In addition, an estimated 23 million people in the United States listened to a podcast in a given month that year. This statistic is expected to increase to 65 million by 2012, with 25 million of these listeners deemed "active users," those who listen to a podcast at least once a week (eMarketer, 2008). Listening to podcasts is eased by the spread of listening devices. Podcasts are most commonly listened to via personal computers or MP3 player devices; over one third of U.S. adults owned an MP3 player in 2008. The ease by which a podcast can be listened to is further bolstered by the mobile phone technology allowing for downloading and listening to podcasts.

Beyond ease of listening, a number of factors have contributed to the emergence of podcasting. First, the on-demand aspect of podcasts facilitates their portability. While traditional radio and audio-based content is not available after the original broadcast, podcasts are archived and accessible online at any time after release. Second, podcasts are easily accessible for both listeners and creators. Podcasts are easy to download, as the only requirements are a computer and an Internet connection, or a broadband enabled mobile phone. In addition, podcasts are easy to create as a selection of user-friendly software including Audacity and GarageBand can be downloaded to craft, edit, and upload a podcast. This

accessibility and ease then correspond with low costs as podcasts are typically free for listeners, and do not cost a great deal to create. Finally, podcasts are censure free with few rules and regulations in place regarding content. This has appealed to an alternative audience and content providers, and a large number of bloggers have turned to podcasting as an extension of their blogging.

Similar to the profile of bloggers, the young, Internet savvy, educated, and relatively wealthy profile of podcasters and those who listen to podcasts makes this group attractive to sport organizations and aligns with the profile of sport fans. Podcasts have emerged as valuable assets for various sport organizations. ESPN represents the most heavily involved sports media company with regard to podcasts. As of May 2009, ESPN was producing 125 different podcasts, and 9.6 million of the organization's podcasts were downloaded in that single month. This number represented a 40% increase from 2008. ESPN offers podcasts for some of its more popular television programs including *Pardon the Interruption*. ESPN has incorporated sponsorship and advertising within many of its podcasts, with sponsor ads before and after content, along with sponsorship of specific content segments.

Sport teams have also embraced podcasts as a means to reach out to fans and provide insights to further bolster relationships. NBA teams such as the Phoenix Suns offer free subscriptions to a collection of both audio and video podcasts (*vodcasts*) created by the team and media partners. The content of these podcasts varies from press conferences, coach's shows, and player interview shows, to content providing inside information concerning the organization. In addition, fan-created podcasts have become an increasingly popular form of expression for dedicated followers of teams. For instance, fans of the Philadelphia Phillies have developed a variety of podcasts focused on the team that include: Philcast, Phillies Weekly, Phillies Nation, and Phightin' Phils. These podcasts provide fans with a forum to discuss the team and share their opinions on recent team activities with other fans. These fan-created podcasts also represent additional promotion of the organization. Teams such as the Vancouver Canucks highlight fan-created podcasts such as The Crazy Canucks on the team's official Web site, while also providing a designated section of their Web site where fans can upload and publicize their podcasts.

The on-demand nature and overall accessibility of podcasts contribute to the popularity of podcasts as a mechanism to discuss and promote sport. Consumers have demonstrated a willingness to download and listen to podcasts, while both organizations and consumers are willing and able to produce podcasts. As podcasts continue to increase in popularity, a number of challenges confront sport managers and podcast creators. These challenges include providing consistent and compelling content to listeners; ensuring that podcast content complements existing content; and facilitating, monitoring, and promoting fan-created podcasts that focus on the organization. Additional challenges include raising awareness of podcasts, tracking listeners, and incorporating sponsorship. Podcasts as well as blogs can be integral to effective communication with sport fans. In addition, podcasts can connect individuals with similar interests and reflect the technological developments that have facilitated these connections. Similarly, technological developments in online video have contributed to the popularity and pervasiveness of online video content as a valuable resource for sport organizations.

Online Video Content

In 2008, the average U.S. consumer spent 3,800 hours per year consuming media of all kinds. Television, radio, and Internet combine for 80% of all media consumption. The Internet remains third among these three content providers, but this medium is growing rapidly. Overall media time has been growing at 2.5% per year, while online media time is growing at 5% per year (U.S. Census Bureau, 2009). Consumer usage of the Internet continues to grow, and a corresponding increase in willingness to consume **online video content**. In 2003, consumers spent 34% of their time online watching video content. In 2008, 78.5% of the total U.S. Internet audience viewed online video (GRABstats.com, 2010). YouTube is the leading advertiser-supported video content site and has an online audience of 70 million unique visitors per month (The Future Buzz, 2009). By comparison, the most popular television shows generate an audience of around 10 million viewers.

Business leaders and developers did not initially identify showing video on a computer as a primary objective of new media technologies. In the early stages of the Internet, consumers simply were not watching video online. However, a number of technological developments have led to the current consumption levels for online video content. First, the processing power of personal computers continues to escalate. Second, with this increase in processing power, levels of bandwidth have also increased. Third, media and media consumption has become increasingly digitized. Finally, the quality of video players available on personal computers has improved considerably, and continues to evolve. Collectively, these developments have contributed to a proliferation of video content available online. Meanwhile, consumers are willing, and nearly demanding, to view this content via their personal computers and mobile phones. This has presented a variety of challenges for content providers, broadcasters, and consumers alike.

As content providers and broadcasters address these challenges, a number of distribution models have been developed for online video content, and these models have been adopted in the sport context. The broadcast model is an advertising-based model in which content providers attempt to broadcast to as many people as possible through relatively straightforward access to users, while not charging users a subscription fee. The lack of subscription fees and easy access result in content providers attempting to sell as many advertisements as possible to generate revenue. NCAA March Madness on Demand represents one of the more successful examples of this model. Users can stream all Men's NCAA Basketball Tournament games online at no cost. Hulu.com represents another successful example of the broadcast model, and Hulu currently has partnerships in place with sport entities such as The NFL Network, The Big Ten Network, The Tennis Channel, and the Dew Winter Tour.

The subscription model provides content to consumers at a fee. Often, these subscription fees vary based on the amount and quality of content offered to users. National Association of Stock Car Auto Racing (NASCAR) has aligned with Turner Sports and Entertainment Digital to provide a variety of online content offerings and access at different price points. MLB.tv is an additional subscription-based offering that allows fans to view out-of-market MLB games and additional supplementary content. The traditional affiliate model facilitates a relationship among content providers, networks, and cable companies. In this model, individuals who subscribe to certain cable providers are granted access to broadband channels from select cable networks. ESPN3, originally known as ESPN Broadband then ESPN360, is one of the most successful examples of this model. ESPN3 allows subscribers to the cable provider Comcast to view ESPN content online, while ESPN3 receives a portion of the profits from the cable fees. The video content provided through ESPN3 includes both content airing on the various ESPN networks, as well as content exclusive to the online provider.

The provision of online video content, and the process behind it, will continue to evolve.

North American professional sport organizations such as MLB and the NHL have been proactive and successful in streaming out-of-market games for fans. Also, the NBA has advanced efforts for streaming both in-market and out-of-market games, while teams such as the Philadelphia 76ers have launched a traditional affiliate initiative to stream their games. In addition, global sport events such as the FIFA World Cup and the Olympic and Paralympic Games (through ParalympicSport.TV) have benefited to a great extent from effective online distribution of video content. These successes have included not only streaming live games, but also include users viewing highlight packages as well as re-watching events. Meanwhile, leagues such as the NFL have been slow to adapt and struggle with illicit online pirating of games.

Both paid and free online content models have been viable for the time being. Free content has demonstrated an ability to drive consumers to paid content. Consumer preference is to not pay to view online video content, while consumers have demonstrated tolerance towards ads before videos in exchange for free viewing. However, consumers are also willing to pay for specific, high quality content presented in a convenient manner. Sport managers must confront the challenges to provide video content to their consumers where, when, and how consumers want it. This has become increasingly important as mobile technology continues to advance.

Mobile Technology

Mobile telephones are now the largest providers of wireless access to the Internet today. Initially, the challenges for mobile phones and Internet access had been quality and speed. Mobile phones have developed from First Generation phones providing basic cell phone service with limited availability and no text messaging, to Third (3G) and Fourth (4G) Generation phones incorporating high speed mobile and broadband service, while also holding the capacity for browsing, instant messaging, and e-mail. These *smartphones* combine the functionality of a personal digital assistant with the functionality of a cell phone as well as a laptop with Wi-Fi access (Laudon & Guercio Traver, 2009). Examples of smartphones include the iPhone, BlackBerry, and Droid.

A distinguishing characteristic of smartphones is that users can download applications to their phones. These applications provide users with information, entertainment, games, and interactivity. The Apple iPhone has developed applications most effectively through an open source system that encourages independent developers to produce their own applications that can then be sold to iPhone users. As a result, over 90,000 iPhone applications are available to users. The Droid has a similar open source system, and the companies behind the Droid, Verizon and Motorola, have organized challenges for developers with cash prizes for application submissions judged to be the best across a variety of categories.

A number of sport-based mobile applications have been successful. MLB At Bat is a by-product of MLB.tv and represents the trendsetter in live game tracking with rich graphics and live game audio from both home and away markets, in-game highlights, news, and fantasy tracking and statistics. In July 2009, video streaming of live games via this application was launched with one free game of the day as well as single games available for purchase. The NFL has launched an application that features scores and updates, along with select video content from the NFL Network. The NBA and CBS Sports have applications that place an emphasis on scores, news, and real-time updates. In addition, Sportacular, from the Citizen Sports Network, and SI Golf Nation are examples of mobile phone applications that connect users via social networking functionality. Sportacular allows users to chat during games via Facebook, while SI Golf Nation

encourages users to connect with other golfers through equipment reviews, course descriptions, and practice tips (Fisher, 2009).

Beyond the ability to more closely follow sports, **mobile phone technology** has implications for the delivery of the game experience. Both during broadcasts and at live games, a number of organizations have adopted sponsored text-to-win contests or polls, in which fans can submit a text message in an effort to win a prize. Frequently, these contests include an opportunity for the fan to opt-in to receive further marketing communication from the organization. The Phoenix Coyotes developed an application in which fans receive a package of highlights, interviews, and post-game press conferences delivered via mobile phones immediately following games. In addition, many stadiums encourage fans to text to report incidents in the stands. This allows fans to anonymously report unruly behavior among other fans to the stadium's security personnel. Furthermore, mobile ticketing is becoming increasingly popular. Mobile ticketing allows for tickets to be delivered to a fan's mobile phone via text message. This 'ticket' is then validated at a specified gate at the stadium. Mobile ticketing allows fans to avoid lines at Will Call, while sport teams can avoid the printing costs associated with traditional tickets. The Oakland Athletics were the first team to utilize mobile ticketing, and as of 2009, 13 MLB teams allow fans to purchase and receive tickets through their mobile phones (*SportsBusiness Journal*, 2009).

Mobile phones represent a $650 billion industry worldwide. The technology behind mobile phones continues to advance at an amazing rate. At the same time, consumer reliance on mobile phones is increasing further. Sport managers must continue to develop mechanisms to communicate to, and provide for, consumers via mobile technology. Overall, new media technologies have introduced a variety of new responsibilities for sport organizations. These responsibilities have translated to new jobs and career opportunities.

■ CAREER OPPORTUNITIES

New media technologies present a variety of means by which organizations can engage a vast audience, but in order for this to be successful, effective management of these technologies must be in place. The development, implementation, and management of new media strategies has created many employment opportunities within the sport industry. Increasingly, organizations are introducing positions to direct, manage, or coordinate social media initiatives. In addition, new media technologies have fostered opportunities in online and digital marketing communications. New media technologies have also impacted careers in sponsorship sales, sponsorship activation, and sponsor relations. Furthermore, new media developments have opened up new opportunities within traditional media relations positions, along with corporate communications.

New media has also introduced a variety of mechanisms by which prospective employees can market themselves to potential employers. Job seekers create their own personal Web sites and blogs to complement their traditional business cards, resumes, and cover letters. These new media platforms allow individuals to further communicate their qualifications for positions. Furthermore, online video presentations provide another channel to reach out to employers, while sport organizations such as Major League Soccer have employed online video to screen candidates for ticket sales positions. Lastly, new media technologies have transformed the ways that job candidates network and learn about opportunities. Employment listings such as Tweetmyjobs utilize Twitter to post job openings, while facilitating the efficient search for job opportunities. Social media platforms such as Facebook allow for professional networking, while LinkedIn represents a business-specific social networking site designed for professional networking and building connections among users.

Finally, new media's most pronounced impact with regard to career development could be providing job candidates with a platform to showcase their abilities. While a resume and cover letter can highlight and describe an individual's ability to write, an actual blog conveys this much more directly. The open source system used by platforms such as Facebook, the iPhone, and the iPad allow developers to create their own applications to demonstrate their skills to potential employers. Meanwhile, instead of talking about one's creativity as it relates to a job opportunity in marketing, a job applicant can provide tangible evidence of his or her creativity by crafting a viral video for an organization as part of his or her application materials. Recently, a large shoe brand challenged the two finalists for a Social Media Strategist position to design a social media campaign for the brand. The decision of who to hire was made based upon a voting system of users who viewed and voted on the respective campaigns online. New media technologies, particularly social media technologies, are characterized by the emotion, passion, and self-expression inherent to their usage. Job applicants can leverage these characteristics to market themselves to potential employers in creative and innovative ways in an effort to bolster their career.

■ CURRENT ISSUES

As new media technologies evolve and innovation continues, the possibilities for sport organizations and sport fans seem endless. However, new media presents a number of challenges to the sport industry. Sport managers must continue to develop and maintain destination Web sites that drive traffic, highlight sponsors, and provide relevant information and features to consumers. As social media continues to evolve and become an important aspect of consumers' everyday activities, sport managers should complement their sport organizations' destination Web sites with social media strategies that encourage engagement and interaction among consumers, while strengthening relationships between the organization and fans through compelling content. These efforts can channel the collective power of social networks. Meanwhile, the infinite amount of data provided by new media must be mined to effectively leverage technologies such as blogs and podcasts, while facilitating these online conversations. Furthermore, sport managers must adapt to ongoing advances in video content and work with content providers, advertisers, and traditional broadcasters to ensure that content is provided to users as conveniently and efficiently as possible. Finally, the proliferation of mobile phones and the innovation of smartphones translate to increased importance placed upon the delivery of all content via handheld devices.

Beyond the opportunities and challenges presented by the new media developments described above, sport managers can utilize a number of emerging technologies. Viral marketing campaigns conducted online can provide sport brands with a cost effective means to promote their products and raise awareness exponentially. Ongoing improvements in not only online video quality, but also High Definition (HD) and 3-D television have implications for delivering the game experience and distinguishing in-game attendance from viewing games at home or in sports bars. Also, technological developments, such as the Slingbox or tablets such as the iPad, must be accounted for as additional mechanisms to deliver content to consumers.

■ SUMMARY

This chapter has outlined and described a number of new media technologies that can bolster the relationship between sport organizations and consumers. Technological development in concert with an emphasis on user-generated content has led to consumers increasingly sharing their attitudes and opinions. Meanwhile, new media technologies provide a relatively easy and cost-effective means for sport organizations to promote their product and reach a wide audience. The sport industry has been significantly altered by new media technologies. These developments have made it simpler and more cost effective for sport managers to reach a diverse audience from around the world. However, establishing real and deep connections with this audience can be increasingly difficult due to the sheer number of choices consumers have to entertain themselves. Sport organizations must continue to evolve, just as new media technologies are evolving, to best leverage the endless opportunity provided by these developments.

■ RESOURCES

Mashable: The Social Media Guide
  http://www.mashable.com
  http://www.facebook.com/mashable
  http://www.twitter.com/mashable

Sports and New Media Blog
  http://sportsandnewmedia.wordpress.com/

SportPost
  http://www.sportpost.com

TechCrunch
  http://techcrunch.com/
  http://www.facebook.com/techcrunch
  http://twitter.com/techcrunch

eMarketer
  http://www.emarketer.com/
  http://www.facebook.com/eMarketer
  http://twitter.com/emarketer

CASE STUDY: Manchester United Ban Players from Twitter and Facebook

In January 2010, an update on the official Manchester United Web site read as follows (as cited in O'Neil, 2010):

> "The club wishes to make it clear that no Manchester United players maintain personal profiles on social networking websites. Fans encountering any web pages purporting to be written by United players should treat them with extreme scepticism. Any official news relating to Manchester United or its players will be communicated via ManUtd.com."

In short, Club officials were implementing an all-out ban on social networking activities among players. Shortly after this announcement, players' Facebook profiles were emptied, and Twitter accounts were removed. Wayne Rooney, Ryan Giggs, and Darren Fletcher had their Twitter accounts removed. Wes Brown had his Facebook profile removed. Meanwhile, the contents of the Facebook Walls of Ryan Giggs and Rio Ferdinand were cleared of any content.

The Club framed the policy as a means to protect their players. Specifically, the language concerning "scepticism" (sic) towards any existing pages intended to communicate that the ban guarded players against fans creating faux pages that may contain content deemed unbecoming. In addition, driving traffic to the Club's official Web site was no doubt a motivation for the policy. However, many critics saw directly through the policy and its intent. They believed the policy represented a knee-jerk reaction to social media issues related to other clubs. Ryan Bent, a former striker for Tottenham Hotspur, expressed his frustration with the Club's handling of his transfer negotiations with Sunderland via Twitter during the summer of 2009. In addition, Liverpool forward Ryan Babel tweeted a critique of his manager's decision to drop him from the lineup for a game at Stoke. The latter incident occurred just prior to Manchester United's policy announcement.

Critics proclaimed that the social media ban was a not-so-transparent means to prevent players from making comments on social networking sites that could potentially create a media firestorm. In addition, concern over sensitive matters, such as the Club's current financial standing, being discussed on various social media platforms was also cited. Beyond questions concerning the motivation behind the policy, many critics deemed the policy as short-sighted. Observers understood the Club's desire to protect its brand, and attempt to control the social media conversation. However, the policy was deemed limited and a potential obstacle to fostering loyalty among fans. Furthermore, many wondered why a brand such as Manchester United would elect to shut down social media, considering its potential for generating revenue. Nonetheless, the social media ban was adopted by rival Manchester City, and as noted earlier in the chapter, similar policies were put in place during the 2010 FIFA World Cup.

Questions for Discussion

1. Do you believe that it is reasonable for sport organizations to ban employees from social media? Explain.
2. Assume you are an owner of a professional sport organization. What type of policy would you implement with regard to employee use of social media? Would you have any restrictions? If so, what restrictions would you put in place? How would you enforce this policy?
3. As an owner of a professional sport organization, are there any social media platforms and new media technologies you would encourage your employees to utilize? Any you would discourage? Explain.

Technorati

    http://technorati.com/

    http://twitter.com/technorati

The Future Buzz: Social Media Marketing and Digital PR

    http://thefuturebuzz.com/

    http://www.facebook.com/thefuturebuzz

The Long Tail: Why the Future of Business is Selling Less of More, **by Chris Anderson**

    Anderson, C. (2006). *The Long Tail: Why the Future of Business is Selling Less of More.* Upper New York, NY: Hyperion.

Googled: The End of the World As We Know It, **by Ken Auletta**

    Aueletta, K. (2009). *Googled: The End of the World As We Know It.* New York, NY: Penguin Press, HC

Creating Podcasts

    http://www.how-to-podcast-tutorial.com/

    http://audacity.sourceforge.net/

    http://www.apple.com/ilife/garageband/

Creating Blogs

    https://www.blogger.com/start

    http://wordpress.com/

■ KEY TERMS

blogs, destination Web sites, Internet, Internet marketing communication, mobile phone technology, new media, online video content, podcasts, social media, social network

■ REFERENCES

Athletic Business. (2009). Twitter rivals. Retrieved November 19, 2010, from http://athleticbusiness.com/articles/article.aspx?articleid=2716&zoneid=40

Beech, J., Chadwick, S., & Tapp, A. (2000). Surfing in the Premier League: Key issues for football club marketers using the Internet. *Managing Leisure, 5,* 51–64.

Bozich, R. (2007). Louisville reporter ejected for blogging at NCAA game. *USA Today.* Retrieved November 19, 2010, from http://www.usatoday.com/sports/college/baseball/2007-06-11-reporter-ejected_N.htm

Brady, E., & Libit, D. (2006). Alarms sound over athletes' Facebook time. *USA Today.* Retrieved November 19, 2010, from http://www.usatoday.com/tech/news/internetprivacy/2006-03-08-athletes-websites_x.htm

Croteau, D., & Hoynes, W. (2003). *Media society: Industries, images, and audiences* (3rd ed.). Thousand Oaks, CA: Sage Publications

eMarketer (2008, February 4). Heard the latest about podcasting? Retrieved November 19, 2010, from http://www.emarketer.com/Article.aspx?R=1005869

Fisher, E. (2009). Mobile apps we like. *Sports-Business Journal.* Retrieved November 19, 2010, from http://www.sportsbusinessjournal.com/article/62691

Flew, T. (2008). *New media: An introduction.* Melbourne, Australia: Oxford University Press, p. 17.

Gaudin, S. (2010). Twitter now has 75m users; most asleep at the mouse. *Computerworld.* Retrieved November 19, 2010, from http://www.computerworld.com/s/article/9148878/Twitter_now_has_75M_users_most_asleep_at_the_mouse

GRABstats.com (2010). Online video sharing statistics/online video sharing stats. Retrieved on December 16, 2010, from http://www.grabstats.com/statcategorymain.asp?StatCatID=1

Hambrick, M.E., Simmons, J.M., Greenhalgh, G.P., & Greenwell, T.C. (2010, May). Examining the use of Twitter in sport: A content analysis of professional athlete tweets. Presented at the annual North American Society for Sport Management, Tampa, FL. *International Journal of Sport Communication,* in press.

Hessert, K. (2009). Five secrets of unlocking the power of Twitter for college sports. College Sports Information Directors of America. Retrieved November 19, 2010, from http://www.cosida.com/documents/2009/2/19/Secrets_of_Unlocking_Power_of_Twitter.pdf

Internet World Stats (2010). Internet usage statistics: The big picture. Retrieved from http://www.internetworldstats.com/stats.htm

Kruse, M. (2009). For SEC, tech-savvy fans might be biggest threats to media exclusivity. *St. Petersburg Times*. Retrieved November 19, 2010, from http://www.tampabay.com/news/science/personaltech/for-sec-tech-savvy-fans-might-be-biggest-threats-to-media-exclusivity/1027680

Laudon, K. C., & Guercio Traver, C. (2009). *E-commerce* (5th ed.). Upper Saddle River, NJ: Pearson Prentice Hall.

McClusky, M. (2010). Athletes confused by Olympic social media rules. *Wired*. Retrieved November 19, 2010, from http://www.wired.com/epicenter/2010/02/athletes-confused-by-olympic-social-media-rules/

Nielsen (2009). Global faces and networked places: A Nielsen report on social networking's new global footprint. Retrieved November 19, 2010, from http://blog.nielsen.com/nielsenwire/wp-content/uploads/2009/03/nielsen_globalfaces_mar09.pdf

O'Neil, N. (2010). World's most valuable soccer team doesn't get social media. *Social Times*. Retrieved November 19, 2010, from http://www.socialtimes.com/2010/01/manchester-united-fail/

Qualman, E. (2009, August 10). Social media: Fad or revolution. SearchEngineWatch.com. Retrieved November 19, 2010, from http://searchenginewatch.com/3634651

Reynolds, T. (2007, March 9). USC player in trouble over "racist" Facebook. Retrieved on December 16, 2010, from http://mycrimespace.com/2007/03/09/usc-player-in-trouble-over-racist-facebook/

SportsBusiness Journal (2009, November 9). Ticketing. Going paperless. Retrieved November 19, 2010, from http://www.sportsbusinessjournal.com/article/63994

Stamm, D. (2009, March 10). Report: Eagles fire employee over Facebook vent. Retrieved November 19, 2010, from http://www.nbcphiladelphia.com/news/sports/Report-Eagles-Fire-Employee-Over-Facebook-Vent.html

TechCrunch (2008, December 31). Top social media sites of 2008. Retrieved from http://www.techcrunch.com/2008/12/31/top-social-media-sites-of-2008-facebook-still-rising/

Technorati (2009). State of the blogosphere 2009. Retrieved November 19, 2010, from http://technorati.com/blogging/feature/state-of-the-blogosphere-2009/

The Future Buzz (2009). Social media, Web 2.0, and Internet stats. Retrieved November 19, 2010, from http://thefuturebuzz.com/2009/01/12/social-media-web-20-internet-numbers-stats/

United States Census Bureau (2009). Media usage and consumer spending: 2001 to 2011. Retrieved November 19, 2010, from http://www.census.gov/compendia/statab/2009/tables/09s1089.pdf

Van den Poel, D., & Leunis, J. (1999). Consumer acceptance of the Internet as a channel of distribution. *Journal of Business Research, 45*, 249–256.

CHAPTER 19

The Sporting Goods and Licensed Products Industries

Dan Covell and Mary A. Hums

■ INTRODUCTION

This chapter presents information on two related segments of the sport industry: sporting goods and licensed products. According to Hardy (1997), an analysis of sport products reveals its triple commodity nature: the activity or game form, the service, and the goods. Hardy defines **sporting goods** as the physical objects necessary for the game form. The development and sale of such goods serve as the focus of this chapter. The sporting goods industry has a long history, and the segment encompasses equipment, apparel, and footwear. **Licensed products**, those items of clothing or products bearing the name or logo of a popular collegiate or professional sport team, have been around for a comparatively short period of time and constitute a specialized subset of the sporting

goods industry. Both of these areas produce revenues in the billions of U.S. dollars and euros worldwide and are a major source of domestic revenue for major sport properties (Adams, 2003).

So how do these areas impact sport organizations? Consider that in 2006, the University of Oregon, with assistance from uniform supplier Nike, unveiled for its football team a redesign of game uniform helmets (green or white), jerseys, pants and socks (green, black, yellow, or white), and shoes (black or white) that would allow it 384 different combinations. The redesign was the program's fourth over the previous ten years. During the 2010 season, which saw Oregon lose to Auburn University for the BCS Championship on a last-second field goal, the Ducks sported a different uniform for every game. Nike's creative director for apparel stated that Nike was always presenting Oregon with innovations and ideas, some of which Oregon would embrace, while saying "no" to others regardless of protests and negative reviews of many fans and alumni. Of the color schemes, Nike calls the yellow color "lightning yellow," but critical wags called it "jaundiced," "urine," or "banana peel" (Murphy, 2003; Taylor, 2003b).

Initially, then-head coach Mike Bellotti allowed team seniors to decide on what combination would be worn for each game, but for the 2006 season he and his equipment manager made the call, because, as Bellotti said, "to get 22 guys to agree on something is tough enough. I have trouble myself" (McCarthy & Whiteside, 2006, p. 1C). Nike claims the new uniforms are 28% lighter and help wick away moisture. Nike has partnered with Oregon on this initiative in large part due to the influence of Nike founder Phil Knight, a graduate of the school and former track athlete there. Knight has also donated millions to the school and has a significant impact on how the athletic department is managed. Knight regularly talks with university officials and coaches, dons a headset at football games to listen to coaches' play-calling, and is allowed to roam the sidelines (Fain, 2007).

So why 384 combinations, when some criticize the colors, designs, and the fact that 384 combinations is hardly uniform? Belotti claims the garb draws national attention (which it did, through the various media reports consulted for this citation) and helps draw recruits. To this point, said Bellotti, "My wife hated it, but my players loved it. I guess you know who won that one" (Taylor, 2003a, p. 54). And speaking of getting attention, women's lingerie company Victoria's Secret introduced a new line of officially licensed products with college logos on tank tops, sweats, and underwear. At its introduction, 32 schools were part of the line, including the University of California at Berkeley, Harvard University, the University of Nebraska, and Penn State University. Nebraska spokesperson Kelly

Bartling said of the items, "Looking at the garments, everything is cute, and they portray the Big Red spirit in a totally unobjectionable way ... Certainly undergarments are things everyone needs to wear" (Moser, 2008, p. A4).

The unveiling of the new Ducks multifaceted uniform combinations and Victoria Secret's new lines are just examples of the market impact of sporting goods and licensed products. The following statistics provide a larger sense of the revenues associated with these segments.

- Total outdoor sporting goods products year-to-date sales through March 2010 rose to $1.17 billion, up 11.7% from 2009. Sales in outdoor chains like Cabela's were up 14% over March 2009.
- With double-digit growth in March 2010 pushing sales to $130.9 million, athletic apparel 2010 year-to-date sales rose 15.1% to $338 million. The category covers athletic sportswear, licensed apparel, outerwear, and base layers.

With sales of $74.2 million in March 2010, running products year-to-date sales rose 14.8% to $180.8 million. Footwear, with 74% of total sales, maintained the positive trends seen in previous months' sales ("Topline," 2010). The remainder of this chapter examines the specifics of these related segments.

■ HISTORY

Sporting Goods

The French economic philosopher J. B. Say (1964) created the term **entrepreneur** to describe those who created ideas for better uses of existing technology, and the early sporting goods industry in the United States is replete with entrepreneurial innovation. As early as 1811, George Tryon, a gunsmith, began to carve out a niche with people interested in sport. After expanding into the fishing tackle business, Tryon's company became a major wholesaler of sporting goods east of the Mississippi River. In the late 1840s and 1850s, Michael Phelan and John Brunswick each established production of billiards equipment. Brunswick, a Swiss immigrant, established billiard parlors across the country, and by 1884 had merged with his two largest competitors, creating a $1.5 million operation that was larger than all of its competitors combined. The company moved into bowling in the 1890s. Hillerich and Bradsby began in 1859 as a wood-turning shop in Louisville and expanded to baseball bat production in 1884. Former professional baseball player George Wright, along with partner H. A. Ditson, operated Wright and Ditson beginning in the late 1880s. In 1888, Rawlings began operations in St. Louis, promoting itself as offering a "full-line emporium" of all sporting goods (Funding Universe, n.d.; Hardy, 1995).

But it was Albert G. Spalding who typified the early sporting goods entrepreneur. Spalding, a standout professional baseball pitcher in the late nineteenth century, parlayed his baseball reputation and a loan of $800 to create a sporting goods manufacturing giant based on selling to the expanding middle class in the United States. While also owning the Chicago White Stockings of the National League, Spalding adopted technological advances to manufacture bats, baseballs, gloves, uniforms, golf clubs, bicycles, hunting goods, and football equipment (Levine, 1985). Many other manufacturers also focused on sporting goods production, but Spalding understood that he had to create and foster the markets for these products as the newly affluent middle class sought to find uses for their leisure time. Spalding produced guides on how to play and exercise, promoted grassroots sport competitions, and gained credibility with consumers by claiming official supplier status with baseball's National League. Spalding also

created a profitable distribution system in which the company sold directly to retailers at a set price with the guarantee retailers would sell at a price that Spalding set. This technique created stable markets for Spalding goods and eliminated price cutting at the retail level (Levine, 1985). Spalding's connection with the National League helped establish the value of endorsements and licensing connections, which would become industry staples.

The twentieth century saw continued developments in the industry as consumer demands continued to grow. In 1903, Harvard football coach Bill Reid devoted many pages in his diary to his efforts working with local merchants to design and manufacture pads to protect his players (Smith, 1994). The Sporting Goods Manufacturers Association (SGMA) was founded in 1906 as intercollegiate football leaders and athletic equipment manufacturers sought to make the sport safer and less violent. In the 1920s a number of famous sport personalities

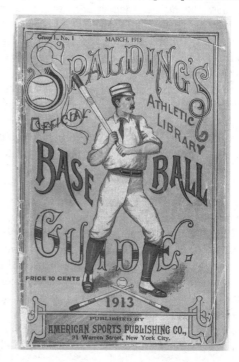

began to endorse sporting goods products, including Knute Rockne, Honus Wagner, and Nap Lajoie. During this time, adidas established a strong international presence. Founded in the 1920s by Adolph "Adi" Dassler (from whose name the company name would derive) from a family shoe business, the firm made strong inroads through producing soccer cleats and track spikes. Dassler established his product in part by convincing U.S. track Olympian Jesse Owens to wear his spikes in the 1936 Berlin Summer Olympic Games. Adi's brother, Rudolf, would later go on to found Puma after a falling out between the two brothers. The two companies would compete for international market share for the remainder of the century, with adidas ultimately prevailing, in part through its close partnership with FIFA (Fédération Internationale de Football Association), soccer's international governing body (Smit, 2008). In the 1940s there was a retrenchment in spending on sporting goods, but after the Korean War in the 1950s, as prosperity returned to the United States, spending on sporting goods increased. Tennis greats Fred Perry and Jean Rene Lacoste (Izod) helped launch the fashion-sportswear segment in the 1950s. In the 1960s, imported products arrived in greater numbers in the U.S. market, especially Japanese baseball products. The 1970s also brought increased recognition of product liability and the injuries associated with sports equipment. This recognition engendered increased concern for risk management by teachers, coaches, and administrators. As the industry moved through the 1980s and 1990s, there was continuing growth as products and consumer demographics became more diverse (O'Brien, 2002).

In the 1980s and 1990s, the industry experienced the emergence of several industry giants, most notably Nike and Reebok. Nike, the brainchild of Phil Knight, began as an offshoot of Knight's original Blue Ribbon Sports company. The Nike name came from one of Knight's colleagues in 1971. By 1980, Nike had pulled in $269 million and replaced adidas as the United States' top sneaker maker. Although Nike temporarily lost its top ranking to Reebok in 1986, the advent of the "Air Jordan" and "Bo Knows" marketing campaigns in the late 1980s propelled Nike back to the top, and Nike was a $2 billion company by 1990 (Katz, 1993). During the second quarter of fiscal year 2007 (September 1, 2006, to November 30, 2006), Nike claimed revenues of $3.8 billion ($1.4 billion in the United States), with a net income of $325.6 million. By the end of 2009, net sales had reached $19.1 billion (although the period's severe global economic downturn forced the company to lay off 1,700 employees) (Horovitz, 2009). Adidas countered Nike's ascendance in 2005 when it purchased Reebok for $3.8 billion, in part to gain control over Reebok's licensing agreements with the National Football League (NFL) and the National Basketball Association (NBA) (Smit, 2008).

Licensed Products

Baseball historian Warren Goldstein (1989) noted that many early baseball teams (e.g., the Cincinnati Red Stockings in 1869) got their names from their distinctive apparel. Uniforms created a sense of apartness and defined who was a player and who was not. Davis (1992) commented that clothing styles are a transmitted code that can impart meanings of identity, gender, status, and sexuality. Licensed apparel communicates on each of these levels and is based on the notion that fans will purchase goods to draw them closer to their beloved organizations and athletes. Writer Bill Simmons describes the early days of buying player-specific licensed products this way: "Fans bought them because they wanted to dress like players on the team. Not only were we supporting our guys, but the player we chose became an expression of sorts" (2004, p. 12).

The industry was slow to realize the financial potential of such connections. In 1924, while walking past shops down Fifth Avenue in Manhattan, sportswriter Francis Wallace observed displays and neckties in the colors of what he termed the aristocracy of the gridiron: Army, Harvard, Notre Dame, Princeton, and Yale. In 1947 University of Oregon Athletic Director Leo Harris and Walt Disney agreed to allow Oregon to use Disney's Donald Duck image for the university's mascot. While these were some early steps toward the development of licensable properties, the University of California–Los Angeles (UCLA) is generally credited with being the first school to enter into a licensing agreement with a manufacturer when its school bookstore granted a license to a watch manufacturer in 1973. The National Collegiate Athletic Association (NCAA) formed its properties division to license championship merchandise in 1975, but it does not administer licensing programs for member schools. Significant revenue growth began in the late 1980s, when the University of Notre Dame, which began its licensing program in 1983, experienced growth of 375% from 1988 to 1989. Collegiate licensed product sales totaled $100 million in the early 1980s. In 1995, sales reached $2.5 billion, and 10 years later sales were estimated at $2.7 billion (Collegiate Licensing Company, 2005). The peak for licensed sales for major college and pro licensed products was 1996, with sales of $13.8 billion. That statistic had slipped to $11.8 billion by 2001 (Sperber, 1993; Nichols, 1995; Plata, 1996; Hiestand, 2002). SportsMedia (2010) reported the following numbers for different sport properties: MLB, $2.5 billion; NBA, $2.5 billion; NFL, $3.0 billion; NHL, $1.0 billion; and college sport, $2.7 billion.

The licensing programs in professional sport leagues are administered by a for-profit branch of each league, generally referred to as a **properties division**. Properties divisions approve licensees, police trademark infringement, and distribute licensing revenues equally among league franchises. Properties divisions usually handle marketing and sponsorship efforts as well. The NFL was the first professional league to develop a properties component in 1963, under the leadership of then-commissioner Alvin "Pete" Rozelle. The first license was granted to Sport Specialties. David Warsaw, the founder of the company, had worked with Chicago Bears owner George Halas in the 1930s in selling Bears merchandise and later developed licensing agreements with the Los Angeles Dodgers and the then–Los Angeles Rams ("Sports Merchandising," 1996). By the late 1970s, each NFL team's licensing share was believed to be nearly half a million dollars annually.

Major League Baseball (MLB) followed with the creation of its properties division (MLB Properties) in 1966, although many teams that had strong local sales were reluctant to give up their licensing rights to the league. Indeed, some teams were loathe to share their marks with licensees because of their perceptions that such actions would cheapen the product. George Weiss, general manager of the New York Yankees, recoiled at the notion of licensing agreements, saying, "Do you think I want every kid in this city walking around with a Yankees cap?" National Hockey League (NHL) Enterprises

began formal league-governed licensing in 1969, and NBA Properties initiated activities in 1982 (Helyar, 1994; Lipsey, 1996).

Players associations also administer licensing programs. The Major League Baseball Players Association (MLBPA) was the first to enter into such an agreement when then Executive Director Marvin Miller entered into a two-year, $120,000 pact with Coca-Cola in the late 1960s to permitting the beverage manufacturer to put players' likenesses on bottle caps. Such royalties helped fund the emerging union's organizing activities. Miller also negotiated a comprehensive agreement with trading card manufacturer Topps Company in 1968. Topps was permitted to continue manufacturing trading cards bearing player likenesses for double the player's previous yearly fees (from $125 to $250), and it paid the union 8% on annual sales up to $4 million and 10% on all subsequent sales. In the first year, the contract earned the MLBPA $320,000 (Helyar, 1994).

In September 2000, the NFL Players Association (NFLPA) and the NFL entered into a unique partnership that provides group licensing rights of NFL players to NFL sponsors. In addition, through this program, NFL Players provides numerous licensing and marketing services to companies. Any program utilizing six or more NFL players in conjunction with consumer products, marketing, advertising, or sales initiatives requires a license from NFL Players. NFL Players works with more than 65 licensees whose products include trading cards, video games, apparel, and collectibles ("NFL Players," 2010).

■ INDUSTRY STRUCTURE

Sporting Goods

The Sporting Goods Manufacturers Association (SGMA), an industry trade association (see below), defines the sporting goods industry as in-

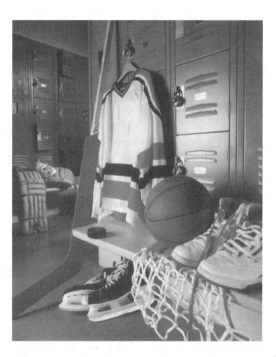

cluding manufacturers of sporting goods equipment, athletic footwear, and sports apparel as well as manufacturers of accessory items to the sport and recreation market. **Sporting goods equipment** includes fitness products as well as sport-specific products for golf, soccer, tennis, in-line skating, and so on. In recent years, participation rates in sport and physical activities have remained constant, as have accompanying sales of sporting goods equipment. The second segment is athletic footwear. **Athletic footwear** is defined as branded and unbranded athletic shoes for casual wear or active usage, outdoor/hiking sports boots, and sport sandals. The third segment is sports apparel. Broadly defined, **sports apparel** encompasses garments which are designed for, or which could be used in, active sports (SGMA, 2002a, 2002b).

■ SPORTING GOODS TRADE ASSOCIATIONS

Within the industry, there are a number of **trade associations** for sporting goods professionals.

One of these is the previously mentioned SGMA. The SGMA is the trade association for manufacturers, producers, and distributors of sports apparel, athletic footwear, and sporting goods equipment, serving more than 1,000 sporting goods manufacturers, retailers, and marketers in the sports products industry, and representing over 3,000 business locations, plants and distribution centers. According to the SGMA, the industry employs more than 375,000 people, and generates $60 billion in domestic revenue and $15 billion in international revenue (wholesale) ("About SGMA," 2010).

Licensing

The manufacturers of licensed products, the **licensees**, include well-known sport-product companies such as adidas, Reebok, and Nike; prominent electronics and video game manufacturers Electronic Arts and Sony; and smaller firms such as Artcarved (jewelry), Mead (stationery), and Topps (trading cards and memorabilia). Licensees pay teams and leagues, the **licensors**, for the right to manufacture products bearing team and school names, nicknames, colors, and logos. If these names and logos are registered with the U.S. Patent and Trademark Office, they are referred to as **trademarks**. A trademark is defined under the Federal Trademark Act of 1946, commonly referred to as the Lanham Act, as "any word, name, symbol, or device or combination thereof adopted and used by a manufacturer or merchant to identify his goods and distinguish them from those manufactured or sold by others." The law defines trademark infringement as the reproduction, counterfeiting, copying, or imitation in commerce of a registered mark, and bars companies that do not pay for the right to use these trademarks from manufacturing products bearing those marks (Lanham Act, 15 U.S.C. §§ 1051–1127, 1946).

Licensing enables schools and teams to generate brand recognition and interest and to increase revenues with very little financial risk. The licensees assume the risk by manufacturing the product, then pay a fee to the licensor, called a **royalty**, for the use of specific trademarks on specific products. Royalty fees generally range from 4% (for toys and games) to 20% (for trading cards and video games) and are based on gross sales at wholesale costs. Apparel royalties range from 11% for on-field items to 15% for player-identified items (Adams, 2003). Wholesale costs are those paid by the retailer, not the price paid by consumers. Licensees use the established images and popularity of sport teams to boost their sales.

Collegiate Sport

Some NCAA Division I schools administer their own licensing programs. The benefit of self-maintenance is that schools can retain a greater portion of sales revenues. The remainder of Division I Bowl Subdivision schools, like the smaller pro leagues and many Championship Subdivision schools, enlist the services of independent licensing companies to manage their programs. The Collegiate Licensing Company (CLC), formed in 1981, and recently purchased by sport marketing company IMG (formerly International Marketing Group) and now known as IMG College, articulates licensing agreements on behalf of approximately 200 colleges and universities, bowls, conferences, the Heisman Trophy, and the NCAA as their independent licensing company. Client colleges pay a portion of the royalties (usually 50%) to CLC for their efforts. According to Pat Battle, Senior Corporate Vice President of IMG College, by 2008 the retail market for collegiate merchandise had grown to more than $3.5 billion in annual sales, with apparel accounting for 62%, with less than 20% of the sales now taking place on college campuses. Non-apparel, which continues to close the gap each year, is led by the college market's number one licensee Electronic Arts

(EA). The EA Sports NCAA Football video game has become the number two selling sports game in North America (Covell & Barr, 2010).

■ CAREER OPPORTUNITIES

A number of career opportunities exist in these segments, ranging from entrepreneurs with an idea for a specific product or store to employment with firms such as Callaway, Russell, Under Armour, or New Balance. There are also sporting goods stores, which include locally owned single-unit stores, large chains such as Champs Sports, Dick's, or Academy Sports, and niche retailers such as Lids (which specializes in sales of licensed and branded headwear). The potential career opportunities in the licensing industry include employment with league licensing departments, collegiate licensing offices, and licensees as well as with retail sales outlets and product manufacturers.

Large companies such as footwear and apparel manufacturer New Balance are composed of divisions for each product line, such as basketball, tennis, cross-training/fitness, and children. New Balance has created a niche in the highly competitive footwear market by providing customers with footwear with extensive width sizing. It has done this, the company states, through a commitment to domestic manufacturing (the company employs more than 4,000 workers and maintains manufacturing facilities in Massachusetts and Maine) and leadership in technological innovation. In 2004, the company acquired lacrosse equipment manufacturer Warrior, and by 2006 the company reported worldwide sales of $1.55 billion (New Balance, 2008). New Balance has staff positions in manufacturing, research and development, sales and marketing, and promotions.

Sporting goods stores operate on many levels. Locally owned specialty retailers operate sporting goods stores in the traditional model

of a family-owned and operated store located for a number of years in the same town. These stores offer a somewhat limited variety of different types of sporting goods depending on the location. Some have more than one location. Consider the various specialty running shoe stores across the United States such as Metro Run & Walk (three stores in the Washington, DC area), soundRunner With No Boundaries (two stores in southern Connecticut), and Super Runners Shops in New York City and Long Island. According to industry surveys, the 700 specialty running stores in the United States account for about $700 million a year in sales. Gary Muhrcke of Super Runners says his business survives in the face of competition from online running shoe retailers like Road Runner Sports and larger chains like Fleet Feet because of personal service. "I can't see the shape of a person's foot over the phone. I can't look at a person's body structure or size or whether they're bowlegged over the Internet. The basic reason why we're still here—we're needed." Julie Francis of soundRunner notes that her stores survive because of running shoe sales (which account for 60% of all store sales), the fact that they can accommodate customer segments like fitness walkers and runners, not just elite runners, and that these stores are more involved in the communities in which they are located, sponsoring races, clinics, medical referrals, and social networking. Manufacturers also like the specialty stores, because, according to Jim Weber of Brooks, which places 80% of its product in such stores, "It's introducing our brand to people a pair of feet at a time, and that usually happens in specialty stores ... No one does it better than a specialty store" (Spiegel, 2008, p. C6).

The larger chain stores tend to offer a wider selection of products. Some of these stores, such as Champs or Lady Foot Locker, are usually located in malls, where people stop in if they go to the mall to shop. Others, such as Academy

Sports and Dick's, are freestanding "big box" stores considered a final destination for shoppers. As opposed to the mall stores, where people stop in if they are shopping at the mall, people go to a Dick's with the intention of buying sporting goods and nothing else. Each of these stores needs sales staff as well as managers who oversee the financial, marketing, and personnel aspects of the store. Larger chains need store managers as well as people to work on the corporate level. Depending on the size of a store, buyers may be needed to make decisions about which products to stock in the upcoming seasons. Buyers, the people who deal directly with the sporting goods companies, often attend events such as the Super Show or the World Sports Expo to see which new products will be on the market in the approaching year and place their store orders accordingly.

■ APPLICATION OF KEY PRINCIPLES

Management

As long as society, the economy, and technology remain somewhat stable or change only slowly, management has time to adjust to maintain and improve performance. However, rapid change is the rule in the sporting goods and licensed products industries, and industry managers face new challenges brought on by a very fluid environment. These challenges include intense competition and new performance standards that every management team must now achieve. These standards include competition, quality, speed and flexibility, innovation, and sustainable growth (Covell, Walker, Siciliano, & Hess, 2007).

Innovation is a key performance standard affecting sporting goods and licensed products. According to industry experts, it is a critical factor for survival, let alone success. As noted earlier, entrepreneurs such as Albert Spalding and John Brunswick significantly impacted these

industries by creating new products and services to meet the needs and wants of consumers. This trend continues today through the efforts of individuals such as Kevin Plank, the founder of Under Armour, and James Smith Moore, creator of "Jimmy Kicks," an online company that produces limited edition sneakers.

As a running back and business major at the University of Maryland in 1995, Plank saw teammates suffer from heat stress during practice and wondered whether their sweat-soaked T-shirts contributed to their maladies, so he developed a performance undershirt that wicked moisture away from the skin. Plank could not convince large manufacturers to back him, so he took to selling directly to team equipment managers out of the trunk of his car (much like Phil Knight first did with Blue Ribbon Sports). In 1996, he booked $17,000 in sales, and after establishing official supplier agreements with MLB, NHL, and the U.S. Ski Team (like Spalding had with MLB over a century before), sales topped $100 million in 2003 (Hiestand, 2003). By 2008, Under Armour launched its first line of running shoes, and achieved annual earnings of $765 million (McCarthy, 2008). Total sales revenue topped the $1 billion mark in 2010 (Sharrow, 2011).

Described by writer Pamela Ryckman as "a hustler," Moore, the son of a single mother who grew up on the east side of Detroit, Michigan, started a lizard breeding business at age 15, selling more than 500 hatchlings online for as much as $80 a piece. One year later, when a local store ran out of a popular Nike shoe, he hired a manufacturer in China to supply him with knockoffs (shoes that looked like the Nikes but were not authentic), which he then sold for as much as $200 a pair on his own Web site and other online auction sites. Nike soon sent him a cease-and-desist letter, but by then Moore had made $14,000 (Ryckman, 2010, p. B6).

Moore got Jimmy Kicks off the ground with the support of Bizdom U, founded in 2006 by

Cleveland Cavaliers owner Dan Gilbert to aid young entrepreneurs. The Detroit-based program gives enrollees training, technical support and a $1,500-a-month living stipend to foster their ideas in exchange for labor (e.g., to teach sales and marketing, students sell memberships to the Detroit Zoo). Bizdom U also offers start-up grants for those with promising business plans. Moore created a Web site that produces limited-edition hip-hop style–influenced sneakers. Anyone can log on to the site and create blueprints for original shoes, and users vote on the designs. Winners are named quarterly (earning them $500), and the designs are manufactured in numbered pairs and sold on the site for $79.99, more than four times the cost of production. Moore carries no inventory, and the shoes are sent directly to buyers from manufacturers overseas (Ryckman, 2010).

Marketing

■ ENDORSEMENTS

The heart of the sporting goods industry, as Albert Spalding first demonstrated, is the concept that expert usage helps overcome the risk factors that customers assess when deciding on a purchase. Spalding sold consumers on the fact that his ball was the one used by the best baseball league in the world, conveying to buyers that if it was good enough for the best, it was good enough for them. The concept of endorsements in sport was born.

Today, this concept continues. Most athletic footwear companies sink huge investments into star athletes (e.g., Michael Jordan and "Air Jordan"). The trend is slightly different in certain niche sports, like the so-called board (skateboard, snowboard, surfing) sports. The companies manufacturing products for these sports (an $11 billion industry) have thwarted entry from mainstream giants like Nike, which has usually gained entrée to most any mar-

ket it has sought to capture. Some companies hinder themselves trying to get in the door, as did PacSun (a retailer of board sports apparel with 850 locations in malls across the United States) when it recently ran print ads in skateboarding magazines featuring a skateboard with the trucks (axels) on backwards. Consider the case of Grenade, a glove and outwear company founded in 2000 by brothers Danny (a two-time Olympic silver medal winner in the snowboard half-pipe) and Matt Kass (himself an ex-pro snowboarder). Since its founding, the company's sales have doubled each year, topping $6.2 million in 2006. While its revenues are nowhere near Nike's, the company succeeds because of its image, described by writer Matt Higgins as "rider-owned, exclusive, with an iconoclast's bent" (2006, p. C13). Danny Kass describes his company this way: "We were all in our early 20s and teens when this started. It was something that made us stand apart. We didn't want to do what other companies were doing. A lot of companies can't figure out the formula for our success. What we have is organic" (Higgins, 2006, p. C13). The Kass's mother, Joanne, describes the brothers' partnership this way: "Matt was the entrepreneur, the visionary. Danny was the entertainer," as evidenced when Matt collected 50 cents apiece from neighborhood kids who came to watch Danny skate on their backyard ramp (Roenigk, 2007, p. 62). Matt was looking to start his own business in 2000 because "we wanted to get more from snowboarding than just riding for people and collecting paychecks." Danny has sponsorships from Gnu Snowboards and Quicksilver, and as he put it, "we didn't want to do something that would conflict with our sponsors. Gloves made sense." With funding from Danny's contest earnings and Matt's real estate investments, they started the company, operating out of a renovated gas station in June Lake, California. By 2004 the company had expanded into outwear, videos, and t-shirts, seeking to hit $15 million in sales by 2012. Of the company's current position, writer Alyssa Roenigk commented, "gloves remain the company's signature product—Grenade thrives more on aesthetics than technology, with gloves designed by artists and riders" (2007, p. 64, 66).

Bob Klein, a former professional snowboarder and now an agent, captured the endorsement credibility link, "He's such an icon. When he wears the newest product, it becomes popular instantly. It's hard to top that marketing." Kass has resisted selling the business to the industry giants (like he did with Quicksilver in 2005) because "it's hard to get [credibility]. When you lose it, you can get it back" (Higgins, 2006, p. C13). The company initially developed some of its image at the 2001 X Games in Aspen through a "guerilla" marketing campaign, using spray paint and stencils to tag trees, snowboards, and halfpipe walls. It would later include a stencil in glove packs to encourage buyers to do the same, and sponsored a contest in 2004, awarding prizes to those who submitted evidence of innovative stenciling. Photos of stenciled police cars and a wall at the Kass's former high school in New Jersey soon rolled in. After a visit from local police to their California offices, the company stopped shipping the stencils. The company also got a call from Federal Homeland Security officials because of its name. "They thought we were a grassroots (terrorist) movement," said Matt (Roenigk, 2007, p. 66).

The Challenges of Creating a Brand

Throughout the chapter we have discussed some of the iconic sport figures who influenced the sporting goods and licensed product industries. Most of the names are familiar to you and others across the globe. But what about Li-Ning? Doesn't ring a bell? Li-Ning, a male gymnast, is described by writer Joe Nocera as "a Michael Jordanesque figure" in his home country of China, having won three gold medals in the 1984 Los Angeles Summer Olympic Games.

Six years later, he used his image to found an eponymous athletic footwear company. In 2008, the company generated $700 million a year in revenues. Nocera describes a visit to the company's headquarters this way:

Almost everything about Li-Ning feels like your basic modern sneaker company: the airy, wide-open campus; the casually dressed young executives bustling about; the rows of basketball and tennis courts under construction; the huge posters of Chinese Olympians and other athletes who have endorsed Li-Ning shoes and clothing like the tennis player Ivan Ljubicic and, believe it or not, Shaquille O'Neal (2008, p. B1).

The company has even adopted a positioning statement (a.k.a., slogan) "Anything is possible," seeming like a corrected Chinese translation of adidas's grammatically off-kilter "Impossible is nothing," and a logo that, according to Nocera, looks like Nike's swoosh "except with a checkmark stuck at the front of it." In addition, the Shaq figure stamped on his branded line of Li-Ning shoes (costing $120) looked to Nocera "an awful lot like Nike's Air Jordan figure" (2008, p. B8). Those who have seen Shaq lately know that to believe the play of the two is equal would truly mean that "Anything is possible."

According to chief operations officer (COO), Guo Jianxin, of Li Ning (China), by 2013 the company wants to achieve revenues of $2 billion, with 20% of that coming from international sales (in 2008, only 1% came from outside China). "But to get there, Li-Ning will have to become a brand like Nike or adidas" (Nocera, 2008, p. B8). But what does that mean? A **brand's image** is defined as "the cumulative impact of all the associations with a particular brand" (Keller, 1998, p. 93), and is formed for sport organizations by a collection of elements that can include logos, players, traditions, facilities, rivalries, and ownership (Gladden, 2007). Li-Ning may have positive scores on all of these factors for Chinese consumers, but what about for people in the United States? Or Brazil, Germany, or South Africa?

Nocera writes:

It's easy when you live in the West to take brands–their power, their ability to conjure up feelings of status among consumers, the loyalty they can generate–completely for granted ... But go to China, and you get a whole new appreciation for brands ... What is the car of choice in China if you have some money? Surprisingly, an Audi. Why? Because Audi got (there) early and did the best job among foreign car manufacturers of persuading the Chinese that an Audi is a symbol that you've made it ... There is a powerful sense among Chinese consumers that domestic brands are inferior–and a distinct lack of confidence among Chinese companies in the allure of their own brands (2008, p. B8).

This has been a problem for Li-Ning because its domestic market share has dropped to third against Nike and adidas since the late 1990s when each were first allowed to sell products in China. So if Chinese companies like Li-Ning have trouble connecting with their own consumers against established foreign brands, how will they compete against these brands in international markets? Li-Ning officials hired a branding consultant to help with its' branding challenges. "I said to the Li-Ning executives, 'What does it mean to you when you wear a Li-Ning shoe?'" trying to show them that branding wasn't just about copying Nike, but to create a distinct identity. "They couldn't define it," the consultant said (Nocera, 2008, p. B8). So for the time being, the company has put its international plans on hold, focusing instead on domestic markets in cities that Nike and adidas haven't penetrated with shoes that have a patriotic Chinese focus (one new shoe is named for Lei Feng, a famous Chinese soldier glorified by the Chinese gov-

ernment after his death in 1962 (allegedly the soldier had kept a diary which showed how he had been inspired by Communist party head Mao Tse-Tung to do good deeds and to hate "class enemies") (Chang, 2006; Nocera, 2008). However, it won't be easy, because industry giant Nike is also setting its sights on the Chinese market, investing $1.5 billion in marketing there in 2009, with plans to double or triple that statistic in 2010. Of these efforts, Nike CEO Mark Parker stated, "No matter how much you're investing (in China), it's not enough" (Horovitz, 2009, p. 2B).

Ethics

■ MANUFACTURER AND LICENSEE CONDUCT

One of the most basic forms of global involvement occurs when a business turns to a foreign company to manufacture one or more of its products. This practice is called **global sourcing** because the company turns to whatever manufacturer or source around the world will most efficiently produce its products. Companies that engage in global sourcing take advantage of manufacturing expertise or lower wage rates in foreign countries, and then sell their products either just in their home market or in markets around the world. Global sourcing is common in the clothing and footwear industries, for example, where companies in countries such as Mexico, China, and Malaysia have much lower production costs because workers are paid at much lower wage rates than workers in the United States. The foreign producer or source manufactures the product to a particular company's specifications and then attaches the company's label or logo to the product. Nike, Reebok, Benetton, and Banana Republic are examples of companies that engage in a great deal of global sourcing. Many sport apparel and shoe manufacturers have come under fire for paying unfairly low wages and having unsafe working conditions in their overseas operations, particularly in Asian nations. Reports indicated, for example, that Nike was paying workers in Indonesian plants $1.35 per day (Katz, 1993). Wages have not risen greatly over the years; some factories in India that produce Nike products pay $2.75 per day (Worker Rights Consortium, 2010). Nike answered these charges with a report issued by Andrew Young, spokesperson for GoodWorks International. After six months of visiting 12 Asian factories and interviewing workers in Indonesia, China, and Vietnam about labor practices, Young concluded, "It is my sincere belief that Nike is doing a good job ... but can and should do better" (Nike, 2002, p. 1).

An additional factor that can potentially complicate such apparel agreements is the behavior of licensees, specifically with manufacturing products in factories with poor working conditions. We learned above of the importance of licensed products in terms of revenues and branding, but schools can incur negative reactions from consumers and interest groups should the companies with which they sign licensing agreements have a history of exploiting workers. Because of the mission and nature of education environments, colleges and universities have been particularly vulnerable to criticism on this score, especially from student-run groups on their own campuses. Recently, the United Students Against Sweatshops, a national coalition of students critical of sweatshop factory conditions, lobbied to convince 96 schools (including Columbia University, the University of Michigan, the University of North Carolina, and Stanford University) to end or suspend licensing agreements (some as valuable as $1 million in sales) with Russell Athletic (owned by parent company Fruit of the Loom) after the company closed a factory in Honduras when its workers unionized, leaving 1,200 jobless. As a result of the actions, Russell agreed to rehire the workers and not to fight unionization efforts in its seven other Honduran factories, in response to which Mel

Tenen, who oversees licensing agreements at the University of Miami (Florida)—the first school to end its agreement with Russell—commented, "It's not often that a major licensee will take such a necessary and drastic step to correct the injustices that affected its workers" (Greenhouse, 2009, p. B4). The victory for the movement came after a decade of convincing multiple schools to adopt codes of conduct for their licensees. Scott Nova, executive director of the Workers Rights Consortium, to which more than 170 schools belong, sees the move as a "maturation of the universities' codes of conduct," and that schools now could exercise their ability to influence the actions of companies and licensees. The union president at the closed plant in Honduras praised the actions of the student groups, stating, "For us, it was very important to receive the support of the universities. We are impressed by the social consciousness of the students in the United States" (Greenhouse, 2009, p. B4).

Finance

■ REVIVING A FLAGGING SEGMENT

Probably the most venerated of all licensed products is the trading card. Millions of youths in the United States grew up collecting cards bearing the likenesses and statistics of their favorite baseball and other sports stars. Author Josh Wilker wrote of his youthful devotion to collecting cards growing up in rural Vermont in the mid-1970s in these terms:

> For a long time, I knew how to find happiness. All I needed was a quarter. I lived in the country, far away from almost everything ... Far away from clear television signals. Far away from my favorite place in the world, where the baseball team I loved played its games ... But I was close enough to one thing. If I had a quarter, I could walk a

half-mile to the general store and buy a pack of baseball cards (2010, p. 7).

Wilker would wait until he got home to his room to open the newly purchased pack, and recalled the experience as:

the boundless possibilities in that slim moment when I levered my fingernail below the flap of an unopened pack ... And in the tiny clicking sound of the flap disconnecting. And in the first strong whiff of gum. And in the first glimpse of some unidentifiable piece of a card, a swatch of grass in the photo on the front, a row of numbers on the back ... I looked for the first time directly at a brand-new card and felt the sunshine coming up from it as if from some better world, some wider moment suddenly so close I could hold it in my hand (pp. 8–9).

The industry that instilled this reaction from Wilker as he collected the cards of the era's greats (like Johnny Bench and Steve Carlton), the ill-fated near-greats (like Mark Fidrych and J.R. Richard), the forgotten (like Rudy Meoli and Rowland Office), and the reviled (like Bucky Dent by Red Sox fans), as well as generations of children in the United States, which was long-dominated by Topps. The Topps company began in 1890 as the American Leaf Tobacco Company, an importer of tobacco for independent cigar manufacturers. The company switched to making chewing gum during the Great Depression of the 1930s, then in 1951 started to use sports trading cards, specifically baseball cards, to sell bubble gum. Card collecting was popular as early as the late nineteenth century, and companies included sets of Civil War generals and Native American chiefs inserted in cigar packs. The most valuable card of all-time, a Honus Wagner card issued by the Sweet Caporal Company in 1910, was discontinued after Wagner, a nonsmoker whose likeness was used without his permission,

objected. Other companies such as Goudy Gum and Bowman specialized in cards, and had most of the market sewed up through deals with star players. As noted above, the company entered the market by signing contracts with legitimate minor league prospects, first with as little as one dollar, later increased to five. Topps negotiated a comprehensive agreement with the MLBPA in 1968, where the company was permitted to continue manufacturing trading cards bearing player likenesses for double the player's previous yearly fees (from $125 to $250, now up to $500), and it paid the union eight percent on annual sales up to $4 million and 10% on all subsequent sales. Company personnel would do all the photography and write all the copy for the backs (Boyd & Harris, 1991; Helyar, 1994; Rushin, 2002).

Topps ruled the baseball card market until 1981, when a federal court antitrust decision broke its stranglehold, leading to an explosion of competition. By the late 1980s, new card companies like Upper Deck and expanded card varieties such as rookie cards developed a speculative market, with consumers flooding the market with cash seeking to buy cards as investments. The market bubble grew until 1991, when sports cards sales topped $1.2 billion, then burst, settling to annual sales of $300 million by 2004, and to $200 million by 2008. Card shops closed at a rapid rate as well, from 5,000 in the early 1990s to 500 in 2009. In response, card makers have struggled to regain market share with new products and sets, such as cards with pieces of bats or game-worn uniforms affixed to them. In 2003, four separate card companies released 87 separate sets of cards, and by 2005, brands such as Fleer, Pacific, and Sky Box folded, and Topps concluded that the trading card market was going to shrink 25% a year. According to one industry expert, "There was too much money going into competition and not enough into marketing, especially to younger kids" (Duerson, 2007, p. 30; Forman, 2004; "Scorecard: Go Figure," 2004).

Bruce Gershenoff, who runs the original Upper Deck store from which the card line emerged, described the bust this way:

> My sales from '88 to '92 were $10,000 to $13,000 a month, and the cost of goods was only $1,000 to $2,000 a month. Then (the companies) started putting out so much product, raising the price on packs and putting in chaser cards that caused people to stop trying to make sets. Kids ran away. Hobbyists got aggravated because they couldn't afford everything, and speculators backed off because of oversaturation. By '94 my sales were $3,000 a month, and my products were up to $5,000. I had to get out (Winn, 2009, p. 53).

But in 2007, Topps was purchased by a group led by former Disney CEO Michael Eisner (whose company at the time owned the then-Anaheim Angels), after Topps' net income quadrupled to $8.7 million in 2006. Part of the reason is that Major League Baseball's properties division reduced trading card licensees to two—Topps and Upper Deck—clearing out much of the competition in a formerly crowded market. In addition, MLB has helped trading card companies through efforts such as National Baseball Card Day, first held on June 17, 2006. The initial reports are good. *Card Trade* magazine, an industry trade journal, reported that dealers saw a 43.2% increase in gross sales, the biggest jump in six years. Industry insiders see Eisner's plan to run Topps as a private company as wise, and his marketing experience with Disney and the Angels is lauded. Said Scott Keinhofer, editor of *Card Trade*, "Michael Eisner has some potential to do big things ... to Topps and to (trading cards) in general" (Duerson, 2007, p. 30). Maybe the next generation's Josh Wilker can find happiness all over again through the likes of Evan Longoria, Mark Prior, Gio Gonzalez, and Manny Ramirez.

Legal

■ ANTITRUST AND LICENSING AGREEMENTS

In 2000, the NFL signed a 10-year, $250 million deal with Reebok to be its exclusive provider of licensed apparel, ending deals with other companies. But one of the companies spurned in the wake of the Reebok deal, American Needle (founded in 1918 and the first company to sell licensed headwear, and also a former official supplier to many MLB teams beginning in the 1940s), sued the NFL, arguing that based on Section 1 of the Sherman Act, the NFL and Reebok were conspiring to stifle competition and inflate prices. American Needle argued that immediately after the Reebok deal was signed, prices for NFL licensed products quickly rose. In 2008, a unanimous three-judge panel of the United States Court of Appeals for the Seventh Circuit, in Chicago, ruled for the NFL on the ground that the league is a single entity (Belson, 2010; Belson & Schwarz, 2010). The case ended up at the Supreme Court, and its finding will be reported in the paragraphs below.

As we learned above, professional league properties divisions have for decades negotiated such deals on behalf of all member franchises. These actions have been based on an exemption granted by the federal government to work as a single entity to negotiate broadcast deals. This "single entity" approach is the concept American Needle sought to challenge in its suit, especially because its sales dropped 25% after the Reebok deal. But according to company president Robert Kronenberger (grandson of the company's founder who had convinced reluctant Chicago Cubs owner Philip Wrigley to let him sell Cubs caps at Wrigley Field on consignment) said of the suit: "For me, it's a principled thing. We just want to be competitive. I understand that it's probably a business decision. It's just black and white and this is wrong ... It's not just headwear. It could be beyond that: television, concessions, food, beer. It's not just about me" (Belson, 2010, p. B15; Belson & Schwarz, 2010, p. B15).

Kronenberger's comments are not merely the rhetoric of a jilted plaintiff. Industry experts believed that if the NFL was successful in defending its status in the case, and it was found exempt from Section 1 of the Sherman Act, it could extend its League-wide deals to stadium concessionaires, vendors, and parking operators, agreements that are currently managed by individual franchises. This could, potentially, drive up the cost of attending games. It could also mean that, according to legal experts, professional leagues could be empowered to unilaterally impose labor agreements when bargaining with players' unions. But legal experts also believed the case, if decided in favor of American Needle, would cause all professional leagues to lose their single entity status exemption in negotiating labor agreements with players' unions and broadcast agreements. However, one legal scholar doesn't think an NFL win would mean a future with $200 licensed fleece sweatshirts, because "people would just go buy a baseball sweatshirt instead" (Belson & Schwarz, 2010, p. B15).

In January 2010, after the NFL won at the trial and appeals court level, the U.S. Supreme Court heard arguments from both sides on the case. The NFL had actually joined with American Needle in asking for the review, an action taken, according to one legal expert, "because they think they can win" (King, 2010, p. 9). Some experts felt that the NFL could count on four of the nine sitting justices—Chief Justice John Roberts, and Justices Samuel Aleto, Antonin Scalia, and Clarence Thomas—and would not get two others, Justices John Paul Stevens and Ruth Bader Ginsberg, leaving the league only needing to convert one of the remaining three (Justices Stephen Breyer, Anthony Kennedy, and Sonia Sotomayor). Sotomayor, named to the high court in 2009 by President Barack Obama, has the most direct contact with pro league sports

issues, having issued an injunction as an appeals court judge against MLB owners in 1995, ending the player lockout that led to the cancellation of the 1994 World Series. She was also part of a three-judge appeals court panel that upheld the NFL's draft eligibility rule, which had been challenged by former Ohio State University running back Maurice Clarett.

American Needle drew support from the existing players' unions and the NFL Coaches Association, while the NFL had support from the NCAA, the NBA, the NHL, and video game manufacturer Electronic Arts, which expressed concerns about the difficulty in negotiating agreements with each individual team, a move it believed would result in higher costs to consumers. Writer Bill King noted that a reversal in favor of American Needle would be in line with 30 years of lower court rulings which have found leagues to be joint ventures, even as most courts have upheld the single entity structure in those instances where it is seen to have benefitted consumers. An unsigned op-ed piece in the *New York Times* the day of the hearing sided with American Needle, stating, "the league is actually a cooperative effort of 32 separately owned, profit-making teams. They compete in everything from hiring to ticket sales. They should have to comply with Section 1" (Broughton, 2010; "Football," 2010, p. A26; Kaplan, 2010; King, 2010).

At the hearing, which lasted one hour and 11 minutes, eight justices chose to ask questions (not including Justice Thomas, who customarily remains silent). The justices sought to get each side to suggest, as in the words of Justice Kennedy: "a zone where we are sure a rule of reason inquiry ... would be inappropriate?" Neither side was willing to set parameters on how the court should act, and one observer remarked after the hearing, "Both sides have to walk away from that argument not knowing what's going to come out of it because the questions were ... off the wall (and) unfocused ... There are simply no principle standards for deciding when sports leagues should be allowed to cooperate and when they should be allowed to compete." Indeed, Justice Sotomayor said to NFL lead attorney Gregg Levy, "I am very much swayed by your arguments, but I can very much see a counter argument that promoting t-shirts is only to make money. It doesn't really promote the game. It promotes the making of money. And once you fix prices for making money, that's a ... violation" (King & Kaplan, 2010, p. 28).

On May 23, 2010, the court unanimously found in favor of American Needle. "The league's decision to license independently owned trademarks collectively to a single vendor," Justice Stevens wrote for the court, deprived the marketplace "of actual or potential competition." "Although NFL teams have common interests such as promoting the NFL brand," Stevens continued, "they are still separate, profit-maximizing entities ... Each of the teams is a substantial, independently owned and independently managed business. The teams compete with one another, not only on the playing field, but to attract fans, for gate receipts and for contracts with managerial and playing personnel." In addition, Stevens wrote that teams certainly compete in the market for intellectual property: "To a firm making hats, the (New Orleans) Saints and the (Indianapolis) Colts are two potentially competing suppliers of valuable trademarks" (Liptak & Belson, 2010, p. 1).

The ruling did not resolve the lawsuit. The court said American Needle's claims were not barred at the outset but must rather be analyzed under a standard that antitrust lawyers call the "rule of reason" to determine whether the league's licensing practices harmed competition. The case will be returned to the lower courts. Robert Kronenberger said of the decision: "This is to protect competition and consumers and right a wrong. We hope to prevail, but we'll see what happens" (Liptak & Belson, 2010, p. 1).

■ SUMMARY

This chapter considered two growing and expanding segments of the sport industry: sporting goods and licensed products. Three product categories compose the sporting goods industry segment: equipment, athletic footwear, and apparel. Several trade associations assist sporting goods professionals, the largest of which is the SGMA.

The licensed product industry continues to generate significant revenues. Teams and leagues earn a certain percentage of sales, called royalties, on items bearing logos. Leagues and players associations administer licensing programs on the professional level. Colleges may administer their own licensing programs or may enlist the services of organizations such as IMG College. Individuals are needed to work in many capacities in both the sporting goods and licensed products industries. These areas cut across many other segments of the sport industry, including professional sport, intercollegiate athletics, recreational sport, and the health and fitness industry. Wherever there is a need for equipment to play a sport or a need for the right clothing to announce that a person is a fan of a particular team, the sporting goods industry and the licensed product industry become pivotal.

■ RESOURCES

adidas
5055 N. Greeley Ave.
Portland, OR 97217
http://www.adidas.com

IMG College
546 East Main Street
Lexington, KY 40508
859-226-4678
http://www.imgcollege.com

CASE STUDY: Om Means Om

Although only 29 years old, Bronwen Morrison was an industry veteran. When she first came out of her undergrad sport management degree program, she took a job with the Liberty Sports Group, where she had interned while in college, and managed the launch of the "Beckster," a skateboarding shoe targeted toward the market's smaller grassroots segment, where companies like Grenade tend to dominate. The shoe was a modest success, so much so that Morrison, when spotted wearing a throwback 1976 San Diego Padres jersey at the sporting goods SuperShow in Atlanta, was asked to head the creation of a line of throwback-inspired urban fashion clothes for women by Trey Luce, creator and owner of Thugstaz. The line, which would be dubbed "Hugstaz," was also a solid market success, and put the line in positive competition with similar products by Ecko and other urban fashion companies.

But Bronwen was feeling that she had done all she could do with Hugstaz. While it was a fun challenge to take on, doing the research and meeting with designers and working with retailers, she had never really loved the products she was working with. Plus, she had begun to look for some challenges in her life outside of work. She was still in decent shape nearly a decade after college—she had played soccer and lacrosse in high school, but only intramural sports in college—but the basic cardio and gym routines were getting stale. About this same time, Bronwen's mother, Fantasia had introduced her to yoga. For her mom to practice (and that was the term; one didn't *do* or *work at* yoga, one *practiced* it) was not a stretch (no pun intended). Demographically, yoga had become a real fitness trend with those like her mom: white, female, 40 to 60 years old, relatively affluent, and educated. Sure, there were others who took part in yoga "classes," but four out of five were like her mom. While skeptical at first (Bronwen had always been drawn to the traditional competitive sports she played growing up and, like many, had believed yoga to be the province of hippies and pseudo-mystics), she had to admit it was a lot tougher than it looked. After holding poses for the first one-hour class in a studio in which the temperature was 97°, she felt like a wrung-out dishrag. But it was also invigorating. She was challenged physically, but there was also an opportunity for mental focus and an inner calming.

As she attended more classes, she started to do some research on the industry. Sixteen million people in the United States now practice yoga, and spending on yoga products and classes had increased 87% since 2004, to $5.7 billion a year. She read about John Friend, the founder of Anusara, what writer Mimin Swartz called one of the fastest-growing styles of yoga. Friend sponsored teaching seminars that drew 800 people, organized the yoga-and-music "Wanderlust" festival, has publishing and DVD ventures, and produced a line of clothing in cooperation with adidas (which is promoted to his 200,000 students in 70 countries by his 1,200 licensed yoga teachers). His company, Anusara, Inc., generates $2 million a year in revenue (Swartz, 2010).

She found that one apparel retail chain, Lululemon Athletica (which described its products as "yoga-inspired athletic apparel"), reported sales of $81.7 million in its 100-plus stores in 2009. The company was founded in 1998 in Vancouver, British Columbia, by Chip Wilson, who had worked in the snowboard-surfboard industry. According to sources she consulted, the company's promotional strategies included working with yoga instructors and offering free classes to non-practitioners. The company has since branched out to include products for runners and other activities as well as items like rain jackets (for $128) and $48 t-shirts that are "yoga-inspired." CEO Christine Day calls the company's principle: "yoga and ..." (Walker, 2009, p. 18). Writer Rob Walker described the thinking behind this approach in an article Bronwen found: "One lesson of the 'action sports' niche is the power of the lifestyle crossover. Just as you don't have to skateboard to wear skateboard sneakers, you don't have to be able to nail a sun-saturation pose to wear yoga pants" (Walker, 2009, p. 30).

So Bronwen visited a Lululemon Athletica store in a nearby mall, nestled in between an Anthropolgie and a J.Crew. She sorted through some of the items, including garments made of a seaweed-derived material that claimed to release "minerals and vitamins" into the wearer's sweaty skin. "Really," she said out loud, laughing. "I'd like to see some scientific tests that support that." She then thought back to something she read during her research, the criticism of a long-time yoga practitioner, lamenting that yoga had been transformed by the company into something that was upper class, female, and mostly about lifestyle and clothes. "Well, all apparel manufacturers do that," Bronwen thought. "We did that at Liberty; we did that at Hugstaz. We wanted customers to think of our brand and our products as something more than just clothes."

As she walked through the store, assessing the merchandise and observing the customers—and they *were* all female, white and upper class, she noticed—she also was wondering why they were the segment most drawn to yoga. She started to think other niches were out there—she had seen men and some non-white women in the few classes she had taken—that a retailer or apparel company could reach. Nike or adidas wouldn't be interested, she thought, as the segment was too small to impact their bottom lines. And not many guys—at least guys she knew—were going to walk into a store called "Lulu" or "Lemon." So could it be done? Could she start something "yoga-inspired" for men? She walked out of the store, and headed to her car, thinking.

Questions for Discussion

1. What would be the initial steps Bronwen should take to establish a retail outlet for a company meant to reach the untapped segments identified above?
2. Does it make more sense to start a retail outlet or a line of apparel to be sold through existing retailers? Explain.
3. What factors identified in this chapter would impact Bronwen's efforts to manufacture apparel?
4. How might existing retailers and manufacturers provide challenging competition?
5. Can licensing and endorsements be utilized by Bronwen in getting her firm off the ground?

New Balance Athletic Shoes, Inc.
Corporate Headquarters
Brighton Landing
20 Guest Street
Boston, MA 02135
617-783-4000
http://www.newbalance.com

Nike—World Headquarters
One Bowerman Drive
Beaverton, OR 97005
503-671-6453
http://www.nike.com

Reebok International
1895 JW Foster Blvd.
Canton, MA 02021
781-401-5000
http://corporate.reebok.com

Sporting Goods Manufacturers Association (SGMA)
8505 Fenton Street
Suite 211
Silver Spring, MD 20910
301-495-6321
http://www.sgma.com

Under Armour
  1020 Hull Street
  Baltimore, MD 21230
  www.underarmour.com

■ KEY TERMS

athletic footwear, brand's image, entrepreneur, global sourcing, licensed products, licensees, licensors, properties division, royalty, sporting goods, sporting goods equipment, sports apparel, trade associations, trademarks

■ REFERENCES

About SGMA. (2010). *Sporting Goods Manufacturers Association.* Retrieved November 22, 2010, from http://www.sgma.com/about/

Adams, R. (2003, July 7–13). Leagues favor fewer deals, higher quality. *Street & Smith's SportsBusiness Journal*, pp. 21–22.

Belson, K. (2010, January 7). American Needle: From green celluloid visors to caps of all kinds. *New York Times*, p. B15.

Belson, K., & Schwarz, A. (2010, January 7). Antitrust case has implications far beyond N.F.L. *New York Times*, pp. B13, B15.

Boyd, B.C., & Harris, F.C. (1991). *The great American baseball card flipping, trading and bubble gum book.* New York: Ticknor & Fields.

Broughton, D. (2010, January 4–10). Sports and this court: How the nine sitting justices have ruled on industry-related cases. *Street & Smith's SportsBusiness Journal*, p. 10.

Chang, J., with Halliday, J. (2006). *Mao: The unknown story.* New York: Anchor Books.

Collegiate Licensing Company. (2005). Media FAQs. Retrieved February 10, 2010, from http://www.clc.com/clcweb/publishing.nsf/Content/faq-media.html?open&faqtype=media#WRID-6E3GQP

Covell, D., & Barr, C.A. (2010). *Managing intercollegiate athletics.* Scottsdale, AZ: Holcomb Hathaway.

Covell, D., Walker, S., Siciliano, J., & Hess, P. (2007). *Managing sport organizations: Responsibility for performance* (2nd ed.). Burlington, MA: Butterworth Heineman.

Davis, F. (1992). *Fashion, culture and identity.* Chicago, IL: University of Chicago Press.

Duerson, A. (2007, March 10). Back on Topps. *Sports Illustrated*, p. 30.

Fain, P. (2007, October 26). Oregon debates role of big sports donors. *The Chronicle of Higher Education*, pp. A38–A41.

Football and antitrust. (2010, January 13). *New York Times*, p. A26.

Forman, R. (2004, June 8). New basketball cards go for $500 a pack. *USA Today*, p. 3C.

Funding Universe. (n.d.). Brunswick Corporation. Retrieved February 10, 2011, from http://www.fundinguniverse.com/company-histories/Brunswick-Corporation-Company-History.html

Gladden, J.M. (2007). Managing sport brands. In B.J. Mullin, S. Hardy, & W.A. Sutton, *Sport marketing* (3rd Ed.) (pp. 171–187). Champaign, IL: Human Kinetics.

Goldstein, W. (1989). *Playing for keeps: A history of early baseball.* Ithaca, NY: Cornell University Press.

Greenhouse, S. (2009, November 18). Labor fight ends in win for students. *New York Times*, pp. B1, B4.

Hardy, S. (1995). Adopted by all the leading clubs: Sporting goods and the shaping of leisure. In D. K. Wiggins (Ed.), *Sport in America* (pp. 133–150). Champaign, IL: Human Kinetics.

Hardy, S. H. (1997). Entrepreneurs, organizations, and the sports marketplace. In S.W. Pope (Ed.), *The new American sports history* (pp. 341–365). Champaign, IL: University of Illinois Press.

Helyar, J. (1994). *Lords of the realm.* New York: Random House.

Hiestand, M. (2002, August 19). Sports gear so out of style it's in style. *USA Today*, p. 3C.

Hiestand, M. (2003, March 27). Underwear getting noticed at tournament. *USA Today*, p. 2C.

Higgins, M. (2006, November 24). In board sports, credibility sells along with gear. *New York Times*, pp. A1, C13.

Horovitz, B. (2009, December 7). Nike CEO knows how to just do it. *USA Today*, pp. 1B–2B.

Kaplan, D. (2010, January 4–10). All four unions, credit-card issuers among the 'friends of the court' filing briefs in the case. *Street & Smith's SportsBusiness Journal*, p. 9.

Katz, D. (1993, August 16). Triumph of the swoosh. *Sports Illustrated*, pp. 54–73.

Keller, K.L. (1998). *Strategic brand management: Building, measuring and managing brand equity*. Upper Saddle River, NJ: Prentice Hall.

King, B. (2010, January 4–10). Supreme Court weighs a game changer. *Street & Smith's SportsBusiness Journal*, pp. 1, 8–11.

King, B., & Kaplan, D. (2010, January 18–24). NFL, Needle, get their high court moment. *Street & Smith's SportsBusiness Journal*, pp. 1, 28.

Lanham Act, 15 U.S.C. § 1051–1127 (1946).

Levine, P. (1985). *A. G. Spalding and the rise of baseball: The promise of American sport*. New York: Oxford University Press.

Lipsey, R. (Ed.). (1996). *Sports market place*. Princeton, NJ: Sportsguide.

Liptak, A., & Belson, K. (2010, May 24). N.F.L. fails in its request for antitrust immunity. *New York Times*. Retrieved November 22, 2010, from http://www.nytimes.com/2010/05/25/sports/football/25needle.html

McCarthy, M. (2008, December 9). Under Armour is making a run at Nike. *USA Today*, p. 1C.

McCarthy, M., & Whiteside, K. (2006, September 13). What to wear? Oregon has 384 game-day choices. *USA Today*, p. 1C.

Moser, K. (2008, July 11). College pride, briefly. *The Chronicle of Higher Education*, p. A4.

Murphy, A. (2003, September 29). Make way for Ducks. *Sports Illustrated*, pp. 53–59.

New Balance. (2008). New Balance. Retrieved February 10, 2011, from http://www.newbalance.com/assets/corporate/NB_Corporate_Overview.pdf

NFL Players (2010). Licensees. Retrieved November 22, 2010, from http://www.nflplayers.com/About-us/Sponsors–Licensees/

Nichols, M.A. (1995, April). A look at some of the issues affecting collegiate licensing. *Team Licensing Business, 7*(4), 18.

Nike, Inc. (2002). Frequently asked questions. Retrieved November 22, 2010, from http://swoosh.custhelp.com/

Nocera, J. (2008, April 12). China tries to solve its Brand X blues. *New York Times*, pp. B1, B8.

O'Brien, G. (2002, June). Elements of style: A smashing shirt. *GQ*, p. 61.

Plata, C. (1996, September/October). Ducks & dollars. *Team Licensing Business, 8*(6), 38.

Roenigk, A. (2007, January 29). The power of glove. *ESPN Magazine*, pp. 61–66.

Rushin, S. (2002, May 13). Sweet smell of innocence. *Sports Illustrated*, p. 17.

Ryckman, P. (2010, June 24). Fostering entrepreneurs and trying to revive a city. *New York Times*, p. B6.

Say, J.B. (1964). *A treatise on political economy*. New York: Sentry Press.

Scorecard: Go figure. (2004, July 5). *Sports Illustrated*, p. 20.

Sharrow, R. (2011, July 27). Under Armour sales hit $1 billion in 2010, preps for cotton launch. *Baltimore Business Journal*. Retrieved from http://www.bizjournals.com/baltimore/news/2011/01/27/under-armour-sales-hit-1b-in-2010.html

Simmons, B. (2004, December 20). The sports guy. *ESPN Magazine*, p. 12.

Smit, B. (2008). *Sneaker wars: The enemy brothers who founded Adidas and Puma and the family feud that forever changed the business of sport*. New York: Ecco.

Smith, R.A. (Ed.) (1994). *Big-time football at Harvard, 1905: The diary of coach Bill Reid*. Urbana, IL: University of Illinois Press.

Sperber, M. (1993). *Shake down the thunder: The creation of Notre Dame football*. New York: Henry Holt.

Spiegel, J.E. (2008, February 7). Competition gaining on a niche market. *New York Times*, p. C6.

Sporting Goods Manufacturers Association (SGMA). (2002a). Outdoor recreation in America. North Palm Beach, FL: Author.

Sporting Goods Manufacturers Association (SGMA). (2002b). The SGMA report: Sports apparel monitor. North Palm Beach, FL: Author.

SportsMedia. (2010). SportsMedia product licensing. Retrieved February 10, 2011, from http://www.sportsmedia.net/MediaKit/Collegiate_Licensing/collegiate_licensing.htm

Sports merchandising industry loses its creator, David Warsaw. (1996, July/August). *Team Licensing Business, 8*(5), 18.

Swartz, M. (2010, July 26). The yoga mogul. *New York Times Magazine*, pp. 40–43.

Taylor, P. (2003a, September 8). Wild Ducks. *Sports Illustrated*, p. 54.

Taylor, P. (2003b, October 27). Phil Taylor's sidelines. *Sports Illustrated*, p. 57.

Topline reports on outdoor, athletic apparel, running, dive, paddlesports. (2010, May 10). *Sport Business Research Network*. Retrieved from http://0-www.sbrnet.com.wildpac.wnec.edu/publication.asp?function=detail&magid=183116

Walker, R. (2009, July 19). Marketing pose. *New York Times Magazine*, p. 18.

Wilker, J. (2010). *Cardboard gods: An All-American tale told through baseball cards*. New York: Seven Footer Press.

Winn, L. (2009, August 24). The last iconic baseball card. *Sports Illustrated*, pp. 49–53.

Worker Rights Consortium. (2010). Preliminary report on minimum wage violations in Bangalore, India. Retrieved February 10, 2011, from http://www.workersrights.org/linkeddocs/Bangalore%20Minimum%20Wage_Preliminary%20Report.pdf

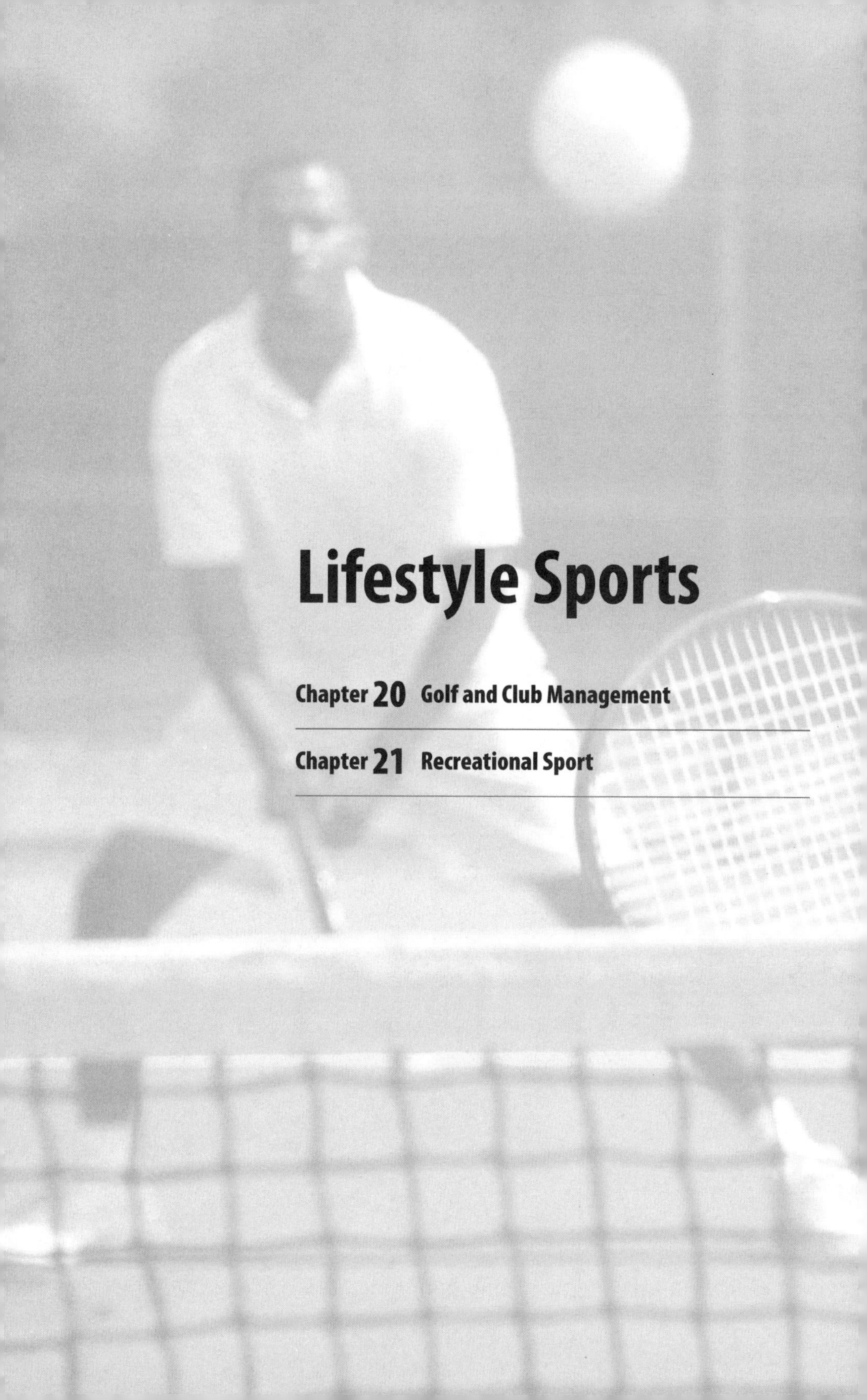

Lifestyle Sports

CHAPTER

20

Golf and Club Management

Rod Warnick

■ INTRODUCTION

Golf courses and country clubs are a significant sport attraction in the United States. Within the last decade, close to 30 million Americans played golf on nearly 16,000 courses. Few sports leave as distinctive an imprint on the landscape as the golf course and the country club. This is also one of the few sports where the playing field is not standardized, but differs from course-to-course and even from day-to-day. These large open green spaces are easily recognized in flyovers due to their size, distinct holes, and manicured turf layouts. During the last quarter of the twentieth century, the number of golfers increased four times faster than the nation's population, from 10 million golfers to over 30 million (Napton and Laingen, 2008). The courses they play on occupy a land mass as large as the states of Rhode Island and Delaware combined (Santiago and Rodewald, 2005).

Golf courses and country clubs come in two major varieties: public and private facilities. There are a number of variations of clubs and courses; however, these two major distinctions are important. Private courses, especially country club facilities, outnumbered public courses until 1960. These private courses were popular because the game had evolved from being played solely by the American social elite who had brought it here from Scotland in the late 1800s. The evolution of the country club and development of more public access courses and facilities created periods of rapid growth and a coming of age for the modern era of golf and club management. The game and its management for the general public at both private and public facilities are now considered to be in a mature phase of its life cycle (IBISWorld, 2010).

So where did the idea for these clubs come from? The modern American country club movement has a direct ancestry in city clubs, but the clubs that evolved in the United States were uniquely American. Golf was not part of the early club movement; however, the popularity of golf did spur their growth at the turn of the nineteenth century. First was the **city club** concept evolved from the nineteenth century dining clubs in major cities, which stemmed from earlier men's clubs in Britain. The American movement in clubs, though, was distinctly different and, as Americans' use of leisure time increased, the game of golf grew in popularity. The profession of club management also arose to professionally operate these facilities for their members and participants. This movement led to the development of the iconic institution of the American country club.

As John Steele Gordon (1990) wrote in his article entitled, "The Country Club":

> *The country club has had a profound effect on the development of American society and on the most dynamic part of the American social scene in the twentieth century, the suburbs. Thus it is no surprise that the country club has fascinated the American creative establishment ... (Gordon, 1990, p. 75).*

■ HISTORY

The **country club** originated about 120 years ago and was conceived by affluent Americans, the overwhelming majority whom were of Protestant and British ancestry. Today's exclusive private country club has spread to virtually every ethnic and religious group in a very heterogeneous country and to most other nations around the world (Gordon, 1990).

The American economic and political climate of the nineteenth century respected individualism and eschewed inherited nobility and the caste system of Europe. Many Americans had generated wealth and independence during the Industrial Revolution and from them rose a new entrepreneurial class. Rockefeller, Carnegie, Morgan, Vanderbilt families, and others became the names of legend. By the 1880s, the U.S. banks had become the international headquarters of the banking system. Banks that were originally branch offices were now lending money, capital, and advice back to the British and other Europeans. As America had arrived as the world banking center, this created a moneyed class of individuals who sought to spend time with people of their own kind, away from average citizens of modest means. This new economic elite class was built on entrepreneurship and the principles of freedom and hard work. These wealthy businessmen began to emulate the behaviors of formerly scorned privileged and noble classes of their British ancestors (Moss, 2001; Gordon, 1990; Miller, 1978).

Ironically, the American country club got its start because the economically elite also lacked one central social institution of the British aristocracy: the country house or estate. The British upper classes had long resided in the rural countryside. Its elite ventured into London and other metropolitan areas for politics, business, or the social season for a portion of the year, but most months were spent living on vast estates in the rural countryside. These estates were the sources of wealth and privilege and also where they entertained members of their elite class. In contrast, American commerce was centered in the city and the wealthy entrepreneurs resided there. While they possessed no rural roots, they yearned for the peaceful environments outside the hectic, dirty, and polluted central cities. The American wealthy class began to seek destinations outside the metropolitan areas, and built private estates and summer homes in such places as Newport, Rhode Island, along the Hudson River north of New York City in the Catskill Mountains, and at the end of rail lines near urban areas. Thus, the interest and timing were set for a new movement for America's wealthy entrepreneurial class to enjoy the pleasures of success. Opportunities and facilities were needed where they could express their wealth and engage in recreational activities, and the country club concept was the solution (Moss, 2001; Gordon, 1990; Miller, 1978).

The Game of Golf and Golf Course and Club Development

The game of golf originated with the Scottish players and founders of the Royal and Ancient Golf Club of St. Andrews, Scotland. Construction of facilities for the sport of golf evolved quickly in the United States. Napton and Laingen (2008) document four major periods of golf course construction and development from 1878 through 2000. The game was first introduced to the U.S. market in Yonkers, New York with the Apple Tree Gang, where the first small, three-hole course was built, also named St. Andrews. In 1895, the United States Golf Association (USGA) was formed, and contributed greatly to the transformation of golf from a game to that of a competitive sport. From 1878 to 1919, the growth of new golf courses and country clubs primarily were concentrated in *golf club villages* located on urban fringes. During this time, 962 courses were built, mostly private country clubs (Napton and Laingen, 2008). In 1914 the Club Managers Association of Boston was formed. At the same time in New York a similar organizational effort among club managers was taking place. These organizations ultimately formed the **Club Managers Association of America (CMAA)** and the **Professional Golfers Association (PGA)** (Morris, 2002). Today over 28,000 golf professionals are members of the PGA (PGALinks, 2010).

Three-fifths of 2,689 new golf courses were built after World War I in the 1920s, but this growth spurt was slowed by World War II and the subsequent worldwide economic depression from 1929 to the early 1940s. Construction of the classic Augusta National golf course occurred in Georgia in 1932, setting a new standard in golf course design (Napton and Laingen, 2008). Golf was well positioned for a dramatic growth period corresponding with the increase in leisure time and affluence of the 1950s and 1960s. During these two decades an upwardly mobile, wealthy growing population wanted to leave behind the Great Depression, war memories, and the polluted and decaying central cities in favor of open areas of land and the game of golf. During this period, 5,558 new golf courses were built (Napton and Laingen, 2008). The 1970s saw a maturation and subsequent saturation of golf and the country club. Great professionals such as Jack Nicklaus and Arnold Palmer played to ever larger crowds and the PGA Tour and USGA Championships grew in popularity as well. The general public's interest in playing golf, however, slowed as the economy stagnated and declined in the early 2000s (Napton and Laingen, 2008).

The National Golf Foundation (NGF) (Beditz, 2008) reported the number of private golf clubs today is the same as it was on the eve of the Great Depression: 4,400 clubs. While the total number of clubs has remained relatively constant, considerable conversion activity has taken place. These conversions reflect the growing need for these facilities to be more carefully managed. From 2000 to 2008, 288 private clubs converted to public facilities and 387 converted from public to private status. A large number of these facilities were converted to a management contract, in that they were taken over by large golf management companies such as American Golf. Considering the 343 new club openings and the 39 that closed their doors, this produced a net growth of only 205 clubs. One reason for this shift is that a drop in memberships and associated revenues, such as initiation fees, dues, and food/beverage, left some clubs unable to meet operating costs and debt service. The majority of public-to-private conversions are also real estate–related course conversions, where a membership or home-sale threshold was met, which prompted change.

Largely due to high entry barrier costs for equipment, membership, or even the daily play cost, the middle and lower class players have simply reduced or dropped out of the game entirely. Furthermore, those middle-aged adults who took up the game at a younger age found time restrictions in family obligations constraining their playing time and volume. For those who play frequently and those who play at private country clubs and exclusive golf clubs, interest remains stable. With an aging American population and a large number of Baby Boomers reaching retirement age, the game is likely to rebound and stabilize in the next two decades.

The Country Club Concept: How it Evolved and Brought Forth the Sportsmanship Ideal

Founded in 1882, The Country Club of Brookline, located near Boston, Massachusetts, is considered to be the first country club in the United States. It offered outdoor activities such as horseback riding, and built a small golf course in 1893 that members expanded to 18 holes in 1899. While indeed the *country club movement* was a novel concept in the 1880s, members and guests of Brookline and other country clubs also sought another concept, that of *sportsmanship*. The rules of sportsmanship were established in the 1880s at Yale, but the concept was perfected and played out on the golf course.

Professional sports in the late 1800s were mired in an environment of festering disagreements mixed with rather unfair contest outcomes. Contest fixing was very common, bribery was rampant, most sports had few standardized rules, and gamblers appeared to run professional sports. There was a need for a gentlemen's outlet where true sportsmanship could be observed and played regularly, and not only by gifted athletes or hired professionals.

The country club became a highly successful concept that was copied in record numbers throughout the United States. The successful formula remains largely intact today. A *country club* is a place located in a country-like setting, with open areas and lots of green space, that has a standard meeting facility: the clubhouse. This is where members go to enjoy sports and sportsmanship, engage in activities for the pursuit of happiness, develop friendships and comingle with friends and like-minded others in peaceful surroundings, and to celebrate life and its wonderful occasions. These are truly places of relaxation, recreation, and rejuvenation. The Country Club in Brookline epitomized this formula for success. Its membership emphasized "true sport promoted and practiced by true sportsmen, true gentlemen and true friends" (Gordon, 1990; Miller, 1978).

Today The Country Club in Brookline is best known as the place that popularized the game of golf in the United States, including serving as the site of the 1913, 1963, and 1988 U.S. Open Tournaments, the site of a number of U.S. amateur events, and most recently the site of one of the greatest comebacks in golf history, the 1999 Ryder Cup. But its brightest achievement and perhaps most glorious memory in the sporting world was the 1913 U.S. Open. This event was recently re-enacted in the movie, "The Greatest Game Ever Played," and featured the accomplishments of a little known caddie at the time, Francis Ouimet, who then beat Harry Vardon and Ted Ray, two of the greatest golfers in the world. Francis Ouimet was merely an enthusiastic, working class caddie who loved the game of golf and who just barely qualified for the Open. He pulled off the biggest upset of a lifetime and was a true American sportsman. It has been said that no other winner of a golf tournament did more to popularize the game of golf than Ouimet (Hardin, 2008). He also can be called America's *first gentleman golfer*, as his behavior built on the concept of true sportsmanship. Ouimet went on to become a legendary golfer, and the Francis Ouimet Scholarship still exists today. An annual scholarship dinner is held each spring in Boston, where scholarships are awarded for golfers, caddies, grounds keepers, and young professionals. Golf legends are honored by the Ouimet name and legacy for the professionalism they have brought to the game.

Clubs today, however, face challenges that did not exist a century ago. Life is more complex and so are clubs and their management. Students looking to be involved in events will find that the typical country or city club is an ever changing venue. This requires employees to be well educated and professional, who may specialize in food and beverage management, event management, sport and/or golf management, grounds and facility management, and/or club governance.

■ WHAT IS A CLUB?

There are basically two major categories of clubs where recreational activities such as golf, tennis, or other sports are pursued, the public club and the private club. These two distinctions are important in terms of access, membership, operation philosophy, profit motive, market orientations, and organizational structure.

A **public club** is like any typical business that is open to the public. Some of these clubs aggressively compete for members or business in a public setting. Individuals and members are welcomed to play or use the facilities if they can pay. Some are members, but the club is largely a public accommodation facility, that is, it welcomes participants from nearly all types of backgrounds to play golf and enjoy the offerings of the club. Public golf facilities are typically just golf courses with very limited services. Some offer additional revenue-producing facilities such as tennis or swimming, and a limited food and beverage outlet(s). They may have some banquet areas to support golf outings. A **private club**, though, restricts it membership and may either be a private for profit entity or a private, nonprofit entity. **Private exclusive clubs** go one step further by restricting membership to only those who are invited to join or become a member by a vote of the current existing membership. While money may be an important factor in why a person joins a country club, it is not the sole reason. Compatibility and like-mindedness with the membership are equally as important.

A *private club* is a place where people hold a common bond of special type interests, experiences, backgrounds, professions, and desires for coming together in a standard meeting place to co-mingle for social and recreational purposes. A private club can be defined as follows:

1. A place that is not open to the public.
2. A member or an individual must be accepted by the rest of the membership before he or she can join. Once someone is accepted, he or she usually must pay an initiation fee and monthly membership dues. Some clubs also have minimum spending requirements for members (e.g., members must spend a certain amount of money each month or year in the club's food and beverage outlets).
3. It has a standard meeting place, typically a clubhouse, critical to its operation.
4. It is a place where co-mingling of social, recreational, or educational purposes occur (Premier Club Services, 2010).

A *public accommodation club* or *private for-profit club*, on the other hand, is open to the public, may have special membership plans, may advertise and compete readily for the public to use and enjoy its facilities, and typically does not restrict the number of potential users except for capacity issues. Private exclusive clubs are provided tax breaks and have restrictions on how they may compete in the public marketplace.

For example, private exclusive clubs may not advertise (Premier Club Services, 2010).

People join private clubs for a variety of reasons. Some like the exclusive atmosphere of the club and see membership as a statement of social position or social class. Others join because of the recreational facilities, the club is convenient for their types of interests, or it is part of or close by their neighborhood. Members may appreciate that, with their fast paced two-income households and busy family schedules, they do not have to wait to be seated at the club's dining facilities or don't have to schedule well in advance a golf tee time as they would, for example, at a public golf or dining facility.

Others view club membership as a way to get ahead in business because people in their professions are also members or because their clubs give them an impressive place to entertain clients. However, most private exclusive clubs are not places where business occurs formally. As the past president of The Country Club in Brookline, Thomas Frost, said,

> *"Any person wishing to join the club for business purposes probably would not be elected [or admitted]. To my knowledge, no business has ever paid for a membership"* *(Miller, 1978, p. 41).*

While discussions about business likely do take place, most country clubs are formed as refuges from business activities. In fact, some clubs will go as far as to restrict business papers, business meetings, and the operation of cell phones and PDAs on site. However, while business meetings, reviews of contracts, and business conferences are restricted at exclusive private clubs, major companies may give individuals a club membership as an employment incentive or perk. But there are even restrictions here on what types of clubs can accept corporate memberships. Exclusively private,

non-profit clubs do not accept corporate memberships; they accept only individuals and families. Other people join clubs because their parents and grandparents were club members and club membership is a family tradition. These are typically called **legacy members**. Others simply enjoy the personal recognition and service they receive at a private club.

Private clubs are built for a variety of reasons. U.S. clubs that began in the nineteenth century or earlier were often started by a small group of individuals who decided to each put up a sum of money to buy a piece of land or an already-existing building, and begin a club for purely social reasons. Modern-day private clubs are built by developers (residential, resort, and free standing facilities) as a way to help them sell homes, attract visitors, or target high-level playing communities. In this instance the club and its golf course are the centerpiece of a housing development, and individuals who buy the homes surrounding it either are automatically members or have the option to become members. A resort type of course may be one of several centerpiece attractions to attract people to a vacation destination.

The unique environment of a signature designed golf course and the historic sighting of the facility are all part of the major appeal for the club members. Private clubs tend to have the best furnishings in a state-of-the-art golf facility as well as impressive, well-kept grounds designed especially for playability, and other recreational facilities. Furthermore, the goal of most private clubs is to provide a level of service that is rarely found elsewhere, which is created to keep the individual in a membership experience that will last a lifetime. This is where the member is called by name, relationships are formed and enjoyed, and where the individual is treated as someone special. A club is the member's home-away-from-home and often is where the household's major life events (e.g., weddings, birthdays, anniversaries, dedications) are celebrated.

Not all clubs are private or exclusive. There are public, private for-profit, high-end daily fee, resort, and destination clubs for nearly all socioeconomic classes to enjoy. Golf clubs and courses are defined as an industry sector today. IBISWorld *Industry Reports* (2010) identifies the club industry as a $26.1 billion sector of the U.S. economy with a special Standard Industrial Classification (SIC) code—71391—and labels the sector "Golf Courses & Country Clubs in the US." This *Industry Report* includes firms that operate golf courses as their primary activity and country clubs with dining and other recreational facilities (i.e., exclusive private clubs like The Country Club in Brookline). These establishments provide food and beverage services, equipment rental services, and golf instruction plus the opportunity to play golf and/or other recreational activities. Golf courses can be public, private, semiprivate or an exclusive, private membership country club. This industry, as monitored and followed by IBISWorld (2010), excludes golf driving ranges, miniature golf facilities, and golf courses associated with resorts and hotels. However, a golf learning center and driving range may be a part of the golf course operation if these facilities are not operated as separate or stand-alone complexes.

Today, all of a private club's facilities face competition from public and resort facilities. Clubs are also restricted in some of the services they can provide to their members due to tax regulations and other competitive advantages. Still, there is demand for the private club and the typical food service and recreation it offers. Competitors for a club's food and beverage outlets include high-end gourmet restaurants, corporate chain restaurants, sports bars, and even fast-food restaurants. Private clubs typically have multiple food outlets that may include a fine dining room(s), a casual pub or grill room,

and snack bars at the pool complexes and quick service outlets on the golf course or in mobile units roaming the course. Public golf courses compete with a club's golf facilities. In fact, until recently one of the fastest growing concepts in the golf sector was the high-end, daily fee public course.

Public health clubs, day spas, and health spas, including many large hotel chains that have club concepts in their operations, now compete aggressively with the recreational facilities of private clubs. Luxury resorts, time share community club concepts, and hotels now are replicating the *club experience* and compete aggressively for this business. These competitive pressures on clubs today have created a different environment from the past decades. Private clubs must be led by professional managers who can assure quality club facilities, experiences, and an extraordinary level of service its members demand, and do so at a high level of value for the dollars invested.

Ownership and Types of Clubs

There are basically two types of ownerships in the golf and club management industry: member-owned clubs called **equity clubs** and non-member owned clubs called **non-equity clubs**. Equity clubs are owned by the members and typically hold a private non-profit status. This does not mean the clubs are not profitable, rather it means that no individual or group of individuals or corporate entity may benefit from the income or profit from the club. The money earned must be reinvested back into the club. Most private exclusive clubs are **non-profit 501c7 clubs** as regulated by the U.S. Internal Revenue Service (IRS). These are not open to the general public and are typically governed by a Board of Directors who are elected by the membership. Members are not only the customers and guests, they are also the owners or shareholders (i.e., they own equity in the club). Each member has a vote when deciding major club issues and admitting new members (unless the member has a type of membership that restricts voting privileges). Managers of these private exclusive clubs work directly for the members (Premier Club Services, 2010).

There are five key components to the operations of a 501c7 club. IRS regulations allow it to be tax exempt from federal tax income liabilities, which provides substantial cost savings in taxes on an annual basis. For example, if a club earns $1 million in revenue after all expenses and is in a 46% corporate tax rate level based on revenues, it would save 46% or $460,000 in federal income taxes. These regulations include:

1. The club must be a club and organized for club purposes.
2. The club's purposes include being organized for pleasure, recreation, and other non-profit purposes, and such purposes must be clearly stated in the articles of incorporation and in the club's bylaws.
3. Substantially all of the club's activities must be for pleasure, recreation, or other non-profitable purposes (now called *the substantial rule* replacing the exclusive rule in IRS standards).
4. There may be no inurnment, meaning no net earnings may benefit any one individual or group of shareholders.
5. The club's charter must not contain a provision that discriminates on the basis of race, color, or religion. Single gender clubs (all male or all female) are permitted under the IRS rules (Premier Club Services, 2010; Part VII, Chapter 1, p. 2).

The regulations further require that a club files each year to retain and declare its 501c7 status and must prove that its income is from member services. Failure to file or violation of these standards would require the club to pay back taxes on the previous three operating years at the prevailing rate and the club would be taxed on full gross revenues, not the earnings after expenses and before taxes. Private exclusive clubs are permitted to engage in some outside income opportunities and this typically falls under the 15-35 rule. This rule states that a club may earn no more than 15% of its gross income from outside, non-member business. In addition, no more than 35% of all non-member income including functions, investments, and other income sources may not total more than 35% of all gross income. This is a two-step rule, which means that a club may not violate either the 15% or the 35% limits. General managers are responsible for monitoring, booking, and approving all types of outside income and this income is typically labeled as *unrelated business income (UBI)* (Premier Club Services, 2010).

Consequently, a 501c7 private exclusive club is very highly regulated; detailed function sheets listing all members, non-members, and income must be maintained for each club event. Separate records for all member and non-member income must be kept and losses in event income may not be used to offset income or avoid taxes. If audited, the club must prove that each event held at the club was a member event. If there is no proof, then the IRS counts the event as a non-member event and the income from the event is taxable. Clubs do have to pay taxes on the non-member income and, because it is so tightly and aggressively regulated by the IRS, the 501c7 exclusive club usually is managed to limit the number of non-member events. Charitable events such as charitable golf tournaments are permissible and do not count as non-member income (Premier Club Services, 2010).

Additional strict regulations also apply to what can and cannot be provided to members either on or off premises (noted as traditional and non-traditional services), and how land holdings and sales of capital items (land, parking lots, residential lots, etc.) may be disposed of. When they host a major public event, such as a PGA Tour event or Ryder Cup Tournament, 501c7 clubs such as The Country Club are required to forego their 501c7 status for the year, and pay the appropriate taxes for the revenue realized during the income year. A 501c7 club must be documented and applied for each year, and being such a club one year does not automatically qualify that club to remain such forever (Premier Club Services, 2010). Public courses and clubs operated by government entities are also exempted from taxes, but function at a lower operating budget and attract a different profile of the golf playing public.

Private for-profit equity clubs typically have a membership and are owned by an individual, group of individuals, partnership, or corporation and operated in such a manner as to earn a profit for the owners/investors. Members can sell their memberships for a profit or claim a loss should they leave the club during their lifetimes, but the income or loss is taxable. Non-equity clubs are owned by real-estate developers, corporations, individuals, or investment firms. These are taxed as a regular business according to their for-profit ownership type (Premier Club Services, 2010).

■ CLUB ORGANIZATIONAL STRUCTURE

A club's organizational structure depends in part on whether the club is an equity club, private or non-profit club, a private non-equity club, or a public club.

Non-Equity and Public Course Clubs' Management Structure

The organizational structure of a non-equity club differs from an equity club's structure in that it is not owned by their members but is owned by an individual, group of investors, or a corporation. There is no board of directors made up of club members but there may be an advisory board. The club is managed and directed by the club's general manager, who follows the owner's policies rather than policies established by the club's members (Perdue, 2007).

Some clubs have an advisory board (sometimes called a *board of governors*) and other member committees for the more important club areas (e.g., the clubhouse, golf course, and tennis facilities). However, these bodies typically have no policy making authority, power, or direct authority. Depending on the scope of the advisory committee's recommendations, the management team and staff may act on the recommendations or simply pass them on to the owner(s) or ownership team for review. The general manager is usually given complete authority to operate the club and accept new members, subject to the owner's oversight and review.

Public golf courses and clubs operate in much the same way, with the general manager or management team typically reporting to a parks and recreation director who then reports to a government body entity that may be a board of selectmen, city manager, mayor, or county commissioner(s). Public courses may have an advisory board or committee that helps set policy and these members may be appointed, elected, or volunteers.

Equity Clubs' Management Structure

To govern an equity private exclusive club, which involves providing assistance and policy direction to club managers and carrying out various other functions, its members typically elect those from its membership to serve on the club's board of directors. These elected officers have various responsibilities, the most important of which is to establish club policy and hire the management team and general manager, who then will perform the day-to-day operational aspects of the club. The elected president appoints members to serve on the club's committees and calls and sets board meetings. The club's department managers, assistant management team, and professionals (i.e., the golf and tennis professionals and course superintendent) report directly to the general manager. The general manager then reports to the board. The board reports directly to the members. At the top of the management hierarchy are the members. In the equity private exclusive club, the organizational structure is typically an inverted pyramid or hourglass shape with the members at the top and the general manager at the mid-point of the hour glass who then overseas a management team and staff (Perdue, 2007).

■ BOARD OF DIRECTORS

Generally speaking, an equity club's **board of directors** (called a **board of governors** at some clubs) establishes club policies and governs the club. A club board is made up of directors (the number varies from club to club) and the club's officers, which include the president, vice president, secretary, and treasurer. The club's general manager attends board meetings but is not considered a board member and does not vote on policy. A board's specific duties and responsibilities are spelled out in each club's bylaws. Typical responsibilities include: establishing general operating policies; overseeing the financial stability of the club (which includes reviewing the club's financial statements, approving its operating budget, taking action if the budget is not being followed, and so on); voting on new member candidates; and handling member discipline problems, including voting on whether to suspend or expel members. Another very important responsibility of the board is to hire the club's general manager. The general manager does work very closely with the board, makes recommendations, helps develop the agendas, keeps records, and orients new members to the board and club, but only typically carries out the policies decided by the board in the day-to-day operations of the club.

Executive Committee

If a club has an **executive committee**, it is usually composed of the club's officers. Sometimes the club's immediate past president is included, and the bylaws of some clubs permit the current president to appoint additional members if necessary. An executive committee usually has duties and responsibilities similar to those of the board of directors. It essentially is a "mini-board" that acts in lieu of the club's full board between board meetings and responds to issues that do not necessitate calling the whole board together (Perdue, 2007). The club's general manager typically participates in executive committee meetings as well as in meetings of the entire board, unless the committee is in executive session and/or reviewing the manager's or management team's performance(s).

■ OTHER CLUB COMMITTEES

In addition to these two major organizational structure components, there are a wide variety of other committees that involve club members in decision-making and policy directives. These club committees exist to: 1) carry out the responsibilities assigned to them by the club's board or bylaws, 2) advise the board and help it carry out certain responsibilities and duties, 3) provide input and assistance to club managers, and 4) listen for suggestions and other feedback from members and act as liaisons between club members and the club's board and managers or management team.

There are two types of club committees: standing and ad hoc. **Standing committees** are permanent committees that help the club conduct ongoing activities. **Ad hoc committees** are formed for a special purpose, such as assisting with a bigger-than-usual golf tournament, researching the club's history to prepare for a club's centennial celebration, or helping to plan and conduct a planning process for a major club renovation. An ad hoc committee is usually focused on a single problem or issue and remains in existence until that problem or issue is resolved. The club's board dissolves an ad hoc committee once its purpose is served.

Club committees can be very positive forces and provide an opportunity for the members to be more highly involved in the policy directives in the club and its operations. These committees can generate enthusiasm in the policy directives as best practices; or as worse practices can become so involved and micromanage all decisions in a club so as to limit the management team's effectiveness. All club committee members should be provided orientations to the club's policies and management team parameters to ensure the best possible working relationship between the committees, the board, and management. Some or all of these committees may or may not be found in a typical equity club and there may be many other committees in larger, more complex and diverse full-service clubs. The following standing committees are typically found in private exclusive clubs: strategic or long-range planning, finance, bylaws, nominating, membership, house, social, athletic, and golf course. Other ad hoc committees in a private, exclusive club may include strategic planning, renovation, building, or a professional tour event committee. The ad hoc committees are formed for only the short-term needs and for special reasons.

■ GOLF AND COUNTRY CLUB INDUSTRY PERFORMANCE

Depending upon the source and method of data collection, the number of golf facilities in the United States varies. The latest statistics from IBISWorld listed 11,427 golf courses (18 hole equivalent courses; 9 hole facilities are counted as half courses and multiple golf courses count as one facility) and country club facilities in the United States that generate $21.6 billion in annual revenues (IBISWorld, 2010). The number of facilities is down from the peak of slightly over 12,000 facilities earlier in this decade (IBISWorld, 2010). In fact, the recession has hit some clubs hard. In 2009, about 140 of the overall 16,000 courses (of all types) closed and only 15 new facilities opened. The recession and downturn in the economy and a slight decline in the number of golfers has contributed to this downturn since 2005 (**Figure 20-1**). With this overall decline in number of golfers, the number of rounds played has declined, too. In the first half of 2010, rounds of golf were down 2.7% from the previous year. IBISWorld *Industry Reports* projects the number of facilities to increase to about 12,400 by 2015 with annual revenues of $23.51 billion (IBISWorld, 2010).

Market Drivers

The market demand, called *market drivers*, in the golf and country club industry are influenced by a number of factors, including:

- Participation
- Number of courses and types of courses available to the playing public and private club members
- Condition of the course and the playing experience
- Demand for quality experiences and services, restricted to high-end or unique courses
- Price to play a round of golf
- Available time to play a full 18-hole round of golf
- Seasonal play and weather patterns
- Turf grass conditions

Golf participation is a key driving factor in the demand for golf. As more people play, more facilities and services are needed, more equipment is purchased, and more soft goods (balls, shoe, clothing, etc.) are consumed. The growth in recent years of junior, women, and minority

FIGURE 20-1 Golf Participation in the United States: 1993–2009.

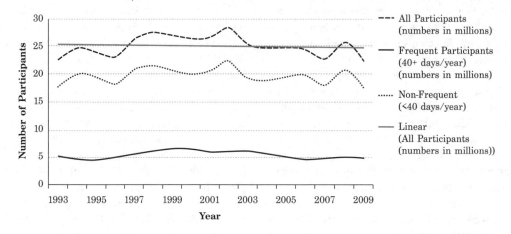

Source: Courtesy of National Sporting Goods Association (NSGA) (1993–2009). Source: Sports Business Research Network (www.SBRnet.com). Data compiled by Rod Warnick, PhD, University of Massachusetts at Amherst.

golfers also cannot be overlooked as these trends may influence current and future demand for the game and facilities (IBISWorld, 2010). Women continue to comprise about 25% of all golfers and, as noted here, of the youth and young adult golfers, the only segment growing in numbers is the 7- to 11-year-old demographic.

The number of golf courses and country clubs available for participation also influences demand. A greater supply of facilities or the development of new ones will encourage golfers to join and participate in the industry's activities.

The overall condition of golf courses will also affect how regularly people play. As competition for the consumer has increased, clubs are striving to provide quality conditions and services to gain a competitive edge. This has directly led to golf course condition improvements and the demand from the golfing public for course beauty and action similar to what they have observed on televised PGA Tournaments. New golf course maintenance technology improvements have enhanced the overall course design, layout, and playing conditions. These fac-

tors have contributed to a general demand for high quality courses over the past few decades, and correspondingly the cost of golf course maintenance by hole has also greatly increased (IBISWorld, 2010).

The ability to afford and be associated with a high quality or unique, long-standing exclusive club also influences membership demand. With this type of demand comes the status of being associated with a country club, especially a prestigious club with a waiting list. This status will influence overall demand for membership and, although membership of a country club may include both negative and positive connotations, the demand for these private exclusive, unique golf services, courses and experiences has increased strongly over the past two decades. The long-standing tradition of a country club membership that drove the evolution of the country club cannot be underestimated (Perdue 2007, IBISWorld, 2010).

The price to participate in a typical round of golf may also affect demand. If fee increases are too rapid or too high, people may reduce or withhold paying for the increased costs, reduce their playing volume, trade down to lower cost alternatives, and/or simply seek different recreational pursuits.

Other market drivers of demand include the popularity of other sports including tennis and exercise activities, including use of a fitness center at country clubs and more full service facilities; amount and level of leisure time available to people who play golf and other activities; impact of weather on participation; the latent demand factor or desire to increase sport participation and fitness levels; and the success of U.S. golfers on the professional golf circuit (i.e., the "win on Sunday, play on Monday" syndrome) (IBISWorld, 2010). The demand for tennis has increased from 2002 through 2008 as has the demand for fitness activities. The influx of day spas throughout the United States is a trend to be noted as it potentially affects full-service country clubs, some private clubs, and resort clubs.

The seasonal use of clubs and the opportunity to play throughout the year varies substantially across various regions of the United States. Generally, usage of country club and golf facilities declines during the first (January to March) and fourth (October to December) quarters of the year in the northern climates, when colder temperatures and shorter days reduce the demand for golf. Usage may also decline in southern climates when temperatures become too hot to play, due to extremely high heat indices, humidity, threat of thunderstorms, and overall heat stress conditions. Typically, country clubs generate a greater share of their yearly revenues in the third and fourth quarters, which includes end of the year tournaments, holidays, and year-end party season. As a result, firms usually generate a disproportionate share of revenues and cash flows in the second, third, and fourth quarters of each year and have lower revenues and profits in the first quarter (Perdue, 2007; IBISWorld, 2010).

Golf demand may also be affected by nonseasonal and severe weather patterns. Periods of extremely hot, cold, or rainy weather in a given region can be expected to reduce golf-related revenue. Droughts and extended periods of low or reduced rainfall may affect the availability and cost of water needed to irrigate golf courses and to keep fairways, tee boxes, and especially greens in optimal playing conditions. Optimal playing conditions require turf grass to remain at a stable growing cycle to retain color and speed to carry the golf ball across playing surfaces. This requires significant amounts of water, fertilization, and maintenance. Conversely, too much rain, floods, and high winds or violent storms may reduce or interrupt golf playing opportunities.

Market Segmentation

The average golfer is about 37 years old and is likely to keep playing as he or she ages. The influx of new young golfers over the last two decades has also slowed the statistical aging of the golf public. Participation profile by gender finds about 75% of the golfers to be men and 25% women. Participation in golf is directly related to income levels. For example, participation rates for those with income levels between $25,000 and $60,000 vary between 8% to 20% of their respective income brackets, while the biggest declines in golf participation in the last two decades have been with those in the household incomes of under $75,000 per year category (**Figure 20-2**). Those households with income levels over $150,000 have participation rates that reach nearly 30%. One segment that has stabilized the golf participation rates have been the frequent or highly involved golfing segment, defined as those who play golf more often. There has been a steady base of approximately 5 to 6 million frequent golfers who play golf more than 40+ days per year (National Sporting Goods Association, 2009); however, this portion of golfers who are frequent participants has declined slightly in the past decade as well. In 1993, 22%

FIGURE 20-2   Distribution of Golfers by Household Income: 1993–2006.

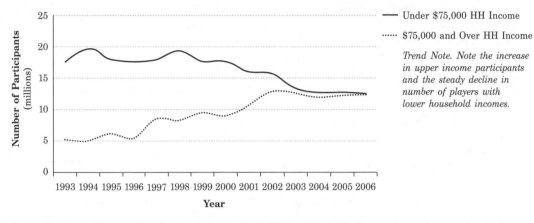

Source: Courtesy of National Sporting Goods Association (NSGA) (1993–2009). Source: Sports Business Research Network (www.SBRnet.com). Data compiled by Rod Warnick, PhD, University of Massachusetts at Amherst.

were frequent players, those who golfed over 40 times per year. In 2000, this percent had grown to 24%; however, by 2006, the percentage of frequent golfers had fallen back to 19% with this distribution of an overall smaller golfing population **(Figure 20-3)**. In 2006 the NGF noted at the Golf 2020 Summit that the distribution of the frequent golf-playing segment (NGF calls them *core golfers*) had also declined slightly during the decade, resulting in the overall flatness and slight decline in the number of rounds played (Beditz, 2006). This is likely a result of some golfers simply not playing as much by dropping below the 40 times per year threshold.

Market Segmentation Product Types

As stated above, consumers can choose from at least three viable facility options: public golf courses, private golf courses, and private exclusive country clubs. Public golf courses account for the dominant share of the market types, comprising 38.5% of the market courses/facilities (IBISWorld, 2010). These courses tend to attract individual golfers who play on an occasional basis and do not want to pay a yearly membership to a private club or a country club. These courses generally undertake lower levels of marketing and lower levels of investment in

FIGURE 20-3   Distribution of Golf Player Types: 1993, 2000 and 2005.

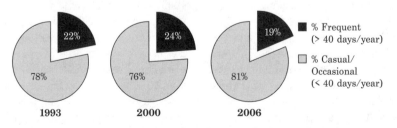

Source: Courtesy of National Sporting Goods Association (NSGA) (1993–2009). Source: Sports Business Research Network (www.SBRnet.com). Data compiled by Rod Warnick, PhD, University of Massachusetts at Amherst.

upkeep and maintenance, and typically attract only a limited number of special outings and tournaments. According to IBISWorld *Industry Reports* (2010), the size of the segment has increased by about 2% since 2000 due to a greater proportion of public and daily fee golf courses being built.

Private golf courses or golf clubs without the full-scale offerings of a country club's facilities account for 34.1% of the market types of courses (IBISWorld, 2010). Yearly memberships are available and charged to those who prefer them, but the courses are also open to the public and do charge greens fees and cart rentals that are higher than public courses for non-members and visitors. Because these facilities are often focused specifically on golf, some are of equal quality to private country clubs while others provide basic, above-average quality golfing experiences. These courses are more expensive than public facilities and more serious golfers with higher skills or lower handicaps tend to play there. Due to the higher quality golf experience and a private for-profit motive, these courses not only charge more but also attract more corporate or business golfing days and tournaments. According to IBISWorld *Industry Reports* (2010), the number of private clubs has not increased and, as a result of overbuilding in some U.S. regions, this segment has actually declined by about 2% since 2000.

Private exclusive country clubs account for the remaining 27.4% of the market types (IBISWorld, 2010). These were the dominant type of U.S. golf operations existing through the 1960s, but as golf became a game played by a more diverse clientele and spread into the middle and lower classes, the demand for public, private, and semiprivate courses increased. Membership fees at private country clubs are generally the highest and typically include a large initiation fee in addition to annual or monthly dues. These facilities are also more full service and offer the highest level of quality services and facility standards. This segment of the golf course and club field has been relatively stable in numbers since 2000, with some downturn in smaller and older country clubs.

Course Locations and Participation Levels

Over the years the bulk of new golf course and club construction has moved both west and south. The number of golf facilities are now more heavily concentrated in the southeast, where 25.1% of the establishments are located, and in the Great Lakes region where 20.7% are located (IBISWorld, 2010). The playing season is simply longer in the southeast, and more private communities, resorts and local governments now offer golf facilities, courses, and clubs in these areas. Florida has the most golf facilities of any state with 1,054, followed by California with 937 as of 2010 (IBISWorld, 2010). The warm weather, longer playing season, and the reduced level of days subjected to cold or poor playing conditions contribute to more demand for golf in these areas. Growing population centers in the southeast, particularly in cities such as Charlotte, Raleigh/Durham, and Atlanta are driving a stronger demand for golf. Florida, South Carolina, and Georgia's warm coastal areas have seen an increase in construction of new facilities in this region as well. The Great Lakes region traditionally has had a large number of establishments due to lower land prices and high water levels, which help lower overall maintenance costs. The upper Midwest states show sustained and higher household participation rates and a greater concentration of frequent golfers than elsewhere in the United States.

Not surprisingly, the southeastern region holds the highest percentage level of revenue at 29.8% (IBISWorld, 2010). This is due to several reasons: 1) the larger number of golf courses and country clubs; 2) an increase in the golf playing population; 3) more golfing vacation days or visits to the region to play golf; and, 4) an older and aging population and longer-term residents who migrated from the northern climates who have increased leisure time availability (**Figure 20-4**).

Golf and Country Club Firms

There are no dominant players in the golf course and country club industry. This sector of the economy is highly fragmented. Only a few large firms operate hundreds of courses, several medium size companies own and/or operate between five and 20 courses, and dozens of companies operate two to four courses. Thousands are stand-alone, single course operations.

The largest golf course operators are: Club-Corp (estimated market share 2.5%), American

Golf Corporation (estimated 1.2% market share), Century Golf Partners (estimated 1.0% market share), Troon Golf (estimated 1.0% market share), and Palmer Golf (estimated < 1.0% market share). These same operators accounted for about 8% market share in 2002 (IBISWorld, 2010). The level of market share within the industry will likely not change substantially in the future. There are a number of reasons for this, including: 1) the high fragmentation of the industry; 2) geographic challenges in achieving economies of scale via mergers and acquisitions; 3) operations that are not standardized; 4) higher investment costs to acquire both large parcels of undeveloped land and existing golf courses and

FIGURE 20-4 Distribution of Golf Courses by State, 2010.

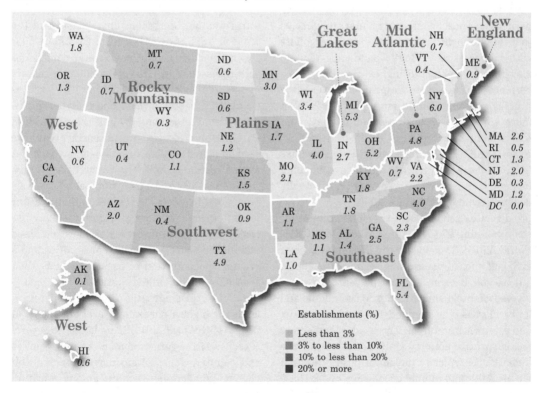

Source: Courtesy of IBISWorld Industry Report 71391, *Golf Courses & Country Clubs in the United States.* (IBISWorld 2010.)

country clubs; and 5) the development costs to build new state-of-the-art golf complexes. These combined factors are likely to force slower overall growth in this sector. Consolidation is likely to continue to occur and may accelerate in the short term as small establishments, particularly those under financial pressure with declining revenues and members and high debt loads, seek to sell or merge with other larger operations. Larger profitable golf operations will likely be able to purchase golf courses at much lower or distressed values, and these firms will increase their portfolio, potential profitability, and stature (e.g., Trump National).

Cost Factor Benchmarks

The cost structure and benchmarks to monitor in the operation of golf courses and country clubs are dependent upon the type of facilities and experiences being offered, and the structure and size of the respective operation. Overall, this sector observes a relative poor level of growing profitability. This is due to the current economic downturn but also because a significant portion of the industry is comprised of private exclusive clubs that are a 501c7 non-profit organization. These facilities seek to break even, so any profits are retained and re-invested back into the operation. Because many costs are relatively fixed from year to year, profits are largely based on achieving membership goals, maintaining or increasing attendance at various functions, and maintaining or increasing participation (use) benchmarks. In the early years of the current performance period (the last decade), golf operations averaged a pretax profit margin of about 2% to 4%. Since the recession hit in 2008–2009, household wealth and spending have declined, and show a sharp decline in some regions. Profitability for some operations are into the red, which requires further reductions in costs, special assessments in private exclusive clubs of the membership, or consolidation or reduction

of services in other public or private for-profit operations. While earnings in clubs are expected to improve in the coming years, the overall short-term picture suggests that some losses for certain types of clubs will continue, especially for those clubs that do not take aggressive budgetary corrections (IBISWorld, 2010).

The major cost factors in golf and country club operations are direct purchases for fertilizers, plants, food, beverages, golf equipment for rent and resale, and other miscellaneous materials. This accounts for 40% of the operations' expenses. These cost proportions are variable based on the size and structure of the individual golf operation but remain relatively stable from year to year. Labor costs also comprise a large proportion of the operation's expenses at approximately 36% (IBISWorld, 2010). Golf operations are highly labor intensive due to regular course maintenance, development requirements, and service positions (including food and golf playing services) to meet the needs of golfing and club patrons/members.

Capital costs are relatively small in this industry, as depreciation amounts to about 2% of overall revenue. These expenses are allocated for vehicles, golf carts, lawnmowers, and other maintenance machinery as well as kitchen and computer equipment, all of which have longer life cycles with the improved production and manufacturing techniques over the last two decades (IBISWorld, 2010).

Miscellaneous costs amount to 20% of this sector's expenses. For those clubs trying to obtain competitive advantages in the marketplace, all market, advertising, and promotion costs tend to increase. Investment or discretionary capital to expand existing properties, facilities, and offerings, as well as entering into new business opportunities varies greatly. There are no clear patterns as these expenses fluctuate substantially from year to year and across the variety of golf operations (IBISWorld, 2010).

Basis of Competition in the Marketplace

The success of golf and country club operations depends on their ability to attract new members, retain existing members, sell the club's amenities and golf outing business for tournaments, charitable, and special events, and to maintain or increase the level of club usage by both the members and guests.

Although most golf and country club operations in the profit sector devote significant resources to promote their facilities and services, a number of the factors affecting club membership and usage are beyond the establishment's control. In addition, private exclusive clubs are not permitted to advertise and must seek members through referrals, incentives, and other means. Local and federal government laws for 501c7 clubs, including income tax regulations, are applicable to club members and the number of guests who may use the club; this can adversely influence membership activity and income potential. Furthermore, changes in consumer tastes and preferences, local, regional and national economic conditions—including levels of disposable income, weather, and demographic trends—may also affect demand for club membership and daily usage.

These golf operations also experience strong competition from comparable and non-comparable rivals. Establishments compete primarily on the basis of the management and professionals' expertise, their reputation, featured facilities, quality and breadth of services, golfing and recreational/entertainment experiences, and price.

For potential patrons and members, the geographic location of the facility may be a major influence when choosing a golf course to play. This factor alone can be particularly influential when one is deciding to join the club as well as considering the substantial monetary outlay for the initiation and ongoing membership fees. The level of competition varies from region to region and locale to locale, and is subject to

change as existing facilities are renovated or new facilities are developed. An increase in the number or quality of clubs and other facilities in a particular region could significantly increase competition and steal away existing members from one operation to another in the same locale (Perdue, 2007; National Club Association 2010; and IBISWorld, 2010).

For business and corporate usage, facilities such as conference rooms, business facilities, reciprocal rights, restaurants, bars, cafes, other complimentary sports facilities, and unique features can influence the choice of venue (Perdue, 2007).

Competition can also be based on the skill level of particular players. A golfer with either a high handicap or low playing ability is less likely to regularly play on a very expensive golf course. Similarly, a golf course that is particularly challenging to play is less likely to attract low-skilled players. The quality of the course that provides a high quality playing experience tends to attract higher demand and if the course is perceived to be a good value for the quality and is priced reasonably then demand should go up. Golfers are reluctant to play on a high-priced golf course that is not maintained to a superior standard or is overly difficult to play. Players with high skills or low handicaps are more likely to pay to play on a high-quality golf course. Courses that offer mid-week pricing discounts can attract additional patronage during slow periods. Average prices for a round of golf at the lower end of the market are between $20 and $25 for an 18 hole round. For top of the range courses, fees are upwards of $80 to $100 for an 18-hole round (IBISWorld, 2010). Value pricing and packaging of meals/dinner, cart rental, and lessons with a round of golf are now much more commonplace. Resorts are packaging golf experiences into their vacation plans as well.

Finally, based on evidence of a moderate level of consolidation in the last few years, there will be considerable opportunities in the coming years for consolidation in this fragmented sector. Will this continue? Through the acquisition of golf course operations, companies will continue to compete primarily on the basis of price, competitive location, and reputation for delivering quality experiences through their golf course operations. The marketing and management of golf courses and country clubs that deliver quality experiences at a higher perceived value will impact the choice of facilities and activity level selected. When a golf operation has the opportunity to acquire other facilities and become a bigger and more recognized market player, then it is easier to break through this clutter and gain a competitive edge. An excellent current example would be Trump National's acquisitions of clubs over the last few years.

■ PROFESSIONAL STAFF POSITIONS IN A PRIVATE GOLF CLUB

The management team of a golf club is made up of a group of highly skilled and trained professionals. This was not always the case. In the past, members of the club often tried to manage and operate the club or course on their own. However, due to the size and lack of volunteers, more clubs have hired staff and given the day-to-day operations over to professional management teams, who are specialists in a variety of skill areas. The following describes the types of positions available in golf course and country club operations.

Management Team

Private equity clubs, because the members own them, can operate as the members desire; but, these clubs, along with non-equity clubs and public clubs, now typically involve professional managers and industry specialists. The preferred organizational management structure employs a management team endorsed by the Club Managers Association of America (CMAA) that is comprised of club professionals; department heads; certified professionals in food and beverage management (including chefs, cooks, and bartenders); sport management professionals (golf, tennis, and aquatics professionals); grounds and golf course superintendents; building and engineering technicians/specialists, and other specialty staff members who report to a general manager (Perdue, 2007; CMAA, 2010).

The official executive management position in the club is the general manager. This person's title may vary from club to club; he or she can be referred to as an executive director, director of club operations, or chief operating officer or executive (COO), but most refer to the lead executive of the management team as simply the general manager. The general manager is hired by the club's board of directors or owners and is responsible to the entire board but usually reports directly to the club president or owner(s). It is the general manager's duty to carry out the policies set by the board (Perdue, 2007).

The general manager's salary and fringe benefits are negotiable but usually correlate with the size of the club and the manager's experience. Fringe benefits for general managers might include all or some of the following: vacation (usually 2 to 4 weeks per year); sick leave; insurance (health, disability, life); pension or investment retirement plan; use of the club's facilities or a membership at a nearby sister club; housing or living quarters; automobile or club-leased car arrangement; paid professional association membership; and continuing education for professional development (Perdue, 2007).

Club Professionals

Professionals commonly found at country or city clubs are golf, tennis, and fitness club/center professionals. In recent years, spa professionals are being added as clubs expand their services to members. A club's golf course superintendent is not considered a club professional, though, but instead a professional in turf, agronomy, or plant and soil sciences. The golf course or grounds superintendent position works very closely with golf professionals and is considered to be at a similar organizational level. Because of its sports-related nature, an aquatic director's position may or may not be considered a club professional but is in a typical administrative function area overseeing a sport facility, which is the swimming center, pool area(s), or beach, and sport-related staff that include the lifeguards and water safety instructors (Perdue, 2007).

■ GOLF PROFESSIONAL

A club's golf professional, also referred to as a *golf pro* or *director of golf*, is in charge of all activities related to the club's golf program, such as working with the general manager to prepare the golf budget, teaching golf to members, supervising other teaching pros on staff, conducting club golf tournaments, overseeing the club's handicap system, overseeing the tee-time reservation system, maintenance and liaison on the locker room operations, arranging a tee-time schedule, supervising the use and maintenance of the club's golf cars, equipment rentals and repair, and running the golf pro shop. The golf pro may or may not own the pro shop merchandise, depending on the club and the administrative appointment as a club staff or professional, or act in a service role as an independent contractor. Golf professionals are certified through the Professional Golfers Association (PGA) and are likely graduates of a professional golf management school or program. These professionals are typically trained in all aspects of golf instruction and golf business techniques, and most often begin their careers as interns, progressing to assistant golf professionals before rising to the level of golf

professional in increasingly responsible positions. Some eventually become the director of golf in single large or multiple club operations. Others aspire and conclude their careers by being managers or eventually general managers of their operations, but this is more typical in a large golf club operation with multiple courses or locations as opposed to a full service country club or full service resort club operation. In seasonal clubs, assistant golf professionals may split their time between seasonal clubs in a northern and southern climate (Perdue, 2007; PGALinks, 2010).

■ TENNIS PROFESSIONAL

A club's tennis professional manages the club's tennis program. He or she gives individual lessons to members, establishes clinics for members of all ages, oversees the maintenance of the tennis courts, actively works with the club's tennis committee or tennis advisory committee, and works with the general manager to prepare a budget for the program. If the club is seasonal and lacks both indoor and outdoor or platform tennis facilities, then the tennis professional may be a part-time seasonal position. Some tennis professionals work *swing jobs,* where their season is split between two different locations such as a New England club during the summer and a Florida club in the winter. Tennis professionals are certified through the U.S. Tennis Association (USTA) and most likely played tennis competitively. Upon completion of their competitive careers, these tennis professionals evolved into teaching and management responsibilities, first interning and later as a teaching assistant professional before promotion to a head tennis professional position (Perdue, 2007; United States Tennis Association, 2010).

■ GOLF COURSE SUPERINTENDENT

A club's golf course superintendent is in charge of maintaining the golf course's green environment and playing areas in an ideal playing condition. The golf course superintendent's expertise is basically in the business of keeping the grass green, in top playing condition, and disease-free. A superintendent typically has a degree in turf grass management or agronomy and works to mold the natural elements of grass, trees, hills, streams, and ponds, or in a dry climate, rock formations, native plants, and topography, into a beautiful golf course that works with the existing landscape. The superintendent must constantly monitor the environment to protect the course including carefully tracking the weather conditions. The superintendent and his or her staff develop integrated pest and disease management programs to aid against plant disease, insects, pests, adverse weather conditions, and other environmental factors that threaten the prime playing and turf conditions. The golf course superintendent also works with the club's general manager and golf course committee to develop the golf course budget. Most golf course superintendents begin their careers as a grounds staff member, and then acquire an assistant golf course superintendent position before advancing to a head golf course superintendent position. The Golf Course Superintendents Association of America (GCSAA) offers golf course superintendents a professional certification program enabling them to be recognized for their achievements in golf course management. The professional designation Certified Golf Course Superintendent (CGCS) is bestowed upon those who meet the association's stringent certification requirements. This designation is the most widely recognized in the golf industry and is the highest level of recognition to be achieved in grounds and turf management.

■ AQUATICS DIRECTOR

A club's aquatics director, also known as the head swim professional in some clubs, is an important water safety professional. An aquatic

director's responsibility is substantial and life preserving, because he or she is constantly dealing with members in situations where bad judgment or lack of skill might end in tragedy. The aquatics director is professionally trained in physical education and possesses superior administrative abilities and aquatics skills. Aquatics directors typically begin their careers as a lifeguard, a water safety instructor, and then assistant aquatics director before eventually becoming an aquatics director. An aquatics director should be friendly but at the same time command respect so that he or she can effectively enforce the club's safety rules and maintain a safe swimming environment. While most are employed in facilities with pools, some clubs also have waterfront access and a beach where the larger bodies of water may require additional water safety skills and oversight. Depending upon the types of facilities, such as pools versus waterfront locations (lakes, ponds, rivers, or oceans), local chapters of the American Red Cross offer specialized training and certification for lifeguards, water safety, and waterfront directors that is specific to their locales (Perdue, 2007; American Red Cross, 2010).

■ SPA DIRECTORS

With the addition of new spa complexes to private clubs and country clubs, spa management and staff positions are becoming more prominent. The rapid development of new day, resort, and club spas has been a fast evolving trend in recent years. As traditionally occurs in emerging growth industries, a corresponding demand for qualified employees to occupy key management and support positions within the facilities that were built to capture a hot market has intensified. Spa directors should be certified and able to identify and hire qualified massage therapists to be able to meet the needs of clientele who may not be entirely familiar with the tasks and massage techniques. He or she must also be able to balance the competing needs of club's management staff, therapists employed, and the members served. The National Certification Board certifies spa directors and therapists for Massage and Bodywork (NCBMB).

DEPARTMENT MANAGERS

The number and type of department managers a club has depends on the type and size of the club. For example, a very small city club might have only an executive chef and a catering or banquet manager in addition to the general manager. At the other extreme, a very large country club might have a food and beverage director, an executive chef, banquet manager, beverage manager, clubhouse manager, director of security, executive housekeeper, controller, membership director, director of human resources, spa and/or fitness director, an events and communications director, and a director of purchasing in the main clubhouse in addition to the sport professionals and administrators of the sport facilities (Perdue, 2007).

CLUBHOUSE MANAGER

The clubhouse manager is usually the general manager's second in command. He or she is in charge of managing the clubhouse and its personnel and enforcing clubhouse policies and operating procedures. An assistant manager, in some clubs, might assume the second-in-command role and have more extensive duties and the clubhouse manager may report to this manager (Perdue, 2007).

CONTROLLER

A club's controller develops and oversees policies to control and coordinate accounting, auditing, budgeting, and related duties; prepares or oversees the preparation of the club's financial statements; and analyzes and forecasts financial information for the club's managers, board of directors, and committees. This person is typically a certified public accountant (CPA) or a degreed accountant (Perdue, 2007).

EXECUTIVE CHEF

The executive chef is responsible for all food production in a club's food and beverage outlets. Executive chefs develop menus, develop food purchase specifications and recipes, supervise food-production staff members, and develop budget reports to monitor food and labor costs for the department. He or she is also responsible for maintaining the highest food quality and sanitation standards. At some clubs, a food and beverage director oversees the executive chef and other food and beverage department managers, in which case the executive chef's role may be restricted. The executive chef is typically trained as a culinary chef and certified by the American Culinary Federation (ACF, 2010). This credential requires a considerable amount of education and work experience, requiring a freshly educated chef to move up through the chain of command in order to obtain the Certified Executive Chef (CEC) position. This usually requires a formal culinary education, but in some cases work experience may offset formal educational training (Perdue, 2007; ACF, 2010).

BANQUET OR EVENT MANAGER

A club's banquet manager promotes the club's dining facilities for private banquets, business and social meetings, and other activities. This person oversees all administrative and operational aspects of preparing and serving food at banquets, and works with the executive chef to put together banquet menus. This person typically has a formal education in hospitality and food service management with a concentration in food, restaurant, or event management. Some event management professionals may have education training in sport event management if the club is heavily involved in outings and tournaments (Perdue, 2007).

■ MEMBERSHIP DIRECTOR

A membership director may work closely with the membership committee in a private equity club to help identify, close and/or introduce, and oversee club membership categories and the club's waitlist. In a private non-equity for-profit club, the membership director may have a highly active role in membership recruitment and retention. There may also be incentives and a commission paid to the individual in recruiting new members. This person may help manage and coordinate member guest events and invitations, and assist the event manager and the banquet manager on special membership events. This person typically has a sales management or marketing background and/or education, and must promote the facility through direct personal contact and one-to-one sales and membership meetings. They may hold a degree in marketing, sport management, or hospitality management.

■ EMPLOYEES

A club's employees report to department managers (or intermediate supervisors) and create products and services for club members. As with a club's managers and professionals, the number and types of employees a club has depends on the type and size of the club. For example, at a small city club, the kitchen might only have a few cooks in addition to the executive chef. A large country club might employ an executive chef, sous chef, sauce cook, fry cooks, line prep persons, breakfast cooks, chef-de-garde manger (cold station), butcher, broiler cooks, sauté cooks, and salad prep persons. The same organizational issues may also affect other departments such as grounds, golf operations, sport facilities, maintenance staff, and housekeeping.

■ STRATEGIES FOR ENTERING GOLF MANAGEMENT AND CLUB OPERATIONS

The club management field provides opportunities for career development and advancement for those who choose to pursue the club management career path. This is largely achieved by following the strategy to become a certified club manager (CCM).

Students may begin their career path by accumulating certification points while still in school. Students may seek to work for independent, stand alone, private; or private non-profit clubs as one entry path into club management. One specific way is to pursue club management internships during the summer months at independent, stand alone, or private or private non-profit clubs. Those pursuing a corporate career path should seek summer employment and internships created at a number of larger companies, such as ClubCorp, American Golf, or Troon Golf. These large corporations oversee multiple club facilities and offer employees potential career paths into well-paying management positions.

On the sport professional side, students who have a passion for such sports as golf, tennis, racquetball, and other sports may pursue positions as assistant professionals who teach and direct these sports for the membership. The PGA (golf), USTA (tennis), and ARC (swimming) offer career paths for those who love the game and would like to teach the game as part of their career. Those wanting to work outdoors may pursue a career as a golf course superintendent. Students may find an internship involving turf and course grounds and recreational facilities maintenance; certification would be through the GCSAA (discussed previously).

Success in this industry requires a combination of club management expertise, sport and food service knowledge, and general business skills. Club professionals must be able to do what is expected of managers in general: know how to read and analyze an income statement and balance sheet properly; prepare budgets; develop and implement membership and marketing plans; manage, hire, and train employees; plan and execute events; and use excellent member service skills. Knowledge in food service, food safety, inventory control, beverage management, and banquet and dining room management are essential in the clubhouse. Additionally, sport professionals guide the sport and fitness activities of club members, so their depth of knowledge and expertise in specific sport or fitness activities increases the attractiveness of candidates for permanent jobs.

Educational preparation for careers in club management is derived from college and professional associations. Because success in this field requires an understanding of business and club management skills and sport professional concepts, degree programs in club management in a hospitality program, sport management, and exercise science or professional golf management are particularly relevant. These areas of study may be viewed as complementary, and colleges that offer courses in each of these professional areas offer the best opportunity for the widest choices and preparation for the club management field.

Understanding and responding to the sport and special event needs of club members requires specific knowledge sport instruction and event planning. Coursework in human anatomy and physiology, kinesiology, and nutrition is particularly helpful for those seeking to break into this industry through the sport side. Courses in turf management, plant and soil sciences, pest management, and grounds maintenance are essential for those destined for a career in golf course turf management. Those seeking entry through the clubhouse side of the industry must take management courses in club, events, food and beverage, and banquet management, plus related

hospitality management courses. A background in club management can prepare a person to face the myriad of management, legal, marketing, accounting, and financial issues involved in the successful operation of a golf or country club.

Beyond earning a college degree in the above-named fields, a person on the club management career track can connect with the Club Managers Association of America (CMAA), the PGA, or the USTA for advanced educational opportunities and certification programs. CMAA offers the appropriate education training for entry-level managers to advance in a club management career as well as the Certified Club Manager (CCM) program.

Students wishing to pursue a career in the golf side of the business as a golf professional may pursue a golf management degree at one of the 20 Professional Golf Management (PGM) programs located at various universities across the country (http://www.pgalinks.com). The PGA Golf Management University Program is a 4.5- to 5-year college curriculum for aspiring PGA professionals requiring 600 hours of work experience; four specifically designed golf internships are offered. Existing college students may also become PGA professional members by becoming registered apprentices and going through the PGA Professional Golf Management (PGA PGM) program. This program provides the opportunity to acquire the knowledge and skills necessary for success in the golf industry through extensive classroom studies and internship experiences. The PGA claims a 100% job placement rate for those who complete the PGA PGM University Program (PGALinks, 2010).

Students seeking a career in the turf management side of the business can gain a turf management degree generally in an agronomy, plant, soils, or turf management from an agricultural college or university across the country. A list of schools is on the PGALinks Web site (http://www.pgalinks.com). To be a golf course superintendent, a student must master agronomy and turf grass management practices; possess a working knowledge of golf facility construction principles, practices, and methods; and possess a thorough understanding of the rules and strategies of the game of golf.

Other positions in the golf course maintenance operations include assistant golf course superintendent, equipment manager, and assistant equipment manager. Occasionally, a golf course superintendent may aspire to become a club general manager. This is more likely to occur in a public or private golf club where the emphasis is entirely on golf and less on the social functions and full-service aspects of a larger country club or resort club. Students interested in learning more about the golf maintenance side of the industry should become involved with the GCSAA by visiting the association's Web site (http://www.gcsaa.org) or becoming involved with a local university student chapter.

Pay Scales and Salaries

Club staff and employees often enjoy wages and benefits competitive with or even higher than those of other employees in the hospitality industry. Many club employees stay with their clubs for extended periods or return seasonally because of the pleasant surroundings and competitive wages. It is not unusual to find club line employees who have worked at their clubs for decades. These employees often appreciate the uniqueness of the upscale club environment, job security, family atmosphere, fringe benefits, and seasonal nature that are typical of these facility operations.

The CMAA conducts one of the more comprehensive wage and compensation surveys in the club industry every two years. These surveys go out to controllers and general managers working at about 900 clubs. Their responses provide an overview of the types of salaried and staff positions and the pay scales and benefits offered to such operations. These surveys, though, represent private exclusive country, city, and yacht clubs and not semi-private or public facilities where the wages are typically lower, but these statistics are a useful benchmark for those seeking a career in club and golf operations management. The survey examines pay scales for a wide selection of job types in clubs from the Chief Operating Officers to the entry-level staff positions. The most recent study covers the 2009 operating year (CMAA, 2009).

■ ENTRY LEVEL AND MID-MANAGEMENT SALARY SCALES

Table 20-1 compares the average salaries for entry level and mid-management salaries in club management in 2007 and 2009. These salaries represent clubs that are primarily private exclusive non-profit clubs. Salaries in private for-profit clubs would be expected to be comparable; however, public clubs and semi-private club salaries would be slightly lower. The positions students might seek to fill with internship and management-in-training experiences would include assistant manager, dining room manager, membership assistant or director, food and beverage manager, catering manager, and director or assistant technology manager. The two fastest growing positions in clubs are membership manager/director and director of technology. In some clubs, event or dining room managers are being hired and may report to the banquet or catering manager or be part of staff in these departments. Assistant manager positions are also being expanded in larger clubs to spread the work effort and improve the quality of life for young managers in the profession as well as to prepare them for promotions.

In private club management, managers and nearly all staff receive a salary and, depending upon the performance of the club, an annual bonus. These bonuses are substantial as noted in Table 20-1 and often carry through to staff and hourly positions. For example, the average salary

TABLE 20-1   Salaried Staff Positions for Entry and Mid-Level Managers in Club Management 2007–2009

Salaried Staff Salaries and Bonuses

	Total Compensation		Average Salary		Additional Income (Incl. Bonuses and Lessons)	
	2009	2007	2009	2007	2009	2007
Assistant Manager	$68,257	$65,211	$57,355	$56,673	$9,594	$6,139
Clubhouse Manager	$87,322	$77,769	$74,897	$68,725	$11,198	$7,717
Food and Beverage Director	$72,279	$62,356	$59,139	$51,414	$11,512	$6,323
Catering Manager	$57,457	$53,493	$46,324	$45,000	$11,519	$7,996
Executive Chef	$89,853	$87,091	$76,740	$77,483	$10,720	$7,374
Director of Technology	$80,674	$64,500	$67,575	$57,028	$8,894	$6,221
Human Resources Manager	$66,666	$58,678	$54,224	$49,368	$8,863	$4,469
Chief Financial Officer	$122,862	$106,996	$108,157	$95,518	$14,944	$10,459
Accountant/Controller	$80,226	$72,101	$68,041	$62,208	$9,031	$5,288
Office Manager	$55,380	$48,820	$44,474	$42,180	$9,123	$3,275
Secretary/Administrative Assistant	$41,496	$36,636	$35,107	$35,162	$4,682	$2,027
Membership/Marketing Director	$64,907	$62,199	$48,818	$47,267	$16,154	$14,184
Golf Course Superintendent	$121,874	$114,049	$103,555	$99,493	$14,232	$9,840
Head of Building Maintenance	$59,545	$57,064	$51,415	$48,722	$6,194	$3,914
Health and Fitness Director	$70,185	$63,716	$49,040	$46,228	$20,934	$17,865
Head Golf Professional	$107,161	$102,237	$82,446	$81,969	$24,882	$18,706
Assistant Golf Professional	$46,806	$43,863	$33,563	$34,121	$12,855	$9,281
Head Tennis Professional	$81,859	$77,378	$41,562	$46,451	$36,229	$29,800
Assistant Tennis Professional	$45,009	$53,958	$19,681	$27,293	$25,679	$23,627

Source: Courtesy of CMAA 2009 Compensation and Benefits Report (Market Connect, 2009).

for a clubhouse manager in 2009 was $74,897 with an annual average bonus of $11,198. This average salary was up from $68,725 in 2007 with an annual average bonus of $7,717.

Golf and tennis professionals in private clubs also earn competitive salaries. An average salary for head golf professional in 2009 was $82,466 with an annual average bonus of $18,706. This average salary was up from $81,969 in 2007 with an annual average bonus of $24,882 including both bonuses and lesson revenue. An average salary for a head tennis professional in 2009 was $41,562 with an annual average bonus of $36,229.

Golf course superintendent professionals earn very competitive salaries. An average salary for a head golf course superintendent in 2009 was $103,555 with an annual average bonus of $14,232. Building and grounds professionals in clubs earned an average $51,415 in 2009 with an annual average bonus of $6,194 (Table 20-1).

■ PROFESSIONAL EXECUTIVE CLUB MANAGEMENT POSITIONS

Professional career managers at the highest levels in clubs earn highly competitive salaries. The top management positions in clubs are typically labeled: chief operating officer (COO); general manager (GM), manager, or clubhouse manager. In 2009, the average total compensation package for a COO was $229,248; for a GM $167,766, for a manager $121,212, and for a club manager $110,168. The overall average total compensation package for a career club management professional in 2009 was $182,176 (**Table 20-2**).

Staffing clubs for managers is a challenge when the open hours for clubs may require up to two to three 40-hour shifts per week. Managers should be prepared to cover over 100 hours in an average work week. Club managers and staff members in country clubs and those within sport and golf operations are required to work weekends, early morning, or evening shifts. Managers on salary may be required to work 60- to 80-hour work weeks during the busy season. Despite the long hours in the club field, there are bonuses and the opportunity to experience other clubs, extended benefit and bonus packages, plus other benefits such as housing and meals provided. Managers and staff may also be provided with free golf, tennis, and other sport and fitness privileges at their club or a nearby comparable club. Entry level managers and staff are typically very supportive of each other and are pursuing these careers for the lifestyles and overall quality of life compared to some other professions as well as helping others live healthy and productive lives. This industry is definitely for people who like being surrounded by high-energy, like-minded people.

Finally, club managers who do advance their careers through the certification process are rewarded for such efforts. The CCM certification process has a dramatic impact on salaries. The average salary of a certified manager across all manager types in the club management field is $204,231 versus a non-certified manager receiving $162,932.

■ CURRENT AND FUTURE ISSUES FOR GOLF AND CLUB MANAGEMENT

The Golf 2020 Summit was convened in 2006 when concerns for the game of golf were mounting. Since 2000, clear indications of an industry plateau present a number of challenges for the

TABLE 20-2 Average Compensation by Management Title in Clubs, 2009					
	Components of Total Compensation				
Title	Total Compensation	Base Salary	Deferred Compensation	Total Bonuses	Total Benefits
CEO/COO	**$229,248**	$161,322	$15,198	$24,467	$39,126
General Manager	**$167,766**	$128,679	$12,975	$15,716	$23,298
Manager	**$121,212**	$92,542	$6,146	$8,100	$19,292
Club manager	**$110,168**	$94,924	$3,833	$8,520	$14,506
Overall	**$182,176**	**$136,075**	**$13,046**	**$18,377**	**$27,525**

Source: Courtesy of CMAA 2009 Compensation and Benefits Report (Market Connect, 2009).

industry in the coming decade. This is not to say that golf and club management are in a major decline phase of the activity's life cycle, but rather it may be due to the related factors of intense growth and impacts of a recessionary economy. Plenty of evidence suggests there was too much supply for a declining playing public. When and where the activity and markets will bottom out are not yet clear.

Kennedy (2006), presenting at the Golf 2020 Summit, indicated six major trends affecting the game. Major threats included the time crunch trends that included more child-centered activities; the media trap of 24-7 connections with intrusive media devices; people consuming more experiences; the marketplace trap of endless choices and continuous improvements; and changing lifestyles and pace of living. These trends were affecting golf participation and had intensified. However, Kennedy also gave considerable attention to five other threats to the golf industry, including:

- *connected-ness*—defined as ending loneliness and isolation and being part of and consuming more of a larger web of connections in life (the Facebook, MySpace, or LinkedIn trend)
- *the new power of women*—defined as shift from stealth to overt power in all areas including the workplace, marketplace, politics, home, society, and culture
  - Key question: Will golf be embraced as an important activity in the new and evolving power base of women?
- *a winner/loser society*—defined as a two class system in society with a growing poor or lower class, a very wealthy upper class growing, and a middle class being downsized considerably or squeezed out
  - Key questions: How does this affect the industry? What if the losers can't afford the cost of golf, the "exhausted affluent" don't have time to play, and the

newly rich gravitate to newer sports/activities?
- *child preparation*—defined as a willingness to sacrifice time, energy and money now for the preparation of our children for their successful adulthood; the belief that children come first and self comes second
  - Key question: What if parents siphon their golf resources (time and money) towards their kid(s) and as a result the parents never develop "the golf habit"?
- *the health imperative*—defined as a sophisticated understanding that health, in all its aspects, is crucial for a valuable and meaningful life
  - Key questions: What if golf isn't seen as active enough? What if golf courses are viewed as being environmentally unhealthy with their high levels of chemicals and pesticides as well as being water hogs?

Other challenges for the golf and club management industry include the need for better benchmarking and data reporting. Prior to commissioning the Golf 2020 Summit, there was only sporadic golf data monitoring. No standard industry definition existed for some measures of golf demand nor was there complete agreement about demand terminology. Interest in golf participation was measured only mostly by private organizations such as Simmons Market Research Bureau and the Sporting Goods Manufacturing Association (SGMA). Nielsen ratings assessed television viewership of golfing events and various tour groups tracked tournament attendance. There were various marketing analysis and feasibility studies conducted for developers but only sporadic measurement of economic impact of the game, clubs, and tournament events. The charitable impact of golf tournaments was also only sporadically reported, although many perceived it to be substantial.

In moving the industry forward, Hughes (2006) reported that more sophisticated measurement and reporting was needed with particular focus on trends and outside factors affecting the field. These include socioeconomic issues, demography, diversity, and youth introduction as well as overall player and member retention in the game. It was suggested that more specifically detailed revenue information needed to be captured at the course level and a more unified data collection effort was needed to successfully monitor and benchmark the industry.

The PGA indicated that more performance tracking was needed and the National Golf Course Owners Association (NGCOA) agreed to do more financial benchmarking. Since then NGCOA and the PGA have worked to track rounds and revenue more closely and are leveraging larger multi-course operations to participate and to model their reporting after the Smith Travel Report, which analyzes trends in the travel and hotel industry. The NGCOA benchmarking allows for the development of the *Competitive Golf Marketplace (CGM) Report* that has now evolved into a program called "PerformanceTrak." PerformanceTrak is a collaborative service of the NGCOA and PGA of America that provides participants with local market benchmark data on golf fee revenues and monthly rounds-played data. The service is available to NGCOA members as well as PGA Professionals free-of-charge and allows comparison and marketplace data on rounds played, available tee times, and golf revenue (green and cart fees) to golf course operators at the local and market areas while keeping their individual and respective numbers confidential. New measures are also being produced to measure such new benchmark statistics as Revenue Per Available Tee Time (RevPATT) and Revenue Per Utilized Round (RevPUR) index for every participant facility. These measures are similar to RevPAR (Revenue Per Available Room) in the hotel industry.

The industry is also striving to develop new programs to introduce the game, bring new players into the game and club facilities, continue to focus on benchmarking/measurement at the facility level, to develop more consistency and coordination among all golf allied groups, to provide more emphasis on golf industry's economic impact nationally and at the state levels, and to more rigorously measure the outcomes of specific programs and their effects. For example, in 2010 an alliance of golf organization launched the "We Are Golf" campaign, a new coalition led by the NGCOA, The PGA of America, GCSAA, and CMAA to change the face of golf and to represent the economic, human, and environmental benefits of the industry at federal, state, and local levels of government. The promoted perception is that golf is a major industry that has a profound impact on America's economic, environmental, and social agendas. There are those who believe the industry remains misunderstood by many influential policymakers in Washington, D.C. and around the nation. The "We Are Golf" campaign aims to change their perceptions by better illustrating the stories of golf's diverse businesses and their employees, the tax revenues it creates, the tourism it spawns, the charity it generates, and the environmental leadership it provides (Golf Course Superintendents Association of America, 2010).

Finally, golf course and club management are solely driven by golf participation. The key question for the coming decades as golf moves towards 2020 is: will golf demand grow, stabilize, or decline? An important assessment of the golf playing public is to analyze the golfers who play most often and understand more of their reasons for playing the game. These are the private sector golfers. The NGF (Beditz, 2008) conducted an extensive survey of private country club and golf club only operations and players of private facilities. They found in 2008 there were approximately 2.1 million private club golfers in the United States ages 18 and older. This segment represents about 9% of all adult golfers, while private golf and the clubs they join represent 30% of all golf facilities. This also indicates that these golfers are private club members for a reason and are willing to pay a premium for less crowded courses. Why are these types of players and members important to the industry? Private golfers are disproportionately avid players and spenders versus public golfers. Private golfers play three times as much as public golfers and spend three times as much on an annual basis. The majority of these individuals joined their clubs before they turned age 50. Private club golfers also indicate significantly different reasons for joining a private club that varied with the type of club they actually join. While members of both country clubs and golf-only clubs join for the convenience and quality of the golf course, country club members also placed a high priority on other amenities for themselves and their families **(Figure 20-5)**.

The NGF study also surveyed the overall financial health of clubs and found that about 1

FIGURE 20-5   Reasons for Joining a Private Club—Country Club versus Golf Club.

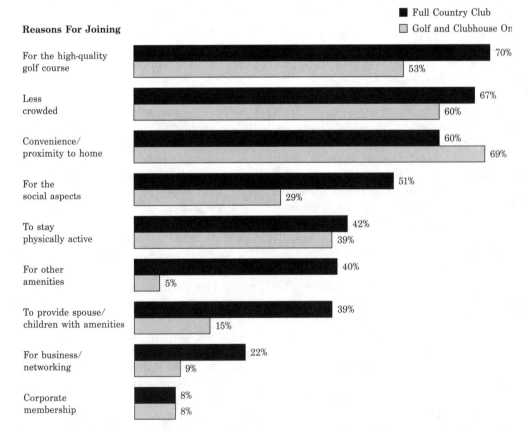

Source: Beditz, J. (2008). "What's in Store? The Future of America's Private Golf Clubs." *Club Director*, July/August 2008, Vol. 26, Issue 4, p. 29. © National Club Association. [Note: Joseph F. Beditz, PhD, is president and CEO of the National Golf Foundation.]

in 5 clubs, or an estimated 750 golf clubs, were seriously challenged financially and that all clubs regardless of financial health had experienced a drop in membership and rounds played in 2008 from the peak periods earlier in the decade (Beditz, 2008). The reasons for reducing or dropping membership were most often noted as 1) relocation and 2) money factors. Desires to pursue a variety of leisure pursuits, and work and family obligations were also stated; however, there was little attrition in membership and volume of play linked to the condition of the club's golf course and facility, the lack of family activities, or health reasons. To respond to the financial stress put on clubs, private golf facilities are implementing a variety of methods to improve their overall financial well-being. Clubs at the highest risk levels are more likely to discount green fees and membership fees; utilize expanded sales, marketing, and incentive programs; broaden opportunities for trial memberships; and implement special financing or interest-free membership initiation fees. Healthier clubs that have higher financial capability are more likely to invest in improving the golf course, clubhouse, and overall course conditioning. The at-risk clubs simply do not have the capital for such investments and therefore suffer from a competitive disadvantage (Beditz, 2008).

This survey also examined the future outlook for demand and examined two additional future dimensions of golf: participation and membership. It also asked how likely they would be to still enjoy the membership at a private club in five years. Two thirds expressed a high likelihood that they would still be members. Of the remaining respondents, 21% were on the fence and 10% to 15% were at risk of giving up their membership entirely. The reasons other than relocation or health were driven primarily by the cost of the membership. However, having a spouse who plays golf significantly improved the chances that the couple would retain their membership (Beditz, 2008).

Non-members were also surveyed to determine their latent demand for golf participation. One way to measure latent demand is to also ask current markets if they intend or desire to play golf more in the future. Those non-members who are attracted to joining a golf club responded that they would join for the same reasons as current members: privilege and convenience. The study also found that the age paradigm for club membership appears to be shifting from a large proportion of members who join when they are between the ages of 30 and 45 to a high proportion of potential members joining between the ages of 45 and 60. Target marketing of Baby Boomers is still highly viable for club membership in the coming decade. The study also indicated that there are still 1 to 2 million qualified and potential golf households that will consider golf memberships. The key target markets for the future from this study indicated two primary groups: those with household incomes of $100,000 or more and those who play golf who are in the prime target age groups of 30 to 60 years. The NGF study also highlighted significant lifestyle segments that would make significant prospective golf club members including older, upper-class, college-educated professionals, middle-aged couples in satellite cities, and couples with dual incomes and no children (Beditz, 2008). Finally, the NGF recommended for the future that golf course facilities undertake several proactive options. These included: 1) an honest business assessment of the operation on key financial terms with specific attention to membership, participation, and participation volume; 2) a competitive analysis of the market areas including both direct and indirect competitive assessment and differentiation assessments; 3) an assessment of current and latent demand in the immediate market area with particular emphasis upon key target market profiles; 4) development of a financial forecast to evaluate the potential for a club's financial health to be maintained or restored and the time commitment for the adjustments; and 5) a well-developed strategic plan including surveys of current members and potential non-members; reviews of the best business models to remain viable; and successful or well-designed strategies for positioning the club to remain viable for a sufficiently longer term basis, a recommended five-year plan.

The NGF is concerned about the future of golf and its implications for the operation of golf courses and country clubs. The National Club Association has also been tracking trends in its latest publication, *2010 Trends and Issues*, and has identified the following six major areas for careful monitoring in the future: 1) economic outlook, more specifically the job market, the luxury market, consumer confidence, and tax increases; 2) demographics, include age profiles and changes in multi-generational diversity; 3) lifestyle and club membership issues, with particular attention to "living local" and "cocooning"; 4) leisure and recreation trends, including attention to the main club sports such as golf and tennis, but also general and specific fitness trends; 5) hospitality and lodging trends, regarding overnight stay business; and 6) food and beverage, meaning the support of and use of seasonal, local, healthy, and organic menu and diet options/issues and environmentally-friendly practices.

Country clubs today are basically organized and structured either according to a public role and function or as a private club. Membership at these clubs varies depending on the public or private nature of the club itself. The types of ownership of these country clubs also varies from a member-owned club, called an equity club, to a non-member owned club called a non-equity club. The type of ownership has implications as to whether a club is considered non-profit by the Internal Revenue Service. Within the golf club industry segment, there are a small number of larger firms who operate hundreds of golf courses. The largest segment, though, is the stand-alone, single golf course operation.

The club management field provides opportunities for career development and advancement for those who choose to pursue the club management career path. Students interested in a career in club management should perform research and collect information on certification programs and the various organizations associated with this field, such as the Club Managers Association of America. Students wishing to pursue a career in the golf side of the business as a golf professional may pursue a golf management degree at one of the 20 Professional Golf Management (PGM) programs located at various universities across the country.

■ SUMMARY

Golf courses and country clubs are a significant sport attraction in the United States. During the last quarter of the twentieth century the growth in the number of golfers increased at a faster rate than that of the growth in the nation's population. The game of golf originated with the Scottish players and founders of the Royal and Ancient Golf Club of St. Andrews, Scotland. The Country Club of Brookline located near Boston, Massachusetts is considered to be the first country club in the United States, founded in 1882.

■ KEY TERMS

ad hoc committees, board of directors, board of governors, city club, Club Managers Association of America (CMAA), country club, equity club, executive committee, legacy members, non-equity club, non-profit 501c7 clubs, private club, private exclusive club, Professional Golfers Association (PGA), public club, standing committees

CASE STUDY: Event Planning at Augusta National

Every year the Masters Golf Tournament is held at Augusta National Golf Course in Augusta, Georgia. It is considered to be one of the major U.S. golf tournaments of the year. Admission to the grounds is highly restricted and in 2010 was even tighter with return to the golf scene of Tiger Woods after a four-month hiatus from the game due to personal issues.

The 18-hole Augusta National course features 7,270 yards of golf from the longest tees for a par of 72. The course rating is 74.0 and its slope rating is 135. Designed by Alister MacKenzie and Robert Trent Jones, Jr., American Society of Gold Course Architects (ASGCA), the Augusta National Golf Course opened in 1933. James Armstrong currently manages the course as the Executive Director. However, the food and beverage operations at the clubhouse are sparse and in the past was not well managed for special events and tournaments.

Recently, managers from two clubs in New England have helped operate the food and beverage outlets at the main clubhouse during the week prior to and during the tournament. These managers are Phil Koretski from the Misquamicut Club in Rhode Island, who has served as the Hospitality Manager, and Brent Tartamella from the Westmoor Club on Nantucket, who has served as the Manager of the Player/Member area. With their coordination, the service and responsibilities for this prestigious event and set of accompanying venues have improved greatly. This year a special challenge was dealt to the managers. In addition to the standard venues that they must oversee, they were asked to assist in the staging of two special events: an evening event and dinner called the "Legends of Golf" and another evening event called the "Future of Golf." The sponsors were the same as those for The Masters event and included AT&T, Mobil/Exxon, IBM, Mercedes, Rolex, and CBS Sports. The managers' plates were full with their assigned tasks, so they asked two young entry level managers to assist in staging these events. Nicole was from the Misquamicut Club in Rhode Island and Jamie was from Sebonak Club of Long Island, New York. Both had experience with staging and servicing clientele from high end clubs, but this challenged the best of their abilities.

So, Phil and Brent invited Nicole and Jamie into Phil's office at the Misquamicut Club for a meeting in late October and indicated that they would like both Nicole and Jamie to coordinate these two special events. There were some guidelines for each and the events would require some special staffing. In the past, Phil had used students in club and sport management programs from around the country to supplement the staff for a portion of the week for each of these events.

Phil says, "OK ladies, we have this special request for two events that the PGA and USGA would like us to stage and help develop for them at The Masters in April. The first event, 'The Legends of Golf' will be held on Monday evening of the week of the tournament from 6 to 9 PM. It will include a cocktail reception from 6 to 7 PM and a formal evening dinner and program from 7 to 9 PM. The event will need to have a theme in keeping with the integrity of The Masters and Augusta, and will have a very restricted 'by invitation only' guest list. We expect approximately 300 people at this event. The second event, 'The Future of Golf' is expected to be a more upbeat and up tempo event held on Tuesday evening from 6 to 9 PM. It will include a cocktail hour from 6 to 7 PM with a short program honoring the up and coming golfers of this decade and it will be less formal, buffet style food setup with some soft, trendy but not flashy entertainment. We are expecting a much lighter turnout for this event—about 200 people. We will need to theme both according to the parameters set forth by the PGA, USGA, and Augusta National."

"Both of these events, due to their size, will require us to bring in some extra help early in that week. We have had some success with student help from the hospitality programs, but this needs more structure and I would like you to determine the staff size you will need, reach out, and bring in students from the best institutions. You will need to carefully train them and orient them to Augusta. Background checks will be important, too. You may select the type of training you believe will be appropriate. We would like them to be on site the Friday before the event ready to go with training if necessary at that time, and we will provide off site housing from Thursday through the following Wednesday. We will use them to prep and setup on Saturday and Sunday and then for full implementation for each of the events on Monday and Tuesday evening."

Brent stated, "We expect the normal large crowd at Augusta but with the economy in such a downturn, this year the crowd is expected to be about 10% smaller than normal. However, it has been our experience that you should always expect the unexpected when staging these events and attendance at these events are expected to probably be at 90 to 95% capacity."

Brent continued, "So here is the charge: theme these events, staff them up with projections of the staff you will need, and provide appropriate training methods to deliver the very best service. You may choose the venue where it would be best to stage these events and you can check with us on what might be available. Full competitive play does not begin until Wednesday and crowds and use of the facility will be lighter the first two days. But remember, the crowd on Monday night will be much older and some may be physically challenged at their age. So, choice of a venue is important. Second, it will require table service. The event on Tuesday is totally different, but needs to be appropriate for the traditions of Augusta. Please come back with tentative plans by the first week in December."

A month went by and both Nicole and Jamie were hard at work planning the two special events. They met again with Phil and Brent at the Wianno Club on Cape Cod prior to an NECMA monthly meeting. Planning appeared to be going well. However, the news just broke in the last week that the game of golf will take a major blow with a situation surrounding the personal life of one of the top golfers in the field. Most believed that attendance would suffer greatly at The Masters that year due to both the economy and the absence of this top golfer from the tournament. The planning committee at Augusta for the event suggested that "The Legends of Golf" event continue with its planning but to plan for a reduced attendance of 25%. They also suggested that the "Future of Golf" be scaled back considerably by cutting the meal service, while still implementing a short program to honor the amateur players and offer a number of food stations with the event going from 6 to 8 PM. Nicole and Jamie were frustrated but planning went ahead with the adjustments.

Fast forward two more months to early March, about one month out from the Masters. The unexpected happens! The top player announced that he will return to play at The Masters. Demand for tickets and access to the special events suddenly doubled. The Legends event appeared to be under control, but planning for the Futures event seemed out of control. Demand for tickets more than tripled with the announcement of this top player's return and his attendance at that event. This ran the gamut from news media to tabloid requests for credentials to others hoping to attend.

Brent and Phil exclaimed to both Nicole and Jamie. "Expect the unexpected!"

Questions for Discussion

1. Why is the Masters such a prestigious event? Who sponsors the Masters? What are the differences between the PGA Tour and the PGA? What are the four major golf events?

2. Who should be on the guest list for the "Legends of Golf" event? (Identify the living legends of golf here.)
3. Who should be on the guest lists for the "Upcoming Stars of Golf" for the last decade (2000–2010)? (Identify the up and coming stars of the game.) Who would be the top ten up and coming stars you would highlight or honor at this event? What is the difference between an amateur golfer and a professional golfer?
4. How many staff members should Nicole and Jamie plan to bring in for these events? What are the factors you would use to determine this staffing requirement?
5. What is the best training method to bring the student workers up to speed? (There are at least two service styles here and potentially a third. There also are a number of guest services issues to deal with in clearance and press issues for this event.)
6. A complicated planning aspect has been the changing numbers for the event. How does this change your event planning and hosting for both events?
7. How should Nicole and Jamie work together to make the best use of their time in planning for these two separate but equally important events?
8. Design the appropriate theme focusing on the details of each of these events, including an enhanced theme title, venue type setup, colors, table settings, gift mementos, food theme (i.e., menu items and beverages), logistics, staffing and staff appearances, security, and transportation issues.

■ REFERENCES

American Culinary Federation (ACF). (2010). Who We Are. Retrieved December 3, 2010, from http://www.acfchefs.org//AM/Template.cfm?Section=Home6

American Red Cross (ARC). (2010). Preparing and getting trained. Retrieved December 3, 2010, from http://www.redcross.org

Beditz, J.F. (2006). Golf's vital signs: 2000–2006. Presented at the Seventh Annual Golf Summit 2020, October 30–31, 2006, St. Augustine, Florida. Retrieved December 3, 2010, from http://www.golf2020.com/PowerPoint/2006/VitalSigns.ppt

Beditz, J.F. (2008, July/August). What's in store?: The future of America's private golf clubs. *Club Director*, 28–32.

Club Managers Association of America (CMAA). (2010). CMAA–Who we are. Retrieved December 3, 2010, from http://www.cmaa.org/template.aspx?id=216

Club Managers Association of America (CMAA). (2009). *Compensation and Benefits Report.* Alexandria, VA: Club Managers Association of America.

Golf Course Superintendents Association of America (GCSAA). (2010, January 25). WE ARE GOLF initiative announced as industry initiative for changing perceptions. Retrieved December 3, 2010, from http://www.gcsaa.org/news/NewsReleases.aspx?id=2e5c97a8-e110-4d16-bd15-3915f6479dc2

Gordon, J.S. (1990). The Country Club. *American Heritage, 41*(6), 75–84.

Hardin, R. (2008). America's first golf hero: Francis Ouimet and the 1913 U.S. Open. *International Social Science Review, 83*(3), 158–170.

Hughes, M. (2006). Golf's financial metrics. Presented at the Seventh Annual Golf Summit 2020, October 30–31, 2006, St. Augustine, Florida. Retrieved December 3, 2010, from http://www.golf2020.com/PowerPoint/2006/GolfMetrics.ppt

Kennedy, C. (2006). Five key trends impacting the future of golf. Presented at the Seventh Annual Golf Summit 2020, October 30–31, 2006, St. Augustine, Florida. Retrieved December 3, 2010, from http://www.golf2020.com/PowerPoint/2006/FiveKeyTrends.ppt

IBISWorld. (2010, September). *IBIS World Industry Report 71391: Golf Courses and Country Clubs in the U.S.* (SIC 71391). Retrieved December 3, 2010, from http://www.ibisworld.com/industry/default.aspx?indid=1652

Miller, D. (1978). The saga of the American country club. *Town & Country, 132*, 41.

Morris, R.R. (2002). In Martin J. (Ed.), *Club Managers Association of America: Celebrating seventy-five years of service, 1927–2002* [Club Managers Association of America: Celebrating Seventy-Five Years of Service, 1927–2002] (English Trans.). (1st ed.). Virginia Beach, VA: Donning Company Publishers.

Moss, R.J. (2001). *Golf and the American Country Club.* Urbana, IL: University of Illinois Press.

Napton, D.E., & Laingen, C.R. (2008). "Expansion of golf courses in the United States." *Geographical Review, 98*(1), 24–41.

National Club Association. (2010). *2010 Trends and Issues.* (Executive Summary). Washington, DC: National Club Association.

National Sporting Goods Association (NSGA). (2009). Golf participation in the U.S. 1993–2009. Data retrieved from http://www.sbrnet.com.silk.library.umass.edu:2048/

Perdue, J. (2007). *Contemporary Club Management* (2nd ed.). East Lansing, MI: Educational Institute.

PGALinks (2010). *The Official Member Site of the PGA of America.* Retrieved December 3, 2010, from http://www.pgalinks.com/

Premier Club Services (2010). Your Club and the Law. Club Managers Association of America. Retrieved December 21, 2010, from http://www.cmaa.org/uploadedFiles/PCS/Governance/ycltoc.pdf

Santiago, M.J., & Rodewald, A.D. (2005). Considering wildlife in golf course management. Retrieved December 3, 2010, from http://ohioline.osu.edu/w-fact/0015.html

United States Tennis Association (USTA). (2010). Home. Retrieved December 3, 2010, from http://www.usta.com/

CHAPTER 21

Recreational Sport

Laurie Gullion

■ INTRODUCTION

An interest in recreation is integral to the lives of most people in the United States from childhood through adulthood. Whether the arena is indoors or outdoors, people seek to be involved directly or indirectly with recreational activities for a variety of reasons: fun, excitement, relaxation, social interaction, challenge, and lifestyle enhancement.

The roots of involvement with organized recreation may begin in childhood with Little League baseball and softball. It can be nurtured through involvement in Young Men's Christian Association (YMCA) aquatics programs and summer camp experiences. In adulthood people explore enjoyable activities such as the thrill of whitewater kayaking and summer vacations with families in national parks. Through retirement a person can embrace a range of "masters" activi-

ties such as "70-plus" ski clubs that encourage lifelong participation in an activity.

The recreation industry in the United States is extensive and diverse, although the various segments usually share a common mission. Organizations strive to provide activities that offer personal and social benefits to individuals during their leisure time. A characteristic of recreation that sets it apart from other segments of the sport industry is that there is often **direct participation** by people through active performance in an activity, such as sea kayaking classes, a mountain bike race, or fishing with a certified guide. However, **indirect participation** by spectators may also occur in recreation and also contributes to the economic base, a strategy effective in the tourism industry, which seeks to promote recreation-based events such as triathlons that draw spectators to a particular region.

HISTORY: THE MODERN RECREATIONAL MOVEMENT

Leisure time in the nineteenth century emerged as a result of the urbanization and industrialization of U.S. society. Technological innovations in factories made work more monotonous and prompted citizens to seek diversions. The recreation movement sought to address social issues affecting a population faced with a 66-hour workweek (6 days a week, 11 hours a day). Public attitudes toward work and leisure changed from a more Puritan ethic, which valued work over play, to a perception of recreation as important to the growth and health of the individual and as a means to improve community well-being.

By mid-century, a number of developments helped expand and formalize recreation. In reaction to accelerating urban development, the **parks movement** resulted in the establishment of public lands, such as Central Park in New York City, open free of charge to all people. Boston's famous Emerald Necklace of parkways began to surround and provide an escape from its urban center. Technology also brought innovations such as the bicycle and golf ball, and the moderate price of sporting goods such as canoes and rowboats opened these activities to all economic classes. Social and religious institutions

such as the Young Men's and Young Women's Christian Associations (YMCA, YWCA) and the Young Men's and Young Women's Hebrew Associations organized in local cities.

An increasing fascination with the wilderness in the United States prompted an interest in outdoor travel and construction of the famous mountain houses and wilderness camps of the Northeast, mostly popular in the Adirondacks of New York. Only the most daring ventured to the uncivilized West, yet in 1872 President Ulysses S. Grant was able to convince the federal government to establish Yellowstone as the first national park in the world. This act established the U.S. commitment to preserving public lands, a unique philosophy later exported to European countries. The creation of the National Park Service (NPS) in 1916 by Theodore Roosevelt escalated the preservation of extraordinary geologic and cultural sites, including national seashores, historic battlefields and monuments, and wildlife areas. The NPS recorded 276 million visits in 2008, activities that generated nearly $12 billion in economic benefits to local communities (Stynes, 2009).

By the end of the twentieth century, the recreation movement had created formal organizations in the form of local clubs and national associations devoted to recreation and committed to developing standards for activities. Organizations such as the American Canoe Association, established in 1880, began to shape not only recreational participation through the development of instructional guidelines but also competition rules for races and regattas. Early in the twentieth century, the interest in recreation continued to accelerate with the establishment of well-known organizations such as the Boy Scouts in 1910 and the Girl Scouts in 1912.

A phenomenon unique to the United States also emerged during this time when organized summer camps for children began to proliferate. In the nineteenth century, the camping movement often focused on gatherings of a religious nature for adults. Concerned about the effect of urbanization on children, advocates developed the first fresh air camps in the latter half of the 1800s to allow urban children to travel to the country. By the early 1900s, the camping movement had gained momentum in attracting children to these popular outdoor experiences. Today specialty camps for sports and recreational activities have been added to the mix. The American Camping Association (ACA) reported in 2007 that an estimated 12,000 camps existed nationwide, served 11 million children and adults, and employed 1.2 million adults (ACA, 2010). Between 1990 and 2010, the number of day camps increased by 90% (ACA, 2010).

Following World War II, an expanding U.S. economy broadened the scope of the recreation industry. This economic growth led to the creation of local parks and recreation departments, the establishment of armed forces recreation to improve the morale of individuals and families, and the emergence of commercial recreation enterprises such as the skiing industry. The federal government also approved legislation that created the National Wilderness Preservation System, the National Wild and Scenic Rivers System, the National Trails System, a system of National Recreation Areas, and the Land and Water Conservation Fund, which provides matching grants to states and local governments for acquiring and developing public outdoor recreation areas. People in the United Sates recreated outdoors in growing numbers, especially women and older adults. Walking continued as the most popular activity, with 83% of the population walking in 2000 compared to 67% in 1994–1995 (Cordell, 2008).

Technological improvements continued to develop new sporting goods, generating growing interest in other activities such as snowboarding, artificial wall climbing, kayaking, and wake boarding. As other emerging technologies such as electronic entertainment sought to capture the public's leisure time in the twenty-first century, President Barack Obama established America's Great Outdoors Initiative in 2010 to reconnect people in the United States, particularly children, to the nation's natural and cultural heritage. He directed a consortium of federal agencies to promote community-based recreation and conservation, create job and volunteer opportunities related to conservation and outdoor recreation, and support existing programs and projects that educate people in the United States about the country's history, culture, and natural resources (Obama, 2010).

■ TRENDS IN PARTICIPATION

An appreciation of the outdoors is central to the American lifestyle, and recent trends in participation support the enduring value of outdoor recreation. The total number of people who participated in one or more outdoor activities grew by 4.4% from an estimated 208 million in 2000 to 217 million in 2007. At the same time, the total number of participation days in all activities increased from 67 billion to 84 billion, representing growth of approximately 25% (Cordell, Betz, Green, & Mou, 2008).

The 2007 National Survey on Recreation and the Environment, conducted by the USDA Forest Service and Interagency National Survey Consortium, shows the top outdoor recreation activities for people aged 16 years and older (**Table 21-1**). Viewing and photographing activities remain strong and continue to grow along with family-centered outdoor activities, kayaking, surfing, and orienteering. Extreme sports continue to grow among a variety of ages (**Figure 21-1**), along with some long-lasting favorites such as skateboarding and newer activities like paintball (RCC Associates, 2009). The U.S. Fish and Wildlife Service (2007) reported that 38% of all U.S. residents 16 years and older participated in hunting, fishing, or wildlife observation in 2006 and spent $180 billion on wildlife-related

TABLE 21-1   Top 10 Outdoor Recreation Activities, 2005–2007

Activity	Number (in millions)
Walk for pleasure	193.4
Family gathering	164.7
Gardening/landscaping for pleasure	153.7
View/photograph natural scenery	145.8
Visit nature centers, etc.	128.4
View/photograph wildflowers, trees, etc.	118.6
Attend outdoor sports events	118.1
Picnicking	116.0
View/photograph other wildlife	115.0
Swimming in an outdoor pool	97.7

Source: National Survey on Recreation and the Environment, USDA Forest Service, Southern Research Station, Athens, GA (H. Ken Cordell, Project Leader).

recreation—a statistic said to approximate the total amount people in the United States spent on spectator sports, casinos, motion pictures, golf courses and country clubs, amusement parks, and arcades combined.

As the U.S. population ages and the 76 million people in the baby boomer generation approach retirement, the recreation industry can capitalize on this generation's optimism about their retirement and their popularizing of the fitness movement in the 1960s (Sporting Goods Manufacturers Association [SGMA], 2010a). Approximately 68% of baby boomers say they expect to participate in recreational activities during retirement (American Association of Retired People [AARP], 2004). Short-term experiences that are available relatively close to home at a low cost are gaining in popularity (SGMA, 2010b). The age distribution among the United States population is shifting from younger to older. In 1900, the median age was 23 years, but it is expected to reach 39 by 2030

FIGURE 21-1   Most Popular Extreme Sports in the United States.

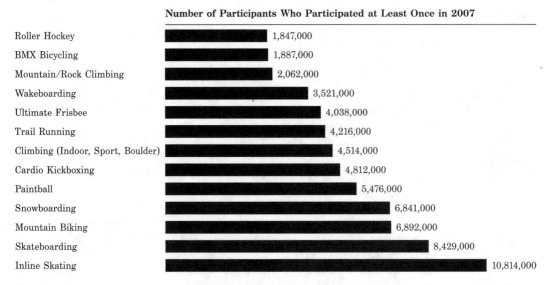

Number of Participants Who Participated at Least Once in 2007

Roller Hockey	1,847,000
BMX Bicycling	1,887,000
Mountain/Rock Climbing	2,062,000
Wakeboarding	3,521,000
Ultimate Frisbee	4,038,000
Trail Running	4,216,000
Climbing (Indoor, Sport, Boulder)	4,514,000
Cardio Kickboxing	4,812,000
Paintball	5,476,000
Snowboarding	6,841,000
Mountain Biking	6,892,000
Skateboarding	8,429,000
Inline Skating	10,814,000

Source: Sporting Goods Manufacturing Association. (2008). Extreme sports: An ever-popular attraction. Retrieved February 19, 2011, from http://www.sgma.com/press/2_Extreme-Sports-An-Ever-Popular-Attraction

(U.S. Department of Commerce, 2010). The largest segment of the country's population will be middle-aged or older, most likely with diverse interests and a range of fitness levels. Recreation professionals will need to respond to the needs of these participants.

Increased racial and ethnic diversity is anticipated with related growth in urban areas. Between 2000 and 2030, the U.S. population is expected to increase by 82 million (U.S. Department of Commerce, 2010). The Hispanic population "would contribute 32 percent of the nation's population growth from 1990 to 2000, 39 percent from 2000 to 2010, 45 percent from 2010 to 2030, and 60 percent from 2030 to 2050" (Cheeseman-Day, n.d.). Researchers from several universities completed a project for the National Park Service that examined the use of Rocky Mountain National Park by ethnic minority visitors and non-minority visitors (Rodriguez, Bright, & Roberts, 2004). Not only will the recreation industry need to respond to the needs of a more diverse population, but it must also address the impact of demographic shifts on recreation areas near cities.

A challenge for the recreation industry will be to continue to attract younger ages to activities so as to sustain growth. An Outdoor Foundation study (2010) found an overall downward slide in outdoor recreation participation for children 6–12 years old, although the decrease was not as significant as in past studies. Children are also changing their relationship to recreation as "pick-up" or casual play in team sports continues to suffer. In 2009, only five team "pick-up" activities exceeded organized/sanctioned play: basketball, ice hockey, field hockey, touch football, and beach volleyball (SGMA, 2010b). One reason organized/sanctioned play dominates is because more young athletes specialize in one sport at an earlier age. Also, SGMA research found a person is more than three times more likely to stay active in team sports if that individual participates in physical education in

school, which has implications for financially strapped school system officials trying to decide which programs to eliminate. Outdoor activities, running, cycling, water sports, winter sports, and racquet sports show similar increases in participation among those who take physical education classes (SGMA, 2010b).

Economic challenges like the recession early in the twenty-first century are affecting different segments of the recreation industry in other ways. For instance, the overall number of golfers dropped 3% between 2007 and 2008, with a drop of 4.5% among core golfers, defined as those who play eight or more rounds a year (Swartz, 2010). Contributing factors include increases in the cost of a round, less time for 18 holes of golf, a drop in business-related golf, and a drop in golfing vacations. The industry is aware it needs to target women, African Americans, and Hispanics to sustain any growth in the sport (National Golf Foundation [NGF], 2006).

Women are participating in increasing numbers in a variety of outdoor activities. According to an Outdoor Industry Association study (2005), 64% of women age 16 years or older (or 73.2 million women) participated in a human-powered activity during 2004. However, the challenge involves girls and younger women, because 33% of women in the survey were 45 years or older. The largest growth activity among women in 2004 was fly fishing. This increased participation is also evident in the emergence of women's-only programming such as the popular "Becoming an Outdoorswoman" series run by state fish and wildlife divisions.

Participation rates vary greatly by activity, and a newcomer to the recreation field would be wise to examine the demographic trends in each area. As national demographics shift, managers will be faced with the difficult task of changing recreation facilities and programs to meet participants' needs. Overall, participants will be more likely be women, older, more racially and ethnically diverse, or come from urban areas. These factors will shape the industry in the coming years as recreation managers modify strategies for designing facilities, marketing programs, and hiring staff to deliver recreational opportunities responsive to this changing population.

■ SEGMENTS OF THE RECREATION INDUSTRY

Today the recreation industry offers people a wealth of opportunities for participation across its many segments. Consumers can find many intriguing activities to suit their needs. Competent recreational professionals are needed to staff the industry, and interested people would be wise to explore the variety of options in what has become a very competitive job market. The industry is so diverse that it can appear very fragmented because it is divided into a myriad of professional associations specific to certain activities. The categories presented in the next few sections were selected as a means to explore major segments, but a prospective employee must realize that a particular recreation business may fit into two or three of the basic segments.

Community-Based Recreation

The term **community-based recreation** implies that participants are united by a common interest in recreation at the local level. Local parks and recreation departments and community agencies such as the YMCA, YWCA, Jewish Community Centers, Girls and Boys Clubs, and Scouts offer general community services. Some agencies may target specific ages through youth centers and senior centers. Parks and recreation departments are supported through a mix of local property tax monies and user fees from participants. These programs are no longer free to the public, given the increased competition for budgetary support among all town services

(e.g., fire and police departments). As a result, recreation managers are becoming increasingly creative in soliciting private sponsorships from local companies to sponsor special programs to keep program costs low for the public. To support their programs, agencies like the YMCA, Jewish Community Centers, and Boys and Girls Clubs often rely on a greater mix of funding sources, including user fees and memberships, private donations (such as United Way), grant programs from public and private sources, and in-house fund-raising events.

Public Recreation

Public recreation reaches beyond the local level to state and federal agencies. State forest and parks departments, the National Park Service (a division of the U.S. Department of the Interior), and the National Forest Service (a division of the U.S. Department of Agriculture [USDA]) manage recreational opportunities on public lands. Interest in national forests and parks remains high, with an explosion of visits to the 390 areas in the national park system and the 155 national forests in recent years. The National Park Service recorded 285 million visits to national parks, seashores, monuments, and historic sites in 2009, an increase of 10 million from the previous year (U.S. NPS, 2009). This high use continues to affect a system beleaguered by federal budget constraints. The park service is grappling with policy issues concerning vehicle congestion, recreational vehicle access, a deteriorating infrastructure, and control of visitor volume and duration. The National Park Service has identified the need to conduct a comprehensive study of public use of the park system (Lee, 2003).

The National Forest Service employs 30,000 permanent employees to manage the nation's 191 million acres of forest lands (USDA Forest Service, 2003b). Traditionally, available positions focused on resource management, but the agency has added recreation employees to its national forest system offices and examines forest recreation through its research and development teams. Its Job Corps program employs 900 people at 18 centers on forest lands. The programs train 9,000 enrollees annually in vocational and social skills as well as basic educational training that leads to college or the military (USDA Forest Service, 2003b).

Military Recreation

The U.S. Department of Defense maintains extensive **military recreation** programs through branches of the armed services. Although an overriding mission is the fitness and military readiness of personnel, the armed services also seek to provide an array of recreational opportunities for families on bases in the United States and abroad as a means of improving overall morale and a sense of community. Facilities include but are not limited to ski areas, marinas, recreation centers, fitness centers, youth centers, golf courses, and bowling centers. The military is also creating new programs for enlisted personnel and veterans with disabilities who have returned from war, such as the Wounded Warriors Project at Fort Carson, Colorado. Since 1948 the armed services have also supported the training of athletes for the Olympic Games and other major international competitions, and more than 400 active-duty personnel have achieved Olympic status as a result (Quigley, 2004). Nine American veterans with disabilities represented the United States at the 2008 Summer Paralympic Games in Beijing, China (Paralyzed Veterans of America, n.d.).

Military recreation organizations face the same challenges as other government-funded recreation programs. Recent decreases in appropriated funds have challenged the armed services to maintain program quality and improve their economic performance. The majority of recreation employees at military facilities are civilians rather than military personnel, which

creates job opportunities for trained people from the local communities.

Outdoor Recreation

Outdoor recreation attracts those who enjoy natural environments in different seasons, and people's increasing passion for the outdoors continues to expand this already large segment of the industry. The Outdoor Industry Association (2006) reported the active outdoor recreation economy as a $730 billion business with three out of four people in the United States participating annually. The industry creates more than 6.5 million jobs, sustains growth in many rural economies, and touches about 8% of personal consumption expenditures in the United States. Bicycling tops the list of popular activities with 60 million participants.

The outdoor industry is highly diverse, with a mix of for-profit and not-for-profit ventures in each subcategory. Segments include but are not limited to skiing and snowboarding, boating (rafting, canoeing, kayaking, and sailing), golf, summer camps, backpacking and camping, natural resource management, and tourist travel. Adventurous programs modeled after Outward Bound are also popular among people seeking high degrees of challenge in the outdoors.

University Outdoor Programs

Extracurricular **university outdoor programs** and clubs provide excellent opportunities for students to participate in a variety of outdoor activities and develop instructional and leadership skills through instructor training programs. They provide an excellent vehicle to obtain college work experience and begin creating a network in the recreation industry. The Association for Experiential Education (AEE) has accredited 10 university programs that provide training and activities for prospective leaders. The AEE has a broad outreach to more than 3,000 members, including international outdoor organizations (AEE, 2010). Almost 40 universities and colleges belong to the Association for Outdoor Recreation and Education (AORE, 2010), which also has strong links to military recreation programs. Some college activity programs, such as those at Princeton and Cornell, are larger than many commercial recreation centers. Academic programs offer excellent training to students in related management areas such as marketing, accounting, and finance as well as experience in instruction and leadership.

Therapeutic Recreation

The **therapeutic recreation** field uses recreational activities as a means to improve a participant's physical, emotional, and mental health. The activities can be offered as part of an overall treatment or rehabilitation program that may have evolved from medical care at a hospital, psychiatric facility, or nursing home. Therapeutic recreation services are also offered through park and recreation departments, independent living centers, schools, community mental health agencies, specialty recreation organizations, and social service agencies. Such services may also include programs for individuals who may be at risk of entering or are already in the judicial system. The programs vary widely, from hospital-based cardiac rehabilitation, for

which recreation is used to improve physical fitness, to a wilderness camp sponsored by a state division of youth services, which seeks to change the behaviors of court-referred youth.

Therapeutic recreation organizations often seek personnel with experience in recreation, counseling, or social work. Most important, they need employees whose specific skills and experience match the needs of a specific population, such as trained chemical dependency counselors. Therapists who do not have specialized training in recreational activities such as ropes/challenge courses or water sports work in conjunction with other recreation professionals who can offer that leadership. As the population of the United States ages, prospective employees should explore the opportunities available in adult day care, outpatient programs, psychiatric rehabilitation, and physical rehabilitation, especially services for people with disabilities.

■ CAREER OPPORTUNITIES

The recreation field offers individuals an excellent opportunity to work indoors and outdoors in pleasant surroundings, enjoy a healthy lifestyle, and introduce others to the benefits of participation at any age and any ability level. A number of common positions exist at recreation organizations, whether public or private, for-profit, or not-for-profit (**Table 21-2**). Recreation consumers, particularly those ready to pay a fee for participation, are increasingly savvy customers who expect a high degree of professional service in instruction and overall service delivery. From the moment they contact an organization to inquire about recreation programs and services, customers often seek to be reassured that they will obtain an educational, enjoyable, and safe experience. Some recreational activities can be very exciting with higher degrees of risk than other activities. After all, the challenging nature of outdoor sports such as whitewater

TABLE 21-2 Typical Recreation Positions

Activity director (cruise ships, senior centers)

Aquatics director

Aquatics specialist (town summer programs,
    YMCAs, YWCAs)

Armed forces recreation leader

Camp counselor

Camp director

Facilities manager (bowling, marinas, rafting)

Guide (river, fishing, hunting)

Instructor (skiing, swimming, canoeing,
    kayaking, scuba diving, wilderness)

Naturalist

Outdoor travel/tour leader

Park ranger

Park superintendent

"Pro" (golf, tennis)

Program director

Recreation director (town, community center)

Recreation therapist

Retail manager

Youth coordinator

---

kayaking or rock climbing is the very element that intrigues participants. Recreation professionals have a responsibility to deliver these programs with a high degree of skill and manage them with an eye to providing acceptable degrees of risk.

Job Search Strategies

Recreation managers are always seeking effective instructors, leaders, or guides who can create and execute programs, deliver excellent instruction tailored to the participants' needs, and provide leadership in challenging situations. A recreation manager wants people-oriented employees who know how to communicate well with the public, who work well with a variety of customers and staff, and who are responsible individuals committed to delivering quality programs and services. A recreation agency is often a small, lean operation that also needs employees

who bring business skills to the workplace. As recreation professionals move into managerial positions, they may need to supervise programs and staff, monitor risk management concerns in programs, create innovative marketing campaigns, develop and administer budgets, act as a liaison with public and private agencies, and develop alternative sources of funding beyond user fees.

Finding a recreation job requires a general understanding of all segments of the industry and a sense of where expansion in this highly competitive industry is occurring or is likely to occur. A prospective employee should analyze the specialized instructional and managerial skills necessary in specific areas of interest. A multifaceted approach should be adopted to successfully obtain a recreation position:

1. *Participate in a variety of activities.* Explore both popular and relatively uncommon activities (such as backpacking, scuba diving, sailing, or rock climbing). Share your interests and hobbies during interviews, whether they include music, travel, or other useful experiences. Employers and clients want to see staff with active experience in a variety of interesting undertakings.

2. *Develop general instructional and programming skills.* Working with a wide variety of ages, genders, abilities, and types of programming is helpful, particularly for those who aspire to an administrative position as a coordinator or director. Recreation managers seek employees with tangible skills, and a useful strategy is to obtain training and hands-on experience through internships, cooperative education, summer employment, and volunteer opportunities.

3. *Refine skills in several specific programming areas.* Recreation is becoming increasingly specialized, and prospective employers may want an employee with a set of skills unique to a specific activity. Obtaining spe-

cific training and certification from a designated national governing body such as the Professional Ski Instructors of America, the American Red Cross, or the American Canoe Association is necessary. First aid and emergency preparedness skills are essential parts of this training.

4. *Consider associated skills that can strengthen a resume.* A versatile candidate also offers a base of knowledge and skills useful to a business office, including marketing, accounting, public relations, business computer applications, writing, knowledge of legal issues, and computer-aided promotional design. Academic programs enable a prospective candidate to develop this more extensive background.

Professional Preparation

Two approaches to professional preparation exist in the recreation field. The recreation skills approach provides shorter, more intensive preparation in a particular area, often resulting in certification. The other approach is to select an academic program of one, two, or four years' duration at a college or university, which provides a broader knowledge base. It is important to realize that not every prospective employee has a recreation or outdoor recreation degree. Other related, useful degrees include forestry, social work, sport management, business, early childhood education, criminal justice, environmental education, and public administration.

The skills approach enables a person to obtain training and experience through organizations such as the National Outdoor Leadership School (NOLS) or Outward Bound, two of the largest outdoor organizations that provide specialized leadership development. A person might also participate in the certification processes offered by national governing bodies such as the American Canoe Association or Professional

Ski Instructors of America. Other nationally recognized agencies also provide training. Project Adventure, for example, teaches people to use structured activities on challenge/obstacle courses in environments ranging from summer camps to corporate training and development. Project Adventure provides a short-term, focused program at a lower cost (than other training avenues) that develops an individual's instructional and leadership skills in one specific activity.

Academic programs at colleges and universities offer a broader base of knowledge through expanded curricula for bachelor's and master's degrees. Individuals who seek to advance to managerial positions in program development or general administration would be wise to seek a master's degree. These programs vary in their alignments within the institution, and such alignments may flavor the curriculum. For instance, they may be housed in schools of health, physical education, recreation, or education as well as departments of sport management, forestry and natural resources, regional planning, or travel and tourism.

Interested students would be wise to establish a foundation of knowledge through general courses and select a focus in a particular segment that provides deeper knowledge and skills. **Table 21-3** provides an overview of some basic courses that can be useful in the recreation field. Because industry segments overlap, it is difficult to strictly divide academic courses into the various segments. A blend of courses from those listed for specific segments is useful preparation for the field.

■ CURRENT ISSUES

The traditional roots of the recreation industry continue to shape the modern profession. The worth of recreation programming is still judged in terms of its ability to build better human

TABLE 21·3 Academic Course Preparation for the Recreation Industry

General Recreation Courses Useful for Any Industry Segment

Introduction to Recreation and Leisure Services
History of Recreation
Recreation and Society
Program Planning and Organization
Group Leadership and Supervision
Risk Management in Recreation
Recreation Facilities Planning and Design
Internship/Cooperative Education Placement

General Business Courses Useful for Any Industry Segment

Financial Accounting
Introduction to Marketing
Fundamentals of Finance
Management Principles
Personnel Management
Public Relations
Computer Business Applications

Courses for Public Recreation

Park and Recreation Administration
Public Administration
Recreation Resource Management
Conservation Law and Enforcement

Courses for Outdoor Recreation

Introduction to Outdoor Recreation
Commercial Recreation
Travel and Tourism
Environmental Education and Interpretation

Courses for Therapeutic Recreation

Introduction to Therapeutic Recreation
Recreation and Rehabilitation
Special Populations in Therapeutic Recreation

beings and enhance community life. Today recreation professionals are faced with additional challenges in fulfilling their missions because of changing factors in our society. Managers will need to monitor shifting demographic trends to adequately handle the impact of continuing financial constraints facing the recreation industry.

A fundamental shift in financing recreation has occurred in an era in which federal, state, and local governments have reduced their proportionate shares of recreation budgets. Public recreation now competes for funding in an economic climate shadowed by a rising federal deficit, the emergence of state tax reform initiatives, and constrained local budgets. The recreation professional is often faced with the task of finding alternatives to government funding or user fees to support recreation services.

Park and recreation officials at local, state, and federal levels face challenges that include deteriorating park and recreation infrastructures, increasing crime, and declining federal, state, and local tax resources. Professionals must determine creative methods for capital development while simultaneously controlling operating expenses and establishing spending priorities in light of increasingly reduced budgets. Recreation managers must also strategize how to make parks and recreation areas safe from vandalism, crime, gangs, and substance abuse so they do not have an image that prevents citizens from enjoying them. They must advocate for the essential role that public recreation plays in promoting individual and community health and well-being (National Recreation and Park Association [NRPA], 2010).

Public and Private Sectors

Gone are the days when a recreation programmer could simply take a group onto public lands with little understanding of pertinent regulatory agencies. The **public sector**, or government, owns or manages the trails, beaches, information centers, and wildlife that attract people to a particular region. The **private sector**, or nongovernment arena, often provides the jobs and services that enable people to enjoy their experience while they are there. The relationship can be very complex and often requires an understanding of land management plans, regulatory processes, permit requirements, and natural heritage constraints, such as endangered species. Interactions may be quite formal, as when the government contracts with concessionaires to provide food services or run hotels in national parks or when ski areas use national forest land for their operations. The effects of this interaction can be far-reaching. For instance, proposals by ski areas to expand their snow-making capacity on federal lands require review by a host of government agencies, including federal, state, and local environmental protection divisions. To be successful, a commercial operator must have knowledge of public laws, policies, and practices.

Many private or nonprofit businesses not related to recreation also use public lands, as in the case of ranchers who graze cattle on public lands or logging companies that cut timber in national forests. Effective government coordination is needed among all interested parties to promote a viable recreation and tourism industry. Although an awareness of public policy is essential at every government level, it is particularly crucial for managers grappling with controversial issues. Proposed resource management plans—particularly changes in forest practices—often attract the attention of diverse groups, including logging interests, recreational users, and environmental or conservation agencies. Today's park managers need to be politically savvy to balance a variety of constituents' interests in public lands and handle the public scrutiny inherent in their positions.

Commercial outdoor recreation organizations grapple with continuing challenges in achieving financial security. As segments of the industry expand rapidly, they may face a shakedown similar to that occurring in the maturing ski industry. The National Ski Areas Association (2006) reported that 485 ski areas operated in 2006–2007, compared with 727 in 1984–1985. Skier/snowboarder visits totaled 55.1 million in 2006–2007, a decline of 6.5% from the previous year, due largely to unfavorable weather conditions. The ski industry is also grappling with an aging skier population and the flattening of expansion in snowboarding, which has been declining since participation peaked in 2004 (Lewis, 2008). Anticipating and planning for the adverse effects of unfavorable weather is necessary in outdoor recreation and affects financial stability. For instance, snow-making costs at ski areas have increased to cover fluctuations in snow conditions, and increased insurance premium costs have also contributed to rising costs in the industry.

As the number of visitors to public lands increases, recreation professionals have a responsibility to monitor and control use of those areas to prevent destruction of natural resources and enhance participant safety. Improved **environmental awareness** is necessary as instructors, guides, and managers need to abide by the increasingly strict regulations that control public use and educate their participants about those guidelines. Users must understand recommended environmental practices for minimizing impact upon trails, rivers, and camping areas, particularly in high-traffic areas, and must abide by the restrictions in group numbers levied by federal and state agencies. Leaders need to minimize conflicts between diverse users, such as hikers and mountain bikers, skiers, snowmobilers, and users of personal watercraft and off-road vehicles. They also need to conduct activities in accordance with recognized safe practices in the activity to minimize accidents and rescues. Although client safety itself is an issue, cost is a concern as well. The public cannot afford to underwrite the costs of rescues, which are increasing as the total number of visitors escalates in the outdoors. Managers need to consider how sustainable or "green" practices for facilities can promote ethical use of natural resources, such as the National Ski Areas Association's Sustainable Slopes project, which has been endorsed by almost 200 ski areas (National Ski Areas Association, 2010).

Beyond increased environmental awareness, recreation professionals need to develop **cultural awareness** in an industry that has become more global. Travel companies now attract customers to trekking in Nepal, sea kayaking in New Zealand, bird watching in Central America, and skiing in Scandinavia, among many other opportunities. For recreational professionals who do their work abroad, understanding local customs, laws, and the environment is important in providing successful experiences. For instance, Norway has a heritage of land use for recreation that allows a visitor to camp on private lands as long as the camping is unobtrusive, but this practice would not be advisable in a place such as the province of Quebec, where certain rivers are strictly regulated and reserved for private salmon fishing and guiding.

Americans with Disabilities Act

Access to recreational facilities and services is being reexamined in light of the **Americans with Disabilities Act** (ADA) of 1990, which creates a unique set of challenges and opportunities to the industry. Recreation programmers need to adapt their programs to meet a variety of needs as people with physical disabilities grow more interested in enhancing their lifestyle with physical activity. For instance, water sports offer freedom of movement to people who use wheelchairs, enabling them to access the outdoors more easily. However, the rugged terrain, remote wilderness environments, and

necessary safety equipment inherent in some outdoor activities require a manager to be creative and practical in developing programs accessible to people with disabilities. The USDA Forest Service noted that early federal ADA task forces addressed the high level of modifications necessary in urban areas but did not take into consideration how those standards in an outdoor recreation area could change the setting and the experience for all people (USDA Forest Service, 2003a). As a result, its Outdoor Recreation Accessibility Guidelines (2003a) strive to protect unique characteristics of natural settings while integrating universal designs in facilities and programs to maximize accessibility.

The Forest Service guidelines address outdoor recreation access routes, beach access routes, camping and picnicking areas, and other constructed features. A separate section outlines guidelines for pedestrian hiking trails. The document addresses issues beyond the Forest Service's 1993 *Universal Access to Outdoor Recreation: A Design Guide*, which means it may apply in situations such as primitive areas that the *Design Guide* would have exempted. Rapid advances in technology are enabling use of outdoor resources by those with disabilities and interested participants with disabilities are becoming increasingly savvy about accessible opportunities.

Park managers, recreation programmers, outdoor outfitters, and guides must keep abreast of developments in this area as they create frameworks for improved access to programs and activities such as rafting, canoeing, hiking, and horseback riding. They must be aware of unique issues that can affect programming, such as how to accommodate assistive devices (including service dogs) and how to review regulations and policies for inadvertent discrimination against people with disabilities, such as group size restrictions. More specific resources are now available for programmers, such as the

American Canoe Association's *Teaching Paddling to People with Disabilities.*

A good example of an organization that is doing great work in promoting recreational activities for people with disabilities is the National Ability Center in Park City, Utah. It offers a broad range of activities, including skiing, snowboarding, horseback riding, swimming, cycling, sled hockey, and quad rugby. The National Ability Center serves thousands of people with disabilities on a yearly basis (National Ability Center, 2009).

Therapeutic recreation professionals need to study the economic restructuring of the healthcare system and understand how a shift from institutional care to home-based care will affect delivery of services. As the population of the United States ages and the number of people with disabilities increases, the demand for services is likely to increase as well. The therapeutic recreation professional may be asked to integrate recreation services as a part of a comprehensive home healthcare plan. He or she might also explore respite care, wherein caregivers provide for older citizens at a central facility during the day, providing stimulating programs to involve and challenge participants.

In therapeutic recreation, staff may also need specialized training to effectively meet the needs of a particular population. A professional may need to understand substance abuse, eating disorders, attention deficit and hyperactivity disorders, mental health issues such as depression and post-traumatic stress syndrome, and physical health issues such as cardiac problems and disability challenges. Understanding the range of medications and their side effects in combination with exercise and environment effects is also important. Developing an accurate and positive portrait of each participant's capability is necessary, and recreation staff must work with agency personnel prior to establishing programs to develop program goals that meet participants' needs.

Risk Management

Understanding the role of **risk management** in recreation is integral to all segments of the industry. Employees have a responsibility to develop enjoyable programming at appropriate sites and conduct it prudently without eliminating the challenge and excitement that originally attracted people to the activity. Administrators and staff who understand the laws affecting recreation and are familiar with the elements of risk management can mitigate the increase in lawsuits against recreational professionals and in settlements by the courts and insurance companies.

Recreation programs need written, well-defined risk management plans to establish guidelines for equipment and facility use, program development and operation, management of changing environmental conditions, and emergency preparedness. An organization's recommended practices should be reflected in its risk management plan, and an ongoing review of the plan is necessary to ensure employees abide by the guidelines and that the guidelines are still appropriate in light of current standards in the field. Many programs have designated risk management committees that review procedures and accident reports and use outside evaluators to help target areas for improvement. Smaller businesses conduct internal reviews among staff and administrators to improve their practices. Many use advisory boards comprised of industry experts to review new programs and general operations.

Elements of a risk management program include but are not limited to the following:

- Participant health screening prior to participation to determine the appropriate level of involvement, if any

- Preprogram information to inform participants about an activity
- Equipment and facility safety checks
- Criteria for staff hiring, including necessary activity certifications or experience and first aid credentials
- Continuing education and training for staff
- Recommended progressions of activities that meet current national standards
- Adequate staff–student ratios and protocols for general and specific supervision of groups
- Emergency response protocols, including first aid response, evacuation, and search and rescue
- Critical accident protocols, including those covering interaction with families and the press.

Informed participant consent is an important legal issue in recreation programming. Participants must be made aware of the potential risks inherent in activities before they begin so they can make informed decisions about the nature of their participation. Organizations often provide preprogram activity information, recommended clothing and equipment lists, and an assumption-of-risk/waiver-of-liability form in an effort to inform people about the upcoming experience. Safety education is an integral part of a program plan, and individual and group responses and rescues in emergency situations are often practiced in recreational activities as a part of a participant's education. As the popularity of adventurous activities increases, professionals have a responsibility to train participants in rescue so that they do not have to rely on agencies to execute rescues on their behalf.

Greater degrees of risk are inherent in some recreational activities, which make them exciting, but organizations have a responsibility to use this element wisely. Leaders have a legal responsibility to develop programs that do not involve unreasonable risks, and they should only ask participants to perform activities with a clear benefit. For more information on risk management, refer to Chapter 5, Legal Principles Applied to Sport Management.

■ SUMMARY

The complexity of modern life is likely to promote a continuing need for enjoyable, safe, and challenging recreational activities as a diversion for the public and as a partial solution to social problems in our society. Just as lifestyles have become more complex in the United States, so has the nature of the recreation profession. Industry professionals face numerous challenges as they seek to provide quality recreational experiences for diverse participants.

Technological changes in equipment and communications require employees to understand the impact of these changes upon recreation businesses. Such things as cellular and satellite phones on wilderness trips and marketing through Internet Web sites and social media have changed the face of the industry. The ease of international travel and the emergence of popular eco-vacations overseas have prompted professionals to gain an understanding of different cultures and physical environments. Increasing government regulation, particularly in the area of safety, means professionals must be aware of and comply with new laws, policies, and procedures. As specific industry segments mature, employees will be held to higher and higher standards of training and performance. These challenges require employees to bring a broad range of skills to their positions and continue their education to deliver quality experiences that meet current standards in the field. The reward is involvement in enriching experiences that enhance the recreation employee's life and can effect social change.

CASE STUDY: Blazing New Trails

The Appalachian Mountain Club's Galehead Hut is 4.6 miles from the nearest road and considered its most remote hut in the White Mountains system in New Hampshire. The 67-year-old facility underwent a major and controversial rebuilding in 2000, when the USDA Forest Service requested that the hut be made wheelchair accessible to comply with the Americans with Disabilities Act of 1990. The reason: Any new construction on federal lands must be ADA compliant, and the Appalachian Mountain Club (AMC) had decided that the tired Galehead Hut needed a complete rebuilding rather than another round of renovations. The AMC had begun work on a new facility without accessible features because it believed that a backcountry hut did not have to meet ADA regulations. However, the USDA Forest Service, which awards the AMC its permit to operate the huts in the national forest, required that the building be redesigned to meet federal standards. Ultimately, the costs of a wheelchair access ramp, accessible bunkroom, bathroom renovations, and stair removal added approximately $50,000 to the $400,000 renovation—in part because the change in design happened after the project was under way. The AMC designed the facility to be an environmental model for the new century, with new composting technology and solar electric generation in a ridge-top location where human waste was previously carried off by helicopters. Now it was state of the art on many levels, including accessibility to people with a wide range of physical abilities.

Public sentiment regarding the project generated countless letters to regional newspapers and *AMC Outdoors*, the AMC's membership magazine. One AMC member wrote: "When will the AMC start to fight such insane regulations instead of meekly acquiescing?" New Hampshire's largest newspaper, the *Manchester Union-Leader*, asked in a July 1, 2000, cover story, "What might [legendary hutmaster] Joe Dodge think of the Appalachian Mountain Club's new Galehead Hut, if he stopped laughing about the handicap-access ramp leading up to the porch at 3,800 feet?" Another writer in *AMC Outdoors* asked: "Just how many disabled people and their wheelchairs are planning to be brought in and out by helicopter? There certainly isn't any other way for them to get there."

However, on August 16 three hikers in wheelchairs and two on crutches climbed the rugged trail to Galehead, negotiating narrow bridges, endless boulders, mud, and streams with the help of friends, family, and volunteers. They received little help from the able-bodied hiker who cursed at the group for blocking the trail and questioned their right to be hiking. An able-bodied hiker can complete the ascent in 3.5 hours. It took 12 hours for the group to tackle the 2,000-foot elevation gain and earn a well-deserved resting place on the easily accessible front porch. The hike made the front page of the *New York Times* on August 17 in a story entitled "For These Trailblazers, Wheelchairs Matter."

The Galehead Trek 2000 began as a casual idea at Northeast Passage, a nonprofit program at the University of New Hampshire that offers programming to people with physical disabilities. Northeast Passage offers a popular series of recreation programs to people with disabilities, including sled hockey, wheelchair basketball, sea kayaking, hand cycling, water skiing, and more. When critical opinion surfaced in the media, Northeast Passage participants objected to the public sentiment that they couldn't complete the climb and became determined to do it. Among the committed group was a mother, a Paralympic cross-country skier, a college wheelchair racer, a doctor with a goal of climbing

Mt. Katahdin in Maine, and a ski instructor. They used new wheelchairs with frames and tires designed for rugged terrain, long poles that turned the wheelchairs into rickshaws, tethers that allowed volunteers to pull their chairs, planks for stream crossings—and a strong spirit of experimentation that allowed them to be creative problem solvers on the trail. One participant with limited use of his legs because of polio walked on his hands across some streams. Asked if they would attempt the hike again, some said yes. And a year later, they ascended Mt. Lafayette in Franconia Notch.

The hikers' achievements brought a spotlight to the bigger challenge facing the nation's wilderness areas—namely, how to make outdoor facilities more friendly to people with disabilities. How can campgrounds, information and education centers, bathrooms and outhouses, and trails be made more accessible? During the media coverage of Galehead Trek 2000 the USDA Forest Service allayed some concerns about the intent of ADA regulations, still being interpreted by a consortium of agencies that administer federal lands. No, the trails will not be paved to the huts, said the Forest Service's national accessibility coordinator. But beyond the natural features of the landscape, the person-built facilities need to have standardized features that allow accessibility. Changes in mobility technology are rapid, and what may seem impossible today may be quite possible in upcoming decades. Some say the real barriers are the attitudes and misconceptions of those who believe that people with disabilities do not want or do not deserve access to wilderness areas. Some people believe the money spent on hut modifications could be better spent on trail maintenance. However, one man wrote to Northeast Passage after the event, saying: "Having climbed up to that hut by a couple of different routes, I would have said there is no way you could do what you did. In fact, I am one of those Appalachian Club Members who deplored the wheelchair accessible expenditures as ridiculous. I stand magnificently corrected."

Questions for Discussion

1. As a recreation programmer who has created accessible activities, how can you educate other people about how to adapt activities? Develop fact sheets that focus on the abilities of people with specific disabilities. Create an educational seminar that provides tips for adapting some sample programs (pick one or several specific activities).
2. Federal agencies, particularly the USDA Forest Service, are continuing to interpret the impact of the ADA upon wilderness areas in the United States. You are a recreation manager with clients who have physical disabilities and are interested in outdoor recreation opportunities. Find out the current guidelines and issues so that you know the rights of your clients.
3. As a recreation programmer, you have participants with disabilities who are inspired by the Galehead Trek 2000 story. How do you plan and execute a hike for a similar team in your local area?
4. Assume you are the executive director of the AMC. What impact does the Galehead project have on future renovations of any backcountry facilities in New Hampshire's White Mountains system? What advice would you offer directors of other trail systems in the United States who plan to construct new backcountry facilities?

■ RESOURCES

American Alliance for Health, Physical Education, Recreation and Dance (AAHPERD)
1900 Association Drive
Reston, VA 22191
703-476-3400
http://www.aahperd.org/

American Camp Association (ACA)
5000 State Road, 67 North
Martinsville, IN 46151
765-342-8456
http://www.acacamps.org/

American Recreation Coalition
1225 New York Avenue NW, Suite 450
Washington, DC 20005-6405
202-682-9530
http://www.funoutdoors.com/arc

Association for Experiential Education
3775 Iris Avenue, Suite 4
Boulder, CO 80301
303-440-8844
http://www.aee.org/

Disabled Sports USA
451 Hungerford Drive, Suite 100
Rockville, MD 20850
301-217-0960
http://www.dsusa.org

Jewish Community Centers of North America
520 Eighth Avenue
New York, NY 10018
212-532-4949
http://www.jcca.org/index.lasso

National Golf Foundation (NGF)
1150 South US Highway One, Suite 401
Jupiter, FL 33477
561-744-6006
http://www.ngf.org

National Park Service (NPS)
1849 C Street, NW
Washington, DC 20240
202-208-6834

General information: http://www.nps.gov/
Job information: http://www.nps.gov/
    gettinginvolved/employment/index.htm

National Recreation and Park Association
22377 Belmont Ridge Road
Ashburn, VA 20148
703-858-0784
http://www.nrpa.org

Resort and Commercial Recreation Association
P.O. Box 1564
Dubuque, IA 52004
http://www.r-c-r-a.org/

USDA Forest Service
1400 Independence Avenue, SW
Washington, DC 20250
202-205-8333
http://www.fs.fed.us/

Young Men's Christian Association of the USA
101 North Wacker Drive
Chicago, IL 60606
800-872-9622
http://www.ymca.net/

Young Women's Christian Association of the USA
1015 18th Street, NW, Suite 1100
Washington, DC 20036
202-467-0801
http://www.ywca.org/539

■ KEY TERMS

Americans with Disabilities Act (ADA), community-based recreation, cultural awareness, direct participation, environmental awareness, indirect participation, informed participant consent, military recreation, outdoor recreation, parks movement, private sector, public recreation, public sector, risk management, therapeutic recreation, university outdoor programs

■ REFERENCES

American Association for Retired People (AARP). (2004). Baby boomers envision retirement II: Survey of baby boomers' expectations for retirement. Washington, DC: Author.

American Camping Association (ACA). (2010). Trend fact sheet. Retrieved December 6, 2010, from http://www.acacamps.org/media-center/camp-trends/fact

Association for Experiential Education (AEE). (2010). Accredited programs. Retrieved December 6, 2010, from http://www.aee.org/accreditation/programs

Association for Outdoor Recreation and Education (AORE). (2010). Current AORE organizational members. Retrieved December 6, 2010, from http://www.aore.org/organizations-and-vendors/organizational-members/default.aspx

Cheeseman-Day, J. (n.d.). Population profile of the United States. Retrieved December 20, 2010, from http://www.census.gov/population/www/pop-profile/natproj.html

Cordell, H.K. (2008). The latest on trends in nature-based outdoor recreation. *Forest History Today*. Retrieved December 6, 2010, from http://www.foresthistory.org/publications/FHT/FHTSpring2008/Cordell.pdf

Cordell, H.K., Betz, C., Green, G., & Mou, S. (2008). Iris Internet Research Information Series. Outdoor recreation activity trends: What's growing, what's slowing? Retrieved December 6, 2010, from http://warnell.forestry.uga.edu/nrrt/nsre/IRISRec/IRISRec7rpt.pdf

Lee, R.F. (2003). *Public use of the national park system 1872–2000*. Washington, DC: National Park Service.

Lewis, M. (2008). 2007/2008 snowboard sales summary. Retrieved December 18, 2010, from http://business.transworld.net/11825/features/200708-sia-snowboard-sales-summary/

National Ability Center (NAC). (2009). Sports programs. Retrieved December 6, 2010, from http://www.discovernac.org/programs.htm

National Golf Foundation (NGF). (2006). *A strategic perspective on the future of golf*. Retrieved December 6, 2010, from http://www.ngf.org/pages/golf-industry-report

National Recreation and Park Association. (2010). Why parks and recreation are essential public services [pdf]. Retrieved December 6, 2010, from http://www.google.com/search?sourceid=navclient&ie=UTF-8&rlz=1T4ADFA_enUS376&q=Why+parks+and+recreation+are+essential+public+services

National Ski Areas Association. (2006). 2006/2007 ski resort industry research compendium. Retrieved December 6, 2010, from http://www.nsaa.org/nsaa/marketing/docs/0607-research-compendium.pdf

National Ski Areas Association (NSAA). (2010). Environmental charter. Retrieved December 6, 2010, from http://www.nsaa.org/nsaa/environment/sustainable_slopes/Charter.pdf

Obama, B. (2010). A 21st century strategy for America's great outdoors. Retrieved December 6, 2010, from http://www.doi.gov/americasgreatoutdoors/upload/2010outdoors-mem-rel-2.pdf

Outdoor Foundation. (2010). 2010 outdoor recreation participation report. Retrieved December 20, 2010, from http://www.outdoorindustry.org/images/researchfiles/TOF_ResearchParticipation2010.pdf?121

Outdoor Industry Association. (2005). Outdoor recreation participation study (7th edition for 2004): Female participation. Retrieved December 6, 2010, from http://www.outdoorfoundation.org/pdf/ParticipationStudy2005Females.pdf

Outdoor Industry Association. (2008). Outdoor recreation participation report 2008. Retrieved December 6, 2010, from http://www.outdoorfoundation.org/research.participation.2008.html

Outdoor Industry Foundation. (2006). The active outdoor recreation economy. Retrieved December 6, 2010, from http://www.outdoorindustry.org/images/researchfiles/RecEconomy_State%20final403.pdf?52

Paralyzed Veterans of America. (n.d.). Nine Paralyzed Veterans of America athletes depart for China in search of Olympic gold. Retrieved December 6, 2010, from http://pva.convio.net/site/News2?page=NewsArticle&id=9055&security=1&news_iv_ctrl=0

Quigley, S. (2004). Military athletes have proud Olympic history. Retrieved December 6, 2010, from http://www.defense.gov/news/newsarticle.aspx?id=25521

Rodriguez, D., Bright, A., & Roberts, N. (2004). Ethnic minority visitors and non-visitors: An examination of constraints regarding outdoor recreation participation in Rocky Mountain National Park. Retrieved December 6, 2010, from http://www .nature.nps.gov/helpyourparks/diversity/pdf/ RMNP_FinalTechnicalRpt_Dec04.pdf

RRC Associates. (2009). New Mexico statewide comprehensive outdoor recreation plan (SCORP) update survey final results. Retrieved December 6, 2010, from http://www.emnrd.state.nm.us/ PRD/scorp/documents/AppendixD-SCORPSurvey FinalReport.pdf

Sporting Goods Manufacturers Association (SGMA). (2010a). SGMA's 2010 state of the industry report released. Retrieved from December 6, 2010, from http://www.sgma.com/press/224_SGMA's-2010- State-of-the-Industry-Report-Released

Sporting Goods Manufacturers Association (SGMA). (2010b). SGMA study identifies active segments of U.S. population. Retrieved December 18, 2010, from http://www.sgma.com/press/237_ SGMA-Study-Identifies-Active-Segments-of-U.S.- Population

Swartz, J. (2010, August 3). Recessions and golf don't mix. *USA Today*, pp. 1B-2B.

Stynes, D. (2009). National park visitor spending and payroll impact 2008. Retrieved December 20, 2010, from http://web4.canr.msu.edu/mgm2/

U.S. Department of Commerce (2010). U.S. Census. [Tables A1, B1]. Retrieved from http://www .census.govpopulation/www/projections/projection sagesex//html

USDA Forest Service. (2003a). Outdoor recreation accessibility guidelines. Retrieved December 6, 2010, from http://www.fs.fed.us/recreation/ programs/accessibility

USDA Forest Service. (2003b). Jobs. What we do. Retrieved December 6, 2010, from http://www. fs.fed.us/fsjobs/whatdo.html

USDA Forest Service and Interagency National Survey Consortium. (2000–2002). *National survey on recreation and the environment*. Washington, DC: Author.

U.S. Fish and Wildlife Service. (2007). 2006 national survey of fishing, hunting, and wildlife-associated recreation. Retrieved December 18, 2010, from http://www.census.gov/prod/2008pubs/fhw06-nat .pdf

U.S. National Park Service. (2009). NPS stats. Retrieved December 6, 2010, from http://www.nature .nps.gov/stats/viewReport.cfm?selectedReport= SystemSummaryReport.cfm

Career Preparation

Chapter 22   Strategies for Career Success

Strategies for Career Success

Mary A. Hums and Virginia R. Goldsbury

■ INTRODUCTION

What is your dream job in sport management? General Manager of the Los Angeles Lakers? Director of Stadium Operations at Yankee Stadium? Athletic Director at University of Florida? Marketing Director for the U.S. Olympic Committee? How do you begin to climb the sport industry ladder? What are the realities of trying to break into the sport industry? This chapter deals with these questions and gives you suggestions on how to market your most valuable resource—you!

Myths About Careers in Sport Management: A Reality Check

People are drawn to the sport management profession for a great number of reasons. The reason most often given is a love of sport. To be very honest, many people love sport, but a love of sport is simply not enough to land a job in the industry. As a matter of fact, if you gave that as your answer to a prospective sport employer in an interview, it would be a very short interview! Prospective employers look for people who want to work in the business of sport. An often used expression is, "It's nice that you love sports, but can you put people in seats?" In other words, sport employers look for people who are business people first and sports enthusiasts second.

People seeking careers in the sport industry often have misperceptions about what working in the industry will be like, and there are a number of common myths about working in the sport industry. This section is not meant to discourage students from going into the industry but rather is intended to present a realistic picture of what the job market is like for people trying to break in.

■ MYTH 1: A SPORT MANAGEMENT DEGREE IS A TICKET TO SUCCESS

As pointed out in Chapter 1, History of Sport Management, the number of sport management programs in the country is growing, with more than 200 colleges and universities currently offering sport management as a major on either the undergraduate or graduate levels. All of these graduates are seeking employment in the sport industry. In addition, some students graduating with degrees in management, marketing, public relations, communications, or exercise science, as well as many from MBA programs and law schools, are vying to land jobs in the field. People currently working in industries outside of sport, such as advertising agencies, banks, or financial services, are increasingly considering career changes into the sport industry, showcasing the transferable skills, such as sales or merchandising, they acquired in those other industries.

A couple of examples illustrate the demand for jobs in the industry. On average, 450 to 550 job openings are posted each year at the Professional Baseball Employment Opportunities (PBEO) Job Fair held in conjunction with the Winter Baseball Meetings (North American Professional Baseball League [NAPBL], 2010). When the New Orleans Hornets had an opening for a $25,000 Community Relations position, the opening drew 1,000 applications in one week (Helyar, 2006). Positions with the organizing committee for the Chicago 2016 Olympic bid drew thousands of applications, and once the bid was awarded to Rio de Janeiro, those working for the bid committee found themselves unemployed (Chicago Press Release Services, 2009). The large volume of job applicants has caused a number of sport organizations to incorporate electronic databases and Web sites to gather job applicant information. Obviously, competition for jobs is intense, and a sport management degree does not guarantee a job in the industry. It is important to note, however, that the sport industry is broader than just professional sport. A myriad of employment opportunities exist in health and fitness, facility management, colleges, recreational sport, sport for people with disabilities, youth sports, and the other areas mentioned throughout this book. Also, the more willing a person is to relocate, the better the chance he or she has of finding employment.

What, then, are the advantages to earning a degree in sport management? First, one learns about the application of business principles to the sport industry. Taking a marketing class, for example, provides groundwork in basic marketing concepts. As we know from Chapter 3, Marketing Principles Applied to Sport Management, sport marketing is inherently different from traditional marketing because the sport product is unpredictable and perishable, and the sport marketer has very little, if any, control over the core product. A sport management major will have a solid understanding of this difference. A sport management degree also gives a student working knowledge of the industry. Because classes are geared specifically toward sport, students are immersed in industry happenings in the classroom, constantly learning about current issues and current events. Students read publications such as *Street & Smith's SportsBusiness Journal* and *Athletic Business*.

Many sport management degree programs allow initial access to the industry via **internship** opportunities with sport organizations. These hands-on learning experiences give students the chance to live the sport industry firsthand, gaining valuable work experience. Beyond this, the internship allows students to meet people working in the industry and begin establishing a professional **network**. In addition, a good number of sport management academic programs have professors who have come to academia after working in the industry and who actively maintain industry ties, giving students another way to access a network of sport industry professionals. The importance of networking is discussed later in this chapter. Finally, when working on a sport management degree, students learn about opportunities to build their resumes. What will make your resume stand out from all the others? Being involved in as many sport management–related opportunities as possible! Sport management programs often stage campus events such as 3-on-3 basketball tournaments and golf tournaments. Sport management programs routinely receive requests from sport organizations for event volunteers. Students are wise to take advantage of these opportunities and get involved. Having these experiences on a resume makes a difference, because they indicate one's commitment to the industry. People who do not major in sport management do not necessarily have access to these advantages.

■ MYTH 2: IT'S NOT WHO YOU KNOW, IT'S WHAT YOU KNOW

The truth is, "It's not what you know, it's who you know." Actually, we could take this a step further and say, "It's not who you know, it's who knows you." Having a degree is simply not enough. In the sport industry, as much or perhaps more than in just about any other industry, people hire someone because of a personal recommendation from someone else. The importance of networking cannot be overstated.

Sport managers have to actively work to expand their networks to include all kinds of people. It is easy and comfortable for people to build networks with others like themselves, but for the sport industry to continue to thrive and to serve all constituents, sport managers must diversify their networks so that opportunities will be available to all.

■ MYTH 3: MOST EMPLOYMENT OPPORTUNITIES ARE IN PROFESSIONAL SPORT OR NCAA DIVISION I ATHLETIC DEPARTMENTS

When people hear the term *sport management*, the jobs that most often come to mind are in professional sport or National Collegiate Athletic Association (NCAA) Division I college athletics. To the question, "What do you want to do with your sport management degree?" a common answer is, "I want to be the general manager of the (name of the nearest major professional sport franchise)" or "I want to be the athletic director at (name of the school that won the most recent national football or basketball championship)." The fact is the number of jobs in professional sport is limited. For example, at present there are only 30 Major League Baseball (MLB) general managers, and although that number may vary slightly via expansion or contraction, it will never be very high. The same is true for the other major league professional sports. Professional sport front offices tend to be relatively small compared with other employers. Minor league offices employ minimal staff as full-time employees. A minor league baseball franchise at the A level may have as few as 10 to 12 full-time employees, while an AAA franchise may have 20 to 25. Also, there tends to be a relatively low turnover rate in these positions. People who get jobs in professional sport tend to stay in their jobs. In addition, people already in the industry tend to get "recycled" when positions come open. If a ball club is looking for a new general manger, for example, it will look to former general managers or current assistant general managers to fill the position.

Many colleges and universities are currently dealing with economic setbacks or concerns unrelated to sport that in turn affect the amount of money spent on athletic programs. If funding is not available to athletic departments, those departments will be unable to hire staff. State universities are especially susceptible to this problem, because state lawmakers make decisions about where limited state funding will go. If the state legislature cuts the amount of dollars available to a university, the cutbacks will be felt throughout all areas of the institution, including athletics. This makes it difficult for college and university athletic departments to create new positions. To make up for this shortfall in personnel, however, a number of college and university athletic departments are offering more graduate assistantships and internships. These positions offer opportunities for those trying to enter the field to gain experience.

As this textbook has pointed out, someone entering the sport industry needs to look beyond professional and college sport for job opportunities. The multibillion-dollar segments of the industry include sporting goods and apparel, recreational sport, and the health and fitness area, to name a few. The purpose of a book such as this is to help students broaden their horizons to see the vast opportunities that lie in front of them in all different segments of the industry.

■ MYTH 4: SPORT MANAGEMENT JOBS ARE GLAMOROUS AND EXCITING

Many people have the impression that working in the sport industry is glamorous and exciting. They have visions of "hanging out" with famous athletes, driving around in chauffeured limousines, and being in the glare of the spotlight. However, when it comes to working in the sport industry, nothing could be further from the truth. No one goes to an Ohio State football game to watch the ticket manager do his or her job. People do not go to a Pacers game in Conseco Fieldhouse to watch the event coordinator organize the details of the game. The bottom line is that sport managers labor in the background so that others can enjoy the spotlight. A typical work schedule for that event coordinator is 60 to 70 hours per week, including lots of late nights and long weekends. Remember, when other people are going out to be entertained they are coming to the place where the sport manager is hard at work. Although it is exciting to work at games or events, a sport manager very seldom—if ever—gets to see any of the action of the game or event itself. There

are too many behind-the-scenes details to take care of to be a fan.

To a large degree, the work of sport managers is similar to jobs in the corporate world, but they are unique in that they require industry-specific knowledge. Someone who is an accountant for the Kansas City Royals, for example, is doing the same job as someone who is an accountant for any large business, but the sport accountant needs to understand player salary concerns such as deferred compensation. A sport lawyer works with the same legal issues as a non-sport lawyer, such as contracts or licensing agreements, but the sport lawyer has to understand salary caps and luxury taxes. General business knowledge is important, but specific knowledge of the sport industry is essential. Another distinction is the affiliation with a team or league. People just feel differently about working in sport. It is more fun to say, "I work in sales for the Detroit Pistons" than it is to say, "I work in the business office for Artisan Steel Fabrication." There is just something special about going to your office when your office is in a ballpark or an arena.

■ MYTH 5: SPORT MANAGEMENT JOBS PAY WELL

The expression, "You have to pay your dues" is as true in the sport industry as in other parts of the business world. In general, salaries—especially starting salaries—tend to be low in the sport industry. Because of the high number of applicants for these jobs, salaries can stay low and people are thankful for the opportunites when they do get jobs. Demand for the jobs far outstrips the supply. How many times have you heard someone say something like, "I'd work for the Atlanta Braves for free!" The starting salaries tend to be rather low, although there is potential for increased earnings as you move up in the industry.

Now that you are aware of some of the barriers you may encounter on the way to finding your place in the sport industry, how do you go about starting down the road to your sport management career? How do you begin undertaking a successful job search? The remainder of this chapter gives you some tools to work with—tools such as informational interviews, job interview skills, and resume writing. Good luck!

■ FINDING A JOB

Finding a job, any job, is a difficult, time-consuming, and challenging process. At this time, you are dealing with building a career; therefore, your first job in the sport industry is just that—your first job, the first step in what it is hoped will be a satisfying career. To prepare yourself, you need to begin early in your collegiate experience, as early as your first year!

You need to have a plan when seeking a job. **Figure 22-1** shows you the various phases of this process. The following section provides details that will help guide you along the way.

Steps to Finding the Best First Job

■ 1. KNOW YOURSELF

Analyze your skills, abilities, interests, and preferred workplace environment. Before you know anything else, you must know yourself. Your goal is to find a job utilizing your strengths, challenging yourself where you want to be challenged, and minimizing your frustrations. A variety of instruments can help you with this exercise. Although many are online, do not use such assessments in a vacuum. Use your college's career office to help you.

■ 2. CAREER EXPLORATION

Exploring career jobs, although time-consuming, can prove to be interesting and valuable. This

FIGURE 22-1 The Job Search Process.

STEP 4: Job Search Strategy

- Prepare your resume.
- Contact 3–5 individuals to write letters of reference.
- Draft a cover letter to accompany your resume.
- Check job listings.
- Talk to people in the industry about job leads.
- Follow-up with prospective employers after sending application materials.

STEP 3: Gaining Experience

- Check out internship opportunities.
- Serve on a committee.
- Become a leader in a club on campus.
- Volunteer to help out at sports events on campus.
- Volunteer to help out at community events.

STEP 2: Career Exploration

- Identify jobs that might interest you.
- Begin to gather information about those jobs.
- Check Web sites for information.
- Read books, journals, magazines, and newspapers.
- Talk to people who work in those organizations.

STEP 1: Know Yourself!

- Who are you?
- What are your skills?
- What are your abilities?
- What are your interests?
- Who can help you find these answers?

text has exposed you to all aspects of the sport industry. Now select those most interesting to you and begin your research. The more informed you are, the better prepared you will be to make a decision about your own career. The first step is to learn as much as you can about each area. Read books, professional journals, magazines, newspapers, and online resources. Once you can speak intelligently regarding your field of interest, begin informational interviewing. Talk to people who work in positions or in organizations that interest you. This is a wonderful way to utilize and expand your network while gaining valuable insight into a variety of career paths. Informational interviewing will be discussed in detail later in the chapter.

■ 3. GAIN EXPERIENCE

It is a well-known fact that with experience comes marketability. What do employers mean when they ask if you have experience? What kind of experience are they expecting? One way to begin to answer these questions is to learn what makes a valuable candidate for employment. Ask yourself what you would expect from someone you were going to pay. How do you gain this valuable experience? As a student, you have numerous opportunities to experiment with different segments of the sport industry, gain new skills, and improve the skills you have. You have access to people in all segments of the sport industry as well as volunteer opportunities. In many cases you can earn college credit while experiencing a portion of the industry or a particular department within the area and making valuable connections. Professional sport franchises, marketing agencies, health clubs, facilities, and your college or university athletic department all offer internships. The work is demanding and the pay often nonexistent, but you will gain valuable experience. An internship can occasionally lead to permanent employment, but even if it does not, you will be increasing your marketability.

In addition to an organized internship, take advantage of as many opportunities to expand your horizons as you can. Many organizations such as the Professional Golfers Association (PGA), the Ladies Professional Golfers Association (LPGA), the United States Tennis Association (USTA), the Special Olympics, and local sports commissions need hoards of volunteers for their events. Take the initiative and create your own volunteer opportunities if none currently exist. Remember, on-campus organizations also offer leadership opportunities. Student government associations, fraternities or sororities, and other student-run organizations always need people. You can gain valuable—and transferable—leadership skills working with these groups. Each experience will help define your long-term goals and in the process make you more interesting to potential employers. Get involved early and often!

■ 4. JOB SEARCH STRATEGY

Finding a job requires time, energy, and thoughtful preparation. Now that you have a clearer picture of your skills, abilities, and goals, you are in a position to begin writing an effective resume and accompanying cover letter. These documents should reflect the energy you have expended preparing for a management career and demonstrate a professional attitude. You may have heard the comment that "Looking for a job is a full-time job." This can certainly be true. However, you may not be able to spend 40 hours per week on your job search, so make sure to set up a schedule that works for you and stick to it. Decide to make a certain number of phone calls, send a certain number of e-mails, mail or e-mail a certain number of applications, and/or research particular organizations each week. Keep a well-documented journal of your job search activities. Follow up each application with a phone call a week or two later. There is a fine line between being persistent and being aggressive, but you want your prospective employers to know you are interested in working with them.

Where should you look for job openings in the sport industry? As a sport management student, your college or university sport management program is a good place to start. Sport organizations routinely send information about job and internship openings to these programs. Check with your departmental faculty, who may have connections in the industry and may know of some openings that are not publicly advertised. Also check the Web sites for teams and sport organizations. For example, *NCAA News*, which lists openings in intercollegiate athletics, is available online. Organizations such as Nike, the United States Olympic Committee, and the International Paralympic Committee also list job and internship opportunities online. Traditional job Web sites such as Monster.com may also have a selection of sport jobs. Your career services office also may have a jobs database where employers who list employment opportunities may be particularly interested in students from your school. While a number of Web sites provide information specifically about job opportunities in the sport industry, remember that these are not free services, and there will be a cost associated with using them.

■ INFORMATIONAL INTERVIEWING

One effective means of expanding your understanding of an industry, an organization, or a particular job or department is to speak to someone who is already there. The information you glean from **informational interviewing** serves as a foundation for making your own career decisions, while simultaneously building a valuable

network of professional connections. You may choose to interview relatives, friends, acquaintances, or alumni of your college or university. Alumni are often an overlooked resource; however, they are often very willing to help students from their school. Check with your career center or the alumni relations office, which may maintain a database of alumni who have offered their services for just this purpose. Your academic department or specific faculty may also be able to supply you with a list of helpful alumni.

First you need to schedule an appointment for a phone interview or in-person meeting. Have your questions prepared before you call in case the person you are trying to reach is available

immediately. You want to present yourself as an aspiring professional, so have your questions written down. You have 20 minutes to talk to the person who has a job you may like to have. What is it you really want to know? If you feel you need more time, excuse yourself and ask if you might talk to him or her again if you have additional questions. You might also ask for suggestions of someone else to contact.

What Do I Ask?

Only you can decide what is truly important to you. Some suggestions to consider are as follows:

- Please briefly describe what you do. What tasks take most of your time? How would you describe your working conditions, including hours, pressure, pace, and so on? How does your position relate to the rest of the organization?
- What particular character and personality traits would you suggest one needs to be successful in your position in this industry?
- What experiences, education, and other training would prepare me to enter this field?
- What kind of lifestyle choices have you had to make because of your job and how do you feel about them?
- What about your job do you find most satisfying? What is the most challenging or frustrating?
- I know that the sport industry is very difficult to break into. What two pieces of career advice would you offer to help me successfully enter this world?
- During the course your career, did you have a mentor? If so, who was it and how did that person help you?
- Can you recommend two or three other people who would be worthwhile for me

to speak with? May I use your name when writing or calling them?

Additional Hints About the Informational Interviewing Process

- Conduct your interview at the interviewee's place of business if possible.
- Dress appropriately. This is a business meeting, so wear business attire.
- Be professional and articulate in your presentation.
- Observe the setting, the overall culture of the organization, and the relationships among the employees.
- Bring copies of your resume and business cards (if you have them).
- While there, ask yourself if you would be comfortable working in this environment.
- Get business cards from each person you meet.
- Send a personally written thank-you note immediately afterward. It can be handwritten if your handwriting is legible; otherwise, it should be typed. E-mail is also acceptable if you have been communicating that way. Remember: appropriate grammar is expected in an e-mail, not text messaging or chat abbreviations!
- Keep accurate notes of your interviews, as you may need to refer to them later.

Other Sources of Information

Professional journals, relevant books, and industry publications are valuable sources of career information. They provide current trends and plans for the future. Many of these have been discussed in previous chapters. Know the sources for your particular segment of interest, whether it is college athletics, professional sports, event management, facility management, marketing, health and fitness, or recreation. Most industry segments have an association that provides support for the profession. For example, the National Intramural Recreational Sports Association (NIRSA) is the professional organization for campus recreation. The National Association of Collegiate Directors of Athletics (NACDA) serves this purpose in intercollegiate athletics. The National Federation of State High School Associations (NFSHSA) provides information for people working in scholastic sport. These associations provide valuable connections, current relevant information, and sometimes job postings. Some have student memberships, which is a convenient way to begin your professional affiliations.

◼ MARKETING YOURSELF

Writing an Effective Resume

Before you begin to write your **resume**, make a list of your previous jobs and extracurricular activities. Evaluate your activities relative to your career goals. You will need to discuss each experience with prospective employers, demonstrating its significance to you as well as the organization for which you worked. Present yourself as a potential colleague, not "just" a student.

◼ TIPS TO EFFECTIVELY INTERPRET YOUR EXPERIENCES

- Your experience counts! Acknowledge your accomplishments in activities, internships, and jobs.
- Use the language of the industry when appropriate. This is not to be confused with slang. Each industry has vocabulary, including acronyms that may be specific to it. Using these terms demonstrates your knowledge of the industry.
- Present your experiences through the lens of your career goal. Draw connections between your work and your field of interest.

- Convey your learning as well as your duties. Did you attend marketing strategy meetings, brainstorming sessions, or other relevant meetings? Demonstrate insights gained and information acquired.
- Quantify whenever appropriate. That means monetary amounts, percentages, and numbers. How many participants were part of the event you organized? How many additional corporate sponsors participated this year because of your efforts? How much money was raised? Figures give the reader a clearer picture of the depth and breadth of your experience.
- Demonstrate the value you brought to the environment: the job, internship, volunteer, or extracurricular activity.
- Be prepared with "talking points" demonstrating the valuable personal attributes you bring to the workplace, such as time management, conflict resolution, decision making, adaptability, and leadership.
- Assemble a portfolio of projects and documents showcasing your skills and talents related to your career goals.

◼ RESUME OUTLINE

1. *Heading: Name, address, telephone number, e-mail address.* Remember, you want to be easy to reach while presenting a professional image. Therefore, provide a phone number where you will get messages if you are not home, and an e-mail address that you regularly check. Be sure to set up a professional-sounding e-mail address. What professional image do you convey to a potential employer if your e-mail address is partygirl@myschool.edu or partyboy@school.com?

   If you have your own Web site or an account on a social network like Facebook, Twitter, or MySpace, make sure the information you have on it presents an image that you want a prospective employer to see. There is no way to be sure exactly who is looking at your online profile. You may think if you allow only your "friends" to have access, your information is secure. However, there are always cracks. For example, government agencies can access your profile under the auspices of the Patriot Act. Consider using LinkedIn for your professional networking.

Understand the ramifications of posting questionable material. Even if the material is intended for friends, it can be viewed by anyone with Internet access. What is funny or cute to friends may have a very different (and negative) impact on potential employers. If you are in a photo that someone else posts with your name on it, you will come up in a search! According to a recent poll conducted by the National Association of Colleges and Employers (NACE), more than one-fourth of employers have "Googled" candidates or reviewed their profiles on social networking sites. There is only one way to ensure that no one has access to potentially damaging information or photographs online: Don't put them online in the first place!

2. *Objective: Your resume needs a focus.* This section is optional, but if you choose to include a written objective on your resume, then it must be well thought out and constructed. Be specific but not limiting. You may write a summary statement that includes your long-term goals.

3. *Education.* Include the college or university you are attending or have graduated from, your degree, major, and minor. Do not include high school information. If your university grade point average (GPA) is a 3.00 or better, you should include it. Employers may think it is less than that if they do not see it on the resume.

Include any national or international student exchange experience. Students sometimes list honors with education; some have a separate section. In either case, they should be listed. Honors include scholarships, dean's list, honor societies, and academic awards.

Students sometimes include a selection of the courses they have taken, which may not be obvious to the reader, but are related to the position for which they are applying.

4. *Experience.* When writing about your experiences, think in terms of your accomplishments, what you brought to the organization, and any positive changes resulting from your work there. Use impact statements. Begin each statement with an action verb or skill. Never just restate the job description.

Experiences can be grouped to ensure the employer focuses on those most relevant to your career goals, such as "Sport Experience" and "Other Experience." By using this format, you can highlight all the sport activities in which you have participated (excluding varsity and intramural athletics). Be sure to list experiences in reverse chronological order, listing your most recent experiences first.

5. *Accomplishments.* Include major accomplishments demonstrating the qualities an employer looks for in a potential employee (e.g., self-financed 100% of my educational expenses; salesperson of the month three consecutive months; hiked the entire Appalachian Trail, Spring 2010). This should include at least two entries. The placement of this section depends on the types of accomplishments listed.

6. *Skills.* In this section you may include foreign languages you speak, including a level of understanding: fluent, intermediate, basic. You may include specific computer

packages and systems (e.g., desktop publishing, Web design, ticketing systems), particularly if you have advanced skills.

7. *Activities.* These are activities organized by the school, the local area, or region (athletics, student government, band member) independent of the things you do by yourself (reading, playing music, fitness).

■ FINAL RESUME TIPS

- Organize information logically.
- Use a simple, easy-to-read font.
- Tailor the information to the job you are seeking.
- Pay attention to spelling, punctuation, and grammar. Making even one spelling error means the employer will not consider you any further.
- Have several people proofread your document.
- Consult the professionals in your campus career services office.
- Typically, a resume for someone just graduating with an undergraduate degree is one page. A resume can be two pages, but the information on the second page must be important enough for the reader to turn the page. Therefore, one-page-only resumes are encouraged.
- If you are mailing your resume, use good-quality white or off-white paper, and be sure to mail it in a large, flat envelope so you do not have to fold your resume.
- E-mailed resumes: Copy and paste your document into the body of the e-mail. Never submit your resume as an attachment unless specifically requested to do so. Not all e-mail programs can read all attachments. The same is true for the cover letter. Resumes submitted as Word documents are easier for employers to access but also may be modified by others. If you choose to submit

your application materials in PDF format, they will have a higher level of security, but may present a barrier to being read.

For your information, a typical one-page resume is presented in **Figure 22-2**. This document is a good example of how the information in this chapter can be utilized to create a winning resume. You can also visit Web sites such as Monster.com or Forbes.com to find additional examples and suggestions for resumes.

References

Assume that employers will want to check your **references** before they make you a job offer. Who should you ask to serve as a reference? How many references do you need?

Most employers will want to speak to at least three references; therefore, your list should include five or six people. Include their titles and contact information. Your references should be able to speak articulately and comfortably about you. If someone seems uncomfortable with the idea of a verbal interview, give them an "out" by suggesting that perhaps they would prefer to write a letter instead. It is not just what your references say, but how they say it that makes the difference.

As an undergraduate, your references should include faculty, coaches, and previous employers. Unless they specify otherwise, potential employers are not interested in personal references. Choose people who know you well enough to address your true abilities to perform the job successfully.

You want to have conversations with all people who will serve as your references, so make an appointment to see them or speak to them on the phone. You want your references to have a good idea of the work you are seeking and why you are qualified for the position. They should also have a sense of your personality,

FIGURE 22-2 Sample Resume.

JEFFREY CHARLES SENIOR

416 Someplace Road
Highland Park, IL 60035
847-555-3554
hpgiants55@aol.com

EDUCATION

Pennsylvania State University
B.S. Sport Management, May 2011 G.P.A. 3.48

HIGHLIGHTS

- Studied in Sydney, Australia, from January 2009 through April 2009.
- Accepted into New Balance Haigis Hoopla Event Management class.
- Made $36,170 for the athletic ticket office of Northwestern University.
- Dean's List, four semesters.
- Inducted into the National Society of Collegiate Scholars.
- Inducted into the Golden Key International Honour Society.

EXPERIENCE

U.S. Soccer Federation, Chicago, IL   Summer 2009

INTERN
- Assisted in all aspects of U.S. Open Cup Tournament.
- Contributed to other event operation projects, including media coordination and signage set-up.

**Pennsylvania State University Athletic
Department, State College, PA**   September 2009

INTERN
- Managed ticket call booth at two home football games.

**Northwestern University Athletic
Department, Evanston, IL**   Summer 2008

INTERN
- Generated $5,000 in season ticket sales through telephone solicitation.
- Sold individual game tickets for football, men's and women's basketball.
- Promoted Northwestern University's football program throughout the community.

Chicago Rush, Rosemont, IL   June 2008

VOLUNTEER
- Implemented game-day promotion at eight home games.
- Monitored pre-game festivities.

Chicago Wolves, Glenview, IL   Summer 2007

INTERN
- Contacted customers to encourage season ticket purchases.
- Represented the Wolves at 12 charity events.
- Contributed game promotional ideas, which were subsequently used.

ACTIVITIES

- Vice President of Recruitment, Inter Fraternity Council.
- Alumni Co-chairperson, Beta Epsilon Chapter of Sigma Alpha Mu Fraternity.
- Volunteer, New Balance Haigis Hoopla; student-run three-on-three basketball tournament involving 450 teams, 20,000 spectators, and 15 vendors.

your goals, and your strengths and weaknesses as they apply to the job.

Make sure your references have a copy of your resume and keep them informed of your progress. They should have an expectation that someone will be calling about you—the employer's contact should not come as a surprise. It is also important that you tell your references whether you receive an offer and if you accept it.

Employers check references only if they are seriously considering making an offer. References do have an influence on the outcome, so choose yours wisely.

The Cover Letter

Each resume must be accompanied by a **cover letter**. This document must also be professional and informative without being identical to your resume. There is no one model for a particular job application. Each letter should address the specific concerns of the organization to which you are applying. Consequently, you should expect to thoroughly research each organization and, after careful analysis, write a letter that demonstrates your value to the prospective employer.

Structure your letters of application with three or four paragraphs:

1. Why are you writing? How did you learn of the position? Why is it of interest to you? Demonstrate your knowledge of the organization. By including a reference to the company, you form a positive connection from the start.
2. Discuss your strongest qualifications that match the position as you understand it. Provide concrete evidence of your related experience.
3. Reinforce qualifications presented in your resume, but do not repeat them exactly. Show your strong writing skills.

4. Request an interview. Mention that you will call within a specific period of time to discuss an appointment, and follow up accordingly.

Always generate your own job search correspondence. This is an opportunity to demonstrate your value to the employer, your professionalism, and your strong writing abilities. Be sure to address the letter to a specific individual with his or her appropriate business title and address. Some job opening postings will ask you to send your materials to the human resources office, and there will be no specific person's name listed. If this is the case, when you send your materials you should address the person as "Dear Hiring Manager" or "Dear Internship Director" and avoid using "Dear Sir" or "To Whom It May Concern." Adapt your letter for each situation and always be able to offer specific examples to confirm the main points of your experiences. Finally, always produce error-free copy. As with your resume, one spelling mistake in a cover letter can mean that the employer will no longer consider your application.

Use the cover letter to enhance your resume, not restate it. If the job search is a marketing campaign, then this letter is an integral part of it. You are the product, and, unlike the sport product, you want to be positively predictable. You do have total control over the product. Show this in your application package by making it professional and confident.

The Job Interview

The job **interview** is your opportunity to demonstrate to the prospective employer that you are the best candidate for the position. It is also a chance to learn more about the organization, the position, and opportunities for advancement—in short, to determine if you are interested in continuing to pursue employment with the organization. The keys to an effective interview are threefold: preparation, the interview, and follow-up.

■ PREPARATION

The interview preparation phase is critical and should be given the same respect the actual interview receives. It will take more energy and time than either of the other two phases. To be effective in the interview, you must be very well prepared. A football team practices for hours each day of the week for Saturday's three-hour game. The harder and more efficiently the players practice, the better and more successful they will be in the game and the greater the chance of a win. The same principle is true for the interview. The more time you spend in preparation, the more comfortable you will be in the interview; consequently, the greater your opportunity for a successful interaction.

To present a clear picture of whom you are and what you have to offer, you must take time to assess yourself. Be honest with yourself. Evaluate the person you are, not the person you would like to be. Assess your strengths and weaknesses. We all have them. You should be able to discuss your strengths with confidence and your weaknesses with a plan for improvement. In assessing the appropriate industry, organizations, and job, ask yourself questions such as the following:

- Do I prefer working independently or with a group?
- How do I deal with stress and frustration?
- What kind of supervision works best for me?
- Do I like to write? Am I good at it?
- Am I energetic and good-humored?
- Am I happy in competitive, fast-paced situations?
- Am I persuasive and able to motivate others?
- Is salary a top priority for me?

- Am I flexible, able to work long hours or on changeable projects?

The interviewer will assume you know something about his or her organization. Do not disappoint him or her; learn as much as you can. Here are some potential information sources:

- Make use of the Internet, which is a prime information source for almost every industry. Most sport organizations have their own home page. It is also possible to use the Internet to gather valuable information regarding the competition.
- Call the public relations office of the sport organization and request written information, such as media guides.
- Read newspapers and professional journals.
- Talk to someone who currently works for the organization. Perhaps that person had the job for which you are applying or worked with the person who did.
- Speak to clients, customers, and competitors.

■ THE INTERVIEW

Behavior is the foundation of the interview process. The best predictor of future performance is past performance in a similar situation. Interviewers are looking not just for particular skills, but also for personal attributes of a successful professional. What is it an employer wants to know about a candidate that is relative to the job? Characteristics of a successful employee include oral and written communication skills, adaptability, ability to learn, analysis, initiative, creativity and innovation, integrity, interpersonal skills, decisiveness, leadership, planning and organizing, sensitivity, stress tolerance, tenacity, and high standards of performance.

Interviews are limited in time; therefore, it is important to begin appropriately. Remember the old cliché: "You only get one chance to make a first impression." As in any new relationship, the first goal is to establish rapport.

- Dress appropriately. Appropriate attire for an interview is a suit. The sport industry may seem like a casual industry, but it is a business.
- Be early—it is better to be ten minutes early than one minute late!
- Shake hands firmly and smile, making eye contact with the person.
- Engage in conversation.
- Be friendly, warm, and interested.

One common interview method is known as behavioral interviewing. During a behavioral interview, the interviewer will ask questions probing for examples of specific, relevant behaviors. Questions may be phrased to extract the most telling response from the interviewee. Here are some sample questions from a behavioral interview:

- We've all experienced times when we felt over our heads in a class or a project. Tell me about a time when that happened to you. How did you handle the situation?
- What would you identify as the biggest achievement of your college career? What did you do to contribute to that achievement?
- Have you ever had trouble getting along with a classmate or teacher? How did you deal with the situation so you could continue to work with that person?

In each of these examples, the interviewer is asking the interviewee to describe a specific situation or task, the action that took place, and the outcome or consequence of that action. Quality responses are not feelings or opinions. They are not plans for the future, nor are they vague statements. If you spend some time

identifying situations representing each of the characteristics mentioned earlier, you should be prepared for any questions. If the employer asks a theoretical question such as "Describe your strengths and weaknesses," you can still respond with a situation demonstrating the strengths you want to showcase or how you make accommodations for your weaknesses.

In addition to questions you can answer using the behavioral format, be ready for some of the old standards: "Tell me about yourself." "How would your friends describe you?" Be honest. When answering interview questions, honesty is the best policy. An interviewer can always tell when a candidate is being less than honest. It is not only what you say that impresses an interviewer but also how you conduct yourself. The recruiter is trying to find out how well you know yourself and how comfortable you are with who you are.

Again, the best predictor of future performance is past performance in a similar situation. Be prepared with anecdotes demonstrating your behaviors in a positive light.

Once the actual interview begins, concentrate on communicating effectively:

- Listen attentively. Restate the question if you are unsure what the interviewer is actually asking.

- Answer questions directly, providing examples.
- Make good eye contact with the interviewer.
- Talk openly about yourself, your accomplishments, and your goals.
- Maintain a positive, interested demeanor.
- Ask appropriate questions. Demonstrate interest in, and knowledge of, the organization.
- Make certain you have a clear idea of the position for which you are interviewing.
- Always get a business card or a means of connecting with the interviewer later.

Illegal Questions There are laws regulating the questions employers may ask in an interview situation. Interviewers must limit themselves to gathering information that will help them decide whether a person can perform the functions of a particular job. Therefore, questions seeking more personal information—for example, marital status, sexual orientation, national origin or citizenship, age, disability, or arrest record— do not have to be answered. The decision to answer or not is the interviewee's. Although most interviewers will not ask these questions, you should think about how you will respond if the situation arises. If you feel particularly uncomfortable, discuss this issue with a counselor in your campus career center before your first interview.

■ FOLLOW-UP

The follow-up to an interview is an indication of your interest and maturity. As part of the follow-up, do the following:

- Assess the interview. Were all your questions answered? Was there anything you could have presented more clearly?
- Write a thank-you note immediately, reinforcing your interest and qualifications for the position.
- Call the interviewer if you have something to add or if you have additional questions. This shows you are enthusiastic, persistent, and interested.
- Call the sport organization if you have not heard from someone there in the designated time.

If you are well prepared, aware of your competencies and areas requiring development, understand the type of work environment you would prefer, and believe you have the necessary skills and abilities, you will be successful. When qualifications of competing candidates are relatively equal, interviewers are inclined to hire people who have been honest and straightforward. Be yourself.

■ WHAT MAKES A SUCCESSFUL CANDIDATE?

A successful candidate exhibits certain traits and skills. Some of these include the following:

- *Preparation:* Knowledge of and interest in the employer and the specific job opening
- *Personal or soft skills:* Confidence, adaptability, flexibility, maturity, energy, drive, enthusiasm, initiative, and empathy
- *Goal orientation:* Ability to set short- and long-term goals
- *Communication skills:* Written and oral, including listening and nonverbal communication skills
- *Organizational skills:* Teamwork, leadership, problem identification and solving, and time management
- *Experience:* Ability to articulate the relevance of previous experience to the position for which you are interviewing.

- *Professional appearance:* Business suits for men and women alike. Remember, some people have allergic reactions to perfumes and colognes, so it is best not to use them prior to your interview.
- *Cross-cultural awareness:* Multiple languages, international, or intercultural experience
- *Computer skills:* Web site development, statistical packages, word processing, spreadsheets, and desktop publishing

■ SUMMARY

Finding a job in the sport industry is an arduous task, but the results can be rewarding. This chapter presents information about the realities of looking for a job in the sport industry. Make no mistake; this is a difficult industry to break into. This chapter, while informing you about some of the barriers you will face, also gives you some tools to use to help you along the way. Incorporating the techniques included in this chapter, such as networking, informational interviewing, resume and cover letter writing, and interviewing skills, will help increase your marketability in the sport industry.

■ KEY TERMS

cover letter, informational interviewing, internship, interview, network, references, resume

■ REFERENCES

Chicago Press Release Services. (2009). Chicago 2016 Olympic bid team now unemployed, in search of new jobs. Retrieved December 7, 2010, from http://chicagopressrelease.com/news/chicago-2016-olympic-bid-team-now-unemployed-in-search-of-new-jobs

Helyar, J. (2006, September 16). Are universities' sport management programs a ticket to a great job? Not likely. Retrieved December 28, 2010, from http://www.gamefacesportsjobs.com/breaking_in/WSJ/prwsjflngeffrt.htm

North American Professional Baseball League (NAPBL). (2010). Take the plunge and find new staff members at the 17th annual PBEO Job Fair. Retrieved December 7, 2010, from http://www.pbeo.com/10_job_fair.aspx

Glossary

absolutism The belief that moral precepts are universal, that is, applicable to all circumstances.

Academic Progress Rate (APR) An academic reform initiated by the NCAA; it collects data on a team's academic results based on graduation rates, eligibility, and retention of student-athletes from the previous year. Results are then tied to recruiting opportunities, number of athletic scholarships, postseason eligibility, and NCAA revenue distribution.

academic reform Movement toward the improvement of student athletes' academic performance, including satisfactory academic progress requirements in order to maintain eligibility.

academics The educational environment.

activation The commitment of financial resources in support of a company's sponsorship through promotion and advertising that thematically includes the sport property's imagery.

ad hoc committees Formed for a special purpose, usually focused on a single problem or issue and remains in existence until that problem or issue is resolved. The club's board dissolves an ad hoc committee once its purpose is served.

administrative law The body of law created by rules, regulations, orders, and decisions of administrative bodies.

aftermarketing Customer retention activities that take place after a purchase has been made; the process of providing continued satisfaction and reinforcement to individuals or organizations who are past or current customers.

Age Discrimination in Employment Act (ADEA) A 1967 law that prohibits employment discrimination on the basis of age.

agency A relationship in which one party (the agent) agrees to act for and under the direction of another (the principal).

agent A party acting for and under the direction of another (the principal).

Agents, Gambling and Amateurism (AGA) Division of the NCAA that works not only to investigate alleged violations of involvement of student-athletes with agents, but also to inform and educate student-athletes and agents themselves about acceptable and unacceptable practices.

ambush marketing A strategy that involves placement of marketing material and promotions at an event that attracts consumer and media attention, without becoming an official sponsor of that event.

Americans with Disabilities Act (ADA) A 1990 law that has as its intent the prevention of discrimination against people with disabilities in employment, public services, transportation, public accommodations, and telecommunications services; it protects employees with disabilities at all stages of the employment relationship.

ancillary revenue Occurs from the sale of food and beverage, merchandise, parking charges, ticket fees, and sponsorships.

antitrust law The body of state and federal law designed to protect trade and commerce from unlawful restraint, monopolies, price fixing, and price discrimination.

arenas Indoor facilities that host sporting and entertainment events; they are usually built to accommodate one or more prime sports tenants.

Arledge, Roone An executive at ABC TV who was responsible for the development of sport broadcasting so that it appealed as entertainment to an audience beyond hard-core fans.

assets Things that an organization owns that can be used to generate future revenues, such as equipment, stadiums, and league memberships.

Association for Intercollegiate Athletics for Women (AIAW) A governance organization for women's athletics, established in 1971, that emphasized the educational needs of students and rejected the commercialized men's athletics model. It became effectively defunct in 1982.

athletic footwear Branded and unbranded athletic shoes for casual wear or active usage, outdoor/hiking sports boots, and sport sandals.

audience research The collection of data regarding the audience for a broadcast.

balance sheet A financial statement that shows the assets, liabilities, and owners' equity of an organization.

barnstorming tours The travel and appearances at events of star athletes and teams to promote the popularity of a particular sport.

beat reporter A writer or media personality from a local media outlet who is specifically assigned to cover a sport organization, its games, and its practices; also known as a *beat writer*.

beat writer See *beat reporter*.

benefit selling A sales approach that involves the promotion and creation of new benefits or the promotion and enhancement of existing benefits to offset existing perceptions or assumed negatives related to the sport product or service.

Big Ten Conference An athletic conference formed in 1895 by college and university faculty representatives (under the name Intercollegiate Conference of Faculty Representatives) to create student eligibility rules for football. The athletic conference has a 100-year tradition of shared practices and policies that enforce the priority of academics and emphasize the values of integrity, fairness, and competitiveness in all aspects of its student-athletes' lives.

blog A personal Web site featuring a series of chronological entries by an author.

board of directors Also called a board of governors at some clubs, this select group of people establishes club policies and governs the club.

board of governors See *board of directors*.

bona fide occupational qualification (BFOQ) An employment qualification that, although it may discriminate against a protected class (i.e., sex, religion, or national origin), relates to an essential job duty and is considered reasonably necessary for the normal operation of a business or organization and therefore not illegal.

bonds Financial instruments typically issued by large corporate entities or governments that allow the borrower to borrow large dollar amounts, usually for a relatively long period of time.

booking director A person responsible for scheduling events for a facility.

Boras, Scott Founder of the Scott Boras Corporation and an innovator in baseball representation. He is known for his free market philosophy, the use of data in negotiations, his level of preparation, and his knowledge of the game and rules.

box office director A person responsible for the sale of all tickets to events as well as the collection of all ticket revenue.

branded apparel Clothing that has a brand name.

brand's image The cumulative view, beliefs, and associations of consumers and others about a brand. It evokes the idea that a consumer is not just purchasing a product or a service, but also the impression of that product or service.

breach The breaking of a promise in a contract.

broadcast rights The property interest possessed under law that allows an entity to broadcast sound and/or images of an event.

b-roll A film, DVD, or videotape of raw footage chosen by the organization to accompany a written news release; it is not a finished segment ready for broadcast.

budgeting The process of developing a written plan of revenues and expenses for a particular accounting cycle; the budget specifies available funds among the many purposes of an organization to control spending and achieve organizational goals.

business development A business function focused on strategy, creating strategic partnerships, and relationships with suppliers and customers. The business development function focuses on strategic deal-making with a goal of increasing sales, attracting new clients, and expanding a company's long-term business success or scope.

call-to-action ad An advertisement that aims to encourage consumers to do something, such as buy a ticket to a sport event.

capacity The ability to understand the nature and effects of one's actions; generally, individuals over the age of 18 possess capacity.

Carnegie Reports of 1929 Documents by the Carnegie Foundation that examined intercollegiate athletics and identified many academic abuses, recruiting abuses, payments to student-athletes, and commercialization of athletics. These reports pressured the NCAA to evolve from a group that developed rules for competition into an organization for overseeing all aspects of intercollegiate athletics.

cash-flow budgeting Accounting for the receipt and timing of all sources and expenditures of money.

cause-related marketing effort An event sponsored by a corporation for the purpose of generating money for a particular cause.

city club Concept evolved from the nineteenth century dining clubs in major cities, which stemmed from earlier men's clubs in Britain. Precursor to today's country club.

club Sport management structures composed of a limited number of members who organize events, standardize rules, and settle disputes.

Club Managers Association of America (CMAA) Organization composed of club professionals, department heads, and certified professionals in food and beverage management (including chefs, cooks, and bartenders); sport management professionals (golf, tennis, and aquatics professionals); grounds and golf course superintendents; building and engineering technicians/specialists; and other specialty staff members who report to a club's general manager.

coaches People who instruct or train players in the fundamentals of a sport and directs team strategy.

codes of conduct Statements of a company, business, organization, or profession that explicitly outline and explain the principles under which it operates and provide guidelines for employee behavior; also called codes of ethics.

codes of ethics See *codes of conduct*.

collective bargaining agreement (CBA) A legal agreement between an employer and a labor union that regulates the hours, wages, and terms and conditions of employment.

commissioner The administrative head of a professional sport league.

Commission on Intercollegiate Athletics for Women (CIAW) A governance organization for women's athletics created in 1966; forerunner of the Association for Intercollegiate Athletics for Women (AIAW).

communications All methods used by an organization to proactively deliver its key messages to a diverse universe of constituencies.

communication skills Oral and written skills for presenting facts and information in an organized, courteous fashion.

community-based recreation Recreational activities at the local level, such as those offered by community agencies and local parks and recreation departments.

community relations Activities and programs that have the objective of having a positive impact on the community and thereby improving an organization's public image.

competitive balance The notion that the outcome of a competition is uncertain, and thus provides greater entertainment value for spectators.

compliance Adherence to NCAA and conference rules and regulations. The compliance coordinator in an athletic department is responsible for educating coaches and student-athletes about the rules and regulations, overseeing the initial and continuing eligibility of student-athletes, and preventing or investigating any violations that occur.

concerts Musical events.

conference call A method of communication that allows an arranged call by telephone or internet connection between multiple parties.

conference realignment A school wanting to join a conference or change conference affiliation. An issue that occurs periodically, effectively changing the landscape of college athletics.

conference rules Standards set forth by particular conferences that require member institutions to abide by, in addition to NCAA regulation.

conflicts of interest Situations in which one's own interests may be furthered over those of the principal to whom one owes a fiduciary duty (e.g., the athlete being represented by the agent).

consideration The inducement to a contract represented by something of value, such as money, property, or an intangible quality.

constitutional law The body of law developed from precedents established by courts applying the language of the U.S. Constitution and state constitutions to the actions and policies of governmental entities.

content providers An organization or individual that creates information, educational or entertainment content for the Internet, CD-ROMs, software-based products, or television.

contests Competitions that award prizes based on contestants' skills and abilities; a purchase may be required as a condition of entering the contest.

contract A written or oral agreement between two or more parties that creates a legal obligation to fulfill the promises made by the agreement.

convention centers Facilities built and owned by a public entity and used to lure conventions and business meetings to a particular municipality.

convocations An assembly of people for a specific purpose (i.e., graduation, speaking engagement).

Corcoran, Fred The architect of the professional golf tournament.

corporate governance model A model of league leadership in which owners act as the board of directors, and the commissioner acts as the chief executive officer.

corporate ownership The ownership of a team by a corporation.

cost per thousand (CPM) A measure of advertising efficiency that allows advertisers to gauge the relative cost-effectiveness of ads. It determines the relative cost of each advertising medium to reach 1,000 prospects.

country club An exclusive private facility to socialize, network, and participate in leisure activities.

coupons Certificates that generally offer a reduction in price for a product or service.

cover letter A document accompanying a resume that introduces yourself and demonstrates your value to the prospective employer.

crisis plan A strategy for handling a crisis; it should include a system to notify key members of the organization as soon as possible of a crisis situation and should identify roles and responsibilities for members of the organization.

crisis team A group of key organizational individuals who will be responsible for managing any crises.

cross-ownership Ownership of more than one sport franchise.

cross-promotion A joining together of two or more companies to capitalize on a sponsorship or expand its scope.

crowd management plan A document that assesses the type of event, surrounding facilities and/or environment, team or school rivalries, threats of violence, and details emergency contingencies, taking crowd size and seating configuration, and the use of security personnel and ushers into consideration.

cultural awareness Understanding of local customs, laws, and the environment.

cultural differences Differences between the customs, values, and traditions of cultures.

cume Cumulative unduplicated audience over time.

Curt Flood Act This Act granted major league baseball players, but not minor leaguers, the legal right to sue their employers under the Sherman Act. It confirmed that baseball's exemption from federal antitrust laws applies to business areas including the minor leagues; the minor league player reserve clause; the amateur draft; franchise expansion, location or relocation; franchise ownership issues; marketing and sales of the entertainment product of baseball; and licensed properties.

customer relationship management The implementation of relationship marketing practices.

database marketing A type of marketing that involves creating a database (usually consisting of names, addresses, phone numbers, and other demographic information related to current and potential customers) and then using it to maintain or gain customers.

debt An amount of money that an organization borrows.

decision making A process of gathering and analyzing information so as to make a choice on how to pursue an opportunity or solve a problem.

de Coubertin, Pierre Founder of the modern Olympics.

default Occurs when a borrower is unable to repay a debt.

defendant The person or organization against whom a lawsuit is brought.

delegation Assigning responsibility and accountability for results to employees.

delivery systems The means over which content is provided to consumers in the cable or broadcasting industries.

demographic   Related to the statistical characteristics of a group of people (i.e., age, income, gender, social class, or educational background).

demographic segments   Parts of an audience that have been divided along age, gender, and ethnic lines as well as according to income, purchasing habits, and other lifestyle factors.

designated market areas (DMAs)   Discrete units (groups of counties) into which the A. C. Nielsen Company has divided the United States, based on which local stations residents most often watch.

destination Web site   An official site on the Internet employed by a sport organization for communication and commerce.

D.I.M. Process   A three-step process for risk management that entails 1) developing the risk management plan, 2) implementing the plan, and 3) managing the plan.

direct mail   A type of marketing solicitation sent via the U.S. Mail to targeted lists of current or potential clients.

direct marketing   A method of communication that uses material sent directly to a specific target audience either via mail or e-mail.

direct participation   Active performance of an activity.

disaffirm   To opt out of a contract.

diversity   Any differences between individuals, including age, race, gender, sexual orientation, disability, education, and social and economic background, that affect how people perform and interact with each other.

Division I   A subgroup of NCAA institutions that, in general, supports the philosophy of competitiveness, generating revenue through athletics, and national success; this organization offers athletic scholarships.

Division II   A subgroup of NCAA institutions that, in general, attracts student-athletes from the local or in-state area, who may receive some athletic scholarship money but usually not a full amount.

Division III   A subgroup of NCAA institutions that does not allow athletic scholarships, and that encourages participation in athletics by maximizing the number and variety of opportunities available to students; the emphasis is on the participants' experience rather than that of spectators.

due process   The right to notice and a hearing before life, liberty, or property may be taken away.

duty of care   A legal obligation that a person acts toward another as a reasonable person would in the circumstances. This duty arises from one's relationship to another, a voluntary assumption of the duty of care, or from a duty mandated by law.

eduselling   An evolutionary form of selling that combines needs assessment, relationship building, customer education, and aftermarketing in a process that originates at the prospect-targeting stage and progresses to an ongoing partnership agreement.

electronic newsletters   A newsletter sent via e-mail rather than by being printed and mailed to subscribers.

emotional intelligence   The ability of workers to identify and acknowledge people's emotions and, instead of having an immediate emotional response, to take a step back and allow rational thought to influence their actions.

empowerment   The encouragement of employees to use their initiative and make decisions within their areas of operations, and the provision of resources to enable them to do so.

enforcement   An area within the NCAA administrative structure, created in 1952, that deals with enforcing the NCAA's rules and regulations.

entrepreneur A person who creates an idea for a better use of existing technology.

environmental awareness Knowledge of the regulations that control public use of lands, and the responsibility to monitor and control human relationships with natural environment use to prevent destruction of natural resources.

Equal Pay Act (EPA) A 1963 law that prohibits an employer from paying one employee less than another on the basis of sex when the two are performing jobs of equal skill, effort, and responsibility and are working under similar conditions.

equal protection The Fourteenth Amendment guarantee that no person or class of persons shall be denied the protection of the laws that is enjoyed by other persons or other classes in like circumstances in their enjoyment of personal rights and the prevention and redress of wrongs.

equity club Clubs owned by the members; typically hold a private nonprofit status.

ESPN A cable TV sports channel; it was the first all-sports channel.

ethical dilemma A practical conflict involving more or less equally compelling values or social obligations.

ethical reasoning The process of making a fair and correct decision; it depends on one's values or the values of the organization for which one works.

ethics The systematic study of the values guiding decision making.

ethnic marketing Advertising that targets an ethnic group, such as Hispanics or African Americans.

evaluating A functional area of management that measures and ensures progress toward organizational objectives by establishing reporting systems, developing performance standards, observing employee performance, and designing reward systems to acknowledge successful work on the part of employees.

event director A person involved in planning, organizing, and executing projects, celebrations, sporting contests, etc. Management of the show from start to finish may involve dealing with ushers, security, and medical personnel, show promoters, patrons, and coping with crises that may occur.

event marketing The process of promoting and selling a sport or special event; it encompasses nine areas: sales of corporate sponsorship, advertising efforts, public relations activities, hospitality, ticket sales, broadcasting, Web site development and management, licensing/merchandising, and fund-raising.

executive committee A group that usually has duties and responsibilities similar to those of the board of directors, but it acts as a "mini-board" between board meetings by responding to issues that do not necessitate bringing the entire board together.

expenses The costs incurred by an organization in an effort to generate revenues.

faculty athletics representative (FAR) A member of an institution's faculty or administrative staff who is designated to represent the institution and its faculty in the institution's relationships with the NCAA and its conference.

family events Products geared toward the toddler and through the "tween" markets. Often these are acts produced from television or movie programs that are run on mainstream television or theaters, such as Sesame Street Live or Disney on Ice.

fan identification The personal commitment and emotional involvement that customers have with a sport organization.

fiduciary duties Obligation to act in the best interest of another party.

Football Bowl Subdivision (FBS) A category of Division I institutions that are large football-playing schools; they must meet minimum attendance requirements for football. Formerly known as Division I-A.

Football Championship Subdivision (FCS) A category of Division I institutions that play football at a level below that of Division I-A; they are not held to any attendance requirements. Formerly known as Division I-AA.

franchise free agency A strategy in which team owners move their teams to cities that provide them newer facilities with better lease arrangements and more revenues.

franchise rights The privileges afforded to owners of a sport franchise.

freestanding inserts Separately printed advertising or coupon sections that are inserted into a newspaper.

freestanding sport management firm A full-service sport management firm providing a wide range of services to the athlete, including contract negotiations, marketing, and financial planning.

full-service agencies Sport management/marketing agencies that perform a complete set of agency functions.

fund development An area of responsibility within a collegiate athletic department that seeks new ways to increase revenues, oversees alumni donations to the athletic department, and oversees fundraising events.

gate receipts Revenue from ticket sales.

general manager The official executive management position in a club.

global sourcing The use of whatever manufacturer or source around the world that will most efficiently produce a company's products.

global strategy A corporate strategy of creating products that have the same appeal and generate the same demand worldwide.

governing bodies Groups that create and maintain rules and guidelines and handle overall administrative tasks.

government relations Activities conducted to influence public officials toward a desired action; also known as *lobbying*.

grassroots efforts Programs and activities undertaken to increase sport participation and interest in a particular region.

grassroots programs Activities and events that target individuals at the most basic level of involvement, sport participation.

hospitality Providing a satisfying experience for all stakeholders in an event (participants, spectators, media, and sponsors).

Hulbert, William The "Czar of Baseball"; he developed the National League of Professional Baseball Players.

human relations movement Management theory focusing on the behavior and motivations of people in the workplace.

image ad An advertisement created to reinforce an organization's brand imagery in the minds of consumers.

impasse A breakdown in negotiations.

income The difference between revenues and expenses, also called *profit*.

income mismanagement A form of unethical behavior by a sports agent that consists of mishandling a client's money, whether by incompetence or criminal intent.

income statement A summary of the revenues, expenses, and profits of an organization over a given time period.

independent contractor A worker who is not under the employer's supervision and control.

indirect participation Participating in an activity as a spectator.

informational interviewing Asking questions of someone employed in a particular career or organization in an effort to expand one's understanding of that industry, organization, or career.

informed participant consent Making participants aware of the potential risks inherent in activities before they begin so they can make informed decisions about the nature of their participation.

in-house agencies Separate departments or divisions within a major corporation that deal with event management.

in-kind sponsorship Sponsorship benefits given to a newspaper, magazine, radio station, or television station in exchange for a specified number of free advertising spots or space, rather than money.

initiative Going beyond one's formal job description to help the organization.

injunction An order from a court to do or not to do a particular action.

integrated marketing Long-term strategic planning for managing functions in a consistent manner.

integrated marketing communications (IMC) The symbiosis of advertising, marketing, and public relations.

intellectual property Refers to creations of the mind.

interactivity The ability for a viewer to partake in an event through such things as requesting and receiving customized information and purchasing products via the Internet while watching the event on television.

intercept interviews See *pass-by interviews.*

interest Money that is paid for the use of money lent, or principal, according to a set percentage (rate).

Intercollegiate Athletic Association of the United States (IAAUS) The forerunner of the National Collegiate Athletic Association (NCAA); formed in 1905 by 62 colleges and universities to formulate rules making football safer and more exciting to play.

Intercollegiate Conference of Faculty Representatives See *Big Ten Conference.*

Intercollegiate Football Association An athletic association formed in 1876 and made up of students from Harvard, Yale, Princeton, and Columbia who agreed on consistent playing and eligibility rules for football.

internal communications Communication with and to an organization's staff.

International Association of Auditorium Managers (IAAM) The professional trade association for the facility management field.

international federations (IFs) Organizations responsible for managing and monitoring the everyday running of the world's various sports disciplines, including the organization of events during the Olympic Games, and the supervision of the development of athletes practicing these sports at every level. Each IF governs its sport at world level and ensures its promotion and development.

International Olympic Committee (IOC) A nongovernmental, nonprofit organization that is the legal and business entity; entrusted with the control, development, and operation of the modern Olympic Games.

Internet Worldwide web of information that transcends geographic boundaries.

Internet marketing communication Information provided to consumers through the Internet concerning marketing mix variables (i.e., product, price, promotion, place, public relations).

internship A job position in which students or graduates gain supervised practical experience.

interview A formal meeting between an employer and a prospective employee to evaluate the latter's qualifications for a job.

invasion of privacy   An unjustified intrusion into one's personal activity or an unjustified exploitation of one's personality.

inverted pyramid   A style of writing used for press releases, in which the most important facts are presented in the lead paragraph and then the remaining paragraphs are arranged in a descending order of importance.

Jockey Club, the   A group established in Newmarket, England, around 1850 to settle disputes, establish rules, determine eligibility, designate officials, regulate breeding, and punish unscrupulous participants in the sport of thoroughbred racing.

judges   See *officials*.

judicial review   Evaluation by a court that occurs when a plaintiff challenges a rule, regulation, or decision.

key messages   The messages that an organization wants to convey to the media during an interview or press conference.

Knight Commission   A commission created in 1989 by the Trustees of the Knight Foundation, composed of university presidents, CEOs and presidents of corporations, and a congressional representative, to propose a reform agenda for intercollegiate athletics.

labor exemption   An exception that states that terms agreed to in a collective bargaining agreement are immune from antitrust scrutiny during the term of the agreement.

Lanham Act   A federal law that governs trademarks and service marks and gives protection to the owner of a name or logo.

law practice only   A type of sport management firm that deals only with the legal aspects of an athlete's career, such as contract negotiation, dispute resolution, legal representation in arbitration or other proceedings, and the preparation of tax forms.

leading   A functional area of management that is the "action" part of the management process; it involves a variety of activities, including delegating, managing differences, managing change, and motivating employees.

league   A profit-oriented legal and business entity organized so that teams can compete against each other, but also operate together in areas such as rule making, broadcasting, licensing, and marketing.

"league think"   A term coined by NFL Commissioner Pete Rozelle to describe the need for owners to think about what was best for the NFL as a whole rather than what was best for their individual franchises.

legacy members   People who join clubs because their parents and grandparents were club members and club membership is a family tradition.

legality   Concept that the subject matter of a contract cannot violate laws or public policy.

legislation and governance   An area within the NCAA administrative structure that deals with interpreting NCAA legislation.

legitimate interest   Refers to a reason for upholding the use of separate-gender teams.

liabilities   The sum of debts that an organization owes.

licensed merchandise   See *licensed products*.

licensed products   Items bearing the logo or trademark of a sport organization; their sale generates a *royalty* (percentage of the net or wholesale selling price) for the sport organization.

licensees   The manufacturers of licensed products.

licensors   Teams and leagues that own the rights to logos, names, and so forth.

local/civic venues   Typically located in towns or small cities, these locations offer small capacity.

luxury tax   A fee that a team incurs when it exceeds a set payroll threshold.

managing change   Effectively implementing change in the workplace and being aware of employees' natural resistance to change.

managing technology   Being familiar with technology and using it to one's advantage.

marketing director   A person involved with analyzing and purchasing media (e.g., TV, radio, print, billboards), coordinating promotions, and designing marketing materials (e.g., brochures, flyers).

marketing fund   A pool of money that is set aside from the profits of other shows. The concessionaire and the venue director each agree to a certain share of the percentage of sold goods, and they use the pool to help invest in future programs.

marketing mix   The controllable variables a company puts together to satisfy a target market group, including product, price, place, and promotion.

Mason, James G.   Co-inventor, with Walter O'Malley, of the idea of a sport management curriculum.

McCormack, Mark   Founder of IMG (International Management Group) who invented the modern sports agency. He built IMG from one client in 1960 to a global sports, entertainment, and media company with 2,200 employees in 70 offices in 30 countries at the time of his death in 2003. IMG at the time billed itself as the world's largest, most diverse, truly global company dedicated to the marketing and management of sport and leisure lifestyle.

media buyer   A person who purchases advertising for clients.

media guide   An annual publication containing all of the information a reporter will need to know about an organization, including staff directories; biographies of all coaches, players, owners, and front office staff; and team and individual records and statistics.

media list   A list of members of the media, such as beat writers, editors, columnists, and news directors.

media notes   A packet of information for the press containing all the statistical information and biographical information on the teams competing in a game, from both an individual and a team perspective.

media planning   Choosing the correct medium in which to place advertising in an effort to reach the most people fitting the target audience's demographic profile.

media training   Education of players, coaches, athletic directors, and so forth about interview techniques, handling hostile interviewers, and shaping messages into sound bites.

member conferences   Groupings of institutions within the NCAA that provide many benefits and services to their members. Conferences have legislative power over their member institutions in the running of championship events and the formulation of conference rules and regulations. Member conferences must have a minimum of six member institutions within a single division to be recognized as a voting member conference of the NCAA.

metropolitan facilities   Venues located in large cities with very large capacities, such as Madison Square Garden in New York, The Wells Fargo Center complex in Philadelphia, and the Staples Center in Los Angeles.

military recreation   Recreational programs offered by the armed services for military personnel and their families on bases in the United States and abroad.

mobile phone technology   Portable/cellular telephones are now the largest providers of wireless access to the Internet today and provide users with information, entertainment, games, and interactivity.

modern Olympic Games, the An international athletic event, started in 1896, based on ancient Greek athletic games.

monopoly A business or organization that faces no direct competition for its products or services, and as a result possesses high bargaining power.

morality Concerned with the values guiding behavior; a specific type of ethical issue.

moral principles Virtues or moral precepts.

morals The fundamental baseline values dictating appropriate behavior within a society.

motivation The reasons why individuals strive to achieve organizational and personal goals and objectives.

multi-box A device that allows multiple cameramen and radio reporters to plug into an audio feed without having to place too many microphones on the podium.

National Association of Intercollegiate Athletics (NAIA) An athletic governance organization for small colleges and universities, founded in 1940.

National Association of Professional Baseball Players (NAPBP) A group of professional baseball teams formed in 1871; any ball club that was willing to pay its elite players could join.

National Collegiate Athletic Association (NCAA) A voluntary association that is the primary rule-making body for college athletics in the United States. It oversees academic standards for student-athletes, monitors recruiting activities of coaches and administrators, and establishes principles governing amateurism.

National Federation of State High School Associations (NFHS) A nonprofit organization that serves as the national coordinator for high school sports as well as activities such as music, debate, theater, and student council.

national governing bodies (NGBs) Organizations that administer a specific sport in a given country, operating within the guidelines set forth by their respective international federations; also known as *national federations (NFs)*.

nationalism A feeling of pride in one's nation.

National Junior College Athletic Association (NJCAA) An athletic association founded in 1937 to promote and supervise a national program of junior college sports and activities.

National Labor Relations Act (NLRA) A 1935 law that establishes the procedures for union certification and decertification and sets forth the rights and obligations of union and management once a union is in place.

National League of Professional Baseball Players (NLPBP) The successor to the National Association of Professional Baseball Players; formed in 1876, it was a stronger body in which authority for the management of baseball rested.

National Olympic Committees (NOCs) The organizations responsible for the development and protection of the Olympic Movement in their respective countries.

national youth league organizations Organizations that promote participation in a particular sport among children and are not affiliated with schools.

NCAA National Office The main office of the National Collegiate Athletic Association, located in Indianapolis, Indiana; it enforces the rules the NCAA membership passes and provides administrative services to all NCAA committees, member institutions, and conferences.

negligence An unintentional tort that occurs when a person or organization commits an act or omission that causes injury to a person to whom he, she, or it owes a duty of care.

new media The emergence of digital, computerized, or networked information and communication technologies in the later part of the twentieth century.

new media industry An industry that combines elements of computing, technology, telecommunications, and content to create products and services that can be used interactively by consumers and business users.

news release See *press release*.

niche sports Sports that are unique and appealing to a distinct segment of the market, whether defined by age demographics, such as the Millennial Generation or Generation Y (the teenagers and 20-somethings of today), or socioeconomic class, as is seen with sailing and polo's appeal to a higher income level.

non-equity clubs Non-member owned clubs.

non-profit 501(c)(7) clubs Private exclusive social and recreational clubs not open to the general public and typically governed by a Board of Directors who are elected by the membership. Members are not only the customers and guests, they are also the owners or shareholders (i.e., they own equity in the club).

non-school agencies Organizations that are not affiliated with a school system.

North American Society for Sport Management (NASSM) An organization that promotes, stimulates, and encourages study, research, scholarly writing, and professional development in the area of sport management, in both its theoretical and applied aspects.

not-for-profit A classification of an event or organization; most often, not-for-profit events focus on raising money for a charitable enterprise.

officials/judges Individual contractors employed by schools or leagues to supervise athletic competitions.

off-the-record comments Remarks made to the media that are not meant to be published or broadcast.

Ohio University The first university to establish a master's program in sport management, in 1966.

Olympism The philosophy behind the Olympic Games, which seeks "to create a way of life based on the joy found in effort, the educational value of good example and respect for universal fundamental ethical principles."

O'Malley, Walter Co-inventor, with James G. Mason, of the idea of a sport management curriculum. Also owner of the Brooklyn and Los Angeles Dodgers from 1943 until his death in 1979.

one-school/one-vote A structure of organization in the NCAA from 1973 to 1997 in which each member school and conference had one vote at the NCAA's annual convention, which was assigned to the institution's president or CEO.

online video content Consumer usage of video content on the Internet.

operations director A person who supervises facility preparation for all types of events, and coordinates, schedules, and supervises the numerous changeovers that take place as one event moves in and another moves out.

organizational behavior (OB) A field involved with the study and application of the human side of management and organizations.

organizational politics The use of power or other resources outside of the formal definition of a person's job to achieve a preferred outcome in the workplace.

organizing A functional area of management that focuses on putting plans into action by determining which types of jobs need to be performed and who will be responsible for doing these jobs.

organizing committees for the Olympic Games (OCOGs) The organizations primarily responsible for the operational aspects of the Olympic Games; such an organization is formed once a city has been awarded the Games.

outdoor recreation Type of activities that take place in natural environments (e.g., camping, canoeing, golfing, etc.).

overly aggressive client recruitment A form of unethical behavior by sports agents that includes such behaviors as paying athletes to encourage them to sign with agents early and promising athletes things that may not be achievable.

owners' equity The amount of their own money that owners have invested in the firm.

parks movement A political movement in the nineteenth century to permanently set aside lands for preservation, conservation, multiuse, and/or public use in the United States. The concept of preserving wilderness, important geomorphological formations, wildlife habitat and fragile ecosystems, and/or areas of great beauty or scientific interest as well as land dedicated towards public recreation and tourism has spread worldwide.

participative decision making Involving employees or members of an organization in the decision-making process.

pass-by interviews On-site interviews in heavy-traffic areas (such as malls) that utilize visual aids and assess the interviewee's reaction to the visual aids.

people skills Knowing how to treat all people fairly, ethically, and with respect.

personal selling Face-to-face, in-person selling.

physical therapists See *trainers.*

plaintiff The person or organization that initiates a lawsuit.

planning A functional area of management that includes defining organizational goals and determining the appropriate means by which to achieve those desired goals.

podcasts A series of digital audio files that can be downloaded through online syndication.

point-of-sale/point-of-purchase marketing Display materials used by marketers to attract consumers' attention to their product or service and their promotional campaign at the retail level.

premium seating Personal seat licenses, luxury suites, and club seating.

premiums Merchandise offered free or at a reduced price as an inducement to buy a different item or items.

press conference A formal invitation for the press to gather at a specific location to hear an announcement and ask questions concerning it.

press release A written announcement sent to editors and reporters to let people know what an organization is doing and to stimulate stories about the organization; also known as a *news release.*

principal The original amount that an organization borrows (Chapter 4). One who authorizes another to act on his or her behalf as an agent (Chapter 5).

private club A place where people hold a common bond of special interests, experiences, backgrounds, professions, and desires for coming together in a standard meeting place to gather for social and recreational purposes; not open to the public.

private exclusive clubs A specific type of private club restricting membership to only those who are invited to join or become a member by a vote of the current existing membership.

private schools Institutions that do not receive government assistance. In the United States, they were the first schools to provide athletic participation opportunities.

private sector Nongovernment population.

Professional Golfers Association (PGA) An organization comprised of more than 28,000 golf professionals who work at golf courses and country clubs.

professional tournaments Sporting events that are sponsored by community groups, corporations, or charities; players earn their income through prize money and endorsements.

profits The difference between an organization's revenues and expenses.

Progressive Movement An early twentieth-century social and political movement that believed in social improvement by governmental action and advocated economic, political, and social reforms.

properties division A for-profit branch of a league that administers the league's licensing program; such divisions approve licensees, police trademark infringement, and distribute licensing revenues.

psychographic Related to the preferences, beliefs, values, attitudes, personalities, and behavior of an individual or group.

public club A public accommodation facility welcoming participants from nearly all types of backgrounds to play golf and enjoy the offerings of the club.

public ownership Ownership by stockholders via shares that can be freely traded on the open market.

public policy Pertains to a service important to the public.

public recreation Recreational activities or opportunities offered at the state and federal level, such as state and federal forest and parks departments.

public relations (PR) director A person who works with the media, including TV and radio news directors, newspaper editors, and reporters to establish or promote a person, corporation/manufacturer, or product.

public school A free tax-supported school controlled by a local governmental authority.

public sector Government.

rating The percentage of television households in the survey universe that is tuned in to a particular program.

rational basis Lowest standard of review in a discrimination case and focuses on any basis other than race, religion, national origin, or gender. Examples include economic or social background, sexual orientation, physical or mental disability, or athletic team membership.

registration system A system for registering participants in events and collecting and disseminating the appropriate information.

relationship marketing Marketing that aims to build mutually satisfying long-term relations with key parties (e.g., customers, suppliers, and distributors) in an attempt to earn and retain their business.

references People who know you well enough to speak on your behalf.

relativism The belief that what is moral depends on the specific situation.

release of liability Contract that parties sign after an injury occurs, by which a party gives up the right to sue later (usually in return for a financial settlement).

religious events Encompass mass worship.

reserve clause   A clause in a player's standard contract that gives a team the option to renew the player for the following season.

reserve list   A list of reserved players that was sent to each team in Major League Baseball; the teams had a gentleman's agreement not to offer contracts to any player on this list, thus keeping players bound to their teams.

reserve system   A restrictive system used to limit a free and open market so that owners retain the rights to players and control salary expenditures.

resume   A short summary of one's career and qualifications prepared by an applicant for a position.

retainer   A fee paid monthly to an agency or individual to retain their services.

return on investment (ROI)   1) The expected dollar-value return on the financial cost of an investment, usually stated as a percentage (Chapter 4). 2) The achievement of specific marketing and sales objectives from a sport sponsorship (Chapter 15).

revenues   The funds that flow into an organization and constitute its income.

revenue sharing   A system in which each team receives a percentage of various league-wide revenues.

rights agreement   Specified national or regional telecasts with various over-the-air networks and cable networks. Networks will negotiate permission to broadcast specific leagues or teams for a certain period of time.

rights and production   A type of rights arrangement in which the network pays the rights holder a rights fee, is responsible for all costs and expenses associated with producing the game(s) or event(s) for television, sells all of the advertising time itself, and retains all the revenue.

rights holder   The person or entity that owns or controls the rights to an event.

rights only   A type of rights arrangement in which the network pays a rights fee, and the organizer is responsible for production that must meet network standards of quality.

risk   The uncertainty of the future benefits of an investment made today.

risk management   Protecting a business or organization from anything that could possibly go wrong and lead to a loss of revenues or customers; developing a management strategy to prevent legal disputes from arising and to deal with them if they do occur.

rival leagues   Leagues that compete directly with established leagues.

roster management   Capping the roster sizes for men's teams in an effort to comply with Title IX gender equity provisions.

royalty   A fee paid to the licensor for the use of specific trademarks on specific products.

Rozelle, Alvin "Pete"   A commissioner of the National Football League (NFL) and shrewd promoter of the league who is largely credited with building the NFL into the model professional sport league. While commissioner, Rozelle increased shared broadcasting and marketing revenues, restructured the revenue sharing system, and negotiated the merger of the American Football League into the NFL.

salary cap   A financial mechanism that limits team payroll to a percentage of league revenues, thereby preventing large market teams from exploiting their financial advantage to buy the best teams.

sales inventory   The products available to the sales staff to market, promote, and sell through a range of sales methodologies.

sales promotion   A short-term promotional activity that is designed to stimulate immediate product demand.

sampling Giving away free samples of a product to induce consumers to try it.

school athletic director An administrator of a school athletic program whose responsibilities include risk management, researching and purchasing insurance, handling employment issues, ensuring gender equity, and fund-raising.

scientific management The idea that there is one best way to perform a job most efficiently that can be discovered through scientific studies of the tasks that make up a job, and the belief that managers can get workers to perform the job in this best way by enticing them with economic rewards. Also known as *Taylorism*.

script A specific, detailed, minute-by-minute schedule of activities throughout an event's day, including information on a) the time of day and the activities taking place then, b) the operational needs (equipment and setup) surrounding each activity, and c) the event person or persons in charge of the various activities.

seasonal events Events that take place during a specific time frame.

secondary meaning Refers to the protection afforded geographic or descriptive terms in a product that a producer has used through advertising and media to lead the public to identify the producer or that product with the trade or service mark, thus permitting the user to protect an otherwise unprotectable mark.

segmentation Identifying subgroups of the overall marketplace based on a variety of factors, such as age, income level, ethnicity, geography, and lifestyle.

self-governance System in which leagues organize themselves (opposite of corporate governance).

senior women's administrator (SWA) The highest-ranking female administrator involved with the conduct of an NCAA member institution's intercollegiate athletics program.

service mark A word, name, or symbol used to identify the source of an intangible service.

share The percentage of all television households watching television at the time that are tuned into a particular program.

single entity Meaning one person, place, thing, business, and so on.

single-entity structure A model of league ownership in which the league is considered as a single entity to avoid antitrust liability and to create some centralized fiscal control.

soccer-specific stadium (SSS) Facilities built solely for soccer teams. SSS has become the legacy of soccer investor, Lamar Hunt, owner of the Columbus Crew, whose soccer specific stadium in Columbus, Ohio, was the first venue of its size to be built in the United States and has fueled SSS growth.

social media Platform for engaging consumers and allowing for user-generated content.

social network An online area in which people who share common ties can engage and interact with one another.

specialized agency A sport management/marketing agency that limits the scope of services performed or the type of clients serviced.

speculation A guess or answer to a hypothetical question or situation.

sponsorship The acquisition of rights to affiliate or directly associate with a product or event for the purpose of deriving benefits related to that affiliation.

sport events Games or tournaments in facilities that typically take place on a seasonal basis and can be scheduled up to eight months in advance.

sporting goods The physical objects necessary to play a sport.

sporting goods equipment Fitness products and sport-specific products.

sport law The application of existing laws to the sport setting.

sport management firm affiliated with a law firm A type of arrangement in which a freestanding sport management has a working relationship with a law firm so that each entity can fill a void by providing the services the other does not offer.

sport management/marketing agencies A business that acts on behalf of a sport property (i.e., a person, company, event, team, or place).

sport management structures Structures that help managers organize and run sports; they are conceived and evolve in response to broad social changes or to address specific issues within a segment of the sport industry.

sport property An athlete, company, event, team, or place.

sports agent A person who acts as a representative of an athlete or coach to further the client's interests.

sports apparel Garments that are designed for, or could be used in, active sports.

sports event managers Personnel who administer, promote, and operate any type of events related to sport.

sports marketing representative A person who coordinates all of the marketing and sponsorship activities for sport properties, which include sporting events run by the agency firm and the athletes represented by the firm.

stadiums Outdoor or domed facilities that provide sites for sports teams and other nonsport events, such as outdoor concerts.

stakeholders Groups and individuals who have a direct or indirect interest in an organization.

standard or uniform player contract An individual contract used by a league for its professional athlete employees in which all terms are standardized except for the time period and salary.

standing committees Permanent committees that help a club to conduct ongoing activities.

state actor A private entity that is so enmeshed with a public entity that the private entity is considered a governmental one for purposes of subjecting the private entity to the rights protected by the United States and state constitutions.

state associations Nonprofit groups that have a direct role in organizing state championships and competitions in athletics and activities and are the final authority in determining athlete eligibility.

statutes Legislatively created laws codified in an act or a body of acts collected and arranged according to a particular theme or session of a legislature.

strict scrutiny First standard of review in a discrimination case. Applies where one discriminates on the basis of race, religion, or national origin.

student-athlete services An area of responsibility within a collegiate athletic department that addresses the academic concerns and welfare of student-athletes, overseeing such areas as academic advising, tutoring, and counseling.

subscriber fees Additional revenue that cable networks earn from the money individuals pay to receive cable television in their homes.

sweepstakes A game of chance or luck in which everyone has an equal chance to win; no purchase may be required to enter a sweepstakes.

target market A group of consumers to whom a product is marketed.

telecast rights Include broadcast (cable) and narrowcast (all other developing distribution media) rights.

telemarketing Sales efforts conducted over the phone.

territorial rights Rules that limit a competitor franchise from moving into another team's territory without league permission or without providing compensation.

theaters Public assembly facilities that are primarily used for the presentation of live artistic entertainment; they are usually constructed by universities, public entities, and private (usually nonprofit) groups.

The Olympic Partner Program (TOP) A sponsorship program established by the International Olympic Committee, in which corporations pay millions of dollars for status as an official Olympic sponsor for a four-year period and are granted exclusivity in a sponsorship category.

therapeutic recreation Recreational activities that are offered as a means to improve a participant's physical, emotional, and mental health.

ticket rebate Part of the surcharge that the consumer must pay when they purchase a ticket to an event. This is an additional fee that is structured based on the ticket price and returned to the facility or venue as a result of the sale.

time buy A type of rights arrangement in which the organizer buys time on the network and, subject to the network's quality control, is responsible for production of the event and handling sales.

Title VII of the Civil Rights Act A statute that specifically prohibits any employment decision, practice, or policy that treats individuals unequally due to race, color, national origin, sex, or religion; it covers employers with 15 or more employees.

Title IX A comprehensive statute aimed at eliminating sex discrimination in any educational program or activity that receives federal funding.

tort An injury or wrong suffered as the result of another's improper conduct.

total return Benefits that do not appear on a financial balance sheet, such as generating goodwill and favorable public relations.

tournament operations Pre-event, actual event, and post-event activities for staging an event.

trade associations Organizations dedicated to promoting the interests of and assisting the members of a particular industry.

trade shows Multiple-day events held annually in the same location.

trademark A word, name, or symbol used by a manufacturer or merchant to identify and distinguish its goods from those manufactured and sold by others.

trainers/physical therapists Individuals who treat the ailments and injuries of the members of an athletic team.

university outdoor programs Programs that provide opportunities for college students to participate in a variety of outdoor activities and develop instructional and leadership skills.

university venues Consist of stadiums, arenas, and theaters. The market for university and college venues is generally dictated by the student population.

unreasonable searches and seizures Searches and seizures conducted without probable cause or other considerations that would make them legally permissible.

up-selling   Persuading an existing customer to move up to the next more expensive sales level.

variable pricing   Charging a premium price for tickets to events or games in greater demand.

vertical integration   The effort of a sport management/marketing agency to control all aspects of an event.

video news release (VNR)   A preproduced video piece that is edited for broadcast and includes a written story summary or press release.

volunteer management   The supervision of volunteers involved with an event; it involves two areas: 1) working with event organizers and staff to determine the areas in which volunteers are needed and the quantity needed, and 2) soliciting, training, and managing the volunteers.

waivers   A contract in which parties agree to give up their right to sue for negligence before participating in the activity for which they are waiving the right to sue.

Web conferencing   The real-time exchange of audio, video, and text-based messages via the Internet.

Web site   A public relations outlet on the Internet that allows an organization to get its message out in an unfiltered manner and to interact with stakeholders.

youth league director   A supervisor of a youth league, whose responsibilities may include hiring, supervising, and evaluating coaches; coordinating nearly all facets of contest management, including the hiring and paying of officials and event staff; setting league training and disciplinary policies; determining league budgets; overseeing all associated fund-raising; determining and verifying game scheduling and athlete eligibility; transmitting relevant publicity; and handling public relations.

zero-base budgeting   Reviewing all activities and related costs as if the event were being produced or occurring for the first time; previous budgets and actual revenues and expenses are ignored.

About the Authors

Editors

Lisa P. Masteralexis, JD

Lisa P. Masteralexis is the Department Head and an Associate Professor in the Mark H. McCormack Department of Sport Management in the Isenberg School of Management at the University of Massachusetts, Amherst. She holds a JD from Suffolk University School of Law and a BS in Sport Management from the University of Massachusetts Amherst. She teaches courses in sport law and labor relations in professional sport. Her primary research interests are in legal issues and labor relations in the sport industry.

Her scholarly work includes contributions to *Marquette Sport Law Review*, the *Journal of College and University Law*, *Journal of the Legal Aspects of Sport*, *Journal of Sport Management*, *Journal of Sport and Social Issues*, *New England Law Review*, and *European Journal for Sport Management*. She has written book chapters in *Sport Law: A Managerial Approach*, *Law for Recreation and Sport Managers*, *Management for Athletic/Sport Administration*, and *Sport in the Global Village*. In 2000, Professor Masteralexis co-authored an amicus brief to the U.S. Supreme Court on behalf of professional golfer Casey Martin. She has made more than 50 presentations in the United States and abroad before the American Bar Association, the Academy of Legal Studies in Business, the Sport and Recreation Law Association, the North American Society for Sport Management, the European Association for Sport Management, and numerous universities and law schools.

Professor Masteralexis has received the University of Massachusetts's College Outstanding Teacher Award three times and was a Lilly Foundation Teaching Fellow. She is on the Advisory Board of the National Sports Law Institute. She is a member of the Massachusetts and U.S. Supreme Court Bars, and she is also a certified player agent with the Major League Baseball Players Association.

Carol A. Barr, PhD

Carol A. Barr currently serves as Associate Dean for Undergraduate Programs and Campus Relations in the Isenberg School of Management at the University of Massachusetts Amherst. In this role, she serves as the Academic Dean for all business school students at UMass Amherst, oversees the undergraduate programs area within the Isenberg School, and represents the Isenberg School on various committees throughout the University. She holds a BS in Athletic Administration from the University of Iowa (four year letter winner in field hockey), and an MS and PhD in Sport Management from the University of Massachusetts, Amherst.

Dr. Barr also holds an Associate Professor position in the Department of Sport Management. Her research interests lie in the areas of management issues and gender equity within collegiate athletics. She has published articles in the *Journal of Sport Management*, *Sport Marketing Quarterly*, *Journal of Higher Education*, *Journal of Business Ethics*, *Sex Roles*, and the *International Sports Journal*. Dr. Barr has published more than 40 articles for sport practitioners in publications such as *Athletic Business* and *Street & Smith's SportsBusiness Journal*. Dr. Barr is also the co-author of *Managing Intercollegiate Athletics*, a textbook that provides unique, relevant course material on intercollegiate athletic management. She has performed consulting work for the National

Collegiate Athletic Association, and has been involved in legal research surrounding gender equity concentrating on its application to the collegiate athletic arena.

Within her academic association, Dr. Barr has served on the Executive Council of the North American Society for Sport Management (NASSM), serving as President from 2006 to 2007, and served on the editorial board of the *Journal of Sport Management*.

Mary A. Hums, PhD

Mary A. Hums is a Professor in the Sport Administration Program at the University of Louisville. She holds a PhD in Sport Management from Ohio State University, an MA in Athletic Administration and an MBA from the University of Iowa, and a BBA in Management from the University of Notre Dame. In addition to being a past President of the Society for the Study of Legal Aspects of Sport and Physical Activity (SSLASPA; now Sport and Recreation Law Society [SRLA]), Dr. Hums is an active member of the North American Society for Sport Management (NASSM); the European Association of Sport Management (EASM); the American Alliance for Health, Physical Education, Recreation, and Dance (AAHPERD); and the International Olympic Academy Participants Association (IOAPA). Prior to coming to the University of Louisville, Dr. Hums served on the Sport Management faculty at the University of Massachusetts, Amherst; directed the Sport Management Program at Kennesaw State University in Atlanta; and was Athletic Director at St. Mary-of-the-Woods College in Terre Haute, Indiana. She worked as a volunteer for the 1996 Summer Paralympic Games in Atlanta, 2002 Winter Paralympic Games in Salt Lake City, and 2010 Winter Paralympic Games in Vancouver. In 2004, she lived in Athens, Greece, for five months, working at both the Olympic (softball) and Paralympic (goalball) Games. In 2006, Hums was selected by the United States Olympic Committee to represent the United States at the International Olympic Academy's Educators' Session.

Contributors

Gregory Bouris

Gregory Bouris is the Director of Communications for the Major League Baseball Players Association, where he is responsible for developing and managing all internal and external communications activities. His responsibilities include media relations, marketing communications, advertising, publications, and promotional and cause-related marketing. Bouris holds a BS in Sport Management from the University of Massachusetts. In his 27-year professional career, he has established himself as one of the industry's most experienced public relations and communications professionals, witnessing the growth of the sport industry from the inside. When the New York Islanders named him publicity director in 1986, he became the youngest such director in professional sports. Since then, he has acquired experience dealing with many of the top issues that face the industry, including expansion, franchise development, ownership transfers, arena construction, collective bargaining, licensing, cause-related marketing initiatives, the Internet, and broadcasting, in his similar roles at 1-800-FLOWERS.com, SportsChannel New York, the Florida Panthers, and the New York Islanders. Bouris also teaches part-time at Adelphi University in Garden City, New York, and has served on the board of the Nassau County Sports Commission.

Dan Covell, PhD

Dan Covell is an Associate Professor of Sport Management in the School of Business at Western New England College. He holds a BA in studio art from Bowdoin College. After working in secondary education as a coach, teacher, and athletic administrator, Covell earned his MS in Sport Management from the University of Massachusetts, Amherst. Covell earned his PhD in 1999, while he worked as an administrative intern in the Harvard University Athletic Department. Dr. Covell's research interests focus mainly on management issues in intercollegiate and secondary school athletics. His scholarly contributions include articles in the *International Sports Journal, Sport Management Review,* and *Sport Marketing Quarterly*.

Todd W. Crosset, PhD

Todd W. Crosset is an Associate Professor in the Mark H. McCormack Department of Sport Management in the Isenberg School of Management at the University of Massachusetts, Amherst. He holds an MA and PhD in Sociology from Brandeis University, as well as a BA from the University of Texas Austin where he was an All-American Swimmer and a member of a national championship team. Prior to arriving at the University of Massachusetts, he held positions as Head Coach of Swimming at Northeastern University and Assistant Athletic Director at Dartmouth College. Dr. Crosset's academic interests include gender and racism in sport management, and sexual assault in sport. His book, *Outsiders in the Clubhouse,* which is about life on the LPGA golf tour, won the North American Society for Sport Sociology Book of the Year Award in 1995. Dr. Crosset may be best known for his work on the issue of athlete sexual assault on college campuses. Dr. Crosset was one of the first scholars to identify and name coach–athlete abuse as a problem. In this area of study his focus is on prevention. Currently, Dr. Crosset is consulting on legal issues exploring the intersection between athlete sexual assault and Title IX. Dr. Crosset has developed a course on sport community relations.

This is the first undergraduate course of its kind and is a partnership between the Springfield Armor of the NBA's D-League and commu-

nity groups in the Springfield (Massachu. community of color.

Sheranne Fairley, PhD

Dr. Sheranne Fairley is an Assistant Professor in the Mark H. McCormack Department of Sport Management at the University of Massachusetts, Amherst. She holds a PhD in Business from Griffith University in Australia. Dr. Fairley's primary research interests focus on the consumer behavior of sport fans, sport tourism, volunteerism, event management, and destination promotion. She has published her research in the *Journal of Sport Management, Sport Management Review, Sport in Society, Event Management, Journal of Sport & Tourism,* and the *Journal of Legal Aspects of Sport*. Dr. Fairley has presented her work at international conferences including the North American Society for Sport Management (NASSM), the European Association of Sport Management (EASM), and the Sport Management Association of Australia and New Zealand (SMAANZ). She has also acted as an ad hoc reviewer for numerous journals and conferences. She is currently on the Advisory Board of the United States Australian Football League.

Kevin Filo, PhD

Kevin Filo is a Research Fellow at Griffith University within the Centre for Tourism, Sport, and Service Innovation (TSSI). Kevin completed his PhD in Sport Management at Griffith University in December 2008. He was most recently an Assistant Professor of Sport Marketing at University of Massachusetts in the Isenberg School of Management where he taught courses in Sport Marketing, Sport Consumer Behavior, and Sport and New Media.

Dr. Filo's primary research interest focuses on the synergy that exists between sport and charity. He is currently involved in research projects with charitable organizations including the Lance Armstrong Foundation, Movember,

MS Canada, and Back on My Feet. His secondary research interest examines sport and new media technologies. He has published his research in the *Journal of Sport Management, Sport Marketing Quarterly*, and *International Journal of Sport Management and Marketing*, among others. From 2004 to 2005, he served as Merchandising Coordinator for the Lance Armstrong Foundation (LAF), managing the supply chains for the highly successful LIVESTRONG wristband campaign, a cause-related marketing campaign between Nike and the LAF, which has raised over $70 million for the LAF.

Troy Flynn

Troy Flynn began his career in the sports and entertainment industry in the Operations Department with Global Spectrum, based out of Philadelphia, at the company headquarters: the Wells Fargo Dome. Troy specialized in the Operations field of Arena management working in venues throughout the United States. As a Director of Operations in Trenton, New Jersey, Troy was involved in several corporate initiatives to support and open various venues throughout the United States. Troy was promoted to Assistant General Manager of the Sun National Bank Center in 2007, and shortly after promoted to General Manager of the Spaladium Arena in Split, Croatia. Troy Flynn Became the first acting General Manager for Global Spectrum Europe, the European expansion company associated with Global Spectrum. His duties were to establish routing, book events, and provide an operational structure for transition. Troy also worked as the General Manager of the Mullins Center at the University of Massachusetts Amherst. He is currently the Vice President of Operations for the Devil's Arena Entertainment group at the Prudential Center in Newark, New Jersey.

Betsy Goff, JD

Betsy Goff is a Lecturer and the Director of Internships at the University of Massachusetts, Amherst. Professor Goff holds a BS from the Wharton School of the University of Pennsylvania and a JD from Temple University. Her area of expertise is sports and the media, most particularly sports television and the relationship sport organizers and television rights' holders should have with the international broadcast community. She has written several position papers for IOC television workshops and has served on various panels for Practicing Law Institute. She has consulted with such organizations as the All England Club (Wimbledon), The Royal and Ancient Golf Club of St. Andrews (British Open Golf), the USTA, the IOC, and several Olympic Game Organizing Committees on the structure of their television agreements with broadcasters throughout the world. In addition, she has participated in negotiating, drafting, and administering those and other contracts for television broadcast rights to sporting events throughout the world. Professor Goff also has hands-on experience in sports law, sports agency, event management, integrated sales and marketing, product licensing and merchandising, and sports on the Internet through her years of experience at ABC, IMG, and ESPN.

Virginia R. Goldsbury, MEd

Virginia R. Goldsbury has been associated with the field of career development for the past 31 years. She holds a BA from the Pennsylvania State University and a MEd from the University of Massachusetts, Amherst. She is currently retired from her most recent position as Associate Director of Career Services for the University of Massachusetts, Amherst. Ms. Goldsbury worked closely with the Sport Management Department for 14 years. She was highly involved with her professional association, the Eastern Association of Colleges and Employers, having served on the executive board for more than two years. She was also a member of the National Association of Colleges and Employers (NACE).

Laurie Gullion, MS

Laurie Gullion is an assistant clinical professor in the Kinesiology Department of the University of New Hampshire, Durham. Professor Gullion holds a BA in Communications and an MS in Sport Management from the University of Massachusetts, Amherst. She has published six books on recreational sport, including the national instructional text for the American Canoe Association, and has edited its recent *Teaching Paddling to People with Disabilities*. She is the former coordinator of the Outdoor Leadership Program at Greenfield Community College, and director of the undergraduate program of the Sport Management Department at the University of Massachusetts, Amherst. An outdoor writer, she has completed 11 whitewater canoeing expeditions to Arctic and sub-Arctic rivers in the United States, Canada, Norway, and Finland, having paddled almost 12,000 miles in remote regions since 1980.

Neil Longley, PhD

Neil Longley is a Professor in the Sport Management Department in the Isenberg School of Management at the University of Massachusetts, Amherst. Dr. Longley holds a bachelor's degree in Administration and an MA in Economics from the University of Regina, an MBA from the University of Manitoba, and a PhD in Economics from Washington State University. Dr. Longley's primary academic interests are in the areas of sport economics and sport finance. He has published sport-related articles in such journals as *Social Science Journal, American Journal of Economics and Sociology, Law and Business Review of the Americas, Journal of Sports Economics*, and *Canadian Public Policy*. His research on discrimination in the National Hockey League has been particularly influential. His article "Salary Discrimination in the National Hockey League: The Effects of Team Location," originally published in the journal *Canadian Public Policy*, was reprinted in *Interna-*

tional Library of Critical Writings in Economics: The Economics of Sport—a book that reprints the most important articles in the field of sport economics over the past 50 years. Most recently, Dr. Longley has written a chapter for the book *International Sports Economics Comparisons*, which is a collection of articles from leading sports economists around the world that compares and contrasts the sport industry across various countries.

Dr. Longley also has an extensive publication record outside the sport area, particularly in the areas of investment finance, public policy analysis, and international trade policy. He has published in such journals as *Columbia Journal of World Business, Canadian Investment Review, Contemporary Economic Policy, International Journal of Public Administration, Canadian Public Policy, Public Choice, Journal of World Trade*, and *Law and Policy in International Business*. During his career, Dr. Longley has also done considerable consulting work—particularly in the areas of market impact studies and cost-benefit analyses—for clients in both the private and public sectors.

Stephen McKelvey, JD

Stephen McKelvey is an Assistant Professor in the Sport Management Department in the Isenberg School of Management at the University of Massachusetts, Amherst. Professor McKelvey holds a BA from Amherst College, an MS in Sport Management from the University of Massachusetts, Amherst, and a JD from Seton Hall School of Law. He brings a unique offering to his teaching, combining an expertise in both sport law and sport marketing to provide students with exposure to important legal issues in sport marketing and management. His research and writing focus primarily on the legal and practical applications of intellectual property issues to the industry. He has authored articles for a wide range of publications including *Journal of Legal Aspects of Sport, Journal of Sport Management,*

Sport Marketing Quarterly, Seton Hall Journal of Sport Law, Entertainment and Sports Lawyer, Brand Week, and *Street & Smith's SportsBusiness Journal,* among others. A noted authority on ambush marketing, he has previously served as an adjunct professor at both Seton Hall School of Law and Seton Hall Stallman School of Business. Professor McKelvey has more than 15 years of experience as a practitioner within the sport industry, on both the property and the agency sides, as head of Major League Baseball's Corporate Sponsorship Department, as Vice President of PSP Sports' successful in-house sport marketing and promotions agency, and as President of Fan Guide, Inc.

Tracy Schoenadel, EdD, ABD, MS

Tracy Schoenadel is Director of the Center for Spectator Sport Research at the Mark H. McCormack Department of Sport Management in the Isenberg School of Management at the University of Massachusetts. Drawing on her extensive industry contacts and experience, Tracy and the Center are currently attracting industry partners that offer the McCormack Sport Management Department's students one challenging research assignment after another.

The Center divides its research among market studies, customized marketing research, and the creation of strategic marketing plans. Prior to her appointment at the Center, Tracy was a Vice President at TNS and directed the sponsorship research division. She was also the Executive Director of the industry-leading ESPN Sports Poll.

Rod Warnick

Dr. Rod Warnick is a Professor and former Department Head of Hospitality and Tourism Management in the Isenberg School of Management at the University of Massachusetts. Currently, he is a Special Assistant to the Dean of the School of Management for accreditation learning outcome assessments.

Dr. Warnick has published numerous articles dealing with recreational and sport activity and tourism trends, volume segmentation, market share analysis, quality of life and recreation, consumer behavior in recreation and tourism settings, and trend analysis studies. Rod has been a consultant to the Professional Golfers Association of America (PGA), Ladies Professional Golf Association (LPGA), and major resort complexes such as Smugglers Notch Resort and The Breakers. His co-authored publication *Recreation Trends and Markets* has been quoted in numerous research and recreation planning and management publications. He is also the co-author of the Massachusetts Statewide Comprehensive Outdoor Recreation Plan – *Massachusetts Outdoors: For Our Common Good,* Volumes I and II. Rod is also a founding member of the Northeast's largest recreation and tourism research conference, NERR (Northeast Recreation Research Conference). Rod teaches courses in club management, tourism marketing, hospitality marketing, hospitality sales and advertising, and recreation/resort management. He is a member of CMAA and NECMA and also serves as the co-chair of the UMass Athletic Council, the UMass NCAA Accreditation Review Team, and the UMass Campus Planning Committee. Rod has received awards in teaching, research and service/outreach and was UMass Amherst TeachNology Fellow, and a Club Foundation Faculty Intern. His students have won numerous awards and scholarships in the club management field. He holds graduate research degrees from the Pennsylvania State University and the University of Montana.

Glenn Wong, JD

Glenn Wong is a Professor in the Sport Management Department in the Isenberg School of Management at the University of Massachusetts, Amherst. He received a BA in Economics and Sociology from Brandeis University and a JD from Boston College Law School. While at the

University of Massachusetts, he has served as the Sport Management Department Head, Interim Director of Athletics, and Acting Dean of the School of Physical Education. Professor Wong is currently the Faculty Athletics Representative for the university to the National Collegiate Athletic Association. A lawyer, he is author of *The Essentials of Sports Law, Third Edition* (2002). He has co-authored *Law and Business of the Sports Industries*, Volumes I and II, and *The Sport Lawyer's Guide to Legal Periodicals*. He contributed book chapters in *The Management of Sport: Its Foundation and Application, Successful Sport Management,* and *Law and Sport: Contemporary Issues.* He has contributed publications to *Case Studies, Athletic Business, Seton Hall Legislative Journal, Entertainment and Sports Lawyer, Detroit College of Law Review, Gonzaga Law Review, Entertainment and Sports Law Journal, Arbitration Journal,* and *Nova Law Review.* Professor Wong is a member of the Massachusetts Bar and the American Arbitration Association, where he is a member of the Labor Arbitration Panel. He is also a member of the Arbitration Panel of the International Council of Arbitration for Sport. He has served as a salary arbitrator for Major League Baseball. Professor Wong has been on the board of directors of the Sports Lawyers Association, the Massachusetts Sports Partnership, the Governor's Sports Advisory Council, and the Faculty Athletics Representatives Association, and he is a former member of the

NCAA's Committee on Competitive Safeguards and Medical Aspects of Sports.

There are many other contributors who have added to the text in prior years and whose work is still present in this edition. We are grateful for their contributions and have kept their names on the chapters where they have made significant contributions. We acknowledge their work and thank them here:

- Kevin Barrett, General Manager, Coral Springs Center for the Arts, Coral Springs, FL
- Nancy Beauchamp, General Manager, Finance, Rhode Island Convention Center, Providence, RI
- James M. Gladden, Dean, School of Physical Education and Tourism Management, Indiana University, Purdue University, Indianapolis, IN
- Michael Graney, Senior VP of Business Development, Economic Development Council of Western Mass, Springfield, MA
- Mireia Lizandra, International Sport Marketing Consultant, Philadelphia, PA
- Andrew McGowan, Director of Communications, Firethorn, Atlanta, GA
- Robert Newman, Chief Operations Officer, AEG Facilities, Los Angeles, CA
- William Sutton, Associate Director and Professor, DeVos Sport Business Management Program, University of Central Florida, Orlando, FL

Index

Photo Credits

APPLIED
PHYSICS

APPLIED PHYSICS

Third Edition

Paul E. Tippens

Department of Physics
Chairperson, Department of Special Studies
Southern Technical Institute

Gregg Division · McGraw-Hill Book Company

New York   Atlanta   Dallas   St. Louis   San Francisco

Auckland   Bogotá   Guatemala   Hamburg   Johannesburg   Lisbon

London   Madrid   Mexico   Montreal   New Delhi   Panama   Paris

San Juan   São Paulo   Singapore   Sydney   Tokyo   Toronto

To my brother, Dr. Jack Tippens

Sponsoring Editor: D. Eugene Gilmore
Editing Supervisor: Larry Goldberg
Design and Art Supervisor/Text Designer: Patricia Lowy
Production Supervisor: Frank Bellantoni

Cover Photographer: Geoffrey Gove

Library of Congress Cataloging in Publication Data

Tippens, Paul E.
  Applied physics.

  Includes index.
  1. Physics. I. Title.
QC21.2.T55 1984   530   83-12007
ISBN 0-07-064977-4

CONTENTS

PREFACE

The response to the first two editions of *Applied Physics* has been gratifying, and it indicates that the general tone and level of the text has been appealing to students. This new edition, therefore, has maintained the same readability and liberal use of illustrations which were so popular in the previous editions. The major changes have been directed toward the improvement of the text as an instructional agent. Recognizing that students are largely responsible for their own learning, and that a textbook is the major source of information, the following improvements have been made in the third edition:

1. **Clearly stated objectives are provided at the beginning of each chapter.**
2. **The opening paragraphs have been revised to provide a brief statement of rationale and applications.**
3. **Several sections have been entirely rewritten to present a more logical and instructive approach.**
4. **A new section has been added to each chapter which summarizes the basic concepts and formulas applicable to each instructional unit.**
5. **Many problems at the end of each chapter have been revised and the total number has been expanded. There are now approximately 1100 problems and over 500 questions contained in this edition.**
6. **A review of the right-triangle trigonometry necessary for working with vectors has been added to the math review as an appendix.**

After significant discussion with reviewers and several visits to industrial and engineering firms, it was decided to shift the emphasis more toward the use of the International System of Units (SI) but to retain the mixture of U.S. Customary System (USCS) units in the early chapters. Many of these older units will, unfortunately, be used by American industries for at least another decade. Technicians must be able to recognize and convert units from one system to the other, especially in the fields of mechanics and thermodynamics. The SI system is used exclusively in this text for all other fields of physics.

A conscious effort has been made to expand and to clarify essential physical concepts. The text is profusely illustrated with line drawings, and many examples are given in each chapter to show applications. Where possible, each chapter has been written as an independent unit, permitting the instructor to select only those chapters needed for a particular class or to alter the sequence of topics. For example, some instructors begin with the chapter on acceleration and then proceed to the more difficult presentation of vector mechanics. The only prerequisites assumed by this text are a general understanding of the algebra necessary for formula rearrangement and a limited acquaintance with right-triangle trigonometry. A study guide is available for students, and a detailed solutions manual has been prepared for instructors.

The author wishes to acknowledge the assistance and valuable input provided by the many instructors and students who have used the earlier editions. Suggestions and recommendations for improvement are always welcome.

Paul E. Tippens

Mechanics

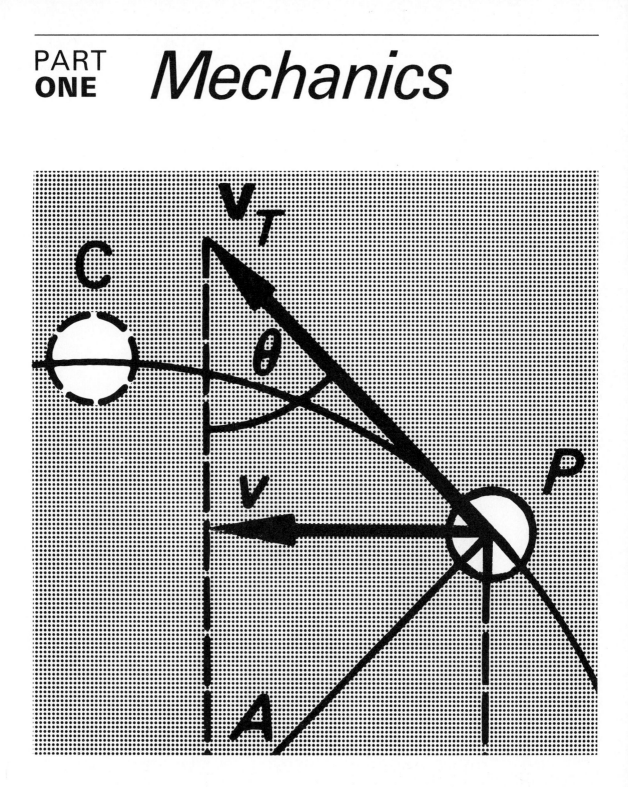

1 *Introduction*

You are about to embark on one of the most important courses of study you will ever attempt. You may be planning to work in the fields of civil, mechanical, or electrical technology. You may decide to pursue one of the many vocational or trade careers which require some math and science background. Quite likely, you are unsure at this point about your ultimate employment goals. And even if you stick with your original choice, technology is changing rapidly. So much is uncertain, in fact, that you must be at least a little pleased to hear that *one* course will benefit you regardless of what happens later.

Regardless of your career choices, it's difficult to imagine any technical courses of study that do not build on an underlying foundation of basic physics. With a thorough understanding of mechanics, heat, sound, and electricity, you carry with you the building blocks for almost any technical career. Should you find it necessary or desirable to change careers either before or after graduation, you will be able to draw from a general base of science and mathematics. By taking this physics course seriously and by devoting an unusual amount of time and energy, you will have less trouble in the future. In your later coursework and on the job, you will be riding the crest of the wave instead of merely staying afloat in an angry sea.

WHAT IS PHYSICS?

Even if you are among the very few lucky enough to have taken high school physics, you still probably have a rather fuzzy view of what *physics* really means and how it might differ, for example, from *science*. For our purpose, the sciences may be divided between *biological* and *physical*. The biological sciences deal with living things. The physical sciences deal primarily with the nonliving sides of nature.

Physics can be defined as the science which investigates the fundamental concepts of matter, energy, and space, and the relationships between them.

In terms of this broad definition, there are no clear boundaries between the many physical sciences. This is evident from the overlapping fields of biophysics, chemical physics, astrophysics, geophysics, electrochemistry, and so forth.

In this book it is our goal to provide a very basic introduction to the world of physics. The emphasis is definitely on application and the broad field of physics will be narrowed to the essential concepts which underlie all technical knowledge. You will study mechanics, heat, light, sound, electricity, and atomic structure. The most basic of these topics, and probably the most important for beginning students, is mechanics.

Mechanics is concerned with the position (*statics*) and motion (*dynamics*) of matter in space. Statics represents the study of physics associated with bodies at rest. Dynamics is concerned with a description of motion and its causes. In each case, the engineer or technician is concerned with measuring and describing physical quantities in terms of their cause and effect.

An engineer, for example, uses physical principles to determine which type of bridge structure will be the most efficient for a given situation. The concern is for the *effect* of forces. If the completed bridge should fail, the *cause* of failure must be analyzed in order to apply this knowledge to future construction. It is important to note that by *cause* the scientist means the sequence of physical events leading to an *effect*.

WHAT PART IS PLAYED BY MATHE- MATICS?

Mathematics serves many purposes. It is philosophy, art, metaphysics, and logic. However, these values are subordinate to its main value as a tool for the scientist, engineer, or technician. One of the rewards of a first course in physics is the growing awareness of the relevance of mathematics. Finally, you will begin to see very specific applications of basic mathematics.

Suppose you wish to predict how long it takes to stop a car traveling at a given speed. You might record the weight of the car, the initial speed, the change in speed, and the distance and time required to stop the car. When all these facts are recorded, the next step is to relate them to each other. We cannot do so without the tools of mathematics.

If you completed such an experiment, your measurements plus a knowledge of mathematics would lead you to the following relationship:

$$s = vt + \tfrac{1}{2}at^2$$

where s = stopping distance
v = initial speed
t = stopping time
a = rate of change in speed

This statement is a *workable hypothesis*. From this equation we can predict the stopping time of other vehicles. When it has been used long enough for us to be reasonably sure that it is true, we call it a *scientific theory*. In other words, any scientific theory is just a workable hypothesis which has stood the test of time.

Thus, we see that mathematics is useful in deriving formulas which describe physical events accurately. Mathematics plays an even larger role in solving such formulas for specific quantities.

For instance, in the above formula it would be a relatively simple matter to find values for s, v, and a when the other quantities are given, but the solution for t involves a more specialized knowledge of mathematics. How easily you derive or solve a theoretical relationship depends on your background in mathematics.

A review of the mathematics required for applied physics is presented in App. A. If you are unfamiliar with any of the topics discussed, study this appendix. Regardless of your background, you should review the concepts of powers of ten and literal equations. Skill in using the tools of mathematics will make the solution of physical problems an enjoyable challenge rather than a mystery to be avoided.

HOW SHOULD I STUDY PHYSICS?

Reading technical material is different from other reading. Attention to specific meanings of words must be given if the material is to be understood. Graphs, drawings, charts, and photographs are often included in technical literature. They are always helpful and even essential to the description of physical events. You should study them thoroughly so that you understand the principles clearly.

Much of what you learn will be from classroom lectures and experiments. The beginning student often asks: How can I concentrate fully on the lecture and at the same time take good notes? Of course, it may not be possible to understand fully all the concepts presented and still take complete notes. You must learn to note only the significant portions of each lesson. Make sure you listen attentively to the explanation of various topics. Learn to recognize *key words* like *work*, *force*, *energy*, and *momentum*.

Adequate preparation before class should give you a good idea of which portions of the lecture are covered in the text and which are not. If a problem or definition is in the text, it is usually better to jot down a key word and concentrate fully on what the instructor is saying.

Notes written during a lecture are necessarily brief and untidy. Therefore, you should compile a neat and comprehensive lecture notebook, using both class notes and the text as source material. Do this as soon as possible after each lecture while the concepts are still fresh. This serves three purposes: (1) it provides a set of neat, understandable review notes; (2) it shows you those areas in which you are weak; and (3) it encourages regular and organized study habits. Probably the most important part of a notebook is the problems. Work out all the examples presented in class or assigned as homework.

2 *Technical Measurement and Vectors*

OBJECTIVES: After completing this chapter, you should be able to:

1. **Write the fundamental units for mass, length, and time in SI and U.S. Customary System (USCS) units.**
2. **Define and apply the SI prefixes which indicate multiples of base units.**
3. **Convert from one unit to another unit for the same quantity when given the necessary definitions.**
4. **Define a vector quantity and a scalar quantity and give examples of each.**
5. **Determine the components of a given vector.**
6. **Find the resultant of two or more vectors.**

The application of physics, whether in the shop or in a technical laboratory, always requires measurements of some kind. An automobile mechanic might be measuring the diameter or *bore* of an engine cylinder. Refrigeration technicians might be concerned with volume, pressure, and temperature measurements. Electricians use instruments which measure electric resistance and current, and mechanical engineers are concerned about the effects of forces whose magnitudes must be accurately determined. In fact, it is difficult to imagine any occupation that is not involved with the measurement of some physical quantity.

In the process of physical measurement, the technician is often concerned with the direction as well as the magnitude of a particular quantity. The length of a wooden rafter is determined by the angle it makes with the horizontal. The direction of an applied force determines its effectiveness in producing a displacement. The direction in which a conveyor belt moves is often just as important as the speed with which it moves. Such physical quantities as *displacement*, *force*, and *velocity* are often encountered in industry. In this chapter, the concept of *vectors* is introduced to permit the study of both the magnitude and the direction of physical quantities.

2-1 PHYSICAL QUANTITIES

The language of physics and technology is universal. Facts and laws must be expressed in an accurate and consistent manner if everyone is to mean exactly the same thing by the same term. For example, suppose an engine is said to have a piston displacement of 3.28 liters (200 cubic inches). Two questions must be answered if this statement is to be understood: (1) How is the *piston displacement* measured, and (2) what is the *liter*?

Piston displacement is the volume that the piston displaces, or "sweeps out," as it moves from the bottom of the cylinder to the top. It is really not a displacement in the usual sense of the word; it is a volume. A standard measure for volume that is easily recognized throughout the world is the liter. Therefore, when an engine has a label on it that reads "piston displacement = 3.28 liters," all mechanics will give the same meaning to the label.

In the above example, the piston displacement (volume) is an example of a *physical quantity*. Notice that this quantity was defined by describing the procedure for its measurement. In physics, all quantities are defined in this manner. Other examples of physical quantities are length, weight, time, speed, force, and mass.

A physical quantity is measured by comparison with some known standard. For example, we might need to know the length of a metal bar. With appropriate instruments we might determine the length of the bar to be 12 feet. The bar does not contain 12 things called "feet"; it is merely compared with the length of some standard known as a "foot." The length could also be represented as 3.66 meters or 4 yards if we used other known measures.

The *magnitude* of a physical quantity is given by a *number* and a *unit* of measure. Both are necessary because either the number or the unit by itself is meaningless. Except for pure numbers and fractions, it is necessary to include the unit with the number when listing the magnitude of any quantity.

> The **magnitude** of a physical quantity is completely specified by a number and a unit, e.g., 20 meters or 40 liters.

Since there are many different measures for the same quantity, we need a way of keeping track of the exact size of particular units. To do this, it is necessary to establish standard measures for specific quantities. A standard is a permanent or easily determined physical record of the size of a unit of measurement. For example, the standard for measuring electrical resistance, the *ohm*, might be defined by comparison with a standard resistor whose resistance is accurately known. Thus, a resistance of 20 ohms would be 20 times as great as that of a standard 1-ohm resistor.

Remember that every physical quantity is defined by telling how it is measured. Depending on the measuring device, each quantity can be expressed in a number of different units. For example, some distance units are *meters*, *kilometers*, *miles*, and *feet*, and some speed units are *meters per second*, *kilometers per hour*, *miles per hour*, and *feet per second*. Regardless of the units chosen, however, distance must be a *length* and speed must be *length* divided by *time*. Thus, *length* and *length/time* are the *dimensions* of the physical quantities *distance* and *speed*.

Note that speed is defined in terms of two lesser quantities (length and time). Length and time, on the other hand, cannot be defined in lesser terms. Therefore, we say that length and time are *fundamental* quantities and that speed is not a fundamental quantity.

From this discussion, we are led to the notion that there may be a limit to the number of fundamental quantities. If we can reduce all physical measurements to a small number of fundamental measures with standard base units for each quantity, then there will be much less confusion in their application.

2-2 THE INTERNATIONAL SYSTEM

The international system of units is called *Système International d'Unités* (SI) and is essentially the same as what we have come to know as the *metric system*. The International Committee on Weights and Measures has established seven fundamental quantities and has assigned official base units to each quantity. A summary of these quantities, their base units, and the symbols for the base units is given in Table 2-1.

Table 2-1 The SI Base Units for Seven Fundamental Quantities and Two Supplemental Quantities

Quantity	Unit	Symbol
Base units		
Length	meter	m
Mass	kilogram	kg
Time	second	s
Electric current	ampere	A
Temperature	kelvin	K
Luminous intensity	candela	cd
Amount of substance	mole	mol
Supplemental units		
Plane angle	radian	rad
Solid angle	steradian	sr

Each of the units listed in Table 2-1 has a specific measurable definition which can be duplicated anywhere in the world. Of these base units only one, the *kilogram*, is currently defined in terms of a single physical sample. This standard specimen is kept at the International Bureau of Weights and Measures in France. Copies of the original specimen have been made for use in other

Fig. 2-1 The U.S. standard kilogram. A platinum–iridium cylinder housed in the National Bureau of Standards.

nations. The United States prototype is shown in Fig. 2-1. All other units are defined in terms of reproducible physical events and can be accurately determined at a number of locations throughout the world.

We can measure many quantities, such as volume, pressure, speed, and force, which are combinations of two or more fundamental quantities. However, no one has ever encountered a measurement that cannot be expressed in terms of length, mass, time, current, temperature, luminous intensity, or amount of substance. Combinations of these quantities are referred to as *derived* quantities, and they are measured in derived units. Several common derived units are listed in Table 2-2.

Unfortunately, the SI units are not fully implemented in many industrial applications. The United States is making progress toward the adoption of SI units. However, wholesale conversions are costly, particularly in many mechanical and thermal applications, and total conversion to the international system will require some time. For this reason it is necessary to be familiar with older units for physical quantities. The USCS units for several important quantities are listed in Table 2-3.

It should be noted that even though the foot, pound, and other units are frequently used in the United States, they have been redefined in terms of the SI standard units. Thus, all measurements are presently based on the same standards.

Table 2-2 Derived Units for Common Physical Quantities

Quantity	Derived units	Symbol	
Area	square meter	m^2	
Volume	cubic meter	m^3	
Frequency	hertz	Hz	s^{-1}
Mass density (density)	kilogram per cubic meter	kg/m^3	
Speed, velocity	meter per second	m/s	
Angular velocity	radian per second	rad/s	
Acceleration	meter per second squared	m/s^2	
Angular acceleration	radian per second squared	rad/s^2	
Force	newton	N	$kg \cdot m/s^2$
Pressure (mechanical stress)	pascal	Pa	N/m^2
Kinematic viscosity	square meter per second	m^2/s	
Dynamic viscosity	newton-second per square meter	$N \cdot s/m^2$	
Work, energy, quantity of heat	joule	J	$N \cdot m$
Power	watt	W	J/s
Quantity of electricity	coulomb	C	
Potential difference, electromotive force	volt	V	J/C
Electric field strength	volt per meter	V/m	
Electric resistance	ohm	Ω	V/A
Capacitance	farad	F	C/V
Magnetic flux	weber	Wb	$V \cdot s$
Inductance	henry	H	$V \cdot s/A$
Magnetic flux density	tesla	T	Wb/m^2
Magnetic field strength	ampere per meter	A/m	
Magnetomotive force	ampere	A	
Luminous flux	lumen	lm	$cd \cdot sr$
Luminance	candela per square meter	cd/m^2	
Illuminance	lux	lx	lm/m^2
Wave number	1 per meter	m^{-1}	
Entropy	joule per kelvin	J/K	
Specific heat capacity	joule per kilogram kelvin	$J/(kg \cdot K)$	
Thermal conductivity	watt per meter kelvin	$W/(m \cdot K)$	
Radiant intensity	watt per steradian	W/sr	
Activity (of a radioactive source)	1 per second	s^{-1}	

Table 2-3 U.S. Customary System Units

Quantity	SI unit	USCS unit
Length	meter (m)	foot (ft)
Mass	kilogram (kg)	slug (slug)
Time	second (s)	second (s)
Force (weight)	newton (N)	pound (lb)
Temperature	kelvin (K)	degree Rankine (R)

2-3 MEASURE-MENT OF LENGTH

The standard SI unit of length, the *meter* (m), was originally defined as one ten-millionth of the distance from the North Pole to the equator. For practical reasons, this distance was marked off on a standard platinum–iridium bar. In 1960, the standard was changed to allow greater access to a more accurate measure of the meter. Presently, the meter is defined as follows:

> One **meter** *is the length of exactly 1,650,763.73 wavelengths of the orange-red light from krypton-86.*

Of course, we do not need to know this definition in order to make accurate measurements. Many tools, such as simple meter sticks and calipers, are calibrated to agree with the standard measure.

A distinct advantage of the metric system over other systems of units is the use of prefixes to indicate multiples of the base unit. Table 2-4 defines the accepted prefixes and demonstrates their use to indicate multiples and subdivisions of the meter.

Table 2-4 Multiples and Submultiples for SI Units

Prefix	Symbol	Multiplier	Use
tera	T	$1,000,000,000,000 = 10^{12}$	1 terameter (Tm)
giga	G	$1,000,000,000 = 10^{9}$	1 gigameter (Gm)
mega	M	$1,000,000 = 10^{6}$	1 megameter (Mm)
kilo	k	$1,000 = 10^{3}$	1 kilometer (km)
centi	c	$0.01 = 10^{-2}$	1 centimeter (cm)*
milli	m	$0.001 = 10^{-3}$	1 millimeter (mm)
micro	μ	$0.000001 = 10^{-6}$	1 micrometer (μm)
nano	n	$0.000000001 = 10^{-9}$	1 nanometer (nm)
—	Å	$0.0000000001 = 10^{-10}$	1 angstrom (Å)*
pico	p	$0.000000000001 = 10^{-12}$	1 picometer (pm)

* The use of the centimeter and the angstrom is discouraged, but they are still widely used.

From the table, you can determine that

$$1 \text{ meter (m)} = 1000 \text{ millimeters (mm)}$$
$$1 \text{ meter (m)} = 100 \text{ centimeters (cm)}$$
$$1 \text{ kilometer (km)} = 1000 \text{ meters (m)}$$

The relationship between the centimeter and the *inch* can be seen in Fig. 2-2. By definition, 1 inch is equal to exactly 25.4 millimeters. This definition and other useful definitions are as follows (symbols for the units are in parentheses):

$$1 \text{ inch (in.)} = 25.4 \text{ millimeters (mm)}$$
$$1 \text{ foot (ft)} = 0.3048 \text{ meter (m)}$$
$$1 \text{ yard (yd)} = 0.914 \text{ meter (m)}$$
$$1 \text{ mile (mi)} = 1.61 \text{ kilometers (km)}$$

Fig. 2-2 A comparison of the inch to the centimeter as a measure of length.

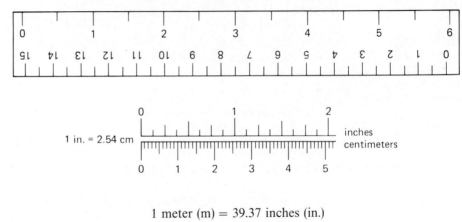

1 in. = 2.54 cm

1 meter (m) = 39.37 inches (in.)
1 meter (m) = 3.281 feet (ft)
1 meter (m) = 1.094 yards (yd)
1 kilometer (km) = 1.621 mile (mi)

In reporting data, it is preferable to use the prefix that will allow the number to be expressed in the range from 0.1 to 1000. For example, 7,430,000 meters should be expressed as 7.43×10^6 m, and then it should be reported as 7.43 megameters, abbreviated 7.43 Mm. It would not usually be desirable to write this measurement as 7430 kilometers (7430 km) unless the distance is being compared with other distances measured in kilometers. In the case of the quantity 0.00064 ampere, it is proper to write either 0.64 milliampere (0.64 mA) or 640 microamperes (640 μA). Normally, prefixes are chosen for multiples of a thousand.

2-4
MEASURING INSTRUMENTS

The choice of a measuring instrument is determined by the accuracy required and by the physical conditions surrounding the measurement. A basic choice for the mechanic or machinist is most often the steel rule, such as the one shown in Fig. 2-3. This rule is often accurate enough when you are measuring openly accessible lengths. Steel rules may be graduated as fine as thirty-seconds or even sixty-fourths of an inch. Metric rules are usually graduated in millimeters.

Fig. 2-3 Six-inch (15-cm) steel scales. (a) Scales $\frac{1}{32}$ in. and 0.5 mm. *(The L. S. Starrett Company.)* (b) Scales $\frac{1}{100}$ and $\frac{1}{50}$ in. *(Brown and Sharpe Mfg. Co.)*

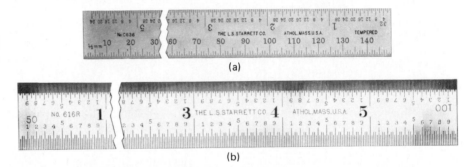

(a)

(b)

For the measurement of inside and outside diameters, calipers such as those shown in Fig. 2-4 may be used. The caliper itself cannot be read directly and therefore must be set to a steel rule or a standard size gauge.

Fig. 2-4 Using calipers to measure an inside diameter. *(Kostel Enterprises, Ltd.)*

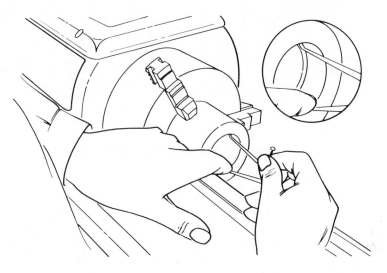

The best accuracy possible with a steel rule is determined by the size of the smallest graduation and is of the order of 0.01 in. or 0.1 mm. For greater accuracy the machinist often uses a standard micrometer caliper, such as the one shown in Fig. 2-5 or a standard vernier caliper, as in Fig. 2-6. These instru-

Fig. 2-5 A micrometer caliper, showing a reading of 0.250 in. *(The L. S. Starrett Company.)*

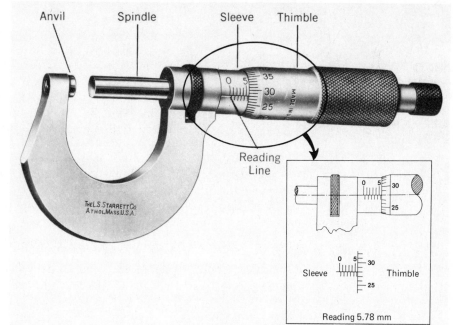

Fig. 2-6 The
vernier caliper
*(The L. S. Starrett
Company.)*

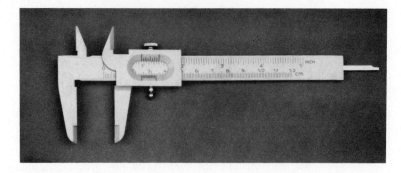

ments make use of sliding scales to record very accurate measurements. Micrometer calipers can measure to the nearest ten-thousandth of an inch (0.002 mm), and vernier calipers are used to measure within 0.001 in. or 0.02 mm.

The depth of blind holes, slots, and recesses is often measured with a micrometer depth gauge. Figure 2-7 shows such a gauge being used to measure the depth of a shoulder.

Fig. 2-7 Measuring
the depth of a
shoulder with a
micrometer depth
gauge. *(The L. S.
Starrett Company.)*

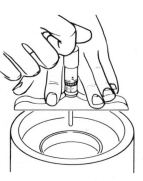

2-5
UNIT CON-
VERSIONS

Because so many different units are required for a variety of jobs, it is often necessary to convert a measurement from one unit to another. For example, suppose that a machinist records the outside diameter of a pipe as $1\frac{3}{16}$ in. To order a fitting for the pipe, the machinist may need to know this diameter in millimeters. Such conversions can easily be accomplished by treating units algebraically and using the principle of cancellation.

In the above case, the machinist should first convert the fraction to a decimal.

$$1\tfrac{3}{16} \text{ in.} = 1.19 \text{ in.}$$

Next, the machinist should write down the quantity to be converted, giving both the number and the unit (1.19 in.). The definition which relates inches to millimeters is recalled:

$$1 \text{ in.} = 25.4 \text{ mm}$$

Since this statement is an equality, we can form two ratios, each equal to 1.

$$\frac{1 \text{ in.}}{25.4 \text{ mm}} = 1 \qquad \frac{25.4 \text{ mm}}{1 \text{ in.}} = 1$$

Note that the number 1 does not equal the number 25.4, but the *length* of 1 in. is equal to the *length* of 25.4 mm. Thus, if we multiply some other length by either of these ratios, we will get a new number, but we will not change the length. Such ratios are called *conversion factors*. Either of the above conversion factors may be multiplied by 1.19 in. without changing the length represented. Multiplication by the first ratio does not give a meaningful result. Note that units are treated as algebraic quantities.

$$(1.19 \text{ in.})\left(\frac{1 \text{ in.}}{25.4 \text{ mm}}\right) = \left(\frac{1.19}{25.4}\right)\left(\frac{\text{in.}^2}{\text{mm}}\right) \qquad Wrong!$$

Multiplication by the second ratio, however, gives the following result:

$$(1.19 \text{ in.})\left(\frac{25.4 \text{ mm}}{1 \text{ in.}}\right) = \frac{(1.19)(25.4)}{(1)} \text{mm} = 30.2 \text{ mm}$$

Therefore, the outside diameter of the pipe is 30.2 mm.

The following procedure is used in unit conversions:

1. **Write down the quantity to be converted.**
2. **Define each unit appearing in the quantity to be converted in terms of the desired unit(s).**
3. **For each definition, form two conversion factors, one being the reciprocal of the other.**
4. **Multiply the quantity to be converted by those factors which will cancel all but the desired units.**

Sometimes it is necessary to work with quantities which have multiple units. For example, *speed* is defined as *length* per unit *time* and may have units of *meters per second* (m/s), *feet per second* (ft/s), or other units. The same algebraic procedure can help with conversion of multiple units.

EXAMPLE 2-1   Convert a speed of 60 km/h to units of meters per second.

Solution   We recall two definitions which might result in four possible conversion factors.

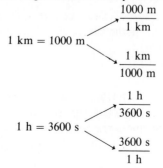

We write down the quantity to be converted, then choose conversion factors which will cancel nondesired units.

$$60 \ \frac{\text{km}}{\text{h}} \left(\frac{1000 \text{ m}}{1 \text{ km}} \right) \left(\frac{1 \text{ h}}{3600 \text{ s}} \right) = 16.7 \ \frac{\text{m}}{\text{s}}$$

Additional examples of the procedure are as follows:

$$30 \ \frac{\text{mi}}{\text{h}} \left(\frac{5280 \text{ ft}}{1 \text{ mi}} \right) \left(\frac{1 \text{ h}}{60 \text{ min}} \right) \left(\frac{1 \text{ min}}{60 \text{ s}} \right) = 44 \text{ ft/s}$$

$$20 \ \frac{\text{lb}}{\text{in.}^2} \left(\frac{1550 \text{ in}^2}{1 \text{ m}^2} \right) \left(\frac{0.454 \text{ kg}}{1 \text{ lb}} \right) = 1.41 \times 10^4 \text{ kg/m}^2$$

The required definitions can be found in App. B, if they are not available in this chapter.

When working with technical formulas, it is always helpful to substitute units as well as numbers. For example, the formula for speed v is

$$v = \frac{s}{t}$$

where s is the distance traveled in a time t. Thus, if a car travels 400 m in 10 s, its speed will be

$$v = \frac{400 \text{ m}}{10 \text{ s}} = 40 \ \frac{\text{m}}{\text{s}}$$

Notice that the units of velocity are meters per second, written m/s.

Whenever velocity appears in a formula, it must always have units of *length* divided by *time*. These are said to be the *dimensions* of velocity. There may be many different units for a given physical quantity, but the dimensions result from a definition, and they do not change.

In working with formulas, it will be useful to remember two rules concerning dimensions:

Rule 1 *If two quantities are to be added or subtracted, they must be of the same dimensions.*

Rule 2 *The quantities on both sides of an equals sign must be of the same dimensions.*

EXAMPLE 2-2   Show that the formula

$$s = v_0 t + \tfrac{1}{2}at^2$$

is dimensionally correct. The symbol s represents the distance traveled in a time t while accelerating at a rate a from an initial speed v_0. Assume that acceleration has units of meters per second squared (m/s^2).

Solution

Since the units of a are given, the unit of length must be meters (m) and the unit of time must be seconds (s). Ignoring the factor $\frac{1}{2}$, which has no dimensions, we substitute units for the quantities in the equation.

$$\text{m} = \frac{\text{m}}{\cancel{s}} \cancel{(s)} + \frac{\text{m}}{\cancel{s^2}} \cancel{(s)^2}$$

Notice that both Rule 1 and Rule 2 are satisfied. Therefore, the equation is dimensionally correct.

The fact that an equation is dimensionally correct is a valuable check. Such an equation still may not be a *true* equation, but at least it is consistent dimensionally.

2-6 VECTOR AND SCALAR QUANTITIES

Some quantities can be totally described by a number and a unit. Only the *magnitudes* are of interest in an area of 12 m², a volume of 40 ft³, or a distance of 50 km. Such quantities are called *scalar* quantities.

A scalar quantity is completely specified by its magnitude—a number and a unit. Examples are speed (15 mi/h), distance (12 km), and volume (200 cm³).

Scalar quantities which are measured in the same units may be added or subtracted in the usual way. For example,

$$14 \text{ mm} + 13 \text{ mm} = 27 \text{ mm}$$
$$20 \text{ ft}^2 - 14 \text{ ft}^2 = 6 \text{ ft}^2$$

Some physical quantities, such as force and velocity, have direction as well as magnitude. In such cases, they are called *vector* quantities. The direction must be a part of any calculations involving such quantities.

A vector quantity is completely specified by a magnitude and a direction. It consists of a number, a unit, and a direction. Examples are displacement (20 m N) and velocity (40 mi/h, 30°N of W).

The direction of a vector may be given by reference to conventional north, east, west, and south directions. Consider, for example, the vectors 20 m, W and 40 m at 30°N of E, as shown in Fig. 2-8. The expression "north of east" indicates that the angle is formed by rotating a line northward from the easterly direction.

Another method of specifying direction which will be particularly useful later on is to make reference to perpendicular lines called *axes*. These imaginary lines are usually chosen to be horizontal and vertical, but they may be oriented along other directions as long as the two lines remain perpendicular. An imaginary horizontal line is usually called the x axis, and an imaginary vertical line is called the y axis. (See Fig. 2-9.) Directions are given by angles measured counterclockwise from the positive x axis. The vectors 40 m at 60° and 50 m at 210° are shown in the figure.

Fig. 2-8 Indicating the direction of a vector by reference to north (N), south (S), east (E), or west (W).

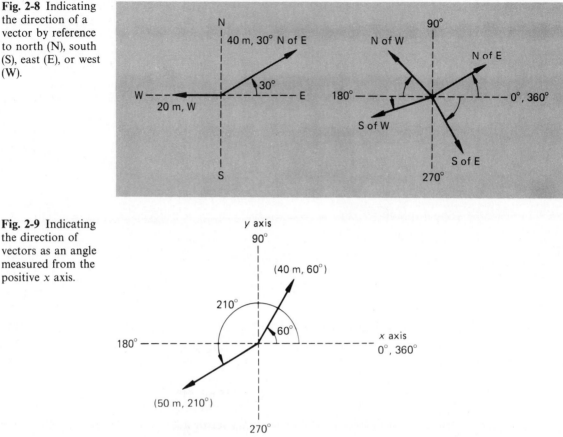

Fig. 2-9 Indicating the direction of vectors as an angle measured from the positive x axis.

Assume a person travels by car from Atlanta to St. Louis. The *displacement* from Atlanta can be represented by a line segment drawn to scale from Atlanta to St. Louis (see Fig. 2-10). An arrowhead is drawn on the St. Louis end to denote the direction. It is important to note that the displacement, represented by the vector $\mathbf{D}_1$, is completely independent of the actual path or the

Fig. 2-10 Displacement is a vector quantity. Its direction is indicated by a solid arrow. Distance is a scalar quantity, indicated above by a dashed line.

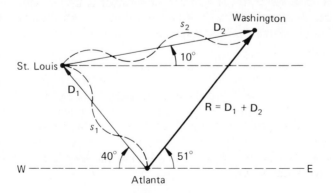

mode of transportation. The odometer would show that the car had actually traveled a scalar distance s_1 of 541 mi. The magnitude of the displacement is only 472 mi.

Another important difference is that the vector displacement has a constant direction of 140° (or 40°N of W). However, the direction of the car at any instant on the trip is not important when considering the scalar distance.

Now, let us suppose that our traveler continues the drive to Washington. This time the vector displacement D_2 is 716 mi at a constant direction of 10°N of E. The corresponding ground distance s_2 is 793 mi. The total distance traveled for the entire trip from Atlanta is the arithmetic sum of the scalar quantities s_1 and s_2.

$$s_1 + s_2 = 541 \text{ mi} + 793 \text{ mi} = 1334 \text{ mi}$$

However, the *vector sum* of the two displacements D_1 and D_2 must take note of direction as well as magnitudes. The question now is not the distance traveled but the resulting displacement from Atlanta. This vector sum is represented in Fig. 2-10 by the symbol R, where

$$R = D_1 + D_2$$

Methods we will discuss in the next section will allow us to determine the magnitude and direction of R. Using a ruler and a device for measuring angles, we would see that

$$R = 545 \text{ mi, } 51°$$

Remember that in performing vector additions, both the magnitude and direction of the displacements must be considered. The additions are geometric instead of algebraic. It is possible for the magnitude of a vector sum to be less than the magnitude of either of the component displacements.

A vector is usually denoted in print by boldface type. For example, the symbol D_1 denotes a displacement vector in Fig. 2-10. A vector can be denoted conveniently in handwriting by underscoring the letter or by putting an arrow over it. In print, the magnitude of a vector is usually indicated by italics; thus, D denotes the magnitude of the vector D. A vector is often specified by a pair of numbers (R, θ). The first number and unit gives the magnitude, and the second number gives the angle measured counterclockwise from the positive x axis. For example,

$$R = (R, \theta) = (200 \text{ km, } 114°)$$

Note that the magnitude R of a vector is always positive. A negative sign before the symbol of a vector merely reverses its direction; i.e., it interchanges the arrow tip without affecting the length. If $A = (20 \text{ m E})$, then $-A$ would be (20 m W).

2-7 ADDITION OF VECTORS BY GRAPHICAL METHODS

In this section we discuss two common graphical methods for finding the geometric sum of vectors. The *polygon method* is the more useful, since it can be readily applied to more than two vectors. The *parallelogram method* is useful for the addition of two vectors at a time. In each case the magnitude of a vector is indicated to scale by the length of a line segment. The direction is denoted by an arrow tip at the end of the line segment.

EXAMPLE 2-3

A ship travels 100 mi due north on the first day of a voyage, 60 mi northeast on the second day, and 120 mi due east on the third day. Find the resultant displacement by the polygon method.

Solution

A suitable scale might be 20 mi = 1 cm, as in Fig. 2-11. Using this scale, we note that

$$100 \text{ mi} = 100 \text{ mi} \times \frac{1 \text{ cm}}{20 \text{ mi}} = 5 \text{ cm}$$

$$60 \text{ mi} = 60 \text{ mi} \times \frac{1 \text{ cm}}{20 \text{ mi}} = 3 \text{ cm}$$

$$120 \text{ mi} = 120 \text{ mi} \times \frac{1 \text{ cm}}{20 \text{ mi}} = 6 \text{ cm}$$

By measuring with a ruler, we find from the scale diagram that the arrow for the resultant is 10.8 cm long. Therefore, the magnitude is

$$10.8 \text{ cm} = 10.8 \text{ cm} \times \frac{20 \text{ mi}}{1 \text{ cm}} = 216 \text{ mi}$$

Fig. 2-11 The polygon method of vector addition.

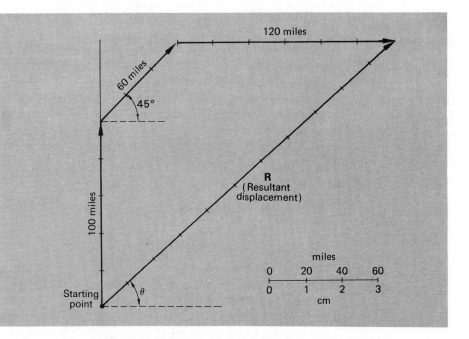

Measuring the angle θ with a protractor shows the direction to be 41°. The resultant displacement is therefore

$$\mathbf{R} = (216 \text{ mi}, 41°)$$

Note that the order in which the vectors are added does not change the resultant in any way. We could have begun with any of the three distances traveled by the ship.

The polygon method can be summarized as follows:

1. **Choose a scale and determine the length of the arrows which correspond to each vector.**
2. **Draw to scale an arrow representing the magnitude and direction of the first vector.**
3. **Draw the arrow of the second vector so that its tail is joined to the tip of the first vector.**
4. **Continue the process of joining tail to tip until the magnitude and direction of all vectors have been represented.**
5. **Draw the resultant vector with its tail at the origin (starting point) and its tip joined to the tip of the last vector.**
6. **Measure with ruler and protractor to determine the magnitude and direction of the resultant.**

Graphical methods can be used to find the resultant of all kinds of vectors. They are not restricted to measuring displacement. In the next example we determine the resultant of two *forces* by the parallelogram method.

In the parallelogram method, which is useful only for two vectors at a time, these vectors are drawn to scale with their tails at a common origin (see Fig. 2-12). The two arrows then form two adjoining sides of a parallelogram.

Fig. 2-12 The parallelogram method of vector addition.

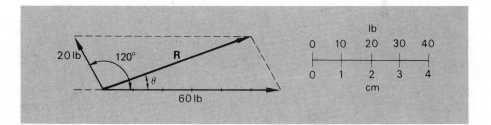

The other two sides are constructed by drawing parallel lines of equal length. The resultant is represented by the diagonal of the parallelogram included between the two vector arrows.

EXAMPLE 2-4 A rope is wrapped around a telephone pole, making an angle of 120°. If one end is pulled with a force of 60 lb and the other with a force of 20 lb, what is the resultant force on the telephone pole?

Solution

Using a scale of 1 cm = 10 lb gives

$$60 \text{ lb} \times \frac{1 \text{ cm}}{10 \text{ lb}} = 6 \text{ cm}$$

$$20 \text{ lb} \times \frac{1 \text{ cm}}{10 \text{ lb}} = 2 \text{ cm}$$

A parallelogram is constructed in Fig. 2-12 by drawing the two forces to scale from a common origin with 120° between them. Completing the parallelogram allows the resultant to be drawn as a diagonal from the origin. Measurement of R and θ with a ruler and protractor gives 53 lb for the magnitude and 19° for the direction. Hence,

$$\mathbf{R} = (53 \text{ lb}, 19°)$$

**2-8
FORCE AND
VECTORS**

A push or pull that tends to cause motion is called a *force*. A stretched spring exerts forces on the objects to which its ends are attached; compressed air exerts forces on the walls of its container; and a tractor exerts a force on the trailer it is pulling. Probably the most familiar force is the force of gravitational attraction exerted on every body by the earth. This force is called the *weight* of the body. A definite force exists even though there is no contact between the earth and the bodies it attracts. Weight is a vector quantity that is directed toward the center of the earth.

The SI unit of force is the *newton* (N). Its relationship to the U.S. customary unit, the *pound* (lb), is

$$1 \text{ N} = 0.225 \text{ lb} \qquad 1 \text{ lb} = 4.45 \text{ N}$$

A 120-lb woman has a weight of 534 N. If the weight of a pipe wrench is 20 N, it would weigh about 4.5 lb in USCS units. Until all industries have converted completely to SI units, the pound will still be with us, and frequent conversions are necessary.

Two of the measurable effects of forces are (1) changing the dimensions or shape of a body and (2) changing a body's motion. If in the first case there is no resultant displacement of the body, the push or pull causing the change in shape is called a *static force*. If a force changes the motion of a body, it is called a *dynamic force*. Both types of forces are conveniently represented by vectors, as in Example 2-4.

The effectiveness of any force depends on the direction in which it acts. For example, it is easier to pull a sled along the ground with an inclined rope, as shown in Fig. 2-13, than to push it. In each case, the applied force is pro-

Fig. 2-13 The force **F** acting at an angle θ can be replaced by its horizontal and vertical components.

ducing more than a single effect. That is, the pull on the cord is both lifting the sled and moving it forward. Similarly, pushing the sled would have the effect of adding to the weight of the sled. We are thus led to the idea of *components* of a force, i.e., the effective values of a force in directions other than that of the force itself. In Fig. 2-13, the force **F** can be replaced by its horizontal and vertical components $\mathbf{F}_x$ and $\mathbf{F}_y$.

If a force is represented graphically by its magnitude and an angle (R, θ), its components along the x and y directions can be determined. A force **F** acting at an angle θ above the horizontal is drawn in Fig. 2-14. The meaning

Fig. 2-14 Graphical representation of x and y components of **F**.

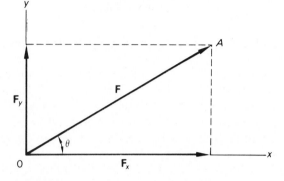

of the x and y components, $\mathbf{F}_x$ and $\mathbf{F}_y$, can be seen in this diagram. The segment from O to the perpendicular dropped from A to the x axis is called the x component of **F** and is labeled $\mathbf{F}_x$. The segment from O to the perpendicular line from A to the y axis is called the y component of **F** and is labeled $\mathbf{F}_y$. By drawing the vectors to scale, we can determine the magnitudes of the components graphically. These two components acting together would have the same effect as the original force **F**.

EXAMPLE 2-5

A lawn mower is pushed downward with a force of 40 N at an angle of 50° with the horizontal. What is the magnitude of the horizontal effect of this force?

Solution

A sketch is drawn, as in Fig. 2-15a, to translate the word problem into a picture. This approach often aids in understanding the problem. The 40-N force is transmitted through the handle to the body of the lawn mower. A vector diagram is shown in Fig. 2-15b. A ruler and protractor are used to draw the diagram accurately. A scale of 1 cm = 10 N is convenient for this example. The horizontal effect of the 40-N force is the x component, as labeled in the figure. Measurement of this line segment gives

$$\mathbf{F}_x = 2.57 \text{ cm}$$

Since 1 cm = 10 N, we obtain

$$\mathbf{F}_x = 2.57 \text{ cm} \frac{10 \text{ N}}{1 \text{ cm}} = 25.7 \text{ N}$$

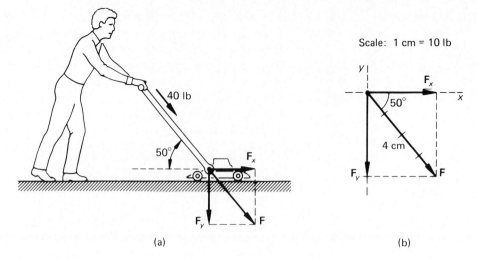

(a)   (b)

Notice that the effective force is quite a bit less than the applied force. As an additional exercise, you should show that the magnitude of the *downward* component of the 40-N force is $\mathbf{F}_y = 30.6$ N.

2-9
THE RESULTANT FORCE

When two or more forces act at the same point on an object, they are said to be *concurrent forces*. The combined effect of such forces is called the *resultant force*.

> *The **resultant force** is that single force which will produce the same effect in both magnitude and direction as two or more concurrent forces.*

Resultant forces may be calculated graphically by representing each concurrent force as a vector. The polygon or parallelogram method of vector addition will then give the resultant force.

Often forces act in the same line, either together or in opposition to each other. If two forces act on a single object in the same direction, the resultant force is equal to the sum of the magnitudes of the forces. The direction of the resultant would be the same as that of either force. Consider, for example, a 15-N force and a 20-N force acting in the same easterly direction. Their resultant is 35 N, E, as demonstrated in Fig. 2-16a.

If the same two forces act in opposite directions, the magnitude of the resultant force is equal to the *difference* of the magnitudes of the two forces, and it acts in the direction of the larger force. Suppose the 15-N force in our example were changed so that it pulled to the west. As seen in Fig. 2-16b, the resultant would be 5 N, E.

If forces act at an angle between 0 and 180° to each other, their resultant is the vector sum. The polygon method or the parallelogram method of vector addition may be used to find the resultant force. In Fig. 2-16c, our two forces of 15 and 20 N act at an angle of 60° with each other. The resultant force, calculated by the parallelogram method, is found to be 30.4 N at 34.7°.

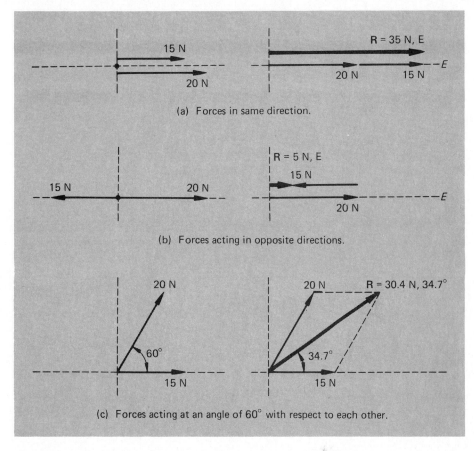

Fig. 2-16 The effect of direction on the resultant of two forces.

(a) Forces in same direction.

(b) Forces acting in opposite directions.

(c) Forces acting at an angle of 60° with respect to each other.

2-10 TRIGO-NOMETRY AND VECTORS

Graphical treatments of vectors are good for visualizing forces, but they are usually not very accurate. A much more useful approach is to take advantage of simple right-triangle trigonometry, and today's calculators have simplified the process considerably. A brief review is provided in App. A-4 for those who feel such a review is necessary. Familiarity with the *pythagorean theorem* and some experience with the *sine*, *cosine*, and *tangent* functions is all you will need for this unit of study.

Trigonometric methods can improve your accuracy and speed in determining the resultant vector or in finding the components of a vector. In most cases, it is helpful to use imaginary x and y axes when working with vectors in an analytical way. Any vector can then be drawn with its tail at the center of these imaginary lines. Components of the vector might be seen as effects along the x or y axis.

EXAMPLE 2-6

What are the x and y components of a force of 200 N at an angle of 60°?

Solution

A diagram is drawn placing the tail of the 200-N vector at the center of the x and y axes (see Fig. 2-17).

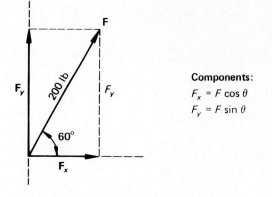

Fig. 2-17 Using trigonometry to find the x and y components of a vector.

Components:
$F_x = F \cos \theta$
$F_y = F \sin \theta$

We first compute the x component, F_x, by noting that it is the side adjacent. The 200-N vector is the hypotenuse. Using the cosine function, we obtain

$$\cos 60° = \frac{F_x}{200 \text{ N}}$$

from which

$$F_x = (200 \text{ N}) \cos 60° = 100 \text{ N}$$

For purposes of calculation, we recognize that the side opposite to 60° is equal in length to F_y. Thus, we may write

$$\sin 60° = \frac{F_y}{200 \text{ N}}$$

or

$$F_y = (200 \text{ N}) \sin 60° = 173.2 \text{ N}$$

In general we may write the x and y components of a vector in terms of its magnitude F and direction θ:

$$\boxed{\begin{aligned} \mathbf{F}_x &= F \cos \theta \\ \mathbf{F}_y &= F \sin \theta \end{aligned}}$$
  Components of a Vector (2-1)

where θ is the angle between the vector and the positive x axis, measured in a counterclockwise direction.

The sign of a given component can be determined from a vector diagram. The four possibilities are shown in Fig. 2-18. The magnitude of the component can be found by using the small angle ϕ when angle θ is greater than 90°.

Fig. 2-18 (a) In the first quadrant, the angle θ is between 0 and 90°; both F_x and F_y are positive. (b) In the second quadrant, the angle θ is between 90 and 180°; F_x is negative and F_y is positive. (c) In the third quadrant, the angle θ is between 180 and 270°; both F_x and F_y are negative. (d) In the fourth quadrant, the angle θ is between 270 and 360°; F_x is positive and F_y is negative.

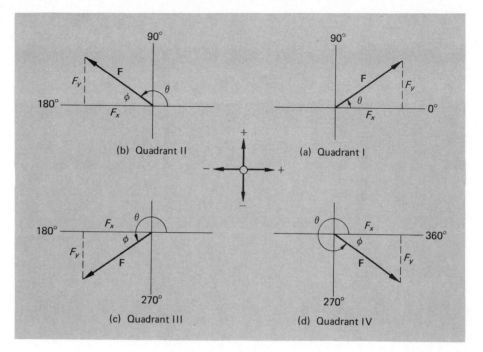

(b) Quadrant II

(a) Quadrant I

(c) Quadrant III

(d) Quadrant IV

EXAMPLE 2-7

Find the x and y components of a 400-N force at an angle of 220° from the positive x axis.

Solution

Refer to Fig. 2-18c, which describes this problem when $\theta = 220°$. The small angle ϕ is found by reference to 180°.

$$\phi = 220° - 180° = 40°$$

From the figure, both F_x and F_y will be negative.

$$F_x = -|F \cos \phi| = -(400 \text{ N}) \cos 40°$$

$$= -(400 \text{ N})(0.766) = -306 \text{ N}$$

$$F_y = -|F \sin \phi| = -(400 \text{ N}) \sin 40°$$

$$= -(400 \text{ N})(0.643) = -257 \text{ N}$$

Note that the signs were determined from the figure. With many electronic calculators, both the magnitude and the sign of $\mathbf{F}_x$ and $\mathbf{F}_y$ can be found directly from Eq. (2-1) using $\theta = 220°$. You should verify this fact.

Trigonometry is also useful in calculating the resultant force. In the special case for two forces $\mathbf{F}_x$ and $\mathbf{F}_y$ at right angles to each other, as in Fig. 2-19, the resultant (R, θ) may be found from

$$R = \sqrt{F_x^2 + F_y^2} \qquad \tan \theta = \frac{F_y}{F_x} \tag{2-2}$$

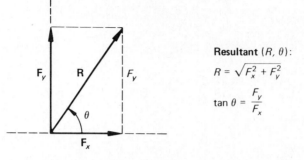

Fig. 2-19 The resultant of two perpendicular vectors.

Resultant (R, θ):

$$R = \sqrt{F_x^2 + F_y^2}$$

$$\tan \theta = \frac{F_y}{F_x}$$

If either F_x or F_y is negative, it is usually easier to determine the small angle ϕ, as described in Fig. 2-18. The sign (or direction) of the forces F_x and F_y determines which of the four quadrants is used. Then, Eq. (2-2) becomes

$$\tan \phi = \left| \frac{F_y}{F_x} \right|$$

Only the absolute values of F_x and F_y are needed. If desired, the angle θ from the positive x axis may be determined. In any case, the direction must be clearly identified.

EXAMPLE 2-8

What is the resultant of a 5-N force directed horizontally to the right and a 12-N force directed vertically downward?

Solution

Label the two forces $F_x = 5$ N and $F_y = -12$ N (downward). Draw a diagram for the situation described by Fig. 2-18d. The magnitude of the resultant R is found from Eq. (2-2)

$$R = \sqrt{F_x^2 + F_y^2} = \sqrt{(5 \text{ N})^2 + (-12 \text{ N})^2}$$

$$= \sqrt{25 \text{ N}^2 + 144 \text{ N}^2} = \sqrt{169 \text{ N}^2} = 13 \text{ N}$$

To find the direction of R, we first find the small angle ϕ:

$$\tan \phi = \left| \frac{-12 \text{ N}}{5 \text{ N}} \right| = 2.4$$

$$\phi = 67.4° \text{ below positive } x \text{ axis}$$

The angle θ measured counterclockwise from the positive x axis is

$$\theta = 360° - 67.4° = 292.6°$$

The resultant force is 13 N at 292.6°.

2-11
THE COM-
PONENT
METHOD OF
VECTOR
ADDITION

Often a body is acted on by a number of forces having different magnitudes, directions, and points of application. Forces which intersect at a common point or have the same point of application are said to be *concurrent* forces. When such forces are not at right angles with each other, calculating the resultant can be more difficult. The vectors would not fall along either the x or the y axis in all cases. The component method of addition of vectors is needed for these more general cases. Consider the vectors **A**, **B**, and **C** in Fig. 2-20. The resultant

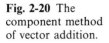

Fig. 2-20 The component method of vector addition.

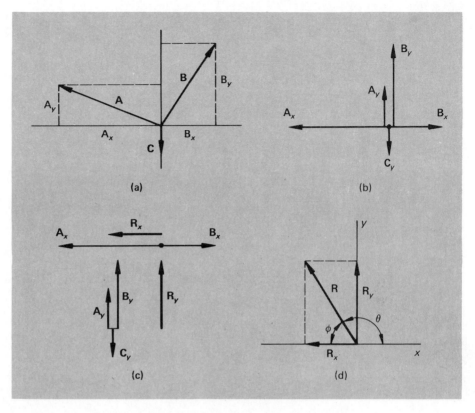

R is the vector sum **A** + **B** + **C**. However, **A** and **B** are not along an axis and cannot be added in the usual manner. The following procedure may be used:

1. Draw each vector from the center of imaginary x and y axes.
2. Find the x and y components of each vector.
3. Find the x component of the resultant by adding the x components of all vectors. (Components to the right are positive and those to the left are negative.)

$$R_x = A_x + B_x + C_x$$

4. Find the y component of the resultant by adding the y components of all vectors. (Upward components are positive and downward components are negative.)

$$R_y = A_y + B_y + C_y$$

5. Find the magnitude and direction of the resultant from its perpendicular components R_x and R_y.

$$R = \sqrt{R_x^2 + R_y^2} \qquad \tan \phi = \frac{R_y}{R_x}$$

The above steps are shown graphically in Fig. 2-20.

EXAMPLE 2-9   Three ropes are tied to a stake, and the following forces are exerted: $\mathbf{A} = 20$ lb, E; $\mathbf{B} = 30$ lb, 30°N of W; and $\mathbf{C} = 40$ lb, 52°S of W. Determine the resultant force.

Solution   Follow the steps described above.

1. Draw a figure representing each force (Fig. 2-21a). Two things should be noticed from the figure: (a) all angles are determined from the x axis, and (b) the components of each vector are labeled opposite and adjacent to known angles.

Fig. 2-21 Calculating the x and y components of all vectors.

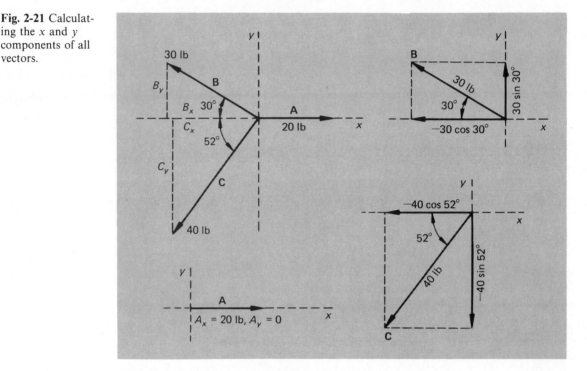

2. Find the x and y components of each vector. (Refer to Fig. 2-21b, c, and d.) Note that the force A has no y component. Care must be taken to obtain the correct sign for each component. For example, B_x, C_x, and C_y are each negative. The results are listed in Table 2-5.

Table 2-5 A Table of Components

Force	ϕ_x	x component	y component
$A = 20$ lb	0°	$A_x = 20$ lb	$A_y = 0$
$B = 30$ lb	30°	$B_x = -(30 \text{ lb})(\cos 30°)$	$B_y = (30 \text{ lb})(\sin 30°)$
		$= -26.0$ lb	$= 15$ lb
$C = 40$ lb	52°	$C_x = -(40 \text{ lb})(\cos 52°)$	$C_y = (-40 \text{ lb})(\sin 52°)$
		$= -24.6$ lb	$= -31.5$ lb
		$R_x = \sum F_x = -30.6$ lb	$R_y = \sum F_y = -16.5$ lb

3. Add the x components to obtain R_x.

$$R_x = A_x + B_x + C_x$$

$$= 20 \text{ lb} - 26 \text{ lb} - 24.6 \text{ lb} = -30.6 \text{ lb}$$

4. Add the y components to obtain R_y.

$$R_y = A_y + B_y + C_y$$

$$= 0 + 15 \text{ lb} - 31.5 \text{ lb} = -16.5$$

5. Now we find R and θ from R_x and R_y (see Fig. 2-22)

$$R = \sqrt{R_x^2 + R_y^2} = \sqrt{(-30.6)^2 + (-16.5)^2}$$

$$= \sqrt{936.4 + 272.2} = 34.8 \text{ lb}$$

$$\tan \phi = \left| \frac{R_y}{R_x} \right| = \left| \frac{-16.5}{-30.6} \right| = 0.539$$

$$\phi = 28.3°\text{S of E (or } 208.3°)$$

Thus, the resultant force is 34.8 lb at 28.3°S of E.

Fig. 2-22

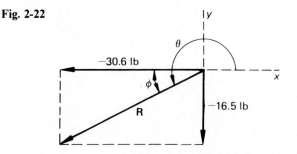

2-12 VECTOR DIFFERENCE

When we study relative velocity, acceleration, and certain other quantities, we must be able to find the difference of two vector quantities. The difference between two vectors is obtained by adding one vector to the negative of the other. The negative of a vector is found by constructing a vector equal in magnitude but opposite in direction. For example, if **A** is a vector whose magnitude is 40 m and whose direction is east, then the vector −**A** is a displacement of 40 m directed to the west. Just as we have in algebra that

$$a - b = a + (-b)$$

we have in vector subtraction that

$$\mathbf{A} - \mathbf{B} = \mathbf{A} + (-\mathbf{B})$$

The process of subtracting vectors is illustrated in Fig. 2-23. The given vectors are shown in Fig. 2-23a; Fig. 2-23b shows the vectors **A** and −**B**. The vector sum by the polygon method is pictured in Fig. 2-23c.

Fig. 2-23 Finding the difference of two vectors.

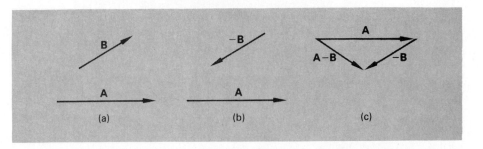

(a)   (b)   (c)

SUMMARY

Technical measurement is essential for the application of physics. You have learned that there are seven fundamental quantities and that each has a single approved SI unit. In mechanics, the three fundamental quantities of length, mass, and time are the only ones required for most applications. Some of these applications involve *vectors* and some involve *scalars*. Since vector quantities have direction, they must be added and subtracted by special methods. The following points summarize this unit of study:

- The SI prefixes used to express multiples and subdivisions of the base units are given below:

giga (G) = 10^9	centi (c) = 10^{-2}	nano (n) = 10^{-9}
mega (M) = 10^6	milli (m) = 10^{-3}	pico (p) = 10^{-12}
kilo (k) = 10^3	micro (μ) = 10^{-6}	

- To convert one unit to another,
  a. Write down the quantity to be converted (number and unit).
  b. Recall the necessary definitions.
  c. Form two conversion factors for each definition.
  d. Multiply the quantity to be converted by those conversion factors which cancel all but the desired units.
- The **polygon method** of vector addition: The **resultant** vector is found by drawing each vector to scale, placing the tail of one vector to the tip of another until all vectors are drawn. The resultant is the straight line drawn from the starting point to the tip of the last vector (Fig. 2-24).

Fig. 2-24

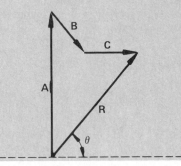

- The **parallelogram method** of vector addition: The resultant of two vectors is the diagonal of a parallelogram formed by the two vectors as adjacent sides. The direction is away from the common origin of the two vectors (Fig. 2-25).

Fig. 2-25

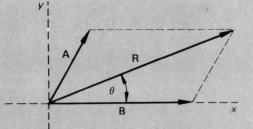

- The x and y **components** of a vector (R, θ):

$$R_x = R \cos \theta \qquad R_y = R \sin \theta$$

- The **resultant** of two perpendicular vectors (R_x, R_y):

$$R = \sqrt{R_x^2 + R_y^2} \qquad \tan \phi = \frac{R_y}{R_x}$$

- The **component method** of vector addition:

$$R_x = A_x + B_x + C_x + \cdots \qquad R_y = A_y + B_y + C_y + \cdots$$

$$R = \sqrt{R_x^2 + R_y^2} \qquad \tan \phi = \frac{R_y}{R_x}.$$

QUESTIONS

2-1. Define the following terms:
   a. fundamental quantity
   b. SI units
   c. conversion factor
   d. dimensions
   e. vector quantity
   f. scalar quantity
   g. components
   h. resultant vector
   i. concurrent forces
   j. polygon method
   k. parallelogram method
   l. component method

2-2. Express the following measurements in proper SI form using the appropriate prefixes. The symbol for the base unit is given in parentheses:
   a. 298,000 meters (m)
   b. 7600 volts (V)
   c. 0.000067 amperes (A)
   d. 0.0645 newtons (N)
   e. 43,000,000 grams (g)
   f. 0.00000065 farads (F)

2-3. What three fundamental quantities appear in the definition of most laws of mechanics? Name the three fundamental units associated with each quantity in the SI and USCS units.

2-4. A unit of specific heat capacity is cal/g · C°. How many definitions are needed to convert these units to their corresponding units in the USCS, where the units are Btu/lb · F°? Show by a series of products how you would perform such a conversion.

2-5. Given that the units of s, v, a, and t are meters (m), meters per second (m/s), meters per second squared (m/s^2), and second (s), respectively, what are the dimensions of each quantity? Accept or reject the following equations on the basis of dimensional analysis:

a. $s = vt + \frac{1}{2}at^2$ **c.** $v_f = v_0 + at^2$

b. $2as = v_f^2 - v_0^2$ **d.** $s = vt + 4at^2$

2-6. Distinguish between vector and scalar quantities, and give examples of each. Explain the difference between adding vectors and adding scalars. Is it possible for the sum of two vectors to have a magnitude less than either of the original vectors?

2-7. What are the minimum and maximum resultants of two forces of 10 N and 7 N if they act on the same object?

2-8. Look up a section on rectangular and polar coordinates in a math book. What are the similarities between components of a vector and the rectangular and polar coordinates of a point?

2-9. If a vector has a direction of 230° from the positive x axis, what are the signs of its x and y components? If the ratio R_y/R_x is negative, what are the possible angles for R as measured from the positive x axis?

PROBLEMS

2-1. Perform the following conversions:

a. 28.3 cm to meters

b. 90,500 mg to kilograms

c. 367 mi/h to feet per second

d. 875 mi to kilometers

e. 86 mm to kilometers

f. 470,000 mm to inches

g. 16 cm^2 to square meters

h. 300 ft^3 to cubic meters

i. 55 mi/h to kilometers per hour

j. 240 mm/s to meters per minute

Ans. **(a)** 0.283 m **(b)** 9.05×10^{-2} kg **(c)** 538 ft/s **(d)** 1408 km **(e)** 86,000 km **(f)** 1.85×10^4 in. **(g)** 1.6×10^{-3} m^2 **(h)** 8.50 m^3 **(i)** 88.5 km/h **(j)** 14.4 m/min.

2-2. An electrician must install an underground cable from the highway to a home. If the home is located 1.2 mi into the woods, how many feet of cable will be needed? How many meters?

2-3. A Datsun engine has a piston displacement (volume) of 1595 cm^3 and a bore diameter of 83 mm. Express these measurements in cubic inches and in inches. *Ans.* 97.3 in.^{3}, 3.27 in.

2-4. A unit commonly used to measure cross sections of wire is the square mil, where 1 mil = 0.001 in. The diameter of 16-gauge electrical wire is 50.82 mils. What is the cross section (area) of this wire in square inches? In square millimeters?

2-5. One U.S. gallon is a volume equivalent to 231 in.^{3}. Suppose a gasoline tank in an automobile is roughly equivalent to a rectangular solid 24 in. long, 18 in. wide, and 12 in. high. How many gallons will this tank hold? *Ans.* 22.4 gal.

2-6. A woman weighs 130 lb and is 5 ft and 9 in. tall. Express her weight and height in newtons and in meters.

2-7. A large block of metal weighing 600 N causes a wooden beam to sag 2 cm at its midpoint. Express these measurements in pounds and in inches.

Ans. 135 N, 0.787 in.

2-8. The outside dimensions of a freezer are listed as $65\frac{7}{8}$ by $29\frac{3}{4}$ by $30\frac{1}{8}$ inches. What is the volume of space occupied by the freezer in cubic feet and in liters (L)? (1 L = 1000 cm^3.)

2-9. Atmospheric pressure is listed at 14.7 lb/in.^{2}. The SI unit for pressure is pascals (Pa) where 1 Pa = 1 N/m^2. What is atmospheric pressure in pascals?

Ans. 1.014×10^5 Pa.

2-10. The density of a material is its mass per unit volume. Convert a density of 125 g/cm^3 to kilograms per cubic meter.

2-11. A boat sails 200 km west, then 500 km south. Represent each of these displacements as a vector, choosing a scale of 1 cm = 50 km. Construct a parallelogram, and using a ruler and protractor show that the resultant displacement is 539 km at an angle of 68.2° S of W (248.2°).

2-12. A motorboat heads straight across a river at a speed of 20 km/h. The river current flows parallel to the bank at a speed of 16 km/h. Represent each of these velocities as a vector. Draw the river-speed vector first (to scale) along a horizontal *x* axis. Now, using the polygon method of vector addition, draw in the boat-speed vector. What is the resultant speed of the boat (vector sum)? What angle does the boat make with the river bank as it crosses?

2-13. What are the horizontal and vertical components of **(a)** a 600-N force directed 41° S of E? **(b)** a 520-m displacement directed 110° from the positive *x* axis?

Ans. **(a)** 453 N, −394 N **(b)** −178 m, 489 m.

2-14. Determine the *x* and *y* components of the following vectors: **(a)** 360 N at 35° N of W; **(b)** 240 km/h at 320°; and **(c)** 730 m, 210°.

2-15. An upward lift of 80 N is required to raise a window. What force exerted along a pole, making an angle of 34° with the wall, is needed to raise the window?

Ans. 96.5 N.

2-16. A team of surveyors mark off successive displacements of **A** = (80 m, 60°), **B** = (40 m, 0°), and **C** = (20 m, 330°). Determine the resultant displacement by the polygon method.

2-17. Find the resultant of the following forces by the polygon method: **A** = (450 N, 150°); **B** = (200 N, 270°); and **C** = (300 N, 320°).

Ans. 232 N, 226°.

2-18. An engine is held from the ceiling by two ropes. Rope *A* exerts a 60-lb force and rope *B* exerts a 90-lb force. The angle between the two ropes is 35°. The resultant of these forces is the weight of the engine. Find the weight by the polygon method or by the parallelogram method.

2-19. Find the resultant force **R** = **A** + **B** by any method when **(a)** **A** = (520 N, south) and **B** = (260 N, west); **(b)** **A** = (18 m/s, north) and **B** = (15 m/s, west).

Ans. **(a)** 581 N, 243.4° **(b)** 23.4 N, 129.8°.

2-20. In removing a nail, a force of 260 lb is applied by a hammer in the direction shown in Fig. 2-26. What are the horizontal and vertical components of this force?

Fig. 2-26

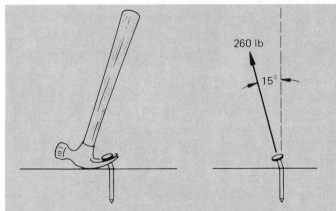

2-21. A force of 60 lb is exerted along the handle of a lawn mower which makes an angle of 40° with the ground. What is the effective horizontal push? What must the force be if the horizontal force needs to be increased to 50 lb?

Ans. 46 lb, 65.3 lb.

2-22. Find the resultant of the following perpendicular forces: **(a) A** = (400 N, 0°) and **B** = (820 N, 270°); **(b) A** = (650 N, 180°) and **B** = (500 N, 90°).

2-23. A chain is wrapped around the bumper of an automobile, and forces of 400 N and 280 N are exerted at right angles to each other. What is the magnitude of the resultant force?

Ans. 488 N.

2-24. A rope is tied to the edge of a large box. What force at an angle of 38° with the horizontal will produce an effective upward pull of 80 lb?

2-25. Determine the resultant force on the bolt in Fig. 2-27.

Ans. 69.6 lb, 154.1°.

Fig. 2-27

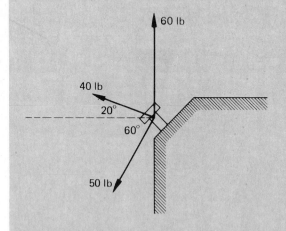

2-26. A boat heads directly across a stream with a velocity of 20 km/h. The current perpendicular to the bank is 15 km/h. What is the resulting direction and speed of the boat?

2-27. In Fig. 2-28, what force F at what angle θ is needed to pull the car directly east with a resultant force of 400 lb?

Ans. 223 lb, 17.9°.

Fig. 2-28

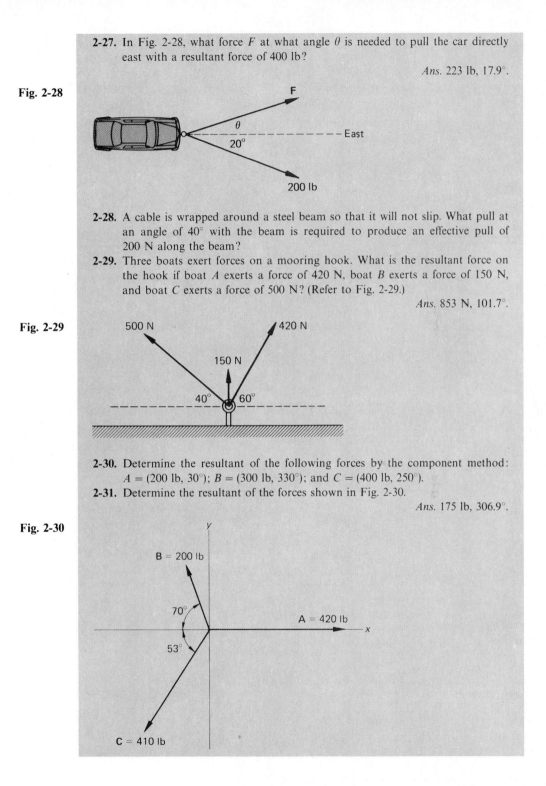

2-28. A cable is wrapped around a steel beam so that it will not slip. What pull at an angle of 40° with the beam is required to produce an effective pull of 200 N along the beam?

2-29. Three boats exert forces on a mooring hook. What is the resultant force on the hook if boat A exerts a force of 420 N, boat B exerts a force of 150 N, and boat C exerts a force of 500 N? (Refer to Fig. 2-29.)

Ans. 853 N, 101.7°.

Fig. 2-29

2-30. Determine the resultant of the following forces by the component method: $A = (200 \text{ lb}, 30°)$; $B = (300 \text{ lb}, 330°)$; and $C = (400 \text{ lb}, 250°)$.

2-31. Determine the resultant of the forces shown in Fig. 2-30.

Ans. 175 lb, 306.9°.

Fig. 2-30

2-32. Determine the resultant of the forces in Fig. 2-31.

Fig. 2-31

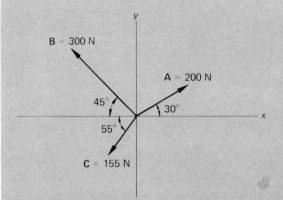

2-33. An airplane is trying to keep on a due west course toward an airport. The airspeed of this plane is 600 km/h. If the wind has a speed of 40 km/h and is blowing in a direction of 30° S of W, what direction should the aircraft be pointed and what will be its speed relative to the ground?

Ans. 1.9° N of W, 634 km/h.

2-34. Compute the resultant of the following forces: 220 lb, 60°; 125 lb, 210°; and 175 lb, 340°.

2-35. A force table is a laboratory apparatus with a circular top graduated from 0 to 360°. Weights **A**, **B**, and **C** are suspended from pulleys attached to the edge of the table at various angles. Determine the resultant (R, θ) for each case:

a. $A = 10$ N at 0° $B = 30$ N at 120° $C = 20$ N at 323°
b. $A = 20$ N at 0° $B = 30$ N at 225° $C = 10$ N at 300°
c. $A = 20$ N at 0° $B = 10$ N at 127° $C = 30$ N at 225°
d. $A = 20$ N at 0° $B = 30$ N at 150° $C = 15$ N at 233°

Ans. **(a)** 17.8 N, 51.8° **(b)** 30.1 N, 277.2° **(c)** 15.1 N, 241.3° **(d)** 15.3 N, 168.7°.

3

Translational Equilibrium

OBJECTIVES: After completing this chapter, you should be able to:

1. **Demonstrate by example or experiment your understanding of Newton's first and third laws of motion.**

2. **State the first condition for equilibrium, give a physical example, and demonstrate graphically that the first condition is satisfied.**

3. **Construct a free-body diagram representing all forces acting on an object which is in translational equilibrium.**

4. **Solve for unknown forces by applying the first condition for equilibrium.**

5. **Apply your understanding of kinetic and static friction to the solution of equilibrium problems.**

Forces may act in such a manner as to cause motion or to prevent motion. Large bridges must be designed so that the overall effect of forces is to prevent motion. Every truss, girder, beam, and cable must be in *equilibrium*. In other words, the resultant forces acting at any point on the entire structure must be balanced. Shelves, chain hoists, hooks, lifting cables, and even large buildings must be constructed so that the effects of forces are controlled and understood. In this chapter we will continue our study of forces by studying objects at rest. The friction force which is so essential for equilibrium in many applications will also be introduced in this chapter as a natural extension of our work with all forces.

**3-1
NEWTON'S
FIRST LAW**

We know from experience that a stationary object remains at rest unless acted on by some outside force. A can of oil will stay on a workbench until someone tips it over. A suspended weight will hang until it is released. We know that forces are necessary to cause anything to move if it is originally at rest.

Less obvious is the fact that an object in motion will continue in motion until an outside force changes the motion. For example, a steel bar that slides on the shop floor soon comes to rest because of its interaction with the floor. The same bar would slide much farther on ice before stopping. This is because the horizontal interaction, called *friction*, between the floor and the bar is much greater than the friction between the ice and the bar. This leads to the idea that a sliding bar on a perfectly frictionless horizontal plane would stay in motion forever. These ideas are a part of Newton's first law of motion.

Newton's First Law: *A body at rest remains at rest and a body in motion remains in uniform motion in a straight line unless acted on by an external unbalanced force.*

Due to the existence of friction, no actual body is ever completely free from external forces. But there are situations in which it is possible to make the resultant force zero or approximately zero. In such cases, the body will behave in accordance with the first law of motion. Since we recognize that friction can never be eliminated completely, we also recognize that Newton's first law is an expression of an *ideal* situation. A flywheel rotating on lubricated ball bearings tends to keep on spinning, but even the slightest friction will eventually bring it to rest.

Newton called the property of a particle that allows it to maintain a constant state of motion or rest *inertia*. His first law is sometimes called the *law of inertia*. When an automobile is accelerated, the passengers obey this law by tending to remain at rest until the external force of the seat compels them to move. Similarly, when the automobile stops, the passengers continue in motion with constant speed until they are restrained by their seat belts or through their own efforts. All matter has inertia. The concept of *mass* is introduced later as a measure of a body's inertia.

**3-2
NEWTON'S
THIRD LAW**

There can be no force unless two bodies are involved. When a hammer strikes a nail, it exerts an "action" force on the nail. But the nail must also "react" by pushing back against the hammer. In all cases there must be an *acting* force and a *reacting* force. Whenever two bodies interact, the force exerted by the second body on the first (the reaction force) is equal in magnitude and opposite in direction to the force exerted by the first body on the second (the action force). This principle is stated in *Newton's third law*:

Newton's Third Law: *To every action there must be an equal and opposite reaction.*

Therefore, there can never be a single isolated force. Consider the examples of action and reaction forces in Fig. 3-1.

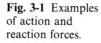 **Fig. 3-1** Examples of action and reaction forces.

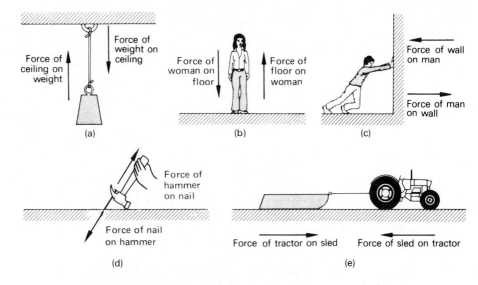

Note that the acting and reacting forces do not cancel each other. They are equal in magnitude and opposite in direction, but they act on *different* objects. For two forces to cancel, they must act on the same object. It might be said that the action forces create the reaction forces.

For example, someone starting to climb a ladder begins by putting one foot on the rung and pushing on it. The rung must exert an equal and opposite force on the foot if it is not to collapse. The greater the force exerted by the foot on the rung, the greater the reaction against the foot must be. Of course the rung cannot create a reaction force until the force of the foot is applied. The action force acts on the object, and the reacting force acts on the agent which applies the force.

**3-3
EQUILIBRIUM**

The resultant force was defined as a single force whose effect is the same as a given system of forces. If the tendency of a number of forces is to cause motion, the resultant will also produce this tendency. A condition of equilibrium exists where the resultant of all external forces is zero. This is the same as saying that each external force is balanced by the sum of all the other external forces when equilibrium exists. Therefore, according to Newton's first law, a body in equilibrium must be either at rest or in motion with constant velocity since there is no unbalanced force.

Consider the system of forces in Fig. 3-2a. The vector polygon solution shows that regardless of the sequence in which the vectors are added, their resultant is always zero. The tip of the last vector lands on the tail of the first vector (see Sec. 2-7).

A system of forces not in equilibrium can be put in equilibrium by replacing their resultant force with an equal but opposite force called the *equili-*

Fig. 3-2 Forces in equilibrium.

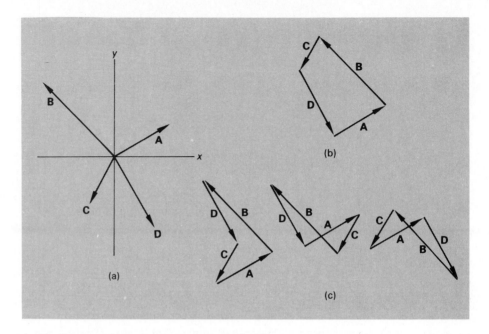

brant. For instance, the two forces **A** and **B** in Fig. 3-3*a* have a resultant **R** in a direction 30° above the horizontal. If we add **E**, which is equal in magnitude to **R** but which has an angle 180° greater, the system will be in equilibrium, as shown in Fig. 3-3*b*.

We have shown in the previous chapter that the magnitudes of the *x* and *y* components of any resultant **R** are given by

$$R_x = \sum F_x = A_x + B_x + C_x + \cdots$$
$$R_y = \sum F_y = A_y + B_y + C_y + \cdots$$

Fig. 3-3 The equilibrant.

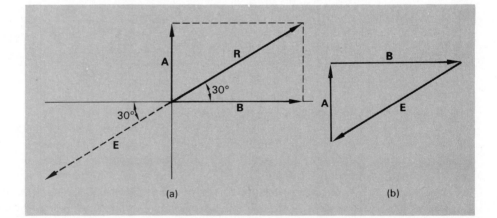

When a body is in equilibrium, the resultant of all forces acting on it is zero. In this case, both R_x and R_y must be zero; hence, for a body in equilibrium,

$$\boxed{\sum F_x = 0 \qquad \sum F_y = 0}$$ (3-1)

These two equations represent a mathematical statement of the *first condition for equilibrium*, which can be stated as follows:

> *A body is in translational equilibrium if and only if the vector sum of the forces acting upon it is zero.*

The term *translational equilibrium* is used to distinguish the first condition from the second condition for equilibrium, which involves rotational motion, discussed in Chap. 4.

3-4 FREE-BODY DIAGRAMS

Before applying the first condition for equilibrium to the solution of physical problems, you must be able to construct vector diagrams. Consider, for example, the 40-lb weight suspended by ropes shown in Fig. 3-4a. There are three forces acting on the knot—those exerted by the ceiling, by the wall, and by the earth (weight). If each of these forces is labeled and represented as a vector, we can draw a vector diagram such as the one in Fig. 3-4b. Such a diagram is called a *free-body diagram*.

Fig. 3-4 Free-body diagrams showing the action and reaction forces.

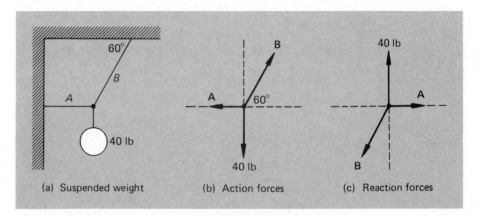

(a) Suspended weight (b) Action forces (c) Reaction forces

A **free-body diagram** is a vector diagram which describes all forces acting on a particular body or object. Note that in the case of concurrent forces, all vectors point away from the center of the x and y axes, which cross at a common origin.

In drawing free-body diagrams, it is important to distinguish between action and reaction forces. In our example, there are forces *on* the knot, but there are also three equal and opposite reaction forces exerted *by* the knot.

From Newton's third law, the reaction forces exerted *by* the knot *on* the ceiling, wall, and earth are shown in Fig. 3-4*c*. To avoid confusion, it is important to pick a point at which all forces are acting and draw those forces which act *on* the body at that point.

When solving equilibrium problems, we will find it useful to also indicate the components of forces on the vector diagram. A complete procedure for drawing a free-body diagram is as follows:

1. From the given conditions of a problem, draw a neat sketch representing the situation. Label it sufficiently to indicate all known and unknown forces.
2. Isolate each body of the system to be studied. Do this either mentally or by drawing a light circle around the point of application of the forces.
3. Construct a force diagram for each body to be studied. The forces are represented as vectors with their tails placed at the center of a rectangular coordinate system. (See examples in Figs. 3-5 and 3-7.)
4. Represent the *x* and *y* axes with dotted lines. These axes need not necessarily be drawn horizontally and vertically, as we shall see.
5. Dot in rectangles corresponding to the *x* and *y* components of each vector, and determine known angles from given conditions.
6. Label all known and unknown components opposite and adjacent to known angles.

Although this process may appear laborious, it is helpful and sometimes necessary for a clear understanding of a problem. As you gain practice drawing free-body diagrams, their use will become routine.

The two types of forces which act on a body are *contact forces* and *field forces*. Both must be considered in the construction of a force diagram. For example, the gravitational attraction on a body by the earth, called its *weight*,

Fig. 3-5 (*a*) A sketch is drawn to clarify the problem. (*b*) A free-body diagram is constructed.

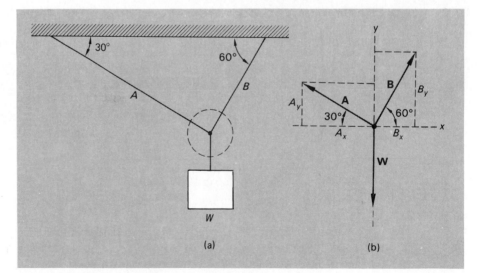

Fig. 3-6 Rotation of x and y axes to coincide with the perpendicular vectors **A** and **B**.

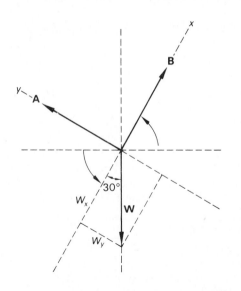

does not have a point of contact with the body. Nevertheless, it exerts a very real force and must be considered an important factor in any force problem. The direction of the weight vector should always be assumed to be downward.

EXAMPLE 3-1

A block of weight W hangs from a cord which is knotted to two other cords, A and B, fastened to the ceiling. If cord B makes an angle of 60° with the ceiling and cord A forms a 30° angle, draw the free-body diagram of the knot.

Solution

Following the procedure above, we construct the diagram shown in Fig. 3-5. This free-body diagram is valid and workable, but choosing the x and y axes along the vectors **B** and **A**, instead of horizontally and vertically, simplifies the diagram. Thus, in Fig. 3-6 we need only resolve one force **W** into components since **A** and **B** would now lie entirely along a particular axis.

Hint: Whenever possible choose x and y axes so that as many forces as possible are completely specified along them.

Probably the most difficult part of constructing vector diagrams is the visualization of forces. In drawing free-body diagrams, it is helpful to imagine that the forces are acting on *you*. Become the knot in a rope or the block on a table and try to see the forces you would experience. Two additional examples are shown in Fig. 3-7. Note that the force exerted by the light boom in Fig. 3-7a is outward and not toward the wall. This is because we are interested in forces exerted *on* the end of the boom and not those exerted *by* the end of the boom. We pick a point at the end of the boom where the two ropes are attached. The 60-N weight and the tension **T** are action forces exerted by the ropes at this point. If the end of the boom is not to move, these forces must be balanced by a third force—the force exerted by the wall (through the boom). This third force **B**, acting on the end of the boom, must not be confused with the inward reaction force which acts *on* the wall.

Fig. 3-7 Examples of free-body diagrams. Note that the components of vectors are labeled opposite and adjacent to known angles.

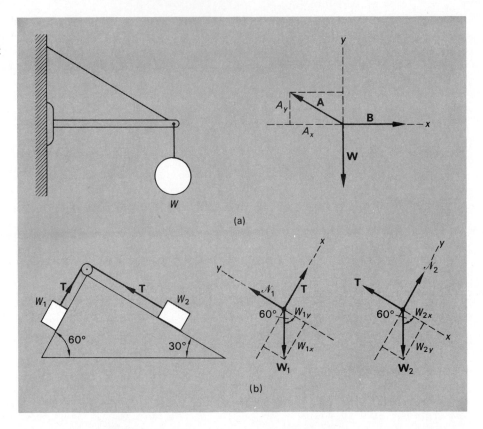

(a)

(b)

The second example (Fig. 3-7b) also shows action forces acting on two weights connected by a light cord. Friction forces, which are discussed later, are not included in these diagrams. The tension in the cord on either side is shown as T, and the normal forces $\mathcal{N}_1$ and $\mathcal{N}_2$ are perpendicular forces exerted by the plane on the blocks. If these forces were absent, the blocks would swing together. (Note the choice of axes in each diagram.)

3-5 SOLUTION OF EQUILIBRIUM PROBLEMS

In Chap. 2 we discussed a procedure for finding the resultant of a number of forces by rectangular resolution. A similar procedure can be used to add forces which are in equilibrium. In this case the first condition for equilibrium tells us that the resultant is zero, or

$$R_x = \sum F_x = 0 \qquad R_y = \sum F_y = 0 \qquad (3-2)$$

Thus we have two equations which can be used to find unknown forces.

The following steps should be followed in solving for unknown forces in equilibrium:

1. Sketch and label the conditions of the problem.
2. Draw a free-body diagram (Sec. 3-4).

3. Resolve all forces into their x and y components even though they may contain unknown factors, such as $A \cos 30°$ or $B \sin 45°$. (You may wish to construct a table of forces like Table 3-1.)
4. Use the first condition for equilibrium [Eq. (3-1)] to set up two equations in terms of the unknown forces.
5. Solve algebraically for the unknown factors.

Table 3-1

Force	θ_x	x component	y component
A	$60°$	$A_x = -A \cos 60°$	$A_y = A \sin 60°$
B	$0°$	$B_x = B$	$B_y = 0$
W	$-90°$	$W_x = 0$	$W_y = -100$ N
		$\sum F_x = B - A \cos 60°$	$\sum F_y = A \sin 60° - 100$ N

EXAMPLE 3-2

A 100-N ball suspended by a rope A is pulled aside by a horizontal rope B and held so that rope A forms an angle of $30°$ with the vertical wall. (See Fig. 3-8.) Find the tensions in ropes A and B.

Fig. 3-8 Forces acting on the knot are represented in a free-body diagram.

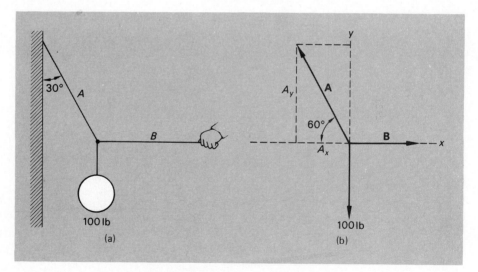

Solution

We solve by following the above steps illustrated in Fig. 3-8.

1. Draw a sketch. (Fig. 3-8a.)
2. Draw a free-body diagram. (Fig. 3-8b.)
3. Resolve all forces into their components (Table 3-1). Note from the figure that A_x and W_y are negative.

4. We now apply the first condition for equilibrium. Summing the forces along the x axis yields

$$\sum F_x = B - A \cos 60° = 0$$

from which we obtain

$$B = A \cos 60° = 0.5A \qquad (3\text{-}3)$$

since $\cos 60° = 0.5$. A second equation results from summing the y components.

$$\sum F_y = A \sin 60° - 100 \text{ N} = 0$$

from which

$$A \sin 60° = 100 \text{ N} \qquad (3\text{-}4)$$

5. Finally, we solve for the unknown forces. Since $\sin 60° = 0.866$, we have from Eq. (3-4)

$$0.866A = 100 \text{ N}$$

or

$$A = \frac{100 \text{ N}}{0.866} = 115 \text{ N}$$

Now that the value of A is known, Eq. (3-3) can be solved for B as follows:

$$B = 0.5A = (0.5)(115 \text{ N})$$

$$B = 57.5 \text{ N}$$

EXAMPLE 3-3   A 200-N ball hangs from a cord knotted to two other cords, as shown in Fig. 3-9. Find the tensions in ropes A, B, and C.

Fig. 3-9

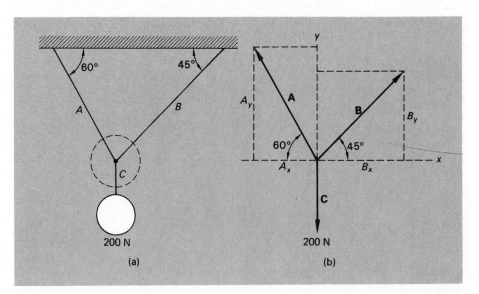

Solution
Since a sketch is already provided, the first step is to construct a free-body diagram, as illustrated in Fig. 3-9b. The x and y components for each vector as calculated from the figure are:

x component	y component
$A_x = -A \cos 60°$	$A_y = A \sin 60°$
$B_x = B \cos 45°$	$B_y = B \sin 45°$
$C_x = 0$	$C_y = -200$ N

Summing the forces along the x axis, we obtain

$$\sum F_x = -A \cos 60° + B \cos 45° = 0$$

which can be simplified by substituting known trigonometric functions. Hence

$$-0.5A + 0.707B = 0 \tag{3-5}$$

More information is needed to solve this equation. We obtain a second equation by summing the forces along the y axis giving

$$0.866A + 0.707B = 200 \text{ N} \tag{3-6}$$

Equations (3-4) and (3-5) are now solved simultaneously for A and B by the process of substitution. Solving for A in Eq. (3-4) gives

$$A = \frac{0.707B}{0.5} \quad \text{or} \quad A = 1.414B \tag{3-7}$$

Now we substitute this equality into Eq. (3-6) obtaining

$$0.866(1.414B) + 0.707B = 200 \text{ N}$$

which can be solved for B as follows:

$$1.225B + 0.707B = 200 \text{ N}$$

$$1.93B = 200 \text{ N}$$

$$B = \frac{200 \text{ N}}{1.93} = 104 \text{ N}$$

The tension A can now be found by substituting $B = 104$ N into Eq. (3-7):

$$A = 1.414(104 \text{ N}) = 147 \text{ N}$$

The tension in cord C is, of course, 200 N since it must be equal to the weight.

EXAMPLE 3-4
A 200-lb block rests on a frictionless inclined plane of slope angle 30°. A cord attached to the block passes over a frictionless pulley at the top of the plane and is attached to a second block. What must the weight of the second block be if the system is to be in equilibrium? (Neglect the weight of the cord.)

Solution After sketching the system, a free-body diagram is constructed for each body, as shown in Fig. 3-10. Applying the first condition for equilibrium to the second block (Fig. 3-10c), we find that

$$T - W = 0$$

or

$$T = W$$

Since the rope is continuous and the system is frictionless, the tension in Fig. 3-10b for the 200-lb block must also be equal to the weight W.

Fig. 3-10 A free-body diagram is drawn for each body in the problem.

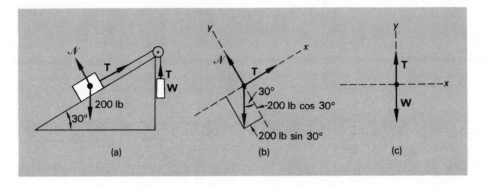

(a)   (b)   (c)

Considering the diagram for the 200-lb block, we determine the components of each force as follows:

x component	y component
$T_x = T = W$	$T_y = 0$
$\mathcal{N}_x = 0$	$\mathcal{N}_y = \mathcal{N}$
$(200 \text{ lb})_x = (-200 \text{ lb})(\sin 30°)$	$(200 \text{ lb})_y = (-200 \text{ lb})(\cos 30°)$

Applying the first condition yields

$$\sum F_x = 0 \qquad T - (200 \text{ lb})(\sin 30°) = 0 \qquad (3\text{-}8)$$

$$\sum F_y = 0 \qquad \mathcal{N} - (200 \text{ lb})(\cos 30°) = 0 \qquad (3\text{-}9)$$

From Eq. (3-8) we obtain

$$T = (200 \text{ lb})(\sin 30°) = 100 \text{ lb}$$

and, therefore, $W = 100$ lb since $T = W$. Thus a 100-lb weight is required to maintain equilibrium.

The normal force exerted by the plane on the 200-lb block can be found from Eq. (3-9), although this calculation was not necessary to determine the weight W. Hence

$$\mathcal{N} = (200 \text{ lb})(\cos 30°) = (200 \text{ lb})(0.866)$$

$$= 173 \text{ lb}$$

3-6 FRICTION

Whenever a body moves while it is in contact with another object, frictional forces oppose the relative motion. These forces are caused by the adhesion of one surface to the other and by the interlocking of irregularities in the rubbing surfaces. It is friction that holds a nail in a board, allows us to walk, and makes automobile brakes work. In all these cases friction has a desirable effect.

In many other instances, however, friction must be minimized. For example, it increases the work necessary to operate machinery, it causes wear, and it generates heat, which often causes additional damage. Automobiles and airplanes are streamlined in order to decrease air friction, which is large at high speeds.

Whenever one surface moves past another, the frictional force exerted by each body on the other is parallel or tangent to the two surfaces and acts in such a manner as to oppose relative motion. It is important to note that these forces exist not only when there is relative motion but even when one object only *tends* to slide past another.

Suppose a force is exerted on a block which rests on a horizontal surface, as shown in Fig. 3-11. At first the block will not be moved because of the action of a force called the *force of static friction* $\mathscr{F}_s$. But as the applied force is increased, motion eventually occurs, and the frictional force exerted by the horizontal surface while the block is moving is called the *force of kinetic friction* $\mathscr{F}_\kappa$.

Fig. 3-11 (*a*) In static friction motion is impending. (*b*) In kinetic friction the two surfaces are in relative motion.

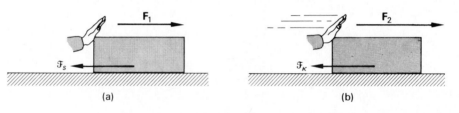

(a)   (b)

The laws governing frictional forces can be determined experimentally in the laboratory by using an apparatus similar to the one shown in Fig. 3-12a. A box of weight W is placed on a horizontal table, and a string attached to the box is passed over a light frictionless pulley and attached to a weight hanger. All forces acting on the box and hanger are shown in their corresponding free-body diagrams (Fig. 3-12b and c).

Let us consider that the system is in equilibrium, which requires the box to be stationary or moving with a constant velocity. In either case, we may apply the first condition for equilibrium. Consider the force diagram of the box as shown in Fig. 3-12c.

$$\sum F_x = 0 \qquad \mathscr{F} - T = 0$$
$$\sum F_y = 0 \qquad \mathscr{N} - W = 0$$

or

$$\mathscr{F} = T \qquad \text{and} \qquad \mathscr{N} = W$$

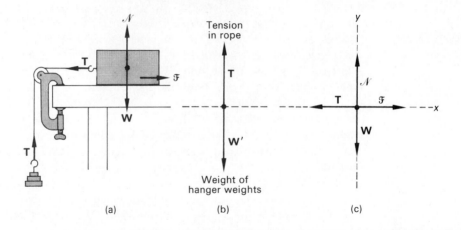

Fig. 3-12 Experiment to determine force of friction.

(a)   (b)   (c)

Thus the force of friction is equal in magnitude to the tension in the string, and the normal force exerted by the table on the box is equal to the weight of the box. Note that the tension in the string is determined by the weight of the hanger plus the weights placed on the hanger.

We begin the experiment by slowly adding weights to the hanger, thus gradually increasing the tension in the string. As the tension is increased, the equal but oppositely directed force of static friction is also increased. If $\mathbf{T}$ is increased sufficiently, the box will start to move, indicating that $\mathbf{T}$ has overcome the *maximum* force of static friction $\mathscr{F}_{s,max}$. Thus, although the force of static friction $\mathscr{F}_s$ will vary according to values of tension in the string, there exists a single maximum value $\mathscr{F}_{s,max}$. Only this maximum value will be useful in the solution of problems involving friction. Therefore, in this text $\mathscr{F}_s$ will be understood to represent $\mathscr{F}_{s,max}$.

To continue the experiment, suppose we add weights to the box, thereby increasing the normal pressure between the box and the table. Our normal force will now be

$$\mathscr{N} = W + \text{added weights}$$

Repeating the above procedure will show that a *proportionately* larger value of $\mathbf{T}$ will be necessary to overcome $\mathscr{F}_s$. In other words, if we double the normal force between two surfaces, the maximum force of static friction which must be overcome is also doubled. If $\mathscr{N}$ is tripled, $\mathscr{F}_s$ is tripled, and so it will be for other factors. Therefore it can be said that the maximum force of static friction is directly proportional to the normal force between the two surfaces. We can write this proportionality as

$$\mathscr{F}_s \propto \mathscr{N}$$

which can be stated as an equation:

$$\boxed{\mathscr{F}_s = \mu_s \mathscr{N}} \tag{3-10}$$

where μ_s is a proportionality constant called the *coefficient of static friction*. Since μ_s is the constant ratio of two forces, it is a dimensionless quantity.

In the above experiment it will be noticed that after $\mathcal{F}_s$ has been overcome, the box will increase its speed, or accelerate, until it is stopped by the pulley. This indicates that a lesser value of **T** would be necessary to keep the box moving with a constant speed. Thus the force of kinetic friction $\mathcal{F}_\kappa$ must be smaller than the value of $\mathcal{F}_s$ for the same surfaces. In other words, it requires more force to start a block moving than it does to keep it moving with constant speed. In the latter case, the first condition for equilibrium is still satisfied; hence the same reasoning which led to Eq. (3-10) for static friction will yield the following proportionality for kinetic friction:

$$\mathcal{F}_\kappa \propto \mathcal{N}$$

which can be stated as an equation. As before,

$$\boxed{\mathcal{F}_\kappa = \mu_\kappa \mathcal{N}} \tag{3-11}$$

where μ_κ is a proportionality constant called the *coefficient of kinetic friction*.

The proportionality coefficients μ_s and μ_κ can be shown to depend on the roughness of the surfaces but not on the area of contact between the two surfaces. It can be seen from the equations above that μ depends only on the frictional force $\mathcal{F}$ and the normal force $\mathcal{N}$ between the surfaces. Of course, it must be realized that Eqs. (3-10) and (3-11) are not fundamentally rigorous, like other physical equations. Many variables interfere with the general application of these formulas. No one who has experience in automobile racing, for instance, will believe that the friction force is *completely* independent of the contact area. Nevertheless, the equations are useful tools for estimating resistive forces in specific cases.

Table 3-2 shows some representative values for the coefficients of static and kinetic friction for different types of surfaces. These values are approximate and depend upon the condition of the surfaces.

Table 3-2 Approximate Coefficients of Friction

Material	μ_s	μ_κ
Wood on wood	0.7	0.4
Steel on steel	0.15	0.09
Metal on leather	0.6	0.5
Wood on leather	0.5	0.4
Rubber on concrete, dry	0.9	0.7
wet	0.7	0.57

Problems involving friction are solved like other force problems, except that the following points should be considered:

1. Frictional forces are parallel to the surfaces and directly oppose motion of the surfaces across each other.
2. The force of static friction is larger than the force of kinetic friction for the same materials.
3. In drawing free-body diagrams, it is usually more expedient to choose the x axis along the plane of motion and the y axis normal to the plane of motion.
4. The first condition for equilibrium can be applied to set up two equations representing forces along the plane of motion and normal to it. (The more complicated problem, which involves a resultant force, will be treated in a later chapter.)
5. The relations $\mathscr{F}_s = \mu_s \mathscr{N}$ and $\mathscr{F}_\kappa = \mu_\kappa \mathscr{N}$ can be applied to solve for the desired quantity.

EXAMPLE 3-5

A 50-lb block rests on a horizontal surface. A horizontal pull of 10 lb is required to just start the block moving. After motion is started, only a 5-lb force is required to move the block with a constant speed. Find the coefficients of static and kinetic friction.

Solution

The key words which should be recognized are *just start moving* and *move with constant speed*. The former implies static friction whereas the latter implies kinetic friction. In each case a condition of equilibrium exists. The correct free-body diagrams are shown in Fig. 3-13a and b. Let us first consider the force which overcomes static friction. Applying the first condition for equilibrium to Fig. 3-13a gives

$$\sum F_x = 0 \qquad\qquad\qquad 10 \text{ lb} - \mathscr{F}_s = 0$$
$$\sum F_y = 0 \qquad\qquad\qquad \mathscr{N} - 50 \text{ lb} = 0$$

from which we note that

$$\mathscr{F}_s = 10 \text{ lb} \qquad \mathscr{N} = 50 \text{ lb}$$

Fig. 3-13 (*a*) A force of 10 lb is required to overcome the maximum force of static friction. (*b*) A force of only 5 lb is required to move the block with constant speed.

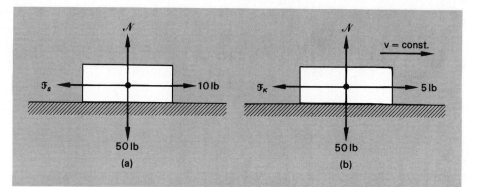

Thus we can find the coefficient of static friction from Eq. (3-8).

$$\mu_s = \frac{\mathscr{F}_s}{\mathscr{N}} = \frac{10 \text{ lb}}{50 \text{ lb}} = 0.2$$

The force which overcomes kinetic friction is 5 lb. Hence, summing the forces along the x axis yields

$$5 \text{ lb} - \mathscr{F}_\kappa = 0$$

or

$$\mathscr{F}_\kappa = 5 \text{ lb}$$

The normal force is still 50 lb, and so

$$\mu_\kappa = \frac{\mathscr{F}_\kappa}{\mathscr{N}} = \frac{5 \text{ lb}}{50 \text{ lb}} = 0.1$$

EXAMPLE 3-6   What force **T** at an angle of 30° above the horizontal is required to drag a 40-lb block to the right at constant speed if $\mu_\kappa = 0.2$?

Solution   We shall first sketch the problem and then construct a free-body diagram, as shown in Fig. 3-14. Applying the first condition for equilibrium yields

$$\begin{aligned} \sum F_x = 0 &\qquad T_x - \mathscr{F}_\kappa = 0 \\ \sum F_y = 0 &\qquad \mathscr{N} + T_y - 40 \text{ lb} = 0 \end{aligned} \qquad (3\text{-}12)$$

The latter equation shows the normal force to be

$$\mathscr{N} = 40 \text{ lb} - T_y \qquad (3\text{-}13)$$

Fig. 3-14 The force **T** at an angle above the horizontal reduces the normal force, resulting in a smaller force of friction.

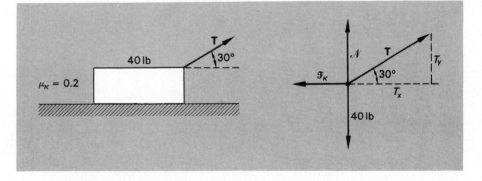

It should be noted that the normal force is decreased by the y component of **T**. Substituting $\mathscr{F}_\kappa = \mu_\kappa \mathscr{N}$ into Eq. (3-12) gives

$$T_x - \mu_\kappa \mathscr{N} = 0$$

But $\mathscr{N} = 40 \text{ lb} - T_y$ from Eq. (3-13), and so

$$T_x - \mu_\kappa(40 \text{ lb} - T_y) = 0 \qquad (3\text{-}14)$$

From the free-body diagram it is noted that

$$T_x = T \cos 30° = 0.866T$$

and

$$T_y = T \sin 30° = 0.5T$$

Thus, recalling that $\mu_\kappa = 0.2$, we can write Eq. (3-14) as

$$0.866T - (0.2)(40 \text{ lb} - 0.5T) = 0$$

which can be solved for T as follows:

$$0.866T - 8 \text{ lb} + 0.1T = 0$$

$$0.966T - 8 \text{ lb} = 0$$

$$0.966T = 8 \text{ lb}$$

$$T = \frac{8 \text{ lb}}{0.966} = 8.3 \text{ lb}$$

Therefore a force of 8.3 lb is required to pull the block with constant speed if the rope makes an angle of 30° above the horizontal.

EXAMPLE 3-7   A 100-lb block rests on a 30° inclined plane. If $\mu_\kappa = 0.1$, what push **P** parallel to the plane and directed up the plane will cause the block to move (a) up the plane with constant speed and (b) down the plane with constant speed?

Solution (a)   The general problem is sketched in Fig. 3-15a. For motion up the plane, the force of friction is directed down the plane, as shown in Fig. 3-15b. Applying the first condition for equilibrium, we obtain

$$\sum F_x = 0 \qquad P - \mathscr{F}_\kappa - W_x = 0 \qquad\qquad (3\text{-}15)$$

$$\sum F_y = 0 \qquad\qquad \mathscr{N} - W_y = 0 \qquad\qquad (3\text{-}16)$$

From the figure, the x and y components of the weight are

$$W_x = (100 \text{ lb})(\sin 30°) = 50 \text{ lb}$$

$$W_y = (100 \text{ lb})(\cos 30°) = 86.6 \text{ lb}$$

Fig. 3-15 Friction on the inclined plane.

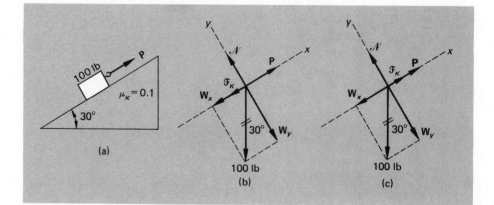

(a)

(b)

(c)

Substitution of the latter into Eq. (3-16) allows us to solve for the normal force. Hence

$$\mathscr{N} - 86.6 \text{ lb} = 0$$

$$\mathscr{N} = 86.6 \text{ lb}$$

The push required to move up the plane is, from Eq. (3-15),

$$P = \mathscr{F}_\kappa + W_x$$

But $\mathscr{F}_\kappa = \mu_\kappa \mathscr{N}$, so that

$$P = \mu_\kappa \mathscr{N} + W_x$$

Substituting known values for μ_κ, $\mathscr{N}$, and W_x, we obtain

$$P = (0.1)(86.6 \text{ lb}) + 50 \text{ lb}$$

$$= 58.7 \text{ lb}$$

Note that the push up the plane in this case must overcome both the frictional force of 8.66 lb and the 50-lb component of the weight down the plane.

Solution (b)   Now we must consider the push **P** required to retard the downward motion. The only difference between this problem and the problem in part *a* is that the friction force is now directed up the plane. The normal force does not change, and the components of the weight do not change. Therefore, if we sum the forces along the *x* axis in Fig. 3-15c, we have

$$\sum F_x = 0 \qquad P + \mathscr{F}_\kappa - W_x = 0$$

from which

$$P = W_x - \mathscr{F}_\kappa$$

or

$$P = 50 \text{ lb} - 8.66 \text{ lb}$$

$$= 41.3 \text{ lb}$$

The force of 41.3 lb directed up the plane retards the downward motion of the block so that its speed is constant. If this force **P** were not exerted, the block would accelerate down the plane of its own accord.

EXAMPLE 3-8   What is the maximum slope angle θ for an inclined plane such that a block of weight W will not slide down the plane?

Solution   A sketch and free-body diagram are constructed as shown in Fig. 3-16. The maximum value of θ would be that value which overcomes static friction $\mathscr{F}_s = \mu_s \mathscr{N}$. Applying the first condition for equilibrium gives

$$\sum F_x = 0 \qquad \mathscr{F}_s - W_x = 0$$

$$\sum F_y = 0 \qquad \mathscr{N} - W_y = 0$$

from which we transpose to obtain

$$\mathscr{F}_s = W_x \qquad \mathscr{N} = W_y \tag{3-17}$$

Fig. 3-16 The limiting angle of repose.

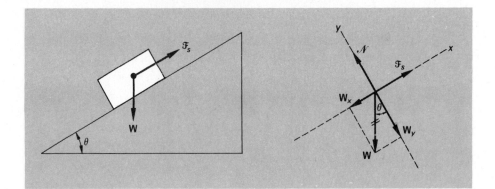

From Fig. 3-16 we note that θ is an angle whose tangent is W_x/W_y; hence, from Eq. (3-17), we have

$$\tan \theta = \frac{W_x}{W_y} = \frac{\mathscr{F}_s}{\mathscr{N}}$$

But $\mathscr{F}_s/\mathscr{N}$ is equal to the coefficient of static friction μ_s. Hence

$$\boxed{\tan \theta = \mu_s}$$

Thus a block, regardless of its weight, will remain at rest on an inclined plane unless $\tan \theta$ equals or exceeds μ_s. The angle θ in this case is called the *limiting angle* or the *angle of repose*.

It is left as an exercise for you to show that a block will slide down the plane with the constant speed if

$\tan \theta = \mu_\kappa$.

SUMMARY

In this chapter, we have defined objects which are at rest or in motion with constant speed to be in equilibrium. Through the use of vector diagrams and Newton's laws, we have found it possible to determine unknown forces for systems which are known to be in equilibrium. The following items will summarize the more important concepts to be remembered:

- *Newton's first law of motion* states that an object at rest and an object in motion with constant speed will maintain the state of rest or constant motion unless acted on by a resultant force.
- *Newton's third law of motion* states that every action must produce an equal and opposite reaction. The action and reaction forces do not act on the same body.
- Free-body diagrams: From the conditions of the problem a neat sketch is drawn and all known quantities are labeled. Then a force diagram indicating all forces and their components is constructed. All information such as that given in Fig. 3-17 should be a part of the diagram.

Fig. 3-17

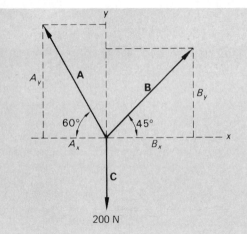

200 N

- Translational equilibrium: A body in translational equilibrium has no resultant force acting on it. In such cases, the sum of all the x components is zero, and the sum of all the y components is zero. This is known as the first condition for equilibrium and is written

$$\boxed{R_x = \sum F_x = 0} \qquad \boxed{R_y = \sum F_y = 0}$$

- Applying these conditions to Fig. 3-1, for example, we obtain two equations in two unknowns:

$$B \cos 45° - A \cos 60° = 0$$

$$B \sin 45° + A \sin 60° - 200 \text{ N} = 0$$

These equations can be solved to find A and B.
- Static friction exists between two surfaces when motion is impending; kinetic friction occurs when the two surfaces are in relative motion. In either case, the friction forces are proportional to the normal force. They are given by

$$\boxed{\mathscr{F}_s = \mu_s \mathscr{N}} \qquad \boxed{\mathscr{F}_\kappa = \mu_\kappa \mathscr{N}}$$

These forces must often be considered in equilibrium problems.

QUESTIONS

3-1. Define the following terms:

a. Inertia	**f.** Friction force
b. Reaction force	**g.** Coefficient of friction
c. Equilibrium	**h.** Normal force
d. Equilibrant	**i.** Angle of repose
e. Free-body diagram	

3-2. A popular magic trick consists of placing a coin on a card and the card on the top of a glass. The edge of the card is flipped briskly with the forefinger, causing the card to fly off the top of the glass as the coin drops into the glass. Explain. What law does this illustrate?

3-3. When the head of a hammer becomes loose, you can reseat it by holding the hammer vertically and tapping the base of the handle against the floor. Explain. What law does this illustrate?

3-4. Explain the part played by Newton's third law of motion in the following activities: **(a)** walking, **(b)** rowing, **(c)** rockets, and **(d)** parachuting.

3-5. Can a moving body be in equilibrium? Give several examples.

3-6. Can a moving body be in equilibrium? Give several examples.

3-6. According to Newton's third law of motion, every force has an equal and oppositely directed reaction force. Therefore, the concept of a resultant unbalanced force must be an illusion that really does not hold under close examination. Do you agree with this statement? Give the reasons for your answer.

3-7. A brick is suspended from the ceiling by a light string. A second identical string is attached to the bottom of the brick and hangs within the reach of a student. When the student pulls the lower string slowly, the upper string breaks, but when the lower string is jerked, it breaks. Explain.

3-8. A long steel cable is stretched between two buildings. Show by diagrams and discussion why it is not possible to pull the cable so taut that it will be perfectly horizontal with no sag in the middle.

3-9. We have seen that it is always advantageous to choose the x and y axes so that as many forces as possible are completely specified along an axis. Suppose that no two forces are perpendicular to each other. Will there still be an advantage to rotating axes to align an unknown force with an axis as opposed to aligning a known force? Test this approach by applying it to one of the text examples.

3-10. Discuss a few beneficial uses of the force of friction.

3-11. Why do we speak of a *maximum* force of static friction? Why do we not discuss a maximum force of kinetic friction?

3-12. Why is it easier to pull a sled at an angle than it is to push a sled at the same angle? Draw free-body diagrams to show what the normal force would be in each case.

3-13. Is the normal force acting on a body always equal to its weight?

3-14. When walking across a frozen pond, should you take short steps or long ones? Why? If the ice were completely frictionless, would it be possible for you to get off the pond? Explain.

PROBLEMS

3-1. Consider the suspended weight in Fig. 3-18. Visualize the forces acting on the knot and draw a free-body diagram. Label all forces and indicate known angles. Apply the first condition for equilibrium to get two equations, and solve for the tensions in ropes A and B.

Ans. $A = 1374$ N, $B = 1462$ N.

Fig. 3-18

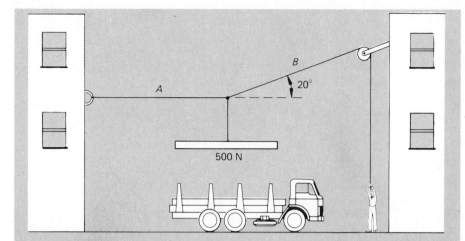

3-2. A mechanic pulls with a force of 80-lb in the direction shown in Fig. 3-19. Draw a free-body diagram of all the forces acting on the pulley. What are the magnitudes of the forces *A* and *B*?

Fig. 3-19

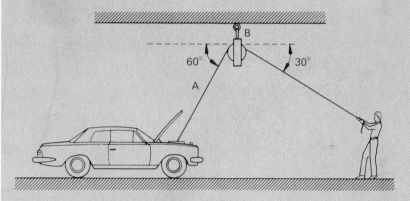

3-3. Determine the tension in rope *A* and the compression *B* in the strut in Fig. 3-20. The compression in the strut is equal in magnitude but opposite in direction to the force exerted by the strut on its end.

Ans. $A = 231$ N, $B = 462$ N.

Fig. 3-20

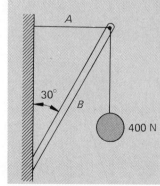

3-4. If the breaking strength of cable A in Fig. 3-21 is 200 N, what is the maximum weight W which can be supported by this apparatus?

Fig. 3-21

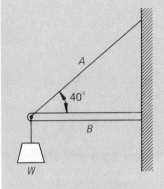

3-5. A 90-N wagon with frictionless wheels is rolled up a 37° inclined plane by a push P directed parallel to the plane. Draw a free-body diagram of the forces acting on the wagon. What is the minimum push P required to roll the wagon up the plane? What push P directed horizontally is needed to hold the wagon at rest?

Ans. 54.2 N, 67.8 N.

3-6. A 70-lb block of steel is at rest on a 41° incline. What is the magnitude of the static friction force directed up the incline?

3-7. Find the tension in ropes A and B for the arrangements shown in Fig. 3-22.

Ans. **(a)** $A = 170$ N, $B = 294$ N **(b)** $A = 134$ N, $B = 209$ N
(c) $A = 1410$ N, $B = 1150$ N.

Fig. 3-22

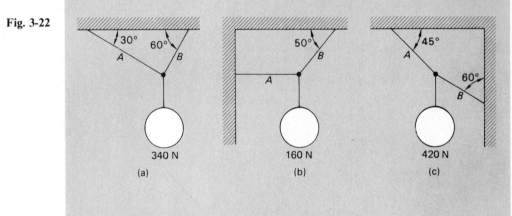

(a) (b) (c)

3-8. Find the tension in the cable and the compression in the boom for the arrangements of Fig. 3-23.

Fig. 3-23

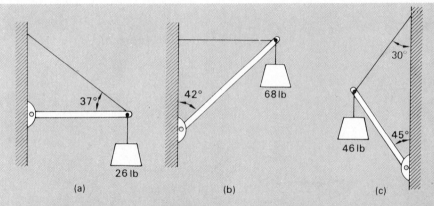

(a)   (b)   (c)

3-9. A cable is stretched horizontally across the top of two vertical poles which are separated by a horizontal distance of 20 m. A traffic light weighing 250 N is attached to the midpoint of the cable causing the center to sag a distance of 1.2 m. What is the tension in the cable?

Ans. 1049 N.

3-10. Assume that the cable in Prob. 3-9 has a breaking strength of 1200 N. What is the maximum weight of the traffic light if the system is not to fail?

3-11. Determine the compression in the center strut B and the tension in the rope A for the situation described by Fig. 3-24.

Ans. $A = 643$ N, $B = 940$ N.

Fig. 3-24

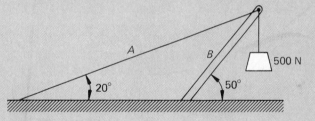

3-12. Find the tension in each cord of Fig. 3-25 if the weight W is 476 N.

Fig. 3-25

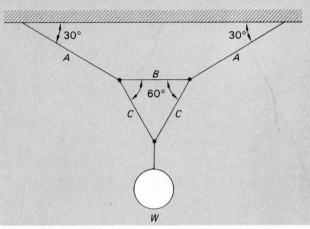

3-13. A horizontal force of 40 lb will just start an empty 600-lb sled moving across packed snow. **(a)** What is the coefficient of static friction? **(b)** What force is required to start the sled moving if 200 lb of supplies are placed in the sled?

Ans. **(a)** 0.0667 **(b)** 53.3 lb.

3-14. Once the sled of Prob. 3-13 starts moving a force of only 25 lb will keep it moving at constant speed when the sled is empty. What is the coefficient of sliding friction? What force is required to continue the constant sliding speed after 200 lb of supplies are added to the sled?

3-15. The coefficient of kinetic friction between wood and wood is 0.4, and the coefficient of static friction is 0.7. What horizontal force is required to just start motion of a 12-lb wooden block on a horizontal wooden floor? What force will cause it to move with constant speed once motion has begun?

Ans. 8.4 lb, 4.8 lb.

3-16. A steel block weighing 240 N rests on a level steel beam. If $\mu_k = 0.09$, what horizontal force will move the block with constant speed?

3-17. A 180-lb man stands on a wooden floor in leather-soled shoes. Assume that $\mu_s = 0.5$ and $\mu_k = 0.4$. What horizontal force will just start the man sliding on the floor? What force will move him with constant speed?

Ans. 90 lb, 72 lb.

3-18. A 2-N eraser is pressed against a vertical blackboard with a horizontal push of 12 N. The coefficient of static friction is 0.25. **(a)** Find the force required to move the eraser parallel to the base of the blackboard. **(b)** Find the upward force needed to start vertical motion.

3-19. A 200-lb refrigerator is placed on a blanket and dragged across a tile floor. If $\mu_s = 0.4$ and $\mu_k = 0.2$, what horizontal force is required to just start motion, and what force will move the refrigerator with constant speed?

Ans. 80 lb, 40 lb.

3-20. A cake of ice slides with constant speed across a wooden floor when a horizontal force of 8 lb is applied. What is the weight of the cake of ice if $\mu_k = 0.15$?

3-21. It is determined experimentally that a 20-lb horizontal force will move a 60-lb lawn mower with constant speed. The handle of the mower makes an angle of 40° with the ground. What force along the handle will move the mower forward at constant speed? What is the normal force?

Ans. 36.2 lb, 83.3 lb.

3-22. Suppose the lawn mower of Prob. 3-21 is to be moved backward at constant speed by *pulling* on the handle at 40°. What pull is required in this case? What is the normal force?

3-23. A 46-N sled has a pole attached to it at an angle of 30° above the horizontal. **(a)** If $\mu_k = 0.1$, find the force required to pull the sled at constant speed. **(b)** Find the force required to push the sled with the pole at the same angle.

Ans. **(a)** 5.02 N **(b)** 5.64 N.

3-24. A 300-lb wooden box rests on a horizontal plane. A 76-lb push applied at an angle of 37° below the horizontal just starts the block moving. What is the coefficient of static friction?

3-25. In Fig. 3-26, assume that $W = 400$ N, $\theta = 37°$, and $\mu_s = 0.2$. **(a)** Determine the magnitude of the normal force. **(b)** Find the maximum force of static friction. **(c)** What push P directed up the plane is required to just start the block moving up the plane?

Ans. **(a)** 319 N **(b)** 63.9 N **(c)** 305 N.

Fig. 3-26

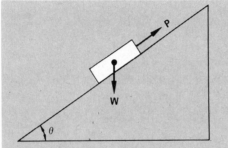

3-26. Assume that $W = 60$ lb, $\theta = 43°$, and $\mu_k = 0.3$ in Fig. 3-26. What push directed up the plane will move the block with constant speed **(a)** up the plane and **(b)** down the plane?

3-27. What horizontal push P is required to just hold a 200-N block on a 60° inclined plane if $\mu_s = 0.4$?

Ans. 157 N.

3-28. In Prob. 3-27, what horizontal push would just start the block moving up the plane?

3-29. Two weights are hung over two frictionless pulleys, as shown in Fig. 3-27. What weight W will cause the 300-lb block to just start moving to the right?

Ans. 108 lb.

Fig. 3-27

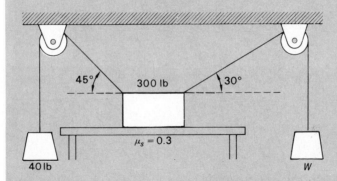

3-30. In the arrangement of Fig. 3-28, assume that the coefficient of static friction between the 200-lb block and the surface is 0.3. Find the maximum weight which can be hung at point O equilibrium.

Fig. 3-28

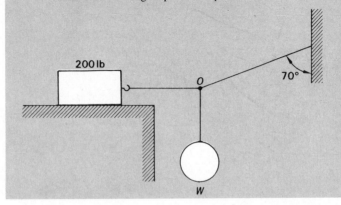

3-31. A mobile conveyor belt is used to load crates into a cargo plane. If $\mu_s = 0.5$, what is the maximum elevation angle to avoid sliding?

Ans. 26.6°.

3-32. A wooden roof is sloped at a 40° angle. What is the minimum coefficient of static friction between the sole of a roofer's shoe and the roof to avoid slippage?

4 *Torque and Rotational Equilibrium*

OBJECTIVES: After completing this chapter, you should be able to:

1. Illustrate by example and definition your understanding of the terms *moment arm* and *torque*.

2. Calculate the *resultant torque* about any axis when given the magnitude and position of forces on an extended object.

3. Solve for unknown forces or distances by applying the *first and second conditions for equilibrium*.

4. Define and illustrate by example what is meant by the *center of gravity*.

In previous chapters, we have discussed forces which act at a single point. Translational equilibrium exists when the vector sum of forces is zero. However, there are many cases in which the forces acting on an object do not have a common point of application. Such forces are said to be *nonconcurrent*. For example, a mechanic exerts a force on the handle of a wrench to tighten a bolt. A carpenter uses a long lever to pry the lid from a wooden box. The engineer considers twisting forces which tend to snap a beam attached to a wall. The steering wheel of an automobile is turned by forces which do not have a common point of application. In such cases, there may be a *tendency to rotate* which we will define as *torque*. If we learn to measure or predict the torques produced by certain forces, we can obtain desired rotational effects. If no rotation is desired, there must be no resultant torque. This leads naturally to a condition for *rotational equilibrium* which is very important for industrial and engineering applications.

4-1
CONDITIONS FOR EQUILIBRIUM

When a body is in equilibrium, it is either at rest or in uniform motion. According to Newton's first law, only the application of a resultant force can change this condition. We have seen that if all forces acting on such a body intersect at a single point and their vector sum is zero, the system must be in equilibrium. When a body is acted on by forces which do not have a common *line of action*, it may be in translational equilibrium but not in rotational equilibrium. In other words, it may not move to the right or left or up or down, but it may still rotate. In studying equilibrium, we must consider the point of application of each force as well as its magnitude.

Consider the forces exerted on the lug wrench in Fig. 4-1a. Two equal opposing forces **F** are applied to the right and to the left. The first condition for equilibrium tells us that the vertical and horizontal forces are balanced. Hence, the system is said to be in equilibrium. However, if the same two forces are

Fig. 4-1 (*a*) Equilibrium exists; forces have the same line of action. (*b*) Equilibrium does not exist because opposing forces do not have same line of action.

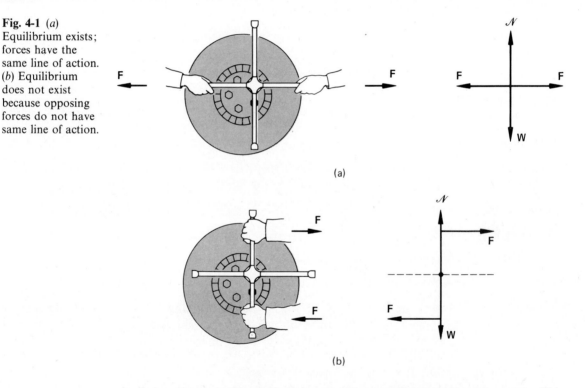

applied as shown in Fig. 4-1*b*, the wrench has a definite tendency to rotate. This is true even though the vector sum of the forces is still zero. Clearly, we need a second condition for equilibrium to cover rotational motion. A formal statement of this condition will be given later.

In Fig. 4-1*b*, the forces **F** do not have the same *line of action*.

The **line of action** *of a force is an imaginary line extended indefinitely along the vector in both directions.*

When the lines of action of forces do not intersect at a common point, rotation may occur about a point called the *axis of rotation.* In our example, the axis of rotation is an imaginary line passing through the stud perpendicular to the page.

4-2 THE MOMENT ARM

The perpendicular distance from the axis of rotation to the line of action of a force is called the *moment arm* of that force. It is the moment arm that determines the effectiveness of a given force in causing rotational motion. For example, if we exert a force **F** at increasing distances from the center of a large wheel, it becomes easier and easier to rotate the wheel about its center. (See Fig. 4-2.)

> The **moment arm** of a force is the *perpendicular* distance from the *line of action* of the force to the *axis of rotation.*

Fig. 4-2 The unbalanced force **F** has no rotational effect about the center at point *A* but becomes increasingly effective as the moment arm gets longer.

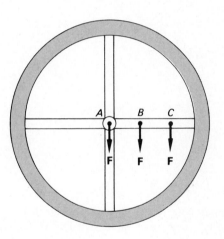

If the line of action of a force passes through the axis of rotation (point *A* of Fig. 4-2), the moment arm is zero. No rotational effect is observed regardless of the magnitude of the force. In this simple example, the moment arms at points *B* and *C* are simply the distance from the axis of rotation to the point of application of the force. Note, however, that the line of action of a force is a mere geometrical construction. The moment arm is drawn perpendicular to this line. It may be equal to the distance from the axis to the point of application of a force, but this is true only when the applied force is directed perpendicular to this distance. In the examples of Fig. 4-3, *r* represents the moment arm and *O* represents the axis of rotation. Study each example, observing how the moment arms are drawn and reasoning whether the rotation is clockwise or counterclockwise about *O*.

Fig. 4-3 Some examples of moment arms.

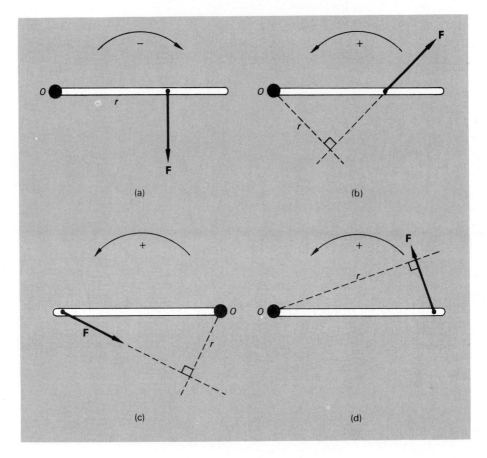

(a) (b) (c) (d)

Force has been defined as a push or pull that tends to cause motion. *Torque* τ can be defined as the tendency to produce a change in rotational motion. It is also called the *moment of force* in some textbooks. As we have seen, rotational motion is affected by both the magnitude of a force F and by its moment arm r. Thus, we will define torque as the product of a force and its moment arm.

$$Torque = force \times moment\ arm$$

$$\boxed{\tau = Fr} \tag{4-1}$$

It must be understood that r in Eq. (4-1) is measured perpendicular to the line of action of the force **F**. The units of torque are the units of force times distance, for example, *newton-meters* (N · m) and *pound-feet* (lb · ft).

Earlier, we established a sign convention to indicate the direction of forces. The direction of torque depends on whether it tends to produce clockwise (cw) or counterclockwise (ccw) rotation. We shall follow the same convention we used for measuring angles. If the force **F** tends to produce counterclockwise rotation about an axis, the torque will be considered positive. Clockwise torques will be considered negative. In Fig. 4-3, all the torques are positive (ccw) except for that in Fig. 4-3*a*.

EXAMPLE 4-1   A force of 20 N is exerted on a cable wrapped around a drum which has a diameter of 120 mm. What is the torque produced about the center of the drum? (See Fig. 4-4.)

Fig. 4-4 The tangential force exerted by a cable wrapped around a drum.

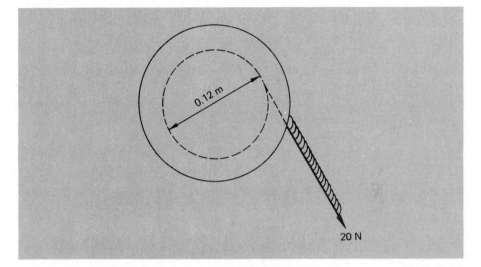

Solution   Notice that the line of action of the 20-N force is perpendicular to the diameter of the drum. The moment arm, therefore, is equal to the radius of the drum. Converting the diameter to meters (0.12 m), the radius is 0.06 m. The torque is found from Eq. 4-1:

$$\tau = Fr = -(20 \text{ N})(0.06 \text{ m}) = -1.20 \text{ N} \cdot \text{m}$$

The torque is negative because it tends to cause clockwise rotation.

EXAMPLE 4-2   A mechanic exerts a 20-lb force at the end of a 10-in. wrench, as shown in Fig. 4-5. If this pull makes an angle of 60° with the handle, what is the torque produced on the nut?

Fig. 4-5 Calculating torque.

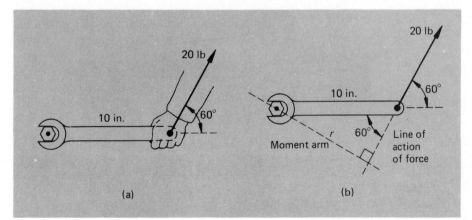

Solution   First, we draw a neat sketch, extend the line of action of the 20-lb force, and draw in the moment arm as shown. Note that the moment arm r is perpendicular to both the line of action of the force and to the axis of rotation. You must remember that the moment arm is a geometrical construction and may or may not be along some physical structure such as the handle of the wrench. From the figure we obtain

$$r = (10 \text{ in.}) \sin 60° = 8.66 \text{ in.}$$

$$\tau = Fr = (20 \text{ lb})(8.66 \text{ in.}) = 173 \text{ lb} \cdot \text{in.}$$

If desired, this torque can be converted to 14.4 lb · ft.

In some applications, it is more useful to work with the *components* of a force to obtain the resultant torque. In the preceding example, for instance, we could have resolved the 20-lb vector into its horizontal and vertical components. Instead of finding the torque of a single force, we would then need to find the torque of two component forces. As shown in Fig. 4-6, the 20-lb vector has components F_x and F_y which are found from trigonometry:

$$F_x = (20 \text{ lb})(\cos 60°) = 10 \text{ lb}$$

$$F_y = (20 \text{ lb})(\sin 60°) = 17.3 \text{ lb}$$

Fig. 4-6 The component method of calculating torque.

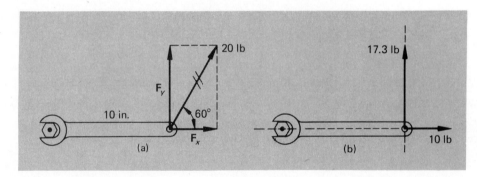

Notice from Fig. 4-6*b* that the line of action of the 10-lb force passes through the axis of rotation. It does not produce any torque because its moment arm is zero. The entire torque is, therefore, due to the 17.3-lb component perpendicular to the handle. The moment arm of this force is the length of the wrench, and the torque is

$$\tau = Fr = (17.3 \text{ lb})(10 \text{ in.}) = 173 \text{ lb} \cdot \text{in.}$$

Note that the same result is obtained using this method. No more calculations are required because the horizontal component has a zero moment arm. If we choose the components of a force along and perpendicular to a known distance, we need only concern ourselves with the torque of this perpendicular component.

In Chap. 2, we demonstrated that the resultant of a number of forces could be obtained by adding the x and y components of each force to find the components of the resultant.

$$R_x = A_x + B_x + C_x + \cdots \qquad R_y = A_y + B_y + C_y + \cdots$$

This procedure applies to forces which have a common point of intersection. Forces which do not have a common line of action may produce a resultant torque in addition to a resultant translational force. When the applied forces act in the same plane, the resultant torque is the algebraic sum of the positive and negative torques due to each force.

$$\boxed{\tau_R = \sum \tau = \tau_1 + \tau_2 + \tau_3 + \cdots} \qquad (4\text{-}2)$$

Remember that counterclockwise torques are positive and clockwise torques are negative.

EXAMPLE 4-3

A piece of angle iron is hinged at point A as shown in Fig. 4-7. Determine the resultant torque at A due to the 60- and 80-N forces.

Fig. 4-7

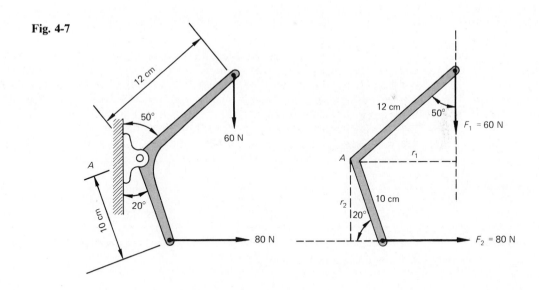

Solution

A free-body diagram is drawn and the moment arms r_1 and r_2 are constructed as in Fig. 4-7b. The lengths of the moment arms are:

$$r_1 = (12 \text{ cm}) \sin 50° = 9.19 \text{ cm}$$

$$r_2 = (10 \text{ cm}) \sin 70° = 9.40 \text{ cm}$$

Considering A as the axis of rotation, the torque due to F_1 is negative (cw) and the torque due to F_2 is positive (ccw). The resultant torque is found as follows:

$$\tau_R = \tau_1 + \tau_2 = F_1 r_1 + F_2 r_2$$
$$= -(60 \text{ N})(9.19 \text{ cm}) + (80 \text{ N})(9.40 \text{ cm})$$
$$= -552 \text{ N} \cdot \text{cm} + 752 \text{ N} \cdot \text{cm}$$
$$= 200 \text{ N} \cdot \text{cm}$$

The resultant torque is 200 N · cm, counterclockwise. This answer is best expressed as 2.00 N · m in SI units.

4-5
EQUILIBRIUM

We are now ready to discuss the necessary condition for rotational equilibrium. The condition for translational equilibrium was stated in equation form as

$$\boxed{\sum F_x = 0 \qquad \sum F_y = 0} \qquad (4\text{-}3)$$

If we are to ensure that the rotational effects are also balanced, we must stipulate that there is no resultant torque. Hence the second condition for equilibrium is:

The algebraic sum of all the torques about any axis must be zero.

$$\boxed{\sum \tau = \tau_1 + \tau_2 + \tau_3 + \cdots = 0} \qquad (4\text{-}4)$$

The second condition for equilibrium simply tells us that the clockwise torques are exactly balanced by the counterclockwise torques. Moreover, since rotation is not occurring about any point, we may choose whatever point we wish as an axis of rotation. As long as the moment arms are measured to the same point for each force, the resultant torque will be zero. By choosing the axis of rotation at the point of application of an unknown force, problems may be simplified. If a particular force has a zero moment arm, it does not contribute to torque regardless of its magnitude.

EXAMPLE 4-4

Consider the arrangement diagramed in Fig. 4-8. A uniform beam weighing 200 N is held up by two supports A and B. Given the distances and forces listed in this figure, what are the forces exerted by the supports?

Solution

A free-body diagram is drawn to show clearly all forces and distances between forces. Note that all of the weight of the uniform beam is considered as acting at the center of the board. Next we will apply the first condition for equilibrium, Eq. (4-3):

$$\sum F_y = A + B - 300 \text{ N} - 200 \text{ N} - 400 \text{ N} = 0$$

or

$$A + B = 900 \text{ N}$$

Since this equation has two unknowns, we must have more information. Therefore, we will apply the second condition for equilibrium.

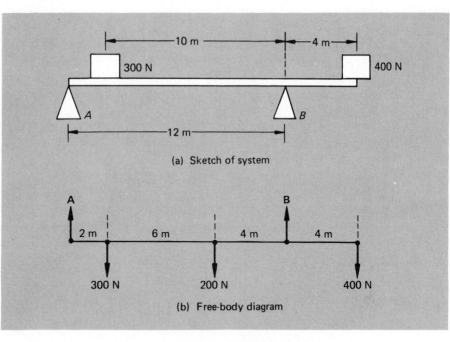

Fig. 4-8 The solution of torque problems is aided by first drawing a rough sketch of the system. A free-body diagram can then be drawn to indicate forces and distances.

(a) Sketch of system

(b) Free-body diagram

First, we must select an axis about which we can measure moment arms. The logical choice is at the point of application of some unknown force. Choosing the axis at *B* gives this force a zero moment arm. The sum of the torques about *B* results in the following equation:

$$\sum \tau_B = -A(12 \text{ m}) + (300 \text{ N})(10 \text{ m}) + (200 \text{ N})(4 \text{ m}) - (400 \text{ N})(4 \text{ m}) = 0$$

Note that the 400-N force and the force *A* tend to produce clockwise rotation about *B*. (Their torques were negative.) Simplifying gives

$$-(12 \text{ m})A + 3000 \text{ N} \cdot \text{m} - 1600 \text{ N} \cdot \text{m} + 800 \text{ N} \cdot \text{m} = 0$$

Adding (12 m)*A* to both sides and simplifying, we obtain

$$2200 \text{ N} \cdot \text{m} = (12 \text{ m})A$$

Dividing both sides by 12 m, we find that

$$A = 183 \text{ N}$$

Now to find the force exerted by support *B*, we can return to the equation obtained from the first condition for equilibrium.

$$A + B = 900 \text{ N}$$

Solving for *B*, we obtain

$$B = 900 \text{ N} - A = 900 \text{ N} - 183 \text{ N}$$

$$= 717 \text{ N}$$

As a check on this solution, we could choose the axis of rotation at *A*, then apply the second condition for equilibrium to find *B*.

EXAMPLE 4-5   A uniform 200-lb boom, 24 ft long, is supported by a cable as shown in Fig. 4-9. The boom is hinged at the wall, and the cable makes a 30° angle with the boom, which is horizontal. If a load of 500 lb is hung from the right end, what is the tension T in the cable? What are the horizontal and vertical components of the force exerted by the hinge?

Fig. 4-9 Forces on a horizontal boom.

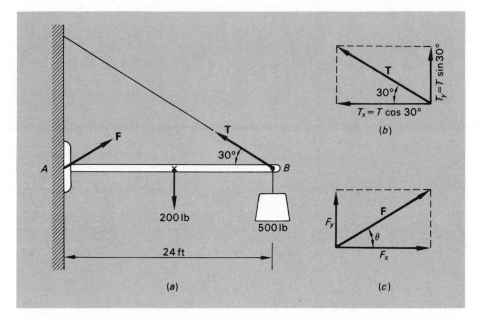

Solution   Let us consider the boom as the object in equilibrium. Of the two unknown forces F and T, we know least about the force F. Therefore it is logical to choose the hinge as our axis of rotation when summing torques. In this manner, the unknown force F will have zero moment arm, rendering its torque about point A zero also. (Do not make the mistake of assuming that the force exerted by the hinge is entirely along the boom.) We can determine the cable tension from the second condition of equilibrium.

$$\sum \tau_A = F(0) - (200 \text{ lb})(12 \text{ ft}) - (500 \text{ lb})(24 \text{ ft}) + T_x(0) + T_y(24 \text{ ft}) = 0$$

$$= 0 - 2400 \text{ lb} \cdot \text{ft} - 12,000 \text{ lb} \cdot \text{ft} + T_y(24 \text{ ft}) = 0$$

$$T_y(24 \text{ ft}) = 14,400 \text{ lb} \cdot \text{ft}$$

From Fig. 4-8b,

$$T_y = T \sin 30° = 0.5 \ T$$

so that

$$(0.5T)(24 \text{ ft}) = 14,400 \text{ lb} \cdot \text{ft}$$

$$12T = 14,400 \text{ lb}$$

$$T = 1200 \text{ lb}$$

In order to find the horizontal and vertical components of **F**, we can apply the first condition for equilibrium. The horizontal component is found by summing forces along the x axis.

$$\sum F_x = 0 \qquad F_x - T_x = 0$$

from which

$$F_x = T_x = T \cos 30°$$

$$= (1200 \text{ lb})(\cos 30°) = 1040 \text{ lb}$$

The vertical component is found by summing the forces along the y axis.

$$\sum F_y = 0 \qquad F_y + T_y - 200 \text{ lb} - 500 \text{ lb} = 0$$

Solving for F_y, we obtain

$$F_y = 700 \text{ lb} - T_y$$

or

$$F_y = 700 \text{ lb} - (1200 \text{ lb})(\sin 30°)$$

$$= 700 \text{ lb} - 600 \text{ lb} = 100 \text{ lb}$$

It is left as an exercise for you to show that the magnitude and direction of the force **F** from its components is 1045 lb at 5.5° above the boom.

4-6 CENTER OF GRAVITY

Every particle on the earth has at least one force in common with every other particle—its *weight*. In the case of a body made up of many particles, these forces are essentially parallel and directed toward the center of the earth. Regardless of the shape and size of the body, there exists a point at which the entire weight of the body may be considered to be concentrated. This point is called the *center of gravity* of the body. Of course, the weight does not in fact all act at this point. But we would calculate the same torque about a given axis if we considered the entire weight to act at that point.

The center of gravity of a regular body, such as a uniform sphere, cube, rod, or beam, is located at its geometric center. This fact was used in the examples of the previous section, where we considered the weight of an entire beam as acting at its center. Although the center of gravity is a fixed point, it does not necessarily lie within the body. For example, a hollow sphere, a circular hoop, and a rubber tire all have centers of gravity outside the material of the body.

From the definition of the center of gravity, it is recognized that any body which is suspended at this point will be in equilibrium. This is true because the weight vector, which represents the sum of forces acting on each portion of the body, will have a zero moment arm. Thus, we can compute the center of gravity of a body by determining the point at which an upward force will produce rotational equilibrium.

EXAMPLE 4-6

Compute the center of gravity of the two spheres in Fig. 4-10 if they are connected by a 30-in. rod of negligible weight.

Fig. 4-10 Computing the center of gravity.

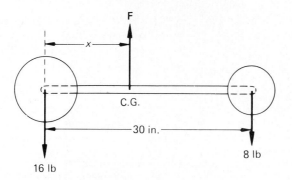

Solution

We first draw an upward vector indicating the force at the center of gravity which would balance the system. Suppose we choose to locate this vector at a distance from the center of the 16-lb sphere. The distance x would be drawn and labeled on the figure. Since the upward force must equal the sum of the downward forces, the first condition for equilibrium tells us that

$$F = 16 \text{ lb} + 8 \text{ lb} = 24 \text{ lb}$$

Now we will choose our axis of rotation at the center of the 16-lb sphere. This is the best choice because the distance x is measured from this point. The second condition for equilibrium is applied as follows:

$$\sum \tau = (24 \text{ lb})x - (8 \text{ lb})(30 \text{ in.}) = 0$$

$$(24 \text{ lb})x = 240 \text{ lb} \cdot \text{in.}$$

$$x = 10 \text{ in.}$$

If the rod joining the two spheres is suspended from the ceiling at a point 10 in. from the center of the 16-lb sphere, the system will be in equilibrium. This point is the center of gravity. You should show that the same conclusion follows if you sum torques about the right end or about any other point.

SUMMARY

When forces acting on a body do not have the same line of action or do not intersect at a common point, rotation may occur. In this chapter, we introduced the concept of torque as a measure of the tendency to rotate. The major concepts are summarized below:

- The **moment arm** of a force is the perpendicular distance from the line of action of the force to the axis of rotation.
- The **torque** about a given axis is defined as the product of the magnitude of a force and its moment arm:

$Torque = force \times moment \; arm$

$$\boxed{\tau = Fr}$$

It is positive if it tends to produce counterclockwise motion and negative if the motion produced is clockwise.

$+$ ccw

$-$ cw

- The **resultant torque** τ_R about a particular axis a is the algebraic sum of the torques produced by each force. The signs are determined by the above convention.

$$\tau_R = \sum \tau_A = F_1 r_1 + F_2 r_2 + F_3 r_3 + \cdots$$

- **Rotational equilibrium:** A body in rotational equilibrium has no resultant torque acting on it. In such cases, the sum of all the torques about *any* axis must equal zero. The axis may be chosen anywhere because the system is not tending to rotate about any point. This is called the second condition for equilibrium and may be written

$$\sum \tau = 0 \qquad \textit{the sum of all torques about any point is zero}$$

- **Total equilibrium** exists when the first and second conditions are satisfied. In such cases, three independent equations can be written:

$$\text{(a) } \sum F_x = 0 \qquad \text{(b) } \sum F_y = 0 \qquad \text{(c) } \sum \tau = 0$$

By writing these equations for a given situation, unknown forces, distances, or torques can be found.

- The **center of gravity** of a body is the point through which the resultant weight acts regardless of how the body is oriented. For applications involving torque, the entire weight of the object may be considered as acting at this point.

QUESTIONS

4-1. Define the following terms:
    a. line of action   **d.** torque
    b. axis of rotation   **e.** rotational equilibrium
    c. moment arm   **f.** center of gravity

4-2. You lift a heavy suitcase with your right hand. Describe and explain the position of your body.

4-3. A parlor trick consists of asking you to stand against a wall with your feet together so that the side of your right foot rests against the wall. You are then asked to raise your left foot off the floor. Why can't you do this without falling?

4-4. Why is a Volkswagen bus more likely to turn over than a Corvette or some other sports car?

4-5. If you know the weight of a brick to be 6 lb, describe how you could use a meterstick and a pivot to measure the weight of a baseball.

4-6. Describe and explain the arm and leg motions used by a tightrope walker to maintain balance.

4-7. Discuss the following items and their use of the principle of torque: **(a)** screwdriver, **(b)** wrench, **(c)** pliers, **(d)** wheelbarrow, **(e)** nutcracker, and **(f)** crowbar.

PROBLEMS

4-1. A leather belt is wrapped around a pulley 12 in. in diameter. A force of 6 lb is applied to the belt. What is the torque at the center of the shaft?

                                              Ans. 3 lb · ft.

4-2. The rod in Fig. 4-11 is 20 in. long, and the axis of rotation is A. Determine the moment arm if the angle θ is **(a)** 90°, **(b)** 60°, **(c)** 30°, and **(d)** 0°.

Fig. 4-11

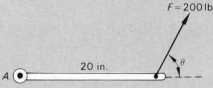

4-3. Determine the torque produced for each of the angles in Prob. 4-2. Neglect the weight of the rod.

Ans. **(a)** 333 lb · ft **(b)** 289 lb · ft **(c)** 167 lb · ft **(d)** 0.

4-4. In Fig. 4-12, what is the resultant torque **(a)** about point A and **(b)** about the left end of the wooden beam? Neglect the weight of the beam.

Fig. 4-12

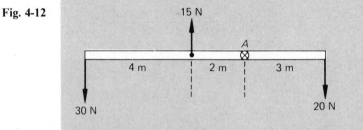

4-5. Determine the resultant torque about point A and about point C in Fig. 4-13.

Ans. $\tau_{A} = 6.19$ lb · ft, $\tau_{C} = -6.67$ lb · ft.

Fig. 4-13

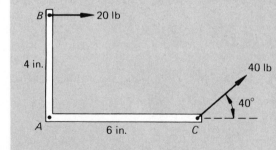

4-6. A V belt is wrapped around a pulley 16 in. in diameter. If a resultant torque of 4 lb · ft is required, what force must be applied along the belt?

4-7. Determine the unknown forces for the arrangements in Fig. 4-14. Assume that equilibrium exists and that the weight of the bar is negligible in each case.

Ans. **(a)** $A = 26.7$ lb, $F = 107$ lb **(b)** $F_{1} = 198$ lb, $F_{2} = 87.5$ lb **(c)** $A = 50.9$ N, $B = 49.1$ N.

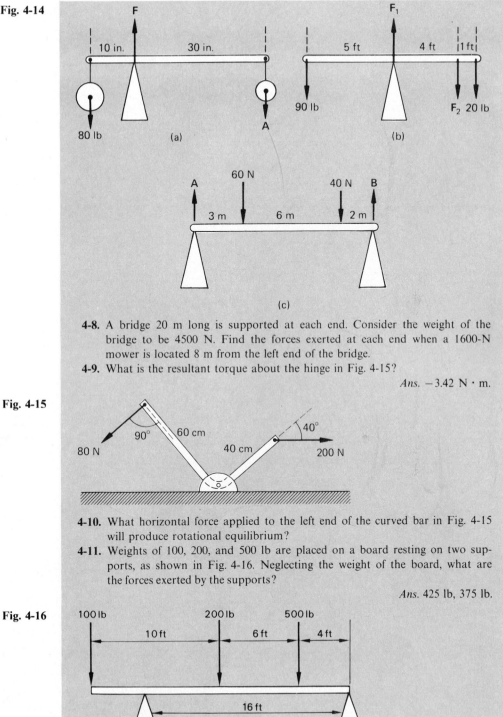

Fig. 4-14

(a)

(b)

(c)

4-8. A bridge 20 m long is supported at each end. Consider the weight of the bridge to be 4500 N. Find the forces exerted at each end when a 1600-N mower is located 8 m from the left end of the bridge.

4-9. What is the resultant torque about the hinge in Fig. 4-15?

Ans. -3.42 N · m.

Fig. 4-15

4-10. What horizontal force applied to the left end of the curved bar in Fig. 4-15 will produce rotational equilibrium?

4-11. Weights of 100, 200, and 500 lb are placed on a board resting on two supports, as shown in Fig. 4-16. Neglecting the weight of the board, what are the forces exerted by the supports?

Ans. 425 lb, 375 lb.

Fig. 4-16

4-12. A uniform bar 8 m long and weighing 2400 N is supported by a fulcrum 3 m from the right end. If a 9000-N weight is placed on the right end what downward force must be exerted at the left end in order to balance the system?

4-13. A 30-lb box and a 50-lb box are positioned at opposite ends of a 16-ft board. The board is supported only at its midpoint. Where should a third box weighing 40 lb be placed to balance the system?

Ans. 4 ft left of center.

4-14. Weights of 2, 5, 8, and 10 N are hung from a 10-m rod, of negligible weight, at distances of 2, 4, 6, and 8 m from the left end. What are the magnitude and location of a single upward force which will balance the system?

4-15. A uniform horizontal bar is 800 mm long and is of negligible weight. A weight of 40 N is hung from the left end of the rod and an 84-N weight is hung from the right end. Where should a single upward support be positioned to balance the system?

Ans. 542 mm from left end.

4-16. Find the forces F_1, F_2, and F_3 such that the system in Fig. 4-17 is in equilibrium.

Fig. 4-17

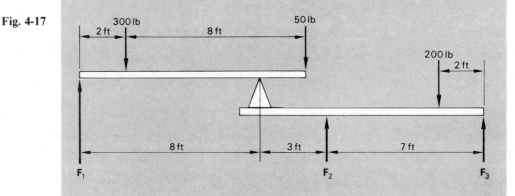

4-17. Find the resultant torque about A in Fig. 4-18. What is the resultant torque if the axis of rotation is at point B instead?

Ans. -1.61 N · m.

4-18. A 10-ft platform is placed across two stepladders, one at each end. The platform weighs 40 lb, and a painter located 4 ft from the right end weighs 180 lb. What are the forces exerted by each of the ladders?

4-19. Consider the boom arrangement of Fig. 4-19. The boom weighs 400 N and is 6 m long. The cable AC is attached to the boom at a distance of 4.5 m from the wall. If the weight W is 1200 N, what is the tension in the cable? What are the horizontal and vertical components of the force exerted by the hinge on the boom? What is the magnitude and direction of this force?

Ans. $T = 2340$ N, $F_x = 1410$ N, $F_y = -267$ N, $F = 1430$ N, $\theta = 349.3°$.

4-20. In Fig. 4-19, the boom weighs 80 lb and is 12 ft long, and the cable is attached at a point 10 ft from the wall. The breaking strength of the cable is 800 lb. What is the maximum weight W that can be hung at the right end?

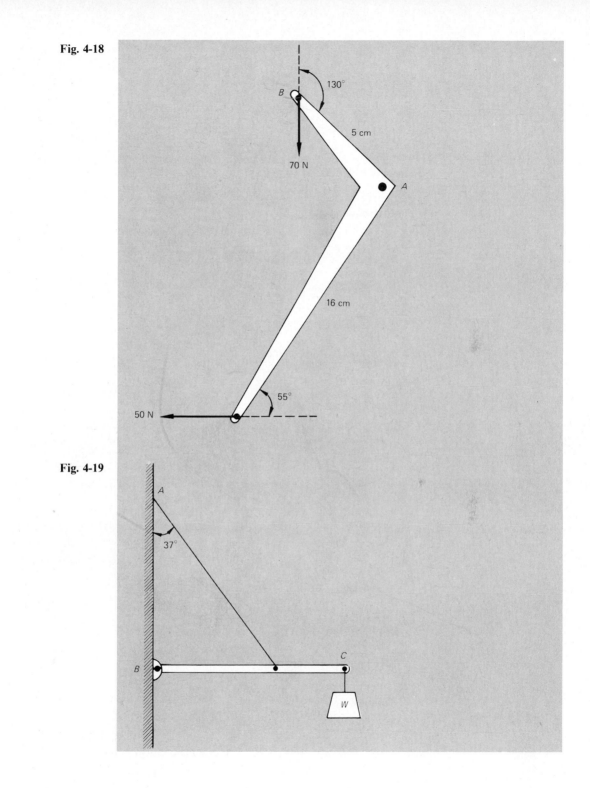

Fig. 4-18

Fig. 4-19

4-21. If the weight of the boom in Fig. 4-20 is neglected and the weight W is 2000 lb, **(a)** what is the tension in the horizontal cable? **(b)** what are the magnitude and direction of the resultant force acting on the boom at its lower end?

Ans. $T = 5770$ lb, $F = 6110$ lb, $\theta = 19.1°$.

Fig. 4-20

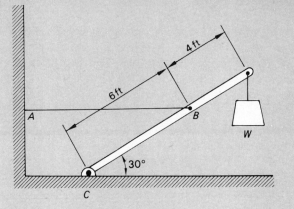

4-22. If the weight of the boom in Fig. 4-20 is neglected, **(a)** what weight W will produce a tension of 400 lb in the horizontal cable? **(b)** what are the magnitude and direction of the force acting on the boom at its lower end?

4-23. Compute the center of gravity of a sledgehammer if the metal head weighs 12 lb and the 32-in. supporting handle weighs 2 lb. Assume that the handle is of uniform construction and weight.

Ans. 2.29 in. from head.

4-24. Find the center of gravity for two spheres connected by a rod, as in Fig. 4-10. In this example, assume that the rod is 200 mm long and of negligible weight. The left sphere weighs 40 N and the right sphere weighs 12 N.

4-25. Assume that the boom in Fig. 4-20 weighs 80 lb and that the suspended weight W is 200 lb. At what distance from the supporting pivot C must a 100-lb weight be attached in order to produce a cable tension of 900 lb?

Ans. 7.18 ft.

5 *Uniformly Accelerated Motion*

OBJECTIVES: After completing this chapter, you should be able to:

1. Define and give formulas for *average speed* and *average acceleration*.

2. Solve problems involving *time, distance, average speed,* and *average acceleration*.

3. Apply one of the four general equations for uniformly accelerated motion to solve for one of the five parameters: *initial speed, final speed, acceleration, time,* and *distance*.

4. Solve acceleration problems involving free-falling bodies in a gravitational field.

Everything in the physical world is in motion, from the largest galaxies in the universe to the elementary particles within atoms. We must study the motions of objects if we are to understand their behavior and learn to control them. Uncontrolled or erratic motion, as in falling buildings, destructive vibrations, or a runaway car, can create dangerous situations, but controlled motion often serves our convenience. It is important to be able to analyze motion and to represent it in terms of fundamental formulas.

**5-1
SPEED AND
VELOCITY**

The simplest kind of motion an object can experience is uniform motion in a straight line. If the object covers the same distances in each successive unit of time, it is said to move with *constant speed*. For example, if a train covers 26 ft of track every second that it moves, we say that it has a constant speed of

26 ft/s. Whether the speed is constant or not, the average speed of a moving object is defined by

$$\text{Average speed} = \frac{\text{distance traveled}}{\text{time elapsed}}$$

$$\bar{v} = \frac{s}{t} \tag{5-1}$$

The bar over the symbol v means that the speed represents an average value for the time interval t.

Remember that the dimension of speed is the ratio of a length to a time interval. Hence, the units of miles per hour, feet per second, meters per second, and centimeters per second are all typical units of speed.

EXAMPLE 5-1 A golfer sinks a putt 3 s after the ball leaves the club face. If the ball traveled with an average speed of 0.8 m/s, how long was the putt?

Solution Solving Eq. (5-1) for s, we have

$$s = \bar{v}t = (0.8 \text{ m/s})(3 \text{ s})$$

Therefore, the distance of the putt is

$$s = 2.4 \text{ m}$$

It is important to recognize that speed is a scalar quantity which is completely independent of direction. In Example 5-1, it was not necessary for us to know either the speed of the golf ball at any instant or the nature of its path. Similarly, the average speed of a car traveling from Atlanta to Chicago is a function only of the distance registered on its odometer and the time required to make the trip. It makes no difference as far as computation is concerned whether the driver of the car took the direct or scenic route or even if he stopped for meals.

We must make a clear distinction between the scalar quantity *speed* and its directional counterpart *velocity*. This is best done by recalling the difference between *distance* and *displacement*, as discussed in Chap. 2. Suppose, in Fig. 5-1, an object moves along the broken path from A to B. The actual distance traveled is denoted by s, whereas the displacement is represented by the polar coordinates

$$\mathbf{D} = (D, \theta)$$

As an example, suppose the distance s in Fig. 5-1 is 500 mi, and the displacement is 350 mi at 45°. If the actual traveling time is 8 h, the average speed is

$$\bar{v} = \frac{s}{t} = \frac{500 \text{ mi}}{8 \text{ h}} = 62.5 \text{ mi/h}$$

Fig. 5-1 Displacement and velocity are vector quantities, whereas distance and speed are independent of direction: *s*, distance; **D**, displacement; **v**, velocity; *t*, time.

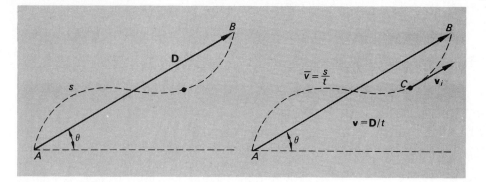

However, the average *velocity* must consider the displacement magnitude and direction. The average velocity is given by

$$\bar{\mathbf{v}} = \frac{\mathbf{D}}{t} = \frac{350 \text{ mi}, 45°}{8 \text{ h}}$$

$$\bar{\mathbf{v}} = 43.8 \text{ mi/h}, 45°$$

Therefore, if the path of the moving object is curved, the difference between speed and velocity is one of direction as well as magnitude.

Automobiles cannot always travel at constant speeds for long periods of time. In traveling from the point *A* to *B*, we may be required to slow down or speed up because of road conditions. For this reason, it is sometimes useful to talk of *instantaneous speed* or *instantaneous velocity*.

The **instantaneous speed** is a scalar quantity representing the speed at the instant the car is at an arbitrary point *C*. It is, therefore, the time rate of change in distance.

The **instantaneous velocity** is a vector quantity representing the velocity at any point *C*. It is the time rate of change in displacement.

In this chapter we shall be concerned primarily with average speed and average velocity. Note that if the motion is along a straight path (no change in direction), the terms *speed* and *velocity* may be used interchangeably. However, it is a good practice to reserve the term *velocity* for the more complete description of motion.

5-2 ACCELERATED MOTION

In most cases, the velocity of a moving object changes as motion continues. This type of motion is called *accelerated motion*. The time rate at which velocity changes is called the *acceleration*. For example, suppose we observe the motion of a body for a period of time *t*. The initial velocity $\mathbf{v}_0$ of the body will be defined as its velocity at the beginning of the time interval, i.e., when $t = 0$. The final velocity is defined as the velocity $\mathbf{v}_f$ the body has at the end of the time interval, when $t = t$. Thus, if we are able to measure the initial and final velocities of a moving object, we can say that its acceleration is given by

$$Acceleration = \frac{change\ in\ velocity}{time\ interval}$$

$$\mathbf{a} = \frac{\mathbf{v}_f - \mathbf{v}_0}{t} \tag{5-2}$$

Acceleration written in the above manner is a vector quantity and thus depends upon changes in direction as well as changes in magnitude. If the direction of motion is in a straight line, only the speed of the object is changing. If it follows a curved path, both magnitude and directional changes occur and the acceleration is no longer in the same direction as the motion. In fact, if the curved path follows a perfect circle, the acceleration will always be at right angles to the motion. In this case, only the direction of motion is changing while the speed at any point on the circle is constant. The latter type of motion will be treated in a later chapter.

5-3 UNIFORMLY ACCELERATED MOTION

The simplest kind of acceleration is motion in a straight line in which the speed changes at a constant rate. This special kind of motion is generally referred to as *uniformly accelerated motion or constant acceleration*. Since there is no change in direction, the vector difference in Eq. (5-2) becomes simply the algebraic difference between the magnitude of the final velocity $\mathbf{v}_f$ and the magnitude of the initial velocity $\mathbf{v}_0$. Hence, for uniform acceleration

$$a = \frac{v_f - v_0}{t} \tag{5-3}$$

For example, consider a car which moves with constant acceleration from point A to point B, as in Fig. 5-2. The car's speed at A is 40 ft/s, and its speed at B is 60 ft/s. If the increase in speed requires 5 s, the acceleration can be determined from Eq. (5-3). Hence

$$a = \frac{v_f - v_0}{t} = \frac{60\ \text{ft/s} - 40\ \text{ft/s}}{5\ \text{s}}$$

$$= \frac{20\ \text{ft/s}}{5\ \text{s}} = 4\ \text{ft/s}^2$$

The answer is read as *four feet per second per second* or *four feet per second squared*. It means that every second the car increases its speed by 4 ft/s. Since the car had already reached a speed of 40 ft/s when we started our time ($t = 0$), 1, 2, and 3 s later it would have speeds of 44, 48, and 52 ft/s, respectively.

Fig. 5-2 Uniformly accelerated motion.

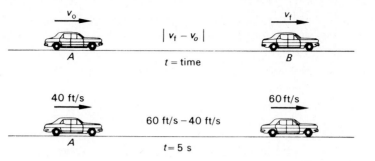

EXAMPLE 5-2

A train reduces its speed from 60 to 20 mi/h in 8 s. Find the acceleration.

Solution

We first note that there is an inconsistency of units between velocity in miles per hour and time in seconds. The velocity is converted to feet per second as follows:

$$60 \, \frac{mi}{h} \times \frac{5280 \text{ ft}}{1 \text{ mi}} \times \frac{1 \text{ h}}{3600 \text{ s}} = 88 \text{ ft/s}$$

Similarly, it is determined that 20 mi/h is equal to 29.3 ft/s. Substitution into Eq. (5-3) gives

$$a = \frac{v_f - v_0}{t} = \frac{29.3 \text{ ft/s} - 88 \text{ ft/s}}{8 \text{ s}}$$

$$a = -7.33 \text{ ft/s}^2$$

The minus sign tells us that the speed is *reduced* by 7.33 ft/s every second. This type of acceleration is sometimes referred to as *deceleration*.

Many times the same equation is used to solve for different quantities. You should, therefore, solve each equation literally for each symbol in the equation. A very convenient form arises for Eq. (5-3) when it is solved explicitly for the final speed. Thus

$$v_f = v_0 + at \qquad\qquad (5\text{-}4)$$

Final speed = initial speed + change in speed

EXAMPLE 5-3

An automobile maintains a constant acceleration of 8 m/s². If its initial speed was 20 m/s, what will its speed be after 6 s?

Solution

The final speed is obtained from Eq. (5-4).

$$v_f = v_0 + at = 20 \text{ m/s} + (8 \text{ m/s}^2)(6 \text{ s})$$

or

$$v_f = 20 \text{ m/s} + 48 \text{ m/s}$$

Hence the final speed is

$$v_f = 68 \text{ m/s}$$

Now that the concept of initial and final velocities is understood, let us return to the equation for average speed and express it in terms of initial and final states. The average velocity of an object moving with uniform acceleration is found just like the arithmetic mean of two numbers. Given an initial speed and a final speed, the average speed is simply

$$\bar{v} = \frac{v_f + v_0}{2} \tag{5-5}$$

Utilizing this relation in Eq. (5-1) gives us a more useful expression for computing distance:

$$s = \bar{v}t = \frac{v_f + v_0}{2} t \tag{5-6}$$

EXAMPLE 5-4   A moving object increases its speed uniformly from 200 to 400 cm/s in 2 min. (*a*) What is its average speed, and (*b*) how far did it travel in the 2 min?

Solution   The average speed is found by direct substitution into Eq. (5-5).

$$\bar{v} = \frac{v_f + v_0}{2} = \frac{400 \text{ cm/s} + 200 \text{ cm/s}}{2}$$

or

$$\bar{v} = \frac{600 \text{ cm/s}}{2} = 300 \text{ cm/s}$$

The distance traveled is then found from Eq. (5-1).

$$s = \bar{v}t = (300 \text{ cm/s})(2 \text{ min})$$

The units of time are inconsistent, but since 2 min = 120 s, we have

$$s = (300 \text{ cm/s})(120 \text{ s}) = 36{,}000 \text{ cm}$$

**5-4
OTHER
USEFUL
RELATIONS**

Thus far we have presented two fundamental relations. One arises from the definition of velocity and the other from the definition of acceleration. They are

$$s = \bar{v}t = \frac{v_f + v_0}{2} t \tag{5-6}$$

and

$$v_f = v_0 + at \tag{5-4}$$

Although these are the only formulas necessary to attack the many problems presented in this chapter, two other very useful relationships can be obtained from them. The first is derived by eliminating the final velocity from Eqs. (5-6) and (5-4). Substituting the latter into the former yields

$$s = \frac{(v_0 + at) + v_0}{2} t$$

Simplifying gives

$$s = \frac{(2v_0 + at)t}{2} = \frac{2v_0 t + at^2}{2}$$

or

$$\boxed{s = v_0 t + \tfrac{1}{2}at^2} \tag{5-7}$$

The second relation is derived by eliminating t from the basic equations. Solving Eq. (5-4) for t yields

$$t = \frac{v_f - v_0}{a}$$

which on substitution into Eq. (5-6) gives

$$s = \left(\frac{v_f + v_0}{2}\right)\left(\frac{v_f - v_0}{a}\right)$$

from which

$$\boxed{2as = v_f^2 - v_0^2} \tag{5-8}$$

Although these two equations add no new information, they are very useful in solving problems in which either the final velocity or time is not given and you need to find one of the other parameters.

**5-5
SOLUTION
OF ACCEL-
ERATION
PROBLEMS**

Although the solution to problems involving constant acceleration depends primarily upon choosing the correct formula and substituting known values, there are several suggestions to help the beginning student. Physical problems of this kind frequently involve motion which either started from rest or is brought to a stop from some initial speed. In either case, the formulas discussed can be simplified by the substitution of either $v_0 = 0$ or $v_f = 0$, as the case may be. Table 5-1 summarizes the general formulas.

**Table 5-1 Summary of
Acceleration Formulas**

(1) $\quad s = \dfrac{v_f + v_0}{2}\, t$

(2) $\quad v_f = v_0 + at$
(3) $\quad s = v_0 t + \tfrac{1}{2}at^2$
(4) $\quad 2as = v_f^2 - v_0^2$

A close look at the four general equations will reveal a total of five parameters: s, v_0, v_f, a, and t. Given any three of these quantities, the remaining two can be found from the general equations. Therefore, a good starting point in solving any problem is to read it thoroughly with a view to establishing the three quantities required for solution. It is also important to choose a direction to call positive and apply it consistently to speed, distance, and acceleration when inserting the values into equations.

If you have difficulty in deciding which equation should be used, it may help to recall the conditions such an equation must satisfy. First, it must contain the unknown parameter. Second, all other parameters that appear in the equation must be known. For example, if a problem gives you values for v_f, v_0, and t, you may solve for a in Eq. (2) of Table 5-1. The following examples will illustrate a technique for solving even the more difficult problems.

EXAMPLE 5-5   A motorboat starting from rest attains a speed of 30 mi/h in 15 s. What was its acceleration, and how far did it travel?

$$\text{Given: } v_0 = 0 \qquad\qquad \text{Find: } a = ?$$

$$v_f = 30 \text{ mi/h} = 44 \text{ ft/s} \qquad s = ?$$

$$t = 15 \text{ s}$$

Solution   In solving for acceleration, we must choose an equation which contains a but not s. Equation (2) can be used where $v_0 = 0$. Hence

$$v_f = at$$

from which

$$a = \frac{v_f}{t} = \frac{44 \text{ ft/s}}{15 \text{ s}}$$

$$= 2.93 \text{ ft/s}^2$$

The distance can be found from Eq. (1), as follows:

$$s = \frac{v_f}{2} t = \frac{44 \text{ ft/s}}{2} (15 \text{ s})$$

$$= 330 \text{ ft}$$

EXAMPLE 5-6   An airplane lands on a carrier deck at 200 mi/h and is brought to a stop in 600 ft. Find the acceleration and the time required to stop.

$$\text{Given: } v_0 = 200 \text{ mi/h} = 294 \text{ ft/s} \qquad \text{Find: } a = ?$$

$$v_f = 0 \qquad\qquad t = ?$$

$$s = 600 \text{ ft}$$

Solution   Choosing Eq. (4), we solve for a as follows:

$$2as = v_f^2 - v_0^2$$

$$(2a)(600 \text{ ft}) = 0 - (294 \text{ ft/s})^2$$

$$a = \frac{-(294 \text{ ft/s})^2}{(2)(600 \text{ ft})} = \frac{-86{,}400 \text{ ft}^2/\text{s}^2}{1200 \text{ ft}}$$

$$= -72 \text{ ft/s}^2$$

Then, solving for the time in Eq. (2) yields

$$t = \frac{v_f - v_0}{a} = \frac{-v_0}{a} = \frac{-294 \text{ ft/s}}{-72 \text{ ft/s}^2}$$

or

$$t = 4.08 \text{ s}$$

EXAMPLE 5-7 A train traveling initially at 16 m/s is under constant acceleration of 2 m/s². How far will it travel in 20 s? What will its final velocity be?

$$\text{Given: } v_0 = 16 \text{ m/s} \qquad \text{Find: } s = ?$$
$$a = 2 \text{ m/s}^2 \qquad\qquad v_f = ?$$
$$t = 20 \text{ s}$$

Solution From Eq. (3) we have

$$s = v_0 t + \tfrac{1}{2}at^2$$
$$= (16 \text{ m/s})(20 \text{ s}) + \tfrac{1}{2}(2 \text{ m/s}^2)(20 \text{ s})^2$$
$$= 320 \text{ m} + 400 \text{ m} = 720 \text{ m}$$

The final velocity is found from Eq. (2).

$$v_f = v_0 + at = 16 \text{ m/s} + (2 \text{ m/s}^2)(20 \text{ s})$$
$$= 56 \text{ m/s}$$

**5-6
GRAVITY
AND
FREELY
FALLING
BODIES**

Much of our knowledge about the physics of falling bodies originated with the Italian scientist Galileo Galilei (1564–1642). He was the first to demonstrate that in the absence of friction all bodies, large or small, heavy or light, fall to the earth with the same acceleration. This was a revolutionary idea, for it contradicted what a person might expect. Until the time of Galileo, people followed the teachings of Aristotle that heavy objects fall proportionally faster than lighter objects. The classic explanation for the paradox rests with the fact that heavier bodies are proportionately more difficult to accelerate. This resistance to motion is a property of a body called its *inertia*. Thus, in a vacuum, a feather will fall at the same rate as a steel ball because the larger inertial effect of the steel ball compensates exactly for its larger weight. (See Fig. 5-3.)

In the treatment of falling bodies given in this chapter, the effects of air friction are neglected entirely. Under these circumstances, gravitational acceleration is uniformly accelerated motion. At sea level and 45° latitude, this acceleration has been measured to be 32.17 ft/s², or 9.806 m/s², and is denoted by g. For our purposes, the following values will be sufficiently accurate:

$$\boxed{\begin{aligned} g &= 32 \text{ ft/s}^2 \\ g &= 9.8 \text{ m/s}^2 \end{aligned}} \tag{5-9}$$

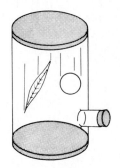

Fig. 5-3 All bodies fall with the same acceleration in a vacuum.

Since gravitational acceleration is constant acceleration, the same general equations of motion apply. However, one of the parameters is known in advance and need not be stated in the problem. If the constant g is inserted into the general equations (Table 5-1) the following modified forms will result:

$$(1a) \quad s = \frac{v_f + v_0}{2} t \qquad s = \bar{v}t$$

$$(2a) \quad v_f = v_0 + gt$$
$$(3a) \quad s = v_0 t + \tfrac{1}{2}gt^2$$
$$(4a) \quad 2gs = v_f^2 - v_0^2$$

Before utilizing these equations, a few general comments are in order. In problems dealing with free-falling bodies, it is extremely important to choose a direction to call positive and to follow through consistently in the substitution of known values. The sign of the answer is necessary to determine the location of a point or the direction of the velocity at specific times. For example, the distance s in the above equations represents the distance above or below the origin. If the upward direction is chosen as positive, a positive value for s indicates a distance above the starting point; if s is negative, it represents a distance below the starting point. Similarly, the signs of v_0, v_f, and g indicate their directions.

EXAMPLE 5-8   A rubber ball is dropped from rest, as shown in Fig. 5-4. Find its velocity and position after 1, 2, 3, and 4 s.

Solution   Since all parameters will be measured downward, it will be more convenient to choose the downward direction as positive. Organizing the data, we have

Given: $v_0 = 0$ $\qquad\qquad$ Find: $v_f = ?$

$$g = +32 \text{ ft/s}^2 \qquad\qquad s = ?$$

$$t = 1, 2, 3, \text{ and } 4 \text{ s}$$

The velocity as a function of time is given by Eq. (2a), where $v_0 = 0$.

$$v_f = v_0 + gt = gt$$

$$= (32 \text{ ft/s}^2)t$$

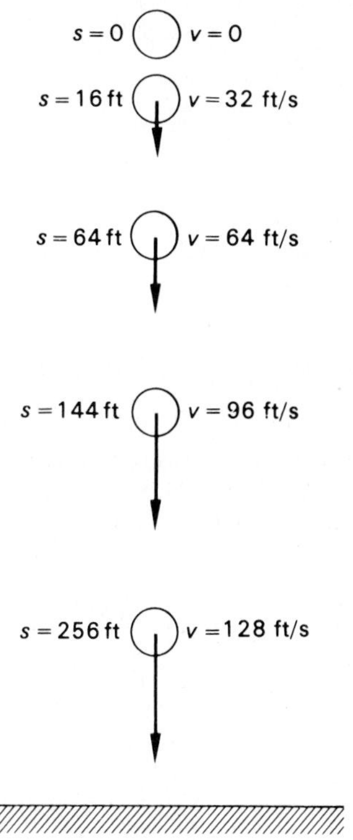

Fig. 5-4 A freely falling body has a constant downward acceleration of 32 ft/s².

$s = 0$ ◯ $v = 0$

$s = 16\,\text{ft}$ ◯ $v = 32$ ft/s

$s = 64\,\text{ft}$ ◯ $v = 64$ ft/s

$s = 144\,\text{ft}$ ◯ $v = 96$ ft/s

$s = 256\,\text{ft}$ ◯ $v = 128$ ft/s

After 1 s we have

$$v_f = (32\ \text{ft/s}^2)(1\ \text{s}) = 32\ \text{ft/s} \qquad \text{downward}$$

Similar substitution of $t = 2$, 3, and 4 s will yield final velocities of 64, 96, and 128 ft/s. All these velocities are directed downward since that direction was chosen as positive.

The position as a function of time is calculated from Eq. (3a). Since the initial velocity is zero, we write

$$s = v_0 t + \tfrac{1}{2}gt^2 = \tfrac{1}{2}gt^2$$

from which

$$s = \tfrac{1}{2}(32\ \text{ft/s}^2)t^2 = (16\ \text{ft/s}^2)t^2$$

After 1 s the body will fall a distance

$$s = (16\ \text{ft/s}^2)(1\ \text{s})^2 = (16\ \text{ft/s}^2)(1\ \text{s}^2)$$

$$= 16\ \text{ft}$$

After 2 s

$$s = (16\ \text{ft/s}^2)(2\ \text{s})^2 = (16\ \text{ft/s}^2)(4\ \text{s}^2)$$

$$= 64\ \text{ft}$$

Similarly, calculations give 144 and 256 ft for the positions after 3 and 4 s. The above results are summarized in Table 5-2.

Table 5-2

Time t, s	Speed at the end of time t, ft/s	Position at the end of time t, ft
0	0	0
1	32	16
2	64	64
3	96	144
4	128	256

EXAMPLE 5-9

Assuming a ball is projected upward with an initial velocity of 96 ft/s, explain without using equations how its upward motion is just the reverse of its downward motion.

Solution

We shall assume the upward direction to be positive, making the acceleration due to gravity equal to -32 ft/s². The negative sign indicates that the speed of an object projected vertically will have its speed reduced by 32 ft/s every second it rises. (Refer to Fig. 5-5.) If its initial speed is 96 ft/s, its speed after 1 s will be reduced to 64 ft/s. After 2 s its speed will be 32 ft/s, and after 3 s its speed will be reduced to zero. When the speed becomes zero, the ball has reached its maximum height and begins to fall freely from

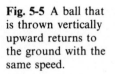

Fig. 5-5 A ball that is thrown vertically upward returns to the ground with the same speed.

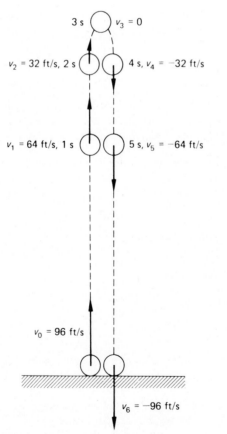

3 s $\quad v_3 = 0$

$v_2 = 32$ ft/s, 2 s $\qquad 4$ s, $v_4 = -32$ ft/s

$v_1 = 64$ ft/s, 1 s $\qquad 5$ s, $v_5 = -64$ ft/s

$v_0 = 96$ ft/s

$v_6 = -96$ ft/s

rest. However, now the speed of the ball will be *increasing* by 32 ft/s every second since both the direction of motion and the acceleration of gravity are in the negative direction. Its speed after 4, 5, and 6 s will be −32, −64, and −96 ft/s, respectively. Except for the sign, which indicates the direction of motion, the speeds are the same at equal heights above the ground.

EXAMPLE 5-10

A baseball thrown vertically upward from the roof of a tall building has an initial velocity of 20 m/s. (*a*) Calculate the time required to reach its maximum height. (*b*) Find the maximum height. (*c*) Determine its position and velocity after 1.5 s. (*d*) What are its position and velocity after 5 s? (See Fig. 5-6.)

Fig. 5-6 A ball projected vertically upward rises until its velocity is zero; then it falls with increasing velocity.

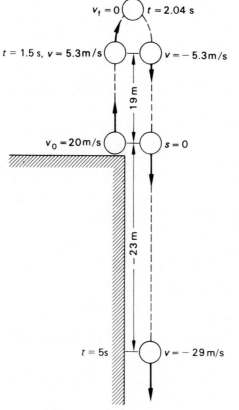

$v_f = 0$ $t = 2.04$ s

$t = 1.5$ s, $v = 5.3$ m/s $v = -5.3$ m/s

19 m

$v_0 = 20$ m/s $s = 0$

−23 m

$t = 5$ s $v = -29$ m/s

Solution (*a*)

Let us choose the upward direction as positive since the initial speed is directed upward. At the highest point, the final velocity of the ball will be zero. Organizing the known data, we have

$$\text{Given: } v_0 = 20 \text{ m/s} \qquad \text{Find: } t = ?$$
$$v_f = 0 \qquad\qquad s = ?$$
$$g = -9.8 \text{ m/s}^2$$

The time required to reach the maximum height can be determined from Eq. (2a):

$$t = \frac{v_f - v_0}{g} = -\frac{v_0}{g}$$

$$= \frac{-20 \text{ m/s}}{-9.8 \text{ m/s}^2} = 2.04 \text{ s}$$

Solution (b)   The maximum height is found by setting $v_f = 0$ in Eq. (1a).

$$s = \frac{v_f + v_0}{2} t = \frac{v_0}{2} t$$

$$= \frac{20 \text{ m/s}}{2} (2.04 \text{ s}) = 20.4 \text{ m}$$

Solution (c)   To find the position and velocity after 1.5 s, we must establish new conditions.

Given: $v_0 = 20$ m/s   Find: $s = ?$

$g = -9.8$ m/s^2 $v_f = ?$

$t = 1.5$ s

We can now calculate the position as follows:

$$s = v_0 t + \tfrac{1}{2}gt^2$$

$$= (20 \text{ m/s})(1.5 \text{ s}) + \tfrac{1}{2}(-9.8 \text{ m/s}^2)(1.5 \text{ s})^2$$

$$= 30 \text{ m} - 11 \text{ m} = 19 \text{ m}$$

The velocity after 1.5 s is given by

$$v_f = v_0 + gt$$

$$= 20 \text{ m/s} + (-9.8 \text{ m/s}^2)(1.5 \text{ s})$$

$$= 20 \text{ m/s} - 14.7 \text{ m/s} = 5.3 \text{ m/s}$$

Solution (d)   The same equations apply to find the position and velocity after 5 s. Thus

$$s = v_0 t + \tfrac{1}{2}gt^2$$

$$= (20 \text{ m/s})(5 \text{ s}) + \tfrac{1}{2}(-9.8 \text{ m/s}^2)(5 \text{ s})^2$$

$$= 100 \text{ m} - 123 \text{ m} = -23 \text{ m}$$

The negative sign indicates that the ball is located 23 m below the point of release. The speed after 5 s is given by

$$v_f = v_0 + gt$$

$$= 20 \text{ m/s} + (-9.8 \text{ m/s}^2)(5 \text{ s})$$

$$= 20 \text{ m/s} - 49 \text{ m/s} = -29 \text{ m/s}$$

In this case, the negative sign indicates that the ball is traveling downward.

SUMMARY

A convenient way of describing objects in motion is to discuss their *velocity* or their acceleration. In this chapter, a number of applications have been presented which involve these physical quantities.

- **Average velocity** is the distance traveled per unit of time, and **average acceleration** is the change in velocity per unit of time.

$$\bar{v} = \frac{s}{t} \qquad a = \frac{v_f - v_0}{t}$$

- The definitions of velocity and acceleration result in the establishment of four basic equations involving uniformly accelerated motion:

$$s = \left(\frac{v_0 + v_f}{2}\right)t$$

$$v_f = v_0 + at$$

$$s = v_0 t + \tfrac{1}{2}at^2$$

$$2as = v_f^2 - v_0^2$$

Given any three of the five parameters (v_0, v_f, a, s, and t), the other two can be determined from one of these equations.

- To solve acceleration problems, read the problem with a view to establishing the three given parameters and the two which are unknown. You might set up columns like

$$\text{Given: } a = 4 \text{ m/s}^2 \qquad \text{Find: } v_f = ?$$
$$s = 500 \text{ m} \qquad\qquad v_0 = ?$$
$$t = 20 \text{ s}$$

This procedure helps you choose the appropriate equation. Remember to choose a direction as positive and to apply it consistently throughout the problem.

- **Gravitational acceleration:** Problems involving gravitational acceleration can be solved like other acceleration problems. In this case, one of the parameters is known in advance to be

$$a = g = 9.8 \text{ m/s}^2 \text{ or } 32 \text{ ft/s}^2$$

The sign of the gravitational acceleration is + or − depending on whether you choose up or down as the positive direction.

QUESTIONS

5-1. Define the following terms:

a. Constant speed	**e.** Instantaneous velocity
b. Average speed	**f.** Instantaneous speed
c. Velocity	**g.** Uniformly accelerated motion
d. Acceleration	**h.** Acceleration due to gravity

5-2. Distinguish clearly between the terms *speed* and *velocity*. A stock-car racer drives 500 laps around a 1-mi track in a time of 5 h. What was the average speed? What was the average velocity?

5-3. A bus driver travels a distance of 200 mi in 4 h. At the same time, a tourist travels the 200 mi by car but stops twice for a 30-min rest along the route. Nevertheless, the tourist arrives at the destination at the same instant as the bus driver. Compare the average speed of the bus driver with the average speed of the tourist.

5-4. Give some examples of motion in which the speed is constant but the velocity is not.

5-5. Two evenly spaced bowling balls are rolling along a level return trough at constant speed. Describe their later speed and separation in view of the fact that the first ball starts uphill to the rack before the second ball.

5-6. A sports announcer states, "The newly designed race car negotiated the 500-mi obstacle course in a record-breaking endurance run, reaching average speeds of 150 mi/h along the way." What is wrong with this statement?

5-7. A long strip of pavement is marked off in 100-ft intervals. Students stationed on a nearby ridge use their stopwatches to measure the time required for a car to cover the distance. The following data are obtained:

Distance, ft	0	100	200	300	400	500
Time, s	0	2.1	4.3	6.4	8.4	10.5

Plot a graph with distance as the ordinate and time as the abscissa. What is the significance of the slope of the curve? What is the speed of the car?

5-8. The acceleration of gravity on a distant planet is one-fourth of the acceleration experienced on the earth. Does this mean that a rock dropped from a height of 4 ft will hit the ground in one-fourth the time required on the earth? Explain.

5-9. A spring-loaded gun fires a Ping-Pong ball vertically upward. On the moon the ball is observed to rise to a height of six times that observed on the earth. What can we say about the acceleration of gravity on the surface of the moon?

5-10. The symbol g is sometimes referred to as *gravity* or the *acceleration of gravity*. Comment on the appropriateness of these expressions.

PROBLEMS

5-1. A transfer truck traveled 640 mi on a run from Atlanta to New York (state) The entire trip took 14 h, but the driver made two 30-min stops for meals. What was the average speed for the trip?

Ans. 45.7 mi/h.

5-2. A dump truck gets about 9 mi on a gallon of fuel, which is priced at a dollar a gallon. What will be the cost of driving this truck for 2 h if its average speed is 30 mi/h?

5-3. An arrow leaves the bow 0.5 s after being released from a cocked position. If it has reached a speed of 40 m/s in this time, what was the average acceleration?

Ans. 80 m/s².

5-4. An automobile traveling at a constant speed of 50 km/h accelerates at a rate of 4 m/s^2 for 3 s. What is its speed at the end of the 3-s interval?

5-5. A truck traveling at a speed of 60 mi/h suddenly brakes to a stop. The skid marks are observed to be 180 ft long. What was the average acceleration, and how much time was required to stop the truck after the brakes were applied?

Ans. -21.5 ft/s^2, 4.09 s.

5-6. An arresting device is used to land airplanes on a carrier deck. The average acceleration produced by this device is -150 ft/s^2, and the airplanes are generally stopped in a time of 3 s. Under these conditions, what would be the approach velocity and the stopping distance?

5-7. A car travels at a constant speed of 55 mi/h. If the driver's mind wanders for a couple of seconds, how far will the car have traveled?

Ans. 161 ft.

5-8. A truck travels for 2 h at an average speed of 60 km/h. Then, it travels for 3 h at an average speed of 40 km/h. What was the total distance traveled and the average speed for the entire trip?

5-9. An elevator is lifted at a constant speed of 40 ft/s. How much time is required for the elevator to be lifted 200 ft?

Ans. 5 s.

5-10. Two cities are 2000 km apart. What must be the average speed of a light plane if it is to make the trip in 10 h?

5-11. A bullet leaves a 28-in. rifle barrel with a muzzle velocity of 2700 ft/s. What was its average acceleration in the barrel, assuming that it started from rest? How long did the bullet remain in the barrel after the rifle was fired?

Ans. 1.56×10^6 ft/s^2, 0.00173 s.

5-12. A monorail train traveling at 80 km/h must be brought to a stop in a distance of 40 m. What average acceleration is required, and what is the stopping time?

5-13. In a braking test, a car is observed to come to rest in 3 s. What were the acceleration and the stopping distance if the initial speed of the car was 60 km/h?

Ans. -5.56 m/s^2, 25.0 m.

5-14. A rocket traveling at 400 ft/s in space is given a sudden acceleration. If it reaches a speed of 600 ft/s in 4 s, what was its average acceleration? How far did it travel in this time?

5-15. A railroad car loaded with coal starts from rest and coasts freely down a gentle slope. If the average acceleration is 4 ft/s^2, what will be the speed of the car in 5 s? What distance will be covered in this period of time?

Ans. 20 ft/s, 50 ft.

5-16. A crane is used to lift a steel I-beam to the top of a 100-ft building. For the first 2 s, the beam is lifted from rest with an upward acceleration of 8 ft/s^2. If the speed remains constant for the remainder of the trip, how much total time was required to raise the beam from the ground to the roof?

5-17. A rocket starting from rest on the launching pad acquires a vertical velocity of 140 m/s in 9 s. Find **(a)** the acceleration, **(b)** the distance above the ground at the end of 9 s, and **(c)** the velocity at the end of 3 s.

Ans. **(a)** 15.6 m/s^2 **(b)** 630 m **(c)** 46.7 m/s.

5-18. A train accelerates from rest at 4 ft/s^2. After covering a distance of 200 ft, the train then travels at a constant velocity for 4 s. At that instant, the train is braked to a stop in 6 s. What is the total distance traveled, and how much total time was required?

5-19. A brick is dropped from the top of the bridge 80 m above the water. **(a)** How long is the brick in the air? **(b)** With what velocity does the brick strike the water?

Ans. **(a)** 4.04 s **(b)** 39.6 m/s.

5-20. A bolt is accidentally dropped from the top of a building. Five seconds later it strikes the street below. **(a)** How high is the building? **(b)** What is the final speed?

5-21. An arrow is shot vertically upward with an initial velocity of 80 ft/s. **(a)** How long will it rise? **(b)** How high will it rise? **(c)** What are its position and velocity after 2 s? **(d)** What are its position and velocity after 6 s?

Ans. **(a)** 2.5 s **(b)** 100 ft **(c)** 96 ft, 16 ft/s **(d)** −96 ft, −112 ft/s.

5-22. A hammer is thrown vertically upward to the top of a roof 50 ft high. **(a)** What was the minimum initial velocity required? **(b)** How much time was required?

5-23. A ball is dropped from the window of a skyscraper, and 2 s later a second ball is thrown vertically downward. What must the initial velocity of the second ball be if it is to overtake the first ball just as it strikes the ground 400 m below?

Ans. 22.3 m/s.

5-24. A stone is thrown vertically downward from the top of a bridge. Four seconds later it strikes the water below with a final velocity of 60 m/s. **(a)** What was the initial velocity of the stone? **(b)** How high is the bridge above the water?

5-25. A balloonist rising vertically with a velocity of 4 m/s releases a sandbag at the instant when the balloon is 16 m above the ground. **(a)** Compute the position and velocity of the sandbag (relative to the ground) after 0.3 s and after 2 s. **(b)** How many seconds after its release will it strike the ground? **(c)** With what speed does it strike the ground?

Ans. **(a)** 16.76 m, 1.06 m/s, 4.4 m, −15.6 m/s **(b)** 2.26 s **(c)** −18.2 m/s.

5-26. A baggage lift is accelerating upward at 5 ft/s². At the instant its upward speed is 8.0 ft/s a bolt drops from the top of the lift 10 ft from its floor. **(a)** Find the time until the bolt strikes the floor. **(b)** What distance has the bolt fallen relative to the ground?

5-27. An arrow is shot vertically upward with a speed of 40 m/s and 3 s later another is shot upward with a velocity of 60 m/s. At what time and position will they meet?

Ans. 4.54 s, 80.6 m.

6 *Projectile Motion*

OBJECTIVES: After completing this chapter, you should be able to:

1. **Explain with equations and diagrams the horizontal and vertical motion of a projectile launched at various angles.**

2. **Determine the position and velocity of a projectile when its initial velocity and position are given.**

3. **Determine the range, the maximum height, and the time of flight for a projectile when the initial speed and angle of projection are given.**

We have seen that objects projected vertically upward or downward or dropped from rest are accelerated uniformly in the earth's gravitational field. In this chapter, we consider the more general problem of an object projected freely into a gravitational field in a nonvertical direction, as shown in Fig. 6-1.

An object launched into space without motive power of its own is called a *projectile*. If we neglect air resistance, the only force acting on a projectile is its weight **W**, which causes its path to deviate from a straight line. It receives constant downward acceleration due to gravity, but it differs from the motion studied previously. The direction of the acceleration usually differs from that of the initial velocity. The projectile has a constant horizontal velocity and a vertical velocity that changes uniformly under the influence of gravity.

6-1 HORIZONTAL PROJECTION

If an object is projected horizontally, its motion can best be described by considering its horizontal and vertical motion separately. For example, in Fig. 6-2, a ball is dropped vertically at the same instant that another ball is projected horizontally. The horizontal velocity for the latter ball is unchanged, as

Fig. 6-1 A projectile is an object launched freely into space under the influence of gravity alone. The only force acting on such an object is its weight **W**.

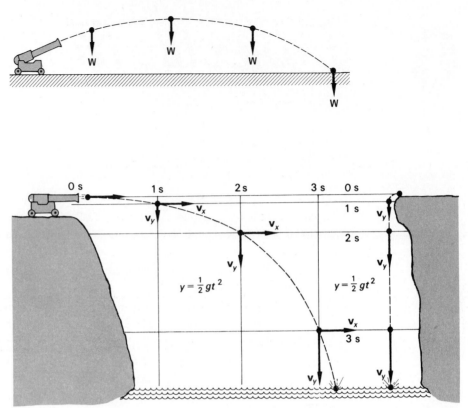

Fig. 6-2 Motion of a projectile fired horizontally. The vertical velocity and position increase with time like those of a free-falling body. Note that the horizontal distance increases linearly with time, indicating a constant horizontal velocity.

indicated by arrows of the same length throughout its trajectory. The vertical velocity, on the other hand, is initially zero and increases uniformly, in accordance with equations derived in Chap. 5 for freely falling bodies. The balls will strike the water at the same instant, even though one is also moving horizontally. Thus problems are greatly simplified by finding separate solutions for horizontal and vertical components.

A comparison of the general equations for uniformly accelerated motion with those used for projectile motion is given in Table 6-1. For example, the equation relating distance to initial velocity and time

$$s = v_0 t + \tfrac{1}{2}at^2$$

can be written

$$y = v_{0y} t + \tfrac{1}{2}gt^2$$

where y = vertical position
v_{0y} = initial vertical velocity
g = acceleration of gravity

For problems in which the initial velocity is horizontal, the final position will be below the origin, and the final velocity will be directed downward.

Table 6-1 Uniformly Accelerated Motion and Projectiles

Uniformly accelerated motion	Projectile motion	
(1) $s = \bar{v}t = \dfrac{v_0 + v_f}{2}t$	$x = \bar{v}_{0x}t$	$y = \dfrac{v_{0y} + v_y}{2}t$
(2) $v_f = v_0 + at$	$v_y = v_{0y} + gt$	
(3) $s = v_0 t + \frac{1}{2}at^2$	$y = v_{0y}t + \frac{1}{2}gt^2$	
(4) $2as = v_f^2 - v_0^2$	$2gy = v_y^2 - v_{0y}^2$	

Since gravity is also directed vertically downward, it is more convenient to choose the downward direction as positive. It should also be noted that for horizontal projection

$$v_{0x} = \bar{v}_x \qquad v_{0y} = 0$$

since the horizontal velocity is constant and the initial vertical velocity is zero. Therefore, the horizontal and vertical positions at any instant can be found from

$$\boxed{\begin{aligned} x &= v_{0x}t \\ y &= \tfrac{1}{2}gt^2 \end{aligned}} \qquad \begin{aligned} &\textit{Horizontal Position} \\ &\textit{Vertical Position} \end{aligned} \qquad \text{(6-1)}$$

Similarly, the horizontal and vertical components of the final velocity at any instant are given by

$$\boxed{\begin{aligned} \bar{v}_x &= v_{0x} \\ v_y &= gt \end{aligned}} \qquad \begin{aligned} &\textit{Horizontal Velocity} \\ &\textit{Vertical Velocity} \end{aligned} \qquad \text{(6-2)}$$

The final position and velocity can be found from their components. In all the above equations, the positive value must be substituted for g if we choose the downward direction as positive.

EXAMPLE 6-1

A cannonball is projected horizontally with an initial velocity of 120 m/s from the top of a cliff 250 m above a lake, as illustrated in Fig. 6-3. (*a*) In what time will it strike the water at the foot of the cliff? (*b*) What is the horizontal distance from the foot of the cliff to the point of impact in the lake? (*c*) What are the horizontal and vertical components of its final velocity?

Solution (a)

The time required to strike the water is a function only of vertical parameters. The initial velocity in the *y* direction is zero, and the ball must fall through a distance of 250 m. Therefore,

$$y = \tfrac{1}{2}gt^2$$

which yields, on substitution,

$$250 \text{ m} = \tfrac{1}{2}(9.8 \text{ m/s}^2)t^2$$

Fig. 6-3

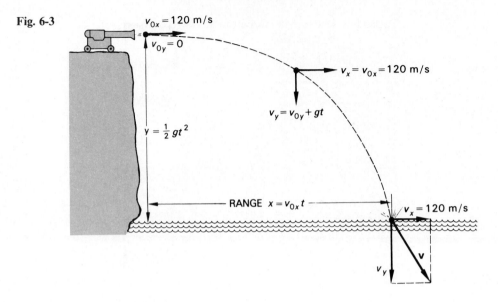

$v_{0x} = 120$ m/s

$v_{0y} = 0$

$v_x = v_{0x} = 120$ m/s

$v_y = v_{0y} + gt$

$y = \frac{1}{2}gt^2$

RANGE $x = v_{0x}t$

$v_x = 120$ m/s

v

v_y

Simplifying, we obtain

$$(4.9 \text{ m/s}^2)t^2 = 250 \text{ m}$$

from which

$$t = \sqrt{\frac{250 \text{ s}^2}{4.9}} = 7.14 \text{ s}$$

Solution (b)   The horizontal distance is a function only of the initial horizontal velocity and the time required to strike the water. Hence

$$x = v_{0x}t = (120 \text{ m/s})(7.14 \text{ s}) = 857 \text{ m}$$

Solution (c)   The horizontal component of the velocity is unchanged and equal to 120 m/s. The vertical component, on the other hand, is given by

$$v_y = gt = (9.8 \text{ m/s})(7.14 \text{ s})$$

$$= 70 \text{ m/s}$$

It is left as an exercise to show that the final velocity at the point of impact is 139 m/s in a direction 30.3° below the horizontal.

**6-2
THE MORE
GENERAL
PROBLEM
OF TRAJEC-
TORIES**

The more general case of projectile motion occurs when the projectile is fired at an angle. This problem is illustrated in Fig. 6-4, where the motion of a projectile fired at an angle θ with an initial velocity $\mathbf{v}_0$ is compared with the motion of an object projected vertically upward. Once again it is easy to see the advantage of treating the horizontal and vertical motions separately. In this case the equations listed in Table 6-1 may be used, and we should consider the upward direction as positive. Thus, if the vertical position y is above the origin, it will

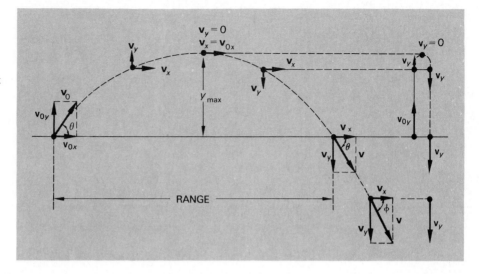

Fig. 6-4 The motion of a projectile fired at an angle is compared with the motion of an object thrown vertically upward.

be positive; if it is below the origin, it will be negative. Similarly, upward velocities will be positive. Since the acceleration is always directed downward, we must substitute a negative value for g.

The following procedure is useful in solving most projectile problems:

1. Resolve the initial velocity $\mathbf{v}_0$ into its x and y components:

$$v_{0x} = v_0 \cos \theta \qquad v_{0y} = v_0 \sin \theta \qquad \text{(6-3)}$$

2. The horizontal and vertical components of its position at any instant are given by

$$x = v_{0x} t$$
$$y = v_{0y} t + \tfrac{1}{2} g t^2 \qquad \text{(6-4)}$$

3. The horizontal and vertical components of its velocity at any instant are given by

$$v_x = v_{0x}$$
$$v_y = v_{0y} + gt \qquad \text{(6-5)}$$

4. The final position and velocity can then be obtained from their components.

The important point to remember in applying these equations is to be consistent throughout with units and sign convention.

EXAMPLE 6-2   An artillery shell is fired with an initial velocity of 400 ft/s at an angle of 30° above the horizontal. Find (*a*) its position and velocity after 8 s, (*b*) the time required to reach its maximum height, and (*c*) the horizontal range R as indicated in Fig. 6-4.

Solution (a)   The horizontal and vertical components of the initial velocity are

$$v_{0x} = v_0 \cos \theta = (400 \text{ ft/s})(\cos 30°) = 346 \text{ ft/s}$$

$$v_{0y} = v_0 \sin \theta = (400 \text{ ft/s})(\sin 30°) = 200 \text{ ft/s}$$

The x component of its position after 8 s is

$$x = v_{0x} t = (346 \text{ ft/s})(8 \text{ s}) = 2770 \text{ ft}$$

The y component of its position at this time is given by

$$y = v_{0y} t + \tfrac{1}{2} g t^2$$

from which

$$y = (200 \text{ ft/s})(8 \text{ s}) + \tfrac{1}{2}(-32 \text{ ft/s}^2)(8 \text{ s})^2$$

$$= 1600 \text{ ft} - 1024 \text{ ft} = 576 \text{ ft}$$

Hence, the position of the shell after 8 s is 2770 ft down range and 576 ft above its initial position.

In computing its velocity at this point, we first recognize that the x component of the velocity does not change. Thus

$$v_x = v_{0x} = 346 \text{ ft/s}$$

The y component must be computed from

$$v_y = v_{0y} + gt$$

so that

$$v_y = 200 \text{ ft/s} + (-32 \text{ ft/s})(8 \text{ s})$$

$$= 200 \text{ ft/s} - 256 \text{ ft/s}$$

$$= -56 \text{ ft/s}$$

The minus sign indicates that the projectile is on its way down. Finally, we can compute the resultant velocity from its components, as shown in Fig. 6-5. The angle ϕ is calculated from

$$\tan \phi = \frac{v_y}{v_x} = \frac{56}{346} = 0.162$$

from which

$$\phi = 9.2°$$

Fig. 6-5

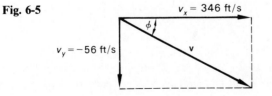

$$v_x = 346 \text{ ft/s}$$

$$v_y = -56 \text{ ft/s}$$

The magnitude of the velocity is

$$v = \frac{v_y}{\sin \phi} = \frac{56}{\sin 9.2°} = 350 \text{ ft/s}$$

Solution (b)

At the maximum point in the shell's trajectory, the y component of its velocity is zero. Hence, the time to reach this height can be computed from

$$v_y = v_{0y} + gt$$

Substituting given values for v_{0y} and g, we obtain

$$0 = 200 \text{ ft/s} + (-32 \text{ ft/s})t$$

from which

$$t = \frac{200 \text{ ft/s}}{32 \text{ ft/s}^2} = 6.25 \text{ s}$$

As an exercise, it is suggested that the student use this result to show that the maximum height in the trajectory is 625 ft.

Solution (c)

The range of the projectile can be computed by recognizing that the total time t' of the entire flight is equal to twice the time to reach the highest point. Hence

$$t' = 2t = (2)(6.25 \text{ s}) = 12.5 \text{ s}$$

and the range is

$$R = v_{0x} t' = (346 \text{ ft/s})(12.5 \text{ s})$$

$$= 4325 \text{ ft}$$

Therefore, the projectile rises for 6.25 s to a height of 625 ft and then falls to the ground at a horizontal distance of 4325 ft from the point of release.

SUMMARY

The key to problems involving projectile motion is to treat the horizontal motion and the vertical motion separately. Most projectile problems are solved using the following approach:

- Resolve the initial velocity v_0 into its x and y components:

$$\boxed{v_{0x} = v_0 \cos \theta} \qquad \boxed{v_{0y} = v_0 \sin \theta}$$

- The horizontal and vertical components of its position at any instant are given by

$$\boxed{x = v_{0x} t} \qquad \boxed{y = v_{0y} t + \tfrac{1}{2}gt^2}$$

- The horizontal and vertical components of its velocity at any instant are given by

$$\boxed{v_x = v_0} \qquad \boxed{v_y = v_0 + gt}$$

- The final position and velocity can then be obtained from their components.

The important point to remember in applying these equations is to be consistent throughout with units and sign conversion.

6-1. Define the following terms:
a. Projectile
b. Trajectory
c. Range

6-2. Is the motion of a projectile fired at an angle an example of uniformly accelerated motion? What if the projectile is fired vertically upward? Explain.

6-3. At what angle should a baseball be thrown if it is to reach its maximum range? At what angle must it be thrown to attain maximum height? Plot the trajectories you would expect for a ball thrown at **(a)** 90°, **(b)** 60°, **(c)** 45°, **(d)** 30°, and **(e)** 0°.

6-4. Suppose a hunter shoots an arrow directly at a squirrel on a tree limb, and the squirrel begins to fall at the instant the arrow leaves the bow. Will the arrow hit the squirrel? Why? Draw a sketch showing their relative motions.

6-5. A child drops a rubber ball from the window of a car traveling at a constant speed of 60 mi/h. What is the initial velocity of the ball relative to the ground? Describe its motion.

6-6. A toy car is pulled across the floor with uniform speed. If a marble is projected vertically upward from the car, describe its motion in relation to the car. Describe its motion in relation to the floor.

6-7. Explain the adjustment of sights on a rifle for increasing target distances.

6-8. Explain the reasoning behind the use of high or low trajectories for punting in a football game.

PROBLEMS

6-1. A box of supplies is dropped from an airplane which is located a vertical distance of 340 m above a lake. If the plane has a horizontal velocity of 70 m/s, what horizontal distance will the box travel before striking the water?

Ans. 583 m.

6-2. Logs are discharged horizontally from a greased shute which is located 20 m above a millpond. If the logs leave the shute with a horizontal speed of 15 m/s, how far will the logs travel horizontally before striking the water?

6-3. An overhead crane has an electromagnet which is 80 ft above the ground. The crane operator wants to drop a piece of scrap metal at a spot 60 ft beyond the end of the crane's track. What horizontal speed must the crane have when it reaches the end of its track?

Ans. 26.8 ft/s.

6-4. A steel ball rolls off the edge of a table top 6 ft high. If the ball strikes the floor at a distance of 5 ft from the base of the table, what was its velocity at the instant it left the table?

6-5. A stone is thrown horizontally from the top of a building with an initial velocity of 200 m/s. At the same instant another stone is dropped from rest. **(a)** Compute the position and velocity of the second stone after 3 s. **(b)** How far has the first stone traveled horizontally during this 3 s? **(c)** How far has it traveled vertically? **(d)** What are the horizontal and vertical components of its velocity after 3 s?

Ans. **(a)** −44.1 m, −29.8 m/s **(b)** 600 m **(c)** −44.1 m **(d)** 200 m/s, −29.8 m/s.

6-6. A marble is thrown horizontally with an initial speed of 1000 ft/s. Another marble is dropped at the same instant. Answer the same questions as in Prob. 6-5.

6-7. Two tall buildings are 400 ft apart. A ball is thrown horizontally from the roof of the first building 1700 ft from the ground. With what horizontal speed must the ball be thrown if it is to enter a window of the second building 800 ft from the ground?

Ans. 53.3 ft/s.

6-8. A rifle bullet is fired in a horizontal direction and strikes the bull's-eye 50 m down range. The center of the bull's-eye is 100 mm below the rifle's line of sight. What was the muzzle velocity of the bullet?

6-9. A bomber flying with a horizontal speed of 500 mi/h releases a bomb. Six seconds later the bomb strikes the ocean below. At what altitude was the plane flying? How far did the bomb travel horizontally? What are the magnitude and direction of its final velocity?

Ans. 576 ft, 4400 ft, 758 ft/s, $-14.7°$.

6-10. A stream of water from the nozzle of a hose emerges horizontally with a speed of 12 m/s. If the water strikes the ground 0.5 s later, how high is the nozzle from the ground? What is the horizontal range?

6-11. An arrow is shot into the air with a velocity of 120 ft/s at an angle of 37° with the horizontal. **(a)** What are the horizontal and vertical components of its initial velocity? **(b)** What is its position after 2 s? **(c)** What are the magnitude and direction of its resultant velocity after 2 s?

Ans. **(a)** 96 ft/s, 72 ft/s **(b)** $x = 192$ ft, $y = 80$ ft **(c)** 96 ft/s, 4.77°.

6-12. A stone is thrown at an angle of 58° with an initial speed of 16 km/h. What is its position and velocity after 3 s?

6-13. A projectile is launched at an angle of 30° with an initial speed of 20 m/s. **(a)** What is the highest point in its trajectory? **(b)** What is its horizontal range? **(c)** How much time is it in the air?

Ans. **(a)** 5.10 m **(b)** 35.3 m **(c)** 2.04 s.

6-14. A baseball leaves a bat with a velocity of 35 m/s at an angle of 32°. What is the highest point in its path? When will it strike a billboard in center field 8 m above the playing field?

6-15. A putting green is located 240 ft horizontally and 64 ft vertically from the tee. What must be the magnitude and direction of the initial velocity if a ball is to strike the green at this location after a time of 4 s?

Ans. 100 ft/s, 53.1°.

6-16. An arrow leaves its bow with a velocity of 40 m/s and at an angle of 41° with the horizontal. What is the horizontal range?

6-17. It is desired to strike a target, whose horizontal range is 12 km, with 105-mm howitzer projectiles. The angle of elevation is 35°. **(a)** Find the required muzzle velocity for the gun neglecting air resistance. **(b)** What is the time of flight to the target?

Ans. **(a)** 354 m/s **(b)** 41.4 s.

6-18. Two children ride bicycles toward each other with constant velocities of 20 and 10 ft/s. Each child releases a ball 6 ft from the ground with a forward horizontal velocity of 40 ft/s relative to the bicycle. If the two balls collide 1 ft from the ground, what was their separation when they were released?

6-19. A shot leaves a putter's hand 7 ft from the ground with an initial velocity of 40 ft/s at an angle of 42° with the horizontal. How long will it rise? What is the velocity of the shot at the highest point in its trajectory? What is its acceleration at this instant? How high is it from the ground at this instant? What is the horizontal range?

Ans. 0.836 s, 29.7 ft/s^2, 18.2 ft, 56.5 ft.

6-20. A wild boar charges directly toward a hunter with a constant speed of 60 ft/s. At the instant the boar is 100 yd away, the hunter fires an arrow at 30° with the ground. With what velocity must the arrow leave the hunter if it is to strike its target?

7 *Newton's Second Law*

OBJECTIVES: After completing this chapter, you should be able to:

1. Describe the relationship between force, mass, and acceleration and give the consistent units for each in the metric and U.S. customary systems of units.

2. Define the units *newton* and *slug* and explain why they are derived units rather than fundamental units.

3. Demonstrate by definition and example your understanding of the distinction between mass and weight.

4. Determine mass from weight and weight from mass at a point where the acceleration due to gravity is known.

5. Draw a free-body diagram for objects in motion with constant acceleration, set the resultant force equal to the total mass times the acceleration, and solve for unknown parameters.

According to Newton's first law of motion, an object will undergo a change in its state of rest or motion *only* when acted on by a resultant, unbalanced force. We now know that a change in motion, i.e., a change in speed, results in *acceleration*. In many industrial applications, we need to be able to predict the acceleration that will be produced by a given force. For example, the forward force required to accelerate a car from rest to a speed of 60 km/h in 8 s is of interest to the automotive industry. In this chapter, you will study the relationships between force, mass, and acceleration.

Before studying the relationship between a resultant force and the acceleration it produces in a formal way, let us consider a simple experiment.

A linear air track is an apparatus for studying the motion of objects under conditions that approximate zero friction. Hundreds of tiny air jets create an upward force which balances the weight of the glider in Fig. 7-1. A string is attached to the front of the glider, and a spring scale of negligible weight is used to measure the applied horizontal force as shown. The acceleration the glider receives can be measured by determining the change in speed for a known period of time. The first applied force F_1 in Fig. 7-1a causes an acceleration a_1.

Fig. 7-1 Variation of acceleration with applied force.

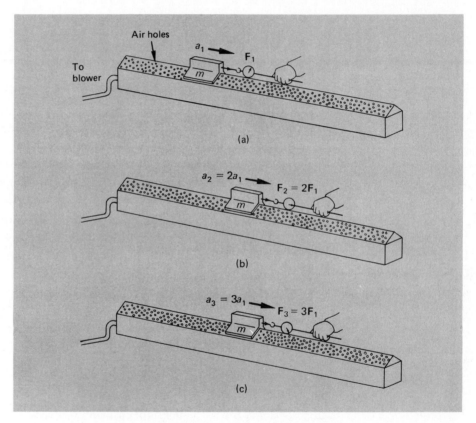

For example, when we apply a force of 4 lb, let's assume that we measure an acceleration of 2 ft/s². Next we double the applied force, as indicated in Fig. 7-1b, and again observe the acceleration.

Our observations will show that twice the force $2F_1$ will produce twice the acceleration $2a_1$. In other words, an 8-lb force would cause an acceleration of 4 ft/s² in our example. Similarly, tripling the force will increase the acceleration by a factor of 3. A force of 12 lb will produce an acceleration of 6 ft/s².

Thus, it is found that the acceleration of a body is directly proportional to the applied force and in the direction of that force. This means that the ratio of force to acceleration is always a constant:

$$\frac{F_1}{a_1} = \frac{F_2}{a_2} = \frac{F_3}{a_3} = \text{constant}$$

In our specific example, for forces of 4, 8, and 12 lb, the constant is equal to $2 \text{ lb} \cdot \text{s}^2/\text{ft}$.

We shall later see that this constant ratio can be considered as a property of the body called its mass m, where

$$m = \frac{F}{a}$$

Newton's second law is a statement of how the acceleration of a body varies with the applied force and the *mass* of the body. For the moment, the mass of an object may be thought of as the amount of matter that makes up the object. To understand the variation of acceleration with mass, let us return to our experiment. This time we shall keep the applied force F constant. The mass will be changed by adding in succession more gliders of equal size and weight. Note from Fig. 7-2 that if the force is unchanged, an increase in mass

Fig. 7-2 Variation of acceleration with mass.

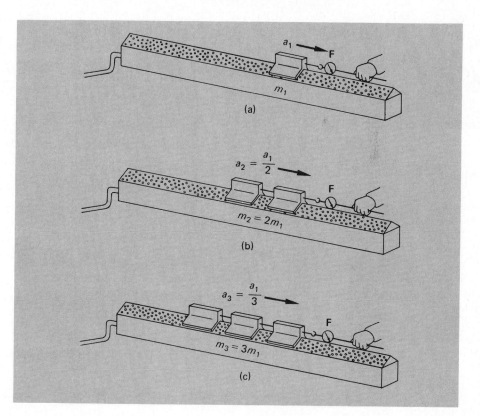

will result in a proportionate *decrease* in the acceleration. If the constant applied force is equal to 12 lb, we shall observe accelerations of 6, 3, and 2 ft/s² for the cases shown in Figs. 7-2*a*, *b*, and *c*, respectively.

From the above observations we are now prepared to state *Newton's second law of motion*:

> *Whenever an unbalanced force acts on a body, it produces in the direction of the force an acceleration that is directly proportional to the force and inversely proportional to the mass of the body.*

Accordingly, we can write the proportion

$$a \propto \frac{F}{m}$$

Whenever mass is held constant, an increase in the applied force will result in a similar increase in acceleration. On the other hand, if the force is unchanged, increasing the mass results in a proportionate decrease of acceleration. By choosing appropriate units, we can write this proportion as an equation:

Resultant force = mass × acceleration

$$\boxed{F = ma}$$

Newton's Second Law (7-1)

In order for a unit of force to be consistent with combined units of mass and acceleration, it is necessary to define one of the three parameters *F*, *m*, and *a* in terms of the other two. For example, we can choose the unit *kilogram* (kg) for mass *m* and the unit *meters per second squared* (m/s²) for acceleration *a*. From Eq. (7-1), the only consistent unit for force would be the kg · m/s². This awkward combination is redefined as a *newton* (N). Because of the use of derived units in Newton's second law, it is important to know the consistent units for each quantity.

1. The fundamental SI unit for mass is the *kilogram* (kg), and the acceleration unit is the *meter per second per second* (m/s²). The SI force unit derived from these units is called the *newton* (N). One **newton** is that resultant force required to give a one-kilogram mass an acceleration of one meter per second per second.

   Force (N) = *mass* (kg) × *acceleration* (m/s²)

2. In USCS, the mass unit is derived from the chosen units of *pound* (lb) for force and *feet per second per second* for acceleration. This new unit for mass is called the *slug* (from the *sluggish* or inertial property of mass). One **slug** (slug) is that mass to which a resultant force of one pound will give an acceleration of one foot per second per second.

   Force (lb) = *mass* (slugs) × *acceleration* (ft/s²)

The SI unit of force is less than the USCS unit, and a mass of one slug is much greater than a mass of one kilogram. The following conversion factors might be helpful:

$$1 \text{ lb} = 4.448 \text{ N} \qquad 1 \text{ slug} = 14.59 \text{ kg}$$

A 1-lb bag of apples might contain four or five apples—each weighing about a newton. A person weighing 160 lb on earth would have a mass of 5 slugs or 73 kg.

It is important to recognize that the F in Newton's second law represents a *resultant* or unbalanced force. If more than one force acts on an object, it will be necessary to determine the resultant force *along the direction of motion*. The resultant force will always be along the direction of motion, since it is the *cause* of the acceleration. All components of forces which are perpendicular to the acceleration will be balanced. If the x axis is chosen along the direction of motion, we can determine the x component of each force and write

$$\boxed{\sum F_x = ma_x} \qquad (7\text{-}2)$$

A similar equation could be written for the y components if the y axis were chosen along the direction of motion.

7-2 THE RELATIONSHIP BETWEEN WEIGHT AND MASS

Before we consider examples of Newton's second law, we must have a clear understanding of the difference between the *weight* of a body and its *mass*. Perhaps no other point is more confusing to the beginning student. The *pound* (lb), which is a unit of force, is often used as a mass unit, the pound-mass (lb_m). The kilogram, which is a unit of mass, is often used in industry as a unit of force, the kilogram-force (kgf). These seemingly inconsistent units result from the fact that there are many different systems of units in use. In this text, there should be less cause for confusion because we use only the SI and U.S. customary (British gravitational) units. Therefore, in this book the *pound* (lb) will always refer to *weight*, which is a force, and the unit *kilogram* (kg) will always refer to the *mass* of a body.

The weight of any body is the force with which the body is pulled vertically downward by gravity. When a body falls freely to the earth, the only force acting on it is its weight **W**. This net force produces an acceleration **g**, which is the same for all falling bodies. Thus, from Newton's second law we can write the relationship between a body's weight and its mass:

$$\boxed{W = mg \qquad \text{or} \qquad m = \frac{W}{g}} \qquad (7\text{-}3)$$

In either system of units (1) the mass of a particle is equal to its weight divided by the acceleration of gravity; (2) weight has the same units as the unit of force; and (3) the acceleration of gravity has the same units as acceleration.

Therefore, we can summarize as follows:

$$\text{SI: } W \text{ (N)} = m \text{ (kg)} \times g \text{ (9.8 m/s}^2)$$

$$\text{USCS: } W \text{ (lb)} = m \text{ (slug)} \times g \text{ (32 ft/s}^2)$$

The values for g, and hence the weights, in the above relations apply only at points on the earth near sea level, where g has these values.

Two things must be remembered in order to understand fully the difference between mass and weight:

Mass is a universal constant equal to the ratio of a body's weight to the gravitational acceleration due to its weight.

Weight is the *force* of gravitational attraction and varies depending upon the acceleration of gravity.

Therefore, the mass of a body is only a measure of its inertia and is not in any way dependent upon gravity. In outer space, a hammer has negligible weight, but it serves to drive nails just the same since its mass is unchanged.

In USCS units a body is usually described by stating its weight **W** in *pounds*. The mass, if desired, is computed from this weight and has the unit of *slugs*. In SI units a body is usually described in terms of its mass in *kilograms*. The weight, if desired, is computed from the given mass and has the units of *newtons*. In the following examples, all parameters are measured at points where $g = 32$ ft/s^2 or 9.8 m/s^2.

EXAMPLE 7-1   Find the mass of a person who weighs 150 lb.

Solution

$$m = \frac{W}{g} = \frac{150 \text{ lb}}{32 \text{ ft/s}^2} = 4.69 \text{ slugs}$$

EXAMPLE 7-2   Find the weight of an 18-kg block.

Solution

$$W = mg = 18 \text{ kg}(9.8 \text{ m/s}^2) = 176 \text{ N}$$

EXAMPLE 7-3   Find the mass of a body whose weight is 100 N.

Solution

$$m = \frac{W}{g} = \frac{100 \text{ N}}{9.8 \text{ m/s}^2} = 10.2 \text{ kg}$$

7-3 APPLICATION OF NEWTON'S SECOND LAW TO SINGLE-BODY PROBLEMS

The primary difference between the problems discussed in this chapter and earlier problems is that a net, unbalanced force is acting to produce an acceleration. Thus, after constructing the free-body diagrams which describe the situation, the first step is to determine the unbalanced force and set it equal to the product of mass and acceleration. The desired quantity can then be determined from the relation

Resultant force = mass × acceleration

$$\boxed{F \text{ (resultant)} = ma} \tag{7-1}$$

The following examples will serve to demonstrate the relationship between force, mass, and acceleration.

EXAMPLE 7-4   What acceleration will a force of 20 N impart to a 10-kg body?

Solution   There is only one force acting, and so

$$F = ma \qquad \text{or} \qquad a = \frac{F}{m}$$

and

$$a = \frac{20 \text{ N}}{10 \text{ kg}} = 2 \text{ m/s}^2$$

EXAMPLE 7-5   What resultant force will give a 32-lb body an acceleration of 5 ft/s²?

Solution   In order to find the resultant force we must first determine the mass of the body from its given weight.

$$m = \frac{W}{g} = \frac{32 \text{ lb}}{32 \text{ ft/s}^2} = 1 \text{ slug}$$

then

$$F = ma = (1 \text{ slug})(5 \text{ ft/s}^2) = 5 \text{ lb}$$

EXAMPLE 7-6   What mass has a body if a force of 60 N will give it an acceleration of 4 m/s?

Solution   Solving for m in Newton's law, we have

$$m = \frac{F}{a} = \frac{60 \text{ N}}{4 \text{ m/s}^2} = 15 \text{ kg}$$

In the preceding examples, the unbalanced forces were easily determined. However, as the number of forces acting on a body increases, the problem of determining the resultant force is less obvious. In these cases, perhaps it is wise to point out a few considerations.

According to Newton's second law, a resultant force always produces an acceleration *in the direction of the resultant force*. This means that the net force and the acceleration it causes are of the same algebraic sign, and they each have the same line of action. Therefore, if the direction of motion (acceleration) is considered positive, less negative factors will be introduced into the equation $F = ma$. For example, in Fig. 7-3b, it is preferable to choose the direction of motion (left) as positive since the equation

$$P - \mathscr{F}_\kappa = ma$$

is preferable to the equation

$$\mathscr{F}_\kappa - P = -ma$$

which would result if we chose the right direction as positive.

Fig. 7-3 The direction of acceleration should be chosen as positive.

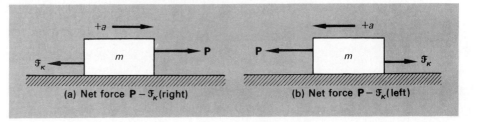

(a) Net force $P - \mathcal{F}_K$ (right)   (b) Net force $P - \mathcal{F}_K$ (left)

Another consideration which results from the above discussion is that the forces acting normal to the line of motion will be in equilibrium if the resultant force is constant. Thus, in problems involving friction, normal forces can be determined from the first condition for equilibrium.

In summary, we apply the following equations to acceleration problems:

$$\sum F_x = ma_x \qquad \sum F_y = ma_y = 0 \qquad (7\text{-}4)$$

where $\sum F_x$ and a_x are taken as positive and along the line of motion and $\sum F_y$ and a_y are taken normal to the line of motion.

EXAMPLE 7-7

A force of 100 lb pulls a 64-lb block horizontally across the floor. If $\mu_k = 0.1$, find the acceleration of the block.

Solution

A free-body diagram is superimposed on the sketch in Fig. 7-4. We will choose right as positive. To avoid confusing the weight of the block with its mass, it is often desirable to calculate each in advance. The weight (64 lb) is given, and the mass is found from $m = W/g$.

$$W = 64 \text{ lb} \qquad m = \frac{64 \text{ lb}}{32 \text{ ft/s}^2} = 2 \text{ slugs}$$

Fig. 7-4

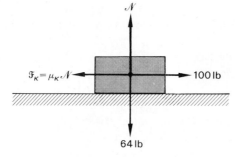

The resultant force along the floor is 100 lb less the force of friction $\mathcal{F}_k$. Applying Newton's second law, we obtain

Resultant force = mass × acceleration

$$100 \text{ lb} - \mathcal{F}_k = ma$$

Recalling that $\mathcal{F}_k = \mu_k \mathcal{N}$, we may write

$$100 \text{ lb} - \mu_k \mathcal{N} = ma$$

Since no motion occurs in the vertical direction, we note from the figure that

$$\mathcal{N} = W = 64 \text{ lb}$$

Substituting $\mathcal{N} = 64$, $\mu_k = 0.1$, and $m = 2$ slugs, we have

$$100 \text{ lb} - (0.1)(64 \text{ lb}) = (2 \text{ slugs})a$$

Simplifying and solving for a yields

$$100 \text{ lb} - 6.4 \text{ lb} = (2 \text{ slugs})a$$

$$a = \frac{93.6 \text{ lb}}{2 \text{ slugs}} = 46.8 \text{ ft/s}^2$$

You should verify that *pounds per slug* is equivalent to *feet per second squared*.

7-4 PROBLEM-SOLVING TECHNIQUES

Solving all physics problems requires an ability to organize the given data and to apply formulas in a consistent manner. Often a procedure is helpful to the beginning student, and this is particularly true for the problems in this chapter. A logical sequence of operations for problems involving Newton's second law is outlined below.

1. Read the problem carefully for general understanding.
2. Draw a sketch, labeling given information.
3. Draw a free-body diagram with an axis along the direction of motion.
4. Indicate the positive direction of acceleration.
5. Determine the mass and weight of each object:

$$W = mg \qquad m = \frac{W}{g}$$

6. From the free-body diagram, determine the resultant force along the direction of motion. $(\sum F)$.
7. Determine total mass $(m_t = m_1 + m_2 + \cdots)$
8. Set the resultant force $\sum F$ equal to total mass (m_t) times acceleration a:

$$\boxed{\sum F = m_t a}$$

9. Solve for the unknown quantity.

EXAMPLE 7-8

A 2000-lb elevator is lifted upward with an acceleration of 4 ft/s². What is the tension in the supporting cable?

Solution

Read the problem, then draw a sketch from which a free-body diagram may be drawn (see Fig. 7-5). Notice that the positive direction of acceleration (upward) is indicated on the free-body diagram.

Fig. 7-5 Upward acceleration in a gravitational field.

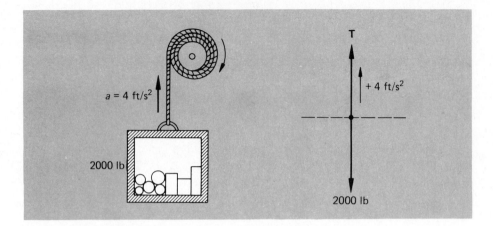

Now we determine the mass and the weight of the 2000-lb elevator. The weight, of course, is 2000 lb. The mass must be calculated from $m = W/g$.

$$W = 2000 \text{ lb} \qquad m = \frac{2000 \text{ lb}}{32 \text{ ft/s}^2} = 62.5 \text{ slugs}$$

Since the elevator is the only object moving, the 62.5 slugs represents the *total* mass m_t.

The resultant force from the free-body diagram is

$$\sum F = T - 2000 \text{ lb}$$

From Newton's second law, we now write

Resultant force = total mass × acceleration

$$T - 2000 \text{ lb} = (62.5 \text{ slugs})(4 \text{ ft/s}^2)$$

$$T - 2000 \text{ lb} = 250 \text{ lb}$$

Finally, we solve for the unknown T by adding 2000 lb to both sides of the equation.

$$T = 250 \text{ lb} + 2000 \text{ lb}$$

$$T = 2250 \text{ lb}$$

EXAMPLE 7-9

A 100-kg ball is lowered by means of a cable with a downward acceleration of 5 m/s². What is the tension in the cable?

Solution

As before, we construct a sketch and a free-body diagram (Fig. 7-6). Note that the downward direction is chosen as positive since that is the direction of motion.

This time the *mass* is given and the *weight* must be calculated from $W = mg$.

$$m = 100 \text{ kg} \qquad W = (100 \text{ kg})(9.8 \text{ m/s}^2) = 980 \text{ N}$$

The resultant force is the *net* downward force, or

$$\sum F = W - T \qquad \text{(remember, down is positive)}$$

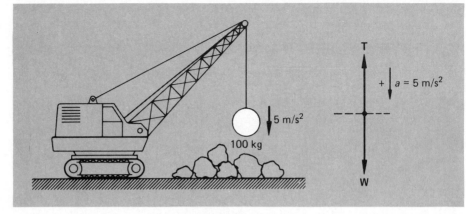

Fig. 7-6 Downward acceleration.

Now, from Newton's second law, we write

Net downward force = total mass × downward acceleration

$$W - T = ma$$

Substituting known quantities, we obtain

$$980 \text{ N} - T = (100 \text{ kg})(5 \text{ m/s}^2)$$

$$980 \text{ N} - T = 500 \text{ N}$$

from which we solve for T by adding T to both sides and subtracting 500 N from both sides:

$$980 \text{ N} - 500 \text{ N} = T$$

$$T = 480 \text{ N}$$

EXAMPLE 7-10   An Atwood machine consists of a single pulley with masses suspended on each side. It is a simplified version of many industrial systems in which counterweights are used for balance. Assume that the mass on the right side is 10 kg and that the mass on the left side is 2 kg. (*a*) What is the acceleration of the system? (*b*) What is the tension in the cord?

Solution (a)   We first draw a sketch and a free-body diagram for each mass (Fig. 7-7). The weight and mass of each object are determined.

$$m_1 = 2 \text{ kg} \qquad W_1 = m_1 g = (2 \text{ kg})(9.8 \text{ m/s}^2) \qquad \text{or} \qquad W_1 = 19.6 \text{ N}$$

$$m_2 = 10 \text{ kg} \qquad W_2 = m_2 g = (10 \text{ kg})(9.8 \text{ m/s}^2) \qquad \text{or} \qquad W_2 = 98 \text{ N}$$

Now the problem is to determine the net unbalanced force on the entire system. Note that the pulley merely changes the direction of the forces. The unbalanced force is, therefore, just the difference in the weights. This is just what we would expect from experience. Notice the tension T is the same on either side, since there is only one rope. Thus, the

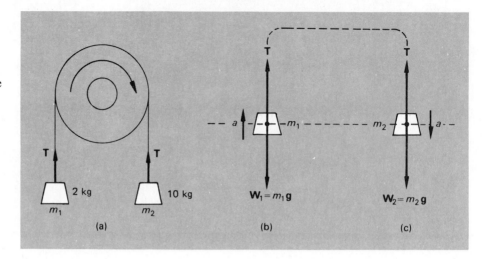

Fig. 7-7 Two masses suspended from a single pulley. Free-body diagrams are drawn; the positive direction of acceleration is chosen to be upward on the left and downward on the right.

tension cancels out and does not figure in the resultant force, which may be written as follows:

$$\sum F = W_2 - T + T - W_1$$
$$\sum F = W_2 - W_1$$

The total mass of the system is simply the sum of all the masses in motion.

$$m_t = m_1 + m_2 = 2 \text{ kg} + 10 \text{ kg}$$
$$m_t = 12 \text{ kg} \qquad \text{(total mass)}$$

From Newton's second law of motion, we have

$$Resultant \ force = total \ mass \times acceleration$$
$$W_2 - W_1 = (m_1 + m_2)a$$

Substituting for W_2, W_1, m_1, and m_2, we have

$$98 \text{ N} - 19.6 \text{ N} = (2 \text{ kg} + 10 \text{ kg})a$$

From which we may solve for a as follows:

$$78.4 \text{ N} = (12 \text{ kg})a$$
$$a = \frac{78.4 \text{ N}}{12 \text{ kg}} = 6.53 \text{ m/s}^2$$

Solution (b)

In order to solve for the tension in the cord, we must consider either of the masses by itself, since considering the system as a whole would not involve cord tension. Suppose we consider the forces acting on m_1:

$$Resultant \ force = mass \times acceleration$$
$$T - W_1 = m_1 a$$

But $a = 6.53$ m/s^2 and the mass and weight are known, so that we have

$$T - 19.6 \text{ N} = (2 \text{ kg})(6.53 \text{ m/s}^2)$$

$$T - 19.6 \text{ N} = 13.06 \text{ N}$$

$$T = 32.7 \text{ N}$$

We would obtain the same value for the tension if we applied Newton's law to the second mass. You should demonstrate this fact as an additional exercise.

EXAMPLE 7-11   A 64-lb block rests on a frictionless table top. A rope attached to it passes over a light frictionless pulley and is attached to a weight **W**, as shown in Fig. 7-8a. (a) What must the value of **W** be to give the system an acceleration of 16 ft/s^2? (b) What is the tension in the rope?

Fig. 7-8

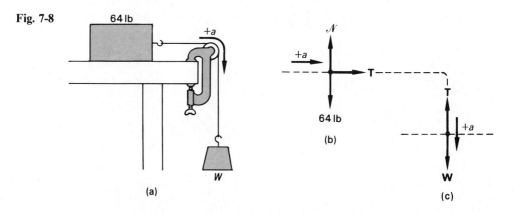

(a)   (b)   (c)

Solution (a)   Draw free-body diagrams for each body in the system, as shown in Fig. 7-8b and c. Since the vertical forces on the 64-lb block are balanced, the net force on the entire system is simply the weight **W**. Hence, applying Newton's law yields

Resultant force on system = total mass × acceleration

$$W = \left(\frac{64 \text{ lb}}{g} + \frac{W}{g} \right) a$$

$$W = \frac{64 \text{ lb} + W}{g} a = (64 \text{ lb} + W) \frac{a}{g}$$

$$W = (64 \text{ lb} + W) \frac{16 \text{ ft/s}^2}{32 \text{ ft/s}^2}$$

$$W = \frac{64 \text{ lb} + W}{2}$$

$$2W = 64 \text{ lb} + W$$

$$2W - W = 64 \text{ lb}$$

$$W = 64 \text{ lb}$$

To solve for the tension in the rope, we may choose either Fig. 7-8b or c since each diagram involves the unknown **T**. The better choice is the former because the net force on the 64-lb body is the tension **T**. Thus

$$Resultant\ force = mass \times acceleration$$

$$T = \frac{64\ lb}{32\ ft/s^2}\ (16\ ft/s^2)$$

$$= 32\ lb$$

One more example will be given in this section to allow you to become more familiar with the reasoning process involved with more complex systems. Since the foundation has been laid in previous examples, we include only the significant steps in the solution.

EXAMPLE 7-12   Consider the masses $m_1 = 20$ kg and $m_2 = 18$ kg in the system represented by Fig. 7-9. If the coefficient of kinetic friction is 0.1 and the inclination angle θ is 30°, find (a) the acceleration of the system and (b) the tension in the cord joining the two masses.

Fig. 7-9

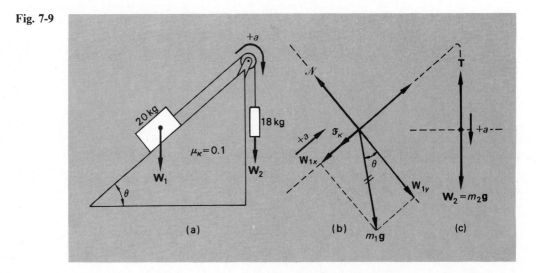

(a)   (b)   (c)

Solution (a)   Using the symbols as defined in Fig. 7-9, we apply Newton's law to the system:

$$Resultant\ force\ on\ system = total\ mass \times acceleration$$

$$W_2 - W_{1x} - \mathscr{F}_\kappa = (m_1 + m_2)a$$

The symbols on the left side are found as follows:

$$W_2 = m_2 g = (18\ kg)(9.8\ m/s^2) = 176\ N$$

$$W_{1x} = m_1 g \sin \theta = (20\ kg)(9.8\ m/s^2)(\sin 30°) = 98\ N$$

$$W_{1y} = m_1 g \cos \theta = (20\ kg)(9.8\ m/s^2)(\cos 30°) = 170\ N$$

$$\mathscr{F}_\kappa = \mu_\kappa N = \mu_\kappa W_{1y} = (0.1)(170\ N) = 17\ N$$

Substitution into the equation of motion yields

$$176 \text{ N} - 98 \text{ N} - 17 \text{ N} = (20 \text{ kg} + 18 \text{ kg})a$$

from which we obtain

$$a = 1.61 \text{ m/s}^2$$

Solution (b) To find the tension in the cord, we apply Newton's law to the 18-kg mass, as shown in Fig. 7-9c:

$$Resultant\ force = mass \times acceleration$$

$$m_2\, g - T = m_2\, a$$

$$T = m_2\, g - m_2\, a = m_2(g - a)$$

$$= (18 \text{ kg})(9.8 \text{ m/s}^2 - 1.61 \text{ m/s}^2)$$

$$= 147 \text{ N}$$

SUMMARY

In this chapter, we have considered the fact that a resultant force will always produce an acceleration in the direction of the force. The magnitude of the acceleration is directly proportional to the force and inversely proportional to the mass, according to Newton's second law of motion. The following concepts are essential to applications of this fundamental law:

- The mathematical formula which expresses Newton's second law of motion may be written as follows:

$$Force = mass \times acceleration$$

$$F = ma \qquad m = \frac{F}{g} \qquad a = \frac{F}{m}$$

In SI units: $1 \text{ N} = (1 \text{ kg})(1 \text{ m/s}^2)$

In USCS units: $1 \text{ lb} = (1 \text{ slug})(1 \text{ ft/s}^2)$

- Weight is the force due to a particular acceleration g. Thus, weight W is related to mass m by Newton's second law:

$$W = mg \qquad m = \frac{F}{g} \qquad g = 9.8 \text{ m/s}^2 \text{ or } 32 \text{ ft/s}^2$$

For example, a mass of 1 kg has a weight of 9.8 N. A weight of 1 lb has a mass of $\frac{1}{32}$ slug. In a given problem you must determine whether weight or mass is given. Then you must determine what is needed in an equation. Conversions of mass to weight and weight to mass are common.

- Application of Newton's second law:
  1. Construct a free-body diagram for each body undergoing an acceleration. Indicate on this diagram the direction of positive acceleration.
  2. Determine an expression for the net resultant force on a body or a system of bodies.

3. Set the resultant force equal to the total mass of the system multiplied by the acceleration of the system.
4. Solve the resulting equation for the unknown quantity.

QUESTIONS

7-1. Define the following terms:
   a. Newton's second law
   b. Mass
   c. Weight
   d. Slug
   e. Newton

7-2. In a laboratory experiment the acceleration of a small car is measured by the separation of spots burned at regular intervals in a paraffin-coated tape. Larger and larger weights are transferred from the car to a hanger at the end of a tape which passes over a light, frictionless pulley. In this manner, the mass of the entire system is kept constant. Since the car moves on a horizontal air track with negligible friction, the resultant force is equal to the weights at the end of the tape. The following data are recorded:

Weight, W	2	4	6	8	10	12
Acceleration, m/s^2	1.4	2.9	4.1	5.6	7.1	8.4

   Plot a graph of weight vs. acceleration. What is the significance of the slope of this curve? What is the mass of the system?

7-3. In the experiment described in Question 7-2, the student places a constant weight of 4 N at the free end of the tape. Several runs are made, increasing the mass of the car each time by adding weights. What happens to the acceleration as the mass of the system is increased? What should the value of the product of the mass of the system and the acceleration be for each run?

7-4. Distinguish clearly between the terms *mass* and *weight*.

7-5. What is the mass of a 160-lb person on the earth? What is the mass on the moon?

7-6. A round piece of brass found in the laboratory is marked 500 g. Is this its weight or its mass? How can you be sure?

7-7. A state of equilibrium is maintained on a force table by hanging masses from pulleys mounted at various positions on the circular edge. In calculating the equilibrant, we sometimes use grams instead of newtons. Are we justified in doing this?

7-8. Does an analytical balance actually measure weight or mass? Explain.

7-9. Two monkeys hang at opposite ends of a rope which passes over a light frictionless pulley. The monkeys are of equal mass and at the same height. The monkey on the left is tied so that it cannot climb. What will happen to the left monkey if the right monkey climbs up the rope? If it climbs down the rope? If it lets go of the rope?

7-10 Suppose that both monkeys in the previous problem are free to climb. The monkey on the right pulls twice as much rope through its hands per unit time as the left monkey does. Which monkey will reach the top first, or will they reach the top together?

PROBLEMS

7-1. A 2-kg mass is acted on by a resultant force of **(a)** 8 N and **(b)** 4 lb. What is the resulting acceleration for each case (in metric units)?

Ans. (a) 4 m/s² (b) 8.9 m/s².

7-2. A resultant force of 200 lb produces an acceleration of 5 ft/s². What is the mass of the object being accelerated? What is its weight?

7-3. Find the mass and the weight of a body if a resultant force of 16 N will give it an acceleration of 5 m/s².

Ans. 3.2 kg, 31.4 N.

7-4. What resultant force is necessary to give a 4-kg hammer an acceleration of 6 m/s²?

7-5. Find the weight of a body whose mass is **(a)** 5 slugs, **(b)** 8 kg, and **(c)** 0.25 kg.

Ans. (a) 160 lb (b) 78.4 N (c) 2.45 N.

7-6. Find the mass of a body whose weight is **(a)** 600 lb, **(b)** 40 N, and **(c)** 0.80 lb.

7-7. A 2500-lb automobile is speeding at 55 mi/h. What retarding force is required to stop the car in 200 ft on a level road?

Ans. −1273 lb.

7-8. What horizontal push is required to drag a 60-kg sled with an acceleration of 4 m/s²? Assume that a horizontal friction force of 20 N opposes the motion.

7-9. A horizontal force of 100 N pulls an 8-kg block horizontally across the floor. If the coefficient of kinetic friction between the block and the floor is 0.2, find the acceleration of the block.

Ans. 10.5 m/s².

7-10. A car's speed increases from 30 to 60 mi/h in 5 s under the action of a resultant force of 1150 lb. What is the mass of the car? What is its weight?

7-11. A 5-ton tractor pulls a 10-ton trailer on a level road and gives it an acceleration of 6 ft/s². If this tractor exerts the same force on an 8-ton trailer, what acceleration will result?

Ans. 6.92 ft/s².

7-12. A net force of 200 N gives a wagon an acceleration of 6 m/s². What are the mass and weight of the wagon? Assume that a 10-kg load is added to the wagon. What resultant force is required to give the same acceleration?

7-13. A 64-lb load hangs at the end of a rope. Find the acceleration of the load if the tension in the cable is **(a)** 64 lb, **(b)** 40 lb, and **(c)** 96 lb.

Ans. (a) 0 (b) 12 ft/s² down (c) 16 ft/s² up.

7-14. A 10-kg mass is lifted upward by a light cable. What is the tension in the cable if the acceleration is **(a)** zero, **(b)** 6 m/s² upward, and **(c)** 6 m/s² downward?

7-15. An 800-kg elevator is lifted vertically by a strong rope. Find the acceleration of the elevator if the tension in the rope is **(a)** 9000 N, **(b)** 7840 N, and **(c)** 2000 N.

Ans. (a) 1.45 m/s² up (b) 0 (c) −7.3 m/s² down.

7-16. An 18-lb block is accelerated upward with a cord whose breaking strength is 20 lb. Find the maximum acceleration which can be given to the block without breaking the cord.

7-17. A 2000-lb elevator is lifted vertically with an acceleration of 8 ft/s². Find the minimum breaking strength of the cable. A 200-lb man standing on a scale will read his weight differently in the moving elevator. What is the weight recorded by the spring scale?

Ans. 2500 lb, 250 lb.

7-18. A 9-kg load of cement is accelerated upward with a cord whose breaking strength is 200 N. What is the maximum upward acceleration such that the cord does not break?

7-19. If the coefficient of friction between the tire and the road is 0.7, what is the minimum distance in which a 1600-kg car can be stopped if it is traveling at 60 km/h?

Ans. 20.2 m.

7-20. A 20-kg box is on the bed of a truck. The coefficient of static friction is 0.4, and the coefficient of sliding friction is 0.3. Find the magnitude and direction of the friction force acting on the box and the acceleration of the box relative to the ground **(a)** when the truck is accelerating at 8 m/s², and **(b)** when the truck is decelerating at 2 m/s².

7-21. A light cord passing over a light frictionless pulley, as in Fig. 7-7, has masses m_1 and m_2 attached to its ends. What will the acceleration of the system and the tension in the cord be if **(a)** $m_1 = 12$ kg and $m_2 = 10$ kg; **(b)** $m_1 = 20$ g and $m_2 = 50$ g?

Ans. **(a)** 0.891 m/s², 105 N **(b)** 4.2 m/s², 0.28 N.

7-22. Suppose the masses in Prob. 7-21 are replaced with the weights $W_1 = 24$ lb and $W_2 = 16$ lb. What will the resultant acceleration and tension in the cord be?

7-23. A 30-kg mass rests on a 37° inclined plane. The coefficient of kinetic friction is 0.3. A push **P** applied parallel to the plane and directed up the plane causes the mass to accelerate at 3 m/s². **(a)** What is the normal force? **(b)** What is the friction force? **(c)** What is the resultant force up the plane? **(d)** What is the magnitude of the push **P**?

Ans. **(a)** 235 N **(b)** 70.5 N **(c)** 90 N **(d)** 338 N.

7-24. A 400-lb sled slides down a hill inclined at 60° with respect to the horizontal. The coefficient of sliding friction is 0.2. **(a)** What is the normal force? **(b)** What is the force of friction? **(c)** What is the resultant force down the hill? **(d)** What is the acceleration?

7-25. Consider the system shown in Fig. 7-10. If $m_1 = 16$ kg and $m_2 = 10$ kg, what is the resultant force on the system? What is the acceleration of the system? What is the tension in the cord? Neglect friction.

Ans. 3.77 m/s², 60.3 N.

Fig. 7-10

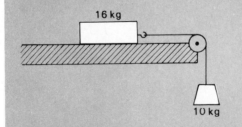

7-26. If the *weight* of m_1 in Fig. 7-10 is 200 lb and if $\mu_k = 0.3$, what must be the weight of m_2 if the system is to have an acceleration of 6 ft/s²?

7-27. If $m_1 = 10$ kg, $m_2 = 8$ kg, and $m_3 = 6$ kg in Fig. 7-11, what is the acceleration of the system? Neglect friction.

Ans. 1.63 m/s^2.

Fig. 7-11

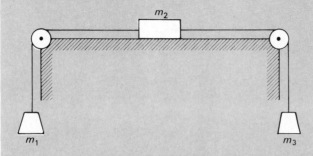

7-28. What weight W_2 must be attached in Fig. 7-12 in order to cause a 64-lb block, W_1, to move with an acceleration of 6 ft/s^2 **(a)** up the plane and **(b)** down the plane? Neglect friction.

Fig. 7-12

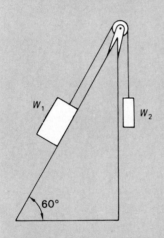

7-29. If the mass of W_1 in Fig. 7-12 is 6 kg and the mass of W_2 is 10 kg, what are the acceleration of the system and the tension in the cord? Neglect friction.

Ans. 2.94 m/s^2, 68.6 N.

7-30. Assume that W_2 is 64 lb and that the coefficient of kinetic friction is 0.4 in Fig. 7-12. What weight W_2 is required to cause the block to move up the plane with an acceleration of 6 m/s^2?

8 *Work, Energy, and Power*

OBJECTIVES: After completing this chapter, you should be able to:

1. **Define and write mathematical formulas for work, potential energy, kinetic energy, and power.**

2. **Apply the concepts of work, energy, and power to the solution of problems similar to those given as examples in the text.**

3. **Define and demonstrate by example your understanding of the following units: *joule, foot-pound, watt, horsepower*, and *foot-pound per second*.**

4. **Discuss and apply your knowledge of the relationship between the performance of work and the corresponding change in kinetic energy.**

5. **Discuss and apply your knowledge of the principle of conservation of mechanical energy.**

6. **Determine the power of a system and understand its relationship to time, force, distance, and velocity.**

The principal reason for the application of a resultant force is to cause a displacement. For example, a large crane lifts a steel beam to the top of a building; the compressor in an air conditioner forces a fluid through its cooling cycle; and electromagnetic forces move electrons across a television screen. Whenever a force acts through a distance, we will learn, *work* is done in a way that can be measured or predicted. The capacity for doing work will be defined as *energy*, and the rate at which it is accomplished will be defined as *power*. The control and use of energy is probably the major concern of industry today, and a thorough understanding of the three concepts of work, energy, and power is essential.

When we attempt to drag a block with a rope, as in Fig. 8-1a, nothing happens. We are exerting a force, but the block has not moved. On the other hand, if we continually increase our pull, eventually the block will be displaced. In this case

Fig. 8-1 The work done by a force **F** undergoing a displacement *s*.

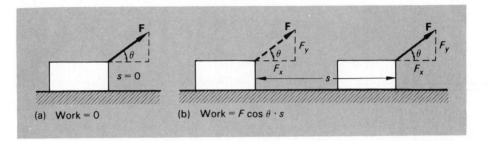

(a) Work = 0   (b) Work = $F \cos \theta \cdot s$

we have actually accomplished something in return for our efforts. This accomplishment is defined in physics as *work*. The term *work* has an explicit, quantitative, operational definition. In order for work to be done, three things are necessary:

1. There must be an applied force.
2. The force must act through a certain distance, called the *displacement*.
3. The force must have a component along the displacement.

Assuming that we are given these conditions, a formal definition of work may be stated:

> **Work** is a scalar quantity equal to the product of the magnitudes of the displacement and the component of the force in the direction of the displacement.

$$Work = Force\ component \times displacement$$

$$\boxed{Work = F_x s} \tag{8-1}$$

In this equation F_x is the component of **F** along the displacement *s*. In Fig. 8-1, only F_x contributes to work. Its magnitude can be found from trigonometry, and work can be expressed in terms of the angle θ between **F** and *s*:

$$Work = (F \cos \theta)s \tag{8-2}$$

Quite often the force causing the work is directed entirely along the displacement. This happens when a weight is lifted vertically or when a horizontal force drags an object along the floor. In these simple cases, $F_x = F$, and the work is the simple product of force and displacement:

$$Work = Fs \tag{8-3}$$

Another special case occurs when the applied force is perpendicular to the displacement. In this instance, the work will be zero, since $F_x = 0$. An example is motion parallel to the earth's surface in which gravity acts vertically downward and is perpendicular to all horizontal displacements. Then the force of gravity does no work.

EXAMPLE 8-1   What work is done by a 60-N force in dragging the block of Fig. 8-1 a distance of 50 m when the force is transmitted by a rope making an angle of 30° with the horizontal?

Solution   We must first determine the component F_x of the 60-N force **F**. Only this component contributes to work. Graphically, this is accomplished by drawing the 60-N vector to scale at a 30° angle. Measuring F_x and converting to newtons gives

$$F_x = 52.0 \text{ N}$$

With trigonometry, we could accomplish the same calculation using the cosine function

$$F_x = (60 \text{ N})(\cos 30°) = 52.0 \text{ N}$$

Now, applying Eq. (8-1), we obtain the work

$$\text{Work} = F_x \cdot s = (52.0 \text{ N})(50 \text{ m})$$

$$= 2600 \text{ N} \cdot \text{m}$$

Note that the units of work are the units of force times distance. Thus, in SI units, work is measured in *newton-meters* ($N \cdot m$). By agreement, this combination unit is renamed the *joule*, which is denoted by the symbol J.

> One **joule** (1 J) is equal to the work done by a force of one newton in moving an object through a parallel distance of one meter.

In Example 8-1, the work done in dragging the block would be written as 2600 J.

In the United States, work is sometimes also given in USCS units. When the force is given in *pounds* (lb) and the displacement is given in *feet* (ft), the corresponding work unit is called the *foot-pound* (ft · lb).

> One **foot-pound** (1 ft · lb) is equal to the work done by a force of one pound in moving an object through a parallel distance of one foot.

No special name is given to this unit.

The following conversion factors will be useful when comparing work units in the two systems:

$$1 \text{ J} = 0.7376 \text{ ft} \cdot \text{lb} \qquad 1 \text{ ft} \cdot \text{lb} = 1.356 \text{ J}$$

8-2 RESULTANT WORK

When we consider the work of several forces acting on the same object, it is often useful to distinguish between positive and negative work. In this text, we will follow the convention that the work of a particular force is positive if the force component is in the same direction as the displacement. Negative work is done by a force component which opposes the actual displacement. Hence, work done by a crane in lifting a load is positive, but the gravitational force exerted by the earth on the load is doing negative work. Similarly, when we stretch a spring, the work on the spring is positive; the work on the spring is negative when the spring contracts, pulling us back. Another important example of negative work is that performed by a frictional force which is opposite to the direction of displacement.

If several forces act on a body in motion, the *resultant work* (total work) is the algebraic sum of the works of the individual forces. This will also be equal to the work of the resultant force. It is seen that the accomplishment of net work requires the existence of a resultant force. These ideas are clarified in the following example:

EXAMPLE 8-2   A push of 200 lb moves a 100-lb block up a 30° inclined plane, as shown in Fig. 8-2. The coefficient of kinetic friction is 0.25, and the length of the plane is 20 ft. (*a*) Compute the work done by each force acting on the block. (*b*) Show that the net work done by these forces is the same as the work of the resultant force.

Fig. 8-2 The work required to push a 100-lb block up a 30°-inclined plane.

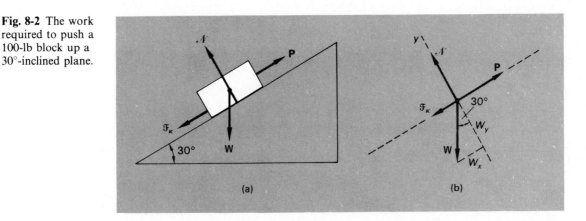

(a)   (b)

Solution (a)   There are four forces acting on the block: $\mathcal{N}$, **P**, $\mathscr{F}_\kappa$, and **W**. (Fig. 8-2*b*.) The normal force $\mathcal{N}$ does no work because it has no component along the displacement.

$$(\text{Work})_{\mathcal{N}} = 0$$

The push **P** is entirely along the displacement and in the direction of the displacement. Hence

$$(\text{Work})_\mathbf{P} = P_s = (200 \text{ lb})(20 \text{ ft}) = 4000 \text{ ft} \cdot \text{lb}$$

The magnitude of the friction force $\mathscr{F}_\kappa$, is computed as follows:

$$\mathscr{F}_\kappa = \mu_\kappa \mathcal{N} = \mu_\kappa W_y = \mu_\kappa W \cos 30°$$

$$= (0.25)(100 \text{ lb})(\cos 30°) = 21.6 \text{ lb}$$

Since this force is directed down the plane in a direction opposite to the displacement, it does negative work, which is given by

$$(\text{Work})_{\mathscr{F}} = (-21.6 \text{ lb})(20 \text{ ft}) = -432 \text{ ft} \cdot \text{lb}$$

The weight **W** of the block also does negative work since its component W_x is directed opposite to the displacement.

$$(\text{Work})_{\mathbf{W}} = -W_x s = -(W \sin 30°)(20 \text{ ft})$$

$$= -(100 \text{ lb})(\sin 30°)(20 \text{ ft})$$

$$= -1000 \text{ ft} \cdot \text{lb}$$

Solution (b) The net work is obtained by summing the works of the individual forces.

$$\text{Net work} = (\text{work})_N + (\text{work})_\mathbf{P} + (\text{work})_{\mathscr{F}} + (\text{work})_\mathbf{W}$$

$$= 0 + 4000 \text{ ft} \cdot \text{lb} - 432 \text{ ft} \cdot \text{lb} - 1000 \text{ ft} \cdot \text{lb}$$

$$= 2568 \text{ ft} \cdot \text{lb}$$

To show that this is also the work of the resultant force, we first compute the resultant force. According to methods discussed in previous chapters,

$$F_R = P - \mathscr{F}_K - W_x$$

$$= 200 \text{ lb} - 21.6 \text{ lb} - 50 \text{ lb}$$

$$= 128.4 \text{ lb}$$

The work of $\mathbf{F}_R$ is therefore

$$(\text{Work})_{\mathbf{F}_R} = F_R s = (128.4 \text{ lb})(20 \text{ ft})$$

$$= 2568 \text{ ft} \cdot \text{lb}$$

which compares with the value obtained by computing the work of each force separately.

It is important to distinguish between the *resultant* or *net* work and the work of an individual force. If we speak of the work required to move a block through a distance, the work done by the pulling force is not necessarily the resultant work. Work may be done by a friction force or by other forces. Resultant work is simply the work done by a resultant force. If the resultant force is zero then the resultant work is zero even though individual forces may be doing positive or negative work.

**8-3
ENERGY**

Energy may be thought of as *anything which can be converted into work.* When we say that an object has energy, we mean that it is capable of exerting a force on another object in order to do work on it. Conversely, if we do work on some object, we have added to it an amount of energy equal to the work done. The units of energy are the same as those for work; the *joule* and the *foot-pound.*

In mechanics we shall be concerned with two kinds of energy:

Kinetic energy E_k : Energy possessed by a body by virtue of its motion.

Potential energy E_p : Energy possessed by a system by virtue of position or condition.

One can readily think of many examples of each kind of energy. For instance, a moving car, a moving bullet, and a rotating flywheel all have the ability to do work because of their motion. Similarly, a lifted object, a compressed spring, and a cocked rifle have the potential for doing work because of position. Several examples are provided in Fig. 8-3.

Fig. 8-3 Examples of (a) kinetic and (b) potential energy.

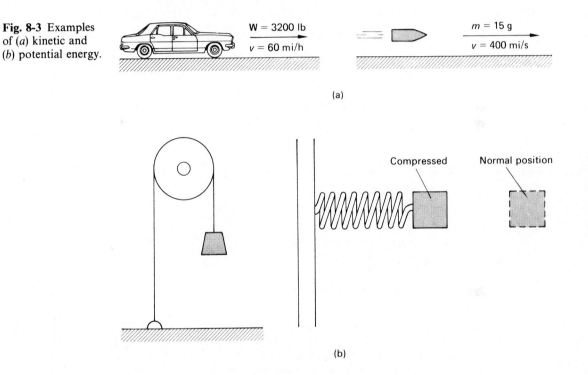

$W = 3200$ lb
$v = 60$ mi/h

$m = 15$ g
$v = 400$ mi/s

(a)

Compressed

Normal position

(b)

**8-4
WORK AND
KINETIC
ENERGY**

We have defined kinetic energy as the capability for performing work as a result of the motion of a body. To see the relationship between motion and work, let's consider a constant force **F** acting on the block in Fig. 8-4. Consider that the block has an initial speed v_0 and that the force **F** acts through a distance s causing the speed to increase to a final value v_f. If the body has a mass m, Newton's second law tells us that it will gain speed, or accelerate, at a rate given by

$$a = \frac{F}{m} \tag{8-4}$$

Fig. 8-4 The work done by the force **F** results in a change in kinetic energy of the mass *m*.

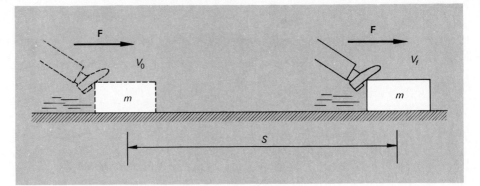

until it reaches the final speed v_f. From Chap. 5, we recall

$$2as = v_f^2 - v_0^2$$

from which

$$a = \frac{v_f^2 - v_0^2}{2s}$$

Substitution of this into Eq. (8-4) yields

$$\frac{F}{m} = \frac{v_f^2 - v_0^2}{2s}$$

which can be solved for the product Fs to obtain

$$Fs = \tfrac{1}{2}mv_f^2 - \tfrac{1}{2}mv_0^2 \tag{8-5}$$

The quantity on the left side of Eq. (8-5) represents the work done on the mass *m*. The quantity on the right side must be the change in kinetic energy as a result of this work. Thus, we can define kinetic energy E_K as

$$\boxed{E_K = \tfrac{1}{2}mv^2} \tag{8-6}$$

Following this notation, $\tfrac{1}{2}mv_f^2$ and $\tfrac{1}{2}mv_0^2$ would represent final and initial kinetic energies, respectively. The important result can be stated as follows:

The work of a resultant external force on a body is equal to the change in kinetic energy of the body.

A close look at Eq. (8-5) will show that an *increase* in kinetic energy ($v_f > v_0$) will result from *positive work, whereas a decrease in kinetic energy* ($v_f < v_0$) will result from *negative* work. In the special case in which zero v is done, the kinetic energy is a constant, given by Eq. (8-6).

EXAMPLE 8-3

Compute the kinetic energy of a 4-kg sledgehammer at the instant its velocity is 24 m/s.

Solution

Applying Eq. (8-6), we obtain

$$E_k = \tfrac{1}{2}mv^2 = \tfrac{1}{2}(4 \text{ kg})(24 \text{ m/s})^2$$

$$= 1152 \text{ N} \cdot \text{m} = 1152 \text{ J}$$

EXAMPLE 8-4   Compute the kinetic energy of a 3200-lb automobile traveling at 60 mi/h (88 ft/s).

Solution   We compute as before except that we must determine the mass from the weight.

$$E_K = \frac{1}{2} mv^2 = \frac{1}{2} \left(\frac{W}{g} \right) v^2$$

Substituting given values for W and v, we have

$$E_K = \frac{1}{2} \left(\frac{3200 \text{ lb}}{32 \text{ ft/s}^2} \right) (88 \text{ ft/s})^2$$

$$= 3.87 \times 10^5 \text{ ft} \cdot \text{lb}$$

EXAMPLE 8-5   What average force F is necessary to stop a 16-g bullet traveling at 260 m/s as it penetrates into wood a distance of 12 cm?

Solution   The total work required to stop the bullet will be equal to the change in kinetic energy. (See Fig. 8-5.) Since the bullet is stopped, $v_f = 0$, and so Eq. (8-5) yields

$$Fs = -\tfrac{1}{2}mv_0^2$$

Substituting gives

$$F(0.12 \text{ m}) = -\tfrac{1}{2}(0.016 \text{ kg})(260 \text{ m/s})^2$$

Dividing by 0.12 m, we have

$$F = \frac{-(0.016 \text{ kg})(260 \text{ m/s})^2}{(2)(0.12 \text{ m})}$$

$$= -4510 \text{ N}$$

The minus sign indicates that the force was opposite to the displacement. It should be noted that this force is about 30,000 times the weight of the bullet.

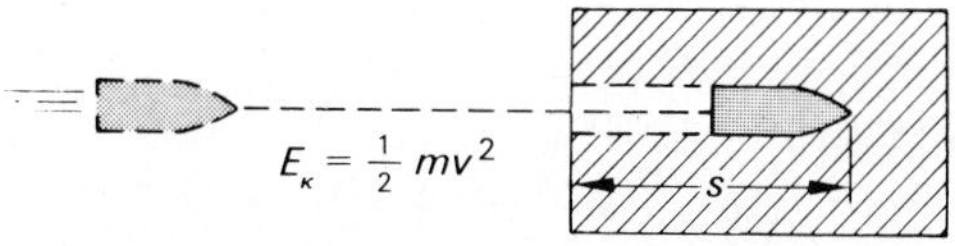

Fig. 8-5 The work done in stopping a bullet is equal to the initial kinetic energy of the bullet.

$$E_K = \tfrac{1}{2} mv^2$$

**8-5
POTENTIAL
ENERGY**

The energy that systems possess by virtue of their positions or conditions is called *potential energy*. Since energy expresses itself in the form of work, potential energy implies that there must be a potential for doing work. For example, suppose the pile driver in Fig. 8-6 is used to lift a body of weight **W** to a height h above the ground stake. We say that the body–earth system has gravitational potential energy. When such a body is released, it will do work when it strikes the stake. If it is heavy enough and if it has fallen from a great enough height, the work done will result in driving the stake through a distance s.

The external force **F** required to lift the body must at least be equal to the weight **W**. Thus, the work done on the system is given by

$$\text{Work} = Wh = mg \cdot h$$

Fig. 8-6 (a) Lifting a mass m to a height h requires the work mgh. (b) The body-earth system, therefore, has a potential energy $E_p = mgh$. (c) When the mass is released, it has the capacity for doing the work mgh on the stake.

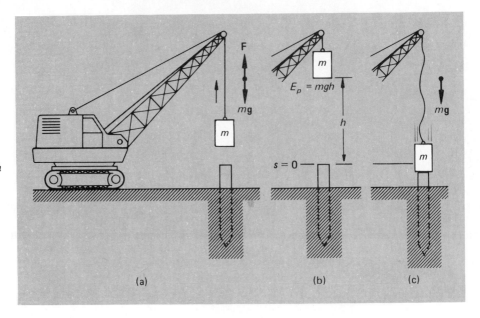

(a)   (b)   (c)

This amount of work can also be done *by* the body after it has dropped a distance h. Thus, the body has potential energy equal in magnitude to the external work required to lift it. This energy does not come from the earth–body system, but results from work done on the system by an external agent. Only *external* forces, such as **F** in Fig. 8-6 or friction, can add energy to or remove energy from the system made up of the body and the earth.

Note from the preceding discussion that potential energy E_p can be found from

$$E_p = Wh = mgh \qquad Potential\ Energy \quad (8\text{-}7)$$

where W and m are the weight and the mass of an object located a distance h above some reference point.

The potential energy depends on the choice of a particular reference level. The gravitational potential energy for an airplane is quite different when measured with respect to a mountain peak, a skyscraper, or sea level. The capacity for doing work is much greater if the aircraft falls to sea level. Potential energy has physical significance only in the event that a reference level is established.

EXAMPLE 8-6   A 250-g carburetor is held 200 mm above a workbench which is 1 m above the floor. Compute the potential energy relative to (a) the bench top and (b) the floor.

Solution (a)   The height h of the carburetor above the bench is 200 mm (or 0.2 m), and the mass is 250 g or (0.25 kg). Thus, the potential energy relative to the bench is

$$E_p = mgh = (0.25\ \text{kg})(9.8\ \text{m/s}^2)(0.2\ \text{m})$$

$$= 0.49\ \text{J}$$

Notice that kilograms, meters, and seconds are the only units of mass, length, and time which are consistent with the definition of a joule.

Solution (b)   The potential energy with reference to the floor is based on a different value of h.

$$E_p = mgh = (0.25 \text{ kg})(9.8 \text{ m/s}^2)(1.2 \text{ m})$$

$$= 2.94 \text{ J}$$

EXAMPLE 8-7   An 800-lb commercial air-conditioning unit is lifted by a chain hoist until it is 22 ft above the floor. What is the potential energy relative to the floor?

Solution   Applying Eq. (8-7), we obtain

$$E_p = Wh = (800 \text{ lb})(22 \text{ ft}) = 17,600 \text{ ft} \cdot \text{lb}$$

We have stated that the potential for doing work is a function only of the weight and the height h above some reference point. The potential energy at a particular position is not dependent on the path taken to reach that position. This is because the same work must be done against gravity regardless of the path. In Example 8-7, work of 17,600 ft · lb was required to lift the air conditioner through a vertical distance of 22 ft. If we chose to exert a lesser force by moving it up an incline, a greater distance would be required. In either case, the work done against gravity is 17,600 ft · lb, because the end result is the placement of an 800-lb weight at a height of 22 ft.

**8-6
CONSERVA-
TION OF
ENERGY**

Quite often, at relatively low speeds, an interchange takes place between kinetic and potential energies. For example, suppose a mass m is lifted to a height h and dropped, as shown in Fig. 8-7. An external force has increased the energy of the system, giving it a potential energy $E_p = mgh$ at the highest point. This is

Fig. 8-7 The total mechanical energy is constant if there is no air resistance.

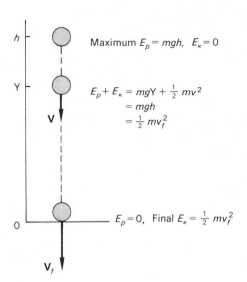

Maximum $E_p = mgh$, $E_\kappa = 0$

$E_p + E_\kappa = mgY + \frac{1}{2}mv^2$
$\qquad\quad = mgh$
$\qquad\quad = \frac{1}{2}mv_f^2$

$E_p = 0$, Final $E_\kappa = \frac{1}{2}mv_f^2$

the total energy available to the system, and it cannot change unless an external resistive force is encountered. As the mass falls, its potential energy decreases because its height above the ground is reduced. The lost potential energy reappears in the form of kinetic energy of motion. In the absence of air resistance, the total energy $(E_p + E_k)$ remains the same. Potential energy continues to be converted into kinetic energy until the mass reaches the ground $(h = 0)$. At this final position, the kinetic energy is equal to the total energy, and the potential energy is zero. The important point to be made is that the sum of E_p and E_k is the same at any point during the fall (see Fig. 8-7).

$$\text{Total energy} = E_p + E_k = \text{constant}$$

We say that mechanical energy is *conserved*. In our example the total energy at the top is mgh and the total energy at the bottom is $\frac{1}{2}mv^2$ if we neglect air resistance. We are now prepared to state the principle of *conservation of mechanical energy*:

> **Conservation of Mechanical Energy:** *In the absence of air resistance or other dissipative forces, the sum of the potential and kinetic energies is a constant provided that no energy is added to the system.*

Under these conditions, the final kinetic energy of a mass m dropped from a height h is equal to the initial potential energy:

$$\tfrac{1}{2}mv_f^2 = mgh \tag{8-8}$$

Solving this relationship for v_f gives a useful equation for determining the final velocity from energy considerations.

$$v_f = \sqrt{2gh} \tag{8-9}$$

A great advantage of this method is that the final velocity is determined from the initial and final energy states. The actual path taken does not matter in the absence of friction.

EXAMPLE 8-8   In Fig. 8-8, a 40-kg ball is pulled to one side until it is 1.6 m above its lowest position. Neglecting friction, what will its velocity be as it passes through its lowest point?

Solution   Conservation of mechanical energy requires that the final kinetic energy be equal to the initial potential energy.

$$\tfrac{1}{2}mv_f^2 = mgh$$

Thus, Eq. (8-9) applies, and we simply solve for v_f.

$$v_f = \sqrt{2gh} = \sqrt{2(9.8 \text{ m/s}^2)(1.6 \text{ m})}$$
$$= 5.60 \text{ m/s}$$

As an additional exercise you should show that the total energy of the system is 627 J.

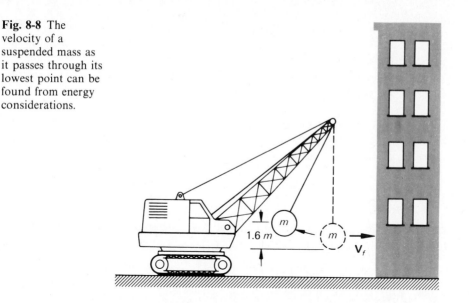

Fig. 8-8 The velocity of a suspended mass as it passes through its lowest point can be found from energy considerations.

1.6 m

V_f

Now let us consider the more general case in which some of the mechanical energy is lost due to friction. The change in mechanical energy resulting from such a force will always be equal to the negative work done by the friction force. The final kinetic energy will be reduced because some of the total energy available initially will be lost in doing work against friction. We may write this fact as follows:

$$\left| \begin{array}{c} Final\ kinetic \\ energy \end{array} \right| = \left| \begin{array}{c} initial\ potential \\ energy \end{array} \right| - \left| \begin{array}{c} work\ against \\ friction \end{array} \right|$$

$$\tfrac{1}{2}mv_f^2 = mgh - Fs \qquad (8\text{-}10)$$

Perhaps a better way of writing this statement would be to express it in terms of the total energy available initially.

$$mgh = \tfrac{1}{2}mv_f^2 + Fs \qquad (8\text{-}11)$$

This equation is a mathematical statement of the principle of conservation of energy, which can now be restated as follows:

Conservation of energy: *The total energy of a system is always constant, although energy changes from one form to another may occur within the system.*

EXAMPLE 8-9

A 64-lb block rests initially at the top of a 300-ft plane inclined at an angle of 30°, as shown in Fig. 8-9. If $\mu_\kappa = 0.1$, find the velocity at the bottom of the plane from energy considerations.

Solution

Let us begin by computing the potential energy at the top of the plane.

$$E_p = Wh = (64\ lb)(300\ ft)(\sin\ 30°)$$

$$= 9600\ ft \cdot lb$$

Fig. 8-9 Some of the initial potential energy at the top of the incline is lost in doing work against friction as the block slides down.

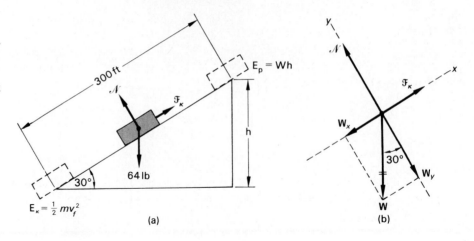

This energy is the total amount available initially. In order to determine how much of it will be lost in doing work against friction, we must first compute the normal force $\mathcal{N}$ exerted by the plane on the block. From Fig. 8-9b

$$\mathcal{N} = W_y = (64 \text{ lb})(\cos 30°) = 55.4 \text{ lb}$$

from which the force of friction must be

$$\mathcal{F}_\kappa = \mu_\kappa \mathcal{N} = (0.1)(55.4 \text{ lb}) = 5.54 \text{ lb}$$

The work done by the friction force is

$$\mathcal{F}_\kappa s = (5.54 \text{ lb})(300 \text{ ft}) = 1660 \text{ ft} \cdot \text{lb}$$

Now, according to Eq. (8-9), the final kinetic energy must equal the initial potential energy less the work done against friction. Thus

$$\tfrac{1}{2}mv_f^2 = 9600 \text{ ft} \cdot \text{lb} - 1660 \text{ ft} \cdot \text{lb}$$
$$= 7940 \text{ ft} \cdot \text{lb}$$

Since the mass of the block is

$$m = \frac{W}{g} = \frac{64 \text{ lb}}{32 \text{ ft/s}^2} = 2 \text{ slugs}$$

we have, on substitution,

$$\tfrac{1}{2}(2 \text{ slugs})v_f^2 = 7940 \text{ ft} \cdot \text{lb}$$

from which

$$v_f^2 = 7940 \text{ ft} \cdot \text{lb/slug} = 7940 \text{ ft}^2/\text{s}^2$$

Taking the square root of both sides, we obtain the final velocity.

$$v_f = 89 \text{ ft/s}$$

You should show that the final velocity would have been 98 ft/s if there had been no frictional forces.

8-7
POWER

In our definition of work, *time* is not involved in any way. The same amount of work is done whether the task takes an hour or a year. Given enough time, even the weakest motor can lift the pyramids of Egypt. However, if we wish to perform a task efficiently, the *rate* at which work is done becomes a very important engineering quantity:

Power is the rate at which work is performed.

$$P = \frac{\text{work}}{t}$$ ft · lb/s or J/s (8-12)

In USCS units, we use foot-pounds per second as a unit of power. The corresponding SI unit has a special name, the *watt* (W), defined as

$$1 \text{ W} = 1 \text{ J/s}$$

The watt and the foot-pound per second are inconveniently small units for most industrial purposes. Therefore, the *kilowatt* (kW) and the *horsepower* (hp) are defined:

$$1 \text{ kW} = 1000 \text{ W}$$

$$1 \text{ hp} = 550 \text{ ft} \cdot \text{lb/s}$$

In the United States, the watt and kilowatt are used almost exclusively in connection with electric power; horsepower is reserved for mechanical power. This practice is purely a convention and by no means necessary. It is perfectly proper to speak of an 0.08-hp light bulb or to brag about a 238-kW engine. The conversion factors are

$$1 \text{ hp} = 746 \text{ W} = 0.746 \text{ kW}$$

$$1 \text{ kW} = 1.34 \text{ hp}$$

Since work is frequently done in a continuous fashion, an expression for power which involves velocity is useful. Thus

$$P = \frac{\text{work}}{t} = \frac{Fs}{t}$$ (8-13)

from which

$$P = F\frac{s}{t} = Fv$$ (8-14)

where v is the velocity of the body on which the parallel force F is applied.

EXAMPLE 8-10

A 40-kg load is raised to a height of 25 m. If the operation requires 1 min, find the power required. What is the power in units of horsepower?

Solution

The work done in lifting the load is

$$\text{Work} = Fs = mgh = (40 \text{ kg})(9.8 \text{ m/s}^2)(25 \text{ m})$$

$$= 9800 \text{ J}$$

The power is then

$$P = \frac{\text{work}}{t} = \frac{9800 \text{ J}}{60 \text{ s}} = 163 \text{ W}$$

Since 1 hp = 746 W, the horsepower developed is

$$P = (163 \text{ W}) \frac{1 \text{ hp}}{746 \text{ W}} = 0.219 \text{ hp}$$

EXAMPLE 8-11   A 60-hp motor provides power for the elevator of a hotel. If the weight of the elevator is 2000 lb, how much time is required to lift the elevator 120 ft?

Solution   The work required is given by

$$\text{Work} = Fs = (2000 \text{ lb})(120 \text{ ft})$$

$$= 2.4 \times 10^5 \text{ ft} \cdot \text{lb}$$

Since 1 hp = 550 ft · lb/s, the power developed is

$$P = (60 \text{ hp}) \frac{550 \text{ ft} \cdot \text{lb/s}}{1 \text{ hp}} = 3.3 \times 10^4 \text{ ft} \cdot \text{lb/s}$$

From Eq. (8-13)

$$P = \frac{Fs}{t}$$

so that

$$t = \frac{Fs}{P} = \frac{2.4 \times 10^5 \text{ ft} \cdot \text{lb}}{3.3 \times 10^4 \text{ ft} \cdot \text{lb/s}}$$

$$= 7.27 \text{ s}$$

Equation (8-12) can be solved for work: Work = Pt. Therefore, the *kilowatthour* (kW · h) unit used by electric companies in billing is a unit of *power* (kilowatt) times *time* (hour), or a unit of work. Quite reasonably, the bill is for the amount of work that has been done. However, the price per kilowatthour may also be determined by the peak power demand of the consumer.

SUMMARY

The concepts of work, energy, and power have been discussed in this chapter. The major points to remember are summarized below:

- The *work* done by a force F acting through a distance s is found from the following equations (refer to Fig. 8-1):

$$\text{Work} = F_x s \qquad \text{Work} = (F \cos \theta)s$$

SI units: *joule* (J)   USCS unit: *foot-pound* (ft · lb)

- *Kinetic energy E_k is the capacity for doing work as a result of motion. It has the same units as work and is found from*

$$E_k = \frac{1}{2} m v_2 \qquad E_k = \frac{1}{2} \left(\frac{W}{g} \right) v^2$$

- Gravitational *potential energy* is the energy which results from the position of an object relative to the earth. Potential energy E_p has the same units as work and is found from

$$E_p = Wh \qquad E_p = mgh$$

where W or mg is the weight of the object and h is the height above some reference position.
- Net work is equal to the change in kinetic energy.

$$Fs = \tfrac{1}{2}mv_f^2 - \tfrac{1}{2}mv_0^2$$

- Conservation of mechanical energy under the action of a dissipative force F:

$$mgh = \tfrac{1}{2}mv_f^2 + Fs \qquad \text{Initial } E_p = \text{final } E_K + \text{work}_F$$

- *Power is the rate at which work is done:*

$$P = \frac{\text{work}}{t} \qquad P = \frac{Fs}{t} \qquad P = Fv$$

SI unit: watt (W)   USCS unit: ft · lb/s
Other units 1 kW = 10^3 W   1 hp = 550 ft · lb/s

QUESTIONS

8-1. Define the following terms:
    a. Work   **f.** Power
    b. Joule   **g.** Horsepower
    c. Potential energy   **h.** Watt
    d. Kinetic energy   **i.** Kilowatthour
    e. Conservation of energy

8-2. Distinguish clearly between the physicist's concept of work and the general concept of work.

8-3. Two teams are engaged in a tug of war. Is work done? When?

8-4. Whenever net work is done on a body, will the body necessarily undergo acceleration? Discuss.

8-5. A diver stands on a board 10 ft above the water. What kind of energy results from this position? What happens to this energy as she dives into the water? Is work done? If so, what is doing the work, and on what is the work done?

8-6. Compare the potential energies for two bodies A and B if **(a)** A is twice as high as B but of the same mass; **(b)** B is twice as heavy as A but at the same height; and **(c)** A is twice as heavy as B, but B is twice as high as A.

8-7. Compare the kinetic energies of two bodies A and B if **(a)** A has twice the speed of B; **(b)** A has half the mass of B; and **(c)** A has twice the mass and half the speed of B.

8-8. In stacking 8-ft boards, you lift an entire board at its center and lay it on the pile. Your helper lifts one end, rests it on the pile, and then lifts the other end. Compare the work done.

8-9. In the light of what you have learned of work and energy, describe the most efficient procedure for ringing the bell with a sledgehammer at the fair. What precautions should you take?

8-10. A roller coaster at the fair boasts "a maximum height of 100 ft with a maximum speed of 60 mi/h." Do you believe the advertisement? Explain.

8-11. A man mows his yard for years using a 4-hp riding lawn mower. One spring he trades the mower in for a 6-hp mower. After using the new mower for a while he proclaims, "I've got more than twice the power that I had with the old mower." Is his statement correct? Why do you think he is convinced of the large increase in power?

PROBLEMS

8-1. A horizontal force of 20 N drags a small sled across the ground at constant speed. The speed is constant because the force of friction exactly balances the 20-N pull. If a distance of 42 m is covered, what is the work done by the pulling force? What is the work of the friction force? What is the total or net work done?

Ans. 840 J, −840 J, 0 J.

8-2. An external work of 400 ft · lb is applied in lifting a 30-lb motor. If all this work contributes to lifting the motor, how high will it be lifted?

8-3. How much work is done in lifting a 6-lb weight to a height of 2 ft and in lifting a 9-kg mass to a height of 8 m?

Ans. 12 ft · lb, 706 J.

8-4. A trunk is pulled 24 m across the floor by a rope making an angle θ with the horizontal, as shown in Fig. 8-10. The tension in the rope is 8 N. Compute the work done when **(a)** $\theta = 0°$, **(b)** $\theta = 30°$, **(c)** $\theta = 60°$.

Fig. 8-10

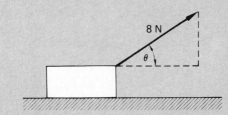

8 N

θ

8-5. An average force of 40 N shortens a coiled spring by 6 cm. **(a)** What is the work done by the 40-N force? **(b)** What is the work done by the reaction force of the spring? **(c)** What is the potential energy after the spring has been compressed?

Ans. **(a)** 2.4 J **(b)** −2.4 J **(c)** 2.4 J.

8-6. A 10-kg block is pushed 8 m along a horizontal surface by a constant force of 26 N. If $\mu_k = 0.2$, what is the resultant work? What acceleration will the block receive?

8-7. A string of freight cars is pulled 300 yd along a track by a switch engine which exerts a force of 3 tons to overcome rolling friction. How much work is done by the switch engine?

Ans. 5.4×10^6 ft · lb.

8-8. A block is pushed 6 m along a horizontal surface by a horizontal force of 6 N. The opposing force of friction is 2 N. **(a)** What is the work done by the 6-N force? **(b)** What is the work done by the friction force? **(c)** What is the net or resultant work?

8-9. A 20-kg sled is pushed up a 34° slope to a vertical height of 140 m above its initial position. **(a)** What is the distance traveled by the sled? **(b)** Neglecting friction, what is the minimum force **P** required to move the sled up the slope? **(c)** How much work is done by the force **P**? **(d)** What is the potential energy at the top?

Ans. **(a)** 250.4 m **(b)** 109.6 N **(c)** 27,440 J **(d)** 27,440 J.

8-10. Assume the same conditions as in Prob. 8-9 except that the coefficient of kinetic friction is 0.2. **(a)** What is the normal force? **(b)** What is the force of kinetic friction? **(c)** What is the minimum push **P** required to move the sled up the slope? **(d)** What is the work done by the force **P**? **(e)** What resultant work was done if the speed remained constant? **(f)** What is the potential energy at the top?

8-11. An 800-lb block is pulled along a horizontal surface by a rope which makes an angle of 37° with the horizontal. The block is dragged through a distance of 200 ft, and the coefficient of kinetic friction is 0.3. The tension in the rope is 400 lb. **(a)** What is the normal force? **(b)** What is the friction force? **(c)** What is the resultant force? **(d)** What is the *net*, or resultant, work?

Ans. **(a)** 559 lb **(b)** −168 lb **(c)** 151 lb **(d)** 30,200 ft · lb.

8-12. A 6-kg mass falls through a distance of 20 m. What is the loss in potential energy?

8-13. An 8-lb hammer head is moving with a speed of 60 ft/s as it strikes the head of a spike. What is its kinetic energy at that instant **(a)** in foot-pounds, **(b)** in joules?

Ans. **(a)** 450 ft · lb **(b)** 610 J.

8-14. An automobile weighs 2200 lb. What is its mass? How much work is necessary to lift this car to a height of 800 ft? What is the potential energy at that height? If it is released, what will its speed be on striking the ground? Verify that its final kinetic energy equals the initial potential energy.

8-15. A 10-kg mass is lifted to a height of 20 m. What are the potential energy, kinetic energy, and total energy? The mass is then released and falls freely. What are the total energy, potential energy, and kinetic energy when the mass is 5 m above the ground? What are the final kinetic energy and the velocity of the mass when it strikes the ground?

Ans. 1960 J, 0 J, 1960 J; 1960 J, 490 J, 1470 J; 1960 J, 19.8 m/s².

8-16. Consider a 64-lb object at a height of 30 ft above a concrete floor. From energy considerations, compute its velocity on impact after dropping from that height. Verify that the same velocity would result if the calculations were made on the basis of a free-falling body according to the methods of Chap. 6.

8-17. The hammer of a pile driver weighs 800 lb and falls a distance of 16 ft before striking the pile. The impact drives the pile 6 in. deeper into the ground. Based on work-energy considerations, what was the average force driving the pile?

Ans. 25,600 lb.

8-18. A 10-kg sled traveling initially at 2 m/s is given a steady push **P** for a distance of 12 m. What must be the value of **P** in order to increase the speed to 4 m/s in this distance? Calculate first from work-energy considerations, then check your answer using Newton's second law.

8-19. A ballistic pendulum is a laboratory device (Fig. 8-11) which might be used to calculate the velocity of a projectile. A 40-g ball is caught by a 500-g suspended mass. After impact, the two masses move together until they stop at a point 45 mm above the point of impact. From energy considerations, what was the velocity of the combined masses just after impact? (Neglect effects of friction.)

Ans. 0.939 m/s.

Fig. 8-11 A ballistic pendulum.

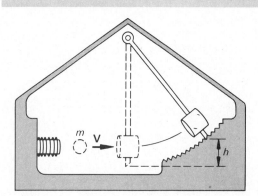

8-20. A 64-lb projectile leaves the ground with a kinetic energy of 4096 ft · lb. Use energy considerations to determine the maximum height the projectile will reach.

8-21. A 20-g bullet leaves a rifle barrel with a muzzle velocity of 1500 m/s. Calculate its kinetic energy. If the bullet penetrates a wooden block a distance of 1.2 cm, what is the average force exerted by the block on the bullet?

Ans. 22,500 J, -1.88×10^6 N.

8-22. A 16-lb shell is fired vertically upward with a muzzle velocity of 400 ft/s. What is the initial kinetic energy, and what is the potential energy at the highest point in its trajectory?

8-23. Find the work required to move a 4-kg box up an incline 20 m long and 16 m high if the coefficient of kinetic friction is 0.3.

Ans. 768 J.

8-24. What will be the kinetic energy of the block in Prob. 8-23 when it reaches the bottom of the incline after being released from the top?

8-25. A sled weighing 20 lb slides from rest at the top of a hill 128 ft high. The slope of the hill is at an angle of 37° with the horizontal. **(a)** What is the component of the weight acting down the plane? **(b)** What is the potential energy when the sled is at the top? **(c)** If the sled encounters a friction force of 2 lb as it slides to the bottom, what is the work done against friction? **(d)** What is the final velocity from energy considerations?

Ans. **(a)** 12.04 lb **(b)** 2560 ft · lb **(c)** 425 ft · lb **(d)** 82.6 ft/s.

8-26. Answer all questions in Prob. 8-25 for a 6-kg sled at the top of a hill 20 m high and 30 m long. Assume that the friction force is equal to 12 N.

8-27. A simple pendulum 1 m long has an 8-kg bob. **(a)** How much work is required to move the pendulum from its vertical position to a horizontal position? **(b)** Compute the velocity and kinetic energy of the bob at the instant it passes through the lowest position in its path.

Ans. **(a)** 78.4 J **(b)** 4.43 m/s.

8-28. A simple pendulum 2 ft long has a wooden bob which weighs 5 lb. As it passes through its lowest point, its velocity is measured to be 10 ft/s. What is its kinetic energy at that point? What is the maximum potential energy that can be attained? What is the maximum height to which the bob can rise?

8-29. A 5-lb hammer is moving horizontally at 25 ft/s when it strikes a nail. If the nail meets an average resistive force of 300 lb, compute the depth of penetration.

Ans. 0.163 ft.

8-30. A water pump feeds water from a well into a watering trough 30 ft higher than the water level of the well. (Water weighs 62.4 lb/ft^3.) If the pump delivers 60 ft^3 of water each minute, how much work is done each minute?

8-31. A 40-kg mass is lifted through a distance of 20 m. If the operation requires 3 s, what is the average power employed?

Ans. 2.61 kW.

8-32. A power-station conveyer belt lifts 500 tons of ore per hour to a height of 90 ft. What average horsepower is required?

8-33. What is the maximum speed at which a 40-hp hoist can lift a 2-ton load?

Ans. 5.5 ft/s.

8-34. A 200-lb man climbs an 800-ft slope in 7 h. How much work does he do in foot-pounds? In joules? What average power must he supply?

8-35. A 300-kg elevator is raised with constant velocity through a vertical distance of 100 m in 2 min. What is the increase in potential energy? What is the useful output power of the hoist?

Ans. 2.94×10^5 J, 2.45 kW.

8-36. What weight can a 40-hp engine pull along a level road at 44 ft/s if the coefficient of friction between the weight and the road is 0.1?

8-37. A 90-hp motor provides power for the elevator of a hotel. If the weight of the elevator is 3000 lb, how much time is required to lift the elevator 200 ft? Assume constant speed.

Ans. 12.1 s.

8-38. An elevator is powered by a 30-hp motor. The weight of the elevator and its load is 2000 lb. If the overall efficiency of the motor is 70 percent, what will be the upward speed of the elevator?

8-39. What is the maximum speed at which a 40-kW engine can hoist an 800-kg load?

Ans. 5.10 m/s.

9 *Impulse and Momentum*

OBJECTIVES: After completing this chapter, you should be able to:

1. Define and give examples of *impulse* and *momentum* as vector quantities.

2. Write and apply a relationship between *impulse* and the resulting *change in momentum*.

3. State the law of *conservation of momentum* and apply it to the solution of physical problems.

4. Define and be able to calculate the *coefficient of restitution* for two surfaces.

5. Distinguish by example and definition between elastic and inelastic collisions.

6. Predict the velocities of two colliding bodies after impact when the coefficient of restitution, masses, and initial speeds are given.

Energy and work are scalar quantities which say absolutely nothing about direction. The law of conservation of energy describes only the relationship between initial and final states; it says nothing about how the energies are distributed.

For example, when two objects collide, we can say that the total energy before collision must equal the energy after collision if we neglect friction and other heat losses. But we need a new concept if we are to determine how the total energy is divided between the objects or even their relative directions after impact.

The concepts of impulse and momentum presented in this chapter add a vector description to our discussion of energy and motion.

<table>
<tr><td>

**9-1
IMPULSE
AND
MOMENTUM**

</td><td>

When a golf ball is driven from the ground, as in Fig. 9-1, a large average force $\mathbf{F}$ acts on the ball during a very short interval of time Δt, causing the ball to accelerate from rest to a final velocity $\mathbf{v}_f$. It is extremely difficult to measure either the force or its duration, but their product $\mathbf{F} \Delta t$ can be determined from the resulting change in velocity of the golf ball. From Newton's second law we have

</td></tr>
</table>

$$\mathbf{F} = m\mathbf{a} = m\frac{\mathbf{v}_f - \mathbf{v}_0}{\Delta t}$$

Fig. 9-1 When a golf club strikes the ball, a force $\mathbf{F}$ acting through a time interval Δt results in a change of momentum.

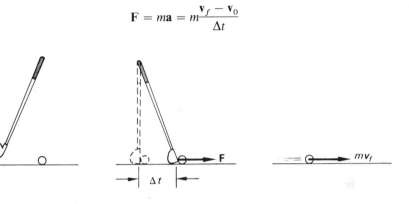

Multiplying by Δt gives

$$\mathbf{F} \Delta t = m(\mathbf{v}_f - \mathbf{v}_0)$$

or

$$\boxed{\mathbf{F} \Delta t = m\mathbf{v}_f - m\mathbf{v}_0} \tag{9-1}$$

This equation is so useful in solving problems involving impact that the terms are given special names.

> The **impulse** $\mathbf{F} \Delta t$ is a vector quantity equal in magnitude to the product of the force and the time interval in which it acts. Its direction is the same as that of the force.

> The **momentum p** of a particle is a vector quantity equal in magnitude to the product of its mass m and its velocity $\mathbf{v}$.

$$\boxed{\mathbf{p} = m\mathbf{v}}$$

Thus Eq. (9-1) can be stated verbally:

Impulse $(\mathbf{F} \Delta t)$ = *change in momentum* $(m\mathbf{v}_f - m\mathbf{v}_0)$

The SI unit of impulse is the *newton-second* $(\mathrm{N} \cdot \mathrm{s})$. The unit of momentum is the *kilogram-meter per second* $(\mathrm{kg} \cdot \mathrm{m/s})$. It is convenient to distinguish these units even though they are actually the same:

$$\mathrm{N} \cdot \mathrm{s} = \frac{\mathrm{kg} \cdot \mathrm{m}}{\mathrm{s}^2} \times \mathrm{s} = \mathrm{kg} \cdot \mathrm{m/s}$$

The corresponding units in the USCS are the *pound-second* (lb · s) and *slug-foot per second* (slug · ft/s).

EXAMPLE 9-1

A 3-kg sledgehammer is moving at a speed of 14 m/s as it strikes a steel spike. It is brought to a stop in 0.02 s. Determine the average force on the spike.

Solution

Since $v_f = 0$, we have from Eq. (9-1),

$$F \, \Delta t = -mv_0$$

If we consider that the hammer is moving downward, we substitute $v_0 = -14$ m/s, giving

$$F = \frac{-mv_0}{\Delta t} = \frac{-(3 \text{ kg})(-14 \text{ m/s})}{0.02 \text{ s}}$$

$$= 2100 \text{ N}$$

This force, exerted on the hammer, is equal in magnitude but opposite in direction to the force exerted on the spike. It must be emphasized that the force found in this manner is an *average* force. At some instants the force will be much greater than 2100 N.

EXAMPLE 9-2

A 0.6-lb baseball moving toward the batter with a velocity of 44 ft/s is struck with a bat which causes it to move in a reversed direction with a velocity of 88 ft/s. (Refer to Fig. 9-2.) Find the impulse and the average force exerted on the ball if the bat is in contact with the ball for 0.01 s.

Fig. 9-2 Impact of a bat with a baseball.

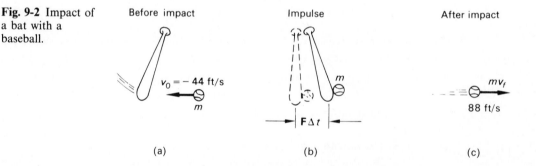

Before impact $\quad$ Impulse $\quad$ After impact

$v_0 = -44$ ft/s

m

m

mv_f

88 ft/s

$F\Delta t$

(a) $\qquad\qquad$ (b) $\qquad\qquad$ (c)

Solution

Consider the final direction of motion as positive. Applying Eq. (9-1), we solve for the impulse as follows:

$$F \, \Delta t = mv_f - mv_0 = m(v_f - v_0)$$

since

$$m = \frac{W}{g} = \frac{0.6 \text{ lb}}{32 \text{ ft/s}} = 0.0188 \text{ slug}$$

$$F \, \Delta t = 0.0188 \text{ slug}[88 \text{ ft/s} - (-44 \text{ ft/s})]$$

$$= 0.0188 \text{ slug}(132 \text{ ft/s})$$

$$\text{Impulse} = F \, \Delta t = 2.48 \text{ lb} \cdot \text{s}$$

The average force is then found by substituting $\Delta t = 0.01$ s.

$$F(0.01 \text{ s}) = 2.48 \text{ lb} \cdot \text{s}$$

$$F = \frac{2.48 \text{ lb} \cdot \text{s}}{0.01 \text{ s}} = 248 \text{ lb}$$

9-2 THE LAW OF CONSERVATION OF MOMENTUM

Let us consider the *head-on* collision of the masses m_1 and m_2, as shown in Fig. 9-3. We denote their velocities before impact as u_1 and u_2 and after impact as v_1 and v_2. The impulse of the force $\mathbf{F}_1$ acting on the right mass is

$$F_1 \, \Delta t = m_1 v_1 - m_1 u_1$$

Fig. 9-3 Head-on collision of two masses.

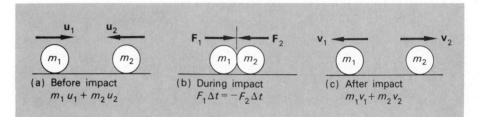

(a) Before impact
$$m_1 u_1 + m_2 u_2$$

(b) During impact
$$F_1 \Delta t = -F_2 \Delta t$$

(c) After impact
$$m_1 v_1 + m_2 v_2$$

Similarly, the impulse of the force $\mathbf{F}_2$ on the left mass is

$$F_2 \, \Delta t = m_2 v_2 - m_2 u_2$$

During the time Δt, $\mathbf{F}_1 = -\mathbf{F}_2$, so that

$$F_1 \, \Delta t = -F_2 \, \Delta t$$

or

$$m_1 v_1 - m_1 u_1 = -(m_2 v_2 - m_2 u_2)$$

and finally, after rearranging,

$$\boxed{m_1 u_1 + m_2 u_2 = m_1 v_1 + m_2 v_2} \qquad (9\text{-}2)$$

Total momentum before impact = total momentum after impact

Thus we have derived a statement of the law of *conservation of momentum*:

The total linear momentum of colliding bodies before impact is equal to their total momentum after impact.

EXAMPLE 9-3

Assume that m_1 and m_2 of Fig. 9-3 have masses of 8 and 6 kg, respectively. The mass m_1 moves initially to the right with a velocity of 4 m/s and collides with m_2, moving to the left at 5 m/s. What is the total momentum before and after the collision?

Solution   We choose the direction to the right as positive, taking care to affix the proper sign to the velocities.

$$p_0(\text{before impact}) = m_1 u_1 + m_2 u_2$$

$$p_0 = (8 \text{ kg})(4 \text{ m/s}) + (6 \text{ kg})(-5 \text{ m/s})$$

$$= 32 \text{ kg} \cdot \text{m/s} - 30 \text{ kg} \cdot \text{m/s} = 2 \text{ kg} \cdot \text{m/s}$$

The same total momentum must exist after impact, and so we can write

$$p_f = m_1 v_1 + m_2 v_2 = 2 \text{ kg} \cdot \text{m/s}$$

If either v_1 or v_2 can be measured after the collision, the other can be determined from this relation.

EXAMPLE 9-4   A rifle weighs 8 lb and fires a bullet weighing 0.02 lb at a muzzle velocity of 2800 ft/s. Compute the recoil velocity if the rifle is freely suspended.

Solution   Since both the rifle m_1 and the bullet m_2 are initially at rest, the total momentum before firing must equal zero. The momentum is unaltered, and so it must also be zero after firing. Hence Eq. (9-2) gives

$$0 = m_1 v_1 + m_2 v_2$$

$$m_1 v_1 = -m_2 v_2$$

$$v_1 = -\frac{m_2 v_2}{m_1}$$

$$= -\frac{(0.02 \text{ lb}/32 \text{ ft/s}^2)(2800 \text{ ft/s})}{8 \text{ lb}/32 \text{ ft/s}^2}$$

$$= -7 \text{ ft/s}$$

An interesting experiment which demonstrates the conservation of momentum can be performed with eight small marbles and a grooved track, as shown in Fig. 9-4. If one marble is released from the left, it will be stopped upon colliding with the others, and one on the right end will roll out with the same velocity. Similarly, when two, three, four, or five marbles are released from the left, the same number will roll out to the right with the same velocity, the others remaining at rest in the center.

You might reasonably ask why two marbles roll off in Fig. 9-4 instead of one with twice the velocity, since this condition would also conserve momentum. For example, if each marble has a mass of 50 g, and if two marbles approach from the left at a velocity of 20 cm/s, the total momentum before impact is 2000 g · cm/s. This same momentum could be achieved after impact if

Fig. 9-4 Conservation of momentum.

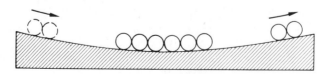

only one marble left, assuming it had a velocity of 40 cm/s. The answer lies in the fact that energy must be conserved. If one marble came off with twice the velocity, its kinetic energy would be much greater than that available from the other two. The kinetic energy put into the system would be

$$E_0 = \tfrac{1}{2}mv^2 = \tfrac{1}{2}(0.1 \text{ kg})(0.2 \text{ m/s})^2$$

$$= 2 \times 10^{-3} \text{ J}$$

The kinetic energy of one marble traveling at 40 cm/s is exactly twice this value.

$$E_f = \tfrac{1}{2}mv^2 = \tfrac{1}{2}(0.05 \text{ kg})(0.4 \text{ m/s})^2$$

$$= 4 \times 10^{-3} \text{ J}$$

Therefore, it is seen that energy as well as momentum is important in describing impact phenomena.

9-3 ELASTIC AND INELASTIC IMPACTS

From the experiment in the previous section, the student might assume that the kinetic energy as well as the momentum is unchanged by a collision. Although this assumption is approximately true for hard bodies like marbles and billiard balls, it is not true for soft bodies, which rebound much more slowly upon impact. During impact, all bodies become slightly deformed, and small amounts of heat are liberated. The vigor with which a body restores itself to its original shape after deformation is a measure of its *elasticity*, or restitution.

If the kinetic energy remains constant in a collision (an ideal case), the collision is said to be *completely elastic*. In this instance no energy is lost through heat or deformation in collision. A hardened steel ball dropped on a marble slab would approximate a completely elastic collision. If the colliding bodies stick together and move off as a unit afterward, the collision is said to be *completely inelastic*. A bullet which becomes embedded in a wooden block is an example of this type of impact. The majority of collisions fall between these two extremes.

In a completely elastic collision between two masses m_1 and m_2, we can say that both energy and momentum will be unaltered. Hence, we can apply two equations:

Energy: $\qquad \tfrac{1}{2}m_1 u_1^2 + \tfrac{1}{2}m_2 u_2^2 = \tfrac{1}{2}m_1 v_1^2 + \tfrac{1}{2}m_2 v_2^2$

Momentum: $\qquad m_1 u_1 + m_2 u_2 = m_1 v_1 + m_2 v_2$

which can be simplified to give

$$m_1(u_1^2 - v_1^2) = m_2(u_2^2 - v_2^2)$$

$$m_1(u_1 - v_1) = m_2(u_2 - v_2)$$

Dividing the first equation by the second gives

$$\frac{u_1^2 - v_1^2}{u_1 - v_1} = \frac{u_2^2 - v_2^2}{u_2 - v_2}$$

Factoring the numerators and dividing out, we obtain

$$u_1 + v_1 = u_2 + v_2$$

or

$$v_1 - v_2 = u_2 - u_1 = -(u_1 - u_2) \tag{9-3}$$

Thus, in the ideal case of a completely elastic collision, the relative velocity after collision, $v_1 - v_2$, is equal to the negative of the relative velocity before collision. The closer these quantities are to being equal, the more elastic the collision. The negative ratio of the relative velocity after collision to the relative velocity before collision provides a means of measuring the elasticity of a collision.

The **coefficient of restitution** e is the negative ratio of the relative velocity after impact to the relative velocity before impact.

$$e = -\frac{v_1 - v_2}{u_1 - u_2}$$

Incorporating the minus sign into the numerator of this equation yields

$$\boxed{e = \frac{v_2 - v_1}{u_1 - u_2}} \tag{9-4}$$

If the collision is completely elastic, $e = 1$. If the collision is completely inelastic, $e = 0$. In the inelastic case the two bodies move off with the same velocity, so that $v_2 = v_1$. In general, the coefficient of restitution has some value between 0 and 1.

A simple method of determining the coefficient of restitution is shown in Fig. 9-5. A sphere of the material being measured is dropped onto a fixed plate from a height h_1. Its rebound is measured to a height h_2. In this case, the mass of the plate is so large that v_2 is approximately 0. Therefore,

$$e = \frac{v_2 - v_1}{u_1 - u_2} = -\frac{v_1}{u_1}$$

Fig. 9-5

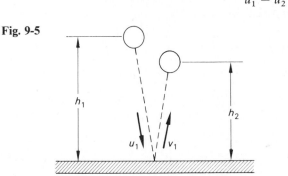

The velocity u_1 is simply the velocity acquired in falling from a height h_1, which is found from

$$u_1^2 - u_0^2 = 2gh_1$$

But the initial velocity $u_0 = 0$, so that

$$u_1^2 = 2gh_1$$

or

$$u_1 = \sqrt{2gh_1}$$

We have considered the downward direction as positive. If the ball rebounds to a height h_2, its rebound velocity v_1 must be $-\sqrt{2gh_2}$. (The minus sign indicates the change in direction.) Hence, the coefficient of restitution is given by

$$e = -\frac{v_1}{u_1} = -\frac{-\sqrt{2gh_2}}{\sqrt{2gh_1}}$$

or

$$\boxed{e = \sqrt{\frac{h_2}{h_1}}} \qquad (9\text{-}5)$$

The resulting coefficient is a joint property of the ball and the rebounding surface.

For a very elastic surface, e has a value of 0.95 or greater (steel or glass), whereas for less resilient substances e may be extremely small. It is interesting to note that the rebound height is a function of the vigor with which the impact deformation is restored. Contrary to popular conception, a steel ball or glass marble will bounce to a greater height than most rubber balls.

EXAMPLE 9-5 A 2-kg ball traveling to the left with a speed of 24 m/s collides head-on with a 4-kg ball traveling to the right at 16 m/s. (a) Find the resulting velocity if the two balls stick together on impact. (b) Find their final velocities if the coefficient of restitution is 0.80.

Solution (a) In this instance $v_2 = v_1$ and $e = 0$. Let us denote their final velocity by v. The law of conservation of momentum tells us that

$$m_1 u_1 + m_2 u_2 = m_1 v_1 + m_2 v_2 = (m_1 + m_2)v$$

since $v_1 = v_2 = v$. Choosing the right direction as positive, we have on substitution

$$(2 \text{ kg})(-24 \text{ m/s}) + (4 \text{ kg})(16 \text{ m/s}) = (2 \text{ kg} + 4 \text{ kg})v$$

$$-48 \text{ kg} \cdot \text{m/s} + 64 \text{ kg} \cdot \text{m/s} = (6 \text{ kg})v$$

$$16 \text{ kg} \cdot \text{m/s} = (6 \text{ kg})v$$

from which

$$v = \tfrac{16}{6} \text{ m/s} = 2.67 \text{ m/s}$$

The fact that this velocity is positive indicates that both bodies move together to the right after collision.

Solution (b)

In this case e is not zero, and the balls rebound after collision with different velocities. Therefore, more information is needed than that derived from the momentum equation alone. We resort to the given value of $e = 0.80$ and Eq. (9-4) to give us more information.

$$e = 0.80 = \frac{v_2 - v_1}{u_1 - u_2}$$

or

$$v_2 - v_1 = (0.80)(u_1 - u_2)$$

Substituting the known values for u_1 and u_2, we obtain

$$v_2 - v_1 = (0.80)(-24 \text{ m/s} - 16 \text{ m/s})$$

$$= (0.80)(-40 \text{ m/s})$$

or finally

$$v_2 - v_1 = -32 \text{ m/s}$$

We can now use the momentum equation to arrive at another relation between v_2 and v_1, allowing us to solve the two equations simultaneously.

$$m_1 u_1 + m_2 u_2 = m_1 v_1 + m_2 v_2$$

The left side of this equation has already been found in part **a** to equal 16 kg · m/s. Therefore, we have on substitution for m_1 and m_2 on the right side

$$16 \text{ kg} \cdot \text{m/s} = (2 \text{ kg})v_1 + (4 \text{ kg})v_2$$

from which

$$2v_1 + 4v_2 = 16 \text{ m/s}$$

or

$$v_1 + 2v_2 = 8 \text{ m/s}$$

Hence we have two equations:

$$v_2 - v_1 = -32 \text{ m/s} \qquad v_1 + 2v_2 = 8 \text{ m/s}$$

Solving simultaneously, we obtain

$$v_1 = 24 \text{ m/s} \qquad v_2 = -8 \text{ m/s}$$

Thus, after colliding, the balls reverse their directions, m_1 moving to the right with a velocity of 24 m/s and m_2 moving to the left with a velocity of 8 m/s.

EXAMPLE 9-6

A 12-g bullet is fired into a 2-kg block of wood suspended from a cord, as shown in Fig. 9-6. The impact of the bullet causes the block to swing 10 cm above its original level. Compute the velocity of the bullet as it strikes the block.

Solution

We can compute the combined velocity after impact from energy considerations. The kinetic energy of the block and bullet immediately after the collision is converted into potential energy as they rise to a height h. Hence, if v is the initial velocity of the block and bullet, we have

$$\tfrac{1}{2}(m_1 + m_2)v^2 = (m_1 + m_2)gh$$

Fig. 9-6 Computing the muzzle velocity u from energy and momentum considerations.

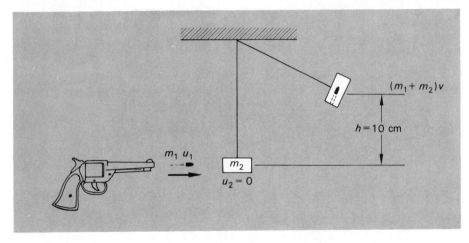

Dividing by $m_1 + m_2$, we obtain

$$v^2 = 2gh$$

from which

$$v = \sqrt{2gh}$$

Therefore, the combined velocity after collision is

$$v = \sqrt{(2)(9.8 \text{ m/s}^2)(0.1 \text{ m})} = 1.4 \text{ m/s}$$

The momentum equation then becomes

$$m_1 u_1 + m_2 u_2 = (m_1 + m_2)v$$

or, since $u_2 = 0$,

$$(0.012 \text{ kg})u_1 = (0.012 \text{ kg} + 2 \text{ kg})(1.4 \text{ m/s})$$

$$= (2.012 \text{ kg})(1.4 \text{ m/s})$$

$$0.012u_1 = 2.82 \text{ m/s}$$

which gives an entrance velocity of

$$u_1 = 235 \text{ m/s}$$

SUMMARY

In this chapter you learned the relationship between impulse and momentum. Physical problems were then introduced to deal with elastic and inelastic collisions. The major concepts are summarized below:

- The *impulse* is the product of the average force F and the time interval Δt through which it acts.

    Impulse $= F \Delta t$ SI units: N · s   USCS units: lb · s

- The *momentum* of a particle is its mass times its velocity.

  Momentum $p = mv$ SI units: kg · m/s   USCS units: slug · ft/s

- The impulse is equal to the change in momentum:

$$F \, \Delta t = mv_f - mv_0$$

     Note: N · s = kg · m/s (equivalent units)

- *Conservation of momentum*: The total momentum before impact is equal to the total momentum after impact (see Fig. 9-3).

$$m_1 u_1 + m_2 u_2 = m_1 v_1 + m_2 v_2$$

- The *coefficient of restitution* is found from relative velocities before and after collision or from the rebound height:

$$e = \frac{v_2 - v_1}{u_1 - u_2}$$

$$e = \sqrt{\frac{h_2}{h_1}}$$

- For a completely elastic collision, $e = 1$.
  For a completely inelastic collision, $e = 0$.

QUESTIONS

9-1. Define the following terms:
  a. Impulse   **d.** Elastic impact
  b. Momentum   **e.** Inelastic impact
  c. Conservation of momentum   **f** Coefficient of restitution

9-2. Show the equivalence of the units of impulse with the units of momentum in USCS units.

9-3. Discuss the vector nature of impulse and momentum.

9-4. How does the magnitude of the impulse 1 lb · s compare with the magnitude of the impulse 1 N · s?

9-5. Discuss the conservation of energy and momentum for **(a)** an elastic collision and **(b)** an inelastic collision.

9-6. If you hold a weapon loosely when firing, it appears to give a greater kick than when you hold it tight against your shoulder. Explain. What effect does the weight of the weapon have?

9-7. A mortar shell explodes in midair. How is momentum conserved? How is energy conserved?

9-8. Suppose you hit a tennis ball into the air with a racket. The ball first strikes the concrete court and then bounds over the fence, landing in the grass. How many impulses were involved, and which impulse was the greatest?

9-9. A father and his daughter stand facing each other on a frozen pond. If the girl pushes her father backward, describe their relative motion and velocities. Would they differ if the father pushed the daughter?

9-10. Two small cars of masses m_1 and m_2 are tied together with a compressed spring between them. The cord is burned with a match, releasing the spring and imparting an equal impulse to each car. Compare the ratio of their displacements to the ratio of their masses at some later instant.

PROBLEMS

9-1. Compute the momentum and kinetic energy of a 3200-lb car moving north at 60 mi/h.

Ans. 8800 slug · ft/s, 3.87×10^5 ft · lb.

9-2. What is the momentum of a 0.003-kg bullet moving at 600 m/s in a direction 30° above the horizontal? What are the horizontal and vertical components of this momentum?

9-3. A 2500 kg truck traveling at 40 km/h strikes a brick wall and comes to a stop in 0.2 s. **(a)** What is the impulse? **(b)** Find the average force on the truck during the crash.

Ans. **(a)** -2.78×10^4 lb · s **(b)** 1.39×10^5 lb.

9-4. A 400-g rubber ball is dropped from a window which is 12 m from the pavement below. Find the speed of the ball just before impact. What is its momentum just before impact? If it leaves the pavement with a speed of 12 m/s, what is its momentum after impact? What is the total change in momentum? If the ball is in contact with the pavement for 0.01 s, what is the average force exerted on the ball?

9-5. A 0.2-kg baseball reaches the batter with a speed of 20 m/s. After it has been struck, it leaves the bat at 35 m/s in a reversed direction. If the ball exerts an average force of 8400 N, how long was it in contact with the bat?

Ans. 1.31 m/s.

9-6. A train travels with a speed of 60 mi/h and weighs 8×10^6 lb. **(a)** What impulse will the train exert while stopping? **(b)** If the train comes to a dead stop in 600 ft, how long will it take? **(c)** What is the required braking force?

9-7. An empty truck weighing 3 tons rolls freely at 5 ft/s along level ground and collides with a loaded truck weighing 5 tons, standing at rest and free to move. If the two trucks couple together, find their velocity after collision. Compare the kinetic energy before collision with that after impact. How do you account for the decrease in energy?

Ans. 1.88 ft/s, $E_{k0} = 2344$ ft · lb, $E_{kf} = 879$ ft · lb.

9-8. A 24-g bullet is fired with a muzzle velocity of 900 m/s from a 5-kg rifle. Find the recoil velocity of the rifle. Find the ratio of the kinetic energy of the bullet to that of the rifle.

9-9. A 4-kg ball moving with a velocity of 8 m/s collides head-on with another ball of 2-kg mass which is initially at rest. After impact, the first mass is still moving in the same direction but with a velocity of 4 m/s. Find **(a)** the velocity of the 2-kg mass after the collision, **(b)** the initial kinetic energy, **(c)** the total energy after impact, and **(d)** the energy loss during impact.

Ans. **(a)** 8 m/s **(b)** 128 J **(c)** 96 J **(d)** 32 J.

9-10. Two children, weighing 80 and 50 lb, are at rest on roller skates. If the larger child pushes the other so that the smaller one moves away at a speed of 6 mi/h, what will the velocity of the large child be?

9-11. The coefficient of restitution of steel is 0.90. If a steel ball is dropped from a height of 7 m, how high will it rebound?

Ans. 5.67 m.

9-12. In Prob. 9-11, what is the time between the first contact with the surface and the second contact?

9-13. A ball dropped from rest onto a fixed horizontal plate rebounds to a height which is 81 percent of its original height. **(a)** Find the coefficient of restitution. **(b)** Determine the vertical velocity of impact required to cause the ball to rebound to a height of 8 m.

Ans. **(a)** 0.9 **(b)** 13.9 m/s.

9-14. A 12-kg block is at rest on a frictionless horizontal surface. A 400-g ball traveling with a speed of 16 m/s in a direction 30° below the horizontal strikes and embeds itself in the block. What are the horizontal and vertical components of the ball's incident momentum? With what speed does the block slide along the surface after impact?

9-15. A 5-lb ball and a 12-lb ball approach each other with equal speeds of 25 ft/s. **(a)** What will their combined speed after impact be if the collision is completely inelastic? **(b)** What will their respective speeds be after impact if the collision is completely elastic?

Ans. **(a)** -10.3 ft/s **(b)** $v_5 = 4.41$ ft/s, $v_{12} = -45.6$ ft/s.

9-16. A 60-g body has an initial velocity of 100 cm/s to the right, and a 150-g body has an initial velocity of 30 cm/s to the left. If the coefficient of restitution is 0.80, find their respective speeds and directions after impact. What percentage of the initial kinetic energy is lost during the collision?

9-17. A 7.2-kg bowling ball traveling at 12 m/s overtakes another ball of the same mass traveling at 7 m/s. Assume that $e = 0.9$. What are the respective velocities after impact?

Ans. 7.25 m/s, 11.8 m/s.

9-18. An atomic particle of mass 20×10^{-28} kg moving with a velocity of 4×10^6 m/s collides head-on with a particle of mass 12×10^{-28} kg initially at rest. Assuming that the collision is completely elastic, find **(a)** the total momentum before impact and **(b)** the velocity of the incident particle after impact.

9-19. If the block in Fig. 9-6 weighs 36 lb, how high will it be raised above its initial level if a 1-lb projectile enters it with a velocity of 200 ft/s and remains lodged in the block?

Ans. 0.457 ft.

9-20. Two perfectly elastic balls of masses $m_1 = 0.3$ kg and $m_2 = 0.8$ kg are supported by strings 120 cm long. The smaller mass is pulled aside until it has been raised through a vertical distance of 6 cm and then released. What is the velocity of each ball after the first impact?

9-21. A 0.2-kg projectile is fired with a horizontal speed of 500 m/s into a 30-kg block of wood. The block is suspended at the end of a long cord and is initially at rest. What is the speed of the block and projectile after impact? Assume the collision to be completely inelastic. How high will the block rise after the collision?

Ans. 3.31 m/s, 0.559 m.

9-22. An 8-kg block of ice is supported by a long cord. A bullet is fired into the ice causing it to rise to a vertical height of 18 cm. If the mass of the bullet was 3 g, what was its velocity just before becoming embedded in the ice?

9-23. Two wooden 2-kg balls rest on a frictionless track 5 m apart. If a third ball of the same mass strikes the first with a velocity of 30 m/s, how long will it take for the first ball to strike the second? Assume $e = 1$.

Ans. 0.167 s.

9-24. An astronaut in orbit outside his capsule uses a revolver to control his motion. The astronaut with all his gear weighs 200 lb on earth. If the revolver fires 0.05-lb bullets with a muzzle velocity of 2700 ft/s, and if the astronaut fires 10 shots, what will his final velocity be? Compute the kinetic energy of the astronaut and the kinetic energy of the 10 bullets. Account for the difference between the two energies.

10 *Uniform Circular Motion*

OBJECTIVES: After completing this chapter, you should be able to:

1. Demonstrate by definition and examples your understanding of the concepts of *centripetal acceleration* and *centripetal force*.

2. Apply your knowledge of centripetal force and centripetal acceleration to the solution of problems similar to those in this text.

3. Define and apply the concepts of *frequency* and *period* of rotation, and relate them to the linear speed of an object in uniform circular motion.

4. Apply your knowledge of centripetal force to problems involving *banking angles*, the *conical pendulum*, and motion in a *vertical circle*.

5. State and apply the universal law of gravitation.

In previous chapters we considered primarily motion in a straight line. This approach is sufficient to describe and apply most mechanical concepts. Unfortunately, bodies in the natural world generally move along curved paths. Artillery shells travel along parabolic paths under the influence of the earth's gravitational field. Planets revolve about the sun in paths which are nearly circular. On the atomic level electrons circle about the nucleus of an atom. In fact, it is difficult to imagine any phenomenon in physics which does not involve motion in at least two dimensions.

**10-1
MOTION
IN A
CIRCULAR
PATH**

Newton's first law tells us that all bodies moving in a straight line with constant speed will maintain their velocity unaltered unless acted on by an external force. The velocity of a body is a vector quantity consisting of both its speed and its direction. Just as a resultant force is required to change its speed, a resultant force must be applied to change its direction. Whenever this force acts in a direction other than the original direction of motion, the path of a moving particle is changed.

The simplest kind of two-dimensional motion occurs when a constant external force always acts at right angles to the path of a moving particle. In this case the resultant force will produce an acceleration which alters only the direction of motion, leaving the speed constant. This simple type of motion is referred to as *uniform circular motion.*

> **Uniform circular motion** is motion in which there is no change in speed, only a change in direction.

An example of uniform circular motion is afforded by swinging a rock in a circular path with a string, as shown in Fig. 10-1. As the rock revolves with constant speed, the inward force of the tension in the string constantly changes the direction of the rock, causing it to move in a circular path. If the string should break, the rock would fly off at a tangent perpendicular to the radius of its circular path.

Fig. 10-1 (*a*) The inward pull of the string on the rock causes it to move in a circular path. (*b*) If the string breaks, the rock will fly off at a tangent to the circle.

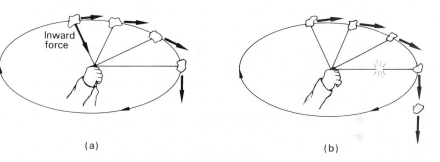

Inward force

(a)

(b)

**10-2
CENTRIP-
ETAL
ACCELERA-
TION**

Newton's second law of motion states that a resultant force must produce an acceleration in the direction of the force. In uniform circular motion, the acceleration changes the velocity of a moving particle by altering its direction.

The position and velocity of a particle moving in a circular path of radius R are shown at two instants in Fig. 10-2. When the particle is at point A, its velocity is represented by the vector $\mathbf{v}_1$. After a time interval Δt, its velocity is represented by the vector $\mathbf{v}_2$. The acceleration by definition is the change in velocity per unit time. Thus

$$\mathbf{a} = \frac{\Delta \mathbf{v}}{\Delta t} = \frac{\mathbf{v}_2 - \mathbf{v}_1}{\Delta t} \tag{10-1}$$

The change in velocity $\Delta \mathbf{v}$ is represented graphically in Fig. 10-2*b*. The difference between the two vectors $\mathbf{v}_2$ and $\mathbf{v}_1$ is constructed according to the methods

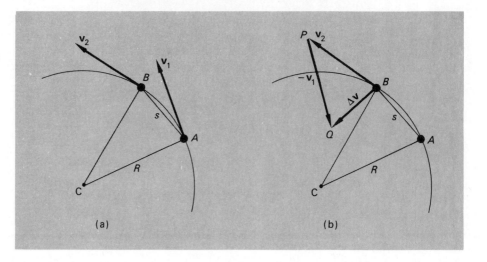

(a)   (b)

introduced in Chap. 2. Since the velocities $\mathbf{v}_2$ and $\mathbf{v}_1$ have the same magnitude, they form the legs of an isosceles triangle *BPQ* whose base is Δ**v**. If we construct a similar triangle *ABC*, it can be noted that the magnitude of Δ**v** has the same relationship to the magnitude of either velocity as the chord *s* has to the radius *R*. This proportionality is stated symbolically as

$$\frac{\Delta v}{v} = \frac{s}{R} \tag{10-2}$$

where *v* represents the absolute magnitude of either $\mathbf{v}_1$ or $\mathbf{v}_2$.

The distance the particle actually covers in traveling from point *A* to point *B* is not the distance *s* but the length of the arc from *A* to *B*. The shorter the time interval Δ*t*, the closer these points are until in the limit the chord length becomes equal to the arc length. In this case, the length *s* is given by

$$s = v\,\Delta t$$

which when substituted into Eq. (10-2) yields

$$\frac{\Delta v}{v} = \frac{v\,\Delta t}{R}$$

Since the acceleration from Eq. (10-1) is Δ*v*/Δ*t*, we can rearrange terms and obtain

$$\frac{\Delta v}{\Delta t} = \frac{v^2}{R}$$

Therefore, the rate of change in velocity, or the *centripetal acceleration*, is given by

$$\boxed{a_c = \frac{v^2}{R}} \tag{10-3}$$

where *v* is the linear speed of a particle moving in a circular path of radius *R*.

The term *centripetal* means that the acceleration is always directed toward the center. Notice in Fig. 10-2b the vector $\Delta \mathbf{v}$ does not point toward the center. This is because we have considered a long time interval between the measurements at A and B. If we restrict the separation of these points to an infinitesimal distance, the vector $\Delta \mathbf{v}$ would point toward the center.

The units of centripetal acceleration are the same as those for linear acceleration. For example, in the SI, v^2/R would have the units

$$\frac{(\text{m/s})^2}{\text{m}} = \frac{\text{m}^2/\text{s}^2}{\text{m}} = \text{m/s}^2$$

EXAMPLE 10-1   A 4-lb body is tied to the end of a cord and whirled in a horizontal circle of radius 6 ft. If the body makes three complete revolutions every second, determine its linear speed and its centripetal acceleration.

Solution   If the body makes 3 rev/s, the time to travel one complete circle (a distance $2\pi R$) is $\frac{1}{3}$ s. Hence, the linear speed is

$$v = \frac{2\pi R}{0.333 \text{ s}} = \frac{2\pi(6 \text{ ft})}{0.333 \text{ s}}$$

$$= 113 \text{ ft/s}$$

Therefore, the centripetal acceleration, from Eq. (10-3), is

$$a_c = \frac{v^2}{R} = \frac{(113 \text{ ft/s})^2}{6 \text{ ft}}$$

$$= \frac{12.8 \times 10^3 \text{ ft}^2/\text{s}^2}{6 \text{ ft}} = 2130 \text{ ft/s}^2$$

The procedure used to compute linear speed in the above example is so useful that it is worth remembering. If we define the *period* as the time for one complete revolution and designate it by the letter T, the linear speed can be computed by dividing the period into the circumference. Thus

$$\boxed{v = \frac{2\pi R}{T}} \tag{10-4}$$

Another useful parameter in engineering problems is the rotational speed, expressed in *revolutions per minute* (rpm) or *revolutions per second* (rev/s). This quantity is called the *frequency* of rotation and is given by the reciprocal of the period.

$$f = \frac{1}{T} \tag{10-5}$$

The validity of this relation is demonstrated by noting that the reciprocal of seconds per revolution (s/rev) is revolutions per second (rev/s). Substitution of this definition into Eq. (10-4) yields an alternative equation for determining the linear speed.

$$v = 2\pi f R \qquad (10\text{-}6)$$

For example, if the frequency is 1 rev/s and the radius 1 ft, the linear speed would be 2π ft/s.

**10-3
CENTRIP-
ETAL
FORCE**

The inward force necessary to maintain uniform circular motion is defined as the *centripetal force*. From Newton's second law of motion, the magnitude of this force must equal the product of mass and centripetal acceleration. Thus

$$F_c = ma_c = \frac{mv^2}{R} \qquad (10\text{-}7)$$

where m is the mass of an object moving with a speed v in a circular path of radius R. The units chosen for the quantities F_c, m, v, and R must be consistent for the system chosen. For example, the USCS units for mv^2/R are

$$\frac{\text{slug} \cdot \text{ft}^2/\text{s}^2}{\text{ft}} = \frac{\text{slug} \cdot \text{ft}}{\text{s}^2} = \text{lb}$$

An inspection of Eq. (10-7) reveals that the inward force $\mathbf{F}_c$ is directly proportional to the square of the velocity of the moving object. This means that increasing the linear speed to twice its original value will require four times the original force. Similar reasoning will show that doubling the mass or halving the radius will require twice the original centripetal force.

For problems in which the rotational speed is expressed in terms of the frequency, the centripetal force can be determined from

$$F_c = \frac{mv^2}{R} = 4\pi^2 f^2 mR \qquad (10\text{-}8)$$

This relation results from substitution of Eq. (10-6) which expresses the linear speed in terms of the frequency of revolution.

EXAMPLE 10-2

A 4-kg ball is swung in a horizontal circle by a cord 2 m long. What is the tension in the cord if the period is 0.5 s?

Solution

The tension in the cord will be equal to the centripetal force necessary to hold the 4-kg body in a circular path. The linear speed is obtained by dividing the period into the circumference.

$$v = \frac{2\pi R}{T} = \frac{2\pi(2 \text{ m})}{0.5 \text{ s}} = 25.1 \text{ m/s}$$

from which the centripetal force is

$$F_c = \frac{mv^2}{R} = \frac{(4 \text{ kg})(25.1 \text{ m/s})^2}{2 \text{ m}}$$

$$= 1260 \text{ N}$$

EXAMPLE 10-3   Two 4-lb weights rotate about the center axis at 12 rev/s, as shown in Fig. 10-3. (*a*) What is the resultant force acting on each weight? (*b*) What is the tension in the rod?

Solution (*a*)   The total downward force of the weights and rod is balanced by the upward force of the center support. Therefore, the resultant force acting on each revolving weight is a pull toward the center equal to the centripetal force. The mass of each weight is

$$m = \frac{W}{g} = \frac{4 \text{ lb}}{32 \text{ ft/s}^2} = 0.125 \text{ slug}$$

Substituting the given values of frequency, mass, and radius into Eq. (10-8), we obtain

$$F_c = 4\pi^2 f^2 mR = 4\pi^2(12 \text{ rev/s})^2(0.125 \text{ slug})(1.5 \text{ ft})$$

$$= 1066 \text{ lb}$$

The same calculations hold for the other weight.

Fig. 10-3 Objects traveling in a circular path. The resultant force of the rod on the objects provides the necessary centripetal force. According to Newton's third law, the objects exert an equal and opposite reaction force on the rod. This reaction force is called the *centrifugal force.* These forces do not cancel each other because they act on different objects.

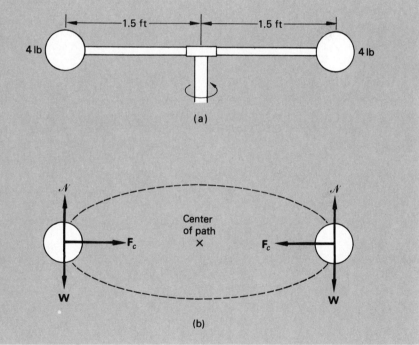

Solution (*b*)   The resultant force just computed represents the centripetal force exerted by the rod on the weights. According to Newton's third law, there must be an equal and opposite reaction force exerted by the weight on the rod. Remember that although these forces are equal in magnitude and opposite in direction, they do not act on the same body. Because the outward force exerted on the rod is *fleeing the center*, it is sometimes referred to as the *centrifugal force.* It is this centrifugal force that causes the tension in the rod. Since it is equal in magnitude to the centripetal force, the tension in the rod must also be 1066 lb.

When an automobile is driven around a sharp turn on a perfectly level road, friction between the tires and the road provides centripetal force (see Fig. 10-4). If this centripetal force is not adequate, the car may slide off the road. The maximum value of the force of friction determines the maximum speed with which a car can negotiate a turn of a given radius.

Fig. 10-4 The centripetal force of friction. Note that there is no outward force on the car.

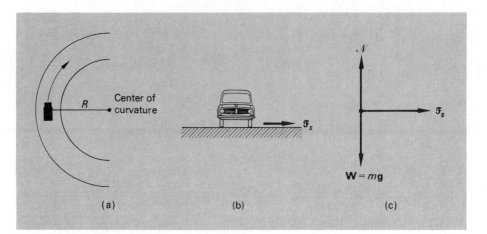

EXAMPLE 10-4

What is the maximum speed at which an automobile can negotiate a curve of radius 300 ft without sliding if the coefficient of static friction is 0.7?

Solution

As the car increases its speed, the force of static friction required to hold it gets larger. Finally, the car attains a speed so great that the centripetal force equals the maximum force of static friction. At that instant

$$\mathscr{F}_s = F_c = \frac{mv^2}{R}$$

and since $\mathscr{F}_s = \mu_s \mathscr{N}$, we can write

$$\frac{mv^2}{R} = \mu_s \mathscr{N}$$

Applying the first condition for equilibrium to the vertical forces in Fig. 10-4 reveals that the normal force is equal to the weight of the car

$$\mathscr{N} = W = mg$$

Hence

$$\frac{mv^2}{R} = \mu_s mg \qquad \text{or} \qquad v^2 = \mu_s gR$$

from which

$$\boxed{v = \sqrt{\mu_s gR}} \qquad\qquad (10\text{-}9)$$

Substituting known values for μ_s, g, and R, we can now compute the maximum speed.

$$v = \sqrt{(0.7)(32 \text{ ft/s}^2)(300 \text{ ft})} = 82 \text{ ft/s}$$

or approximately 56 mi/h.

It is quite surprising that the weight of the automobile was not considered in determining the maximum speed. Our own experience tends to contradict the independence of weight. The answer to this paradox does not lie in the validity of the above equations but in the fact that the friction force acts on the wheels below the center of gravity of the car. There is also an uneven distribution of weight. Since the center of gravity of heavy cars is usually lower than for light cars, the difference in stability and distribution of weight will affect the turning speed. However, if we stipulate that the weight is uniformly distributed and neglect problems of vertical stability, the above equations are valid.

Now let us consider the effects of banking a turn to eliminate the friction force. As seen from Fig. 10-5, a road can be banked in such a manner that the normal force $\mathcal{N}$ has vertical and horizontal components:

$$\mathcal{N}_x = \mathcal{N} \sin \theta \qquad \mathcal{N}_y = \mathcal{N} \cos \theta$$

Fig. 10-5 Effects of banking a turn. The horizontal component of the normal force, $\mathcal{N} \sin \theta$, provides the necessary centripetal acceleration.

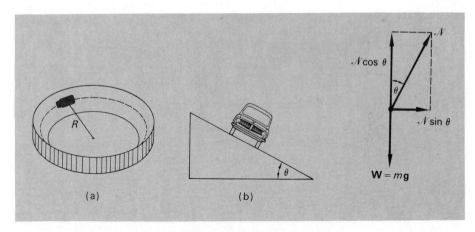

(a) (b)

The horizontal component provides the necessary centripetal force. Therefore, if we represent the linear velocity by v and the radius of the turn by R, the banking angle θ required to eliminate the need for friction is obtained from

$$\mathcal{N} \sin \theta = \frac{mv^2}{R}$$

Since the vertical forces are balanced,

$$\mathcal{N} \cos \theta = mg$$

Dividing the first equation by the second yields

$$\tan \theta = \frac{v^2}{Rg}$$

(10-10)

EXAMPLE 10-5   Find the required banking angle for a curve of radius 480 ft if it is to be negotiated at a speed of 80 mi/h without the need of a friction force.

Solution   The linear speed is first converted to feet per second:

$$v = 80 \text{ mi/h} = 117 \text{ ft/s}$$

Substituting in Eq. (10-10) yields

$$\tan \theta = \frac{v^2}{Rg} = \frac{(117 \text{ ft/s})^2}{(480 \text{ ft})(32 \text{ ft/s}^2)} = 0.89$$

from which the required banking angle must be

$$\theta = 41.7°$$

10-5
THE
CONICAL
PENDULUM

A conical pendulum consists of a mass m revolving in a horizontal circle with constant speed v at the end of a cord of length L. A comparison of Fig. 10-6 with Fig. 10-5 shows that the formula derived for the banking angle also applies for the angle the cord makes with the vertical in a conical pendulum. In the latter problem, the necessary centripetal force is provided by the horizontal component of the tension in the cord. The vertical component is equal to the weight of the revolving mass. Hence

$$T \sin \theta = \frac{mv^2}{R} \qquad T \cos \theta = mg$$

Fig. 10-6 The conical pendulum.

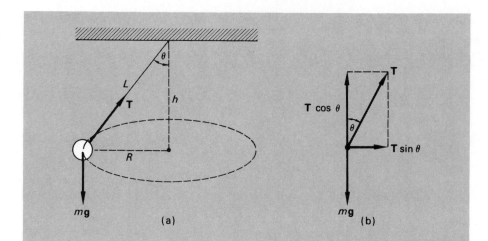

(a)   (b)

from which

$$\tan \theta = \frac{v^2}{Rg} \qquad (10\text{-}10)$$

is obtained as in the previous section.

A careful study of Eq. (10-10) will show that as the linear speed increases, the angle that the cord makes with the vertical also increases. Therefore, the vertical position of the mass (indicated in Fig. 10-6) is raised, causing a reduction in the distance h below the point of support. If we wish to express Eq. (10-10) in terms of the vertical position h, we should note that

$$\tan \theta = \frac{R}{h}$$

from which we obtain

$$\frac{R}{h} = \frac{v^2}{gR}$$

Thus, the distance of the weight below the support is a function of the linear speed and is given by

$$h = \frac{gR^2}{v^2} \qquad (10\text{-}11)$$

This principle operates governors used on some engines (Fig. 10-7). The position of the weight can be used to open or close fuel valves. Note that all the forces do not act at a single point in this case.

A more useful form for Eq. (10-11) can be obtained by expressing the linear speed in terms of the rotational frequency. Since $v = 2\pi fR$, we can write

$$h = \frac{gR^2}{4\pi^2 f^2 R^2} = \frac{g}{4\pi^2 f^2}$$

Fig. 10-7 The centrifugal governor. Why is the term *centripetal governor* not appropriate.

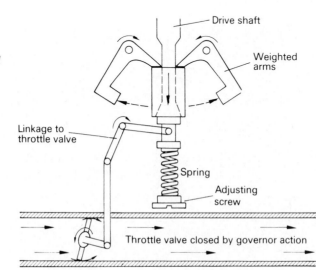

Drive shaft

Weighted arms

Linkage to throttle valve

Spring

Adjusting screw

Throttle valve closed by governor action

Solving for f, we obtain

$$f = \frac{1}{2\pi} \sqrt{\frac{g}{h}}$$

(10-12)

This form has the advantage of eliminating the radius of revolution R from consideration.

10-6 CENTRIPETAL FORCE IN AVIATION

With increased maneuverability of aircraft, it has become necessary to design wings of exceptional strength. When we consider a plane weighing around 20 tons and flying with a speed of 600 mi/h, we can easily see that a tremendous centripetal force will be required in order to negotiate a sharp turn. This force must be supplied by the reaction of air on the wings and fuselage of the plane.

Since the problem of banking in a horizontal turn is identical with cases already discussed, in this section we consider motion in a vertical circle. Referring to Fig. 10-8, let us assign $\mathbf{v}_1$ as the velocity of the aircraft as it passes

Fig. 10-8 Forces exerted on an airplane at the upper and lower limits of a vertical loop.

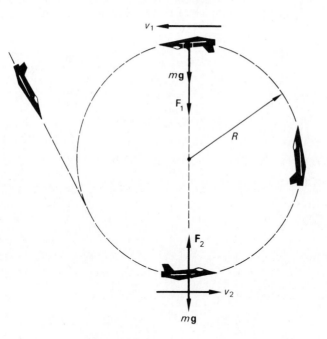

through the highest point in its path. The forces acting on it at this point are its weight $m\mathbf{g}$ and the force $\mathbf{F}_1$ exerted by the air against its wings. Both of these contribute to the required centripetal force. Hence

$$F_1 + mg = \frac{mv_1^2}{R}$$

(10-13)

at the highest point in the circular turn. On the other hand, when the aircraft passes through the lowest point in the loop, its weight opposes the reaction of the air against its wings so that the centripetal force is

$$F_2 - mg = \frac{mv_2^2}{R} \tag{10-14}$$

where v_2 and F_2 represent the magnitudes of the velocity and air-lift force at the bottom of the loop.

EXAMPLE 10-6   With what force does a 200-lb test pilot press downward in his seat at the bottom of a circular loop of radius 2500 ft if it is negotiated at 420 mi/h (616 ft/s)?

Solution   Although the above equations were derived for the aircraft, they apply to any body moving in a vertical circle. Applying them to the test pilot, we must solve Eq. (10-14) for F_2, obtaining

$$F_2 = \frac{mv_2^2}{R} + mg$$

This force represents the push exerted by the seat on the pilot. It will, of course, be equal to the force that the pilot exerts on the seat. Since the mass $m = W/g$ and $W = mg$, we have

$$F_2 = \frac{Wv_2^2}{gR} + W = \frac{(200 \text{ lb})(616 \text{ ft/s})^2}{(32 \text{ ft/s}^2)(2500 \text{ ft})} + 200 \text{ lb}$$

$$= 949 \text{ lb} + 200 \text{ lb} = 1149 \text{ lb}$$

Thus, the pilot will experience a force nearly 6 times his own weight. It is easy to see that this factor must be taken into consideration.

10-7 GRAVITA-TION

The earth and planets follow approximately circular orbits around the sun. Newton suggested that the inward force which maintains planetary motion is only one example of a universal force called *gravitation*, which acts between all masses in the universe. He stated his thesis in the following *universal law of gravitation*:

> *Each particle in the universe attracts each other particle with a force that is directly proportional to the product of their masses and inversely proportional to the square of the distance between them.*

The proportionality is usually stated in the form of an equation:

$$\boxed{F = G\,\frac{m_1 m_2}{r^2}} \tag{10-15}$$

where m_1 and m_2 are the masses of any two particles separated by a distance r, as shown in Fig. 10-9.

The proportionality constant G is a universal constant equal to

$$G = 6.67 \times 10^{-11} \text{ N} \cdot \text{m}^2/\text{kg}^2$$

$$= 3.44 \times 10^{-8} \text{ lb} \cdot \text{ft}^2/\text{slug}^2$$

Fig. 10-9 The universal law of gravitation.

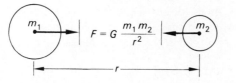

EXAMPLE 10-7

Two lead balls, weighing 16 lb and 8 lb, are 2 ft apart. With what force do they attract each other?

Solution

The masses are first computed from the given weights as follows:

$$m_1 = \frac{16 \text{ lb}}{32 \text{ ft/s}^2} = 0.5 \text{ slug}$$

$$m_2 = \frac{8 \text{ lb}}{32 \text{ ft/s}^2} = 0.25 \text{ slug}$$

The force of attraction is computed as follows:

$$F = G \frac{m_1 m_2}{r^2}$$

$$= (3.44 \times 10^{-8} \text{ lb} \cdot \text{ft}^2/\text{slug}^2) \frac{(0.5 \text{ slug})(0.25 \text{ slug})}{(2 \text{ ft})^2}$$

$$= (3.44 \times 10^{-8} \text{ lb} \cdot \text{ft}^2/\text{slug}^2)(3.12 \times 10^{-2} \text{ slug}^2/\text{ft}^2)$$

$$= 1.08 \times 10^{-9} \text{ lb}$$

It is seen that the gravitational force is actually a very small force. Because of the relatively large mass of the earth in comparison with objects on its surface, we often assume that gravitational forces are strong. However, if we consider two marbles closely separated on a horizontal surface, our experience certainly substantiates that the gravitational attraction is very weak.

EXAMPLE 10-8

At the surface of the earth, the acceleration of gravity is 9.8 m/s². If the radius of the earth is 6.38×10^6 m, compute the mass of the earth.

Solution

Suppose we consider a mass m near the surface of the earth. The gravitational force which attracts this mass is equal to its weight given by

$$W = mg = G \frac{mm_e}{r^2}$$

Solving for m_e, we obtain

$$m_e = \frac{gr^2}{G}$$

from which the mass of the earth is found to be

$$m_e = \frac{(9.8 \text{ m/s}^2)(6.38 \times 10^6 \text{ m})^2}{6.67 \times 10^{-11} \text{ N} \cdot \text{m}^2/\text{kg}^2} = 5.98 \times 10^{24} \text{ kg}$$

or approximately 6.59×10^{21} tons.

SUMMARY

We have defined uniform circular motion as motion in a circle where the speed is constant and only the direction changes. The change in direction produced by a central force is referred to as *centripetal acceleration*. The major concepts presented in this chapter are as follows:

- The linear speed v of an object in uniform circular motion can be calculated from the period T or frequency f:

$$v = \frac{2\pi R}{T}$$

$$v = 2\pi f R$$

- The centripetal acceleration a_c is found from the linear speed, the period, or the frequency as follows:

$$a_c = \frac{v^2}{R}$$

$$a_c = \frac{4\pi^2 R}{T^2}$$

$$a_c = 4\pi^2 f^2 R$$

- The centripetal force F_c is equal to the product of the mass m and the centripetal acceleration a_c. It is given by

$$F_c = \frac{mv^2}{R}$$

$$F_c = 4\pi^2 f^2 mR$$

- Other useful formulas are as follows:

$$v = \sqrt{\mu_s g R}$$

Maximum Speed without Slipping

$$\tan \theta = \frac{v^2}{gR}$$

Banking Angle or Conical Pendulum

$$f = \frac{1}{2\pi}\sqrt{\frac{g}{h}}$$

Frequency of a Conical Pendulum

QUESTIONS

10-1. Define the following terms:

a. Uniform circular motion   **f.** Linear speed

b. Centripel acceleration   **g.** Period

c. Centripetal force   **h.** Frequency

d. Gravitational constant   **i.** Critical speed

e. Universal law of gravitation   **j.** Conical pendulum

10-2. Explain with diagrams why the acceleration of a body moving in a circle at constant speed is directed toward the center.

10-3. A bicyclist leans to the side when negotiating a turn. Why? Describe with a free-body diagram the forces acting on the rider.

10-4. In negotiating a circular turn, a car hits a patch of ice and skids off the road. According to Newton's first law, the car will move forward in a direction tangent to the curve, not outward at right angles to it. Why?

10-5. If the force causing circular motion is directed toward the center of rotation, why is water thrown off clothes during the spin cycle of a washing machine?

10-6. When a ball tied at the end of a string is revolved in a circle at constant speed, the inward centripetal force is equal in magnitude to the outward centrifugal force. Does this represent a condition of equilibrium? Explain.

10-7. What factors contribute to the most desirable banking angles on roadways?

10-8. Does the centripetal force do work in uniform circular motion?

10-9. A motorcyclist negotiates a circular track at constant speed. What exerts the centripetal force, and on what does the force act? What exerts the centrifugal reaction force, and on what does it act?

10-10. A rock at the end of a string moves in a vertical circle. Under what conditions can its linear speed be constant? On what does the centripetal force act? On what does the centrifugal force act?

10-11. What is the value of the gravitational constant G on the moon?

10-12. Given the mass of the earth, its distance from the sun, and its orbital speed, explain how you would determine the mass of the sun.

PROBLEMS

10-1. A ball having a mass of 0.05 kg is attached to the end of a cord 1.5 m long. The ball is swung in a circular path at the end of the cord with a speed of 8.0 m/s. What is the centripetal force?

Ans. 2.13 N.

10-2. An 8-lb weight moves in a horizontal circle with a linear speed of 95 ft/s. What is the centripetal force if the radius is 3.2 ft?

10-3. A 4-lb object is tied to a cord and swung in a horizontal circle of radius 3 ft. Neglect the effects of gravity and assume a frequency of revolution of 80 rpm. Determine **(a)** the linear speed, **(b)** the centripetal acceleration, **(c)** the centripetal force, and **(d)** what happens if the cord breaks.

Ans. **(a)** 25.1 ft/s **(b)** 211 ft/s^2 **(c)** 52.6 lb
(d) the object moves off at a tangent.

10-4. Answer the same questions as in Prob. 10-3 for a 2-kg mass whirled in a circle of radius 1.6 m at 3 rev/s.

10-5. Two 8-kg masses are attached to the end of a thin rod 400 mm long. The rod is supported in the middle and whirled in a circle. Assume that the rod can support a maximum tension of only 80 N. What is the maximum frequency of revolution in rpm?

Ans. 67.5 rpm.

10-6. A record 12 in. in diameter is set to revolve at 45 rpm. What is the linear speed of a point on the record **(a)** 2 in. from the center, **(b)** 4 in. from the center, and **(c)** at the edge?

10-7. A drive shaft 6 cm in diameter rotates at 9 rev/s. What is the centripetal acceleration at the surface of the shaft?

Ans. 95.9 m/s^2.

10-8. A merry-go-round revolves with a period of 6 s. How far from the center should you sit to experience a centripetal acceleration of 12 ft/s^2?

10-9. A 4-kg mass swings in a horizontal circle of radius 2 m. If it revolves at 6 rev/s, what is its period of revolution? What is its linear speed? Find its centripetal acceleration and the tension in the cord.

Ans. 0.167 s, 2840 m/s², 11,400 N.

10-10. At what frequency should a 6-lb ball be revolved in a radius of 3 ft in order to produce a centripetal acceleration of 12 ft/s²? What will the tension in the cord be?

10-11. What centripetal acceleration is required to move a 2.6-kg mass in a horizontal circle of radius 300 mm if its linear speed is 15 m/s? What is the centripetal force?

Ans. 750 m/s², 1950 N.

10-12. What must the speed of a satellite be just above the surface of the earth if it is to travel in a circular orbit about the earth? Assume that the radius of the earth is 4000 mi. What is the nature of the centripetal force in this case?

10-13. An electron revolves in an orbit about the nucleus in a circular path of radius 6×10^{-9} cm. If the mass of an electron is 9.11×10^{-31} kg and its linear speed is 3.2×10^{6} m/s, compute the centripetal acceleration and the centripetal force.

Ans. 1.71×10^{23} m/s², 1.56×10^{-7} N.

10-14. The breaking strength of a cord is 12 N. What is the maximum frequency of revolution that can be sustained if a 5-kg mass is to be moved in a horizontal circular orbit of radius 2 m? (The weight is supported by a frictionless surface.) Now suppose that the cord is lengthened to move the mass in a 4-m radius. What must the new frequency be to maintain the same tension in the rope?

10-15. The radius of the earth is approximately 6.4×10^{6} m. Objects at the equator are moving with a linear speed of 465 m/s. What is the centripetal acceleration?

Ans. 3.39×10^{-2} m/s².

10-16. A bus negotiates a curve of radius 487 m. What force will be exerted on an 80-kg passenger by the outside wall of the bus when it is traveling at 60 km/h?

10-17. A 9-kg block rests on the bed of a truck as its turns a curve of radius 86 m. The coefficient of sliding friction between the block and the truck bed is 0.3, and the coefficient of static friction is 0.4. **(a)** Does the friction force act toward the center of the curve or away from it? **(b)** What is the maximum speed with which the truck can move if the block is to remain at rest? **(c)** If the truck were able to negotiate the turn at a much greater speed without turning over, what would the resultant acceleration of the block be?

Ans. **(a)** toward center **(b)** 18.4 m/s **(c)** 2.94 m/s.

10-18. A 10-in.-diameter record turns on a record player at 78 rpm. A bug rests on the record 1 in. from the outside edge. **(a)** If the bug weighs 0.02 lb, what force acts on him? **(b)** What exerts this force? **(c)** Where should the bug crawl if he wishes to reduce this force by one-half?

10-19. On a rainy day the coefficient of friction between the tires and roadway is 0.4. What is the maximum speed at which a car can go around a curve of 80 m radius?

Ans. 63.7 km/h.

10-20. Find the banking angle θ in Prob. 10-19 necessary to eliminate the friction force at a speed of 60 mi/h.

10-21. Find the required banking angle θ if a car is to make a 180° U turn in a circular distance of 600 ft at 50 mi/h without friction.

Ans. 41.3°.

10-22. A curve in a road 9 m wide has a radius of 96 m. How much higher than the inside edge should the outside edge be for an automobile to travel safely at 30 mi/h?

10-23. **(a)** What is the linear speed of the flyweights in Fig. 10-10 if $\theta = 60°$? **(b)** Calculate the rate of revolution of the shaft in revolutions per minute.

Ans. **(a)** 4.9 ft/s **(b)** 108 rpm.

Fig. 10-10

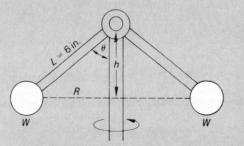

10-24. If the flyweights in Fig. 10-10 weigh 1.5 lb apiece, **(a)** what is the tension in the rod when the shaft is rotating at 100 rpm? **(b)** What is the angle θ? **(c)** What is the distance h?

10-25. What frequency of revolution is required to raise the flyweights in Fig. 10-10 a distance of 25 mm above their equilibrium position? Assume that $L = 150$ mm.

Ans. 86.3 rpm.

10-26. A 24-kg body is whirled in a horizontal circle by a cord with a breaking strength of 300 N. When the speed of the body is 8.0 m/s, the string breaks. Find the angle the cord makes with the vertical at that instant and the length of the cord if the radius of the path is 9 m.

10-27. In Fig. 10-10 find the angular speed in revolutions per minute required to cause the rope to make an angle of 30° with the vertical.

Ans. 82.1 rpm.

10-28. A test pilot goes into a dive at 620 ft/s and pulls out in a curve of radius 2800 ft. If the pilot weighs 160 lb, what force is exerted on her by the seat? What acceleration will be experienced at the lowest point in the dive? How many times greater is this value than the acceleration of gravity g?

10-29. Since the actual force acting on a pilot depends on the pilot's own weight, the centripetal effects are usually measured in terms of acceleration. If the maximum acceleration a human being can withstand is 7 times the acceleration of gravity ($7g$), what is the maximum velocity for pulling out of a dive of radius 3000 ft?

Ans. 759 ft/s.

10-30. A mass m is tied to a rope and whirled in a vertical circle of radius R, as shown in Fig. 10-11. Show that the resulting tension in the rope when the ball is at the top of the circle is given by

$$T_1 = \frac{mv_1^2}{R} - mg$$

and that the tension at the bottom of the circle is

$$T_2 = \frac{mv_2^2}{R} + mg$$

Fig. 10-11

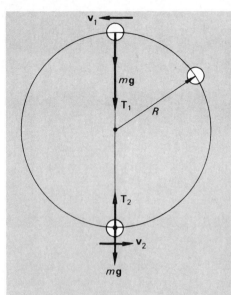

where v_1 is the velocity at the top of the loop and v_2 is the velocity at the bottom of the loop.

10-31. With motion in a vertical circle, as discussed in Prob. 10-30, there exists a *critical velocity* v_c (at the highest point) below which the cord becomes slack. Show that it is given by $v_c = \sqrt{gR}$.

10-32. The combined mass of a motorcycle and driver is 210 kg. If the driver is to negotiate a loop-the-loop of 6-m radius, what must the minimum speed be to ensure that the cyclist does not fall away from the loop at the top of the vertical circle? If the speed is 12 m/s, what force do the driver and motorcycle exert on the top of the loop?

10-33. A 36-kg girl rides on the seat of a swing attached to chains 20 m long. If she is released from a position 8 m lower than the top of the swing, what is her linear speed when she passes the lowest point? What force does she exert on the swing at this point? Should we refer to this force as centripetal or centrifugal?

Ans. 15.3 m/s, 776 N, centrifugal.

10-34. A cord is tied to a pail of water, and the pail is swung in a vertical circle of 5-ft radius. What must the minimum velocity of the pail be at the highest point of the circle if no water is to spill from the pail?

10-35. A 4-kg mass is separated from a 2-kg mass by a distance of 8 m. Compute the gravitational force of attraction between the two masses.

Ans. 8.34×10^{-12} N.

10-36. How far apart should a 2-ton weight be from a 3-ton weight if their mutual force of attraction is to be 4×10^{-4} lb?

10-37. The mass of the earth is about 81 times the mass of the moon. If the radius of the earth is 4 times that of the moon, what is the acceleration of gravity on the moon's surface?

Ans. 1.94 m/s².

11 *Rotation of Rigid Bodies*

OBJECTIVES: After completing this chapter, you should be able to:

1. Define *angular displacement*, *angular velocity*, and *angular acceleration*, and apply these concepts to the solution of physical problems.

2. Draw analogies relating angular-motion parameters (θ, ω, α) to linear-motion parameters, and solve angular acceleration problems in a manner similar to that learned in Chap. 5 for linear acceleration problems (refer to Table 11-1).

3. Write and apply the relationships between linear speed or acceleration and angular speed or acceleration.

4. Define the *moment of inertia* of a body and describe how this quantity and the angular speed can be used to calculate *rotational kinetic energy*.

5. Apply the concepts of *Newton's second law*, *rotational work*, *rotational power*, and *angular momentum* to the solution of physical problems.

We have been considering only translational motion, in which an object's position is changing along a straight line. But it is possible for an object to move in a curved path, or to undergo rotational motion. For example, wheels, shafts, pulleys, gyroscopes, and many other mechanical devices rotate about their axes without translational motion. The generation and transmission of power is nearly always dependent on rotational motion of some kind. It is essential for you to be able to predict and control such motion. The concepts and formulas presented in this chapter are designed to provide you with these essential skills.

**11-1
ANGULAR
DISPLACE-
MENT**

The angular displacement of a body describes the amount of rotation. If point *A* on the rotating disk in Fig. 11-1 rotates on its axis to point *B*, the angular displacement is denoted by the angle θ. There are several ways of measuring this angle. We are already familiar with the units of degrees and revolutions, which are related according to the definition

$$1 \text{ rev} = 360°$$

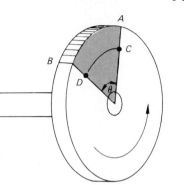

Fig. 11-1 Angular displacement θ is indicated by the shaded portion of the disk. The angular displacement is the same from *C* to *D* as it is from *A* to *B* for a rigid body.

Neither of these units is very useful in describing rotation of rigid bodies. A more applicable measure of angular displacement is the *radian* (rad). An angle of 1 rad is a central angle whose arc *s* is equal in length to the radius *R*. (See Fig. 11-2.) More generally, the radian is defined by the equation

$$\theta = \frac{s}{R} \tag{11-1}$$

where *s* is the arc of a circle described by the angle θ. Since the ratio of *s* to *R* is the ratio of two distances, the radian is a unitless quantity.

The conversion factor which relates radians to degrees is found by considering an arc length *s* equal to the circumference of a circle $2\pi R$. Such an angle in radians is given from Eq. (11-1) by

$$\theta = \frac{2\pi R}{R} = 2\pi \text{ rad}$$

Fig. 11-2 The measure of angular displacement and a comparison of units.

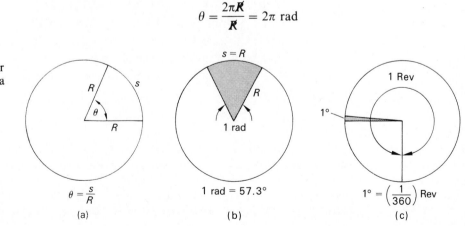

Hence

$$1 \text{ rev} = 360° = 2\pi \text{ rad}$$

from which we note that

$$1 \text{ rad} = \frac{360°}{2\pi} = 57.3°$$

EXAMPLE 11-1   If the arc length s is 6 ft and the radius is 10 ft, compute the angular displacement θ in radians, degrees, and revolutions.

Solution   Substituting directly into Eq. (11-1), we obtain

$$\theta = \frac{s}{R} = \frac{6 \text{ ft}}{10 \text{ ft}} = 0.6 \text{ rad}$$

Converting to degrees yields

$$\theta = (0.6 \text{ rad}) \frac{57.3°}{1 \text{ rad}} = 34.4°$$

and since 1 rev = 360°

$$\theta = (34.4°) \frac{1 \text{ rev}}{360°} = 0.0956 \text{ rev}$$

EXAMPLE 11-2   A point on the edge of a rotating disk of radius 8 m moves through an angle of 37°. Compute the length of the arc described by the point.

Solution   Since Eq. (11-1) was defined for an angle measured in radians, we must first convert 37° to radian units

$$\theta = (37°) \frac{1 \text{ rad}}{57.3°} = 0.646 \text{ rad}$$

The arc length is given by

$$s = R\theta = 8 \text{ m } (0.646 \text{ rad}) = 5.17 \text{ m}$$

The unit radian is dropped because it represents a ratio of length to length (m/m = 1).

**11-2
ANGULAR
VELOCITY**

The time rate of change in angular displacement is called the *angular velocity*. Thus, if an object rotates through an angle θ in a time t, its angular velocity is given by

$$\bar{\omega} = \frac{\theta}{t} \qquad (11\text{-}2)$$

The symbol ω, the Greek letter *omega*, is used to denote rotational velocity. Although angular velocity may be expressed in *revolutions per minute* or *revolutions per second*, in most physical problems it is necessary to use *radians per second* to conform with convenient formulas. Since the rate of rotation in many technical problems is given in terms of the frequency of revolutions, the following relation will be useful:

$$\omega = 2\pi f \tag{11-3}$$

where ω is measured in *radians per second* and f is measured in *revolutions per second*.

EXAMPLE 11-3   Compute the average angular velocity of a long-playing phonograph record ($33\frac{1}{3}$ rpm).

Solution   Note that no mention was made of the distance to the center of the record. The angular velocity depends only on the rate of rotation. The frequency of revolution is

$$f = \left(\frac{33\frac{1}{3}\text{ rev}}{\text{min}}\right)\left(\frac{1\text{ min}}{60\text{ s}}\right) = 0.555\text{ rev/s}$$

or, substituting into Eq. (11-3), the angular velocity is

$$\omega = \left(\frac{2\pi\text{ rad}}{\text{rev}}\right)\left(\frac{0.555\text{ rev}}{\text{s}}\right) = 3.49\text{ rad/s}$$

It is important to realize that the angular velocity discussed in this section represents an *average* velocity. The same distinction must be made between the average and the instantaneous angular velocities as that discussed in Chap. 5 for average and instantaneous linear velocities.

11-3 ANGULAR ACCEL-ERATION   Like linear motion, angular motion may be uniform or accelerated. The rate of rotation may increase or decrease under the influence of a resultant torque. For example, if the angular velocity changes from an initial value ω_0 to a final value ω_f in a time t, the angular acceleration is given by

$$\alpha = \frac{\omega_f - \omega_0}{t}$$

The Greek letter α (*alpha*) denotes angular acceleration. A more useful form for this equation is

$$\boxed{\omega_f = \omega_0 + \alpha t} \tag{11-4}$$

A comparison of Eq. (11-4) with Eq. (5-4) for linear acceleration will show that their forms are identical if we draw analogies between angular and linear parameters.

Now that the concept of initial and final angular velocities has been introduced, we can express the average angular velocity in terms of its initial and final values:

$$\bar{\omega} = \frac{\omega_f + \omega_0}{2}$$

Substituting this equality for $\bar{\omega}$ in Eq. (11-2) yields a more useful expression for the angular displacement:

$$\theta = \bar{\omega}t = \frac{\omega_f + \omega_0}{2}t \qquad (11\text{-}5)$$

This equation is also similar to an equation derived for linear motion. In fact, the equations for angular acceleration have the same basic form as those derived in Chap. 5 for linear acceleration if we draw the following analogies:

$$s \text{ (ft, m)} \leftrightarrow \theta \text{ (rad)}$$

$$v \text{ (ft/s, m/s)} \leftrightarrow \omega \text{ (rad/s)}$$

$$a \text{ (ft/s}^2, \text{ m/s}^2) \leftrightarrow \alpha \text{ (rad/s}^2)$$

Time, of course, is the same for both types of motion and is measured in seconds. Table 11-1 illustrates the similarities between angular and linear motion.

Table 11-1 Comparison of Linear Acceleration and Angular Acceleration

Constant linear acceleration	Constant angular acceleration
$s = \bar{v}t = \dfrac{v_f + v_0}{2}t$	$\theta = \bar{\omega}t = \dfrac{\omega_f + \omega_0}{2}t$
$v_f = v_0 + at$	$\omega_f = \omega_0 + \alpha t$
$s = v_0 t + \frac{1}{2}at^2$	$\theta = \omega_0 t + \frac{1}{2}\alpha t^2$
$2as = v_f^2 - v_0^2$	$2\alpha\theta = \omega_f^2 - \omega_0^2$

In applying these formulas, we must be careful to choose the appropriate units for each quantity. It is also important to choose a direction (clockwise or counterclockwise) as positive and to follow through consistently in affixing the appropriate sign to each quantity.

EXAMPLE 11-4   A flywheel increases its rate of rotation from 6 to 12 rev/s in 8 s. What is its angular acceleration?

Solution   We will first compute the initial and final angular velocities:

$$\omega_0 = 2\pi f_0 = \left(\frac{2\pi \text{ rad}}{\text{rev}}\right)\left(\frac{6 \text{ rev}}{\text{s}}\right) = 12\pi \text{ rad/s}$$

$$\omega_f = 2\pi f_0 = \left(\frac{2\pi \text{ rad}}{\text{rev}}\right)\left(\frac{12 \text{ rev}}{\text{s}}\right) = 24\pi \text{ rad/s}$$

The angular acceleration is

$$\alpha = \frac{\omega_f - \omega_0}{t} = \frac{(24\pi - 12\pi) \text{ rad/s}}{8 \text{ s}}$$

$$= 1.5\pi \text{ rad/s}^2 = 4.71 \text{ rad/s}^2$$

EXAMPLE 11-5 A grinding disk rotating initially with an angular velocity of 6 rad/s receives a constant acceleration of 2 rad/s². (*a*) What angular displacement will it describe in 3 s? (*b*) How many revolutions will it make? (*c*) What is its final angular velocity?

Solution (a) The angular displacement is given by

$$\theta = \omega_0 t + \tfrac{1}{2}\alpha t^2$$

$$= (6 \text{ rad/s})(3 \text{ s}) + \tfrac{1}{2}(2 \text{ rad/s}^2)(3 \text{ s})^2$$

$$= 18 \text{ rad} + (1 \text{ rad/s}^2)(9 \text{ s}^2)$$

$$= 27 \text{ rad}$$

Solution (b) Since 1 rev = 2π rad, we obtain

$$\theta = (27 \text{ rad}) \frac{1 \text{ rev}}{2\pi \text{ rad}} = 4.30 \text{ rev}$$

Solution (c) The final velocity is equal to the initial velocity plus the change in speed. Thus

$$\omega_f = \omega_0 + \alpha t = 6 \text{ rad/s} + (2 \text{ rad/s}^2)(3 \text{ s})$$

$$= 12 \text{ rad/s}$$

11-4 RELATION BETWEEN ANGULAR AND LINEAR MOTION

The *axis of rotation* of a rigid rotating body can be defined as that line of particles which remains stationary during rotation. This may be a line through the body, as with a spinning top, or it may be a line through space, as with a rolling hoop. In any case, our experience tells us that the farther a particle is from the axis of rotation, the greater its linear speed. This fact was expressed in Chap. 10 by the formula

$$v = 2\pi f R$$

where *f* is the frequency of rotation. We now derive a similar relation in terms of angular speed. The rotating particle in Fig. 11-3 turns through an arc *s*, which is given by

$$s = \theta R$$

from Eq. (11-1). If this distance is traversed in a time *t*, the linear speed of the particle is given by

$$v = \frac{s}{t} = \frac{\theta R}{t}$$

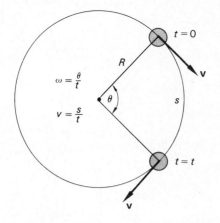

Fig. 11-3 The relation between angular speed and linear speed.

$\omega = \dfrac{\theta}{t}$

$v = \dfrac{s}{t}$

Since $\theta/t = \omega$, the linear speed can be expressed as a function of the angular speed.

$$\boxed{v = \omega R} \tag{11-6}$$

This result also follows from Eq. (11-3), in which the angular velocity is expressed as a function of the frequency of revolution.

EXAMPLE 11-6   A drive shaft has an angular speed of 60 rad/s. At what distance should flyweights be positioned from the axis if they are to have a linear speed of 120 ft/s?

Solution   Solving for R in Eq. (11-6), we obtain

$$R = \frac{v}{\omega} = \frac{120 \text{ ft/s}}{60 \text{ rad/s}} = 2 \text{ ft}$$

Let us now return to a particle moving in a circle of radius R and assume that the linear speed changes from some initial value v_0 to a final value v_f in a time t. The *tangential acceleration* a_T of such a particle is given by

$$a_T = \frac{v_f - v_0}{t}$$

Because of the close relationship between linear speed and angular speed, as represented by Eq. (11-6), we can also express the tangential acceleration in terms of a change in angular velocity.

$$a_T = \frac{\omega_f R - \omega_0 R}{t} = \frac{\omega_f - \omega_0}{t} R$$

or

$$\boxed{a_T = \alpha R} \tag{11-7}$$

where α represents the angular acceleration.

We must be careful to distinguish between the tangential acceleration, as defined in Eq. (11-7), and the centripetal acceleration defined by

$$a_c = \frac{v^2}{R} \tag{11-8}$$

The tangential acceleration represents a change in linear speed whereas the centripetal acceleration represents only a change in the direction of motion. The distinction is shown graphically in Fig. 11-4. The resultant acceleration can be found by computing the vector sum of the tangential and centripetal accelerations.

Fig. 11-4 The relationship between tangential and centripetal accelerations.

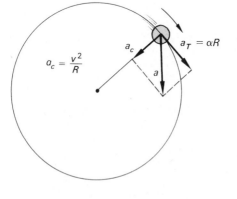

EXAMPLE 11-7   Find the resultant acceleration of a particle moving in a circle of radius 0.5 m at the instant when its angular speed is 3 rad/s and its angular acceleration is 4 rad/s^2.

Solution   The tangential acceleration from Eq. (11-7) is

$$a_T = \alpha R = (4 \text{ rad/s}^2)(0.5 \text{ m}) = 2 \text{ m/s}^2$$

Since $v = \omega R$, the centripetal acceleration is given by

$$a_c = \frac{v^2}{R} = \frac{\omega^2 R^2}{R} = \omega^2 R$$

from which we obtain

$$a_c = (3 \text{ rad/s})^2 (0.5 \text{ m}) = 4.5 \text{ m/s}^2$$

Finally, the magnitude of the resultant acceleration is obtained from Pythagoras' theorem.

$$a = \sqrt{a_T^2 + a_c^2} = \sqrt{2^2 + 4.5^2}$$
$$= 4.92 \text{ m/s}^2$$

The direction of the resultant acceleration can be found from its components in the usual manner.

11-5
ROTATIONAL
KINETIC
ENERGY;
MOMENT OF
INERTIA

We have seen that a particle moving in a circle of radius R has a linear speed given by

$$v = \omega R$$

If the particle has a mass m, it will have a kinetic energy given by

$$E_\kappa = \tfrac{1}{2}mv^2 = \tfrac{1}{2}m\omega^2 R^2$$

A rigid body like that in Fig. 11-5 can be considered as consisting of many particles of varying masses located at different distances from the axis of rotation O. The total kinetic energy of such an extended body will be the sum of the kinetic energies of each particle making up the body. Hence

$$E_\kappa = \sum \tfrac{1}{2}m\omega^2 r^2$$

Fig. 11-5 Rotation of an extended body. The body can be thought of as many individual masses all rotating with the same angular velocity.

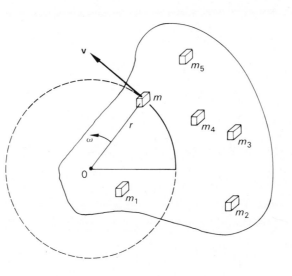

Since the constant $\tfrac{1}{2}$ and the angular velocity ω are the same for all particles, we can rearrange to obtain

$$E_\kappa = \tfrac{1}{2}(\sum mr^2)\omega^2$$

The quantity in parentheses, $\sum mr^2$, has the same value for a given body regardless of its state of motion. We define this quantity as the *moment of inertia* and represent it by I

$$I = m_1 r_1^2 + m_2 r_2^2 + m_3 r_3^2 + \cdots$$

or

$$\boxed{I = \sum mr^2} \tag{11-9}$$

The SI unit for I is the *kilogram–square meter* and the USCS unit is the *slug–square foot.*

Using this definition, we can express the rotational kinetic energy of a body in terms of its moment of inertia and its angular velocity:

$$E_\kappa = \tfrac{1}{2}I\omega^2$$

(11-10)

Note the similarity between the terms m for linear motion and I for rotational motion.

EXAMPLE 11-8

Find the moment of inertia for the system illustrated in Fig. 11-6. The rods joining the masses are of negligible weight, and the system rotates with an angular speed of 6 rad/s. What is the rotational kinetic energy? (Consider the masses to be point masses.)

Fig. 11-6 Computing the moment of inertia.

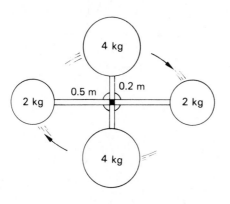

Solution

The moment of inertia from Eq. (11-9) is

$$I = m_1r_1^2 + m_2\,r_2^2 + m_3\,r_3^2 + m_4\,r_4^2$$

$$= (2\ \text{kg})(0.5\ \text{m})^2 + (4\ \text{kg})(0.2\ \text{m})^2 + (2\ \text{kg})(0.5\ \text{m})^2 + (4\ \text{kg})(0.2\ \text{m})^2$$

$$= (0.50 + 0.16 + 0.50 + 0.16)\text{kg} \cdot \text{m}^2$$

$$= 1.32\ \text{kg} \cdot \text{m}^2$$

The rotational kinetic energy is given by

$$E_\kappa = \tfrac{1}{2}I\omega^2 = \tfrac{1}{2}(1.32\ \text{kg} \cdot \text{m}^2)(6\ \text{rad/s})^2$$

$$= 23.8\ \text{J}$$

For bodies which are not composed of separate masses but are actually continuous distributions of matter, the calculation of moments of inertia is more difficult and usually involves calculus. A few simple cases are given in Fig. 11-7, along with the formulas for computing their moments of inertia.

Sometimes it is desirable to express the rotational inertia of a body in terms of its *radius of gyration k*. This quantity is defined as the radial distance from the center of rotation to a circumference at which the total mass of the

Fig. 11-7 Moments of inertia for bodies about their indicated axes.

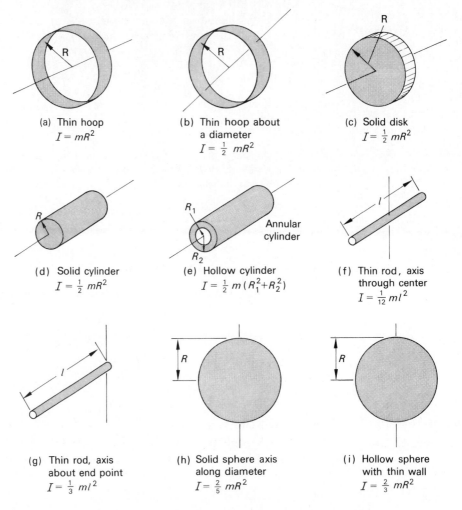

(a) Thin hoop
$I = mR^2$

(b) Thin hoop about a diameter
$I = \frac{1}{2} mR^2$

(c) Solid disk
$I = \frac{1}{2} mR^2$

(d) Solid cylinder
$I = \frac{1}{2} mR^2$

(e) Hollow cylinder
$I = \frac{1}{2} m (R_1^2 + R_2^2)$

Annular cylinder

(f) Thin rod, axis through center
$I = \frac{1}{12} ml^2$

(g) Thin rod, axis about end point
$I = \frac{1}{3} ml^2$

(h) Solid sphere axis along diameter
$I = \frac{2}{5} mR^2$

(i) Hollow sphere with thin wall
$I = \frac{2}{3} mR^2$

body might be concentrated without changing its moment of inertia. According to this definition, the moment of inertia can be found from the formula

$$I = mk^2 \qquad (11\text{-}11)$$

where m represents the total mass of the rotating body and k is its radius of gyration.

**11-6
THE
SECOND
LAW OF
MOTION IN
ROTATION**

Suppose we analyze the motion of the rotating rigid body in Fig. 11-8. Consider a force **F** acting on the small mass m, indicated by a shaded portion of the object, at a distance r from the axis of rotation.

The force **F** applied perpendicular to r causes the body to rotate with a tangential acceleration

$$a_T = \alpha r$$

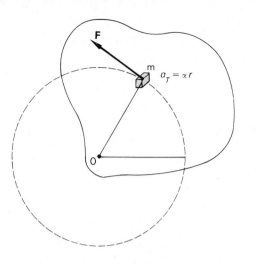

where α is the angular acceleration. From Newton's second law of motion

$$F = ma_T = m\alpha r$$

Multiplying both sides of this relation by r yields

$$Fr = (mr^2)\alpha$$

The quantity Fr is recognized as the torque produced by the force **F** about the axis. Thus, for the mass m we write

$$\tau = (mr^2)\alpha$$

A similar equation may be derived for all other portions of the rotating object. However, the angular acceleration will be constant for every portion, regardless of its mass or distance from the axis. Therefore, the resultant torque on the whole body is

$$\tau = \left(\sum mr^2\right)\alpha$$

or

$$\boxed{\tau = I\alpha} \tag{11-12}$$

Torque = moment of inertia × angular acceleration

Note the similarity of Eq. (11-12) with the second law for linear motion, $F = ma$. Newton's *law for rotational motion* is as follows:

A resultant torque applied to a rigid body will always result in an angular acceleration that is directly proportional to the applied torque and inversely proportional to the body's moment of inertia.

In applying Eq. (11-12), it is important to recall that the torque produced by a force is equal to the product of its distance from the axis and the perpendicular component of the force. It must also be remembered that the angular acceleration is expressed in radians per second per second.

EXAMPLE 11-9   A circular grinding disk of radius 0.6 m and mass 90 kg is rotating at 460 rpm. What frictional force, applied tangent to the edge, will cause the disk to stop in 20 s?

Solution   We first calculate the moment of inertia of the disk from the formula given in Fig. 11-7.

$$I = \tfrac{1}{2}mR^2 = \tfrac{1}{2}(90 \text{ kg})(0.6 \text{ m})^2$$

$$= 16.2 \text{ kg} \cdot \text{m}^2$$

Converting the rotational speed to radians per second, we obtain

$$\omega = \left(\frac{2\pi \text{ rad}}{\text{rev}}\right)\left(\frac{460 \text{ rev}}{\text{min}}\right)\left(\frac{1 \text{ min}}{60 \text{ s}}\right)$$

$$= 48.2 \text{ rad/s}$$

Thus the angular acceleration is

$$\alpha = \frac{\omega_f - \omega_0}{t}$$

$$= \frac{0 - (48.2 \text{ rad/s})}{20 \text{ s}} = -2.41 \text{ rad/s}^2$$

Applying Newton's second law gives

$$\tau = Fr = I\alpha$$

from which

$$F = \frac{I\alpha}{r} = \frac{(16.2 \text{ kg} \cdot \text{m}^2)(-2.41 \text{ rad/s}^2)}{0.6 \text{ m}}$$

$$= -65.0 \text{ N}$$

The negative sign appears because the force must be directed opposite to the direction of rotation of the disk.

**11-7
ROTATIONAL
WORK AND
POWER**

Work was defined in Chap. 8 as the product of a displacement and the component of the force in the direction of the displacement. We now consider the work done in rotational displacement under the influence of a resultant torque.

Consider a force **F** acting at the edge of a pulley of radius r, as shown in Fig. 11-9. The effect of such a force is to rotate the pulley through an angle θ while the point at which the force is applied moves through a distance s. The arc distance s is related to θ by

$$s = r\theta$$

Hence the work of the force **F** is by definition

$$\text{Work} = Fs = Fr\theta$$

but Fr is the torque due to the force, so that we obtain

$$\boxed{\text{Work} = \tau\theta} \tag{11-13}$$

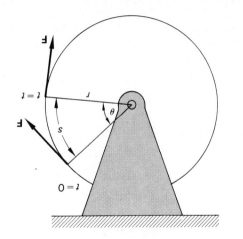

Fig. 11-9 Work and power in rotation.

The angle θ must be expressed in radians for either system of units in order that the work can be expressed in foot-pounds or joules.

Mechanical energy is usually transmitted in the form of rotational work. When we speak of the power output of engines, we are concerned with the rate at which rotational work is done. Thus rotational power can be determined by dividing both sides of Eq. (11-13) by the time t required for the torque τ to effect a displacement θ

$$\text{Power} = \frac{\text{work}}{t} = \frac{\tau\theta}{t} \qquad (11\text{-}14)$$

Since θ/t represents the average angular velocity $\bar{\omega}$, we write

$$\boxed{\text{Power} = \tau\bar{\omega}} \qquad (11\text{-}15)$$

Notice the similarity of this relation with its analog, $P = Fv$, derived earlier for linear motion. Both are measures of *average* power.

EXAMPLE 11-10   A wheel of radius 2 ft has a moment of inertia of 8.2 slug · ft². A constant force of 12 lb is applied at the rim. (*a*) Assuming the wheel starts from rest, what will its angular acceleration be after 4 s? (*b*) What average horsepower is developed?

Solution (a)   We first compute the torque from the product of the tangential force and the radius of the wheel

$$\tau = Fr = (12 \text{ lb})(2 \text{ ft}) = 24 \text{ lb} \cdot \text{ft}$$

Applying Newton's second law, we find the angular acceleration to be

$$\alpha = \frac{\tau}{I} = \frac{24 \text{ lb} \cdot \text{ft}}{8.2 \text{ slug} \cdot \text{ft}^2} = 2.93 \text{ rad/s}^2$$

Solution (b)   The rate at which work is done depends upon the angular displacement θ described by the wheel in 4 s. This displacement is

$$\theta = \omega_0 t + \tfrac{1}{2}\alpha t^2$$

$$= 0 + \tfrac{1}{2}(2.93 \text{ rad/s}^2)(4 \text{ s})^2$$

$$= 23.4 \text{ rad}$$

The average power is, from Eq. (11-4),

$$P = \frac{\tau\theta}{t} = \frac{(24 \text{ lb} \cdot \text{ft})(23.4 \text{ rad})}{4 \text{ s}}$$

$$= (140 \text{ ft-lb/s}) \frac{1 \text{ hp}}{550 \text{ ft} \cdot \text{lb/s}}$$

$$= 0.255 \text{ hp}$$

The same result might be obtained by determining the average angular velocity $\bar{\omega}$ and applying Eq. (11-15).

**11-8
ANGULAR
MOMENTUM**

Consider a particle of mass m moving in a circle of radius r, as shown in Fig. 11-10a. If its linear velocity is v, it will have a linear momentum $p = mv$. With reference to the fixed axis of rotation, we define the *angular momentum* L of the particle as the product of its linear momentum and the perpendicular distance from the axis to the revolving particle.

$$L \text{ (particle)} = mvr \qquad (11\text{-}16)$$

Fig. 11-10 Defining angular momentum.

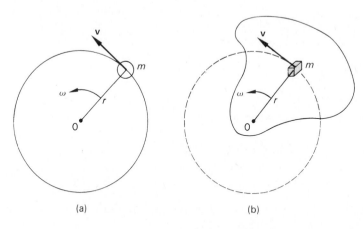

(a)   (b)

Now let us consider the definition of angular momentum as it applies to an extended rigid body. Figure 11-10b describes such a body, which is rotating about its axis O. Each particle in the body has an angular momentum given by Eq. (11-16). Substituting $v = \omega r$, each particle has an angular momentum given by

$$mvr = m\omega r^2 = (mr^2)\omega$$

Since the body is rigid, all particles within the body have the same angular velocity, and the total angular momentum of the body is

$$L = (\sum mr^2)\omega$$

Thus the total angular momentum is equal to the product of a body's angular velocity and its moment of inertia

$$\boxed{L = I\omega} \qquad (11\text{-}17)$$

EXAMPLE 11-11   A thin uniform rod is 1 m long and has a mass of 6 kg. If the rod is pivoted at its center and set into rotation with an angular speed of 16 rad/s, compute its angular momentum.

Solution   The moment of inertia of a thin rod is, from Fig. 11-7,

$$I = \frac{ml^2}{12} = \frac{(6\ \text{kg})(1\ \text{m})^2}{12} = 0.5\ \text{kg} \cdot \text{m}^2$$

Hence its angular momentum is

$$L = I\omega = (0.5\ \text{kg} \cdot \text{m}^2)(16\ \text{rad/s})$$
$$= 8\ \text{kg} \cdot \text{m}^2/\text{s}$$

Notice that the SI unit of angular momentum is $\text{kg} \cdot \text{m}^2/\text{s}$. The USCS unit is $\text{slug} \cdot \text{ft}^2/\text{s}$.

11-9 CONSERVA-TION OF ANGULAR MOMENTUM

We can understand the definition of angular momentum better if we return to the fundamental equation for angular motion, $\tau = I\alpha$. Recalling the defining equation for angular acceleration

$$\alpha = \frac{\omega_f - \omega_0}{t}$$

we can write Newton's second law as

$$\tau = I\frac{\omega_f - \omega_0}{t}$$

Multiplying by t, we obtain

$$\tau t = I\omega_f - I\omega_0 \qquad (11\text{-}18)$$

Angular impulse = change in angular momentum

The product τt is defined as the *angular impulse*. Note the similarity between this equation and the one derived in Chap. 9 for linear impulse.

If no external torque is applied to a rotating body, we can set $\tau = 0$ in Eq. (11-18), yielding

$$0 = I\omega_f - I\omega_0$$

or

$$I\omega_f = I\omega_0 \qquad (11\text{-}19)$$

Final angular momentum = initial angular momentum

Thus we are led to a statement of the *conservation of angular momentum:*

> *If the sum of the external torques acting on a body or system of bodies is zero, the angular momentum remains unchanged.*

This statement holds true even if the rotating body is not rigid but is altered so that its moment of inertia changes. In this case, the angular speed also changes so that the product $I\omega$ is always constant. Skaters, divers, and acrobats all control the rate at which their bodies rotate by extending or retracting their limbs to decrease or increase their angular speed.

An interesting experiment illustrating the conservation of angular momentum is shown in Fig. 11-11. A woman stands on a rotating platform with heavy weights in each hand. She is first set into rotation with her arms fully extended. By drawing her hands closer to her body, she decreases her moment of inertia. Since her angular momentum cannot change, she will notice a considerable increase in her angular speed. By extending her arms, she will be able to decrease her angular speed.

Fig. 11-11 Experiment to demonstrate the conservation of angular momentum. The woman controls her rate of rotation by moving the weights inward to increase rotational speed or outward to decrease rotational speed.

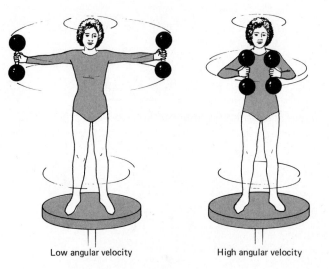

Low angular velocity   High angular velocity

EXAMPLE 11-12   Assume the woman in Fig. 11-11 has a constant moment of inertia equal to 3 slug · ft^2 and that she holds a 16-lb weight in each hand. While holding the weights at a distance $r_1 = 3$ ft from the axis of rotation, she is given an initial velocity $\omega_0 = 3$ rad/s. If she pulls the weights inward until they are at a distance $r_2 = 1$ ft from the center of rotation, what will her resulting angular speed be?

Solution   If we consider the 16-lb weights as point masses, the moment of inertia I_m of the woman will be increased in each case by Mr^2, where $M = 32$ lb/(32 ft/s^2) = 1 slug is the total mass of the two weights and r is the distance of the weights from the center of rotation.

Since the final momentum must equal the initial momentum, we can write

$$(I_m + Mr_2^2)\omega_f = (I_m + Mr_1^2)\omega_0$$

We now solve for the final angular speed as follows:

$$[3 \text{ slug} \cdot \text{ft} + (1 \text{ slug})(1 \text{ ft})^2]\omega_f = [3 \text{ slug} \cdot \text{ft}^2 + (1 \text{ slug})(3 \text{ ft})^2](3 \text{ rad/s})$$

$$(4 \text{ slug} \cdot \text{ft}^2)\omega_f = (12 \text{ slug} \cdot \text{ft}^2)(3 \text{ rad/s})$$

$$\omega_f = 9 \text{ rad/s}$$

Her angular speed has been tripled by bringing the weights in to her chest.

SUMMARY

In this chapter, we extended the concept of circular motion to include the rotation of a rigid body composed of many particles. We found that many problems can be solved by methods discussed earlier for linear motion. The essential concepts are summarized below:

- The similarities between angular and linear motion:

Rotational	θ	ω	α	I	$I\omega$	τ	$I\alpha$	$\tau\theta$	$\frac{1}{2}\alpha\omega^2$	$\tau\omega$
Linear	s	v	a	m	mv	F	ma	Fs	$\frac{1}{2}mv^2$	Fv

- The angle in radians is the ratio of the arc distance s to the radius R of the arc. Symbolically we write:

$$\theta = \frac{s}{R} \qquad s = \theta R$$

The radian is a unitless ratio of two lengths.
- Angular velocity, which is the rate of angular displacement, can be calculated from θ or from the frequency of rotation:

$$\bar{\omega} = \frac{\theta}{t} \qquad \bar{\omega} = 2\pi f \qquad \text{\textit{Average Angular Velocity}}$$

- Angular acceleration is the time rate of change in angular speed:

$$\alpha = \frac{\omega_f - \omega_0}{t} \qquad \text{\textit{Angular Acceleration}}$$

- By comparing θ to s, ω to v, and α to a, the following equations can be utilized for angular acceleration problems:

$$\theta = \frac{\omega_f - \omega_0}{2}t$$
$$\omega_f = \omega_0 + \alpha t$$
$$\theta = \omega_0 t + \frac{1}{2}\alpha t^2$$
$$2\alpha\theta = \omega_f^2 - \omega_0^2$$

When any three of the five parameters θ, α, t, ω_f, and ω_0 are given, the other two can be found from one of these equations. Choose a direction of rotation as being positive throughout your calculations.

- The following equations are useful when comparing linear motion with rotational motion:

$$v = \omega R \qquad a_T = \alpha R$$

- Other useful relationships:

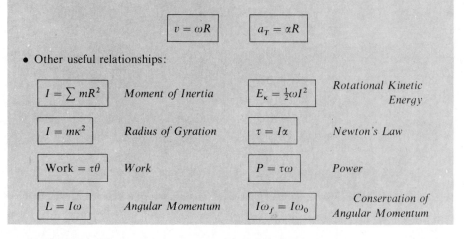

$I = \sum mR^2$ *Moment of Inertia*	$E_\kappa = \frac{1}{2}\omega I^2$ *Rotational Kinetic Energy*
$I = m\kappa^2$ *Radius of Gyration*	$\tau = I\alpha$ *Newton's Law*
$Work = \tau\theta$ *Work*	$P = \tau\omega$ *Power*
$L = I\omega$ *Angular Momentum*	$I\omega_f = I\omega_0$ *Conservation of Angular Momentum*

QUESTIONS

11-1 Define the following terms:
- **a.** Radius of gyration
- **b.** Radian
- **c.** Angular speed
- **d.** Angular momentum
- **e.** Moment of inertia
- **f.** Tangential acceleration
- **g.** Angular displacement
- **h.** Angular acceleration
- **i.** Rotational kinetic energy

11-2. Make a list of the SI and USCS units for angular velocity, angular acceleration, moment of inertia, torque, and rotational kinetic energy.

11-3. State the angular analogies for the following translational equations:
- **a.** $\omega_f = v_0 + at$
- **b.** $s = v_0 t + \frac{1}{2}at^2$
- **c.** $F = ma$
- **d.** $E_\kappa = \frac{1}{2}mv^2$
- **e.** Work $= Fs$
- **f.** Power $=$ work$/t = Fv$

11-4. A sphere, a cylinder, a disk, and a hollow ring all have identical masses and are rotating with constant angular speed about a common axis. Compare their individual rotational kinetic energies, assuming their outside diameters are equal.

11-5. Explain how a diver controls his motion so that he can strike the water feet first or head first.

11-6. A cat held feet up and dropped from any elevation above a few feet will always land feet first. How does he accomplish this?

11-7. When energy is supplied to a body so that both translation and rotation result, its total kinetic energy is given by

$$E_\kappa = \frac{1}{2}mv^2 + I\omega^2$$

How the energy is divided between rotational and translational effects is determined by the distribution of mass (moment of inertia). From these statements, which of the following objects will roll to the bottom of an inclined plane first?
- **a.** A solid disk of mass M
- **b.** A circular hoop of mass M

11-8. Refer to Question 11-7. If a solid sphere, a solid disk, a solid cylinder, and a hollow cylinder are released simultaneously from the top of an inclined plane, in what order will they reach the bottom?

11-9. A disk whose moment of inertia is I_1 and whose angular velocity is ω_1 is meshed with a disk whose moment of inertia is I_2 and whose angular velocity is ω_2. Write the conservation equation by denoting their combined angular velocity by ω.

11-10. Refer to Question 11-9. Suppose $\omega_1 = \omega_2$ and $I_1 = 2I_2$. How would their combined velocity compare with their initial velocity? Suppose $\omega_1 = 3\omega_2$ and $I_1 = I_2$?

PROBLEMS

11-1. A point near the edge of a rotating shaft of radius 3 ft moves through a distance of 2 ft. Compute the angular displacement **(a)** in radians, **(b)** in degrees, and **(c)** in revolutions.

Ans. **(a)** 0.667 rad **(b)** 38.2° **(c)** 0.106 rev.

11-2. A point on the edge of a large wheel 8 m in diameter moves through an angle of 37°. Compute the length of the arc described by the point.

11-3. An electric motor turns at a frequency of 600 rpm. What is its angular speed? What is the angular displacement after 6 s?

Ans. 62.8 rad/s, 377 rad.

11-4. A rotating pulley completes 12 rev in 4 s. Determine the average angular speed **(a)** in revolutions per second, **(b)** in revolutions per minute, and **(c)** in radians per second.

11-5. A rotating flywheel starts from rest and reaches a final rotational speed of 900 rpm in 4 s. Determine the angular acceleration and the angular displacement after 4 s.

Ans. 23.6 rad/s², 189 rad.

11-6. An electric motor rotating at 1900 rpm slows to 300 rpm in 5 s when the power is turned off. Find **(a)** the angular acceleration and **(b)** the angular displacement during the 5 s.

11-7. A grinding stone rotating at 4 rev/s receives a constant angular acceleration of 3 rad/s². **(a)** What angular displacement will it describe in 3 s? **(b)** How many revolutions will it make? **(c)** What will its final angular speed be?

Ans. **(a)** 88.9 rad **(b)** 14.1 rev **(c)** 34.1 rad/s.

11-8. What is the linear speed of a point on the surface of a rotating cylinder if the cylinder makes 10 complete revolutions in 20 s and the diameter of the cylinder is 3 m?

11-9. A cylindrical piece of metal stock 6 in. in diameter rotates in a lathe at 800 rpm. What is the linear velocity of the surface of the cylinder?

Ans. 20.9 ft/s.

11-10. The proper tangential velocity for machining steel stock is about 2.3 ft/s. At what rpm should a steel cylinder 3 in. in diameter be turned in a lathe?

11-11. A pulley 32 cm in diameter and rotating initially at 4 rev/s receives a constant angular acceleration of 2 rad/s². **(a)** Compute the angular speed after 8 s. **(b)** What is the angular displacement during this time? **(c)** What is the linear velocity of a belt wrapped around the pulley after 8 s? **(d)** What is the tangential acceleration of the belt?

Ans. **(a)** 41.1 rad/s **(b)** 265 rad **(c)** 6.58 m/s **(d)** 0.32 m/s².

11-12. A woman standing 4 m from the center of a rotating platform covers a distance of 100 m in 20 s. If she started from rest, what is the angular acceleration of the platform? What is the rpm of the platform after 20 s?

11-13. A 6-kg particle revolves in a circle 1 m in diameter. If the angular speed increases from 600 to 1500 rpm in 12 s, what is the magnitude of the resultant force acting on the particle at the instant the particle is rotating at 1500 rpm?

Ans. 7.4×10^4 N.

11-14. A phonograph turntable revolves at 78 rpm. When the current is shut off, frictional forces bring it to a stop in 3.5 s. What is the tangential acceleration of a point 4 in. from the center of the turntable? What distance does this point travel before stopping?

11-15. A 2-kg mass revolves at 160 rpm on the end of a string 60 cm long. Find **(a)** the moment of inertia, **(b)** the angular speed, **(c)** the angular momentum, and **(d)** the rotational kinetic energy.

Ans. **(a)** 0.72 kg · m² **(b)** 16.8 rad/s **(c)** 12.1 kg · m²/s **(d)** 101 J.

11-16. A uniform ring weighing 16 lb revolves about its center at 6 rev/s. If its rotational kinetic energy is 400 ft · lb, what must the radius of the ring be?

11-17. A uniform 90-kg grinding wheel has a diameter of 0.6 m and rotates at 1200 rpm. Find **(a)** the moment of inertia, **(b)** the rotational kinetic energy, and **(c)** the angular momentum.

Ans. **(a)** 4.05 kg · m² **(b)** 3.21×10^4 J **(c)** 509 kg · m²/s.

11-18. An unbalanced torque of 150 N · m imparts an angular acceleration of 12 rad/s² to the rotor of a generator. What is the moment of inertia of the generator?

11-19. The flywheel on an engine has a moment of inertia of 24 slug · ft². What torque is required to accelerate the wheel from rest to an angular speed of 400 rpm in 10 s?

Ans. 101 lb · ft.

11-20. The radius of gyration of an 8-kg wheel is 50 cm. Find its moment of inertia and kinetic energy if it is rotating at 300 rpm.

11-21. A solid 82-kg cylinder of radius 22 cm has a constant force of 45 N applied tangentially at the rim by a wide leather belt. Find **(a)** the moment of inertia, **(b)** the angular acceleration, **(c)** the angular velocity after 4 s, and **(d)** the angular displacement after 4 s. **(e)** Show that the work done on the wheel in 4 s is equal to the kinetic energy after 4 s.

Ans. **(a)** 1.98 kg · m² **(b)** 5 rad/s² **(c)** 20 rad/s **(d)** 40 rad **(e)** 396 J.

11-22. A large 120-kg turbine wheel has a radius of gyration of 1 m. A frictional torque of 80 N · m opposes rotation of the shaft. What torque must be applied to accelerate the wheel from rest to 300 rpm in 10 s?

11-23. The driving wheel attached to an electric motor has a diameter of 12 in. and makes 1400 rpm. When a belt drive is connected around the wheel, the tension in the belt on the slack side is 40 lb and the tension on the tight side is 110 lb. Find the horsepower transmitted by the belt.

Ans. 9.33 hp.

11-24. **(a)** What is the torque developed by a 1200-kW engine if its output shaft is turning at 2000 rpm? **(b)** If a drum 50 cm in diameter is attached to the output shaft, what is the maximum mass that can be lifted by a rope wrapped around the drum? **(c)** With what velocity would it rise?

11-25. A block is attached to a cord passing over a pulley through a hole in a horizontal frictionless surface, as shown in Fig. 11-12. Initially the block is revolving at 4 rad/s at a distance of 2 ft from the center of the hole. If the cord is pulled from below until it is 0.5 ft from the center, what is the new angular velocity?

Ans. 64 rad/s.

Fig. 11-12

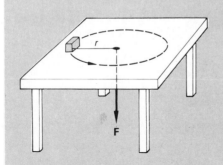

11-26. Suppose the 2-kg mass of the block in Prob. 11-25 is rotating at 3 rad/s at a distance of 1 m from the center of the hole. At what distance r from the hole will the tension in the cord be 45 N?

11-27. A 6-kg disk A rotating at 400 rpm engages with a 3-kg disk B initially at rest. The radius of disk A is 0.4 m, and the radius of disk B is 0.2 m. (See Fig. 11-13.) What is the combined angular speed after the disks are meshed?

Ans. 37.2 rad/s.

Fig. 11-13

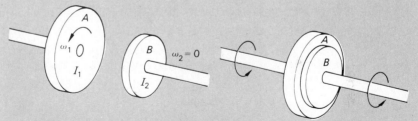

11-28. Assume the same conditions as in Prob. 11-27, except that disk B is rotating at 60 rad/s initially in the direction opposite to disk A. What will the resultant angular velocity be when the two disks are meshed?

12 *Simple Machines*

OBJECTIVES: After completing this chapter, you should be able to:

1. Describe a simple machine and its operation in general terms to the extent that *efficiency* and *conservation of energy* are explained.

2. Write and apply formulas for computing the efficiency of a simple machine in terms of work or power.

3. Distinguish by definition and example between *ideal* mechanical advantage and *actual* mechanical advantage.

4. Draw a diagram of each of the following simple machines and beside each diagram write a formula for computing the ideal mechanical advantage: (*a*) lever, (*b*) inclined plane, (*c*) wedge, (*d*) gears, (*e*) pulley systems, (*f*) wheel and axle, (*g*) screw jack, (*h*) belt drive.

5. Compute the mechanical advantage and the efficiency of each of the simple machines listed in the previous objective.

A simple machine is any device which transmits the application of a force into useful work. With a chain hoist we can transmit a small downward force into a very large upward force for lifting. In industry delicate samples of radioactive material are handled by machines that allow an applied force to be reduced significantly. Single pulleys may be used to change the direction of an applied force without affecting its magnitude. A study of machines and their efficiency is essential for the productive use of energy. In this chapter, you will become familiar with levers, gears, pulley systems, inclined planes, and other machines routinely used for many industrial applications.

12-1 SIMPLE MACHINES AND EFFICIENCY

In a simple machine input work is done by the application of a single force, and the machine performs output work by means of a single force. During any such operation (Fig. 12-1), three processes occur:

1. Work is supplied to the machine.
2. Work is done against friction.
3. Output work is done by the machine.

Fig. 12-1 Three processes occur in the operation of a simple machine: (1) the input of a certain amount of work, (2) the loss of energy in doing work against friction, and (3) the output of useful work.

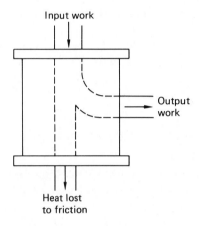

Input work

Output work

Heat lost to friction

According to the principle of conservation of energy, these processes are related as follows:

Input work = work against friction + output work

The amount of useful work performed by a machine can never be greater than the work supplied to it. There will always be some loss due to friction or other dissipative forces. For example, in pumping up a bicycle tire with a small hand pump we exert a downward force on the plunger, causing air to be forced into the tire. That some of our input work is lost to friction can easily be verified by feeling how warm the wall of the hand pump becomes. The smaller we can make the friction loss in a machine, the greater the return for our effort. In other words, the effectiveness of a given machine can be measured by comparing its output work with the work supplied to it.

The **efficiency** E of a machine is defined as the ratio of the work output to the work input.

$$E = \frac{\text{work output}}{\text{work input}} \qquad (12\text{-}1)$$

The efficiency as defined in Eq. (12-1) will always be a number between 0 and 1. Common practice is to express this decimal as a percentage by multiplying by 100. For example, a machine which does 40 J of work when 80 J of work is supplied to it has an efficiency of 50 percent.

Another useful expression for efficiency can be noted from the definition of power as work per unit time. We can write

$$P = \frac{\text{work}}{t} \qquad \text{or} \qquad \text{Work} = Pt$$

The efficiency in terms of power input P_i and power output P_o is given by

$$E = \frac{\text{work output}}{\text{work input}} = \frac{P_o t}{P_i t}$$

or

$$E = \frac{\text{power output}}{\text{power input}} = \frac{P_o}{P_i} \tag{12-2}$$

EXAMPLE 12-1   A 60-hp motor winds a cable around a drum. (a) If the cable lifts a 3-ton load of bricks to a height of 12 ft in 3 s, calculate the efficiency of the motor. (b) At what rate is work done against friction?

Solution (a)   First compute the output power.

$$P_o = \frac{Fs}{t} = \frac{(6000 \text{ lb})(12 \text{ ft})}{3 \text{ s}}$$

$$= (24{,}000 \text{ ft} \cdot \text{lb/s}) \frac{1 \text{ hp}}{550 \text{ ft} \cdot \text{lb/s}}$$

$$= 43.6 \text{ hp}$$

The efficiency is then found from Eq. (12-2):

$$E = \frac{P_o}{P_i} = \frac{43.6 \text{ hp}}{60 \text{ hp}} = 0.727$$

$$= 72.7\%$$

Solution (b)   The rate at which work is done against friction is the difference between the input power and the output power, or 16.4 hp.

**12-2
MECHAN-
ICAL
ADVANTAGE**
Simple machines like the lever, block and tackle, chain hoist, gears, inclined plane, and the screw jack all play important roles in modern industry. We can illustrate the operation of any of these machines by the general diagram in Fig. 12-2. An input force $\mathbf{F}_i$ acts through a distance s_i, accomplishing the work $F_i s_i$. At the same time, an output force $\mathbf{F}_o$ acts through a distance s_o, performing the useful work $F_o s_o$.

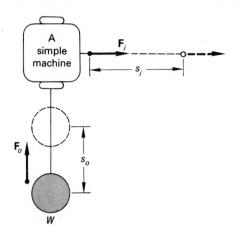

Fig. 12-2 During the operation of a simple machine, an input force $\mathbf{F}_i$ acts through a distance s_i while an output force $\mathbf{F}_o$ acts through a distance s_o.

The **actual mechanical advantage** M_A of a machine is defined as the ratio of the output force F_o to the input force F_i.

$$M_A = \frac{\text{output force}}{\text{input force}} = \frac{F_o}{F_i} \qquad (12\text{-}3)$$

An actual mechanical advantage greater than 1 indicates that the output force is greater than the input force. Although most machines have values of M_A greater than 1, this is not always the case. In handling small, fragile objects, it is sometimes desirable to make the output force smaller than the input force.

In the previous section, we noted that the efficiency of a machine increases as frictional effects become small. Applying the conservation-of-energy principle to the simple machine in Fig. 12-2 yields

Work input = work against friction + work output

$$F_i s_i = (\text{work})_{\mathscr{F}} + F_o s_o$$

The most efficient engine possible would realize no losses due to friction. We can represent this *ideal* case by setting $(\text{work})_{\mathscr{F}} = 0$ in the above equation. Thus

$$F_o s_o = F_i s_i$$

Since this equation represents an ideal case, we define the *ideal mechanical advantage* M_I as

$$M_I = \frac{F_o}{F_i} = \frac{s_i}{s_o} \qquad (12\text{-}4)$$

The **ideal mechanical advantage** of a simple machine is equal to the ratio of the distance the input force moves to the distance the output force moves.

The efficiency of a simple machine is the ratio of output work to input work. Therefore, for the general machine of Fig. 12-2 we have

$$E = \frac{F_o s_o}{F_i s_i} = \frac{F_o/F_i}{s_i/s_o}$$

Finally, utilizing Eqs. (12-3) and (12-4), we obtain

$$E = \frac{M_A}{M_I} \qquad (12\text{-}5)$$

All the above concepts have been treated as they apply to a general machine. In the following sections we shall apply them to specific machines.

12-3 THE LEVER

Possibly the oldest and most generally useful machine is the simple lever. A *lever* consists of any rigid bar pivoted at a certain point called the *fulcrum*. Figure 12-3 illustrates the use of a long rod to lift a weight **W**. We can calculate the ideal mechanical advantage of such a device in two ways. The first method involves the principle of equilibrium, and the second uses the principle of work, as discussed in the previous section. Since the equilibrium method is easier for the lever, we shall apply it first.

Fig. 12-3 The lever.

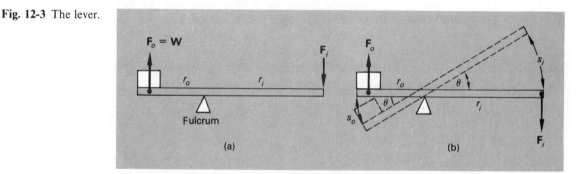

Because no translational motion is involved during the application of a lever, the condition for equilibrium is that the input torque equal the output torque:

$$F_i r_i = F_o r_o$$

The ideal mechanical advantage can be found from

$$M_I = \frac{F_o}{F_i} = \frac{r_i}{r_o} \qquad (12\text{-}6)$$

The ratio F_o/F_i is considered the *ideal* case because no friction forces are considered.

The same result is obtained from work considerations. Note from Fig. 12-3b that the force $\mathbf{F}_i$ moves through the arc distance s_i while the force $\mathbf{F}_o$ moves through the arc distance s_o. However, the two arcs are subtended by the same angle θ, and so we can write the proportion

$$\frac{s_i}{s_o} = \frac{r_i}{r_o}$$

Substitution into Eq. (12-4) will verify the result obtained from equilibrium considerations, that is, $M_I = r_i/r_o$.

EXAMPLE 12-2

An iron bar 3 m long is used to lift a 60-kg block. The bar is used as a lever, as shown in Fig. 12-3. The fulcrum is placed 80 cm from the block. What is the ideal mechanical advantage of the system, and what input force is required?

Solution

The distance $r_o = 0.8$ m; and the distance $r_i = 3$ m $- 0.8$ m $= 2.2$ m. Therefore, the ideal mechanical advantage is

$$M_I = \frac{r_i}{r_o} = \frac{2.2 \text{ m}}{0.8 \text{ m}} = 2.75$$

The output force in this case is equal to the weight of the 60-kg block ($W = mg$). Therefore, the required input force is given by

$$F_i = \frac{F_o}{M_I} = \frac{(60 \text{ kg})(9.8 \text{ m/s}^2)}{2.75}$$

$$= 214 \text{ N}$$

Before leaving the subject of the lever, it should be noted that very little of the input work is lost to friction forces. For all practical purposes, the actual mechanical advantage for a simple lever is equal to the ideal mechanical advantage. Other examples of the lever are illustrated in Fig. 12-4.

12-4 APPLICATIONS OF THE LEVER PRINCIPLE

A serious limitation of the elementary lever is the fact that it operates through a small angle. There are many ways of overcoming this restriction by allowing for continuous rotation of the lever arm. For example, the *wheel and axle* (Fig. 12-5) allows for the continued action of the input force $\mathbf{F}_i$. Applying the reasoning described in Sec. 12-2 for a general machine, it can be shown that

$$\boxed{M_I = \frac{F_o}{F_i} = \frac{R}{r}} \tag{12-7}$$

Thus the ideal mechanical advantage of a wheel and axle is the ratio of the radius of the wheel to the radius of the axle.

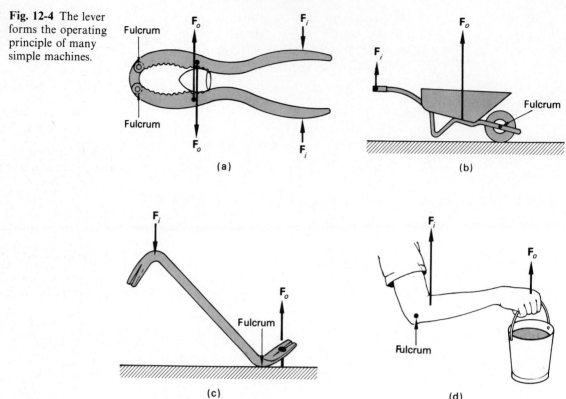

Fig. 12-4 The lever forms the operating principle of many simple machines.

Fulcrum

F_o

F_i

Fulcrum

F_o

F_i

(a)

F_i

F_o

Fulcrum

(b)

F_i

F_o

Fulcrum

(c)

F_i

F_o

Fulcrum

(d)

Fig. 12-5 The wheel and axle.

F_o

R r

F_i

W

Fig. 12-6 A single
fixed pulley serves
only to change the
direction of the
input force.

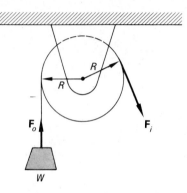

Another application of the lever concept is through the use of *pulleys*. A single pulley, as shown in Fig. 12-6, is simply a lever whose input moment arm is equal to its output moment arm. From the principle of equilibrium, the input force will equal the output force, and the ideal mechanical advantage will be

$$M_I = \frac{F_o}{F_i} = 1 \qquad (12\text{-}8)$$

The only advantage of such a device lies in its ability to change the direction of an input force.

A single movable pulley (Fig. 12-7), on the other hand, has an ideal

Fig. 12-7 A single
movable pulley.
(*a*) The input force
moves through
twice the distance
that the output
force travels.
(*b*) The free-body
diagram shows that
$2F_i = F_o$.

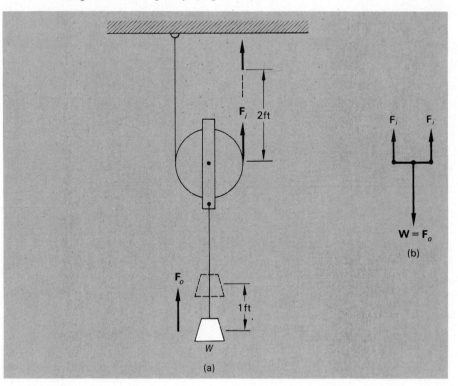

mechanical advantage of 2. Note that the two supporting ropes must each be shortened by 1 ft in order to lift the load through a distance of 1 ft. Therefore, the input force moves through a distance of 2 ft while the output force only moves a distance of 1 ft. Applying the principle of work, we have

$$F_i(2 \text{ ft}) = F_o(1 \text{ ft})$$

from which the ideal mechanical advantage is

$$M_I = \frac{F_o}{F_i} = 2 \tag{12-9}$$

The same result can be shown by constructing a free-body diagram, as in Fig. 12-7b. From the figure it is evident that

$$2F_i = F_o$$

or

$$M_I = \frac{F_o}{F_i} = 2$$

Fig. 12-8 The block and tackle. This arrangement has an ideal mechanical advantage of 4 since four strands support the movable block.

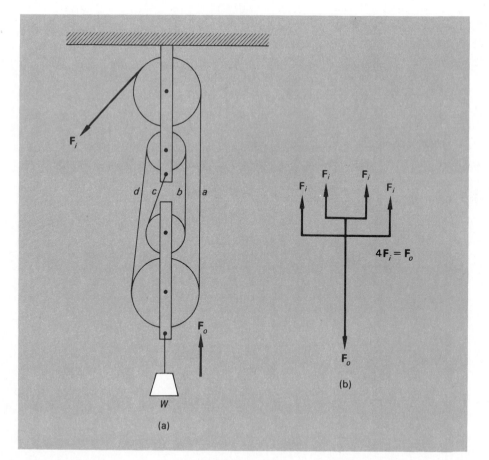

The latter method is usually applied to problems involving movable pulleys since it allows one to associate M_I with the number of strands supporting the movable pulley.

EXAMPLE 12-3   Calculate the ideal mechanical advantage of the block-and-tackle arrangement shown in Fig. 12-8.

Solution   We first construct a free-body diagram, as shown in Fig. 12-8b. From the figure we note that

$$4F_i = F_o$$

from which

$$M_I = \frac{F_o}{F_i} = \frac{4F_i}{F_i} = 4$$

Note that the uppermost pulley serves only to change the direction of the input force. The same M_I would result if $\mathbf{F}_i$ were applied upward at point a.

12-5 THE TRANS- MISSION OF TORQUE

The simple machines discussed so far are used to transmit and apply forces in order to move loads. In most mechanical applications, work is done by transmitting torque from one drive to another. For example, the belt drive (Fig. 12-9) transmits the torque from a driving pulley to an output pulley. The mechanical advantage of such a system is the ratio of the torques between the output pulley and the driving pulley:

$$M_I = \frac{\text{output torque}}{\text{input torque}} = \frac{\tau_o}{\tau_i}$$

Fig. 12-9 The belt drive.

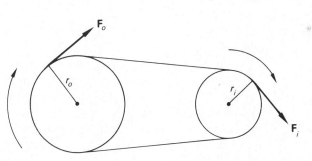

From the definition of torque, we can write this expression in terms of the radii of the pulleys

$$M_I = \frac{\tau_o}{\tau_i} = \frac{F_o r_o}{F_i r_i}$$

If there is no slippage between the belt and pulleys, it is safe to say that the tangential input force F_i is equal to the tangential output force F_o. Thus

$$M_I = \frac{F_o r_o}{F_i r_i} = \frac{r_o}{r_i}$$

Since the diameters of pulleys are usually specified instead of their radii, a more convenient expression is

$$M_I = \frac{D_o}{D_i} \qquad (12\text{-}10)$$

where D_i is the diameter of the driving pulley and D_o is the diameter of the output pulley.

Suppose we now apply the principle of work to the belt drive. Remember that work is defined in rotary motion as the product of torque τ and angular displacement θ. For the belt drive, assuming ideal conditions, the input work equals the output work. Thus

$$\tau_i \theta_i = \tau_o \theta_o$$

The power input must also be equal to the power output. Dividing the above equation by the time t required to rotate through the angles θ_i and θ_o, we obtain

$$\tau_i \frac{\theta_i}{t} = \tau_o \frac{\theta_o}{t} \qquad \text{or} \qquad \tau_i \omega_i = \tau_o \omega_o$$

where ω_i and ω_o are the angular speeds of the input and output pulleys. Note that the ratio τ_o / τ_i represents the ideal mechanical advantage. Therefore, we can add another expression to Eq. (12-10), to obtain

$$\boxed{M_I = \frac{D_o}{D_i} = \frac{\omega_i}{\omega_o}} \qquad (12\text{-}11)$$

This important result shows that the mechanical advantage is achieved at the expense of rotary motion. In other words, if the mechanical advantage is 2, the input shaft must rotate with twice the angular speed of the output shaft. The ratio ω_i / ω_o is sometimes referred to as the *speed ratio*.

If the speed ratio is greater than 1, the machine produces an output torque which is greater than the input torque. As we have seen, this feat is accomplished at the expense of rotation. On the other hand, many machines are designed to increase the rotational output speed. In these cases, the speed ratio is less than 1, and the increased rotational speed is accomplished with reduced torque output.

EXAMPLE 12-4   Consider the belt drive illustrated in Fig. 12-9, where the diameter of the small driving pulley is 6 in. and the diameter of the driven pulley is 18 in. A 6-hp motor drives the input pulley at 600 rpm. Calculate the revolutions per minute and torque delivered to the driven wheel if the system is 75 percent efficient.

Solution   We first calculate the ideal mechanical advantage (100 percent efficiency) of the system. From Eq. (12-11),

$$M_I = \frac{D_o}{D_i} = \frac{18 \text{ in.}}{6 \text{ in.}} = 3$$

Since the efficiency is 75 percent, the actual mechanical advantage is given from Eq. (12-5).

$$M_A = EM_I = (0.75)(3) = 2.25$$

Now the actual mechanical advantage is the simple ratio of output torque τ_o to input torque τ_i. Recalling that the power in rotational motion is equal to the product of torque and angular velocity, we can solve for τ_i as follows:

$$\tau_i = \frac{P_i}{\omega_i} = \frac{(6 \text{ hp})[(550 \text{ ft} \cdot \text{lb/s})/\text{hp}]}{(600 \text{ rev/min})(2\pi \text{ rad/rev})(1 \text{ min/60 s})}$$

$$= \frac{(6)(550 \text{ ft} \cdot \text{lb/s})}{20\pi \text{ rad/s}} = 52.5 \text{ ft} \cdot \text{lb}$$

Since $M_A = \tau_o/\tau_i$, the output torque is given by

$$\tau_o = M_A \tau_i = (2.25)(52.5 \text{ ft} \cdot \text{lb})$$

$$= 118 \text{ ft} \cdot \text{lb}$$

Assuming the belt does not slip, it will move with the same linear velocity v around each pulley. Since $v = \omega r$, we can write the equality

$$\omega_i r_i = \omega_o r_o \qquad \text{or} \qquad \omega_i D_i = \omega_o D_o$$

from which

$$\omega_o = \frac{\omega_i D_i}{D_o} = \frac{(600 \text{ rpm})(6 \text{ in.})}{18 \text{ in.}} = 200 \text{ rpm}$$

Note that the ratio of ω_i to ω_o yields the ideal mechanical advantage and not the actual mechanical advantage. The difference between M_I and M_A is due to friction, both in the belt and in the shaft bearings. Since greater tension on the belt will result in greater friction forces, maximum efficiency is obtained by reducing the belt tension until it just prevents the belt from slipping on the pulleys.

Before leaving our discussion of the transmission of torque, we must consider the application of *gears*. A gear is simply a notched wheel which can transmit torque by meshing with another notched wheel, as shown in Fig. 12-10. A pair of meshing gears differs from a belt drive only in the sense that the gears rotate in opposite directions. The same relationships derived for the belt drive hold for gears:

$$M_I = \frac{D_o}{D_i} = \frac{\omega_i}{\omega_o} \tag{12-12}$$

A more useful expression makes use of the fact that the number of teeth N on the rim of a gear is proportional to its diameter D. Because of this dependence, the ratio of the number of teeth on the driven gear N_o to the number of teeth

Fig. 12-10 Spur gears. The ideal mechanical advantage is the ratio of the number of teeth on the output gear to the number of teeth on the input gear.

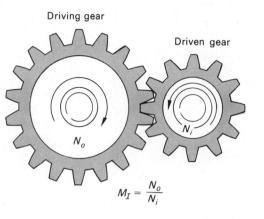

Driving gear

Driven gear

N_o

N_i

$$M_I = \frac{N_o}{N_i}$$

on the driving gear N_i is the same as the ratio of their diameters. Hence we can write

$$M_I = \frac{N_o}{N_i} = \frac{D_o}{D_i} \qquad (12\text{-}13)$$

The use of gears avoids the problem of slippage, which is common with belt drives. It also conserves space and allows for a greater torque to be transmitted.

In addition to the *spur* gears illustrated in Fig. 12-10, there are several other types of gears. Four common types are worm gears, helical gears, bevel gears, and planetary gears. Examples of each are shown in Fig. 12-11. The same general relationships apply for all these gears.

12-6
THE INCLINED PLANE

The only machines we have discussed so far involve application of the lever principle. A second fundamental machine is the *inclined plane.* Suppose you have to move a heavy load from the ground to a truck bed without hoisting equipment. You would probably select a few long boards and form a ramp from the ground to the bed of the truck. Experience has taught you that it takes less effort to push a load up a small elevation than it does to lift the load directly. Since a smaller input force results in the same output force, a mechanical advantage is realized. However, the smaller input force is accomplished at the cost of greater distance.

Consider the movement of a weight **W** up the inclined plane in Fig. 12-12. The slope angle θ is such that the weight must be moved through a distance s to reach a height h at the top of the incline. If we neglect friction, the work required to push the weight up the plane is the same as the work required to lift it up vertically. We can express this equality as

Work input = work output

$$F_i s = Wh$$

Fig. 12-11 Four common types of gears: (*a*) helical, (*b*) planetary, (*c*) bevel, (*d*) worm. (The spur gear which is the most common type is shown in Fig. 12-10.)

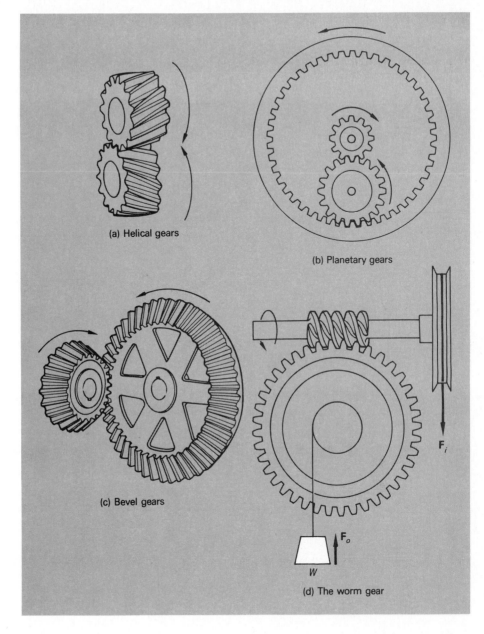

(a) Helical gears

(b) Planetary gears

(c) Bevel gears

(d) The worm gear

where F_i is the input force and W is the output force. The ideal mechanical advantage will be the ratio of the weight to the input force. Stating this symbolically, we have

$$M_I = \frac{W}{F_i} = \frac{s}{h} \qquad (12\text{-}14)$$

Fig. 12-12 The inclined plane. The input force represents the effort required to push the block up the plane; the output force is equal to the weight of the block.

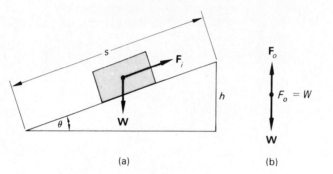

(a)   (b)

EXAMPLE 12-5   The 200-lb wooden crate in Fig. 12-13 is to be raised to a loading platform 6 ft high. A ramp 12 ft long is used to slide the crate from the ground to the platform. Assume that the coefficient of friction is 0.3. (*a*) What is the ideal mechanical advantage of the ramp? (*b*) What is the actual mechanical advantage?

Fig. 12-13 Computing the actual mechanical advantage of an inclined plane.

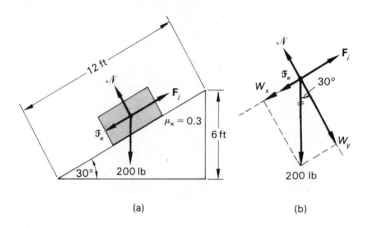

(a)   (b)

Solution (a)   The ideal mechanical advantage, from Eq. (12-14), is

$$M_I = \frac{s}{h} = \frac{12 \text{ ft}}{6 \text{ ft}} = 2$$

This value represents the mechanical advantage of the ramp if it were frictionless.

Solution (b)   The actual mechanical advantage is the ratio of the weight lifted to the required input force, considering friction. Applying the first condition for equilibrium to the free-body diagram (Fig. 12-13*b*), we find that the normal force $\mathcal{N}$ is given by

$$\mathcal{N} = W_y = (200 \text{ lb})(\cos 30°) = 173 \text{ lb}$$

from which the friction force must be

$$\mathcal{F} = \mu \mathcal{N} = (0.3)(173 \text{ lb}) = 51.9 \text{ lb}$$

Summing the forces along the plane, we obtain

$$F_i - \mathcal{F} - W_x = 0$$

But $W_x = (200\ \text{lb})(\sin 30°) = 100\ \text{lb}$, so that we have

$$F_i - 51.9\ \text{lb} - 100\ \text{lb} = 0$$

$$F_i = 51.9\ \text{lb} + 100\ \text{lb} = 152\ \text{lb}$$

We can now compute the actual mechanical advantage:

$$M_A = \frac{F_o}{F_i} = \frac{200\ \text{lb}}{152\ \text{lb}} = 1.32$$

It is left as an exercise for the student to show that the efficiency of the ramp is 66 percent.

12-7 APPLICATIONS OF THE INCLINED PLANE

Many machines apply the principle of the inclined plane. The simplest is the *wedge* (Fig. 12-14), which is actually a double inclined plane. In the ideal case, the mechanical advantage of a wedge of length L and thickness t is given by

$$M_I = \frac{L}{t} \tag{12-15}$$

Fig. 12-14 The wedge is actually a double inclined plane.

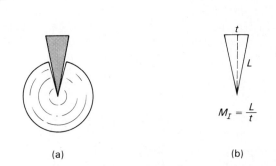

$$M_I = \frac{L}{t}$$

(a)　　　　　　(b)

This equation is a direct consequence of the general relation expressed by Eq. (12-14). The ideal mechanical advantage is always much greater than the actual mechanical advantage because of the large friction forces between the surfaces in contact. The wedge finds its application in axes, knives, chisels, planers, and all other cutting tools. A cam is a kind of rotary wedge which is used to lift valves in internal combustion engines.

One of the most useful applications of the inclined plane is the *screw*. This principle can be explained by examining a common tool known as the *screw jack* (Fig. 12-15). The threads are essentially an inclined plane wrapped

Fig. 12-15 The screw jack.

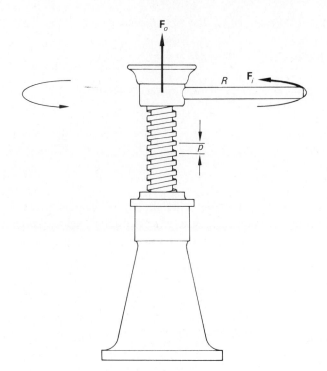

continuously around a cylindrical shaft. When the input force F_i turns through a complete revolution $(2\pi R)$, the output force F_o will advance through the distance p. This distance p is actually the distance between two adjacent threads, and it is called the *pitch* of the screw. The ideal mechanical advantage is the ratio of the input distance to the output distance.

$$M_I = \frac{s_i}{s_o} = \frac{2\pi R}{p} \qquad (12\text{-}16)$$

The screw is an example of a very inefficient machine, but in this case it is usually an advantage since friction forces are needed to hold the load in place while the input force is not being applied.

SUMMARY

A simple machine has been defined as a device which converts a single input force F_i into a single output force F_o. In general, the input force moves through a distance s_i, and the output force moves through a distance s_o. The purpose is to accomplish useful work in a manner suited to a particular application. The major concepts are given below:

- A simple machine is a device which converts a single input force F_i into a single output force F_o. The input force moves through a distance s_i, and the output force moves a distance s_o. There are two mechanical advantages:

$$M_A = \frac{F_o}{F_i} \quad \text{actual mechanical advantage (friction considered)}$$

$$M_I = \frac{s_o}{s_i} \quad \text{ideal mechanical advantage (assumes no friction)}$$

- The efficiency of a machine is a ratio of output work to input work. It is normally expressed as a percentage and can be calculated from any of the following relations:

$$E = \frac{\text{work output}}{\text{work input}} \qquad E = \frac{\text{power output}}{\text{power input}} \qquad E = \frac{M_A}{M_I}$$

- The ideal mechanical advantages for a number of simple machines are given below.

$$M_I = \left(\frac{F_o}{F_i}\right)_{\text{ideal}} = \frac{r_i}{r_o} \qquad \text{\textit{Lever}}$$

$$M_I = \left(\frac{F_o}{F_i}\right)_{\text{ideal}} = \frac{R}{r} \qquad \text{\textit{Wheel and Axle}}$$

$$M_I = \frac{D_o}{D_i} = \frac{\omega_i}{\omega_o} \qquad \text{\textit{Belt Drive}}$$

$$M_I = \frac{W}{F_i} = \frac{s}{h} \qquad \text{\textit{Inclined Plane}}$$

$$M_I = \frac{L}{t} \qquad \text{\textit{Wedge}}$$

$$M_I = \frac{N_o}{N_i} = \frac{D_o}{D_i} \qquad \text{\textit{Gears}}$$

$$M_I = \frac{s_i}{s_o} = \frac{2\pi R}{P} \qquad \text{\textit{Screw Jack}}$$

QUESTIONS

12-1. Define the following terms:
  a. Machine
  b. Efficiency
  c. Lever
  d. Pulley
  e. Gears
  f. Wedge
  g. Screw
  h. Pitch
  i. Inclined plane
  j. Wheel and axle
  k. Actual mechanical advantage
  l. Ideal mechanical advantage
  m. Belt drive

12-2. What is meant by *useful work* or *output work*? What is meant by *input work*? Write the general relationship between input work and output work.

12-3. Two jacks are operated simultaneously to lift the front end of a car. Immediately afterward, it is noted that the left jack feels warmer than the right one. Which jack is more efficient? Explain.

12-4. A machine may alter the magnitude and/or the direction of an input force. **(a)** Name several examples in which both changes occur. **(b)** Give examples in which only the magnitude of the input force is altered. **(c)** Give some examples in which only the direction is altered.

12-5. A machine lifts a load through a vertical distance of 4 ft while the input force moves through a distance of 2 ft. Would this machine be helpful in lifting large weights? Explain.

12-6. A bicycle can be operated in three gear ranges. In *low range* the pedals describe two complete revolutions while the rear wheel turns through one revolution. In *medium range* the pedals and the wheels turn at the same rate. In *high range* the rear wheel of the bicycle completes two revolutions for every complete pedal revolution. Discuss the advantages and disadvantages of each range.

12-7. What happens to the ideal mechanical advantage if a simple machine is operated in reverse? What happens to its efficiency?

12-8. Give several examples of machines which have an actual mechanical advantage less than 1.

12-9. Why do buses and trucks often use larger steering wheels than those found on automobiles? What principle is used?

12-10. Draw diagrams of pulley systems which have ideal mechanical advantages of 2, 3, and 5.

12-11. Usually the road to the top of a mountain winds around the mountain instead of going straight up the side. Why? If we neglect friction, is more work required to reach the top along the spiral road? Is more power required? If we consider friction, would it require less work to drive straight up the side of the mountain? Explain.

PROBLEMS

12-1. A 25 percent efficient machine performs external work of 200 J. What input work is required?

Ans. 800 J.

12-2. During the operation of a 300-hp engine, energy is lost at the rate of 200 hp because of friction. What are the useful output power and the efficiency of the engine?

12-3. A 60-W motor lifts a 2-kg mass to a height of 4 m in 3 s. **(a)** Compute the output power. **(b)** What is the efficiency of the motor? **(c)** What is the rate at which work is done against friction?

Ans. **(a)** 26.1 W **(b)** 43.6% **(c)** 33.9 W.

12-4. One edge of a 200-lb safe is lifted with a 4-ft steel rod. What input force is required at the end of the rod if a fulcrum is placed 6 in. from the safe? (To lift one edge, a force equal to one-half the weight of the safe is required.)

12-5. A frictionless machine lifts a 200-lb load through a distance of 10 ft. If the input force moves through a distance of 30 ft, what is the ideal mechanical advantage of the machine? What is the magnitude of the input force?

Ans. 3, 66.7 lb.

12-6. What would be the required input force if the machine in Prob. 12-5 were 60 percent efficient?

12-7. A 60-N weight is lifted in the three different ways shown in Fig. 12-16. Compute the ideal mechanical advantage and the required input force for each application.

Ans. **(a)** 2, 30 N **(b)** 3, 20 N **(c)** 0.33, 180 N

 Fig. 12-16

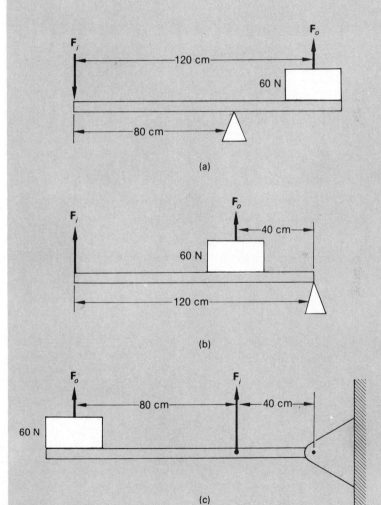

12-8. A 20-kg mass is to be lifted with a rod 2 m long. If you can exert a downward force of 40 N on one end of the rod, where should you place a block of wood to act as a fulcrum?

12-9. A wheel 0.2 m in diameter is attached to an axle with a diameter of 6 cm. If a weight of 400 N is attached to the axle, what force must be applied to the rim of the wheel to lift the weight at constant speed? Neglect friction.

Ans. 120 N.

12-10. What is the mechanical advantage of a screwdriver used as a wheel and axle if its blade is 0.3 in. wide and the handle diameter is 0.8 in.?

12-11. Determine the force F required to lift a 200-N load W with each of the four pulley systems shown in Fig. 12-17.

Ans. **(a)** 100 N **(b)** 50 N **(c)** 40 N **(d)** 50 N.

Fig. 12-17

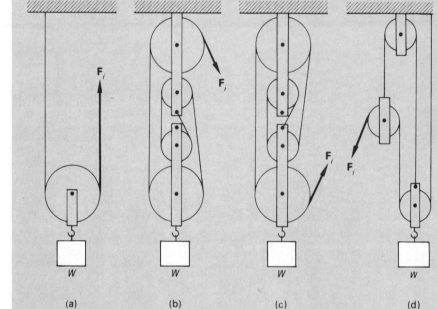

| (a) | (b) | (c) | (d) |

12-12. The *chain hoist* (Fig. 12-18) is a combination of the wheel and axle and the block and tackle. Show that the ideal mechanical advantage of such a device is given by

$$M_I = \frac{2R}{R - r}$$

12-13. A pair of step pulleys (Fig. 12-19) makes it possible to change output speeds merely by shifting the belt. If an electric motor turns the input pulley at 2000 rpm, find the possible angular speeds of the output shaft. The pulley diameters are 4, 6, and 8 in.

Ans. **(a)** Small-input pulley: 2000, 1330, 1000 rpm
(b) middle-input pulley: 3000, 2000, 1500 rpm
(c) large-input pulley: 4000, 2670, 2000 rpm.

Fig. 12-18 The chain hoist.

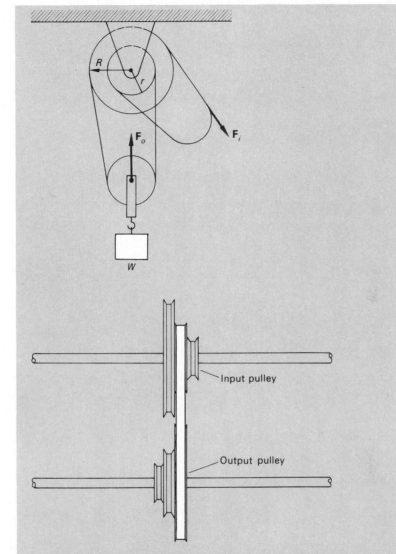

Fig. 12-19 The step pulley.

Input pulley

Output pulley

12-14. An 8-hp motor drives the input pulley of a belt drive at 600 rpm. Compute the revolutions per minute and torque delivered to the driven pulley if the system is 60 percent efficient. The diameters of the input and output pulleys are 4 and 8 in., respectively.

12-15. A worm drive similar to that shown in Fig. 12-11 has n teeth in the gear wheel. (If $n = 80$, one complete turn of the worm will advance the wheel one-eightieth of a revolution.) Derive an expression for the ideal mechanical advantage of the worm gear in terms of the radius of the input pulley R, the radius of the output shaft r, and the number of teeth n in the gear wheel.

Ans. $M_I = nR/r$.

12-16. The worm drive of Prob. 12-15 has 80 teeth in the gear wheel. If the radius of the input wheel is 18 in. and the radius of the output shaft is 3 in., what input force is required to lift a 2-ton load? Assume an efficiency of 80 percent.

12-17. A 37° inclined plane forms a loading ramp for a 40-kg crate. The ramp is 8.2 m long, and the coefficient of friction is 0.2. **(a)** What is the ideal mechanical advantage of the ramp? **(b)** What is the actual mechanical advantage? **(c)** What is the efficiency?

Ans. **(a)** 1.67 **(b)** 1.31 **(c)** 78%.

12-18. The lever of a screw jack is 24 in. long. If the screw has six threads per inch, what is its ideal mechanical advantage? If the jack is 15 percent efficient, what force is needed to lift 2000 lb?

12-19. A wrench with a 6-in. handle acts to tighten a $\frac{1}{4}$-in. diameter bolt having 10 threads per inch. What is the pitch of the bolt? Compare the ideal mechanical advantage. If an input force of 20 lb results in a 600-lb force on the nut, what is the efficiency?

Ans. 0.1 in., 377, 8%.

12-20. A shaft rotating at 800 rpm delivers a torque of 240 N · m to an output shaft which is rotating at 200 rpm. If the efficiency of the machine is 70 percent, compute the output torque. What is the output power in horsepower?

12-21. A screw jack has a screw whose pitch is 0.25 in. Its handle is 16 in. long, and a load of 1.9 tons is being lifted. **(a)** Neglecting friction, what force is required at the end of the handle? **(b)** What is the ideal mechanical advantage of this jack?

Ans. 9.45 lb, 402.

12-22. A certain refrigeration compressor comes equipped with a 250-mm diameter pulley and is designed to operate at 600 rpm. What should the diameter of the motor pulley be if the motor speed is 2000 rpm?

13 *Elasticity*

OBJECTIVES: After completing this chapter, you should be able to:

1. Demonstrate by example and discussion your understanding of *elasticity*, *elastic limit*, *stress*, *strain*, and *ultimate strength*.
2. Write and apply formulas for calculating Young's modulus, shear modulus, and bulk modulus.
3. Define and discuss the meanings of *hardness*, *malleability*, and *ductility* as applied to metals.

Until now we have been discussing objects in motion or at rest. The objects have been assumed to be rigid and absolutely solid. But we know that wire can be stretched, that rubber tires will compress, and that bolts will sometimes break. A more complete understanding of nature requires a study of the mechanical properties of matter. The concepts of *elasticity*, *tension*, and *compression* are analyzed in this chapter. As the kinds of alloys increase and the demands on them become greater, our knowledge of such concepts becomes more important. For example, the stress placed on space ships or on cables in modern bridges is of a magnitude unheard of a few years ago.

**13-1
ELASTIC
PROPERTIES
OF MATTER**

We define an *elastic* body as one which returns to its original size and shape when a deforming force is removed. Rubber bands, golf balls, trampolines, diving boards, footballs, and springs are common examples of elastic bodies. Putty, dough, and clay are examples of inelastic bodies. For all elastic bodies, we shall find it convenient to establish a cause-and-effect relationship between a deformation and the deforming forces.

Consider the coiled spring of length *l* shown in Fig. 13-1. We can study its elasticity by adding successive weights and observing the increase in length.

Fig. 13-1 The
uniform elongation
of a spring.

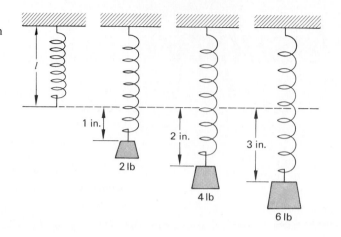

A 2-lb weight lengthens the spring by 1 in.; a 4-lb weight lengthens the spring by 2 in.; and a 6-lb weight lengthens the spring by 3 in. Evidently, there is a direct relationship between the elongation of a spring and the applied force.

Robert Hooke first stated this relationship in connection with the invention of a balance spring for a clock. In general, he found that a force **F** acting on a spring (Fig. 13-2) produces an elongation s that is directly proportional to the magnitude of the force. *Hooke's law* can be written

$$F = ks \qquad (13\text{-}1)$$

The proportionality constant k varies extremely with the type of material and is

Fig. 13-2 The
relation between a
stretching force **F**
and the elongation
s it produces.

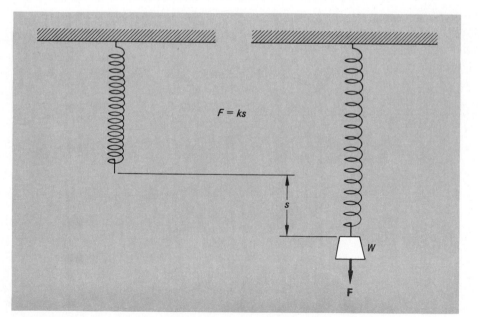

called the *spring constant*. For the example illustrated in Fig. 13-1, the spring constant is

$$k = \frac{F}{s} = 2 \text{ lb/in.}$$

Hooke's law is by no means restricted to coiled springs; it will apply to the deformation of all elastic bodies. In order to make the law more generally applicable, it will be convenient to define the terms *stress* and *strain*. Stress refers to the *cause* of an elastic deformation, whereas strain refers to the *effect*, i.e., the deformation itself.

Three common types of stresses and their corresponding deformations are shown in Fig. 13-3. A *tensile* stress occurs when equal and opposite forces are directed away from each other. A *compressive* stress occurs when equal and opposite forces are directed toward each other. A *shearing* stress occurs when equal and opposite forces do not have the same line of action.

The effectiveness of any force producing a stress is highly dependent upon the area over which the force is distributed. For this reason, a more complete definition of stress can be stated as follows:

Stress is the ratio of an applied force to the area over which it acts, e.g., newtons per square meter or pounds per square foot.

Fig. 13-3 Three common stresses shown with their corresponding deformations: (*a*) tension, (*b*) compression, (*c*) shear.

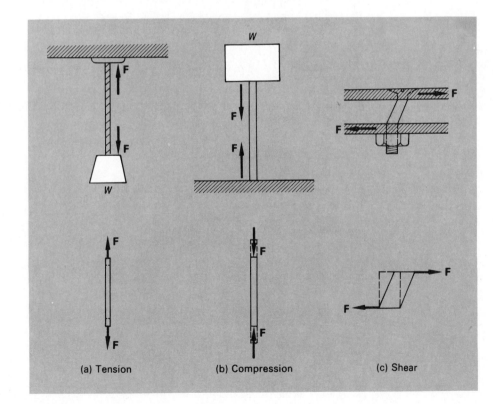

(a) Tension (b) Compression (c) Shear

As mentioned earlier, the term *strain* must represent the effect of a given stress. The general definition of strain might be as follows:

> **Strain** is the relative change in the dimensions or shape of a body as the result of an applied stress.

In the case of a tensile or compressive stress, the strain may be considered a change in length per unit length. A shearing stress, on the other hand, may alter only the shape of a body without changing its dimensions. Shearing strain is usually measured in terms of an angular displacement.

The *elastic limit* is the maximum stress a body can experience without becoming permanently deformed. For example, an aluminum rod whose cross-sectional area is 1 in.^{2} will become permanently deformed by the application of a tensile force greater than 19,000 lb. This does not mean that the aluminum rod will break at this point; it means only that the rod will not return to its original size. In fact, the tension can be increased to about 21,000 lb before the rod breaks. It is this property of metals which allows them to be drawn out into wires of smaller cross sections. The greatest stress a wire can withstand without breaking is known as its *ultimate strength*.

If the elastic limit of a material is not exceeded, we can apply Hooke's law to any elastic deformation. Within the limits of a given material, it has been experimentally verified that the ratio of a given stress to the strain it produces is a constant. In other words, the stress is directly proportional to the strain. *Hooke's law* states:

> *Provided that the elastic limit is not exceeded, an elastic deformation (strain) is directly proportional to the magnitude of the applied force per unit area (stress).*

If we call the proportionality constant the *modulus of elasticity*, we can write Hooke's law in its most general form:

$$Modulus\ of\ elasticity = \frac{stress}{strain} \qquad (13\text{-}2)$$

In the following sections we shall discuss the specific applications of this fundamental relation.

13-2 YOUNG'S MODULUS

In this section we consider longitudinal stresses and strains as they apply to wires, rods, or bars. For example, in Fig. 13-4 a force **F** is applied to the end of a wire of cross-sectional area A. The longitudinal stress is given by

$$Longitudinal\ stress = \frac{F}{A}$$

The metric unit for stress is the *newton per square meter*, which is identical to the *pascal* (Pa).

$$1\ Pa = 1\ N/m^2$$

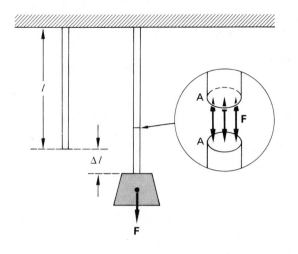

Fig. 13-4
Computing Young's modulus for a wire of cross section A. The elongation Δl is exaggerated for clarity.

The USCS unit for stress is the *pound per square inch* (lb/in.^{2}). Since the pound per square inch remains in common use, it will be helpful to compare it with the SI unit:

$$1 \text{ lb/in.}^2 = 6895 \text{ Pa} = 6.895 \text{ kPa}$$

The effect of such a stress is to stretch the wire, i.e., to increase its length. Hence the longitudinal strain can be represented by the change in length per unit length. We can write

$$\text{Longitudinal strain} = \frac{\Delta l}{l}$$

where l is the original length and Δl is the elongation. Experimentation has shown that a comparable decrease in length occurs for a compressive stress. The same equations will apply whether we are discussing an object under tension or an object under compression.

If we define the longitudinal modulus of elasticity as *Young's modulus* Y, we can write Eq. (13-2) as

$$\textit{Young's modulus} = \frac{\textit{longitudinal stress}}{\textit{longitudinal strain}}$$

$$\boxed{Y = \frac{F/A}{\Delta l / l} = \frac{Fl}{A \, \Delta l}} \tag{13-3}$$

The units of Young's modulus are the same as the units of stress, i.e., pounds per square inch or pascals. This follows since the longitudinal strain is a unitless quantity. Representative values for some of the most common materials are listed in Tables 13-1 and 13-2.

Table 13-1 Elastic Constants for Various Materials in SI Units

Material	Young's modulus Y, MPa*	Shear modulus S, MPa	Bulk modulus B, MPa	Elastic limit, MPa	Ultimate strength, MPa
Aluminum	68,900	23,700	68,900	131	145
Brass	89,600	35,300	58,600	379	455
Copper	117,000	42,300	117,000	159	338
Iron	89,600	68,900	96,500	165	324
Steel	207,000	82,700	159,000	248	489

* (1 MPa = 10^6 Pa)

Table 13-2 Elastic Constants for Various Materials in USCS Units

Material	Young's modulus Y, lb/in.^{2}	Shear modulus S, lb/in.^{2}	Bulk modulus B, lb/in.^{2}	Elastic limit, lb/in.^{2}	Ultimate strength, lb/in.^{2}
Aluminum	10×10^6	3.44×10^6	10×10^6	19,000	21,000
Brass	13×10^6	5.12×10^6	8.5×10^6	55,000	66,000
Copper	17×10^6	6.14×10^6	17×10^6	23,000	49,000
Iron	13×10^6	10×10^6	14×10^6	24,000	47,000
Steel	30×10^6	12×10^6	23×10^6	36,000	71,000

EXAMPLE 13-1

A telephone wire 120 m long and 2.2 mm in diameter is stretched by a force of 380 N. What is the longitudinal stress? If the length after stretching is 120.10 m, what is the longitudinal strain? Determine Young's modulus for the wire.

Solution

The cross-sectional area of the wire is

$$A = \frac{\pi D^2}{4} = \frac{\pi (2.2 \times 10^{-3} \text{ m})^2}{4} = 3.8 \times 10^{-6} \text{ m}^2$$

$$\text{Stress} = \frac{F}{A} = \frac{380 \text{ N}}{3.8 \times 10^{-6} \text{ m}^2}$$

$$= 100 \times 10^6 \text{ N/m}^2 = 100 \text{ MPa}$$

$$\text{Strain} = \frac{\Delta l}{l} = \frac{0.10 \text{ m}}{120 \text{ m}} = 8.3 \times 10^{-4}$$

$$Y = \frac{\text{stress}}{\text{strain}} = \frac{100 \text{ MPa}}{8.3 \times 10^{-4}} = 120,000 \text{ MPa}$$

EXAMPLE 13-2

What is the maximum load which can be hung from a steel wire $\frac{1}{4}$ in. in diameter if its elastic limit is not to be exceeded? Determine the increase in length under this load if the original length is 3 ft.

Solution

From Table 13-2, the elastic limit for steel is 36,000 lb/in.² Since this value represents the limiting stress, we write

$$\frac{F}{A} = 36{,}000 \text{ lb/in.}^2$$

where A is given by

$$A = \frac{\pi D^2}{4} = \frac{\pi (0.25 \text{ in.})^2}{4} = 0.0491 \text{ in.}^2$$

Thus the limiting load is

$$F = (36{,}000 \text{ lb/in.}^2)A$$

$$= (36{,}000 \text{ lb/in.}^2)(0.0491 \text{ in.}^2) = 1770 \text{ lb}$$

The increase in length under such a load is found from Eq. (13-3) as follows:

$$\Delta l = \frac{l}{Y}\frac{F}{A} = \frac{36 \text{ in.}}{30 \times 10^6 \text{ lb/in.}^2}(36{,}000 \text{ lb/in.}^2)$$

$$= 0.0432 \text{ in.}$$

**13-3
SHEAR
MODULUS**

Compressive and tensile stresses produce a slight change in volume as a result of altered dimensions. As mentioned earlier, a shearing stress alters only the shape of a body, leaving its volume unchanged. For example, consider the parallel noncurrent forces acting on the cube in Fig. 13-5. The applied force causes each successive layer of atoms to slip sideways, much like the pages of a book under similar stress. The interatomic forces restore the block to its original shape when the stress is relieved.

The shearing stress is defined as the ratio of the tangential force **F** to the area A over which it is applied. The shearing strain is defined as the angle ϕ (in radians), which is called the *shearing angle* (refer to Fig. 13-5b). Applying Hooke's law, we can now define the *shear modulus S* as follows:

$$S = \frac{\text{shearing stress}}{\text{shearing strain}} = \frac{F/A}{\phi} \tag{13-4}$$

Fig. 13-5 Shearing stress and shearing strain.

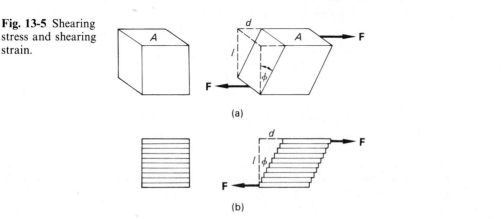

(a)

(b)

The angle ϕ is usually so small that it is approximately equal to tan ϕ. Making use of this fact, we can rewrite Eq. (13-4) in the form

$$S = \frac{F/A}{\tan \phi} = \frac{F/A}{d/l} \qquad (13\text{-}5)$$

Since the value of S is an indication of the rigidity of a body, it is sometimes referred to as the *modulus of rigidity*.

EXAMPLE 13-3 A steel stud (Fig. 13-6) 1 in. in diameter projects 1.5 in. out from the wall. If the end of the bolt is subjected to a shearing force of 8000 lb, compute its downward deflection.

Fig. 13-6 The downward deflection of a stud is an example of shearing strain.

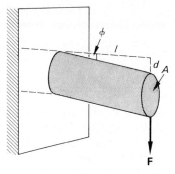

Solution The cross-sectional area is

$$A = \frac{\pi D^2}{4} = \frac{\pi(1 \text{ in.})^2}{4} = 0.785 \text{ in.}^2$$

If we represent the downward deflection by d, we can solve as follows:

$$S = \frac{F/A}{d/l} = \frac{Fl}{Ad}$$

$$d = \frac{Fl}{AS} = \frac{(8000 \text{ lb})(1.5 \text{ in.})}{(0.785 \text{ in.}^2)(12 \times 10^6 \text{ lb/in.}^2)}$$

$$= 1.27 \times 10^{-3} \text{ in.}$$

You should show that this deflection results in a shearing angle of 8.47×10^{-4} rad.

13-4 VOLUME ELASTICITY; BULK MODULUS

So far we have considered stresses which cause a change in the shape of an object or result in primarily one-dimensional strains. In this section we shall be concerned with changes in volume. For example, consider the cube in Fig. 13-7 on which forces are applied uniformly over the surface. The initial volume of the cube is denoted by V, and the area of each face is represented by A. The resultant force $\mathbf{F}$ applied normal to each face causes a change in volume $-\Delta V$. The minus sign indicates that the change represents a volume reduction. The

Fig. 13-7 The bulk modulus. The original volume is reduced by the application of a uniform compressive force on each face.

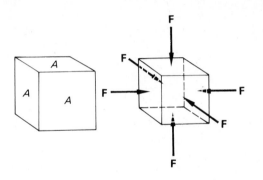

volume stress F/A is the normal force per unit area, whereas the volume strain $-\Delta V/V$ is the change in volume per unit volume. Applying Hooke's law, we define the modulus of volume elasticity, or *bulk modulus*, as follows:

$$B = \frac{\text{volume stress}}{\text{volume strain}} = -\frac{F/A}{\Delta V/V} \qquad (13\text{-}6)$$

This type of strain applies to liquids as well as solids. Table 13-3 lists the bulk moduli for a few of the more common liquids. When working with liquids, it is sometimes more convenient to represent the stress as pressure P, which is defined as the force per unit area F/A. With this definition, we can rewrite Eq. (13-6):

$$B = \frac{-P}{\Delta V/V} \qquad (13\text{-}7)$$

Table 13-3 Bulk Moduli for Liquids

Liquid	Bulk modulus B	
	lb/in.^{2}	MPa
Benzene	1.5×10^5	1,050
Ethyl alcohol	1.6×10^5	1,100
Mercury	40×10^5	27,000
Oil	2.5×10^5	1,700
Water	3.1×10^5	2,100

The reciprocal of the bulk modulus is called the *compressibility k*. Often it is more convenient to study the elasticity of materials by measuring their compressibilities. By definition,

$$k = \frac{1}{B} = -\frac{1}{P}\frac{\Delta V}{V_0} \qquad (13\text{-}8)$$

Equation (13-8) indicates that the compressibility is the fractional change in volume per unit increase in pressure.

EXAMPLE 13-4   A hydrostatic press contains 6 ft³ of water. Find the decrease in volume of the water when it is subjected to a pressure of 2400 lb/in.²

Solution   The initial volume of the water is

$$V = (6 \text{ ft}^3) \frac{1728 \text{ in.}^3}{1 \text{ ft}^3} = 10,370 \text{ in.}^3$$

The decrease in volume is given from Eq. (13-7):

$$\Delta V = -\frac{PV}{B} = -\frac{(2400 \text{ lb/in.}^2)(10,370 \text{ in.}^3)}{3.1 \times 10^5 \text{ lb/in.}^2}$$

$$= -80.3 \text{ in.}^3$$

Since the units of pressure and bulk modulus are the same, it is not necessary to convert the volume from cubic feet to cubic inches, as in the above example, but the decrease in volume is so minute that it is usually better to express the change in the smaller units.

**13-5
OTHER
PHYSICAL
PROPERTIES
OF METALS**

In addition to the elasticity, the tensile strength, and the shearing strength of materials, there are other important properties of metals. A solid consists of molecules arranged so closely together that they attract each other very strongly. This attraction, called *cohesion*, gives a solid a definite shape and size. It also affects its usefulness to industry as a working material. Such properties as hardness, ductility, malleability, and conductivity must be understood before metals are chosen for specific applications. Three of these properties are illustrated in Fig. 13-8.

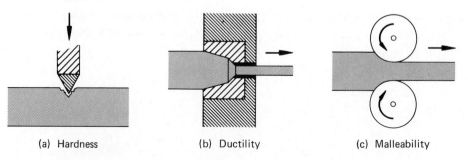

(a) Hardness   (b) Ductility   (c) Malleability

Fig. 13-8 Illustrating the working properties of metals. (*a*) A hard metal resists penetration. (*b*) A ductile metal can be drawn into a wire. (*c*) A malleable metal can be rolled into sheets.

Hardness is an industrial term used to describe the ability of metals to resist forces that tend to penetrate them. Hard materials resist being scratched, worn away, penetrated, or otherwise damaged physically. Some metals such as sodium and potassium are very soft, while iron and steel are two of the hardest materials. The hardness of metals is tested with machines that push a cone-shaped diamond point into test materials. The penetration is measured, and a hardness reading is taken directly from a dial.

Two other special properties of materials are *ductility* and *malleability*. The meaning of each of these terms is seen from Fig. 13-8. Ductility is defined as the ability of a metal to be drawn out into a wire. Tungsten and copper are very ductile. Malleability is the property which enables us to hammer or bend metals into any desired shape or to roll them into sheets. Most metals are malleable, gold being the most malleable.

Conductivity refers to the ability of metals to permit the flow of electricity. The best conductors are silver, copper, gold, and aluminum, in that order. More will be said about this property in later chapters.

SUMMARY

In industry, we must utilize materials effectively and for appropriate situations. Otherwise, metal failures will result in costly damage or serious injury to employees. In this chapter, we have discussed the elastic properties of matter and some of the formulas used to predict the effects of stress on certain solids. The following points will summarize this chapter:

- According to *Hooke's law*, an elastic body will deform or elongate an amount s under the application of a force F. The constant of proportionality k is the *spring constant*:

$$F = ks \qquad k = \frac{F}{s} \qquad \text{Hooke's Law}$$

- *Stress* is the ratio of an applied force to the area over which it acts. *Strain* is the relative change in dimensions which results from the stress. For example,

$$\text{Longitudinal stress} = \frac{F}{A} \qquad \text{Longitudinal strain} = \frac{\Delta l}{l}$$

- The *modulus of elasticity* is the constant ratio of stress to strain:

$$\text{Modulus of elasticity} = \frac{stress}{strain}$$

- *Young's modulus* Y is for longitudinal deformations:

$$Y = \frac{F/A}{\Delta l/l} \qquad \text{or} \qquad Y = \frac{Fl}{A \cdot \Delta l} \qquad \text{Young's Modulus}$$

- A shearing strain occurs when an angular deformation ϕ is produced:

$$S = \frac{F/A}{\tan \phi} \qquad \text{or} \qquad S = \frac{F/A}{d/l} \qquad \text{Shear Modulus}$$

- Whenever an applied stress results in a change in volume ΔV, you will need the *bulk modulus B*, given by

$$B = -\frac{F/A}{\Delta V/V}$$

Bulk Modulus

The reciprocal of the bulk modulus is called the compressibility.

QUESTIONS

13-1. Define the following terms:
  a. Elasticity   **g.** Strain
  b. Hooke's law   **h.** Elastic limit
  c. Spring constant   **i.** Ultimate strength
  d. Tensile stress   **j.** Young's modulus
  e. Compressive stress   **k.** Shear modulus
  f. Shear stress   **l.** Bulk modulus

13-2. Explain clearly the relationship between stress and strain.

13-3. Two wires have the same length and cross-sectional area but are not of the same material. Each wire is hung from the ceiling with a 2000-lb weight attached. The wire on the left stretches twice as far as the one on the right. Which has the greater Young's modulus?

13-4. Does Young's modulus depend on the length and cross-sectional area? Explain.

13-5. Two wires, *A* and *B*, are made of the same material and are subjected to the same loads. Discuss their relative elongations when **(a)** wire *A* is twice as long as wire *B* and has twice the diameter of wire *B* and **(b)** wire *A* is twice as long as wire *B* and has one-half the diameter of wire *B*.

13-6. After studying the various elastic constants given in Tables 13-1 and 13-2, would you say it was usually easier to stretch a material or to shear a material? Explain.

13-7. A 400-lb weight is evenly supported by three wires of the same dimensions, one of copper, one of aluminum, and one of steel. Which wire experiences the greatest stress? Which experiences the least stress? Which wire experiences the greatest strain? Which experiences the least strain?

13-8. Discuss the various stresses resulting when a machine screw is tightened.

13-9. Give several practical examples of longitudinal, shearing, and volume strains.

13-10. For a given metal, would you expect there to be any relation between its modulus of elasticity and its coefficient of restitution? Discuss.

13-11. Which has the greater compressibility, steel or water?

PROBLEMS

13-1. A coil spring is used to support a 1.8-kg mass. If the spring stretches 2 cm, what is the spring constant? What mass would be required to stretch the spring 5 cm?

Ans. 882 N/m, 44.1 N.

13-2. A 10-kg mass is supported by a spring whose constant is 12 N/cm. Compute the elongation of the spring.

13-3. A steel wire 15 ft long and 0.1 in.^{2} in cross section is found to increase its length by 0.01 ft under the tension of a 2000-lb force. What is Young's modulus for the steel wire?

Ans. 30×10^6 lb/in.^{2}

13-4. A wire whose cross section is 4 mm^2 is stretched by 0.1 mm by a certain weight. How far will a wire of the same material and length stretch if its cross-sectional area is 8 mm^2 and the same weight is attached?

13-5. A no. 18 copper wire has a diameter of 0.04 in. and is originally 10 ft long. **(a)** What is the greatest load that can be supported by this wire without exceeding its elastic limit? **(b)** Compute the change in length of the wire under this load. **(c)** What is the maximum load that can be supported without breaking the wire? **(d)** What is the maximum elongation?

Ans. **(a)** 28.9 lb **(b)** 0.0135 ft **(c)** 61.6 lb **(d)** 0.0288 ft.

13-6. An aluminum rivet 12 mm in diameter is subjected to a stress of 31000 kPa. What force is applied to the rivet? If the rivet is initially 30 cm long, how far will it stretch?

13-7. What is the minimum diameter of a brass rod if it is to support a 400-N load without exceeding the elastic limit?

Ans. 1.16×10^{-3} m.

13-8. A solid cylindrical steel column is 12 ft high and 6 in. in diameter. What will its decrease in length be when supporting a load of 90 tons?

13-9. How much will a 600-mm length of brass wire stretch when a 4-kg mass is hung from its end? The wire has a diameter of 1.2 mm.

Ans. 2.32×10^{-4} m.

13-10. A steel piano wire has an ultimate strength of about 35,000 lb/in.^{2} How large a load can a 0.5-in.-diameter steel wire hold before breaking?

13-11. The shear modulus for copper is about 4.2×10^{10} Pa. A 3000-N shearing force is applied to the upper surface of a copper cube which is 40 mm on a side. How large a distortion angle (in degrees) is caused by the force?

Ans. 2.56×10^{-15} deg.

13-12. A cube of aluminum 3 in. on a side is subjected to a shearing force of 20,000 lb. Compute the deflection d of the cube and the shearing angle ϕ in radians.

13-13. A steel plate 0.5 in. thick has an ultimate shearing strength of 50,000 lb/in.^{2} What force must be applied to punch a $\frac{1}{4}$-in. hole through the plate?

Ans. 19,600 lb.

13-14. Two sheets of aluminum on an aircraft wing are to be held together by aluminum rivets of cross-sectional area 0.25 in.^{2} The shearing stress on each rivet must not exceed one-tenth of the elastic limit for aluminum. How many rivets are needed if each rivet supports the same fraction of a total shearing force of 25,000 lb?

13-15. The twisting of a cylindrical shaft (Fig. 13-9) through an angle θ is an example of a shearing strain. An analysis of the situation shows that the angle of twist in radians is given by

$$\theta = \frac{2Ll}{\pi SR^4}$$

where L = applied torque R = radius of cylinder
         l = length of cylinder S = shear modulus for material

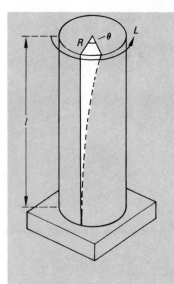

Fig. 13-9 A torque τ applied at one end of a solid cylinder causes it to twist through an angle θ.

If a torque of 100 lb · ft is applied to the end of a cylindrical steel shaft 10 ft long and 2 in. in diameter, what will the angle of twist be in radians?

Ans. 7.64×10^{-3} rad.

13-16. An engine delivers 140 hp at 800 rpm to an 8-ft solid-iron drive shaft 2 in. in diameter. Find the angle of twist in the drive shaft (refer to Prob. 13-15).

13-17. What increase in pressure is required to decrease the volume of 200 L of water by 0.004 percent?

Ans. 4.06×10^{-3} L.

13-18. A piston of surface area 10 in.^{2} exerts a force of 800 lb on 1 liter of benzene. What is the decrease in volume of the benzene?

13-19. Compute the compressibility of glycerin if a pressure of 290 lb/in.^{2} causes a volume of 64 in.^{3} to decrease by 3×10^{-3} in.^{3}

Ans. 1.6×10^{-7} in.^{2}/lb.

14 Simple Harmonic Motion

OBJECTIVES: After completing this chapter, you should be able to:

1. Describe and apply the relationship between force and displacement in simple harmonic motion.

2. Use the reference circle to describe the variation in magnitude and direction of displacement, velocity, and acceleration for simple harmonic motion.

3. Write and apply formulas for the determination of displacement x, velocity v, or acceleration a in terms of time, frequency, and amplitude.

4. Write and apply a relationship between the frequency of motion and the mass of a vibrating object when the spring constant is known.

5. Compute the frequency or period in simple harmonic motion when the position and acceleration are given.

6. Describe the motion of a simple pendulum and calculate the length required to produce a given frequency.

Until now we have discussed the motion of objects under the influence of a constant, unchanging force. Such motion was described by calculating the position and velocity as functions of time. However, the real world often consists of varying forces. Common examples are swinging pendulums, balance wheels of watches, tuning forks, a mass vibrating at the end of a coiled spring, and vibrating air columns in musical instruments. In these cases and many others, we need a more complete description of motion caused by a resultant force which varies in a predictable manner.

14-1 PERIODIC MOTION

Whenever an object is deformed, an elastic restoring force appears which is proportional to the deformation. When released, such an object will vibrate back and forth about its equilibrium position. For example, after a swimmer springs from a diving board (Fig. 14-1), the board continues to vibrate about its normal position for a definite length of time.

Fig. 14-1 The periodic vibration of a diving board.

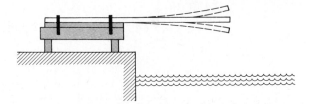

This type of motion is said to be *periodic* because the position and velocity of the moving particles are repeated as a function of time. Since the restoring force is reduced after each vibration, the board eventually comes to rest.

Periodic motion is that motion in which a body moves back and forth over a fixed path, returning to each position and velocity after a definite interval of time.

An ice puck coupled to a spring is shown in Fig. 14-2. The ice puck is a laboratory device which rides on a cushion of carbon dioxide, approximating frictionless motion. Suppose we pull the ice puck to the side and release it so that it oscillates about its initial position O without friction. According to Hooke's law, the restoring force **F** is directly proportional to the displacement x of the ice puck from its equilibrium position O. Since the restoring force is always opposed to the displacement, a negative sign must be introduced. Thus we write

$$F = -kx \tag{14-1}$$

Fig. 14-2 The frictionless ice puck can be used to illustrate simple harmonic motion. The restoring force **F** is always directed toward the center of oscillation O.

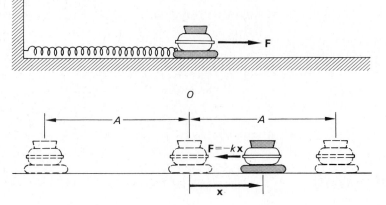

The maximum displacement of the ice puck from its equilibrium position is called the *amplitude A*. It is at this position that the ice puck experiences the maximum restoring force and consequently its maximum acceleration. The force decreases as the puck approaches its center of oscillation, becoming zero at that point. However, the momentum of the puck carries it on past the center, bringing the restoring force of the spring back into play again. This force increases until the puck comes to a stop at its maximum displacement, whereupon it begins its return trip. If there were no loss of energy due to friction, the back-and-forth motion would continue indefinitely. This type of oscillatory motion in the absence of friction is known as *simple harmonic motion* (SHM).

> **Simple harmonic motion** is periodic motion in the absence of friction produced by a restoring force which is directly proportional to the displacement and oppositely directed.

The *period T* is defined as the time for one complete trip, or oscillation. For example, if the ice puck is released from the right at a distance A from its equilibrium position, the time required for it to return to that position is its period of vibration. It must be pointed out, however, that every point in the vibratory path must be covered in measuring a complete oscillation. The time required to move from the center of oscillation to the distance A and back represents only one-half of a period.

The *frequency f* is the number of complete oscillations per unit time. Since the period is the time for one oscillation, the frequency must be the reciprocal of the period, or

$$f = \frac{1}{T}$$

The unit of frequency is often expressed as vibrations per second or as inverse seconds (s^{-1}); the SI unit for frequency is the *hertz* (Hz).

$$1 \text{ Hz} = \frac{1}{s}$$

Thus, a frequency of 500 vibrations per second becomes 500 Hz.

14-2 THE REFERENCE CIRCLE

It has been shown that an object vibrating with SHM is influenced by a restoring force that is directly proportional to its displacement. If we apply Newton's second law to Eq. (14-1), we shall see that the acceleration is also proportional to the displacement. Thus $F = ma = -kx$ from which

$$a = -\frac{k}{m} x \tag{14-2}$$

As long as the mass m remains constant, the ratio k/m will also be constant, indicating that the magnitude of the acceleration increases with the displacement. The minus sign appears because the acceleration is always directed toward the center of oscillation.

Since the acceleration in SHM is not constant, the equations derived in earlier chapters will not apply. To determine new relationships directly requires the use of calculus. Fortunately, these equations can be deduced by geometrical methods. When a body moves in a circular path with uniform speed, its linear projection moves with SHM. This fact is illustrated in Fig. 14-3, where the shadow of a ball attached to a rotating disk oscillates back and forth with periodic motion. This experiment suggests that our knowledge of uniform circular motion may be helpful in describing SHM.

Fig. 14-3 The projection or shadow of a ball attached to a rotating disk moves with SHM.

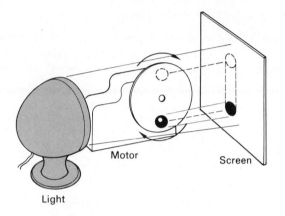

The *reference circle* in Fig. 14-4 is used to compare the motion of an object moving in a circle with its horizontal projection. Since it is the motion of the projection that we wish to study, we shall refer to the position *P* of the object moving in a circle as the *reference point*. The radius of the reference circle is equal to the amplitude of the horizontal oscillation. If the linear speed v_T and

Fig. 14-4 Displacement in SHM.

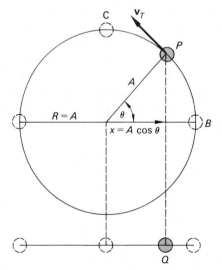

angular speed ω of the reference point are constant, the projection Q will move back and forth with SHM. Time is assigned a zero value when the reference point is at B in Fig. 14-4. At any later time t, the reference point P will have moved through an angle θ. The displacement x of the projection Q is therefore

$$x = A \cos \theta$$

Recalling that the angle $\theta = \omega t$, we can now write the displacement as a function of the angular velocity of the reference point.

$$x = A \cos \theta = A \cos \omega t \qquad (14\text{-}3)$$

Although the angular velocity ω is useful for describing motion of the reference point P, it is not directly applied to the projection Q. However, we should recall that the angular velocity is related to the frequency of revolution by

$$\omega = 2\pi f$$

where ω is expressed in radians per second and f is the number of revolutions per second. It should also be recognized that the projection Q will describe one complete oscillation while the reference point describes one complete revolution. Thus the frequency f is the same for each point. Substituting $\omega = 2\pi f$ into Eq. (14-3), we obtain

$$\boxed{x = A \cos 2\pi f t} \qquad (14\text{-}4)$$

This equation can be applied to compute the displacement of a body moving with SHM of amplitude A and frequency f. Remember that the displacement x is always measured from the center of oscillation.

**14-3
VELOCITY
IN SIMPLE
HARMONIC
MOTION**

Let us consider a body moving back and forth with SHM under the influence of a restoring force. Since the direction of the vibrating body is reversed at the end points of its motion, its velocity must be zero when its displacement is a maximum. It is then accelerated toward the center by the restoring force until it reaches its maximum speed at the center of oscillation, i.e., when its displacement is zero.

In Fig. 14-5 the velocity of a vibrating body is compared at three instants with corresponding points on a reference circle. It will be noticed that the velocity $\mathbf{v}$ of the vibrating body at any instant is the horizontal component of the tangential velocity $\mathbf{v}_T$ of the reference point. At point B the reference point is moving vertically upward and has no horizontal velocity. This point therefore corresponds to the zero velocity of the vibrating body when it reaches its amplitude A. At point C the horizontal component of $\mathbf{v}_T$ is equal to its entire magnitude. This point corresponds to a position of maximum velocity for the vibrating body, i.e., at its center of oscillation. In general, the velocity of the vibrating body at any point Q is determined from the reference circle to be

$$v = -v_T \sin \theta = -v_T \sin \omega t \qquad (14\text{-}5)$$

Fig. 14-5 Velocity and the reference circle.

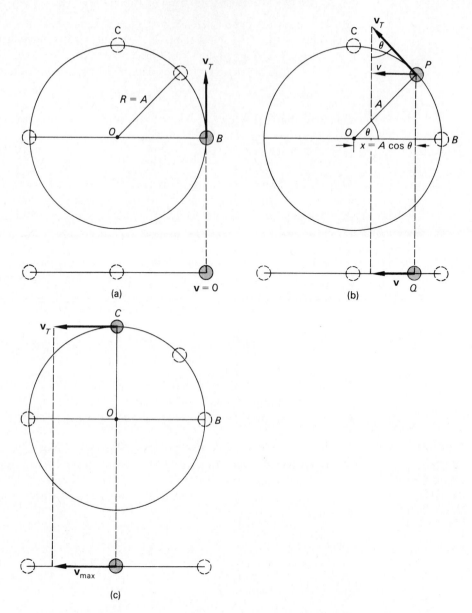

(a)

(b)

(c)

The minus sign appears since the direction of the velocity is toward the left. We can make this equation more useful by recalling the relationship between the tangential velocity v_T and the angular velocity:

$$v_T = \omega A = 2\pi f A$$

Substitution into Eq. (14-5) yields

$$\boxed{v = -2\pi f A \sin 2\pi f t} \tag{14-6}$$

This equation will give the velocity of a vibrating body at any instant if it is remembered that sin θ is negative when the reference point lies below the diameter of the reference circle.

EXAMPLE 14-1 An ice puck attached to a spring, as in Fig. 14-2, is pulled to the right a distance of 6 cm and released. (*a*) If it returns to the point of release in 2 s and continues to vibrate with SHM, compute its position and velocity after 5.2 s. (*b*) What is its maximum velocity?

Solution (*a*) The time for one complete vibration is 2 s. Thus the frequency is given by

$$f = \frac{1}{T} = \frac{1}{2\ s} = 0.5\ \text{Hz}$$

The position after 5.2 s is

$$x = A\ \cos\ 2\pi f t$$
$$= (6\ \text{cm})\ \cos\ [(2\pi)(0.5\ \text{Hz})(5.2\ \text{s})]$$
$$= (6\ \text{cm})\ \cos\ (16.3\ \text{rad})$$

In order to evaluate cos (16.3 rad), we convert to degrees.

$$(16.3\ \text{rad})\ \frac{57.3°}{1\ \text{rad}} = 934°$$
$$\cos\ 934° = \cos\ 214° = -\cos\ 34° = -0.829$$

Thus the displacement x is

$$x = (6\ \text{cm})(-0.829) = -4.97$$

The minus sign indicates that the ice puck is 4.97 cm to the left of its equilibrium position.

The velocity of the puck after 5.2 s is found from

$$v = -2\pi f A\ \sin\ 2\pi f t$$
$$= -2\pi(0.5\ \text{Hz})(6\ \text{cm})(\sin\ 214°)$$
$$= (-18.8\ \text{cm/s})(-\sin\ 34°)$$
$$= 10.5\ \text{cm/s}$$

The velocity is positive, indicating that it is moving to the right.

Solution (*b*) The maximum velocity occurs when the displacement is zero or when the reference angle is 90 or 270°. Thus

$$v_{\text{max}} = -2\pi f A\ \sin\ 90° = -2\pi f A$$
$$= -2\pi(0.5\ \text{Hz})(6\ \text{cm})$$
$$= -18.8\ \text{cm/s}$$

This represents the maximum velocity directed to the left since we chose 90° as a reference angle. If 270° had been chosen, a positive value would have resulted.

**14-4
ACCELERA-
TION IN
SIMPLE
HARMONIC
MOTION**

The velocity of a vibrating body is never constant. Therefore, although it was not often mentioned, acceleration plays a very important role in the equations derived in the previous section. We now attempt to obtain an expression which will allow us to determine the acceleration of objects under the influence of a restoring force.

At the position of maximum displacement, the velocity of a vibrating object is zero. It is at this instant that the body is acted on by the maximum restoring force. Thus the acceleration of the body is a maximum when its veloc-

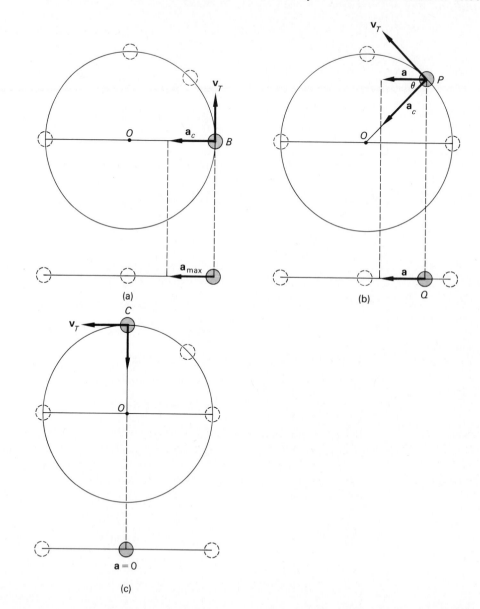

(a)

(b)

(c)

ity is zero. As the object approaches its equilibrium position, the restoring force (and therefore the acceleration) is reduced until it reaches zero at the center of oscillation. At the equilibrium position, the acceleration is zero and the velocity has its maximum value.

Figure 14-6 demonstrates that the acceleration a of a particle moving with SHM is equal to the horizontal component of the centripetal acceleration a_c of the reference point. From the figure,

$$a = -a_c \cos \theta = -a_c \cos \omega t \qquad (14\text{-}7)$$

The minus sign indicates that the acceleration is directed toward the left. Recalling that $a_c = \omega^2 R$ and that $R = A$, we can rewrite Eq. (14-7) as

$$a = -\omega^2 A \cos \omega t$$

Substituting $\omega = 2\pi f$, as in the previous section, we obtain

$$a = -4\pi^2 f^2 A \cos 2\pi f t \qquad (14\text{-}8)$$

Equation (14-8) can be simplified by noting from Eq. (14-3) that

$$\cos \theta = \cos 2\pi f t = \frac{x}{A}$$

from which

$$a = -4\pi^2 f^2 A \, \frac{x}{A}$$

or

$$\boxed{a = -4\pi^2 f^2 x} \qquad (14\text{-}9)$$

Therefore, the acceleration is directly proportional to the displacement and opposite in direction.

14-5 THE PERIOD AND FREQUENCY

From the information now established concerning position, speed, and acceleration of vibrating bodies, we can derive some very useful formulas for computing the period or frequency of vibration. For example, if we solve Eq. (14-9) for the frequency f, we obtain

$$\boxed{f = \frac{1}{2\pi} \sqrt{-\frac{a}{x}}} \qquad (14\text{-}10)$$

Since the displacement x and the acceleration are always opposite in sign, the term $-a/x$ is always positive.

The period T is the reciprocal of the frequency. Making use of this fact in Eq. (14-10), we define the period by

$$T = 2\pi \sqrt{-\frac{x}{a}} \qquad (14\text{-}11)$$

Thus, if the acceleration is known at a particular displacement, the period of vibration can be computed.

When the motion of bodies under the influence of an elastic restoring force is considered, it is more convenient to express the period as a function of the spring constant and mass of the vibrating body. This can be done by comparing Eqs. (14-2) and (14-9):

$$a = -\frac{k}{m}x \qquad a = -4\pi^2 f^2 x$$

Combining these relations, we obtain

$$4\pi^2 f^2 = \frac{k}{m}$$

from which the frequency is

$$f = \frac{1}{2\pi}\sqrt{\frac{k}{m}} \qquad (14\text{-}12)$$

Finally, the period T is given by the reciprocal of the frequency. Thus

$$T = 2\pi \sqrt{\frac{m}{k}} \qquad (14\text{-}13)$$

Note that neither the period nor the frequency depends upon the amplitude (maximum displacement) of the vibrating body. They depend only on the spring constant and the mass of the vibrating body.

EXAMPLE 14-2 A 2-kg steel ball is attached to the end of a flat strip of metal that is clamped at its base, as shown in Fig. 14-7. (*a*) If a force of 5 N is required to displace the ball by 16 cm, what will its period of vibration be upon release? (*b*) What is its maximum acceleration?

Solution (a) A force of 5 N displaces the mass by 16 cm. Thus the spring constant is

$$k = \frac{F}{x} = \frac{5 \text{ N}}{0.16 \text{ m}} = 31.2 \text{ N/m}$$

The period is found from Eq. (14-13).

$$T = 2\pi \sqrt{\frac{m}{k}} = 2\pi \sqrt{\frac{2 \text{ kg}}{31.2 \text{ N/m}}}$$

$$= 2\pi(0.253) = 1.59 \text{ s}$$

Fig. 14-7

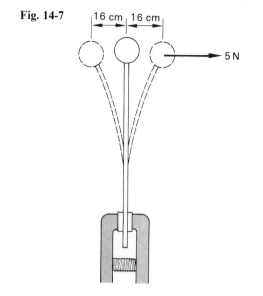

16 cm | 16 cm

5 N

Solution (b)   The maximum acceleration occurs when the displacement is a maximum, i.e., when $x = 0.16$ m. Thus

$$a = -4\pi^2 f^2 x = -\frac{4\pi^2}{T^2} x$$

$$= -\frac{4\pi^2(0.16 \text{ m})}{(1.59 \text{ s})^2} = -2.5 \text{ m/s}^2$$

**14-6
THE
SIMPLE
PENDULUM**

When a heavy pendulum bob is swinging at the end of a light cord or rod, as in Fig. 14-8, it approximates SHM. If we assume that all the mass is concentrated at the center of gravity of the bob and that the restoring force acts at a single point, we refer to this apparatus as a *simple* pendulum. Although this assumption is never strictly true, a close approximation is obtained by making the mass of the connecting rod or cord very small in comparison with the pendulum bob.

Notice that the displacement x of the bob is not along a straight line but lies along the arc subtended by the angle θ. From methods discussed in Chap. 11, the length of the displacement is simply the product of the angle θ and the length of the cord. Thus

$$x = l\theta$$

If the motion of the bob is SHM, the restoring force must be given by

$$F = -kx = -kl\theta \qquad (14\text{-}14)$$

which means that the restoring force should be proportional to θ since the length l is constant. Let us examine the restoring force to see if this is the case.

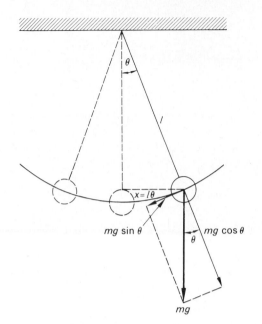

Fig. 14-8 The simple pendulum approximates SHM.

In the back-and-forth movement of the pendulum bob, the necessary restoring force is provided by the tangential component of the weight. From Fig. 14-8, we can write

$$F = -mg \sin \theta \qquad (14\text{-}15)$$

Thus the restoring force is proportional to $\sin \theta$ instead of to θ. The conclusion must be that the bob does not oscillate with SHM. However, if we stipulate that the angle θ is small, $\sin \theta$ will be approximately equal to the angle θ in radians. You can verify this approximation by considering several small angles:

$\sin \theta$	θ (rad)
$\sin 6° = 0.1045$	$6° = 0.1047$
$\sin 12° = 0.208$	$12° = 0.209$
$\sin 27° = 0.454$	$27° = 0.471$

When the approximation $\sin \theta \approx \theta$ is used, Eq. (14-15) becomes

$$F = -mg \sin \theta = -mg\theta$$

Comparing this relation with Eq. (14-14), we obtain

$$F = -kl\theta = -mg\theta$$

from which

$$\frac{m}{k} = \frac{1}{g}$$

Substitution of this proportion into Eq. (14-13) yields an expression for the period of a simple pendulum:

$$T = 2\pi \sqrt{\frac{l}{g}} \tag{14-16}$$

Notice that for small amplitudes the period of a simple pendulum is a function of neither the mass of the bob nor the amplitude of vibration. In fact, since the acceleration of gravity is constant, the period is determined solely by the length of the connecting cord or rod.

EXAMPLE 14-3   In a laboratory experiment a student is given a stop watch, a wooden bob, and a piece of cord. He is then asked to determine the acceleration of gravity g. If he constructs a simple pendulum of length 1 m and measures the period to be 2 s, what value will he obtain for g?

Solution   Squaring both sides of Eq. (14-16) gives

$$T^2 = 4\pi^2 \frac{l}{g}$$

from which

$$g = \frac{4\pi^2 l}{T^2} = \frac{4\pi^2 (1\ \text{m})}{(2\ \text{s})^2}$$

$$= 9.87\ \text{m/s}^2$$

**14-7
THE
TORSION
PENDULUM**

Another example of SHM is afforded by the torsion pendulum (Fig. 14-9), which consists of a solid disk or cylinder supported at the end of a thin rod. If the disk is twisted through an angle θ, the restoring torque τ is directly proportional to the angular displacement. Thus

$$\tau = -k'\theta \tag{14-17}$$

where k' is a constant which depends on the material from which the thin rod is made. (See Prob. 13-11.)

Fig. 14-9 The torsion pendulum.

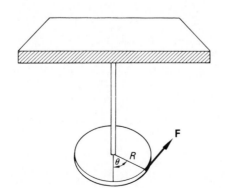

When the disk is released, the restoring torque produces an angular acceleration which is directly proportional to the angular displacement. The period of the simple angular harmonic motion thus produced is given by

$$T = 2\pi \sqrt{\frac{I}{k'}} \qquad (14\text{-}18)$$

where I is the moment of inertia of the vibrating system and k' is the torsion constant defined in Eq. (14-17).

EXAMPLE 14-4   A solid disk of mass 0.16 kg and radius 0.12 m is twisted through an angle of 1 rad and released. (a) If the torsion constant of the wire supporting the disk is 0.025 N · m/rad, calculate the maximum angular acceleration. (b) What is the period of oscillation?

Solution (a)   The moment of inertia of the disk is

$$I = \tfrac{1}{2}mR^2 = \tfrac{1}{2}(0.16 \text{ kg})(0.12 \text{ m})^2$$

$$= 1.15 \times 10^{-3} \text{ kg} \cdot \text{m}^2$$

The angular acceleration is a maximum when the angular displacement is 1 rad. From Eq. (14-17) we have

$$\tau = I\alpha = -k'\theta$$

$$\alpha = -\frac{k'\theta}{I} = \frac{-(0.025 \text{ N} \cdot \text{m/rad})(1 \text{ rad})}{1.15 \times 10^{-3} \text{ kg} \cdot \text{m}^2}$$

$$= -21.7 \text{ rad/s}^2$$

Solution (b)   The period from Eq. (14-18) is

$$T = 2\pi \sqrt{\frac{I}{k'}} = 2\pi \sqrt{\frac{1.15 \times 10^{-3} \text{ kg} \cdot \text{m}^2}{0.025 \text{ N} \cdot \text{m/rad}}}$$

$$= 2\pi(0.214)s = 1.35 \text{ s}$$

Notice that the period is not a function of the angular displacement.

SUMMARY

Simple harmonic motion is periodic motion in which the restoring force is proportional to the displacement. Such vibratory motion without friction produces predictable variations in displacement and velocity. The major concepts discussed in this chapter are summarized below:

- Simple harmonic motion is produced by a *restoring force F* given by:

$$\boxed{F = -kx} \qquad \textit{Restoring Force}$$

- Since $F = ma = -kx$, the acceleration produced by a restoring force is

$$\boxed{a = -\frac{k}{m}x} \qquad \textit{Acceleration}$$

- A convenient way to study simple harmonic motion is to use the *reference circle*. The variations in displacement x, velocity v, and acceleration a can be seen by reference to Figs. 14-4, 14-5, and 14-6.
- For SHM the displacement, velocity, and acceleration may be expressed in terms of the amplitude A, the time t, and the frequency of vibration f:

$$x = A \cos 2\pi f t \qquad\qquad Displacement$$

$$v = -2\pi f A \sin 2\pi f t \qquad\qquad Velocity$$

$$a = -4\pi^2 f^2 x \qquad\qquad Acceleration$$

- The period T and the frequency f in simple harmonic motion are found from

$$f = \frac{1}{2\pi}\sqrt{-\frac{a}{x}} \quad \text{or} \quad f = \frac{1}{2\pi}\sqrt{\frac{k}{m}} \qquad Frequency$$

$$T = 2\pi\sqrt{-\frac{x}{a}} \quad \text{or} \quad T = 2\pi\sqrt{\frac{m}{k}} \qquad Period$$

- For a simple pendulum of length l, the period is given by

$$T = 2\pi\sqrt{-\frac{l}{g}} \qquad Period\ of\ Simple\ Pendulum$$

- A torsion pendulum consists of a solid disk or cylinder of moment of inertia I suspended at the end of a thin rod. If the torsion constant k' is known, the period is given by

$$T = 2\pi\sqrt{\frac{I}{k'}} \qquad Period\ of\ Torsion\ Pendulum$$

QUESTIONS

14-1. Define the following terms:

a. Simple harmonic motion   f. Displacement
b. Spring constant   g. Amplitude
c. Restoring force   h. Frequency
d. Simple pendulum   i. Period
e. Torsion constant   j. Hertz

14-2. Give several examples of motion which in your opinion is SHM.

14-3. What effect will doubling the amplitude A of a body moving with SHM have on **(a)** the period, **(b)** the maximum velocity, and **(c)** the maximum acceleration?

14-4. A 2-kg mass m_1 moves in SHM with a frequency f_1. What mass m_2 will cause the system to vibrate with twice the frequency?

14-5. Explain, with the use of diagrams, why the velocity in SHM is greatest when the acceleration is the least.

14-6. An ice puck is attached to a spring of force constant k and set into vibration of amplitude A, as shown in Fig. 14-2. The spring is then replaced with one with a force constant of $4k$, and the ice puck is set into vibration at the same amplitude. Compare their periods and frequencies of oscillation.

14-7. A pendulum clock runs too slow and loses time. What adjustment should be made?

14-8. Given a spring of known force constant, a meterstick, and a stopwatch, how can you determine the value of an unknown mass?

14-9. How may the principle of the pendulum be used to compute (a) length, (b) mass, and (c) time?

14-10. Explain clearly why the motion of a pendulum is not simple harmonic when the amplitude is large. Is the period larger or smaller than it should be if the motion were strictly simple harmonic?

PROBLEMS

14-1. A rubber ball is swinging in a horizontal circle 200 cm in diameter, making 20 rpm. A shadow of the ball is projected on a wall by a distant light. What is the amplitude of the motion of the shadow? What is its frequency? What is its period?

Ans. 100 cm, 0.33 Hz, 3 s.

14-2. If the rubber ball in Prob. 14-1 describes a circle of radius 12 in. and moves at 300 rpm, what is the frequency of its projection? What is its amplitude? What is its maximum velocity?

14-3. A 10-lb weight stretches a spring 8 in. before reaching a position of equilibrium. (a) What is the spring constant? (b) If the weight is displaced an additional 6 in. and released, what is the maximum restoring force?

Ans. (a) 1.25 lb/in. (b) −17.5 lb.

14-4. A body vibrates with SHM of amplitude 12 cm and frequency 4 Hz. What is the period? What is the displacement of the body after 3.2 s?

14-5. An object is moving with SHM of amplitude 16 cm and frequency 2 Hz. (a) What is the maximum velocity of the body? (b) What is its maximum acceleration? (c) What is its position after 3.2 s? (d) What are the velocity and acceleration after 3.2 s?

Ans. (a) −201 cm/s (b) 25.3 m/s² (c) −12.9 cm (d) −118 m/s, 20.4 m/s².

14-6. A body is vibrating with SHM of amplitude 6 in. and period 1.5 s. (a) What are its maximum velocity and acceleration? (b) What are its position, velocity, and acceleration after it has been vibrating for 7 s?

14-7. A 200-g mass is suspended from a long spiral spring. When displaced 10 cm, the mass is found to vibrate with a period of 2 s. (a) What is the spring constant? (b) What are its velocity and acceleration as it passes upward through the point 5 cm above its equilibrium position?

Ans. (a) 1.97 N/m (b) 27.2 cm/s, −49.3 m/s².

14-8. Show that the velocity of an object in SHM can be written as a function of its amplitude and displacement.

$$v = \pm 2\pi f \sqrt{A^2 - x^2}$$

Apply this formula directly to Prob. 14-7 and compare your results.

14-9. A body describing SHM has a maximum acceleration of 24 m/s² and a maximum speed of 2 m/s. What are its period and amplitude of vibration?

Ans. 0.524 s, 0.167 m.

14-10. A point on a metal string is vibrating at 256 Hz with an amplitude of 1 mm. What is the speed of the string when it passes through the center of its oscillation?

14-11. A 400-g mass stretches a spring 20 cm. The 400-g mass is then removed and replaced with an unknown mass m. When the mass m is pulled down 5 cm and released, it vibrates with a period of 0.1 s. Compute the mass of the vibrating object.

Ans. 4.96 g.

14-12. The prong of a tuning fork vibrates with a frequency of 330 Hz and an amplitude of 2 mm. What is the velocity when the displacement is 1.5 mm?

14-13. What is the length in feet of a pendulum whose period is 2 s?

Ans. 3.24 ft.

14-14. A pendulum has a length of 2 m and executes 21 complete vibrations in 1 min. What is the acceleration of gravity?

14-15. A simple pendulum swings with an amplitude of 2 ft. If the length of the pendulum is 20 ft, what is the velocity of the bob as it passes through its lowest point? What is its maximum acceleration? In order to see how closely the motion approximates SHM, compute the velocity at the lowest point from energy considerations.

Ans. -2.53 ft/s, -3.2 ft/s^2, 2.53 ft/s.

14-16. A pendulum clock beats seconds every time the bob passes through its lowest point. What must be the length of the pendulum at a place where $g = 32$ ft/s^2? If the clock is moved to a point where $g = 31$ ft/s, how much time will it lose in 1 day?

14-17. A disk 20 cm in diameter is suspended in a horizontal position by a wire attached to its center. A force of 20 N applied to the rim of the disk causes it to twist through an angle of 12°. If the period of the angular harmonic motion is 0.5 s when released, determine the moment of inertia of the disk.

Ans. 0.061 kg · m^2.

14-18. An irregularly shaped object is suspended by a wire as a torsion pendulum. A torque of 40 lb · ft causes it to twist through an angle of 15°. When released, the body oscillates with a frequency of 3 Hz. What is the moment of inertia of the irregular body?

14-19. A torsion pendulum has a maximum angular acceleration of 20 rad/s^2 when its displacement is 70°. What is its frequency of vibration?

Ans. 0.644 Hz.

15 *Fluids at Rest*

Liquids and gases are called *fluids* because they flow freely and fill their containers. In this chapter you will learn that fluids may exert forces on the walls of their containers. Such forces acting on definite surface areas create a condition of *pressure*. A hydraulic press utilizes fluid pressure to lift heavy loads. The structure of water basins, dams, and large oil tanks is determined largely by pressure considerations. The design of boats, submarines, and weather balloons must take into account the pressure and density of the surrounding fluid.

15-1 DENSITY

Before discussing the statics and dynamics of fluids, it is important to understand the relation of a body's weight to its volume. For example, we refer to lead or iron as *heavy* whereas wood or cork is considered *light*. What we really mean is that a block of wood is lighter than a block of lead *of similar size*. The terms light and heavy are comparative terms. As illustrated in Fig. 15-1, it is possible for a block of lead to weigh the same as a block of wood if their relative size differs greatly. On the other hand, 1 ft³ of lead weighs more than 6 times as much as 1 ft³ of wood.

Fig. 15-1 The relation between weight and volume compared for lead and wood.

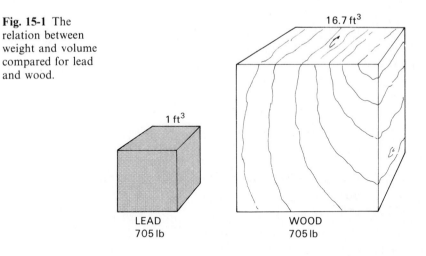

16.7 ft³

1 ft³

LEAD
705 lb

WOOD
705 lb

The quantity which relates a body's weight to its volume is known as its *weight density*.

The **weight density** D of a body is defined as the ratio of its weight W to its volume V. Units are the *newton per cubic meter* (N/m³) and the *pound per cubic foot* (lb/ft³).

$$D = \frac{W}{V} \qquad W = DV \tag{15-1}$$

Thus, if a 20-lb object occupies a volume of 4 ft³, it has a weight density of 5 lb/ft³.

As mentioned in Chap. 7, the weight of a body is not constant but varies according to location. A more useful relation for density takes advantages of the fact that *mass* is a universal constant, independent of gravity.

The **mass density** ρ of a body is defined as the ratio of its mass m to its volume V.

$$\rho = \frac{m}{V} \qquad m = \rho V \tag{15-2}$$

The units of mass density are the ratio of a mass unit to a volume unit, i.e., grams per cubic centimeter, kilograms per cubic meter, or slugs per cubit foot.

The relation between weight density and mass density is found by recalling that $W = mg$. Thus

$$D = \frac{mg}{V} = \rho g \qquad (15\text{-}3)$$

In USCS units, matter is usually described in terms of its weight. For this reason, weight density is more often used when working with this system of units. In SI units mass is the more convenient quantity, and the mass density is preferred. Table 15-1 lists the weight densities and mass densities of some common substances.

Table 15-1 Mass Density and Weight Density

Substance	D, lb/ft^3	ρ g/cm^3	ρ kg/m^3
Solids:			
Aluminum	169	2.7	2,700
Brass	540	8.7	8,700
Copper	555	8.89	8,890
Glass	162	2.6	2,600
Gold	1204	19.3	19,300
Ice	57	0.92	920
Iron	490	7.85	7,850
Lead	705	11.3	11,300
Oak	51	0.81	810
Silver	654	10.5	10,500
Steel	487	7.8	7,800
Liquids:			
Alcohol	49	0.79	790
Benzene	54.7	0.88	880
Gasoline	42	0.68	680
Mercury	850	13.6	13,600
Water	62.4	1.0	1,000
Gases (0°C):			
Air	0.0807	0.00129	1.29
Hydrogen	0.0058	0.000090	0.090
Helium	0.0110	0.000178	0.178
Nitrogen	0.0782	0.00126	1.25
Oxygen	0.0892	0.00143	1.43

EXAMPLE 15-1 A cylindrical tank for gasoline is 3 m long and 1.2 m in diameter. How many kilograms of gasoline will the tank hold?

Solution   First we find the volume:

$$V = \pi r^2 h = \pi(0.6 \text{ m})^2(3 \text{ m}) = 3.39 \text{ m}^3$$

Substituting the volume and mass density into Eq. (15-1), we obtain

$$m = \rho V = (680 \text{ kg/m}^3)(3.39 \text{ m}^3) = 2310 \text{ kg}$$

15-2 PRESSURE

The effectiveness of a given force often depends upon the area over which it acts. For example, a woman wearing narrow heels will do much more damage to floors than she would with flat heels. Even though she exerts the same downward force in each case, with the narrow heels her weight is spread over a much smaller surface area. The *normal force per unit area* is called *pressure*. Symbolically, the pressure P is given by

$$\boxed{P = \frac{F}{A}} \tag{15-4}$$

where A is the area over which the perpendicular force F is applied. The unit of pressure is the ratio of any force unit to a unit of area. Examples are newtons per square meter and pounds per square inch. In SI units, the N/m^2 is renamed the *pascal* (Pa). The *kilopascal* (kPa) is the most appropriate measure for fluid pressure.

$$1 \text{ kPa} = 1000 \text{ N/m}^2 = 0.145 \text{ lb/in.}^2$$

EXAMPLE 15-2   A golf shoe has 10 cleats, each having an area of 0.01 in.² in contact with the floor. Assume that in walking, there is one instant when all 10 cleats support the entire weight of a 180-lb person. What is the pressure exerted by the cleats on the floor? Express the answer in SI units.

Solution   The total area in contact with the floor is 0.1 in.² (10 × 0.01 in.²). Substitution into Eq. (15-4) yields

$$P = \frac{F}{A} = \frac{180 \text{ lb}}{0.1 \text{ in.}^2} = 1800 \text{ lb/in.}^2$$

Converting to SI units, we obtain

$$P = (1800 \text{ lb/in.}^2)\left(\frac{1 \text{ kPa}}{0.145 \text{ lb/in.}^2}\right) = 1.24 \times 10^4 \text{ kPa}$$

As the area of the shoe in contact with the floor decreases, the pressure becomes larger. It is easy to see why this factor must be considered in floor construction.

15-3 FLUID PRESSURE

There is a very significant difference between the way a force acts on a fluid and on a solid. Since a solid is a rigid body, it can withstand the application of a force without a significant change in shape. A liquid, on the other hand, can sustain a force only at an enclosed surface or boundary. If a fluid is not restrained, it will flow under a shearing stress instead of being deformed elastically.

> *The force exerted by a fluid on the walls of its container must always act perpendicular to the walls.*

It is this characteristic property of fluids that makes the concept of pressure so useful. Holes bored in the bottom and sides of a barrel of water (Fig. 15-2) demonstrate that the force exerted by the water is everywhere perpendicular to the surface of the barrel.

Fig. 15-2 The forces exerted by a fluid on the walls of its container are perpendicular at every point.

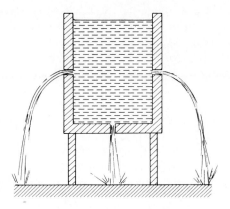

A moment's reflection will show the student that a liquid also exerts an upward pressure. Anyone who has tried to keep a rubber float under the surface of water is immediately convinced of the existence of an upward pressure. In fact, we find that:

> *Fluids exert pressure in all directions.*

Figure 15-3 shows a liquid under pressure. The force acting on the face of the

Fig. 15-3 Fluids exert pressure in all directions.

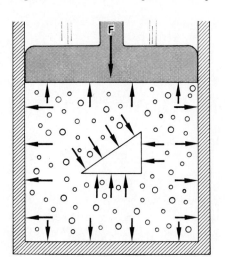

piston, the walls of the enclosure, and the surfaces of a suspended object are shown in the figure.

Just as larger volumes of solid objects exert greater forces against their supports, fluids exert greater pressure at increasing depths. The fluid at the bottom of a container is always under a greater pressure than that near the surface. This is due to the weight of the overlying liquid. However, we must point out a distinct difference between the pressure exerted by solids and that exerted by liquids. A solid object can exert only a *downward* force due to its weight. At any particular depth in a fluid, the pressure is the same in all directions. If this were not true, the fluid would flow under the influence of a resultant pressure until a new condition of equilibrium was reached.

Since the weight of the overlying fluid is proportional to its density, the pressure at any depth is also proportional to the density of the fluid. This can be seen by considering a rectangular column of water extending from the surface to a depth h, as shown in Fig. 15-4. The weight of the entire column acts on the surface area A at the bottom of the column.

Fig. 15-4 The relationship of pressure, density, and depth.

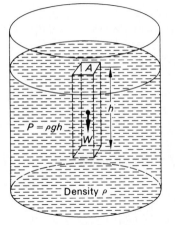

From Eq. (15-1), we can write the weight of the column as

$$W = DV = DAh$$

where D is the weight density of the fluid. The pressure (weight per unit area) at the depth h is given by

$$P = \frac{W}{A} = Dh$$

or, in terms of mass density,

$$\boxed{P = Dh = \rho gh} \tag{15-5}$$

The fluid pressure at any point is directly proportional to the density of the fluid and to the depth below the surface of the fluid.

EXAMPLE 15-3   The water pressure in a certain house is 160 lb/in.² How high must the water level in a reservoir be above the point of release in the house?

Solution   The weight density of water is 62.4 lb/ft³. The pressure is 160 lb/in². To avoid inconsistency in units, we convert the pressure to units of pounds per square foot.

$$P = (160 \text{ lb/in.}^2) \frac{144 \text{ in.}^2}{1 \text{ ft}^2} = 23{,}040 \text{ lb/ft}^2$$

Solving for h in Eq. (15-5), we have

$$h = \frac{P}{D} = \frac{23{,}040 \text{ lb/ft}^2}{62.4 \text{ lb/ft}^3} = 369 \text{ ft}$$

In the above example, no mention was made of the size or shape of the reservoir containing the supply of water. Additionally, no information was given about the path of the water or size of the pipes connecting the reservoir to the home. Can we assume that our answer is correct when it is based only upon the difference in water levels? Doesn't the shape or area of a container have any effect on liquid pressure? In order to answer these questions, we must recall some of the characteristics of fluids already discussed.

Consider a series of vessels of different areas and shapes interconnected, as shown in Fig. 15-5. It would seem at first glance that the greater volume of water in vessel B should develop a greater pressure at the bottom than vessel D. The effect of such a difference in pressure would then force the liquid to rise higher in vessel D. However, filling the vessels with liquid shows the levels to be the same for each vessel.

Fig. 15-5 Water seeks its own level, indicating that the pressure is independent of area or shape of the container.

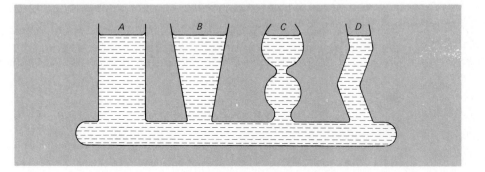

Part of the problem in understanding this paradox results from confusing the terms *pressure* and *total force*. Since pressure is measured in terms of a unit area, we do not consider the *total area* when solving problems involving pressure. For example, in vessel A the area of the liquid at the bottom of the vessel is much greater than the area at the bottom of vessel D. This means that the liquid in vessel A will exert a greater *total force* on the bottom than the liquid in vessel D. But the greater force is applied over a larger area so that the pressure is the same in both vessels.

If the bottoms of vessels *B*, *C*, and *D* have the same area, we can say that the total forces are also equal at the bottoms of these containers. (Of course, the pressures are equal at any particular depth.) You may wonder how the total forces can be equal when vessels *B* and *C* contain a greater volume of water. The additional water in each case is supported by vertical components of forces exerted by the walls of the container on the fluid. (See Fig. 15-6.) When the walls of a container are vertical, the forces acting on the sides have no upward components. The total force at the bottom of a container is therefore equal to the weight of a straight column of water above the base area.

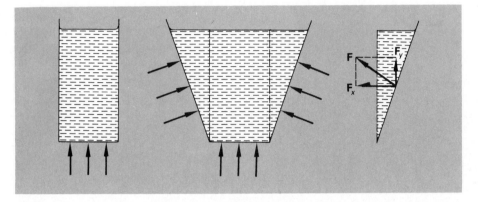

Fig. 15-6 The pressure at the bottom of each vessel is a function only of the depth of the liquid and is the same in all directions. Since the area at the bottom is the same for both vessels, the total force exerted on the bottom of each container is also the same.

EXAMPLE 15-4   Assume that the vessels in Fig. 15-5 are filled with gasoline until the fluid level is 1 ft above the base of each vessel. The areas at the bases of vessels *A* and *B* are 20 and 10 in.^{2}, respectively. Compare the pressure and the total force at the base of each container.

Solution   The pressure is the same at the base of either container and is given by

$$P = Dh = (42 \text{ lb/ft}^3)(1 \text{ ft}) = 42 \text{ lb/ft}^2$$

The total force in each case is the product of the pressure and base area ($F = PA$). Thus

$$F_A = (42 \text{ lb/ft}^2)(20 \text{ in.}^2)\, \frac{1 \text{ ft}^2}{144 \text{ in.}^2} = 5.83 \text{ lb}$$

$$F_B = (42 \text{ lb/ft}^2)(10 \text{ in.}^2)\, \frac{1 \text{ ft}^2}{144 \text{ in.}^2} = 2.92 \text{ lb}$$

Before considering other applications of fluid pressure, let us summarize the principles discussed in this section for fluids at rest.

1. The forces exerted by a fluid on the walls of its container are always perpendicular.

2. The fluid pressure is directly proportional to the depth of the fluid and to its density.
3. At any particular depth, the fluid pressure is the same in all directions.
4. Fluid pressure is independent of the shape or area of its container.

15-4 MEASURING PRESSURE

The pressure discussed in the previous section is due only to the fluid itself and can be calculated from Eq. (15-5). Unfortunately, this is usually not the case. Any liquid in an open container, for example, is subjected to atmospheric pressure in addition to the pressure of its own weight. Since the liquid is relatively incompressible, the external pressure of the atmosphere is transmitted equally throughout the volume of the liquid. This fact, first stated by the French mathematician Blaise Pascal (1623–1662), is called *Pascal's law*. Generally, it can be stated as follows:

An external pressure applied to an enclosed fluid is transmitted uniformly throughout the volume of the liquid.

Most devices which measure pressure directly actually measure the difference between the *absolute pressure* and *atmospheric pressure*. The result is called the *gauge pressure*.

Absolute pressure = gauge pressure + atmospheric pressure

Atmospheric pressure at sea level is 101.3 kPa, or 14.7 lb/in.^{2} Because atmospheric pressure enters into so many calculations, we often use a pressure unit of 1 *atmosphere* (atm), defined as the average pressure exerted by the atmosphere at sea level, that is, 14.7 lb/in.^{2}

A common device for measuring gauge pressure is the open-tube *manometer* (muh-nom'-uh-ter), shown in Fig. 15-7. The manometer consists of a U-shaped tube containing a liquid, usually mercury. When both ends of the tube are open, the mercury seeks its own level because 1 atm of pressure is exerted at each of the open ends. When one end is connected to a pressurized chamber, the mercury will rise in the open tube until the pressures are equal-

Fig. 15-7 The open-tube manometer. Pressure is measured by the height *h* of the mercury column.

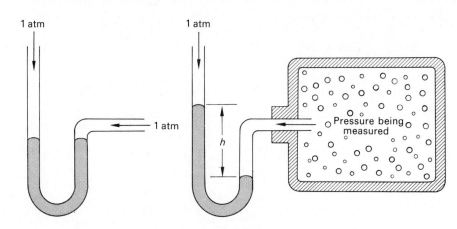

ized. The difference between the two levels of mercury is a measure of the gauge pressure, i.e., the difference between the absolute pressure in the chamber and atmospheric pressure at the open end. The manometer is used so often in laboratory situations that atmospheric pressures and other pressures are often expressed in *centimeters of mercury* or *inches of mercury*.

Atmospheric pressure is usually measured in the laboratory with a mercury barometer. The principle of its operation is shown in Fig. 15-8. A glass

Fig. 15-8 The barometer.

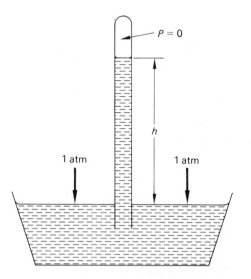

tube, closed at one end, is filled with mercury. The open end is covered, and the tube is inverted in a bowl of mercury. When the open end is uncovered, the mercury flows out of the tube until the pressure exerted by the column of mercury exactly balances atmospheric pressure acting on the mercury in the bowl. Since the pressure in the tube above the column of mercury is zero, the height of the column above the level of mercury in the bowl indicates the atmospheric pressure. At sea level an atmospheric pressure of 14.7 lb/in.^{2} will cause the level of the mercury in the tube to stabilize at a height of 76 cm, or 30 in.

In summary, we can write the following equivalent measures of atmospheric pressure:

$$1 \text{ atm} = 101.3 \text{ kPa} = 14.7 \text{ lb/in.}^2 = 76 \text{ cm of mercury}$$

$$= 30 \text{ in. of mercury} = 2116 \text{ lb/ft}^2$$

EXAMPLE 15-5   The mercury manometer is used to measure the pressure of a gas inside a tank. (Refer to Fig. 15-7.) If the difference between the two mercury levels is 36 cm, what is the absolute pressure inside the tank?

Solution   The gauge pressure is 36 cm of mercury, and atmospheric pressure is 76 cm of mercury. Thus the absolute pressure is found from Eq. (15-5).

$$\text{Absolute pressure} = 36 \text{ cm} + 76 \text{ cm} = 112 \text{ cm of mercury}$$

The pressure in the tank is equivalent to the pressure that would be exerted by a column of mercury 112 cm high.

$$P = Dh = \rho g h$$

$$= (13,600 \text{ kg/m}^3)(9.8 \text{ m/s}^2)(1.12 \text{ m})$$

$$= 1.49 \times 10^5 \text{ N/m}^2 = 149 \text{ kPa}$$

You should verify that this absolute pressure is also 21.6 lb/in.^{2} or 1.47 atm.

**15-5
THE
HYDRAULIC
PRESS**

The most universal application of Pascal's law is found with the hydraulic press, shown in Fig. 15-9. According to Pascal's principle, a pressure applied to the liquid in the left column will be transmitted undiminished to the liquid in the column in the right. Thus, if an input force F_i acts upon a piston of area A_i, it will cause an output force F_o to act on a piston of area A_o so that

Input pressure = output pressure

$$\frac{F_i}{A_i} = \frac{F_o}{A_o} \tag{15-6}$$

Fig. 15-9 The hydraulic press.

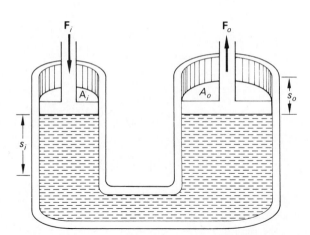

The ideal mechanical advantage of such a device is equal to the ratio of the output force to the input force. Symbolically, we write

$$M_I = \frac{F_o}{F_i} = \frac{A_o}{A_i} \tag{15-7}$$

A small input force can be multiplied to yield a much larger output force simply by having the output piston much larger in area than the input piston. The output force is given by

$$F_o = F_i \frac{A_o}{A_i} \tag{15-8}$$

According to the methods developed in Chap. 12 for simple machines, the input work must equal the output work if we neglect friction. If the input force F_i travels through a distance s_i while the output force F_o travels through a distance s_o, we can write

$$Input\ work = output\ work$$

$$F_i s_i = F_o s_o$$

This relation leads to another useful expression for the ideal mechanical advantage of a hydraulic press.

$$M_I = \frac{F_o}{F_i} = \frac{s_i}{s_o} \tag{15-9}$$

Notice that the mechanical advantage is gained at the expense of input distance. For this reason, most applications utilize a system of valves to permit the output piston to be raised by a series of short input strokes.

EXAMPLE 15-6   The smaller and larger pistons of a hydraulic press have diameters of 2 and 24 in., respectively. (*a*) What input force is required in order to deliver a total output force of 2000 lb at the larger piston? (*b*) How far must the smaller piston travel in order to lift the larger piston 1 in.?

Solution (*a*)   The mechanical advantage is

$$M_I = \frac{A_o}{A_i} = \frac{\pi d_o^2/4}{\pi d_i^2/4} = \left(\frac{d_o}{d_i}\right)^2$$

$$= \left(\frac{24\ \text{in.}}{2\ \text{in.}}\right)^2 = (12)^2 = 144$$

The required input force is given by

$$F_i = \frac{F_o}{M_I} = \frac{2000\ \text{lb}}{144} = 13.9\ \text{lb}$$

Solution (*b*)   Applying Eq. (15-9), we can compute the input distance.

$$s_i = M_I s_o = (144)(1\ \text{in.}) = 144\ \text{in.}$$

The principle of the hydraulic press is found in many engineering and mechanical devices. Power steering, the hydraulic jack, shock absorbers, and automobile braking systems are a few common examples.

15-6 ARCHIMEDES' PRINCIPLE

Anyone familiar with swimming and other water sports has observed that objects seem to lose weight when submerged in water. In fact, the object may even float on the surface because of the upward pressure exerted by the water. An ancient Greek mathematician, Archimedes (287–212 B.C.), first studied the buoyant force exerted by fluids. *Archimedes' principle* can be stated as follows:

> *An object which is completely or partly submerged in a fluid experiences an upward force equal to the weight of the fluid displaced.*

Archimedes' principle can be demonstrated by studying the forces a fluid exerts on a suspended object. Consider a disk of area A and height H which is completely submerged in a fluid, as shown in Fig. 15-10. Recall that the pressure at any depth h in a fluid is given by

$$P = \rho g h$$

Fig. 15-10 The buoyant force on the disk is equal to the weight of the fluid it displaces.

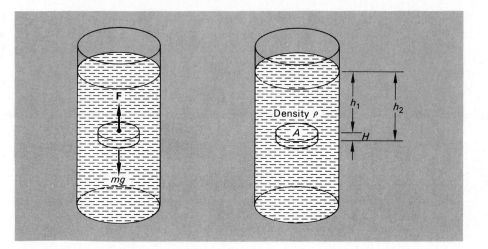

where ρ is the mass density of the fluid and g is the acceleration of gravity. Of course, if we wish to represent the absolute pressure within the fluid, we must add the external pressure exerted by the atmosphere. The total downward pressure P_1 on top of the disk in Fig. 15-10 is therefore

$$P_1 = P_a + \rho g h_1 \qquad \text{downward}$$

where P_a is atmospheric pressure and h_1 is the depth at the top of the disk. Similarly, the upward pressure P_2 on the bottom of the disk is

$$P_2 = P_a + \rho g h_2 \qquad \text{upward}$$

where h_2 is the depth at the bottom of the disk. Since h_2 is greater than h_1, the pressure on the bottom of the disk will exceed the pressure at the top, resulting in a net upward force. If we represent the downward force by F_1 and the upward force by F_2, we can write

$$F_1 = P_1 A \qquad F_2 = P_2 A$$

The net upward force exerted *by* the fluid *on* the disk is called the *buoyant force* and is given by

$$F_B = F_2 - F_1 = A(P_2 - P_1)$$

$$= A(P_a + \rho g h_2 - P_a - \rho g h_1)$$

$$= A \rho g (h_2 - h_1) = A \rho g H$$

where $H = h_2 - h_1$ is the height of the disk. Finally, if we recall that the volume of the disk is $V = AH$, we obtain the important result

$$\boxed{F_B = V\rho g = mg} \tag{15-10}$$

Buoyant force = weight of displaced fluid

which is Archimedes' principle.

In applying this result, it must be recalled that Eq. (15-10) allows us to compute only the *buoyant force* due to the difference in pressures. It does not represent the resultant force. A submerged body will sink if the weight of the fluid it displaces (the buoyant force) is less than the weight of the body. If the weight of the displaced fluid is exactly equal to the weight of the submerged body, it will neither sink nor rise. In this instance, the body will be in equilibrium. If the weight of displaced fluid exceeds the weight of a submerged body, the body will rise to the surface and float. When the floating body comes to equilibrium at the surface, it will displace its own weight of liquid. Figure 15-11 demonstrates this point with the use of an overflow can and a beaker to catch the fluid displaced by a wooden block.

Fig. 15-11 A floating body displaces its own weight of fluid.

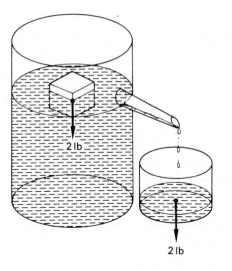

EXAMPLE 15-7   A cork float has a volume of 2 ft³ and a density of 15 lb/ft³. (a) What volume of the cork is beneath the surface when the cork floats in water? (b) What downward force is required to submerge the cork completely?

Solution (a)   The floating cork will displace a volume of water equal to its own weight, which is

$$W = DV = (15 \text{ lb/ft}^3)(2 \text{ ft}^3) = 30 \text{ lb}$$

Since water has a weight density of 62.4 lb/ft³, the volume of water displaced is

$$V = \frac{W}{D} = \frac{30 \text{ lb}}{62.4 \text{ lb/ft}^3} = 0.481 \text{ ft}^3$$

Thus the volume of the cork under the water is also 0.481 ft³.

Solution (b)

In order to submerge the cork, a downward force F must be exerted, in addition to the weight W of the cork, such that their sum equals the buoyant force F_B. Symbolically,

$$F + W = F_B$$

The required force F is therefore equal to the difference between the buoyant force and the weight of the cork:

$$F = F_B - W$$

The buoyant force in this case can be found by computing the weight of 2 ft³ of water (the amount of water displaced when the cork is entirely submerged). We obtain

$$F_B = DV = (62.4 \text{ lb/ft}^3)(2 \text{ ft}^3) = 124.8 \text{ lb}$$

The required force F to submerge the block is

$$F = 124.8 \text{ lb} - 30 \text{ lb} = 94.8 \text{ lb}$$

EXAMPLE 15-8

A weather balloon is to operate at an altitude where the density of air is 0.9 kg/m³. At this altitude, the balloon has a volume of 20 m³ and is filled with hydrogen ($\rho_H = 0.09$ kg/m³). If the balloon bag weighs 118 N, what load can it support at this level?

Solution

The buoyant force is equal to the weight of the displaced air. Thus

$$F_B = \rho g V = (0.9 \text{ kg/m}^3)(9.8 \text{ m/s}^2)(20 \text{ m}^3) = 176 \text{ N}$$

The weight of 20 m³ of hydrogen is

$$W_H = \rho_H g V = (0.09 \text{ kg/m}^3)(9.8 \text{ m/s}^2)(20 \text{ m}^3) = 17.6 \text{ N}$$

The load supported is

$$W_L = F_B - W_H - W_B$$

$$= 176 \text{ N} - 17.6 \text{ N} - 118 \text{ N} = 40.4 \text{ N}$$

Large balloons can maintain a condition of equilibrium at any altitude by adjustment of their weight or buoyant force. The weight can be lightened by releasing the ballast provided for that purpose. The buoyant force can be decreased by releasing the gas from the balloon or increased by pumping more gas into the flexible balloon. Hot-air ballons use the lower density of heated air to provide their buoyancy.

SUMMARY

We have discussed the concepts of fluids and pressure. Density, buoyant forces, and other quantities were defined and applied to many physical examples. The key ideas discussed in this chapter are summarized below:

- A very important physical property of matter is its *density*. The weight density D and the mass density ρ are defined as follows:

$$Weight \; density = \frac{weight}{volume} \qquad \boxed{D = \frac{W}{V}} \qquad \text{N/m}^3 \text{ or lb/ft}^3$$

$$\text{Mass density} = \frac{mass}{volume} \qquad \boxed{\rho = \frac{m}{V}} \qquad \text{kg/m}^3 \text{ or slugs/ft}^3$$

- Since $W = mg$, the relationship between D and ρ is

$$\boxed{D = \rho g} \qquad \text{Weight density} = \text{mass density} \times \text{gravity}$$

- Important points to remember about fluid pressure:
  a. The forces exerted by a fluid on the walls of its container are always perpendicular.
  b. The fluid pressure is directly proportional to the depth of the fluid and to its density.

$$\boxed{P = \frac{F}{A} \qquad P = Dh \qquad P = \rho gh}$$

  c. At any particular depth, the fluid pressure is the same in all directions.
  d. Fluid pressure is independent of the shape or area of its container.
- Pascal's law states that *an external pressure applied to an enclosed fluid is transmitted uniformly throughout the volume of the liquid.*
- When measuring fluid pressure, it is essential to distinguish between *absolute* pressure and *gauge* pressure:

$$\text{Absolute pressure} = \text{gauge pressure} + \text{atmospheric pressure}$$

$$\text{Atmospheric pressure} = 1 \text{ atm} = 1.013 \times 10^5 \text{ N/m}^2$$

$$= 1.013 \times 10^5 \text{ Pa} = 14.7 \text{ lb/in.}^2$$

$$= 76 \text{ cm of mercury}$$

- Applying Pascal's law to the hydraulic press gives the following for the ideal advantage:

$$\boxed{M_I = \frac{F_o}{F_i} = \frac{s_i}{s_o}} \qquad \begin{array}{l} \textit{Ideal Mechanical Advantage} \\ \textit{for Hydraulic Press} \end{array}$$

- Archimedes' principle: *An object which is completely or partly submerged in a fluid experiences an upward force equal to the weight of the fluid displaced.*

$$\boxed{F_B = mg} \qquad \text{or} \qquad \boxed{F_B = V\rho g} \qquad \textit{Buoyant Force}$$

QUESTIONS

15-1 Define the following terms:

a. Weight density	**f.** Absolute pressure
b. Mass density	**g.** Gauge pressure
c. Pressure	**h.** Manometer
d. Total force	**i.** Archimedes' principle
e. Pascal's law	**j.** Buoyant force

15-2. Make a list of the units for weight density and the similar units for mass density.

15-3. Which is numerically larger: the weight density of an object or its mass density?

15-4. The density of water is given in Table 15-1 as 62.4 lb/ft³. In performing an experiment with water on the surface of the moon, would you trust this value? Explain.

15-5. Which is heavier, 870 kg of brass or 3.5 ft³ of copper?

15-6. Why are dams so much thicker at the bottom than at the top? Does the pressure exerted on the dam depend on the length of the reservoir perpendicular to the dam?

15-7. A large block of ice floats in a bucket of water so that the level of the water is at the top of the bucket. Will the water overflow when the ice melts? Explain.

15-8. A tub of water rests on weighing scales which indicate 40 lb total weight. Will the total weight increase when a 5-lb fish is floating on the surface of the water? Discuss.

15-9. Suppose an iron block supported by a string is completely submerged in the tub of Question 15-8. How will the reading on the scales be affected?

15-10. A boy just learning to swim finds that he can float on the surface more easily after inhaling air. He also observes that he can hasten his descent to the bottom of the pool by exhaling air on the way down. Explain his observations.

15-11. A toy sailboat filled with pennies floats in a small tub of water. If the pennies are thrown into the water, what happens to the water level in the tub?

15-12. Is it more difficult to hold a cork float barely under the surface than it is at a depth of 5 ft? Explain.

15-13. Is it possible to construct a barometer using water instead of mercury? How high will the column of water be if the external pressure is 1 atm?

15-14. Discuss the operation of a submarine and a weather balloon. Why will a balloon rise to a definite height and stop? Will a submarine sink to a particular depth and stop if no changes are made after submerging?

PROBLEMS

15-1. What volume does 0.4 kg of alcohol occupy? What is the weight of this volume?

Ans. 5.06×10^{-4} m³, 3.92 N.

15-2. An unknown substance has a volume of 20 ft³ and weighs 3370 lb. Considering its density, what might the substance be?

15-3. What volume of water has the same weight as 1 ft³ of lead? Compute the mass density of the water in slugs per cubic feet.

Ans. 11.3 ft³, 1.95 slugs/ft³.

15-4. An open U-shaped tube containing mercury is 1 cm² in cross section. What volume of water must be poured into the left tube in order to cause the mercury in the right tube to rise 1 cm above its original position?

15-5. Find the pressure in kilopascals due to a column of mercury 60 cm high. What is this pressure in pounds per square inch? In atmospheres?

Ans. 80 kPa, 11.6 lb/in.², 0.79 atm.

15-6. A submarine dives to a depth of 120 ft and levels off. The interior of the submarine is maintained at atmospheric pressure. What total force is exerted against a hatch 2 ft wide and 3 ft long?

15-7. A 20-kg piston rests on a sample of gas in a cylinder 8 cm in diameter. What is the gauge pressure in the gas? What is the absolute pressure?

Ans. 39 kPa, 140.3 kPa.

15-8. A water-pressure gauge indicates a pressure of 50 lb/in.² at the foot of a building. What is the maximum height to which the water will rise in the building?

15-9. The gauge pressure in an automobile tire is 28 lb/in.² If the wheel supports 1000 lb, what area of the tire is in contact with the ground?

Ans. 35.7 in.²

15-10. Two liquids which do not react chemically are placed in a bent tube, as shown in Fig. 15-12. Show that the heights of the liquids above their surface of separation are inversely proportional to their densities:

$$\frac{h_1}{h_2} = \frac{\rho_2}{\rho_1}$$

Fig. 15-12

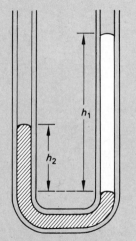

15-11. Assume that the two liquids in the U-shaped tube of Fig. 15-12 are water and oil. Compute the density of the oil if the water stands 19 cm above the interface and the oil stands 24 cm above the interface. Refer to Prob. 15-10.

Ans. 792 kg/m³.

15-12. A cylindrical water tank 50 ft high and 20 ft in diameter is filled with water. **(a)** What is the water pressure on the bottom of the tank? **(b)** What is the total force on the bottom? **(c)** What is the pressure in a water pipe which is located 90 ft below the water surface?

15-13. The *specific gravity* of an object is defined as the ratio of the weight of the object to the weight of an equal volume of water. By definition the specific gravity of water is 1.0. From the table of densities, calculate the specific gravity of copper, lead, and gasoline.

Ans. 8.89, 11.3, 0.673.

15-14. Archimedes' principle may often be used to determine the weight of an equal volume of water. A piece of iron weighs 24 lb in air and 21 lb when submerged in water. **(a)** What is the specific gravity of the iron? **(b)** What is the density?

15-15. The areas of the small and large pistons in a hydraulic press are 0.5 and 2.5 in.^{2}, respectively. What is the ideal mechanical advantage of the press? What force must be exerted in order to lift a 1-ton load? Through what distance must the input force act in order to lift the 1-ton load a distance of 1 in.?

Ans. 50, 40 lb, 50 in.

15-16. A force of 500 lb is applied to the small piston of a hydraulic press. Its diameter is 2 in. What must the diameter of the large piston be if it is to lift a 100-ton load?

15-17. The inlet pipe which supplies air pressure to operate a hydraulic lift is 2 cm in diameter. The output piston is 32 cm in diameter. What air pressure must be used to lift an 1800-kg automobile?

Ans. 219 kPa.

15-18. The area of the piston in a force pump is 10 in.^{2} What force is required to raise water with the piston to a height of 100 ft?

15-19. A 64-lb metal block has a volume of 0.2 ft^3. The block is suspended from a cord and submerged in oil. ($D = 48$ lb/ft^3.) Find the buoyant force and the tension in the cord.

Ans. 9.6 lb., 54.4 lb.

15-20. A stone of unknown composition weighs 82 lb in air. Its apparent weight is 74 lb when submerged in water. What is the volume of the stone, and what is its density?

15-21. A 20-kg balloon is filled with 80 m^3 of hydrogen. What force is required to hold it down?

Ans. 745 N.

15-22. A balloon 40 m in diameter is filled with helium. What total mass can be lifted by this balloon in air of density 0.9 kg/m^3?

15-23. A block of wood weighs 16 lb in air. A lead sinker, which has an apparent weight of 28 lb in water, is attached to the wood, and both are submerged in water. If their combined apparent weight in water is 18 lb, find the density of the wooden block.

Ans. 38.4 lb/ft^3.

15-24. The floor of a river barge is 18 ft wide and 70 ft long. How much deeper will it sink into the water if a 200-ton load of coal is placed in the barge?

15-25. A block of wood which has a volume of 120 cm^3 is found to have a mass of 100 g. Will it float in water? Gasoline?

Ans. Yes, no.

15-26. What percentage of an iceberg will remain below the surface of seawater ($\rho = 1030$ kg/m^3)?

15-27. What is the smallest area of ice 3 m thick that will support a 90-kg man? The ice is floating in fresh water.

Ans. 3.68 m^2.

16 *Fluids in Motion*

OBJECTIVES: After completing this chapter, you should be able to:

1. Define the *rate of flow* of a fluid and solve problems which relate the rate of flow to the velocity and cross-sectional area.

2. Write *Bernoulli's equation* in its general form and describe the equation as it would apply to (*a*) a fluid at rest, (*b*) fluid flow at constant pressure, and (*c*) flow through a horizontal pipe.

3. Apply Bernoulli's equation to the solution of problems involving absolute pressure P, density ρ, fluid elevation h, and fluid velocity v.

In Chap. 15 we studied the properties of fluids at rest. The work of Archimedes, Pascal, and Newton all contributed greatly to our present knowledge of fluids. Unfortunately, the mathematical difficulties encountered when dealing with fluids in motion are formidable. However, the fundamental aspects of fluid flow can be analyzed by making certain assumptions and generalizations. This chapter will give you a working knowledge of the mechanics of fluids in motion.

16-1 FLUID FLOW

In studying the dynamics of fluids, we shall assume that all fluids in motion exhibit *streamline flow*.

Streamline flow is the motion of a fluid in which every particle in the fluid follows the same path (past a particular point) as that followed by previous particles.

Figure 16-1 illustrates the *streamlines* of air flowing past two stationary obstacles. Note that the streamlines break down as air passes over the second obstacle, setting up whirls and eddies. These little whirlpools represent *turbulent flow* and absorb much of the fluid energy, increasing the frictional drag through the fluid.

Fig. 16-1 Streamline and turbulent flow of a fluid in its path.

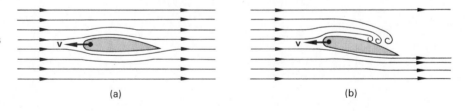

(a)   (b)

We shall further consider that fluids are incompressible and have essentially no internal friction. Under these conditions, certain predictions can be made about the rate of fluid flow through a pipe or other container.

The **rate of flow** is defined as the volume of fluid that passes a certain cross section per unit of time.

In order to express this rate quantitatively, we shall consider a liquid flowing through the pipe of Fig. 16-2 with an average speed v. During a time interval t, each particle in the stream moves through a distance vt. The volume V flowing through a cross section A is given by

$$V = Avt$$

Fig. 16-2 Computing the rate of flow of a fluid through a pipe.

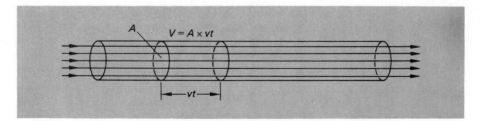

Thus the rate of flow (volume per unit time) can be calculated from

$$R = \frac{Avt}{t} = vA \qquad (16\text{-}1)$$

Rate of flow = velocity × cross section

The units of R express the ratio of a volume unit to a time unit. Common examples are cubic feet per second, cubic meters per second, liters per second, and gallons per minute.

If the fluid is incompressible and we ignore the effects of internal friction, the rate of flow R will remain constant. This means that a variation in the pipe cross section, as illustrated in Fig. 16-3, will result in a change in speed of the liquid so that the product vA remains constant. Symbolically, we write

$$R = v_1 A_1 = v_2 A_2 \qquad (16\text{-}2)$$

Fig. 16-3 In streamline flow the product of the fluid velocity and the cross-sectional area of the pipe is constant at any point.

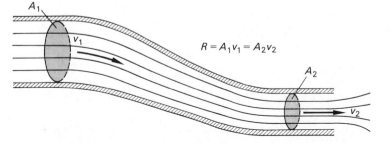

$$R = A_1 v_1 = A_2 v_2$$

A liquid will flow faster through a narrow section of pipe and more slowly through the broad sections. It is this principle which causes water to flow more rapidly when the banks of a small stream suddenly come closer together.

EXAMPLE 16-1   Water flows through a rubber hose 1 in. in diameter at a speed of 4 ft/s. What must the diameter of the nozzle be if water is to emerge with a velocity of 20 ft/s? What is the rate of flow in gallons per minute?

Solution   The rate of flow is constant, so that $A_1 v_1 = A_2 v_2$. Since the area A is proportional to the square of the diameter, we have

$$d_1^2 v_1 = d_2^2 v_2 \qquad \text{or} \qquad d_2^2 = \frac{v_1}{v_2} d_1^2$$

from which

$$d_2^2 = \frac{4 \text{ ft/s}}{20 \text{ ft/s}} (1 \text{ in.})^2 = 0.2 \text{ in.}^2$$

or

$$d_2 = 0.447 \text{ in.}$$

In order to determine the rate of flow, we must first determine the area of the 1-in. hose.

$$A_1 = \frac{\pi d_1^2}{4} = \frac{\pi}{4} (1 \text{ in.})^2 = 0.785 \text{ in.}^2$$

$$= 0.785 \text{ in.}^2 \ \frac{1 \text{ ft}^2}{144 \text{ in.}^2} = 5.45 \times 10^{-3} \text{ ft}^2$$

The rate of flow is $R = A_1 v_1$, so that

$$R = (5.45 \times 10^{-3} \text{ ft}^2)(4 \text{ ft/s}) = 0.0218 \text{ ft}^3/\text{s}$$

Recalling that 1 ft³ = 7.48 gal and that 1 min = 60 s, we can express this rate in the desired units:

$$R = (0.0218 \text{ ft}^3/\text{s})\left(\frac{7.48 \text{ gal}}{1 \text{ ft}^3}\right)\left(\frac{60 \text{ s}}{1 \text{ min}}\right) = 9.78 \text{ gal/min}$$

The same rate would be obtained by considering the product $A_2 v_2$.

16-2 PRESSURE AND VELOCITY

We have noted that a fluid's speed increases when it flows through a constriction. An increase in speed can result only through the presence of an accelerating force. In order to accelerate the liquid as it enters the constriction, the pushing force from the large cross section must be greater than the resisting force from the constriction. In other words, the pressure at points A and C in Fig. 16-4 must be greater than the pressure at B. The tubes inserted into the

Fig. 16-4 The increased velocity of a fluid flowing through a constriction indicates a drop in pressure.

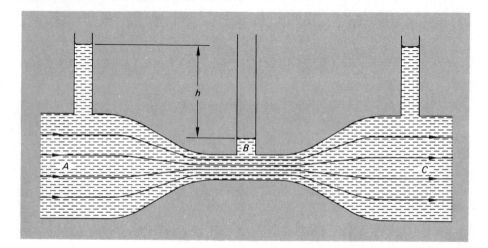

pipe above these points clearly indicate the difference in pressure. The fluid level in the tube above the restriction is lower than the level in the adjacent areas. If h is the difference in height, the pressure differential is given by

$$P_A - P_B = \rho gh \qquad (16\text{-}3)$$

This assumes that the pipe is horizontal and that no pressure changes are introduced because of a change in potential energy.

The above example, as illustrated in Fig. 16-4, shows the principle of the *venturi meter*. From a determination of the difference in pressure, this device makes it possible to calculate the velocity of water in a horizontal pipe.

The venturi effect finds many other applications for both liquids and gases. The carburetor in an automobile utilizes the venturi principle to mix gasoline vapor and air. Air passing through a constriction on its way to the cylinders creates a low-pressure area as its speed increases. The decrease in pressure is used to draw fuel into the air column, where it is readily vaporized.

Figure 16-5 shows two methods you can use to demonstrate the decrease in pressure due to an increase in velocity. The simplest example consists of blowing air past the top surface of a sheet of paper, as shown in Fig. 16-5a. The pressure in the airstream above the paper will be reduced. This allows the excess pressure on the bottom to force the paper upward.

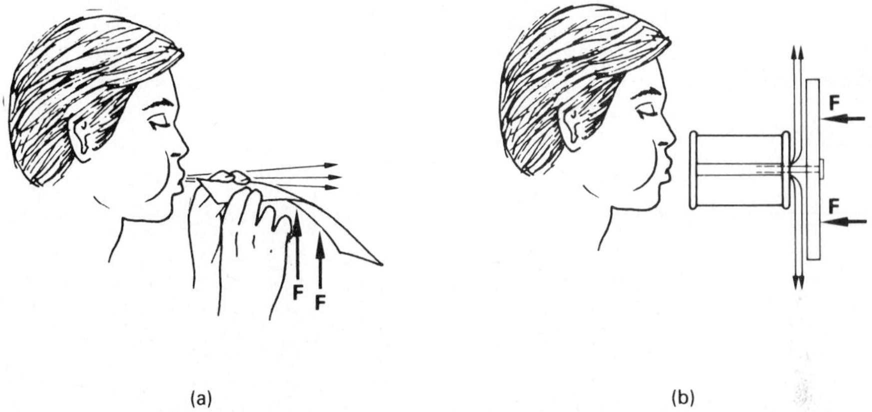

Fig. 16-5 Demonstrations of the decrease in pressure resulting from an increase in fluid speeds.

(a)　　　　　　　　　　　　　　　　　　(b)

A second demonstration requires a hollow spool, a cardboard disk, and a pin (Fig. 16-5b). The pin is driven through the cardboard disk and placed in one end of the hollow spool, as shown in the figure. If you blow through the open end, you will find that the disk becomes more tightly pressed to the other end. One would expect the cardboard disk to fly off immediately. The explanation is that air blown into the spool must escape through the narrow space between the disk and the end of the spool. This action creates a low-pressure area, allowing the external atmospheric pressure to push the disk tight against the spool.

16-3 BERNOULLI'S EQUATION

In our discussion of fluids, we have emphasized four quantities: the pressure P, the density ρ, the velocity v, and the height h above some reference level. The relationship between these quantities and their ability to describe fluids in motion was first established by Daniel Bernoulli (1700–1782), a Swiss mathematician. Steps leading to the development of this fundamental relationship can be understood by considering Fig. 16-6.

Since a fluid has mass, it must obey the same conservation laws established earlier for solids. Consequently, the work required to move a certain volume of fluid through a pipe must equal the total change in kinetic and potential energy. Let us consider the work required to move the fluid from point a to point b in Fig. 16-6a. The net work must be the sum of the work done by the input force F_1 and the negative work done by the resisting force F_2.

$$\text{Net work} = F_1 s_1 - F_2 s_2$$

Fig. 16-6 Deriva-
tion of Bernoulli's
equation.

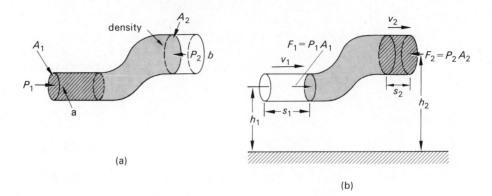

(a)

(b)

But $F_1 = P_1 A_1$ and $F_2 = P_2 A_2$, so that

$$\text{Net work} = P_1 A_1 s_1 - P_2 A_2 s_2$$

The product of area and distance represents the volume V of the fluid moved through the pipe. Since this volume is the same at the bottom and at the top of the pipe, we can substitute

$$V = A_1 s_1 = A_2 s_2$$

obtaining

$$\text{Net work} = P_1 V - P_2 V = (P_1 - P_2)V$$

The kinetic energy E_κ of a fluid is defined as $\frac{1}{2}mv^2$, where m is the mass of the fluid and v is its velocity. Since the mass remains constant, a change in kinetic energy ΔE_κ results only from the difference in fluid speed. In our example, the change in kinetic energy is

$$\Delta E_\kappa = \tfrac{1}{2}mv_2^2 - \tfrac{1}{2}mv_1^2$$

The potential energy of a fluid at a height h above some reference point is defined as mgh, where mg represents the weight of the fluid. The volume of fluid moved through the pipe is constant. Therefore, the change in potential energy ΔE_p results from the increases in height of the fluid from h_1 to h_2:

$$\Delta E_p = mgh_2 - mgh_1$$

We are now prepared to apply the principle of conservation of energy. The net work done on the system must equal the sum of the increases in kinetic and potential energy. Thus

$$\text{Net work} = \Delta E_\kappa + \Delta E_p$$

$$(P_1 - P_2)V = (\tfrac{1}{2}mv_2^2 - \tfrac{1}{2}mv_1^2) + (mgh_2 - mgh_1)$$

If the density of the fluid is ρ, we can substitute $V = m/\rho$, giving

$$(P_1 - P_2)\frac{m}{\rho} = \tfrac{1}{2}mv_2^2 - \tfrac{1}{2}mv_1^2 + mgh_2 - mgh_1$$

Multiplying through by ρ/m and rearranging, we obtain Bernoulli's equation:

$$P_1 + \rho g h_1 + \tfrac{1}{2}\rho v_1^2 = P_2 + \rho g h_2 + \tfrac{1}{2}\rho v_2^2 \qquad (16\text{-}4)$$

Since the subscripts 1 and 2 refer to any two points, Bernoulli's equation can be stated more simply as

$$\boxed{P + \rho g h + \tfrac{1}{2}\rho v^2 = \text{constant}} \qquad (16\text{-}5)$$

Bernoulli's equation finds application in almost every aspect of fluid flow. The pressure P must be recognized as the *absolute* pressure and not the *gauge* pressure. Remember that ρ is the mass density and not the weight density of the fluid. Notice that the units of each term in Bernoulli's equation are units of pressure.

**16-4
APPLICA-
TIONS OF
BERNOULLI'S
EQUATION**

In many physical situations, the speed, height, or pressure of a fluid is constant. In such cases Bernoulli's equation holds in simpler form. For example, when a liquid is stationary, both v_1 and v_2 are zero. Bernoulli's equation will then show that the difference in pressure is

$$P_2 - P_1 = \rho g(h_2 - h_1) \qquad (16\text{-}6)$$

This equation is identical to the relationship discussed in Chap. 15 for fluids at rest.

Another important result occurs when there is no change in pressure ($P_1 = P_2$). In Fig. 16-7 a liquid emerges from a hole, or orifice, near the bottom of an open tank. Its velocity as it emerges from the orifice can be determined from Bernoulli's equation. We shall assume that the liquid level in the tank falls slowly in comparison with the emergent speed so that the speed v_2 at the top can be assumed zero. Additionally, it is noted that the liquid pressure at both

Fig. 16-7 Torricelli's theorem.

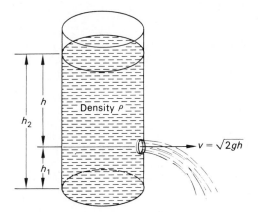

the top and at the orifice is equal to atmospheric pressure. Thus $P_1 = P_2$ and $v_2 = 0$, reducing Bernoulli's equation to

$$\rho g h_1 + \tfrac{1}{2}\rho v_1^2 = \rho g h_2$$

or

$$v_1^2 = 2g(h_2 - h_1) = 2gh$$

This relationship is known as *Torricelli's* (toh-ree-chel'-ees) *theorem*:

$$\boxed{v = \sqrt{2gh}} \qquad (16\text{-}7)$$

Note that the emergent velocity of a liquid at a depth h is the same as that of an object dropped from rest at a height h.

The rate at which a liquid flows from an orifice is given by vA from Eq. (16-1). Torricelli's relation allows us to express the rate of flow in terms of the height of a liquid above the orifice. Hence

$$R = vA = A\sqrt{2gh} \qquad (16\text{-}8)$$

EXAMPLE 16-2   A crack in a water tank has a cross-sectional area of 1 cm². At what rate is water lost from the tank if the water level in the tank is 4 m above the opening?

Solution   The area $A = 1$ cm² $= 10^{-4}$ m² and the height $h = 4$ m. Direct substitution into Eq. (16-8) gives

$$R = A\sqrt{2gh} = (10^{-4} \text{ m}^2)\sqrt{(2)(9.8 \text{ m/s}^2)(4 \text{ m})}$$
$$= (10^{-4} \text{ m}^2)(8.85 \text{ m/s}) = 8.85 \times 10^{-4} \text{ m}^3/\text{s}$$

An interesting example demonstrating Torricelli's principle is shown in Fig. 16-8. The discharge velocity increases with depth. Note that the maximum range occurs when the opening is at the middle of the water column. Although the discharge velocity increases below the midpoint, the water strikes the floor

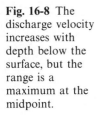

Fig. 16-8 The discharge velocity increases with depth below the surface, but the range is a maximum at the midpoint.

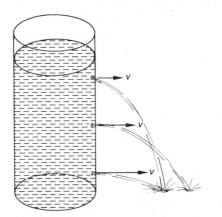

closer. This is because it strikes the floor sooner. Holes equidistant above and below the midpoint will have the same horizontal range.

As a final application, let us return to the venturi effect, which describes the motion of a fluid through a constriction. If the pipe in Fig. 16-9 is horizontal, we can set $h_1 = h_2$ in Bernoulli's equation, giving

$$P_1 + \tfrac{1}{2}\rho v_1^2 = P_2 + \tfrac{1}{2}\rho v_2^2 \tag{16-9}$$

Fig. 16-9 Fluid flow through a constriction in a horizontal pipe.

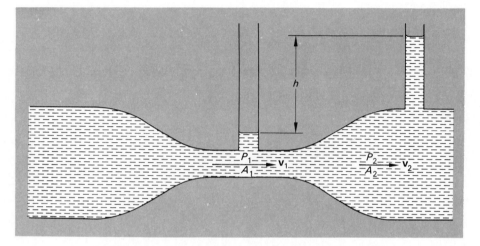

Since v_1 is greater than v_2, it follows that the pressure P_1 must be less than the pressure P_2 in order for Eq. (16-9) to hold. This relationship between velocity and pressure has already been discussed.

EXAMPLE 16-3   Water flowing initially at 10 ft/s passes through a venturi tube like the one in Fig. 16-9. If $h = 4$ in., what is the velocity of the water in the constriction?

Solution   The difference in pressure, from Eq. (16-3), is

$$P_2 - P_1 = \rho g h$$

The pressure difference, from Bernoulli's equation, is

$$P_2 - P_1 = \tfrac{1}{2}\rho v_1^2 - \tfrac{1}{2}\rho v_2^2$$

Combining these two relations, we have

$$\rho g h = \tfrac{1}{2}\rho v_1^2 - \tfrac{1}{2}\rho v_2^2$$

Multiplying through by $2/\rho$ gives

$$2gh = v_1^2 - v_2^2$$

Note that this relation is similar to that for a freely falling body with an initial velocity v_2. Solving for v_1^2, we have

$$v_1^2 = 2gh + v_2^2$$

$$= (2)(32 \text{ ft/s}^2)(0.333 \text{ ft}) + (10 \text{ ft/s})^2$$

$$= 21.3 \text{ ft}^2/\text{s}^2 + 100 \text{ ft}^2/\text{s}^2 = 121.3 \text{ ft}^2/\text{s}^2$$

Therefore, the velocity through the constriction is

$$v_1 = \sqrt{121.3} = 11 \text{ ft/s}$$

In the above example, the density of the fluid did not enter into our calculations because the fluid in the tubes above the pipe was the same as that flowing through the pipe. When considering the density of the fluid, it must be recognized that the symbol ρ is the mass density and not the weight density.

SUMMARY

In this chapter we have discussed the rate of flow of fluids and how it is related to fluid velocity and cross-sectional area. Bernoulli's equation was derived and applied to problems involving the dynamics of fluids. The essential concepts are summarized below:

- The *rate of flow* is defined as the volume of fluid that passes a certain cross section A per unit of time t. In terms of fluid velocity v, we write

$$\boxed{R = \frac{V}{t} = vA}\qquad \textit{Rate of flow = velocity} \times \textit{cross section}$$

- For an incompressible fluid flowing through pipes in which the cross sections vary, the rate of flow is constant:

$$\boxed{v_1 A_1 = v_2 A_2} \qquad \boxed{d_1^2 v_1 = d_2^2 v_2}$$

where v is the fluid velocity, A is the cross-sectional area of the pipe, and d is the diameter of the pipe.

- The net work done on a fluid is equal to the changes in kinetic and potential energy of the fluid. Bernoulli's equation expresses this fact in terms of the pressure P, the density ρ, the height of the fluid h, and its velocity v.

$$\boxed{P + \rho g h + \tfrac{1}{2}\rho v^2 = \text{constant}} \qquad \textit{Bernoulli's Equation}$$

If a volume of fluid changes from a state 1 to a state 2, as shown in Fig. 16-6, we can write

$$\boxed{P_1 + \rho g h_1 + \tfrac{1}{2}\rho v_1^2 = P_2 + \rho g h_2 + \tfrac{1}{2}\rho v_2^2}$$

- Special applications of Bernoulli's equation occur when one of the parameters does not change:

For a stationary liquid $(v_1 = v_2)$

$$\boxed{P_2 - P_1 = \rho g(h_1 - h_2)}$$

If the pressure is constant
$(P_1 = P_2)$

$$v = \sqrt{2gh}$$

For a horizontal pipe
$(h_1 = h_2)$

$$P_1 + \tfrac{1}{2}\rho v_1^2 = P_2 + \tfrac{1}{2}\rho v_2^2$$

QUESTIONS

16-1. Define the following terms:
  a. Streamline flow
  b. Turbulent flow
  c. Rate of flow
  d. Venturi effect
  e. Bernoulli's equation
  f. Torricelli's theorem

16-2. What assumptions and generalizations are made concerning the study of fluid dynamics?

16-3. Why does the flow of water from a faucet decrease when someone turns on another faucet in the same building?

16-4. Two rowboats moving parallel to each other in the same direction are drawn together. Explain.

16-5. Explain what would happen in a modern jet airliner at high speed if a hijacker fired a bullet through the window or broke open an escape hatch.

16-6. During high-velocity windstorms or hurricanes, the roofs of houses are sometimes blown off without otherwise damaging the homes. Explain with the use of diagrams.

16-6. During high-velocity windstorms or hurricanes, the roofs of houses are sometimes blown off without otherwise damaging the homes. Explain with the use of diagrams.

16-7. A small child knocks a balloon over the heating duct in his home and is surprised to find that the balloon remains suspended above the duct, bobbing from one side to the other. Explain.

16-8. What conditions would determine the maximum lift capacity of a stream-lined aircraft wing? Draw figures to justify your answer.

16-9. Explain with diagrams how a baseball pitcher throws a rising fast ball, an outside curve ball, and a sinking fast ball. Would a pitcher prefer to throw into the wind or with the wind when delivering the three pitches discussed above?

16-10. Two identical reservoirs are placed on the floor side by side. One is filled with mercury, and the other is filled with water. A hole is bored in each reservoir at the same depth below the surface. Compare the ranges of the emergent fluids.

PROBLEMS

16-1. Gasoline flows through a 1-in.-diameter hose at an average speed of 5 ft/s. What is the rate of flow in cubic feet per second? How many minutes are required to fill a 20-gal tank? (1 ft^3 = 7.481 gal.)
                                    Ans. 2.73×10^{-2} ft^3/s, 1.63 min.

16-2. Water flows from a terminal 3 cm in diameter and has an average speed of 2 m/s. What is the rate of flow in cubic meters per minute?

16-3. Water flowing from a 2-in. pipe emerges horizontally at the rate of 8 gal/min. What is the horizontal range of the stream of water if the pipe is 4 ft from the ground?

Ans. 0.408 ft.

16-4. What must the area of a hose be if it is to deliver 8 liters of oil in 1 min with an exit speed of 3 m/s? (1 liter = 0.001 m^3.)

16-5. Water flowing at 6 m/s through a 6-cm pipe is connected to a 3-cm pipe. What is the velocity in the small pipe? Is the rate of flow greater in the smaller pipe?

Ans. 24 m/s, no.

16-6. Oil is forced through a pipe at the rate of 6 gal/min. What should the diameter of a connecting tube be for an exit velocity of 4 ft/s?

16-7. What is the difference in pressure in the two connecting pipes of Prob. 16-5? Assume both pipes to be horizontal.

Ans. 270 kPa.

16-8. What is the difference in pressure in the two interconnecting pipes of Prob. 16-6 if the diameter of the entrance pipe is 2 in.? The weight density of the oil is 48 lb/ft^3, and the pipes are horizontal.

16-9. What is the emergent velocity of water from a crack in its container 6 m below the surface? If the area of the crack is 1.3 cm^3, at what rate of flow does water leave the container?

Ans. 10.8 m/s, 1.41 × 10^{-3} m^3/s.

16-10. Water flows at the rate of 2 ft^3/min through an opening at the bottom of a cylindrical tank. The water in the tank is 16 ft deep. What is the rate of escape if an added pressure of 9 lb/in.^{2} is applied to the surface of the water?

16-11. A pump of 2 kW output power discharges water from a cellar into a street 6 m above. At what rate in liters per second is the cellar emptied.

Ans. 34 L/s.

16-12. Water flows steadily through a horizontal pipe. At a point where the pressure is 20 lb/in.^{2} the velocity is 2 ft/s. What will the pressure be if the pipe changes in size causing the speed to increase to 25 ft/s?

16-13. A horizontal pipe of diameter 120 mm has a constriction of diameter 40 mm. The velocity of water in the pipe is 60 cm/s and the pressure is 150 kPa. **(a)** What is the velocity in the constriction? **(b)** What is the pressure in the constriction?

Ans. 540 cm/s, 136 kPa.

16-14. The water column in the container shown in Fig. 16-8 stands at a height H above the base of the container. Show that the depth h required to give the horizontal range x is given by

$$h = \frac{H}{2} \pm \frac{\sqrt{H^2 - x^2}}{2}$$

How does this equation show that holes equidistant above and below the midpoint will have the same horizontal range?

16-15 A column of water stands 16 ft above the base of its container. What are two hole depths at which the emergent water will have a horizontal range of 8 ft?

Ans. 1.07 ft, 14.9 ft.

16-16. Refer to Fig. 16-8 and Prob. 16-10. Show that the horizontal range is given by

$$x = 2\sqrt{h(H - h)}$$

Use this relation to show that the maximum range is equal to the height H of the water column.

16-17. Water flows through a horizontal pipe at the rate of 82 ft³/min. A pressure gauge placed on a 6-in. cross section of the pipe reads 16 lb/in.² What is the pressure in a section of pipe where the diameter is 3 in?

Ans. 11.1 lb/in.²

16-18. An aircraft wing 25 ft long and 5 ft wide experiences a lifting force of 800 lb. What is the difference in pressure between the upper and lower surfaces of the wing?

16-19. Assume that air ($\rho = 1.3$ kg/m³) is flowing past the top surface of an aircraft wing at 36 m/s. The air moving past the lower surface of the wing has a speed of 27 m/s. If the wing has a weight of 3700 N and an area of 3.5 m², what is the buoyant force on the wing?

Ans. 1290 N.

16-20. Benzene ($\rho = 1.71$ slugs/ft³) flows through a venturi meter having a throat diameter of 4 in. and a main-tube diameter of 8 in. If the drop in pressure is 600 lb/ft², what is the rate of flow in cubic feet per minute?

16-21. Water flows through the pipe shown in Fig. 16-10 at the rate of 120 ft³/min. The pressure at section A is 28 lb/in.², and the elevation of section B is 20 ft greater than that of section A. The lower section of pipe has a diameter of 12 in., and the upper section has a diameter of 8 in. **(a)** Find the velocities of the stream at points A and B. **(b)** What is the pressure at point B?

Ans. **(a)** $v_A = 2.55$ ft/s, $v_B = 5.73$ ft/s **(b)** 19.2 lb/in.²

Fig. 16-10

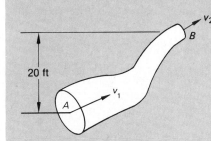

16-22. Seawater ($D = 64$ lb/ft³) is pumped through the system of pipes shown in Fig. 16-11 at the rate of 4 ft³/min. The pipe diameters at the lower and upper sections are 4 and 2 in., respectively. The water is discharged into the atmosphere ($P_a = 14.7$ lb/in.²) at the right end of the upper section, 6 ft above the lower section. **(a)** What are the speeds of flow in the upper and lower pipes? **(b)** What are the pressures in the lower and upper sections?

Fig. 16-11

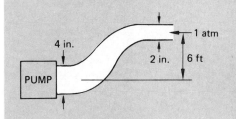

Heat, Light, and Sound

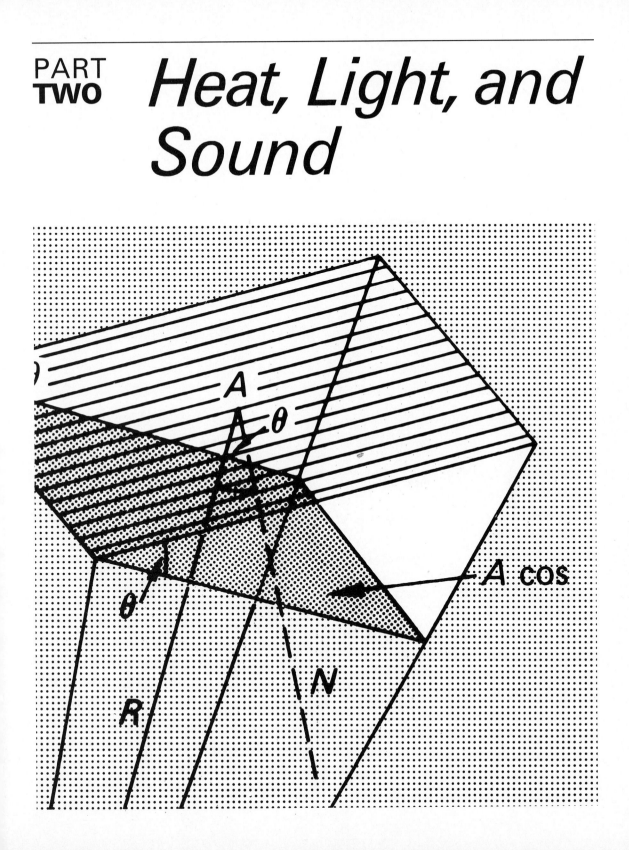

17 *Temperature and Expansion*

OBJECTIVES: After completing this chapter, you should be able to:

1. **Demonstrate your understanding of the Celsius, Fahrenheit, Kelvin, and Rankine temperature scales by converting from specific temperatures on one scale to corresponding temperatures on another scale.**

2. **Distinguish between specific temperatures and temperature intervals and convert an interval on one scale to the equivalent interval on another scale.**

3. **Write formulas for linear expansion, area expansion, and volume expansion and be able to apply them to the solution of problems similar to those given in this chapter.**

We have discussed the behavior of systems at rest and in motion. The fundamental quantities of mass, length, and time were introduced to describe the state of a given mechanical system.

Consider, for example, a 10-kg block moving with a constant speed of 20 m/s. The quantities of mass, length, and time are all present, and we find them sufficient to describe the motion. We can speak of the weight of the block, its kinetic energy, or its momentum, but a complete description of a system requires more than a simple statement of these quantities.

This becomes apparent when our 10-kg block encounters frictional forces. As the block slides to a stop, its energy seems to disappear, but the block and its supporting surface are slightly warmer. If energy is to be conserved, we must assume that the lost energy reappears in some form not yet considered. When energy disappears from the visible motion of objects and does not reappear in the form of visible potential energy, we frequently notice a rise in temperature. In this chapter we introduce the concept of temperature as a fourth fundamental quantity.

17-1 TEMPERA-TURE AND THERMAL ENERGY

Until now we have been concerned only with the causes and the effects of *external* motion. A block resting on a table is in translational and rotational equilibrium insofar as its surroundings are concerned. However, a much closer study of the block reveals that it is active internally. Figure 17-1 shows a simple model of a solid. Individual molecules are held together by elastic forces analogous to the springs in the figure. These molecules oscillate about their equilibrium positions with a particular frequency and amplitude. Thus both potential energy and kinetic energy are associated with the molecular motion.

Fig. 17-1 A simplified model of a solid in which the individual molecules are held together by elastic forces.

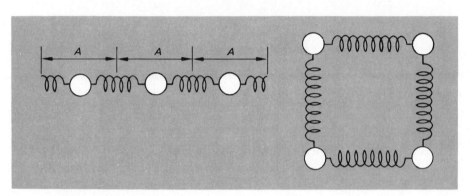

Since this internal energy is related to the hotness or coldness of a body, it is often referred to as thermal energy.

> **Thermal energy** represents the total internal energy of an object, i.e., the sum of its molecular kinetic and potential energies.

When two objects with different temperatures are placed in contact, energy is transferred from one to the other. For example, suppose hot coals are dropped into a container of water, as shown in Fig. 17-2. Thermal energy will be transferred from the coals to the water until the system reaches a stable condition, called *thermal equilibrium*. When touched, the coals and the water produce similar sensations and there is no more transfer of thermal energy.

Such changes in thermal energy states cannot be satisfactorily explained in terms of classical mechanics alone. Therefore, all objects must have a new fundamental property which determines whether they will be in thermal equilibrium with other objects. This property is called *temperature*. In our example, the coals and the water are said to have the same temperature when the transfer of energy is zero.

> *Two objects are said to be in* **thermal equilibrium** *if and only if they are at the same temperature.*

Once we establish a means of measuring temperature, we have a necessary and sufficient condition for thermal equilibrium. The transfer of thermal energy which is due only to a difference in temperature is defined as *heat*.

Fig. 17-2 Thermal equilibrium.

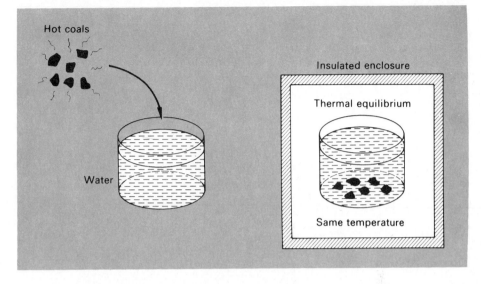

> **Heat** *is defined as the transfer of thermal energy which is due to a difference of temperature.*

Before discussing the measurement of temperature, we should distinguish clearly between temperature and thermal energy. It is possible for two objects to be in thermal equilibrium (same temperature) with very different thermal energies. For example, consider a pitcher of water and a pint cup of water, each having a temperature of 200°F. If they are mixed together, there will be no transfer of energy, but the thermal energy is much greater in the pitcher because it contains many more molecules. Remember that thermal energy represents the *sum* of the kinetic and potential energies of all the molecules. If we pour the water from each container onto separate blocks of ice, as shown in Fig. 17-3, more ice will be melted by the larger volume, indicating that it had more thermal energy.

17-2 THE MEASUREMENT OF TEMPERATURE

Temperature is usually determined by measuring some mechanical, optical, or electrical quantity which varies with temperature. For example, most substances expand as their temperature increases. If a change in any dimension can be shown to have a one-to-one correspondence with changes in temperature, the variation can be calibrated to measure temperature. A device calibrated in this way is called a *thermometer*. The temperature of another object can then be measured by placing the thermometer in close contact with it and allowing the two to reach thermal equilibrium. The temperature indicated by a number on the graduated thermometer also corresponds to the temperature of the surrounding objects.

> A **thermometer** is a device which, through marked scales, can give an indication of its own temperature.

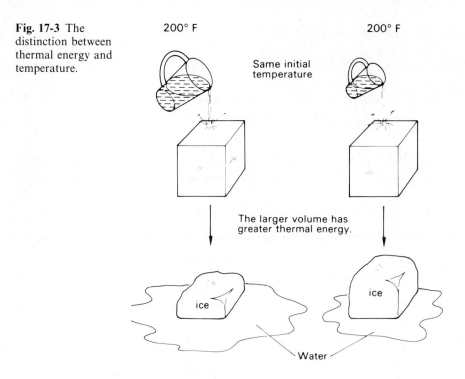

Fig. 17-3 The distinction between thermal energy and temperature.

200° F   200° F

Same initial temperature

The larger volume has greater thermal energy.

ice   ice

Water

Two things are necessary in constructing a thermometer. First, we must have a confirmation that some thermometric property X varies with temperature T. If the variation is linear, we can write

$$T = kX$$

where k is the proportionality constant. The thermometric property should be one that is easily measured, e.g., the expansion of a liquid, the pressure in a gas, or the resistance in an electric circuit. Other quantities which vary with temperature are radiated energy, the color of emitted light, vapor pressure, and magnetic susceptibility. Thermometers have been constructed for each of these thermometric properties. The choice is dictated by the range of temperatures over which the thermometer is linear and by the mechanics of its use.

The second requirement in constructing a thermometer is the establishment of standard temperatures. This is usually accomplished by selecting lower and upper *fixed points*, which are temperatures readily available for laboratory measurement. Two convenient temperatures easily reproduced are:

The **lower fixed point** (ice point) is the temperature at which water and ice coexist in thermal equilibrium under a pressure of 1 atm.

The **upper fixed point** (steam point) is the temperature at which water and steam coexist in equilibrium under a pressure of 1 atm.

The most widely used temperature measurement for scientific work is based on a scale set up by Anders Celsius (1701–1744), a Swedish astronomer. The *Celsius* scale arbitrarily assigns the number 0 to the lower fixed point and the number 100 to the upper fixed point. The 100 units between 0 and 100 represent temperatures between the ice point and the steam point. Since there are 100 divisions between these points, the Celsius scale is sometimes referred to as the *centigrade* scale. Each division or unit on the scale is called a *degree* (°). For instance, we write room temperature as 20°C (*twenty degrees Celsius*).

Sometimes a beginning student working in the laboratory is astonished that the temperature of ice and steam "turn out to be exactly 0 and 100°C." This certainly seems like an indication of order in the world of physics. Of course, the answer is that they have those temperatures simply because we define them in that manner. We may just as well marvel that our ears and nose are perfectly situated for wearing glasses.

Another scale for measuring temperature was developed in 1714 by Gabriel Daniel Fahrenheit. The development of this scale was based on the choice of different fixed points. Fahrenheit chose the temperature of a freezing solution of salt water as his lower fixed point and assigned the number and unit of 0°F. The upper fixed point was chosen to be the temperature of the human body. For some unexplained reason, he assigned the number and unit of 96°F for body temperature. The fact that body temperature is really 98.6°F indicates an experimental error in establishing the scale. Relating the Fahrenheit scale to the universally accepted fixed points on the Celsius scale, we note that 0 and 100°C correspond to 32 and 212°F.

We can compare the two scales by calibrating ordinary mercury-in-glass thermometers. This type of thermometer makes use of the fact that liquid mercury expands with increasing temperature. It consists of an evacuated glass capillary tube with a reservoir of mercury at the bottom and a closed top. Since mercury expands more than the glass tube, the mercury column rises in the tube until the mercury, glass, and its surroundings are in equilibrium.

Suppose we make two ungraduated thermometers and place them in a mixture of ice and water, as in Fig. 17-4. After allowing the mercury columns to stabilize, we mark 0°C on one thermometer and 32°F on the other. Next we place the two thermometers directly above boiling water, allowing the mercury columns to stabilize at the steam point. Again we mark the two thermometers, inscribing 100°C and 212°F adjacent to the mercury level above the marks corresponding to the ice point. The level of mercury is the same in each thermometer. Thus the only difference between the two thermometers will be in how they are graduated. There are 100 divisions, or Celsius degrees (C°), between the ice point and steam point on the Celsius thermometer, and there are 180 divisions, or Fahrenheit degrees (F°), on the Fahrenheit thermometer. Thus 100 Celsius degrees represents the same temperature interval as 180 Fahrenheit degrees. Symbolically,

$$100 \ C° = 180 \ F° \qquad \text{or} \qquad 5 \ C° = 9 \ F° \qquad (17\text{-}1)$$

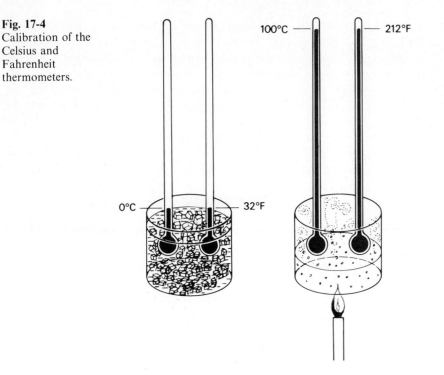

Fig. 17-4
Calibration of the Celsius and Fahrenheit thermometers.

100°C — — 212°F

0°C — — 32°F

The degree mark (°) is placed after the C or F to emphasize that the numbers correspond to temperature intervals and not to specific temperatures. In other words, 20 F° is read "twenty Fahrenheit degrees" and corresponds to a *difference* between two temperatures on the Fahrenheit scale. The symbol 20°F, on the other hand, refers to a specific mark on the Fahrenheit thermometer. For example, suppose a pan of hot food cools from 98 to 76°F. These numbers correspond to specific temperatures, as indicated by the height of a mercury column. However, they represent a temperature interval of

$$\Delta t = 98°F - 76°F = 22 \ F°$$

Δt is used to denote a change in temperature.

The physics which treats the transfer of thermal energy is nearly always concerned with changes in temperature. Thus it often becomes necessary to convert a temperature interval from one scale to the corresponding interval on the other scale. This can best be accomplished by recalling from Eq. (17-1) that an interval of 5 C° is equivalent to an interval of 9 F°. The appropriate conversion factors can be written as

$$\frac{5 \ C°}{9 \ F°} = 1 = \frac{9 \ F°}{5 \ C°} \tag{17-2}$$

When converting F° to C°, the factor on the left should be used; when converting C° to F°, the factor on the right should be used.

EXAMPLE 17-1   During a 24-h period, a steel rail varies in temperature from 20°F at night to 70°F in the middle of the day. Express this range of temperature in Celsius degrees.

Solution   The temperature interval is

$$\Delta t = 70°F - 20°F = 50 \text{ F}°$$

In order to convert the interval to Celsius degrees, we choose the conversion factor which will cancel the Fahrenheit units. Thus

$$\Delta t = 50 \text{ F} \times \frac{5 \text{ C}°}{9 \text{ F}} = 27.8 \text{ C}°$$

It must be remembered that Eq. (17-2) applies for temperature intervals. It can be used only when working with *differences* in temperatures. It is another matter entirely to find the temperature on the Fahrenheit scale which corresponds to the same temperature on the Celsius scale. Using ratio and proportion, we can develop an equation which will convert specific temperatures. Suppose, for example, we place two identical thermometers in a beaker of water, as shown in Fig. 17-5. One thermometer is graduated in Fahrenheit degrees and the other in Celsius degrees. The symbols t_C and t_F represent the same temperature (the temperature of the water), but they are on different scales. It should be apparent from the figure that the difference between t_C and 0°C corresponds to the same interval as the difference between t_F and 32°F. The ratio

Fig. 17-5 Comparison of the Celsius and Fahrenheit scales.

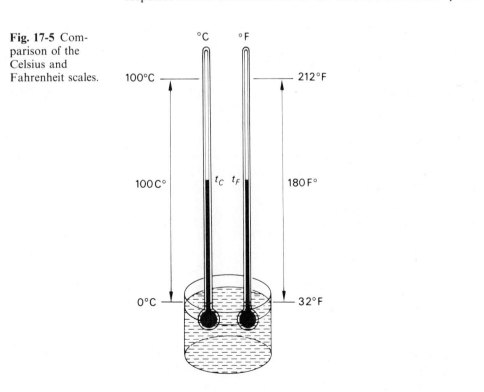

of the former to 100 divisions should be the same as the ratio of the latter to 180 divisions. Hence,

$$\frac{t_C - 0}{100} = \frac{t_F - 32}{180}$$

Simplifying and solving for t_C, we obtain

$$t_C = \tfrac{5}{9}(t_F - 32) \tag{17-3}$$

or, solving for t_F,

$$t_F = \tfrac{9}{5}t_C + 32 \tag{17-4}$$

EXAMPLE 17-2 The melting point of lead is 330°C. What is the corresponding temperature on the Fahrenheit scale?

Solution Substitution into Eq. (17-4) yields

$$t_F = \tfrac{9}{5}t_C + 32 = \tfrac{9}{5}(330) + 32$$

$$= 594 + 32 = 626°F$$

It is important to recognize that the t_F and t_C of Eqs. (17-3) and (17-4) represent identical temperatures. The numbers are different because the origin of each scale was at a different point and the degrees are of different size. What these equations tell us is the relationship between the *numbers* which are assigned to specific temperatures on two *different* scales.

17-3
THE GAS THER-MOMETER

Although the mercury-in-glass thermometer is the best known and most widely used, it is not as accurate as many other thermometers. In addition, mercury freezes at around −40°C, restricting the range over which it can be used. A very accurate thermometer with an extensive measuring range can be constructed by utilizing the properties of a gas. All gases subjected to heating expand in nearly the same manner. If their expansion is prevented by maintaining a constant volume, the pressure will increase in proportion to temperature.

In general, there are two kinds of gas thermometers. One kind maintains a constant pressure and utilizes the increases in volume as an indicator. This type is called a *constant-pressure* thermometer. The other kind, called a *constant-volume* thermometer, measures the increase in pressure as a function of temperature. The constant-volume thermometer is illustrated in Fig. 17-6. The gas is contained in bulb *B*, and the pressure it exerts is measured by the mercury manometer. As the temperature of the gas increases, it expands, forcing the mercury down in the closed tube and up in the open tube. In order to maintain a constant volume of the gas, the open tube must be raised until the level of mercury in the closed tube is brought back to the reference mark *R*.

Fig. 17-6 The
constant-volume
thermometer.

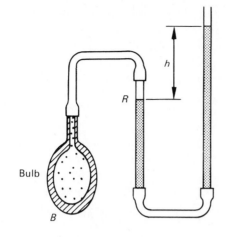

The difference in the two mercury levels is then an indication of the gas pressure at constant volume. The instrument can be calibrated for temperature measurements through the use of fixed points, as in the previous section.

The same apparatus can be used as a constant-pressure thermometer, as illustrated in Fig. 17-7. In this instance the volume of gas in bulb B is allowed to increase at constant pressure. The pressure exerted on the gas is maintained constant at 1 atm by lowering or raising the open tube until the mercury levels are the same in both tubes. The change in volume with temperature can then be indicated by the mercury level in the closed tube. Calibration consists of marking the mercury level at the ice point and again at the steam point.

Gas thermometers are very useful because of their almost unlimited range. For this reason and because they are so accurate, they are commonly used in research laboratories and in bureaus of standards. However, they are also large and bulky, rendering them useless for many minute technical measurements.

Fig. 17-7 The
constant-pressure
thermometer.

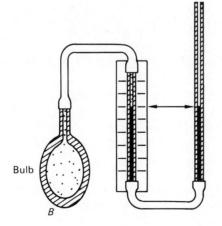

It has probably occurred to the reader that Celsius and Fahrenheit scales have a very serious limitation. Neither 0°C nor 0°F represents a true zero of temperature. Consequently, for temperatures much lower than the ice point a negative temperature results. Even more serious is the fact that a formula involving temperature as a variable will not work with the existing scales. For example, we have discussed the expansion of a gas with an increase in temperature. We can state this proportionality as

$$V = kt$$

where k is the proportionality constant and t is the temperature. Certainly, the volume of a gas is not zero at 0°C or negative at negative temperatures, and yet these conclusions might be drawn from the above relationship.

This example provides a clue for establishing an *absolute* scale. If we can determine the temperature at which the volume of a gas under constant pressure becomes zero, we can establish a true zero of temperature. Suppose we use a constant-pressure gas thermometer, like the one in Fig. 17-7. The volume of the gas in the bulb can be measured carefully, first at the ice point and then at the steam point. These two points can be plotted on a graph, as in Fig. 17-8,

Fig. 17-8 The variation of the volume of a gas as a function of temperature. Absolute zero can be defined by extrapolation to zero volume.

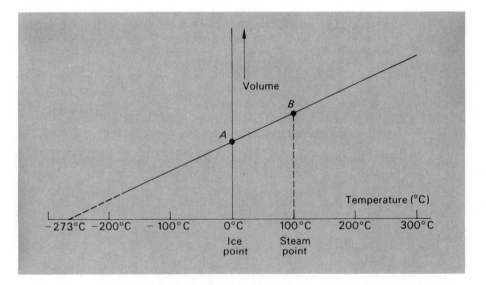

with the volume as the ordinate and the temperature as the abscissa. The points A and B correspond to the gas volume at temperatures of 0 and 100°C, respectively. A straight line through these two points, extended both to the left and to the right, provides a mathematical description of the change in volume as a function of temperature. Note that the line can be extended indefinitely to the right, indicating that there is no upper limit to temperature. However, we cannot extend the line indefinitely to the left because it will eventually intercept the temperature axis. At this theoretical point, the gas would have zero volume.

Further extension of the line would indicate a negative volume, which is meaningless. Therefore, the point at which the line intercepts the temperature axis is called the *absolute zero* of temperature. (Actually, any real gas would liquefy before reaching this point.)

If the above experiment is performed for several different gases, the slope of the curves will vary slightly. But the temperature intercept will always be the same and near $-273°C$. Ingenious theoretical and experimental procedures have established that the absolute zero of temperature is $-273.15°C$. In this text we shall assume that it is $-273°C$ without fear of significant error. Conversion to the Fahrenheit scale shows that absolute zero is $-460°F$ on that scale.

An absolute temperature scale has as its zero point the absolute zero of temperature. One such scale was devised by Lord Kelvin (1824–1907). The standard interval on this scale, the *kelvin*, has been adopted by the international (SI) metric system as the base unit for temperature measurement. The interval on the *Kelvin scale* represents the same change in temperature as the Celsius degree. Thus, an interval of 5 K (read "five kelvins") is exactly the same as 5 C°.

The Kelvin scale is related to the Celsius scale by the formula

$$T_K = t_C + 273$$

(17-5)

For example, 0°C would correspond to 273 K, and 100°C would correspond to 373 K. (See Fig. 17-9.) Hereafter we will reserve the symbol T for absolute temperature and the symbol t for other temperatures.

Fig. 17-9 A comparison of the four common temperature scales.

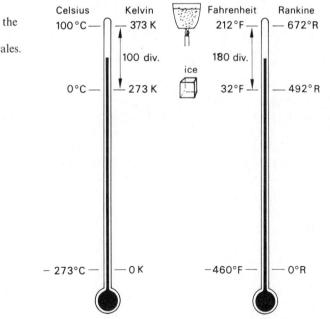

A second absolute scale in widespread use is the *Rankine scale*, which has its zero point at $-460°F$. The degree sizes on this scale are identical to Fahrenheit degrees. The relationship between the temperature in degrees Rankine (°R) and the corresponding temperature in degrees Fahrenheit is

$$T_R = t_F + 460 \tag{17-6}$$

For example, $0°F$ corresponds to $460°R$, and $212°F$ corresponds to $672°R$.

Remember that Eqs. (17-5) and (17-6) apply for specific temperatures. If we are concerned with a change in temperature or a difference in temperature, the absolute change or difference is the same in kelvins as it is in Celsius degrees. It is helpful to recall that

$$1 \text{ K} = 1 \text{ C}° \qquad 1 \text{ R}° = 1 \text{ F}° \tag{17-7}$$

EXAMPLE 17-3   A mercury-in-glass thermometer may not be used at temperatures below $-40°C$. This is because mercury freezes at this temperature. (*a*) What is the freezing point of mercury on the kelvin scale? (*b*) What is the difference between this temperature and the freezing point of water? Express the answer in kelvins.

Solution (a)   Direct substitution of $-40°C$ into Eq. (17-5) yields

$$T_K = -40°C + 273 = 233 \text{ K}$$

Solution (b)   The difference in the freezing points is

$$\Delta t = 0°C - (-40°C) = 40 \text{ C}°$$

Since the size of the kelvin is identical to that of the Celsius degree, the difference is also 40 kelvins.

At this point you may ask why we still retain the Celsius and Fahrenheit scales. When working with heat, one is nearly always concerned with changes in temperature. In fact, there must be a change in temperature in order for heat to be transferred. Otherwise, the system would be in thermal equilibrium. Since the Kelvin and Rankine scales are based on the same intervals as the Celsius and Fahrenheit scales, it makes no difference which scale is used for temperature intervals. On the other hand, if a formula calls for a specific temperature rather than a temperature difference, the absolute scale must be used.

**17-5
LINEAR
EXPANSION**
The most common effect produced by temperature changes is a change in size. With a few exceptions, all substances increase in size with rising temperature. The atoms in a solid are held together in a regular pattern by electric forces. At any temperature the atoms vibrate with a certain frequency and amplitude. As

the temperature is increased, the amplitude (maximum displacement) of the atomic vibrations increases. This results in an overall change in the dimensions of the solid.

A change in any *one* dimension of a solid is called *linear expansion*. It is found experimentally that an increase in a single dimension, for example the length of a rod, is dependent on the original dimension and the change in temperature. Consider, for example, the rod in Fig. 17-10. The initial length is

Fig. 17-10 Linear expansion.

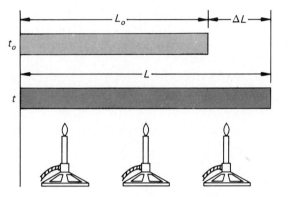

L_0 and the initial temperature is t_0. When heated to a temperature t, the rod's new length is denoted by L. Thus a change in temperature, $\Delta t = t - t_0$, has resulted in a change in length, $\Delta L = L - L_0$. The proportional change in length is given by

$$\Delta L = \alpha L_0 \, \Delta t \qquad (17\text{-}8)$$

where α is the proportionality constant called the *coefficient of linear expansion*. Since an increase in temperature does not produce the same increase in length for all materials, the coefficient α is a property of the material. Solving Eq. (17-8) for α, we obtain

$$\alpha = \frac{\Delta L}{L_0 \, \Delta t} \qquad (17\text{-}9)$$

The coefficient of linear expansion of a substance can be defined as *the change in length per unit length per degree change in temperature*. Since the ratio $\Delta L/L_0$ has no dimensions, the units of α are in inverse degrees, that is, $1/\text{C}°$ of $1/\text{F}°$. The expansion coefficients for many common materials are given in Table 17-1.

EXAMPLE 17-4   An iron pipe is 300 m long at room temperature (20°C). If the pipe is to be used as a steam pipe, how much allowance must be made for expansion, and what will the new length of the pipe be?

Table 17-1 Linear Expansion Coefficients

Substance	$10^{-5}/C°$	$10^{-5}/F°$
	α	
Aluminum	2.4	1.3
Brass	1.8	1.0
Concrete	0.7–1.2	0.4–0.7
Copper	1.7	0.94
Glass, Pyrex	0.3	0.17
Iron	1.2	0.66
Lead	3.0	1.7
Silver	2.0	1.1
Steel	1.2	0.66
Zinc	2.6	1.44

Solution

The temperature of steam is 100°C and $\alpha_{iron} = 1.2 \times 10^{-5}/C°$. Thus the increase in length is

$$\Delta L = \alpha L_0\, \Delta t = (1.2 \times 10^{-5}/C°)(300 \text{ m})(100°C - 20°C)$$

$$= (1.2 \times 10^{-5}/C°)(300 \text{ m})(80 \text{ C}°) = 0.288 \text{ m}$$

Therefore, the length of the pipe at 100°C is

$$L = L_0 + \Delta L = 300.29 \text{ m}$$

We can see from this example that the new length may be calculated by the following relation:

$$\boxed{L = L_0 + \alpha L_0\, \Delta t} \tag{17-10}$$

Remember, when calculating ΔL, that the units of α must be consistent with the units for Δt.

Linear expansion has both useful and destructive properties when applied to physical situations. The destructive effects require engineers to use expansion joints or rollers to make allowances for expansion. The predictable expansion of some materials, on the other hand, can be used to open or close switches at certain temperatures. Such devices are called *thermostats*.

Probably the most common application of the principle of linear expansion is the bimetallic strip. This device, shown in Fig. 17-11, consists of two flat strips of different metals welded or riveted together. The strips are fused together so that they are the same length at a chosen temperature t_0. If we heat the strip, causing a rise in temperature, the material with the larger expansion coefficient will expand more. For example, a brass-iron strip will bend in an arc toward the iron side. When the source of heat is removed, the strip will gradually return to its original position. Cooling the strip below the initial temperature will cause the strip to bend in the other direction. This results because

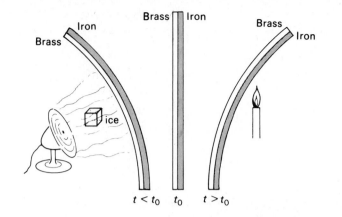

Fig. 17-11 The bimetallic strip.

Brass   Iron

Brass

Brass   Iron

Brass   Iron

ice

$t < t_0$ t_0 $t > t_0$

the material with the higher coefficient of expansion also *decreases* in length at a faster rate. The bimetallic strip has many useful applications, from thermostatic control systems to blinking lights. Since the expansion is in direct proportion to an increase in temperature, the bimetallic strip can also be used as a thermometer.

17-6 AREA EXPANSION

Linear expansion is by no means restricted to the length of a solid. Any line drawn through the solid will increase in length per unit length at the rate given by its expansion coefficient α. For example, in a solid cylinder the length, diameter, and a diagonal drawn through the solid will all increase their dimensions in the same proportion. In fact, the expansion of a surface is exactly analogous to a photographic enlargement, as illustrated in Fig. 17-12. Notice also that if the material contains a hole, the area of the hole expands at the same rate it would if it were filled with material.

Fig. 17-12 Thermal expansion is analogous to a photographic enlargement. Note that the hole gets larger in the same proportion as the material.

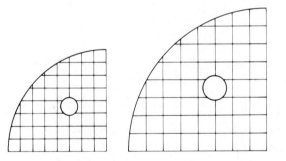

Let us consider the area expansion of the rectangular surface in Fig. 17-13. Both the length and width of the material will expand at the rate given by Eq. (17-10). Thus the new length and width are given, in factored form, by

$$L = L_0(1 + \alpha \, \Delta t)$$

$$W = W_0(1 + \alpha \, \Delta t)$$

Fig. 17-13 Area
expansion.

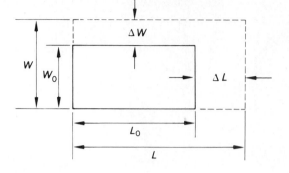

We can now derive an expression for area expansion by finding the product of these two equations.

$$LW = L_0 W_0 (1 + \alpha \, \Delta t)^2$$

$$= L_0 W_0 (1 + 2\alpha \, \Delta t + \alpha^2 \, \Delta t^2)$$

Since the magnitude of α is of the order of 10^{-5}, we may certainly neglect the term containing α^2. Hence we can write

$$LW = L_0 W_0 (1 + 2\alpha \, \Delta t)$$

or

$$A = A_0 (1 + 2\alpha \, \Delta t)$$

where $A = LW$ represents the new area and $A_0 = L_0 W_0$ represents the original area. Rearranging terms, we obtain

$$A - A_0 = 2\alpha A_0 \, \Delta t$$

or

$$\Delta A = 2\alpha A_0 \, \Delta t \qquad (17\text{-}11)$$

The coefficient of area expansion γ is approximately twice the coefficient of linear expansion. Symbolically,

$$\gamma = 2\alpha \qquad (17\text{-}12)$$

where γ (gamma) is the change in area per unit initial area per degree change in temperature. Using this definition, we may write the following formulas for area expansion.

$$\Delta A = \gamma A_0 \, \Delta t \qquad (17\text{-}13)$$

$$A = A_0 + \gamma A_0 \, \Delta t \qquad (17\text{-}14)$$

EXAMPLE 17-5   A brass disk has a hole 80 mm in diameter punched in its center at 70°F. If the disk is placed in boiling water, what will be the new area of the hole?

Solution

We first compute the area of the hole at 70°F.

$$A_0 = \frac{\pi D^2}{4} = \frac{\pi (80 \text{ mm})^2}{4} = 5027 \text{ mm}^2$$

Now the area expansion coefficient is

$$\gamma = 2\alpha = (2)(1.0 \times 10^{-5}/\text{F}°) = 2 \times 10^{-5}/\text{F}°$$

The increase in the area of the hole is found from Eq. (17-13) as follows:

$$\Delta A = \gamma A_0 \, \Delta t$$
$$= (2 \times 10^{-5}/\text{F}°)(5027 \text{ mm}^2)(212°\text{F} - 70°\text{F})$$
$$= 14.3 \text{ mm}^2$$

The new area is found by adding this increase to the original area (see Eq. (17-14)).

$$A = A_0 + \Delta A$$
$$= 5027 \text{ mm}^2 + 14.3 \text{ mm}^2 = 5041.3 \text{ mm}^2$$

17-7
VOLUME
EXPANSION

The expansion of heated material is the same in all directions. Therefore, the volume of a liquid, gas, or solid will have a predictable increase in volume with a rise in temperature. Reasoning similar to that of the previous sections will give us the following formulas for volume expansion.

$$\Delta V = \beta V_0 \, \Delta t \tag{17-15}$$

$$V = V_0 + \beta V_0 \, \Delta t \tag{17-16}$$

The symbol β (beta) is the *volume expansion coefficient*. It represents the *change in volume per unit volume per degree change in temperature*. For solid materials it is approximately three times the linear expansion coefficient.

$$\beta = 3\alpha \tag{17-17}$$

When working with solids, we can compute β from the table of linear expansion coefficients (Table 17-1). For different liquids, the volume expansion coefficients are listed in Table 17-2. The molecular separation in gases is so

Table 17-2 Volume Expansion Coefficients

	β	
Liquid	$10^{-4}/\text{C}°$	$10^{-4}/\text{F}°$
Alcohol, ethyl	11	6.1
Benzene	12.4	6.9
Glycerin	5.1	2.8
Mercury	1.8	1.0
Water	2.1	1.2

great that they all expand at approximately the same rate. Volumetric expansion of gases will be discussed later.

EXAMPLE 17-6 A Pyrex glass bulb is filled with 50 cm³ of mercury at 20°C. What volume will overflow if the system is heated uniformly to a temperature of 60°C? Refer to Fig. 17-14.

Fig. 17-14 The volume overflow is found by subtracting the change in volume of the glass from the change in volume of the liquid.

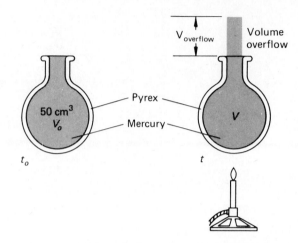

Solution The inside volume of the glass bulb is 50 cm³ initially and will increase according to Eq. (17-15). Remember that $\beta_G = 3\alpha_G$. At the same time, the mercury will increase in volume according to the value of β_M. The overflow will, therefore, be the difference between the two expansions.

$$\begin{pmatrix} \text{Volume} \\ \text{overflow} \end{pmatrix} = \begin{pmatrix} \text{volume increase} \\ \text{in mercury} \end{pmatrix} - \begin{pmatrix} \text{volume increase} \\ \text{in glass} \end{pmatrix}$$

$$V_{\text{overflow}} = \Delta V_M - \Delta V_G$$

$$= \beta_M V_M \,\Delta t - \beta_G V_G \,\Delta t$$

We will compute the volume increases separately.

$$\Delta V_M = \beta_M V_M \,\Delta t = (1.8 \times 10^{-4}/\text{C}°)(50 \text{ cm}^3)(40 \text{ C}°) = 0.36 \text{ cm}^3$$

$$\Delta V_G = 3\alpha_G V_G \,\Delta t = 3(0.3 \times 10^{-5}/\text{C}°)(50 \text{ cm}^3)(40 \text{ C}°) = 0.018 \text{ cm}^3$$

Thus the volume overflow is

$$V_{\text{overflow}} = \Delta V_M - \Delta V_G = 0.36 \text{ cm}^3 - 0.018 \text{ cm}^3$$

$$= 0.342 \text{ cm}^3$$

The volume overflow is 0.342 cm³.

**17-8
THE
ABNORMAL
EXPANSION
OF WATER**

Suppose we fill the bulb of the tube in Fig. 17-15 with water at 0°C so that the narrow neck is partially filled. Expansion or contraction of the water can easily be measured by observing the water level in the narrow tube. As the temperature of the water increases, the water in the tube will gradually sink, indicating a contraction. The contraction continues until the temperatures of the

Fig. 17-15 The irregular expansion of water. As the temperature of water is increased from 0 to 8°C, it first contracts and then expands.

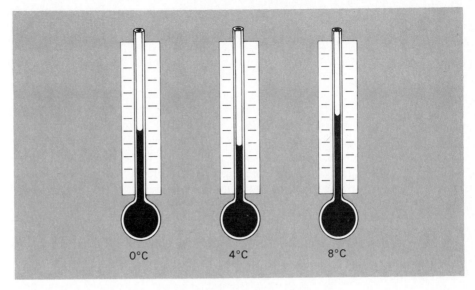

bulb and the water are 4°C. As the temperature increases above 4°C, the water reverses its direction and rises continuously, indicating the normal expansion with an increase in temperature. This means that water has its minimum volume and its maximum density at 4°C.

The variation in the density of water with temperature is shown graphically in Fig. 17-16. If we study the graph from the high-temperature side, we note that the density gradually increases to a maximum of 1.0 g/cm^3 at 4°C. The density then decreases gradually until the water reaches the ice point. Ice occupies a greater volume than water, and its formation sometimes results in cracked water pipes if proper precautions are not taken.

Fig. 17-16 Variation in the density of water near 4°C.

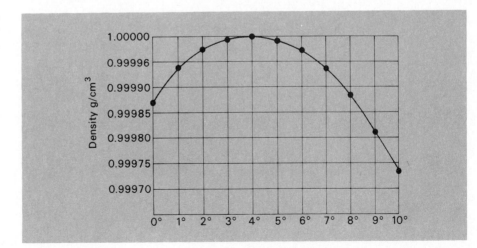

The greater volume in the ice results from the way groups of its molecules are bonded in its crystalline structure. As the ice melts, the water formed still contains groups of molecules bonded in this open crystal structure. As these structures begin to collapse, the molecules move closer together, increasing the density. This is the dominant process until the water reaches a temperature of 4°C. From that point to higher temperatures, the increased amplitude of molecular vibrations takes over and the water expands.

Once again the beginning student may be tempted to marvel that science can be so exact. The very thought that the density of water at 4°C "turns out to be exactly 1.00 g/cm^3" must certainly be a remarkable coincidence. However, like the temperatures of the ice point and steam point, this result is also a consequence of a definition. The scientists who originally devised the metric system defined the kilogram as the mass of 1000 cm^3 of water at 4°C. Later the kilogram was redefined in terms of a platinum–iridium cylinder which serves as a standard.

SUMMARY

We have seen that because of the existence of four commonly used temperature scales, temperature conversions are important. You have also studied one very important effect of changes in temperature of materials, a change in the physical dimensions. The major concepts are summarized below:

- There are four temperature scales with which you should be thoroughly familiar. These scales are compared in Fig. 17-5, giving values for the steam point, the ice point, and absolute zero on each scale. It is very important for you to distinguish between a temperature interval Δt and a specific temperature t. For temperature intervals:

$$\frac{5 \, C°}{9 \, F°} = 1 = \frac{9 \, F°}{5 \, C°} \qquad 1 \, K = 1 \, C° \qquad 1 \, R° = 1 \, F°$$

Temperature Intervals

- For specific temperatures you must correct for the interval difference, but you must also correct for the fact that different numbers are assigned for the same temperatures:

$$t_C = \frac{5}{9}(t_F - 32) \qquad t_F = \frac{9}{5} t_C + 32$$

Specific Temperatures

$$T_K = t_C + 273 \qquad T_R = t_F + 460$$

Absolute Temperatures

- The following relations apply for thermal expansion of solids:

$$\Delta L = \alpha L_0 \, \Delta t \qquad L = L_0 + \alpha L_0 \, \Delta t$$

Linear Expansion

$$\Delta A = \gamma A_0 \, \Delta t \qquad A = A_0 + \gamma A_0 \, \Delta t \qquad \gamma = 2\alpha$$

Area Expansion

$$\Delta V = \beta V_0 \, \Delta t \qquad V = V_0 + \beta V_0 \, \Delta t \qquad \beta = 3\alpha$$

Volume Expansion

- The volume expansion of a liquid uses the same relation as for a solid except, of course, that there is no linear expansion coefficient α for a liquid. Only β is needed.

QUESTIONS

17-1. Define the following terms:

a. Thermal energy
b. Temperature
c. Thermal equilibrium
d. Thermometer
e. Ice point
f. Steam point

g. Celsius scale
h. Fahrenheit scale
i. Absolute zero
j. Kelvin scale
k. Rankine scale
l. Coefficient of linear expansion

17-2. Two lumps of hot iron ore are dropped into a container of water. The system is insulated and allowed to reach thermal equilibrium. Is it necessarily true that the iron ore and the water have the same thermal energy? Is it necessarily true that they have the same temperature? Discuss.

17-3. Distinguish clearly between thermal energy and temperature.

17-4. If a flame is placed underneath a mercury-in-glass thermometer, the mercury column first drops and then rises. Explain.

17-5. What factors must be considered in the design of a sensitive thermometer?

17-6. How good is our sense of touch as a means of judging temperature? Does the "hotter" object always have the higher temperature?

17-7. Given an unmarked thermometer, how would you proceed to graduate it in Celsius degrees?

17-8. A 6-in. ruler expands 0.0014 in. when the temperature is increased 1 C°. How much would a 6-cm ruler expand during the same temperature interval if it is made of the same material?

17-9. A brass rod connects the opposite sides of a brass ring. If the system is heated uniformly, will the ring remain circular?

17-10. A brass nut is used with a steel bolt. How is the closeness of fit affected when the bolt alone is heated? If the nut alone is heated? If they are both heated equally?

17-11. An aluminum cap is screwed tightly to the top of a pickle jar at room temperature. After the pickle jar has been stored in the refrigerator for a day or two, the cap cannot easily be removed. Explain. Suggest a way to remove the cap with very little effort. How might this problem be solved by the manufacturer?

17-12. Describe the expansion of water near 4°C. Why does a lake freeze at the surface first? What temperature is likely to result at the bottom of the lake if its surface is frozen?

17-13. Follow reasoning similar to that for area expansion to derive Eqs. (17-15) and (17-16). In the text it was stated that γ is only approximately equal to twice α. Why is it not exactly twice α? Is the error larger in Eq. (17-13) or in Eq. (17-15)?

PROBLEMS

17-1. Body temperature is normal at 98.6°F. What is the corresponding temperature on the Celsius scale?

Ans. 37°C.

17-2. The boiling point of sulfur is 444.5°C. What is the corresponding temperature on the Fahrenheit scale?

17-3. The boiling point of oxygen is −297.35°F. What is the corresponding temperature on the Celsius scale? The Rankine scale? The Kelvin scale?

Ans. −183°C, 163°R, 90 K.

17-4. Gold melts at 1336 K. What is the corresponding temperature in degrees Rankine? In degrees Celsius? In degrees Fahrenheit?

17-5. A wall of firebrick has an inside temperature of 313°F and an outside temperature of 73°F. Express the difference in surface temperatures in Celsius degrees and in kelvins.

Ans. 133 C°, 133 K.

17-6. Prove that the Celsius and Fahrenheit scales have the same reading at −40°.

17-7. A piece of copper alloy is removed from a furnace at 200°C and cooled to a temperature of 20°C. Express the change in temperature in Fahrenheit degrees. What is the change in kelvins?

Ans. 324 F°, 180 K.

17-8. Acetone boils at 56.5°C. Liquid nitrogen boils at −196°C. Express the difference between these temperatures in Rankine degrees.

17-9. Suppose you wish to make history by setting up your own temperature scale. You choose the boiling point of acetone (56.5°C) as your lower fixed point and the boiling point of sulfur (444.5°C) as your upper fixed point. You call your scale the "Mentius scale" and divide it into 100 graduations between your chosen fixed points. Thus 0°M corresponds to 56.5°C, and 100°M corresponds to 444.5°C. What is the relation between a Mentius degree and a Celsius degree? What is absolute zero on your scale?

Ans. 1 M° = 3.88 C°, −85°M.

17-10. Answer the questions in Prob. 17-9 if your fixed points are chosen as the freezing (−117°C) and boiling (78.5°C) points of ethyl alcohol.

17-11. A piece of copper tubing is 6 m long at 20°C. How much will it increase in length when heated to a temperature of 80°C?

Ans. 6.12 mm.

17-12. A silver bar is 1 ft long at 70°F. How much will it increase in length when it is placed in boiling water?

17-13. The diameter of a hole in a steel plate is 9 cm when the temperature is 20°C. What will the diameter of the hole be at 200°C?

Ans. 9.019 cm.

17-14. A brass rod is 12 ft long at 70°F. If its length after heating is 12.01 ft, what is its temperature?

17-15. The laboratory apparatus for measuring the coefficient of linear expansion is illustrated in Fig. 17-17. The temperature of a metal rod is increased by passing steam through an enclosed jacket. The resulting increase in length is measured with the micrometer screw at one end. Since the original length and temperature are known, the expansion coefficient can be calculated from Eq. (17-8). The following data were recorded during an experiment with a rod of unknown metal:

$$L_0 = 60 \text{ cm} \qquad t_0 = 23°C$$

$$\Delta L = 0.104 \text{ cm} \qquad t_f = 98°C$$

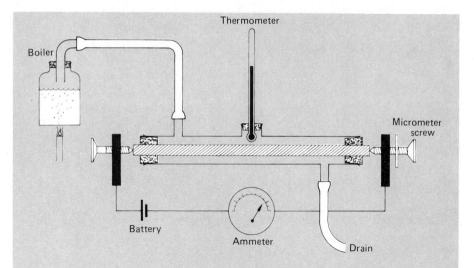

Fig. 17-17 Apparatus for measuring coefficient of linear expansion.

What is the coefficient of linear expansion for this metal? What do you think the metal is?

Ans. $2.3 \times 10^{-5}/C°$, Al.

17-16. Assume that the end points of a rod are rigidly fixed between two walls to prevent expansion with increasing temperature. From the definition of Young's modulus and your knowledge of linear expansion, show that the compressive force F exerted by the walls will be given by

$$F = \alpha A Y \, \Delta t$$

where A = cross section of rod
Y = Young's modulus of rod
Δt = increase in temperature of rod

17-17. The cross section of a steel rod is 2 in.². What force is needed to prevent it from expanding if the temperature is increased from 70 to 120°F?

Ans. 1.98×10^4 lb.

17-18. A rectangular sheet of aluminum measures 6 by 8 cm at 23°C. What is its area at 0°C?

17-19. A round brass plug has a diameter of 8.001 cm at 28°C. To what temperature must the plug be cooled if it is to fit snugly into an 8.000-cm hole?

Ans. 21.1°C.

17-20. The temperature of an iron rod 10.0 ft long and 0.2 in.² in cross section is lowered by 15 F°. What force would be required to stretch it to its original length? (See Prob. 17-16.)

17-21. What is the increase in volume of 16 liters of ethyl alcohol when it is heated from 20 to 50°C?

Ans. 0.528 liter.

17-22. A Pyrex glass beaker is filled to the top with 200 cm³ of mercury at 20°C. How much mercury will overflow if the temperature of the system is increased to 68°C?

17-23. If 200 cm^3 of benzene exactly fills an aluminum cup at 40°C, and if the system is cooled to 18°C, how much benzene (at 18°C) can be added to the cup without overflowing?

Ans. 5.14 cm^3.

17-24. Prove that the density of a material changes with temperature so that the new density ρ is given by

$$\rho = \frac{\rho_0}{1 + \beta \, \Delta t}$$

where ρ_0 = original density
β = volume expansion coefficient
Δt = change in temperature

17-25. The density of mercury at 0°C is 13.6 g/cm^3. What is its density at 60°C?

Ans. 13.5 g/cm^3.

18 *Quantity of Heat*

OBJECTIVES: After completing this chapter, you should be able to:

1. Define quantity of heat in terms of the *calorie*, the *kilocalorie*, the *joule*, and the *British thermal unit* (Btu).

2. Write a formula for the *specific heat capacity* of a material and apply it to the solution of problems involving the loss and gain of heat.

3. Write formulas for calculating the *latent heats of fusion* and *vaporization* and apply them to the solution of problems in which heat produces a change in phase of a substance.

4. Define the *heat of combustion* and apply it to problems involving the production of heat.

Thermal energy is the energy associated with random molecular motion, but it is not possible to measure the position and velocity of every molecule in a substance in order to determine its thermal energy. However, we can measure *changes* in thermal energy by relating it to a change in temperature.

For example, when two systems at different temperatures are placed together, they eventually reach a common intermediate temperature. From this observation it is safe to say that the system at the higher temperature has lost thermal energy to the system at the lower temperature. The thermal energy lost or gained by objects is called *heat*. This chapter is concerned with the quantitative measurement of heat.

**18-1
THE
MEANING
OF HEAT**

It was originally believed that two systems reach thermal equilibrium through the transfer of a substance called *caloric*. It was postulated that all bodies contain an amount of caloric in proportion to their temperature. Thus, when two objects were placed in contact, the object of higher temperature transferred

319

caloric to the object of lower temperature until they reached the same temperature. The idea that a substance is transferred carries with it the implication that there is a limit to the amount of heat energy that can be withdrawn from a body. It was this point that eventually led to the downfall of the caloric theory.

Count Rumford of Bavaria was the first to shed doubt on the caloric theory. He made his discovery in 1798 while supervising the boring of a cannon. The bore of the cannon was kept full of water to prevent overheating. As the water boiled away, it was replenished. According to the existing theory, caloric had to be supplied to boil the water. The apparent production of caloric was explained by supposing that when matter is finely divided, it loses some of its ability to retain caloric. Rumford devised an experiment to show that even a dull boring tool which did not cut the gun metal at all produced enough caloric to boil the water. In fact, it seemed that as long as mechanical work was supplied, the tool was an inexhaustible source of caloric. Rumford ruled out the caloric theory on the basis of his experiments and suggested that the explanation must be related to motion. Hence the idea that mechanical work is responsible for the creation of heat was introduced. The equivalence of heat and work as two forms of energy was established later by Sir James Prescott Joule.

18-2
THE
QUANTITY
OF HEAT

The idea of heat as a substance must be discarded. It is not something that an object *has* but something that it *gives up* or *absorbs*. Heat is simply another form of energy that can be measured only in terms of the effect it produces. We define a unit of heat as the thermal energy required to produce some standard change. Three common units are the *calorie*, the *kilocalorie*, and the *British thermal unit*.

> One **calorie** (cal) is the quantity of heat required to change the temperature of one gram of water through one Celsius degree.

> One **kilocalorie** (kcal) is the quantity of heat required to change the temperature of one kilogram of water through one Celsius degree. (1 kcal = 1000 cal.)

> One **British thermal unit** (Btu) is the quantity of heat required to change the temperature of water with a mass of one standard pound through one Fahrenheit degree.

Before we use these definitions, we must discuss briefly the relationship between the units involved. For instance, the pound unit (lb_m) which appears in the definition of a Btu must be recognized as the *mass of the standard pound*. This represents a departure from USCS units, in which the unit pound was reserved for weight. Therefore, when we refer to 1 lb_m of water, we shall be referring to a *mass* of water equivalent to about $\frac{1}{32}$ slug. This distinction is necessary because the pound of water must represent a constant quantity of matter, independent of location. By definition the pound mass is related to the gram and kilogram as follows:

$$1 \ lb_m = 454 \ g = 0.454 \ kg$$

The difference between the three units of heat results from the difference in masses and the difference in the temperature scales. It is left as an exercise for you to show that

$$1 \text{ Btu} = 252 \text{ cal} = 0.252 \text{ kcal} \tag{18-1}$$

Now that we have defined units for the quantitative measurement of heat, the distinction between quantity of heat and temperature should be clear. For example, suppose we pour 1 lb_m of water into one beaker and 4 lb_m of water into another beaker, as illustrated in Fig. 18-1. The initial temperature of the water in each beaker is measured to be 70°F. A flame is placed under each beaker for the same length of time, delivering 20 Btu of heat energy to the water in each beaker. The temperature of the 1-lb_m quantity of water increases 20 F°, but the temperature of the 4-lb_m quantity increases by only 5 F°. Yet the same quantity of heat was supplied to the water in each beaker.

Fig. 18-1 The same quantity of heat is applied to different masses of water. The larger mass experiences a smaller rise in temperature.

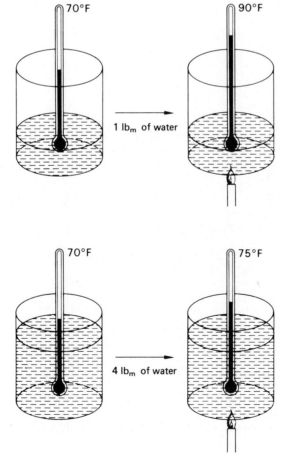

70°F   90°F

1 lb_m of water

70°F   75°F

4 lb_m of water

18-3 HEAT AND MECHANICAL ENERGY

Rumford's experiment demonstrated that as long as mechanical work is supplied, it is possible to obtain a limitless source of heat energy. For example, there is no limit to the heat energy produced by rubbing two wooden sticks together. However, mechanical energy is transformed into heat energy, and there must be a relationship between the units measuring mechanical energy and those measuring heat energy.

The first quantitative relationship between the thermal-energy units and the mechanical-energy units was established by Joule in 1843. Although Joule devised many different experiments to demonstrate the equivalence of heat units and energy units, the apparatus most often remembered is illustrated in Fig. 18-2. Falling weights supplied the mechanical energy, which rotated a set of

Fig. 18-2 Joule's experiment for determining the mechanical equivalent of heat. The falling weights do work in stirring the water and raising its temperature.

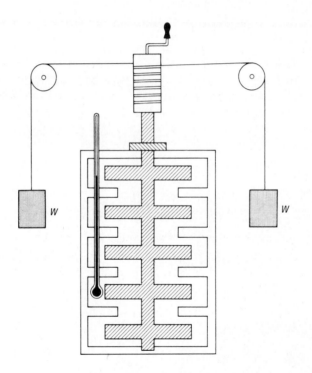

paddles in a water can. The quantity of heat absorbed by the water was measured from the known mass and the measured increase in temperature of the water.

From this experiment and others, Joule published an average result. His estimate was that an 812-lb weight falling through a height of 1 ft would cause the temperature of 1 lb$_m$ of water to rise 1°F. In other words, the thermal unit of 1 Btu was equivalent to the mechanical unit of 812 ft · lb.

In modern times the mechanical equivalent of heat has been accurately established in terms of the electric energy necessary to raise the temperature of water one degree. The accepted results are

$$1 \text{ Btu} = 778 \text{ ft} \cdot \text{lb} \qquad (18\text{-}2)$$
$$1 \text{ cal} = 4.186 \text{ J} \qquad (18\text{-}3)$$
$$1 \text{ kcal} = 4186 \text{ J} \qquad (18\text{-}4)$$

18-4 SPECIFIC HEAT CAPACITY

We have defined a quantity of heat as the thermal energy required to raise the temperature of a given mass. However, the amount of thermal energy required to raise the temperature of a substance varies for different materials. For example, suppose we apply heat to five balls, all of the same size but made of different materials, as shown in Fig. 18-3a. If we want to raise the temperature of each ball to 100°C, we shall find that some of the balls must be heated longer than the others. For illustration, let us assume that each ball has a volume of 1 cm³ and an initial temperature of 0°C. Each ball is heated with a burner capable of delivering thermal energy at the rate of 1 cal/s. The approximate times required to obtain a temperature of 100°C for each ball are given in Fig. 18-3. Notice that the lead ball reaches the final temperature in only 37 s whereas the iron ball requires 90 s of continuous heating. The glass, aluminum, and copper balls require intermediate times.

Fig. 18-3 A comparison of heat capacities for five balls of different materials.

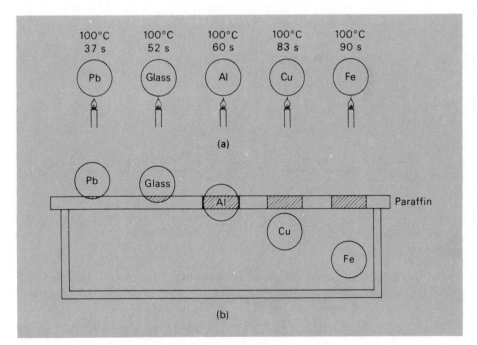

Since more heat was absorbed by the iron and copper balls, it might be expected that they would release more heat on cooling. That this is true can be demonstrated by placing the five balls (at 100°C) simultaneously on a thin strip of paraffin, as in Fig. 18-3b. The iron and copper balls eventually melt through the paraffin and drop into the pan. The lead and glass balls never make it through. Clearly, there must be some property of a material that relates to the quantity of heat absorbed or released during a change in temperature. As a step in establishing this property, we first define *heat capacity*.

The **heat capacity** of a body is the ratio of heat supplied to the corresponding rise in temperature of the body.

$$\text{Heat capacity} = \frac{Q}{\Delta t} \qquad (18\text{-}5)$$

The units of heat capacity are calories per Celsius degree (cal/C°), kilocalories per Celsius degree (kcal/C°), or Btu per Fahrenheit degree (Btu/F°). For the above example, 89.4 cal of heat was required to raise the temperature of the iron ball by 100 C°. Thus the heat capacity of the iron ball is 0.894 cal/C°.

The mass of an object is not included in the definition of heat capacity. Therefore, heat capacity is a property of the object. To make it a property of the material, the *heat capacity per unit mass* is defined. We call this property the *specific heat capacity*, denoted c.

The **specific heat capacity** of a material is the quantity of heat required to raise the temperature of a unit mass through one degree.

$$\boxed{c = \frac{Q}{m\,\Delta t} \qquad Q = mc\,\Delta t} \qquad (18\text{-}6)$$

The SI unit of specific heat assigns the *joule* for heat, the *kilogram* for mass, and the *kelvin* for temperature. Thus c has units of J/kg · K. In industry most temperature measurements are made in C° or F°, and the calorie and the Btu are still the dominant units for the quantity of heat. For the immediate future, this text will emphasize the following units for specific heat in the metric and U.S. customary systems: cal/g · C° and Btu/lb$_m$ · F°. In the example of the iron ball, the mass is found to be 7.85 g. The specific heat of iron is therefore

$$c = \frac{Q}{m\,\Delta t} = \frac{89.4 \text{ cal}}{(7.85 \text{ g})(100 \text{ C°})} = 0.114 \text{ cal/g · C°}$$

Notice that we speak of the heat capacity of the *ball* and the specific heat of *iron*. The former relates to the object itself whereas the latter relates to the material from which the object is made. In our experiment with the balls, we noted only the quantity of heat required to raise their temperature 100 C°. The density of the materials was not considered. If the sizes of the balls were adjusted so that each had the same mass, we would observe different results.

Since the specific heat of aluminum is the highest, more heat would be required for the aluminum ball than for the others. Similarly, the aluminum ball would release more heat in cooling.

We have defined a calorie as the heat required to change the temperature of one gram of water through one Celsius degree. Therefore, the specific heat of water is equal to 1 cal/g $\cdot$ C° (or 1 kcal/kg $\cdot$ C°) by definition. Similar reasoning with the definition of a Btu will show that the specific heat of water is also equal to 1 Btu/lb$_m$ $\cdot$ F°. An important consequence of these definitions is that the specific heat of any object is numerically the same in either system of units. This can be demonstrated by unit conversion:

$$1 \, \frac{Btu}{lb_m \cdot F°} \times \frac{9 \, F°}{5 \, C°} \times \frac{1 \, lb_m}{454 \, g} \times \frac{252 \, cal}{1 \, Btu} = 1 \, cal/g \cdot C°$$

The specific heats of some common substances are listed in Table 18-1.

Table 18-1 Specific Heat Capacities

Substance	c, cal/g $\cdot$ C° or Btu/lb$_m$ $\cdot$ F°
Aluminum	0.22
Brass	0.094
Copper	0.093
Ethyl alcohol	0.60
Glass	0.20
Gold	0.03
Ice	0.50
Iron	0.113
Lead	0.031
Mercury	0.033
Silver	0.056
Steam	0.480
Steel	0.114
Turpentine	0.42
Zinc	0.092

Once the specific heats of a large number of materials have been established, the thermal energy released or absorbed in many experiments can be determined. For example, the quantity of heat Q required to raise the temperature of a mass m through an interval Δt, from Eq. (18-6), is

$$Q = mc \, \Delta t \qquad (18\text{-}7)$$

where c is the specific heat of the mass.

EXAMPLE 18-1   How much heat is required to raise the temperature of 200 g of mercury from 20 to 100°C?

| **Solution** | Substitution into Eq. (18-7) yields |

$$Q = mc\,\Delta t = (200\text{ g})(0.033\text{ cal/g} \cdot \text{C}°)(100°\text{C} - 20°\text{C})$$

$$= (200\text{ g})(0.033\text{ cal/g} \cdot \text{C}°)(80\text{ C}°) = 528\text{ cal}$$

**18-5
THE
MEASURE-
MENT OF
HEAT**

We have often emphasized the distinction between thermal energy and temperature. The term *heat* has now been introduced as the thermal energy *absorbed* or *released* during a temperature change. The quantitative relationship between heat and temperature is best described by the concept of specific heat as it appears in Eq. (18-7). The physical relationships between all these terms are now beginning to fall into place.

The principle of thermal equilibrium tells us that whenever objects are placed together in an insulated enclosure, they will eventually reach the same temperature. This is the result of a transfer of thermal energy from the warmer bodies to the cooler bodies. If energy is to be conserved, we say that *the heat lost by the warm bodies must equal the heat gained by the cool bodies*. That is,

$$\boxed{Heat\ lost = heat\ gained} \tag{18-8}$$

This equation expresses the net result of heat transfer within a system.

The heat lost or gained by an object is not related in a simple way to the molecular energies of the objects. Whenever thermal energy is supplied to an object, it can absorb the energy in many different ways. The concept of specific heat is needed to measure the abilities of different materials to utilize thermal energy to increase their temperatures. The same amount of applied thermal energy does not result in the same temperature increase for all materials. For this reason, we say that temperature is a *fundamental* quantity. Its measurement is necessary in order to determine the quantity of heat lost or gained in a given process.

In applying the general equation for the conservation of thermal energy [Eq. (18-7)], the quantity of heat gained or lost by each item is calculated from the equation

$$Q = mc\,\Delta t \tag{18-7}$$

The term Δt represents the absolute change in temperature when applied to the conservation equation. The procedure is best demonstrated by an example.

EXAMPLE 18-2

A handful of copper shot is heated to 90°C and then dropped into 80 g of water at 10°C. The final temperature of the mixture is 18°C. What was the mass of the shot?

Solution

Applying Eq. (18-8), we write

Heat lost by shot = heat gained by water

$$m_s c_s\,\Delta t_s = m_w c_w\,\Delta t_w$$

$$m_s c_s(t_s - t_e) = m_w c_w(t_e - t_w)$$

The change in temperature of the shot is computed by subtracting the equilibrium temperature t_e from the initial temperature of the shot t_s. On the other hand, the change in temperature of the water is computed by subtracting the initial temperature of the water t_w from the equilibrium temperature. This does not represent an error in sign because the quantity on the left represents a heat *loss* and the quantity on the right represents a heat *gain*. Obtaining the required specific heats from Table 18-1 and substituting other known quantities, we have

$$m_s(0.093 \text{ cal/g} \cdot \text{C}°)(90°\text{C} - 18°\text{C}) = (80 \text{ g})(1 \text{ cal/g} \cdot \text{C}°)(18°\text{C} - 10°\text{C})$$

$$m_s(0.093 \text{ cal/g} \cdot \text{C}°)(72 \text{ C}°) = (80 \text{ g})(1 \text{ cal/g} \cdot \text{C}°)(8 \text{ C}°)$$

$$m_s = 95.6 \text{ g}$$

In this simple example we have neglected two important facts: (1) the water must have a container, which will also absorb heat from the shot; (2) the entire system must be insulated from external temperatures. Otherwise, the equilibrium temperature will always be room temperature. A laboratory device called a *calorimeter* (Fig. 18-4) is used to control these difficulties. The calorimeter consists of a thin metallic vessel K, generally aluminum, held centrally

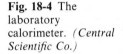

Fig. 18-4 The laboratory calorimeter. *(Central Scientific Co.)*

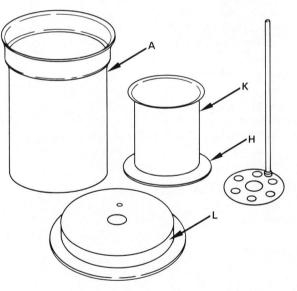

within an outer jacket A by a nonconducting rubber support H. Loss of heat is minimized in three ways: (1) the rubber gasket prevents loss by conduction; (2) the dead air space between the container walls prevents heat loss by air currents; and (3) highly polished metal vessels reduce the loss of heat by radiation. These three methods of heat transfer will be discussed in the following chapter. The wooden cover L has holes in the top for insertion of a thermometer and an aluminum stirrer.

EXAMPLE 18-3 In a laboratory experiment it is desired to use a calorimeter to find the specific heat of iron. Eighty grams of dry iron shot is placed in a cup and heated to a temperature of 95°C. The mass of the inner aluminum cup and of the aluminum stirrer is 60 g. The calorimeter is partially filled with 150 g of water at 18°C. The hot shot is quickly poured into the cup, and the calorimeter is sealed, as shown in Fig. 18-5. After the system has reached thermal equilibrium, the final temperature is 22°C. Compute the specific heat of iron.

Fig. 18-5 A calorimeter can be used to compute the specific heat of a substance.

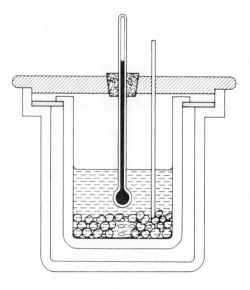

Solution The heat lost by the iron shot must equal the heat gained by the water plus the heat gained by the aluminum cup and stirrer. We can assume that the initial temperature of the cup is the same as that of the water and stirrer (18°C). We will calculate the heat gained by the water and by the aluminum separately.

$$Q_{water} = mc\ \Delta t = (150\ g)(1\ cal/g \cdot C°)(22°C - 18°C)$$

$$= (150\ g)(1\ cal/g \cdot C°)(4\ C°) = 600\ cal$$

$$Q_{Al} = mc\ \Delta t = (60\ g)(0.22\ cal/g \cdot C°)(22°C - 18°C)$$

$$= (60\ g)(0.22\ cal/g \cdot C°)(4\ C°) = 52.8\ cal$$

Now the total heat gained is the sum of these values.

$$\text{Heat gained} = 600\ cal + 52.8\ cal = 652.8\ cal$$

This amount must equal the heat lost by the iron shot:

$$\text{Heat lost} = Q_s = mc_s\ \Delta t = (80\ g)c_s(95°C - 22°C)$$

Setting the heat lost equal to the heat gained gives

$$(80\ g)c_s(73\ C°) = 652.8\ cal$$

Solving for c_s, we obtain

$$c_s = \frac{652.8 \text{ cal}}{(80 \text{ g})(73 \text{ C}°)} = 0.11 \text{ cal/g} \cdot \text{C}°$$

In this experiment the heat gained by the thermometer was neglected. In an actual experiment, the portion of the thermometer inside the calorimeter would absorb about the same amount of heat as an extra 0.5 g of water. This quantity, called the *water equivalent* of the thermometer, should be added to the mass of water in an accurate experiment.

18-6 CHANGE OF PHASE

When a substance absorbs a given amount of heat, the speed of its molecules usually increases and its temperature rises. Depending on the specific heat of the substance, the rise in temperature is directly proportional to the quantity of heat supplied and inversely proportional to the mass of the substance. However, a curious thing happens when a solid melts or when a liquid boils. In these cases, the temperature remains constant until all the solid melts or until all the liquid boils.

To understand what happens to the applied energy, let us consider a simple model, as illustrated in Fig. 18-6. Under the proper conditions of temperature and pressure, all substances can exist in three *phases*, solid, liquid, or

Fig. 18-6 A simplified model showing the relative molecular separations in the solid, liquid, and gaseous phases. During a change of phase, the temperature remains constant.

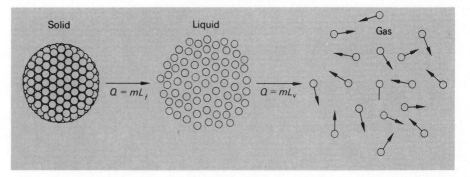

gas. In the solid phase, the molecules are held together in a rigid, crystalline structure so that the substance has a definite shape and volume. As heat is supplied, the energies of the particles in the solid gradually increase and its temperature rises. Eventually, the kinetic energy becomes so great that some of the particles overcome the elastic forces that hold them in fixed positions. The increased separation gives them the freedom of motion which we associate with the liquid phase. At this point, the energy absorbed by the substance is used in separating the molecules more than in the solid phase. The temperature does not increase during such a change of phase. The change of phase from a solid to a liquid is called *fusion*, and the temperature at which this change occurs is called the *melting point*.

The quantity of heat required to melt a unit mass of a substance at its melting point is called the *latent heat of fusion* for that substance.

The **latent heat of fusion** L_f of a substance is the heat per unit mass required to change the substance from the solid to the liquid phase at its melting temperature.

$$L_f = \frac{Q}{m} \qquad Q = mL_f \tag{18-9}$$

The latent heat of fusion L_f is expressed in Btu per pound, calories per gram, or kilocalories per kilogram. The term *latent* arises from the fact that the temperature remains constant during the melting process. The heat of fusion for water is 80 cal/g or 144 Btu/lb$_m$. This means that 1 g of ice absorbs 80 cal of heat energy in forming 1 g of water at 0°C.

After all the solid melts, the kinetic energy of the particles in the resulting liquid increases in accordance with its specific heat, and the temperature rises again. Eventually the temperature will level off as the thermal energy is used to change the molecular structure, forming a gas or vapor. The change of phase from a liquid to a vapor is called *vaporization*, and the temperature associated with this change is called the *boiling point* of the substance.

The quantity of heat required to vaporize a unit mass is called the *latent heat of vaporization*.

The **latent heat of vaporization** L_v of a substance is the heat per unit mass required to change the substance from a liquid to a vapor at its boiling temperature.

$$L_v = \frac{Q}{m} \qquad Q = mL_v \tag{18-10}$$

The heat of vaporization for water is 540 cal/g or 970 Btu/lb$_m$. In other words, 1 g of water absorbs 540 cal of heat energy in forming 1 g of water vapor at 100°C.

Values for the heat of fusion and the heat of vaporization of other substances are given in Table 18-2. It should be noted that the numerical difference between the *calorie per gram* and the *Btu per pound mass* arises only because of the difference between temperature intervals. Consequently, the unit of 1 Btu/lb$_m$ is equivalent to nine-fifths that of 1 cal/g.

It is often helpful in studying the changes of phase of a substance to plot a graph showing how the temperature of the substance varies as thermal energy is applied. Such a graph is shown in Fig. 18-7 for water. If a quantity of ice is taken from a freezer at -20°C and heated, its temperature will increase gradually until the ice begins to melt at 0°C. For each degree rise in temperature, each gram of ice will absorb 0.5 cal of heat energy. During the melting process, the temperature remains constant, and each gram of ice will absorb 80 cal of heat energy in forming 1 g of water.

Table 18-2 Heats of Fusion and Heats of Vaporization for Various Substances

Substance	Melting point, °C	Heat of fusion, cal/g	Boiling point, °C	Heat of vaporization, cal/g
Alcohol, ethyl	−117.3	24.9	78.5	204
Aluminum	658	76.8	2057	
Ammonia	−75	108.1	−33.3	327
Copper	1080	42	2310	
Helium	−269.6	1.25	−268.9	5
Lead	327.3	5.86	1620	208
Mercury	−39	2.8	358	71
Oxygen	−218.8	3.3	−183	51
Silver	960.8	21	2193	558
Water	0	80	100	540
Zinc	420	24	918	475

Once all the ice has melted, the temperature begins to rise again at a uniform rate until the water begins to boil at 100°C. For each degree increase in temperature, each gram will absorb 1 cal of heat energy. During the vaporization process, the temperature remains constant. Each gram of water absorbs 540 cal of heat energy in forming 1 g of water vapor at 100°C. If the resulting water vapor is contained and the heating is continued until all the water is gone, the temperature will again start to rise. The specific heat of steam is 0.48 cal/g · C°.

Fig. 18-7 The variation of temperature with a change in thermal energy for water.

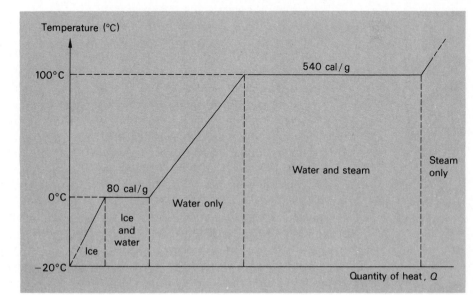

EXAMPLE 18-4   What quantity of heat is required to change 20 lb_m of ice at 12°F to steam at 212°F?

Solution   The heat necessary to raise the temperature of the ice to its melting point is

$$Q_1 = mc\,\Delta t = (20 \text{ lb}_m)(0.5 \text{ Btu/lb}_m \cdot \text{F}°)(32°\text{F} - 12°\text{F})$$

$$= 200 \text{ Btu}$$

The heat required to melt the ice is given from Eq. (18-9).

$$Q_2 = mL_f = (20 \text{ lb}_m)(144 \text{ Btu/lb}_m) = 2880 \text{ Btu}$$

The heat necessary to raise the temperature of the resulting water to 212°F is

$$Q_3 = mc\,\Delta t = (20 \text{ lb}_m)(1 \text{ Btu/lb}_m \cdot \text{F}°)(212°\text{F} - 32°\text{F})$$

$$= 3600 \text{ Btu}$$

The heat required to vaporize the water is, from Eq. (18-10),

$$Q_4 = mL_v = (20 \text{ lb}_m)(970 \text{ Btu/lb}_m) = 19{,}400 \text{ Btu}$$

The total heat required is

$$Q = Q_1 + Q_2 + Q_3 + Q_4$$

$$= (200 + 2880 + 3600 + 19{,}400) \text{ Btu}$$

$$= 26{,}080 \text{ Btu}$$

When heat is removed from a gas, its temperature drops until it reaches the temperature at which it boiled. As more heat is removed, the vapor returns to the liquid phase. This process is referred to as *condensation*. In condensing, a vapor gives up an amount of heat equivalent to the heat required to vaporize it. Thus the *heat of condensation* is equivalent to the heat of vaporization. The difference lies only in the direction of heat transfer.

Similarly, when heat is removed from a liquid, its temperature will drop until it reaches the temperature at which it melted. As more heat is removed, the liquid returns to its solid phase. This process is called *freezing* or *solidification*. The heat of solidification is exactly equal to the heat of fusion. Thus the only distinction between freezing and melting lies in whether heat is being released or absorbed.

Under the proper conditions of temperature and pressure, it is possible for a substance to change from the solid phase directly to the gaseous phase without passing through the liquid phase. This process is referred to as *sublimation*. Solid carbon dioxide (dry ice), iodine, and camphor (mothballs) are examples of substances which are known to sublime at normal temperatures. The quantity of heat absorbed per unit mass in changing from a solid to a vapor is called the *heat of sublimation*.

Before we leave the subject of fusion and vaporization, it will be instructive to offer examples of their measurement. In any given mixture, the quantity of heat absorbed must equal the quantity of heat released. This principle holds even if a change of phase occurs. The procedure is demonstrated in the examples below.

EXAMPLE 18-5   After 12 g of crushed ice at $-10°C$ is dropped into a 50-g aluminum calorimeter cup containing 100 g of water at 50°C, the system is sealed and allowed to reach thermal equilibrium. What is the resulting temperature?

Solution   The heat lost by the calorimeter and water must equal the heat gained by the ice, including any changes of phase that take place. Let us assume that all the ice melts, leaving only water at the equilibrium temperature t_e.

$$Total\ heat\ lost = heat\ lost\ by\ calorimeter + heat\ lost\ by\ water$$

$$= m_c\, c_c(50°C - t_e) + m_w\, c_w(50°C - t_e)$$

$$= (50)(0.22)(50°C - t_e) + (100)(1)(50°C - t_e)$$

$$= 550°C - 11t_e + 5000°C - 100t_e$$

$$= 5550°C - 111t_e$$

$$Total\ heat\ gained = heat\ gained\ by\ ice + heat\ to\ melt\ ice + heat\ to\ bring\ water\ to\ t_e$$

$$= m_i\, c_i\, \Delta t_i + m_i\, L_f + m_i\, c_w(t_e - 0°C)$$

$$= (12)(0.5)(10) + (12)(80) + (12)(1)t_e$$

$$= 1020 + 12t_e$$

$$Total\ heat\ lost = total\ heat\ gained$$

$$5550 - 111t_e = 1020 + 12t_e$$

$$123t_e = 4530$$

$$t_e = 36.8°C$$

EXAMPLE 18-6   If 10 g of steam at 100°C is introduced into a mixture of 200 g of water and 120 g of ice, find the final temperature and composition of the mixture.

Solution   The rather small amount of steam in comparison with ice and water makes us wonder whether enough heat can be released by the steam to melt all the ice. To check this suspicion, we shall compute the heat required to melt the 120 g of ice completely at 0°C.

$$Q_1 = m_i\, L_f = (120\ g)(80\ cal/g) = 9600\ cal$$

The maximum heat we can expect the steam to give up is

$$Q_2 = m_s\, L_v + m_s\, c_w(100°C - 0°C)$$

$$= (10)(540) + (10)(1)(100) = 6400\ cal$$

Since 9600 cal was needed to melt all the ice and only 6400 cal can be delivered by the steam, the final mixture must consist of ice and water at 0°C.

To determine the final composition of the mixture, note that 3200 additional calories would be required to melt the remaining ice. Hence

$$m_i\, L_f = 3200\ cal$$

$$m_i = \frac{3200\ cal}{80\ cal/g} = 40\ g$$

Therefore, there must be 40 g of ice in the final mixture. The amount of water remaining is

$$Water\ remaining = initial\ water + melted\ ice + condensed\ steam$$

$$= 200\ g + 80\ g + 10\ g = 290\ g$$

The final composition consists of a mixture of 40 g of ice in 290 g of water at 0°C.

Suppose we had assumed in the above example that all the ice melted, attempting to solve for t_e as in Example 18-5. In this case, we would have obtained a value for the equilibrium temperature which was below the freezing point (0°C). Clearly, this kind of answer could result only from a false assumption.

An alternative procedure for solving Example 18-6 would be to solve directly for the number of grams of ice which must have melted in order to balance the 6400 cal of heat energy released by the steam. It is left as an exercise for you to show that the same results are obtained.

18-7 HEAT OF COMBUSTION

Whenever a substance is burned, it releases a definite quantity of heat. The quantity of heat per unit mass, or per unit volume, when the substance is completely burned is called the *heat of combustion*. Commonly used units are Btu per pound mass, Btu per cubic foot, calories per gram, and kilocalories per cubic meter. For example, the heat of combustion of coal is approximately 13,000 Btu/lb$_m$. This means that each pound of coal, when completely burned, should release 13,000 Btu of heat energy.

SUMMARY

In this chapter you have studied the quantity of heat as a measurable quantity that is based on a standard change. The British thermal unit and the calorie are measures of the heat required to raise the temperature of a unit mass of water by a unit degree. By applying these standard units to experiments with a variety of materials, we have learned to predict heat losses or heat gains in a constructive fashion. The essential concepts presented in this chapter are as follows:

- The **British thermal unit** (Btu) is the heat required to change the temperature of one pound-mass of water one Fahrenheit degree.
- The **calorie** is the heat required to raise the temperature of one gram of water by one Celsius degree.
- Several conversion factors may be useful for problems involving thermal energy:

$$\boxed{1\ Btu = 252\ cal = 0.252\ kcal} \qquad \boxed{1\ cal = 4.186\ J}$$

$$\boxed{1\ Btu = 778\ ft \cdot lb} \qquad \boxed{1\ kcal = 4186\ J}$$

- The **specific heat capacity** c is used to determine the quantity of heat Q absorbed or released by a unit mass m as the temperature changes by an interval Δt.

$$c = \frac{Q}{m \, \Delta t} \qquad Q = mc \, \Delta t \qquad \textit{Specific Heat Capacity}$$

- Conservation of thermal energy requires that in any exchange of thermal energy the heat lost must equal the heat gained.

$$\textit{Heat lost} = \textit{heat gained} \qquad \sum (mc \, \Delta t)\text{loss} = \sum (mc \, \Delta t)\text{gain}$$

As an example, suppose body 1 transfers heat to bodies 2 and 3 as the system reaches an equilibrium temperature t_e:

$$m_1 c_1(t_1 - t_e) = m_2 c_2(t_e - t_2) + m_3 c_3(t_e - t_3)$$

- The latent **heat of fusion** L_f and the latent **heat of vaporization** L_v are heat losses or gains by a unit mass m during a phase change. There is no change in temperature.

$$L_f = \frac{Q}{m} \qquad Q = mL_f \qquad \textit{Latent Heat of Fusion}$$

QUESTIONS

18-1. Define the following terms:
- **a.** Heat
- **b.** Temperature
- **c.** Calorie
- **d.** British thermal unit
- **e.** Mechanical equivalent of heat
- **f.** Heat capacity
- **g.** Specific heat capacity
- **h.** Conservation of heat energy
- **i.** Calorimeter
- **j.** Water equivalent
- **k.** Fusion
- **l.** Melting point
- **m.** Heat of fusion
- **n.** Vaporization
- **o.** Boiling point
- **p.** Heat of vaporization
- **q.** Condensation
- **r.** Freezing
- **s.** Sublimation
- **t.** Heat of combustion

18-2. Discuss the caloric theory of heat. In what ways is it successful in explaining heat phenomena? Where does it fail?

18-3. Blocks of five different metals—aluminum, copper, zinc, iron, and lead—are constructed with the same mass and the same cross-sectional area. Each block is heated to a temperature of 100°C and placed on a block of ice. Which will melt the ice to the greatest depth? List the remaining four metals in the order of decreasing penetration depths.

18-4. On a winter day the snow is observed to melt from the concrete sidewalk before it melts from the road. Which has the higher heat capacity?

18-5. If two objects have the same heat capacity, are they necessarily constructed of the same material? What if they have the same specific heat capacities?

18-6. Why is temperature considered a *fundamental quantity*?

18-7. A mechanical analogy to the concept of thermal equilibrium is given in Fig. 18-8. When the valve is opened, the water will flow until it has the same level in each tube. What are the analogies to temperature and thermal energy?

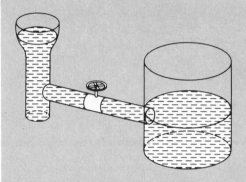

Fig. 18-8 A mechanical analogy to the equalization of temperature.

18-8. The mechanical equivalence of heat is established so that heat and work can be expressed in the same units. How then can we distinguish between the terms *work* and *heat*?

18-9. Discuss the change of phase from solid to liquid to vapor in terms of the molecular theory of matter.

18-10. In a mixture of ice and water, the temperature of both the ice and the water is 0°C. Why then does the ice feel colder to the touch?

18-11. Why does steam at 100°C produce a far worse burn than water at 100°C?

18-12. The temperature of 1 g of iron is raised by 1 C°. How much more heat would be required to raise the temperature of 1 lb_m of iron by 1 F°?

PROBLEMS

18-1. How much heat in calories is required to raise the temperature of 200 g of lead from 20 to 100°C? From 40 to 90°F?

Ans. 496 cal, 172 cal.

18-2. What quantity of heat will be released when 40 lb_m of copper cools from 78 to 32°F?

18-3. A lawn mower engine does work at the rate of 7 hp. What equivalent amount of heat energy will the engine give off in 1 h?

Ans. 1.78×10^4 Btu.

18-4. The mechanical output of an electric motor is 2 kW. This represents 80 percent of the input electric energy; the remainder is lost to heat. Express this loss in kilocalories per second.

18-5. A waterfall is 500 ft above the base of a cliff. If all the potential energy lost in the fall is converted into heat, how much is the temperature of the water raised?

Ans. 0.643 F°.

18-6. How much heat is developed by the brakes of a 4000-lb_m car in order to bring it to a rest from a speed of 60 mi/h?

18-7. Hot coffee is poured into an 0.5-kg ceramic cup with a specific heat of 0.21 cal/g · C°. How much heat is absorbed by the cup if its temperature increases from 78 to 178°F?

Ans. 5.83 kcal.

18-8. When 450 cal of heat is applied to a brass ball, its temperature increases from 20 to 70°C. What is the mass of the ball?

18-9. A 4-lb copper sleeve must be heated from 70 to 250°F so that it will expand enough to slip over a shaft. How much heat is needed?

Ans. 67.0 Btu.

18-10. In a heat-treating operation, a hot copper part is cooled quickly in water (quenched). If the temperature of the part drops from 400 to 30°C and the part loses 80 kcal of heat, what was the mass of the copper part?

18-11. A foundry has an electric furnace that can completely melt 540 kg of copper. If the temperature of the copper was initially 20°C, how much heat is required?

Ans. 75,900 kcal.

18-12. How much heat is needed to completely melt 20 g of silver at its melting temperature?

18-13. A heating element supplies heat at the rate of 20 kcal per minute. How much time is required to completely melt a 3-kg block of aluminum?

Ans. 11.5 min.

18-14. How much heat does an electric freezer absorb in lowering the temperature of 1900 g of water from 80 to 10°C?

18-15. A 450-g cylinder of lead is heated to 100°C and dropped into a 50-g copper calorimeter. The calorimeter contains 100 g of water initially at 10°C. Find the specific heat of lead if the equilibrium temperature of the mixture is 21.1°C.

Ans. 0.033 cal/g · C°.

18-16. How much iron (at 212°F) must be mixed with 10 lb_m of water at 68°F to bring the equilibrium temperature to 100°F?

18-17. A workman needs to know the temperature inside an oven. He removes a 2-kg iron bar from the oven and places it in a 1-kg aluminum container partially filled with 2 kg of water. If the temperature of the water rises from 21 to 50°C, what was the oven temperature?

Ans. 292°C.

18-18. Suppose that 200 g of copper at 300°C is dropped into 310 g of water at 15°C contained in a 310-g copper calorimeter cup. Compute the equilibrium temperature.

18-19. What quantity of heat is required to convert 2 kg of ice at −25°C to steam at 100°C?

Ans. 1465 kcal.

18-20. How much heat will be released by converting 0.5 lb_m of steam to ice at 10°F?

18-21. In an experiment to determine the latent heat of vaporization for water, a student determines the mass of an aluminum calorimeter cup to be 50 g. After a quantity of water is added, the combined mass of the water and calorimeter is 120 g. The initial temperature of the water and calorimeter is 18°C. A quantity of steam at 100°C is passed into the calorimeter, and the system is allowed to reach thermal equilibrium. The equilibrium temperature is 47.4°C, and the total mass of the final mixture is 124 g.

(a) What is the mass of water in the cup before the steam was introduced? **(b)** What mass of steam condensed? **(c)** What value will the student obtain for the heat of vaporization?

Ans. **(a)** 70 g **(b)** 4 g **(c)** 543 cal/g.

18-22. If 4 g of steam at 100°C is mixed with 20 g of ice at −5°C, what will the equilibrium temperature be?

18-23. If 10 g of ice at −5°C is mixed with 6 g of steam at 100°C, find the final temperature and composition of the mixture.

Ans. 13.38 g of H_2O, 2.62 g of steam at 100°C.

18-24. What equilibrium temperature is reached when 2 lb_m of ice at 0°F is dropped into 7.5 lb_m of water at 200°F in a 3-lb_m aluminum calorimeter?

18-25. How many pounds of coal must be burned to melt completely 50 lb_m of ice in a heater that is 60 percent efficient?

Ans. 0.923 lb_m.

18-26. If 100 g of water at 20°C is mixed with 100 g of ice at 0°C and 4 g of steam at 100°C, find the final temperature and composition of the mixture.

18-27. How much fuel oil (15,000 Btu/lb_m) is needed to raise the temperature of 120 lb_m of steel from 75 to 900°F?

Ans. 0.746 lb_m.

Table 19-1 Thermal Conductivities

Substance	k Btu $\cdot$ in./ft^2 $\cdot$ h $\cdot$ F$^\circ$	kcal/m $\cdot$ s $\cdot$ C$^\circ$
Aluminum	1451	5.0×10^{-2}
Brass	750	2.6×10^{-2}
Copper	2660	9.2×10^{-2}
Silver	2870	9.9×10^{-2}
Steel	320	1.1×10^{-2}
Asbestos	4.0	1.4×10^{-4}
Brick	5.0	1.7×10^{-4}
Concrete	12.0	4.1×10^{-4}
Corkboard	0.3	1.0×10^{-5}
Glass	7.3	2.5×10^{-4}
Air	0.16	5.3×10^{-6}
Water	4.15	1.4×10^{-4}

EXAMPLE 19-1

The outside wall of a brick barbecue pit is 3 in. thick. The inside surface is at 300°F, and the outside surface is 85°F. How much heat is lost in 1 h through an area of 1 ft^2?

Solution

Solving for Q in Eq. (19-1), we obtain

$$Q = kA\tau \frac{\Delta t}{L}$$

$$= (5 \text{ Btu} \cdot \text{in./ft}^2 \cdot \text{h} \cdot \text{F}^\circ)(1 \text{ ft}^2)(1 \text{ h}) \frac{300°\text{F} - 85°\text{F}}{3 \text{ in.}}$$

$$= 358 \text{ Btu}$$

It is always a good idea to carry the units of each quantity throughout the entire solution of a problem. This practice will save many needless errors. For example, it is sometimes easy to forget that in USCS units the thickness must be expressed in inches and the area in square feet. If the units of thermal conductivity are given with their numerical value in the equation, these errors will not be made.

When two materials of different thermal conductivities and similar cross sections are connected, the rate at which heat is conducted through each material must be constant. If there are no sources or sinks of heat energy within the materials and the end points are maintained at a constant temperature, a steady flow will eventually be reached. The heat cannot "pile up" or "speed up" at any point.

EXAMPLE 19-2

The wall of a freezing plant is composed of 10 cm of corkboard inside 14 cm of solid concrete (Fig. 19-3). (a) If the temperature of the inner wall of the corkboard is $-20°$C and that of the outer wall is 24°C, find the temperature of the corkboard–concrete interface. (b) Calculate the heat flow in kilocalories per square meter per second.

Fig. 19-3 Heat conduction through a compound wall.

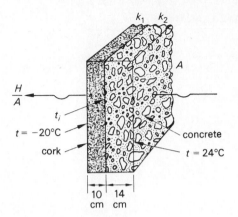

Solution (a)

For steady flow, the rate of heat flow through the corkboard is equal to the rate of heat flow through the concrete. We shall use the subscript 1 to refer to the corkboard and the subscript 2 to refer to the concrete. Thus, letting t_i be the temperature at the interface, we have

$$\frac{H}{A} \text{ (corkboard)} = \frac{H}{A} \text{ (concrete)}$$

$$\frac{k_1[t_i - (-20°C)]}{L_1} = \frac{k_2(24°C - t_i)}{L_2}$$

$$\frac{(1 \times 10^{-5})(t_i + 20)}{0.10 \text{ m}} = \frac{(4.1 \times 10^{-4})(24 - t_i)}{0.14 \text{ m}}$$

Now if we multiply through by 1.4×10^4, we obtain

$$1.4(t_i + 20) = 41(24 - t_i)$$

$$1.4t_i + 28 = 984 - 41t_i$$

$$t_i = 22.5°C$$

Solution (b)

The heat flow per unit area per unit time can now be found from

$$\frac{H_1}{A_1} = \frac{k_1(t_i + 20°C)}{0.10 \text{ m}}$$

$$= \frac{(1 \times 10^{-5} \text{ kcal/m} \cdot \text{s} \cdot \text{C}°)(22.5 + 20) \text{ C}°}{0.10 \text{ m}}$$

$$= 4.25 \times 10^{-3} \text{ kcal/m}^2 \cdot \text{s}$$

The same rate would be calculated through the concrete. Note that the difference in temperature between the end points of the corkboard is 42.5 C° whereas the temperature difference in the concrete is only 1.5 C°. The very different temperature intervals result primarily from the difference in thermal conductivities of the walls.

19-3 CONVECTION

Convection has been defined as the process in which heat is transferred by the actual mass motion of a material medium. A current of liquid or gas that absorbs energy at one place and then moves to another place, where it releases heat to a cooler portion of the fluid, is called a *convection current*. A laboratory demonstration of a convection current is illustrated in Fig. 19-4. A rectangular

Fig. 19-4 An example of natural heat convection.

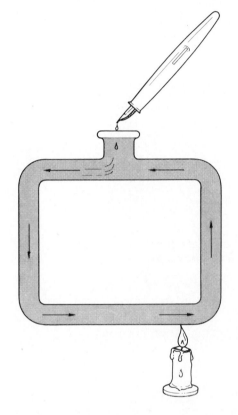

section of glass tubing is filled with water and heated at one of the lower corners. The water near the flame is heated and expands, becoming less dense than the cooler water above it. As the heated water rises, it is replaced by cooler water from the lower tube. This process continues until a counterclockwise convection current is circulating throughout the tubing. The existence of such a current is vividly demonstrated by dropping ink into the opening at the top. The ink will be carried along by the convection current until it finally returns to the top from the right section of the tube.

If the motion of a fluid is caused by a difference in density that accompanies a change in temperature, the current produced is referred to as *natural convection*. The water flowing through the glass tubing in the above example represents a natural-convection current. When a fluid is caused to move by the action of a pump or fan, the current produced is referred to as *forced convection*. Many homes are heated by using fans to force hot air from a furnace throughout the rooms.

Both forced- and natural-convection currents occur in the process of heating a room with a radiator. (Refer to Fig. 19-5.) A circulating water pump

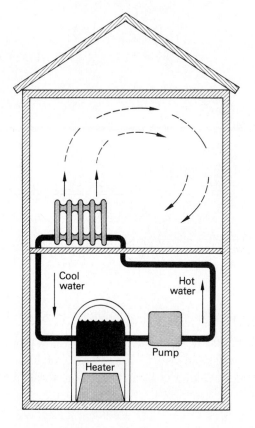

Fig. 19-5 Forced convection currents circulate the heated water and return it to the furnace. The room is heated by natural convection currents in the air.

forces hot water through the pipes to the radiator and back to the heater or furnace. The heat from the water is conducted through walls of the radiator to the air in contact with it. The heated air rises and displaces the cooler air, thus establishing natural-convection currents throughout the room. Although some heating occurs by the process of radiation, conduction and convection play the large heating roles. The name "radiator" is a misnomer.

The calculation of heat transferred by convection is an enormously difficult task. So many physical properties of a fluid depend upon temperature and pressure that we can hope for only an estimate in most situations. We present a working relationship based on experimental observations. Suppose we consider a conducting slab of material of area A and temperature t_s. If this vertical slab is completely submerged in a cooler fluid at a temperature t_f, natural-convection currents will be set up in the fluid, as illustrated in Fig. 19-6. The fluid which comes in contact with the walls will rise and displace the cooler air. Experimental observation shows that the rate H at which heat is transferred by convection is proportional to the area A and to the difference in temperature Δt between the wall and the fluid. We write

$$H = \frac{Q}{\tau} = hA\,\Delta t \qquad\qquad (19\text{-}3)$$

where h is the proportionality constant called the *convection coefficient*.

Fig. 19-6 When a heated slab is placed in a cool fluid, convection currents transfer heat away from the slab at a rate proportional to the difference in temperatures and to the area of the slab.

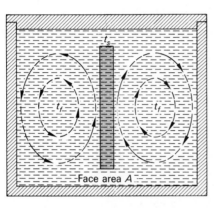

Unlike thermal conductivity, the convection coefficient is not a property of the solid or fluid but depends upon many parameters of the system. It is known to vary with the geometry of the solid and its surface finish, the velocity of the fluid, the density of the fluid, and the thermal conductivity. Differences in the temperature and pressure of the fluid also affect the value for h. Convection coefficients for certain geometries are given in Table 19-2. Commonly accepted units for h are $\text{kcal/m}^2 \cdot \text{s} \cdot \text{C}°$ in the metric system and $\text{Btu/h} \cdot \text{ft}^2 \cdot \text{F}°$ in the USCS.

Table 19-2 Convection Coefficients

Geometry	$h,\ \text{kcal/m}^2 \cdot \text{s} \cdot \text{C}°$
Vertical plate	$(4.24 \times 10^{-4})\sqrt[4]{\Delta t}$
Horizontal plate	
Facing up	$(5.95 \times 10^{-4})\sqrt[4]{\Delta t}$
Facing down	$(3.14 \times 10^{-4})\sqrt[4]{\Delta t}$
Pipe of diameter D	$(1.0 \times 10^{-3})\sqrt[4]{\dfrac{\Delta t}{D}}$

EXAMPLE 19-3

A flat vertical wall 6 m² in area is maintained at a constant temperature of 116°C, and the surrounding air on both sides is at 35°C. How much heat is lost from the wall to both sides in 1 h by natural convection?

Solution

We must first compute h for a vertical wall. From Table 19-2 we have

$$h = (4.24 \times 10^{-4})\sqrt[4]{116 - 35}$$

$$= (4.24 \times 10^{-4})\sqrt[4]{81} \text{ kcal/m}^2 \cdot \text{s} \cdot \text{C}°$$

$$= 1.27 \times 10^{-3} \text{ kcal/m}^2 \cdot \text{s} \cdot \text{C}°$$

The quantity of heat transferred from each wall can be found by solving for Q in Eq. (19-3).

$$Q = hA\tau \, \Delta t$$

$$= (1.27 \times 10^{-3} \text{ kcal/m}^2 \cdot \text{s} \cdot \text{C}°)(6 \text{ m}^2)(3600 \text{ s})(81 \text{ C}°)$$

$$= 2.22 \times 10^3 \text{ kcal}$$

Since there are two walls, the total heat transferred is

$$Q = (2)(2.22 \times 10^3 \text{ kcal}) = 4.44 \times 10^3 \text{ kcal}$$

19-4 RADIATION

The term radiation refers to the continuous emission of energy in the form of electromagnetic waves originating at the atomic level. Gamma-rays, x-rays, light waves, infrared rays, radio waves, and radar waves are all examples of electromagnetic radiation; they differ only in their wavelength. In this section, we shall be concerned with *thermal radiation*.

Thermal radiation consists of electromagnetic waves emitted by a solid, liquid, or gas by virtue of its temperature.

All objects are continuously emitting radiant energy. At low temperatures the rate of emission is small, and the radiation is predominantly of long wavelengths. As the temperature is increased, the rate of emission increases very rapidly, and the predominant radiation shifts to shorter wavelengths. If an iron rod is heated continuously, it will eventually give off radiation in the visible region; hence the terms *red hot* and *white hot*.

Experimental measurements have shown that the rate at which thermal energy is radiated from a surface *varies directly with the fourth power of the absolute temperature of the radiating body.* Thus, if the temperature of an object is doubled, the rate at which it emits thermal energy will be increased sixteenfold.

An additional factor which must be considered in computing the rate of heat transfer by radiation is the nature of the exposed surfaces. Objects that are good emitters of thermal radiation are also good absorbers of radiation. An object which absorbs all the radiation incident on its surface is called an *ideal absorber*. Such an object will also be an *ideal radiator*. There is no such thing as an *ideal* absorber; but, in general, the blacker a surface is, the better it absorbs thermal energy. For example, a black shirt absorbs more of the sun's radiant energy than a lighter shirt. Since the black shirt is also a good emitter, its external temperature will be higher than our body temperature, making us uncomfortable.

An ideal absorber or an ideal radiator is sometimes referred to as a *blackbody* for the reasons mentioned above. The radiation emitted from a blackbody is called *blackbody radiation*. Although such bodies do not actually exist, the concept is very useful as a standard for comparing the abilities of various surfaces to absorb or emit thermal energy.

> **Emissivity** e is a measure of a body's ability to absorb or emit thermal radiation.

The emissivity is a unitless quantity which has a numerical value between 0 and 1, depending upon the nature of the surface. For a blackbody, the emissivity is equal to unity. For a highly polished silver surface, it is near zero.

The rate of radiation R of a body is formally defined as the radiant energy emitted per unit area per unit time, i.e., the power per unit area. Symbolically,

$$R = \frac{E}{\tau A} = \frac{P}{A} \qquad (19\text{-}4)$$

If the radiant power P is expressed in watts and the surface area A in square meters, the rate of radiation will be in watts per square meter. As we have discussed earlier, this rate depends on two factors, the absolute temperature T and the emissivity e of the radiating body. The formal statement of this dependence, known as the *Stefan–Boltzmann law*, can be written

$$\boxed{R = \frac{P}{A} = e\sigma T^4} \qquad (19\text{-}5)$$

The proportionality constant σ is a universal constant completely independent of the nature of the radiation. If the radiant power is expressed in watts and the surface in square meters, σ has the value of 5.67×10^{-8} W/m$^2 \cdot$ K^4. The emissivity e has values from 0 to 1, depending upon the nature of the radiating surface. A summary of the symbols and their definitions is given in Table 19-3.

Table 19-3 Definition of Symbols in the Stefan–Boltzmann law $(R = e\sigma T^4)$

Symbol	Definition	Comment
R	Energy radiated per unit time per unit area	$\dfrac{E}{\tau A}$ or $\dfrac{P}{A}$
e	Emissivity of the surface	0–1
σ	Stefan's constant	5.67×10^{-8} W/m$^2 \cdot$ K^4
T^4	The fourth power of the absolute temperature	K^4

EXAMPLE 19-4   What power will be radiated from a spherical silver surface 10 cm in diameter if its temperature is 527°C? The emissivity of the surface is 0.04.

Solution   We must first compute the surface area from the known diameter of the sphere.

$$A = 4\pi R^2 = \pi D^2 = \pi(0.1 \text{ m})^2 = 0.0314 \text{ m}^2$$

The absolute temperature is

$$T = 527 + 273 = 800 \text{ K}$$

Solving for P in Eq. (19-5), we obtain

$$P = e\sigma A T^4$$

$$= (0.04)(5.67 \times 10^{-8} \text{ W/m}^2) \cdot (\text{K})^4(0.0314 \text{ m}^2)(800 \text{ K})^4$$

$$= 29.2 \text{ W}$$

We have said that all objects continuously emit radiation, regardless of their temperature. If this is true, why don't the objects eventually run out of fuel? The answer is that they *would* run down if no energy were supplied to them. The filament in an electric light bulb cools rather quickly to room temperature when the supply of electric energy is shut off. It does not cool further because, at this point, the filament is absorbing radiant energy at the same rate that it is emitting radiant energy. The law covering this phenomenon is known as *Prevost's law of heat exchange*:

> *A body at the same temperature as its surroundings radiates and absorbs heat at the same rates.*

Figure 19-7 shows an isolated object in thermal equilibrium with the walls of its container.

The rate at which energy is absorbed by a body is also given by the Stefan–Boltzmann law [Eq. (19-5)]. Thus we can figure the net transfer of radiant energy by an object surrounded by walls at a different temperature. For

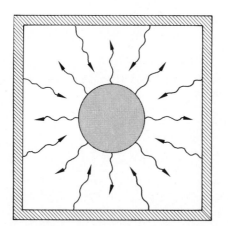

Fig. 19-7 When an object and its surroundings are at the same temperature, the radiant energy emitted is the same as that absorbed.

example, consider a thin wire filament in a lamp which is covered with an envelope, as shown in Fig. 19-8. Let the temperature of the filament be denoted by T_1 and the temperature of the surrounding envelope be denoted by T_2. The emissivity of the filament is e, and only radiative processes are considered. In this example, we note that

Net rate of radiation = rate of energy emission − rate of energy absorption

$$R = e\sigma T_1^4 - e\sigma T_2^4$$

$$\boxed{R = e\sigma(T_1^4 - T_2^4)}$$

(19-6)

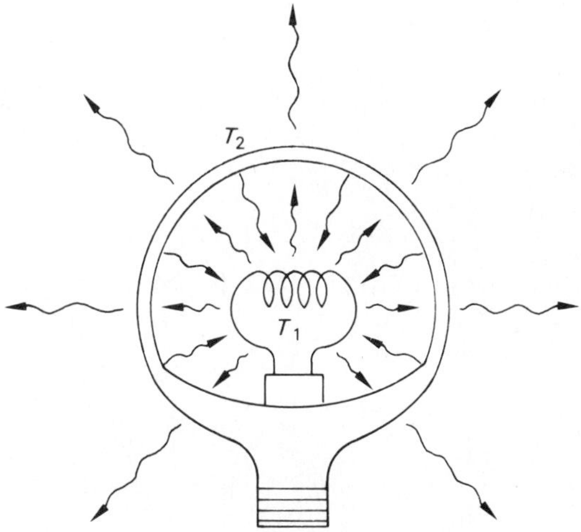

Fig. 19-8 The net energy emitted by a radiator in surroundings of a different temperature.

Equation (19-6) can be applied to any system for computing the net energy emitted by a radiator of temperature T_1 and emissivity e in the presence of surroundings at a temperature T_2.

SUMMARY

Heat is the transfer of thermal energy from one place to another. We have seen that the *rate* of transfer by conduction, convection, and radiation can be predicted from experimental formulas. The effects of material, surface areas, and temperature differences must be understood for many industrial applications of heat transfer. The major concepts presented in this chapter are:

- In the transfer of heat by conduction, the quantity of heat Q transferred per unit time τ through a wall or rod of length L is given by

$$H = \frac{Q}{\tau} = kA\frac{\Delta t}{L}$$ *Conduction*   *Metric Units:* kcal/s
USCS Units: Btu/h

where A is the area and Δt is the difference in surface temperatures. From this relation, the thermal conductivity is

$$k = \frac{QL}{A\tau \, \Delta t}$$

Metric Units: kcal/m · s · C°
USCS Units: Btu · in./ft² · h · F°

- The heat transferred by convection for a surface A is given by

$$H = \frac{Q}{\tau} = hA \, \Delta t$$

Convection

In this case Δt is the difference in temperature between the surface and the fluid. The convection coefficient for several cases is given below:

Geometry	kcal/m² · s · C°
Vertical plate	$(4.24 \times 10^{-4})\sqrt[4]{\Delta t}$
Horizontal plate	
Facing upward	$(5.95 \times 10^{-4})\sqrt[4]{\Delta t}$
Facing downward	$(3.14 \times 10^{-4})\sqrt[4]{\Delta t}$

- For heat transfer by radiation, we define the rate of radiation as the energy emitted per unit area per unit time (or simply the power per unit area):

$$R = \frac{E}{\tau A} = \frac{P}{A}$$

Rate of Radiation, W/m²

According to *Stefan–Boltzmann's law*, this rate is given by

$$R = \frac{P}{A} = e\sigma T^4$$

$\sigma = 5.67 \times 10^{-8}$ W/m² · K⁴

- Prevost's law of heat exchange states that *a body at the same temperature as its surroundings radiates and absorbs heat at the same rates.*

QUESTIONS

19-1. Define the following terms:
  a. Conduction
  b. Thermal conductivity
  c. Natural convection
  d. Forced convection
  e. Convection coefficient
  f. Thermal radiation
  g. Blackbody
  h. Emissivity
  i. Stefan–Boltzmann law
  j. Stefan's constant σ
  k. Prevost's law

19-2. Discuss the vacuum bottle and explain how it minimizes transfer of heat by conduction, convection, and radiation.

19-3. What determines the *direction* of heat transfer?

19-4. Heat flows both by conduction and by radiation. In what ways are they different? In what ways are they similar?

19-5. A hot chunk of iron is suspended centrally within an evacuated calorimeter. Can we determine the specific heat of iron by the techniques introduced in Chap. 18? Discuss.

19-6. Discuss the analogies that exist between steady state heat flow and the flow of an incompressible fluid.

19-7. A pan of water is placed over a gas burner on a kitchen stove until the water boils vigorously. Discuss the heat transfers which take place. How would you explain the fact that the bubbles forming in the water are carried to the surface in the form of a pyramid instead of rising directly to the surface?

19-8. By placing a flame underneath a paper cup filled with water it is possible to bring the water to a boil without burning the bottom of the cup. Explain.

19-9. When a piece of paper is wrapped around a stick of wood and the system is heated with a flame, the paper will begin to burn. But if the paper is wrapped tight around a copper rod and heated in the same manner, it does not burn. Why?

19-10. On a very cold day, a piece of iron feels colder to the touch than a piece of wood. Explain.

19-11. Copper has about twice the thermal conductivity of aluminum, but its specific heat is a little less than half that of aluminum. A rectangular block is made from each material so that they have identical masses and the same surface area at their bases. Each block is heated to 300°C and placed on the top of a large cube of ice. Which block will stop sinking first? Which will sink deeper?

19-12. Distinguish between thermal conductivity and specific heat as they relate to heat transfer.

19-13. The term *absorptivity* is sometimes used in place of the term *emissivity*. Can you justify this practice?

19-14. Why is more air conditioning required to cool the inside of a navy-blue car than a white car of the same size?

19-15. If a house is to be designed for maximum comfort in both summer and winter, would you prefer a light roof or a dark roof? Explain.

19-16. If you are interested in the number of kilocalories transferred by radiation in a unit of time, the Stefan–Boltzmann law can be written in the form

$$\frac{Q}{\tau} = e\sigma A T^4$$

Show that Stefan's constant σ is equal to 1.35×10^{-11} kcal/m$^2 \cdot$ s $\cdot$ K^4 for this form of the law.

19-17. When a liquid is heated in a glass beaker, a wire gauze is usually placed between the flame and the bottom of the beaker. Why is this a wise practice?

19-18. Does the warm air over a burning fire rise, or is it forced upward by the flames?

19-19. Should a hot-water or steam radiator be painted with a good emitter or a poor one? If it is painted black, will it be more efficient? Why?

19-20. Which is a faster process, conduction or convection? Give an illustration to justify your conclusion.

PROBLEMS

19-1. The bottom of a metal pan has an area of 86 cm². The pan is filled with boiling water (100°C) and is placed on top of a cork board 5 mm thick. The formica table top underneath the corkboard maintains a constant temperature of 20°C. How much heat is conducted through the cork in 2 min?

Ans. 0.165 kcal.

19-2. A steel plate has a cross section of 600 cm². One side is at 170°C and the other is at 120°C. If the steel is 20 mm thick, what is the rate of heat transfer in kilocalories per second?

19-3. A glass window is $\frac{1}{8}$ in. thick and has a length of 3 ft and a height of 2 ft. How much heat will be conducted through the glass in 1 day if the surface temperatures are 48 and 45°F?

Ans. 2.52 × 10⁴ Btu.

19-4. How much heat will be lost in 12 h by conduction through a 3-in. brick firewall if one side is at 330°F and the other at 78°F? The area of the wall is 10 ft².

19-5. One end of an iron rod 30 cm long and 4 cm² in cross section is placed in a bath of ice and water. The other end is placed in a steam bath. How much time in minutes is required to transfer 1.0 kcal of heat energy? In what direction does the heat flow?

Ans. 11.4 min, toward ice bath.

19-6. A solid wall of concrete is 80 ft high, 100 ft wide, and 6 in. thick. The temperature of one side is 30°F, and the temperature of the other side is 100°F. How many minutes will pass before 400,000 Btu of heat is transferred by conduction?

19-7. The bottom of an aluminum pan is 3 mm thick and has a surface area of 120 cm². How many calories per minute are conducted through the bottom of the pan if the temperature of the outer surface is 114°C and that of the inner surface is 117°C?

Ans. 36 kcal.

19-8. What thickness of copper is required to have the same insulating value as 2 in. of corkboard? What thicknesses of aluminum and brass are required?

19-9. A steel rod 30 cm long is rigidly attached to a silver rod 60 cm long. Both rods have a cross-sectional area of 4 cm². The free end of the silver rod is maintained at 5°C, and the free end of the steel rod is maintained at 95°C. **(a)** What is the temperature at the interface? **(b)** How much heat is conducted in 1 min?

Ans. **(a)** 21.4°C **(b)** 64.6 cal.

19-10. The wall of a freezing plant consists of 6 in. of concrete and 4 in. of corkboard. The temperature of the inside cork surface is −15°F, and the temperature of the outside concrete surface is 70°F. **(a)** What is the temperature at the interface? **(b)** How much heat is conducted through 1 ft² in 1 h?

19-11. A plate-glass window in an office building measures 2 by 6 m and is 1.2 cm thick. When its outer surface is at a temperature of 23°C and the inner surface at 25°C, how much heat is transferred through the glass in 1 h?

Ans. 1.8 × 10³ kcal.

19-12. A wooden icebox 4 cm thick has an overall effective area of 2 m². How many grams of ice will be melted in 1 min if the inside temperature is 4°C and the outside temperature is 26°C? ($k = 2.5 \times 10^{-5}$ kcal/m · s · C°.)

19-13. A flat vertical wall 4 by 6 m in size is maintained at a temperature of 90°C. The surrounding air on both sides is at 30°C. How much heat is lost from both sides of the wall in 1 h?

Ans. 1.22×10^4 kcal.

19-14. Assume the wall in Prob. 19-13 is horizontal instead of vertical. How much heat is lost from both sides in 1 h?

19-15. The air in a room at 26°C is separated from the outside air at −4°C by a vertical glass window 3 mm thick and 10 m² in area. We must expect a small difference in temperature between the inner and outer surfaces of the glass. This is due to the fact that in steady state heat flow the rate of heat transfer by convection inside, the rate of heat conduction through the glass, and the rate of heat transfer by convection outside must all be equal. For the purposes of calculation, assume that the center of the glass is at the midway point in temperature (11°C). **(a)** What is the steady state rate of heat flow? **(b)** What are the inner and outer surface temperatures of the glass window?

Ans. **(a)** 0.125 kcal/s **(b)** $t_i = 11.075$°C, $t_0 = 10.925$°C.

19-16. A vertical steam pipe has an outside diameter of 8 cm and a height of 5 m. The outside temperature of the pipe is 94°C, and the room temperature is 23°C. How much heat is released to the air by convection in 1 h? (Refer to Table 19-2.)

19-17. What is the rate of radiation of a blackbody at a temperature of 327°C?

Ans. 7.35 kW/m².

19-18. Thermal radiation is incident upon a body at the rate of 100 W/m². If the body absorbs 20 percent of the incident radiation, what is its emissivity? What energy in joules will be emitted by this body in 1 min if its surface area is 1 m² and its temperature is 727°C?

19-19. The operating temperature of the filament in a 25-W lamp is 1727°C. If the emissivity of the filament is 0.3, what is its surface area?

Ans. 0.918 cm².

19-20. Find the rate of radiation of a blackbody when its temperature is 60°C and compare it with the rate from the same body when its temperature is doubled.

19-21. The filament in a lamp operates at a temperature of 727°C and is surrounded by an envelope at 227°C. If the filament has an emissivity of 0.25 and a surface area of 0.30 cm², what is the operating power of the lamp?

Ans. 0.399 W.

20 *Thermal Properties of Matter*

OBJECTIVES: After completing this chapter, you should be able to:

1. Write and apply the relationship between the volume and the pressure of a gas at constant temperature (*Boyle's law*).

2. Write and apply the relationship between the volume and the temperature of a gas under conditions of constant pressure (*Charles' law*).

3. Write and apply the relationship between the temperature and pressure of a gas under conditions of constant volume (Gay-Lussac's law).

4. Apply the *general gas law* to the solution of problems involving changes in mass, volume, pressure, and temperature of gases.

5. Define *vapor pressure*, *dew point*, and *relative humidity*, and apply these concepts to the solution of problems.

Now that we have an understanding of the concepts of heat and temperature, we proceed to study the thermal behavior of matter. Four measurable quantities are of interest: the pressure, volume, temperature, and mass of a sample. Together, these variables determine the *state* of a given sample of matter. Depending upon its state, matter may exist in the liquid, solid, or gaseous phase. Thus it is important to distinguish between the terms *state* and *phase*. We begin by studying the thermal behavior of gases.

20-1
IDEAL
GASES AND
BOYLE'S
LAW

In a gas the individual molecules are so far apart that the cohesive forces between them are usually very small. Even though the molecular structure of different gases may vary considerably, their behavior is affected little by the size of the individual molecules. It is usually safe to say that when a large quantity of gas is confined in a rather small volume, the volume occupied by the molecules is still a tiny fraction of the total volume.

One of the most useful generalizations about gases is the concept of an *ideal gas*, whose behavior is completely unaffected by cohesive forces or molecular volumes. Of course, no real gas is *ideal*, but under ordinary conditions of temperature and pressure, the behavior of any gas conforms very closely to the behavior of an ideal gas. Therefore, experimental observations of many real gases can lead to the derivation of general physical laws governing their thermal behavior. The degree to which any real gas obeys these relations is determined by how closely it approximates an ideal gas.

The first experimental measurements of the thermal behavior of gases were made by Robert Boyle (1627–1691). He made an exhaustive study of the changes in the volume of gases as a result of changes in pressure. All other variables, such as mass and temperature, were kept constant. In 1660, Boyle demonstrated that the volume of a gas is inversely proportional to its pressure. In other words, doubling the volume *decreases* the pressure to one-half its original value. This finding is now known as *Boyle's law*.

> **Boyle's law:** *Provided that the mass and temperature of a sample of gas are held constant, the volume of the gas is inversely proportional to its absolute pressure.*

Another way of stating Boyle's law is to say that the product of the pressure P of a gas and its volume V will be constant as long as the temperature does not change. Consider, for example, a closed cylinder equipped with a movable piston, as shown in Fig. 20-1. In Fig. 20-1a, the initial state of the gas is described by its pressure P_1 and its volume V_1. If the piston is pressed

Fig. 20-1 When a gas is compressed at constant temperature, the product of its pressure and its volume is always constant, that is, $P_1 V_1 = P_2 V_2$.

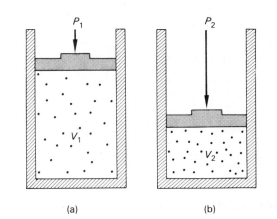

(a)   (b)

downward until it reaches the new position shown in Fig. 20-1*b*, its pressure will increase to P_2 while its volume decreases to V_2. This process is shown graphically in Fig. 20-2. If the process occurs without a change in temperature, Boyle's law reveals that

$$\boxed{P_1 V_1 = P_2 V_2}$$

With Constant
  m and T   (20-1)

In other words, the product of pressure and volume in the initial state is equal to the product of pressure and volume in the final state. Equation (20-1) is a mathematical statement of Boyle's law. The pressure P must be the *absolute* pressure and not *gauge* pressure. (See Chap. 15.)

Fig. 20-2 A *P-V* diagram illustrating that the pressure of an ideal gas varies inversely with its volume.

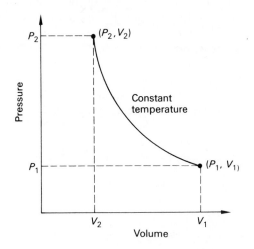

EXAMPLE 20-1   What volume of hydrogen gas at atmospheric pressure is required to fill a 2-ft^3 tank under an absolute pressure of 2500 lb/in.^{2}?

Solution   Recalling that atmospheric pressure is equal to 14.7 lb/in.^{2}, we apply Eq. (20-1).

$$P_1 V_1 = P_2 V_2$$

$$(14.7 \text{ lb/in.}^2)\, V_1 = (2500 \text{ lb/in.}^2)(2 \text{ ft}^3)$$

$$V_1 = 340 \text{ ft}^3$$

Notice that it was not necessary to convert pressure in pounds per square inch to units of pounds per square foot in order to be consistent with volume in cubic feet. Since P and V appear on both sides of the equation, it is only necessary to use consistent units for P and consistent units for V. The unit for P does not have to be consistent with the unit chosen for V.

In Chap. 17 we used the fact that the volume of a gas increased directly with its temperature to help us define absolute zero. We found the result ($-273°$C) by extending the line on the graph in Fig. 20-3. Of course, any real gas will become a liquid before its volume reaches zero. But the direct relationship is a valid approximation for most gases which are not subjected to extreme conditions of temperature and pressure.

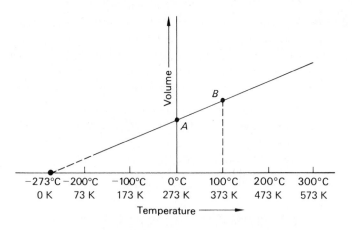

Fig. 20-3 The variation of volume as a function of temperature. When the volume is extrapolated to zero, the temperature of a gas is at absolute zero (0 K).

This direct proportionality between volume and temperature was first experimentally tested by Jacques Charles in 1787. *Charles' law* may be stated as follows:

Charles' Law: *Provided that the mass and pressure of a gas are held constant, the volume of the gas is directly proportional to its absolute temperature.*

If we use the subscript 1 to refer to an initial state of a gas and the subscript 2 to refer to the final state, a mathematical statement of Charles' law is obtained.

$$\frac{V_1}{T_1} = \frac{V_2}{T_2} \qquad \begin{array}{c} \textit{With Constant} \\ \textit{m and P} \end{array} \quad (20\text{-}2)$$

In this equation V_1 refers to the volume of a gas at the *absolute* temperature T_1, and V_2 is the later volume of the same sample of gas when its absolute temperature is T_2.

EXAMPLE 20-2

A large balloon filled with air has a volume of 200 liters at 0°C. What will its volume be at 57°C if the pressure is unchanged?

Solution

Since Charles' law applies only for absolute temperatures, we must first convert the given temperatures to kelvins.

$$T_1 = 273 \text{ K} \qquad T_2 = 57 + 273 = 330 \text{ K}$$

Now we may substitute and solve Eq. (20-2) for V_2.

$$\frac{V_1}{T_1} = \frac{V_2}{T_2}$$

$$\frac{200 \text{ liters}}{273 \text{ K}} = \frac{V_2}{330 \text{ K}}$$

$$V_2 = \frac{(200 \text{ liters})(330 \text{ K})}{273 \text{ K}} = 242 \text{ liters}$$

**20-2
GAY-
LUSSAC'S
LAW**

The three quantities which determine the state of a given mass of gas are its pressure, its volume, and its temperature. Boyle's law deals with changes in pressure and volume under constant temperature, and Charles' law applies for volume and temperature under constant pressure. The variation in pressure as a function of temperature is described in a law attributed to Gay-Lussac.

> **Gay-Lussac's Law:** *If the volume of a sample of gas remains constant, the absolute pressure of the gas is directly proportional to its absolute temperature.*

This means that doubling the pressure applied to a gas will cause its absolute temperature to double also. In equation form, Gay-Lussac's law may be written as

$$\boxed{\frac{P_1}{T_1} = \frac{P_2}{T_2}} \qquad \begin{array}{c}\textit{With Constant} \\ \textit{m and V}\end{array} \quad (20\text{-}3)$$

EXAMPLE 20-3

An automobile tire is inflated to a gauge pressure of 30 lb/in.^{2} at a time when the surrounding pressure is 14.4 lb/in.^{2} and the temperature is 70°F. After driving, the temperature of the air in the tire increases to 100°F. Assuming that the volume changes only slightly, what will be the new gauge pressure in the tire?

Solution

Gay-Lussac's law applies for constant volume, but we must first convert to absolute pressure and to absolute temperature.

$$P_1 = 30 \text{ lb/in.}^2 + 14.4 \text{ lb/in.}^2 = 44.4 \text{ lb/in.}^2$$

$$T_1 = 70 + 460 = 530°\text{R} \qquad T_2 = 100 + 460 = 560°\text{R}$$

Now we calculate the new pressure P_2 from Eq. (20-3).

$$\frac{P_1}{T_1} = \frac{P_2}{T_2}$$

$$\frac{44.4 \text{ lb/in.}^2}{530°\text{R}} = \frac{P_2}{560°\text{R}}$$

$$P_2 = \frac{(44.4 \text{ lb/in.}^2)(560°\text{R})}{530°\text{R}} = 46.9 \text{ lb/in.}^2$$

Note that 46.9 lb/in.^{2} will be the absolute pressure. The gauge pressure will be 14.4 lb/in.^{2} less.

$$\text{Gauge pressure} = 46.9 \text{ lb/in.}^2 - 14.4 \text{ lb/in.}^2 = 32.5 \text{ lb/in.}^2$$

**20-3
GENERAL
GAS LAWS**

Thus far, we have discussed three laws which can be used to describe the thermal behavior of gases. Boyle's law, as given by Eq. (20-1) applies for a sample of gas whose temperature is unchanged. Charles' law, as given by Eq. (20-2) applies for a gas sample under a constant pressure. Gay-Lussac's law, in Eq. (20-3), is for a gas sample under constant volume. Unfortunately, none of these conditions is usually satisfied. Normally, a system undergoes changes in volume, temperature, and pressure as a result of a thermal process. A more general relation combines the three laws as follows:

$$\boxed{\frac{P_1 V_1}{T_1} = \frac{P_2 V_2}{T_2}} \qquad \text{With Constant } m \quad \text{(20-4)}$$

where (P_1, V_1, T_1) may be considered coordinates of the initial state and (P_2, V_2, T_2) the coordinates of the final state. In other words, for a given mass the ratio PV/T is constant for any ideal gas. Equation (20-4) can be remembered by "a private (PV/T) is always a private."

EXAMPLE 20-4

An oxygen tank with internal volume of 20 liters is filled with oxygen under an absolute pressure of 6×10^6 N/m^2 at 20°C. The oxygen is to be used in a high-flying aircraft, where the absolute pressure is 7×10^4 N/m^2 and the temperature is -20°C. What volume of oxygen can be supplied by the tank under these conditions?

Solution

After converting the temperatures to the absolute kelvin scale, we apply Eq. (20-4)

$$\frac{P_1 V_1}{T_1} = \frac{P_2 V_2}{T_2}$$

$$\frac{(6 \times 10^6 \text{ N/m}^2)(20 \text{ liters})}{293 \text{ K}} = \frac{(7 \times 10^4 \text{ N/m}^2)V_2}{253 \text{ K}}$$

$$V_2 = 1480 \text{ liters}$$

Let us now consider the effect of a change in mass on the behavior of gases. If the temperature and volume of an enclosed gas are held constant, the addition of more gas will result in a proportional increase in pressure. Similarly, if the pressure and temperature are fixed, an increase in the mass will result in a proportional increase in the volume of the container. We can combine these experimental observations with Eq. (20-4) to obtain the general relation:

$$\boxed{\frac{P_1 V_1}{m_1 T_1} = \frac{P_2 V_2}{m_2 T_2}} \qquad \text{(20-5)}$$

where m_1 is the initial mass and m_2 is the final mass. A study of this relation will reveal that Boyle's law, Charles' law, Gay-Lussac's law, and Eq. (20-4) are all special cases of the more general equation (20-5).

EXAMPLE 20-5

The pressure gauge on a helium storage tank reads 2000 lb/in.^{2} when the temperature is 27°C. The container develops a leak overnight, and the gauge pressure the next morning is found to be 1500 lb/in.^{2} at a temperature of 17°C. What percentage of the original mass of helium remains inside the container?

Solution

Since the volume of the container remains constant, $V_1 = V_2$ and Eq. (20-5) gives

$$\frac{P_1}{m_1 T_1} = \frac{P_2}{m_2 T_2}$$

The ratio m_2/m_1 represents the fraction of the helium mass remaining. Hence

$$\frac{m_2}{m_1} = \frac{P_2 T_1}{P_1 T_2}$$

The pressures and temperatures are adjusted to their absolute values as follows:

$$P_1 = 2000 \text{ lb/in.}^2 + 14.7 \text{ lb/in.}^2 = 2014.7 \text{ lb/in.}^2$$

$$P_2 = 1500 \text{ lb/in.}^2 + 14.7 \text{ lb/in.}^2 = 1514.7 \text{ lb/in.}^2$$

$$T_1 = 27 + 273 = 300 \text{ K}$$

$$T_2 = 17 + 273 = 290 \text{ K}$$

Substitution of these values yields

$$\frac{m_2}{m_1} = \frac{(1514.7)(300)}{(2014.7)(290)} = 0.778 \qquad ($$

Therefore, 77.8 percent of the helium still remains inside the container.

Equation (20-5) is very general because it accounts for variance in the pressure, volume, temperature, and mass of a gas. However, the quantity which affects pressure and volume is not the mass of a gas but the number of molecules in the gas. According to the kinetic theory of gases, the pressure is due to molecular collisions with the walls of the container. Increasing the number of molecules will increase the number of particles impacting per second, and the pressure of the gas will become greater. If we are considering a thermal process involving quantities of the same gas, it is safe to apply Eq. (20-5) because the mass is proportional to the number of molecules.

When dealing with different kinds of gas, such as hydrogen compared with oxygen, it is necessary to refer to equal numbers of molecules rather than equal masses. When they are placed in similar containers, 6 g of hydrogen will yield a much greater pressure than 6 g of oxygen. There are many more hydrogen molecules in 6 g of H_2 than there are oxygen molecules in 6 g of O_2. To be more general, we must revise Eq. (20-5) to account for differences in the number of gas molecules instead of the difference in mass. However, first we must develop methods of relating the quantity of a gas to the number of molecules present.

20-4 MOLECULAR MASS AND THE MOLE

Although the mass of individual atoms is difficult to determine because of their size, experimental methods have been successful in measuring atomic mass. For example, we know that one atom of helium has a mass of 6.65×10^{-24} g. When working with macroscopic quantities, such as volume, pressure, and temperature, it is much more convenient to compare the *relative masses* of individual atoms.

The relative atomic masses are based upon the mass of a reference atom known as *carbon 12*. By arbitrarily assigning exactly 12 *atomic mass units* (u) to this atom, we have a standard for comparison of other atomic masses.

The **atomic mass** of an element is the mass of an atom of that element compared with the mass of an atom of carbon taken as 12 atomic mass units.

On this basis, the atomic mass of hydrogen is approximately 1 u, and the atomic mass of oxygen is approximately 16 u.

A molecule consists of two or more atoms in chemical combination. The definition of molecular mass follows from the definition of relative atomic mass.

The **molecular mass** M is the sum of the atomic masses of all the atoms making up the molecule.

For example, a molecule of oxygen (O_2) contains two atoms of oxygen. Its molecular mass is 16 u × 2 = 32 u. A molecule of carbon dioxide (CO_2) contains one atom of carbon and two atoms of oxygen. Thus the molecular mass of CO_2 is 44 u:

$$1 \ C = 1 \times 12 = 12 \ u$$
$$\underline{2 \ O = 2 \times 16 = 32 \ u}$$
$$CO_2 = 44 \ u$$

In dealing with gases, we have noted that it is more meaningful to treat the amount of substance present in terms of the number of molecules present. This is accomplished by establishing a new unit of measure called the *mole* (mol).

A **mole** is that quantity of a substance which contains the same number of particles as there are atoms in 12 g of carbon 12.

On the basis of this definition, 1 mol of carbon must be equal to 12 g by definition. Since the molecular mass of any substance is based on carbon 12 as a standard, it follows that:

One mole is the mass in grams equal numerically to the molecular mass of a substance.

For example, 1 mol of hydrogen (H_2) is 2 g; 1 mol of oxygen (O_2) is 32 g; and 1 mol of carbon dioxide (CO_2) is 44 g. In other words, 2 g of H_2, 32 g of O_2, and 44 g of CO_2 all have the same number of molecules. This number N_A is known as *Avogadro's number*.

The ratio of the number of molecules N to the number of moles n must equal Avogadro's number N_A. Symbolically,

$$N_A = \frac{N}{n} \qquad \textit{Molecules per Mole} \quad (20\text{-}6)$$

There are several experimental methods of determining Avogadro's number. The accepted value for N_A is

$$N_A = 6.023 \times 10^{23} \text{ molecules per mole} \qquad (20\text{-}7)$$

The easiest way to determine the number of moles n contained in a gas is to divide its mass m in grams by its molecular mass M. Thus

$$n = \frac{m}{M}$$

Number of Moles (20-8)

EXAMPLE 20-6 (a) How many moles of gas are present in 200 g of CO_2? (b) How many molecules are present?

Solution (a) The molecular mass of CO_2 is 44 u or 44 g/mol. Therefore,

$$n = \frac{m}{M} = \frac{200 \text{ g}}{44 \text{ g/mol}} = 4.55 \text{ mol}$$

Solution (b) From Eq. (20-9),

$$n = \frac{N}{N_A} = 4.55 \text{ mol}$$

$$N = (6.023 \times 10^{23} \text{ molecules/mol})(4.55 \text{ mol})$$

$$= 2.74 \times 10^{24} \text{ molecules}$$

**20-5
THE
IDEAL-GAS
LAW**

Let us now return to our search for a more general gas law. If we substitute the number of moles n for the mass m in Eq. (20-5), we can write

$$\frac{P_1 V_1}{n_1 T_1} = \frac{P_2 V_2}{n_2 T_2}$$

(20-9)

This equation represents the most useful form of a general gas law when all the parameters of an initial state and of a final state are known except for a single quantity.

An alternative expression of Eq. (20-9) is

$$\frac{PV}{nT} = R$$

(20-10)

where R is known as the *universal gas constant*. If we can evaluate R under certain known values of P, V, n, and T, Eq. (20-10) can be used directly without information concerning initial and final states. This is accomplished by computing the value of R for 1 mol of a gas at standard temperature and pressure (STP) of 0°C and 1 atm. Since 1 mol of any gas contains the same number of molecules, the molar volume is dependent upon the temperature and pressure of the gas.

At a temperature of 273 K and a pressure of 1 atm, 1 mol of any gas occupies a volume of 22.4 liters.

Thus the universal gas constant R is found to be

$$\frac{PV}{nT} = \frac{(1 \text{ atm})(22.4 \text{ liters})}{(1 \text{ mol})(273 \text{ K})}$$

$$\boxed{R = 0.0821 \text{ liter} \cdot \text{atm/mol} \cdot \text{K}} \qquad (20\text{-}11)$$

The numerical value for R depends upon the units chosen for P, V, and T. Other values are

$$R = 8.32 \times 10^7 \text{ ergs/mol} \cdot \text{K}$$

$$= 8.32 \text{ J/mol} \cdot \text{K}$$

$$= 2.0 \text{ cal/mol} \cdot \text{K}$$

Equation (20-10) is known as the *ideal-gas law* and is usually written in the form

$$\boxed{PV = nRT} \qquad (20\text{-}12)$$

EXAMPLE 20-7   How many grams of oxygen will occupy a volume of 1600 liters at a pressure of 2 atm and a temperature of 190°C?

Solution   Solving for n in the ideal-gas law, we obtain

$$n = \frac{PV}{RT} = \frac{(2 \text{ atm})(1600 \text{ liters})}{(0.0821 \text{ atm} \cdot \text{liter/mol} \cdot \text{K})(463 \text{ K})}$$

$$= 84.2 \text{ mol}$$

The mass of 84.2 mol of oxygen is found from Eq. (20-8):

$$m = nM = (84.2 \text{ mol})(32 \text{ g/mol}) = 2694 \text{ g}$$

**20-6
LIQUEFAC-
TION OF
A GAS**

We have defined an ideal gas as one whose thermal behavior is completely unaffected by cohesive forces or molecular volume. Such a gas compressed at a constant temperature will remain a gas no matter how great a pressure is supplied to it. In other words, it will obey Boyle's law at any temperature. The binding forces necessary for liquefaction are never present.

All real gases experience intermolecular forces. However, at rather low pressures and high temperatures, real gases behave very like an ideal gas. Boyle's law applies because the intermolecular forces under these conditions are practically negligible. A real gas at high temperatures can be compressed in a cylinder, as in Fig. 20-4, to relatively high pressures without liquefying. By plotting the increase in pressure as a function of the volume, the curve $A_1 B_1$ is obtained. Note the similarity between this curve and that for an ideal gas, as shown in Fig. 20-2.

Fig. 20-4 (*a*) Compression of an ideal gas at any temperature or a real gas at high temperature. (*b*) Liquefaction of a real gas when it is compressed at lower temperatures.

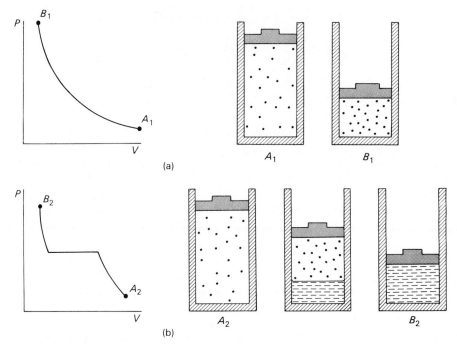

If the same gas is compressed at a much lower temperature, it will begin to condense at a particular pressure and volume. Further compression will continue to liquefy the gas at essentially constant pressure until all the gas has condensed. At that point, a sharp rise in pressure occurs with a slight decrease in volume. The entire process is shown graphically as the curve $A_2 B_2$ in Fig. 20-4.

Let us now begin with the high-temperature compression and perform the experiment at lower and lower constant temperatures. Eventually, a temperature will be reached at which the gas will just begin to liquefy under compression. The highest temperature at which this liquefication occurs is called the *critical temperature.*

> The **critical temperature** of a gas is that temperature above which the gas will not liquefy regardless of the amount of pressure applied to it.

If any gas is to be liquefied, it must first be cooled below its critical temperature. Before this concept was understood, scientists attempted to liquefy oxygen by subjecting it to extreme pressures. Their attempts failed because the critical temperature of oxygen is $-119°C$. After cooling the gas below this temperature, it can be easily liquefied by compression.

20-7 VAPORIZATION

In Chap. 18 we discussed at length the process of vaporization in which a definite quantity of heat is required to change from the liquid phase to the vapor phase. There are three ways in which such a change may occur: (1) evaporation,

(2) boiling, and (3) sublimation. During evaporation, vaporization occurs at the surface of a liquid as the more energetic molecules leave the surface. In the process of boiling, vaporization occurs within the body of the liquid. Sublimation occurs when a solid vaporizes without passing through the liquid phase. In each case, an amount of energy equal to the latent heat of vaporization or sublimation must be lost by the liquid or solid.

The molecular theory of matter assumes that a liquid consists of molecules crowded fairly close together. These molecules have an average kinetic energy which is related to the temperature of the liquid. However, because of random collisions or vibratory motion, not all the molecules move at the same rate of speed; some move faster than others.

Because the molecules are so close together, the forces between them are relatively large. As a molecule approaches the surface of a liquid, as in Fig. 20-5, it experiences a resultant downward force. The net force results from the fact that there are no liquid molecules above the surface to offset the downward attraction of those below the surface. Only the *faster-moving* particles can approach the surface with sufficient energy to overcome the retarding forces. These molecules are said to *evaporate* because, upon leaving the liquid, they become typical gas particles. They have not changed chemically; the only difference between a liquid and its vapor is the distance between molecules.

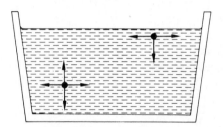

Fig. 20-5 A molecule near the surface of a liquid experiences a net downward force. Only the more energetic molecules are able to overcome this force and leave the liquid.

Since only the most energetic molecules are able to break away from the surface, the average kinetic energy of the molecules remaining in the liquid is reduced. Hence *evaporation is a cooling process.* (If you place a few drops of alcohol on the back of your hand, you will feel a cooling sensation.) The rate of evaporation is affected by the temperature of the liquid, the number of molecules above the liquid (the pressure), the exposed surface area, and the extent of ventilation.

**20-8
VAPOR
PRESSURE**

A jar is partially filled with water, as shown in Fig. 20-6. The pressure exerted by the molecules above the surface of the water is measured by an open-tube mercury manometer. In Fig. 20-6a there are as many molecules of air inside the jar as are contained in an equal volume of air outside the jar. In other words,

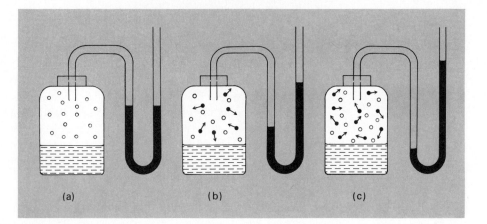

Fig. 20-6 Measuring the vapor pressure of a liquid. (*a*) Air pressure only. (*b*) Partial vapor pressure. (*c*) Saturated vapor pressure.

the pressure inside the jar is equal to 1 atm, as indicated by the equal levels of mercury in the manometer.

When a high-energy liquid molecule breaks away from the surface, it becomes a vapor molecule and mixes with the air molecules above the liquid. These vapor molecules collide with air molecules, other vapor molecules, and the walls of the jar. The additional vapor molecules cause a rise in pressure inside of the jar, as indicated in Fig. 20-6*b*. The vapor molecules may also rebound back into the liquid, where they are held as liquid molecules. This process is called *condensation*. Eventually the rate of evaporation will equal the rate of condensation, and a condition of equilibrium will exist, as shown in Fig. 20-6*c*. Under these conditions, the space above the liquid is said to be *saturated*. The pressure exerted by the saturated vapor against the walls of the jar, over and above that exerted by the air molecules, is called the *saturated vapor pressure*. It is characteristic of the substance and the temperature but independent of the volume of the vapor.

> The **saturated vapor pressure** of a substance is the additional pressure exerted by vapor molecules on the substance and its surroundings under a condition of saturation.

Once a condition of saturation is obtained for a substance and its vapor at a particular temperature, the vapor pressure remains essentially constant. If the temperature is increased, the molecules in the liquid will acquire more energy and evaporation will occur more rapidly. The condition of equilibrium remains upset until once again the rate of condensation has caught up with the rate of evaporation. The saturated vapor pressure of a substance therefore increases with a rise in temperature.

The saturated-vapor-pressure curve for water is plotted in Fig. 20-7. Note that the vapor pressure increases rapidly with temperature. At room temperature (20°C), it is around 17.5 mm of mercury; at 50°C it has increased to 92.5 mm; and at 100°C it is equal to 760 mm, or 1 atm. The latter point is of importance in distinguishing between *evaporation* and *boiling*.

Fig. 20-7 The vaporization curve for water. Any point on the curve represents a condition of pressure and temperature which allows water to boil. The curve ends abruptly at the critical temperature because water can exist only as a gas beyond that point.

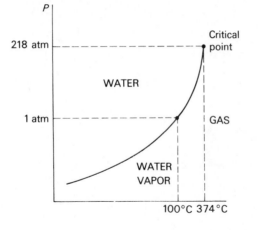

When a liquid boils, bubbles of its vapor can be seen rising toward the surface from within the liquid. The fact that these bubbles are stable and do not collapse indicates that the pressure inside the bubble is equal to the pressure outside the bubble. The pressure inside the bubble is the vapor pressure at that temperature; the pressure on the outside is the pressure at that depth in the liquid. Under this condition of equilibrium, vaporization occurs freely throughout the liquid, causing the liquid to become agitated.

> **Boiling** is defined as vaporization within the body of a liquid when its vapor pressure equals the pressure in the liquid.

If the pressure on the liquid surface is 1 atm, as it would be in an open container, the temperature at which boiling occurs is called the *normal boiling point* for that liquid. The normal boiling point for water is 100°C because that is the temperature at which the vapor pressure of water is 1 atm (760 mm of mercury). If the pressure on any liquid surface is lower than 1 atm, boiling will occur at a temperature lower than the normal boiling point. If the external pressure is greater than 1 atm, boiling will occur at a higher temperature.

20-9 TRIPLE POINT

We have discussed in detail the process of vaporization, and in Fig. 20-7 we constructed a vaporization curve for water. This curve is represented by the line *AB* in the general phase diagram of Fig. 20-8. Any point on this curve represents a temperature and pressure at which water and its vapor can coexist in equilibrium.

A similar curve can be plotted for the temperatures and pressures at which a substance in the solid phase can coexist with its liquid phase. Such a curve is called a *fusion curve*. The fusion curve for water is represented by the line *AC* in the phase diagram. At any point on this curve, the rate at which ice is melting is equal to the rate at which water is freezing. Note that as the pressure increases, the melting temperature (or freezing temperature) is lowered.

Fig. 20-8 Triple-point phase diagram for water or other substance which expands on freezing.

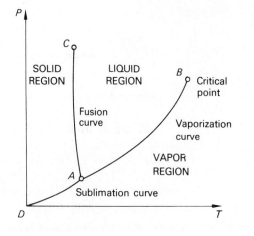

A third graph, called the *sublimation curve*, can be plotted to show the temperatures and pressures at which a solid may coexist with its vapor. The sublimation curve for water is represented by line *AD* of Fig. 20-8.

Let us now study the phase diagram for water more closely to illustrate the usefulness of such a graph for any substance. The coordinates of any point on the graph represent a particular pressure *P* and a particular temperature *T*. The volume must be considered constant for any thermal change indicated by the graph. For any point which falls in the fork between the vaporization and fusion curves, water will exist in its liquid phase. The vapor and the solid regions are also indicated on the diagram. The point *A*, at which all three curves intersect, is called the *triple point* for water. This is the temperature and pressure at which ice, liquid water, and water vapor coexist in equilibrium. Careful measurements have shown that the triple point for water is at 0.01°C and 4.62 mm of mercury (Hg).

20-10 HUMIDITY

The air in our atmosphere consists largely of nitrogen and oxygen with small amounts of water vapor and other gases. It is often useful to describe the water-vapor content of the atmosphere.

> The **absolute humidity** is defined as the mass of water vapor per unit volume of air.

For example, if 7 g of water vapor is contained in every cubic meter of air, the absolute humidity is 7 g/m³. Other units of absolute humidity are pounds per cubic foot and grains per cubic foot (7000 grains = 1 lb).

A more useful method of expressing the water-vapor content in air is to compare the actual vapor pressure at a particular temperature with the saturated vapor pressure at that temperature. When the atmosphere is holding all the water possible for a certain temperature, it is saturated. The addition of more vapor molecules will simply result in an equal amount of condensation.

The **relative humidity** is defined as the ratio of the actual vapor pressure in the air to the saturated vapor pressure at that temperature.

$$Relative\ humidity = \frac{actual\ vapor\ pressure}{saturated\ vapor\ pressure} \qquad (20\text{-}13)$$

The relative humidity is usually expressed as a percentage.

If the air in a room is not already saturated, it can be made so either by adding more water vapor to the air or by lowering the room temperature until the vapor already present is sufficient. *The temperature to which the air must be cooled at constant pressure in order to produce saturation is called the dew point.* Thus, if ice is placed in a glass of water, moisture will eventually collect on the outside walls of the glass when its temperature reaches the dew point. Given the temperature and the dew point, the relative humidity can be computed from saturated-vapor-pressure tables. Table 20-1 lists the saturated vapor pressure for water at various temperatures.

Table 20-1 Saturated Vapor Pressure for Water

Temperature		Pressure,	Temperature		Pressure,
°C	°F	mmHg	°C	°F	mmHg
0	32	4.62	50	122	92.5
5	41	6.5	60	140	149.4
10	50	9.2	70	158	233.7
15	59	12.8	80	176	355.1
17	62.6	14.5	85	185	433.6
19	66.2	16.5	90	194	525.8
20	68	17.5	95	203	633.9
22	71.6	19.8	98	208.4	707.3
24	75.2	22.4	100	212	760.0
26	78.8	25.2	103	217.4	845.1
28	82.4	28.3	105	221	906.1
30	86	31.8	110	230	1074.6
35	95	42.2	120	248	1489.1
40	104	55.3	150	302	3570.5

EXAMPLE 20-8 On a clear day, the air temperature is 86°F, and the dew point is 50°F. What is the relative humidity?

Solution The pressure of saturated vapor at 50°F is 9.2 mm, from Table 20-1. The pressure of saturated vapor at 86°F is 31.8 mm. From Eq. (20-13),

$$Relative\ humidity = \frac{9.2}{31.8} = 0.29$$

Thus the relative humidity is 29 percent.

SUMMARY

The thermal properties of matter must be understood if we are to apply the many laws discussed in this chapter. The relationships between mass, temperature, volume, and pressure allow us to explain and predict the behavior of gases. The major concepts discussed in this chapter are summarized below:

- A useful form of the general gas law which does not involve the use of moles is written on the basis that PV/mT is constant. When a gas in state 1 changes to another state 2, we may write

$$\frac{P_1 V_1}{m_1 T_1} = \frac{P_2 V_2}{m_2 T_2}$$

P = pressure V = volume

m = mass T = absolute temperature

When one or more of the parameters m, P, T, or V is constant that factor disappears from both sides of the above equation. *Boyle's law, Charles' law,* and *Gay-Lussac's law* are the following special cases:

$$P_1 V_1 = P_2 V_2 \qquad \frac{V_1}{T_1} = \frac{V_2}{T_2} \qquad \frac{P_1}{T_1} = \frac{P_2}{T_2}$$

- When applying the general gas law in any of its forms, it must be remembered that the pressure is *absolute pressure* and the temperature is *absolute temperature.*

Absolute pressure = gauge pressure + atmospheric pressure

$$T_K = t_C + 273 \qquad T_R = t_F + 460$$

For example, a pressure measured in an auto tire is 30 lb/in.^{2} at 37°C. These values must be adjusted before substitution into the gas laws:

$$P = 30 \text{ lb/in}^2 + 14.7 \text{ lb/in.}^2 = 44.7 \text{ lb/in.}^2 \qquad \text{(absolute)}$$

$$T = 37 + 273 = 310 \text{ K}$$

- A more general form of the gas law is obtained by using the concepts of molecular mass M, and the number of *moles n* for a gas. The number of molecules in 1 mol is Avogadro's number N_A.

$$N_A = \frac{m}{M} \qquad\qquad N_A = 6.023 \times 10^{23} \text{ molecules/mol}$$

Avogadro's Number

The number of moles is found by dividing the mass of a gas (in grams) by its molecular mass M:

$$n = \frac{m}{M}$$

Number of Moles

Often it is desired to determine the mass, pressure, volume, or temperature of a gas in a single state. The ideal-gas law uses the molar concept to arrive at a more specific equation:

$$PV = nRT \qquad R = 0.0821 \text{ liter} \cdot \text{atm/mol} \cdot \text{K}$$

It should be noted that use of the constant given above restricts the units of P, V, T, and n to those which are in the constant.

- The *relative humidity* can be computed from saturated-vapor-pressure tables according to the following definition:

$$\text{Relative humidity} = \frac{actual\ vapor\ pressure}{saturated\ vapor\ pressure}$$

Remember that the *actual* vapor pressure at a particular temperature is the same as the *saturated* vapor pressure for the dew-point temperature. Refer to the example in the text.

QUESTIONS

20-1. Define the following terms:

a. Ideal gas	**j.** Molecular mass
b. Boyle's law	**k.** Avogadro's number
c. Charles' law	**l.** Ideal-gas law
d. Atomic mass	**m.** Critical temperature
e. Mole	**n.** Vapor pressure
f. Evaporation	**o.** Triple point
g. Boiling	**p.** Absolute humidity
h. Sublimation	**q.** Relative humidity
i. Saturation	**r.** Dew point

20-2. Distinguish between *state* and *phase*.

20-3. Explain Boyle's law in terms of the molecular theory of matter.

20-4. Explain Charles' law in terms of the molecular theory of matter.

20-5. Why must the absolute temperature be used in Charles' law?

20-6. A closed steel tank is filled with an ideal gas and heated. What happens to the **(a)** mass, **(b)** volume, **(c)** density, and **(d)** pressure of the enclosed gas?

20-7. Prove the accuracy of the following equations which involve the density ρ of an ideal gas.

(a) $\dfrac{P_1}{\rho_1 T_1} = \dfrac{P_2}{\rho_2 T_2}$

(b) $\rho = \dfrac{PM}{RT}$

20-8. Suppose we wish to express the pressure of an ideal gas in millimeters of mercury and the volume in cubic centimeters. Show that the universal gas constant will be equal to 6.23×10^4 mm $\cdot$ cm^3/mol $\cdot$ K.

20-9. A mole of any gas occupies 22.4 liters at STP. Can we also say that the same mass of any gas will occupy the same volume? Explain.

20-10. Distinguish between evaporation, boiling, and sublimation.

20-11. From your experience, would you expect alcohol to have a higher vapor pressure than water? Why?

20-12. Explain the principle of operation for the pressure cooker and the vacuum pan in cooking.

20-13. Can a solid have a vapor pressure? Explain.

20-14. If evaporation is a cooling process, is condensation a heating process? Explain.

20-15. Explain the cooling effects of evaporation in terms of the latent heat of vaporization.

20-16. Distinguish between a vapor and a gas by discussing critical temperature.

20-17. Will it take longer to cook an egg by boiling it in water on Mt. Everest or at the seashore? Why?

20-18. Water is brought to a vigorous boil in an open flask. When the flask is removed from the flame and tightly stoppered, the boiling stops. Why? The stoppered flask is then inverted and held under a stream of cold running water. The boiling begins again. Explain. As soon as the flask is removed from the water, boiling stops. If the flask is cooled, boiling begins again. How long can the process of making the water boil by cooling be continued?

20-19. On a cool day, the relative humidity inside a house is the same as the relative humidity outside the house. Are the dew points necessarily the same? Explain.

20-20. Explain what is meant by *critical pressure*.

20-21. Is it possible for ice to exist in equilibrium with boiling water? Explain.

20-22. The formation of moisture on the walls and windows inside a home can cause considerable damage. What causes this moisture? Discuss several ways of reducing or preventing the formation of moisture.

20-23. Discuss the formation of fog and clouds. Why are fog conditions usually worse in the fall and early spring?

PROBLEMS

20-1. The air inside an automobile tire is under a gauge pressure of 30 lb/in.^{2} and occupies a volume of 120 in.^{3}. What volume would this air occupy at the same temperature under an absolute pressure of 14.7 lb/in.^{2} (1 atm)?

Ans. 365 in.^{3}.

20-2. How much air at atmospheric pressure can be stored in a 12-ft^3 tank which can withstand an absolute pressure of 120 lb/in.^{2}?

20-3. A tank with a capacity of 14 liters contains helium gas at 24°C under a gauge pressure of 2700 kPa. **(a)** What will be the volume of a balloon filled with this gas if the helium expands to an internal pressure of 1 atm and if its temperature drops to −35°C? Eventually, the whole system returns to the original temperature of 24°C. **(b)** What is the final volume of the balloon?

Ans. **(a)** 310 liters **(b)** 387 liters.

20-4. A 6-liter container holds a sample of gas under an absolute pressure of 600 kPa and a temperature of 57°C. What will be the new pressure if the same sample of gas is placed into a 3-liter container at 7°C?

20-5. A 6-ft^3 container is filled with a gas at an absolute pressure of 300 lb/in.^{2} and a temperature of 27°C. What is the new pressure if the temperature is raised to 127°C?

Ans. 400 lb/in.^{2}.

20-6. A given mass of gas occupies 12 liters at 7°C and a pressure of 102 kPa. Calculate its temperature when its volume is reduced to 10 liters and the pressure is increased to 230 kPa.

20-7. An air compressor takes in 2 m^3 of air at 20°C and atmospheric pressure (101.3 kPa). If the compressor discharges into a 0.3-m^3 tank at an absolute pressure of 1500 kPa, what is the temperature of the discharged air?

Ans. 651 K.

20-8. If 0.8 liters of a gas at 10°C is heated to 90°C at constant pressure, what will the new volume be?

20-9. At 70°F the gauge pressure of a gas in a steel container is indicated as 80 lb/in.^{2}. What will the pressure gauge read when the tank is heated uniformly to 150°F?

Ans. 94.3 lb/in.^{2}.

20-10. Five liters of a gas at an absolute pressure of 200 kPa and a temperature of 25°C is heated to 60°C and the absolute pressure is reduced to 120 kPa. What volume will the gas occupy under these conditions?

20-11. A compressed-air storage tank whose volume is 120 liters contains 3 kg of air at a pressure of 16 atm. How much more air would have to be forced into the tank to increase the pressure to 18 atm, assuming there is no change in temperature?

Ans. 0.375 kg.

20-12. A sealed tank contains air at 24°C and at a pressure of 4×10^5 N/m^2. What will the pressure be if the temperature increases to 124°C?

20-13. A tractor tire contains 2.8 ft^3 of air at a gauge pressure of 70 lb/in.^{2} What volume of atmospheric air is required to fill this tire assuming there is no change in temperature?

Ans. 16.1 ft^3.

20-14. A tank containing 0.2 m^3 of nitrogen at room temperature and at 8×10^6 N/m^2 pressure is connected through a valve to an empty tank of volume 0.5 m^3. The valve is opened, and the gas is allowed to expand. What is the pressure in the tank after the system returns to room temperature?

20-15. How many moles of helium gas are in a 6-liter tank when the pressure is 2×10^5 N/m^2 and the temperature is 27°C? What is the mass of the helium?

Ans. 0.481 mol, 1.92 g.

20-16. The weight density of nitrogen at STP is 0.0781 lb/ft^3. What is the density of nitrogen at 18 atm and 200°F?

20-17. The molecular mass of sulfur dioxide (SO_2) gas is 64 u. What volume will 8 g of SO_2 occupy at 10 atm and 27°C? If 10^{12} molecules leak from this volume every second, how long will it take to reduce the pressure by one-half?

Ans. 0.308 liter, 3.76×10^{10} s.

20-18. A 5000-cm^3 tank is filled with carbon dioxide at 1 atm of pressure and at a temperature of 27°C. How many grams of CO_2 can be added to the tank if the maximum pressure is 60 atm and there is no change in temperature?

20-19. What mass of oxygen will fill a 16-liter cylinder at a pressure of 20 atm and a temperature of 27°C?

Ans. 0.416 kg.

20-20. The molecular mass of methane gas is 16 u. What is the density of methane in grams per liter at 27°C and 6 atm? How many molecules are contained in 4 liters of methane at this temperature and pressure?

20-21. A flask contains 2 g of helium at a pressure of 12 atm and a temperature of 57°C. What is the volume of the flask? The system is checked at a later time when the temperature is 17°C and the pressure is found to be only 7 atm. How many grams of helium have leaked out of the flask?

Ans. 1.13 liters, 0.672 g.

20-22. The molecular mass of air is 29.0. How many grams of air must be pumped into an automobile tire if it is to have a gauge pressure of 31 lb/in.²? Consider the volume of the tire to be a constant 5000 cm³ and the temperature to remain at 27°C.

20-23. If the air temperature is 20°C and the dew point is 12°C, what is the relative humidity?

Ans. 60.8%.

20-24. The relative humidity in a room is 65 percent at 26°C. What is the relative humidity if the temperature drops to 22°C?

20-25. What is the pressure of water vapor in the air on a day when the temperature is 86°F and the relative humidity is 80 percent?

Ans. 25.4 mm of mercury.

20-26. When room temperature is 28°C, the relative humidity is 77 percent. What is the dew point?

21 *Thermodynamics*

OBJECTIVES: After completing this chapter, you should be able to:

1. Demonstrate by definition and examples your understanding of the *first* and *second laws of thermodynamics*.

2. Define and give illustrated examples of *adiabatic, isochoric*, and *isothermal* processes.

3. Write and apply a relationship for determining the *ideal efficiency* of a heat engine.

4. Define the *coefficient of performance* for a refrigerator and solve refrigeration problems similar to those discussed in the text.

Thermodynamics treats the transformation of heat energy into mechanical energy and the reverse process, the conversion of work into heat. Since almost all the energy available from raw materials is liberated in the form of heat, it is easy to see why thermodynamics plays such an important role in science and technology.

In this chapter, we shall study two basic laws which must be obeyed when heat energy is used to accomplish work. The first law is simply a restatement of the principle of conservation of energy. The second law places restrictions on the efficient use of the available energy.

21-1 HEAT AND WORK

The equivalence of heat and work as two forms of energy has been clearly established. Rumford destroyed the caloric theory of heat by showing that it is possible to remove heat indefinitely from a system so long as external work is supplied. Joule then sealed the case by demonstrating the mechanical equivalence of heat.

Work, like heat, involves a transfer of energy, but there is a very important distinction between the two terms. In mechanics, we define work as a scalar quantity, equal in magnitude to the product of a force and a displacement. Temperature plays no role in this definition. Heat, on the other hand, is energy that flows from one body to another because of a difference in temperature. A temperature difference is a necessary condition for the transfer of heat. Displacement is the necessary condition for the performance of work.

The important point in this discussion is to recognize that both heat and work represent changes which occur in a given process. Usually these changes are accompanied by a change in internal energy. Consider the two situations illustrated in Fig. 21-1. In Fig. 21-1a the internal energy of the water is increased by the performance of mechanical work. In Fig. 21-1b the internal energy of the water is increased through the flow of heat.

Fig. 21-1 Increasing the internal energy of a system (a) by the performance of work and (b) by supplying heat to the system.

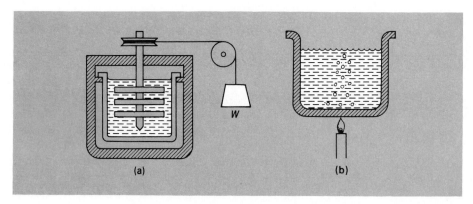

21-2 THE INTERNAL-ENERGY FUNCTION

A system is said to be in *thermodynamic equilibrium* if there is no resultant force on the system and if the temperature of the system is the same as its surroundings. This condition requires that no work be done on or by the system and that there be no exchange of heat between the system and its surroundings. Under these conditions, the system has a definite internal energy U. Its *thermodynamic state* can be described by three coordinates: (1) its pressure P, (2) its volume V, and (3) its temperature T. Whenever energy is absorbed or released by such a system, either in the form of heat or work, it will reach a new state of equilibrium in such a way that energy is conserved.

In Fig. 21-2, let us consider a general thermodynamic process in which a system is caused to change from an equilibrium state 1 to an equilibrium state 2. In Fig. 21-2a the system is in thermodynamic equilibrium, with an initial internal energy U_1 and thermodynamic coordinates (P_1, V_1, T_1). In Fig. 21-2b the system reacts with its surroundings. Heat Q may be absorbed by the system and/or released to its environment. The heat transfer is considered positive for heat input and negative for heat output. The net heat *absorbed* by the system is represented by ΔQ. Work W may be done *by* the system and/or *on* the system.

Fig. 21-2 A
schematic diagram
of a thermo-
dynamic process.

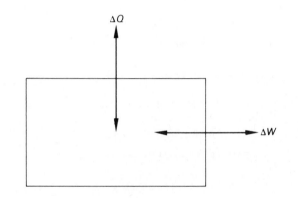

(a) Initial state of system (P_1, V_1, T_1)

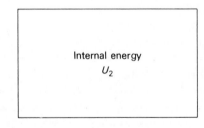

(b) System undergoing thermodynamic process

(c) Final state of system (P_2, V_2, T_2)

Output work is considered positive, and input work is considered negative.
Thus ΔW represents the net work done *by* the system (output work). In Fig.
21-2c the system has reached its final state 2 and is again in equilibrium, with a
final internal energy U_2. Its new thermodynamic coordinates are (P_2, V_2, T_2).

If energy is to be conserved, the change in internal energy

$$\Delta U = U_2 - U_1$$

must represent the difference between the net heat ΔQ absorbed by the system and the net work ΔW done by the system on its surroundings.

$$\Delta U = \Delta Q - \Delta W \qquad (21\text{-}1)$$

Thus the change in internal energy is uniquely defined in terms of the measurable quantities heat and work. Equation (21-1) states the existence of an *internal energy function* which is determined by the thermodynamic coordinates of a system. Its value at the final state minus its value at the initial state represents the change in energy of the system.

21-3 THE FIRST LAW OF THERMO-DYNAMICS

The *first law of thermodynamics* is simply a restatement of the principle of *conservation of energy*:

> *Energy cannot be created or destroyed but can change from one form to another.*

Applying this law to a thermodynamic process, we note from Eq. (21-1) that

$$\boxed{\Delta Q = \Delta W + \Delta U} \qquad (21\text{-}2)$$

This equation represents a mathematical statement of *the first law of thermodynamics* which can be stated as follows:

> *In any thermodynamic process, the net heat absorbed by a system is equal to the sum of the thermal equivalent of the work done by the system and the change in the internal energy of the system.*

EXAMPLE 21-1

In a certain process, a system absorbs 400 cal of heat and at the same time does 80 J of work on its surroundings. What is the increase in the internal energy of the system?

Solution

Applying the first law, we have

$$\Delta U = \Delta Q - \Delta W$$

$$= 400 \text{ cal} - 80 \text{ J}\,\frac{1 \text{ cal}}{4.186 \text{ J}}$$

$$= 400 \text{ cal} - 19.1 \text{ cal} = 380.9 \text{ cal}$$

Thus the 400 cal of input thermal energy is used to perform 19.1 cal of work while the internal energy of the system is increased by 380.9 cal. Energy is conserved.

21-4 THE *P-V* DIAGRAM

Many thermodynamic processes involve energy changes which occur to gases enclosed in cylinders. At this point, it will be useful to derive an expression for computing the work done by an expanding gas. We consider a system consisting of a gas in a cylinder equipped with a movable piston, as shown in Fig. 21-3a. The piston has a cross-sectional area A and rests on a column of gas under a pressure P. Heat can flow in or out of the gas through the cylinder walls. Work can be done on or by the gas by pushing the piston down or by allowing it to expand upward.

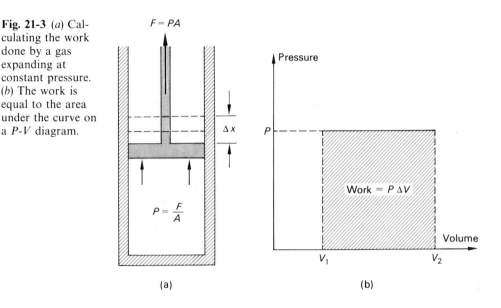

Fig. 21-3 (*a*) Calculating the work done by a gas expanding at constant pressure. (*b*) The work is equal to the area under the curve on a *P-V* diagram.

Let us first consider the work done by the gas when it expands at a constant pressure P. The force exerted by the gas on the piston will be equal to PA. If the piston moves upward through a distance Δx, the work ΔW of this force will be given by

$$\Delta W = F \, \Delta x = PA \, \Delta x$$

But $A \, \Delta x = \Delta V$, where ΔV represents the change in volume of the gas. Hence

$$\boxed{\Delta W = P \, \Delta V} \tag{21-3}$$

In other words, the work done by a gas expanding at constant pressure is equal to the product of the pressure and the change in volume of the gas.

The process can be shown graphically by plotting the increase in volume as a function of pressure (Fig. 21-3*b*). This representation, called a *P-V diagram*, is extremely useful in thermodynamics. In the above example, the pressure was constant, so that the graph is a straight line. Note that the area under the line, indicated by the shaded portion in the figure, is

$$\text{Area} = P(V_2 - V_1) = P \, \Delta V$$

which is equal to the work ΔW, from Eq. (21-3). This leads us to a very important principle:

When a thermodynamic process involves changes in volume and/or pressure, the work done by the system is equal to the area under the curve on a P-V diagram.

In general, the pressure will not be constant during a piston displacement. For example, in the power stroke of a gasoline engine, the fluid is ignited under high pressure, and the pressure decreases as the piston is displaced downward. The P-V diagram in this case is a sloping curve, as shown in Fig. 21-4a. The volume increases from V_1 to V_2 while the pressure decreases from P_1 to P_2. To compute the work in such a process, we must resort to a graphical analysis and measure the area under the P-V curve.

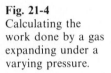

Fig. 21-4
Calculating the work done by a gas expanding under a varying pressure.

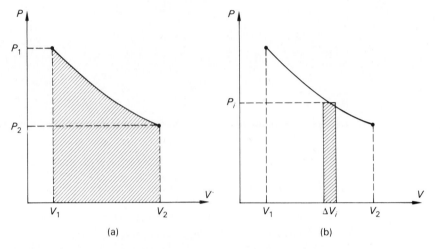

(a)   (b)

That the area under the curve is equal to the work when the pressure is not constant can be demonstrated in Fig. 21-4. The area of the narrow shaded rectangle represents the work done by the gas in expanding by an increment ΔV_i under a constant pressure P_i. If the area under the entire curve is split up into many of these rectangles, we can sum all the products $P_i \Delta V_i$ to obtain the total work. Thus one can see that the total work is simply the area under the P-V diagram between the points V_1 and V_2 on the volume axis.

**21-5
THE
GENERAL
CASE FOR
THE FIRST
LAW**

The first law of thermodynamics stipulates that energy must be conserved in any thermodynamic process. In the mathematical formulation

$$\Delta Q = \Delta W + \Delta U$$

There are three quantities which may undergo changes. The most general process is one in which all three quantities are involved. For example, the fluid in Fig. 21-5 is expanded while in contact with a hot flame. Considering the gas as a system, there is a net heat transfer ΔQ imparted to the gas. This energy is used in two ways: (1) the internal energy ΔU of the gas is increased by a portion of the input thermal energy, and (2) the gas does an amount of work ΔW on the piston which is equivalent to the remainder of the available energy.

Special cases of the first law arise when one or more of the three quantities—ΔQ, ΔW, or ΔU—do not undergo change. In these instances, the first law is considerably simplified. In the following sections we consider several of these special processes.

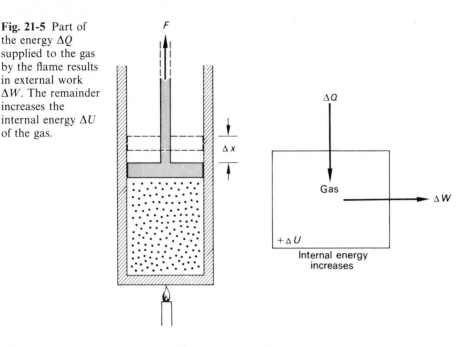

Fig. 21-5 Part of the energy ΔQ supplied to the gas by the flame results in external work ΔW. The remainder increases the internal energy ΔU of the gas.

21-6
ADIABATIC
PROCESSES

Suppose a system is completely isolated from its surroundings so that there can be no exchange of thermal energy Q. Any process which occurs completely inside such an isolated chamber is called an *adiabatic process*, and the system is said to be surrounded by *adiabatic* walls.

> An **adiabatic process** is one in which there is no exchange of thermal energy ΔQ between a system and its surroundings.

Applying the first law to a process in which $\Delta Q = 0$, we obtain

$$\Delta W = -\Delta U \qquad\qquad Adiabatic \quad (21\text{-}4)$$

Equation (21-4) tells us that in an adiabatic process the work is done at the *expense* of internal energy. The decrease in thermal energy is usually accompanied by a decrease in temperature.

As an example of an adiabatic process, consider Fig. 21-6, in which a piston is lifted by an expanding gas. If the walls of the cylinder are insulated and the expansion occurs rapidly, the process will be approximately adiabatic. As the gas expands, it does work on the piston but loses internal energy and experiences a drop in temperature. If the process is reversed by forcing the piston back down, work is done *on* the gas $(-\Delta W)$ and there will be an increase in internal energy (ΔU) such that

$$-\Delta W = +\Delta U$$

In this instance the temperature will rise.

Fig. 21-6 In an adiabatic process there is no transfer of heat, and work is done at the *expense* of internal energy.

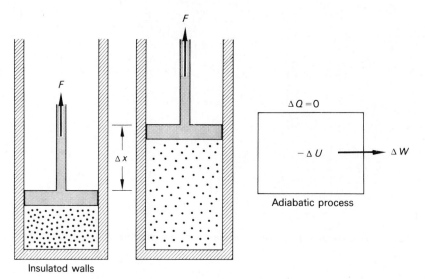

Insulated walls

Another example of an adiabatic process which finds very useful applications in industrial refrigeration is referred to as a *throttling process.*

A **throttling process** is one in which a fluid at high pressure seeps adiabatically through a porous wall or narrow opening into a region of low pressure.

Consider a gas forced by a pump to circulate through the apparatus in Fig. 21-7. Gas from the high-pressure side of the pump is forced through the narrow constriction, called the *throttling valve*, to the low-pressure side. The valve is heavily insulated, so that the process is adiabatic and $\Delta Q = 0$. According to the first law, $\Delta W = -\Delta U$, and the net work done by the gas in passing through the valve is accomplished at the expense of internal energy. In refrigeration, a liquid coolant undergoes a drop in temperature and partial vaporization as a result of the throttling process.

Fig. 21-7 The throttling process.

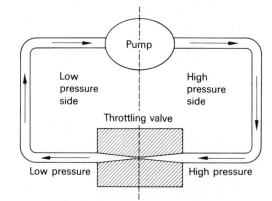

Another special case for the first law occurs when there is no work done, either *by* the system or *on* the system. This type of process is referred to as an *isochoric process*. It is also referred to as an *isovolumic process* since there can be no change in volume without the performance of work.

> An **isochoric process** is one in which the volume of the system remains constant.

Applying the first law to a process in which $\Delta W = 0$, we obtain

$$\Delta Q = \Delta U \qquad\qquad Isochoric \quad (21\text{-}5)$$

Therefore, in an isochoric process all the thermal energy absorbed by a system goes to increase its internal energy. In this instance there is usually a rise in the temperature of the system.

An isochoric process occurs when water is heated in a container of fixed volume, as shown in Fig. 21-8. As heat is supplied, the increase in internal energy results in a rise in the temperature of the water until it begins to boil. Further increases in internal energy go into the process of vaporization. However, the volume of the system, consisting of the water and its vapor, remains constant, and no external work is done.

Fig. 21-8 In an isochoric process, the volume of the system (water and vapor) remains constant.

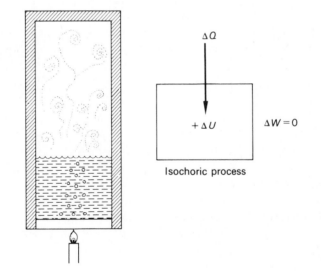

When the flame is removed, the process is reversed as heat leaves the system through the bottom of the cylinder. The water vapor will condense, and the temperature of the resulting water will eventually drop to room temperature. This process represents a loss of heat and a corresponding decrease in internal energy, but, once again, no work is done.

21-8 ISOTHERMAL PROCESSES

It is possible for the pressure and volume of a gas to vary without a change in temperature. In Chap. 20 we introduced Boyle's law to describe volume and pressure changes during such a process. A gas can be compressed in a cylinder so slowly that it will essentially remain in thermal equilibrium with its surroundings. The pressure increases as the volume decreases, but the temperature is essentially constant.

> An **isothermal process** is one in which the temperature of the system remains constant.

If there is no change of phase, a constant temperature indicates that there is no change in the internal energy of the system. Applying the first law to a process in which $\Delta U = 0$, we obtain

$$\Delta Q = \Delta W \qquad \qquad \textit{Isothermal} \quad (21\text{-}6)$$

Thus, in an isothermal process all the energy absorbed by a system is converted into output work.

21-9 THE SECOND LAW OF THERMO-DYNAMICS

When we rub our hands together vigorously, the work done against friction increases the internal energy and causes a rise in temperature. The surrounding air forms a large reservoir at a lower temperature, and the heat energy is transferred to the air without changing its temperature appreciably. When we stop rubbing, our hands return to the same state as before. According to the first law, mechanical energy has been transformed into heat with 100 percent efficiency.

$$\Delta W = \Delta Q$$

Such a transformation can be continued indefinitely as long as work is supplied.

Let us now consider the reverse process. Is it possible to convert heat energy into work with 100 percent efficiency? In the above example, is it possible to capture all the heat transferred to the air and return it to our hands, causing them to rub together indefinitely of their own accord? On a cold winter day, this process would be a boon to hunters with cold hands. Unfortunately, such a process cannot occur even though it does not violate the first law. Neither is it possible to retrieve all the heat lost in braking a car in order to start the wheels rolling again.

We shall see that the conversion of heat energy into mechanical work is a losing process. The first law of thermodynamics tells us that we cannot win in such an experiment. In other words, it is impossible to get more work out of a system than the heat put into the system. It does not, however, preclude us from breaking even. Clearly, we need another rule which states that the 100 percent conversion of heat energy into useful work is not possible. This rule forms the basis for the *second law of thermodynamics*.

The Second Law of Thermodynamics: *It is impossible to construct an engine which, operating continuously, produces no effect other than the extraction of heat from a reservoir and the performance of an equivalent amount of work.*

To give more insight and application to this principle, suppose we study the operation and efficiency of heat engines. A particular system might be a gasoline engine, a jet engine, a steam engine, or even the human body. The operation of a heat engine is best described by a diagram similar to that shown in Fig. 21-9. During the operating of such a general engine, three processes occur:

1. A quantity of heat Q_{in} is supplied to the engine from a reservoir at a high temperature T_{in}.
2. Mechanical work W_{out} is done by the engine through the use of a portion of the heat input.
3. A quantity of heat Q_{out} is released to a reservoir at a low temperature T_{out}.

Fig. 21-9 A schematic diagram for a heat engine.

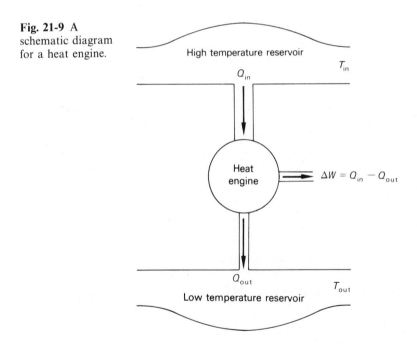

Since the system is periodically returned to its initial state, the net change in internal energy is zero. Thus, the first law tells us that

Work output = heat input − heat output

$$W_{out} = Q_{in} - Q_{out}$$

(21-7)

The efficiency of a heat engine is defined as the ratio of the useful work done by the engine to the heat put into the engine, and it is usually expressed as a percentage.

$$\text{Efficiency} = \frac{\text{work output}}{\text{heat input}}$$

$$E = \frac{Q_{in} - Q_{out}}{Q_{in}} \tag{21-8}$$

For example, an engine that is 25 percent efficient ($E = 0.25$) might absorb 1000 Btu, perform 250 Btu of work, and reject 750 Btu as wasted heat. A 100 percent efficient engine is one in which all the input heat is converted to useful work. In this case, no heat would be rejected to the environment ($Q_{out} = 0$). Although such a process would conserve energy, it violates the second law of thermodynamics. The most efficient engine is the one which rejects the *least* possible heat to the environment.

21-10 THE CARNOT CYCLE

All heat engines are subject to many practical difficulties. Friction and the loss of heat through conduction and radiation prevent actual engines from obtaining their maximum efficiency. An idealized engine free of such problems was suggested by Sadi Carnot in 1824. The *Carnot engine* has the maximum possible efficiency for an engine which absorbs heat from a high-temperature reservoir, performs external work, and deposits heat to a low-temperature reservoir. The effectiveness of a given engine can therefore be determined by comparing it with the Carnot engine operating between the same temperatures.

The Carnot cycle is illustrated in Fig. 21-10. A gas contained in a cylinder equipped with a movable piston is placed in contact with a reservoir at a high temperature T_{in}. A quantity of heat Q_{in} is absorbed by the gas which expands isothermally as the pressure decreases. This first stage of a Carnot cycle is shown graphically as the curve AB in the P-V diagram (Fig. 21-11). The

Fig. 21-10 The Carnot cycle: (*a*) isothermal expansion, (*b*) adiabatic expansion, (*c*) isothermal compression, and (*d*) adiabatic compression.

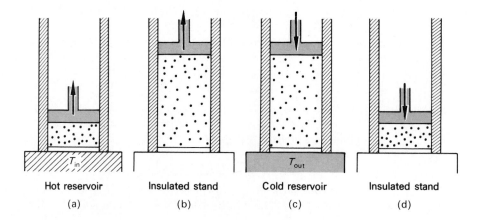

Hot reservoir   Insulated stand   Cold reservoir   Insulated stand

(a)   (b)   (c)   (d)

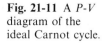

Fig. 21-11 A *P-V* diagram of the ideal Carnot cycle.

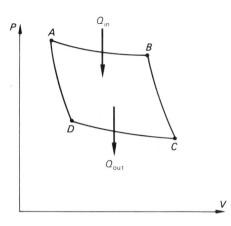

cylinder is next placed on an insulated stand, where it continues to expand adiabatically as the pressure drops to its lowest value. This stage is represented graphically by the curve *BC*. In the third stage the cylinder is removed from the insulated pad and placed on a reservoir at a low temperature T_{out}. A quantity of heat Q_{out} is exhausted from the gas as it is compressed isothermally from point *C* to point *D* in the *P-V* diagram. Finally, the cylinder is again placed on the insulated pad, where it is compressed adiabatically to its original state along the path *DA*. The engine does external work during the expansion processes and returns to its initial state during the compression processes.

21-11 THE EFFICIENCY OF AN IDEAL ENGINE

The efficiency of a real engine is difficult to predict from Eq. (21-8) because the quantities Q_{in} and Q_{out} are difficult to calculate. Frictional and heat losses through the cylinder walls and around the piston, incomplete burning of the fuel, and even the physical properties of different fuels all frustrate our attempts to measure the efficiency of such engines. However, we can imagine an *ideal engine*, one which is not restricted by these practical difficulties. The efficiency of such an engine depends only on the quantities of heat absorbed and rejected between two well-defined heat reservoirs. It does not depend on the thermal properties of the working fuel. In other words, regardless of the internal changes in pressure, volume, length, or other factors, all ideal engines have the same efficiency when they are operating between the same two temperatures (T_{in} and T_{out}).

> An **ideal engine** is one which has the highest possible efficiency for the temperature limits within which its operates.

If we can define the efficiency of an engine in terms of input and output temperatures instead of in terms of the input and output of heat, we will have a more useful formula. For an ideal engine it can be shown that the ratio of Q_{in}/Q_{out} is the same as the ratio of T_{in}/T_{out}. The actual proof is beyond the scope of this text. The efficiency of an ideal engine can, therefore, be expressed as a function of the absolute temperatures of the input and output reservoirs. Equation (21-8), for an ideal engine, becomes

$$E = \frac{T_{in} - T_{out}}{T_{in}} \qquad (21\text{-}9)$$

It can be shown that no engine operating between the same two temperatures can be more efficient than would be indicated by Eq. (21-9). This ideal efficiency thus represents an upper limit to the efficiency of any practical engine. The greater the difference in temperature between two reservoirs, the greater the efficiency of any engine.

EXAMPLE 21-2   (*a*) What is the efficiency of an ideal engine operating between two heat reservoirs at 400 and 300 K? (*b*) How much work is done by the engine in one complete cycle if 800 cal of heat is absorbed from the high-temperature reservoir? (*c*) How much heat is delivered to the low-temperature reservoir?

Solution (*a*)   The ideal efficiency is found from Eq. (21-9).

$$E = \frac{T_{in} - T_{out}}{T_{in}} = \frac{400\text{ K} - 300\text{ K}}{300\text{ K}} = 0.25$$

Thus, the ideal efficiency is 25 percent.

Solution (*b*)   The efficiency is the ratio of W_{out}/Q_{in}, so that

$$\frac{W_{out}}{Q_{in}} = 0.25 \qquad \text{or} \qquad W_{out} = (0.25)Q_{in}$$

$$W_{out} = (0.25)(800\text{ cal}) = 200\text{ cal}$$

A 25 percent efficient engine delivers one-fourth of the input heat to useful work. The rest must be lost (Q_{out}).

Solution (*c*)   The first law of thermodynamics requires that

$$W_{out} = Q_{in} - Q_{out}$$

Solving for Q_{out} we obtain

$$Q_{out} = Q_{in} - W_{out} = 800\text{ cal} - 200\text{ cal} = 600\text{ cal}$$

The work output is usually expressed in joules. Conversion to these units gives

$$W_{out} = (200\text{ cal})(4.186\text{ J/cal}) = 837\text{ J}$$

**21-12
INTERNAL
COM-
BUSTION
ENGINES**
An internal combustion engine generates the input heat within the engine itself. The most common engine of this variety is the four-stroke gasoline engine, in which a mixture of gasoline and air is ignited by a spark plug in each cylinder. The thermal energy released is converted into useful work by the pressure exerted on a piston by the expanding gases. The four-stroke process is illustrated in Fig. 21-12. During the *intake stroke* (Fig. 21-12*a*), a mixture of air and

Fig. 21-12 The
four-stroke gasoline
engine: (*a*) intake
stroke; (*b*) com-
pression stroke;
(*c*) power stroke;
and (*d*) exhaust
stroke.

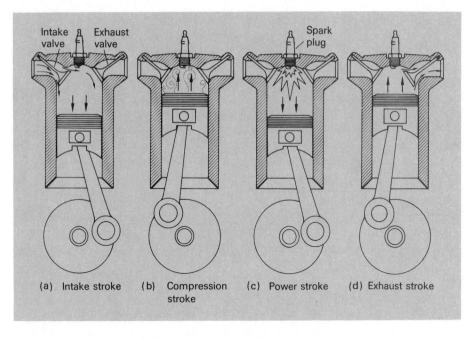

(a) Intake stroke   (b) Compression   (c) Power stroke   (d) Exhaust stroke
stroke

gasoline vapor enters the cylinder through the intake valve. Both valves are
closed during the *compression stroke* (Fig. 21-12*b*) as the piston moves upward,
causing a rise in pressure. Just before the piston reaches the top, the mixture is
ignited, causing a sharp increase in temperature and pressure. In the power
stroke (Fig. 21-12*c*) the expanding gases force the piston downward, performing
external work. The fourth stroke (Fig. 21-12*d*) pushes the burned gases out of
the cylinder through the exhaust valve. The entire cycle is then repeated for as
long as the combustible fuel is supplied to the cylinder.

    The ideal cycle used by the engineer to perfect the gasoline engine is
shown in Fig. 21-13. It is named the *Otto cycle* after its inventor. The compres-

Fig. 21-13 The
Otto cycle for a
four-stroke gasoline
engine.

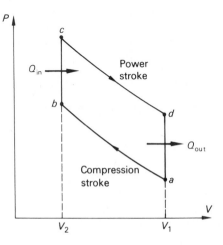

sion stroke is represented by the curve *ab*. The pressure increases adiabatically as the volume is reduced. At point *b* the mixture is ignited, supplying a quantity of heat Q_{in} to the system. This causes the sharp rise in pressure indicated by the line *bc*. In the power stroke (*cd*), the gases expand adiabatically, performing external work. The system then cools at constant volume to point *a*, releasing a quantity of heat Q_{out}. The burned gases are exhausted on the next upward stroke, and more fuel is drawn in on the next downward stroke. Then the cycle begins all over again. The volume ratio V_1/V_2, as indicated in the *P-V* diagram, is called the *compression* ratio and is about 8 for most automobile engines.

The efficiency of the ideal Otto cycle can be shown to be

$$E = 1 - \frac{1}{(V_1/V_2)^{\gamma - 1}} \tag{21-10}$$

where γ is the adiabatic constant for the working substance. The adiabatic constant is defined by

$$\gamma = \frac{c_p}{c_v}$$

where c_p is the specific heat of the gas at constant pressure and c_v is the specific heat at constant volume. For monatomic gases $\gamma = 1.67$, and for diatomic gases $\gamma = 1.4$. In the gasoline engine the working substance is mostly air, for which $\gamma = 1.4$. In the ideal case, Eq. (21-10) shows that the higher compression ratios yield higher efficiencies since γ is always greater than 1.

EXAMPLE 21-3

Compute the efficiency of a gasoline engine for which the compression ratio is 8 and $\gamma = 1.4$.

Solution

From the given information, we note that

$$\frac{V_1}{V_2} = 8 \quad \text{and} \quad \gamma - 1 = 1.4 - 1 = 0.4$$

Thus, from Eq. (21-3),

$$E = 1 - \frac{1}{8^{0.4}} = 1 - \frac{1}{2.3} = 57\%$$

In the above example, 57 percent represents the maximum possible efficiency of a gasoline engine with the parameters given. Actually, the efficiency of such an engine is normally around 30 percent because of uncontrolled heat losses.

A second type of internal combustion engine is the diesel engine. In this engine the air is compressed to a high temperature and pressure near the top of the cylinder. Diesel fuel, which is injected into the cylinder at this point, ignites and forces the piston downward. The idealized diesel cycle is shown by the *P-V* diagram in Fig. 21-14. Starting at *a*, air is compressed adiabatically to point *b*

Fig. 21-14 The ideal diesel cycle.

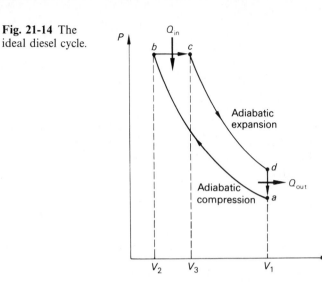

where the diesel fuel is injected. The diesel fuel, ignited by the hot air, delivers a quantity of heat Q_{in} at nearly constant pressure (line bc). The remainder of the power stroke consists of an adiabatic expansion to point d, performing external work. During the exhaust and intake strokes, the gas cools at constant volume to point a, losing a quantity of heat Q_{out}. The efficiency of a diesel engine is a function of the compression ratio (V_1/V_2) and the *expansion ratio* (V_1/V_3).

21-13 REFRIGER-ATION

A refrigerator can be thought of as a heat engine operated in reverse. A schematic diagram of a refrigerator is shown in Fig. 21-15. During every cycle, a compressor or similar device supplies mechanical work W to the system, extracting a quantity of heat Q_{cold} from a cold reservoir and depositing a quantity of heat Q_{hot} to a hot reservoir. According to the first law, the input work is given by

$$W = Q_{hot} - Q_{cold}$$

The effectiveness of any refrigerator is determined by the amount of heat Q_{cold} extracted for the least expenditure of mechanical work W. The ratio Q_{cold}/W is therefore a measure of the cooling efficiency of a refrigerator and is called its *coefficient of performance* η. Symbolically,

$$\eta = \frac{Q_{cold}}{W} = \frac{Q_{cold}}{Q_{hot} - Q_{cold}} \tag{21-11}$$

The maximum efficiency can be expressed in terms of absolute temperatures:

$$\eta = \frac{T_{cold}}{T_{hot} - T_{cold}} \tag{21-12}$$

Fig. 21-15 A
schematic diagram
for a refrigerator.

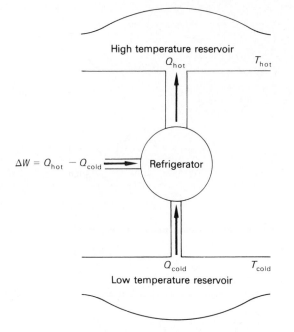

To understand the refrigeration process better let us consider the general schematic in Fig. 21-16. This diagram may refer to a number of refrigeration devices, from a commercial plant to a household refrigerator. The working substance, called the *refrigerant*, is a gas which is easily liquefied by an increase in pressure or a drop in temperature. In the liquid phase it can be vaporized readily by passing it through a throttling process (see Sec. 21-6) near room temperature. Common refrigerants are ammonia, Freon 12, methyl chloride, and sulfur dioxide. Ammonia, the most common industrial refrigerant, boils at $-28°F$ under a pressure of 1 atm. Freon 12, the most common household refrigerant, boils at $-22°F$ at atmospheric pressure. Variation in pressure radically affects the condensation and evaporation temperatures of all refrigerants.

As shown in the schematic, a typical refrigeration system consists of a *compressor*, a *condenser*, a *liquid storage tank*, a *throttling valve*, and an *evaporator*. The compressor provides the necessary input work to move the refrigerant through the system. As the piston moves to the right, it sucks in the refrigerant through the intake valve at a little above atmospheric pressure and near room temperature. During the power stroke, the intake valve closes and the discharge valve opens. The emergent refrigerant, at high temperature and pressure, passes into the condenser where it is cooled until it liquefies. The condenser may be cooled by running water or by an electric fan. It is during this phase that a quantity of heat Q_{hot} is rejected from the system. The condensed liquid refrigerant, still under a condition of high pressure and temperature, is collected in a liquid reservoir. Then the liquid refrigerant is drawn from the storage tank through a throttling valve, causing a sudden drop in temperature

Fig. 21-16 The basic components of a refrigeration system.

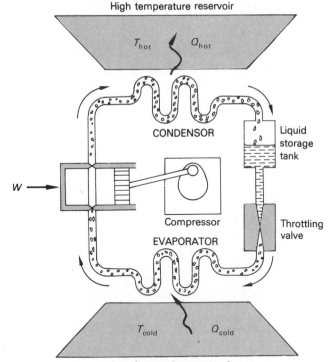

and pressure. As the cold liquid refrigerant flows through the evaporator coils, it absorbs a quantity of heat Q_{cold} from the space and products being cooled. This heat boils the liquid refrigerant and is carried away by the gaseous refrigerant as latent heat of vaporization. This phase is the "payoff" for the entire operation, and all components just contribute to the effective transfer of heat to the evaporator. Finally, the refrigerant vapor leaves the evaporator and is sucked into the compressor to begin another cycle.

SUMMARY

Thermodynamics is the science which treats the conversion of heat into work or the reverse process, the conversion of work into heat. We have seen that not only must energy be conserved in such processes, but also there are limits on the efficiency. The major concepts presented in this chapter are summarized below:

- The *first law of thermodynamics* is a restatement of the conservation-of-energy principle. It says that the net heat ΔQ put into a system is equal to the net work ΔW done by the system plus the net change in internal energy ΔU of the system. Symbolically,

$$\Delta Q = \Delta W + \Delta U$$

First Law of Thermodynamics

- In thermodynamics, work ΔW is often done on a gas. In such cases the work is often represented in terms of pressure and volume. A *P-V* diagram is also useful for measuring ΔW.

$$\boxed{\Delta W = P\,\Delta V} \qquad \Delta W = \text{area under } P\text{-}V \text{ curve}$$

- Special cases of the first law occur when one of the quantities doesn't undergo a change.

  (a) *Adiabatic process:* $\Delta Q = 0$ $\Delta W = -\Delta U$
  (b) *Isochoric process:* $\Delta V = 0$ $\Delta W = 0$ $\Delta Q = \Delta U$
  (c) *Isothermal process:* $\Delta T = 0$ $\Delta U = 0$ $\Delta Q = \Delta W$

- The *second law of thermodynamics* places restrictions on the possibility of satisfying the first. In short, it points out that in every process there is some loss of energy due to frictional forces or other dissipative forces. A 100 percent efficient engine, one which converts all input heat to useful output work, is not possible.
- A heat engine is represented generally by Fig. 21-9. The meaning of the symbols used in the equations below can be taken from that figure. The work done by the engine is the difference between input heat and output heat.

$$\boxed{W = Q_{\text{in}} - Q_{\text{out}}} \qquad\qquad\qquad \textit{Work (kcal or J)}$$

- The *efficiency* E of an engine is the ratio of the work output to the heat input. It can be calculated for an ideal engine from either of the following relations:

$$\boxed{E = \frac{Q_{\text{in}} - Q_{\text{out}}}{Q_{\text{in}}}} \qquad \boxed{E = \frac{T_{\text{in}} - T_{\text{out}}}{T_{\text{in}}}} \qquad \textit{Efficiency}$$

- A *refrigerator* is a heat engine operated in reverse. A measure of the performance of such a device is the amount of cooling you get for the work you must put into the system. Cooling occurs as a result of the extraction of heat Q_{cold} from the cold reservoir. The coefficient of performance η is given by either

$$\boxed{\eta = \frac{Q_{\text{cold}}}{Q_{\text{hot}} - Q_{\text{cold}}}} \qquad \text{or} \qquad \boxed{\eta = \frac{T_{\text{cold}}}{T_{\text{hot}} - T_{\text{cold}}}}$$

QUESTIONS

21-1. Define the following terms:

a. Thermodynamics
b. *P-V* diagram
c. Adiabatic process
d. Isochoric process
e. Heat engine
f. Refrigerator
g. Refrigerant
h. Compressor
i. Condenser
j. Evaporator

k. Internal-energy function
l. First law of thermodynamics
m. Throttling process
n. Isothermal process
o. Second law of thermodynamics
p. Thermal efficiency
q. Carnot cycle
r. Carnot efficiency
s. Coefficient of performance

21-2. The latent heat of vaporization of water is 540 cal/g. However, when 1 g of water is completely vaporized at constant pressure, the internal energy of the system increases by only 500 cal. What happened to the remaining 40 cal? Is this an isochoric process? Is it an isothermal process?

21-3. If both heat and work can be expressed in the same units, why is it necessary to distinguish between them?

21-4. Is it necessary to use the concept of molecular energy in order to describe and use the internal-energy function? Explain.

21-5. A gas undergoes an adiabatic expansion. Does it perform external work? If so, what is the source of energy?

21-6. What happens to the internal energy of a gas undergoing **(a)** adiabatic compression, **(b)** isothermal expansion, and **(c)** a throttling process?

21-7. A gas performs external work during an isothermal expansion. What is the source of energy?

21-8. In the text, only one statement was given for the second law of thermodynamics. Discuss each of the following statements, showing them to be equivalent to that given in the text:
   (a) It is impossible to construct a refrigerator which, working continuously, will extract heat from a cold body and exhaust it to a hot body without the performance of work on the system.
   (b) The natural direction of heat flow is from a body at high temperature to a body at a low temperature, regardless of the size of each reservoir.
   (c) All natural spontaneous processes are irreversible.
   (d) Natural events always proceed in the direction from order to disorder.

21-9. It is energetically possible to extract the heat energy contained in the ocean and use it to power a steamship across the sea. What objections can you offer?

21-10. In an electric refrigerator, heat is transferred from the cool interior to warmer surroundings. Why isn't this in violation of the second law of thermodynamics?

21-11. Consider the performance of external work by the isothermal expansion of an ideal gas. Why isn't this process of converting heat into work in violation of the second law of thermodynamics?

21-12. If natural processes tend to decrease order in the universe, how can you explain the evolution of biological systems to a highly organized state? Does this violate the second law of thermodynamics?

21-13. Will keeping the door of an electric refrigerator open warm or cool a room? Explain.

21-14. What temperature must the cold reservoir have if a Carnot engine is to be 100 percent efficient? Can this ever happen? If it is impossible for a Carnot engine to have a 100 percent efficiency, why is it called the *ideal* engine?

21-15. What determines the efficiency of heat engines? Why is it generally so low?

PROBLEMS

21-1. A piston does 3000 ft · lb of work on a gas, which then expands, performing 2500 ft · lb of work on its surroundings. What is the change in internal energy of the gas in Btu?

Ans. 0.643 Btu.

21-2. A 100-lb block slides down a plane through a vertical distance of 10 ft. If the block is moving with a velocity of 15 ft/s when it reaches the bottom of the plane, how many Btu of heat were lost because of friction?

21-3. A gas expands against a movable piston, lifting it through 2 in. at constant speed. **(a)** How much work is done by the gas if the piston weighs 200 lb and has a cross-sectional area of 12 in.²? **(b)** If the expansion is adiabatic, what is the change in internal energy in Btu? **(c)** Does ΔU represent an increase or a decrease in internal energy?

Ans. **(a)** 33.3 ft · lb **(b)** 0.043 Btu **(c)** decrease.

21-4. During the isothermal expansion of an ideal gas, 3 Btu of heat energy is absorbed. The piston weighs 2000 lb. How high will it rise above its initial position?

21-5. A steam engine operates with an efficiency of 12 percent. How much heat must be supplied per hour in order to develop 4 hp?

Ans. 8.48×10^4 Btu.

21-6. The heat of combustion for coal is 12,000 Btu/lb. An engine burns 2 lb of coal in lifting 4 tons of water through a height of 100 ft. What is the efficiency of the engine?

21-7. At atmospheric pressure 1 g of water has a volume of 1.0 cm³. The heat of vaporization for water at 1 atm is 540 cal/g. When 1 g of water is completely vaporized at atmospheric pressure, it has a final volume of 1671 cm³ in its vapor form. **(a)** Compute the external work done by the system in expanding against its surroundings. **(b)** What is the increase in internal energy of the system?

Ans. **(a)** 40.4 cal **(b)** 499.6 cal.

21-8. In a thermodynamic process, 2000 cal of heat is supplied to a system, allowing the system to perform 3350 J of external work. What is the increase in thermal energy during the process?

21-9. A steam engine takes steam from a boiler at 200°C and exhausts directly into the air at 100°C. What is its deal efficiency?

Ans. 21%.

21-10. In a Carnot cycle, the isothermal expansion of a gas takes place at 400 K, and 500 cal of heat energy is absorbed by the gas. **(a)** How much heat is rejected by the system during the isothermal compression if the process occurs at 300 K? **(b)** What external work is performed by the system?

21-11. A Carnot engine absorbs heat from a reservoir at 500 K and rejects heat to a reservoir at 300 K. In each cycle the engine receives 1200 cal of heat from the high-temperature reservoir. **(a)** What is the Carnot efficiency? **(b)** How many calories are rejected to the low-temperature reservoir? **(c)** How much external work is done in joules?

Ans. **(a)** 40% **(b)** 720 cal **(c)** 2010 J.

21-12. If the engine in Prob. 21-11 is operated in reverse (as a refrigerator) and extracts 1200 cal of heat from the low-temperature reservoir, how many calories will be delivered to the high-temperature reservoir? How much input mechanical work is required?

21-13. The Otto efficiency for a gasoline engine is 50 percent, and the adiabatic constant is 1.4. Compute the compression ratio.

Ans. 5.66.

21-14. A heat pump takes heat from a water reservoir at 41°F and delivers it to a system of pipes in a house at 78°F. The energy required to operate the heat pump is about twice that required to operate a Carnot pump. How much mechanical work must be supplied by the pump in order to deliver 10^6 Btu of heat energy to the house?

21-15. A Carnot engine has an efficiency of 48 percent. If the working substance enters the system at 400°C, what is the exhaust temperature?

Ans. 77°C.

21-16. During the compression stroke of an automobile engine, the volume of the combustible mixture decreases from 18 to 2 in.^{3} If the adiabatic constant is 1.5, what is the maximum possible efficiency for the engine?

21-17. How many joules of work must be done by the compressor in a refrigerator in order to change 1 kg of water at 20°C to ice at −10°C? The coefficient of performance is 3.5.

Ans. 1.26×10^5 J.

21-18. In a mechanical refrigerator the low-temperature coils of the evaporator are at −30°C, and the compressed gas in the condenser has a temperature of 60°C. What is the maximum possible coefficient of performance?

21-19. Consider a specific mass of gas which is forced through an adiabatic throttling process. Before entering the valve, it has internal energy U_1, pressure P_1, and volume V_1. After passing through the valve, it has internal energy U_2, pressure P_2, and volume V_2. The net work is the work done *by* the gas minus the work done *on* the gas. Show that

$$U_2 + P_2 V_2 = U_1 + P_1 V_1$$

The quantity $U + PV$, called the *enthalpy*, is conserved during a throttling process.

21-20. A compression refrigeration system has a coefficient of performance of 4.0. If the evaporating temperature is −12°C, what is the condensing temperature?

21-21. An engine has a thermal efficiency of 27% and an exhaust temperature of 230°C. What is the lowest possible input temperature?

Ans. 416°C.

22 *Wave Motion*

OBJECTIVES: After completing this chapter, you should be able to:

1. Demonstrate by definition and example your understanding of *transverse* and *longitudinal* wave motion.
2. Define, relate, and apply the meaning of the terms *frequency*, *wavelength*, and *speed* for wave motion.
3. Solve problems involving the *mass*, *length*, *tension*, and *wave velocity* for transverse waves in a string.
4. Write and apply an expression for determining the *characteristic frequencies* for a vibrating string with fixed end points.

Energy can be transferred from one place to another by several means. In driving a nail, the bulk kinetic energy of a hammer is converted into useful work on the nail. Wind, projectiles, and most simple machines also perform work at the expense of material motion. Even the conduction of heat and electricity involves the motion of elementary particles called electrons. In this chapter we study the transfer of energy from one point to another without the physical transfer of material between the points.

22-1 MECHANICAL WAVES

When a stone is dropped into a pool of water, it creates a disturbance which spreads out in concentric circles, eventually reaching all parts of the pool. A small stick, floating on the surface of the water, bobs up and down as the disturbance passes. Energy has been transferred from the point of impact of the stone into the water to the floating stick some distance away. This energy is passed along by the agitation of neighboring water particles. Only the disturbance moves through the water. The actual motion of any particular water particle is comparatively small. Energy propagation by means of a disturbance in a medium instead of the motion of the medium itself is called *wave motion*.

The example above is referred to as a *mechanical* wave because its existence depends upon a mechanical source and a material medium.

A **mechanical wave** is a physical disturbance in an elastic medium.

It is important to recognize that all disturbances are not necessarily mechanical. For example, light waves, radio waves, and heat radiation propagate their energy by means of electric and magnetic disturbances. No physical medium is necessary for the transmission of electromagnetic waves. However, many of the basic ideas presented in this chapter for mechanical waves are also applicable to electromagnetic waves.

22-2 TYPES OF WAVES

Waves are classified according to the motion of a local part of a medium with respect to the direction of wave propagation.

In a **transverse wave** the vibration of the individual particles of the medium is perpendicular to the direction of wave propagation.

For example, suppose we fasten one end of a rope to a post and grasp the other end with the hand, as shown in Fig. 22-1. By moving the free end up and down quickly, we send a single disturbance called a *pulse* down the length of rope.

Fig. 22-1 In a transverse wave the individual particles move perpendicular to the direction of propagation.

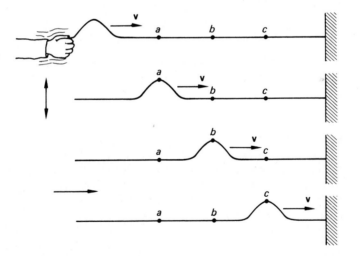

Three equally spaced knots at points *a*, *b*, and *c* demonstrate that the individual particles move up and down while the disturbance moves to the right with velocity **v**.

Another type of wave, which may occur in a coiled spring, is illustrated in Fig. 22-2. The coils near the left end are pinched closely together to form a *condensation*. When the distorting force is removed, a condensation pulse is propagated throughout the length of the spring. No part of the spring moves very

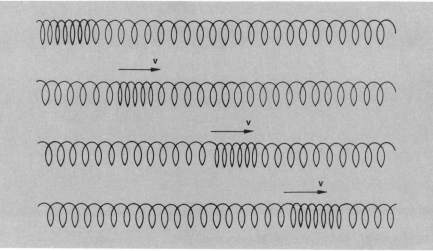

far from its equilibrium position, but the pulse continues to travel along the spring. Such a wave is called a *longitudinal wave* because the spring particles are displaced along the same direction in which the disturbance is traveling.

In a **longitudinal wave** the vibration of the individual particles is parallel to the direction of wave propagation.

If the coils of the spring in our example were forced apart at the left, a *rarefaction* would be formed, as shown in Fig. 22-3. Upon removal of the disturbing force, a longitudinal rarefaction pulse would be propagated along the spring. In general, a longitudinal wave consists of a series of condensations and rarefactions moving in a determined direction.

Fig. 22-3 Longitudinal motion of a rarefaction pulse in a coiled spring.

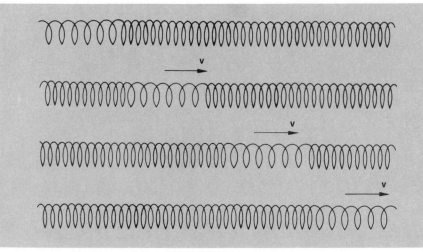

22-3
CALCU-
LATING
WAVE SPEED

The speed with which a pulse moves through a medium depends upon the elasticity of the medium and the inertia of its particles. The more elastic materials yield greater restoring forces when distorted. The less dense materials offer less resistance to motion. In either case, the ability of particles to pass on a disturbance to neighboring particles is improved, and a pulse will travel at a greater speed.

Let us consider the motion of a transverse pulse down the string in Fig. 22-4. The string of mass m and length l is maintained under a constant tension

Fig. 22-4 Computing the speed of a transverse pulse in a string.

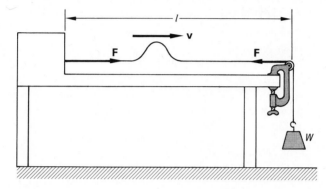

F by the suspended weight. When the string is plucked near the left end, a transverse pulse is propagated along the string. The elasticity of the string is measured by the tension F in the string. The inertia of the individual particles is determined by the *mass per unit length* μ of the string. It can be shown that the speed of a transverse pulse in a string is given by

$$v = \sqrt{\frac{F}{\mu}} = \sqrt{\frac{F}{m/l}} \qquad (22\text{-}1)$$

The mass per unit length μ is usually referred to as the *linear density* of the string. If F is expressed in newtons and μ in kilograms per meter, the speed is in meters per second.

EXAMPLE 22-1

The length l of the string in Fig. 22-4 is 2 m, and the string has a mass of 0.3 g. Calculate the speed of a transverse pulse in the string if it is under a tension of 20 N.

Solution

We first compute the linear density of the string.

$$\mu = \frac{m}{l} = \frac{0.3 \times 10^{-3} \text{ kg}}{2 \text{ m}}$$

$$= 1.5 \times 10^{-4} \text{ kg/m}$$

Then Eq. (22-1) yields

$$v = \sqrt{\frac{F}{\mu}} = \sqrt{\frac{20 \text{ N}}{1.5 \times 10^{-4} \text{ kg/m}}}$$

$$= 365 \text{ m/s}$$

Calculation of the speed of a longitudinal pulse will be reserved for the following chapter, in connection with sound waves.

22-4 PERIODIC WAVE MOTION

So far we have been considering single, nonrepeated disturbances called pulses. What happens if similar disturbances are repeated periodically?

Suppose we attach the left end of a string to the end point of an electromagnetic vibrator, as shown in Fig. 22-5. The end of the metal vibrator is driven with harmonic motion by an oscillating magnetic field. Since the string is attached to the end of the vibrator, a series of periodic transverse pulses is sent down the string. The resulting waves consist of many crests and troughs, which move down the string at a constant rate of speed. The distance between any two adjacent crests or troughs in such a wave train is called the *wavelength*, denoted by λ.

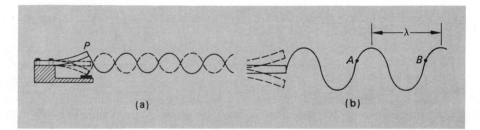

Fig. 22-5 (*a*) Production and propagation of periodic transverse wave. (*b*) The wave length λ is the distance between any two particles in phase, such as those at adjacent crests or at *A* and *B*.

As a wave travels along the string, each particle of the string vibrates about its equilibrium position with the same frequency and amplitude as the vibrating source. However, the particles of the string are not in corresponding positions at the same times. Two particles are said to be *in phase* if they have the same displacement and if they are moving in the same direction. The particles *A* and *B* of Fig. 22-5*b* are in phase. Since particles at the crests of a given wave train are also in phase, we can provide a more general definition for the wavelength.

The **wavelength** λ of a periodic wave train is the distance between any two adjacent particles which are in phase.

Each time the end point *P* of the vibrator makes a complete oscillation, the wave will move through a distance of one wavelength. The time required to cover this distance is therefore equal to the period T of the vibrating source. Hence the wave speed v can be related to the wavelength λ and period T by the equation

$$v = \frac{\lambda}{T} \qquad (22\text{-}2)$$

The frequency f of a wave is the number of waves that pass a particular point in a unit of time. It is the same as the frequency of the vibrating source and is therefore equal to the reciprocal of the period ($f = 1/T$). The units of frequency may be expressed in waves per second, oscillations per second, or cycles per second. The SI unit for frequency is the *hertz* (Hz), which is defined as a cycle per second.

$$1 \text{ Hz} = 1 \text{ cycle/s} = \frac{1}{s}$$

Thus, if 40 waves pass a point every second, the frequency is 40 Hz.

The speed of a wave is more often expressed in terms of its frequency rather than its period. Thus Eq. (22-2) can be written

$$\boxed{v = f\lambda} \qquad (22\text{-}3)$$

Equation (22-3) represents an important physical relationship between the speed, frequency, and wavelength of *any* periodic wave. An illustration of each quantity is given in Fig. 22-6 for a periodic transverse wave.

Fig. 22-6
Relationship between the frequency, wavelength, and speed of a transverse wave.

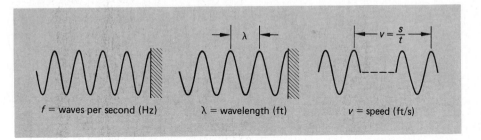

f = waves per second (Hz) λ = wavelength (ft) v = speed (ft/s)

EXAMPLE 22-2   A man sits near the end of a fishing dock and counts the water waves as they strike a supporting post. In 1 min he counts 80 waves. If a particular crest travels 20 m in 8 s, what is the wavelength of the waves?

Solution   The frequency and velocity of the waves are calculated as follows:

$$f = \frac{80 \text{ waves}}{60 \text{ s}} = 1.33 \text{ Hz}$$

$$v = \frac{20 \text{ m}}{8 \text{ s}} = 2.5 \text{ m/s}$$

From Eq. (22-3), the wavelength is

$$\lambda = \frac{v}{f} = \frac{2.5 \text{ m/s}}{1.33 \text{ Hz}} = 1.88 \text{ m}$$

A longitudinal periodic wave can be generated by the apparatus shown in Fig. 22-7. The left end of a coiled spring is connected to a metal ball supported at the end of a clamped hacksaw blade. When the metal ball is displaced to the left and released, it vibrates with harmonic motion. The resulting condensations and rarefactions are passed along the spring, producing a periodic longitudinal wave. Each particle of the coiled spring oscillates back and forth horizontally with the same frequency and amplitude as the metal ball. The distance between any two adjacent particles which are in phase is the wavelength. As indicated in Fig. 22-7, the distance between adjacent condensations or adjacent rarefactions is a convenient measure of the wavelength. Equation (22-3) also applies for a periodic longitudinal wave.

Fig. 22-7 Production and propagation of a periodic longitudinal wave.

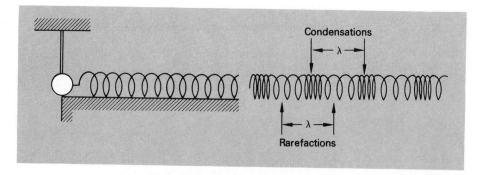

22-5 ENERGY OF A PERIODIC WAVE

We have seen that each particle in a periodic wave oscillates with simple harmonic motion determined by the source of the wave. The energy content of a wave can be analyzed by considering the harmonic motion of the individual particles. For example, consider a periodic transverse wave in a string at the instant shown in Fig. 22-8. Particle *a* has reached its maximum amplitude; its velocity is zero, and it is experiencing its maximum restoring force. Particle *b* is passing through its equilibrium position, where the restoring force is zero. At

Fig. 22-8 Restoring forces which act on particles of a vibrating string.

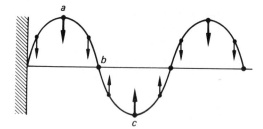

this instant, particle b has its greatest speed and hence its maximum energy. Particle c is at its maximum displacement in the negative direction. As the periodic wave passes along the string, each particle oscillates back and forth through its own equilibrium position.

In Chap. 14 on harmonic motion, we found that the maximum velocity of a particle oscillating with frequency f and amplitude A is given by

$$v_{max} = 2\pi f A$$

When a particle has this speed, it is passing through its equilibrium position, where its potential energy is zero and its kinetic energy is a maximum. Thus the total energy of the particle is

$$E = E_p + E_\kappa = (E_\kappa)_{max}$$
$$= \tfrac{1}{2}mv^2_{max} = \tfrac{1}{2}m(2\pi f A)^2$$
$$= 2\pi^2 f^2 A^2 m \tag{22-4}$$

As a periodic wave passes through a medium, each element of the medium is continuously doing work on adjacent elements. Therefore, the energy transmitted along the length of a vibrating string is not confined to one position. Let us apply the result obtained for a single particle to the entire length of a vibrating string. The energy content of the entire string is the sum of the individual energies of its constituent particles. If we let m refer to the entire mass of the string instead of the mass of an individual particle, Eq. (22-4) represents the total wave energy in the string. In a string of length l, the wave energy per unit length is given by

$$\frac{E}{l} = 2\pi^2 f^2 A^2 \frac{m}{l}$$

Substituting μ for the mass per unit length, we can write

$$\boxed{\frac{E}{l} = 2\pi^2 f^2 A^2 \mu} \tag{22-5}$$

The wave energy is proportional to the square of the frequency f, to the square of the amplitude A, and to the linear density μ of the string. It must be recognized that the linear density is not a function of the length of string. This is true because the mass increases in proportion to the length l, so that μ is constant for any length.

Suppose that a wave travels down a length l of a given string with a speed v. The time t required for the wave to travel this length is

$$t = \frac{l}{v}$$

If the energy in this length of string is represented by E, the power P of the wave is given by

$$P = \frac{E}{t} = \frac{E}{l/v} = \frac{E}{l} v \qquad (22\text{-}6)$$

This represents the *rate* at which energy is propagated down the string. Substitution from Eq. (22-5) yields

$$\boxed{P = 2\pi^2 f^2 A^2 \mu v} \qquad (22\text{-}7)$$

The wave power is directly proportional to the energy per unit length and to the wave speed.

The dependence of wave energy and wave power on f^2 and A^2, as found in Eqs. (22-5) and (22-7), is a general conclusion for all kinds of waves. The same ideas will be applied in the following chapter when the energy of a sound wave is discussed.

22-6 THE SUPER-POSITION PRINCIPLE

Until now we have been considering the motion of a single train of pulses passing through a medium. We now consider what happens when two or more wave trains pass simultaneously through the same medium. Let us consider transverse waves in a vibrating string. The speed of a transverse wave is determined by the tension of the string and its linear density. Since these parameters are a function of the medium and not the source, any transverse wave will have the same speed for a given string under constant tension. However, the frequency and amplitude may vary considerably.

When two or more wave trains exist simultaneously in the same medium, each wave travels through the medium as though the other were not present.

The resultant wave is a superposition of the component waves. In other words, the resultant displacement of a particular particle on the vibrating string is the algebraic sum of the displacements each wave would produce independently of the other. This is the *superposition principle*:

When two or more waves exist simultaneously in the same medium, the resultant displacement at any point and time is the algebraic sum of the displacements of each wave.

It should be noted that the superposition principle, as stated here, applies only for *linear* media, i.e., those for which the response is directly proportional to the cause. Also, the sum of displacements is *algebraic* only if the waves have the same plane of polarization. For our purposes, a vibrating string will be assumed to satisfy both these conditions.

The application of this principle is shown graphically in Fig. 22-9. Two waves, indicated by the solid and dashed lines, superpose to form the resultant wave indicated by the heavy line. In Fig. 22-9*a* the superposition results in a

Fig. 22-9 The superposition principle.

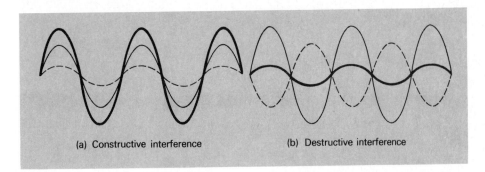

(a) Constructive interference (b) Destructive interference

wave of larger amplitude. These waves are said to interfere *constructively*. *Destructive interference* occurs when the resulting amplitude is smaller, as in Fig. 22-9*b*.

22-7 STANDING WAVES

Let us consider the reflection of a transverse pulse, as shown for the string in Fig. 22-10. When the end of the string is rigidly fixed to a support, the arriving pulse strikes the support, exerting an upward force on it. The reaction force exerted by the support kicks downward on the string, setting up a reflected pulse. Both the displacement and velocity are reversed in the reflected pulse. In other words, a pulse which arrives as a crest is reflected as a trough with the same speed traveling in the opposite direction, and vice versa.

Fig. 22-10 Reflection of a transverse pulse at a fixed boundary.

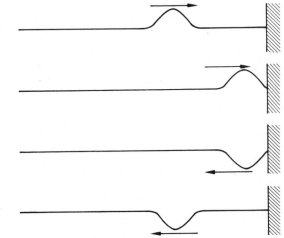

Suppose we consider the wave set up by a vibrating string whose end points are fixed, as in Fig. 22-11. We can use the superposition principle to analyze the resultant waveform at any instant. In Fig. 22-11*a*, we consider the incident and reflected waves at a particular time $t = 0$. The incident wave, traveling to the right, is indicated by a light solid line. The reflected wave, traveling

Fig. 22-11 Produc-
tion of a standing
wave.

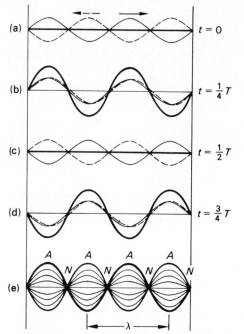

to the left, is indicated by a dotted line. The two waves have the same speed and wavelength, but they are oppositely directed. At this instant all particles of the string lie in a straight horizontal line, as shown by the heavy line. Note that the heavy line is a superposition of the incident and reflected waves at a moment when their displacements add to zero. A snapshot of the string an instant later will show that, with a few exceptions, the particles have all changed positions. This is because the component waves have moved a finite distance.

Let us now consider the resultant wave at time t equal to one-fourth of a period later ($t = \frac{1}{4}T$), as in Fig. 22-11b. The component wave indicated by a solid line will have moved to the *right* a distance of one-fourth wavelength. The component wave indicated by a dashed line will have moved to the *left* a distance of one-fourth wavelength. The resultant wave and hence the shape of the string at this time are indicated by the heavy solid line. Constructive interference has resulted in a wave with twice the amplitude of either of the component waves. When the time t is one-half a period ($t = \frac{1}{2}T$), total destructive interference occurs, and once again the shape of the string is a straight line, as in Fig. 22-11c. At $t = \frac{3}{4}T$ the shape of the string reaches its maximum amplitude in the opposite direction. This constructive interference is shown by the heavy line in Fig. 22-11d.

A series of snapshots of the vibrating string at closely spaced time intervals would reveal a number of loops, as shown in Fig. 22-11e. Such a wave is called a *standing wave*. Notice that there are certain points along the string which remain at rest. These positions, called *nodes*, are labeled N in the figure.

A flea resting on the vibrating string at these points would not be moved up and down by the wave motion.

Between the nodal points, the particles of the string move up and down with simple harmonic motion. The points of maximum amplitude occur midway between the nodes and are called *antinodes*. A flea resting on the string at any of these points, labeled *A*, would experience maximum speeds and displacements in the upward and downward oscillation of the string.

The distance between alternate nodes or alternate antinodes in a standing wave is a measure of the wavelength of the component waves.

Longitudinal standing waves may also occur by the continuous reflection of condensation and rarefaction pulses. In this case the nodes exist where the particles of the medium are stationary, and the antinodes occur where the particles of the medium oscillate with maximum amplitude in the direction of propagation. Longitudinal standing waves will be discussed in the following chapter in connection with sound waves.

22-8 CHARACTERISTIC FREQUENCIES

Let us now consider the possible standing waves which can be set up in a string of length *l* whose ends are fixed, as in Fig. 22-12. When the string is set into vibration, the incident and reflected wave trains travel in opposite directions with the same wavelength. The fixed end points represent *boundary conditions*

Fig. 22-12 Possible standing-wave patterns in a vibrating string.

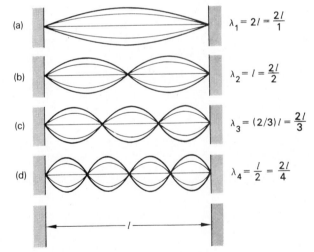

(a) $\lambda_1 = 2l = \dfrac{2l}{1}$

(b) $\lambda_2 = l = \dfrac{2l}{2}$

(c) $\lambda_3 = (2/3)l = \dfrac{2l}{3}$

(d) $\lambda_4 = \dfrac{l}{2} = \dfrac{2l}{4}$

which restrict the possible wavelengths that will produce standing waves. These end points must be displacement nodes for any resulting wave pattern.

The simplest possible standing wave occurs when the wavelengths of incident and reflected waves are equal to twice the length of the string. The standing wave consists of a single loop with nodal points at each end, as shown in Fig. 22-12a. This pattern of vibration is referred to as the *fundamental mode of oscillation.* The *higher modes* of oscillation occur for shorter and shorter wavelengths. From the figure, it is noted that the allowable wavelengths are

$$\frac{2l}{1}, \frac{2l}{2}, \frac{2l}{3}, \frac{2l}{4}, \ldots$$

or, in equation form,

$$\lambda_n = \frac{2l}{n} \qquad n = 1, 2, 3, \ldots \qquad (22\text{-}8)$$

The corresponding frequencies of vibration are, from $v = f\lambda$,

$$f_n = \frac{nv}{2l} = n\frac{v}{2l} \qquad n = 1, 2, 3, \ldots \qquad (22\text{-}9)$$

where v is the speed of the transverse waves. This speed is the same for all wavelengths because it depends only upon the characteristics of the vibrating medium. The frequencies given by Eq. (22-9) are called the *characteristic frequencies of vibration*. In terms of string tension F and linear density μ, the characteristic frequencies are

$$\boxed{f_n = \frac{n}{2l}\sqrt{\frac{F}{\mu}} \qquad n = 1, 2, 3, \ldots} \qquad (22\text{-}10)$$

The lowest possible frequency $(v/2l)$ is called the *fundamental frequency* f_1. The others, which are integral multiples of the fundamental, are known as the *overtones*. The entire series,

$$f_n = nf_1 \qquad n = 1, 2, 3, \ldots \qquad (22\text{-}11)$$

consisting of the fundamental and its overtones, is known as the *harmonic series*. The fundamental is the first harmonic, the first overtone $(f_2 = 2f_1)$ is the second harmonic, the second overtone $(f_3 = 3f_1)$ is the third harmonic, and so on.

EXAMPLE 22-3   A steel piano wire 50 cm long has a mass of 5 g and is under a tension of 400 N. What are the frequencies of its fundamental mode of vibration and the first two overtones?

Solution   The fundamental is found by setting $n = 1$ in Eq. (22-10).

$$f_1 = \frac{1}{2l}\sqrt{\frac{F}{\mu}} = \frac{1}{2l}\sqrt{\frac{F}{m/l}}$$

$$= \frac{1}{(2)(0.5\text{ m})}\sqrt{\frac{400\text{ N}}{(0.005\text{ kg})/(0.5\text{ m})}}$$

$$= 200\text{ Hz}$$

The first and second overtones are

$$f_2 = 2f_1 = 400\text{ Hz}$$

$$f_3 = 3f_1 = 600\text{ Hz}$$

We shall see in the following chapter that as a string vibrates in one or more of its possible modes, energy is transmitted to the surrounding air in the form of sound waves. These longitudinal waves consist of condensations and rarefactions of the same frequency as the vibrating strings. The human ear interprets these waves as sound.

SUMMARY

We have investigated mechanical wave motion in which energy is transferred by a physical disturbance in an elastic medium. The fundamental laws developed in this chapter are very important because they also apply for many other types of waves which will be studied later. The essential concepts are summarized below:

- The velocity of a transverse wave in a string of mass m and length l is given by

$$v = \sqrt{\frac{F}{\mu}} \qquad \mu = \sqrt{\frac{m}{l}} \qquad v = \sqrt{\frac{Fl}{m}} \qquad \textit{Wave Speed}$$

	Force F	Mass m	Length l	Speed v
SI units	N	kg	m	m/s
USCS units	lb	slug	ft	ft/s

- For any wave of period T or frequency f, the speed v can be expressed in terms of the wavelengths λ as follows:

$$v = \frac{\lambda}{T} \qquad v = f\lambda \qquad \textit{Frequency is in } \mathrm{Hz} = 1/s$$

- The *energy per unit length* and the *power* of wave propagation can be found from

$$\frac{E}{l} = 2\pi^2 f^2 A^2 \mu \qquad P = 2\pi^2 f^2 A^2 \mu v$$

- The characteristic frequencies for the possible modes of vibration in a stretched string are found from:

$$f_n = \frac{n}{2l}\sqrt{\frac{F}{\mu}} \qquad n = 1, 2, 3, \dots \qquad \textit{Characteristic Frequencies}$$

- The series $f_n = nf_1$ is called the *harmonics*. They are integral multiples of the fundamental f_1. These are mathematical values and all harmonics may not exist. The actual possibilities beyond the fundamental are called *overtones*. Since all harmonics are possible for the vibrating string, the first overtone is the second harmonic, the second overtone is the third harmonic, and so on.

QUESTIONS

22-1. Define the following terms:
- **a.** Wave motion
- **b.** Wave speed
- **c.** Wavelength
- **d.** Frequency
- **e.** Phase
- **f.** Nodes
- **g.** Antinodes
- **h.** Fundamental
- **i.** Overtone
- **j.** Harmonic
- **k.** Mechanical wave
- **l.** Transverse wave
- **m.** Longitudinal wave
- **n.** Linear density
- **o.** Amplitude
- **p.** Superposition principle
- **q.** Constructive interference
- **r.** Destructive interference
- **s.** Standing waves
- **t.** Characteristic frequencies

22-2. Explain how a water wave is both transverse and longitudinal.

22-3. Describe an experiment to demonstrate that energy is associated with wave motion.

22-4. In a *torsional wave* the individual particles of the medium vibrate with angular harmonic motion about the axis of propagation. Give a mechanical example of such a wave.

22-5. Discuss the interference of waves. Is there a loss of energy when waves interfere? Explain.

22-6. A transverse pulse is sent down a string of mass m and length l under a tension F. How will the speed of the pulse be affected if **(a)** the mass of the string is quadrupled, **(b)** the length of the string is quadrupled, and **(c)** the tension is reduced by one-fourth?

22-7. Draw graphs of a periodic transverse wave and a periodic longitudinal wave. Indicate on the figures the wavelength and amplitude of each wave.

22-8. Which harmonic is indicated by Fig. 22-12d? Which overtone is present?

22-9. We have seen that boundary conditions determine possible modes of vibration. Draw a diagram of the fundamental and of the first two overtones for a vibrating rod **(a)** clamped at one end and **(b)** clamped at its midpoint.

22-10. A vibrating string has a fundamental frequency of 200 Hz. If the length is reduced by one-fourth, what will the new fundamental frequency be? Has the wave speed been altered by shortening the string? Assume constant tension.

22-11. Show graphically the superposition of two waves traveling in the same direction. The second wave has three-fourths the amplitude and one-half the wavelength of the first wave.

22-12. In an experiment with the vibrating string, one end of the string is attached to the tip of a vibrator and the other end passes over a pulley. Suspended weights are used to produce the fundamental and the first three overtones. What effect will stretching the string have on frequency calculations?

PROBLEMS

22-1. A metal wire of mass 500 g and length 50 cm is under a tension of 80 N. What is the speed of a transverse wave in the wire? If the length is reduced by one-half, what will the new mass of the wire be? Show that the speed of a wave in the wire is unchanged.

Ans. 8.94 m/s, 250 g.

22-2. A 1.2-kg rope is stretched over a distance of 5.2 m and placed under a tension of 120 N. Compute the speed of a transverse wave in the rope.

22-3. A 30-m cord under a tension of 200 N sustains a wave whose speed is 72 m/s. What is the mass of the cord?

Ans. 1.16 kg.

22-4. A string 200 cm long has a mass of 500 g. What string tension is required to produce a wave speed of 120 cm/s?

22-5. A longitudinal wave has a frequency of 200 Hz and a wavelength of 4.2 m. What is the speed of the waves?

Ans. 840 m/s.

22-6. A wooden float at the end of a fishing line makes eight complete oscillations in 10 s. If it takes 3.6 s for a single wave to travel 11 m, what is the wavelength of the water waves?

22-7. The steel guy wire supporting a pole is 18.9 m long and 9.5 mm in diameter. It has a linear density of 0.474 kg/m. It is struck at one end by a hammer, and the pulse returns in 0.3 s. What is the tension in the wire?

Ans. 7525 N.

22-8. A bass guitar string 750 mm long is stretched with sufficient tension to produce a fundamental vibration of 220 Hz. What is the velocity of the transverse waves in this string?

22-9. One end of a long horizontal rope oscillates with a frequency of 2 Hz and an amplitude of 50 mm. A 2-m length of the string has a mass of 0.3 kg. If the rope is under a tension of 48 N, how much energy per second must be supplied to the rope?

Ans. 9.47 W.

22-10. A source of a transverse wave train has a frequency of 8 Hz and an amplitude of 4 cm. If the string is 40 m long and has a mass of 80 g, how much energy per unit length passes along the string? If the wavelength of the transverse wave is 1.6 m, what power must be supplied by the source?

22-11. A string 4 m long has a mass of 10 g and a tension of 64 N. What is the frequency of its fundamental mode of vibration? What are the frequencies of the first and second overtones?

Ans. 20, 40, and 60 Hz.

22-12. The second harmonic of a vibrating string is 200 Hz. If the length of the string is 3 m and its tension is 200 N, compute the linear density.

22-13. A 4.3-m string has a tension of 300 N, and a mass of 0.5 g. If it is fixed at each end and vibrates in three segments, what is the frequency of the standing waves?

Ans. 560 Hz.

22-14. A 30-m cable weighing 400 N is stretched between two telephone poles with a tension of 1800 N. What length of time is required for a pulse to make a round trip if the cable is struck?

22-15. In a laboratory experiment, an electromagnetic vibrator is used as the source of standing waves in a string. The linear density of the string is measured to be 0.006 g/cm. One end of the string is connected to the tip of the vibrator. The other end passes over a pulley 1 m away and is attached to a weight hanger. It is found that a mass of 392 g hanging from the free end causes the string to vibrate in three segments. What is the frequency of the vibrator?

Ans. 120 Hz.

22-16. Refer to Prob. 22-15. What mass would be required to cause the string to vibrate in four segments?

23 *Sound*

OBJECTIVES: After completing this chapter, you should be able to:

1. Define *sound* and solve problems involving its velocity in metal, in a liquid, and in a gas.

2. Use boundary conditions to derive and apply relationships for calculating the *characteristic frequencies* for an open pipe and for a closed pipe.

3. Compute the intensity level in *decibels* for a sound whose intensity is given in *watts per square meter*.

4. Use your understanding of the *Doppler effect* to predict the apparent change in sound frequency which occurs as a result of relative motion between a source and an observer.

When a periodic disturbance takes place in air, longitudinal *sound* waves travel out from it. For example, if a tuning fork is struck with a hammer, the vibrating prongs send out longitudinal waves, as shown on Fig. 23-1. An ear, acting as a receiver for these periodic waves, interprets them as sound.

Is the ear necessary for sound to exist? If the tuning fork were struck in the atmosphere of a distant planet, would there be sound even though no ear could interpret the disturbance? The answer depends upon the definition of sound.

The term *sound* is used in two different ways. Physiologists define sound in terms of the auditory sensations produced by longitudinal disturbances in air. For them, sound does not exist on a distance planet. In physics, on the other hand, we refer to the disturbances themselves rather than the sensations produced.

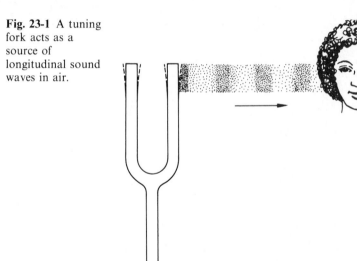

Fig. 23-1 A tuning fork acts as a source of longitudinal sound waves in air.

Sound is a longitudinal mechanical wave which travels through an elastic medium.

In this case, sound does exist on the planet. In this chapter *sound* will be used in its physical sense.

23-1 PRODUCTION OF A SOUND WAVE

Two things must exist in order to produce a sound wave. There must be a source of mechanical vibration, and there must be an elastic medium through which the disturbance can travel. The source may be a tuning fork, a vibrating string, or a vibrating air column in an organ pipe. *Sounds are produced by vibrating matter*. The requirement of an elastic medium can be demonstrated by placing an electric bell inside an evacuable flask, as shown in Fig. 23-2. With the bell connected to a battery so that it rings continuously, the flask is slowly

Fig. 23-2 A bell ringing in a vacuum cannot be heard. A material medium is necessary for the production of sound.

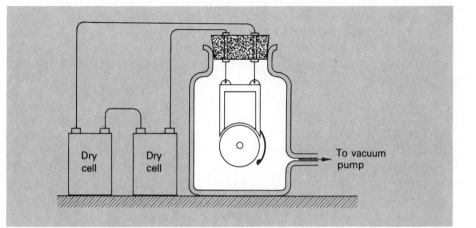

Dry cell

Dry cell

To vacuum pump

evacuated. As more and more of the air is pumped from the flask, the sound of the bell becomes fainter and fainter until finally it cannot be heard at all. When air is allowed to reenter the flask, the sound of the bell returns. Thus, air is necessary to transmit sound.

Let us now examine more closely the longitudinal sound waves in air as they proceed from a vibrating source. A thin strip of metal clamped tight at its base is pulled to one side and released. As the free end oscillates to and fro with simple harmonic motion, a series of periodic, longitudinal sound waves spreads through the air away from the source. The air molecules in the vicinity of the metal strip are alternately compressed and expanded, sending out a wave like that illustrated in Fig. 23-3a. The dense regions where many molecules are

Fig. 23-3 (*a*) Compressions and rarefactions in a sound wave in air at a particular instant. (*b*) The sinusoidal variation in pressure as a function of displacement.

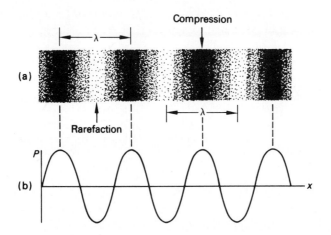

packed tightly together are called *compressions*. They are exactly analogous to the *condensations* discussed for longitudinal waves in a coiled spring. The regions with relatively few molecules are referred to as *rarefactions*. The compressions and rarefactions alternate throughout the medium as the individual air particles oscillate to and fro in the direction of wave propagation. Since a compression corresponds to a high-pressure region and a rarefaction corresponds to a low-pressure region, a sound wave can also be represented by plotting the change in pressure *P* as a function of the distance *x*. (See Fig. 23-3*b*.) The distance between two successive compressions or rarefactions is the wavelength.

23-2 THE SPEED OF SOUND

Anyone who has seen a weapon being fired at a distance has observed the smoke from the weapon before hearing the report. Similarly, we observe the flash of lightning before hearing the thunder. Even though both light and sound travel with finite speeds, the speed of light is so much greater in comparison that it can' be considered instantaneous. The speed of sound can be measured directly by observing the time required for the waves to move through a known distance. In air at 0°C, sound travels at a speed of 331 m/s or 1087 ft/s.

In Chap. 22 we established the idea that wave speed depends upon the elasticity of the medium and the inertia of its particles. The more elastic materials sustain greater wave speeds whereas the denser materials retard wave motion. The following empirical relationships are based on these proportionalities.

For longitudinal sound waves in a wire or rod, the wave speed is given by

$$v = \sqrt{\frac{Y}{\rho}}$$ Rod (23-1)

where Y is Young's modulus for the solid and ρ is its density. This relation is valid only for rods whose diameter are small in comparison with the longitudinal wavelengths of sound passing through them.

In an *extended* solid, the longitudinal wave speed is a function of the shear modulus S, the bulk modulus B, and the density ρ of the medium. The wave speed can be calculated from

$$v = \sqrt{\frac{B + \frac{4}{3}S}{\rho}}$$ Extended Solid (23-2)

For longitudinal waves in a fluid, the wave speed is found from

$$v = \sqrt{\frac{B}{\rho}}$$ Fluid (23-3)

where B is the bulk modulus for the fluid and ρ is its density.

In computing the speed of sound in a gas, the bulk modulus is given by

$$B = \gamma P$$

where γ is the adiabatic constant ($\gamma = 1.4$ for air and diatomic gases) and P is the pressure of the gas. Thus the speed of longitudinal waves in a gas, from Eq. (23-3), is given by

$$v = \sqrt{\frac{B}{\rho}} = \sqrt{\frac{\gamma P}{\rho}}$$ (23-4)

But for an ideal gas

$$\frac{P}{\rho} = \frac{RT}{M}$$ (23-5)

where R = universal gas constant
T = absolute temperature of gas
M = molecular mass of gas

Substitution of Eq. (23-5) into Eq. (23-4) yields

$$v = \sqrt{\frac{\gamma P}{\rho}} = \sqrt{\frac{\gamma RT}{M}}$$ *Gas* (23-6)

EXAMPLE 23-1 Compute the speed of sound in an aluminum rod.

Solution Young's modulus and the density for aluminum are

$$Y = 68,900 \text{ MPa} = 6.89 \times 10^{10} \text{ N/m}^2$$

$$\rho = 2.7 \text{ g/cm}^3 = 2.7 \times 10^3 \text{ kg/m}^3$$

From Eq. (23-1)

$$v = \sqrt{\frac{Y}{\rho}} = \sqrt{\frac{6.89 \times 10^{10} \text{ N/m}^2}{2.7 \times 10^3 \text{ kg/m}^3}}$$

$$= \sqrt{2.55 \times 10^7 \text{ m}^2/\text{s}^2} = 5050 \text{ m/s}$$

This speed is approximately 15 times the speed of sound in air.

EXAMPLE 23-2 Compute the speed of sound in air on a day when the temperature is 27°C. The molecular mass of air is 29.0, and the adiabatic constant is 1.4.

Solution From Eq. (23-6)

$$v = \sqrt{\frac{\gamma RT}{M}} = \sqrt{\frac{(1.4)(8.31 \text{ J/mol} \cdot \text{K})(300 \text{ K})}{29 \times 10^{-3} \text{ kg/mol}}}$$

$$= 347 \text{ m/s}$$

The speed of sound is significantly greater at 27°C than at 0°C. At standard temperature and pressure (0°C, 1 atm) the speed of sound is 331 m/s. For each Celsius degree rise in temperature (above 0°C) the speed of sound in air increases by approximately 0.6 m/s. Hence the speed v of sound can be approximated by

$$v = 331 \text{ m/s} + \left(0.6 \frac{\text{m/s}}{\text{C}°}\right)t$$ (23-7)

where t is the Celsius temperature of the air.

EXAMPLE 23-3 What is the approximate speed of sound in air at room temperature (20°C)?

Solution From Eq. (23-7),

$$v = 331 \text{ m/s} + \left(0.6 \frac{\text{m/s}}{\text{C}°}\right)(20°\text{C}) = 343 \text{ m/s}$$

**23-3
VIBRATING
AIR
COLUMNS**

In the previous chapter we described the possible modes of vibration for a string fixed at both ends. The frequency of the sound waves set up in the air surrounding the string is identical with the frequency of the vibrating string. Thus the possible frequencies, or the *harmonics*, of sound waves produced by a vibrating string are given by

$$f_n = \frac{nv}{2l} \qquad n = 1, 2, 3, \ldots \tag{23-8}$$

where v is the velocity of transverse waves in the string.

Sound can also be produced by the longitudinal vibrations of an air column in an open or closed pipe. As in the vibrating string, the possible modes of vibrations are determined by the boundary conditions. The possible modes of vibration for the air in a closed pipe are illustrated in Fig. 23-4. When a compressional wave is set up in the pipe, the displacement of the air particles at the closed end must be zero.

Fig. 23-4 Possible standing waves in a closed pipe.

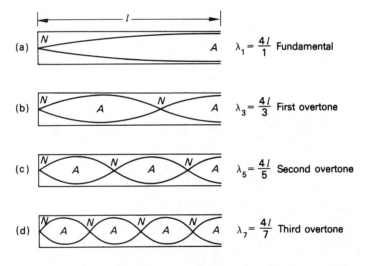

(a) $\lambda_1 = \frac{4l}{1}$ Fundamental

(b) $\lambda_3 = \frac{4l}{3}$ First overtone

(c) $\lambda_5 = \frac{4l}{5}$ Second overtone

(d) $\lambda_7 = \frac{4l}{7}$ Third overtone

The closed end of a pipe must be a displacement node.

The air at the open end of a pipe has the greatest freedom of motion, and so the displacement is free at an open end.

The open end of a pipe must be a displacement antinode.

The sinusoidal curves in Fig. 23-4 represent maximum displacements.

The fundamental mode of oscillation for an air column in a closed pipe has a node at the closed end and an antinode at the open end. Thus the wavelength of the fundamental is 4 times the length l of the pipe (Fig. 23-4*a*). The next possible mode, which is the first overtone, occurs when there are two nodes and two antinodes, as shown in Fig. 23-4*b*. The wavelength of the first overtone is therefore equal to $4l/3$. Similar reasoning will show that the second and third overtones occur for wavelengths equal to $4l/5$ and $4l/7$, respectively. In summary, the possible wavelengths are

$$\lambda_n = \frac{4l}{n} \qquad n = 1, 3, 5, \ldots \qquad (23\text{-}9)$$

The speed of the sound waves is given by $v = f\lambda$, so that the possible frequencies for a *closed pipe* are

$$f_n = \frac{nv}{4l} \qquad n = 1, 3, 5, \ldots \qquad \textit{Closed Pipe} \quad (23\text{-}10)$$

Notice that only the *odd harmonics* are allowed for a closed pipe. The first overtone is the third harmonic, the second overtone is the fifth harmonic, and so on.

An air column vibrating in a pipe open at *both* ends must be bounded by displacement antinodes. Figure 23-5 shows the fundamental and first three

Fig. 23-5 Possible standing waves in an open pipe.

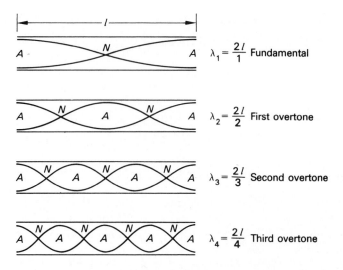

overtones for an open pipe. Note that the fundamental wavelength is twice the length l of the pipe. When the number of nodes is increased one at a time, it is seen that the possible wavelengths in an open pipe are

$$\lambda_n = \frac{2l}{n} \qquad n = 1, 2, 3, \ldots \qquad (23\text{-}11)$$

The possible frequencies are therefore

$$f_n = \frac{nv}{2l} \qquad n = 1, 2, 3, \ldots \qquad \textit{Open Pipe} \quad (23\text{-}12)$$

where v is the velocity of the sound waves. Thus all the harmonics are possible for a vibrating air column in an open pipe. Open pipes of varying lengths are used in many musical instruments, e.g., organs, flutes, and trumpets.

EXAMPLE 23-4　　What are the frequencies of the fundamental and first two overtones for a 12-cm closed pipe? Air temperature is 30°C.

Solution　　The velocity of the sound is

$$v = 331 \text{ m/s} + \left(0.6 \frac{\text{m/s}}{\text{C}^\circ} \right)(30^\circ\text{C}) = 349 \text{ m/s}$$

Thus, from Eq. (23-10),

$$f_1 = \frac{1v}{4l} = \frac{349 \text{ m/s}}{(4)(0.12 \text{ m})} = 727 \text{ Hz}$$

The first and second overtones are the third and fifth harmonics. Hence

$$\text{First overtone} = 3f_1 = 2181 \text{ Hz}$$
$$\text{Second overtone} = 5f_1 = 3635 \text{ Hz}$$

EXAMPLE 23-5　　What length of open pipe will have a frequency of 1200 Hz as its first overtone? Take the speed of sound as 340 m/s.

Solution　　The first overtone in an open pipe is equal to the second harmonic. Thus we can set $n = 2$ in Eq. (23-12)

$$f_2 = \frac{2v}{2l} = \frac{v}{l}$$

$$l = \frac{v}{f_2} = \frac{340 \text{ m/s}}{1200 \text{ Hz}} = 0.283 \text{ m}$$

**23-4
FORCED
VIBRATION
AND
RESONANCE**

When a vibrating body is placed in contact with another body, the second body is forced to vibrate with the same frequency as the original vibrator. For example, if a tuning fork is struck with a hammer and then placed with its base against a wooden table top, the intensity of the sound will suddenly be increased. When the tuning fork is removed from the table, the intensity decreases to its original level. The vibrations of the particles in the table top in contact with the tuning fork are called *forced vibrations*.

We have seen that elastic bodies have certain natural frequencies of vibration which are characteristic of the material and boundary conditions. A taut string of a particular length can produce sounds of characteristic frequencies. An open or closed pipe also has natural frequencies of vibration. Whenever a body is acted on by a series of periodic impulses having a frequency nearly equal to one of the natural frequencies of the body, the body is set into vibration with a relatively large amplitude. This phenomenon is referred to as *resonance* or *sympathetic vibration*.

An example of resonance is offered by a child sitting in a swing. Experience tells us that the swing can be set into vibration with large amplitude by a series of small pushes at just the right intervals. Such resonance occurs only when the pushes are in phase with the natural frequency of vibration for the swing. A slight variation of the input pulses would result in little or no vibration.

Reinforcement of sound by resonance has many useful applications as well as many unpleasant consequences. The resonance of an air column in an organ pipe amplifies the weak sound of a vibrating air jet. Many musical instruments are designed with resonant cavities to produce varying sounds. Electrical resonance in radio receivers enables the listener to hear weak signals clearly. When tuned to the frequency of a desired station, the signal is amplified by electrical resonance. In poorly designed auditoriums or long hallways, music and voices may have a hollow sound which is unpleasant to the ear. Bridges have been known to collapse because of sympathetic vibrations set up by gusts of wind.

23-5 AUDIBLE SOUND WAVES

We have defined sound as a *longitudinal mechanical wave traveling through an elastic medium.* This is a very broad definition that makes no restriction whatsoever on the frequencies of sound. The physiologist is concerned primarily with sound waves which are capable of affecting the sense of hearing. Thus it is useful to divide the spectrum of sound according to the following definitions:

Audible sound refers to sound waves in the frequency range from 20 to 20,000 Hz.

Sound waves having frequencies below the audible range are termed **infrasonic.**

Sound waves having frequencies above the audible range are termed **ultrasonic.**

When studying audible sound, the physiologist uses the terms *loudness, pitch,* and *quality* to describe the sensations produced. Unfortunately, these terms represent sensory magnitudes and are therefore subjective. What is *loud* to one person is moderate to another. What one person perceives as quality, another considers inferior. As always, the physicist must deal with explicit measurable definitions. The physicist therefore attempts to correlate the sensory effects with the physical properties of waves. These correlations can be summarized as follows:

Sensory effects		Physical property
Loudness	↔	Intensity
Pitch	↔	Frequency
Quality	↔	Waveform

The meaning of the terms on the left may vary considerably among individuals. The terms on the right are measurable and objective.

Sound waves constitute a flow of energy through matter. The intensity of a given sound wave is a measure of the rate at which energy is propagated through a given volume of space. A convenient method of specifying sound intensity is in terms of the rate at which energy is transferred through a unit area normal to the direction of wave propagation (see Fig. 23-6). Since the rate at which energy flows is the *power* of a wave, the intensity can be related to the power per unit area passing a given point.

Fig. 23-6 The intensity of a sound wave is a measure of the power transmitted per unit of area perpendicular to the direction of propagation.

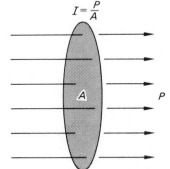

$$I = \frac{P}{A}$$

Sound **intensity** is the power transferred by a sound wave through a unit of area normal to the direction of propagation.

$$I = \frac{P}{A}$$ (23-13)

The units of intensity are the ratio of a power unit to a unit of area. The most common unit of intensity is the watt per square centimeter (W/cm^2), but since the rate of energy flow in sound waves is extremely small, the microwatt (μW) is frequently substituted as the power unit. By definition,

$$1 \ \mu W = 10^{-6} \ W$$

It can be shown, by methods similar to those utilized for a vibrating string, that the sound intensity varies directly with the square of the frequency f and with the square of the amplitude A of a given sound wave. Symbolically, the intensity I is given by

$$I = 2\pi^2 f^2 A^2 \rho v$$ (23-14)

where v is the sound velocity in a medium of density ρ. The symbol A in Eq. (23-14) refers to the amplitude of the sound wave and not the unit area, as in Eq. (23-13).

The intensity I_0 of the faintest audible sound is of the order of 10^{-16} W/cm^2. This intensity, which is referred to as the *hearing threshold*, has been adopted by acoustic experts as the zero of sound intensity.

The **hearing threshold** represents the standard zero of sound intensity. Its value is 10^{-10} μW/cm^2 at a frequency of 1000 Hz.

$$I_0 = 10^{-10} \ \mu\text{W/cm}^2 = 10^{-16} \ \text{W/cm}^2 \qquad (23\text{-}15)$$

The range of intensities over which the human ear is sensitive is enormous. It extends from the hearing threshold I_0 to an intensity 10^{12} times as great. The upper extreme represents the point at which the intensity is intolerable for the human ear. The sensation becomes one of feeling or pain instead of simply hearing.

The **pain threshold** represents the maximum intensity that the average ear can record without feeling or pain. Its value is 100 μW/cm^2 or 10^{-4} W/cm^2.

$$I_p = 100 \ \mu\text{W/cm}^2 = 10^{-4} \ \text{W/cm}^2 \qquad (23\text{-}16)$$

In view of the wide range of intensities over which the ear is sensitive, it is more convenient to set up a logarithmic scale for the measurement of sound intensities. Such a scale is established by the following rule:

When the intensity I_1 of one sound is 10 times as great as the intensity I_2 of another, the ratio of intensity is said to be 1 bel (**B**).

Thus, when comparing the intensities of two sounds, we refer to a difference in intensity levels given by

$$B = \log \frac{I_1}{I_2} \qquad \text{bels (B)} \qquad (23\text{-}17)$$

where I_1 is the intensity of one sound and I_2 is the intensity of the other.

EXAMPLE 23-6 Two sounds have intensities of 25.0 and 1000 μW/cm^2. Compute the difference in intensity levels in bels.

Solution From Eq. (23-17)

$$B = \log \frac{I_1}{I_2} = \log \frac{1000 \ \mu\text{W/cm}^2}{25 \ \mu\text{W/cm}^2}$$

$$= \log 40 = 1.6021 \ \text{B}$$

In practice, the unit of 1 B is too large. To obtain a more useful unit, we define a *decibel* (dB) as one-tenth of a bel. Thus the answer to Example 23-6 can also be expressed as 16.021 dB.

By using the standard zero of intensity I_0 as a standard for comparing all intensities, a general scale has been devised for rating any sound. The intensity level in decibels of any sound of intensity I can be found from the general relation

$$\boxed{\beta = 10 \log \frac{I}{I_0}} \qquad \text{decibels (dB)} \qquad (23\text{-}18)$$

where I_0 is the intensity at the hearing threshold (10^{-16} W/cm^2).

EXAMPLE 23-7   Compute the intensity level in decibels of a sound whose intensity is at the pain threshold (10^{-4} W/cm^2).

Solution   From Eq. (23-18)

$$\beta = 10 \log \frac{10^{-4} \text{ W/cm}^2}{10^{-16} \text{ W/cm}^2} = 10 \log 10^{12}$$

$$= (10)(12) = 120 \text{ dB}$$

Through the logarithmic decibel notation, we have reduced the wide range of intensities to intensity levels from 0 to 120 dB. However, we must remember that the scale is not linear but logarithmic. A 40-dB sound is much more than twice as intense as a 20-dB sound. A sound which is 100 times as intense as another is only 20 dB larger. Several examples of the intensity levels for common sounds are given in Table 23-1.

Table 23-1 Intensity Levels for Common Sounds

Sound	Intensity level, dB
Hearing threshold	0
Rustling leaves	10
Whisper	20
Quiet radio	40
Normal conversation	65
Busy street corner	80
Subway car	100
Pain threshold	120
Jet engine	140–160

23-6 PITCH AND QUALITY

The effect of intensity on the human ear manifests itself as *loudness*. In general, sound waves which are more intense are also louder, but the ear is not equally sensitive to sounds of all frequencies. Therefore, a high-frequency sound may not seem as loud as one of lower frequency which has the same intensity.

The frequency of a sound determines what the ear judges as the *pitch* of the sound. Musicians designate pitch by letters corresponding to key notes on the piano. For example, the C note, D note, and F note each refer to a specific pitch, or frequency. A siren disk, shown in Fig. 23-7, can be used to demonstrate how the pitch is determined by the frequency of a sound. A stream of air is directed against a row of evenly spaced holes. By varying the rate of rotation of the disk the pitch of the resulting sound is increased or decreased.

Two sounds of the same pitch can easily be distinguished. For example, suppose we sound a C note (256 Hz) successively on a piano, a flute, a trumpet, and a violin. Even though each sound has the same pitch, there is a marked difference in the tones. This distinction is said to result from a difference in the *quality* of sound.

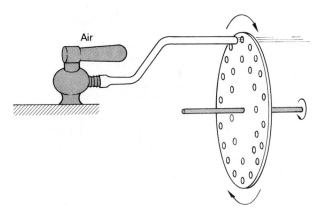

Fig. 23-7 Demonstrating the relationship between pitch and frequency.

Regardless of the source of vibration in musical instruments, several modes of oscillation are usually excited simultaneously. Therefore, the sound produced consists not only of the fundamental but also many of the overtones. *The quality of a sound is determined by the number and relative intensities of the overtones present.* The difference in quality between two sounds can be observed objectively by analyzing the complex *waveforms* resulting from each sound. In general, the more complex the wave, the greater the number of harmonics that contribute to it.

23-7 INTER-FERENCE AND BEATS

In Chap. 22 we discussed the superposition principle as a method for studying interference in transverse waves. Interference also occurs in longitudinal sound waves, and the superposition principle can be applied for them also. A common example of the interference in sound waves occurs when two tuning forks (or other single-frequency sound sources) whose frequencies differ only slightly are struck simultaneously. The sound produced fluctuates in intensity, alternating between loud tones and virtual silence. These regular pulsations are referred to as *beats*. The *vibrato* effect obtained on some organs is an application of this principle. Every vibrato note is produced by two pipes tuned to slightly different frequencies.

To understand the origin of beats, let us examine the interference set up between sound waves proceeding from two tuning forks of slightly different frequency, as shown in Fig. 23-8. The superposition of waves A and B illustrates the origin of beats. The loud tones occur when the waves interfere constructively and the quiet tones when the waves interfere destructively. Observation and calculation show that the two waves interfere constructively $f - f'$ times per second. Thus we can write

$$\text{Number of beats per second} = |f - f'| \qquad (23\text{-}19)$$

For example, if tuning forks of frequencies 256 and 259 Hz are struck simultaneously, the resulting sound will pulsate three times every second.

Fig. 23-8 Diagram illustrating the origin of beats. The wave *C* is a superposition of waves *A* and *B*.

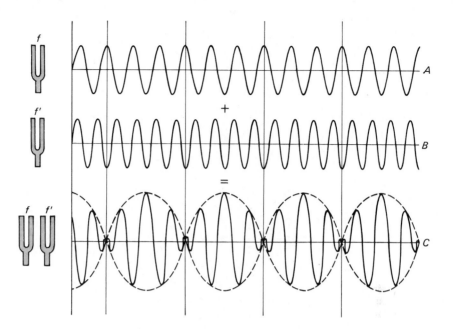

23-8 THE DOPPLER EFFECT

Whenever a source of sound is moving relative to an observer, the pitch of the sound, as heard by the observer, may not be the same as that perceived when the source is at rest. For example, if we stand near a railway track as a train blowing its whistle approaches, we notice that the pitch of the whistle is *higher* than the normal one when the train is stationary. As the train recedes, the pitch is observed to be *lower* than normal. Similarly, at the race tracks the sound of cars driving toward the stands is considerably higher in pitch than the sound of cars driving away from the stands.

The phenomenon is not restricted to the motion of the source. If the source of sound is stationary, a listener moving toward the source will observe a similar increase in pitch. A listener leaving the source of sound, will hear a lower-pitched sound. The change in frequency of sound resulting from relative motion between a source and an observer is called the *Doppler effect*.

> The **Doppler effect** refers to the apparent change in frequency of a source of sound when there is relative motion of the source and the listener.

The origin of the Doppler effect can be demonstrated graphically by representing the periodic waves emitted by a source as concentric circles moving radially outward, as in Fig. 23-9. The distance between any two circles represents the wavelength λ of the sound traveling with a velocity *V*. The frequency with which these waves strike the ear determines the pitch of sound heard.

Let us first consider that the source is moving to the right toward a stationary observer *A*, as in Fig. 23-10. As the moving source emits sound waves, it tends to overtake waves traveling in the same direction as the source.

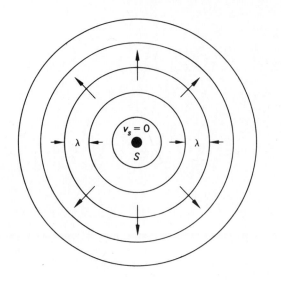

Fig. 23-9 Graphic representation of sound waves emitted from a stationary source.

Fig. 23-10 Illustration of the Doppler effect. The waves in front of a moving source are closer together than the waves behind a moving source.

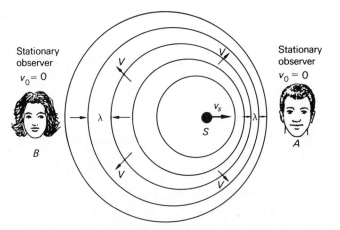

Each successive wave is emitted from a point closer to the observer than its predecessor. The result is that the distance between successive waves, or the wavelength, is smaller than usual. A smaller wavelength results in a higher frequency of waves, which increases the pitch of the sound heard by observer A. Similar reasoning will show that an *increase* in the length of waves reaching observer B will cause B to hear a *lower*-frequency sound.

We can now derive a relationship for predicting the change in observed frequency. During one complete vibration of a stationary source (a time equal to the period T), each wave will move through a distance of one wavelength. This distance is represented by λ in Fig. 23-11a and is given by

$$\lambda = VT = \frac{V}{f_s} \qquad \textit{Stationary Source}$$

Fig. 23-11 Computing the magnitude of the wavelength of sound emitted from a moving source. The source velocity v_s is considered positive for speeds of approach and negative for speeds of recession.

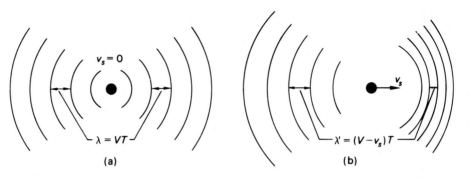

(a)   (b)

where V is the velocity of sound and f_s is the frequency of the source. If the source is moving to the right with a velocity v_s, as in Fig. 23-11b, the new wave-length λ' in front of the source will be given by

$$\lambda' = VT - v_s T = (V - v_s)T$$

But $T = 1/f_s$, so that we write

$$\lambda' = \frac{V - v_s}{f_s} \qquad \textit{Moving Source} \quad (23\text{-}20)$$

This equation will also apply for the wavelength on the left of the moving source if we follow the convention that speeds of approach are considered positive and speeds of recession are considered negative. Thus, if we were computing λ' on the left of our moving source, the negative value would be substituted for v_s, resulting in a larger wavelength.

     The velocity of sound in a medium is a function of the properties of the medium and does not depend upon the motion of the source. Thus the frequency f_o heard by a stationary observer from a moving source of frequency f_s is given by

$$\boxed{f_o = \frac{V}{\lambda'} = \frac{Vf_s}{V - v_s}} \qquad \textit{Moving Source} \quad (23\text{-}21)$$

where V is the speed of sound and v_s is the speed of the source. *The speed v_s is reckoned as positive for speeds of approach and negative for speeds of recession.*

EXAMPLE 23-8

A train whistle emits sound at a frequency of 400 Hz. (a) What is the pitch of the sound heard when the train is moving toward a stationary observer at a speed of 20 m/s? (b) What is the pitch heard when the train is moving away from the observer at this speed? Assume that the speed of sound is 340 m/s.

Solution (a)

Since the train is approaching the observer, its speed v_s is positive. Substitution into Eq. (23-21) yields

$$f_o = \frac{Vf_s}{V - v_s} = \frac{(340 \text{ m/s})(400 \text{ Hz})}{340 \text{ m/s} - 20 \text{ m/s}}$$

$$= \frac{1.36 \times 10^5}{320} = 425 \text{ Hz}$$

Solution (b) Now v_s represents a speed of recession, so that -20 m/s should be substituted in Eq. (23-21).

$$f_o = \frac{Vf_s}{V - v_s} = \frac{(340 \text{ m/s})(400 \text{ Hz})}{340 \text{ m/s} - (-20 \text{ m/s})}$$

$$= \frac{1.36 \times 10^5}{360} = 378 \text{ Hz}$$

Now let us examine the situation in which a source is stationary and the observer moves toward the source with a velocity v_o. In this case, the wavelength of the sound received does not change, but the number of waves encountered per unit of time (the frequency) increases as a result of the observer's speed v_o. Hence the observer will hear the frequency

$$\boxed{f_o = \frac{f_s(V + v_o)}{V}} \qquad \textit{Moving Observer} \quad \text{(23-22)}$$

Here *the speed v_o of the observer should be reckoned as positive for speeds of approach and negative for speeds of recession.*

EXAMPLE 23-9 A stationary source of sound has a frequency of 800 Hz on a day when the speed of sound is 340 m/s. What pitch is heard by a person who is moving from the source at a speed of 30 m/s?

Solution Since v_o represents a speed of recession, $v_o = -30$ m/s must be used in Eq. (23-21). Therefore,

$$f_o = \frac{f_s(V + v_o)}{V} = \frac{(800 \text{ Hz})(340 \text{ m/s} - 30 \text{ m/s})}{340 \text{ m/s}}$$

$$= \frac{(800)(310)}{340} = 729 \text{ Hz}$$

If both the observer and the source are moving Eqs. (23-21) and (23-22) are combined to yield

$$\boxed{f_o = f_s \frac{V + v_o}{V - v_s}} \qquad \textit{General Motion} \quad \text{(23-23)}$$

The same sign convention must be used for this general equation as that developed earlier. Note that Eq. (23-23) will reduce to Eq. (23-21) or to Eq. (23-22) if the observer is stationary ($v_o = 0$) or if the source is stationary ($v_s = 0$).

SUMMARY

We have defined sound as a longitudinal mechanical wave in an elastic medium. Thus the elasticity and density of a medium will affect the speed of sound as it travels in that medium. Under certain conditions we have seen that standing sound waves can produce characteristic frequencies which we observe as the pitch of the sound. The intensity of sound and the Doppler effect were also discussed in this chapter. The major concepts are summarized below:

- Sound is a longitudinal wave traveling through an elastic medium. Its speed in air at 0°C is 331 m/s or 1087 ft/s. At other temperatures the speed of sound is approximated by

$$v = 331 \text{ m/s} + \left(0.6 \frac{\text{m/s}}{\text{C}°}\right) t_C \qquad \textit{Speed of Sound in Air}$$

- The speed of sound in other media can be found from the following:

$$v = \sqrt{\frac{Y}{\rho}} \qquad \textit{Rod} \qquad\qquad v = \sqrt{\frac{\gamma P}{\rho}} = \sqrt{\frac{\gamma RT}{M}} \qquad \textit{Gas}$$

$$v = \sqrt{\frac{B}{\rho}} \qquad \textit{Fluid} \qquad\qquad v = \frac{B + (4/3)S}{\rho} \qquad \textit{Extended Solid}$$

- Standing longitudinal sound waves may be set up in a vibrating air column for a pipe that is open at both ends or for one that is closed at one end. The characteristic frequencies are

$$f_n = \frac{nv}{2l} \qquad n = 1, 2, 3, \ldots \qquad \textit{Open Pipe of Length l}$$

$$f_n = \frac{nv}{4l} \qquad n = 1, 3, 5, \ldots \qquad \textit{Closed Pipe of Length l}$$

Note that *only the odd harmonics are possible for a closed pipe*. In this case, the first overtone is the third harmonic, the second overtone is the fifth harmonic, and so on.

- The intensity of a sound is the power P unit area A perpendicular to the direction of propagation.

$$I = \frac{P}{A} = 2\pi^2 f^2 A^2 \rho v \qquad \textit{Intensity, W/m}^2$$

- The intensity level in decibels is given by

$$\beta = 10 \log \frac{I}{I_0} \qquad I_0 = 1 \times 10^{-12} \text{ W/m}^2 \qquad \textit{Intensity level}$$

- Whenever two waves are nearly the same frequency and exist simultaneously in the same medium, beats are set up such that

Number of beats per second $= f - f'$

- The general equation for the Doppler effect is

$$f_o = f_s \frac{V + v_o}{V - v_s}$$

Doppler Effect

where f_o = observed frequency
f_s = frequency of source
V = velocity of sound
v_o = velocity of observer
v_s = velocity of source

Note: Speeds are reckoned as positive for approach and negative for recession.

QUESTIONS

23-1. Define the following terms:
   a. Sound
   b. Compression
   c. Condensation
   d. Resonance
   e. Infrasonic
   f. Ultrasonic
   g. Loudness
   h. Intensity
   i. Decibels
   j. Pitch
   k. Forced vibration
   l. Audible sound
   m. Hearing threshold
   n. Pain threshold
   o. Intensity level
   p. Frequency
   q. Quality
   r. Waveform
   s. Beats
   t. Doppler effect

23-2. What is the physiological definition of sound? What is the meaning of sound in physics?

23-3. Why must astronauts on the surface of the moon communicate by radio? Can they hear another spacecraft as it lands nearby? Can they hear by touching helmets?

23-4. How is the sound of a person's voice affected by inhaling helium gas? Is the effect one of pitch, loudness, or quality?

23-5. Vocal sounds originate with the vibration of vocal cords. The mouth and nasal openings act as a resonant cavity to amplify and distinguish sounds. Suppose you hum at a constant pitch equal to the C note on a piano. By opening and closing your mouth, what physiological property of the sound is affected?

23-6. The distance in miles to a thunderstorm can be estimated by counting the number of seconds elapsing between the flash of lightning and the arrival of a clap of thunder and dividing the result by 5. Explain why this is a reasonable approximation.

23-7. A store window is broken by an explosion several miles away. A glass of thin crystal shatters when a high note is reached on a violin. Are the causes of damage similar? What physical property of sound was principally responsible in each case?

23-8. Compare the speeds of sound in solids, liquids, and gases. Explain the reason for differences in speed.

23-9. Perform a unit analysis of Eq. (23-1) showing that $\sqrt{Y/\rho}$ will yield units of speed.

23-10. How will the speed of sound in a gas be affected if the temperature of the gas is quadrupled?

23-11. An electric bell operates inside an evacuated flask. No sound is heard because of the absence of a medium. Explain what happens if the flask is tilted until the bell touches the walls of the flask.

23-12. Draw diagrams to demonstrate the differences between a progressive longitudinal wave and a standing longitudinal wave.

23-13. A standing wave is set up in a vibrating string. How are the harmonics of the possible sounds related to the number of loops in the string? How are the harmonics related to the number of nodes?

23-14. What effect will closing one end of an open pipe have on the frequency of a vibrating air column?

23-15. Compare the quality of sound produced by a violin with that produced by tuning fork.

23-16. If the average ear cannot hear sounds of frequencies much in excess of 15,000 Hz, what is the advantage of building stereo music systems which have frequency responses much higher than 15,000 Hz?

23-17. A vibrating tuning fork mounted on a resonating box is moved toward a wall and away from an observer. The resulting sound pulsates in intensity. Explain.

23-18. An instructor attempts to explain the Doppler effect by using baseballs and a bicycle. He proceeds as follows: "Suppose I am at rest, and I release one baseball in the same direction every second at constant speed. Consider me as the source of sound waves and the baseballs as advancing wavefronts. The spacing between the balls at any instant will be constant and analogous to the wavelength of sound waves. Now, suppose I ride a bicycle in the forward direction at a constant speed and continue to release balls in the forward direction and in the backward direction at the same rate and at the same speed. The spacing of the balls in front of me will be closer together because each time I release a ball in that direction I will have also moved in that direction. Similarly, the balls released in the backward direction will be spaced further apart than normal." Give a careful analysis of his explanation. In what ways is his analogy correct? In what very important aspect does his analogy fail? Why would an equation similar to Eq. (23-20) fail as a means of predicting the spacing of the baseballs? Why does it work for sound waves?

PROBLEMS

23-1. Compute the speed of sound in a copper rod of density 8.8 g/cm^3. Young's modulus for copper is 11×10^{10} N/m^2.

Ans. 3.54 km/s.

23-2. The speed of longitudinal waves in a certain metal rod of density 7850 kg/m^3 is measured to be 3380 m/s. **(a)** What is Young's modulus for the metal? **(b)** If the frequency of the waves is 312 Hz, what is the wavelength?

23-3. Compare the theoretical speeds of sound in hydrogen ($\gamma = 1.4$) and helium ($\gamma = 1.66$) at 0°C. The molecular masses for hydrogen and helium are $M_H = 20$ and $M_{He} = 4.0$.

Ans. $v_{He} = 0.77 v_H$.

23-4. A sound wave is sent from a ship to the ocean floor, where it is reflected and returned. If the round trip takes 0.6 s, how deep is the ocean floor? Consider the bulk modulus for seawater to be 2.1×10^9 N/m² and its density 1.03 g/cm³.

23-5. On a day when the air temperature is 27°C, a stone is dropped down a mine shaft 200 m deep. How much later will the impact at the bottom be heard? (Allow for time to drop.)

Ans. 6.96 s.

23-6. When a sound wave enters a medium of different density, its speed changes but the frequency remains constant. Compute the change in wavelength when the sound passes from air to hydrogen. The frequency of the sound is 1000 Hz, and the velocity in air is 331 m/s.

23-7. Find the fundamental frequency and the first three overtones for a 20-cm pipe at 20°C **(a)** if the pipe is open at both ends and **(b)** if the pipe is closed at one end.

Ans. **(a)** 857.5, 1715, 2572, and 3430 Hz **(b)** 429, 1286, 2144, and 3001 Hz.

23-8. What length of closed pipe is required to produce a fundamental frequency of 256 Hz? What length of open pipe will have this fundamental frequency? Assume the temperature to be 0°C.

23-9. The laboratory apparatus shown in Fig. 23-12 is used to measure the speed of sound in air by the resonance method. A vibrating tuning fork of frequency f is held over the open end of a tube partly filled with water. The length of the air column can be varied by changing the water level. As the water level is gradually lowered from the top of the tube, the sound intensity reaches a maximum at the three levels shown in the figure. The maxima occur whenever the air column resonates with the tuning fork. Thus the distance between successive resonance positions is the distance between adjacent modes for the standing waves in the air column. The frequency of the fork is 512 Hz, and the resonance positions occur at 17, 51, and 85 cm

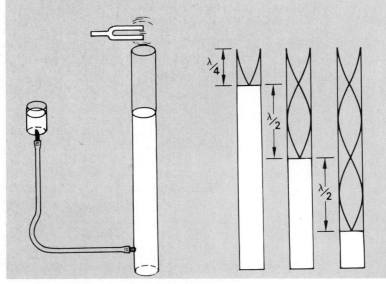

Fig. 23-12 Laboratory apparatus for computing the velocity of sound by resonance methods.

from the top of the tube. **(a)** What is the velocity of sound in the air? **(b)** What is the approximate temperature of the room?

Ans. **(a)** 348 m/s **(b)** 28.3°C.

23-10. In a resonance experiment, the air in a closed tube of variable length is found to resonate with a tuning fork when the air column is first 6 cm, and then 18 cm, long. Assuming that the temperature of the air is 10°C, find the frequency of the tuning fork.

23-11. A closed pipe and an open pipe are each 3 m long. Compute the wavelength of the fourth overtone of each pipe.

Ans. Open = 1.2 m, closed = 1.33 m.

23-12. How many beats per second are heard when two tuning forks of 256 and 259 Hz are sounded together?

23-13. Compute the intensity levels in decibels of sounds of the following intensities: **(a)** 10^{-7} W/cm^2, **(b)** 100 μW/cm^2, **(c)** 4000 μW/cm^2, and **(d)** 2 $\times 10^{-8}$ W/cm^2.

Ans. **(a)** 90 dB **(b)** 120 dB **(c)** 136 dB **(d)** 83 dB.

23-14. How much more intense is a sound 20 dB higher than the hearing threshold?

23-15. What is the difference in decibels between two sounds of intensities 20 and 400 μW/cm^2?

Ans. 13.01 dB.

23-16. Find the ratio of the intensities of two sounds if one is 12 dB louder than the other.

23-17. The fundamental frequency of a train whistle is 300 Hz, and the speed of the train is 60 km/h. On a day when the temperature is 20°C, what frequencies will be heard by a stationary observer as the train passes with its whistle blowing?

Ans. 315, 300, and 286 Hz.

23-18. The noon whistle at a textile mill has a frequency of 360 Hz. What are the frequencies heard by the driver of a car passing the mill? The speed of sound is 343 m/s, and the velocity of the car is 30 m/s.

23-19. A tuning fork of frequency 512 Hz is moved away from an observer and toward a flat wall with a speed of 3 m/s. The speed of sound in the air is 340 m/s. **(a)** What is the apparent frequency of the unreflected sound waves? **(b)** What is the apparent frequency of the reflected sound waves? **(c)** How many beats per second are heard?

Ans. **(a)** 507.5 Hz **(b)** 516.5 Hz **(c)** 9 beats/s.

24 *The Nature of Light*

OBJECTIVES: After completing this chapter, you should be able to:

1. **Discuss the historical investigation into the nature of light and explain how light sometimes behaves as a wave and sometimes as particles.**

2. **Describe the broad classifications in the electromagnetic spectrum on the basis of frequency, wavelength, or energy.**

3. **Write and apply formulas for the relationship between velocity, wavelength, and frequency, and between energy and frequency for electromagnetic radiation.**

4. **Describe experiments which will result in a reasonable estimation of the speed of light.**

An iron bar resting on a table is in thermal equilibrium with its surroundings. From its outward appearance one would never guess that it is very active internally. All objects are continuously emitting radiant heat energy which is related to their temperature. The bar is in thermal equilibrium only because it is radiating and absorbing energy at the same rates. If the balance is upset by placing one end of the bar in a hot flame, the bar becomes more active internally and emits heat energy at a greater rate. As the heating continues to around 600°C, some of the radiation emitted from the bar becomes *visible*. That is, it affects our sense of sight. The color of the bar becomes a dull red, which turns brighter as more heat is supplied.

The radiant energy emitted by the object before this effect is visible consists of electromagnetic waves of longer wavelengths than red light. Such waves are referred to as *infrared rays*, meaning "beyond the red." If the temperature of the bar is increased to around 3000°C, it becomes white hot, indicating a further extension of the radiant energy into the visible region.

This example sets the stage for our discussion of light. The nature of light is no different fundamentally from the nature of other electromagnetic radiations, e.g., heat, radio waves, or ultraviolet radiation. The characteristic which distinguishes light from the other radiations is its energy.

Light is electromagnetic radiation which is capable of affecting the sense of sight.

The energy content of visible light varies from about 2.8×10^{-19} J to around 5.0×10^{-19} J.

24-1 WHAT IS LIGHT?

The answer to that question has been extremely elusive throughout the history of science. The long search for an answer provides an inspiring example of the scientific approach to the solution of a problem. Every hypothesis put forth to explain the nature of light was tested both by logic and by experimentation. The ancient philosophers' contention that visual rays are emitted from the eye to the seen object failed the test of both logic and experience.

By the latter part of the seventeenth century, two theories were being advanced to explain the nature of light, the particle (corpuscular) theory and the wave theory. The principal advocate of the corpuscular theory was Sir Isaac Newton. The wave theory was upheld by Christiaan Huygens (1629–1695), Dutch mathematician and scientist, 13 years older than Newton. Each theory set out to explain the characteristics of light observed at that time. Three important characteristics can be summarized as follows:

1. *Rectilinear propagation:* Light travels in straight lines.
2. *Reflection:* When light is incident on a smooth surface, it turns back into the original medium.
3. *Refraction:* The path of light changes when it enters a transparent medium.

According to the corpuscular theory, tiny particles of unsubstantial mass were emitted by light sources such as the sun or a flame. These particles traveled outward from the source in straight lines at enormous speeds. When the particles entered the eye, the sense of sight was stimulated. Rectilinear propagation was easily explained in terms of particles. In fact, one of the strongest arguments for the corpuscular theory was based on this property. It was reasoned that particles cast sharp shadows, as illustrated in Fig. 24-1a, whereas waves can bend around edges. Such bending of waves, as shown in Fig. 24-1b, is called *diffraction*.

The sharp shadows formed by light beams indicated to Newton that light must consist of particles. Huygens, on the other hand, explained that the bending of water waves and sound waves around obstacles is easily noticed because of the long wavelengths. He reasoned that if light were a wave with a very short wavelength it would appear to cast a sharp shadow because the amount of bending would be very small.

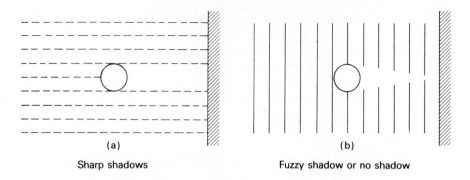

Fig. 24-1 A strong argument for the particle theory of matter is the formation of sharp shadows. Waves were known to bend around obstacles in their path.

(a) Sharp shadows   (b) Fuzzy shadow or no shadow

It was also difficult to explain why particles traveling in straight lines from many directions could cross without impeding one another. In a paper published in 1690, Huygens wrote:

> If, furthermore, we pay attention to, and weigh up, the extraordinary speed with which light spreads in all directions, and also the fact that coming, as it does, from quite different, indeed from opposite, directions, the rays interpenetrate without impeding one another, then we may well understand that whenever we see a luminous object, this cannot be due to the transmission of matter which reaches us from the object, as for instance a projectile or an arrow flies through the air.

Huygens explained the propagation of light in terms of the motion of a disturbance through the distance between a source and the eye. He based his argument on a simple principle which is still useful today in describing the propagation of light. Suppose we drop a stone into a quiet pool of water. A disturbance is created which moves outward from the point of impact in a series of concentric waves. The disturbance continues even after the stone has struck the bottom of the pool. Such an example prompted Huygens to postulate that disturbances existing at all points along a moving wavefront at one instant can be considered sources for the wavefront at the next instant. Huygens' principle states:

> *Every point on an advancing wavefront can be considered a source of secondary waves called wavelets. The new position of the wavefront is the envelope of the wavelets emitted from all points of the wavefront in its previous position.*

The application of this principle is illustrated in Fig. 24-2 for the common cases of a plane wave and a circular wave.

Huygens' principle was particularly successful in explaining reflection and refraction. Figure 24-3 shows how the principle can be used to explain the bending of light as it passes from air to water. When the plane waves strike the water surface at an angle, points *A*, *C*, and *E* become the sources of new wavelets. The envelope of these secondary wavelets indicates a change in direction. A similar construction can be made to explain reflection.

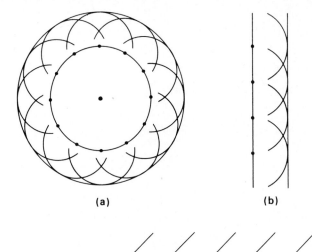

Fig. 24-2 Illustration of Huygens' principle (*a*) for a spherical wave and (*b*) for a plane wave.

(a)

(b)

Fig. 24-3 Huygens' explanation of refraction in terms of the wave theory.

Air

A B C D E

Water

Reflection and refraction were also easily explained in terms of the particle theory. Figures 24-4 and 24-5 illustrate models which can be used to explain reflection and refraction on the basis of tiny corpuscles. Perfectly elastic particles of unsubstantial mass rebounding from an elastic surface could explain the regular reflection of light from smooth surfaces. Refraction could be analogous to the change in direction of a rolling ball as it encounters an incline. This explanation required that the particles of light travel faster in the refracted

Fig. 24-4 Explanation of reflection in terms of the particle theory of light.

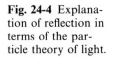

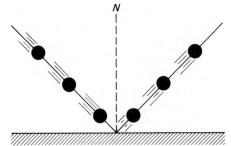

N

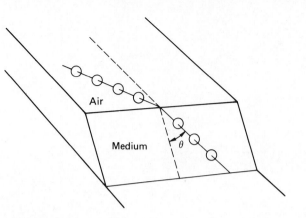

Fig. 24-5 Refraction of light as it passes from air to another medium was explained by this mechanical example.

Air

Medium

θ

medium, whereas the wave theory required light to travel more slowly in the refracted medium. Newton recognized that if it could ever be shown that light travels more slowly in a material medium than it does in air, he would have to abandon the particle theory. It was not until the middle of the nineteenth century that Jean Foucault successfully demonstrated that light travels more slowly in water than it does in air.

24-2 THE PROPAGATION OF LIGHT

The discovery of interference and diffraction in 1801 and 1816 swung the debate solidly toward Huygens' wave theory. Clearly, interference and diffraction could be explained only in terms of a wave theory. However, there still remained one problem. All wave phenomena were thought to require the existence of a medium. How, for example, could light waves travel through a vacuum if there were nothing to "vibrate"? Indeed, how could light reach the earth from the sun or other stars through millions of miles of empty space? In order to avoid this contradiction, physicists postulated the existence of a "light-carrying ether." This all-penetrating universal medium was thought to fill all the space between and within all material bodies. But what was the nature of this ether? Certainly it could not be a gas, solid, or liquid that obeyed the physical laws known at that time. And yet the wave theory could not be denied in light of the evidence of interference and diffraction. No other choice seemed possible except for the definition of ether as "that which carries light."

In 1865 a Scottish physicist, James Clerk Maxwell, set out to determine the properties of a medium which would carry light and also account for the transmission of heat and electric energy. His work demonstrated that *an accelerated charge can radiate electromagnetic waves into space.* Maxwell explained that the energy in an electromagnetic wave is equally divided between electric and magnetic fields which are mutually perpendicular. Both fields oscillate perpendicular to the direction of wave propagation, as shown in Fig. 24-6. Thus a light wave would not have to depend on the vibration of matter. It could be propagated by oscillating transverse fields. Such a wave could "break off" from the region around an accelerating charge and fly off into space with the velocity

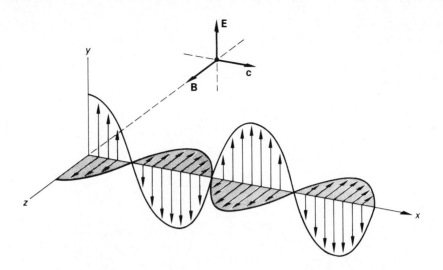

Fig. 24-6
Electromagnetic theory holds that light is propagated as oscillating transverse fields. The energy is equally divided between electric **E** and magnetic **B** fields, which are mutually perpendicular.

of light. Maxwell's equations predicted that heat and electric action, as well as light, were propagated at the speed of light as electromagnetic disturbances.

Experimental confirmation of Maxwell's theory was achieved in 1885 by H. R. Hertz, who proved that radiation of electromagnetic energy can occur *at any frequency*. In other words, light, heat radiation, and radio waves are of the same nature, and they all travel at the speed of light (3×10^8 m/s). All types of radiation can be reflected, focused by lenses, polarized, and so forth. It seemed that the wave nature of light could no longer be doubted.

Confirmation of the electromagnetic theory paved the way for the eventual downfall of the "light-carrying ether" postulate. In 1887, A. A. Michelson, an American physicist, showed conclusively that the velocity of light is a constant, independent of the motion of the source. He could not establish any difference between the speed of light traveling in the direction of the earth's motion and traveling opposite to the earth's motion. Those who are interested in a thorough discussion of the subject should look up the *Michelson–Morley experiment*. Einstein later interpreted Michelson's results to mean that the notion of ether must be abandoned in favor of a completely empty space.

24-3 THE ELECTROMAGNETIC SPECTRUM

Today, the electromagnetic spectrum is known to spread over a tremendous range of frequencies. A chart of the electromagnetic spectrum is presented in Fig. 24-7. The wavelength λ of electromagnetic radiation is related to its frequency f by the general equation

$$c = f\lambda \qquad (24\text{-}1)$$

where c is the velocity of light (3×10^8 m/s). In terms of wavelengths, the tiny segment of the electromagnetic spectrum referred to as the *visible region* lies between 0.00004 and 0.00007 cm.

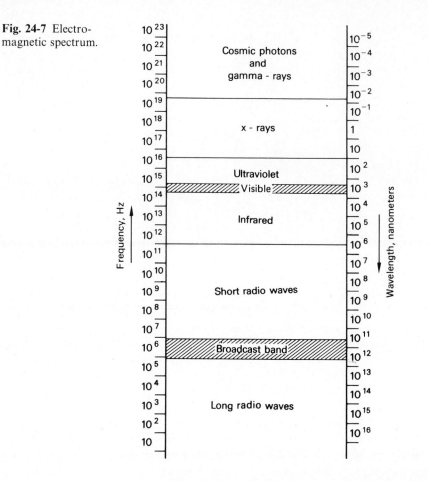

Fig. 24-7 Electromagnetic spectrum.

Because of the small wavelengths of light radiation, it is more convenient to define smaller units of measure. The SI unit is the *nanometer* (nm).

One **nanometer** (1 nm) is defined as one-billionth of a meter.

$$1 \text{ nm} = 10^{-9} \text{ m} = 10^{-7} \text{ cm}$$

Other older units are the *millimicron* (mμ), which is the same as a nanometer, and the *angstrom* (Å), which is 0.1 nm.

The visible region of the electromagnetic spectrum extends from 400 nm for violet light to approximately 700 nm for red light.

EXAMPLE 24-1 The wavelength of yellow light from a sodium flame is 589 nm. Compute its frequency.

Solution The frequency is found from Eq. (24-1).

$$f = \frac{c}{\lambda} = \frac{3 \times 10^8 \text{ m/s}}{589 \times 10^{-9} \text{ m}}$$

$$= 5.09 \times 10^{14} \text{ Hz}$$

Newton was the first to make detailed studies of the visible region by dispersing "white light" through a prism. In order of increasing wavelength, the spectral colors are violet (450 nm), blue (480 nm), green (520 nm), yellow (580 nm), orange (600 nm), and red (640 nm). Anyone who has seen a rainbow has seen the effects that different wavelengths of light have on the human eye.

The electromagnetic spectrum is continuous; there are no gaps between one form of radiation and another. The boundaries we set are purely arbitrary, depending upon our ability to sense one small portion directly and to discover and measure those portions outside the visible region.

The first discovery of radiation of wavelengths longer than those of red light was accomplished in 1800 by William Herschel. These waves are now known as thermal radiation and are referred to as *infrared waves*.

Shortly after the discovery of infrared waves, radiation of wavelengths shorter than visible light were noticed. These waves, now known as *ultraviolet waves*, were discovered in connection with their effect on certain chemical reactions.

How far the infrared region might extend in the direction of longer wavelengths was not known throughout most of the nineteenth century. Fortunately, Maxwell's electromagnetic theory opened the door for the discovery of many other classifications of radiation. The spectrum of electromagnetic waves is now conveniently divided into the eight major regions shown in Fig. 24-7: (1) long radio waves, (2) short radio waves, (3) the infrared region, (4) the visible region, (5) the ultraviolet region, (6) x-rays, (7) gamma-rays, and (8) cosmic photons.

**24-4
THE
QUANTUM
THEORY**

The work of Maxwell and of Hertz in establishing the electromagnetic nature of light waves was truly one of the most important events in the history of science. Not only was the wave nature of light explained, but the door was opened to an enormous range of electromagnetic waves. Remarkably, only 2 years after Hertz' verification of Maxwell's wave equations, the wave theory of light was again challenged. In 1887, Hertz noticed that an electric spark would jump more readily between two charged spheres when their surfaces were illuminated by the light from another spark. This phenomenon, known as the *photoelectric effect*, is demonstrated by the apparatus in Fig. 24-8. A beam of light strikes a metal surface A in an evacuated tube. Electrons ejected by the light are drawn to the collector B by external batteries. The flow of electrons is indicated by a device called an *ammeter*. The photoelectric effect defied explanation in terms of the wave theory. In fact, the ejection of electrons could be accounted for more easily in terms of the old particle theory. Still, there could be no doubt of the wave properties either. Science faced a remarkable paradox.

The photoelectric effect, along with several other experiments involving the emission and absorption of radiant energy, could not be accounted for purely in terms of Maxwell's electromagnetic wave theory. In an attempt to bring experimental observation into agreement with theory, Max Planck, a

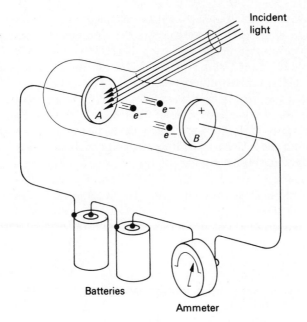

Incident
light

Batteries

Ammeter

German physicist, published his *quantum* hypothesis in 1901. He found that the problems with the radiation theory lay with the assumption that energy is radiated continuously. It was postulated that electromagnetic energy is absorbed or emitted in discrete packets, or *quanta*. The energy content of these quanta, or *photons* as they were called, is proportional to the frequency of the radiation. Planck's equation can be written

$$E = hf \qquad (24\text{-}2)$$

where E = energy of photon
f = frequency of photon
h = proportionality factor called Planck's constant (6.625×10^{-34} J/Hz)

In 1905, Einstein extended the idea proposed by Planck and postulated that the energy in a light beam does not spread continuously through space. By assuming that light energy is concentrated in small packets (photons) whose energy content is given by Planck's equation, Einstein was able to predict the photoelectric effect mathematically. At last, theory was reconciled with experimental observation.

Thus it appears that light is *dualistic*. The wave theory is retained by considering the photon to have a frequency and an energy proportional to the frequency. The modern practice is to use the wave theory when studying the propagation of light. The corpuscular theory, on the other hand, is necessary to describe the interaction of light with matter. We may think of light as radiant energy transported in photons carried along by a wave field.

The origin of light photons was not understood until Niels Bohr in 1913 devised a model of the atom based on quantum ideas. Bohr postulated that electrons can move about the nucleus of an atom only in certain orbits or *discrete energy levels*, as shown in Fig. 24-9. Atoms were said to be *quantized*. If the atoms are somehow energized, as by heat, the orbital electrons may be caused to jump into a *higher* orbit. At some later time, these excited electrons will fall back to their original level, releasing as photons the energy which was originally absorbed. Although Bohr's model was not strictly correct, it provided a basis for understanding the emission and absorption of electromagnetic radiation in quantum units.

Fig. 24-9 Bohr's theory of the atom.

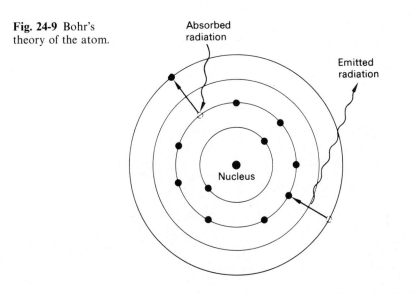

Absorbed radiation

Emitted radiation

Nucleus

24-5 THE SPEED OF LIGHT

The speed of light is probably the most important constant used in physics, and its accurate determination represents one of the most precise measurements accomplished by man. Its magnitude is so great (about 186,000 mi/s) that experimental measurements were entirely unsuccessful until the latter part of the seventeenth century. It was generally believed that the transmission of light must be instantaneous.

The first attempts to measure the speed of light experimentally were made in 1667 by Galileo. Briefly, his method consisted of stationing two observers in towers separated by a known distance. Signals were to be made at night with lanterns. The second experimenter was to uncover his lantern as soon as he received a light signal from the first experimenter. The speed of light could then be determined from the time required for the light to travel between the two towers. The experiment was inconclusive, and Galileo merely added to the prevailing opinion that light transmission was instantaneous. Such an experiment seems humorous to us only because of our present understanding of the true magnitude of the velocity of light.

Eight years later, a Danish astronomer, Olaus Roemer, made the first measurement of the speed of light. He based his calculations on irregularities in the predicted eclipses of one of the moons of the planet Jupiter. Roemer had been measuring the time interval between successive eclipses for several years. He noticed a consistent variation in his computations when measurements were made from different portions of the earth's orbit about the sun. Roemer correctly concluded that the irregularities in his measurements were due to the distance which light traveled to reach the earth. On the basis of his rather inaccurate measurements, Roemer calculated that the speed of light was 140,000 mi/s.

The first successful terrestrial measurement of the speed of light was made by A. H. L. Fizeau, a French scientist. In 1849, his experiment involved the simple computation of the time required for light to traverse a known distance. A schematic diagram of the apparatus is shown in Fig. 24-10. A rotating

Fig. 24-10 Fizeau's apparatus for measuring the speed of light.

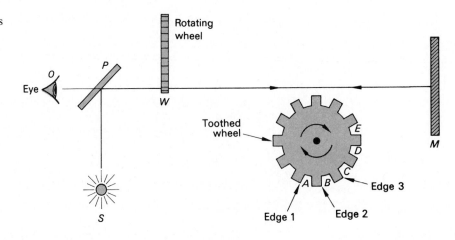

toothed wheel *W* allows light coming from the source to be interrupted, producing a series of short flashes. Let us assume first that the wheel is stationary and that light passes through one of the openings between the teeth. Light from the source *S* is reflected by the half-silvered plate glass *P* through the opening in the wheel and onto the plane mirror *M* located a few miles away. The reflected light returns through the opening and passes through the glass *P* and to the observer *O*.

Now suppose the toothed wheel is rotated at a constant frequency. Light from the source will pass through the opening *A* to the distant mirror and back to the wheel. The rotational frequency of the wheel is adjusted so that the returning light will just pass through the opening *B*. Under these conditions light from the source passes by edge 1 onto the mirror and returns past edge 2. Thus the time required for the light to travel the known distance is the same as the time for the wheel to rotate through the combined width of one opening and one tooth. The speed of light is therefore a function of the known frequency of rotation of the wheel and can be calculated. If the frequency is gradually increased, the light will eventually be blocked again until it reappears past edge 3. The speed of light calculated by Fizeau was 3.13×10^8 m/s. The error is attributed to inaccurate measurements.

In 1850, Foucault refined the apparatus developed by Fizeau by replacing the toothed wheel with a rotating mirror. He is remembered primarily for his measurements of the velocity of light in water. It was the first conclusive evidence that light travels more slowly in water than in air.

Probably no other scientist is more remembered for his work on measuring the speed of light than Albert A. Michelson (1852–1931). Using the Foucault method, he was able to obtain measurements which were extremely accurate. A schematic diagram of his apparatus is shown in Fig. 24-11. The light source, the eight-sided rotating mirror, and the telescope were located on Mt. Wilson, California. The reflecting mirrors were located approximately 22

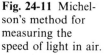

Fig. 24-11 Michelson's method for measuring the speed of light in air.

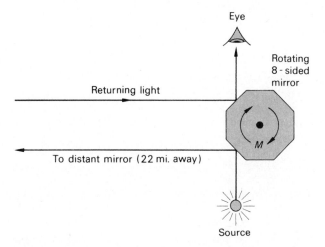

miles away on the top of Mt. San Antonio. From the known distances and the time required for light to complete the trip, Michelson determined that the speed of light in air is 2.997×10^8 m/s. This value is accepted as one of the most precise measurements made using the Foucault principle.

The accepted value for the speed of light in a vacuum is presently

$$c = 2.997925 \times 10^8 \text{ m/s}$$

Useful approximations are 3×10^8 m/s and 186,000 mi/s. These values may be used in most physical calculations without fear of significant error.

SUMMARY

The investigation of the nature of light is still continuing, but experiments show that it sometimes behaves as particles and sometimes as a wave. Modern theory holds that light is electromagnetic radiation, and that its radiant energy is transported in photons carried along by a wave field. The main ideas and formulas presented in this chapter are summarized below:

- The wavelength λ of electromagnetic radiation is related to its frequency f by the general equation

$$c = f\lambda$$ $$c = 3 \times 10^8 \text{ m/s}$$

- The range of wavelengths for visible light goes from 400 nm for violet to 700 nm for red.

$$1 \text{ nm} = 10^{-9} \text{ m}$$

The Nanometer is Used for Wavelengths.

- The energy of light photons is proportional to the frequency.

$$E = hf$$ $$E = \frac{h\lambda}{c}$$ $$h = 6.626 \times 10^{-34} \text{ J/Hz}$$

The constant h is *Planck's constant.*

QUESTIONS

24-1. Define the following terms:
   a. Light
   b. Reflection
   c. Refraction
   d. Diffraction
   e. Ether
   f. Nanometer
   g. Millimicron
   h. Angstrom
   i. Rectilinear propagation
   j. Huygens' principle
   k. Infrared rays
   l. Ultraviolet rays
   m. Photoelectric effect
   n. Quantum theory
   o. Speed of light
   p. Electromagnetic waves

24-2. Discuss the contributions made by each of the following men to our understanding of light.
   a. Sir Isaac Newton
   b. Jean Foucault
   c. H. R. Hertz
   d. Max Planck
   e. Niels Bohr
   f. Olaus Roemer
   g. Christiaan Huygens
   h. James Clerk Maxwell
   i. A. A. Michelson
   j. William Herschel
   k. Albert Einstein
   l. Galileo Galilei
   m. A. H. L. Fizeau

24-3. In what ways does light behave like particles? In what ways does it behave like a wave?

24-4. How do radio waves compare with x-rays with reference to their (a) energy, (b) wavelength, and (c) frequency?

24-5. Use Huygens' principle to construct a figure explaining the phenomenon of reflection.

24-6. Explain the advantages of an eight-sided mirror over a four-sided mirror in Michelson's measurements of the speed of light.

24-7. Write a brief report on the famous Michelson–Morley experiment.

PROBLEMS

24-1. An infrared spectrophotometer scans the wavelengths from 1 to 16 μm. Express this range in terms of the frequencies of the infrared rays.

Ans. 30×10^{13} to 1.88×10^{13} Hz.

24-2. What is the frequency of violet light of wavelength 410 nm?

24-3. A microwave radiator used in measuring automobile speeds emits radiation of frequency 1.2×10^9 Hz. What is the wavelength in nanometers? In angstroms?

Ans. 2.5×10^8 nm, 2.5×10^9 Å.

24-4. What is the range of the frequencies of visible light?

24-5. When light of wavelength 550 nm passes from air into a thin glass plate and out again into the air, the frequency remains constant, but the speed through the glass is reduced to 2×10^8 m/s. What is the wavelength inside the glass?

Ans. 367 nm.

24-6. The wavelength changes from 660 to 455 nm as light passes through a material medium. What is the velocity of light in the medium if the frequency is unaltered?

24-7. If Planck's constant is $h = 6.625 \times 10^{-34}$ J/Hz, what is the energy content of yellow light (600 nm)?

Ans. 3.313×10^{-19} J.

24-8. What is the frequency of light whose energy content is 5×10^{-19} J?

24-9. The sun is approximately 93 million miles from the earth. How much time is required for the light emitted by the sun to reach us on earth?

Ans. 8.33 min.

24-10. If the two experimenters in Galileo's experiment were separated by a distance of 5 km, how much time would have passed between the instant the lantern was opened until the light was observed?

24-11. The light reaching us from the nearest star, Alpha Centauri, requires 4.3 years to reach us. How far is this in miles? In kilometers?

Ans. 2.53×10^{13} mi, 4.05×10^{13} km.

24-12. A spacecraft circling the moon at a distance of 384,000 km from the earth communicates by radio with a base on earth. **(a)** How much time elapses between the sending and receiving of a signal? **(b)** How long would be required for a TV signal to reach the earth from Venus when it is 4×10^7 km from earth?

24-13. In Fizeau's experiment, the plane mirror was located at a distance of 8630 m. He used a wheel containing 720 teeth (and 720 voids). Every time the rotational speed of the wheel was increased by 24.2 rev/s, the light came through to his eye. What value did he obtain for the speed of light?

Ans. 3.01×10^8 m/s.

24-14. In Michelson's measurements of the speed of light, as shown in Fig. 24-11, he obtained a value of 2.997×10^8 m/s. If the total light path was 35 km, what was the rotational frequency of the eight-sided mirror?

25 *Light and Illumination*

OBJECTIVES: After completing this chapter, you should be able to:

1. Illustrate with drawings your understanding of the formation of shadows, and be able to predict the dimensions of the *umbra* or *penumbra* regions.
2. Demonstrate your understanding of the concepts of *luminous flux, luminous intensity*, and *illumination*, and solve problems similar to those in the text.
3. Explain and apply the inverse square law for the illumination of surfaces.

In Chap. 24 we discussed the nature of light and the origin of the modern quantum theory. It was discovered that light is dualistic in nature, sometimes acting as particles and sometimes as waves. The wave characteristics are adequately explained in terms of Maxwell's electromagnetic theory of radiation, in which light occupies only a narrow portion of a much broader spectrum.

Light, traveling at the phenomenal ultimate speed of 3×10^8 m/s, is responsible for all that we perceive directly through the sense of sight. In this chapter we discuss two aspects of the study of light which affect our senses directly. The first is concerned with the rectilinear propagation of light; the second provides a basis for studying light intensity and the illumination of surfaces.

25-1 LIGHT RAYS AND SHADOWS

One of the first properties of light to be studied was rectilinear propagation and the formation of shadows. Instinctively, we rely quite heavily on this property for estimating distances, directions, and shapes. The formation of sharp shadows on a sundial is used to estimate time. In this section we discuss how we can predict the formation of shadows.

According to Huygens' principle, every point on a moving wavefront can be considered a source for secondary wavelets. The wavefront at any time is the envelope of these wavelets. Thus the light emitted in all directions by the point source of light in Fig. 25-1 can be represented by a series of spherical wavefronts moving away from the source at the speed of light. For our purposes, a *point source* of light is one whose dimensions are small in comparison with the distances studied. Note that the spherical wavefronts become essentially plane wavefronts in any specific direction at a long distance away from the source. An imaginary straight line drawn perpendicular to the wavefronts in the direction of the moving wavefronts is called a *ray*. There are, of course, an infinite number of rays starting from the point source.

Fig. 25-1 A ray is an imaginary line, drawn perpendicular to advancing wavefronts, which indicates the direction of light propagation.

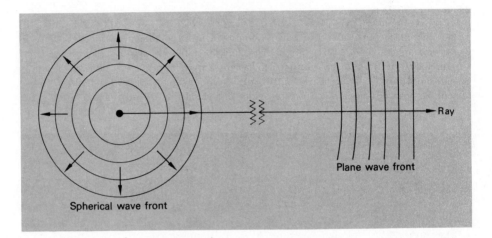

Any dark-colored object absorbs light, but a black one absorbs nearly all the light it receives. Light that is not absorbed upon striking an object is either reflected or transmitted. If all the light incident upon an object is reflected or absorbed, the object is said to be *opaque*. Since light cannot pass through an opaque body, a shadow will be produced in the space behind the object. The shadow formed by a point source of light is illustrated in Fig. 25-2. Since light

Fig. 25-2 Shadow formed by a point source of light.

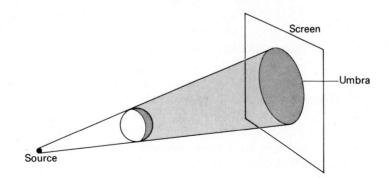

is propagated in straight lines, rays drawn from the source past the edges of the opaque object form a sharp shadow proportional to the shape of the object. Such a region in which no light has entered is called an *umbra*.

If the source of light is an extended one rather than a point, the shadow will consist of two portions, as shown in Fig. 25-3. The inner portion receives no light from the source and is therefore the umbra. The outer portion is called the *penumbra*. An observer within the penumbra would see a portion of the source but not all the source. An observer located outside both regions would see all the source. Solar and lunar eclipses can be studied by similar construction of shadows.

Fig. 25-3 Shadow formed by an extended source of light.

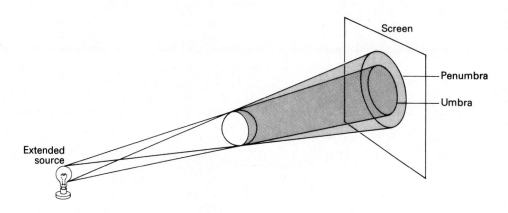

25-2 LUMINOUS FLUX

Most sources of light emit electromagnetic energy distributed over many wavelengths. Electric power is supplied to a lamp, and radiation is emitted. The radiant energy emitted per unit of time by the lamp is called the radiant power or the *radiant flux*. Only a small portion of this radiant power is in the visible region, i.e., in the region between 400 and 700 nm. The sensation of sight depends only on the visible, or *luminous*, energy radiated per unit of time.

> The **luminous flux** F is that part of the total radiant power emitted from a light source which is capable of affecting the sense of sight.

In a common incandescent light bulb, only about 10 percent of the energy radiated is luminous flux. The bulk of the radiant power is nonluminous.

The human eye is not equally sensitive to all colors. In other words, equal radiant power of different wavelengths does not produce equal brightness. A 40-W green light bulb appears brighter than a 40-W blue light bulb. A graph portraying the response of the eye to various wavelengths is shown in Fig. 25-4. Note that the sensitivity curve is bell-shaped around the center of the visible spectrum. Under normal conditions, the eye is most sensitive to yellow-green light of wavelength 555 nm. The sensitivity falls off rapidly for longer and shorter wavelengths.

Fig. 25-4 Sensitivity curve.

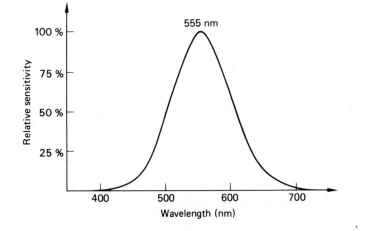

If the unit chosen for luminous flux is to correspond to the sensual response of the human eye, a new unit must be defined. The watt (W) is not sufficient because the visual sensations are not the same for different colors. What is needed is a unit which measures *brightness*. Such a unit is the *lumen* (lm), which is determined by comparison with a standard source.

To understand the definition of a lumen in terms of the standard source, we must first develop the concept of a solid angle. A solid angle in steradians (sr) is defined the same way a plane angle is defined in radians. In Fig. 25-5 the angle θ in radians is

$$\theta = \frac{S}{R} \qquad \text{rad}$$

where S is the arc length and R is the radius. The solid angle Ω is similarly defined by Fig. 25-6. It may be thought of as the opening from the tip of a cone which is subtended by a segment of area on the spherical surface.

One **steradian** (sr) is the solid angle subtended at the center of a sphere by an area A on its surface that is equal to the square of its radius R.

Fig. 25-5 Definition of a plane angle θ expressed in radians.

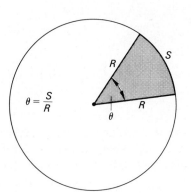

Fig. 25-6 Definition
of a solid angle Ω
in steradians.

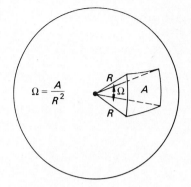

In general, the solid angle in steradians is given by

$$\boxed{\Omega = \frac{A}{R^2}} \qquad \text{sr}$$

(25-1)

The steradian, like the radian, is a unitless quantity.

Just as there are 2π rad in a complete circle, it can be shown by Eq. (25-1) that there are 4π sr in a complete sphere.

$$\Omega = \frac{A}{R^2} = \frac{4\pi R^2}{R^2} = 4\pi \qquad \text{sr}$$

Notice that the solid angle is independent of the distance from the source. There are 4π sr in a sphere regardless of the length of its radius.

EXAMPLE 25-1   What solid angle is subtended at the center of an 8-m-diameter sphere by a 1.5-m^2 area on its surface?

Solution   Equation (25-1) yields

$$\Omega = \frac{1.5 \text{ m}^2}{(4 \text{ m})^2} = 0.0938 \text{ sr}$$

We are now in a position to clarify the definition of a unit which measures luminous flux. The *lumen* is defined by comparison with an internationally recognized standard source.

> One **lumen** (lm) is the luminous flux (or visible radiant power) emitted from a $\frac{1}{60}$-cm^2 opening in a standard source and included within a solid angle of 1 sr.

The standard source consists of a hollow enclosure maintained at the temperature of solidification of platinum, about 1773°C. In practice it is more convenient to use standard incandescent lamps which have been rated by comparison with the standard.

Another convenient definition of the lumen utilizes the sensitivity curve (Fig. 25-4) as a basis for establishing luminous flux. By referring to the standard source, 1 lm is defined in terms of the radiant power of yellow-green light.

One lumen is equivalent to $\frac{1}{680}$ W of yellow-green light of wavelength 555 nm.

To determine the luminous flux emitted by light of a different wavelength, the luminosity curve must be used to compensate for visual sensitivity.

EXAMPLE 25-2 A source of monochromatic red light (600 nm) produces a visible radiant power of 4 W. What is the luminous flux in lumens?

Solution If the light were yellow-green (555 nm) instead of red, it would have a luminous flux F given by

$$F = (680 \text{ lm/W})(4 \text{ W}) = 2720 \text{ lm}$$

From the sensitivity curve, red light of wavelength 600 nm evokes about 59 percent of the response obtained with yellow-green light. Hence the luminous flux issuing from the red light source is

$$F = (0.59)(2720 \text{ lm}) = 1600 \text{ lm}$$

The luminous flux is often calculated in the laboratory by determining the illumination it produces on a known surface area.

25-3 LUMINOUS INTENSITY

Light travels radially outward in straight lines from a source which is small in comparison with its surroundings. For such a source of light, the luminous flux included in a solid angle Ω remains the same at all distances from the source. Therefore, it is frequently more useful to speak of the *flux per unit solid angle* than simply to express the total flux. The physical quantity which expresses this relationship is called the *luminous intensity*.

The **luminous intensity** I of a source of light is the luminous flux F emitted per unit solid angle Ω.

$$\boxed{I = \frac{F}{\Omega}} \tag{25-2}$$

The unit for intensity is the *lumen per steradian* (lm/sr), called a *candela* (cd). The candela, or *candle* as it was sometimes called, originated when the international standard was defined in terms of the quantity of light emitted by the flame of a certain make of candle. This standard was found unsatisfactory, and eventually it was replaced by the platinum standard.

EXAMPLE 25-3 Most light sources have different luminous intensities in different directions. An *isotropic* source is one which emits light uniformly in all directions. What is the total luminous flux emitted by an isotropic source of intensity I?

Solution

From Eq. (25-2), the flux is given by

$$F = \Omega I$$

The total solid angle Ω for an isotropic source is 4π sr. Thus

$$\boxed{F = 4\pi I}$$

Isotropic Source (25-3)

EXAMPLE 25-4

A spotlight is equipped with a 40-cd bulb which concentrates a beam on a vertical wall. The beam covers an area of 9 m^2 on the wall, and the spotlight is located 20 m from the wall. Calculate the luminous intensity of the spotlight.

Solution

The total flux emitted by the 40-cd bulb is

$$F = 4\pi I = (4\pi)(40 \text{ cd}) = 160\pi \text{ lm}$$

This total flux is concentrated by reflectors and lens into a solid angle given by

$$\Omega = \frac{A}{R^2} = \frac{9 \text{ m}^2}{(20 \text{ m})^2} = 0.0225 \text{ sr}$$

The intensity of the beam is now found from Eq. (25-2).

$$I = \frac{F}{\Omega} = \frac{160\pi \text{ lm}}{0.0225 \text{ sr}} = 2.23 \times 10^4 \text{ cd}$$

Note that the units of intensity (cd) and the units of flux (lm) are the same dimensionally. This is true because the solid angle in steradians is dimensionless.

**25-4
ILLUMI-
NATION**

If the intensity of a source is increased, the luminous flux transmitted to each unit of surface area in the vicinity of the source is also increased. The surface appears brighter. In the measurement of light efficiency, the engineer is concerned with the density of luminous flux falling on a surface. We are therefore led to a discussion of the *illumination* of a surface.

The **illumination** E of a surface A is defined as the luminous flux F per unit area.

$$\boxed{E = \frac{F}{A}}$$

(25-4)

When the flux F is measured in lumens and the area A in square meters, the illumination E has the units of *lumens per square meter* or *lux* (lx). When A is expressed in square feet, E is expressed in *lumens per square foot*. The lumen per square foot is sometimes loosely referred to as the footcandle.

Direct application of Eq. (25-4) requires a knowledge of the luminous flux falling on a given surface. Unfortunately, the flux of common light sources is difficult to determine. For this reason, Eq. (25-4) is most often used to calculate the flux when A is known and E is computed from the measured intensity.

To see the relationship between intensity and illumination, let us consider a surface A at a distance R from a point source of intensity I, as shown in Fig. 25-7. The solid angle Ω subtended by the surface at the source is

$$\Omega = \frac{A}{R^2}$$

Fig. 25-7 Computing the illumination of a surface which is perpendicular to the incident flux.

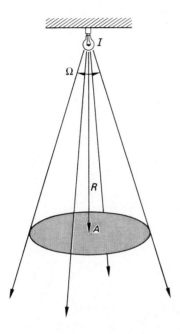

where the area A is perpendicular to the emitted light. If the luminous flux makes an angle θ with the normal to the surface, as shown in Fig. 25-8, we must consider the projected area $A \cos \theta$. This represents the effective area that the flux " sees." Therefore, the solid angle, in general, can be found from

$$\Omega = \frac{A \cos \theta}{R^2}$$

Solving for the luminous flux F in Eq. (25-2), we obtain

$$F = I\Omega = \frac{IA \cos \theta}{R^2} \qquad (25\text{-}5)$$

We are now ready to express the illumination as a function of intensity. Substituting Eq. (25-5) into the defining equation for illumination gives

$$E = \frac{F}{A} = \frac{IA \cos \theta}{AR^2}$$

Fig. 25-8 When a surface makes an angle with the incident flux, the illumination is proportional to the component of the surface perpendicular to the flux.

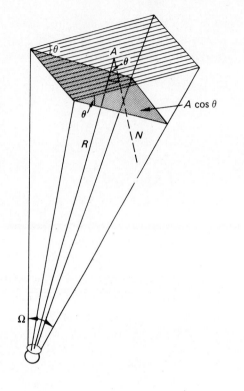

or

$$E = \frac{I \cos \theta}{R^2} \qquad (25\text{-}6)$$

For the special case in which the surface is normal to the flux, $\theta = 0°$, and Eq. (25-6) is simplified to

$$E = \frac{I}{R^2} \qquad \textit{Normal Surface} \quad (25\text{-}7)$$

You should verify that the units of *candela per square meter* are equivalent dimensionally to the units of *lumens per square meter* or *lux*.

EXAMPLE 25-5   A 100-W incandescent lamp has a luminous intensity of 125 cd. What is the illumination of a surface located 3 ft below the lamp?

Solution   By direct substitution into Eq. (25-7) we obtain

$$E = \frac{I}{R^2} = \frac{125 \text{ cd}}{(3 \text{ ft})^2} = 13.9 \text{ lm/ft}^2$$

EXAMPLE 25-6   A tungsten-filament lamp of intensity 300 cd is located 2.0 m away from a surface whose area is 0.25 m². The luminous flux makes an angle of 30° with the normal to the surface. (*a*) What is the illumination? (*b*) What is the luminous flux striking the surface? (Refer to Fig. 25-8.)

Solution (*a*)   The illumination is found directly from Eq. (25-6).

$$E = \frac{I \cos \theta}{R^2} = \frac{(300 \text{ cd})(\cos 30°)}{(2 \text{ m})^2} = 65 \text{ lx}$$

Solution (*b*)   The flux falling on the surface is found by solving for *F* in Eq. (25-3). Thus

$$F = EA = (65 \text{ lx})(0.25 \text{ m}^2)$$

$$= 16.2 \text{ lm}$$

The equations above involving illumination and luminous intensity are mathematical formulations of the *inverse-square law*, which can be stated as follows:

> *The illumination of a surface is proportional to the luminous intensity of a point light source and is inversely proportional to the square of the distance.*

If a light which is illuminating a surface is raised to twice the original height, the illumination will be only one-fourth as great. If the lamp distance is tripled, the illumination is reduced by one-ninth. This inverse-square relationship is illustrated in Fig. 25-9.

Fig. 25-9 Illumination of a surface varies inversely with the square of the distance from a point source.

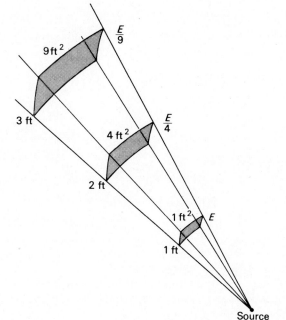

SUMMARY

Luminous flux has been defined as that portion of the total radiant power emitted from a light source which is capable of affecting the sense of sight. Since visual brightness and sensitivity varies for different individuals, it was necessary to define luminous intensity in terms of a standard source and a well-defined solid angle (the steradian). By comparison to such standards, we are able to treat the illumination of surfaces, which is so important for the design of industrial workplaces. The basic concepts are summarized below:

- The *luminous intensity* of a light source is the luminous flux F per unit solid angle Ω. *Luminous flux* is the radiant power in the visible region. It is measured in *lumens*.

$$1 \text{ lm} = \frac{1}{680} \text{ W} \qquad \text{for 555 nm light} \qquad \textit{The Lumen}$$

$$1 \Omega = \frac{A}{R^2} \qquad \textit{Solid Angle in Steradians}$$

$$I = \frac{F}{\Omega} \qquad \textit{Luminous Flux (1 cd = 1 lm/sr)}$$

- For an isotropic source, one emitting light in all directions, the luminous flux is

$$F = 4\pi I \qquad \textit{Isotropic Source}$$

- The *illumination E* of a surface A is defined as the luminous flux per unit area.

$$E = \frac{F}{A} \qquad E = \frac{I \cos \theta}{R^2} \qquad \textit{Illumination (lm/m}^2\textit{), lx}$$

QUESTIONS

25-1. Define the following terms:
- **a.** Umbra
- **b.** Penumbra
- **c.** Lumen
- **d.** Steradian
- **e.** Candle
- **f.** Opaque
- **g.** Ray
- **h.** Luminous flux
- **i.** Luminous intensity
- **j.** Illumination
- **k.** Inverse-square law
- **l.** Isotropic source
- **m.** Point source
- **n.** Standard source

25-2. Can you justify the following definition for a *lumen*? A lumen is equal to the luminous flux falling on a surface of one square meter, all points of which are one meter from a uniform point source of one candle. Explain.

25-3. Draw a diagram illustrating a solar eclipse, labeling the umbra and penumbra formed on the earth.

25-4. Describe the distribution of luminous flux from an incandescent lamp. Why is it not an isotropic source?

25-5. What factors contribute to the illumination of a surface?

25-6. In the illumination of a plane surface by an isotropic point, do we introduce any error by computing the solid angle Ω from the area and location of the plane surface? Explain.

25-7. Photometry is the science of measuring light. The intensity of a light source can be determined by the *photometer*, illustrated in Fig. 25-10. The luminous intensity I_x of the unknown source is found by visual comparison with

Fig. 25-10 Grease-spot photometer used to measure light intensity.

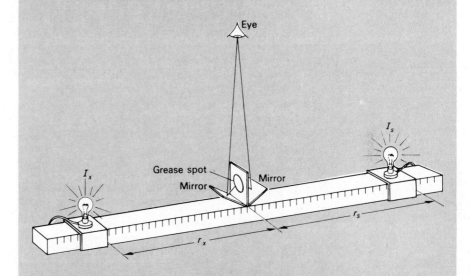

a standard source of known intensity I_s. If the distances of each source are adjusted so that the grease spot is equally illuminated by each source, the unknown intensity can be calculated from the inverse-square law. Derive the photometer equation

$$\frac{I_x}{r_x^2} = \frac{I_s}{r_s^2}$$

where r_x is the distance to the unknown source and r_s is the distance to the standard.

PROBLEMS

25-1. A point source of light is placed 15 cm from an upright 6-cm ruler. Calculate the length of the shadow formed by the ruler on a wall 40 cm from the ruler.

Ans. 22 cm.

25-2. How far must an 80-mm diameter plate be placed in front of a point source of light if it is to form a shadow 400 mm in diameter at a distance of 2 m from the light source?

25-3. A point source of light is approximated by placing a box over a lamp and punching a tiny hole in the box. A screen is positioned at a distance of 1.8 m from the hole in the box. How far from the screen must an 18-mm high object be placed in order to form a shadow that is 60-mm tall?

Ans. 1.26 m.

25-4. How far must a point light source be placed from a circular disk 20 mm in diameter to form a shadow 120 mm in diameter on a screen 1 m from the disk?

25-5. A lamp is covered with a box, and a 20-mm long narrow slit is cut in the box so that light shines through. An object 30 mm tall blocks the light from the slit at a distance of 500 mm. Calculate the length of the umbra and penumbra formed on a screen located 1.5 m from the slit.

Ans. 50 mm, 130 mm.

25-6. A source of light 40 mm in diameter shines through a pinhole in the top of a cardboard box 2 m from the source. What is the diameter of the image formed on the bottom of the box if the height of the box is 60 mm?

25-7. A source of light emits 2 W of luminous flux through a small opening surrounding the source. If the light is of a wavelength which is 20 percent as sensitive as yellow–green light (555 nm), how many lumens are emitted from the opening?

Ans. 272 lm.

25-8. If 400 lm of yellow–green light are emitted through a small opening, how many watts of luminous flux does this represent?

25-9. What is the solid angle subtended at the center of a 3.2-m-diameter sphere by a 0.5-m² area on its surface?

Ans. 0.195 sr.

25-10. A point source of light is placed at the center of a sphere 70 mm in diameter. A hole is cut in the surface of the sphere allowing the flux to pass through a solid angle of 0.12 sr. What is the diameter of the opening?

25-11. An $8\frac{1}{8}$ by 11 cm sheet of metal is illuminated by a source of light located 1.3 m directly above it. **(a)** Compute the luminous flux falling on the metal if the source has an intensity of 200 cd. **(b)** What is the total luminous flux emitted by the light?

Ans. **(a)** 1.11 lm **(b)** 2513 lm.

25-12. A 40-W monochromatic source of yellow–green light (555 nm) illuminates a 0.5-m² surface at a distance of 1 m. **(a)** What is the luminous intensity of the source? **(b)** How many lumens fall on the surface?

25-13. What is the illumination produced by a 200-cd light source on a small surface 4 m away?

Ans. 12.5 lx.

25-14. A lamp 2 m from a small surface produces an illuminance of 100 lx on the surface. What is the intensity of the source?

25-15. A point source of light is 2.3 m from a screen in which a circular hole 80 mm in diameter is cut. The luminous flux passing through the hole is determined to be 0.04 lm. **(a)** What is the solid angle subtended at the source by the hole? **(b)** What is the intensity of the source in the direction of the hole? **(c)** What is the illumination of a piece of paper placed behind the hole?

Ans. **(a)** 9.5×10^{-4} sr **(b)** 42.1 cd **(c)** 7.96 lx.

25-16. A light is suspended 9 m above a street and provides an illumination of 36 lx at a point directly below it. Determine the luminous intensity of the light.

25-17. A 30-cd standard-light source is compared with a lamp of unknown intensity with a grease-spot photometer (refer to Fig. 25-10). The two light sources are placed 1 m apart, and the grease spot is moved toward the standard light. When the grease spot is 25 cm from the standard-light source, the illumination is equal on both sides. Compute the unknown intensity.

Ans. 270 cd.

25-18. Where should the grease spot in Prob. 25-13 be placed for the illumination by the unknown light source to be exactly twice the illumination of the standard source?

25-19. At what distance from a wall will a 35-cd lamp provide the same illumination as an 80-cd lamp located 4 m from the wall?

Ans. 2.65 m.

25-20. What angle θ between the flux and a line drawn normal to a surface will cause the illumination of the surface to be reduced by one-half when the distance to the surface has not changed?

25-21. Compute the illumination of a surface 140 cm from a 74-cd light source if the normal to the surface makes an angle of 38° with the flux.

Ans. 29.8 lx.

25-22. A circular table top is located 4 m below and 3 m to the left of a lamp which emits 1800 lm. What illumination is provided on the surface of the table? What is the area of the table top if 3 lm of flux falls on its surface?

26 *Reflection and Mirrors*

OBJECTIVES: After completing this chapter, you should be able to:

1. Define and illustrate with drawings your understanding of the following terms: *virtual images*, *real images*, *converging mirror*, *diverging mirror*, *magnification*, *focal length*, and *spherical aberration*.

2. Use ray-tracing techniques to construct images formed by spherical mirrors.

3. Predict mathematically the nature, size, and location images formed by spherical mirrors.

4. Determine the *magnification* and/or the *focal length* of spherical mirrors by mathematical and experimental methods.

The eye responds to light. Every object viewed is seen with light—either the light emitted by the object or light that is reflected from it. We now have a general understanding of the nature of light, and in Chap. 25 we studied luminous objects and methods of measuring the light emitted from them.

Although all light can be traced to sources of energy, e.g., the sun, an electric light bulb, or a burning candle, most of what we see in the physical world is a result of reflected light. In this chapter we treat the laws describing how light is turned back into its original medium as a result of striking a surface. Although this phenomenon, called *reflection*, can be interpreted in terms of Maxwell's electromagnetic wave theory, it is much simpler to describe it by tracing *rays*.

The ray treatment, generally referred to as *geometrical optics*, is based on the application of Huygens' principle. Remember that light rays are imaginary lines drawn perpendicular to advancing wavefronts in the direction of light propagation.

When light strikes the boundary between two media, such as air and glass, one or more of three things can happen. As illustrated in Fig. 26-1, some of the light incident on a glass surface is reflected, and some passes into the glass. The light that enters the glass is partially absorbed and partially transmitted. The transmitted light usually undergoes a change in direction, called *refraction*. In this chapter we shall concern ourselves only with the phenomenon of reflection.

Fig. 26-1 When light strikes the boundary between two media, it may be reflected, refracted, or absorbed.

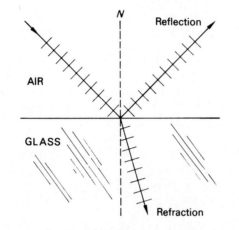

The reflection of light obeys the same general law of mechanics that governs other bouncing phenomena; i.e., the angle of incidence equals the angle of reflection. For example, let us consider the pool table in Fig. 26-2a. In order to hit the black ball on the right, we must aim at a point on the rail such that the incident angle θ_i is equal to the reflected angle θ_r. Similarly, light reflected

Fig. 26-2 Reflection of light follows the same path as that expected for a bouncing billiard ball. The angle of incidence is equal to the angle of reflection.

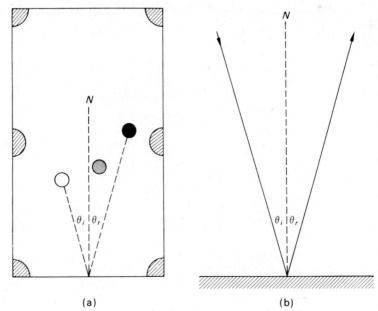

(a)　　　　　　　　　　　(b)

from a smooth surface, as in Fig. 26-2*b*, has equal angles of incidence and reflection. The angles θ_i and θ_r are measured with respect to the normal to the surface. Two basic laws of reflection can be stated:

The angle of incidence is equal to the angle of reflection.

The incident ray, the reflected ray, and the normal to the surface all lie in the same plane.

Light reflection from a smooth surface, in Fig. 26-3*a*, is called *regular* or *specular* reflection. Light striking the surface of a mirror or glass is specularly reflected. If all the incident light which strikes a surface were reflected in this manner, we could not see the surface. We would see only images of other objects. It is *diffuse* reflection (Fig. 26-3*b*) that enables us to see a surface. A rough or irregular surface will spread out and scatter the incident light, resulting in illumination of the surface. Reflection of light from brick, concrete, or newsprint provides examples of diffuse reflection.

Fig. 26-3 (*a*) Specular reflection; (*b*) diffuse reflection.

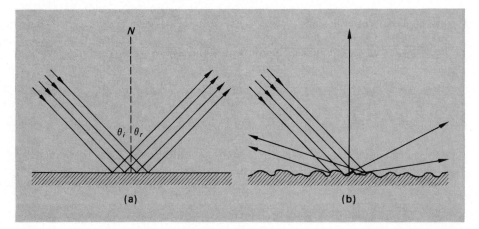

26-2
PLANE
MIRRORS

A highly polished surface which forms images by specular reflection of light is called a *mirror*. The mirrors hanging on the walls of our homes are usually flat, or *plane*, and we all have a certain familiarity with the images formed by plane mirrors. In every case, the image appears to be as far behind the mirror as the actual object is in front of it. As shown in Fig. 26-4, the images also appear

Fig. 26-4 Images formed by mirrors are right–left reversed.

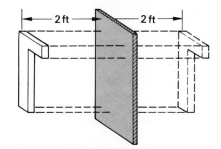

right–left reversed. Anyone who has learned to tie a necktie by looking in a mirror is well aware of these effects.

In order to understand the formation of images by a plane mirror, let us first consider image I formed by rays emitted from a point O in Fig. 26-5. Four light rays are traced from the point source of light. The light ray OV is reflected back on itself at the mirror. Since the reflected light appears to have

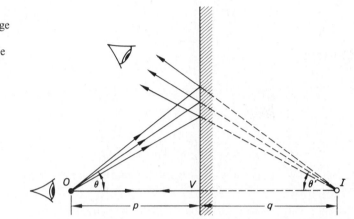

traveled the same distance as the incident light, the image will appear to be an equal distance behind the mirror when viewed along the normal to the reflecting surface. When the reflected light is viewed at an angle to the mirror, the same conclusion results; i.e., the image distance q is equal to the object distance p. This is true because the angle θ is equal to the angle θ' in the figure. Thus we can say that:

The object distance is equal in magnitude to the image distance for a plane mirror.

$$p = q$$

Plane Mirror (26-1)

We now consider the image formed by an extended object, as shown in Fig. 26-6. An extended object may be thought of as consisting of many point objects arranged according to the shape and size of the object. Each point on the object will have an image point located an equal distance behind the mirror. It follows that the image will have the same size and shape as the object. However, right and left will be reversed, as discussed earlier.

Notice that the images formed by a plane mirror are, in truth, reflections of real objects. The images themselves are not real because no light passes through them. These images which *appear* to the eye to be formed by rays of light but which in truth do not exist are called *virtual* images. A *real* image is an image formed by actual light rays.

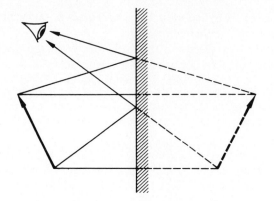

Fig. 26-6 Image of an extended object.

A **virtual image** is one which seems to be formed by light coming from the image, but no light rays actually pass through it.

A **real image** is formed by actual light rays which pass through it. Real images can be projected on a screen.

Since virtual images are not formed by real light rays, they cannot be projected on a screen.

Real images cannot be formed by a plane mirror because the light reflected at a plane surface diverges. But if a plane mirror forms virtual images which do not physically exist, how can we see them? The full answer to this question must wait for a discussion of refraction and lenses. A preliminary answer is illustrated by Fig. 26-7, which also serves to demonstrate the two types of images. The eye makes use of the principle of refraction to reconverge the reflected light which *seems* to come from the virtual image. A *real* image is therefore projected on the retina of the eye. This image, which is formed by real, reflected light rays, is interpreted by the brain to have originated from a point behind the mirror. The brain is conditioned to the rectilinear propagation of light. It is fooled when light is somehow caused to change directions. Men who do not believe the brain can be conditioned to interpret images should try to tie

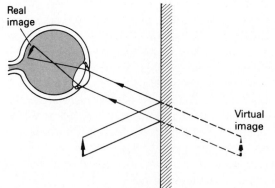

Fig. 26-7 Image formed by a plane mirror is virtual. Such images appear to the eye to be located behind the mirror.

Real image

Virtual image

someone's necktie without looking in a mirror. In this case, the real object seems less natural than its virtual image.

26-3 SPHERICAL MIRRORS

The same geometrical methods applied for the reflection of light from a plane mirror can be used for a curved mirror. The angle of incidence is still equal to the angle of reflection, but the normal to the surface changes at every point along the surface. A complicated relation between the object and its image results.

Most curved mirrors used in practical application are spherical. A *spherical mirror* is a mirror which may be thought of as a portion of a reflecting sphere. The two kinds of spherical mirrors are illustrated in Fig. 26-8. If the

Fig. 26-8 Definition of terms in spherical mirrors.

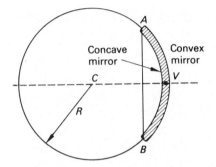

inside of the spherical surface is the reflecting surface, the mirror is said to be *concave*. If the outside portion is the reflecting surface, the mirror is *convex*. In either case, R is the radius of curvature, and C is the *center of curvature* for the mirrors. The segment AB, often useful in optical problems, is called the *linear aperture* of the mirror. The dashed line CV which passes through the center of curvature and the topographical center, or *vertex*, of the mirror is known as the *axis* of the mirror.

Let us now examine the reflection of light from a spherical surface. As a simple case, suppose a beam of parallel light rays to be incident on a concave surface, as shown in Fig. 26-9. Since the mirror is perpendicular to the axis at its vertex V, a light ray CV is reflected back on itself. In fact, any light ray which proceeds along a radius of the mirror will be reflected back along itself. The parallel light ray MN is reflected so that the angle of incidence θ_i is equal to the angle of reflection θ_r. Both angles are measured with respect to the radius CN. The geometry of the reflection is such that the reflected ray passes through a point F on the axis halfway between the center of curvature C and the vertex V. The point F, to which parallel light rays converge, is called the *focal point* of the mirror. The distance from F to V is called the *focal length f*. It is left as an exercise to show from Fig. 26-9a that

$$f = \frac{R}{2} \qquad (26\text{-}2)$$

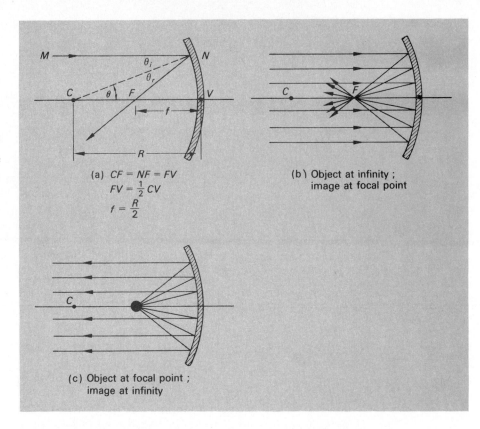

Fig. 26-9 Focal point of a concave mirror. (a) The focal length is one-half the radius of curvature. (b) The object at infinity; the image at the focal point. (c) The object at the focal point; the image at infinity.

(a) $CF = NF = FV$

$FV = \frac{1}{2}CV$

$f = \frac{R}{2}$

(b) Object at infinity; image at focal point

(c) Object at focal point; image at infinity

The focal length f of a concave mirror is one-half of its radius of curvature R.

All light rays from a distant object, such as the sun, will converge at the focal point F, as shown in Fig. 26-9b. For this reason, concave mirrors are frequently called *converging mirrors*. The focal point can be found experimentally by converging sunlight to a point on a piece of paper. The point along the axis of the mirror where the image formed on the paper is brightest will correspond to the focal point of the mirror.

Since light rays are reversible, a source of light placed at the focal point of a converging mirror will form its image at infinity. In other words, the emerging light beam will be parallel to the axis of the mirror, as shown in Fig. 26-9c.

A similar discussion holds for a convex mirror, as illustrated in Fig. 26-10. Note that a parallel light beam incident on a convex surface diverges. The reflected light rays *appear* to come from a point F located behind the mirror, but no light rays actually pass through it. Even though the focal point is virtual, the distance VF is still called the focal length of the convex mirror. Since the actual light rays diverge when striking such a surface, a convex mirror

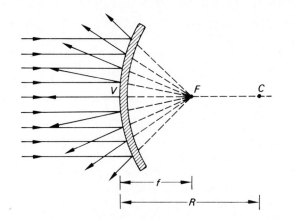

Fig. 26-10 Focal point of a convex mirror.

is called a *diverging mirror*. Equation (26-2) also applies for a convex mirror. However, in order to be consistent with theory to be developed later, the focal length f and the radius R must be reckoned as negative for diverging mirrors.

26-4 IMAGES FORMED BY SPHERICAL MIRRORS

The best method for understanding the formation of images by mirrors is through geometrical optics, or *ray tracing*. This method consists of considering the reflection of a few rays diverging from some point of an object O which is *not* on the mirror axis. The point at which all these reflected rays will intersect determines the image location. We shall discuss three rays whose path can easily be traced. Each ray is illustrated for a converging (concave) mirror in Fig. 26-11 and for a diverging (convex) mirror in Fig. 26-12.

Fig. 26-11 Principal rays for constructing images formed by concave mirrors.

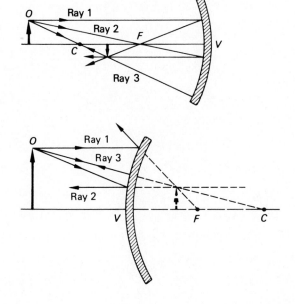

Fig. 26-12 Principal rays for constructing images formed by convex mirrors.

Ray 1 A ray parallel to the mirror axis passes through the focal point of a concave mirror or seems to come from the focal point of a convex mirror.

Ray 2 A ray which passes through the focal point of a concave mirror or proceeds toward the focal point of a convex mirror is reflected parallel to the mirror axis.

Ray 3 A ray which proceeds along a radius of the mirror is reflected back along its original path.

In any given situation, only two of these rays are necessary to locate the image of a point. By choosing rays from an extreme point of the object, the remainder of the image can usually be filled in by symmetry. In the figures, dashed lines are used to identify virtual rays and virtual images.

To illustrate the graphical method and at the same time to visualize some of the possible images, let us consider several images formed by a concave mirror. Figure 26-13a illustrates the image formed by an object *O* which is

Fig. 26-13 Images formed by a converging mirror for the following object distances: (*a*) beyond the center of curvature *C*; (*b*) at *C*; (*c*) between *C* and the focal length *F*; (*d*) at *F*; and (*e*) inside *F*.

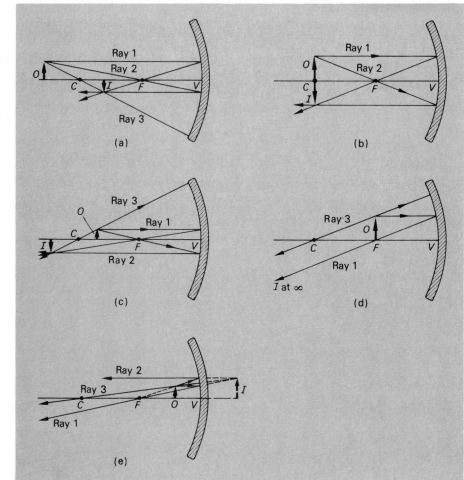

located outside the center of curvature of the mirror. Note that the image is between the focal point F and the center of curvature C. The image is *real*, *inverted*, and *smaller* than the object.

In Fig. 26-13b the object O is located at the center of curvature C. The concave mirror forms an image at the center of curvature which is *real*, *inverted*, and the *same size* as the object.

In Fig. 26-13c the object O is located between C and F. Ray tracing shows that the image is located beyond the center of curvature. It is *real*, *inverted*, and *larger* than the object.

When the object is at the focal point F, all reflected rays are parallel (see Fig. 26-13d). Since the reflected rays will never intersect when extended in either direction, no image will be formed. (Some prefer to say that the image distance is infinite.)

When the object is located inside the focal point F, as shown in Fig. 26-13e, the image *appears* to be behind the mirror. This can be seen by extending the reflected rays to a point behind the mirror. Thus the image is *virtual*. Notice also that the image is *enlarged* and erect (right side up). The magnification in this instance is the principle behind shaving mirrors and other mirrors which form enlarged virtual images.

On the other hand, all images formed by *convex* mirrors have the same characteristics. As was illustrated in Fig. 26-12, such images are *virtual*, *erect*, and *reduced in size*. This results in a wider field of view and accounts for many of the uses of convex mirrors. Automobile rear-view mirrors are usually convex to give maximum viewing capability. Some stores have large convex mirrors conveniently located to give them a panoramic view to help detect shoplifters.

26-5 THE MIRROR EQUATION

Now that we have a feel for the characteristics and formation of images, it will be useful to develop an analytical approach to image formation. Consider the reflection of light from a point object O, as illustrated in Fig. 26-14 for a concave mirror. The ray OV is incident along the axis of the mirror and is

Fig. 26-14 Converging mirror forms a point image of a point object.

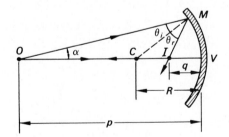

reflected back on itself. Ray OM is selected arbitrarily and proceeds toward the mirror at an angle α with the axis of the mirror. This ray is incident at an angle θ_i and reflected at an equal angle θ_r. The light rays reflected at M and V cross at the point I, forming an image of the object. The object distance p and image distance q are measured from the vertex of the mirror and indicated in the figure. The image at I is a *real* image since it is formed by actual light rays which pass through it.

Now, let us consider the image formed by an extended object OA, as shown in Fig. 26-15. The image of the point O is found to be I, as before. By tracing rays from the top of the arrow, we are able to draw the image of A at B. The ray AM passes through the center of curvature and is reflected back on itself. A ray AV which strikes the vertex of the mirror forms equal angles θ_i and θ_r. Rays VB and AM cross at B, forming an image of the top of the arrow at that point. The rest of the image IB can be constructed by tracing similar rays for corresponding points on the object OA. Notice that the image is *real* and *inverted*.

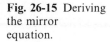

Fig. 26-15 Deriving the mirror equation.

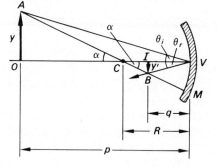

The following quantities are identified in Fig. 26-15.

$$\text{Object distance} = OV = p$$

$$\text{Image distance} = IV = q$$

$$\text{Radius of curvature} = CV = R$$

$$\text{Object size} = OA = y$$

$$\text{Image size} = IB = y'$$

We now attempt to relate these quantities. From the figure, it is noted that angles OCA and VCM are equal. Labeling this angle by α, we can write

$$\tan \alpha = \frac{y}{p - R} = \frac{-y'}{R - q}$$

from which

$$\frac{-y'}{y} = \frac{R - q}{p - R} \tag{26-3}$$

The image size y' is negative because it is inverted in the figure. Similarly, angles θ_i and θ_r in the figure are equal, so that

$$\tan \theta_i = \tan \theta_r, \qquad \frac{y}{p} = \frac{-y'}{q} \tag{26-4}$$

Combining Eqs. (26-3) and (26-4), we have

$$\frac{-y'}{y} = \frac{q}{p} = \frac{R-q}{p-R} \qquad (26\text{-}5)$$

Rearranging terms, we obtain the important relation

$$\boxed{\frac{1}{p} + \frac{1}{q} = \frac{2}{R}} \qquad (26\text{-}6)$$

This relationship is known as the *mirror equation*. It is more often written in terms of the focal length f of the mirror, instead of the radius of curvature. Recalling that $f = R/2$, we can rewrite Eq. (26-6) as

$$\boxed{\frac{1}{p} + \frac{1}{q} = \frac{1}{f}} \qquad (26\text{-}7)$$

A similar derivation can be made for a convex mirror, and the same equations apply if the proper sign convention is adopted. Object and image distances, p and q, must be considered *positive* for real objects and images and *negative* for virtual objects and images. The radius of curvature R and focal length f must be considered *positive* for converging (concave) mirrors and *negative* for diverging (convex) mirrors.

EXAMPLE 26-1   What is the focal length of a converging mirror whose radius of curvature is 20 cm? What are the nature and location of an image formed by the mirror if an object is placed 15 cm from the vertex of the mirror?

Solution   The focal length is one-half of the radius of curvature, and the radius is positive for a converging mirror.

$$f = \frac{R}{2} = \frac{+20 \text{ cm}}{2} = +10 \text{ cm}$$

The location of the image is found from the mirror equation.

$$\frac{1}{p} + \frac{1}{q} = \frac{1}{f}$$

Solving explicitly for q yields

$$q = \frac{pf}{p-f}$$

from which

$$q = \frac{(15 \text{ cm})(10 \text{ cm})}{15 \text{ cm} - 10 \text{ cm}} = +30 \text{ cm}$$

Therefore, the image is real and located 30 cm from the mirror. Ray tracing similar to that of Fig. 26-13c shows that the image will also be inverted.

It is usually easier to solve the mirror equation explicitly for the unknown quantity than to substitute directly. The student will find the following forms useful in most mirror problems:

$$p = \frac{qf}{q-f} \qquad q = \frac{pf}{p-f} \qquad f = \frac{pq}{p+q} \qquad (26\text{-}7)$$

The sign convention is summarized below:

1. The object distance p is positive for real objects and negative for virtual objects.
2. The image distance q is positive for real images and negative for virtual images.
3. The radius of curvature R and focal length f are positive for converging mirrors and negative for diverging mirrors.

This convention applies only to the *numerical* values substituted into Eq. (26-7). The quantities q, p, and f should maintain their signs unchanged until the substitution is made.

EXAMPLE 26-2   Find the position of the image if an object is located 4 cm from a convex mirror whose focal length is 6 cm.

Solution   In this case, $p = 4$ cm and $f = -6$ cm. The minus sign is necessary because a convex mirror is a diverging mirror.

$$q = \frac{pf}{p-f} = \frac{(4 \text{ cm})(-6 \text{ cm})}{4 \text{ cm} - (-6 \text{ cm})}$$

$$= \frac{-24 \text{ cm}^2}{4 \text{ cm} + 6 \text{ cm}} = -2.4 \text{ cm}$$

The image distance is negative, indicating that the image is virtual.

26-6 MAGNIFI-CATION   The images formed by spherical mirrors may be larger, smaller, or equal in size to the objects. The ratio of the image size to the object size is the *magnification* M of the mirror.

$$\text{Magnification} = \frac{\text{image size}}{\text{object size}} = \frac{y'}{y} \qquad (26\text{-}8)$$

The *size* refers to any linear dimension, e.g., height or width. Referring to Eq. (26-5) and to Fig. 26-15, we obtain the useful relation

$$\boxed{M = \frac{y'}{y} = \frac{-q}{p}} \qquad (26\text{-}9)$$

where q is the image distance and p is the object distance. A convenient feature of Eq. (26-9) is that *an inverted image will always have a negative magnification, and an erect image will have a positive magnification.*

EXAMPLE 26-3 A source of light 6 cm high is located 60 cm from a concave mirror whose focal length is 20 cm. Find the position, nature, and size of the image.

Solution We first find the image distance q, as follows:

$$q = \frac{pf}{p-f} = \frac{(60 \text{ cm})(20 \text{ cm})}{60 \text{ cm} - 20 \text{ cm}}$$

$$= \frac{1200 \text{ cm}^2}{40 \text{ cm}} = 30 \text{ cm}$$

Since q is positive, the image is real. The image size is found from Eq. (26-9).

$$M = \frac{y'}{y} = -\frac{q}{p}$$

$$y' = -\frac{qy}{p} = -\frac{(30 \text{ cm})(6 \text{ cm})}{60 \text{ cm}}$$

$$= -3 \text{ cm}$$

The negative sign indicates that the image is inverted. Note that the magnification is $-\frac{1}{2}$.

EXAMPLE 26-4 How far should a pencil be held from a convex mirror to form an image one-half the size of the pencil? The radius of the mirror is 40 cm.

Solution The focal length of the mirror is

$$f = \frac{R}{2} = \frac{-40 \text{ cm}}{2} = -20 \text{ cm}$$

The minus sign occurs because of the diverging mirror. Such a mirror always forms an erect image, reduced in size. (See Fig. 26-12.) The magnification in this case is $+\frac{1}{2}$. Thus

$$M = -\frac{q}{p} = +\frac{1}{2}$$

$$q = -\frac{p}{2}$$

From the mirror equation, q is also

$$q = \frac{pf}{p-f}$$

Combining the two equations for q, we have

$$\frac{pf}{p-f} = -\frac{p}{2}$$

Dividing by p gives

$$\frac{f}{p-f} = -\frac{1}{2}$$

$$2f = -p + f$$

$$p = -f = -(-20 \text{ cm}) = 20 \text{ cm}$$

Thus when an object is held at a distance equal to the focal length from a convex mirror, the image size is one-half of the object size.

26-7
SPHERICAL
ABERRATION

In practice, spherical mirrors form reasonably sharp images as long as their apertures are small compared with their focal lengths. However, when large mirrors are used, some of the rays from objects strike near the outer edges and are focused to different points on the axis. This focusing defect, illustrated in Fig. 26-16, is known as *spherical aberration*.

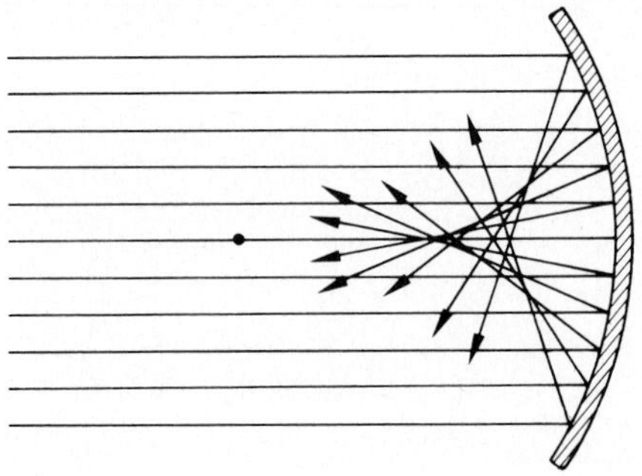

Fig. 26-16 Spherical aberration.

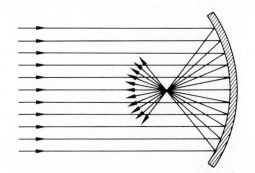

A parabolic mirror does not exhibit this defect. Theoretically, parallel light rays incident on a parabolic reflector will focus at a single point on the mirror axis. (See Fig. 26-17.) A small source of light located at the focal point of a parabolic reflector is the principle used in many spotlights and searchlights. The beam emitted from such a device is parallel to the axis of the reflector.

Fig. 26-17 The optical lever.

SUMMARY

In this chapter we have studied the reflective properties of converging and diverging spherical mirrors. The focal length and radius of curvature of such mirrors determine the nature and size of the images they form. Application of the formulas and ideas given in this chapter are necessary for understanding the operation and use of many technical instruments. The main concepts are summarized below:

- The formation of images by spherical mirrors can be visualized more easily with ray-tracing techniques. The three principal rays are listed below. You should refer to Fig. 26-18a for converging mirrors and to Fig. 26-18b for diverging mirrors.

Fig. 26-18 (*a*) Ray tracing for a converging mirror. (*b*) Ray tracing for a diverging mirror.

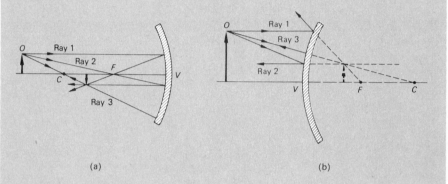

(a)

(b)

Ray 1 A ray parallel to the mirror axis passes through the focal point of a concave mirror or seems to come from the focal point of a convex mirror.

Ray 2 A ray which passes through the focal point of a concave mirror or proceeds toward the focal point of a convex mirror is reflected parallel to the mirror axis.

Ray 3 A ray which proceeds along a radius of the mirror is reflected back along its original path.

- Before listing the mirror equations, you should review what the symbols mean and the sign conventions.

R = radius of curvature   + for converging, − for diverging
f = focal length   + for converging, − for diverging
p = object distance   + for real object, − for virtual
q = image distance   + for real images, − for virtual
y = object size   + if erect, − if inverted
y' = image size   + if erect, − if inverted
M = magnification   + if both erect or both inverted

- The mirror equations can be applied to either converging (concave) or diverging (convex) spherical mirrors:

$$f = \frac{R}{2} \qquad R = 2f \qquad M = \frac{y'}{y} \qquad \frac{1}{p} + \frac{1}{q} = \frac{1}{f}$$

Mirror Equations

- Alternative forms for the last equation are:

$$p = \frac{qf}{q - f} \qquad q = \frac{pf}{p - f} \qquad f = \frac{pq}{p + q}$$

QUESTIONS

26-1. Define the following terms:

a. Plane mirror
b. Spherical mirror
c. Linear aperture
d. Focal length
e. Real image
f. Virtual image
g. Diverging mirror
h. Magnification

i. Specular reflection
j. Diffuse reflection
k. Geometrical optics
l. Radius of curvature
m. Converging mirror
n. Mirror equation
o Spherical aberration
p. Parabolic mirror

26-2. Discuss the statement: One cannot "see" the surface of a perfect mirror.

26-3. Prove by a diagram that rays diverging from a point source of light appear to diverge from a virtual point after reflection from a plane surface.

26-4. Can an image of a real object be projected on a screen by a plane mirror? By a convex mirror? By a concave mirror?

26-5. State the laws of reflection and show how they may be demonstrated in a laboratory.

26-6. Use the mirror equation to show that the image of an infinitely distant object is formed at the focal point of a spherical mirror.

26-7. Use the mirror equation to show that the image of an object placed at the focal point of a concave mirror is located at infinity.

26-8. Use the mirror equation to show that for a plane mirror the image distance is equal in magnitude to the object distance. What is the magnification of a plane mirror?

26-9. In a concave shaving mirror, will greater magnification be achieved when the object is closer to the focal point or when it is closer to the vertex? Use diagrams to verify your conclusion.

26-10. Do objects moving closer to the vertex of a convex mirror form larger or smaller virtual images? Explain with diagrams.

26-11. Without looking at Fig. 26-13 in the text, construct the images formed by a concave mirror when the object is (a) beyond C, (b) at C, (c) between C and F, (d) at F, and (e) between F and V. Discuss the nature and relative size of each image.

26-12. Several small spherical mirrors are lying on a laboratory table. Describe how you would distinguish the diverging mirrors from the converging mirrors without touching them.

26-13. For real objects, is it possible to construct an inverted image by using a diverging mirror? What can you say about the magnification of diverging mirrors?

26-14. You wish to choose a shaving mirror which will give maximum magnification with an erect image. Does the focal length of the mirror play a part in determining its magnification? Explain.

26-15. Two concave spherical mirrors have the same focal length, but one has a larger linear aperture. Which forms the sharper image? Why?

26-16. Show how it is possible for a plane mirror to form a real image if light from the object is first converged by a concave mirror.

PROBLEMS

26-1. A man 1.8 m tall stands 1.2 m from a large plane mirror. **(a)** How tall is his image? **(b)** How far is he from his image? **(c)** What is the shortest mirror length required to enable him to see his entire image?

Ans. **(a)** 1.8 m **(b)** 2.4 m **(c)** 0.9 m.

26-2. A woman 1.68 m tall wants to buy a plane mirror long enough to reflect her full-length image. What should be the length of the mirror? Does it matter what distance she stands from the mirror? Explain, using diagrams.

26-3. A plane mirror moves away from a stationary man at a speed of 30 km/h. How fast does the man's image appear to be moving away from him?

Ans. 60 km/h.

26-4. The *optical lever* is a very sensitive measuring device which utilizes minute rotations of a plane mirror to measure small deflections. The device is illustrated in Fig. 26-19. When the mirror is in position 1, the light ray follows the path IVR_1. If the mirror is rotated through an angle θ to position 2, the ray will follow the path IVR_2. Show that the reflected beam turns through an angle 2θ, which is twice the angle through which the mirror itself turns.

Fig. 26-19 Optical lever.

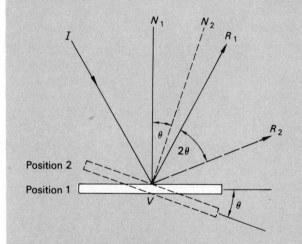

26-5. A light bulb 3 cm high is placed 20 cm in front of a concave mirror with a radius of curvature of 15 cm. Determine the nature, size, and location of the image formed. Sketch the ray-tracing diagram.

Ans. Real, $y' = -1.8$ cm, $q = +12$ cm.

26-6. An object 3 cm tall is placed halfway between the focal point and the center of curvature of a concave spherical mirror. If the radius of the mirror is 30 cm, determine the nature, size, and location of the image formed. Sketch the ray-tracing diagram.

26-7. A 4-cm-high source of light is placed in front of a spherical concave mirror whose radius is 40 cm. Determine the nature, size, and location of the images formed for the following object distances: **(a)** 60 cm, **(b)** 40 cm, **(c)** 30 cm, **(d)** 20 cm, and **(e)** 10 cm.

Ans. **(a)** $q = 30$ cm, $y^1 = -2$ cm, real, inverted, diminished
(b) $q = 40$ cm, $y^1 = -4$ cm, real, inverted, same size
(c) $q = 60$ cm, $y^1 = -8$ cm, real, inverted, enlarged
(d) $q = \infty$, no image formed
(e) $q = -20$ cm, $y^1 = 8$ cm, virtual, erect, enlarged.

26-8. A 60-mm high source of light is placed in front of a spherical concave mirror whose radius is 80 mm. Determine the nature, size, and location of the images formed for the following object distances: **(a)** 100 mm, **(b)** 80 mm, **(c)** 60 mm, **(d)** 40 mm, and **(e)** 20 mm.

26-9. A concave shaving mirror has a focal length of 520 mm. How far away from it should an object be placed for the image to be erect and twice its actual size?

Ans. 260 mm.

26-10. If a magnification of $+3$ is desired, how far should the mirror of Prob. 26-9 be placed from the face?

26-11. An image 60 mm long is formed on a wall located 2.3 m away from a source of light 20 mm high. What must the focal length of a concave mirror be and where should it be placed in order for this to occur?

Ans. $p = 1.15$ m, $f = +862$ mm.

26-12. The diameter of the moon is 3480 km, and it is 3.84×10^5 km from the earth. A telescope on the earth utilizes a spherical concave mirror, whose radius is 8 m, to form an image of the moon. What is the diameter of the image formed? What is the magnification?

26-13. A certain mirror placed 2 m from an object produces an erect image enlarged 3 times. **(a)** Is the mirror a diverging or converging mirror? **(b)** What is the radius of the mirror?

Ans. **(a)** Converging **(b)** $+12$ m.

26-14. The magnification of a mirror is $-\frac{1}{3}$. **(a)** Is it a diverging mirror or a converging mirror? **(b)** Where is the object if its image is formed on a card 540 mm from the vertex of the mirror? **(c)** What is the focal length of the mirror?

26-15. An object is placed 200 mm from the vertex of a convex spherical mirror whose radius is 400 mm. What is the magnification of the mirror?

Ans. $+\frac{1}{2}$.

26-16. A convex mirror has a radius of -60 cm. How far away should an object be held if the image is to be one-third the size of the object?

26-17. An object 6 cm tall is placed in front of a convex mirror of radius -40 cm. Determine the nature, size, and location of the images at object distances of **(a)** 60 cm, **(b)** 40 cm, and **(c)** 20 cm.

Ans. **(a)** $q = -15$ cm, $y^1 = 1.5$ cm, virtual, erect, diminished
(b) $q = -13.3$ cm, $y^1 = 2.0$ cm, virtual, erect, diminished
(c) $q = -10$ cm, $y^1 = 3$ cm, virtual, erect, diminished.

26-18. An object 80 mm tall is placed in front of a convex mirror of radius -600 mm. Determine the nature, size, and location of the images at object distances of **(a)** 1 m, **(b)** 600 mm, and **(c)** 400 mm.

26-19. What should be the radius of curvature of a convex spherical mirror in order to produce an image one-fourth as large as an object 50 cm away?

Ans. -20 cm.

26-20. A convex mirror has a focal length of -500 mm. If an object is placed 400 mm from the vertex, what is the magnification?

26-21. What should the focal length of a shaving mirror be to produce an image twice normal size when a man stands 60 cm in front of it?

Ans. 1.2 m.

26-22. A spherical mirror forms a real image 18 cm from the mirror. The image is twice as large as the object. **(a)** Find the position of the object. **(b)** Find the focal length of the mirror.

26-23. A silver Christmas tree ornament is 4 cm in diameter. Locate the image of a 6-cm object placed 9 cm from the surface of the ornament. What is the magnification?

Ans. $q = 9$ mm, $M = +0.1$.

26-24. A concave mirror of radius 800 mm is placed 600 mm from a plane mirror which faces it. A source of light placed midway between the mirrors is shielded so that light is first reflected from the concave surface. What are the position and magnification of the image formed after reflection from the plane mirror? *Hint:* Treat the image formed by the first mirror as the object for the second mirror.

27 *Refraction*

OBJECTIVES: **After completing this chapter, you should be able to:**

1. **Define the *index of refraction* and state three laws which describe the behavior of refracted light.**

2. **Apply Snell's law to the solution of problems involving the transmission of light in two or more media.**

3. **Determine the change in velocity or wavelength of light as it moves from one medium into another.**

4. **Explain the concepts of *total internal reflection* and the *critical angle* and use these ideas to solve problems similar to those in the text.**

Light travels in straight lines at a constant speed in a uniform medium. If the medium changes, the speed will also change and the light will travel in a straight line along a new path. The bending of a light ray as it passes obliquely from one medium to another is known as *refraction*. The principle of refraction is illustrated in Fig. 27-1 for a light wave entering water from the air. The angle θ_i that the incident beam makes with the normal to the surface is referred to as the *angle of incidence*. The angle θ_r between the refracted beam and the normal is called the *angle of refraction*.

Refraction explains such familiar phenomena as the apparent distortion of objects partially submerged in water. The stick appears to be bent at the surface of the water in Fig. 27-2a, and the fish in Fig. 27-2b appears to be closer to the surface than it really is. In this chapter we study the properties of refractive media and develop equations to predict their effect on incident light rays.

Fig. 27-1 Refraction of a wavefront at the boundary between two media.

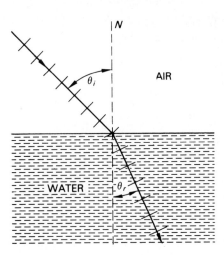

Fig. 27-2 Refraction is responsible for the distortion of images. (*a*) The stick appears to be bent; (*b*) the fish seems to be closer to the surface than it actually is.

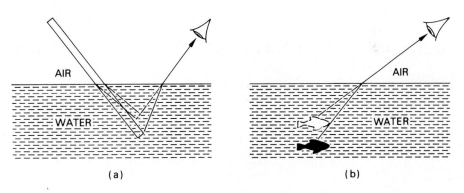

(a)

(b)

27-1 INDEX OF REFRACTION

The velocity of light in a material substance is generally less than the free-space velocity of 3×10^8 m/s. In water the speed of light is almost 2.25×10^8 m/s, which is just about three-fourths of its velocity in air. Light travels about two-thirds as fast in glass, or around 2×10^8 m/s. The ratio of the velocity c of light in a vacuum to the velocity v of light in a particular medium is called the *index of refraction n* for that material.

> The **index of refraction** n of a particular material is the ratio of the free-space velocity of light to the velocity of light through the material.

$$n = \frac{c}{v}$$

Index of Refraction (27-1)

The index of refraction is a unitless quantity, which is generally greater than unity. For water, $n = 1.33$, and for glass, $n = 1.5$. Table 27-1 lists the index of refraction for several common substances. Note that the values given apply for yellow light of wavelength 589 nm. The velocity of light in material substances

Table 27-1 Index of Refraction for Yellow Light of Wavelength 589 nm

Substance	n	Substance	n
Benzene	1.50	Glycerin	1.47
Carbon disulfide	1.63	Ice	1.31
Diamond	2.42	Quartz	1.54
Ethyl alcohol	1.36	Rock salt	1.54
Fluorite	1.43	Water	1.33
Glass		Zircon	1.92
Crown	1.52		
Flint	1.63		

is different for different wavelengths. This effect, known as *dispersion*, will be discussed in a later section. When the wavelength of light is not specified, the index is usually assumed to correspond to that for yellow light.

EXAMPLE 27-1

Compute the velocity of yellow light in a diamond whose refractive index is 2.42.

Solution

Solving for v in Eq. (27-1) gives

$$v = \frac{c}{n} = \frac{3 \times 10^8 \text{ m/s}}{2.42} = 1.24 \times 10^8 \text{ m/s}$$

It is the exceptionally large refractive index which provides one of the most positive tests for the identification of diamonds.

It should be noted from Eq. (27-1) that light travels more slowly through an object of high refractive index. This property is sometimes referred to as the *optical density* of the material.

Optical density is a property of a transparent material which is a measure of the speed of light through the material.

When light passes into a medium of greater optical density, the speed is reduced. When light passes into a medium of smaller optical density, its speed is increased.

27-2
THE
LAWS OF
REFRACTION

Two basic laws of refraction have been known and observed since ancient times. These laws are stated as follows (refer to Fig. 27-3):

The incident ray, the refracted ray, and the normal to the surface all lie in the same plane.

The path of a ray refracted at the interface between two media is exactly reversible.

Fig. 27-3 (*a*) The
incident ray, the
refracted ray, and
the normal to the
surface are in the
same plane.
(*b*) Refracted rays
are reversible.

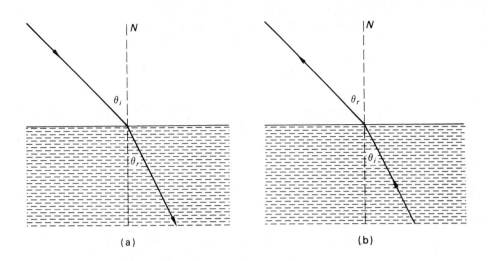

(a)   (b)

These two laws are easily demonstrated by observation and experiment.
However, it is of much more importance, in a practical sense, to understand and
predict the *degree* of bending which occurs.

In order to understand how a change in the velocity of light can alter
its path through a medium, let us consider the mechanical analogy shown in
Fig. 27-4. In Fig. 27-4*a* light incident on the glass plate is first bent toward the

Fig. 27-4 (*a*) The
lateral displacement
of light passing
through glass.
(*b*) A mechanical
analogy.

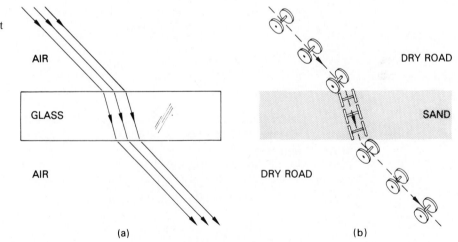

(a)   (b)

normal as it passes through the denser medium, and then it is bent away from
the normal as it returns to the air. In Fig. 27-4*b* the action of wheels encounter-
ing a patch of sand resembles the behavior of light. As they approach the sand,
one wheel strikes first and slows down. The other wheel continues at the same
speed, causing the axle to assume a new angle. When both wheels are in the

sand, the wheels again move in a straight line with uniform speed. The first wheel to enter the sand is also the first to leave, and it speeds up as it leaves the patch of sand. Thus the axle swings around to its original direction. The path of the axle is analogous to the path of a wavefront.

The change in direction of light as it enters another medium can be analyzed with the help of the wavefront diagram in Fig. 27-5. A plane wave in a medium of refractive index n_1 meets at the plane surface of a medium whose index is n_2. The angle of incidence is labeled θ_1, and the refracted angle is

Fig. 27-5 Deriving Snell's law.

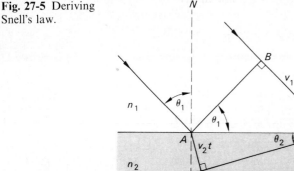
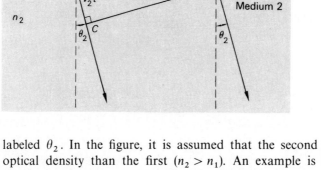

labeled θ_2. In the figure, it is assumed that the second medium has a greater optical density than the first ($n_2 > n_1$). An example is light passing from air ($n_1 = 1$) to water ($n_2 = 1.33$). The line AB represents the wavefront at time $t = 0$ when it just comes into contact with medium 2. The line CD represents the same wavefront after the time t required to enter the second medium completely. Light travels from B to D in medium 1 in the same time t required for light to travel from A to C in medium 2. Assuming the velocity v_2 in the second medium is smaller than the velocity v_1 in the first medium, the distance AC will be shorter than the distance BD. These lengths are given by

$$AC = v_2 t \qquad BD = v_1 t$$

It can be shown from geometry that angle BAD is equal to θ_1 and that angle ADC is equal to θ_2, as indicated in Fig. 27-5. The line AD forms a hypotenuse that is common to the two triangles ADB and ADC. From the figure,

$$\sin \theta_1 = \frac{v_1 t}{AD} \qquad \sin \theta_2 = \frac{v_2 t}{AD}$$

Dividing the first equation by the second, we obtain

$$\frac{\sin \theta_1}{\sin \theta_2} = \frac{v_1}{v_2} \qquad (27\text{-}2)$$

The ratio of the sine of the angle of incidence to the sine of the angle of refraction is equal to the ratio of the velocity of light in the incident medium to the velocity of light in the refracted medium.

This rule was first discovered by the seventeenth-century Dutch astronomer Willebrord Snell and is called *Snell's law* in his honor. An alternative form for the law can be obtained by expressing the velocities v_1 and v_2 in terms of the indexes of refraction for the two media. Recall that

$$v_1 = \frac{c}{n_1} \quad \text{and} \quad v_2 = \frac{c}{n_2}$$

Utilizing these relations in Eq. (27-2), we write

$$n_1 \sin \theta_1 = n_2 \sin \theta_2 \qquad (27\text{-}3)$$

Since the sine of an angle increases as the angle increases, we see that an increase in the index of refraction results in a decrease in the angle and vice versa.

EXAMPLE 27-2   Light passes at an angle of incidence of 35° from water into the air. What is the angle of refraction if the index of refraction for water is 1.33?

Solution   The angle θ_a can be found from Snell's law.

$$n_w \sin \theta_w = n_a \sin \theta_a$$

$$1.33 \sin 35° = 1.0 \sin \theta_a$$

$$\sin \theta_a = 1.33 \sin 35° = 0.763$$

$$\theta_a = 49.7°$$

The index of refraction *decreased* from 1.33 to 1.0, and so the angle *increased.*

EXAMPLE 27-3   A ray of light in water ($n_w = 1.33$) is incident upon a plate of glass ($n_g = 1.5$) at an angle of 40°. What is the angle of refraction into the glass? Refer to Fig. 27-6.

Fig. 27-6

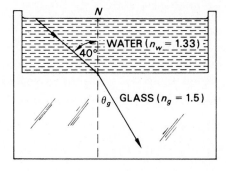

Solution

Applying Snell's law at the interface, we obtain

$$n_w \sin \theta_w = n_g \sin \theta_g$$

$$1.33 \sin 40° = 1.5 \sin \theta_g$$

$$\sin \theta_g = \frac{1.33}{1.5} \sin 40° = 0.57$$

$$\theta_g = 34.7°$$

This time n increased, and so θ decreased.

As an additional exercise, you should show that the ray is reversible.

27-3 WAVE-LENGTH AND REFRACTION

We have seen that light slows down when passing into a medium of greater optical density. What happens to the wavelength of light entering a new medium? In Fig. 27-7, light traveling in air at a velocity c encounters a medium through which it travels at the reduced speed v_m. Upon returning to the air, it again travels at the speed c of light in air. This does not violate the conservation of energy because the energy of a light wave is proportional to its frequency (see Sec. 24-4). The frequency f is the same inside the medium as it is

Fig. 27-7 The wavelength of light is reduced when it enters a denser medium.

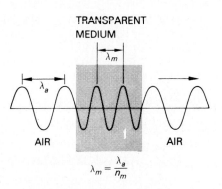

$$\lambda_m = \frac{\lambda_a}{n_m}$$

outside the medium. That this is true will be realized if you consider that the frequency is the number of waves passing any point per unit of time. The same number of waves leaves the medium in a second as enters the medium in a second. Thus the frequency inside the medium cannot change. The velocity is related to the frequency and wavelength by

$$c = f\lambda_a \qquad \text{and} \qquad v_m = f\lambda_m \qquad (27\text{-}4)$$

where c and v_m are the speeds in air and inside the medium and λ_a and λ_m are the respective wavelengths. Since the velocity decreases inside the medium, the wavelength inside the medium must decrease proportionately for the frequency to remain constant. Dividing the first equation by the second in Eq. (27-4) yields

$$\frac{c}{v_m} = \frac{f\lambda_a}{f\lambda_m} = \frac{\lambda_a}{\lambda_m}$$

If we substitute $v_m = c/n_m$, we obtain

$$n_m = \frac{\lambda_a}{\lambda_m}$$

Therefore the wavelength λ_m inside the medium is reduced by

$$\lambda_m = \frac{\lambda_a}{n_m} \tag{27-5}$$

where n_m is the index of refraction of the medium and λ_a is the wavelength of the light in air.

EXAMPLE 27-4   Monochromatic red light of wavelength 640 nm passes from air into a glass plate of refractive index 1.5. What is the wavelength of the light inside the medium?

Solution   Direct substitution into Eq. (27-5) yields

$$\lambda_m = \frac{\lambda_a}{n_m} = \frac{640 \text{ nm}}{1.5} = 427 \text{ nm}$$

As a summary of the relations discussed so far, we can write

$$\boxed{\frac{\sin \theta_1}{\sin \theta_2} = \frac{v_1}{v_2} = \frac{n_2}{n_1} = \frac{\lambda_1}{\lambda_2}} \tag{27-6}$$

where the subscripts 1 and 2 refer to different media. Here we see the relationship between all the important quantities affected by refraction.

**27-4
DISPERSION**

We have already mentioned that the velocity of light in different substances varies with different wavelengths. We defined the index of refraction as the ratio of the free-space velocity c to the velocity inside a medium.

$$n = \frac{c}{v_m}$$

The values given in Table 27-1 are strictly valid for monochromatic yellow light (589 nm). A different wavelength of light, such as blue light or red light, results in a slightly different index of refraction. Red light travels faster through a particular medium than blue light. This can be shown by passing white light through a glass prism, as in Fig. 27-8. Because of the different speeds inside the medium, the beam is *dispersed* into its component colors.

Dispersion is the separation of light into its component wavelengths.

From such an experiment we conclude that white light is actually a mixture of light, consisting of several colors. The projection of a dispersed beam is called a *spectrum*.

Fig. 27-8 Disper-
sion of light by a
prism.

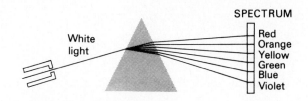

A fascinating phenomenon, known as *total internal reflection*, can occur when light passes obliquely from one medium to a medium with a lower optical density. To understand this phenomenon, consider a source of light submerged in medium 1, as illustrated in Fig. 27-9. Consider the four rays A, B, C, and D, which diverge from the submerged source. Ray A passes into medium 2 normal to the interface. The angle of incidence and the angle of refraction are both zero

Fig. 27-9 Critical angle of incidence.

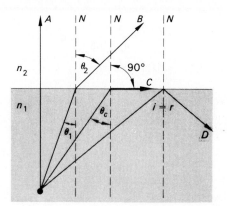

for this special case. Ray B is incident at an angle θ_1 and refracted away from the normal at an angle θ_2. The angle θ_2 is greater than θ_1 because the index of refraction for medium 1 is greater than that for medium 2 ($n_1 > n_2$). As the angle of incidence θ_1 increases, the angle of refraction θ_2 also increases until the refracted ray C emerges tangent to the surface. The angle of incidence θ_c for which this occurs is known as the *critical angle*.

The **critical angle** θ_c is the limiting angle of incidence in a denser medium which results in an angle of refraction of 90°.

A ray approaching the surface at an angle greater than the critical angle is reflected back inside medium 1. The ray D in Fig. 27-9 does not pass into the upper medium at all but is *totally internally reflected* at the interface. This type of reflection follows the same laws as any other reflection; i.e., the angle of incidence is equal to the angle of reflection. Total internal reflection can occur only when light is incident from a denser medium ($n_1 > n_2$).

The critical angle for two given media can be calculated from Snell's law.

$$n_1 \sin \theta_c = n_2 \sin \theta_2$$

where θ_c is the critical angle and $\theta_2 = 90°$. Simplifying, we write

$$n_1 \sin \theta_c = n_2(1)$$

or

$$\boxed{\sin \theta_c = \frac{n_2}{n_1}} \qquad\qquad \textit{Critical Angle} \quad (27\text{-}7)$$

Since $\sin \theta_c$ can never be greater than 1, n_1 must be greater than n_2.

EXAMPLE 27-5

What is the critical angle for a glass-to-air surface if the refractive index of the glass is 1.5?

Solution

Direct substitution yields

$$\sin \theta_c = \frac{n_a}{n_g} = \frac{1.0}{1.5} = 0.667$$

$$\theta_c = 42°$$

The fact that the critical angle for glass is 42° makes it possible to use 45° prisms in many optical instruments. Two such uses are illustrated in Fig. 27-10. In Fig. 27-10a a 90° reflection can be obtained with very little loss of intensity. In Fig. 27-10b a 180° deflection is obtained. In each case, total internal reflection occurs because the angles of incidence are all 45° and therefore greater than the critical angle.

Fig. 27-10 Right-angle prisms make use of the principle of total internal reflection to deviate the path of light.

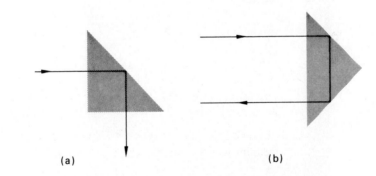

(a)   (b)

**27-6
IS SEEING
THE SAME
AS
BELIEVING?**

Because we are accustomed to light traveling in straight lines, refraction and total internal reflection often present us with pictures we do not believe. Atmospheric refraction accounts for many illusions which are referred to as *mirages*. Figure 27-11 provides two examples of such occurrences. In Fig. 27-11a a layer of hot air in contact with the heated ground is less dense than the cool layers of air above it. Consequently, light from distant objects is refracted upward, making them appear inverted.

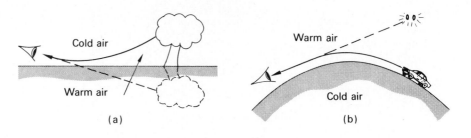

Fig. 27-11 Atmospheric refraction accounts for the mirage in (*a*) and explains the phenomenon of looming in (*b*).

Cold air

Warm air

Warm air

Cold air

(a)

(b)

At night the situation is sometimes reversed; i.e., the cool layer of air is beneath warmer layers. The headlights of the car in Fig. 27-11*b* appear to be *looming* in the air. Many scientists believe that some of the unidentified flying objects (UFOs) reported for centuries can be explained in terms of atmospheric refraction.

Combinations of refraction and total internal reflection account for the bizarre photograph in Fig. 27-12. The picture was taken by an underwater

Fig. 27-12 A photograph taken by an underwater camera presents a bizarre picture of a girl sitting at the edge of a swimming pool. (*From the film Introduction to Optics, Education Development Center.*)

camera looking upward at a girl sitting on the edge of a pool with her legs dangling in the water. An explanation is given in Fig. 27-13. The upper portion of the picture results from refraction at the surface. The inverted legs in the middle of the picture are due to total internal reflection at the surface of the water. The bottom of the picture represents the only undistorted image since the legs are viewed directly and in the same medium.

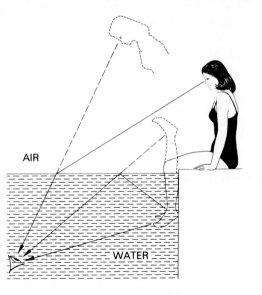

Fig. 27-13 Combinations of refraction and total internal reflection serve to deceive the eye.

AIR

WATER

27-7 APPARENT DEPTH

Refraction causes an object submerged in a liquid of higher index of refraction to appear closer to the surface than it actually is. This shallowing effect is illustrated in Fig. 27-14. The object O appears to be at I because of the refraction of light from the object. The apparent depth is denoted by q, and the actual depth is denoted by p. Snell's law applied at the surface gives

$$\frac{\sin \theta_1}{\sin \theta_2} = \frac{n_2}{n_1} \qquad (27\text{-}8)$$

Fig. 27-14 Relation between apparent depth and actual depth.

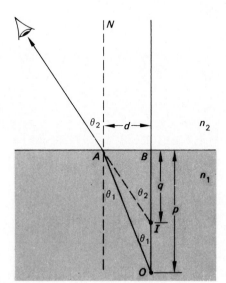

If we can relate the ratio of the indexes of refraction to actual and apparent depths, a useful relation can be obtained for predicting the apparent depths of submerged objects. From Fig. 27-14, it is noted that

$$\angle AOB = \theta_1 \qquad \text{and} \qquad \angle AIB = \theta_2$$

and that

$$\sin \theta_1 = \frac{d}{OA} \qquad \sin \theta_2 = \frac{d}{IA}$$

Using this information in Eq. (27-8), we obtain

$$\frac{\sin \theta_1}{\sin \theta_2} = \frac{d/OA}{d/IA} = \frac{IA}{OA} \tag{27-9}$$

If we restrict ourselves to rays that are nearly vertical, the angles θ_1 and θ_2 will be small, so that the following approximations apply:

$$OA \approx p \qquad \text{and} \qquad IA \approx q$$

Applying these approximations to Eqs. (27-8) and (27-9), we can write

$$\frac{\sin \theta_1}{\sin \theta_2} = \frac{n_2}{n_1} = \frac{q}{p}$$

$$\boxed{\frac{\text{Apparent depth } q}{\text{Actual depth } p} = \frac{n_2}{n_1}} \tag{27-10}$$

EXAMPLE 27-6

A coin rests on the bottom of a container filled with water ($n_w = 1.33$). The apparent distance of the coin from the surface is 9 cm. How deep is the container?

Solution

In this problem, $n_1 = 1.33$ and $n_2 = 1.0$ are the indexes of refraction of water and air, respectively. The actual depth p is found by solving for p in Eq. (27-10).

$$p = \frac{qn_1}{n_2} = \frac{(9 \text{ cm})(1.33)}{1.0} = 12 \text{ cm}$$

The apparent depth is approximately three-fourths of the actual depth.

SUMMARY

Refraction has been defined as the bending of a light ray as it passes obliquely from one medium to another. We have seen that the degree of bending can be predicted based on either the change in velocity or the known index of refraction for each medium. The concepts of refraction, critical angle, dispersion, and internal reflection play important roles in the operation of many instruments. The major concepts covered in this chapter are summarized below:

- The index of refraction of a particular material is the ratio of the free-space velocity of light c to the velocity v of light through the medium.

$$n = \frac{c}{v} \qquad c = 3 \times 10^8 \text{ m/s} \qquad \textit{Index of Refraction}$$

- When light enters from medium 1 and is refracted into medium 2, Snell's law can be written in the following two forms (see Fig. 27-15):

$$n_1 \sin \theta_1 = n_2 \sin \theta_2 \qquad \frac{v_1}{v_2} = \frac{\sin \theta_1}{\sin \theta_2} \qquad \textit{Snell's Law}$$

Fig. 27-15 Snell's law.

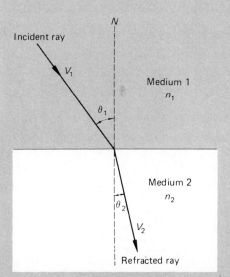

- When light enters medium 2 from medium 1, its wavelength is changed by the fact that the index of refraction is different.

$$\frac{\lambda_1}{\lambda_2} = \frac{n_2}{n_1} \qquad \lambda_2 = \frac{n_1 \lambda_1}{n_2}$$

- The critical angle θ_c is the maximum angle of incidence from one medium which will still produce refraction (at 90°) into a bordering medium. From the definition, we obtain

$$\sin \theta_c = \frac{n_2}{n_1} \qquad \textit{Critical Angle}$$

- Refraction causes an object in one medium to be observed at a different depth when viewed from above in another medium.

$$\frac{\text{Apparent depth } q}{\text{Actual depth } p} = \frac{n_2}{n_1}$$

QUESTIONS

27-1. Define the following terms:
  a. Refraction
  b. Optical density
  c. Snell's law
  d. Dispersion
  e. Index of refraction
  f. Total internal reflection
  g. Critical angle
  h. Apparent depth

27-2. State three laws of refraction and show how they can be demonstrated in the laboratory.

27-3. Is the index of refraction a constant for a particular medium? Explain.

27-4. Explain how the day is lengthened by atmospheric refraction.

27-5. A coin is placed on the bottom of a bucket so that it is just out of sight when viewed at an angle from the top. Show by the use of diagrams why the coin becomes visible if the bucket is filled with water.

27-6. Will objects of higher optical density have greater or smaller critical angles when surrounded by air?

27-7. On the basis of topics discussed in this chapter, explain why a diamond is much more brilliant than a glass replica.

27-8. Explain why right-angle prisms are more efficient reflectors than mirrored surfaces.

27-9. Why are colors observed in the light from a diamond?

27-10. A child stands waist deep in a swimming pool whose depth is uniform throughout. Why does it appear to him that he is standing in the deepest part of the pool?

27-11. The wavelength λ of a certain source of radiation is increased to 2λ. If the index of refraction was originally measured to be 1.5, what will it be when the wavelength is doubled?

27-12. What is the critical angle for an irregular-shaped piece of glass submerged in a liquid of the same index of refraction? Why would the glass be invisible in this case?

PROBLEMS

27-1. The speed of light through a certain medium is measured to be 1.6×10^8 m/s. What is the index of refraction for the medium?

Ans. 1.88.

27-2. If the speed of light is to be reduced by one-third, what must the index of refraction be for the medium through which it travels?

27-3. Compute the speed of light in **(a)** crown glass, **(b)** diamond, **(c)** water, and **(d)** ethyl alcohol.

Ans. **(a)** 1.97×10^8 m/s **(b)** 1.24×10^8 m/s **(c)** 2.26×10^8 m/s **(d)** 2.21×10^8 m/s.

27-4. If light travels at 2.10×10^8 m/s in a transparent medium, what is the index of refraction for that medium?

27-5. Light is incident at an angle of $37°$ from air to flint glass ($n = 1.6$). What is the angle of refraction into the glass? What is the speed in the glass?

Ans. $22°$, 1.88×10^8 m/s.

27-6. A beam of light is incident of the surface of water at an angle of $30°$ with the normal to the surface. What is the angle of refraction into the water?

27-7. Light strikes from medium A into medium B at an angle of $35°$ with the horizontal boundary between the two media. If the angle of refraction is also $35°$, what is the *relative* index of refraction between the two media?

Ans. 1.43.

27-8. Light incident from air at $45°$ is refracted into a transparent medium at an angle of $34°$. What is the index of refraction for the material?

27-9. A beam of light is incident on a plane surface separating two media of indexes 1.6 and 1.4. The angle of incidence is $30°$ in the medium of higher index. What is the angle of refraction?

Ans. 34.8°.

27-10. A ray of light strikes a pane of glass at an angle of incidence of $60°$. If the angle of refraction is $30°$, what is the index of refraction of the glass?

27-11. A light ray originating in air (Fig. 27-16) is incident on water ($n = 1.33$) in a glass ($n = 1.5$) container at an angle of $60°$. The ray continues through the water and glass bottom, emerging into the air again. Compute the angle of emergence.

Ans. 60°.

Fig. 27-16

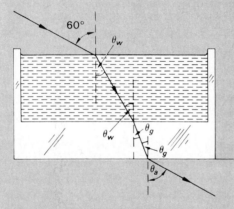

27-12. Prove that, no matter how many parallel layers of different media are traversed by light, the entrance angle and the emergent angle will be equal when the initial and final media are the same.

27-13. What is the critical angle for **(a)** diamond, **(b)** water, and **(c)** ethyl alcohol if the exterior surface is air?

Ans. **(a)** 24.4° **(b)** 48.8° **(c)** 47.3°.

27-14. The critical angle for a certain substance is $38°$ when it is surrounded by air. What is the index of refraction for the substance?

27-15. A right-angle prism like the one shown in Fig. 27-10a is submerged in water. What is the minimum index of refraction for the material in order to achieve total internal reflection?

Ans. 1.88.

27-16. What is the critical angle for flint glass immersed in ethyl alcohol?

27-17. Light passing through a plate of transparent material of thickness t suffers a sidewise displacement d, as shown in Fig. 27-17. Compute the lateral displacement if the light passes through glass surrounded by air. The angle of incidence θ_1 is $40°$, the index of refraction for the glass is 1.5, and the glass is 2 cm thick.

Ans. 5.59 mm.

Fig. 27-17

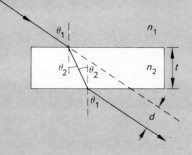

27-18. Prove that the lateral displacement in Fig. 27-17 can be calculated from

$$d = t \sin \theta_1 \left(1 - \frac{n_1 \cos \theta_1}{n_2 \cos \theta_2} \right)$$

Use this relation to verify your answer to Prob. 27-17.

27-19. The water in a swimming pool is 2 m deep. How deep does it appear to a person looking vertically down?

Ans. 1.5 m.

27-20. A plate of glass ($n = 1.5$) is placed over a coin on a table. The coin appears to be 3 cm below the top of the glass plate. What is the thickness of the glass plate?

27-21. The index of refraction of a certain glass is 1.5 for light whose wavelength is 600 nm in air. What is the wavelength of this light as it passes through the glass?

Ans. 400 nm.

28 Lenses and Optical Instruments

OBJECTIVES: After completing this chapter, you should be able to:

1. Determine mathematically or experimentally the focal length of a lens and state whether it is converging or diverging.

2. Apply the lensmaker's equation to solve for unknown parameters related to the construction of lenses.

3. Use ray-tracing techniques to construct images formed by diverging and converging lenses for various object locations.

4. Predict mathematically or determine experimentally the nature, size, and location of images formed by converging and diverging lenses.

A *lens* is a transparent object that alters the shape of a wavefront passing through it. Lenses are usually constructed of glass and shaped so that refracted light will form images similar to those discussed for mirrors. Anyone who has examined objects through a magnifying glass, observed distant objects through a telescope, or experimented in photography knows something of the effects lenses have on light. In this chapter we study the images formed by lenses and discuss their application.

28-1
SIMPLE LENSES

The simplest way of understanding how a lens works is to consider the refraction of light by prisms, as illustrated in Fig. 28-1. When Snell's law is applied to each surface of a prism, it will be seen that light is bent toward the normal when entering a prism and away from the normal on leaving. The effect, in either case, is to cause the light beam to be deviated toward the base of the

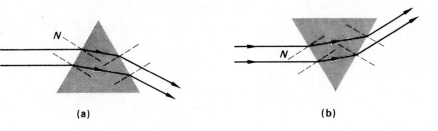

(a)   (b)

prism. The light rays remain parallel because both the entrance and emergent surfaces are planes forming equal angles with all rays passing the prism. Thus a prism merely alters the direction of a wavefront.

Suppose we place two prisms base to base, as shown in Fig. 28-2a. Light incident from the left will converge, but it will not come to a focus. In order to focus the light rays to a point, the extreme rays must be deviated more than the central rays. This is accomplished by grinding the surfaces so that they have a uniformly curved cross section, as indicated in Fig. 28-2b. A lens which

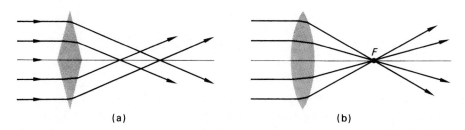

(a)   (b)

Fig. 28-2 (a) Two prisms placed base to base will converge rays but will not bring all rays to a common focus. (b) A converging lens can be constructed by curving the surfaces uniformly.

brings a parallel beam of light to a point focus in this fashion is called a *converging lens.*

> A **converging lens** is one which refracts and converges parallel light to a point focus beyond the lens.

The curved surfaces of lenses may be of any regular shape, such as spherical, cylindrical, or parabolic. Since spherical surfaces are easier to make, most lenses are constructed with two spherical surfaces. The line joining the centers of the two spheres is known as the *axis* of the lens. Three examples of converging lenses are shown in Fig. 28-3, *double convex, plano-convex,* and *converging meniscus.* Note that converging lenses are thicker in the middle than at the edge.

A second type of lens can be constructed by making the edges thicker than the middle, as shown in Fig. 28-4. Parallel light rays passing through such

Fig. 28-3 Examples of converging lenses: (*a*) double convex, (*b*) plano-convex, and (*c*) converging meniscus.

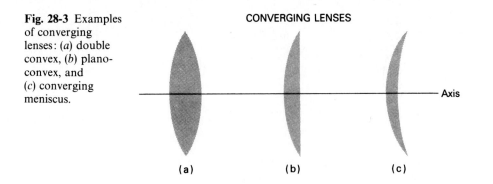

CONVERGING LENSES

Axis

(a)   (b)   (c)

Fig. 28-4 Diverging lens refracts light so that it appears to come from a point in front of the lens.

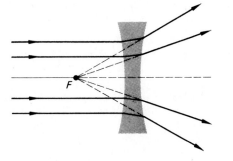

a lens bend toward the thicker part, causing the beam to diverge. Projection of the refracted light rays shows that the light appears to come from a virtual focal point in front of the lens.

A **diverging lens** is one which refracts and diverges parallel light from a point located in front of the lens.

Examples of diverging lenses are *double concave, plano-concave,* and *diverging meniscus.* See Fig. 28-5.

Fig. 28-5 Examples of diverging lenses: (*a*) double concave, (*b*) plano-concave, and (*c*) diverging meniscus.

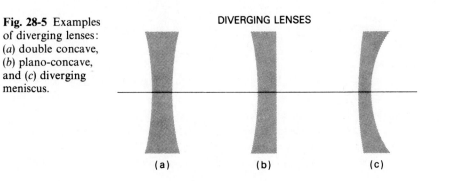

DIVERGING LENSES

(a)   (b)   (c)

28-2
**FOCAL
LENGTH
AND THE
LENS-
MAKER'S
EQUATION**

A lens is regarded as "thin" if the thickness is small in comparison with the other dimensions involved. As with mirrors, image formation by thin lenses is a function of the focal length. However, there are very important differences. One obvious difference is that light may pass *through* a lens in two directions. This results in two focal points for each lens, as shown in Fig. 28-6 for a converging lens and in Fig. 28-7 for a diverging lens. The former has a *real focus F*, and the latter has a *virtual focus F'*. The distance between the optical center of a lens and the focus on either side of the lens is the *focal length f*.

The **focal length** *f* of a lens is reckoned as the distance from the optical center of the lens to either focus.

Fig. 28-6 Demonstrating the focal length of a converging lens. The focal point is real because actual light rays pass through it.

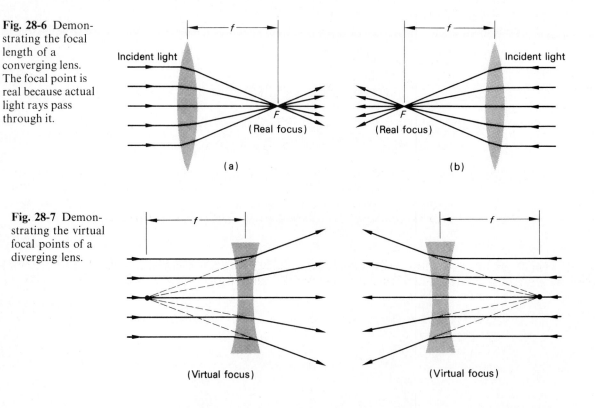

Since light rays are reversible, a source of light placed at either focus of a converging lens results in a parallel light beam. This can be seen by reversing the direction of the rays illustrated in Fig. 28-6.

The focal length *f* of a lens is not equal to one-half the radius of curvature, as for spherical mirrors; it depends on the index of refraction *n* of the material from which it is made. It also is determined by the radii of curvature

R_1 and R_2 of its surfaces, as defined in Fig. 28-8a. For thin lenses, these quantities are related by the equation

$$\frac{1}{f} = (n-1)\left(\frac{1}{R_1} + \frac{1}{R_2}\right)$$ (28-1)

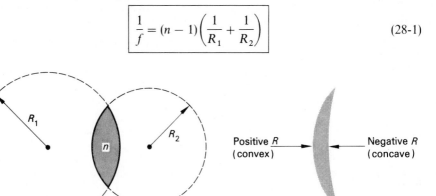

Fig. 28-8 (a) The focal point of a lens is determined by the radii of its surfaces and the index of refraction. (b) The sign convention for the radius of a lens surface.

(a)

Positive R (convex)   Negative R (concave)

(b)

Because Eq. (28-1) involves the construction parameters for a lens, it is referred to as the *lensmaker's equation*. It applies equally to converging and diverging lenses if the following sign convention is followed:

1. The radius of curvature (either R_1 or R_2) is considered positive if the surface is curved outward (convex) and as negative if the surface is curved inward (concave). (Refer to Fig. 28-8b.)
2. The focal length f of a converging lens is considered positive, and the focal length of a diverging lens is considered negative.

EXAMPLE 28-1   A lensmaker plans to construct a plano-concave lens out of glass with an index of refraction of 1.5. What should the radius of its curved surface be if the desired focal length is -30 cm?

Solution   The radius of curvature R_1 for a plane surface is infinity. The radius R_2 of the concave surface is found from Eq. (28-1):

$$\frac{1}{f} = (n-1)\left(\frac{1}{\infty} + \frac{1}{R_2}\right) = (n-1)\frac{1}{R_2}$$

$$R_2 = (n-1)f = (1.5-1.0)(-30 \text{ cm})$$

$$= -15 \text{ cm}$$

By convention, the minus sign shows that the curved surface is concave.

EXAMPLE 28-2   A meniscus lens has a convex surface whose radius of curvature is 10 cm and a concave surface whose radius is -15 cm. If the lens is constructed from glass with an index of refraction of 1.52, what will its focal length be?

Solution   Substitution into the lensmaker's equation yields

$$\frac{1}{f} = (n - 1)\left(\frac{1}{R_1} + \frac{1}{R_2}\right)$$

$$= (1.52 - 1)\left(\frac{1}{10 \text{ cm}} - \frac{1}{15 \text{ cm}}\right)$$

$$= 0.52\left(\frac{3 - 2}{30 \text{ cm}}\right) = \frac{0.52}{30 \text{ cm}}$$

$$f = \frac{30 \text{ cm}}{0.52} = 57.7 \text{ cm}$$

The fact that the focal length is positive indicates that it is a *converging* meniscus lens.

28-3 IMAGE FORMATION BY THIN LENSES

To understand how images are formed by lenses, we now introduce ray-tracing methods similar to those discussed for spherical mirrors. The method consists of tracing two or more rays from a chosen point on the object and using the point of intersection as the image of that point. The entire deviation of a ray passing through a thin lens can be considered to take place at a plane through the center of the lens. In a previous section it was noted that a lens has two focal points. We define the *first focal point* F_1 as the one located on the same side of the lens as the incident light. The *second focal point* F_2 is located on the opposite, or far, side of the lens. With these definitions in mind, there are three principal rays which can easily be traced through a lens. These rays are illustrated in Fig. 28-9 for a converging lens and in Fig. 28-10 for a diverging lens:

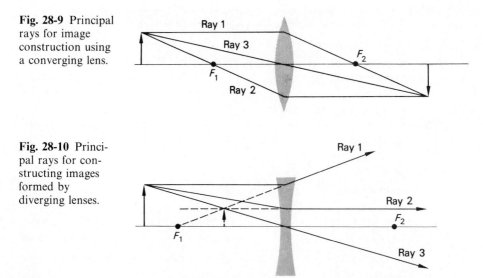

Fig. 28-9 Principal rays for image construction using a converging lens.

Fig. 28-10 Principal rays for constructing images formed by diverging lenses.

Ray 1 A ray parallel to the axis passes through the second focal point F_2 of a converging lens or appears to come from the first focal point F_1 of a diverging lens.

Ray 2 A ray that passes through the first focal point F_1 of a converging lens or proceeds toward the second focal point F_2 of a diverging lens is refracted parallel to the lens axis.

Ray 3 A ray that passes through the geometrical center of a lens will not be deviated.

The intersection of any two of these rays (or their extensions) from an object point represents the image of that point. Since a real image produced by a lens is formed by rays of light which actually pass through the lens, *a real image is always formed on the side of the lens opposite the object. A virtual image will appear to be on the same side of the lens as the object.*

To illustrate the graphical method and, at the same time, to understand the various images formed by lenses, we shall consider several examples. Images formed by a converging lens are shown in Fig. 28-11 for the following object locations:

(*a*) Object located at a distance beyond twice the focal length. A real, inverted, and diminished image is formed between F_2 and $2F_2$ on the opposite side of the lens.

(*b*) Object at a distance equal to twice the focal length. A real, inverted image the same size as the object is located at $2F_2$ on the opposite side of the lens.

(*c*) Object located at a distance between one and two focal lengths from the lens. A real, inverted, and enlarged image is formed beyond $2F_2$ on the opposite side of the lens.

(*d*) Object at the first focal point F_1. No image is formed. The refracted rays are parallel.

(*e*) Object located inside the first focal point. A virtual, erect, and enlarged image is formed on the same side of the lens as the object.

Notice that the images formed by a *convex* lens are similar to those formed by *concave* mirrors. This is true because they both converge light. Since concave lenses diverge light, we would expect them to form images similar to those formed by a diverging mirror (convex mirror). Figure 28-12 demonstrates this similarity.

Images of real objects formed by diverging lenses are always virtual, erect, and diminished in size.

To avoid confusion, one should identify both lenses and mirrors as either *converging* or *diverging*. Diverging lenses are often used to reduce or neutralize the effect of converging lenses.

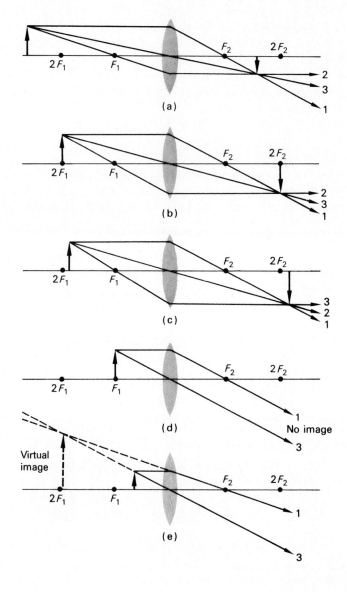

Fig. 28-11 Image construction is shown for the following object distances: (a) beyond $2F_1$; (b) at $2F_1$; (c) between $2F_1$ and F_1; (d) at F_1; and (e) inside F_1.

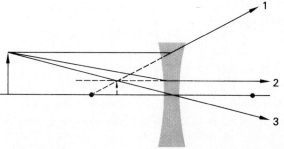

Fig. 28-12 Images formed by diverging lenses are always virtual, erect, and reduced in size.

28-4
THE LENS EQUATION AND MAG-NIFICATION

The characteristics, size, and location of images can also be determined analytically from the *lens equation*. This important relation can be deduced by applying plane geometry to Fig. 28-13. The derivation is similar to the one used to derive the mirror equation, and the final form is exactly the same. The lens equation can be written

$$\frac{1}{p} + \frac{1}{q} = \frac{1}{f}$$

(28-2)

where p = object distance
q = image distance
f = focal length of lens

Fig. 28-13 Deriving the lens equation and the magnification.

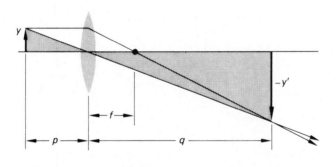

The same sign conventions established for mirrors can be used in the lens equation if converging and diverging lenses are compared with converging and diverging mirrors. This convention is summarized as follows:

1. The object distance p and the image distance q are considered positive for real objects and images and negative for virtual objects and images.
2. The focal length f is considered positive for converging lenses and negative for diverging lenses.

The following alternative forms of the lens equation are useful in solving optical problems:

$$p = \frac{fq}{q-f} \qquad q = \frac{fp}{p-f}$$

$$f = \frac{qp}{p+q}$$

(28-2)

You should verify each of these forms by solving the lens equation explicitly for each parameter in the equation.

The *magnification* of a lens is also derived from Fig. 28-13 and has the same form as discussed for mirrors. Recalling that the magnification M is defined as the ratio of image size y' to the object size y, we can write

$$M = \frac{y'}{y} = -\frac{q}{p} \qquad (28\text{-}3)$$

where q is the image distance and p is the object distance. *A positive magnification indicates that the image is erect whereas a negative magnification occurs only when the image is inverted.*

EXAMPLE 28-3   An object 4 cm high is located 10 cm from a thin converging lens having a focal length of 20 cm. What are the nature, size, and location of the image?

Solution   This situation corresponds to that illustrated in Fig. 28-11e. The image distance is found from Eq. (28-2).

$$q = \frac{pf}{p-f} = \frac{(10 \text{ cm})(20 \text{ cm})}{10 \text{ cm} - 20 \text{ cm}}$$

$$= \frac{200 \text{ cm}^2}{-10 \text{ cm}} = -20 \text{ cm}$$

The minus sign indicates that the image is virtual. The magnification relation [Eq. (28-3)] now allows us to compute the image size.

$$M = \frac{y'}{y} = -\frac{q}{p}$$

$$y' = \frac{-qy}{p} = \frac{-(-20 \text{ cm})(4 \text{ cm})}{10 \text{ cm}}$$

$$= +8 \text{ cm}$$

The positive sign indicates that the image is erect. This example illustrates the principle of a magnifying glass. A converging lens held closer to an object than its focal point produces an erect and enlarged virtual image.

EXAMPLE 28-4   A diverging meniscus lens has a focal length of -16 cm. If the lens is held 10 cm from an object, where is the image located? What is the magnification of the lens?

Solution   Direct substitution yields

$$q = \frac{pf}{p-f} = \frac{(10 \text{ cm})(-16 \text{ cm})}{10 \text{ cm} - (-16 \text{ cm})}$$

$$= \frac{-160}{10 + 16} = -6.15 \text{ cm}$$

The minus sign again indicates that the image is virtual. The magnification is

$$M = -\frac{q}{p} = \frac{-(-6.15 \text{ cm})}{10 \text{ cm}} = +0.615$$

The positive magnification means that the image is erect.

28-5 COMBINATIONS OF LENSES

When light passes through two or more lenses, the combined action can be determined by considering the image that would be formed by the first lens as the object for the second lens, and so on. Consider, for example, the lens arrangement illustrated in Fig. 28-14. Lens 1 forms a real, inverted image I_1 of the object O. By considering this intermediate image as a real object for lens 2, the final image I_2 is seen to be real, erect, and enlarged. The lens equation can be applied successively to the two lenses to determine the location of the final image analytically.

Fig. 28-14 Combinations of lenses.

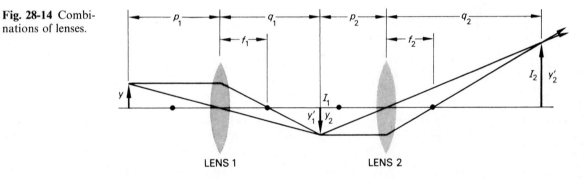

LENS 1   LENS 2

The total magnification produced by a system of lenses is the product of the magnifications produced by each lens in the system. That this is true can be seen from Fig. 28-14. The magnifications in this case are

$$M_1 = \frac{y_1'}{y_1} \qquad M_2 = \frac{y_2'}{y_2}$$

Since $y_1' = y_2$, the product $M_1 M_2$ yields

$$\frac{y_1'}{y_1} \frac{y_2'}{y_2} = \frac{y_2'}{y_1}$$

But y_2'/y_1 is the overall magnification M. In general, we can write

$$\boxed{M = M_1 M_2} \tag{28-4}$$

Applications of the above principles are found for the microscope, the telescope, and other optical instruments.

28-6
THE COMPOUND MICRO-SCOPE

A compound microscope consists of two converging lenses, arranged as shown in Fig. 28-15. The left lens is of short focal length and is called the *objective lens*. This lens has a large magnification and forms a real, inverted image of the object being studied. The image is further enlarged by the *eyepiece*, which forms a virtual final image. The total magnification achieved is the product of the magnifications of the objective lens and the eyepiece.

Fig. 28-15 Microscope.

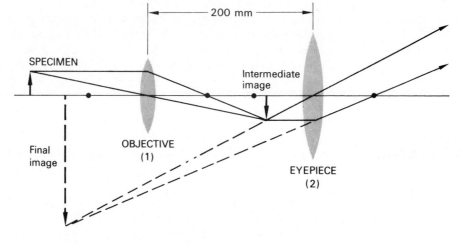

EXAMPLE 28-5

In a compound microscope, the objective lens has a focal length of 8 mm, and the eyepiece has a focal length of 40 mm. The distance between the two lenses is 200 mm, and the final image appears to be at a distance of 250 mm from the eyepiece. (*a*) How far is the object from the objective lens? (*b*) What is the total magnification? (Refer to Fig. 28-15.)

Solution (a)

We begin by labeling the objective lens as 1 and the eyepiece as 2. Since more information is given about parameters that affect the second lens, we shall compute the position of the intermediate image first. From the lens equation, the distance p_2 of this image from the second lens is

$$p_2 = \frac{f_2 q_2}{q_2 - f_2} = \frac{(40 \text{ mm})(-250 \text{ mm})}{-250 \text{ mm} - 40 \text{ mm}}$$

$$= 34.5 \text{ mm}$$

The minus sign was used for the image distance q_2 because it was measured to a virtual image. Now that p_2 is known, we can compute the image distance q_1 for the first image.

$$q_1 = 200 \text{ mm} - 34.5 \text{ mm} = 165.5 \text{ mm}$$

Thus the object distance p_1 must be

$$p_1 = \frac{q_1 f_1}{q_1 - f_1} = \frac{(165.5 \text{ mm})(8 \text{ mm})}{165.5 \text{ mm} - 8 \text{ mm}}$$

$$= 8.41 \text{ mm}$$

Solution (b)   The total magnification is the product of the individual magnifications:

$$M_1 = \frac{-q_1}{p_1} \qquad M_2 = \frac{-q_2}{p_2}$$

Applying Eq. (28-4), we obtain

$$M = M_1 M_2 = \frac{+q_1 q_2}{p_1 p_2}$$

$$= \frac{(165.5 \text{ mm})(-250 \text{ mm})}{(8.41 \text{ mm})(34.5 \text{ mm})} = -143$$

The negative magnification indicates that the final image is inverted. This microscope would be rated $143 \times$, and the object under study should be placed 8.41 mm from the objective lens.

28-7 TELESCOPE

The optical system of a refracting telescope is essentially the same as that of a microscope. Both instruments use an eyepiece, or *ocular*, to enlarge the image produced by an objective lens, but a telescope is used to examine large distant objects and a microscope is used for small nearby objects.

The refracting telescope is illustrated in Fig. 28-16. The objective lens forms a real, inverted, and diminished image of the distant object. As with the microscope, the eyepiece forms an enlarged and virtual final image of the distant object.

Fig. 28-16 Refracting telescope.

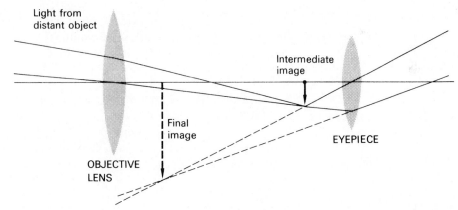

A telescope image is usually smaller than the object being observed. Linear magnification is therefore not a very meaningful way to describe the effectiveness of a given telescope. A better measure would be to compare the size of the final image with the size of the object observed without the telescope. If the image seen by the eye is larger than it would be without the telescope, the effect will be to make the object appear closer to the eye than it actually is.

Spherical lenses often fail to produce perfect images because of defects inherent in their construction. Two of the most common defects are known as *spherical aberration* and *chromatic aberration*. Spherical aberration, as discussed earlier for mirrors, is the inability of a lens to focus all parallel rays to the same point. (See Fig. 28-17.)

> **Spherical aberration** is a lens defect in which the extreme rays are brought to a focus nearer the lens than rays entering near the optical center of the lens.

Fig. 28-17 Spherical aberration.

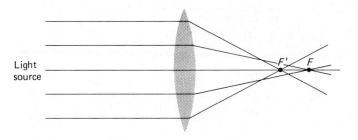

This effect can be minimized by placing a *diaphragm* in front of the lens. The diaphragm blocks off the extreme rays, producing a sharper image along with a reduction in light intensity.

In Chap. 27 we discussed the fact that the index of refraction for a given transparent material varies with the wavelength of the light passing through it. Thus, if white light is incident upon a lens, the rays of the component colors are not focused at the same point. The defect, known as chromatic aberration, is illustrated in Fig. 28-18a, where blue light is shown to focus nearer the lens than red light.

> **Chromatic aberration** is a lens defect which reflects its inability to focus light of different colors to the same point.

The remedy for this defect is the *achromatic lens*, illustrated in Fig. 28-18b. Such a lens can be constructed by combining a converging lens of crown glass

Fig. 28-18 (*a*) Chromatic aberration. (*b*) An achromatic lens.

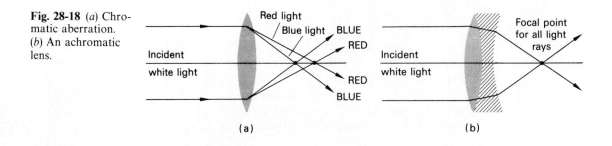

($n = 1.52$) with a diverging lens of flint glass ($n = 1.63$). These lenses are chosen and constructed so that the dispersion of one is equal and opposite to that of the other.

SUMMARY

A lens is a transparent device which converges or diverges light to or from a focal point. Lenses are used extensively in the design of many industrial instruments, and an understanding of how they form images is valuable. A summary of the major concepts discussed in this chapter is provided below:

- Image formation by thin lenses can be understood more easily through ray-tracing techniques as shown in Fig. 28-9 for converging lenses and in Fig. 28-10 for diverging lenses. Remember that the first focal point F_1 is the one on the same side of the lens as the incident light. The second focal point F_2 is on the far side.

    Ray 1 A ray parallel to the axis passes through the second focal point F_2 of a converging lens or appears to come from the first focal point F_1 of a diverging lens.

    Ray 2 A ray that passes through F_1 of a converging lens or proceeds toward F_2 of a diverging lens is refracted parallel to the lens axis.

    Ray 3 A ray which passes through the geometrical center of a lens will not be deviated.

- The *lensmaker's equation* is a relationship between the focal length, the radii of the two lens surfaces, and the index of refraction of the lens material. The meaning of these parameters is seen from Fig. 28-8.

$$\frac{1}{f} = (n - 1)\left(\frac{1}{R_1} + \frac{1}{R_2}\right) \qquad \textit{Lensmaker's Equation}$$

R_1 or R_2 is positive if outside surface is convex, negative if concave.
f is considered positive for converging lens and negative for diverging.

- The equations for object and image locations and for the magnification are the same as for the mirror equations.

$$\frac{1}{p} + \frac{1}{q} = \frac{1}{f} \qquad p = \frac{qf}{q - f} \qquad q = \frac{pf}{p - f} \qquad f = \frac{pq}{p + q}$$

$$\textit{Magnification} = \frac{\textit{image size}}{\textit{object size}} \qquad M = \frac{y'}{y} = \frac{-q}{p}$$

p or q is positive for real and negative for virtual
y or y' is positive if erect and negative if inverted

QUESTIONS

28-1. Define the following terms:

a. Lens
b. Meniscus lens
c. Lens equation
d. Magnification
e. Microscope
f. Objective lens
g. Eyepiece
h. Telescope

i. Converging lens
j. Diverging lens
k. Lensmaker's equation
l. Spherical aberration
m. Chromatic aberration
n. Achromatic lens
o. Diaphragm
p. Virtual focus

28-2. Illustrate by diagrams the effect of a converging lens on a plane wavefront passing through it. What would the effect of a diverging lens be?

28-3. Explain why olives appear to be larger when viewed through their cylindrical glass container. Is the magnification due to the liquid, the glass, or both?

28-4. What happens to the focal length of a converging lens when it is immersed in water? What happens to the focal length of a diverging lens?

28-5. Distinguish between a *real* focus and a *virtual* focus. Which is on the same side of the lens as the incident light?

28-6. Distinguish between the first focal point and the second focal point as defined in the text.

28-7. The focal length of a converging lens is 20 cm. Choose a suitable scale and determine by graphical construction the nature, location, and magnification for the following object distances: **(a)** 15 cm, **(b)** 20 cm, **(c)** 30 cm, **(d)** 40 cm, **(e)** 60 cm, and **(f)** infinity.

28-8. An object is moved from the surface of a lens to the focal point of the lens. Explain what happens to the image if the lens is **(a)** converging; **(b)** diverging.

28-9. Describe what happens to the magnification and location of an image as the object moves from infinity to the surface of **(a)** a converging lens; **(b)** a diverging lens.

28-10. Discuss the similarities and the differences between lenses and mirrors.

28-11. A camera uses a diaphragm to control the amount of light reaching the film. On a bright day, the diaphragm is almost closed, whereas on a dark day it must be opened wide to expose the film properly. Discuss the quality of the images produced in each case if the lens is not corrected for aberrations.

28-12. In a microscope the objective lens has a short focal length, whereas in a telescope the objective lens has a long focal length. Explain the reason for the difference in focal lengths.

28-13. Derive the lens equation with the help of Fig. 28-13.

28-14. Derive the magnification relation [Eq. (28-3)] with the help of Fig. 28-13.

28-15. Describe two methods you might use to determine the focal point of a converging lens experimentally.

28-16. Describe an experiment to determine the focal length of a double-concave lens.

28-17. Without referring to the text, write down the various sign conventions which must be applied when working with thin lenses.

28-18. According to convention, the object distance is considered negative when measured to a *virtual object*. Suggest some examples of virtual objects.

PROBLEMS

28-1. A light source is 600 mm from a converging lens of focal length 180 mm. What are the nature and the location of the image?

Ans. Real, 257 mm.

28-2. A plano-convex lens is held 40 mm from an object? What are the nature and location of the image formed if the focal length is 60 mm?

28-3. A converging thin lens has a focal length of -20 cm. An object is placed 15 cm from the lens. Find the image distance and the nature of the image?

Ans. Virtual, -8.57 cm.

28-4. How far from a source of light must a lens be placed if it is to form an image 800 mm from the lens? The focal length of the lens is 200 mm.

28-5. An object is held 40 mm from a diverging meniscus lens of focal length -240 mm. What are the image distance and what is the magnification?

Ans. $q = -60$ mm, $M = +0.75$.

28-6. What is the magnification of a lens if the focal length is 40 cm and the object distance is 65 cm?

28-7. A magnifying glass is held 40 mm from a specimen. What must the focal length of the lens be in order to produce an erect image twice the size of the specimen?

Ans. $f = +80$ mm.

28-8. How far should the glass of Prob. 28-7 be held from the specimen if the erect image is to be three times as large as the specimen?

28-9. A source of light 36 cm from a lens projects an image on a screen 18 cm from the lens. What is the focal length of the lens? Is it diverging or converging?

Ans. 12 cm, converging.

28-10. An object 450 mm from a converging lens forms a real image 900 mm from the lens. **(a)** What is the focal length of the lens? **(b)** What is the size of the image if the height of the object is 30 mm?

28-11. The focal length of a converging lens is 200 mm. An object 60 mm high is mounted on a movable track so that the distance from the lens can be varied. Calculate the nature, size, and location of the image formed for the following object distances: **(a)** 150 mm, **(b)** 200 mm, **(c)** 300 mm, **(d)** 400 mm, and **(e)** 600 mm.

Ans. **(a)** $q = -600$ mm, $y' = 240$ mm, virtual, erect, enlarged
(b) $q = \infty$, no image formed
(c) $q = 600$ mm, $y' = -120$ mm, real, inverted, enlarged
(d) $q = 400$ mm, $y' = -60$ mm, real, inverted, same size
(e) $q = 300$ mm, $y' = -30$ mm, real, inverted, diminished.

28-12. What are the size and location of an image formed when an object 3 cm high is placed 50 cm from **(a)** a diverging lens of focal length -25 cm and **(b)** a converging lens of focal length 25 cm?

28-13. When parallel light strikes a lens the light diverges, apparently coming from a point 80 mm behind the lens. How far from an object should this lens be held to form an image one-fourth the size of the object?

Ans. $p = 240$ mm.

28-14. What is the minimum film size needed to project the image of a student who is 2 m tall? Assume that the student is located 2.5 m from a camera lens of focal length 55 mm.

28-15. A plano-convex lens is ground from crown glass ($n = 1.52$). What should the radius of the curved surface be if the desired focal length is 400 mm?

Ans. 208 mm.

28-16. The concave surface of a glass lens ($n = 1.5$) has a radius of 200 mm. The convex surface has a radius of 600 mm. What is the focal length? Is it diverging or converging?

28-17. A plastic lens ($n = 1.54$) has a convex surface of radius 250 mm and a concave surface of 700 mm. What is the focal length? Is it diverging or converging?

Ans. 720 mm, converging.

28-18. It is desired to construct a symmetrical, double convex lens out of crown glass ($n = 1.52$). Assume that each surface has the same radius of curvature. What must this radius be if the resulting lens is to have a focal length of 25 cm?

28-19. A camera consists of a converging lens of focal length 50 mm mounted in front of a light-sensitive film as shown in Fig. 28-19. **(a)** When photographing infinite objects, how far should the lens be from the film? **(b)** How far from the film should the lens be to photograph a flower 500 mm from the lens? **(c)** What is the magnification?

Ans. **(a)** $q = 50$ mm **(b)** $q = 55.5$ mm **(c)** $M = -0.111$.

Fig. 28-19 Camera.

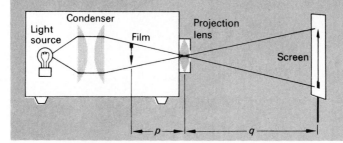

28-20. An object is placed 30 cm from a screen. At what points between the object and the screen can a lens of focal length 5 cm be placed to obtain an image on the screen?

28-21. A simple projector is illustrated in Fig. 28-20. The condenser provides even illumination of the film by the light source. The frame size of regular 8-mm

Fig. 28-20 Projector.

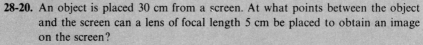

film is 5 by 4 mm. It is desired to project an image 600 by 480 mm on a screen located 6 m from the projection lens. **(a)** What should be the focal length of the projection lens? **(b)** How far should the film be from the lens?

Ans. **(a)** $f = 49.6$ mm **(b)** 50 mm.

28-22. Two thin converging lenses are placed 60 cm apart and have the same axis. The first lens has a focal length of 10 cm, and the second has a focal length of 15 cm. If an object 6 cm high is placed 20 cm in front of the first lens, what are the location and size of the final image? Is it real or virtual?

28-23. A converging lens of focal length 25 cm is placed 50 cm in front of a diverging lens whose focal length is -25 cm. If an object is placed 75 cm in front of the converging lens, what is the location of the final image? What is the total magnification? Is the final image real or virtual?

Ans. $q_2 = -8.33$ cm in front of diverging lens, $M = -0.333$, virtual.

28-24. A telescope has an objective lens of focal length 900 mm and an eyepiece of focal length 50 mm. The telescope is used to examine a rabbit 30 cm high at a distance of 60 m. **(a)** What is the distance between the lenses if the final image is 25 cm in front of the eyepiece? **(b)** What is the apparent height of the rabbit as seen through the telescope?

28-25. The focal length of the eyepiece of a particular microscope is 3 cm, and the focal length of the objective lens is 19 mm. The separation of the two lenses is 26.5 cm, and the final image formed by the eyepiece is at infinity. How far should the objective lens be placed from the specimen being studied?

Ans. $p_1 = 20.7$ mm.

28-26. The Galilean telescope consists of a diverging lens as the eyepiece and a converging lens as the objective. The focal length of the objective is 30 cm, and the focal length of the eyepiece is -2.5 cm. An object 40 m away from the objective has a final image located 25 cm in front of the diverging lens. What is the separation of the lenses? What is the total magnification?

29 Interference, Diffraction, and Polarization

OBJECTIVES: After completing this chapter, you should be able to:

1. Demonstrate by definition and drawings your understanding of the terms *constructive interference*, *destructive interference*, *diffraction*, *polarization*, and *resolving power*.

2. Describe Young's experiment and be able to use the results to predict the location of bright and dark fringes.

3. Discuss the use of a diffraction grating, derive the grating equation, and apply it to the solution of optical problems.

Light is dualistic in nature, sometimes exhibiting the properties of particles and sometimes those of waves. The demonstrative proof of the wave nature of light came with the discovery of interference and diffraction. Then polarization studies showed that, unlike sound waves, light waves are transverse instead of longitudinal.

In this chapter we study these phenomena and their significance in physical optics. We shall find that the neat geometrical-ray approach, which was so helpful in studying mirrors and lenses, must be discarded in favor of a more rigorous wave analysis.

29-1 DIFFRACTION

When light waves pass through an aperture or past the edge of an obstacle, they always bend to some degree into the region not directly exposed to the light source. This phenomenon is called *diffraction*.

Diffraction is the ability of waves to bend around obstacles placed in their path.

To understand this bending of waves, let us consider what happens when water waves strike a narrow opening. A plane-wave generator can be used in a ripple tank, as shown in Fig. 29-1. The vibrating strip of metal serves as a source of waves at one end of a tray of water. The plane waves strike the barrier, spreading out into the region behind the gap. The diffracted waves appear to originate at the gap in accordance with Huygens' wave principle: *each point on a wavefront can be regarded as a new source of secondary waves.*

Fig. 29-1 Schematic diagram illustrating the diffraction of plane water waves through a narrow gap.

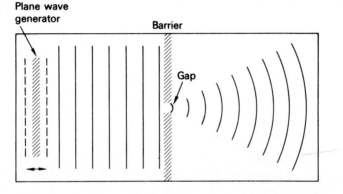

A similar experiment can be performed with light, but for the diffraction to be observable, the slit in the barrier must be very narrow. In fact, diffraction is pronounced only when the dimensions of an opening or an obstacle are comparable to the wavelength of the waves striking it. This explains why diffraction of water waves and sound waves is often observed in nature and the diffraction of light is not.

29-2 YOUNG'S EXPERI-MENT: INTER-FERENCE

The first convincing evidence of diffraction was demonstrated by Thomas Young in 1801. A schematic diagram of Young's apparatus is shown in Fig. 29-2. Light from a monochromatic source falls on a slit A, which acts as a source of secondary waves. Two more slits S_1 and S_2 are parallel to A and equidistant from it. Light from A passes through both S_1 and S_2 and then on to a viewing screen. If light were not diffracted, the viewing screen would be completely dark. Instead, the screen is illuminated, as shown in Fig. 29-3. Even the point B located behind the barrier in direct line with slit A is illuminated. It is easy to see why this experiment caused early physicists to doubt that light consisted of particles traveling in straight lines. The results could be explained only in terms of the wave theory.

The illumination of the screen in alternate bright and dark lines can also be explained in terms of the wave theory. To understand their origin, we recall the *superposition principle*, introduced in Chap. 22 for the study of interference in waves:

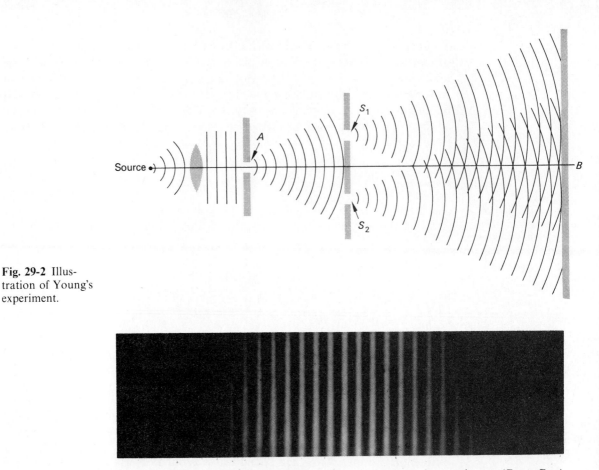

Fig. 29-2 Illustration of Young's experiment.

Fig. 29-3 Photograph of an interference pattern in Young's experiment. (*From F. A. Jenkins and H. E. White, "Fundamentals of Optics," 4th ed., McGraw-Hill Book Company, New York, 1976. Reprinted by permission.*)

> *When two or more waves exist simultaneously in the same medium, the resultant amplitude at any point is the sum of the amplitudes of the composite waves at that point.*

Two waves are said to interfere *constructively* when the amplitude of the resultant wave is greater than the amplitudes of either component wave. *Destructive interference* occurs when the resultant amplitude is smaller.

In Young's experiment, light waves from slit A reach slits S_1 and S_2 at the same time and originate from a single source of one wavelength. Therefore, the secondary wavelets leaving slits S_1 and S_2 are *in phase*. The sources are said to be *coherent*. Figure 29-4 shows how the light and dark bands are produced. The bright bands occur whenever the waves arriving from the two slits interfere constructively. Dark bands occur when destructive interference takes place. At point B in the center of the screen, light travels the same distances p_1 and p_2

Fig. 29-4 Origin of light and dark bands in an interference pattern.

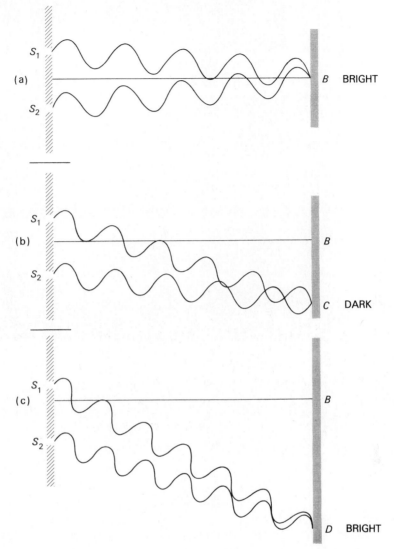

from each slit. The difference in path length $\Delta p = 0$, and constructive interference results in a bright central band. At point C the difference in path lengths Δp causes the waves to interfere destructively. Another bright band occurs at point D when the waves from each slit again reinforce each other. The overall interference pattern is similar to that produced by the water waves in Fig. 29-5.

Let us now consider the theoretical conditions necessary for the production of bright and dark bands. Consider light reaching the point D at a distance y from the central axis AB, as shown in Fig. 29-6. The separation of the two slits is represented by d, and the screen is located at a distance x from

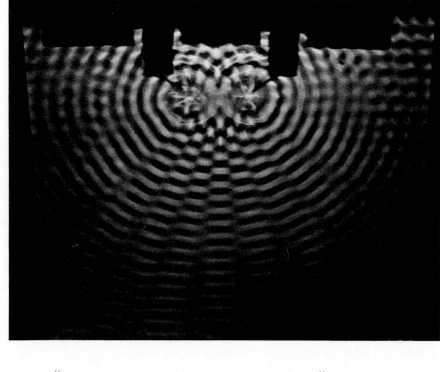

Fig. 29-5 Inter-ference pattern set up in water waves by two coherent sources. (*From "PSSC Physics,"* D. C. Heath and Company, Lexington, Mass., 1965.)

Fig. 29-6 Theoreti-cal interpretation of the double-slit experiment.

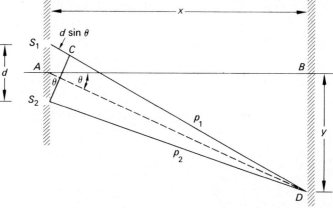

the slits. The point D on the screen makes an angle θ with the axis of the system. The line $S_2 C$ is drawn so that the distances CD and p_2 are equal. As long as the distance x to the screen is much greater than the slit separation d, we may consider that p_1, p_2, and DA are all approximately perpendicular to the line $S_2 C$. Therefore, the angle $S_1 S_2 C$ is equal to the angle θ, and the difference Δp in path lengths of light coming from S_1 and S_2 is given by

$$\Delta p = p_1 - p_2 = d \sin \theta$$

Constructive interference will occur at D when this difference in path length is equal to

$$0, \lambda, 2\lambda, 3\lambda, \ldots, n\lambda$$

where λ is the wavelength of the light. Therefore, the conditions for bright fringes are given by

$$d \sin \theta = n\lambda \qquad n = 0, 1, 2, 3, \ldots \qquad (29\text{-}1)$$

where d is the slit separation and θ is the angle the fringe makes with the axis.

The conditions required for the formation of dark fringes at D will be satisfied when the path difference is

$$\frac{\lambda}{2}, \frac{3\lambda}{2}, \frac{5\lambda}{2}, \ldots$$

Under these conditions, destructive interference will cancel the waves. Thus dark fringes will occur when

$$d \sin \theta = n \frac{\lambda}{2} \qquad n = 1, 3, 5, \ldots \qquad (29\text{-}2)$$

The above equations can be put into a more useful form by expressing them in terms of the measurable distances x and y. For small angles

$$\sin \theta \approx \tan \theta = \frac{y}{x}$$

Substitution of y/x for $\sin \theta$ in Eqs. (29-1) and (29-2) yields

Bright fringes:
$$\frac{yd}{x} = n\lambda \qquad n = 0, 1, 2, \ldots \qquad (29\text{-}3)$$

Dark fringes:
$$\frac{yd}{x} = n \frac{\lambda}{2} \qquad n = 1, 3, 5, \ldots \qquad (29\text{-}4)$$

In experiments designed to measure the wavelength of light, x and d are known initially. The distance y to any particular fringe can be measured and used to determine the wavelength.

EXAMPLE 29-1   In Young's experiment, the two slits are 0.04 mm apart, and the screen is located 2 m away from the slits. The third bright fringe from the center is displaced 8.3 cm from the central fringe. (a) Determine the wavelength of the incident light. (b) Where will the second dark fringe appear?

Solution (a)   For the third bright fringe, $n = 3$ in Eq. (29-3). Thus

$$\frac{yd}{x} = 3\lambda$$

$$\lambda = \frac{yd}{3x} = \frac{(8.3 \times 10^{-2} \text{ m})(4 \times 10^{-5} \text{ m})}{3(2 \text{ m})}$$

$$= 5.53 \times 10^{-7} \text{ m} = 553 \text{ nm}$$

Solution (b)   The displacement of the second dark fringe is found by setting $n = 3$ in Eq. (29-4).

$$\frac{yd}{x} = \frac{3\lambda}{2}$$

$$y = \frac{3\lambda x}{2d} = \frac{(3)(5.53 \times 10^{-7} \text{ m})(2 \text{ m})}{2(4 \times 10^{-5} \text{ m})}$$

$$= 4.15 \times 10^{-2} \text{ m}$$

**29-3
THE DIF-
FRACTION
GRATING**

If many parallel slits similar to those in Young's experiment are regularly spaced and of the same width, a brighter and sharper diffraction pattern can be obtained. Such an arrangement is known as a *diffraction grating*. Gratings are made by ruling thousands of parallel grooves on a glass plate with a diamond point. The grooves act as opaque barriers to light, and the clear spaces form the slits. Most laboratory gratings are ruled from 10,000 to 30,000 lines/in.

A parallel beam of monochromatic light striking a diffraction grating, as shown in Fig. 29-7, is diffracted in a manner similar to that in Young's experiment. Only a few slits are shown in the figure, each separated by a distance d. Each slit acts as a source of secondary Huygens' wavelets, producing an interference pattern. A lens is used to focus the light from the slits on a screen.

Fig. 29-7 The diffraction grating.

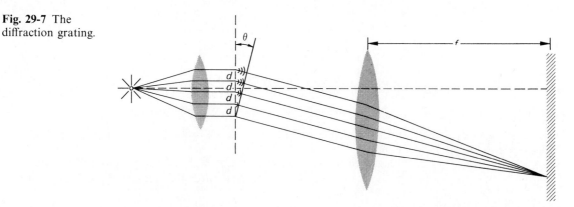

The diffracted rays leave the slits in many directions. In the forward direction, the paths of all rays will be of the same length, setting up a condition for constructive interference. A central bright image of the source is formed on the screen. In certain other directions, the diffracted rays will also be in phase, giving rise to other bright images. One of these directions θ is illustrated in Fig. 29-7. The first bright line formed on either side of the central image is called the *first-order* image. The second bright line on either side of the central maximum is called the *second-order* fringe, and so forth. The condition for the formation of these bright fringes is the same as that derived for Young's experiment. (Refer to Fig. 29-8.) Therefore, we can write the grating equation as

$$d \sin \theta_n = n\lambda \qquad n = 1, 2, 3, \ldots \qquad (29\text{-}5)$$

Fig. 29-8

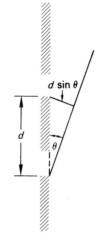

where d = spacing of slits
  λ = wavelength of incident light
  θ_n = deviation angle for nth bright fringe

The first-order bright fringe occurs when $n = 1$. As illustrated in Fig. 29-9a, this image occurs when the paths of diffracted rays from each slit differ by an amount equal to one wavelength. The second-order image occurs when the paths differ by two wavelengths (Fig. 29-9b).

Fig. 29-9

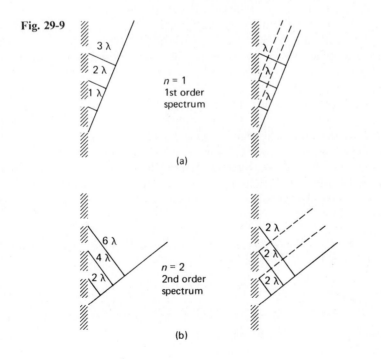

EXAMPLE 29-2   A diffraction grating having 20,000 lines/in. is illuminated by parallel light of wavelength 589 nm. What are the angles at which the first- and second-order bright fringes are formed?

Solution   The slit spacing d that corresponds to 20,000 lines/in. is

$$d = \frac{2.54 \text{ cm/in.}}{20,000 \text{ lines/in.}} = 1.27 \times 10^{-4} \text{ cm}$$

The first-order bright fringe occurs for $n = 1$, and the angle θ_1 is found from Eq. (29-5).

$$\sin \theta_1 = 1 \frac{\lambda}{d} = \frac{5.89 \times 10^{-5} \text{ cm}}{1.27 \times 10^{-4} \text{ cm}} = 0.464$$

$$\theta_1 = 27.6°$$

The second-order fringe occurs when $n = 2$. Thus,

$$\sin \theta_2 = (2)(0.464) = 0.928$$

$$\theta_2 = 68.1°$$

The third-order fringe will not be formed because $\sin \theta_n$ cannot exceed 1.00. (The beam will not be deviated by an angle greater than 90°.)

29-4 RESOLVING POWER OF INSTRUMENTS

We have learned that light passing through a small opening or past an obstacle is diffracted so that the images formed are fuzzy. Interference fringes near the edges of images sometimes make it difficult to determine the exact shape of the source. Figure 29-10 shows the diffraction pattern formed by passing light through a small circular opening. Notice the large central maximum surrounded by dark and bright interference bands. This diffraction is of extreme importance in optical instruments because it sets the ultimate limit on the possible magnification.

To understand this limitation, consider light from the two sources in Fig. 29-11, passing through a small circular opening in an opaque barrier. In Fig. 29-11a the images of the sources A and B are distinguished as separate images. The sources are said to be *resolved*. However, if they are brought closer together, as in Fig. 29-11b, their images overlap, resulting in a confused image. When the sources are so close together (or the opening is so small) that the separate images can no longer be distinguished, the sources are said to be *unresolved*.

The **resolving power** of an instrument is a measure of its ability to produce well-defined separate images.

A useful method of expressing the resolving power of an instrument is in terms of the angle θ subtended at the opening by the objects being resolved. (See Fig. 29-11.) The smallest angle θ_0 for which the images can be distinguished separately is a measure of the resolving power.

Fig. 29-10
Photograph of the interference pattern formed by passing light through a small circular opening. (*Reprinted from Cagnet et al., "Atlas of Optical Phenomena," with permission from Springer-Verlag.*)

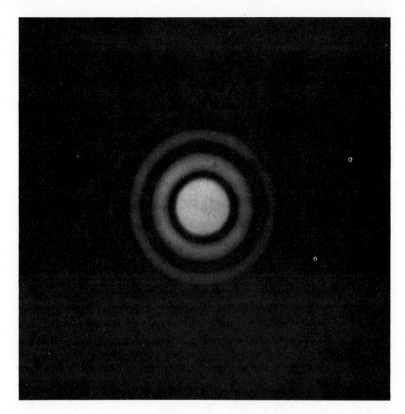

Fig. 29-11 (*a*) The images of the sources *A* and *B* are easily distinguished. (*b*) As the sources are brought closer together, the images overlap, resulting in a confused image.

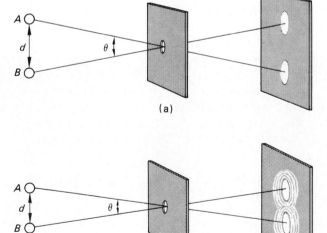

No matter how perfectly a lens is constructed, the image of a point source of light will not be focused at a point. It will appear as only a tiny bright dot with light and dark fringes around it. Resolution improves as the diameter of a lens is increased. It can be shown that for a given lens of diameter D (see Fig. 29-12) the optimum resolution occurs for the angular width θ_0, subtended by the radius of the central image in the diffraction pattern. In a telescope this limiting angle is

$$\theta_0 = \frac{1.22\lambda}{D} \qquad (29\text{-}6)$$

where λ is the wavelength of the light and D is the diameter of the objective lens.

Fig. 29-12 Limit of resolution.

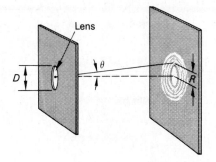

Figure 29-13 illustrates the resolution of two point sources of light. In Fig. 29-13a the two images can still be distinguished; in Fig. 29-13b the images are at the limit of resolution. From the criterion used to obtain Eq. (29-6), two such images are just resolved when the central maximum of one pattern coincides with the first dark fringe of the other pattern.

Fig. 29-13 (a) Separate images formed from two point sources. (b) The images of two sources at the limit of resolution. (*From Cagnet et al., "Atlas of Optical Phenomena," Springer-Verlag. Reprinted by permission.*)

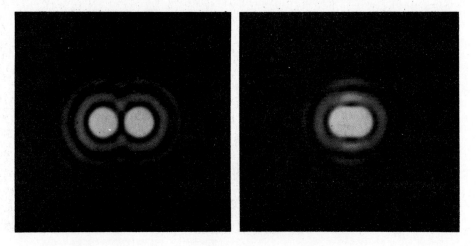

To illustrate the topics we have been discussing in this section, consider a telescope. In Fig. 29-14 two objects are separated by a distance s_0 and are located at a distance p from the objective lens in the telescope. The angle between the objects, in radians, is approximately

$$\theta_0 = \frac{s_0}{p} \qquad (29\text{-}7)$$

Fig. 29-14 Resolution of two distant objects by a spherical lens.

The subscript 0 is used to show that θ_0 and s_0 represent the minimum conditions for resolution. Thus we can rewrite Eq. (29-6) as

$$\boxed{\theta_0 = 1.22 \frac{\lambda}{D} = \frac{s_0}{p}} \qquad (29\text{-}8)$$

Since s_0 represents the minimum separation of objects which can be resolved, this distance is also used to indicate the resolving power of an instrument.

EXAMPLE 29-3   One of the largest refracting telescopes in the world is the 40-in.-diameter instrument at Yerkes Observatory in Wisconsin; its objective lens has a focal length of 19.8 m (65 ft). (a) What is the minimum separation of two features of the moon's surface such that they are just resolved by this telescope? (b) What is the radius of the central maximum in the diffraction pattern set up by the objective lens? (For white light, the central wavelength of 500 nm can be used for computing the resolution. The moon is 3.84×10^5 km from the earth.)

Solution (a)   We must first convert all distances to meters. Thus

$$p = 3.84 \times 10^5 \text{ km} = 3.84 \times 10^8 \text{ m}$$

$$\lambda = 500 \text{ nm} = 5 \times 10^{-7} \text{ m}$$

$$D = 40 \text{ in.}(2.54 \times 10^{-2} \text{ m/in.}) = 1.02 \text{ m}$$

The minimum separation s_0 is found by solving for s_0 in Eq. (29-8).

$$s_0 = 1.22 \frac{\lambda p}{D}$$

$$= \frac{(1.22)(5 \times 10^{-7} \text{ m})(3.84 \times 10^8 \text{ m})}{1.02 \text{ m}} = 230 \text{ m}$$

Solution (b)

From Eq. (29-8), the radius R of the central maximum is

$$R = f\theta_0 = f\,\frac{s_0}{p}$$

$$= \frac{(19.8 \text{ m})(230 \text{ m})}{3.84 \times 10^8 \text{ m}} = 1.19 \times 10^{-5} \text{ m}$$

The 200-in. reflecting telescope at Mt. Palomar in California can distinguish features on the moon 46.3 m (or 152 ft) apart.

29-5 POLARIZATION

All the phoenomena discussed so far can be explained on the basis of either transverse or longitudinal waves. Interference and diffraction occur in sound waves, which are longitudinal, as well as in water waves, which are transverse. More experimental evidence is needed to determine whether light waves are longitudinal or transverse. In this section we introduce a property of light waves that can be interpreted only in terms of transverse waves.

Let us first consider a mechanical example of transverse waves in a vibrating string. If the source of the wave causes each particle of the rope to vibrate up and down in a single plane, the waves are *plane-polarized*. If the rope is vibrated in such a manner that each particle moves in a random manner at all possible angles, the waves are *unpolarized*.

> **Polarization** is the process by which the transverse oscillations of a wave motion are confined to a definite pattern.

As an illustration of the polarization of a transverse wave, consider the rope passing through slotted frames, as shown in Fig. 29-15. The unpolarized vibrations pass through slot *A* and emerge polarized in the vertical plane. This frame is called the *polarizer*. Only waves with vertical vibrations can pass through the slot; all other vibrations will be blocked. The slotted frame *B* is called the *analyzer* because it can be used to test whether the incoming waves are plane-

Fig. 29-15 Mechanical analogy explaining the polarization of a transverse wave.

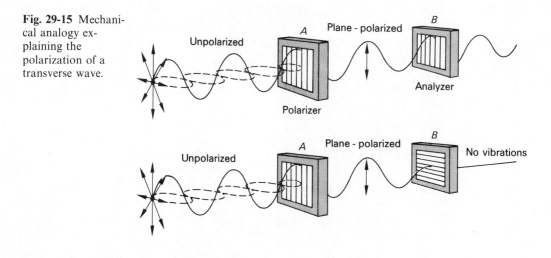

polarized. If the analyzer is rotated so that the slots in *B* are perpendicular to those in *A*, all the incoming waves are stopped. This can happen only if the waves reaching *B* are polarized in a plane perpendicular to the slots in *B*.

Polarization is a characteristic of *transverse* waves. Should the rope in our example be replaced by a spring, as in Fig. 29-16, the longitudinal waves would pass on through the slots, regardless of their orientation.

Fig. 29-16 A longitudinal wave cannot be polarized.

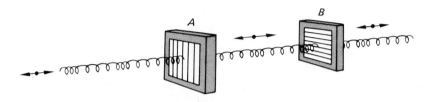

Now, let us consider light waves. In Chap. 24 we discussed the electromagnetic nature of light waves. Recall that such a wave consists of an oscillating electric field and an oscillating magnetic field perpendicular to each other and to the direction of propagation. Therefore, light waves consist of *oscillating fields* rather than of vibrating particles, as was the case for the waves in a rope. If it can be shown that these oscillations can be polarized, we can state conclusively that the oscillations are transverse.

A number of substances exhibit different indexes of refraction for light with different planes of polarization relative to their crystalline structure. Some examples are calcite, quartz, and tourmaline. Plates can be constructed from these materials that transmit light in only a single plane of oscillation. Thus they can be used as polarizers for incident light whose oscillations are randomly oriented. Analogous to the vibrating rope passing through slots, two polarizing plates can be used to determine the transverse nature of light waves.

As shown in Fig. 29-17, light emitted by most sources is unpolarized. Upon passing through a tourmaline plate (the polarizer), the light beam emerges plane-polarized but with reduced intensity. Another plate serves as the analyzer. As this plate is rotated with respect to the polarizer, the intensity of the light passing through the system is gradually reduced until relatively no light is transmitted. It is therefore demonstrated that light waves are transverse rather than longitudinal.

Polarization has demonstrated the transverse nature of light in laboratories for many years, but, the useful applications of the principle were not realized until the development of *Polaroid* sheets. These sheets are constructed by sandwiching a thin layer of iodosulfate crystals between two sheets of plastic. The crystals are aligned by a strong electric field. Two such sheets can be used to control the intensity of light. Photographers use Polaroid filters to vary the intensity and to reduce the glare from reflected light. Complex engineering studies can be made by examining stress patterns in certain plastic tool models. The light and dark fringes set up by polarized light give an indication of the areas of varying stress.

Fig. 29-17 (*a*) Proof that light can be polarized. (*b*) The reduction of transmitted light intensity as the analyzer is rotated from 0 to 90°.

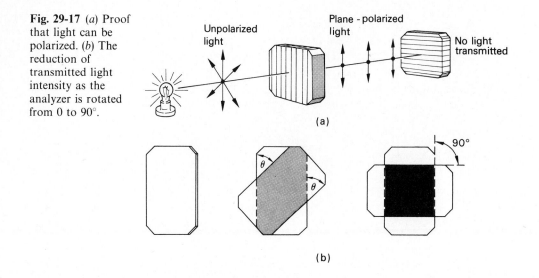

Unpolarized light

Plane - polarized light

No light transmitted

(a)

90°

θ

θ

(b)

SUMMARY

In this chapter we have discussed several ways in which light behaves as a wave. The bending of light around obstacles placed in its path is called diffraction. A combination of diffraction and interference of light waves led to Young's experiment and to the diffraction grating. Modern industrial instruments use these concepts for a variety of applications. The major ideas presented in this chapter are summarized below:

- In Young's experiment interference and diffraction account for the production of bright and dark fringes. The location of these fringes is given by the following equations (see Fig. 29-6):

$$\text{Bright fringes:} \quad \frac{yd}{x} = n\lambda \qquad n = 0, 1, 2, 3, \ldots$$

$$\text{Dark fringes:} \quad \frac{yd}{x} = n\frac{\lambda}{2} \qquad n = 1, 3, 5, 7, \ldots$$

- In a diffraction grating of slit separation d, the wavelengths of the nth order fringes are given by

$$\boxed{d \sin \theta_n = n\lambda} \qquad \boxed{n = 1, 2, 3, \ldots}$$

- The resolving power of an instrument is a measure of its ability to produce well-defined separate images. The minimum conditions for resolution are illustrated in Fig. 29-14. For this situation the resolution equation is

$$\boxed{\theta_0 = 1.22\frac{\lambda}{D} = \frac{s_0}{p}} \qquad \textit{Resolving Power}$$

QUESTIONS

29-1. Define the following terms:
- **a.** Diffraction
- **b.** Interference
- **c.** Coherent
- **d.** Resolving power
- **e.** Resolution
- **f.** Polarization
- **g.** Polarizer
- **h.** Analyzer
- **i.** Young's experiment
- **j.** Huygens' principle
- **k.** Superposition principle
- **l.** Interference fringes
- **m.** Diffraction grating
- **n.** Order of an image
- **o.** Plane-polarized
- **p.** Polaroid sheets

29-2. Radio waves and light waves are both electromagnetic radiations. Explain why radio waves can be received behind tall buildings whereas light cannot reach these areas.

29-3. Consider plane water waves striking a gap in a barrier, as in Fig. 29-1. Explain how the diffraction varies as **(a)** the slit width is decreased and **(b)** the wavelength of incoming waves is reduced.

29-4. Which effects in Young's experiment are due to diffraction and which are due to interference?

29-5. In a diffraction grating, how does the spacing of the lines affect the separation of the fringes in the interference pattern?

29-6. If white light were incident upon a diffraction grating, instead of monochromatic light, what would the resulting interference pattern look like?

29-7. In Young's experiment, what effect will reducing the wavelength of incident light have on the interference pattern?

29-8. What effect does increasing the aperture of a lens have on its resolving power? Will a larger wavelength of light result in increased resolution if other conditions are kept constant?

29-9. The resolving power of some microscopes is increased by illuminating the object with ultraviolet light. Explain.

29-10. A polarizing plate absorbs about 50 percent of the intensity of an unpolarized beam. What accounts for this?

29-11. Assume that a beam of unpolarized light passes through a polarizer and an analyzer, as shown in Fig. 29-17. The analyzer has been rotated by an angle θ from the position for maximum transmission. Only the component of the amplitude A in the plane-polarized beam that lies along the axis is transmitted by the analyzer. This component is given by $A \cos \theta$. The intensity I of light is proportional to the square of the amplitude A. Show that the intensity I of the beam transmitted by the analyzer is given by

$$I = I_0 \cos^2 \theta \qquad (29-9)$$

where θ is the angle at which the analyzer is placed relative to the position for maximum transmitted intensity I_0.

29-12. Which of the following waves can be polarized: **(a)** x-rays, **(b)** water waves, **(c)** sound waves, and **(d)** radio waves?

29-13. When white light falls on a prism, it is dispersed, forming a spectrum of colors with the red component receiving the least deviation. Compare this spectrum with that produced by a diffraction grating.

29-14. Give a strong argument for the wave theory of light.

29-15. Suppose you are using a diffraction grating with a spacing of 3000 lines/cm. Discuss the usefulness of this grating for examining **(a)** infrared radiation of wavelength 3 nm; **(b)** ultraviolet radiation of wavelength 100 nm.

PROBLEMS

29-1. Monochromatic light illuminates two parallel slits 0.2 mm apart. On a screen 1 m from the slits, the first bright fringe is separated from the central fringe by 2.5 mm. What is the wavelength of the light?

Ans. 500 nm.

29-2. Monochromatic light from a sodium flame illuminates two slits separated by 1 mm. A viewing screen is 1 m from the slits, and the distance from the central bright fringe to the bright fringe nearest it is 0.589 mm. What is the frequency of the light?

29-3. Two slits 0.05 mm apart are illuminated by green light of wavelength 520 nm. A diffraction pattern is formed on a viewing screen 2 m away. **(a)** Determine the distance from the center of the screen to the first bright fringe and the distance to the third dark fringe. **(b)** What is the separation between the two first-order bright fringes located on each side of the central band?

Ans. **(a)** 2.08 cm **(b)** 5.2 cm **(c)** 4.16 cm.

29-4. If the separation of the two slits in Young's experiment is 0.1 mm and the distance to the screen is 50 cm, find the distance between the first dark fringe and the third bright fringe when the slits are illuminated with light of wavelength 600 nm.

29-5. A small sodium lamp emits light of wavelength 589 nm, which illuminates a diffraction grating having 5000 lines/cm. Calculate the angular deviations of the first- and second-order images.

Ans. 17.1°, 36°.

29-6. A parallel beam of light illuminates a diffraction grating with 6000 lines/cm. The second-order image is located 32 cm from the central image on a screen 500 cm from the grating. Calculate the wavelength of the light.

29-7. The visible-light spectrum ranges in wavelength from 400 to 700 nm. Find the angular width of the first-order spectrum produced by passing white light through a grating having 20,000 lines/in.

Ans. $\Delta\theta = 15°$.

29-8. An infrared spectrophotometer uses gratings to disperse infrared light. One grating is ruled with 240 lines/mm. What is the maximum range of wavelengths in nanometers that can be studied with this grating?

29-9. A transmission grating ruled with 6000 lines/cm forms a second-order bright fringe at an angle of 53° from the central fringe. What is the wavelength of the incident light?

Ans. 666 nm.

29-10. Light from a mercury-arc lamp is incident on a diffraction grating ruled with 7000 lines/in. The spectrum consists of a yellow line (579 nm) and a blue line (436 nm). Compute the angular separation of these lines in the third-order spectrum.

29-11. What is the minimum separation of two points on the moon's surface that can just be resolved by the Mt. Palomar 200-in. telescope? Assume the reflected light from the moon has a wavelength of 500 nm and that it travels a distance of 384,000 km.

Ans. 46.1 m.

29-12. What is the angular limit of resolution of a man's eye when the diameter of the opening is 0.3 cm? Assume that $\lambda = 500$ nm. At what distance could these eyes resolve the wires in a door screen which are separated by $\frac{1}{4}$ cm?

29-13. A certain radiotelescope has a parabolic reflector which is 70 m in diameter. Radio waves from outer space have a wavelength of 21 cm. Calculate the theoretical limit of angular resolution.

Ans. 3.66×10^{-3} rad.

29-14. It is planned to use a telescope to resolve two points on a mountain 160 km away. If the separation of the points is 2 m, what is the minimum diameter for the objective lens? Assume that $\lambda = 500$ nm.

29-15. The intensity of unpolarized light is reduced by one-half when it passes through a polarizer. In the case of the plane-polarized light reaching the analyzer, the intensity I of the transmitted beam is given by

$$I = I_0 \cos^2 \theta$$

where I_0 is the maximum intensity transmitted and θ is the angle through which the analyzer has been rotated. Three Polaroid plates are stacked so that the axis of each is turned 30° with respect to the preceding plate. By what percentage will incident light be reduced in intensity when it passes through all three plates?

Ans. 28.1%.

PART THREE Electricity and Magnetism

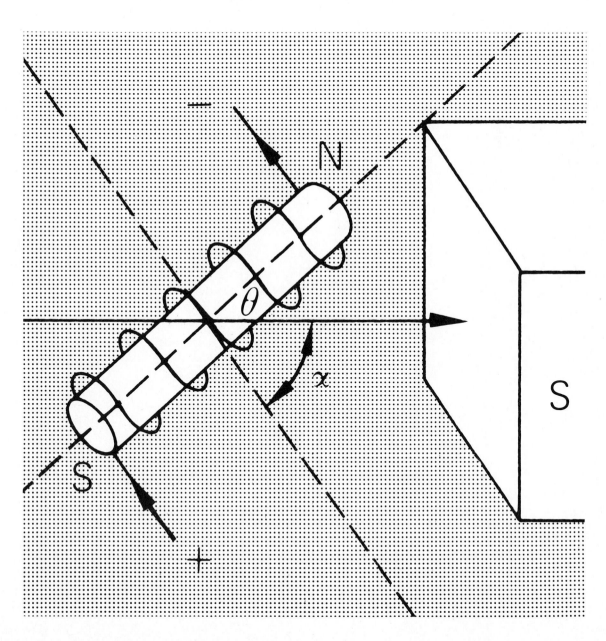

30 *The Electric Force*

OBJECTIVES: After completing this chapter, you should be able to:

1. Demonstrate the existence of two kinds of electric charge and verify the *first law of electrostatics* using laboratory materials.

2. Explain and demonstrate the processes of charging by *contact* and by *induction*, and use an *electroscope* to determine the nature of an unknown charge.

3. State *Coulomb's law* and apply it to the solution of problems involving electric forces.

4. Define the *electron*, the *coulomb*, and the *micro-coulomb* as units of electric charge.

A hard-rubber comb or a plastic rod acquires a strange ability to attract other objects after it is rubbed on a coat sleeve. An annoying *shock* is sometimes experienced when you touch the handle of a car door after sliding across the seat. Stacked sheets of paper tend to resist separation. All these occurrences are examples of *electrification*, a phenomenon which frequently occurs as a result of rubbing objects together. Long ago, the name *charging* was given to the rubbing process, and the electrified object was said to be charged. This chapter begins our study of *electrostatics*, the science which treats electric charges at rest.

30-1 THE ELECTRIC CHARGE

The best way to begin a study of electrostatics is to experiment with objects which become electrified by rubbing. The materials illustrated in Fig. 30-1 are commonly found in the physics laboratory. In the order of their appearance in the figure, they are a hard-rubber rod resting on a piece of cat's fur, a glass rod resting on a piece of silk, the pith-ball electroscope, suspended pith balls, and

Fig. 30-1 Laboratory materials for studying electrostatics: (*a*) a hard-rubber rod resting on a piece of cat's fur; (*b*) a glass rod resting on a piece of silk; (*c*) the pith-ball electroscope; (*d*) suspended pith balls; and (*e*) the gold-leaf electroscope.

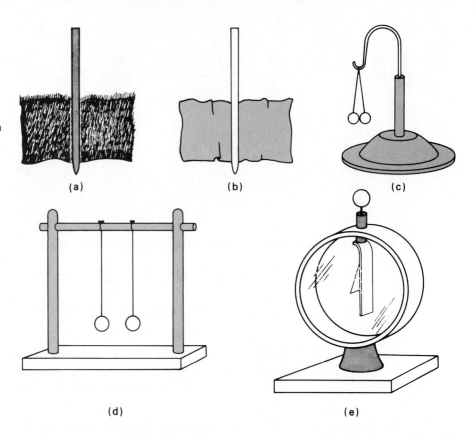

(a)　　　　(b)　　　　(c)

(d)　　　　(e)

the gold-leaf electroscope. A pith ball is a very light sphere of wood pith painted with metallic paint and usually suspended from a silk thread. An *electroscope* is a sensitive laboratory instrument used to detect the presence of an electric charge.

The pith-ball electroscope can be used to study the effects of electrification. Two metallic-coated pith balls are suspended by silk threads from a common point. We begin by vigorously rubbing the rubber rod with cat's fur (or wool). Then if the rubber rod is brought near the electroscope, the suspended pith balls will be attracted to the rod, as shown in Fig. 30-2*a*. After remaining in contact with the rod for an instant, the balls will be repelled from the rod and from each other. When the rod is removed, the pith balls remain separated, as shown in the figure. The initial attraction (due to a redistribution of charge on the neutral pith balls) will be explained later. The repulsion must be due to some property acquired by the pith balls as a result of their contact with the charged rod. We may reasonably assume that some of the *charge* has been transferred from the rod to the pith balls and that all three objects become similarly charged. From these observations, we can state the conclusion that:

> *A force of repulsion exists between two substances which are electrified in the same way.*

Fig. 30-2
(*a*) Charging the pith-ball electroscope with a rubber rod.
(*b*) Charging the pith balls with a glass rod.

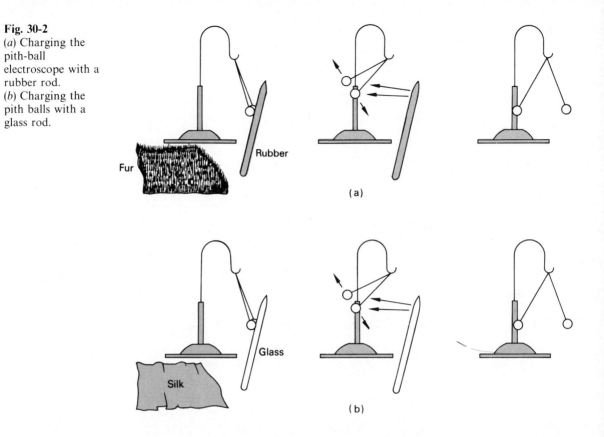

Fur

Rubber

(a)

Glass

Silk

(b)

Let us continue our experimentation by picking up the glass rod and rubbing it vigorously on a silk cloth. When the charged rod is brought near the pith balls, the same sequence of events occurs as with the rubber rod. See Fig. 30-2*b*. Does this mean that the nature of the charge is the same on both rods? Our experiment neither proves nor disproves this assumption. In each case, the rod and balls were electrified in the same way, and so repulsion occurs in each case.

To test whether the two processes are identical, let us charge one pith ball with a glass rod and the other with a rubber rod. As shown in Fig. 30-3, a force of *attraction* exists between the balls charged in this manner. We conclude that the charges produced on the glass and rubber rods are opposite.

Similar experimentation with many different materials demonstrates that all electrified objects can be divided into two groups: (1) those which have a charge like that produced on glass and (2) those which have a charge like that produced on rubber. According to a convention established by Benjamin Franklin, objects in the former group are said to have a *positive* (+) charge, and objects belonging to the latter group are said to have a *negative* (−) charge. These terms have no mathematical significance; they simply denote the two opposite kinds of electric charge.

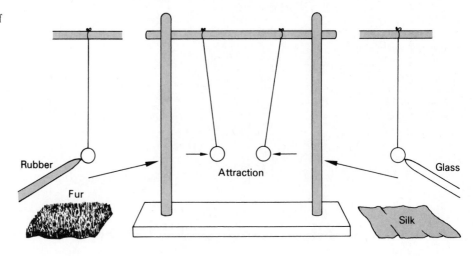

We are now in a position to state the *first law of electrostatics*, which is based on our experimentation:

Like charges repel and unlike charges attract.

Two negatively charged objects or two positively charged objects repel each other, as demonstrated by Fig. 30-2a and b, respectively. Figure 30-3 demonstrates that a positively charged object attracts a negatively charged object.

30-2
THE
ELECTRON

What actually occurs during a rubbing process that causes the phenomenon of electrification? Benjamin Franklin thought that all bodies contained a specified amount of electric fluid which served to keep them in an uncharged state. When two different substances were rubbed together, he postulated that one accumulated an excess of fluid and became positively charged whereas the other lost fluid and became negatively charged. It is now known that the substance transferred is not a fluid but very small amounts of negative electricity called *electrons*.

The modern atomic theory of matter holds that all substances are made up of atoms and molecules. Each atom has a positively charged central core, called the *nucleus*, which is surrounded by a cloud of negatively charged electrons. The nucleus consists of a number of *protons*, each with a single unit of positive charge, and (except for hydrogen) one or more *neutrons*. As the name suggests, a neutron is a neutral particle. Normally, an atom of matter is in a *neutral* or *uncharged* state because it contains the same number of protons in its nucleus as there are electrons surrounding the nucleus. A schematic diagram of the neon atom is shown in Fig. 30-4. If, for some reason, a neutral atom loses one or more of its outer electrons, the atom has a net positive charge and is referred to as a positive *ion*. A negative ion is an atom which has gained one or more additional charges.

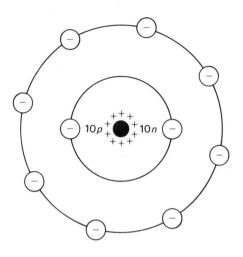

Fig. 30-4 The neon atom consists of a tightly packed nucleus containing 10 protons (*p*) and 10 neutrons (*n*). The atom is electrically neutral because it is surrounded by 10 electrons.

When two particular materials are brought in close contact, some of the loosely held electrons may be transferred from one material to the other. For example, when a hard-rubber rod is rubbed against fur, electrons are transferred from the fur to the rod, leaving an *excess* of electrons on the rod and a *deficiency* of electrons on the fur. Similarly, when a glass rod is rubbed on a silk cloth, electrons are transferred from the glass to the silk. We can now state:

An object which has an excess of electrons is negatively charged, and an object which has a deficiency of electrons is positively charged.

A laboratory demonstration of the transfer of charge is illustrated in Fig. 30-5. A hard-rubber rod is rubbed vigorously on a piece of fur. One pith ball is charged negatively with the rod, and the other is touched with the fur. The resulting attraction shows that the fur is oppositely charged. The process of rubbing has left a deficiency of electrons on the fur.

Fig. 30-5 Rubbing a hard-rubber rod on a piece of fur transfers electrons from the fur to the rod.

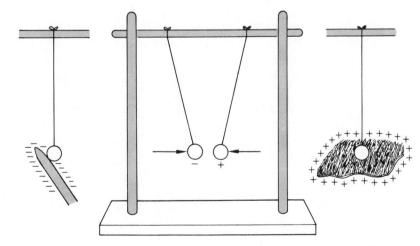

A solid piece of matter is composed of many atoms arranged in a manner peculiar to that material. Some materials, primarily metals, have a large number of *free electrons*, which can move about through the material. These materials have the ability to transfer charge from one object to another, and they are called *conductors*.

A **conductor** is a material through which charge can easily be transferred.

Most metals are good conductors. In Fig. 30-6 a copper rod is supported by a glass stand. The pith balls can be charged by touching the right end of the copper with a charged rubber rod. The electrons are transferred or *conducted* through the rod to the pith balls. Note that none of the charge is transferred to the glass support or to the silk thread. These materials are poor conductors and are referred to as *insulators*.

An **insulator** is a material which resists the flow of charge.

Fig. 30-6 Electrons are conducted by the copper rod to charge the pith balls.

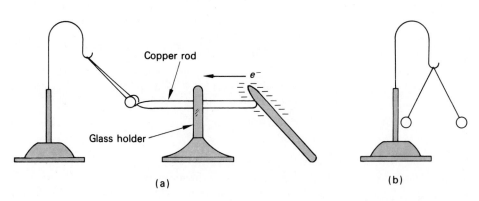

Copper rod

e^-

Glass holder

(a)

(b)

Other examples of good insulators are rubber, plastic, mica, Bakelite, sulfur, and air.

A **semiconductor** is a material intermediate in its ability to carry charge.

Examples are silicon, germanium, and gallium arsenide. The ease with which a semiconductor carries charge can be greatly varied by the addition of impurities or by a change in temperature.

The gold-leaf electroscope shown in Fig. 30-7 consists of a strip of gold foil attached to a conducting rod. The rod and the foil are protected from air currents by a cylindrical metal case with glass windows. The rod is fitted with a spherical knob at the top and is insulated from the case by a block of hard rubber or amber. Whenever the knob is given a charge, the repulsion of like charges on the rod and the gold leaf causes the leaf to diverge away from the rod.

Figure 30-8 illustrates charging the electroscope by *contact*. When the knob is touched with the negatively charged rod, electrons flow from the rod to

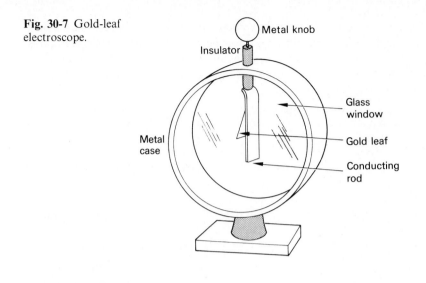

Fig. 30-7 Gold-leaf electroscope.

Metal knob

Insulator

Glass window

Gold leaf

Metal case

Conducting rod

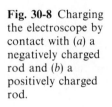

Fig. 30-8 Charging the electroscope by contact with (a) a negatively charged rod and (b) a positively charged rod.

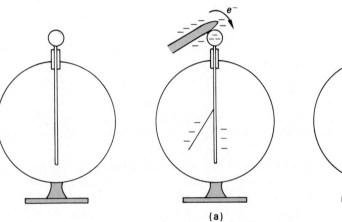

e^-

(a)

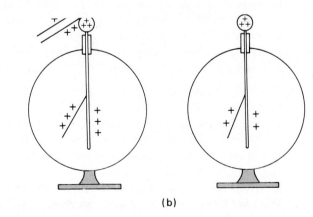

(b)

the leaves, leaving an excess of electrons on the electroscope. When the knob is touched with a positively charged rod, electrons are transferred from the knob to the rod, leaving the electroscope deficient in electrons. Note that the residual charge on the electroscope is of the same sign as that of the charging rod.

Once the electroscope is charged, either negatively or positively, it can be used to detect the presence and nature of other charged objects. (See Fig. 30-9.) For example, consider what happens to the leaf of a negatively charged

Fig. 30-9 The negatively charged electroscope can be used to detect the presence of other charge.

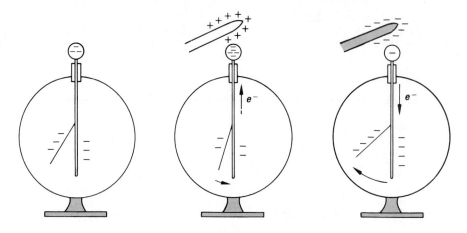

electroscope as a positively charged rod is brought near the knob. Some electrons are drawn from the leaf and rod up into the knob. As a result, the leaf converges. Bringing the rod closer produces a proportionately greater convergence of the leaf as more and more electrons are attracted to the knob. There appears to be a direct proportion between the number of charges on the leaf and rod and the force of repulsion between them. Moreover, there must be some *inverse* relation between the separation of the charged rod and the knob and the force attracting the electrons from the leaf and rod of the electroscope. This force becomes stronger as the separation decreases. These observations will help us understand Coulomb's law, developed in a later section.

Similar reasoning will show that the leaf of a negatively charged electroscope will be repelled further from the rod when the knob is placed near a negatively charged object. Thus a charged electroscope can be used to indicate both the nature and the presence of nearby charges.

30-5 REDISTRIBUTION OF CHARGE

When a negatively charged rod is brought close to an uncharged pith ball, there is an initial attraction, as shown in Fig. 30-10. The attraction of the uncharged object is due to the separation of positive and negative electricity within the neutral body. The proximity of the negatively charged rod repels loosely held electrons to the opposite side of the uncharged object, leaving a deficiency (positive charge) on the near side and an excess (negative charge) on the far side. Since the unlike charge is nearer to the rod, the force of attraction will

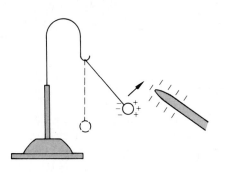

Fig. 30-10
Attraction of a
neutral body due to
a redistribution of
charge.

exceed the force of repulsion and the electrically neutral object will be attracted
to the rod. No charge is gained or lost during this process; the charge on the
neutral body is simply redistributed.

**30-6
CHARGING
BY
INDUCTION**

The redistribution of charge due to the presence of a nearby charged object can
be useful in charging objects without contact. This process, called charging by
induction, can be accomplished without any loss of charge from the charging
body. For example, consider the two neutral metal spheres placed in contact as
shown in Fig. 30-11. When a negatively charged rod is brought near the left

Fig. 30-11
Charging two metal
spheres by
induction.

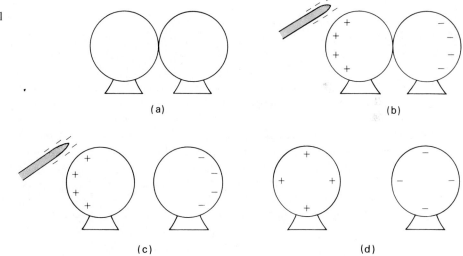

sphere (without touching it), a redistribution of charge occurs. Electrons are
forced from the left sphere to the right sphere through the point of contact.
Now, if the spheres are separated in the presence of the charging rod, the electrons cannot return to the left sphere. Thus the left sphere will have a deficiency
of electrons (a positive charge), and the right sphere will have an excess of
electrons (a negative charge).

A charge can also be induced on a single sphere. This process is illustrated with the electroscope in Fig. 30-12. A negatively charged rod is placed near the metal knob, causing a redistribution of charge. The repelled electrons cause the leaf to diverge, leaving a deficiency of electrons on the knob. By touching the knob with a finger or by connecting a wire from the knob to the earth a path is provided for the repelled electrons to leave the electroscope. The body or the ground will acquire a negative charge equal to the positive charge (deficiency) left on the electroscope. When the charging rod is removed, the leaf of the electroscope will again diverge, as shown in the figure. Charging by induction always leaves a residual charge which is opposite that of the charging body.

Fig. 30-12
Charging an electroscope by induction. Note that the residual charge is opposite that of the charging body.

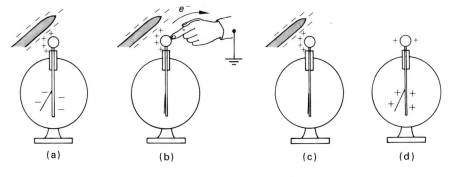

(a) (b) (c) (d)

30-7 COULOMB'S LAW

As usual, the task of the physicist is to measure the interactions between charged objects in some quantitative fashion. It is not sufficient to state that an electric force exists; we must be able to predict its magnitude.

The first theoretical investigation of the electric forces between charged bodies was accomplished by Charles Augustin de Coulomb in 1784. His studies were made with a torsion balance to measure the variation in force with separation and quantity of charge. The separation r of two charged objects is reckoned as the straight-line distance between their centres. The quantity of charge q can be thought of as the excess number of electrons or protons in the body.

Coulomb found that the force of attraction or repulsion between two charged objects is inversely proportional to the square of their separation distance. In other words, if the distance between two charged objects is reduced by one-half, the force of attraction or repulsion between them will be increased fourfold.

The concept of a quantity of charge was not clearly understood in Coulomb's time. There was no established unit of charge and no means for measuring it, but his experiments clearly showed that the electric force between two charged objects is directly proportional to the product of the quantity of charge on each object. Today, his conclusions are stated in *Coulomb's law*:

> *The force of attraction or repulsion between two point charges is directly proportional to the product of the two charges and inversely proportional to the square of the distance between them.*

In order to arrive at a mathematical statement of Coulomb's law, let us consider the charges in Fig. 30-13. In Fig. 30-13a the force F of attraction between two like charges in indicated, and in Fig. 30-13b a force of repulsion is shown for like charges. In either case, the magnitude of the force is determined by the magnitudes of the charges q and q' and by their separation r. From Coulomb's law, we can write

$$F \propto \frac{qq'}{r^2}$$

or

$$F = \frac{kqq'}{r^2} \qquad (30\text{-}1)$$

The proportionality constant k takes into account the properties of the medium separating the charged bodies and has the dimensions dictated by Coulomb's law.

Fig. 30-13
Illustrating
Coulomb's law.

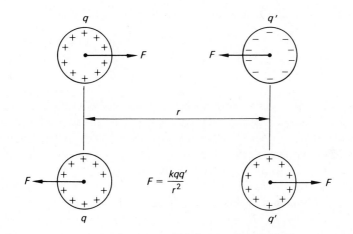

In SI units, the practical system for the study of electricity, the unit of charge is expressed in *coulombs* (C). In this case, the quantity of charge is not defined by Coulomb's law but is related to the flow of charge through a conductor. We shall find later that this rate of flow is measured in *amperes*. A formal definition of the coulomb is as follows:

> One **coulomb** is the charge transferred through any cross section of a conductor in one second by a constant current of one ampere.

Since current theory is not a part of this chapter, it will suffice to compare the coulomb with the charge of an electron.

$$1 \text{ C} = 6.25 \times 10^{18} \text{ electrons}$$

Obviously the coulomb is an enormously large unit from the standpoint of most problems in electrostatics. The charge of one electron expressed in coulombs is

$$e^- = -1.6 \times 10^{-19} \text{ C} \qquad (30\text{-}2)$$

where e^- is the symbol for the electron and the minus sign denotes the nature of the charge.

A more convenient unit for electrostatics is the microcoulomb (μC), defined by

$$1 \ \mu\text{C} = 10^{-6} \text{ C} \qquad (30\text{-}3)$$

Since the SI units of force, charge, and distance do not depend on Coulomb's law, the proportionality constant k must be determined by experiment. A large number of experiments have shown that when the force is in newtons, the distance is in meters, and the charge is in coulombs the proportionality constant is approximately

$$k = 9 \times 10^9 \text{ N} \cdot \text{m}^2/\text{C}^2 \qquad (30\text{-}4)$$

When applying Coulomb's law in SI units, one must substitute this value for k in Eq. (30-1):

$$\boxed{F = \frac{(9 \times 10^9 \text{ N} \cdot \text{m}^2/\text{C}^2)qq'}{r^2}} \qquad (30\text{-}5)$$

It must be remembered that **F** represents the force on a charged particle and is, therefore, a vector quantity. The direction of the force is determined solely by the nature of the charges q and q'. Therefore, it is easier to use the absolute values of q and q' in Coulomb's law, Eq. (30-5). Then remember that like charges repel and opposite charges attract to get the direction of the force. When more than one force acts on a charge, the resultant force is the vector sum of the separate forces.

EXAMPLE 30-1   A -3-μC charge is placed 100 mm from a $+3$-μC charge. Calculate the force between the two charges.

Solution   First we convert to appropriate units.

$$3 \ \mu\text{C} = 3 \times 10^{-6} \text{ C} \qquad 100 \text{ mm} = 100 \times 10^{-3} \text{ m} = 0.1 \text{ m}$$

Then we use the absolute values, so that both q and q' are equal to 3×10^{-6} C. Applying Coulomb's law, we obtain

$$F = \frac{kqq'}{r^2} = \frac{(9 \times 10^9 \text{ N} \cdot \text{m}^2/\text{C}^2)(3 \times 10^{-6} \text{ C})(3 \times 10^{-6} \text{ C})}{(0.1 \text{ m})^2}$$

$$F = 8.1 \text{ N} \qquad\qquad\qquad\qquad\qquad\qquad\qquad\qquad \textit{Attraction}$$

This is a force of *attraction* because the charges had opposite signs.

EXAMPLE 30-2　Two charges $q_1 = -8\ \mu C$ and $q_2 = +12\ \mu C$ are placed 120 mm apart in the air. What is the resultant force on a third charge $q_3 = -4\ \mu C$ placed midway between the other two charges?

Solution　We convert the charges to coulombs ($1\ \mu C = 1 \times 10^{-6}$ C), use their absolute values, and convert the distance to meters (120 mm = 0.12 m). One-half of 0.12 m is 0.06 m. A sketch is drawn in Fig. 30-14 to help visualize the forces. The force on q_3 due to q_1 is directed to the right and is calculated from Coulomb's law.

$$F_1 = \frac{kq_1q_3}{r^2} = \frac{(9 \times 10^9\ \text{N} \cdot \text{m}^2/\text{C}^2)(8 \times 10^{-6}\ \text{C})(4 \times 10^{-6}\ \text{C})}{(0.06\ \text{m})^2}$$

$$F_1 = \frac{0.288\ \text{N} \cdot \text{m}^2}{0.0036\ \text{m}^2} = 80\ \text{N} \qquad\qquad \textit{Repulsion, to the Right}$$

Fig. 30-14
Computing the resultant force on a charge placed midway between two other charges.

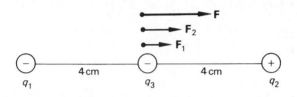

Similarly, the force F_2 on q_3 due to q_2 is equal to

$$F_2 = \frac{kq_2q_3}{r^2} = \frac{(9 \times 10^9\ \text{N} \cdot \text{m}^2/\text{C}^2)(12 \times 10^{-6}\ \text{C})(4 \times 10^{-6}\ \text{C})}{(0.06\ \text{m})^2}$$

$$F_2 = 120\ \text{N} \qquad\qquad \textit{Attraction, Also to the Right}$$

The resultant force **F** is the vector sum of $\mathbf{F}_1$ and $\mathbf{F}_2$. Thus

$$\mathbf{F} = 80\ \text{N} + 120\ \text{N}$$

$$= 200\ \text{N} \qquad\qquad \textit{Directed to the Right}$$

Note that the signs of the charges were used only to determine the direction of the forces; they were not substituted into the calculations.

EXAMPLE 30-3　Three charges $q_1 = +4 \times 10^{-9}$ C, $q_2 = -6 \times 10^{-9}$ C, and $q_3 = -8 \times 10^{-9}$ C are arranged as shown in Fig. 30-15. What is the resultant force on q_3 due to the other two charges?

Solution　Let $\mathbf{F}_1$ be the force on q_3 due to q_1, and let $\mathbf{F}_2$ be the force on q_3 due to q_2. $\mathbf{F}_1$ is a force of attraction and $\mathbf{F}_2$ is a force of repulsion, as shown in the figure. Their magnitudes are found from Coulomb's law.

$$F_1 = \frac{(9 \times 10^9\ \text{N} \cdot \text{m}^2/\text{C}^2)(4 \times 10^{-9}\ \text{C})(8 \times 10^{-9}\ \text{C})}{(0.1\ \text{m})^2}$$

$$= 2.88 \times 10^{-5}\ \text{N} \qquad (37° \text{ north of west})$$

$$F_2 = \frac{(9 \times 10^9\ \text{N} \cdot \text{m}^2/\text{C}^2)(6 \times 10^{-9}\ \text{C})(8 \times 10^{-9}\ \text{C})}{(8 \times 10^{-2}\ \text{m})^2}$$

$$= 6.75 \times 10^{-5}\ \text{N} \qquad \text{east}$$

Fig. 30-15

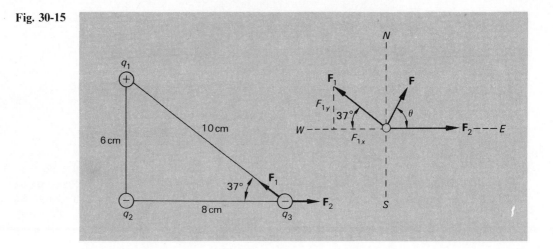

We must now find the resultant **F** of the forces $\mathbf{F}_1$ and $\mathbf{F}_2$. From the free-body diagram, we note that

$$F_x = F_2 - F_{1x} = F_2 - F_1 \cos 37°$$

$$= (6.75 \times 10^{-5} \text{ N}) - (2.88 \times 10^{-5} \text{ N})(0.8)$$

$$= 4.45 \times 10^{-5} \text{ N}$$

$$F_y = F_1 \sin 37° = 1.73 \times 10^{-5} \text{ N}$$

From the components we find

$$\tan \theta = \frac{F_y}{F_x} = \frac{1.73 \times 10^{-5} \text{ N}}{4.45 \times 10^{-5} \text{ N}} = 0.389$$

$$\theta = 21°$$

$$F = \frac{F_y}{\sin \theta} = \frac{1.73 \times 10^{-5} \text{ N}}{\sin 21°} = 4.80 \times 10^{-5} \text{ N}$$

Therefore, the resultant force on q_3 is 4.8×10^{-5} N directed 21° north of east.

SUMMARY

Electrostatics is the science which treats charges at rest. We have seen that there are two kinds of charge that exist in nature. If an object has an excess of electrons it is said to be *negatively* charged; if it has a deficiency of electrons it is *positively* charged. Coulomb's law was introduced to provide a quantitative measure of electrical forces between such charges. The major concepts are:

- The first law of electrostatics states that *like charges repel each other and unlike charges attract each other.*

- Coulomb's law states that *the force of attraction or repulsion between two point charges is directly proportional to the product of the two charges and inversely proportional to the separation of the two charges*

$$F = \frac{kqq'}{r^2}$$

$$k = 9 \times 10^9 \text{ N} \cdot \text{m}^2/\text{C}^2$$

Coulomb's Law

The force F is in newtons (N) when the separation r is in meters (m) and the charge q is measured in coulombs (C).
- When solving the problems in this chapter, it is important to use the *sign* of the charges to *determine* the direction of forces and Coulomb's law to determine their *magnitudes*. The resultant force on a particular charge is then found by the methods of vector mechanics.

QUESTIONS

30-1. Define the following terms:
   a. Electrostatics
   b. Charging
   c. Electron
   d. Negative charge
   e. Positive charge
   f. Ion
   g. Induced charge
   h. Conductor
   i. Insulator
   j. Semiconductor
   k. Coulomb's law
   l. Coulomb
   m. Microcoulomb
   n. Electroscope

30-2. Discuss several examples of static electricity in addition to those mentioned in the text.

30-3. In the process of rubbing a glass rod with a silk cloth, is charge *created*? Explain.

30-4. What is the nature of the charge on the silk cloth in Question 30-3?

30-5. An insulated stand supports a charged metal ball in the laboratory. Describe several procedures of determining the nature of the charge on the ball.

30-6. During an experiment in the laboratory, two bodies are seen to attract each other. Is this conclusive proof that they are both charged? Explain.

30-7. Two bodies are found to repel each other with an electric force. Is this conclusive proof that they are both charged? Explain.

30-8. One of the fundamental principles of physics is the principle of the conservation of charge which states that *the total quantity of electric charge in the universe does not change.* Can you offer reasons for accepting this law?

30-9. Describe what happens to the leaf of a positively charged electroscope as **(a)** a negatively charged rod is brought closer and closer to the knob without touching it; **(b)** a positively charged rod is brought closer and closer to the knob.

30-10. When charging the leaf electroscope by induction, should the finger be removed before the charging rod is taken away? Explain.

30-11. List the units for each parameter in Coulomb's law for SI units.

30-12. Coulomb's law is valid only when the separation r is large in comparison with the radii of the charge. What accounts for this limitation?

30-13. How many electrons would be required to give a metal sphere a negative charge of **(a)** 1 C, **(b)** 1 μC?

PROBLEMS

30-1. Two balls each having a charge of 3 μC are separated by 20 mm. What is the force of repulsion between them?

Ans. 202 N.

30-2. Two point charges of -3 and $+4$ μC are 12 mm apart in a vacuum. What is the electrostatic force between them?

30-3. An alpha particle consists of two protons and two neutrons. What is the repulsive force between two alpha particles separated by a distance of 2 nm?

Ans. 2.3×10^{-10} N.

30-4. The radius of the electron's orbit around the proton in a hydrogen atom is approximately 52 pm (1 pm = 1×10^{-12} m). What is the electrostatic force of attraction?

30-5. What is the separation of two -4 μC charges if the force of repulsion between them is 20 N?

Ans. 84.9 mm.

30-6. Two identical unknown charges experience a 48 N repulsive force when separated by 60 mm. What is the magnitude of each charge?

30-7. A small metal sphere is given a charge of $+40$ μC, and a second sphere located 8 cm away is given a charge of -12 μC. **(a)** What is the force of attraction between them? **(b)** If the two spheres are allowed to touch and are again placed 8 cm apart, what electric force exists between them?

Ans. **(a)** 675 N **(b)** 276 N (repulsion).

30-8. Two charges attract each other with a force of 6×10^{-5} N when they are a certain distance apart in a vacum. If their separation is decreased to one-third of the original distance, what is the new force of attraction?

30-9. The repulsive force between two pith balls is found to be 60 μN. If each pith ball carries a charge of 8 nC, what is their separation?

Ans. 98 mm.

30-10. What should be the separation of two $+5$ μC charges in order that the force of repulsion is 4 N?

30-11. A $+60$ μC charge is placed 60 mm to the left of a $+20$ μC charge. What is the resultant force on a -35 μC charge placed midway between the first two charges?

Ans. 1.4×10^4 N, left.

30-12. A point charge of $+36$ μC is placed 80 mm from a second point charge of -22 μC. **(a)** What force is exerted on each charge? **(b)** What is the result-ant force on a third charge of $+12$ μC placed between the other charges and located 60 mm from the $+36$ μC charge?

30-13. Two charges of $+25$ and $+16$ μC are 80 mm apart in air. A third charge of $+60$ μC is placed 30 mm from the $+25$ μC charge and between the two charges. What is the resultant force on the third charge?

Ans. 1.15×10^4 N.

30-14. A -40 nC charge is placed 40 mm to the left of a $+6$ nC charge. What is the resultant force on a -12 nC charge placed 8 mm to the right of the $+6$ nC charge?

30-15. Two charges of $+16$ and $+9$ μC are 80 mm apart in air. Where should a third charge be placed in order that the resultant force on it be zero? Why is it not necessary to specify either the magnitude or the sign of the third charge?

Ans. 34.3 mm from the 9-μC charge.

30-16. A charge of $+8$ nC is placed 40 mm to the left of a -14 nC charge. Where should a third charge of $+4$ nC be placed if the resultant force on it is to be zero?

30-17. Three point charges, $q_1 = +8$ μC, $q_2 = -4$ μC, and $q_3 = +2$ μC are placed at the corners of an equilateral triangle. Each side of the triangle is 80 mm long. What are the magnitude and direction of the resultant force on the 8-μC charge? Assume that the base of the triangle is formed by a line joining the 8- and 4-μC charges.

Ans. 39 N at 330°.

30-18. A charge of $+60$ nC is located 80 mm above a -40-nC charge. What is the resultant force on a -50-nC charge located 45 mm horizontally to the right of the -40-nC charge?

30-19. A 64-μC charge is located 30 mm to the left of a 16-μC charge. What is the resultant force on a -12-μC charge positioned exactly 50 mm below the 16-μC charge?

Ans. 2650 N, 113.3°.

30-20. A 0.02-g pith ball is suspended freely. The ball is given a charge of $+20$ μC and placed 0.6 m from a charge of $+50$ μC. What will be the initial acceleration of the pith ball?

30-21. Two 8-g pith balls are suspended from silk threads 60 cm long and attached to a common point. When the spheres are given equal quantities of negative charge, the balls come to rest 30 cm apart. Calculate the magnitude of the charge on each pith ball.

Ans. 450 nC.

30-22. What is the resultant force on a $+2$-μC charge at a distance of 60 mm from each of two -4-μC charges which are 80 mm apart in air?

30-23. Two charges q_1 and q_2 are separated by a distance r. They experience a force F at this distance. If the initial separation is decreased by only 40 mm, the force between the two charges is doubled. What was the initial separation?

Ans. 137 m.

30-24. If it were possible to place 1 C of charge on each of two spheres separated by a distance of 1 m, what would be the repulsive force in newtons? How many electrons must be added to each of two metal spheres (1 m apart) if the repulsive force is to be 1 N?

30-25. Two 3-g spheres are suspended from the ceiling by light silk threads of negligible mass. The threads are each 80 mm long and are attached at a common point on the ceiling. What charge must be placed on each sphere if the resulting horizontal separation is to be 50 mm?

Ans. 51.8 nC.

31 *The Electric Field*

OBJECTIVES: After completing this unit of study, you should be able to:

1. **Define the electric field and explain what determines its magnitude and direction.**

2. **Write and apply an expression which relates the electric field intensity at a point to the distance(s) from the known charge(s).**

3. **Explain and illustrate the concept of electric field lines, and discuss the two rules which must be followed in the construction of such lines.**

4. **Explain the concept of the *permittivity* of a medium, and how it affects the field intensity and the construction of field lines.**

5. **Write and apply Gauss' law as it applies to the electric fields surrounding surfaces of known charge density.**

In our study of mechanics we discussed force and motion at great length. Newton's laws of motion were normally used to describe the application and consequences of *contact* forces. A moment's reflection on the universe as a whole convinces us of the enormous number of objects which are *not* in contact.

A projectile experiences a downward force which cannot be explained in terms of its interaction with air particles; planets revolve continuously through the void surrounding the sun; and the sun is pulled along an elliptical path by forces which do not touch it. Even at the atomic level, there are no "strings" to hold the electrons in their orbits about the nucleus.

If we are really to understand our universe, we must develop laws to predict the magnitude and direction of forces which are not transmitted by contact. Two such laws have already been discussed:

1. Newton's law of universal gravitation:

$$F_g = G \frac{m_1 m_2}{r^2} \tag{31-1}$$

2. Coulomb's law for electrostatic forces:

$$F_e = k \frac{q_1 q_2}{r^2} \tag{31-2}$$

Newton's law predicts the force which exists between two masses separated by a distance r; Coulomb's law deals with the electrostatic force, as discussed in Chap. 30. In applying such laws, we find it useful to develop certain properties of the space surrounding masses or charges.

31-1 THE CONCEPT OF A FIELD

Both the electric force and the gravitational force are examples of *action-at-a-distance forces*, which are extremely difficult to visualize. To overcome this fact, early physicists postulated the existence of an invisible material, called *ether*, which was thought to pervade all space. The gravitational force of attraction could then be due to strains in the ether caused by the presence of various masses. Certain optical experiments have now shown the ether theory to be untenable (see Sec. 24-2), and we are forced to consider whether space itself possesses properties of interest to the physicist.

It may be postulated that the mere presence of a mass alters the space surrounding it so as to produce a gravitational force on another nearby mass. We describe this alteration in space by introducing the concept of a *gravitational field* which surrounds all masses. Such a field may be said to exist in any region of space where a test mass will experience a gravitational force. The strength of the field at any point would be proportional to the force a given mass experiences at that point. For example, at every point in the vicinity of the earth, the gravitational field could be represented quantitatively by

$$\mathbf{g} = \frac{\mathbf{F}}{m} \tag{31-3}$$

where $\mathbf{g}$ = acceleration due to gravity
$\quad \mathbf{F}$ = gravitational force
$\quad m$ = test mass (see Fig. 31-1)

If $\mathbf{g}$ is known at every point above the earth, the force $\mathbf{F}$ which will act on a given mass m placed at that point can be determined from Eq. (31-3).

The concept of a field can also be applied to electrically charged objects. The space surrounding a charged object is altered by the presence of the charge. We may postulate the existence of an *electric field* in this space.

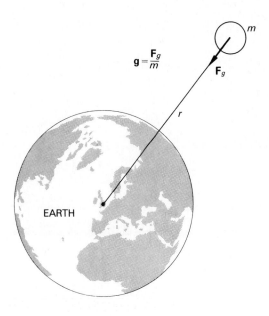

Fig. 31-1 Gravitational field at any point above the earth can be represented by the acceleration g that a small mass m would experience if it were placed at that point.

$g = \dfrac{F_g}{m}$

F_g

m

r

EARTH

An electric field is said to exist in a region of space in which an electric charge will experience an electric force.

This definition provides a test for the existence of an electric field. Simply place a charge at the point in question. If an electric force is observed, an electric field exists at that point.

Just as the force per unit mass provides a quantitative definition of a gravitational field, the strength of an electric field can be represented by the force per unit charge. We define the electric field intensity **E** at a point in terms of the force **F** experienced by small positive charge $+q$ when it is placed at that point (see Fig. 31-2). The magnitude of the electric field intensity is given by

$$E = \frac{F}{q} \tag{31-4}$$

In the metric system, a unit of electric field intensity is the newton per coulomb (N/C). The usefulness of this definition rests with the fact that if the field is known at a given point, we can predict the force which will act on any charge placed at that point.

Since the electric field intensity is defined in terms of a *positive* charge, its direction at any point is the same as the electrostatic force on a positive charge at that point.

*The direction of the electric field intensity **E** at a point in space is the same as the direction in which a positive charge would move if it were placed at that point.*

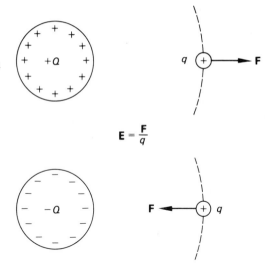

Fig. 31-2 Direction of the electric field intensity at a point is the same as the direction in which a positive charge $+q$ would move when placed at that point. Its magnitude is the force per unit charge (F/q).

$$E = \frac{F}{q}$$

On this basis, the electric field in the vicinity of a positive charge $+Q$ would be outward, or away from the charge, as indicated by Fig. 31-3a. In the vicinity of a negative charge $-Q$, the direction of the field would be inward, or toward the charge (Fig. 31-3b).

It must be remembered that the electric field intensity is a property assigned to the *space* which surrounds a charged body. A gravitational field exists above the earth whether or not a mass is positioned above the earth. Similarly, an electric field exists in the neighborhood of a charged body whether or not a second charge is positioned in the field. If a charge *is* placed in the field, it will experience a force **F** given by

$$\mathbf{F} = q\mathbf{E} \tag{31-5}$$

Fig. 31-3 (*a*) The field in the vicinity of a positive charge is directed radially outward at every point. (*b*) The field is directed inward, or toward a negative charge.

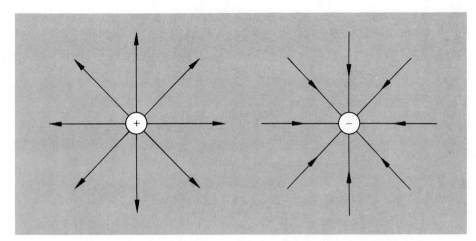

where $\mathbf{E}$ = field intensity

q = magnitude of charge placed in field

If q is positive, $\mathbf{E}$ and $\mathbf{F}$ will have the same direction; if q is negative, the force $\mathbf{F}$ will be directed opposite to the field $\mathbf{E}$.

EXAMPLE 31-1

The electric field intensity between the two plates in Fig. 31-4 is constant and directed downward. The magnitude of the electric field intensity is 6×10^4 N/C. What are the magnitude and the direction of the electric force exerted on an electron projected horizontally between the two plates?

Fig. 31-4 An electron projected into an electric field of constant intensity.

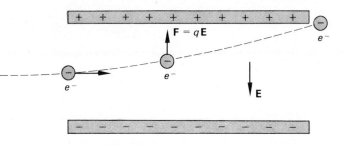

Solution

Since the direction of the field intensity $\mathbf{E}$ is defined in terms of a positive charge, the force on an electron will be upward, or opposite to the field direction. The charge on an electron is -1.6×10^{-19} C. Thus the electric force is given by Eq. (31-5).

$$F = qE = (1.6 \times 10^{-19} \text{ C})(6 \times 10^4 \text{ N/C})$$

$$= 9.6 \times 10^{-15} \text{ N} \qquad \text{upward}$$

Remember that the absolute value of the charge is used. The directions of $\mathbf{F}$ and $\mathbf{E}$ are the same for positive charges and opposite for negative charges.

EXAMPLE 31-2

Show that the gravitational force on the electron in Example 31-1 may be neglected. (The mass of an electron is 9.1×10^{-31} kg.)

Solution

The downward force due to the weight of the electron is

$$F_g = mg = (9.1 \times 10^{-31} \text{ kg})(9.8 \text{ m/s}^2)$$

$$= 8.92 \times 10^{-30} \text{ N}$$

The electric force is larger than the gravitational force by a factor of 1.08×10^{15}.

**31-2
COMPUTING
THE
ELECTRIC
INTENSITY**

We have discussed one method of measuring the magnitude of the electric field intensity at a point in space. A known charge is placed at the point, and the resultant force is measured. The force per unit charge is then a measure of the electric intensity at that point. The disadvantage of this method is that it bears no obvious relationship to the charge Q which creates the field. Experimentation will quickly show that the magnitude of the electric field surrounding a charged body is directly proportional to the quantity of charge on the body. It can also be demonstrated that at points farther and farther away from a charge Q a test charge q will experience smaller and smaller forces. The exact relationship is derived from Coulomb's law.

Suppose we wish to calculate the field intensity E at a distance r from a single charge Q, as shown in Fig. 31-5. The force F that Q exerts on a test charge q at the point in question is, from Coulomb's law,

$$F = \frac{kQq}{r^2} \qquad (31\text{-}6)$$

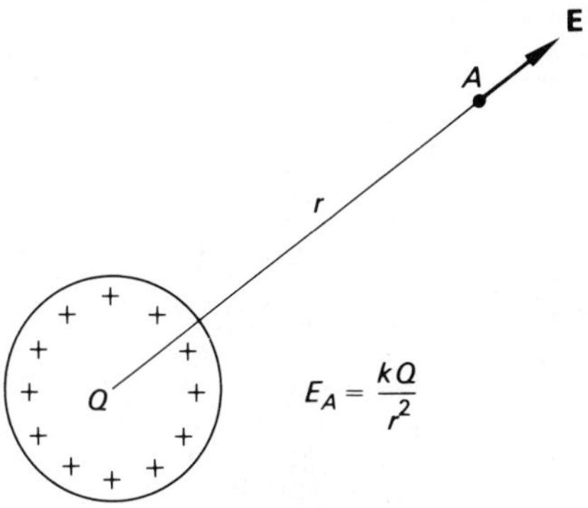

Fig. 31-5 Calculating the electric field intensity at a distance r from the center of a single charge Q.

Substituting this value for F into Eq. (31-4), we obtain

$$E = \frac{F}{q} = \frac{kQq/r^2}{q}$$

$$\boxed{E = \frac{kQ}{r^2}} \qquad (31\text{-}7)$$

where k is equal to 9×10^9 N $\cdot$ m^2/C^2. The direction of the field is away from Q if Q is positive and toward Q if Q is negative. We now have a relation which allows us to compute the field intensity at a point without having to place a second charge at the point.

EXAMPLE 31-3   What is the electric field intensity at a distance of 2 m from a charge of -12 μC?

Solution   Since the charge Q is negative, the field intensity will be directed toward Q. Its magnitude, from Eq. (31-7), is

$$E = \frac{kQ}{r^2} = \frac{(9 \times 10^9 \text{ N} \cdot \text{m}^2/\text{C}^2)(12 \times 10^{-6} \text{ C})}{(2 \text{ m})^2}$$

$$= 27 \times 10^3 \text{ N/C} \qquad \text{toward } Q$$

When more than one charge contributes to the field, as in Fig. 31-6, the resultant field is the vector sum of the contributions from each charge.

$$\mathbf{E} = \mathbf{E}_1 + \mathbf{E}_2 + \mathbf{E}_3 + \cdots$$

$$E = \frac{kQ_1}{r_1^2} + \frac{kQ_2}{r_2^2} + \frac{kQ_3}{r_3^3} + \cdots \qquad \textit{Vector Sum}$$

Fig. 31-6 The field in the vicinity of a number of charges is equal to the vector sum of the fields due to the individual charges.

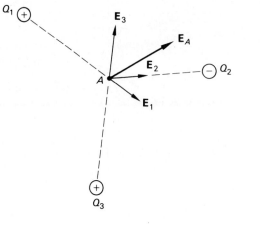

In an abbreviated form, the resultant field at a point in the vicinity of a number of charges is given by

$$\boxed{E = \sum \frac{kQ}{r^2}} \qquad \textit{Vector Sum} \quad (31\text{-}8)$$

It must be remembered that this is a *vector sum* and not an algebraic sum.

EXAMPLE 31-4   Two point charges, $q_1 = -6$ nC and $q_2 = +6$ nC, are 12 cm apart, as shown in Fig. 31-7. Determine the electric field (*a*) at point A and (*b*) at point B.

Solution (a)   By convention, let us consider any vector directed to the right or up as positive and any vector directed to the left or down as negative. The field at A due to q_1 is directed to the left since q_1 is negative, and its magnitude is

$$E_1 = \frac{kq_1}{r_1^2} = \frac{-(9 \times 10^9 \text{ N} \cdot \text{m}^2/\text{C}^2)(6 \times 10^{-9} \text{ C})}{(4 \times 10^{-2} \text{ m})^2}$$

$$= -3.38 \times 10^4 \text{ N/C} \qquad \text{(left)}$$

The electric intensity at A due to q_2 is also directed to the left since q_2 is positive, and it is given by

$$E_2 = \frac{kq_2}{r_2^2} = \frac{-(9 \times 10^9 \text{ N} \cdot \text{m}^2/\text{C}^2)(6 \times 10^{-9} \text{ C})}{(8 \times 10^{-2} \text{ m})^2}$$

$$= -0.844 \times 10^4 \text{ N/C}$$

Fig. 31-7

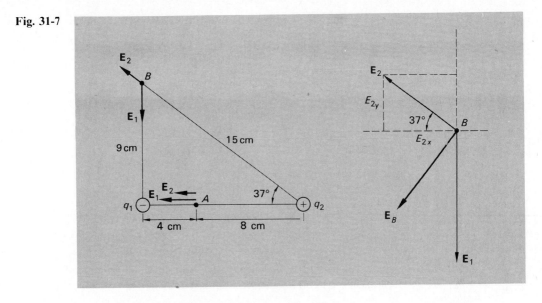

Since the two vectors $\mathbf{E}_1$ and $\mathbf{E}_2$ have the same direction, the resultant intensity at A is simply

$$E_A = E_1 + E_2$$

$$= -3.38 \times 10^4 \text{ N/C} - 0.844 \times 10^4 \text{ N/C}$$

$$= -4.22 \times 10^4 \text{ N/C} \qquad \text{(left)}$$

Solution (b)   The field intensity at B due to q_1 is directed downward and is equal to

$$E_1 = \frac{kq_1}{r_1^2} = \frac{-(9 \times 10^9 \text{ N} \cdot \text{m}^2/\text{C}^2)(6 \times 10^{-9} \text{ C})}{(9 \times 10^{-2} \text{ m})^2}$$

$$= -0.667 \times 10^4 \text{ N/C}$$

Similarly, the field due to q_2 is

$$E_2 = \frac{kq_2}{r_2^2} = \frac{(9 \times 10^9 \text{ N} \cdot \text{m}^2/\text{C}^2)(6 \times 10^{-9} \text{ C})}{(15 \times 10^{-2} \text{ m})^2}$$

$$= 0.240 \times 10^4 \text{ N/C} \qquad \text{at } 37°$$

The resultant intensity at point B is the vector sum of $\mathbf{E}_1$ and $\mathbf{E}_2$. Referring to the vector diagram in Fig. 31-7, we can compute the x and y components of the resultant.

$$E_x = -E_{2x} = -(0.240 \times 10^4 \text{ N/C}) \cos 37°$$

$$= -0.192 \times 10^4 \text{ N/C}$$

$$E_y = E_{2y} - E_1$$

$$= (0.240 \times 10^4 \text{ N/C}) \sin 37° - 0.667 \times 10^4 \text{ N/C}$$

$$= 0.144 \times 10^4 \text{ N/C} - 0.667 \times 10^4 \text{ N/C}$$

$$= -0.523 \times 10^4 \text{ N/C}$$

The resultant intensity can now be calculated from its components:

$$\tan \phi = \frac{E_y}{E_x} = \frac{-0.523 \times 10^4 \text{ N/C}}{-0.192 \times 10^4 \text{ N/C}}$$

$$\phi = 69.8°$$

$$E = \frac{E_y}{\sin \phi} = \frac{0.523 \times 10^4 \text{ N/C}}{\sin 69.8°}$$

$$= 0.557 \times 10^4 \text{ N/C}$$

Therefore, the resultant field intensity at B is 0.557×10^4 N/C directed 69.8° downward and to the left.

31-3 ELECTRIC FIELD LINES

An ingenious aid to the visualization of electric fields was introduced by Michael Faraday (1791–1867) in his early work in electromagnetism. The method consists of representing both the strength and the direction of an electric field by imaginary lines called *electric field lines*.

> **Electric field lines** are imaginary lines drawn in such a manner that their direction at any point is the same as the direction of the electric field at that point.

For example, the lines drawn radially outward from the positive charge in Fig. 31-3a represent the direction of the field at any point on the line. The electric lines in the vicinity of a negative charge would be radially inward and directed toward the charge, as in Fig. 31-3b. We shall see later that the density of these lines in any region of space is a measure of the *magnitude* of the field intensity in that region.

In general, the direction of the electric field in a region of space varies from place to place. Thus the electric lines are normally curved. For instance, let us consider the construction of an electric field line in the region between a positive charge and a negative charge, as illustrated in Fig. 31-8.

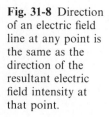 **Fig. 31-8** Direction of an electric field line at any point is the same as the direction of the resultant electric field intensity at that point.

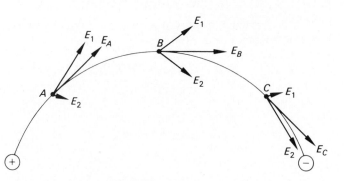

The direction of the electric field line at any point is the same as the direction of the resultant electric field vector at that point. Two rules must be followed when constructing electric field lines:

1. The direction of the field line at any point is the same as the direction in which a positive charge would move if placed at that point.
2. The spacing of the field lines must be such that they are close together where the field is strong and far apart where the field is weak.

Following these very general rules, one can construct the electric field lines for the two common cases shown in Fig. 31-9. As a consequence of how electric lines are drawn, *they will always leave positive charges and enter negative charges*. No lines can originate or terminate in space although one end of an electric line may proceed to infinity.

Fig. 31-9 (*a*) A graphical illustration of the electric field lines in the region surrounding two opposite charges. (*b*) The field lines between two positive charges.

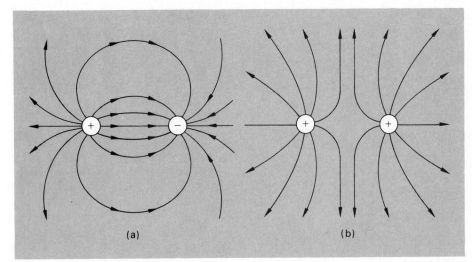

(a)

(b)

31-4
GAUSS' LAW

For any given charge distribution, we can draw an infinite number of electric lines. Clearly, if the spacing of the lines is to be a standardized indication of field strength, we must set a limit on the number of lines drawn in any situation. For example, let us consider the field lines directed radially outward from a positive point charge. (Refer to Fig. 31-10.) We shall use the letter N to represent the number of lines drawn. Now let us imagine a spherical surface surrounding the point charge at a distance r from the charge. The field intensity at every point on such a sphere would be given by

$$E = \frac{kq}{r^2}$$

(31-9)

Fig. 31-10 Electric field intensity at a distance r from a point charge is directly proportional to the number of lines ΔN penetrating a unit area ΔA of an imaginary spherical surface constructed at that distance.

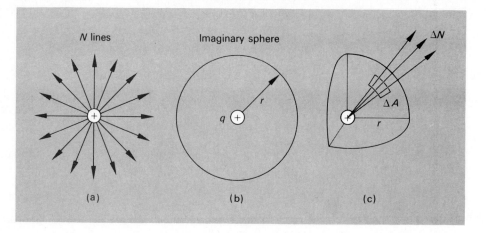

From the way the field lines are drawn, we might also say that the field at a tiny element of surface area ΔA is proportional to the number of lines ΔN penetrating that area. In other words, the density of lines (lines per unit area) is directly proportional to the field strength. Symbolically,

$$\frac{\Delta N}{\Delta A} \propto E_n \qquad (31\text{-}10)$$

The subscript n indicates that the field is everywhere normal to the surface area. This proportionality is true regardless of the total number of lines N which may be drawn. However, once we choose a proportionality constant for Eq. (31-10), we automatically set a limit to the number of lines drawn for any given situation. It has been found that the most convenient choice for this spacing constant is ϵ_0. It is called the *permittivity of free space* and is defined by

$$\boxed{\epsilon_0 = \frac{1}{4\pi k} = 8.85 \times 10^{-12} \text{ C}^2/\text{N} \cdot \text{m}^2} \qquad (31\text{-}11)$$

where $k = 9 \times 10^9$ N $\cdot$ m^2/C^2 from Coulomb's law. Hence Eq. (31-10) can be written

$$\frac{\Delta N}{\Delta A} = \epsilon_0 E_n \qquad (31\text{-}12)$$

or

$$\Delta N = \epsilon_0 E_n \Delta A \qquad (31\text{-}13)$$

When E_n is constant over the entire surface, the total number of lines radiating outward from the enclosed charge is

$$N = \epsilon_0 E_n A \qquad (31\text{-}14)$$

It can be seen that the choice of ϵ_0 is a convenient one by substituting Eq. (31-11) into Eq. (31-9):

$$E_n = \frac{1}{4\pi\epsilon_0} \frac{q}{r^2}$$

Substituting this expression into Eq. (31-14) and recalling that the area of a spherical surface is $A = 4\pi r^2$, we obtain

$$N = \epsilon_0 E_n A$$

$$= \frac{\epsilon_0}{4\pi\epsilon_0} \frac{q}{r^2} 4\pi r^2 = q$$

The choice of ϵ_0 as the proportionality constant has resulted in the fact that *the total number of lines passing normally through a surface is numerically equal to the charge contained within the surface.* Although this result was obtained using a spherical surface, it will apply to any other surface. The more general statement of the result is known as *Gauss' law*:

> *The net number of electric lines of force crossing any closed surface in an outward direction is numerically equal to the net total charge within that surface.*

$$\boxed{N = \sum \epsilon_0 E_n A = \sum q} \tag{31-15}$$

Gauss' law can be used to compute the field intensity near surfaces of charge. This represents a distinct advantage over methods developed so far because the previous equations apply only to point charges. The best way to understand the application of Gauss' law is through examples.

31-5 APPLICATIONS OF GAUSS' LAW

Since most charged conductors have large quantities of charge on them, it is not practical to treat the charges individually. Generally, we speak of the charge density σ, defined as the charge per unit area of surface.

$$\boxed{\sigma = \frac{q}{A} \qquad q = \sigma A} \tag{31-16}$$

EXAMPLE 31-5

Calculate the electric field intensity at a distance r from an infinite sheet of positive charge, as shown in Fig. 31-11.

Solution

The solution of problems using Gauss' law usually necessitates the construction of an imaginary surface of simple geometric form, e.g., a sphere or a cylinder. These are referred to as *gaussian surfaces*. In this example, a cylindrical surface is imagined to penetrate the sheet of positive charge so that it projects a distance r on either side of the

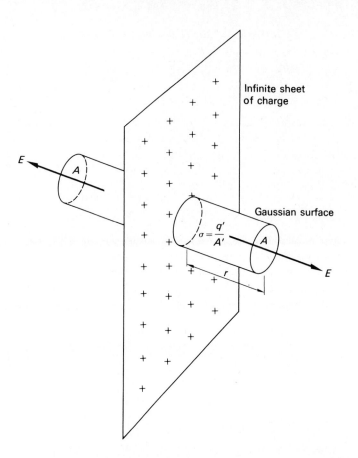

Infinite sheet
of charge

E

A

$\sigma = \dfrac{q'}{A'}$

A

Gaussian surface

r

E

thin sheet. The area A of each end of the cylinder is the same as the area cut on the sheet of charge. Thus the total charge contained inside the cylinder is

$$\sum q = \sigma A$$

where σ represents the charge density. Because of symmetry, the resultant field intensity E must be directed perpendicular to the sheet of charge at any point near the sheet. This means that no field lines will penetrate the curved sides of the cylinder, and the two ends of area A will represent the total area penetrated by the field lines. From Gauss' law,

$$\sum \epsilon_0 E_n A = \sum q$$

$$\epsilon_0 EA + \epsilon_0 EA = \sigma A$$

$$2\epsilon_0 EA = \sigma A$$

$$E = \frac{\sigma}{2\epsilon_0} \qquad (31\text{-}17)$$

Note that the field intensity E is independent of the distance r from the sheet.

Before the reader assumes that the example of an infinite sheet of charge is impractical, it should be pointed out that "infinity" in a practical sense implies only that the dimensions of the sheet are beyond the point of electrical interaction. In other words, Eq. (31-17) applies when the length and width of the sheet are very large in comparison with the distance r from the sheet.

EXAMPLE 31-6   Show by using Gauss' law that all the excess charge resides on the surface of a charged conductor.

Solution   Let us first consider the charged solid conductor in Fig. 31-12. Within such a conductor, charges are free to move if a resultant force is applied to them. After a time, we could safely assume that all charges in the conductor are at rest. Under this condition, the electric field intensity within the conductor must be zero. Otherwise, the charges would be moving. Now, if we construct a gaussian surface just inside the surface of the conductor, as shown in the figure, we can write (for this surface)

$$\sum \epsilon_0 E A = \sum q$$

Substituting $E = 0$, we also find that $\sum q = 0$ or that no charge is enclosed by the surface. Since the gaussian surface can be drawn as close to the outside of the conductor as we wish, we can conclude that all the charge resides on the surface of the conductor. This conclusion holds even if the conductor is hollow on the inside.

Fig. 31-12 Gauss' law demonstrates that all the charge resides on the surface of a conductor.

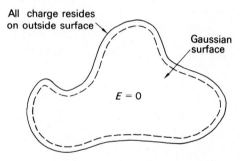

An interesting experiment was devised by Michael Faraday to demonstrate that charge resides on the surface of a hollow conductor. In this experiment, known as the *ice-pail experiment*, a positively charged ball supported by a silk thread is lowered into a hollow metallic conductor. As shown in Fig. 31-13, a redistribution of charge occurs on the walls of the conductor, drawing the electrons to the inner surface. When the ball makes contact with the bottom of the conductor, the induced charge is neutralized, leaving a net positive charge on the outer surface. Probes with an electroscope will show that no charge resides inside the conductor and that a net positive charge remains on the outer surface.

Fig. 31-13 Faraday's ice-pail experiment.

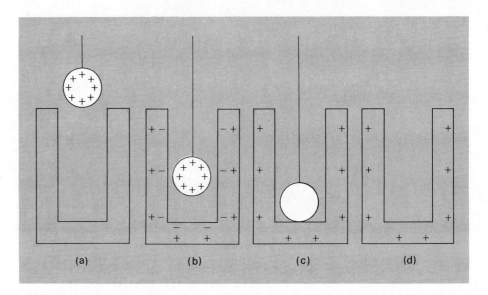

(a) (b) (c) (d)

EXAMPLE 31-7 A capacitor is an electrostatic device consisting of two metallic conductors of area A separated by a distance d. If equal and opposite charge densities σ are placed on the conductors, an electric field E will exist between them. Determine the charge density on either plate. (Refer to Fig. 31-14.)

Solution A gaussian cylinder is constructed as shown in Fig. 31-14 for the inner surface of either plate. There is no field inside the conducting plate, and the only area penetrated by the field lines is the surface A' projecting into the space between the plates. Applying Gauss' law to the left plate, we have

$$\sum \epsilon_0 E A = \sum q$$

$$\epsilon_0 E A' = \sigma A'$$

$$E = \frac{\sigma}{\epsilon_0} \qquad\qquad (31\text{-}18)$$

Fig. 31-14 Electric field in the region between two oppositely charged plates is equal to the ratio of the charge density σ to the permittivity ϵ_0.

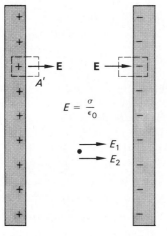

$$E = \frac{\sigma}{\epsilon_0}$$

The same result would be obtained if the gaussian cylinder on the right were used. However, the lines would be directed inward, indicating an enclosed negative charge.

Notice that the field between the two plates in this example is exactly twice the field due to a thin sheet of charge, as given by Eq. (31-17). One can understand this relationship by considering the field $\mathbf{E}$ between the plates as a superposition of the fields due to two oppositely charged sheets.

$$E = E_1 + E_2 = \frac{\sigma}{2\epsilon_0} + \frac{\sigma}{2\epsilon_0} = \frac{\sigma}{\epsilon_0}$$

The field $\mathbf{E}_1$ due to the positive sheet of charge is in the same direction as the field $\mathbf{E}_2$ due to the negative sheet of charge. To the left and right of the two plates $\mathbf{E}_1$ and $\mathbf{E}_2$ are oppositely directed and cancel out.

SUMMARY

The concept of an electric field has been introduced to describe the region surrounding an electric charge. Its magnitude is determined by the force a unit charge will experience at a given location, and its direction is the same as the force on a positive charge at that point. Electric field lines were postulated to give a visual picture of electric fields, and the density of such field lines is an indication of the intensity of the electric field. The major concepts to be remembered are:

- An *electric field* is said to exist in a region of space in which an electric charge will experience an electric force. The *magnitude* of the electric field intensity E is given by the force F per unit of charge q.

$$E = \frac{F}{q} \qquad E = \frac{(9 \times 10^9 \text{ N} \cdot \text{m}^2/\text{C}^2)Q}{r^2}$$

The metric unit for the electric field intensity is the newton per coulomb (N/C). In the above equation, r is the distance from the charge Q to the point in question.
- The resultant field intensity at a point in the vicinity of a number of charges is the *vector* sum of the contributions from each charge.

$$\mathbf{E} = \mathbf{E} + \mathbf{E}_2 + \mathbf{E}_3 + \cdots \qquad E = \sum \frac{kQ}{r^2}$$

It must be emphasized that this is a vector sum and not an algebraic sum. Once the magnitude and direction of each vector is determined, the resultant can be found from vector mechanics.
- The permittivity of free space ϵ_0 is a fundamental constant defined as

$$\epsilon_0 = \frac{1}{4\pi k} = 8.85 \times 10^{-12} \text{ C}^2/\text{N} \cdot \text{m}^2 \qquad \textit{Permittivity}$$

- Gauss' law states that the net number of electric field lines crossing any closed surface in an outward direction is numerically equal to the net total charge within that surface.

$$N = \sum \epsilon_0 E_n A = \sum q$$

Gauss' law

- In applications of Gauss' law the concept of charge density σ as the charge q per unit area A of surface is often utilized:

$$\sigma = \frac{q}{A} \qquad q = \sigma A$$

Charge Density

QUESTIONS

31-1. Define the following terms:
  a. Electric field
  b. Electric field intensity
  c. Electric field lines
  d. Permittivity ϵ_0
  e. Charge density
  f. Gauss' law
  g. Gaussian surface
  h. Faraday's ice pail

31-2. Some texts refer to electric field lines as "lines of force." Discuss the advisability of this description.

31-3. Can an electric field exist in a region of space in which an electric charge would not experience a force? Explain.

31-4. Is it necessary that a charge be placed at a point in order to have an electric field at that point? Explain.

31-5. Using a procedure similar to that for electric fields, show that the gravitational acceleration can be calculated from

$$g = \frac{GM}{r^2}$$

where M = mass of earth
r = distance from center of earth

31-6. Discuss the similarities between electric fields and gravitational fields. In what ways do they differ?

31-7. In Gauss' law the constant ϵ_0 was chosen as the proportionality factor between line density and field intensity. In a theoretical sense, this is a wise choice because it leads to the conclusion that the total number of lines is equal to the enclosed charge. Is such a choice practical for graphically illustrating field lines? According to Gauss' relation, how many field lines would emanate from a charge of 1 C?

31-8. Justify the following statement: the electric field intensity on the surface of any charged conductor must be directed perpendicular to the surface.

31-9. Electric field lines will never intersect. Explain.

31-10. Suppose you connect an electroscope to the outside surface of Faraday's ice pail. Show graphically what will happen to the gold leaf during each of the steps illustrated in Fig. 31-13.

31-11. Can an electric field line begin and end on the same conductor? Discuss.

31-12. What form would Gauss' law take if we had chosen k for the proportionality constant instead of the permittivity ϵ_0?

31-13. In Gauss' law, demonstrate that the units of $\epsilon_0 EA$ are dimensionally equivalent to the units of charge.

31-14. Show that the field in the region outside the two parallel plates in Fig. 31-14 is equal to zero.

31-15. Why is the field intensity constant in the region between two oppositely charged plates? Draw a vector diagram of the field due to each plate at various points between the plates.

PROBLEMS

31-1. A charge of $+2$ μC placed in an electric field experiences a force of 8×10^{-4} N. What is the electric field intensity at that point?

Ans. 400 N/C.

31-2. A charge of -3 nC experiences a force of 6×10^{-5} N. What is the field intensity?

31-3. The uniform electric field between two horizontal plates is 8×10^4 N/C. The top plate is positively charged and the lower plate is negatively charged. What is the magnitude and direction of the force exerted on an electron as it passes through these plates?

Ans. 1.28×10^{-14} N, up.

31-4. An alpha particle consists of two protons and two neutrons, and it has a net positive charge of $+2e$. Assume that the top and lower plates are reversed in Prob. 31-3, but that the magnitude of the electric field is unchanged. What are the magnitude and direction of the force on an alpha particle as it passes between these plates?

31-5. The electric field intensity at a point in space is determined to be 5×10^5 N/C directed due west. What are the magnitude and direction of the force on a -4-μC charge placed at that point?

Ans. 2 N, east.

31-6. What must be the magnitude and direction of the electric field intensity between two horizontal plates if it is desired to produce an upward force of 6×10^{-4} N on a 60-μC charge?

31-7. Find the electric field intensity at a distance of 40 mm from a point charge of 5 nC.

Ans. 2.81×10^4 N/C.

31-8. An electric field intensity of 300 N/C is measured at a distance of 50 mm from an unknown charge. What is the magnitude of the charge?

31-9. How far from a point charge of 80 nC will the field intensity be equal to 5000 N/C?

Ans. 379 mm.

31-10. Determine the electric field intensity at the midpoint between a -60 μC charge and a $+40$ μC charge. The charges are 70 mm apart in air.

31-11. Determine the field intensity at the midpoint between two charges of $+4$ nC and $+8$ nC. Their separation is 80 mm.

Ans. 2.25×10^4 N/C, left.

31-12. Determine the electric field intensity at a point 30 mm to the right of a 16 nC charge and 40 mm to the left of a 9 nC charge.

31-13. Two charges of $+16$ and $+8$ μC are 200 mm apart in air. At what point between the two charges is the field intensity equal to zero?

Ans. 82.8 mm from the 8-μC charge.

31-14. Two charges of $+8$ nC and -5 nC are 40 mm apart in air. At what point on a line joining the two charges will the electric field intensity be equal to zero?

31-15. A charge of -20 μC is placed horizontally at a distance of 50 mm to the right of a 49-μC charge. What is the resultant electric field intensity at a point directly above the -20 μC charge and at a distance of 24 mm?

Ans. 2.82×10^8 N/C, 296.7°.

31-16. Two charges of $+12$ nC and $+18$ nC are separated horizontally by a distance of 28 mm. What is the resultant field intensity at a point 20 mm from each charge and above a line joining the two charges?

31-17. A 20-mg particle is placed in a uniform downward field of intensity 2000 N/C. How many excess electrons must be placed on the particle in order for the electric and gravitational forces to balance?

Ans. 6.12×10^{11} electrons.

31-18. The magnitude of the electric field intensity between the plates in Fig. 31-15 is 4000 N/C. What is the magnitude of the charge on the suspended pith ball whose mass is 3 mg?

Fig. 31-15

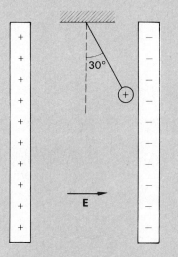

31-19. The electric field intensity between the two plates in Fig. 31-4 is 2 kN/C. The length of the plates is 4 cm, and their separation is 1 cm. An electron is projected into the field from the left with horizontal velocity of 2×10^7 m/s. What is the upward deflection of the electron at the instant it leaves the plates?

Ans. 0.7 mm.

31-20. If the plates in Prob. 31-19 are 1 cm wide, what is the magnitude of the charge on each plate?

31-21. Charges of -2 and $+4$ μC are placed at the corners of an equilateral triangle with 10-cm sides. **(a)** What is the magnitude of the electric field intensity at the third corner? **(b)** What are the magnitude and the direction of the force which would act on a charge of $-2~\mu C$ placed at that corner?

Ans. **(a)** 3.12×10^6 N/C **(b)** 6.24 N, 330°.

31-22. What is the acceleration of an electron placed in a constant field of 4×10^5 N/C?

31-23. Use Gauss' law to show that the field outside a solid charged sphere at a distance r from its center is given by

$$E = \frac{1}{4\pi\epsilon_0} \frac{Q}{r^2}$$

where Q is the total charge on the sphere.

31-24. Use Gauss' law to show that the electric field intensity at a distance R from an infinite line of charge is given by

$$E = \frac{\lambda}{2\pi\epsilon_0 R}$$

where λ is the charge per unit length. Construct a gaussian surface, as shown in Fig. 31-16.

Fig. 31-16

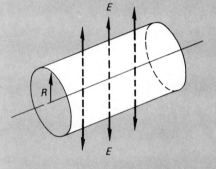

31-25. A uniformly charged conducting sphere has a radius of 24 cm and a surface charge density of $+16~\mu C/m^2$. What is the total number of electric field lines leaving the sphere?

Ans. 1.16×10^{-5} line.

31-26. Use Gauss' law to show that the field just outside any solid conductor is given by

$$E = \frac{\sigma}{\epsilon_0}$$

31-27. What is the electric field intensity 2 m from the surface of a sphere 20 cm in diameter having a surface charge density of $+8$ nC/m²?

Ans. 2.05 N/C.

32 *Electric Potential*

OBJECTIVES: **After completing this chapter, you should be able to:**

1. **Demonstrate by definition and example your understanding of *electric potential energy*, *electric potential*, and *electric potential difference*.**

2. **Compute the potential energy of a known charge at a given distance from other known charges, and state whether the energy is negative or positive.**

3. **Compute the absolute potential at any point in the vicinity of a number of known charges.**

4. **Use your knowledge of potential difference to calculate the work required to move a known charge from any point *A* to another point *B* in an electric field created by one or more point charges.**

5. **Write and apply a relationship between the electric field intensity, the potential difference, and the plate separation for parallel plates of equal and opposite charge.**

In our study of mechanics, many problems were simplified by introducing the concepts of energy. The conservation of mechanical energy allowed us to say certain things about the initial and final states of systems without having to analyze the motion between states. The concept of a change of potential energy into kinetic energy avoids the problem of varying forces.

In electricity, many practical problems can be solved by considering the changes in energy experienced by a moving charge. For example, if a certain quantity of work is required to move a charge against electric forces, the charge should have a *potential* for giving up an equivalent amount of energy when it is released. In this chapter we develop the idea of electric potential energy.

32-1
ELECTRIC
POTENTIAL
ENERGY

One of the best ways to understand the concept of electric potential energy is by comparing it with gravitational potential energy. In the gravitational case, consider that a mass m is moved from level A in Fig. 32-1 to level B. An external force F equal to the weight mg must be applied to move the mass against gravity. The work done by this force is the product of mg and h. When the mass m reaches level B, it has a potential for doing work relative to level A. The system has a *potential energy* (P.E.) which is equal to the work done against gravity.

$$P.E. = mg \cdot h$$

Fig. 32-1 A mass m lifted against a gravitational field **g** results in a potential energy of mgh at level B. When released, this energy will be transformed entirely into kinetic energy as it falls to level A.

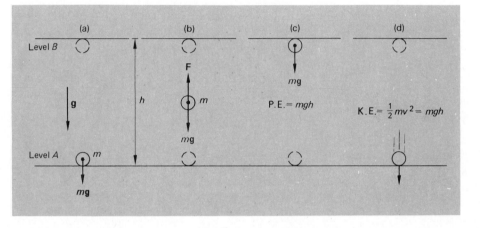

This expression represents the potential for doing work after the mass m is released at level B and falls the distance h. Therefore, the magnitude of the potential energy at B does not depend on the path taken to reach that level.

Now, let us consider a positive charge $+q$ resting at point A in a uniform electric field E between two oppositely charged plates. (See Fig. 32-2.) An electric force qE acts downward on the charge. The work done against the

Fig. 32-2 A positive charge $+q$ is moved against a constant electric field **E** through a distance d. At point B the potential energy will be qEd relative to point A. When released, the charge will gain an equivalent amount of kinetic energy.

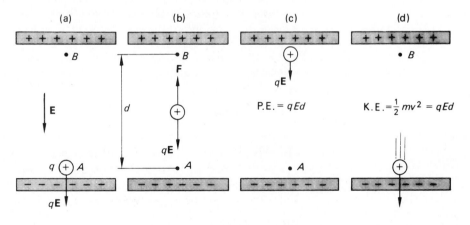

electric field in moving the charge from A to B is equal to the product of the force qE and the distance d. Hence, the electric potential energy at point B relative to point A is

$$\text{P.E.} = qE \cdot d \qquad (32\text{-}1)$$

Before we proceed, we should point out an important difference between gravitational potential energy and electric potential energy. In the case of gravity, there is only one kind of mass, and the forces involved are always forces of attraction. Therefore, a mass at higher elevations always has greater potential energy relative to the earth. This is not true in the electrical case because of the existence of negative charge. In the example, a positive charge, as in Fig. 32-2, has a greater potential energy at point B than at point A. This is true regardless of the reference point chosen for measuring the energy because work has been done *against* the electric field. (Refer to Fig. 32-3.) On the other

Fig. 32-3 A
positive charge
increases its
potential energy
when moved from
A to B; a negative
charge *loses*
potential energy
when it moves from
A to B.

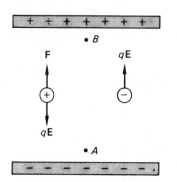

hand, if a negative charge were moved from point A to point B, work would be done *by* the field. A negative charge would have a *lower* potential energy at B, which is exactly opposite to the situation for a positive charge.

> *Whenever a positive charge is moved against an electric field, the potential energy increases; whenever a negative charge moves against an electric field, the potential energy decreases.*

The above rule is a direct consequence of the fact that the direction of the electric field is defined in terms of a positive charge.

**32-2
CALCU-
LATING
POTENTIAL
ENERGY**

In considering the space between two oppositely charged plates, work computations are fairly simple because the electric field is uniform. The electric force that a charge experiences is constant as long as it remains between the plates. In general, however, the field will not be constant, and we must make allowances for a varying force. For example, consider the electric field in the vicinity of a positive charge Q, as illustrated in Fig. 32-4. The field is directed radially outward, and its intensity falls off inversely with the square of the distance from the center of the charge. The field at points A and B is

$$E_A = \frac{kQ}{r_A^2} \qquad E_B = \frac{kQ}{r_B^2}$$

where r_A and r_B are the respective distances to points A and B.

Fig. 32-4 Potential energy due to a charge placed in an electric field is equal to the work done *against* electric forces in bringing the charge from infinity to the point in question.

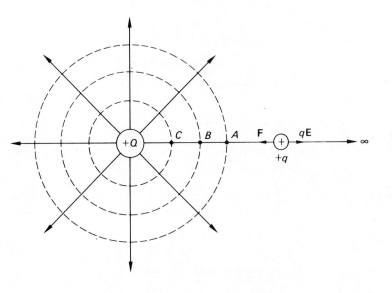

The average electric force experienced by a charge $+q$ when it is moved from point A to point B is

$$F = \frac{kQq}{r_A r_B} \tag{32-2}$$

Thus the work done against the electric field in moving through the distance $r_A - r_B$ is equal to

$$\text{Work}_{A \to B} = \frac{kQq}{r_A r_B}(r_A - r_B)$$

$$= kQq\left(\frac{1}{r_B} - \frac{1}{r_A}\right) \tag{32-3}$$

Note that the work is a function of the distances r_A and r_B. The path traveled is unimportant. The same work would be done against the field in moving a charge from any point on the dashed circle passing through A to any point on the circle passing through B.

Suppose now we compute the work done against electric forces in moving a positive charge from infinity to a point a distance r from the charge Q. From Eq. (32-3), the work is given by

$$\text{Work}_{\infty \to r} = kQq\left(\frac{1}{r} - \frac{1}{\infty}\right)$$

$$= \frac{kQq}{r} \tag{32-4}$$

Since we have shown that the work done against the electric field equals the increase in potential energy, Eq. (32-4) is the potential energy at r relative to infinity. Often potential energy is taken as zero at infinity so that the potential energy of a system composed of a charge q and another charge Q separated by a distance r is

$$\boxed{\text{P.E.} = \frac{kQq}{r}} \tag{32-5}$$

The **potential energy** of the system is equal to the work done against the electric forces in moving the charge $+q$ from infinity to that point.

EXAMPLE 32-1

A charge of $+2$ μC is 20 cm away from another charge of $+4$ μC. (a) What is the potential energy of the system? (b) What is the change in potential energy if the 2-μC charge is moved to a distance of 8 cm from the $+4$-μC charge?

Solution (a)

The potential energy at 20 cm is given by Eq. (32-5).

$$\text{P.E.} = \frac{kQq}{r}$$

$$= \frac{(9 \times 10^9 \text{ N} \cdot \text{m}^2/\text{C}^2)(4 \times 10^{-6} \text{ C})(2 \times 10^{-9} \text{ C})}{0.2 \text{ m}}$$

$$= 36 \times 10^{-5} \text{ J}$$

Solution (b)

The potential energy at a distance of 8 cm is

$$\text{P.E.} = \frac{kQq}{r}$$

$$= \frac{(9 \times 10^9 \text{ N} \cdot \text{m}^2/\text{C}^2)(4 \times 10^{-6} \text{ C})(2 \times 10^{-9} \text{ C})}{0.08 \text{ m}}$$

$$= 90 \times 10^{-5} \text{ J}$$

The change in potential energy is

$$90 \times 10^{-5} \text{ J} - 36 \times 10^{-5} \text{ J} = 54 \times 10^{-5} \text{ J}$$

Notice that the difference is positive, indicating an increase in potential energy. If the charge Q were negative and all other parameters were unchanged, the potential energy would have decreased by this same amount.

32-3
POTENTIAL

When we first introduced the concept of an electric field as force per unit charge, we pointed out that the primary advantage of such a concept was that it allowed us to assign an electrical property to space. If the field intensity is known at some point, the force on a charge placed at that point can be predicted. It is equally convenient to assign another property to the space surrounding a charge that would allow us to predict the potential energy due to another charge placed at any point. This property of space is called *potential* and is defined as follows:

> The **potential** V at a point a distance r from a charge Q is equal to the work per unit charge done against electric forces in bringing a positive charge +q from infinity to that point.

In other words, the potential at some point A, as shown in Fig. 32-5, is equal to *the potential energy per unit charge*. The units of potential are expressed in *joules per coulomb*, defined as a *volt* (V).

$$V_A(\text{V}) = \frac{\text{P.E.(J)}}{q(\text{C})} \tag{32-6}$$

Fig. 32-5 Calculating the potential at a distance r from a charge +Q.

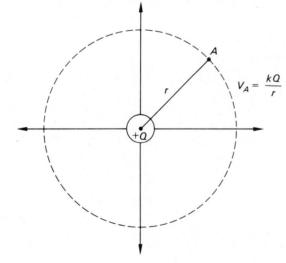

$$V_A = \frac{kQ}{r}$$

Thus, a potential of *one volt* at point A means that *if a charge of one coulomb were to be placed at A, the potential energy would be one joule.* In general when the potential is known at a point A, the potential energy due to a charge q at that point can be found from

$$\boxed{\text{P.E.} = qV_A} \tag{32-7}$$

Substitution of Eq. (32-5) into Eq. (32-6) yields an expression for directly computing the potential.

$$V_A = \frac{P.E.}{q} = \frac{kQq/r}{q}$$

$$V_A = \frac{kQ}{r} \qquad (32\text{-}8)$$

The symbol V_A refers to the potential at point A located at a distance r from the charge Q.

It is noted now that the potential is the same at equal distances from a spherical charge. For this reason, the dashed lines in Figs. 32-4 and 32-5 are called *equipotential lines*. Note that the lines of equal potential are always perpendicular to the electric field lines. If this were not true, work would be done by a resultant force when a charge moved along an equipotential line. Such work would increase or decrease the potential.

Equipotential lines are always perpendicular to electric field lines.

Before offering an example, it must be pointed out that the potential at a point is defined in terms of a positive charge. This means that the potential will be negative at a point in space surrounding a negative charge. As a rule, we must remember that:

The potential due to a positive charge is positive, and the potential due to a negative charge is negative.

Using a negative sign for a negative charge Q in Eq. (32-8) results in a negative value for the potential.

EXAMPLE 32-2 (*a*) Calculate the potential at a point A which is 30 cm distant from a charge of -2 μC. (*b*) What is the potential energy if a $+4$-nC charge is placed at A?

Solution (a) From Eq. (32-8)

$$V_A = \frac{kQ}{r} = \frac{(9 \times 10^9 \text{ N} \cdot \text{m}^2/\text{C}^2)(-2 \times 10^{-6} \text{ C})}{0.3 \text{ m}}$$

$$= -6 \times 10^4 \text{ V}$$

Solution (b) The potential energy due to the $+4$-nC charge is given by direct substitution into Eq. (32-7).

$$P.E. = qV_A = (4 \times 10^{-9} \text{ C})(-6 \times 10^4 \text{ V})$$

$$= -24 \times 10^{-5} \text{ J}$$

A negative potential energy means that work must be done *against* the electric field in moving the charges apart. In the above example, 24×10^{-5} J of work would have to be supplied by an external force in order to remove the charge to infinity.

Now let us consider the more general case, which deals with the potential in the neighborhood of a number of charges. As illustrated in Fig. 32-6:

The potential in the vicinity of a number of charges is equal to the algebraic sum of the potentials due to each charge.

$$V_A = V_1 + V_2 + V_3$$

$$= \frac{kQ_1}{r_1} + \frac{kQ_2}{r_2} + \frac{kQ_3}{r_3}$$

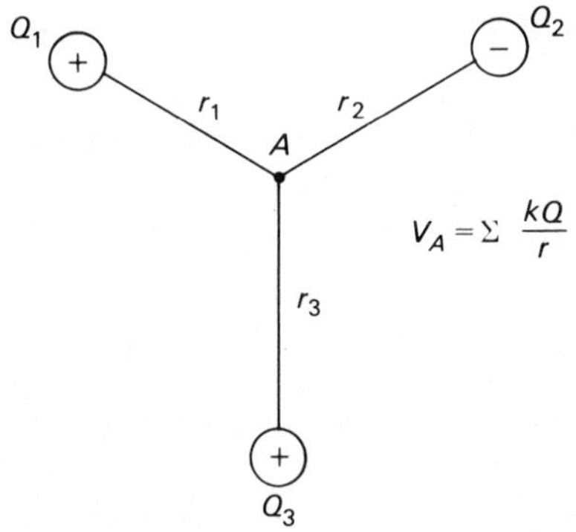

Fig. 32-6 Potential in the vicinity of a number of charges.

$$V_A = \Sigma \frac{kQ}{r}$$

Whenever the charge is negative, as with Q_2 in Fig. 32-6, the sign of the charge is inserted into the calculations. In general,

$$\boxed{V = \Sigma \frac{kQ}{r}} \tag{32-9}$$

This equation is an algebraic sum since potential is a scalar quantity and not a vector quantity.

EXAMPLE 32-3

Two charges, $Q_1 = +6 \ \mu C$ and $Q_2 = -6 \ \mu C$, are separated by 12 cm, as shown in Fig. 32-7. Calculate the potential (a) at point A and (b) at point B.

Solution (a)

The potential at A is found from Eq. (32-9).

$$V_A = \frac{kQ_1}{r_1} + \frac{kQ_2}{r_2}$$

$$= \frac{(9 \times 10^9 \ \text{N} \cdot \text{m}^2/\text{C}^2)(6 \times 10^{-6} \ \text{C})}{4 \times 10^{-2} \ \text{m}} + \frac{(9 \times 10^9 \ \text{N} \cdot \text{m}^2/\text{C}^2)(-6 \times 10^{-6} \ \text{C})}{8 \times 10^{-2} \ \text{m}}$$

$$= 13.5 \times 10^5 \ \text{V} - 6.75 \times 10^5 \ \text{V}$$

$$= 6.75 \times 10^5 \ \text{V}$$

This means that the electric field will do 6.75×10^5 J of work on each coulomb of positive charge that it moves from A to infinity.

Fig. 32-7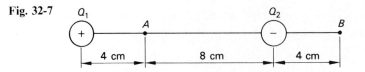

The potential at B is

$$V_B = \frac{kQ_1}{r_1} + \frac{kQ_2}{r_2}$$

$$= \frac{(9 \times 10^9 \ N \cdot m^2/C^2)(6 \times 10^{-6} \ C)}{16 \times 10^{-2} \ m} + \frac{(9 \times 10^9 \ N \cdot m^2/C^2)(-6 \times 10^{-6} \ C)}{4 \times 10^{-2} \ m}$$

$$= 3.38 \times 10^5 \ V - 13.5 \times 10^5 \ V$$

$$= -10.1 \times 10^5 \ V$$

The negative value indicates that the field will hold onto a positive charge. In order to move 1 C of positive charge from A to infinity, another source of energy must perform 10.1×10^5 J of work. The field would perform negative work in this amount.

32-4 POTENTIAL DIFFERENCE

In practical electricity, we are seldom interested in the work per unit charge to remove a charge to infinity. More often, we want to know the work requirements for moving charges between two points. This leads to the concept of *potential difference.*

> The **potential difference** between two points is the work per unit positive charge done by electric forces in moving a small test charge from the point of higher potential to the point of lower potential.

Another way of stating this would be to say that the potential difference between two points is the difference in the potentials at those points. For example, if the potential at some point A is 100 V and the potential at another point B is 40 V, the potential difference is

$$V_A - V_B = 100 \ V - 40 \ V = 60 \ V$$

This means that 60 J of work will be done by the field on each coulomb of positive charge moved from A to B. In general, the work done by the electric field in moving a charge q from point A to point B can be found from

$$\boxed{\text{Work}_{A \to B} = q(V_A - V_B)} \tag{32-10}$$

EXAMPLE 32-4   What is the potential difference between points A and B in Fig. 32-7. How much work is done by the electric field in moving a -2-nC charge from point A to point B?

Solution

The potentials at points A and B were calculated in the previous example. They are

$$V_A = 6.75 \times 10^5 \text{ V} \qquad V_B = -10.1 \times 10^5 \text{ V}$$

Therefore the potential difference between points A and B is

$$V_A - V_B = 6.75 \times 10^5 \text{ V} - (-10.1 \times 10^5 \text{ V})$$

$$= 16.9 \times 10^5 \text{ V}$$

Since A is at a higher potential than B, positive work would be done by the field when a *positive* charge is moved from A to B. If a *negative* charge is moved, the work done by the field in moving it from A to B will be negative. In this example, the work is

$$\text{Work}_{A \to B} = q(V_A - V_B)$$

$$= (-2 \times 10^{-9} \text{ C})(16.9 \times 10^5 \text{ V})$$

$$= -3.37 \times 10^{-3} \text{ J}$$

Since the work done by the field is negative, another source of energy must supply the work to move the charge.

Let us now return to the example of a uniform electric field **E** between two oppositely charged plates, as in Fig. 32-8. We shall assume that the plates are separated by a distance d. A charge q placed in the region between the plates A and B will experience a force given by

$$\mathbf{F} = q\mathbf{E}$$

The work done by this force in moving the charge q from plate A to plate B is given by

$$Fd = (qE)d$$

But this work is also equal to the product of the charge q and the potential difference $V_A - V_B$ between the two plates, so that we can write

$$q(V_A - V_B) = qEd$$

Fig. 32-8 Potential difference between two oppositely charged plates.

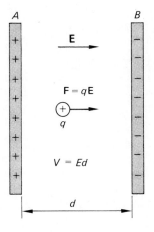

If we divide through by q and represent the potential difference by the single symbol V, we obtain

$$\boxed{V = Ed} \tag{32-11}$$

The potential difference between two oppositely charged plates is equal to the product of the field intensity and the plate separation.

EXAMPLE 32-5 The potential difference between two plates 5 mm apart is 10 kV. Determine the electric field intensity between the plates.

Solution Solving for E in Eq. (32-11) gives

$$E = \frac{V}{d} = \frac{10 \times 10^3 \text{ V}}{5 \times 10^{-3} \text{ m}} = 2 \times 10^6 \text{ V/m}$$

As an exercise, the student should show that the *volt per meter* is equivalent to the *newton per coulomb*. The electric field expressed in volts per meter is sometimes referred to as the *potential gradient*.

32-5 MILLIKAN'S OIL-DROP EXPERIMENT

Now that we have developed the concepts of the electric field and potential difference, we are ready to describe a classic experiment designed to determine the smallest unit of charge. Robert A. Millikan, an American physicist, devised a series of experiments in the early 1900s. A schematic diagram of his apparatus is shown in Fig. 32-9. Very tiny oil droplets are sprayed into the region between the two metallic plates. Electrons are freed from air molecules by passing ionizing x-rays through the medium. These electrons attach themselves to the oil droplets, giving them a net negative charge.

The downward motion of the oil droplets can be observed by a microscope as they fall slowly under the influence of their weight and the upward viscous force of air resistance. (Refer to Fig. 32-9a.) The laws of hydrostatics can be used to calculate the mass m of a particular oil drop from its measured rate of fall.

After the necessary data for determining the mass m have been recorded, and external battery is connected to establish a uniform electric field **E** between the oppositely charged plates. (See Fig. 32-9b.) The magnitude of the field intensity can be controlled by a variable resistor in the electric circuit. The field is adjusted until the upward electric force on the drop is equal to the downward gravitational force, so that the oil drop stops moving. Under these conditions

$$qE = mg$$

where q = net charge of oil drop
m = mass of oil drop
g = acceleration of gravity

Fig. 32-9 Millikan's oil-drop experiment. (*a*) The mass *m* of the droplet is determined from its rate of fall against the viscous force of air resistance. (*b*) The magnitude of of the charge is computed from the equilibrium conditions which suspend the charge between oppositely charged plates.

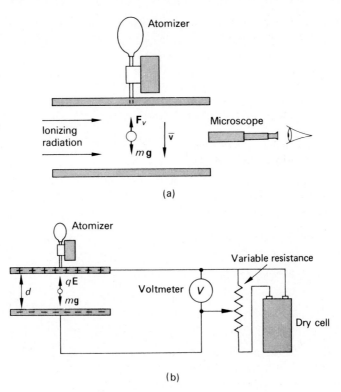

The field intensity **E**, as determined from Eq. (32-11), is a function of the applied voltage V and the plate separation d. Therefore, Eq. (32-12) becomes

$$q \frac{V}{d} = mg$$

and the magnitude of the charge on the oil drop is found from

$$q = \frac{mgd}{V} \qquad (32\text{-}12)$$

The potential difference V can be read directly from an indicating device called a *voltmeter* attached to the circuit. The other parameters are known.

The charges observed by Millikan were not always the same, but he observed that the magnitude of the charge was always an integral multiple of a basic quantity of charge. It was assumed that this *least* charge must be the charge of a single electron and that the other magnitudes resulted from two or more electrons. Computation of the electronic charge by this method yields

$$e = 1.6065 \times 10^{-19} \text{ C}$$

which agrees extremely well with the values obtained by other methods.

32-6
THE
ELECTRON-
VOLT

Let us now consider the energy of a charged particle moving through a potential difference. There are several units in which to measure this energy, but most of the familiar units are inconveniently large. Consider, for example, a charge of 1 C accelerated through a potential difference of 1 V. Its kinetic energy, from Eqs. (32-2) and (32-11), will be

$$\text{K.E.} = qEd = qV$$

$$= (1 \text{ C})(1 \text{ V}) = 1 \text{ C} \cdot \text{V}$$

The coulomb-volt, of course, is a joule. But 1 C of charge is inconveniently large when applied to single particles, and the corresponding unit of energy (the joule) is also large. The most convenient unit of energy in atomic and nuclear physics is the *electronvolt* (eV).

> The **electronvolt** is a unit of energy equivalent to the energy acquired by an electron which is accelerated through a potential difference of one volt.

The electronvolt differs from the coulomb-volt by the same degree as the difference in the charge of an electron and the charge of 1 C. To compare the two units, suppose we compute the energy in joules acquired by an electron which has been accelerated through a potential difference of 1 V:

$$\text{K.E.} = qV$$

$$= (1.6 \times 10^{-19} \text{ C})(1 \text{ V})$$

$$= 1.6 \times 10^{-19} \text{ J}$$

Thus 1 eV is equivalent to an energy of 1.6×10^{-19} J.

SUMMARY

The concepts of potential energy, potential, and potential difference have been extended to electrical phenomena. The many problems dealing with electrostatic potential have been designed to provide a base for direct current electricity which will be discussed later. The essential elements of this chapter are summarized below:

• When a charge q is moved against a constant electric force for a distance d, the potential energy of the system is

$$\boxed{\text{P.E.} = qEd}$$

where E is the constant electric field intensity. If the charge is released, it will acquire a kinetic energy

$$\boxed{\text{K.E.} = \tfrac{1}{2}mv^2 = qEd}$$

as it returns for the same distance.

- Due to the existence of positive and negative charges and the opposite effects produced by the same field, we must remember that:

    The potential energy increases as a positive charge is moved against the electric field, and the potential energy decreases as a negative charge is moved against the same field.

- In general, the potential energy due to a charge q placed at a distance r from another charge Q is equal to the work done against electric forces in moving the charge $+q$ from infinity.

$$V = \frac{kQq'}{r}$$ *Electric Potential Energy*

Note that the distance r is not squared, as it was for the electric field intensity.

- The electric *potential V* at a point a distance r from a charge Q is equal to the work per unit charge done against electric forces in bringing a positive charge $+q$ from infinity.

$$V = \frac{kQ}{r}$$ *Electric Potential*

- The unit of electric potential is the joule per coulomb (J/C), which is renamed the volt (V).

$$1\ V = \frac{1\ J}{1\ C}$$

- The potential at a point in the vicinity of a number of charges is equal to the algebraic sum of the potentials due to each charge:

$$V = \sum \frac{kQ}{r} = \frac{kQ_1}{r_1} + \frac{kQ_2}{r_2} + \frac{kQ_3}{r_3} + \cdots$$ *Algebraic Sum*

- The potential difference between two points A and B is the difference in the potentials at those points.

$$V_{AB} = V_A - V_B$$ *Potential Difference*

- The work done by an electric field in moving a charge q from point A to point B can be found from

$$\text{Work}_{AB} = q(V_A - V_B)$$ *Work and Potential Difference*

- The potential difference between two oppositely charged plates is equal to the product of the field intensity and the plate separation.

$$V = Ed$$ $$E = \frac{V}{d}$$

QUESTIONS

32-1. Define the following terms:
  a. Electric potential energy
  b. Electric work
  c. Potential
  d. Volt
  e. Equipotential lines
  f. Potential difference
  g. Potential gradient
  h. Electronvolt

32-2. Distinguish clearly between positive and negative work. Distinguish between positive and negative potential energy.

32-3. Is it possible for a mass m to increase the potential energy by moving it to a lower elevation? Is it possible for a charged object to increase the potential energy as it is moved to a position of lower potential? Explain.

32-4. Give an example in which the electric potential is zero at some point where the electric field intensity is not zero.

32-5. The electric field inside an electrostatic conductor is zero. Is the electric potential inside the conductor zero also? Explain.

32-6. If the electric field intensity is known at some point, can one determine the electric potential at that point? What information is needed?

32-7. The surface of any conductor is an equipotential surface. Justify this statement.

32-8. Is the direction of the electric field intensity from higher to lower potential? Illustrate.

32-9. Apply the potential concept to the gravitational field to obtain an expression similar to Eq. (32-9) for computing the potential energy per unit mass. Discuss the applications of such a formula.

32-10. Show that the volt per meter is dimensionally equivalent to the newton per coulomb.

32-11. Distinguish between potential difference and a difference in potential energy.

32-12. A potential difference of 220 V is maintained between the ends of a long high-resistance wire. If the center of the wire is grounded ($V = 0$), what is the potential difference between the center and the end points?

32-13. The potential due to a negative charge is negative, and the potential due to a positive charge is positive. Why? Is it also true that the potential energy due to a negative charge is negative? Explain.

32-14. Is potential a property assigned to space or to a charge? What is potential energy assigned to?

PROBLEMS

32-1. Two metal plates are separated by 30 mm and are oppositely charged so that a constant electric field of 6×10^4 N/C exists between them. How much work must be done *against* the electric field in order to move a $+4$-μC charge from the negative plate to the positive plate? How much work is done *by* the electric field? What is the potential energy when the charge is at the negative plate?

Ans. 7.2 mJ, -7.2 mJ, 7.2 mJ.

32-2. The electric field intensity between two parallel plates is 8000 N/C. How much work is done *by* the electric field in moving a -2-μC charge from the negative plate to the positive plate. What is the work done *by* the electric field in moving the same charge back to the positive plate? What is the potential energy when the charge is at the positive plate? What is the potential energy when the charge is at the negative plate? The plates are 25 mm apart.

32-3. A charge of $+6\ \mu C$ is 30 mm away from another charge of 16 μC. **(a)** What is the potential energy of the system? **(b)** What is the *change* in potential energy if the 6-μC charge is moved to a distance of only 5 mm? Is this an increase or decrease in potential energy?

Ans. **(a)** 28.8 J **(b)** 144 J, increase.

32-4. A -3-μC charge is placed 6 mm away from a $+9$-μC charge. What is the potential energy? Is it negative or positive? What is the potential energy if the separation is increased to a distance of 24 mm? Is this an increase or a decrease in potential energy?

32-5. At what distance from a -7-nC charge must a charge of -12 nC be placed if the potential energy is to be 9×10^{-5} J?

Ans. 8.4 mm.

32-6. The potential energy of a system consisting of two identical charges is 4.5 mJ when their separation is 38 mm. What is the magnitude of each charge?

32-7. Calculate the potential at a point A which is 50 mm distant from a charge of $-40\ \mu C$. What is the potential energy if a $+3$-μC charge is placed at A?

Ans. -7.2 MV, -21.6 J.

32-8. What is the potential at a point B located 60 mm away from a charge of $+15\ \mu C$? What is the potential energy of a $+2$-nC charge placed at point B?

32-9. Point A is located 40 mm from a 6-μC charge; point B is located 25 mm from the same charge. Calculate the potential difference between points A and B. How much work is required by an external force if a $+5$-μC charge is moved from A to B?

Ans. 810 kV, 4.05 J.

32-10. How much work is done *by* the electric field in moving a -5-nC charge from a point A to a point B? Point A is 68 mm away from a 90-μC charge and point B is only 26 mm away from the same charge.

32-11. Two charges of $+45$ nC and -9 nC are separated by a distance of 68 mm. What is the potential at a point on a line joining the two charges and located 40 mm from the -9-nC charge?

Ans. 12.4 kV.

32-12. What is the potential at the midpoint of a line joining a -12-μC charge with a $+3$-μC charge. The separation of the two charges is 80 mm.

32-13. Point A is located 90 mm to the right of a -40-μC charge and 30 mm to the left of a $+55$-μC charge. Point B is located 15 mm to the left of the -40-μC charge. What is the potential at A? What is the potential at B? What is the potential difference? How much work is done *by* the electric field in moving a $+4$-nC from point A to point B?

Ans. $+12.5$ MV, -20.3 MV, 32.8 MV, 0.131 J.

32-14. A -60-μC charge is located 45 mm to the right of a $+20$-μC charge. Point A is midway between the two charges. Point B is located a distance of 35 mm directly above the $+20$-μC charge. What is the potential difference between A and B? How much work is done when a -5-μC charge is moved from point A to point B? Will this work be done by the field, or will it have to be supplied by an external force?

32-15. Points A, B, and C are at the corners of an equilateral triangle which is 100 mm on each side. Two charges of $+8$ and -8 μC are located at A and B. What is the potential at C? What is the potential at a point D which is 20 mm from the -8-μC charge on a line joining A and B? How much work is done by the electric field in moving a $+2$-μC charge from point C to point D?

Ans. 0 V, -2.7 MV, 5.4 J.

32-16. Two charges of $+12$ and -6 μC are separated by 160 mm. What is the potential at the midpoint of a line joining the two charges?

32-17. The potential at a certain distance from a point charge is 1200 V, and the electric field intensity at that point is 400 N/C. What is the distance to the charge, and what is the magnitude of the charge?

Ans. 3 m, 400 nC.

32-18. What is the difference in potential between two points 30 and 60 cm away from a -50-μC charge?

32-19. The electric field intensity between two parallel plates 4 mm apart is 6000 N/C. What is the potential difference between the plates?

Ans. 24 V.

32-20. The electric field intensity between two plates separated by a distance of 50 mm is 6×10^5 N/C. What is the potential difference between the plates?

32-21. What must be the separation of two parallel plates if the field intensity is 5×10^4 N/C and the potential difference is 400 V?

Ans. 8 mm.

32-22. The potential difference between two parallel plates is 600 V. A 6-μC charge is accelerated through the entire potential difference. What is the kinetic energy given to the charge?

32-23. Determine the kinetic energy of an alpha particle which is accelerated through a potential difference of 800 kV. (The charge on an alpha particle is $+2e$.)

Ans. 2.56×10^{-13} J.

32-24. A linear accelerator accelerates an electron through a potential difference of 4 MV. What is the energy of an emergent electron in electronvolts? In joules?

32-25. Two large plates are 80 mm apart and have a potential difference of 800 kV. What is the magnitude of the force which would act on an electron placed at the midpoint between the two plates? What would be the kinetic energy of the electron if it moved from one plate to the other?

Ans. 1.6×10^{-12} N, 1.28×10^{-13} J.

32-26. An electron acquires an energy of 2.8×10^{-15} J as it passes from point A to B. What is the potential difference between these points in volts?

32-27. The horizontal plates in Millikan's oil-drop experiment are 20 mm apart. The diameter of a particular drop of oil is 4 μm, and the density of oil is 0.90 g/cm^3. Assuming that two electrons attach themselves to the droplet, what potential difference must exist between the plates in order to establish equilibrium?

Ans. 18.5 kV.

33 *Capacitance*

OBJECTIVES: **After completing this chapter, you should be able to:**

1. **Define *capacitance* and apply a relationship between *capacitance*, applied *voltage*, and total *charge*.**

2. **Compute the capacitance of a *parallel-plate capacitor* when the area of the plates and their separation in a medium of known dielectric constant are given.**

3. **Write and apply expressions for calculating the *dielectric constant* as a function of the voltage, the electric field, or the capacitance before and after insertion of a dielectric.**

4. **Calculate the equivalent capacitance of a number of capacitors connected in *series* and in *parallel*.**

5. **Determine the *energy* of a charged capacitor, given the appropriate information.**

Any charged conductor may be viewed as a reservoir, or source, of electric charge. If a conducting wire is connected to such a reservoir, electric charge can be transferred to perform useful work. In many applications of electricity, large quantities of charge are stored upon a conductor or group of conductors. Any device designed to store electric charge is called a *capacitor*. In this chapter we discuss the nature and application of these devices.

33-1 LIMITA- TIONS ON CHARGING A CONDUCTOR

How much electric charge can be placed on a conductor? Are there practical limits to the number of electrons that can be transferred to or from a conductor? Suppose we connect a large reservoir of positive and negative charges, such as the earth, to a conducting object, as illustrated in Fig. 33-1a. The energy necessary to transfer electrons from the earth to the conductor can be provided

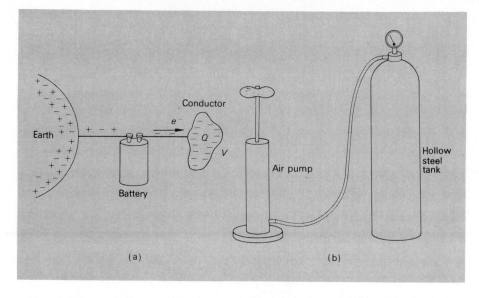

by an electrical device called a *battery*. Charging the conductor is analogous to pumping air into a hollow steel tank. (Refer to Fig. 33-1*b*.) As more air is pumped into the tank, the pressure opposing the flow of additional air becomes greater. Similarly, as more charge Q is transferred to the conductor, the potential V of the conductor becomes higher, making it increasingly difficult to transfer more charge. We can say that the increase in potential V is directly proportional to the charge Q placed on the conductor. Symbolically,

$$V \propto Q$$

Therefore, the ratio of the quantity of charge Q to the potential V produced will be a constant for a given conductor. This ratio reflects the ability of a conductor to store charge and is called its *capacitance C*.

$$C = \frac{Q}{V}$$

(33-1)

The unit of capacitance is the *coulomb per volt* which is redefined as a *farad* (F). Thus, *if a conductor has a capacitance of one farad, a transfer of one coulomb of charge to the conductor will raise its potential by one volt.*

Let us return to our original question about the limitations placed on charging a conductor. We have said that every conductor has a capacitance C for storing charge. The value of C for a given conductor is not a function of either the charge placed on a conductor or the potential produced. In principle, the ratio Q/V will remain constant as charge is added indefinitely, but the capacitance depends on the *size* and *shape* of a conductor as well as on the nature of the *surrounding medium*.

Suppose we try to place an indefinite quantity of charge Q on a spherical conductor of radius r, as illustrated in Fig. 33-2. The air surrounding the conductor is an insulator, sometimes called a *dielectric*, which contains very few charges free to move. The electric field intensity E and the potential V at the surface of the sphere are given by

$$E = \frac{kQ}{r^2} \quad \text{and} \quad V = \frac{kQ}{r}$$

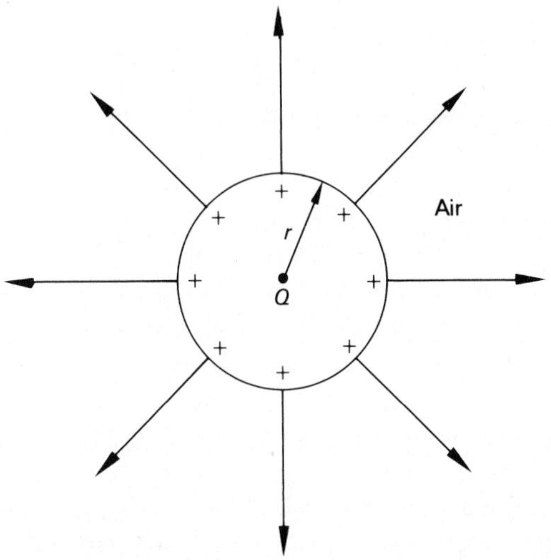

Fig. 33-2 The amount of charge which can be placed on a conductor is limited by the dielectric strength of the surrounding medium.

Since the radius r is constant, both the field intensity and the potential at the surface of the sphere increase in direct proportion to the charge Q. However, there is a limit to the field intensity which can exist on a conductor without ionizing the surrounding air. When this occurs, the air essentially becomes a conductor, and any additional charge placed on the sphere will "leak off" to the air. This limiting value of electric field intensity for which a material loses its insulation properties is called the dielectric strength of that material.

The **dielectric strength** for a given material is that electric field intensity for which the material ceases to be an insulator and becomes a conductor.

The dielectric strength for dry air at 1 atm pressure is around 3 MN/C. Since the dielectric strength of a material varies considerably with environmental conditions, such as pressure, humidity, etc., it is difficult to compute accurate values.

EXAMPLE 33-1   What is the maximum charge that may be placed on a spherical conductor of radius 50 cm?

Solution

The field intensity at the surface of the sphere, at the point of breakdown in the air, is given by

$$E = \frac{kQ}{r^2} = 3 \text{ MN/C}$$

where 3 MN/C is assumed to be the dielectric strength of air. Solving for Q gives

$$Q = \frac{(3 \times 10^6 \text{ N/C})r^2}{k}$$

$$= \frac{(3 \times 10^6 \text{ N/C})(0.5 \text{ m})^2}{9 \times 10^9 \text{ N} \cdot \text{m}^2/\text{C}^2}$$

$$= 8.33 \times 10^{-5} \text{ C} = 83.3 \ \mu\text{C}$$

This example illustrates the enormous magnitude of the coulomb when it is applied as a unit of electrostatic charge.

Note that the amount of charge which can be placed on a spherical conductor decreases with the radius of the sphere. Thus smaller conductors usually can hold less charge. But the shape of a conductor also influences its ability to retain charge. Consider the charged conductors illustrated in Fig. 33-3. If these conductors are tested with an electroscope, it will be discovered

Fig. 33-3 Charge density on a conductor is greatest at regions of greatest curvature.

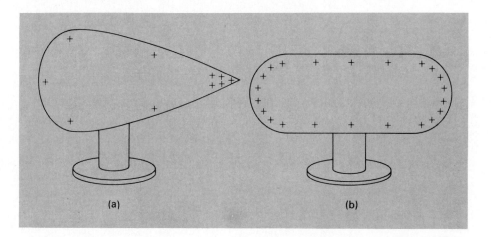

(a) (b)

that the charge on the surface of a conductor is concentrated at points of greatest curvature. Because of the greater charge density in these regions, the electric field intensity is also greater in regions of larger curvature. If the surface is reshaped to a sharp point, the field intensity may become great enough to ionize the surrounding air. A slow leakage of charge sometimes occurs at these locations, producing a *corona discharge*, which is often observed as a faint violet glow in the vicinity of the sharply pointed conductor. It is important to remove all sharp edges from electrical equipment in order to minimize this leakage of charge.

33-2
THE
CAPACITOR

When a number of conductors are placed near one another, the potential of each is affected by the presence of the other. For example, suppose we connect a negatively charged plate A to an electroscope, as in Fig. 33-4. The divergence of the gold leaf in the electroscope provides a measure of the potential of the conductor. Now let us suppose that another conductor B is placed parallel to A a short distance away. When the second conductor is grounded, a positive

Fig. 33-4 A capacitor consists of two closely spaced conductors.

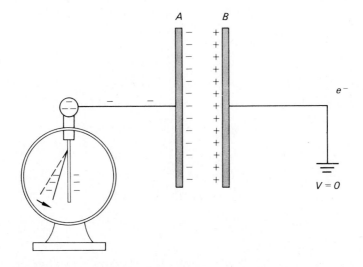

charge will be induced on it as the electrons are forced into the ground. Immediately, the gold leaf will collapse slightly, indicating a drop in the potential of conductor A. Because of the presence of the induced charge on B, less work is required to bring additional units of charge to conductor A. In other words, the capacitance of the system for holding charge has been increased by the proximity of the two conductors. Two such conductors in close proximity, carrying equal and opposite charges, constitute a *capacitor*.

> A **capacitor** consists of two closely spaced conductors carrying equal and opposite charges.

The simplest capacitor is the *parallel-plate capacitor*, illustrated in Fig. 33-4. A potential difference between two such plates can be realized by connecting a battery to them, as shown in Fig. 33-5. Electrons are transferred from plate A to plate B, producing an equal and opposite charge on the plates. The capacitance of this arrangement is defined as follows:

> The **capacitance** between two conductors having equal and opposite charges is the ratio of the magnitude of the charge on either conductor to the resulting potential difference between the two conductors.

Fig. 33-5 Charging a capacitor by transferring charge from one plate to the other.

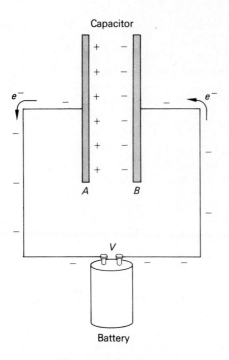

Capacitor

e^-

e^-

A   B

V

Battery

The equation for the capacitance of a capacitor is the same as Eq. (33-1) for a single conductor, except that the symbol V now applies to the *potential difference* and the symbol Q refers to the charge on *either* conductor.

$$C = \frac{Q}{V}$$

(33-2)

$$1 \text{ F} = \frac{1 \text{ C}}{1 \text{ V}}$$

Because of the enormous size of the coulomb as a unit of charge, the farad as a unit of capacitance is usually too large for practical application. Consequently, the following submultiples are commonly used:

$$1 \text{ microfarad } (\mu\text{F}) = 10^{-6} \text{ F}$$

$$1 \text{ picofarad } (\text{pF}) = 10^{-12} \text{ F}$$

Capacitances as low as a few picofarads are not uncommon in some electrical communication applications.

EXAMPLE 33-2

A capacitor having a capacitance of 4 μF is connected to a 60-V battery. What is the charge on the capacitor?

Solution

The charge *on* a capacitor refers to the magnitude of the charge on either plate of the capacitor. From Eq. (33-2),

$$Q = CV = (4 \ \mu\text{F})(60 \text{ V}) = 240 \ \mu\text{C}$$

**33-3
COMPUTING
THE CAPACI-
TANCE**

In general, a larger conductor can hold a greater quantity of charge, and a capacitor can store more charge than a single conductor because of the inductive effect of two closely spaced conductors. The closer the spacing of these conductors, the greater the inductive effect and hence the easier it becomes to transfer additional charge from one conductor to the other. On the basis of these observations, one might suspect that *the capacitance of a given capacitor will be directly proportional to the area of the plates and inversely proportional to their separation.* The exact relationship can be determined by considering the electric field intensity between the capacitor plates.

The electric field intensity between the plates of the charged capacitor in Fig. 33-6 can be found from

$$E = \frac{V}{d} \tag{33-3}$$

where V = potential difference between plates, V
d = separation of plates, m

Fig. 33-6
Capacitance is directly proportional to the area of either plate and inversely proportional to the plate separation.

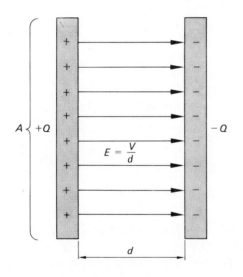

An alternative equation for computing the electric field intensity was derived in Chap. 31, using Gauss' law. It relates the field intensity E to the charge density σ as follows:

$$E = \frac{\sigma}{\epsilon_0} = \frac{Q}{A\epsilon_0} \tag{33-4}$$

where Q = charge on either plate
A = area of either plate
ϵ_0 = permittivity of vacuum (8.85×10^{-2} C^2/N $\cdot$ m^2)

For a capacitor with a vacuum between its plates, we combine Eqs. (33-3) and (33-4) and get

$$\frac{V}{d} = \frac{Q}{A\epsilon_0}$$

Realizing that the capacitance C is the ratio of charge to voltage, we can rearrange terms and obtain

$$C_0 = \frac{Q}{V} = \epsilon_0 \frac{A}{d} \tag{33-5}$$

The subscript 0 is used to indicate that a vacuum exists between the plates of the capacitor. To a very close approximation, Eq. (33-5) can also be used when air is between the capacitor plates.

EXAMPLE 33-3

The plates of a parallel-plate capacitor are 3 mm apart in air. If the area of each plate is 0.2 m^2, what is the capacitance?

Solution

Direct substitution into Eq. (33-5) gives

$$C_0 = \epsilon_0 \frac{A}{d} = \frac{(8.85 \times 10^{-12} \text{ C}^2/\text{N} \cdot \text{m}^2)(0.2 \text{ m}^2)}{3 \times 10^{-3} \text{ m}}$$

$$= 590 \times 10^{-12} \text{ F} = 590 \text{ pF}$$

Parallel-plate capacitors are frequently made with a stack of several plates by connecting alternate plates as shown in Fig. 33-7. By making one of

Fig. 33-7 (*a*) A capacitor consisting of a number of stacked plates, alternating with positive and negative charges. (*b*) A variable capacitor allows one set of plates to be rotated relative to the other, causing a variation in effective area.

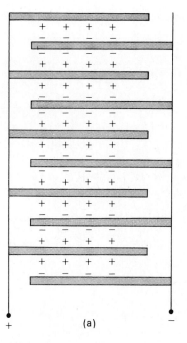

(a)

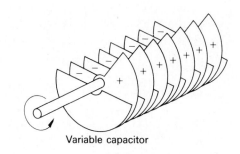

Variable capacitor

(b)

the sets of plates movable a variable capacitor can be constructed. Rotating one set of plates relative to the other set varies the effective area of the capacitor plates, causing a variation in the capacitance. Variable capacitors are often used in the tuning circuits of radios.

33-4 DIELECTRIC CONSTANT; PERMITTIVITY

The amount of charge which can be put on a conductor is determined to a large degree by the dielectric strength of the surrounding medium. Similarly, the dielectric strength of the material between the plates of a capacitor limits its ability to store charge. Most capacitors have a nonconducting material, called a *dielectric*, between the plates to provide a dielectric strength greater than that for air. The following advantages are realized:

1. A dielectric material provides for a small plate separation without contact.
2. A dielectric increases the capacitance of a capacitor.
3. Higher voltages can be used without danger of dielectric breakdown.
4. A dielectric often provides greater mechanical strength.

Common dielectric materials are mica, paraffined paper, ceramics, and plastics. Alternating sheets of metal foil and paraffin-coated paper can be rolled up to provide a compact capacitor with a capacitance of several microfarads.

In order to understand the effect of a dielectric, let us consider the insulating material of Fig. 33-8 placed between capacitor plates having a potential difference V. The electrons in the dielectric are not free to leave their parent atoms, but they do shift toward the positive plate. The protons and electrons of each atom align themselves as shown in the figure. The material is said to

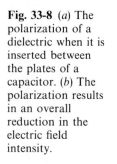

Fig. 33-8 (*a*) The polarization of a dielectric when it is inserted between the plates of a capacitor. (*b*) The polarization results in an overall reduction in the electric field intensity.

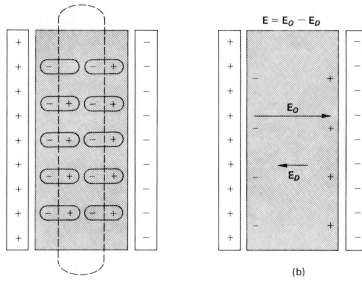

$E = E_O - E_D$

(a)

(b)

become polarized, and the atoms form *dipoles*. All the positive and negative charges inside the dotted ellipse in Fig. 33-8a neutralize each other. However, a layer of negative charge on one surface and a layer of positive charge on the other are not neutralized. An electric field $\mathbf{E}_D$ is set up in the dielectric *opposing* the field $\mathbf{E}_0$ which would exist without the dielectric. The resulting electric field intensity is

$$\mathbf{E} = \mathbf{E}_0 - \mathbf{E}_D \qquad (33\text{-}6)$$

Therefore, insertion of a dielectric results in a reduction of the field intensity between the capacitor plates.

Since the potential difference V between the plates is proportional to the electric field intensity, $V = Ed$, a reduction in the intensity will cause a drop in potential difference. This fact is illustrated by the example shown in Fig. 33-9. The insertion of a dielectric causes a divergence of the gold leaf on the electroscope.

Fig. 33-9 Insertion of a dielectric between the plates of a capacitor causes a drop in potential difference resulting in an increased capacitance.

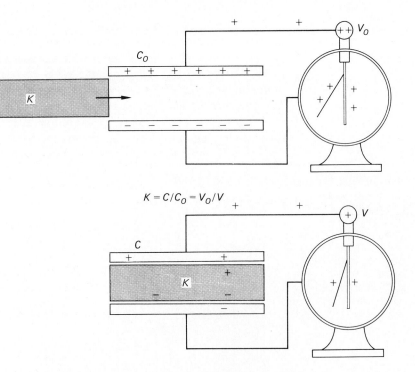

It can be seen from the definition of capacitance, $C = Q/V$, that a drop in voltage will result in an increased capacitance. If we represent the capacitance before insertion of a dielectric by C_0 and the capacitance after insertion by C, the ratio C/C_0 will denote the relative increase in capacitance. Although this ratio varies from material to material, it is constant for a particular dielectric.

The **dielectric constant** K for a particular material is defined as the ratio of the capacitance C of a capacitor with the material between its plates to the capacitance C_0 for a vacuum.

$$K = \frac{C}{C_0}$$
(33-7)

The dielectric constant for various dielectric materials is given in Table 33-1 along with the dielectric strength for the materials. Note that for air K is approximately 1.

Table 33-1 Dielectric Constant and Dielectric Strength

Material	Average dielectric constant	Average dielectric strength, MV/m
Air, dry at 1 atm	1.006	3
Bakelite	7.0	16
Glass	7.5	118
Mica	5.0	200
Nitrocellulose plastics	9.0	2.50
Paper, paraffined	2.0	51
Rubber	3.0	28
Teflon	2.0	59
Transformer oil	4.0	16

On the basis of proportionalities, it can be shown that the dielectric constant is also given by

$$K = \frac{V_0}{V} = \frac{E_0}{E}$$
(33-8)

where V_0, E_0 = voltage and electric field with vacuum between capacitor plates
V, E = respective values after insertion of dielectric material

The capacitance C of a capacitor having a dielectric between its plates is, from Eq. (33-7),

$$C = KC_0$$

Substituting from Eq. (33-5), we have a relation for computing C directly:

$$C = K\epsilon_0 \frac{A}{d}$$
(33-9)

where A is the area of the plates and d is their separation.

The constant ϵ_0 has been defined earlier as the *permittivity* of a vacuum. Recall from our discussions of Gauss' law that ϵ_0 is actually the proportionality constant which relates the density of electric field lines to the electric field intensity in a vacuum. The permittivity ϵ of a dielectric is greater than ϵ_0 by a factor equal to the dielectric constant K. Thus

$$\epsilon = K\epsilon_0 \qquad (33\text{-}10)$$

On the basis of this relation, we can understand why the dielectric constant, $K = \epsilon/\epsilon_0$, is sometimes referred to as the *relative permittivity*. When we substitute Eq. (33-10) into Eq. (33-9), the capacitance for a capacitor containing a dielectric is simply

$$C = \epsilon \frac{A}{d} \qquad (33\text{-}11)$$

This relation is the most general equation for computing capacitance. When a vacuum or air is between the capacitor plates, $\epsilon = \epsilon_0$ and Eq. (33-11) reduces to Eq. (33-5).

EXAMPLE 33-4

A certain capacitor has a capacitance of 4 μF when its plates are separated by 0.2 mm of vacant space. A battery is used to charge the plates to a potential difference of 500 V and is then disconnected from the system. (*a*) What will be the potential difference across the plates if a sheet of mica 0.2 mm thick is inserted between the plates? (*b*) What will the capacitance be after the dielectric is inserted? (*c*) What is the permittivity of mica?

Solution (a)

The dielectric constant of mica is 5. Thus Eq. (33-8) gives

$$V = \frac{V_0}{K} = \frac{500 \text{ V}}{5} = 100 \text{ V}$$

Solution (b)

From Eq. (33-7),

$$C = KC \ = (5)(4\mu F) = 20 \ \mu F$$

Solution (c)

The permittivity is found from Eq. (33-10):

$$\epsilon = K\epsilon_0 = (5)(8.85 \times 10^{-12} \text{ C}^2/\text{N} \cdot \text{m}^2)$$

$$= 44.2 \times 10^{-12} \text{ C}^2/\text{N} \cdot \text{m}^2$$

It should be noted that the charge on the capacitor is the same before and after insertion since the voltage source did not stay connected to the capacitor.

EXAMPLE 33-5

Assume that the source of voltage stays connected to the capacitor in Example 33-4. What will be the increase in charge as a result of insertion of the mica sheet?

Solution

In this instance, the voltage stays at 500 V when the dielectric is inserted. Since the capacitance is increased by the dielectric, an increase in charge must result. The charge across the capacitor initially was

$$Q_0 = C_0 V_0 = (4 \ \mu F)(500 \text{ V}) = 2000 \ \mu C$$

The charge after insertion of the mica is determined by the new capacitance of 20 μF:

$$Q = CV = (20 \ \mu F)(500 \ V) = 10,000 \ \mu C$$

Thus the increase in charge is

$$\Delta Q = Q - Q_0 = 10,000 \ \mu C - 2000 \ \mu C = 8000 \ \mu C$$

This 8000 μC was provided by the voltage source.

**33-5
CAPACITORS
IN PARALLEL
AND IN
SERIES**

Electric circuits often contain two or more capacitors grouped together. In considering the effect of such a grouping, it is convenient to resort to the *circuit diagram*, in which electrical devices are represented by symbols. Four symbols commonly used with capacitors are defined in Fig. 33-10. The high-potential side of a battery is denoted by the longer line. The high-potential side of a

Fig. 33-10 Definition of symbols frequently used with capacitors.

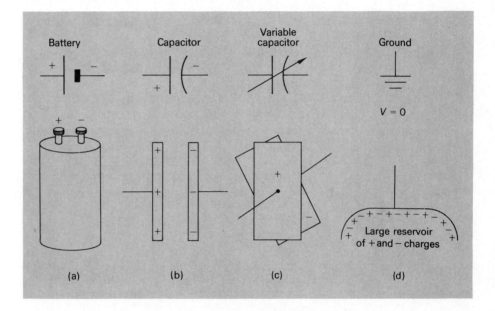

capacitor may be represented as a straight line, with a curved line representing the low-potential side. An arrow indicates a variable capacitor. A *ground* is an electrical connection between the wiring of an apparatus and its metal framework or any other large reservoir of positive and negative charges.

First we consider the effect of a group of capacitors connected along a single path, as shown in Fig. 33-11. Such a connection, in which the positive plate of one capacitor is connected to the negative plate of another, is called a *series connection*. The battery maintains a potential difference V between the positive plate of C_1 and the negative plate of C_3, transferring electrons from one to the other. The charge cannot pass between the plates of a capacitor.

Fig. 33-11
Comput-
ing the equivalent
capacitance of a
group of capacitors
connected in series.

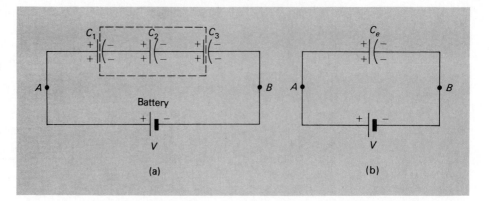

Therefore, all the charge inside the dotted circle in Fig. 33-11a is induced charge. For this reason, the charge on each capacitor is identical. We write

$$Q = Q_1 = Q_2 = Q_3$$

where Q is the effective charge transferred by the battery.

All three capacitors can be replaced by an equivalent capacitance C_e without changing the external effect. We now derive an expression for calculating this equivalent capacitance for the series connection. Since the potential difference between A and B is independent of the path, the battery voltage must equal the sum of the potential drops across each capacitor.

$$V = V_1 + V_2 + V_3 \tag{33-12}$$

If we recall that the capacitance C is defined by the ratio Q/V, Eq. (33-12) becomes

$$\frac{Q}{C_e} = \frac{Q_1}{C_1} + \frac{Q_2}{C_2} + \frac{Q_3}{C_3}$$

For a series connection, $Q = Q_1 = Q_2 = Q_3$, so that we can divide out the charge, yielding

$$\boxed{\frac{1}{C_e} = \frac{1}{C_1} + \frac{1}{C_2} + \frac{1}{C_3}} \qquad \begin{array}{c} \textit{Series} \\ \textit{Connection} \end{array} \tag{33-13}$$

The total effective capacitance for *two* capacitors in series is

$$C_e = \frac{C_1 C_2}{C_1 + C_2} \tag{33-14}$$

The derivation of Eq. (33-14) is left as an exercise.

Now, let us consider a group of capacitors connected so that charge can be shared between two or more conductors. When several capacitors are all connected directly to the same source of potential, as in Fig. 33-12, they are

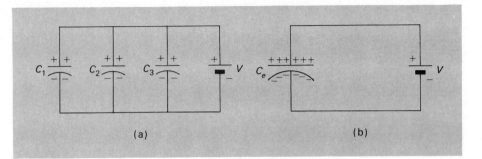

Fig. 33-12 Equivalent capacitance of a group of capacitors connected in parallel.

(a)　　　　　　　　　　(b)

said to be connected in *parallel*. From the definition of capacitance, the charge on each parallel capacitor is

$$Q_1 = C_1 V_1 \qquad Q_2 = C_2 V_2 \qquad Q_3 = C_3 V_3$$

The total charge Q is equal to the sum of the individual charges.

$$Q = Q_1 = Q_2 + Q_3 \qquad\qquad (33\text{-}15)$$

The equivalent capacitance of the entire circuit is $Q = CV$, so that Eq. (33-15) becomes

$$CV = C_1 V_1 + C_2 V_2 + C_3 V_3 \qquad\qquad (33\text{-}16)$$

For a parallel connection,

$$V = V_1 = V_2 = V_3$$

since all capacitors are connected to the same potential difference. Hence the voltages divide out of Eq. (33-16), giving

$$\boxed{C = C_1 + C_2 + C_3}$$ 　　*Parallel Connection* 　(33-17)

EXAMPLE 33-6　　(a) Find the equivalent capacitance of the circuit illustrated in Fig. 33-13a. (b) Determine the charge on each capacitor. (c) What is the voltage across the 4-μF capacitor?

Solution (a)　　The 4- and 2-μF capacitors are in series. Their combined capacitance is found from Eq. (33-14).

$$C_{2,4} = \frac{C_2 C_4}{C_2 + C_4} = \frac{(2\ \mu\text{F})(4\ \mu\text{F})}{2\mu\text{F} + 4\ \mu\text{F}}$$

$$= 1.33\ \mu\text{F}$$

These two capacitors can be replaced by their equivalent capacitance, as shown in Fig. 33-13b. The two remaining capacitors are in parallel. Thus the equivalent capacitance is

$$C_e = C_3 + C_{2,4} = 3\ \mu\text{F} + 1.33\ \mu\text{F}$$

$$= 4.33\ \mu\text{F}$$

Fig. 33-13 Simplifying a problem by substituting equivalent values for capacitance.

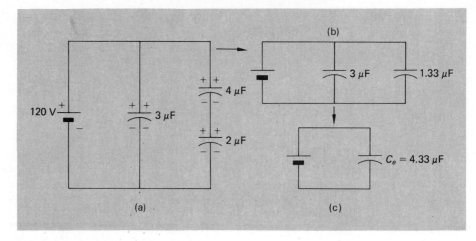

Solution (b) The total charge in the network is

$$Q = C_e V = (4.33 \ \mu\text{F})(120 \ \text{V}) = 520 \ \mu\text{C}$$

The charge Q_3 on the 3-μF capacitor is

$$Q_3 = C_3 V = (3 \ \mu\text{F})(120 \ \text{V}) = 360 \ \mu\text{C}$$

The remainder of the charge,

$$Q - Q_3 = 520 \ \mu\text{C} - 360 \ \mu\text{C} = 160 \ \mu\text{C}$$

must be deposited on the series capacitors. Hence

$$Q_2 = Q_4 = 160 \ \mu\text{C}$$

As a check on these values for Q_2 and Q_4, the equivalent capacitance of the two series capacitors can be multiplied by the voltage drop across it:

$$Q_{2,4} = C_{2,4} V = (1.33 \ \mu\text{F})(120 \ \text{V}) = 160 \ \mu\text{C}$$

Solution (c) The voltage drop across the 4-μF capacitor is

$$V_4 = \frac{Q_4}{C_4} = \frac{160 \ \mu\text{C}}{4 \ \mu\text{F}} = 40 \ \text{V}$$

The remaining 80 V is across the 2-μF capacitor.

**33-6
ENERGY OF
A CHARGED
CAPACITOR**

Consider a capacitor that is initially uncharged. When a source of potential difference is connected to the capacitor, the potential difference between the plates increases as charge is transferred. As more and more charge builds up on the capacitor, it becomes increasingly difficult to transfer additional charge. Suppose we represent the total charge transferred by Q and the final potential difference by V. The *average* potential difference through which the charge is moved is given by

$$V_{\text{av}} = \frac{V_{\text{final}} + V_{\text{initial}}}{2} = \frac{V + 0}{2} = \frac{1}{2} V$$

Since the total charge transferred is Q, the total work done against electric forces is equal to the product of Q and the average potential difference V_{av}. Thus

$$\text{Work} = Q(\tfrac{1}{2}V) = \tfrac{1}{2}QV$$

This work is equivalent to the electrostatic potential energy of a charged capacitor. From the definition of capacitance ($Q = CV$), this potential energy can be written in alternative forms:

$$\boxed{\begin{aligned} \text{P.E.} &= \tfrac{1}{2}QV \\ &= \tfrac{1}{2}CV^2 \\ &= \frac{Q^2}{2C} \end{aligned}}$$

(33-18)

When C is in farads, V is in volts, and Q is in coulombs, the potential energy will be in joules. These equations apply equally to all capacitors regardless of their construction.

SUMMARY

Stored electric charge is a necessity if large quantities of electrical energy are to be delivered on demand to a modern industrial world. We have studied in this chapter the very basic principles which determine the amount of charge that can be stored on capacitors. Further we have discussed the insertion of capacitors into electric circuits and the factors affecting the distribution of charge in such circuits. The fundamental concepts are summarized below:

- Capacitance is the ratio of charge Q to the potential V for a given conductor. For two oppositely charged plates, the Q refers to the charge on either plate and the V refers to the potential difference between the plates.

$$\boxed{C = \frac{Q}{V}} \qquad 1 \text{ farad (F)} = \frac{1 \text{ coulomb (C)}}{1 \text{ volt (V)}} \qquad \textit{Capacitance}$$

- The dielectric strength is that value for E for which a given material ceases to be an insulator and becomes a conductor. For air this value is

$$\boxed{E = \frac{kQ}{r^2} = 3 \times 10^6 \text{ N/C}} \qquad \textit{Dielectric Strength, Air}$$

- For a parallel-plate capacitor, the material between the plates is called the dielectric. The insertion of such a material has an effect on the electric field and the potential between the plates. Consequently, it changes the capacitance. The dielectric constant K for a particular material is the ratio of the capacitance with the dielectric C to the capacitance for a vacuum C_0.

$$K = \frac{C}{C_0}$$ $$K = \frac{V_0}{V}$$ $$K = \frac{E}{E_0}$$ *Dielectric Constant*

- The permittivity of a dielectric is greater than the permittivity of a vacuum by a factor equal to the dielectric constant. For this reason, K is sometimes referred to as the *relative permittivity*.

$$K = \frac{\epsilon}{\epsilon_0}$$ $$\epsilon = K\epsilon_0$$ $$\epsilon_0 = 8.85 \times 10^{-12} \, C^2/N \cdot m^2$$

- The capacitance for a parallel-plate capacitor depends on the surface area A of each plate, the plate separation d, and the permittivity or dielectric constant. The general equation is

$$C = \epsilon \frac{A}{d}$$ $$C = K\epsilon_0 \frac{A}{d}$$ *Capacitance*

For a vacuum, $K = 1$, in the above relationship.

- Capacitors may be connected in series as shown in Fig. 33-11 or in parallel as shown in Fig. 33-12.

(a) For *series connections*, the charge on each capacitor is the same as the total charge, the potential difference across the battery is equal to the sum of the drops across each capacitor, and the net capacitance is found from

$$Q_T = Q_1 = Q_2 = Q_3$$ $$V_T = V_1 + V_2 + V_3$$

$$\frac{1}{C_e} = \frac{1}{C_1} + \frac{1}{C_2} + \frac{1}{C_3}$$ *Series Connections*

(b) For *parallel connections*, the total charge is equal to the sum of the charges across each capacitor, the voltage drop across each capacitor is the same as the drop across the battery, and the effective capacitance is equal to the sum of the individual capacitances.

$$Q_T = Q_1 + Q_2 + Q_3$$ $$V_B = V_1 = V_2 = V_3$$

$$C_e = C_1 + C_2 + C_3$$ *Parallel Connections*

- The potential energy stored in a charged capacitor can be found from any of the following relationships:

$$P.E. = \tfrac{1}{2}QV$$ $$P.E. = \tfrac{1}{2}CV^2$$ $$P.E. = \frac{Q^2}{2C}$$

When C is in *farads*, V is in *volts*, and Q is in *coulombs*, the potential energy will be in *joules*.

QUESTIONS

33-1. Define the following terms:

a. Capacitor   g. Variable capacitor
b. Capacitance   h. Dielectric strength
c. Dielectric   i. Dielectric constant
d. Permittivity   j. Parallel connection
e. Farad   k. Series connection
f. Corona discharge

33-2. Discuss several factors which limit the ability of a conductor to store charge.

33-3. Air is pumped from one metal tank to another, creating a partial vacuum in one tank and a high-pressure in the other. When the pump is removed, potential energy is stored. The energy is released if the two tanks are reconnected and the pressure in each tank becomes equal. In what ways is this mechanical example analogous to charging and discharging a capacitor?

33-4. Large sparks are often seen jumping from the leather belts driving machinery. Explain.

33-5. The Leyden jar is a capacitor which consists of a glass jar coated inside and out with tinfoil, as shown in Fig. 33-14. Contact with the inside coating is made with a metal chain connected to the central metal rod. From the figure, explain how the capacitor becomes charged. What is the function of the ground wire? What purpose does the glass serve?

Fig. 33-14 The Leyden jar.

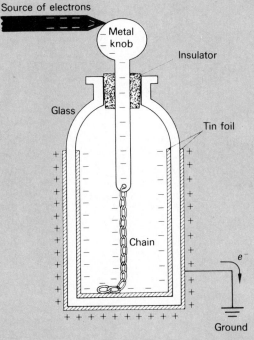

33-6. May lightning be considered a capacitor discharge? Explain.

33-7. Discuss the following statement: the permittivity is a measure of how easily a dielectric will permit the establishment of electric field lines within the dielectric.

33-8. A dielectric with a larger permittivity allows for the storage of greater quantities of charge. Explain.

33-9. Distinguish the dielectric strength of a material from its dielectric constant. What part does each play in the design of a capacitor?

33-10. The term *breakdown voltage* if often used in electronics for capacitors. How would you define such a term? In what way does it differ from the dielectric strength?

33-11. If two point charges are surrounded by a dielectric, will the force each exerts on the other be reduced or increased?

33-12. The unit of permittivity is the $C^2/N \cdot m^2$. Show that the permittivity can be expressed as farads per meter.

33-13. Prove that each of the expressions for potential energy, as given in Eq. (33-18), will yield a proper unit of energy (the joule).

PROBLEMS

33-1. What is the maximum charge that can be placed on a metal sphere 30 mm in diameter?

Ans. 75 nC.

33-2. How much charge can be placed on a metal sphere of radius 40 mm if it is immersed in transformer oil?

33-3. What would be the radius of a metal sphere such that it could theoretically hold a charge of one coulomb in air?

Ans. 54.8 m.

33-4. Write an equation for the potential at the surface of a sphere of radius r in terms of the permittivity of the surrounding medium. Show that the capacitance of such a sphere is given by $C = 4\pi\epsilon r$.

33-5. A parallel-plate capacitor has a capacitance of 28 μF. How much charge will be stored by this capacitor when it is connected to a 120-V source of potential difference?

Ans. 3360 μC.

33-6. Find the capacitance of a parallel-plate capacitor if 1600 μC of charge is on each plate when the potential difference is 80 V.

33-7. A potential difference of 110 V is applied across the plates of a capacitor. If the charge on each plate is 1200 μC, what is the capacitance?

Ans. 10.9 μF.

33-8. What potential difference is required to store a charge of 800 μC on a 40-μF capacitor?

33-9. The plates of a certain capacitor are 3 mm apart and have an area of 0.04 m^2. For a dielectric of air, find **(a)** the capacitance, **(b)** the electric field intensity between the plates, and **(c)** the charge on each plate if 200 V is applied to the capacitor.

Ans. **(a)** 118 pF **(b)** 66.7 kN/C **(c)** 23.6 nC.

33-10. Answer the questions in Prob. 33-9 if mica replaces air as the dielectric. ($K = 5.0$.)

33-11. Find the capacitance of a parallel-plate capacitor if the area of each plate is 0.08 m^2 and the separation of the plates is 4 mm. **(a)** The dielectric is air. **(b)** The dielectric is paraffined paper.

Ans. **(a)** 177 pF **(b)** 354 pF.

33-12. Two parallel plates of a capacitor are 4.6 mm apart and each plate has an area of 0.03 m^2. The capacitor has a dielectric of glass ($k = 7.5$). **(a)** What is the capacitance? **(b)** What is the field intensity between the plates if the plate voltage is 800 V? **(c)** What is the charge on each plate?

33-13. A certain capacitor has a capacitance of 12 μF when its plates are separated by 0.3 mm of vacant space. A battery is used to charge the plates to a potential difference of 400 V and is then disconnected from the system. **(a)** What will be the potential difference across the plates if a sheet of Bakelite ($k = 7$) fills the space between the plates **(b)** What is the capacitance after the Bakelite is inserted? **(c)** What is the permittivity of Bakelite?

Ans. **(a)** 57.1 V **(b)** 84 μF **(c)** 6.20×10^{-11} C^2/N $\cdot$ m^2.

33-14. What voltage will cause a capacitor with a dielectric of glass 4 mm thick to break down?

33-15. What is the breakdown voltage of a capacitor if the plates are separated by 0.5 mm of paraffined paper?

Ans. 25.5 kV.

33-16. A capacitor has a capacitance of 12 μF when the dielectric is air. It is charged to 800 V by means of a battery. **(a)** What is the charge on each plate? The capacitor is now disconnected and immersed in transformer oil. **(b)** What is the new capacitance? **(c)** How much charge is on each plate? **(d)** What is the new potential difference?

33-17. A 6-μF capacitor is connected in series with a 15-μF capacitor. What is the effective capacitance? If it is reconnected in parallel, what will be the effective capacitance?

Ans. 4.29 μF, 21 μF.

33-18. Three capacitors A, B, and C have capacitances of 4, 7, and 12 μF, respectively. What is the equivalent capacitance if they are connected in parallel? In series?

33-19. Find the equivalent capacitance of a 6-μF capacitor if it is connected in series with two parallel capacitors whose capacitances are 5 and 4 μF?

Ans. 3.6 μF.

33-20. Four capacitors A, B, C, and D have capacitances of 12, 16, 20, and 26 μF, respectively. Capacitors A and B are connected in parallel. The combination is then connected in series with C and D. What is the effective capacitance?

33-21. Compute the equivalent capacitance for the circuit shown in Fig. 33-15.

Fig. 33-15

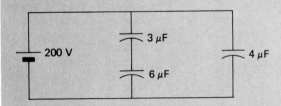

What is the total charge on the equivalent capacitance? What is the voltage across each capacitor?

Ans. $C_e = 6$ μF, $Q_T = 1200$ μC, $Q_4 = 800$ μC, $Q_3 = 400$ μC, $Q_6 = 400$ μC, $V_4 = 200$ V, $V_3 = 133$ V, $V_6 = 67$ V.

33-22. Answer the questions of Prob. 33-21 for the circuit illustrated in Fig. 33-16.

Fig. 33-16

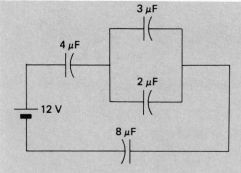

33-23. Three capacitors (A, B, and C) have respective capacitances of 2, 4, and 6 μF. Compute the equivalent capacitance if they are connected in series with an 800-V source of potential difference. What is the charge on each capacitor? What is the voltage on each capacitor?

$Ans.$ $C_e = 1.09$ μF, $Q_T = 873$ μC, $Q_A = Q_B = Q_C = 873$ μC,
$V_A = 436$ V, $V_B = 218$ V, $V_C = 146$ V.

33-24. Compute the equivalent capacitance of the capacitors A, B, and C of Prob. 33-23 if they are connected in parallel. What is the charge on each capacitor?

33-25. What is the potential energy stored in the electric field of a 200-μF capacitor when it is charged to a voltage of 2400 V?

$Ans.$ 576 J.

33-26. What is the energy stored on a 25-μF capacitor when the charge on each plate is 2400 μC?

33-27. How much work is required to charge a capacitor to a potential difference of 30 kV if 800 μC are on each plate?

$Ans.$ 12 J.

33-28. Two identical capacitors C_1 and C_2 are connected in parallel with a 12-V battery. The capacitance of each capacitor with air as the dielectric is 20 μF. What is the charge on each capacitor if a sheet of porcelain ($K = 6$) is inserted between the plates?

33-29. What voltage will cause a parallel-plate capacitor with a dielectric of air 3 mm thick to break down? What is the breakdown voltage if the dielectric is changed to nitrocellulose plastics?

$Ans.$ 9 kV, 750 kV.

33-30. Show that the total capacitance of a multiple-plate capacitor containing N plates separated by air is given by

$$C_0 = \frac{(N - 1)\epsilon_0 A}{d}$$

where A is the area of each plate and d is the separation of each plate.

33-31. A capacitor is formed from 30 parallel plates 20 $\times$ 20 cm. If each plate is separated by 2 mm of dry air, what is the total capacitance?

$Ans.$ 5.13 nF.

34 *Current and Resistance*

OBJECTIVES: After completing this chapter, you should be able to:

1. Demonstrate by definition and example your understanding of *electric current* and *electromotive force*.

2. Write and apply *Ohm's law* to the solution of problems involving electric resistance.

3. Compute *power losses* as a function of voltage, current, and resistance.

4. Define the *resistivity* of a material and solve problems similar to those in the text.

5. Define the *temperature coefficient of resistance* and calculate the change in resistance which occurs with a change in temperature.

We now leave electrostatics and enter a discussion of charges in motion. We have been concerned with forces, electric fields, and potential energies as they relate to charged conductors. For example, excess electrons, evenly distributed over an insulated spherical surface, will remain at rest. However, if a wire is connected from the sphere to ground, the electrons will flow through the wire to the ground. The flow of charge constitutes an *electric current*. In this chapter the foundation is laid for a study of direct currents and electric resistance.

**34-1
THE
MOTION OF
ELECTRIC
CHARGE**

Let us begin our discussion of moving charges by considering the discharge of a capacitor. The potential difference V between the two capacitor plates in Fig. 34-1a is indicated by the electroscope. The total charge Q on either plate is given by

$$Q = CV$$

Fig. 34-1 (*a*) A charged capacitor is a source of current. (*b*) If the capacitor plates are joined by a short, thick wire, the capacitor will discharge instantly. (*c*) A long thin wire allows for a gradual discharge.

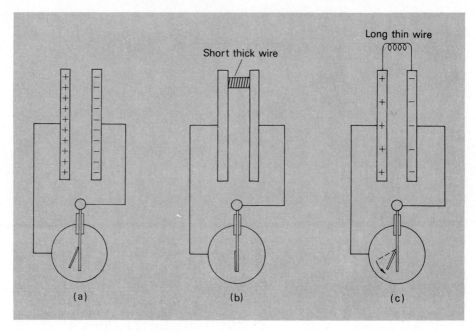

where C is the capacitance. If a path is provided, electrons on one plate will travel to the other, decreasing the net charge and causing a drop in the potential difference. Thus a drop in potential, as indicated by the collapsing leaf of the electroscope, means that charge has been transferred. Any conductor used to connect the plates of a capacitor will cause it to discharge. However, the rate of discharge varies considerably with the size, shape, material, and temperature of the conductor.

If a short, thick wire is connected between the plates of the capacitor, as shown in Fig. 34-1*b*, the electroscope leaf collapses instantly, indicating a very rapid transfer of charge. This current, which exists for a very short time, is called a *transient current*. If we replace the short, thick wire with a long, thin wire of the same material, we shall observe a gradual collapse of the electroscope leaf (Fig. 34-1*c*). Such opposition to the flow of electricity is called electric *resistance*. A quantitative description of electric resistance will be presented in a later section. It is introduced here to illustrate that the rate at which charge flows through a conductor varies. This rate is referred to as the *electric current*.

The **electric current** I is the rate of flow of charge Q past a given point P on an electric conductor.

$$I = \frac{Q}{t}$$

$$(34\text{-}1)$$

The unit of electric current is the *ampere*. One *ampere* (A) represents a flow of charge at the rate of *one coulomb per second* past any point.

$$1 \text{ A} = \frac{1 \text{ C}}{1 \text{ s}}$$

In the example of a discharging capacitor, the current arises from the motion of electrons, as illustrated in Fig. 34-2. The positive charges in a wire

Fig. 34-2 Current arises from the motion of electrons and is a measure of the quantity of charge passing a given point in a unit of time.

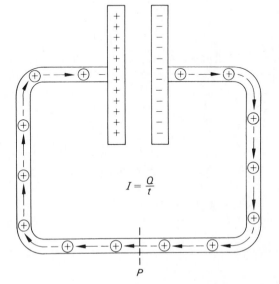

$$I = \frac{Q}{t}$$

P

are tightly bound and cannot move. The electric field created in the wire because of the potential difference between the plates causes the free electrons in the wire to experience a drift toward the positive plate. The electrons are repeatedly deflected or stopped by processes relating to impurities and thermal motions of the atoms. Consequently, the motion of the electrons is not an accelerated one but a drifting or diffusion process. The average drift velocity of electrons is typically of the order of 4 m/h. This velocity of charge, which is a *distance* per unit of time, should not be confused with current, which is a *quantity* of charge per unit of time.

An analogy to water flowing through a pipe is useful in understanding current flow. The rate of flow of the water in gallons per minute is analogous to the rate of flow of charge in coulombs per second. For a current of 1 A, 6.25×10^{18} electrons (1 C) flow past a given point every second. Just as the size and length of a pipe affect the flow of water, the size and length of a conductor affect the flow of electrons.

EXAMPLE 34-1   How many electrons pass a point in 5 s if a constant current of 8 A is maintained in a conductor?

Solution   From Eq. (34-1),

$$Q = It = (8 \text{ A})(5 \text{ s})$$

$$= (8 \text{ C/s})(5 \text{ s}) = 40 \text{ C}$$

$$= (40 \text{ C})(6.25 \times 10^{18} \text{ electrons/C})$$

$$= 2.50 \times 10^{20} \text{ electrons}$$

34-2 THE DIRECTION OF ELECTRIC CURRENT

Thus far, we have discussed only the magnitude of electric current. The choice of direction is purely arbitrary as long as we apply our definition consistently. The flow of charge caused by an electric field in a gas or a liquid consists of a flow of positive ions in the direction of the field or a flow of electrons opposite to the field direction. As we have seen, the current in a metallic material consists of electrons flowing against the field direction. However, a current that consists of negative particles moving in one direction is electrically the same as a current consisting of positive charges moving in the opposite direction.

There are a number of reasons for preferring the motion of positive charge as an indicator of direction. In the first place, all the concepts introduced in electrostatics were defined in terms of positive charges, e.g., the electric field, potential energy, and potential difference. An electron flows contrary to the electric field and "up a potential hill" from the negative plate to the positive plate. If we define current as a flow of *positive* charge, the loss in energy as charge encounters resistance will be from + to − or "down a potential hill." By convention, we consider all currents as consisting of a flow of positive charge.

The direction of conventional current is always the same as the direction in which positive charges would move, even if the actual current consists of a flow of electrons.

For a metallic conducting wire, both electron flow and conventional current are indicated in Fig. 34-3. The zigzag line is used to indicate the electric resistance

Fig. 34-3 In a metallic conductor, the conventional current is in a direction opposite to the flow of electrons.

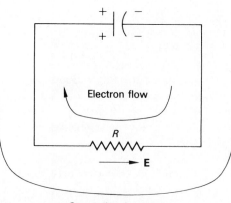

Electron flow

R

E

Conventional current

R. Note that the conventional current flows from the positive plate of the capacitor, neutralizing negative charge on the other plate. Conventional current is in the same direction as the electric field **E** producing the current.

34-3 ELECTRO-MOTIVE FORCE

The currents discussed in the preceding sections were called *transient currents* because they exist only for a short time. Once the capacitor has been completely discharged, there will no longer be a potential difference to promote the flow of additional charge. If some means were available to keep the capacitor continually charged, a continuous current could be maintained. This would require that electrons be continuously supplied to the negative plate to replace those leaving. In other words, energy must be supplied to replace the energy lost by the charge in the external circuit. In this manner, the potential difference between the plates could be maintained, allowing for a continuous flow of charge. A device with the ability to maintain potential difference between two points is called a *source of electromotive force* (emf).

The most familiar sources of emf are batteries and generators. Batteries convert chemical energy into electric energy, and generators transform mechanical energy into electric energy. The detailed nature and operation of these devices will be discussed in a later chapter.

A **source of electromotive force** (emf) is a device which converts chemical, mechanical, or other forms of energy into the electric energy necessary to maintain a continuous flow of electric charge.

In an electric circuit, the source of emf is usually represented by the symbol $\mathscr{E}$.

The function of a source of emf in an electric circuit is similar to the function of a water pump in maintaining the continuous flow of water through a system of pipes. In Fig. 34-4*a* the water pump must perform the work on each

Fig. 34-4 Mechanical analogy of a water pump can be used to explain the function of a source of emf in an electric circuit.

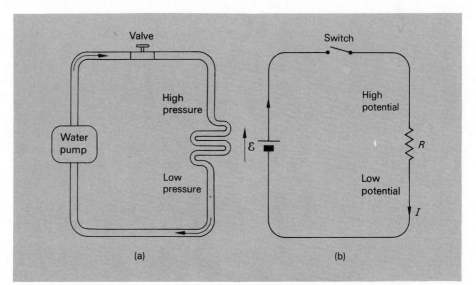

(a) (b)

unit volume of water necessary to replace the energy lost by each unit volume flowing through the pipes. In Fig. 34-4b the source of emf must do work on each unit of charge which passes through it in order to raise it to a higher potential. This work must be supplied at a rate equal to the rate at which energy is lost in flowing through the circuit.

By convention, we have assumed that the current consists of a flow of positive charge even though in most cases it is negative electrons. Therefore, the charge loses energy in passing through the resistor from a high potential to a low potential. In the hydraulic analogy, water passes from high pressure to low pressure. When the shutoff valve is closed, pressure exists but there is no water flow. Similarly, when the electric switch is *open*, there is voltage but no current.

Since emf is work per unit charge, it is expressed in the same unit as potential difference, i.e., the *joule per coulomb*, or *volt*.

> *A source of emf of one volt will perform one joule of work on each coulomb of charge which passes through it.*

For example, a 12-V battery performs 12 J of work on each coulomb of charge transferred from the low-potential side (− terminal) to the high-potential side (+ terminal). An arrow (↑) is usually drawn next to the symbol $\mathscr{E}$ for an emf to indicate the direction in which the source, acting alone, would cause a positive charge to move through the external circuit. The conventional current is directed away from the + terminal of a battery, and the hypothetical positive charge flows "downhill" through external resistance to the − terminal of the battery.

In the following sections, circuit diagrams, like that in Fig. 34-4b, will frequently be used to describe electric systems. Many of the symbols we shall use are defined in Fig. 34-5.

34-4
OHM'S LAW;
RESISTANCE

Resistance (R) is defined as the opposition to the flow of electric charge. Although most metals are good conductors of electricity, all offer some opposition to the surge of electric charge through them. This electric resistance is fixed for many specific materials of known size, shape, and temperature. It is independent of the applied emf and the current passing through it.

The effects of resistance in limiting the flow of charge were first studied quantitatively by Georg Simon Ohm in 1826. He discovered that, *for a given resistor at a particular temperature, the current is directly proportional to the applied voltage.* Just as the rate of flow of water between two points depends on the difference of height between them, the rate of flow of electric charge between two points depends on the difference in potential between them. This proportionality is usually stated as *Ohm's law*:

> *The current produced in a given conductor is directly proportional to the difference of potential between its end points.*

The current I which is observed for a given voltage V is therefore an indication of resistance. Mathematically, the resistance R of a given conductor can be calculated from

$$R = \frac{V}{I} \qquad V = IR \qquad (34\text{-}2)$$

The greater the resistance R, the smaller the current I for a given voltage V. The unit of measurement of resistance is the *ohm*, for which the symbol is the Greek capital letter *omega* (Ω). From Eq. (34-2), it is seen that

$$1\ \Omega = \frac{1\ \text{A}}{1\ \text{V}}$$

A resistance of *one ohm* will allow a current of *one ampere* when a potential difference of *one volt* is impressed across its terminals.

EXAMPLE 34-2   The difference of potential between the terminals of an electric heater is 80 V when there is a current of 6 A in the heater. What will the current be if the voltage is increased to 120 V?

Solution   According to Ohm's law, the resistance of the coils in the heater is

$$R = \frac{V}{I} = \frac{80\ \text{V}}{6\ \text{A}} = 13.3\ \Omega$$

Fig. 34-5 Conventional symbols used in electric-circuit diagrams.

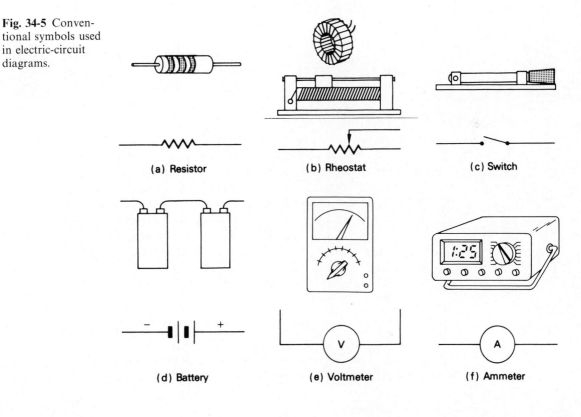

(a) Resistor   (b) Rheostat   (c) Switch

(d) Battery   (e) Voltmeter   (f) Ammeter

Therefore, if the voltage is increased to 120 V, the new current will be

$$I = \frac{V}{R} = \frac{120 \text{ V}}{13.3 \text{ } \Omega} = 9 \text{ A}$$

Here we have neglected any change in resistance due to a rise in temperature of the heating coils.

Four devices commonly used in the laboratory to study Ohm's law are the battery, the voltmeter, the ammeter, and the rheostat. As their names imply, the voltmeter and ammeter are devices to measure voltage and current. The rheostat is simply a variable resistor. A sliding contact changes the number of resistance coils through which charge can flow. A laboratory collection of these electrical devices is illustrated in Fig. 34-6. You should study the circuit diagram in Fig. 34-6a and justify the electrical connections shown pictorially in Fig. 34-6b. Note that the voltmeter is connected in parallel with the battery whereas the ammeter is connected in series. In general, the positive terminals are color-coded red, and the negative terminals are black.

Fig. 34-6 (*a*) A circuit diagram for studying Ohm's law. (*b*) A pictorial diagram showing how the various elements in the circuit are connected in the laboratory.

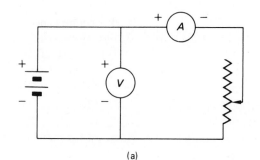

(a)

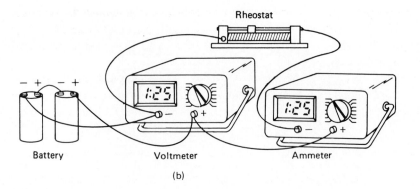

(b)

EXAMPLE 34-3 The apparatus shown in Fig. 34-6 is used to study Ohm's law in the laboratory. The voltage V is determined by the source of emf and remains at 6 V. (*a*) What is the resistance when the rheostat is varied to indicate a current of 0.4 A? (*b*) If this resistance is doubled, what will the new current be?

Solution (a)   From Ohm's law,

$$R = \frac{V}{I} = \frac{6 \text{ V}}{0.4 \text{ A}} = 15 \ \Omega$$

Solution (b)   Doubling the resistance to $30 \ \Omega$ would result in a current given by

$$I = \frac{6 \text{ V}}{30 \ \Omega} = 0.2 \text{ A}$$

Note that doubling the resistance in a circuit reduces the current by one-half.

**34-5
ELECTRIC
POWER AND
HEAT LOSS**

We have seen that electric charge gains energy within a generating source of emf and loses energy in passing through external resistance. Inside the source of emf, work is done *by the source* in raising the potential energy of charge. As the charge passes through the external circuit, work is done *by* the charge on the components of the circuit. In the case of a pure resistor, the energy is dissipated in the form of heat. If a motor is attached to the circuit, the energy loss is divided between heat and useful work. In any case, the energy gained in the source of emf must equal the energy lost in the entire circuit.

Let us examine the work accomplished inside a source of emf more closely. By definition, *one joule* of work is accomplished for each *coulomb* of charge moved through a potential difference of *one volt*. Thus

$$\text{Work} = Vq \tag{34-3}$$

where q is the quantity of charge transferred during a time t. But $q = It$, so that Eq. (34-3) becomes

$$\text{Work} = VIt \tag{34-4}$$

where I is the current in *coulombs per second*. This work represents the energy gained by charge in passing through the source of emf during the time t. An equivalent amount of energy will be dissipated in the form of heat as the charge moves through an external resistance.

The rate at which heat is dissipated in an electric circuit is referred to as the *power loss*. When charge is flowing continuously through a circuit, this power loss is given by

$$P = \frac{\text{work}}{t} = \frac{VIt}{t} = VI \tag{34-5}$$

When V is in volts and I is in amperes, the power loss is measured in watts. That the product of voltage and current will give a unit of power is shown as follows:

$$(V)(A) = \frac{J}{C} \frac{C}{s} = \frac{J}{s} = W$$

Equation (34-5) can be expressed in alternative forms by using Ohm's law ($V = IR$). Substituting for V, we can write

$$P = VI = I^2R \qquad (34\text{-}6)$$

Substitution for I in Eq. (34-6) gives another variation:

$$P = VI = \frac{V^2}{R} \qquad (34\text{-}7)$$

The relation expressed by Eq. (34-6) is so often used in electrical work that heat loss in electrical wiring is often referred to as an "I-squared-R" loss.

EXAMPLE 34-4 A current of 6 A flows through a resistance of 300 Ω for 1 h. What is the power loss? How much heat is generated in joules?

Solution From Eq. (34-6),

$$P = I^2R = (6 \text{ A})^2(300 \text{ } \Omega) = 10{,}800 \text{ W}$$

Since the power represents the heat dissipated per unit of time, we obtain

$$\text{Work} = Pt = (10{,}800 \text{ W})(3600 \text{ s})$$

$$\text{Heat lost} = 3.89 \times 10^7 \text{ J}$$

This represents about 36,900 Btu.

34-6
RESISTIVITY

Just as capacitance is independent of the voltage and quantity of charge, the resistance of a conductor is independent of current and voltage. Both capacitance and resistance are inherent properties of a conductor. The resistance of a wire of uniform cross-sectional area, like the one shown in Fig. 34-7, is determined by the following four factors:

1. The kind of material
2. The length
3. The cross-sectional area
4. The temperature

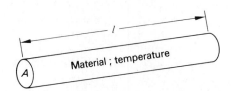

Fig. 34-7 The resistance of a wire depends on the kind of material, the length, the cross-sectional area, and the temperature of the wire.

Ohm, the German physicist who discovered the law that now bears his name, also reported that *the resistance of a conductor at a given temperature is directly proportional to its length, inversely proportional to its cross-sectional area, and dependent upon the material from which it is made.* For a given conductor at a given temperature, the resistance can be computed from

$$R = \rho \frac{l}{A} \tag{34-8}$$

where R = resistance
$\quad\quad l$ = length
$\quad\quad A$ = area

The proportionality constant ρ is a property of the material called its *resistivity*, given by

$$\rho = \frac{RA}{l} \tag{34-9}$$

It varies considerably with different materials and is also affected by changes in temperature. When R is in ohms, A is in square meters, and l is in meters, the unit of resistivity is the ohm-meter ($\Omega \cdot$ m):

$$\frac{(\Omega)(m^2)}{m} = \Omega \cdot m$$

Table 34-1 lists the resistivities of several common metals.

EXAMPLE 34-5   What is the resistance of a 20-m length of copper wire with a diameter of 0.8 mm?

Solution   We first compute the cross-sectional area of the wire in square meters.

$$A = \frac{\pi D^2}{4} = \frac{\pi(8 \times 10^{-4} \text{ m})^2}{4} = 5.03 \times 10^{-7} \text{ m}^2$$

The resistivity of copper is 1.72×10^{-8} $\Omega \cdot$ m. Substitution into Eq. (34-8) gives

$$R = \rho \frac{l}{A} = \frac{(1.72 \times 10^{-8} \ \Omega \cdot \text{m})(20 \text{ m})}{5.03 \times 10^{-7} \text{ m}^2}$$

$$= 0.684 \ \Omega$$

In many engineering applications, the resistivity is given in mixed units. The length is measured in feet, and the area is measured in circular mils (cmil).

One **circular mil** (cmil) is defined as the cross-sectional area of a wire 1 mil (0.001 in.) in diameter.

Table 34-1 Resistivities of Various Materials at 20°C

	Resistivity	
	$\Omega \cdot m$	$\Omega \cdot cmil/ft$
Aluminum	2.8×10^{-8}	17.0
Constantan	49×10^{-8}	295
Copper	1.72×10^{-8}	10.4
Gold	2.2×10^{-8}	13.0
Iron	9.5×10^{-8}	57.0
Nichrome	100×10^{-8}	600
Tungsten	5.5×10^{-8}	33.2
Silver	1.63×10^{-8}	9.6

In order to calculate the area of a wire in circular mils, we first convert its diameter to mils. Since 1 mil is 0.001 in., a diameter can be converted from inches to mils simply by moving the decimal three places to the right. For example,

$$0.128 \text{ in.} = 128.0 \text{ mils}$$

The area of a wire in *square mils* is found from

$$A = \frac{\pi D^2}{4} \quad \text{square mils} \tag{34-10}$$

However, by definition, a wire having a diameter of 1 mil has an area of 1 cmil. Thus

$$1 \text{ cmil} = \frac{\pi}{4} \quad \text{square mils} \tag{34-11}$$

Comparing Eqs. (34-10) and (34-11), it can be seen that *the area in circular mils equals the square of the diameter in mils.* Symbolically,

$$A_{\text{cmils}} = (D_{\text{mils}})^2 \tag{34-12}$$

If the area of a wire is expressed in circular mils and its length in feet, the unit for resistivity from Eq. (34-9) is

$$\rho = \frac{RA}{l} \rightarrow \frac{\Omega \cdot \text{cmil}}{\text{ft}}$$

Table 34-1 also lists the resistivity of materials in the *mil-foot system* of units.

EXAMPLE 34-6   What length of aluminum wire 0.025 in. in diameter is required to construct a 12-Ω resistor?

Solution   The diameter is 25 mils, and the area is found from Eq. (34-12).

$$A_{cmils} = (D_{mils})^2 = (25 \text{ mils})^2 = 625 \text{ cmils}$$

From Eq. (34-8), the length required is

$$l = \frac{RA}{\rho} = \frac{(12 \ \Omega)(625 \text{ cmils})}{17 \ \Omega \cdot \text{cmils/ft}} = 441 \text{ ft}$$

The resistivity ρ was taken from Table 34-1.

**34-7
TEMPERA-
TURE COEF-
FICIENT OF
RESISTANCE**

For most metallic conductors, the resistance tends to increase as the temperature increases. The increased atomic and molecular movement in the conductor hinders the flow of charge. The increase in resistance for most metals is approximately linear when compared with temperature changes. Experiments have shown that the increase in resistance ΔR is proportional to the initial resistance R_0 and the change in temperature Δt. We can write

$$\Delta R = \alpha R_0 \ \Delta t \qquad\qquad (34\text{-}13)$$

The constant α is a characteristic of the material known as the *temperature coefficient of resistance*. The defining equation for α can be found by solving Eq. (34-13):

$$\alpha = \frac{\Delta R}{R_0 \ \Delta t} \qquad\qquad (34\text{-}14)$$

> The **temperature coefficient of resistance** is the change in resistance per unit resistance per degree change in temperature.

Since the units of ΔR and R_0 are the same, the unit of the coefficient α is inverse degrees (1/C°).

EXAMPLE 34-7   An iron wire has a resistance of 200 Ω at 20°C. What will its resistance be at 80°C if the temperature coefficient of resistance is 0.006/C°?

Solution   We first compute the change in resistance from Eq. (34-13):

$$\Delta R = \alpha R_0 \ \Delta t$$

$$= (0.006/\text{C}°)(200 \ \Omega)(80°\text{C} - 20°\text{C})$$

$$= 72 \ \Omega$$

Therefore, the resistance at 80°C is

$$R = R_0 + \Delta R = 200 \ \Omega + 72 \ \Omega = 272 \ \Omega$$

The increase in resistance of a conductor with temperature is large enough to be measured easily. This fact is used in resistance thermometers to measure temperatures very accurately. Because of the very high melting point of some metals, resistance thermometers can be used to measure extremely high temperatures.

SUMMARY

In this chapter, we introduced the *ampere* as a unit of electric current, and we discussed the various quantities which affect its magnitude. Ohm's law described mathematically the relationship between current, resistance, and applied voltage. We also learned the factors which affect electric resistance, and applied these concepts to the solution of basic problems in elementary electricity. The major points are summarized below:

- Electric current I is the rate of flow of charge Q past a given point on a conductor:

$$I = \frac{Q}{t} \qquad 1 \text{ ampere (A)} = \frac{1 \text{ coulomb (C)}}{1 \text{ second (s)}}$$

- By convention, the *direction* of electric current is the same as the direction in which *positive* charges would move, even if the actual current consists of a flow of negatively charged electrons.
- Ohm's law states that *the current produced in a given conductor is directly proportional to the difference of potential between its endpoints:*

$$R = \frac{V}{I} \qquad V = IR \qquad \qquad Ohm's\ Law$$

The symbol R represents the resistance in ohms (Ω) defined as

$$1 \text{ ohm } (\Omega) = \frac{1 \text{ ampere (A)}}{1 \text{ volt (V)}}$$

- The electric power in watts is given by any of

$$P = VI \qquad P = I^2 R \qquad P = \frac{V^2}{R} \qquad \qquad Power$$

- The resistance of a wire depends on four factors: (*a*) the kind of *material*, (*b*) the *length*, (*c*) the cross-sectional *area*, and (*d*) the *temperature*. By introducing a property of the material called its *resistivity* ρ, we can write

$$R = \rho \frac{l}{A} \qquad \rho = \frac{RA}{l} \qquad \qquad SI\ unit\ for\ \rho : \Omega \cdot m$$

- The *temperature coefficient of resistance* α is the change in resistance per unit resistance per degree change in temperature.

$$\alpha = \frac{\Delta R}{R_0 \, \Delta t}$$

$$\Delta R = \alpha R_0 \, \Delta t$$

QUESTIONS

34-1. Define the following terms:
  a. Current
  b. Resistance
  c. Ampere
  d. Emf
  e. Ohm
  f. Rheostat
  g. Ammeter
  h. Voltmeter
  i. Transient current
  j. Source of emf
  k. Electric power
  l. Ohm's law
  m. Resistivity
  n. Circular mil
  o. Temperature coefficient of resistance

34-2. Distinguish clearly between electron flow and conventional current. What are some reasons for preferring the conventional current?

34-3. Use the mechanical analogy of water flowing through pipes to describe the flow of charge through conductors of various lengths and cross-sectional areas.

34-4. A rheostat is connected across the terminals of a battery. What determines the positive and negative terminals on the rheostat?

34-5. Is the electromotive force really a *force*? What is the function of a source of emf?

34-6. What is wrong with the following statement: the resistivity of a material is directly proportional to its length?

34-7. How many circular mils are equivalent to an area of 1 mil^2?

34-8. Use Ohm's law to verify Eqs. (34-6) and (34-7).

PROBLEMS

34-1. How many electrons pass a point every second in a wire carrying a current of 20 A? How much time is needed to transport 40 C of charge past this point?

Ans. 1.25×10^{20} electrons, 2 s.

34-2. If 600 C of charge pass a given point in 3 s, what is the electric current in amperes?

34-3. Find the current in amperes when 690 C of charge pass a given point in 2 min.

Ans. 5.75 A.

34-4. If a current of 24 A exists for 50 s, how many coulombs of charge have passed through the wire?

34-5. **(a)** What is the potential drop across a 4-Ω resistor with a current of 8 A through it? **(b)** What is the resistance of a rheostat if the drop in potential is 48 V and the current through it is 4 A? **(c)** Determine the current through a 5-Ω resistance that has a potential drop of 40 V across it.

Ans. **(a)** 32 V **(b)** 12 Ω **(c)** 8 A.

34-6. A 2-A fuse is placed in a circuit with a battery having a terminal voltage of 12 V. What is the minimum resistance for a circuit containing this fuse?

34-7. What emf is required to pass 60 mA through a resistance of 20 kΩ? If this same emf is applied to a resistance of 300 Ω, what would be the current?

Ans. 1200 V, 4 A.

34-8. A soldering iron draws 0.75 A at 120 V. What is its resistance? How much energy will it use in 15 min?

34-9. An electric lamp has an 80-Ω filament connected to a 110-V direct-current line. What is the current through the filament? What is the power loss in watts?

Ans. 1.38 A, 151 W.

34-10. Assume that the cost of electric energy in a home is 8 cents per kilowatt-hour. A family goes on a 2-week vacation leaving a single 80-W light bulb burning. What is the cost?

34-11. A 120-V, direct-current generator delivers 2.4 kW to an electric furnace. What current is supplied? What is the resistance encountered?

Ans. 20 A, 6 Ω.

34-12. A water turbine delivers 2000 kW to an electric generator. The generator is only 80 percent efficient and has an output terminal voltage of 1200 V. What current is delivered and what is the resistance?

34-13. A 110-V radiant heater draws a current of 6 A. How much heat energy in joules is delivered in 1 hour?

Ans. 2.38 MJ.

34-14. A power line has a total resistance of 4000 Ω. What is the power loss through the wire if the current is reduced to 6 mA?

34-15. The fan motor operating a home cooling system is rated at 10 A for a 110-V line. How much energy is required to operate the fan for a 24-hour period? At a cost of 8 cents per kilowatt-hour, what is the cost of operating this fan continuously for one month (30 days)?

Ans. 95 MW, $63.36.

(*Note:* The current in a home is alternating current instead of direct current, but the same formulas apply.)

34-16. A 20-Ω resistor has a rating of 100 W. Determine the maximum current which can be delivered under these conditions.

34-17. What is the resistance of 200 ft of iron wire with a diameter of 0.002 in. at 20°C?

Ans. 2850 Ω.

34-18. What length of copper wire $\frac{1}{16}$ in. in diameter is required to construct a 20-Ω resistor at 20°C?

34-19. Find the resistance of 40 m of copper wire having a diameter of 0.8 mm at 20°C.

Ans. 1.37 Ω.

34-20. A nichrome wire has a length of 40 m at 20°C. What is its diameter if the total resistance is 500 Ω?

34-21. Determine the resistivity of a wire made of an unknown alloy if its diameter is 0.07 in. and 100 ft of the wire is found to have a resistance of 4 Ω.

Ans. 196 $\Omega \cdot$ cmil/ft.

34-22. How many meters of aluminum wire are needed to construct the windings of a motor if the resistance must be 30 Ω? The diameter of the wire is 0.8 mm.

34-23. The resistance of a length of copper wire is 4 Ω at 20°C. What is its resistance at 80°C? ($\alpha = 0.004/\text{C}°$.)

Ans. 4.96 Ω.

34-24. A length of copper wire has a resistance of 8 Ω at 20°C. What is the resistance at 90°C? At −30°C?

34-25. If the resistance of a conductor is 100 Ω at 60°C, what is its temperature coefficient of resistivity?

Ans. 0.004/C°.

35 *Direct-Current Circuits*

OBJECTIVES: After completing this chapter, you should be able to:

1. Determine the effective resistance of a number of resistors connected in *series* and in *parallel*.

2. Write and apply equations involving *voltage*, *current*, and *resistance* for a circuit containing resistors connected in series and in parallel.

3. Solve problems involving the *emf* of a battery, its *terminal potential difference*, the *internal resistance*, and the *load resistance*.

4. Write and apply *Kirchhoff's laws* for electrical networks similar to those shown in the text.

Two types of current are in use. Direct current (dc) is the continuous flow of charge in only one direction. Alternating current (ac) is a flow of charge continually changing in both magnitude and direction. In this chapter we analyze current, voltage, and resistance for dc circuits. Many of the same methods and procedures can also be applied to ac circuits. The variations required for alternating currents build logically from a strong foundation in dc analysis.

**35-1
SIMPLE
CIRCUITS;
RESISTORS
IN SERIES**

An electric circuit consists of any number of branches joined together so that at least one closed path is provided for current. The simplest circuit consists of a single source of emf joined to a single external resistance, as shown in Fig. 35-1. If $\mathscr{E}$ represents the emf and R indicates the total resistance, Ohm's law yields

$$\mathscr{E} = IR \tag{35-1}$$

where I is the current through the circuit. All the energy gained by charge in passing through the source of emf is lost in flowing through the resistance.

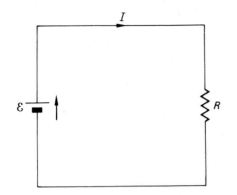

Fig. 35-1 Simple electric circuit.

Let us consider the addition of a number of elements to a circuit. Two or more elements are said to be in *series* if they have only *one* point in common that is not connected to some third element. Current can follow only a single path through elements in series. Resistors R_1 and R_2 of Fig. 35-2a are in series because point A is common to both resistors. However, the resistors in Fig. 35-2b are not in series because point B is common to three current branches. Electric current entering such a junction may follow two separate paths.

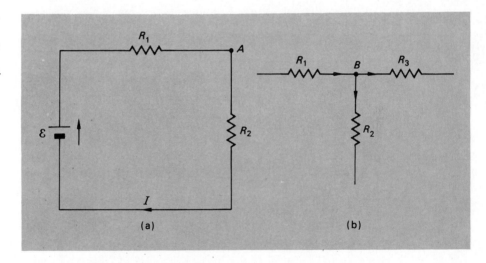

Fig. 35-2 (*a*) Resistors connected in series. (*b*) Resistors which are not connected in series.

Suppose that three resistors (R, R_2, and R_3) are connected in series and enclosed in a box, indicated by the shaded portion of Fig. 35-3. The effective resistance R of the three resistors can be determined from the external voltage V and current I, as recorded by the meters. From Ohm's law

$$R = \frac{V}{I} \tag{35-2}$$

Fig. 35-3 Voltmeter-ammeter method of measuring the effective resistance of a number of resistors connected in series.

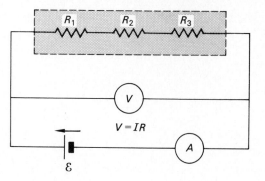

But what is the relationship of R to the three internal resistances? The current through each resistor must be indentical since a single path is provided. Thus

$$I = I_1 = I_2 = I_3 \qquad (35\text{-}3)$$

Utilizing this fact and noting that Ohm's law applies equally well to any part of a circuit, we write

$$V = IR \qquad V_1 = IR_1 \qquad V_2 = IR_2 \qquad V_3 = IR_3 \qquad (35\text{-}4)$$

The external voltage V represents the sum of the energies lost per unit of charge in passing through each resistance. Therefore,

$$V = V_1 + V_2 + V_3$$

Finally, if we substitute from Eq. (35-4) and divide out the current, we obtain

$$IR = IR_1 + IR_2 + IR_3$$

$$\boxed{R = R_1 + R_2 + R_3} \qquad \text{Series} \quad (35\text{-}5)$$

To summarize what has been learned about resistors connected in *series*:

1. The current in all parts of a series circuit is the same.
2. The voltage across a number of resistances in series is equal to the sum of the voltages across the individual resistors.
3. The effective resistance of a number of resistors in series is equivalent to the sum of the individual resistances.

EXAMPLE 35-1

The resistances R_1 and R_2 in Fig. 35-2a are 2 and 4 Ω, respectively. If the source of emf maintains a constant potential difference of 12 V, what is the current delivered to the external circuit? What is the potential drop across each resistor?

Solution

The effective resistance is

$$R = R_1 + R_2 = 2\,\Omega + 4\,\Omega = 6\,\Omega$$

The current is then found from Ohm's law:

$$I = \frac{V}{R} = \frac{12\text{ V}}{6\text{ }\Omega} = 2\text{ A}$$

The voltage drops are therefore

$$V_1 = IR_1 = (2\text{ A})(2\text{ }\Omega) = 4\text{ V}$$

$$V_2 = IR_2 = (2\text{ A})(4\text{ }\Omega) = 8\text{ V}$$

Note that the sum of the voltage drops $(V_1 + V_2)$ is equal to the applied 12 V.

35-2 RESISTORS IN PARALLEL

There are several limitations in the operation of series circuits. If a single element in a series circuit fails to provide a conducting path, the entire circuit is opened and current ceases. It would be quite annoying if all electrical devices in a home were to cease functioning whenever one lamp burned out. Moreover, each element in a series circuit adds to the total resistance of the circuit, thereby limiting the total current which can be supplied. These objections can be overcome by providing alternative paths for electric current. Such a connection, in which current can be divided between two or more elements, is called a *parallel connection*.

A *parallel circuit* is one in which two or more components are connected to two common points in the circuit. For example, in Fig. 35-4, the resistors R_2 and R_3 are in parallel because they both have points A and B in common. Note that the current I, provided by the source of emf, is divided between resistors R_2 and R_3.

Fig. 35-4 Resistors R_2 and R_3 are connected in parallel.

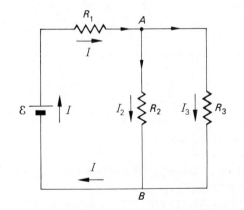

To arrive at an expression for the equivalent resistance R of a number of resistances connected in parallel, we follow a procedure similar to that discussed for a series connection. Assume that three resistors (R_1, R_2, and R_3) are placed inside a box, as shown in Fig. 35-5. The total current I delivered to the box is determined by its effective resistance and the applied voltage:

$$I = \frac{V}{R} \tag{35-6}$$

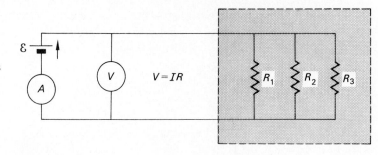

Fig. 35-5 Computing the equivalent resistance of a number of resistors connected in parallel.

In a parallel connection, the voltage drop across each resistor is the same and equivalent to the total drop in voltage.

$$V = V_1 = V_2 = V_3 \qquad (35\text{-}7)$$

That this is true can be realized when we consider that the same energy must be lost by a unit of charge regardless of the path it travels in the circuit. In this example, charge may flow through any one of the three resistors. Thus the total current delivered is divided between the resistors.

$$I = I_1 + I_2 + I_3 \qquad (35\text{-}8)$$

Applying Ohm's law to Eq. (35-8) yields

$$\frac{V}{R} = \frac{V_1}{R_1} + \frac{V_2}{R_2} + \frac{V_3}{R_3}$$

But the voltages are equal, and we can divide them out.

$$\boxed{\frac{1}{R} = \frac{1}{R_1} + \frac{1}{R_2} + \frac{1}{R_3}} \qquad \textit{Parallel} \quad (35\text{-}9)$$

In summary, for parallel resistors:

1. The total current in a parallel circuit is equal to the sum of the currents in the individual branches.
2. The voltage drops across all branches in a parallel circuit must be of equal magnitude.
3. The reciprocal of the equivalent resistance is equal to the sum of the reciprocals of the individual resistances connected in parallel.

In the case of only two resistors in parallel,

$$\frac{1}{R} = \frac{1}{R_1} + \frac{1}{R_2}$$

Solving this equation algebraically for R, we obtain a simplified formula for computing the equivalent resistance.

$$R = \frac{R_1 R_2}{R_1 + R_2} \qquad (35\text{-}10)$$

The equivalent resistance of two resistors connected in parallel is equal to their product divided by their sum.

EXAMPLE 35-2
The total applied voltage to the circuit in Fig. 35-6 is 12 V, and the resistances R_1, R_2, and R_3 are 4, 3, and 6 Ω, respectively. (*a*) Determine the equivalent resistance of the circuit. (*b*) What is the current through each resistor?

Solution (a)
The best approach to a problem which contains both series and parallel resistors is to reduce the circuit by steps to its simplest form, as shown in Fig. 35-6. We first find the equivalent resistance R' of the pair of resistors R_2 and R_3.

$$R' = \frac{R_2 R_3}{R_2 + R_3} = \frac{(3\ \Omega)(6\ \Omega)}{(3 + 6)\Omega} = 2\ \Omega$$

Fig. 35-6 Reducing a complex circuit to a simple equivalent circuit.

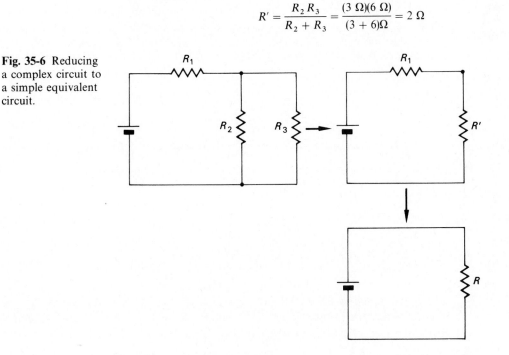

Since the equivalent resistance R' is in series with R_1, the total equivalent resistance is

$$R = R' + R_1 = 2\ \Omega + 4\ \Omega = 6\ \Omega$$

Solution (b)
The total current can be found from Ohm's law:

$$I = \frac{V}{R} = \frac{12\ V}{6\ \Omega} = 2\ A$$

The current through R_1 and R' is therefore 2 A since they are in series. To find the currents I_2 and I_3 we must know the voltage drop V' across the equivalent resistance R'.

$$V' = IR' = (2 \text{ A})(2 \text{ }\Omega) = 4 \text{ V}$$

Thus the potential must drop by 4 V through each of the resistors R_2 and R_3. The currents are found from Ohm's law:

$$I_2 = \frac{V'}{R_2} = \frac{4 \text{ V}}{3 \text{ }\Omega} = 1.33 \text{ A}$$

$$I_3 = \frac{V'}{R_3} = \frac{4 \text{ V}}{6 \text{ }\Omega} = 0.67 \text{ A}$$

Note that $I_2 + I_3 = 2$ A, which is the total current delivered to the circuit.

35-3 EMF AND TERMINAL POTENTIAL DIFFERENCE

In all the preceding problems, we have assumed that all resistance to current flow is due to elements of a circuit which are external to the source of emf. This is not strictly true, however, because there is an inherent resistance within every source of emf. This *internal resistance* is represented by the symbol r and is shown schematically as a small resistance in series with the source of emf. (See Fig. 35-7.) When a current I is flowing through the circuit, there is a loss of

Fig. 35-7 Internal resistance.

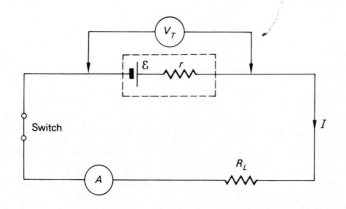

energy through the external load R_L and also there is a heat loss due to the internal resistance. Thus the actual terminal voltage V_T across a source of emf $\mathscr{E}$ with an internal resistance r is given by

$$\boxed{V_T = \mathscr{E} - Ir} \qquad (35\text{-}11)$$

The voltage applied to the external load is therefore less than the emf by an amount equal to the internal potential drop. Since $V_T = IR_L$, Eq. (35-11) can be rewritten

$$V_T = IR_L = \mathscr{E} - Ir \qquad (35\text{-}12)$$

Solving Eq. (35-12) for the current I, we have

$$I = \frac{\mathscr{E}}{R_L + r} \qquad (35\text{-}13)$$

The current in a simple circuit containing a single source of emf is equal to the emf $\mathscr{E}$ divided by the total resistance in the circuit (including internal resistance).

EXAMPLE 35-3 A load resistance of 8 Ω is connected to a battery whose internal resistance is 0.2 Ω. (*a*) If the emf of the battery is 12 V, what current is delivered to the load? (*b*) What is the terminal voltage of the battery?

Solution (a) The current delivered is found from Eq. (35-13).

$$I = \frac{\mathscr{E}}{R_L + r} = \frac{12 \text{ V}}{8 \text{ Ω} + 0.2 \text{ Ω}} = 1.46 \text{ A}$$

Solution (b) The terminal voltage is

$$V_T = \mathscr{E} - Ir = 12 \text{ V} - (1.46 \text{ A})(0.2 \text{ Ω})$$

$$= 12 \text{ V} - 0.292 \text{ V} = 11.7 \text{ V}$$

As a check, we can find the voltage drop across the load R_L:

$$V_T = IR_L = (1.46 \text{ A})(8 \text{ Ω}) = 11.7 \text{ V}$$

35-4 MEASURING INTERNAL RESISTANCE

The internal resistance of a battery can be measured in the laboratory by using a voltmeter, an ammeter, and a known resistance. A voltmeter is an instrument which has an extremely high resistance. When a voltmeter is attached directly to the terminals of a battery, negligible current is drawn from the battery. We can see from Eq. (35-11) that for zero current this terminal voltage is equal to the emf ($V_T = \mathscr{E}$). In fact, the emf of a battery is sometimes referred to as its "open-circuit" potential difference. Thus the emf can be measured with a voltmeter. By connecting a known resistance to the circuit, we can determine the internal resistance by measuring the current delivered to the circuit.

EXAMPLE 35-4 A dry cell gives an open-circuit reading of 1.5 V when a voltmeter is connected to its terminals. When the voltmeter is removed and a load of 3.5 Ω is placed across the terminals of the battery, a current of 0.4 A is measured. What is the internal resistance of the battery?

Solution Solving for r in Eq. (35-12), we obtain

$$r = \frac{\mathscr{E} - IR_L}{I} = \frac{1.5 \text{ V} - (0.4 \text{ A})(3.5 \text{ Ω})}{0.4 \text{ A}}$$

$$= \frac{0.10 \text{ V}}{0.4 \text{ A}} = 0.25 \text{ Ω}$$

As a dry cell ages, its internal resistance increases while its emf remains relatively constant. The increased internal resistance causes a reduction in the current delivered. This fact accounts for the difference in intensity of light between a flashlight using old batteries and one using fresh batteries.

35-5 REVERSING THE CURRENT THROUGH A SOURCE OF EMF

In a battery chemical energy is converted into electric energy in order to maintain current flow in an electric circuit. A generator performs a similar function by converting mechanical energy into electric energy. In either case, the process is reversible. If a source of higher emf is connected in direct opposition to a source of lower emf, the current will pass through the latter from its positive terminal to its negative terminal. Reversing the flow of charge in this manner results in a loss of energy as electric energy is converted into chemical or mechanical energy.

Let us consider the process of charging a battery, as illustrated in Fig. 35-8. As charge flows through the higher source of emf $\mathcal{E}_1$, it gains energy. The terminal voltage for $\mathcal{E}_1$ is given by

$$V_1 = \mathcal{E}_1 - Ir_1$$

in accordance with Eq. (35-12). The output voltage is reduced because of the internal resistance r_1.

Fig. 35-8 Reversing the current through a source of emf.

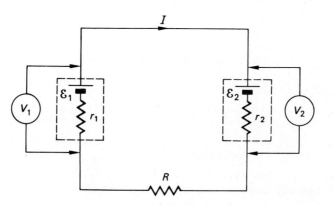

Energy is lost in two ways as charge is forced through the battery against its normal output direction:

1. Electric energy in the amount equal to $\mathcal{E}_2$ is stored as chemical energy in the battery.
2. Energy is lost to the internal resistance of the battery.

Therefore, the terminal voltage V_2, which represents the total drop in potential across the battery, is given by

$$V_2 = \mathcal{E}_2 + Ir_2 \tag{35-14}$$

where r_2 is the internal resistance. Note that in this case the terminal voltage is *greater* than the emf of the battery. The remainder of the potential supplied by the higher source of emf is lost through the external resistance R.

Throughout the entire circuit, the energy lost must equal the energy gained. Thus we can write

Energy gained per unit charge = energy lost per unit charge

$$\mathscr{E}_1 = \mathscr{E}_2 + Ir_1 + Ir_2 + IR$$

Solving for the current I yields

$$I = \frac{\mathscr{E}_1 - \mathscr{E}_2}{r_1 + r_2 + R}$$

The current supplied to a continuous electric circuit is equal to the net emf divided by the total resistance of the circuit, including internal resistance.

$$\boxed{I = \frac{\sum \mathscr{E}}{\sum R}} \qquad (35\text{-}15)$$

For the purposes of applying Eq. (35-15), an emf is considered negative when the current flows against its normal output direction.

EXAMPLE 35-5   Assume the following values for the parameters of the circuit in Fig. 35-8: $\mathscr{E}_1 = 12$ V, $\mathscr{E}_2 = 6$ V, $r_1 = 0.2$ Ω, $r_2 = 0.1$ Ω, and $R = 4$ Ω. (a) What is the current in the circuit? (b) What is the terminal voltage across the 6-V battery?

Solution (a)   From Eq. (35-15), the current is

$$I = \frac{\mathscr{E}_1 - \mathscr{E}_2}{r_1 + r_2 + R} = \frac{12\text{ V} - 6\text{ V}}{0.2\ \Omega + 0.1\ \Omega + 4\ \Omega}$$

$$= \frac{6\text{ V}}{4.3\ \Omega} = 1.40\text{ A}$$

Solution (b)   The terminal voltage of the battery being charged is, from Eq. (35-14),

$$V_2 = \mathscr{E}_2 + Ir_2$$

$$= 6\text{ V} + (1.4\text{ A})(0.1\ \Omega)$$

$$= 6.14\text{ V}$$

**35-6
KIRCH-
HOFF'S
LAWS**

An electrical network is a complex circuit consisting of a number of current loops or meshes. For complex networks containing several meshes and a number of sources of emf, the application of Ohm's law becomes very difficult. A more straightforward procedure for analyzing such circuits was developed in the nineteenth century by Gustav Kirchhoff, a German scientist. His method involves the use of two laws. *Kirchhoff's first law* is:

The sum of the currents entering a junction is equal to the sum of the currents leaving that junction.

$$\sum I_{entering} = \sum I_{leaving} \qquad (35\text{-}16)$$

Kirchhoff's second law states:

The sum of the emfs around any closed current loop is equal to the sum of all the IR drops around that loop.

$$\sum \mathscr{E} = \sum IR \qquad (35\text{-}17)$$

A junction refers to any point in a circuit where three or more wires come together. The first law simply states that charge must flow continuously; it cannot pile up at a junction. In Fig. 35-9, if 12 C of charge enters the junction every second, then 12 C must leave it every second. The current delivered to each branch is inversely proportional to the resistance of that branch.

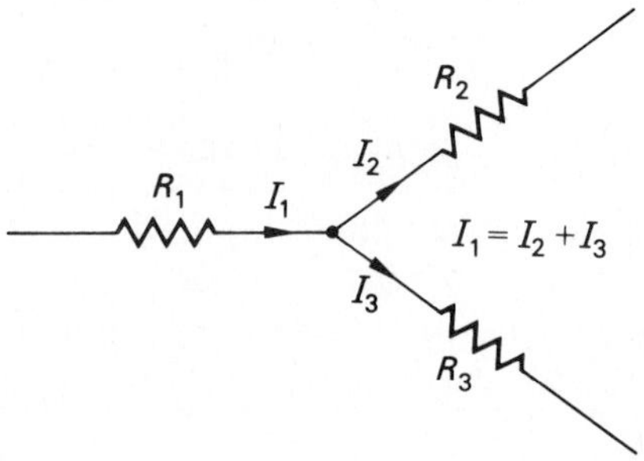

Fig. 35-9 The sum of the currents entering a junction must equal the sum of the currents leaving that junction.

$$I_1 = I_2 + I_3$$

The second law is a restatement of the conservation of energy. If we begin at any point in a circuit and travel around any closed current loop, the energy gained by a unit of charge must equal the energy lost by that charge. Energy is gained through the conversion of chemical or mechanical energy into electric energy by a source of emf. Energy may be lost either in the form of IR potential drops or in the process of reversing the current through a source of emf. In the latter case, electric energy is converted into the chemical energy necessary to charge a battery or electric energy is converted to mechanical energy for the operation of a motor.

In applying Kirchhoff's rules, very definite procedures must be followed. The steps of the general procedure will be presented by considering the example offered by Fig. 35-10a.

1. Assume a current direction for each loop in the network.

The three loops which may be considered are those illustrated in Fig. 35-10b, c, and d. The current I_1 is assumed to flow counterclockwise in the top loop, I_2 is

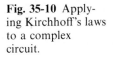

Fig. 35-10 Applying Kirchhoff's laws to a complex circuit.

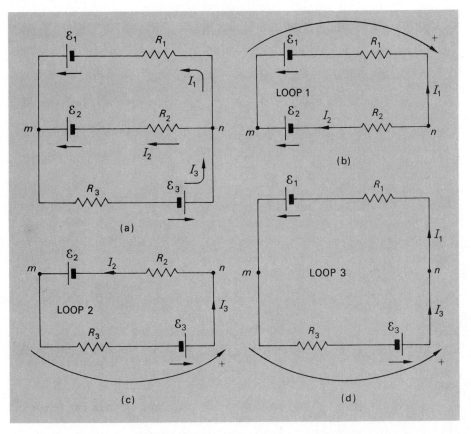

assumed to travel to the left in the middle branch, and I_3 is assumed to flow counterclockwise in the lower loop. If we have guessed correctly, the solution to the problem will give a positive value for the current; if we have guessed wrong, a negative value will indicate that the current is actually in the other direction.

2. Apply Kirchhoff's first law to write a current equation for all but one of the junction points.

Writing the current equation for *every* junction would result in a duplicate equation. In our example, there are two junction points which are labeled *m* and *n*, respectively. The current equation for *m* is

$$\sum I_{\text{entering}} = \sum I_{\text{leaving}}$$

$$I_1 + I_2 = I_3 \tag{35-18}$$

The same equation would result if we considered junction *n*, and no new information would be given.

3. Indicate by a small arrow, drawn next to the symbol for each emf, the direction in which the source, acting alone, would cause a positive charge to move through the circuit.

In our example, $\mathscr{E}_1$ and $\mathscr{E}_2$ are directed to the left, and $\mathscr{E}_3$ is directed to the right.

4. Apply Kirchhoff's second law ($\sum \mathscr{E} = \sum IR$) for one loop at a time. There will be one equation for each loop.

In applying Kirchhoff's second rule, one must begin at a specific point on a loop and *trace* around the loop in a consistent direction back to the starting point. The choice of the *tracing direction* is arbitrary, but, once established, it becomes the positive (+) direction for sign conventions. (Tracing directions for the three loops in our example are labeled in Fig. 35-10.) The following sign conventions apply:

1. When summing the emfs around a loop, the value assigned to the emf is positive if its output (see step 3) is with the tracing direction; it is considered negative if the output is against the tracing direction.
2. An IR drop is considered positive when the assumed current is with the tracing direction and negative when the assumed current opposes the tracing direction.

Let us now apply Kirchhoff's second law to each loop in our example:

Loop 1 Starting at point m and tracing clockwise, we have

$$-\mathscr{E}_1 + \mathscr{E}_2 = -I_1 R_1 + I_2 R_2 \tag{35-19}$$

Loop 2 Starting at point m and tracing counterclockwise, we have

$$\mathscr{E}_3 + \mathscr{E}_2 = I_3 R_3 + I_2 R_2 \tag{35-20}$$

Loop 3 Starting at m and tracing counterclockwise we have

$$\mathscr{E}_3 + \mathscr{E}_1 = I_3 R_3 + I_1 R_1 \tag{35-21}$$

If the equation for loop 1 is subtracted from the equation for loop 2, the equation for loop 3 is obtained, showing that the last loop equation gives no new information.

We now have three independent equations involving only three unknowns. They can be solved simultaneously to find the unknowns, and the third loop equation can be used to check the results.

EXAMPLE 35-6 Solve for the unknown currents in Fig. 35-11, using Kirchhoff's laws.

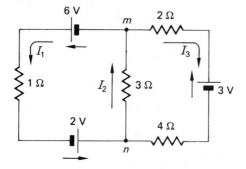

Fig. 35-11

Solution

Current directions are assumed, as indicated in the figure for I_1, I_2, and I_3. If we apply Kirchhoff's first law to junction m, we obtain

$$\sum I \text{ (entering)} = \sum I \text{ (leaving)}$$

$$I_2 = I_1 + I_3 \tag{35-22}$$

Next, the direction of positive output is indicated in the figure, adjacent to each source of emf. Since there are three unknowns, we need at least two more equations from the application of Kirchhoff's second law. Starting at m and tracing counterclockwise around the left loop, we write the voltage equation

$$\sum \mathscr{E} = \sum IR$$

$$6 \text{ V} + 2 \text{ V} = I_1(1 \ \Omega) + I_2(3 \ \Omega)$$

$$8 \text{ V} = (1 \ \Omega)I_1 + (3 \ \Omega)I_2$$

Dividing through by 1 Ω and transposing, we obtain

$$I_1 + 3I_2 = 8 \text{ A} \tag{35-23}$$

The unit ampere arises from the fact that

$$1 \text{ V}/\Omega = 1 \text{ A}$$

Another voltage equation can be written by starting at m and tracing clockwise around the right loop:

$$-3 \text{ V} = I_3(2 \ \Omega) + I_3(4 \ \Omega) + I_2(3 \ \Omega)$$

The negative sign arises from the fact that the output of the source opposes the tracing direction. Simplifying, we have

$$2I_3 + 4I_3 + 3I_2 = -3 \text{ A}$$

$$6I_3 + 3I_2 = -3 \text{ A}$$

$$I_2 + 2I_3 = -1 \text{ A} \tag{35-24}$$

The three equations which must be solved simultaneously for I_1, I_2, and I_3 are

$$I_1 - I_2 + I_3 = 0 \tag{35-22}$$

$$I_1 + 3I_2 = 8 \text{ A} \tag{35-23}$$

$$I_2 + 2I_3 = -1 \text{ A} \tag{35-24}$$

From Eq. (35-22), we note that

$$I_1 = I_2 - I_3$$

which, substituted into Eq. (35-23), yields

$$(I_2 - I_3) + 3I_2 = 8 \text{ A}$$

$$4I_2 - I_3 = 8 \text{ A} \tag{35-25}$$

Now we can solve Eqs. (35-25) and (35-24) simultaneously by eliminating I_3 from the two equations by addition:

$$(35\text{-}24): \quad I_2 + 2I_3 \quad = \quad -1 \text{ A}$$

$$2 \times (35\text{-}25): \quad 8I_2 - 2I_3 \quad = \quad 16 \text{ A}$$

$$9I_2 \quad = \quad 15 \text{ A}$$

$$I_2 = 1.67 \text{ A}$$

Substituting $I_2 = 1.67$ A into Eqs. (35-23) and (35-24) gives values for the other currents:

$$I_1 = 3 \text{ A} \qquad I_3 = -1.33 \text{ A}$$

The negative value obtained for I_3 indicates that our assumed current direction was incorrect. Actually, the current flows opposite the assumed direction. However, in working problems, the minus sign should be retained until all unknowns have been determined.

As a check on the above results, we can write one more voltage equation by applying Kirchhoff's second law to the outside loop. Starting at m and tracing counterclockwise, we obtain

$$(6 + 2 + 3) \text{ V} = I_1(1 \text{ }\Omega) - I_3(4 \text{ }\Omega) - I_3(2 \text{ }\Omega)$$

$$I_1 - 6I_3 = 11 \text{ A}$$

Substituting for I_1 and I_3, we obtain

$$3 \text{ A} - (6)(-1.33 \text{ A}) = 11 \text{ A}$$

$$11 \text{ A} = 11 \text{ A} \qquad\qquad \textit{Check}$$

Note again that the negative value for I_3 was used in the mathematics even though it indicates an incorrect assumption.

35-7
THE WHEAT-
STONE
BRIDGE

A very precise laboratory method for measuring an unknown resistance uses a *Wheatstone bridge*. The circuit diagram for the apparatus is shown in Fig. 35-12. The bridge consists of a battery, a galvanometer, and four resistors. The galvanometer is a highly sensitive instrument which indicates the flow of electric charge. In the diagram, an unknown resistance R_x is balanced with the three known resistances (R_1, R_2, and R_3). Normally, when the switch is closed, the galvanometer will indicate a current between points B and D. By moving the contact point D to the right or left, the resistances R_1 and R_2 can be varied until the galvanometer deflection is zero, indicating zero current between points

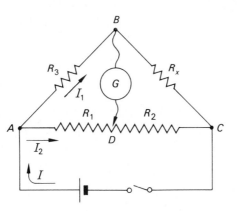

Fig. 35-12 Circuit diagram for the Wheatstone bridge.

B and D. Under these conditions, the bridge is said to be balanced, and points B and D must be at the same potential.

$$V_B = V_D \qquad\qquad Balanced$$

Thus the potential drop from A to B must equal the potential drop from A to D.

$$V_{AB} = V_{AD} \tag{35-26}$$

Similarly,

$$V_{BC} = V_{DC} \tag{35-27}$$

The current I coming from the source of emf splits at point A, sending the current I_1 through the branch ABC and the current I_2 through the branch ADC. Applying Ohm's law to Eqs. (35-26) and (35-27) gives the relations

$$I_1 R_3 = I_2 R_1 \qquad \text{and} \qquad I_1 R_x = I_2 R_2$$

Dividing the second equation by the first and solving for R_x, we have

$$\boxed{R_x = R_3 \, \frac{R_2}{R_1}} \tag{35-28}$$

The laboratory apparatus for the Wheatstone bridge is illustrated in Fig. 35-13. The resistance R_3 is usually a plug-type resistance box, which gives a positive indication of its resistance. Removing plugs will increase the known resistance. The resistances R_1 and R_2 normally consist of a wire of uniform resistance attached to a meterstick. Since the resistance of such a wire is directly proportional to its length, the ratio R_2/R_1 of Eq. (35-28) is equivalent to the ratio of the corresponding wire lengths. If l_1 and l_2 are used to represent the wire segments AD and DC, the unknown resistance can be found from

$$R_x = R_3 \, \frac{l_2}{l_1} \tag{35-29}$$

Thus it is not necessary to know the actual resistance of R_1 and R_2.

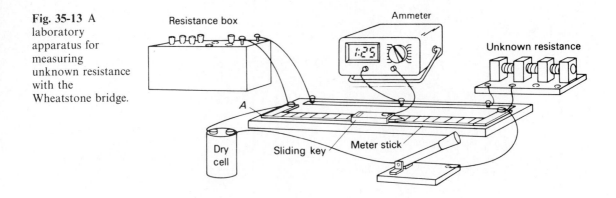

Fig. 35-13 A laboratory apparatus for measuring unknown resistance with the Wheatstone bridge.

Resistance box

Ammeter

Unknown resistance

A

Dry cell

Sliding key

Meter stick

EXAMPLE 35-7

A Wheatstone bridge is used to measure the resistance R_x of a spool of copper wire. It is found that the galvanometer gives a small deflection when 4 Ω is placed on the resistance box. When the contact key is positioned at the 40-cm mark (measured from A), the bridge is balanced. Determine the unknown resistance.

Solution

In this example $l_1 = 40$ cm, $l_2 = 60$ cm, and $R_3 = 4$ Ω. Substitution into Eq. (35-29) yields

$$R_x = R_3 \frac{l_2}{l_1} = (4 \text{ Ω}) \frac{60 \text{ cm}}{40 \text{ cm}} = 6 \text{ Ω}$$

During preliminary adjustments, when the bridge may be far from balanced, a resistor should be placed in series with the galvanometer to protect this extremely sensitive instrument from large currents. The resistor is removed from the circuit when final adjustments are made.

SUMMARY

An understanding of direct-current circuits is essential as an introduction to electrical technology. Most of the advanced study builds on the ideas presented in this chapter. You should review in detail any sections which are not clear to you. A summary of the major relationships is given below:

- In dc circuits, resistors may be connected in series (refer to Fig. 35-3) or in parallel (refer to Fig. 35-5).
  (a) For *series connections*, the current in all parts of the circuit is the same, the total voltage drop is the sum of the individual drops across each resistor, and the effective resistance is equal to the sum of the individual resistances:

$$\boxed{I_T = I_1 = I_2 = I_3} \qquad \boxed{V_T = V_1 + V_2 + V_3}$$

$$\boxed{R_e = R_1 + R_2 + R_3} \qquad \textit{Series Connections}$$

(b) For *parallel connections*, the total current is the sum of the individual currents, the voltage drops are all equal, and the effective resistance is given by

$$I_T = I_1 + I_2 + I_3 \qquad V_T = V_1 = V_2 = V_3$$

$$\frac{1}{R_e} = \frac{1}{R_1} + \frac{1}{R_2} + \frac{1}{R_3}$$ *Parallel Connections*

For two resistors connected in parallel, a simpler form is

$$R_e = \frac{R_1 R_2}{R_1 + R_2}$$ *Two Resistors in Parallel*

- The current supplied to an electric circuit is equal to the *net* emf divided by the total resistance of the circuit, including internal resistances.

$$I = \frac{\sum \mathscr{E}}{\sum R} \qquad \text{for example} \qquad I = \frac{\mathscr{E}_1 - \mathscr{E}_2}{r_1 + r_2 + R_L}$$

The example is for two opposing batteries of internal resistances r_1 and r_2 when the circuit load resistance is R_L.

- According to Kirchhoff's laws, the current entering a junction must equal the current leaving the junction and the net emf around any loop must equal the sum of the *IR* drops. Symbolically,

$$\sum I_{\text{entering}} = \sum I_{\text{leaving}}$$

$$\sum \mathscr{E} = \sum IR$$ *Kirchhoff's Laws*

- The following steps should be applied in solving circuits with Kirchhoff's laws (see Fig. 35-10):

Step 1 *Assume a current direction for each loop in the network.*

Step 2 *Apply Kirchhoff's first law to write a current equation for all but one of the junction points* ($\sum I_{\text{in}} = \sum I_{\text{out}}$).

Step 3 *Indicate by a small arrow the direction in which each emf acting alone would cause a positive charge to move.*

Step 4 *Apply Kirchhoff's second law* ($\sum \mathscr{E} = \sum IR$) *to write an equation for all possible current loops.* An arbitrary positive tracing direction is chosen. An emf is considered positive if its output direction is the same as your tracing direction. An *IR* drop is considered positive when the assumed current direction is the same as your tracing direction.

Step 5 *Solve the equations simultaneously to determine the unknown quantities.*

- A Wheatstone bridge is a device which allows one to determine an unknown resistance R_x by balancing the voltage drops in the circuit. If R_3 is known and the ratio R_2/R_1 can be determined, we have

$$R_x = R_3 \frac{R_2}{R_1}$$ *Wheatstone Bridge*

QUESTIONS

35-1. Define the following terms:

    a. Dc circuit   **e.** Internal resistance

    b. Series connection   **f.** Kirchhoff's first law

    c. Parallel connection   **g.** Kirchhoff's second law

    d. Terminal potential difference   **h.** Wheatstone bridge

35-2. Defend the following statement: the effective resistance of a group of resistors connected in parallel will be less than any of the individual resistances.

35-3. Discuss the advantages and disadvantages of connecting Christmas-tree lights **(a)** in series; **(b)** in parallel.

35-4. What is meant by the "open-circuit" potential difference of a battery?

35-5. Distinguish clearly between terminal potential difference and emf.

35-6. Many electrical devices and appliances are designed to operate at the same voltage. How should such devices be connected in an electric circuit?

35-7. Should elements connected in series be designed to function at a constant current or at a constant voltage?

35-8. In an electric circuit, it is desired to decrease the effective resistance by adding resistors. Should these resistors be connected in parallel or in series?

35-9. Describe a method for measuring the resistance of a spool of wire by using a voltmeter, an ammeter, a rheostat, and a source of emf. Draw the circuit diagram. (The rheostat is used to adjust the current to the range required for the ammeter.)

35-10. In a laboratory experiment with the Wheatstone bridge, the contact key is adjusted for zero galvanometer current. When the key has remained in contact with the wire for a while, a student notes that the bridge becomes unbalanced and there is a slight galvanometer deflection. Suggest a possible explanation.

35-11. Why is it acceptable to use lengths of wire rather than actual resistances when the Wheatstone bridge is balanced?

35-12. Given the emf of a battery, describe a laboratory procedure for determining its internal resistance.

35-13. Compare the formulas for computing equivalent capacitance with the formulas developed in this chapter for resistances in series and in parallel.

35-14. Can the terminal voltage of a battery ever be greater than its emf? Explain.

35-15. Solve Eq. (35-9) explicitly for the equivalent resistance R.

PROBLEMS

35-1. An 18-Ω resistor R_1 and a 9-Ω resistor R_2 are connected in parallel and then in series with a 24-V battery. What is the effective resistance for each connection? Which connection draws more battery current?

                                              Ans. 6 Ω, 27 Ω, parallel.

35-2. A 12-Ω resistor and an 8-Ω resistor are connected in parallel with a 28-V source of emf. What is the effective resistance? What current is delivered by the battery? What are the effective resistance and current if the resistors are reconnected in series?

35-3. An 8-Ω resistor and a 3-Ω resistor are first connected in parallel and then in series with a 12-V source of emf. What are the effective resistance and circuit current for each case? Draw the circuit diagrams for each case.

Ans. 2.18 Ω, 5.5 A, 11 Ω, 1.09 A.

35-4. Given three resistors, $R_1 = 80$ Ω, $R_2 = 60$ Ω, and $R_3 = 40$ Ω, find their effective resistance when connected **(a)** in series, **(b)** in parallel.

35-5. Three resistances of 4, 9, and 11 Ω are connected first in series and then in parallel. Find the effective resistance for each connection.

Ans. 24 Ω, 2.21 Ω.

35-6. A 9-Ω resistor is connected in series with two parallel resistors of 6 and 12 Ω. What is the terminal potential difference if the total current from the battery is 4 A.

35-7. Find the equivalent resistance of the circuit shown in Fig. 35-14.

Ans. 8 Ω.

Fig. 35-14

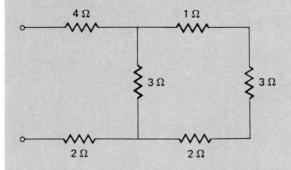

35-8. Determine the effective resistance of the circuit illustrated in Fig. 35-15.

Fig. 35-15

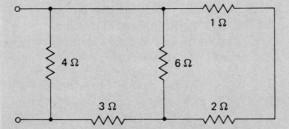

35-9. A resistance of 6 Ω is placed across a 12-V battery whose internal resistance is 0.3 Ω. What is the current delivered to the circuit? What is the terminal voltage?

Ans. 1.9 A, 11.4 V.

35-10. Two resistors of 7 and 14 Ω are connected in parallel with a battery whose emf is 16 V. The internal resistance of the battery is found to be 0.25 Ω. What is the load resistance? What is the external current delivered? What is the terminal potential difference?

35-11. In an experiment to determine the internal resistance of a battery, its open-circuit potential difference is measured as 6 V. The battery is then connected to a 4-Ω resistor, and the current is found to be 1.4 A. What is the internal resistance?

Ans. 0.286 Ω.

35-12. A dc motor draws 20 A from a 120-V line. If the internal resistance is 0.2 Ω, what is the emf of the motor? What is the electric power drawn from the line? What portion of this power is dissipated because of heat losses? What is the power delivered by the motor?

35-13. Determine the total current delivered by the source of emf to the circuit in Fig. 35-16. What is the current through each resistor? Assume that $R_1 = 6\,\Omega$, $R_2 = 3\,\Omega$, $R_3 = 1\,\Omega$, $R_4 = 2\,\Omega$, $r = 0.4\,\Omega$, and $\xi = 24$ V.

Ans. $I_T = 15$ A, $I_1 = 2$ A, $I_2 = 4$ A, $I_3 = 6$ A, $I_4 = 9$ A.

Fig. 35-16

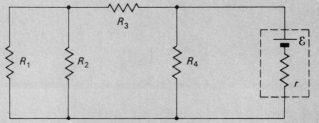

35-14. Answer the same questions as in Prob. 35-13, when $\xi = 50$ V, $R_1 = 12\,\Omega$, $R_2 = 6\,\Omega$, $R_3 = 6\,\Omega$, $R_4 = 8\,\Omega$, $r = 0.4\,\Omega$.

35-15. The circuit illustrated in Fig. 35-7 in this text consists of a 12-V battery, a 4-Ω resistor, and a switch. The internal resistance of the battery is 0.4 Ω. Assume first of all that the switch is left open. **(a)** What would a voltmeter read when placed across the terminals of the battery? **(b)** If the switch is closed, what will the voltmeter reading be? **(c)** With the switch closed, what would the voltmeter read when placed across the 4-Ω resistor?

Ans. **(a)** 12 V **(b)** 10.9 V **(c)** 10.9 V.

35-16. A 6-Ω resistor R_1 and a 4-Ω resistor R_2 are connected in parallel across a 6-V generator whose internal resistance is 0.3 Ω. **(a)** Draw a circuit diagram. **(b)** What is the total current? **(c)** What is the power *developed* by the generator? **(d)** What is the power *delivered* by the generator? **(e)** At what rate is energy lost through R_1? **(f)** At what rate is energy lost through R_2?

35-17. The generator in Fig. 35-17 develops an emf $\mathscr{E}_1$ of 24 V and has an internal resistance of 0.2 Ω. The generator is used to charge a 12-V battery whose internal resistance is 0.3 Ω. The series resistors R_1 and R_2 have resistances of 4 and 6 Ω, respectively. **(a)** What current is delivered to the circuit? **(b)** What is the terminal voltage across the generator? **(c)** What is the terminal voltage across the battery? **(d)** Show that the total drop in voltage in

Fig. 35-17 Charging a battery with a dc generator.

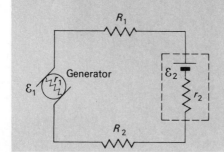

the circuit external to the generator is equal to the terminal voltage of the generator.

Ans. **(a)** 1.14 A **(b)** 23.8 V **(c)** 12.3 V.

35-18. Assume the following values for the parameters of the circuit illustrated in Fig. 35-8: $\mathscr{E}_1 = 100$ V, $\mathscr{E}_2 = 20$ V, $r_1 = 0.3$ Ω, $r_2 = 0.4$ Ω, and $R = 4$ Ω. **(a)** What are the terminal voltages V_1 and V_2? **(b)** What is the drop through the external resistor?

35-19. Use Kirchhoff's laws to solve for the currents through the circuit illustrated in Fig. 35-18.

Ans. $I_1 = 190$ mA, $I_2 = 23.8$ mA, $I_3 = 214$ mA.

Fig. 35-18

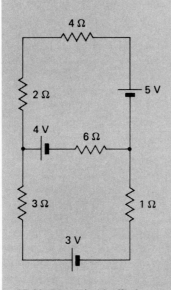

35-20. Use Kirchhoff's laws to solve for the currents through the circuit illustrated in Fig. 35-19.

Fig. 35-19

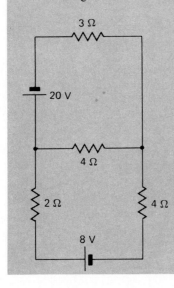

35-21. Apply Kirchhoff's laws to the circuit of Fig. 35-20. What are the currents through each branch?

Ans. $I_1 = 536$ mA, $I_2 = 732$ mA, $I_3 = 439$ mA, $I_4 = 634$ mA.

Fig. 35-20

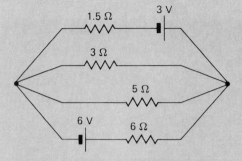

1.5 Ω   3 V

3 Ω

5 Ω

6 V   6 Ω

35-22. A Wheatstone bridge is used to measure the resistance R_x of a coil of copper wire. The resistance box is adjusted for 6 Ω, and the contact key is positioned at the 45-cm mark when measured from point A of Fig. 35-13. Determine R_x.

35-23. Commercially available Wheatstone bridges are portable and have a self-contained galvanometer. The ratio R_2/R_1 can be set at any integral power of 10 between 0.001 and 1000 by a single dual switch. If this ratio is set at 100 and the known resistance R_3 is adjusted to 46.7 Ω, the galvanometer current drops to zero. What is the unknown resistance?

Ans. 4670 Ω.

35-24. In a commercial Wheatstone bridge, R_1 and R_2 have the resistances of 20 and 40 Ω, respectively. If the resistance R_x to be measured is 14 Ω, what must the known resistance R_3 be for zero galvanometer deflection?

36 *Electrochemistry: Thermoelectricity*

OBJECTIVES: After completing this chapter, you should be able to:

1. Demonstrate by definition and example your understanding of *oxidation, reduction,* and the process of *electrolysis.*

2. State *Faraday's three laws* and apply his law of electrolysis to the solution of electroplating problems.

3. Discuss and illustrate your understanding of the process of *charging* and *discharging* a battery.

We have said that batteries convert stored chemical energy into electric energy, but we have not explained how such energy transformations occur. We now discuss some of the reversible processes which allow the interconversion of chemical and electric energy.

In technology, electrochemistry finds its most obvious application in batteries. Another application is found in electrolysis, by which electricity is conducted through a chemical solution. Finally, we shall discuss the conversion of heat energy into electric energy through a device called a thermocouple.

36-1 ELECTRIC CONDUC- TION IN LIQUIDS

In a metallic conductor the electric current consists largely of a movement of electrons in a direction opposite to the electric field. The mechanism for electric conduction is different in liquids and gases because the nature of fluids permits the movement of entire atoms or molecules that are electrically charged. Particles with an excess or a deficiency of electrons are called *ions.* If a potential difference is placed across a fluid containing ions, a current is set up which consists of positive ions moving with the electric field and negative ions moving against the field.

Water is normally a poor conductor of electricity, but many substances, when dissolved in water, break up into charged particles (ions) which react to an electric field. Such substances are called *electrolytes*.

An **electrolyte** is a substance which conducts an electric current when it is dissolved in water or melted.

Common electrolytes are hydrochloric acid (HCl), sulfuric acid (H_2SO_4), sodium chloride (NaCl), sodium hydroxide (NaOH), and barium hydroxide [$Ba(OH)_2$].

A simple apparatus for testing electrolytes is shown in Fig. 36-1. A potential difference is placed across two graphite *electrodes*. The positive electrode is referred to as the *anode*, and the negative electrode is called the *cathode*. The conductivity of a particular solution is indicated by the ammeter reading. Weak electrolytes indicate only a slight current.

Fig. 36-1 Measuring the conductivity of an electrolyte.

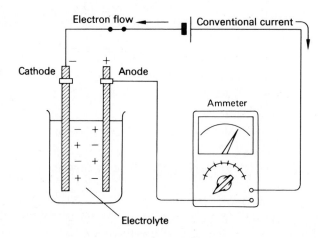

**36-2
ELEC-
TROLYSIS**

What are the effects of passing an electric current through a liquid? Consider ordinary table salt, sodium chloride (NaCl), as an electrolyte. When dissolved in water or melted, NaCl dissociates into sodium (Na^+) ions and chlorine (Cl^-) ions. Remember that the charge on an ion results from the loss or gain of electrons; atoms are neutral in their normal, or ground state. As illustrated in Fig. 36-2, a neutral sodium atom (Na^0) becomes a positive ion (Na^+) when it loses one electron.

$$Na^0 - 1e^- \rightarrow Na^+$$

The atom contains one more proton in the nucleus than there are electrons surrounding the nucleus. The process of losing electrons is referred to as *oxidation*.

Oxidation is a process by which particles lose electrons.

Fig. 36-2 A neutral sodium atom becomes a positive ion by losing an electron.

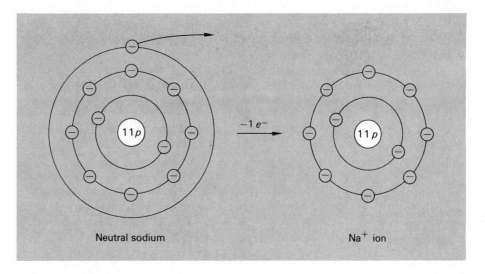

Neutral sodium

Na⁺ ion

A neutral chlorine atom, as shown in Fig. 36-3, becomes a negative ion by gaining an electron.

$$Cl^0 + 1e^- \rightarrow Cl^-$$

The resulting atom is a negative ion because it contains one more electron than it has protons in its nucleus. This reaction is called a *reduction.*

Reduction is a process by which particles gain electrons.

Fig. 36-3 A neutral chlorine atom becomes a negative ion by gaining one electron.

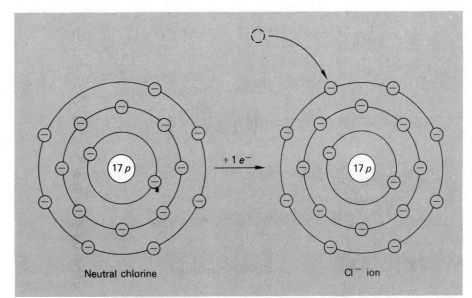

Neutral chlorine

Cl⁻ ion

The disassociation of the neutral salt molecule into sodium and chlorine ions illustrates a very important chemical principle:

When oxidation occurs in a given reaction, it must be accompanied by a corresponding reduction.

In other words, charge is conserved. When one particle loses an electron, another particle gains an electron.

Now, let us consider how a current is conducted through a medium of molten sodium chloride (NaCl), chosen because it is simpler to discuss than a solution of NaCl. The process and the results are the same in either case. Two iron or graphite electrodes are inserted into the molten NaCl, and a battery or generator supplies the necessary potential difference. (See Fig. 36-4.) The

Fig. 36-4 Electrolysis.

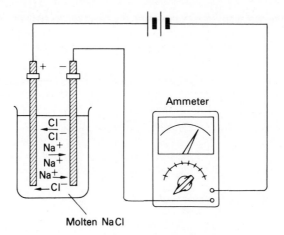

cathode (negatively charged electrode) attracts the positively charged particles, and the Na^+ ions drift to the right. The anode (positively charged electrode) causes the negatively charged Cl^- ions to drift to the left. At the cathode, a sodium ion (Na^+) picks up an electron and becomes a neutral sodium atom. The reaction at the cathode can be represented by

$$Na^+ + e^- \rightarrow Na$$

The neutral sodium atom is not soluble, and it is deposited on the cathode as ordinary metallic sodium. At the same time, a chemical reaction occurs at the anode when a chlorine ion (Cl^-) gives up an electron:

$$Cl^- \rightarrow Cl + e^-$$

The insoluble chlorine atoms thus formed come off the anode as bubbles of chlorine gas. Electrons released at the anode move through the wire under the influence of the emf provided by the battery until they reach the cathode. Thus a current is maintained. Positive and negative ions move in opposite directions through the molten NaCl, and electrons flow in one direction through the wire.

The total charge transferred through a portion of the circuit is the sum of the positive charges moving to the right and the negative charges moving to the left. The entire phenomenon is an example of *electrolysis*.

> **Electrolysis** is the process by which chemical changes are brought about by passing an electric current through a liquid.

In the above example, the chemical changes involved the liberation of chlorine gas at the anode and the deposition of metallic sodium on the electrode.

In the electrolysis of water, a little sulfuric acid (H_2SO_4) is added to water to make it a conductor. The chemical reaction is

$$H_2SO_4 + 2H_2O \rightarrow 2H_3O^+ + SO_4^-$$

The hydronium ions (H_3O^+) and the sulfate ions (SO_4^-) become the charge carriers of the solution. A hydronium ion is simply a hydrogen ion (H^+) attached to a water molecule. Oxygen collects at the anode, and hydrogen collects at the cathode. Two volumes of hydrogen are released for each volume of oxygen.

Another useful product of electrolysis is called *electroplating*. Metallic sodium was deposited on the cathode in the above example. By choosing the proper electrodes and a suitable electrolyte, a thin coating of one metal can be applied to the surface of another. The object to be plated is thoroughly cleaned and attached to the cathode. The plating material (silver, nickel, etc.) is attached to the anode. The electrolyte should be a salt of the plating metal. For example, the plating material was sodium in our earlier example, and the electrolyte was sodium chloride.

36-3 FARADAY'S LAWS

The process of electrolysis was studied in detail by Michael Faraday in the early nineteenth century. In 1830, he experimented primarily to determine the principles relating to the amount of material removed or deposited during electrolysis. His conclusions can be stated in the form of three laws. *Faraday's first law* is:

> *The mass of an element deposited at either electrode during electrolysis is directly proportional to the quantity of charge Q passed through the liquid.*

The quantity of charge transferred depends, of course, on the magnitude of the current I and its duration t:

$$Q = It \tag{36-1}$$

This quantity can be controlled by varying either the current through the circuit or the time interval.

Faraday's second law states:

> *The mass deposited during electrolysis is directly proportional to the atomic mass M of the plating material.*

Recall that the atomic mass M of an element is a number assigned to that element which indicates its *relative* atomic mass. Comparison is made on the basis of the number 12, which is assigned to the carbon 12 atom. Some common examples which may be needed in electrolysis are aluminum (26.98), chromium (51.99), copper (63.54), silver (107.9), and gold (196.97).

Faraday's third law is:

The mass deposited during electrolysis is inversely proportional to the valence of the plating material.

The chemical valence v of an ion is the number of electrons which must be removed or added to an ion to make it electrically neutral. For example, the valence of Na^+ is $+1$ because one electron must be added to the sodium ion to render it neutral. Similarly, the valence of the chlorine ion Cl^- is -1 because one electron must be given up. The valence of copper Cu^{2+} and calcium Ca^{2+} ions is $+2$, and that of the aluminum ion Al^{3+} is $+3$.

The three laws stated above can be combined in a single relation if we introduce the proportionality constant F, called *Faraday's constant*. We can write

$$m = \frac{QM}{Fv} \tag{36-2}$$

where m = mass deposited, kg
 Q = total number of coulombs transferred
 M = atomic mass, kg
 v = valence without regard to sign

Careful experimentation has shown Faraday's constant to be

$$F = 9.65 \times 10^7 \text{ C/kmol} \tag{36-3}$$

The meaning of this constant can be stated as follows. The transfer of 9.65×10^7 C of charge through an electrolytic solution will liberate one kilogram-atomic weight (1 kmol) of a monovalent ($v = \pm 1$) plating material. A valence larger than ± 1 indicates that a greater number of electrons must be added or removed to neutralize the plating material. This means that the same amount of charge will deposit a lesser mass and explains the inverse proportion indicated by Eq. (36-2).

EXAMPLE 36-1 In a laboratory experiment, the apparatus consists of a copper sulfate ($CuSO_4$) solution containing two copper rods as electrodes. How much copper will be deposited in 3 h if a constant current of 4 A is passed through the solution?

Solution The total charge transferred is found from Eq. (36-1).

$$Q = It = (4 \text{ A})(3600 \text{ s/h})(3 \text{ h})$$

$$= 4.32 \times 10^4 \text{ C}$$

The valence of the copper ions Cu^{2+} is $+2$, and the atomic mass is 63.54. Direct substitution into Eq. (36-2) yields

$$m = \frac{QM}{Fv} = \frac{(4.32 \times 10^4 \text{ C})(63.54 \text{ kg})}{(9.65 \times 10^7 \text{ C})(2)}$$

$$= 1.42 \times 10^{-2} \text{ kg}$$

In an actual laboratory experiment, the results of the above calculations could be checked by weighing the cathode before and after the plating operation. The difference in the two values obtained should agree with the mass calculated from Faraday's equation.

36-4 THE VOLTAIC CELL

Two dissimilar metals immersed in an electrolytic solution can cause a chemical reaction capable of producing an electric current. Such an arrangement is called an *electrochemical cell*. To illustrate, let us study the operation of a very primitive cell called the *voltaic cell*. This simple cell is prepared by placing a zinc strip and a copper strip in a jar filled with an aqueous solution of sulfuric acid. (See Fig. 36-5.) When the electrodes are connected through an external circuit, a current will be measured, indicating a constant potential difference.

Fig. 36-5 Voltaic cell.

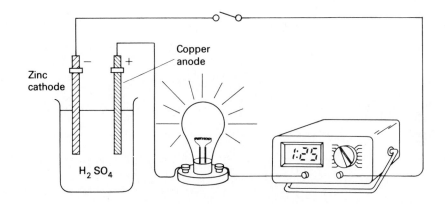

To understand this process, we first consider what happens at the zinc cathode. Oxidation occurs at this electrode as zinc atoms lose electrons and pass into solution. The chemical reaction is

$$Zn^0 \rightarrow Zn^{2+} + 2e^- \tag{36-4}$$

One zinc atom yields one zinc ion and two electrons.

As we discussed for the electrolysis of water, the dilute sulfuric acid ionizes to form hydronium ions (H_3O^+) and sulfate ions (SO_4^{2-}). [Recall that the hydronium ion is simply a hydrogen ion (H^+) attached to a water molecule (H_2O).] The hydronium atoms in the vicinity of the cathode are repelled by the zinc ions and driven toward the copper anode. When the hydronium ions reach the anode, they gain electrons from the copper strip and therefore leave it deficient of electrons, or positively charged. The chemical reduction at the anode is represented by

$$2H_3O^+ + 2e^- \rightarrow 2H_2O + H_2\uparrow$$

Two hydronium atoms accept two electrons from the copper, and hydrogen gas is evolved. Since the copper strip is connected through a wire to the negatively charged zinc strip, electrons flow from the cathode to the anode.

The current from a voltaic cell will be maintained as long as there are reacting materials in solution. After a given amount of energy has been supplied to the external circuit, the reacting materials must be replaced. This type of cell, in which the chemical reactants must be replaced, is called a *primary cell*.

36-5 THE DRY CELL

About the only primary cell still in general use today is the common dry cell, illustrated in Fig. 36-6. It is very practical for providing a convenient source of direct current in the laboratory. The cathode consists of a zinc cylinder, and the anode is a carbon rod. The electrolyte in the dry cell is a moist paste of ammonium chloride (NH_4Cl) and zinc chloride ($ZnCl_2$).

Fig. 36-6 Dry cell.

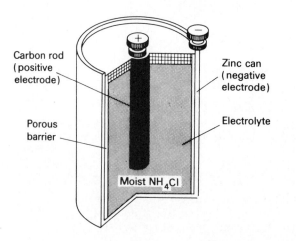

Carbon rod (positive electrode)

Zinc can (negative electrode)

Porous barrier

Electrolyte

Moist NH$_4$Cl

When the electrodes are connected to an external circuit, oxidation occurs at the zinc cathode, and reduction takes place at the carbon anode. At the cathode, zinc ionizes and goes into solution, leaving two electrons, as in the voltaic cell. The reduction process is a little more complicated. Ammonium ions (NH_4^+) in the electrolyte remove electrons from the carbon anode, leaving it positively charged. The hydrogen formed from this reaction is oxidized by the manganese dioxide. Such a cell will generate about 1.5 V. Since this emf is determined by the nature of the reacting materials, it does not depend upon the size of the cell.

Primary cells are very inefficient for long-term use because sooner or later they run out of energy. They are normally used where intermittent currents are required. The *storage cell*, on the other hand, is a rechargeable cell. By reversing the current through a storage cell the chemical processes are also reversed and chemical energy is stored.

The lead–acid storage cells used in automobiles are the most commonly used type of rechargeable cells. In this type of cell, the cathode consists of a plate of spongy lead (Pb), the anode is lead peroxide (PbO_2), and the electrolyte is dilute sulfuric acid (H_2SO_4). Let us first consider what occurs when the cell is discharging. (Refer to Fig. 36-7a.)

Fig. 36-7 A lead–acid storage battery (a) on discharge (b) being charged by a dc generator.

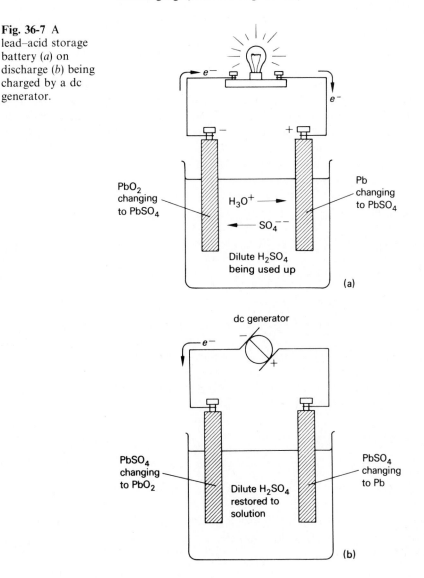

On discharge, the lead atoms of the spongy lead cathode ionize and go into solution, leaving two electrons behind. The oxidation reaction is

$$Pb \rightarrow Pb^{2+} + 2e^- \tag{36-5}$$

These lead ions combine with the sulfate ions in solution to form a deposit of lead sulfate ($PbSO_4$):

$$Pb^{2+} + SO_4^{2-} \rightarrow PbSO_4 \tag{36-6}$$

Thus the cathode is left with a negative charge. At the anode, the hydronium ions H_3O^+ remove oxygen from the lead peroxide, forming water and a deposit of lead sulfate. The anode reaction is

$$4H_3O^+ + 2e^- + PbO_2 + SO_4^{2-} \rightarrow PbSO_4 + 6H_2O \tag{36-7}$$

This reaction gives the anode a positive charge. Because of the difference of potential, a current is maintained as electrons flow through the external circuit from the cathode to the anode. Note that when the cell is discharging, sulfuric acid is being removed from the solution, and water is being added. Also, the electrodes are becoming coated with lead sulfate.

Now suppose that the entire reactions discussed above are reversed by forcing a current through the cell in the opposite direction. This requires a source of higher emf to be connected opposite to the output of the cell, as illustrated in Fig. 36-7b. The reversed chemical action for the cathode and anode can be written

$$\text{Cathode:} \qquad PbSO_4 + 2e^- \rightarrow Pb + SO_4^{2-} \tag{36-8}$$

$$\text{Anode:} \quad PbSO_4 + 6H_2O - 2e^- \rightarrow PbO_2 + SO_4^{2-} + 4H_3O^+ \tag{36-9}$$

Under these conditions, sulfuric acid is restored to the solution, and water is taken from the solution. The electrodes return to their previous composition, the anode becoming lead peroxide and the cathode spongy lead. In this manner, the input electric energy is stored as chemical energy.

The output of a lead–acid storage cell over most of its discharge time is about 2 V. Most automobile batteries consist of six storage cells connected in series to give a 12-V output.

36-7 CAPACITY RATING OF A BATTERY

The capacity rating of a battery is usually given in terms of *ampere-hours* (Ah). A battery having a rating of 80 Ah will theoretically provide a current of 1 A for 80 h, a current of 2 A for 40 h, or a current of 4 A for 20 h. These determinations are made on the basis of the equation

$$Life \ (hours) = \frac{ampere\text{-}hour \ rating}{amperes \ delivered} \tag{36-10}$$

The ampere-hour rating is strongly affected by temperature and the rate of discharge. On very cold mornings when large amperage is required to start an automobile engine, the ampere-hour rating of a battery is reduced sharply.

**36-8
THERMO-
ELECTRIC
EFFECT**

In all the sources of emf discussed in the preceding sections, chemical energy is converted into electric energy or vice versa. Thermoelectric effects involve reversible interchanges between *thermal energy* and *electric energy*. We have already seen how electric energy is converted into heat energy in the I^2R heating of resistors. The reverse effect, on the other hand, is more difficult.

Let us suppose that a circuit is formed of two dissimilar metals and a sensitive galvanometer, as shown in Fig. 36-8. One of the copper–nickel junctions is maintained at a low temperature with ice water, and the other junction is heated by a Bunsen burner. The difference in temperature between the two junctions results in a galvanometer deflection, indicating an electric current. Such junctions are called *thermocouples*. The conversion of heat energy into electric energy by means of a thermocouple is called the *Seebeck effect* after its discoverer, Thomas Johann Seebeck.

The thermocouple is actually a heat engine, heat being absorbed at the hot junction and rejected at the cold junction. The difference between the heat

Fig. 36-8 Seebeck effect.

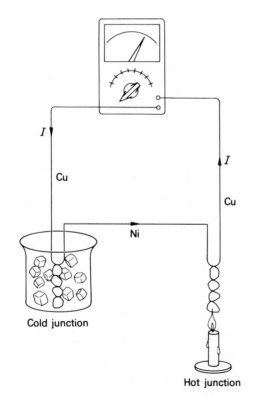

Cold junction

Hot junction

absorbed and rejected is the amount converted into electric energy. The direction of the current is such that it *tends* to equalize the differences in temperature. The current tends to cool the hot junction and to warm the cold junction.

The fact that the emf developed by the Seebeck effect increases with the difference in temperature of the junctions makes the thermocouple useful as a thermometer. The temperature can be read directly by calibrating a sensitive galvanometer. The hot junction can be placed in very remote locations to record temperatures in regions which might normally be inaccessible.

The conversion of heat energy into electric energy is a reversible process. In 1834, Jean Charles Athanase Peltier found that if the galvanometer is replaced with a source of emf, as in Fig. 36-9, one thermocouple junction

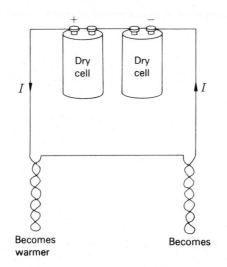

Fig. 36-9 Peltier effect.

tends to become cooler and the other tends to become warmer. The junction on the left becomes warmer as electric energy is converted to thermal energy. At the same time, thermal energy is being converted to electric energy at the other junction. The latter reaction is a cooling process. These differences of temperature observed in the *Peltier effect* are measurable in addition to the normal I^2R heating.

SUMMARY

The study of electrochemical processes helps us to understand the operation of many sources of emf which convert chemical energy into electrical energy. The reverse process of converting electrical energy to chemical energy is used to recharge sources. Today's industrial employees need at the least a general understanding of Faraday's laws even if they are not working directly with the theoretical aspects. A summary of the major topics is given below:

- Faraday's three laws were derived from his study of the electrolytic process. They are:

a. *The mass of an element deposited at either electrode during electrolysis is directly proportional to the quantity of charge Q passed through the liquid.*

b. *The mass deposited during electrolysis is directly proportional to the atomic mass M of the plating material.*

c. *The mass deposited during electrolysis is inversely proportional to the volume of the plating material.*

Faraday's laws can be used to calculate the mass deposited during an electroplating operation. The equation is

$$m = \frac{QM}{Fv}$$

$$F = 9.65 \times 10^7 \text{ C/kmol}$$

Faraday's Equation

where Q = total charge transferred, C

M = atomic mass, kg

v = valence without regard to sign

m = mass deposited, kg

F = Faraday's constant, C/kmol

The capacity rating of a battery is expressed in ampere-hours (A · h) and is defined as

$$\text{Life (h)} = \frac{\text{Ampere-hour rating (A · h)}}{\text{Amperes delivered (A)}}$$

QUESTIONS

36-1. Define the following terms:

a. Thermoelectricity
b. Electrolyte
c. Electrolysis
d. Ionization
e. Cathode
f. Anode
g. Electrolytic cell
h. Electroplating
i. Valence
j. Faraday constant

k. Kilomole
l. Atomic mass
m. Hydronium ion
n. Primary cell
o. Storage cell
p. Oxidation
q. Reduction
r. Seebeck effect
s. Thermocouple
t. Peltier effect

36-2. State and discuss Faraday's three laws for electrolysis.

36-3. Distinguish between emf (open-circuit potential) and terminal voltage of a battery. What is meant by electrode potential? How is the electrode potential affected by an external discharge current?

36-4. The state of charge of a lead–acid storage battery can be determined by a hydrometer, a device which indicates relative density (in comparison with pure water) of the electrolytic solution. Explain how this information is indicative of the state of charge of a storage battery.

36-5. Is the common dry cell really "dry"? Why do you think this term is used?

36-6. The emf of a lead–acid storage battery varies with the state of charge. At one instant, the density of the electrolytic solution is found to be 1.29 g/cm³; at another time, the density is only 1.11 g/cm³. Compare the electromotive forces of the battery for these two instants.

36-7. Compare the voltages of a size D flashlight battery with the large dry cells found in the laboratory. How do their ampere-hour ratings differ?

36-8. Write brief library reports on the following topics:

    a. Fuel cell   **e.** Electromagnetic generator

    b. Piezoelectricity   **f.** Electroluminescence

    c. Photoelectric cell   **g.** Thermionic effect

    d. Solar cell   **h.** Magnetohydrodynamic generator

36-9. Describe the anode, cathode, and electrolytic solution for an electroplating operation.

36-10. In an electrolysis experiment, a silver nitrate ($AgNO_3$) solution contains two silver rods for electrodes. The dissolved silver nitrate contains Ag^+ and NO_3^- ions. Write the chemical reaction for the anode and for the cathode when an external battery is connected to the electrode.

36-11. The *electrochemical equivalent* of an element, denoted by z, represents the mass of that element which is deposited in 1 s by a constant current of 1 A. Show that Faraday's equation can be written in the form

$$m = zIt$$

where m = mass deposited
t = time during which current I flows

36-12. From your answer to Question 36-11 verify that the electrochemical equivalent is given by

$$z = \frac{A}{Fv}$$

36-13. Explain what happens if the current is reversed through the circuit in Fig. 36-9.

36-14. Explain why a car battery "goes dead" faster on a cold morning than on a normal day.

36-15. Lead–acid batteries should never be left in a discharged condition for long periods of time. Why is this a bad practice?

36-16. As a part of routine maintenance, distilled water is sometimes added to a lead–acid storage battery. Why is this necessary? Why should the water be distilled? If some acid is spilled from a battery, what precautions should be taken in replacing the acid?

PROBLEMS

36-1. A current of 40 A flows through a molten NaCl bath for 6 min. How much sodium is deposited at the cathode? (The atomic mass of sodium is 22.91.)

                                                     Ans. 3.42 g

36-2. A current of 50 A flows through a gold (Au^{3+}) electroplating bath for 1 h. If the atomic mass of gold is considered to be 197, how many grams are deposited?

36-3. What current is required to deposit 5 g of zinc from a zinc chloride solution in 30 min? (The atomic mass of zinc is 65.37.)

Ans. 8.2 A

36-4. How many coulombs of charge must be transferred in order to deposit 400 g of copper from a solution of $CuSO_4$?

36-5. How long must a current of 8 A be maintained in an electrolytic cell containing Cu^{2+} ions in order to deposit 2 g of copper?

Ans. 12.66 min.

36-6. A solution of silver nitrate forms Ag^+ and NO_3^- ions. What current should be maintained for 10 min if 100 g of silver is to be deposited?

36-7. For a monovalent ion such as Ag^+, one electron is required to deposit each atom on the cathode. Recalling that Faraday's constant represents the number of coulombs required to deposit 1 kmol of a substance, determine the number of atoms contained in 1 mol of a substance. Verify that this is Avogadro's number.

Ans. 6.03×10^{23} atoms/mol.

36-8. A metal plate having a mass of 102.761 g is placed in an electroplating bath containing copper ions. A steady current is passed through the bath for 20 min. If the mass of the plate is increased to 105.012 g, what was the current in amperes?

36-9. How much time is required for a current of 6 A to plate 1.5 g of silver on a fork?

Ans. 3.73 min.

36-10. How many coulombs are in 1 Ah?

36-11. A 12-V automobile battery is rated at 70 Ah at 3.5 A. How long can it supply this current?

Ans. 20 h.

36-12. On a cold morning, the ampere-hour rating of a 12-V automobile battery drops to 60 Ah. How long will the battery supply a current of 20 A?

36-13. What is the ampere-hour rating of a battery that can provide 800 mA for 70 h?

Ans. 56 Ah.

37 *Magnetism and the Magnetic Field*

OBJECTIVES: After completing this chapter, you should be able to:

1. Demonstrate by definition and example your understanding of *magnetism*, *induction*, *retentivity*, *saturation*, and *permeability*.

2. Write and apply an equation relating the magnetic force on a moving charge to its velocity, its charge, and its direction in a field of known magnetic flux density.

3. Determine the magnetic force on a current-carrying wire placed in a known *B* field.

4. Calculate the magnetic flux density (*a*) at a known distance from a current-carrying wire, (*b*) at the center of a current loop or coil, and (*c*) at the interior of a *solenoid*.

In previous chapters, we saw that electrical charges exert forces on one another. In this chapter, we will study magnetic forces. A magnetic force may be generated by electric charges in motion, and an electric force may be generated by a magnetic field in motion. The operation of electric motors, generators, transformers, circuit breakers, televisions, radios, and most electric meters depends upon the relationship between electric and magnetic forces. We shall begin this chapter by studying the magnetic effects associated with materials and conclude with a discussion of the magnetic effects of charges in motion.

**37-1
MAGNETISM**

The first magnetic phenomena to be observed were associated with rough fragments of lodestone (an oxide of iron) found near the ancient city of Magnesia some 2000 years ago. These *natural magnets* were observed to attract bits and pieces of unmagnetized iron. This force of attraction is referred to as *magnetism*, and the device which exerts a magnetic force is called a *magnet*.

If a bar magnet is dipped into a pan of iron filings and removed, the tiny pieces of iron are observed to cling most strongly to small areas near the ends (see Fig. 37-1). These regions where the magnet's strength appears to be concentrated are called *magnetic poles*.

Fig. 37-1 The strength of a magnet is concentrated near its ends.

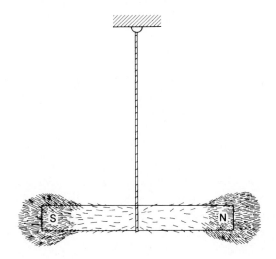

When any magnetic material is suspended from a string, it turns about a vertical axis. As illustrated in Fig. 37-2, the magnet aligns itself in a north–south direction. The end pointing toward the north is called the *north-seeking* pole or the north (N) pole of the magnet. The opposite, *south-seeking*, end is referred to as the south (S) pole of the magnet. It is the polarization of magnetic

Fig. 37-2 (*a*) A suspended bar magnet will come to rest in a north–south direction. (*b*) The top view of a magnetic compass.

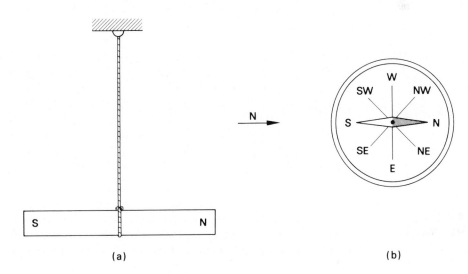

(a) (b)

material that accounts for its usefulness as a compass for navigation. The compass consists of a light magnetized needle pivoted on a low-friction support.

That the north and south poles of a magnet are different can easily be demonstrated. When another bar magnet is brought near a suspended magnet, as in Fig. 37-3, two north poles or two south poles repel each other whereas the north pole of one and the south pole of another attract each other. *The law of magnetic force* states:

> *Like magnetic poles repel each other; unlike magnetic poles attract each other.*

Fig. 37-3 Like poles repel each other; unlike poles attract each other.

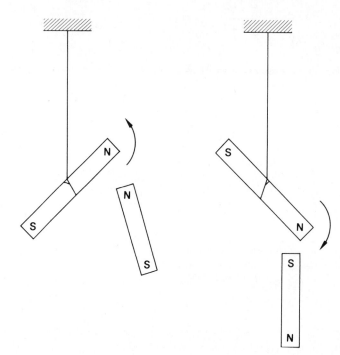

Isolated poles do not exist. No matter how many times a magnet is broken in half, each piece will become a magnet, having both a north and a south pole. We know of no single particle that could create a magnetic field in the same way that a proton or electron can create an electric field.

The attraction of a magnet for unmagnetized iron and the interacting forces between magnetic poles act through all substances. In industry, ferrous materials in trash are separated by magnets for recycling.

37-2 MAGNETIC FIELDS

Every magnet is surrounded by a space in which its magnetic effects are present. Such regions are called *magnetic fields.* Just as electric field lines were useful in describing electric fields, magnetic field lines, called *flux lines,* are useful for visualizing magnetic fields. The direction of a flux line at any point is the same as the direction of the magnetic force on an *imaginary* isolated north pole positioned at that point (see Fig. 37-4a). Accordingly, lines of magnetic flux leave the north pole of a magnet and enter the south pole. Unlike electric field lines, magnetic flux lines do not have beginning or ending points. They form continuous loops, passing through the metallic bar, as shown in Fig. 37-4b. The flux lines in the region between two like or unlike poles are illustrated in Fig. 37-5.

Fig. 37-4 (*a*) Magnetic flux lines are in the direction of the force exerted on an independent north pole. (*b*) The flux lines in the vicinity of a bar magnet.

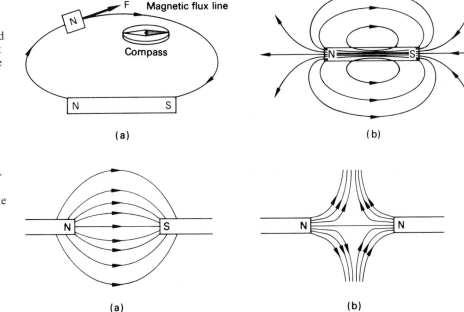

(a)

(b)

Fig. 37-5 (*a*) Magnetic flux lines between two unlike magnetic poles. (*b*) The flux lines in the space between two like poles.

(a)

(b)

37-3 THE MODERN THEORY OF MAGNETISM

Magnetism in matter is currently believed to result from the movement of electrons in the atoms of substances. If this is true, magnetism is a property of *charge in motion* and is closely related to electric phenomena. According to classical theory, individual atoms of a magnetic substance are, in effect, tiny magnets with north and south poles. The magnetic polarity of atoms is thought to arise primarily from the spin of electrons and is due only partially to their orbital motions around the nucleus. Figure 37-6 illustrates the two kinds of electron motion. Diagrams such as this should not be taken too seriously

Fig. 37-6 Two kinds of electron motion responsible for magnetic properties.

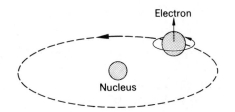

because there is still a lot we do not know about the motion of electrons. But we do firmly believe that magnetic fields of all particles must be caused by charge in motion, and such models help us to describe the phenomena.

The atoms in a magnetic material are grouped into microscopic magnetic regions called *domains*. All the atoms within a domain are believed to be magnetically polarized along a crystal axis. In an unmagnetized material, these domains are oriented in random directions, as indicated by the arrows in Fig. 37-7a. A dot is used to indicate an arrow directed out of the paper, and a cross is used to denote a direction into the paper. If a large number of the domains become oriented in the same direction, as in Fig. 37-7b, the material will exhibit strong magnetic properties.

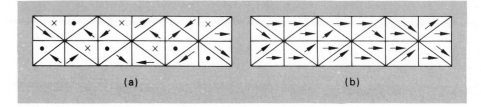

Fig. 37-7 (a) Magnetic domains are randomly oriented in an unmagnetized material. (b) The preferred orientation of domains in a magnetized material.

This theory of magnetism is highly plausible in that it offers an explanation for many of the observed magnetic effects of matter. For example, an unmagnetized iron bar can be made into a magnet simply by holding another magnet near it or in contact with it. This process, called *magnetic induction*, is illustrated by Fig. 37-8. The tacks become temporary magnets by induction. Note that the tacks on the right become magnetized even though they do not actually touch the magnet. Magnetic induction is explained by the domain theory. The introduction of a magnetic field aligns the domains, resulting in magnetization.

Fig. 37-8 Magnetic induction.

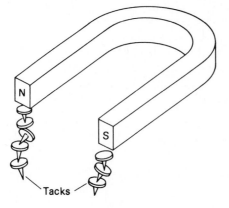

Tacks

Induced magnetism is often only temporary, and when the field is removed, the domains gradually become disoriented. If the domains remain aligned to some degree after the field has been removed, the material is said to be *permanently* magnetized. The ability to retain magnetism is referred to as *retentivity*.

Another property of magnetic materials which is easily explained by the domain theory is *magnetic saturation*. There appears to be a limit to the degree of magnetization experienced by a material. Once this limit has been reached, no greater strength of an external field can increase the magnetization. It is believed that all its domains have been aligned.

37-4 FLUX DENSITY AND PERMEABILITY

In Chap. 31 we stated that electric field lines are drawn so that their spacing at any point will determine the strength of the electric field at that point (refer to Fig. 37-9). The number of lines ΔN drawn through a unit of area ΔA is directly proportional to the electric field intensity E.

$$\frac{\Delta N}{\Delta A} = \epsilon E \tag{37-1}$$

The proportionality constant ϵ, which determines the number of lines drawn, is the permittivity of the medium through which the lines pass.

Fig. 37-9 Electric field intensity is proportional to the electric line density.

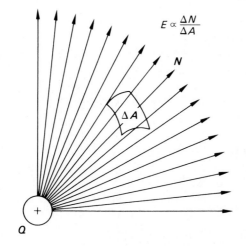

$$E \propto \frac{\Delta N}{\Delta A}$$

An analogous description of a magnetic field can be presented by considering the magnetic flux ϕ passing through a unit of perpendicular area A. This ratio B is called the *magnetic flux density*.

The **magnetic flux density** in a region of a magnetic field is the number of flux lines which pass through a unit perpendicular area in that region.

$$B = \frac{\phi \text{ (flux)}}{A \text{ (area)}} \tag{37-2}$$

The SI unit of magnetic flux is the *weber* (Wb). The unit of flux density would then be webers per square meter, which is redefined as the *tesla* (T). An older unit which remains in use is the *gauss* (G). In summary,

$$1 \text{ T} = 1 \text{ Wb/m}^2 = 10^4 \text{ G} \tag{37-3}$$

EXAMPLE 37-1   A rectangular loop 10 cm wide and 20 cm long makes an angle of 30° with respect to the magnetic flux in Fig. 37-10. If the flux density is 0.3 T, compute the magnetic flux ϕ penetrating the loop.

Fig. 37-10 Computing the magnetic flux through a rectangular conductor.

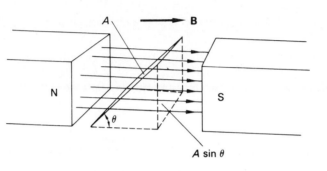

Solution   The effective area penetrated by the flux is that component of the area which is perpendicular to the flux. Thus Eq. (37-2) becomes

$$B = \frac{\phi}{A \sin \theta} \qquad \text{or} \qquad \phi = BA \sin \theta$$

The magnetic flux in webers is found by substitution into this relation.

$$\phi = (0.3 \text{ T})(0.1 \text{ m} \times 0.2 \text{ m})(\sin 30°)$$

$$= (0.3 \text{ T})(0.02 \text{ m}^2)(0.5)$$

$$= 3 \times 10^{-3} \text{ Wb}$$

The flux density at any point in a magnetic field is strongly affected by the nature of the medium or by the nature of a material placed in the medium. For this reason it is convenient to define a new magnetic field vector, the *magnetic field intensity* **H**, which does not depend on the nature of a medium. In any case, the number of lines established per unit area is directly proportional to the magnetic field intensity **H**. We can write

$$B = \frac{\phi}{A} = \mu H \tag{37-4}$$

where the proportionality constant μ is the *permeability* of the medium through which the flux lines pass. Equation (37-4) is exactly analogous to Eq. (37-1), which was developed for electric fields. The permeability of a medium can thus be thought of as a measure of its ability to establish magnetic flux lines. The greater the permeability of a medium, the more flux lines will pass through a unit of area.

The permeability of free space (vacuum) is denoted by μ_0 and has the following magnitude for SI units:

$$\mu_0 = 4\pi \times 10^{-7} \text{ Wb/A} \cdot \text{m} = 4\pi \times 10^{-7} \text{ T} \cdot \text{m/A}$$

The full meaning of the unit webers per ampere-meter will come later. It is determined by the units of ϕ, A, and H of Eq. (37-4), which for a vacuum can be written

$$B = \mu_0 H \qquad\qquad Vacuum \quad (37\text{-}5)$$

If a nonmagnetic material, such as glass, is placed in a magnetic field like that in Fig. 37-11, the flux distribution will not vary appreciably from that established for a vacuum. However, when a highly permeable material, such as soft iron, is placed in the field, the flux distribution will be altered considerably. The permeable material becomes magnetized by induction, resulting in a greater field strength for that region. For this reason, the flux density B is also referred to as the *magnetic induction*.

Fig. 37-11 A permeable material becomes magnetized by induction, resulting in a greater flux density in that region.

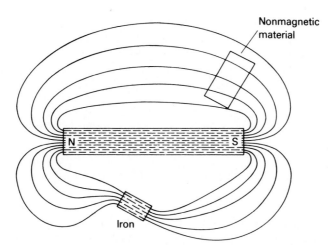

Nonmagnetic material

Iron

Magnetic materials are classified according to their permeability compared with that of free space. The ratio of the permeability of a material to that of a vacuum is called its *relative permeability* and is given by

$$\mu_r = \frac{\mu}{\mu_0} \qquad\qquad (37\text{-}6)$$

Consideration of Eqs. (37-5) and (37-6) shows that the relative permeability of a material is a measure of its ability to change the flux density of a field from its value in a vacuum.

Materials with a relative permeability slightly less than unity have the property of being feebly repelled by a strong magnet. Such materials are said to be *diamagnetic*, and the property is referred to as *diamagnetism*. On the other hand, materials with slightly greater permeability than that of a vacuum are said to be *paramagnetic*. These materials are feebly attracted by a strong magnet.

A few materials, e.g., iron, cobalt, nickel, steel, and alloys of these metals, have extremely high permeabilities, ranging from a few hundred to thousands of times that for free space. Such materials are strongly attracted by a magnet and are said to be *ferromagnetic*.

37-5 MAGNETIC FIELD AND ELECTRIC CURRENT

Although the modern theory of magnetism holds that a magnetic field results from the motion of charges, science has not always accepted this proposition. It is fairly easy to show that a powerful magnet exerts no force on a static charge. In the course of a lecture demonstration in 1820, Hans Oersted set up an experiment to show his students that *moving* charges and magnets also do not interact. He placed the magnetic needle of a compass near a conductor, as illustrated in Fig. 37-12. To his surprise, when a current was sent through the wire,

Fig. 37-12 Oersted's experiment.

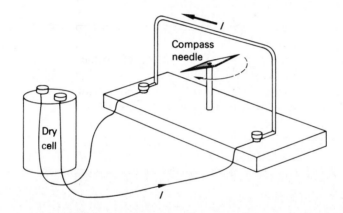

a twisting force was exerted on the compass needle until it pointed almost perpendicular to the wire. Further, the magnitude of the force depended upon the relative orientation of the compass needle and the current direction. The maximum twisting force occurred when the wire and compass needle were parallel before the current was established. If they were initially perpendicular, no force was experienced. Evidently, a magnetic field is set up by the charge in motion through the conductor.

In the same year that Oersted made his discovery. Ampère found that forces exist between two current-carrying conductors. Two wires with current in the same direction were found to attract each other whereas oppositely directed currents caused a force of repulsion. A few years later, Faraday found that the motion of a magnet toward or away from an electric circuit produces a current in the circuit. The relationship between magnetic and electric phenomena could no longer be doubted. Today, all magnetic phenomena can be explained in terms of electric charges in motion.

Let us investigate the effects of a magnetic field by observing the magnetic force exerted on a charge which passes through the field. In studying these effects, it is useful to imagine a positive-ion tube like that in Fig. 37-13. Such a tube allows us to inject a positive ion of constant charge and velocity into a field of magnetic flux density **B**. By pointing the tube in various directions, we can observe the force exerted on the moving charge. The most striking observation

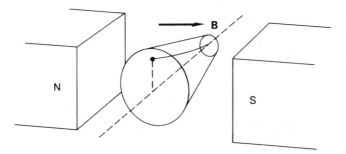

Fig. 37-13 The magnetic force **F** on a moving charge is perpendicular both to the flux density **B** and to the charge velocity **v**.

is that the charge experiences a force which is perpendicular to both the magnetic flux density **B** and to the velocity **v** of the moving charge. Note that when the magnetic flux is directed from the left to the right and the charge is moving toward the reader, the charge is deflected upward. Reversing the polarity of the magnets causes the charge to be deflected downward.

The direction of the magnetic force **F** on a positive charge moving with a velocity **v** in a field of flux density **B** can be reckoned by the *right-hand-screw rule* (see Fig. 37-14):

Fig. 37-14 The right-hand-screw rule.

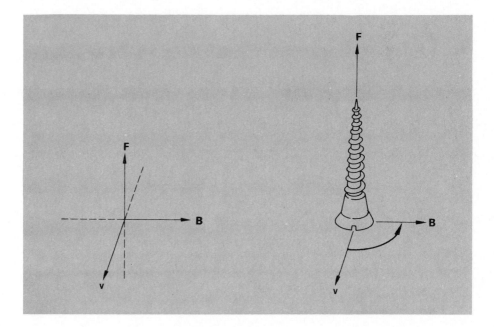

*The direction of the magnetic force **F** on a moving positive charge is the same as the direction of advance of a right-hand screw if rotated from **v** to **B**.*

If the moving charge is negative, as for an electron, the magnetic force will be directed *opposite* to the advance of a right-hand screw.

Let us now consider the magnitude of the force on a moving charge. Experimentation has shown that the magnitude of the magnetic force is directly proportional to the magnitude of the charge q and to its velocity **v**. Greater deflections will be indicated by our positive-ion tube if either of these parameters is increased.

An unexpected variation in the magnetic force will be observed if the ion tube is rotated slowly with respect to the magnetic flux density **B**. As indicated by Fig. 37-15, for a given charge of constant velocity **v**, the magnitude of

Fig. 37-15 Magnitude of the magnetic force varies with the angle the moving charge makes with the direction of the magnetic field.

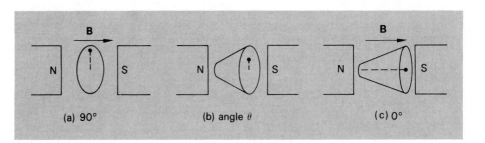

(a) 90°   (b) angle θ (c) 0°

the force varies with the angle the tube makes with the field. Particle deflection is a maximum when the charge velocity is perpendicular to the field. As the tube is slowly rotated toward **B**, the particle deflection becomes less and less. Finally, when the charge velocity is directed parallel to **B**, no deflection occurs, indicating that the magnetic force has dropped to zero. Evidently, the magnitude of the force is a function not only of the magnitude of the charge and its velocity but also varies with the angle θ between **v** and **B**. This variation is accounted for by stating that the magnetic force is proportional to the component of the velocity, **v** sin θ, perpendicular to the field direction. (Refer to Fig. 37-16.)

The above observations are summarized by the proportionality

$$F \propto qv \sin \theta \qquad (37\text{-}7)$$

If the proper units are chosen, the proportionality constant can be equated to the magnetic flux density B of the field causing the force. In fact, this proportionality is often used to *define* magnetic flux density as the constant ratio:

$$\boxed{B = \frac{F}{qv \sin \theta}} \qquad (37\text{-}8)$$

Fig. 37-16

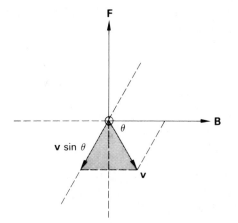

A magnetic field having a flux density of one tesla (one weber per square meter) will exert a force of one newton on a charge of one coulomb moving perpendicular to the field with a velocity of one meter per second.

As a consequence of Eq. (37-8), it can be noted that

$$1 \text{ T} = 1 \text{ N}/(\text{C} \cdot \text{m/s}) = 1 \text{ N/A} \cdot \text{m} \tag{37-9}$$

These unit relationships are useful in solving problems involving magnetic forces.

Solving for the force F in Eq. (37-8), we obtain

$$\boxed{F = qvB \sin \theta} \tag{37-8}$$

which is the more useful form for direct calculation of magnetic forces. The force F is in newtons when the charge q is expressed in coulombs; the velocity v is in meters per second; and the flux density is in teslas. The angle θ indicates the direction of $\mathbf{v}$ with respect to $\mathbf{B}$. The force $\mathbf{F}$ is *always* perpendicular to both $\mathbf{v}$ and $\mathbf{B}$.

EXAMPLE 37-2   An electron is projected from left to right into a magnetic field directed vertically downward. The velocity of the electron is 2×10^6 m/s, and the magnetic flux density of the field is 0.3 T. Find the magnitude and direction of the magnetic force on the electron.

Solution   The electron is moving in a direction perpendicular to $\mathbf{B}$. Thus, $\sin \theta = 1$ in Eq. (37-8), and we find the force F as follows:

$$F = qvB \sin \theta$$

$$= (1.6 \times 10^{-19} \text{ C})(2 \times 10^6 \text{ m/s})(0.3 \text{ T})(1)$$

$$= 9.6 \times 10^{-14} \text{ N}$$

Application of the right-hand-screw rule will show that the direction of the force is *out of the page*, or toward the reader. (It would be into the page for a positive charge like a proton.)

37-7
**FORCE
ON A
CURRENT-
CARRYING
WIRE**

When an electric current passes through a conductor lying in a magnetic field, each charge q flowing through the conductor experiences a magnetic force. These forces are transmitted to the conductor as a whole, causing each unit of length to experience a force. If a total quantity of charge Q passes through the length l of the wire (Figure 37-17) with an average velocity $\bar{v}$, perpendicular to a magnetic field B, the net force on that segment of wire is

$$F = Q\bar{v}B$$

Fig. 37-17 Magnetic force on a current-carrying conductor.

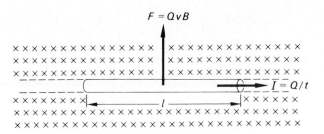

The average velocity for each charge passing through the length l in the time t is l/t. Thus the net force on the entire length becomes

$$F = Q \frac{l}{t} B$$

Rearranging and simplifying, we obtain

$$F = \frac{Q}{t} lB = IlB$$

where I represents the current in the wire.

Just as the magnitude of the force on a moving charge varies with velocity direction, the force on a current-carrying conductor depends on the angle the current makes with the flux density. In general, if a wire of length l makes an angle θ with the **B** field, as illustrated in Fig. 37-18, it will experience a force given by

$$\boxed{F = BIl \sin \theta} \qquad (37\text{-}10)$$

Fig. 37-18

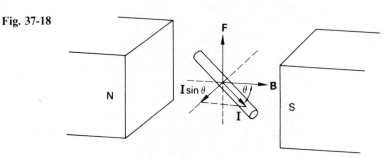

where I is the current through the wire. When B is in *teslas*, l is in *meters*, and I is in *amperes*, the force will be in *newtons*.

The direction of the magnetic force on a current-carrying conductor can be determined by the right-hand-screw rule in the same way as for a moving charge. When **I** is rotated into **B**, the direction of the force **F** is in the same direction as the advance of a right-hand screw. The force **F** is *always* perpendicular to both **I** and **B**.

EXAMPLE 37-3

The wire in Fig. 37-18 makes an angle of 30° with respect to a B field of 0.2 T. If the length of the wire is 8 cm and a current of 4 A passes through it, determine the magnitude and direction of the resultant force on the wire.

Solution

Direct substitution into Eq. (37-10) yields

$$F = BIl \sin \theta$$

$$= (0.2 \text{ T})(4 \text{ A})(0.08 \text{ m})(\sin 30°)$$

$$= 0.032 \text{ N}$$

Application of the right-hand-screw rule shows the direction of the force to be upward, as indicated in Fig. 37-18. If the current direction were reversed, the force would be directed downward.

**37-8
MAGNETIC
FIELD OF
A LONG
STRAIGHT
WIRE**

Oersted's experiment demonstrated that electric charge in motion, or a current, sets up a magnetic field in the space surrounding it. Up to this point, we have been discussing the force that such a field will exert on a second current-carrying conductor or on a charge moving in the field. We shall now begin to calculate the magnetic fields produced by electric currents.

Let us first examine the flux density surrounding a long straight wire carrying a constant current. If iron filings are sprinkled on the paper surrounding the wire in Fig. 37-19, they will become aligned in concentric circles around

Fig. 37-19 Magnetic field surrounding a straight current-carrying conductor.

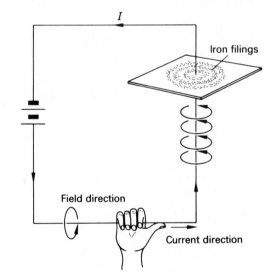

Iron filings

Field direction

Current direction

the wire. Similar investigation of the area surrounding the wire with a magnetic compass will confirm that the magnetic field is circular and directed in a clockwise fashion, as viewed along the direction of conventional (positive) current. A convenient method devised by Ampère to determine the direction of the field surrounding a straight wire is called the *right-hand-thumb rule* (refer to Fig. 37-19).

> *If the wire is grasped with the right hand so that the thumb points in the direction of the conventional current, the curled fingers of that hand will point in the direction of the magnetic field.*

The magnetic induction, or flux density, at a perpendicular distance d from a long straight wire carrying a current I, as shown in Fig. 37-20, can be calculated from

$$B = \frac{\mu I}{2\pi d}$$ *Long Wire* (37-11)

where μ is the permeability of the medium surrounding the wire. In the special cases of a vacuum, air, and nonmagnetic media, the permeability μ_0 is

$$\mu_0 = 4\pi \times 10^{-7} \text{ T} \cdot \text{m/A} \tag{37-12}$$

The units are determined from Eq. (37-11).

Fig. 37-20 Magnetic field B at a perpendicular distance d from a long current-carrying conductor.

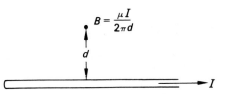

EXAMPLE 37-4   Determine the magnetic induction in the air 5 cm from a long wire carrying a current of 10 A.

Solution   From Eq. (37-11)

$$B = \frac{\mu_0 I}{2\pi d} = \frac{(4\pi \times 10^{-7} \text{ T} \cdot \text{m/A})(10 \text{ A})}{(2\pi)(0.05 \text{ m})}$$

$$= 4 \times 10^{-5} \text{ T}$$

The direction of the magnetic induction is determined from the right-hand-thumb rule. For the case illustrated in Fig. 37-20, it would be out of the paper.

For a derivation of Eq. (37-11) and other relations which follow, the reader is referred to the *Biot-Savart law* or to *Ampère's law*. Many conventional physics texts provide a complete analysis, which usually includes the methods of calculus.

If a wire is bent into a circular loop and connected to a source of current, as shown in Fig. 37-21a, a magnetic field very similar to that for a bar magnet will be set up. The right-hand-thumb rule will still serve to give the field direction in a rough manner, but now the flux lines are no longer circular. The magnetic flux density varies considerably from point to point.

Fig. 37-21 The magnetic field at the center of a circular loop.

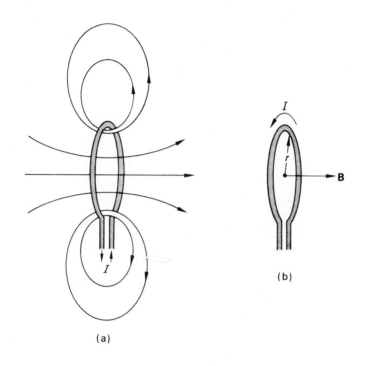

(a)

(b)

The magnetic induction at the center of a circular loop of radius r carrying a current I is given by

$$B = \frac{\mu I}{2r}$$ *Center of Loop*   (37-13)

The direction of B is perpendicular to the plane of the loop. If the wire consists of a coil having N turns, Eq. (37-13) becomes

$$B = \frac{\mu N I}{2r}$$ *Center of Coil*   (37-14)

A *solenoid* consists of many circular turns of wire wound in the form of a helix, as illustrated in Fig. 37-22. The magnetic field produced is very similar

Fig. 37-22 The solenoid.

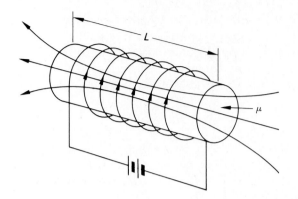

to that of a bar magnet. The magnetic induction in the interior of a solenoid is given by

$$B = \frac{\mu N I}{L}$$

Solenoid (37-15)

where N = number of turns
I = current, A
L = length of the solenoid, m

EXAMPLE 37-5

A solenoid is constructed by winding 400 turns of wire on a 20-cm iron core. The relative permeability of the iron is 13,000. What current is required to produce a magnetic induction of 0.5 T in the center of the solenoid?

Solution

The permeability of the core is

$$\mu = \mu_r \mu_0 = (13,000)(4\pi \times 10^{-7} \text{ T} \cdot \text{m/A})$$

$$= 1.63 \times 10^{-2} \text{ T} \cdot \text{m/A}$$

Solving for I in Eq. (37-15) and substituting known values, we obtain

$$I = \frac{BL}{\mu N} = \frac{(0.5 \text{ T})(0.2 \text{ m})}{(1.63 \times 10^{-2} \text{ T} \cdot \text{m/A})(400 \text{ turns})}$$

$$= 0.015 \text{ A}$$

The diameter of the solenoid is not significant provided that it is small relative to the length L.

One type of solenoid, called a *toroid*, is often used in studying magnetic effects. As will be seen in the following section, the toroid consists of a tightly wound coil of wire in the shape of a doughnut. The magnetic flux density in the core of a toroid is also given by Eq. (37-15).

**37-10
HYSTERESIS**

We have seen that the lines of magnetic flux are more numerous for a solenoid with an iron core than for a solenoid in air. The flux density is related to the permeability μ of the material serving as a core for the solenoid. Recall that the field intensity H and flux density B are related to each other according to the equation

$$B = \mu H$$

Comparison of this relationship with Eq. (37-15) shows that for a solenoid

$$H = \frac{NI}{L} \qquad \text{(37-16)}$$

Note that the magnetic intensity is independent of the permeability of the core. It is a function only of the number of turns N, the current I, and the solenoid length L. The magnetic intensity is expressed in *amperes per meter*.

We can study the magnetic properties of matter by observing the flux density B produced as a function of the magnetizing current or as a function of the magnetic intensity H. This can be more easily done when a substance is fashioned into the form of a toroid, as in Fig. 37-23. The magnetic field set up by a current in the magnetizing windings is confined wholly to the toroid. Such a device is often called a *Rowland ring* after J. H. Rowland, who used it to study the magnetic properties of many materials.

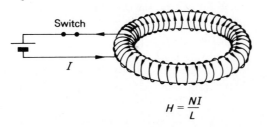

Suppose we begin by studying the magnetic properties of a material with an unmagnetized Rowland ring fashioned out of the substance. Initially, $B = 0$ and $H = 0$. The switch is closed, and the magnetizing current I is gradually increased, producing a magnetic intensity given by

$$H = \frac{NI}{L}$$

where L is the circumference of the ring. As the material is subjected to an increasing magnetic intensity H, the flux density B increases until the material is *saturated*. Refer to the curve AB in Fig. 37-24. Now, if the current is gradually reduced to zero, the flux density B throughout the core does not return to zero but lags behind the magnetic intensity, as illustrated by the curve BC. (This essentially refers to residual magnetism.) The lack of retraceability is known as *hysteresis*.

Hysteresis is the lagging of the magnetization behind the magnetic intensity.

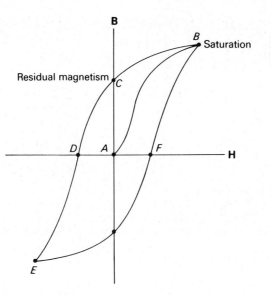

Fig. 37-24 Hysteresis loop.

The only way to bring the flux density B within the ring back to zero is to reverse the direction of the current through the windings. This procedure builds up the magnetic intensity H in the opposite direction, as shown by curve CD. If the magnetization continues to increase in the negative direction, the material will eventually become saturated again with a reversed polarity. Refer to curve DE. Reducing the current to zero again and then increasing it in the positive direction will yield the curve EFB. The entire curve is called the *hysteresis loop*.

The area enclosed by a hysteresis loop is an indication of the quantity of energy that is lost (in the form of heat) by carrying a given material through a complete magnetization cycle. The efficiency of many electromagnetic devices depends on the selection of magnetic materials with low hysteresis. On the other hand, materials which are to remain well magnetized should have large hysteresis.

SUMMARY

We have seen that magnetic fields are created by charge in motion. This very basic principle will underlie much of what follows in your study of electromagnetism. The operation of electric motors, generators, transformers, and an endless variety of industrial instruments requires an understanding of the magnetic field. The major concepts are summarized below:

- The magnetic flux density B in a region of a magnetic field is the number of flux lines which pass through a unit of area perpendicular to the flux.

$$B = \frac{\phi}{A_\perp} = \frac{\phi}{A \sin \theta}$$ *Magnetic Flux Density*

where ϕ = flux, Wb
A = unit area, m²
θ = angle that plane of area makes with flux
B = magnetic flux density, T (1 T = 1 Wb/m²)

- The magnetic flux density **B** is proportional to the magnetic field intensity **H**. The constant of proportionality is the permeability of the medium in which the field exists.

$$B = \frac{\phi}{A_\perp} = \mu H$$

For a Vacuum
$\mu_0 = 4\pi \times 10^{-7}$ T · m/A

- The *relative permeability* μ_r is the ratio of μ/μ_0. We can write

$$B = \mu_0 \mu_r \text{H}$$ where $$\mu_r = \frac{\mu}{\mu_0}$$ *Relative Permeability*

- A magnetic field of flux density equal to 1 T will exert a force of 1 N on a charge of 1 C moving perpendicular to the field with a velocity of 1 m/s. The general case is described by Fig. 37-25 in which the charge moves at an angle θ with the field.

$$F = qvB \sin \theta$$ $$B = \frac{F}{qv \sin \theta}$$ *Magnetic Force on a Moving Charge*

The direction of the magnetic force is given by the right-hand-screw rule, as illustrated in Fig. 37-25.

Fig. 37-25

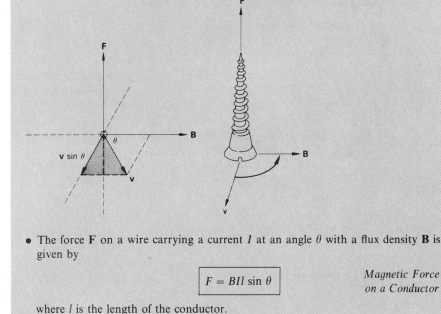

- The force **F** on a wire carrying a current I at an angle θ with a flux density **B** is given by

$$F = BIl \sin \theta$$ *Magnetic Force on a Conductor*

where l is the length of the conductor.

• Equations for many common magnetic fields are given below:

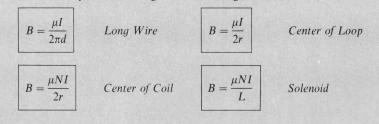

$$B = \frac{\mu I}{2\pi d} \qquad Long\ Wire$$

$$B = \frac{\mu I}{2r} \qquad Center\ of\ Loop$$

$$B = \frac{\mu N I}{2r} \qquad Center\ of\ Coil$$

$$B = \frac{\mu N I}{L} \qquad Solenoid$$

QUESTIONS

37-1. Define the following terms:

a. Magnetism
b. Magnet
c. Domains
d. Retentivity
e. Permeability
f. Weber
g. Tesla
h. Diamagnetic
i. Paramagnetic
j. Ferromagnetic
k. Magnetic poles

l. Law of magnetic force
m. Coulomb's law for magnetic forces
n. Magnetic field
o. Magnetic flux lines
p. Magnetic induction
q. Magnetic saturation
r. Flux density
s. Relative permeability
t. Solenoid
u. Hysteresis

37-2. How can you positively determine whether a piece of steel is magnetized? How would you determine its polarity if magnetized?

37-3. In general, magnetic materials with high permeability have low retentivity. Why do you think this is true?

37-4. The earth acts like a huge magnet with one pole in the Arctic circle and the other in the Antarctic region. Can you justify the following statement: The geographic North Pole is actually near a magnetic south pole? Explain.

37-5. If an iron bar is placed parallel to a north–south direction and is hammered on one end, the bar becomes a temporary magnet. Explain.

37-6. When a bar magnet is broken into several pieces, each part becomes a magnet with a north and a south pole. Apparently, an isolated pole cannot exist. Explain this, using the domain theory of magnetism.

37-7. Heating magnets or passing electric currents through them will cause a reduction in field strength. Explain.

37-8. The strength of a U magnet will be preserved much longer if an iron plate, called a *keeper*, is placed across the north and south poles. Explain.

37-9. A wire lying along a north–south direction supports an electric current from south to north. What happens to the needle of a compass if the compass is placed **(a)** above the wire, **(b)** below the wire, and **(c)** on the right side of the wire?

37-10. Use the right-hand-thumb rule and the right-hand-screw rule to explain why two adjacent wires experience a force of attraction when the currents are in the same direction. Illustrate your point by drawings.

37-11. Explain with the use of diagrams the repulsion of two adjacent wires carrying oppositely directed currents.

37-12. A circular coil in the plane of the paper supports an electric current. Determine the direction of the magnetic flux near the center of the coil when the current is counterclockwise.

37-13. When an electron beam is projected from left to right into a **B** field directed into the paper, the beam is deflected into a circular path. Do the electrons travel clockwise or counterclockwise? Why is the path circular? What if the beam consisted of protons?

37-14. A proton passes through a region of space without being deflected. Can we say positively that no magnetic field exists in that region? Discuss.

37-15. Many sensitive electrical instruments are shielded from magnetic effects by surrounding the device with ferromagnetic material. Explain.

37-16. If B is expressed in teslas and μ is in tesla-meters per ampere, what is the SI unit of H?

37-17. Hardened steel has a thick hysteresis loop whereas soft iron has a thin loop. Which should be used to produce a permanent magnet? Which should be used if strong temporary magnetization is desired?

PROBLEMS

37-1. A constant horizontal field of 0.5 T pierces a rectangular loop 120 mm long and 70 mm wide. Determine the magnetic flux through the loop when its plane makes the following angles with the B field: **(a)** 0°, **(b)** 30°, **(c)** 60°, and **(d)** 90°.

Ans. **(a)** 0 Wb **(b)** 2.1 mWb **(c)** 3.64 mWb **(d)** 4.2 mWb.

37-2. A coil of wire 240 mm in diameter is situated so that its plane is perpendicular to a field of density 0.3 T. Determine the magnetic flux through the coil.

37-3. A magnetic flux of 50 μWb passes through a loop of wire having an area of 0.78 m². What is the magnetic flux density?

Ans. 64.1 μT.

37-4. A rectangular loop 25 × 15 cm is oriented so that its plane makes an angle θ with the **B** field? What is the angle θ if the magnetic flux density is 0.6 T and if the flux linking the loop is 0.015 Wb?

37-5. A proton ($q = +1.6 \times 10^{-19}$ C) is injected from right to left into a **B** field of 0.4 T directed vertically upward. If the velocity of the proton is 2×10^6 m/s, what is the magnitude and direction of the magnetic force on the proton?

Ans. 1.28×10^{-13} N, into paper.

37-6. An alpha particle ($+2e$) is projected in a 0.12 T magnetic field with a velocity of 3.6×10^6 m/s. What is the magnetic force on the charge at the instant its velocity is directed at an angle of 35° with the magnetic flux?

37-7. An electron moves with a speed of 5×10^5 m/s at an angle of 60° with respect to a magnetic field of density **B**. If the electron experiences a force of 3.2×10^{-18} N, what is the flux density?

Ans. 4.62×10^{-5} T.

37-8. A particle having a charge q and a mass m is projected into a **B** field directed into the paper. If the particle has a velocity v, show that it will be deflected into a circular path of radius

$$R = \frac{mv}{qB}$$

Hint: The magnetic force provides the necessary centripetal force.

37-9. A deuteron is a nuclear particle consisting of a proton and a neutron bound together by nuclear forces. The mass of a proton is 1.6724×10^{-27} kg, and its charge is $+1.6 \times 10^{-19}$ C. The mass of a neutron is 1.6747×10^{-27} kg, and it has no charge. A deuteron projected into a magnetic field of flux density 1.2 T is observed to travel in a circular path of radius 300 mm. What is the velocity of the deuteron?

Ans. 1.72×10^7 m/s.

37-10. A proton is moving vertically upward with a speed of 4×10^7 m/s. It passes through a 0.4-T field directed to the right. **(a)** What is the magnitude and direction of the magnetic force? **(b)** Suppose an electron replaces the proton but has the same velocity.

37-11. A sodium ion ($q = +1.6 \times 10^{-19}$ C, $m = 3.818 \times 10^{-27}$ kg) is moving through a **B** field with a velocity of 4×10^4 m/s. What must be the magnitude of the field if the ion is to follow a path with a radius of 200 mm?

Ans. 4.77 mT.

37-12. A *velocity selector* is a device (Fig. 37-26) which utilizes crossed **E** and **B** fields to select ions of only one velocity v. Positive ions of charge q are

Fig. 37-26 Velocity selector.

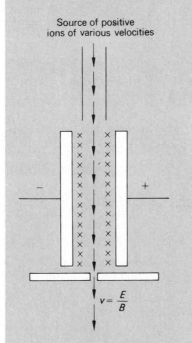

Source of positive ions of various velocities

$$v = \frac{E}{B}$$

projected into the perpendicular fields at varying speeds. Ions with velocities sufficient to make the magnetic force equal and opposite to the electric force pass through the bottom slit undeflected. Show that the speed of these ions can be found from

$$v = \frac{E}{B}$$

37-13. What will be the velocity of protons injected through the velocity selector of Fig. 27-26 if $E = 3 \times 10^5$ N/C and $B = 0.25$ T?

Ans. 1.2×10^6 m/s.

37-14. A wire 1 m long supports a current of 5 A in a direction perpendicular to a magnetic field of flux density 0.034 T. What is the magnetic force on the wire?

37-15. A long wire carries a current of 6 A in a direction 35° north of an easterly magnetic field of flux density 0.04 T. What is the magnitude and direction of the force on each centimeter of wire?

Ans. 1.51×10^{-3} N, into page.

37-16. If 80 mm of a straight wire is at an angle of 53° with a **B** field of 0.23 T, what current is required to give a force of 2 N on this length of wire?

37-17. A 12-cm segment of wire carries a current of 4 A and makes an angle of 41° with horizontal magnetic flux. What must be the magnitude of the flux density to produce a force of 5 N on this wire segment?

Ans. 15.9 T.

37-18. Determine the magnetic induction **B** in air 8 mm from a long wire carrying a current of 14 A.

37-19. What is the magnetic induction **B** in air at a point 4 cm from a long wire carrying a current of 6 A?

Ans. 30 μT.

37-20. Two parallel wires carrying currents I_1 and I_2 are separated by a distance d. Show that the force per unit length F/l each wire exerts on the other is given by

$$\frac{F}{l} = \frac{\mu I_1 I_2}{2\pi d}$$

37-21. Two wires lying in a horizontal plane carry parallel currents of 15 A each and are 200 mm apart in air. If both currents are directed to the right, what are the magnitude and direction of the flux density at a point midway between the wires? What is the force per unit length that each wire exerts on the other? Is it attraction or repulsion?

Ans. 0, 2.25×10^{-4} N/m, attraction.

37-22. A circular loop of radius 50 mm carries a current of 15 A. If the wire is in air, determine the magnetic induction at the center of the loop. What is the magnetic induction if the loop is submerged in a medium whose relative permeability is 3.0?

37-23. A circular loop 240 mm in diameter supports a current of 7.8 A. If it is submerged in a medium of relative permeability 2.0, what is the magnetic induction at the center?

Ans. 81.7 μT.

37-24. A circular coil having 60 turns has a radius of 75 mm. What current must exist in the coil to produce a flux density of 3×10^{-4} T at the center of the coil?

37-25. A circular coil having 40 turns of wire in air has a radius of 6 cm. What current must exist in the coil to produce a flux density of 2×10^{-3} T at its center?

Ans. 4.77 A.

37-26. A solenoid of length 30 cm and diameter 4 cm is closely wound with 400 turns of wire around a nonmagnetic material. If the current in the wire is 6 A, determine the magnetic induction at the center of the solenoid.

37-27. A solenoid has a length of 20 cm and is wound with 220 turns of wire carrying a current of 5 A. What should the relative permeability of the core be to produce a magnetic induction of 0.2 T at the center of the solenoid?

Ans. 29.

38 Forces and Torques in a Magnetic Field

OBJECTIVES: After completing this chapter, you should be able to:

1. Determine the direction of the magnetic force on a current-carrying conductor in a known B field.

2. Write and apply equations for calculating the *magnetic torque* on a coil or a solenoid of known area, number of turns, and current, when located in a magnetic field of known flux density.

3. Explain with drawings the function of each part of a laboratory *galvanometer*; describe how it may be converted to an ammeter and to a voltmeter.

4. Calculate the *multiplier resistance* necessary to increase the range of a dc voltmeter which contains a galvanometer of fixed sensitivity.

5. Calculate the *shunt resistance* necessary to increase the range of a galvanometer or ammeter of constant sensitivity.

6. Explain the operation of a simple *dc motor*, discussing the function of each of its parts, with particular emphasis on the *split-ring commutator*.

We have seen that a current-carrying conductor placed in a magnetic field will experience a force which is perpendicular both to the current I and to the magnetic induction B. A coil suspended in a magnetic field will experience a *torque* due to equal and opposite magnetic forces on the sides of the coil. Such forces and torques provide the operating principle of many useful devices. In this chapter we discuss the galvanometer, the voltmeter, the ammeter, and the dc motor as applications of electromagnetic forces.

A current-carrying conductor suspended in a magnetic field, as illustrated in Fig. 38-1, will experience a magnetic force given by

$$F = BIl \sin \theta = BI_\perp l \tag{38-1}$$

where $I_\perp$ refers to the current perpendicular to the **B** field and l is the length of the conductor. The direction of the force is determined from the right-hand-screw rule.

Fig. 38-1 The force on a current-carrying conductor is directed perpendicular to the magnetic field.

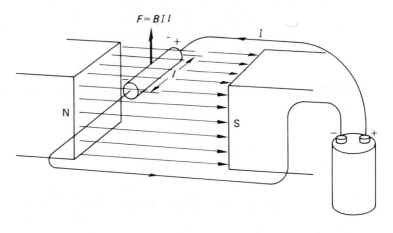

Now let us examine the forces acting on a rectangular current-carrying loop suspended in a magnetic field, shown in Fig. 38-2. The lengths of the sides are a and b, and a current I passes around the loop, as indicated. (The seat of emf and method of leading current into the loop are not shown for simplicity.) Sides mn and op of the loop are each of length a and perpendicular to the magnetic induction **B**. Thus there are exerted on the sides equal and opposite forces of magnitude

$$F = BIa \tag{38-2}$$

The force is directed upward for the segment mn and downward for the segment op.

Fig. 38-2 Magnetic forces on a current-carrying loop.

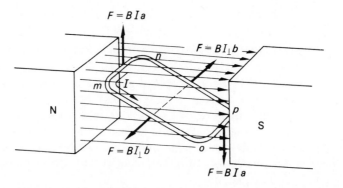

Similar reasoning will show that equal and opposite forces are also exerted on the other two sides. These forces have a magnitude of

$$F = BIb \sin \alpha$$

where α is the angle that the sides *np* and *mo* make with the magnetic field.

Evidently, the loop is in translational equilibrium since the resultant force on the loop is zero. However, the nonconcurrent forces on the sides of length *a* produce a resultant torque which tends to rotate the coil clockwise. As can be seen from Fig. 38-3, each force produces a torque equal to

$$\tau = BIa \frac{b}{2} \cos \alpha$$

Fig. 38-3 Calculating the torque on a current loop.

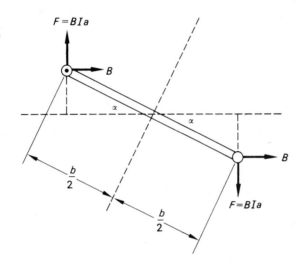

Because the total torque is equal to twice this value, the resultant torque can be found from

$$\tau = BI(a \times b) \cos \alpha \qquad (38\text{-}3)$$

Since $a \times b$ is the area *A* of the loop, Eq. (38-3) can be written

$$\tau = BIA \cos \alpha \qquad (38\text{-}4)$$

Note that the torque is a maximum when $\alpha = 0°$, that is, when the plane of the loop is parallel with the magnetic field. As the coil turns about its axis, the angle α increases, reducing the rotational effect of the magnetic forces. When the plane of the loop is perpendicular to the field, the angle $\alpha = 90°$ and the resultant torque is zero. The momentum of the coil will cause it to pass this point slightly, but the direction of the magnetic forces ensures that it will oscillate until it reaches equilibrium with the plane of the loop perpendicular to the field.

If the loop is replaced with a closely wound coil having N turns of wire, the general equation for computing the resultant torque is

$$\tau = NBIA \cos \alpha \qquad (38\text{-}5)$$

This equation applies to any complete circuit of area A, and its use need not be restricted to rectangular loops. Any plane loop obeys the same relationship.

EXAMPLE 38-1   A rectangular coil consisting of 100 turns of wire has a width of 16 cm and a length of 20 cm. The coil is mounted in a uniform magnetic field of flux density 8 mT, and a current of 20 A is sent through the windings. When the coil makes an angle of 30° with the magnetic field, what is the torque tending to rotate the coil?

Solution   Substituting in Eq. (38-5), we obtain

$$\tau = NBIA \cos \alpha$$

$$= (100 \text{ turns})(8 \times 10^{-3} \text{ T})(20 \text{ A})(0.16 \text{ m} \times 0.2 \text{ m})(\cos 30°)$$

$$= 0.445 \text{ N} \cdot \text{m}$$

**38-2
MAGNETIC
TORQUE ON
A SOLENOID**

The relationship expressed by Eq. (38-5) applies for computing the torque on a solenoid of area A having N turns of wire. However, in applying the relation we must remember that the angle α is the angle that each turn of wire makes with the field. It is the *complement* of the angle θ between the solenoid axis and the magnetic field (refer to Fig. 38-4). An alternative equation for computing the torque on a solenoid is therefore

$$\tau = NBIA \sin \theta \qquad \qquad \textit{Solenoid} \quad (38\text{-}6)$$

You should verify that $\sin \theta$ is equal to $\cos \alpha$ by looking at the figure.

Fig. 38-4 Magnetic torque on a solenoid.

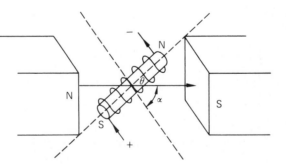

The action of the solenoid in Fig. 38-4 can also be explained in terms of magnetic poles. Applying the right-hand-thumb rule to each turn of wire shows that the solenoid will act as an electromagnet, with north and south poles as indicated.

38-3
THE GALVA-
NOMETER

Any device used to detect an electric current is called a *galvanometer*. The operating principle for the majority of such instruments is based on the torque exerted on a coil in a magnetic field. The essential parts are shown in Fig. 38-5.

Fig. 38-5 Essential components of a galvanometer.

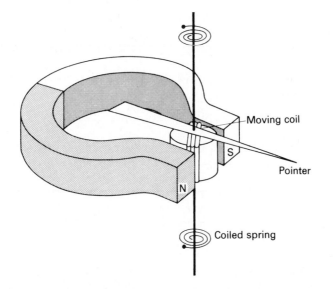

A coil, wrapped around a soft iron core, is pivoted on jeweled bearings between the poles of a permanent magnet. Its rotational motion is restrained by a pair of spiral springs, which also serve as current leads to the coil. Depending upon the direction of the current being measured, the coil and pointer will rotate either in a clockwise or counterclockwise direction.

For the laboratory galvanometer illustrated in Fig. 38-6 the coil and pointer are shown in the equilibrium position. Note that the permanent magnets are shaped to provide a uniform *radial magnetic field*. This ensures that

Fig. 38-6 The laboratory galvanometer.

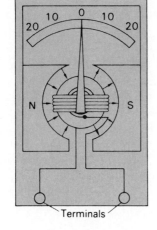

the pointer deflection will be directly proportional to the current in the coil. If the current through the coil passes into the page on the right and out of the page on the left, magnetic forces in the radial field will produce a clockwise torque. The pointer and coil will move clockwise until the resisting counterclockwise spring torque equals the magnetic torque produced by the current. Thus the position of the pointer on the marked scale is a measure of the current magnitude. Reversing the current direction will cause an equal pointer deflection in a counterclockwise direction.

The sensitivity of a galvanometer of the type indicated in Fig. 38-6 is determined by the spring torque, by the friction in the bearings, and by the strength of the magnetic field.

EXAMPLE 38-2   The galvanometer in Fig. 38-6 has a sensitivity of 50 μA per scale division. What current is required to give full deflection of the pointer through 25 scale divisions to the right or left of the equilibrium position?

Solution   The current required is equal to the product of the sensitivity and the number of divisions:

$$I = (50 \ \mu\text{A/div})(25 \ \text{div}) = 1250 \ \mu\text{A}$$

Galvanometers of this type may be designed to read currents as low as 1 μA (10^{-6} A). Greater sensitivities require a modified design. One such design consists of suspending a coil in a magnetic field by thin thread. The motion of the coil is then observed by mounting a mirror on the thread, utilizing the principle of an optical lever.

**38-4
THE DC
VOLTMETER**

Many important dc measuring instruments utilize a galvanometer as an indicating element. Two of the most common are the *voltmeter* and the *ammeter*. The first of these will be discussed in this section as an example of how the galvanometer can be used to measure voltages.

The potential difference across a galvanometer is extremely small even when a large-scale deflection occurs. Thus, if a galvanometer is to be used to measure voltage, it must be converted to a high-resistance instrument. Suppose, for example, it is desired to measure the drop in voltage across the battery in Fig. 38-7. This voltage must be measured without appreciably disturbing the current through the circuit. In other words, the voltmeter must draw negligible current. To accomplish this, a large multiplier resistance R_m is placed in series with the galvanometer as an integral part of a dc voltmeter.

Note that the galvanometer used in a voltmeter is adjusted so that its equilibrium position is to the extreme left on the scale. This allows for a greater range of measurement but unfortunately requires that the current pass through the coils in one direction only. The sensitivity of the galvanometer is determined by the current I_g required for *full-scale deflection* (maximum pointer deflection) as indicated in Fig. 38-7.

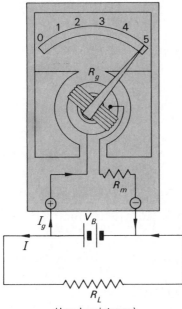

Fig. 38-7 The dc voltmeter.

(Load resistance)

Suppose that the galvanometer coil has a resistance R_g and that the meter is designed to yield full-scale deflection for the current I_g. Such a galvanometer, acting alone, could be calibrated to record voltages from zero up to a maximum value given by

$$V_g = I_g R_g \qquad (38\text{-}7)$$

By properly choosing the multiplier resistance R_m, we can calibrate the meter to read any desired voltage.

Suppose, for example, we want full-scale deflection of the voltmeter for the voltage V_B in Fig. 38-7. The multiplier resistance R_m must be chosen so that only the small current I_g passes through the galvanometer. Under these conditions,

$$V_B = I_g R_g + I_g R_m$$

Solving for R_m, we obtain

$$\boxed{R_m = \frac{V_B}{I_g} - R_g} \qquad (38\text{-}8)$$

Thus we see that the multiplier resistance R_m is equal to the total resistance V_B/I_g less the galvanometer resistance R_g.

EXAMPLE 38-3   A certain galvanometer has an internal resistance of 30 Ω and gives a full-scale deflection for a current of 1 mA. Calculate the multiplier resistance necessary to convert this galvanometer into a voltmeter whose maximum range is 50 V.

Solution

The multiplier resistance R_m must be such that the total drop in voltage through R_g and R_m is 50 V. From Eq. (38-8),

$$R_m = \frac{50 \text{ V}}{1 \times 10^{-3} \text{ A}} - 30 \ \Omega = 50{,}000 \ \Omega - 30 \ \Omega$$

$$= 49{,}970 \ \Omega$$

Note that the total resistance of the voltmeter $(R_m + R_g)$ is 50 kΩ.

A voltmeter must be connected in *parallel* with the part of the circuit whose potential difference is to be measured. This is necessary so that the large resistance of the voltmeter will not greatly alter the circuit.

38-5
THE DC
AMMETER

An ammeter is a device which, through calibrated scales, gives an indication of the electric current without appreciably altering it. A galvanometer is an ammeter, but its range is limited by the extreme sensitivity of the moving coil. The range of the galvanometer, can be extended simply by adding a very low resistance, called a *shunt*, in parallel with the galvanometer coil (refer to Fig. 38-8). Placing the shunt in parallel assures that the ammeter as a whole will have a very low resistance, which is necessary if the current is to be essentially unaltered. The major portion of the current will pass through the shunt. Only the small current I_g required for galvanometer deflection will be drawn from the

Fig. 38-8 The dc ammeter.

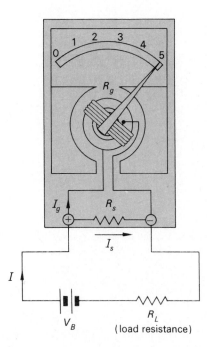

circuit. For example, if 10 A goes through an ammeter, 9.99 A may go through the shunt and only 0.01 A through the coil itself.

Suppose the range of a galvanometer is to be extended to measure a maximum current I of the circuit in Fig. 38-8. A shunt resistance R_s must be chosen such that only the current I_g, required for full-scale deflection, passes through the galvanometer coil. The remainder of the current I_s must pass through the shunt. Since R_g and R_s are in parallel, the IR drop across each resistance must be identical:

$$I_s R_s = I_g R_g \qquad (38\text{-}9)$$

The shunt current I_s is the difference between the circuit current I and the galvanometer current I_g. Thus Eq. (38-9) becomes

$$(I - I_g)R_s = I_g R_g$$

Solving for the shunt resistance R_s, we obtain the following useful relation:

$$R_s = \frac{I_g R_g}{I - I_g}$$

EXAMPLE 38-4   A certain galvanometer has an internal coil resistance of 46 Ω, and a current of 200 mA is required for full-scale deflection. What shunt resistance must be used to convert the galvanometer into an ammeter whose maximum range is 10 A?

Solution   Equation (38-9) gives

$$R_s = \frac{(0.2 \text{ A})(46 \ \Omega)}{10 \text{ A} - 0.2 \text{ A}} = \frac{9.2 \text{ V}}{9.8 \text{ A}}$$

$$= 0.939 \ \Omega$$

It is important to remember that an ammeter must be connected in *series* with the portion of a circuit through which the current is to be measured. The circuit must be opened at some convenient point and the ammeter inserted. If by mistake the ammeter were placed in parallel, the circuit would be shorted across the ammeter because of its extremely low resistance.

**38-6
THE
DC MOTOR**

An electric motor is a device which transforms electric energy into mechanical energy. The dc motor, like the moving coil of a galvanometer, consists of a current-carrying coil in a magnetic field. However, the motion of the coil in a motor is unrestrained by springs. The design is such that the coil will rotate continuously under the influence of magnetic torque.

A very simple dc motor, consisting of a single current-carrying loop suspended between two magnetic poles, is illustrated in Fig. 38-9. Normally, the torque exerted on a current-carrying loop would diminish to zero when its plane becomes perpendicular to the field. In order to provide for continuous rotation of the loop, the current in the loop must be automatically reversed each time it turns through 180°.

The current reversal is accomplished by using a *split-ring commutator*, as shown in Fig. 38-9. The commutator consists of two metal half rings fused to each end of the conducting loop and insulated from each other. As the loop rotates, each brush touches first one half ring and then the other. Thus the electrical connections are reversed every half revolution at times when the loop is perpendicular to the magnetic field. In this manner, the torque acting on the loop is always in the same direction, and the loop will rotate continuously.

Although actual dc motors operate on the principle described for Fig. 38-9, there are a number of designs which increase the available torque and make it more uniform. One such design is shown in Fig. 38-10. A greater magnetic field is established by replacing the permanent magnets with electromagnets. Additionally, the torque can be increased and made more uniform by adding a number of different coils, each having a large number of turns around a slotted iron core called the *armature*. The commutator is an automatic switching arrangement which maintains the currents in the directions shown in the figure, regardless of the orientation of the armature. More will be said about the dc motor in the following chapter.

Fig. 38-9 The dc motor.

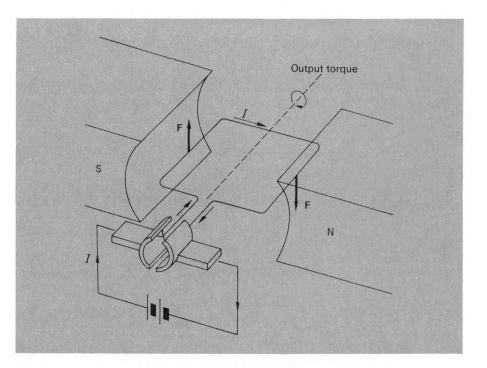

Fig. 38-10 Greater, more uniform torque is possible in commercial motors with many armature coils.

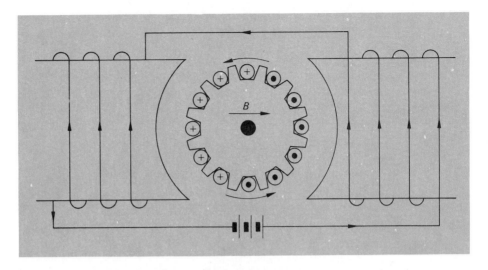

SUMMARY

Magnetic torques on current loops form the basis for so many applications that a strong foundation is essential. The operation of generators, motors, ammeters, voltmeters, and many industrial instruments is directly affected by magnetic forces and torques. The major concepts to be remembered are summarized below:

- The magnetic torque on a current-carrying coil of wire having N turns of wire is given by

$$\tau = NBIA \cos \alpha \qquad \textit{Magnetic Torque}$$

where N = number of turns of wire
B = flux density, T
I = current, A
A = area of the coil of wire, m^2
α = angle plane of coil makes with field

- The same equation applies for a solenoid, except that the angle α is generally replaced with θ, the angle the solenoid axis makes with the field.

$$\tau = NBIA \sin \theta \qquad \textit{Torque on a Solenoid}$$

- The multiplier resistance R_m which must be placed in series with a voltmeter to give full-scale deflection for V_B is found from

$$R_m = \frac{V_B - I_g R_g}{I_g} \qquad \textit{Multiplier Resistance}$$

I_g is the galvanometer current, and R_g is its resistance.

- The shunt resistance R_s which must be placed in parallel with an ammeter to give full-scale deflection for a current I is

$$R_s = \frac{I_g R_g}{I - I_g}$$

Shunt Resistance

QUESTIONS

38-1. Define the following terms:
   a. Magnetic torque
   b. Galvanometer
   c. Voltmeter
   d. Ammeter
   e. Full-scale deflection
   f. Shunt resistance
   g. Multiplier resistance
   h. Sensitivity
   i. Motor
   j. Commutator
   k. Armature

38-2. The equal and opposite forces acting on a current loop in a magnetic field form what is called a *couple.* Show that the resultant torque on such a couple is the product of one of the forces and the perpendicular distance between their lines of action.

38-3. Why is it necessary to provide a *radial* magnetic field for the coil of a galvanometer?

38-4. A coil of wire is suspended by a thread with the plane of the loop coinciding with the plane of the paper. If the coil is placed in a magnetic field directed from left to right, and if a clockwise current is sent through the coil, describe its motion.

38-5. How are the actions of a galvanometer and a motor similar? How are they different?

38-6. How does the core of a galvanometer coil affect the sensitivity of the instrument?

38-7. Explain the torque exerted on a bar magnet suspended in a magnetic field without referring to magnetic poles. Discuss, from an atomic standpoint, how the observed torque may arise from the same cause as the torque on a current loop.

38-8. Suppose the range of an ammeter is to be increased N-fold. Show that the shunt resistance which must be placed across the terminals of the ammeter is given by

$$R_s = \frac{R_a}{N - 1}$$

where R_a is the ammeter resistance.

38-9. Suppose the range of a given voltmeter is to be increased N-fold. Show that the multiplier resistance which must be placed in series with the voltmeter is given by

$$R_m = (N - 1)R_v$$

where R_v is the voltmeter resistance.

38-10. Show by diagrams how an ammeter and a voltmeter should be connected in a circuit. Compare the resistances of the two devices.

38-11. Discuss the error caused by the insertion of an ammeter into an electric circuit. How is this error minimized?

38-12. Discuss the error caused by the insertion of a voltmeter into a circuit. How is the error minimized?

38-13. A voltmeter is connected to a battery, and the reading is taken. An accurate resistance box is then placed in the circuit and adjusted until the voltmeter reading is one-half of its previous value. Show that the voltmeter resistance must be just equal to the added resistance. (This is called the *half-deflection method* for determining voltmeter resistance.)

38-14. Explain what happens when a voltmeter is erroneously placed in series in a circuit. What happens if an ammeter is mistakenly placed in parallel?

38-15. Prepare a short paper on the following topics:
    a. Ballistic galvanometer   **c.** Dynamometer
    b. Ohmmeter   **d.** Wattmeter

38-16. Plot a graph of the torque as a function of time for a single-loop dc motor.

PROBLEMS

38-1. A rectangular loop of wire 6 × 10 cm is placed with its plane parallel to a magnetic field of flux density 0.08 T. What is the resultant torque on the loop if it carries a current of 14 A?

Ans. 0.00672 N · m.

38-2. A rectangular loop of wire has an area of 0.3 m². The plane of the loop makes an angle of 30° with a magnetic field of flux density 0.75 T. What is the resultant torque when the current in the loop is 7 A?

38-3. Calculate the magnetic flux density required to give a loop of 400 turns a torque of 0.5 N · m when its plane is parallel to the field. The dimensions of each turn are 70 × 120 mm, and the current is 9 A.

Ans. 16.5 mT.

38-4. What current is required to produce a maximum torque of 0.8 N · m on a solenoid having 800 turns of area 0.4 m²? The flux density of the field is 3.0 mT. What is the position of the solenoid for maximum torque?

38-5. The axis of a solenoid makes an angle of 34° with a 5-mT magnetic field. If the solenoid has 750 turns, what current is required to produce a torque of 4.0 N · m? The area of each turn is 0.25 m².

Ans. 7.63 A.

38-6. A solenoid consists of 400 turns of wire, each having a radius of 60 mm. What angle does the axis of the solenoid make with the magnetic flux if the current through the wire is 6 A, the flux density is 46 mT, and the resulting torque is 0.80 N · m?

38-7. A galvanometer coil 50 × 120 mm is mounted in a constant radial field of flux density 0.2 T. The coil has 600 turns of wire. What current is required to develop a torque of 3.6×10^{-5} N · m?

Ans. 50 μA.

38-8. A solenoid or 100 turns has a cross-sectional area of 0.25 m². What torque is required to hold the solenoid at an angle of 30° with the field? The current is 10 A and the magnetic field is 42 mT.

38-9. A circular loop consisting of 500 turns carries a current of 10 A in a field of flux density 0.25 T. The area of each turn is 0.2 m². Calculate the torque when the loop makes the following angles with the field: **(a)** 0°, **(b)** 30°, **(c)** 45°, **(d)** 60°, **(e)** 90°.

    Ans. **(a)** 250 N · m **(b)** 217 N · m **(c)** 177 N · m **(d)** 125 N · m **(e)** 0 N · m.

38-10. Plot a curve with torque vs. loop angle for the values obtained in Prob. 38-9.

38-11. A certain voltmeter draws 0.02 mA for full-scale deflection of 50 V. **(a)** What is the resistance of the meter? **(b)** What is the resistance per volt? **(c)** What multiplier resistance must be added to permit the meaurement of 150 V full scale?

    Ans. **(a)** 2.5 MΩ **(b)** 50,000 Ω/V **(c)** 5 MΩ.

38-12. A current of only 90 μA will produce full-scale deflection of a voltmeter which is designed to read 50 mV full scale. **(a)** What is the resistance of the meter? **(b)** What multiplier resistance is required to convert this voltmeter to an instrument that reads a full-scale voltage of 100 mV?

38-13. A galvanometer has a sensitivity of 20 μA per scale division. What current is required to give full-scale deflection with 25 divisions on either side of the equilibrium position?

    Ans. 500 μA.

38-14. A galvanometer has a sensitivity of 15 μA per scale division. How many scale divisions will the galvanometer needle be deflected for a current of 60 μA?

38-15. The coil of an ammeter will burn out if a current of more than 40 mA is sent through it. If the coil resistance is 0.5 Ω, what shunt resistance should be added to permit the measurement of 4 A?

    Ans. 0.00505 Ω.

38-16. An ammeter which has a resistance of 0.1 Ω is connected in a circuit and indicates a current of 10 A. A shunt having a resistance of 0.01 Ω is then connected across the terminals of the meter. What new circuit current is required to produce full-scale deflection of the ammeter?

38-17. A certain galvanometer has an internal resistance of 20 Ω and gives a full-scale deflection for a current of 10 mA. Calculate the multiplier resistance required to convert this galvanometer into a voltmeter whose maximum range is 50 V. What is the total resistance of the resulting voltmeter?

    Ans. 4980 Ω, 5000 Ω.

38-18. A galvanometer having an internal resistance of 35 Ω is to be converted to a voltmeter which will read a maximum voltage of 30 V. What multiplier resistance is needed if full-scale deflection of the galvanometer requires 1 mA?

38-19. What shunt resistance is required to convert the galvanometer of Prob. 38-17 to an ammeter which reads a maximum current of 50 mA?

    Ans. 50 Ω.

38-20. What shunt resistance is required to convert the galvanometer of Prob. 38-18 to an ammeter reading 10 mA full scale?

38-21. A certain voltmeter reads 150 V full scale. The galvanometer coil has a resistance of 50 Ω and produces a full-scale deflection on 20 mV. Find the multiplier resistance in the voltmeter.

    Ans. 374,950 Ω.

38-22. A galvanometer has a coil resistance of 50 Ω and a current sensitivity of 1 mA (full scale). What shunt resistance is needed to convert this galvanometer to an ammeter reading 2 A full scale?

38-23. A laboratory ammeter has a resistance of 0.01 Ω and reads 5 A full scale. What shunt resistance is needed to increase the range of the ammeter tenfold?

Ans. 0.00111 Ω.

38-24. A commercial 3-V voltmeter requires a current of 0.02 mA to produce full-scale deflection. How can it be converted into an instrument with a range of 150 V?

38-25. A voltmeter of range 150 V and 15,000 Ω is connected in series with another voltmeter of range 100 V and 20,000 Ω. What will each meter read when they are connected across a 120-V battery?

Ans. 51.45 V, 68.6 V.

39 *Electromagnetic Induction*

OBJECTIVES: After completing this chapter, you should be able to:

1. Explain and calculate the current or emf induced by a conductor moving through a magnetic field.

2. Write and apply an equation relating the induced emf in a length of wire moving with a velocity *v* directed at an angle θ with a known *B* field.

3. State *Lenz's law* and use it or the *right-hand rule* to determine the direction of induced emf or current.

4. Explain the operation of simple ac and dc generators; calculate the instantaneous and maximum emf or current generated by a simple ac generator.

5. Demonstrate with diagrams your knowledge of *series-wound* and *shunt-wound* motors and solve for starting current and operating voltage in electrical problems.

6. Explain the operation of a *transformer* and solve problems involving changes in current, voltage, or power.

We have seen that an electric field can produce a magnetic field. In this chapter, you will learn that the reverse is also true: a magnetic field can give rise to an electric field. An electric current is *generated* by a conductor which is caused to move relative to a magnetic field. A rotating coil in a magnetic field *induces* an alternating emf, which produces an *alternating current* (ac). This process is called *electromagnetic induction* and it is the operating principle behind many electrical devices. For example, electric ac generators and transformers use electromagnetic induction to produce and distribute electric power economically.

Faraday discovered that when magnetic flux lines are cut by a conductor, an emf is produced between the end points of the conductor. For example, an electric current is induced in the conductor of Fig. 39-1a as it is moved downward across the flux lines. (The lower case symbol i will be used for induced currents and for varying currents.) The faster the movement, the more pronounced the galvanometer deflection. When the conductor is moved upward across the flux lines, a similar observation is made except that the current is reversed (see Fig. 39-1b). If no flux lines are crossed, e.g., the conductor is moved parallel to the field, no current is induced.

Fig. 39-1 When magnetic flux lines are cut by a conductor, an electric current is induced.

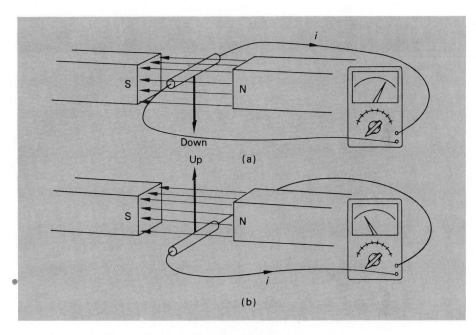

Suppose that a number of conductors are moved through a magnetic field, as illustrated by dropping a coil of N turns across the flux lines in Fig. 39-2. The magnitude of the induced current is directly proportional to the number of coils and to the rate of motion. Evidently, *an emf is induced by the relative motion between the conductor and the magnetic field*. The same effect is observed when the coil is held stationary and the magnet is moved upward.

Summarizing what we have learned from these experiments, we can state that:

1. *Relative motion between a conductor and a magnetic field induces an emf in the conductor.*
2. *The direction of the induced emf depends upon the direction of motion of the conductor with respect to the field.*
3. *The magnitude of the emf is directly proportional to the rate at which magnetic flux lines are cut by the conductor.*

Fig. 39-2 Induced
emf in a coil is
proportional to the
number of turns of
wire passing
through the field.

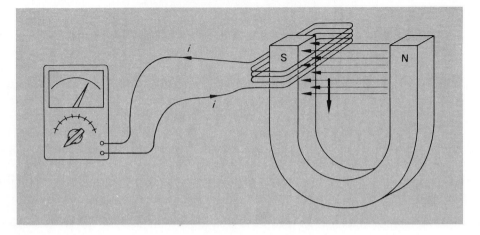

4. *The magnitude of the emf is directly proportional to the number of turns of the
conductor crossing the flux lines.*

A quantitative relationship for computing the induced emf in a coil of
N turns is given by

$$\mathscr{E} = -N\,\frac{\Delta\phi}{\Delta t}$$

$$(39\text{-}1)$$

where $\mathscr{E}$ = average induced emf

$\Delta\phi$ = change in magnetic flux occurring during time interval Δt

*A magnetic flux changing at the rate of one weber per second will induce an emf
of one volt for each turn of the conductor.* The negative sign in Eq. (39-1) means
that the induced emf is in such a direction as to oppose the change that produced it, as will be explained in Sec. 39-3.

Now let us discuss how magnetic flux ϕ linking a conductor may
change. In the simple case of a straight wire moving through lines of flux,
$\Delta\phi/\Delta t$ represents the rate at which the flux linked by the conductor changes.
However, a continuous circuit is necessary for an induced current to exist, and
more often we are interested in the emf induced in a loop or coil of wire.

Recall that the magnetic flux ϕ passing through a loop of effective area
A is given by

$$\phi = BA \qquad\qquad (39\text{-}2)$$

where B is the magnetic flux density. When B is in *teslas* (*webers per square
meter*) and A is in *square meters*, ϕ is expressed in *webers*.

A change in flux ϕ can occur in two principal ways:

1. By changing the flux density **B** going through a constant loop area A:

$$\Delta\phi = (\Delta B)A \qquad\qquad (39\text{-}3)$$

2. By changing the effective area A in a magnetic field of constant flux density $\mathbf{B}$:

$$\Delta\phi = B(\Delta A) \tag{39-4}$$

Two examples of changing flux density through a constant, stationary coil area are given in Fig. 39-3. In Fig. 39-3a, the north pole of a magnet is moved through a circular coil. The changing flux density induces a current in the coil, as indicated by the galvanometer. In Fig. 39-3b no current is induced in coil B so long as the current in coil A is constant. However, by quickly varying the resistance in the left circuit, the magnetic flux density reaching coil B can be increased or decreased. While the flux density is changing, a current is induced in the coil on the right.

Fig. 39-3 (a) Inducing a current by moving a magnet into a coil. (b) A changing current in coil A induces a current in coil B.

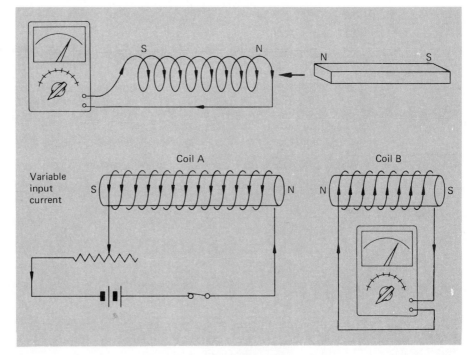

Note that when the north (N) pole of the magnet is moved into the coil in Fig. 39-3a, the current flows in a clockwise direction as viewed toward the magnet. Therefore, the end of the *coil* near the N pole of the magnet becomes an N pole also (from the right-hand-thumb rule of the last chapter). The magnet and the coil will experience a force of repulsion, making it necessary to exert a force to bring them together. If the magnet is removed from the coil, a force of attraction will exist that makes it necessary to exert a force to separate them. We will see in Sec. 39-3 that such forces are a natural consequence of the conservation of energy.

EXAMPLE 39-1   A coil of wire having an area of 10^{-3} m^2 is placed in a region of constant flux density equal to 1.5 T. In a time interval of 0.001 s, the flux density is reduced to 1.0 T. If the coil consists of 50 turns of wire, what is the induced emf?

Solution   The change in flux density is

$$\Delta B = 1.5 \text{ T} - 1.0 \text{ T} = 0.5 \text{ T}$$

From Eq. (39-3), the change in flux is

$$\Delta\phi = (0.5 \text{ T})(10^{-3} \text{ m}^2) = 5 \times 10^{-4} \text{ Wb}$$

Substituting into Eq. (39-1) yields

$$\mathscr{E} = -N \frac{\Delta\phi}{\Delta t}$$

$$= -50 \text{ turns} \frac{5 \times 10^{-4} \text{ Wb}}{0.001 \text{ s}} = -25 \text{ V}$$

The second general way in which the flux linking a conductor may change is by varying the effective area penetrated by the flux. The following example illustrates this point.

EXAMPLE 39-2   A square coil consisting of 80 turns of wire and having an area of 0.05 m^2 is placed perpendicular to a field of flux density 0.8 T. The coil is flipped until its plane is parallel to the field in a time of 0.2 s. What is the average induced emf?

Solution   The area penetrated by the flux varies from 0.05 m^2 to zero. Thus the change in flux is

$$\Delta\phi = B(\Delta A)$$

$$= (0.8 \text{ T})(0.05 \text{ m}^2) = 4 \times 10^{-2} \text{ Wb}$$

The induced emf is

$$\mathscr{E} = -N \frac{\Delta\phi}{\Delta t} = (-80 \text{ turns}) \frac{4 \times 10^{-2} \text{ Wb}}{0.2 \text{ s}}$$

$$= -16 \text{ V}$$

**39-2
EMF
INDUCED
BY A
MOVING
WIRE**

Another example of a changing area in a constant **B** field is illustrated in Fig. 39-4. Imagine that a moving conductor of length l slides along a stationary U-shaped conductor with a velocity v. The magnetic flux penetrating the loop increases as the area of the loop increases. Consequently, an emf is induced in the moving wire, and a current passes around the loop.

The origin of the emf can be understood by recalling that a moving charge in a magnetic field experiences a force given by

$$F = qvB$$

For example, in Fig. 39-4, free charges on the conductor are moved to the right through a magnetic field directed into the paper. The magnetic force **F** acting on the charges moves them through the length l of wire in a direction given by

Fig. 39-4 The emf induced by a wire moving perpendicular to a magnetic field.

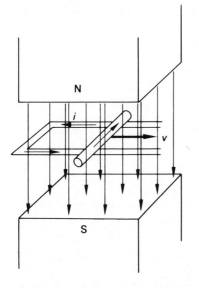

the right-hand-screw rule (away from the reader for conventional current). The work per unit of charge represents the induced emf, which is given by

$$\mathcal{E} = \frac{\text{work}}{q} = \frac{Fl}{q} = \frac{qvBl}{q}$$

$$= Blv \tag{39-5}$$

If the velocity v of the moving wire is directed at an angle θ with the **B** field, a more general form is needed for Eq. (39-5):

$$\boxed{\mathcal{E} = Blv \sin \theta} \tag{39-6}$$

EXAMPLE 39-3   A 0.2-m length of wire moves at a constant velocity of 4 m/s in a direction that is 40° with respect to a magnetic flux density of 0.5 T. Calculate the induced emf.

Solution   Direct substitution into Eq. (39-6) yields

$$\mathcal{E} = (0.5 \text{ T})(0.2 \text{ m})(4 \text{ m/s})(\sin 40°)$$

$$= 0.257 \text{ V}$$

The minus sign does not appear in Eq. (39-6) because the direction of the induced emf is the same as the direction of the magnetic force performing work on the moving charge.

**39-3
LENZ'S LAW**   Throughout the discussions of all physical phenomena, one guiding principle stands out above all the rest: the principle of *conservation of energy*. An emf cannot exist without a cause. Whenever an induced current produces heat or

performs mechanical work, the necessary energy must come from the work done in inducing the current.

Recall the example discussed in Fig. 39-3a. The north pole of a magnet pushed into a coil induces a current which itself gives rise to another magnetic field. The second field produces a force which opposes the original force. Withdrawing the magnet creates a force which opposes the removal of the magnet. This is an illustration of *Lenz's law*:

> **Lenz's Law:** *An induced current will flow in such a direction that it will oppose by its magnetic field the motion of the magnetic field that is producing it.*

The more work that is done in moving the magnet into the coil, the greater will be the induced current and hence, the greater the resisting force. We might have expected this result from the law of conservation of energy. To produce a larger current, we must perform a greater amount of work.

The direction of the current induced in a straight conductor moving through a magnetic field can be determined from Lenz's law. However, there is an easier method, as illustrated in Fig. 39-5. It is known as *Fleming's rule*, or the *right-hand rule*:

> **Fleming's Rule:** *If the thumb, forefinger, and middle finger of the right hand are held at right angles to each other, with the thumb pointing in*

Fig. 39-5 The right-hand rule for determining the direction of induced current.

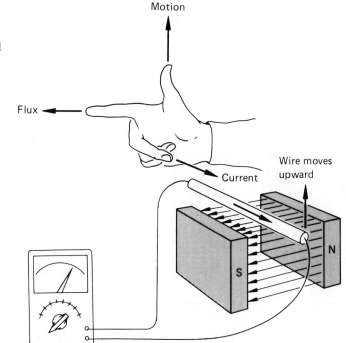

the direction in which the wire is moving and the forefinger pointing in the field direction (N to S), the middle finger will point in the direction of induced conventional current.

Fleming's rule is easy to apply and very useful for studying the currents induced by a simple generator. Students sometimes remember the rule by memorizing *motion—flux—current*. These are the directions given by the thumb, forefinger, and middle finger, respectively.

39-4 THE AC GENERATOR

An electric generator converts mechanical energy into electric energy. We have seen that an emf is induced in a conductor when it experiences a change in flux linkage. When the conductor forms a complete circuit, an induced current can be detected. In a generator, a coil of wire is rotated in a magnetic field, and the induced current is transmitted by wires for long distances from its origin.

The construction of a simple generator is shown in Fig. 39-6. Essentially, there are three components: a *field magnet*, an *armature*, and *slip rings* with *brushes*. The field magnet may be a permanent magnet or an electromagnet. The armature for the generator in Fig. 39-6 consists of a single loop of wire suspended between the poles of the field magnet. A pair of slip rings is fused to each end of the loop; they rotate with the loop as it is turned in the magnetic field. Induced current is led away from the system by graphite brushes which ride on each slip ring. Mechanical energy is supplied to the generator by turning the armature in the magnetic field. Electric energy is generated in the form of an induced current.

Fig. 39-6 The ac generator.

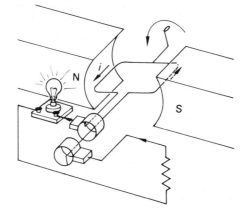

The direction of the induced current must obey Fleming's rule of *motion–flux–current*. In Fig. 39-6, the downward motion of the left wire segment crosses a magnetic flux directed left to right. The induced current is, therefore, toward the slip rings. Similar reasoning shows that the current in the right loop, which is moving upward, will be away from the slip rings.

In order to understand the operation of an ac generator, let us follow the loop through a complete rotation, observing the current generated throughout the rotation. Figure 39-7 shows four positions of the rotating coil and the direction of the current delivered to the brushes in each case. Suppose that the loop is turned mechanically in a counterclockwise direction. In Fig. 39-7a the loop is horizontal, with side M facing the south (S) pole of the magnet. At this point, a maximum current is delivered in the direction shown. In Fig. 39-7b the loop is vertical, with side M facing upward. At this point, no flux lines are being cut, and the induced current drops to zero. When the loop becomes horizontal again, as in Fig. 39-7c, side M is now facing the north (N) pole of the magnet. Therefore, the current delivered to the slip ring M' has changed direction. An induced current flows through the external resistor in a direction opposite to that experienced earlier. In Fig. 39-7d the loop is vertical again, but now side M faces downward. No flux lines are cut, and the induced current again drops to zero. The loop next returns to horizontal as in Fig. 39-7a, and the cycle repeats itself. Thus the current delivered by such a generator alternates periodically, the direction changing twice each rotation.

Fig. 39-7 Production of an alternating current.

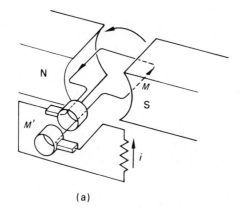

(a)

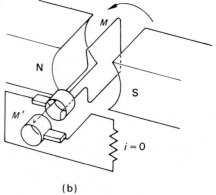

(b)

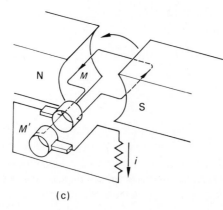

(c)

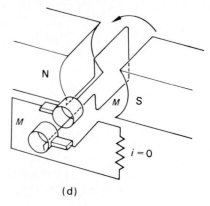

(d)

The emf generated in each segment of a rotating loop must obey the relation

$$\mathcal{E} = Blv \sin \theta \qquad (39\text{-}6)$$

where v is the velocity of a moving wire segment of length l in a magnetic field of flux density **B**. The direction of the velocity v with respect to the **B** field at any instant is denoted by the angle θ. Let us consider the segment M of our rotating current loop when it reaches the position shown in Fig. 39-8. The *instantaneous* emf at that position is given by Eq. (39-6). If the loop rotates in a circle of radius r, the instantaneous velocity v can be found from

$$v = \omega r$$

Fig. 39-8 Calculating induced emf.

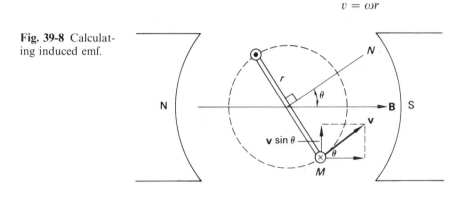

where ω is the angular velocity in radians per second. Substituting into Eq. (39-6) gives the instantaneous emf

$$\mathcal{E} = Bl\omega r \sin \theta \qquad (39\text{-}7)$$

An identical emf is induced in the segment of wire opposite M, and no *net* emf is generated in the other segments. Hence the total instantaneous emf is twice the value given by Eq. (39-7), or

$$\mathcal{E}_{\text{inst}} = 2Bl\omega r \sin \theta \qquad (39\text{-}8)$$

But the area A of the loop is

$$A = l \times 2r$$

and Eq. (39-8) can be further simplified to

$$\boxed{\mathcal{E}_{\text{inst}} = NBA\omega \sin \theta} \qquad (39\text{-}9)$$

where N is the number of turns of wire.

Equation (39-9) expresses a very important principle relating to the study of alternating currents:

> *If the armature is rotating with a constant angular velocity in a constant magnetic field, the magnitude of the induced emf varies sinusoidally with respect to time.*

This fact is illustrated by Fig. 39-9. The emf varies from a maximum value when $\theta = 90°$ to a zero value when $\theta = 0°$. The maximum instantaneous emf is therefore

$$\mathscr{E}_{max} = NBA\omega \tag{39-10}$$

since $\sin 90° = 1$. Stating Eq. (39-9) in terms of the maximum emf, we write

$$\mathscr{E}_{inst} = \mathscr{E}_{max} \sin \theta \tag{39-11}$$

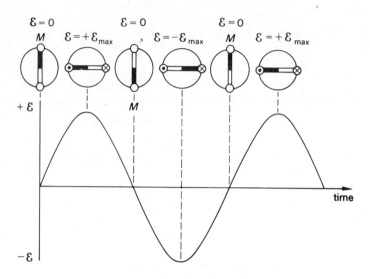

Fig. 39-9 Sinusoidal variation of induced emf with time.

To see the explicit variation of generated emf with time, we should recall that

$$\theta = \omega t = 2\pi ft$$

where f is the number of rotations per second made by the loop. Thus we can express Eq. (39-11) in the following form:

$$\boxed{\mathscr{E}_{inst} = \mathscr{E}_{max} \sin 2\pi ft} \tag{39-12}$$

EXAMPLE 39-4   The armature of a simple ac generator consists of 100 turns of wire, each having an area of 0.2 m². The armature is turned with a frequency of 60 rev/s in a constant magnetic field of flux density 10^{-3} T. What is the maximum emf generated?

Solution   We must first calculate the angular velocity of the coil.

$$\omega = (2\pi \text{ rad/rev})(60 \text{ rev/s}) = 377 \text{ rad/s}$$

Substituting this value and other known parameters into Eq. (39-10), we obtain

$$\mathscr{E}_{max} = NBA\omega$$

$$= (100 \text{ turns})(10^{-3} \text{ T})(0.2 \text{ m}^2)(377 \text{ rad/s})$$

$$= 7.54 \text{ V}$$

Since the induced current is proportional to the induced emf, from Ohm's law, the induced current will also vary sinusoidally according to

$$i_{inst} = i_{max} \sin 2\pi f t$$ (39-13)

The maximum current occurs when the induced emf is a maximum. The sinusoidal variation is similar to that plotted in Fig. 39-9.

The SI unit for frequency is the *hertz* (Hz) which is defined as a cycle per second.

$$1 \text{ Hz} = 1 \text{ cycle/s}$$

Thus a 60-cycle-per-second alternating current has a frequency of 60 Hz.

39-5 THE DC GENERATOR

A simple ac generator can easily be converted to a dc generator by substituting a split-ring commutator for the slip rings, as illustrated in Fig. 39-10. The operation is just the reverse of that discussed earlier for a dc motor (Chap. 38). In the motor, an electric current gives rise to an external torque. In the dc generator, an external torque generates an electric current. The commutator reverses the connections to the brushes twice per revolution. As a result, the current pulsates but never reverses direction. The emf of such a generator varies with time, as shown in Fig. 39-11. Note that the emf is always in the positive direc-

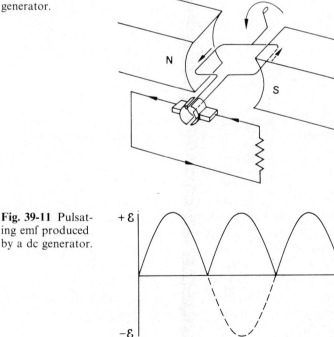

Fig. 39-10 The dc generator.

Fig. 39-11 Pulsating emf produced by a dc generator.

tion, but it rises to a maximum and falls to zero twice per complete rotation. Practical dc generators are designed with many coils in several planes so that the generated emf is larger and nearly constant.

39-6 BACK EMF IN A MOTOR

In an electric motor, a magnetic torque turns a current-carrying loop in a constant magnetic field. We have just seen that a coil rotating in a magnetic field will induce an emf that opposes the cause which gave rise to it. This is true even if a current already exists in the loop. Thus *every motor is also a generator.* According to Lenz's law, such an induced emf must oppose the current delivered to the motor. For this reason, the emf induced in a motor is called *back emf* or *counter emf.*

The effect of a back emf is to reduce the net voltage delivered to the armature coils of the motor. Consider the circuit illustrated in Fig. 39-12. The net voltage delivered to the armature coils is equal to the applied voltage V less the induced voltage $\mathscr{E}_b$.

Applied voltage − induced voltage = net voltage

Fig. 39-12 Back emf in a dc motor.

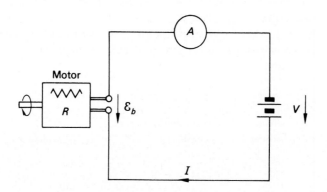

According to Ohm's law, the net voltage across the armature coils is equal to the product of the coil resistance R and the current I. Symbolically, we write

$$V - \mathscr{E}_b = IR \qquad (39\text{-}14)$$

Equation (39-14) tells us that the current through a circuit containing a motor is determined by the magnitude of the back emf. The magnitude of this induced emf, of course, depends on the speed of rotation of the armature. We can show this experimentally by connecting a motor, an ammeter, and a battery in series, as shown in Fig. 39-13. When the armature is rotating freely, a low current is indicated. The back emf reduces the effective voltage. If the motor is stalled by holding the armature stationary, the back emf will drop to zero. The increased net voltage results in a larger circuit current and can cause the motor to overheat and even burn out.

Fig. 39-13 Demonstrating the existence of a back emf in a dc motor.

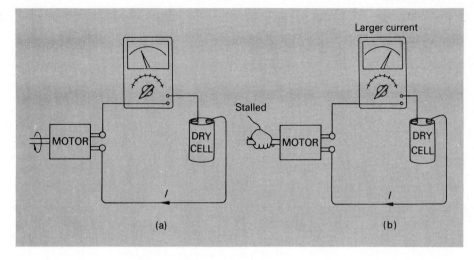

Fig. 39-13 Demonstrating the existence of a back emf in a dc motor.

39-7 TYPES OF MOTORS

Dc motors are classified according to how the field coils and the armature are connected. When the armature coils and the field coils are connected in series, as shown in Fig. 39-14, the motor is said to be *series-wound*. In this type of motor, the current energizes both the field windings and the armature windings. When the armature turns slowly, the back emf is small and the current is large. Consequently, a large torque is developed at low speeds.

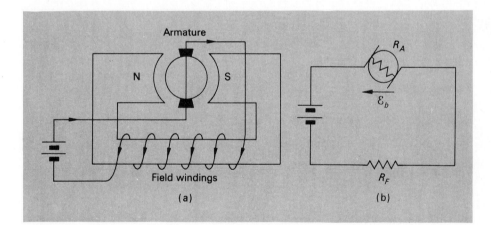

Fig. 39-14 (*a*) The series-wound dc motor. (*b*) Schematic diagram.

In a *shunt-wound* motor, the field windings and the armature windings are connected in parallel, as illustrated by Fig. 39-15. The entire voltage is applied across both windings. The primary advantage of a shunt-wound motor is that it produces more constant torque over a range of speeds. However, the starting torque is usually lower than a similar series-wound motor.

In some applications, the field windings are in two parts, one connected in series with the armature and the other in parallel with it. Such a motor is

Fig. 39-15 (*a*) The shunt-wound dc motor. (*b*) Schematic diagram.

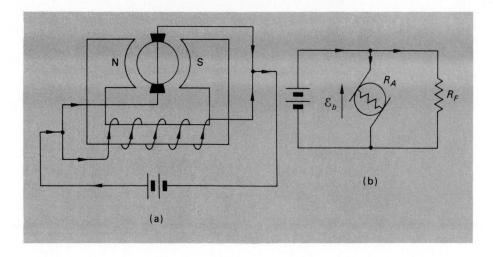

(a)

(b)

called a *compound motor*. The torque produced by a compound motor varies between that of the series and shunt motors.

In *permanent-magnet* motors no field current is necessary. These motors have torque characteristics similar to those of shunt-wound motors.

EXAMPLE 39-5

A 120-Ω dc shunt motor has an armature resistance of 3 Ω and a field resistance of 260 Ω. When the motor is operating at full speed, the total current is 3 A. (*a*) What is the back emf of the motor at full speed? (*b*) Find the current in the motor at the moment its switch is turned on.

Solution (a)

In order to determine the back emf, we must see how the current is divided between the armature and field windings. The current I_F in the field windings can be found by writing the voltage equation for the outside loop in Fig. 39-15*b*:

$$V = I_F R_F$$

from which

$$I_F = \frac{V}{R_F} = \frac{120 \text{ V}}{260 \text{ }\Omega} = 0.46 \text{ A}$$

The current in the armature windings is therefore

$$I_A = 3 \text{ A} - 0.46 \text{ A} = 2.54 \text{ A}$$

Now the voltage equation for the loop containing the battery and the armature is

$$V - \mathscr{E}_b = I_A R_A$$

from which

$$\mathscr{E}_b = V - I_A R_A$$

$$= 120 \text{ V} - (2.54 \text{ A})(3 \text{ }\Omega)$$

$$= 120 \text{ V} - 7.62 \text{ V} = 112.4 \text{ V}$$

Solution (b)

At the instant the switch is turned on, the armature is not yet turning, and consequently $\mathscr{E}_b = 0$. In this case the armature current is

$$I_A = \frac{V}{R_A} = \frac{120 \text{ V}}{3 \; \Omega} = 40 \text{ A}$$

The field current is still 0.46 A, and the total starting current is

$$I = I_A + I_F$$
$$= 40 \text{ A} + 0.46 \text{ A} = 40.5 \text{ A}$$

39-8 THE TRANS-FORMER

It was noted earlier that a changing current in one wire loop will induce a current in a nearby loop. The induced current arises from the changing magnetic field associated with a changing current. Alternating current has a distinct advantage over direct current because of the inductive effect of a current which constantly varies in magnitude and direction. The most common application of this principle is offered by the *transformer*, a device which increases or decreases the voltage in an ac circuit.

A simple transformer is illustrated in Fig. 39-16. There are three essential parts: (1) a primary coil connected to an ac source, (2) a secondary coil, and (3) a soft iron core. As an alternating current is sent through the primary coil, magnetic flux lines move back and forth through the iron core, inducing an alternating current in the secondary coil.

Fig. 39-16 Transformer.

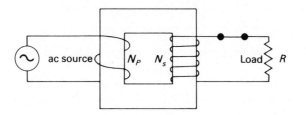

The constantly changing magnetic flux is established throughout the core of the transformer and passes through both primary and secondary coils. The emf $\mathscr{E}_p$ induced in the primary coil is given by

$$\mathscr{E}_p = -N_p \frac{\Delta\phi}{\Delta t} \qquad (39\text{-}15)$$

where N_p = number of primary turns
$\Delta\phi/\Delta t$ = rate at which flux changes

Similarly, the emf $\mathscr{E}_s$ induced in the secondary coil is

$$\mathscr{E}_s = -N_s \frac{\Delta\phi}{\Delta t} \qquad (39\text{-}16)$$

where N_s is the number of secondary turns. Since the same flux changes at the same rate through each coil, we can divide Eq. (39-15) by Eq. (39-16) to obtain

$$\boxed{\frac{\mathscr{E}_p}{\mathscr{E}_s} = \frac{N_p}{N_s}}$$ (39-17)

$$\frac{Primary\ voltage}{Secondary\ voltage} = \frac{primary\ turns}{secondary\ turns}$$

The induced voltage is in direct proportion to the number of turns. If the ratio of secondary turns N_s to primary turns N_p is varied, an input (primary) voltage can provide any desired output (secondary) voltage. For example, if there are 40 times as many turns in the secondary coil, an input voltage of 120 V will be increased to $40 \times 120 = 4800$ V in the secondary coil. A transformer which produces a larger output voltage is called a *step-up transformer*.

A *step-down transformer* can be constructed by making the number of primary turns greater than the number of secondary turns. Using a step-down transformer gives a lower output voltage.

The efficiency of a transformer is defined as the ratio of the power output to the power input. Recalling that electric power is equal to the product of voltage and current, we can write the efficiency E of a transformer as

$$E = \frac{\text{power output}}{\text{power input}} = \frac{\mathscr{E}_s i_s}{\mathscr{E}_p i_p}$$ (39-18)

where i_p and i_s are the currents in the primary coil and the secondary coil, respectively. Most electric transformers are carefully designed for extremely high efficiencies, normally above 90 percent.

It is important to recognize that there is no power gain as a result of transformer action. When the voltage is stepped up, the current must be stepped down, so that the product $\mathscr{E}i$ does not increase. To see this more clearly, let us assume that a given transformer is 100 percent efficient. For this perfect transformer, Eq. (39-18) becomes

$$\mathscr{E}_s i_s = \mathscr{E}_p i_p$$

or

$$\frac{i_p}{i_s} = \frac{\mathscr{E}_s}{\mathscr{E}_p}$$ (39-19)

This equation clearly shows the inverse relationship between current and induced voltage.

EXAMPLE 39-6   An ac generator which delivers 20 A at 6000 V is connected to a step-up transformer. What is the output current at 120,000 V if the transformer efficiency is 100 percent?

Solution   From Eq. (39-19),

$$i_s = \frac{\mathscr{E}_p i_p}{\mathscr{E}_s}$$

$$= \frac{(6000 \text{ V})(20 \text{ A})}{120{,}000 \text{ V}} = 1 \text{ A}$$

Note in the preceding example that the current was reduced to 1 A whereas the voltage was increased twentyfold. Since heat losses in transmission lines vary directly with the square of the current ($i^2 R$), this means that electric power can be transmitted for large distances without significant loss. When the electric power reaches its destination, step-down transformers are used to provide the desired current at lower voltages.

SUMMARY

Electromagnetic induction allows for the production of an electric current in a conducting wire. This is the basic operating principle behind many electrical devices. An understanding of the concepts summarized below is necessary for most applications involving the use of alternating current.

- A magnetic flux changing at the rate of 1 Wb/s will induce an emf of 1 V for each turn of a conductor. Symbolically,

$$\mathscr{E} = -N \frac{\Delta\phi}{\Delta t} \qquad \text{\textit{Induced emf}}$$

- Two principal ways in which the flux changes are

$$\Delta\phi = \Delta B A \qquad \Delta\phi = B \, \Delta A$$

- The induced emf due to a wire of length l moving with a velocity v at an angle θ with a field **B** is given by

$$\mathscr{E} = Blv \sin \theta \qquad \text{\textit{Emf due to Moving Wire}}$$

- According to *Lenz's law*, the induced current must be in such a direction that it produces a magnetic force which opposes the force causing the motion.
- *Fleming's rule:* If the thumb, forefinger, and middle finger of the right hand are held at right angles to each other, with the thumb pointing in the direction in which the wire is moving and the forefinger pointing in the field direction (N to S), the middle finger will point in the direction of induced conventional current. (*Motion–flux–current*).
- The instantaneous emf generated by a coil of N turns moving with an angular velocity ω or frequency f is

$$\mathscr{E}_{\text{inst}} = NBA\omega \sin \omega t \qquad \mathscr{E}_{\text{inst}} = 2\pi f NBA \sin 2\pi f t$$

- The maximum emf occurs when the sin is zero. Thus

$$\mathscr{E}_{max} = NBA\omega \qquad \mathscr{E}_{max} = \mathscr{E}_{max} \sin 2\pi ft$$

- Since the induced current is proportional to $\mathscr{E}$, we also have

$$i_{inst} = i_{max} \sin 2\pi ft \qquad \textit{Instantaneous Current}$$

- The back emf in a motor is the induced voltage which causes a reduction in the net voltage delivered to a circuit.

Applied voltage − induced back emf = net voltage

$$V - \mathscr{E}_b = IR \qquad \mathscr{E}_b = V - IR$$

- For a transformer having N_p primary and N_s secondary turns

$$\frac{Primary\ voltage}{Secondary\ voltage} = \frac{primary\ turns}{secondary\ turns} \qquad \frac{\mathscr{E}_p}{\mathscr{E}_s} = \frac{N_p}{N_s}$$

- The efficiency of a transformer is

$$E = \frac{\text{power output}}{\text{power input}} = \frac{\mathscr{E}_p i_p}{\mathscr{E}_s i_s} \qquad \textit{Transformer Efficiency}$$

QUESTIONS

39-1. Define the following terms:

   a. Induced emf   **i.** Electromagnetic induction

   b. Lenz's law   **j.** Back emf

   c. Ac generator   **k.** Shunt motor

   d. Dc generator   **l.** Series motor

   e. Field magnet   **m.** Compound motor

   f. Armature   **n.** Step-up transformer

   g. Slip rings   **o.** Step-down transformer

   h. Commutator   **p.** Transformer efficiency

39-2. Discuss the various factors which influence the magnitude of an induced emf in a length of wire moving in a magnetic field.

39-3. A bar magnet is held in a vertical position with the north pole facing upward. If a closed-loop coil is dropped over the north end of the magnet, what is the direction of the induced current viewed from the top of the magnet?

39-4. A circular loop is suspended with its plane perpendicular to a magnetic field directed from left to right. The loop is removed from the field by moving it upward quickly. What is the direction of the induced current viewed along the field direction? Is a force required to remove the loop from the field?

39-5. An induction coil is essentially a transformer which operates on direct current. As shown in Fig. 39-17, the induction coil consists of a few primary

Fig. 39-17 Induction coil.

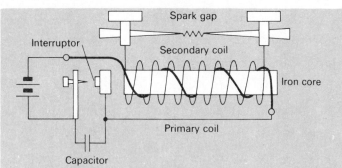

turns wound around an iron core with a large number of secondary turns surrounding the primary. A battery current magnetizes the core so that it attracts the armature of the vibrator and opens the circuit periodically. When the circuit is opened, the field collapses, and a large emf is induced in the secondary coil, producing a spark at the output terminals. What is the function of the capacitor C connected in parallel with the vibrator? Explain how an induction coil is used in the ignition system of an automobile.

39-6. Explain clearly how an ac generator can be converted to a dc generator. How would you proceed to convert an ac generator into an ac motor?

39-7. When the electric motor in a plant is starting, a worker notices that the lights are momentarily dimmed. Explain.

39-8. What type of dc motor should be purchased to operate a winch used to lift heavy objects? Why?

39-9. What type of motor should be used to operate an electric fan where uniform torque is desired at high speeds?

39-10. Explain how the existence of back emf in a motor helps keep its speed constant. *Hint:* What happens to $\mathscr{E}_b$ and I when the armature speed increases or decreases?

39-11. There are three primary ways in which power is lost through the operation of a transformer: (1) wire resistance losses, (2) hysteresis losses, and (3) eddy-current losses. (*Eddy currents* are induced current loops which occur in the mass of a magnetic material resulting from a changing flux.) Explain how energy is wasted by these three processes.

39-12. Explain with the use of diagrams how transformers make it possible to transmit current economically from power installations to homes many miles away.

39-13. An ac generator produces 60 Hz alternating voltage. How many degrees of armature rotation will correspond to one-fourth of a cycle?

39-14. Why is it more economical for power companies to provide alternating current than direct current?

39-15. Prepare a brief report on the following topics and explain the part played by electromagnetic induction.

a. The betatron   **f.** Electric power transmission
b. Induction coil   **g.** The universal motor
c. The telephone   **h.** Induction motor
d. Eddy currents   **i.** Synchronous motor
e. Magnetohydrodynamic generator

PROBLEMS

39-1. A coil of 300 turns moving perpendicular to the flux in a uniform magnetic field experiences a change in flux linkage of 0.23 mWb in 0.002 s. What is the induced emf?

Ans. −34.5 V.

39-2. The magnetic flux linking a loop of wire changes from 5 to 2 mWb in 0.1 s. What is the average induced emf?

39-3. A coil of 120 turns is 90 mm in diameter and has its plane perpendicular to a magnetic field of flux density 60 mT which is produced by a nearby electromagnet. The current in the electromagnet is cut off, and as the field collapses an emf of 6 V is induced in the coil. How long does it take for the field to disappear?

Ans. 7.63 ms.

39-4. A coil of 56 turns has an area of 0.3 m². Its plane is perpendicular to a magnetic field of flux density 7 mT. If this field collapses to zero in 6 ms, what is the induced emf?

39-5. The flux through a coil having 200 turns from 0.06 Wb to 0.025 Wb in 0.5 s. The coil is connected to an electric light, and the combined resistance is 2 Ω. What is the average induced emf and what average current is delivered to the light filament?

Ans. 14 V, 7 A.

39-6. A coil of area 0.2 m² has 80 turns of wire and is suspended with its plane perpendicular to a uniform field. What must the flux density be for an average emf of −2 V to be induced as the coil is flipped parallel to the field in 0.5 s?

39-7. A wire 0.15 m long moves at a constant velocity of 4 m/s in a direction that is 36° with respect to a magnetic field of 0.4 T directed perpendicular to the wire. Determine the induced emf.

Ans. 0.141 V.

39-8. A 0.2 m long wire moves at an angle of 28° with magnetic flux of density 8 mT. The wire length is perpendicular to the flux. What velocity v is required to induce an emf of 60 mV?

39-9. The magnetic field in the air gap between the magnetic poles and the armature of an electric generator has a flux density of 0.7 T. The length of the wires on the armature is 0.5 m. How fast must these wires move in order to generate a maximum emf of 1 V in each armature wire?

Ans. 2.86 m/s.

39-10. A 90-mm length of wire moves with an upward velocity of 35 m/s between the poles of a magnet. The flux is directed from left to right and has a density of 80 mT. If the resistance in the wire is 5 mΩ, what are the magnitude and direction of the induced current?

39-11. An armature in an ac generator consists of 500 turns, each having an area of 60 cm². The armature is rotated at a frequency of 3600 rpm in a uniform field of flux density 2 mT. **(a)** What is the frequency of the alternating voltage? **(b)** What is the maximum emf generated? **(c)** What is the instantaneous emf at the instant when the plane of the coil makes an angle of 60° with the magnetic flux?

Ans. **(a)** 60 Hz **(b)** 2.26 V **(c)** 1.13 V.

39-12. The armature of an ac generator has 800 turns, each having an area of 0.25 m². The coil rotates at a constant 600 rpm in a 3-mT magnetic field. **(a)** What is the maximum induced emf? **(b)** What is the instantaneous emf 0.43 s after the coil passes a position of zero emf?

39-13. A circular coil has 70 turns, each 50 mm in diameter. Assume that the coil rotates about an axis that is perpendicular to a magnetic field of 0.8 T. How fast in revolutions per second must the coil rotate in order to generate a maximum emf of 110 V?

Ans. 159 rev/s.

39-14. A generator develops an emf of 120 V and has a terminal potential difference of 115 V when the armature current is 25 A. What is the resistance of the armature?

39-15. The armature coils of the starting motor in an automobile have a resistance of 0.05 Ω. The motor is driven by a 12-V battery, and when the armature is moving at its operating speed, a back emf of 6V is generated. **(a)** What is the starting current? **(b)** What is the current at operating speed? Ignore the internal resistance and other circuit resistances.

Ans. **(a)** 240 A **(b)** 120 A.

39-16. A 220-V dc motor draws a current of 10 A in operation and has an armature resistance of 0.4 Ω. **(a)** What is the back emf when the motor is operating? **(b)** What is the starting current?

39-17. A 120-V series-wound dc motor has a field resistance of 90 Ω and an armature resistance of 10 Ω. When it is operating at full speed, a back emf of 80 V is generated. **(a)** What is the total resistance of the motor? **(b)** What is the initial current drawn by the motor? **(c)** What is the operating current?

Ans. **(a)** 100 Ω **(b)** 1.2 A **(c)** 0.4 A.

39-18. The efficiency of the motor in Prob. 19-3 is the ratio of the power output to the power input during normal operation. Determine the efficiency based on the known data.

39-19. A 110-V shunt motor has a field resistance of 200 Ω and an armature resistance of 10 Ω. When the motor is operating at full speed, the back emf is 90 V. **(a)** Determine the initial starting current. **(b)** What is the operating current?

Ans. **(a)** 11.55 A **(b)** 2.55 A.

39-20. A 120-V shunt motor has a field resistance of 160 Ω and an armature resistance of 1 Ω. When the motor is operating at full speed, it draws a current of 8 A. **(a)** What is the starting current? **(b)** What series resistance must be added to reduce the starting current to 30 A?

39-21. A shunt generator has a field resistance of 400 Ω and an armature resistance of 2 Ω. The generator delivers a power of 4000 W to an external line at 120 V. What is the emf of the generator?

Ans. 186.3 V.

39-22. A shunt motor connected across a 117-V line generates a back emf of 112 V when the armature current is 10 A. What is the armature resistance?

39-23. A step-up transformer has 400 secondary turns and only 100 primary turns. An alternating voltage of 120 V is connected to the primary coil. What is the output voltage?

Ans. 480 V.

39-24. A step-down transformer is used to drop an alternating voltage from 10,000 to 500 V. What must be the ratio of secondary turns to primary turns? If the input current is 1 A and the efficiency of the transformer is 100 percent, what is the output current?

39-25. A step-up transformer has 80 primary turns and 720 secondary turns. The efficiency of the transformer is 95 per cent. If the primary draws a current of 20 A at 120 V, what are the current and voltage for the secondary?

Ans. 2.11 A, 1080 V.

39-26. A girl wishes to make a transformer that will lower the house voltage from 110 to 11 V in order to operate a small electric bell. She takes a piece of soft iron and some insulated copper wire. What must be the ratio of primary turns to secondary turns? If the current in the primary winding is 0.6 A, what current is delivered to the bell? Assume 100 percent efficiency.

40 *Alternating-Current Circuits*

OBJECTIVES: After completing this chapter, you should be able to:

1. Determine the instantaneous current for charging and discharging a *capacitor* and for the growth and decay of current in an *inductor*.

2. Write and apply equations for calculating the *inductance* and *capacitance* for inductors and capacitors in an ac circuit.

3. Explain with diagrams the phase relationships for a circuit with (*a*) pure resistance, (*b*) pure capacitance, and (*c*) pure inductance.

4. Write and apply equations for calculating the *impedance*, the *phase angle*, and the *effective current* for a series ac circuit containing resistance, capacitance, and inductance.

5. Write and apply an equation for calculating the resonant frequency for an ac circuit.

6. Define and be able to determine the *power factor* for a series ac circuit.

About 99 percent of the energy generated in the United States is in ac form. There are good reasons for the predominant use of ac circuits. A rotating coil in a magnetic field induces an alternating emf in an extremely efficient manner. Besides, the transformer provides a convenient method of transmitting ac currents over long distances with a minimal power loss.

The only element of importance in the dc circuit (besides a source of emf) was the resistor. Since alternating currents behave very differently from direct currents, additional circuit elements become important. In addition to the normal resistance, electromagnetic induction and capacitance play important roles. In this chapter we present a few elementary aspects of alternating current in electric circuits.

In Chap. 33 we discussed the capacitor as an electrostatic device able to store charge. Charging and discharging capacitors in an ac circuit provide an effective means of regulating and controlling the flow of charge. Before discussing the effects of capacitance in an ac circuit, however, it will be useful to describe the growth and decay of charge on a capacitor.

Consider the circuit illustrated in Fig. 40-1, containing only a capacitor and a resistor. When the switch is moved to S_1, the capacitor begins to be

Fig. 40-1 Circuit diagram illustrating a method for charging and discharging a capacitor.

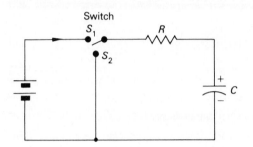

charged rapidly by the current i. However, as the potential difference Q/C between the capacitor plates rises, the rate of flow of charge to the capacitor decreases. At any instant, the iR drop through the resistor must equal the difference between the terminal voltage V_B of the battery and the back emf of the capacitor. Symbolically,

$$V_B - \frac{Q}{C} = iR \qquad (40\text{-}1)$$

where i = instantaneous current
Q = instantaneous charge on capacitor

Initially, the charge Q is zero, and the current i is a maximum. Thus, at time $t = 0$,

$$Q = 0 \qquad \text{and} \qquad i = \frac{V_B}{R} \qquad (40\text{-}2)$$

As the charge on the capacitor builds up, it produces a back emf Q/C opposing the flow of additional charge; the current i decreases. Both the increase in charge and the decrease in current are exponential functions, as shown by the curves in Fig. 40-2. If it were possible to continue charging indefinitely, the limits at $t = \infty$ would be

$$Q = CV_B \qquad \text{and} \qquad i = 0 \qquad (40\text{-}3)$$

Fig. 40-2 (*a*) The charge on a capacitor rises, approaching but never reaching its maximum value. (*b*) The current decreases, approaching zero as the charge builds up to its maximum value.

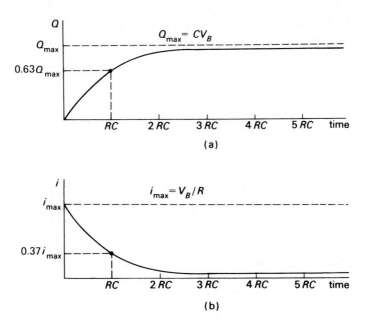

(a)

(b)

The methods of calculus applied to Eq. (40-1) show that the instantaneous charge is given by

$$Q = CV_b(1 - e^{-t/RC})$$ (40-4)

and that the instantaneous current is given by

$$i = \frac{V_B}{R} e^{-t/RC}$$ (40-5)

where t is the time. The logarithmic constant $e = 2.71828$ to six significant figures. Substitution of $t = 0$ and $t = \infty$ into the above relations will yield Eqs. (40-2) and (40-3), respectively.

The equations for computing instantaneous charge and current are simplified at the particular instant when $t = RC$. This time, usually denoted by τ, is called the *time constant* of the circuit.

$$\tau = RC$$ *Time Constant* (40-6)

It is seen from Eq. (40-4) that the charge Q rises to $1 - 1/e$ times its final value in one time constant:

$$Q = CV_B\left(1 - \frac{1}{e}\right) = 0.63CV_B$$ (40-7)

In a capacitance circuit, the charge on a capacitor will rise to 63 percent of its maximum value after charging for a period of one time constant.

Substituting $\tau = RC$ into Eq. (40-5) shows that the current delivered to the capacitor decreases to $1/e$ times its initial value in one time constant:

$$i = \frac{V_B}{R}\frac{1}{e} = 0.37\frac{V_B}{R} \qquad (40\text{-}8)$$

In a capacitive circuit, the current delivered to a capacitor will decrease to 37 percent of its initial value after being charged for a period of one time constant.

Now let us consider the problem of a discharging capacitor. For practical reasons, *a capacitor is considered to be fully charged after a period of time equal to five time constants (5RC).* If the switch in Fig. 40-1 has been in position S_1 for at least this long, it can be assumed that the maximum charge CV_B is on the capacitor. By moving the switch to position S_2 the voltage source is removed from the circuit, and a path is provided for discharge. In this case, the voltage equation (40-1) reduces to

$$-\frac{Q}{C} = iR \qquad (40\text{-}9)$$

Both the charge and the current decay along curves similar to that shown for the charging current in Fig. 40-2b. The instantaneous charge is found from

$$\boxed{Q = CV_B e^{-1/RC}} \qquad (40\text{-}10)$$

and the instantaneous current is given by

$$\boxed{i = \frac{-V_B}{R} e^{-t/RC}} \qquad (40\text{-}11)$$

The negative sign in the current equation indicates that the direction of i in the circuit has been reversed.

After discharging for one time constant, the charge and the current will have decayed to $1/e$ times their initial values. This can be shown by substituting τ into Eqs. (40-10) and (40-11).

In a capacitance circuit, the charge and the current will decay to 37 percent of their initial values after the capacitor has discharged for a length of time equal to one time constant.

The capacitor is considered to be fully discharged after five time constants (5RC).

EXAMPLE 40-1   A 12-V battery having an internal resistance of 1.5 Ω is connected to a 4-μF capacitor through leads having a resistance of 0.5 Ω. (*a*) What is the initial current delivered to the capacitor? (*b*) How long will it take to charge the capacitor fully? (*c*) What is the value of the current after one time constant?

Solution (a)   Initially, there is no back emf from the capacitor. Hence the current delivered to the circuit is the emf of the battery divided by the total resistance in the circuit:

$$i = \frac{\mathscr{E}_B}{R + r} = \frac{12 \text{ V}}{1.5 \ \Omega + 0.5 \ \Omega} = 6 \text{ A}$$

Solution (b)   The capacitor can be considered fully charged after a time

$$t = 5RC = (5)(2 \ \Omega)(4 \ \mu\text{F}) = 40 \ \mu\text{s}$$

Solution (c)   After one time constant RC, the current will have decayed to 37 percent of its initial value. Thus

$$i_\tau = (0.37)(6 \text{ A}) = 2.22 \text{ A}$$

In the preceding discussions, we simplified the approach by using direct currents. When an alternating voltage is impressed upon a capacitor, there are surges of charge into and out of the capacitor plates. Therefore an alternating current is maintained in a circuit even though there is no path between the capacitor plates. The effect of capacitance in an ac circuit will be discussed later.

40-2 THE INDUCTOR

Another important element in an ac circuit is the *inductor*, which consists of a continuous loop or coil of wire. (See Fig. 40-3.) In Chap. 39 we showed that a change in magnetic flux in the region enclosed by such a coil will induce an emf in the coil. Until now, the flux changes originated from sources outside the coil

Fig. 40-3 The inductor.

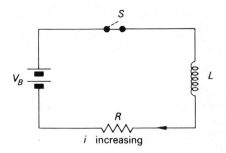

i increasing

itself. We now consider the emf induced in a coil as a result of changes in its *own* current. Regardless of how the flux change occurs, the induced emf must be given by

$$\mathscr{E} = -N \frac{\Delta\phi}{\Delta t} \tag{40-12}$$

where N = number of turns
$\Delta\phi/\Delta t$ = rate at which flux changes

When the current through an inductor increases or decreases, a *self-induced* emf arises in the circuit which *opposes* the change. Consider the circuit illustrated in Fig. 40-3. When the switch is closed, the current rises from zero to its maximum value $i = V_B/R$. The inductor responds to this increasing current by setting up an induced back emf. Since the geometry of the inductor is fixed, the rate of change in flux, $\Delta\phi/\Delta t$, or the induced emf $\mathscr{E}$, is proportional to the rate of change in current, $\Delta i/\Delta t$. This proportionality is expressed in the equation

$$\mathscr{E} = -L\,\frac{\Delta i}{\Delta t} \tag{40-13}$$

The proportionality constant L is called the *inductance* of the circuit. Solving explicitly for the inductance in Eq. (40-13), we write

$$L = -\frac{\mathscr{E}}{\Delta i/\Delta t} \tag{40-14}$$

The unit of inductance is the *henry* (H).

> *A given inductor has an inductance of one henry (H) if an emf of one volt is induced by a current changing at the rate of one ampere per second.*

$$1\ \text{H} = 1\ \text{V} \cdot \text{s/A}$$

The inductance of a coil depends upon its geometry, the number of turns, the spacing of the turns, and the permeability of its core but not upon voltage and current values. In this respect, the inductor is similar to capacitors and resistors.

We shall now consider the growth and decay of current in an inductive circuit. The circuit illustrated in Fig. 40-4 contains an inductor L, a resistor R,

Fig. 40-4 Circuit for studying inductance.

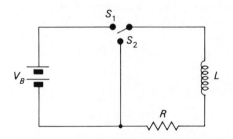

and a battery V_B. The switch is positioned so that the battery can be alternately connected and disconnected from the circuit. When the switch is moved to position S_1, a current begins to grow in the circuit. As the current rises, the induced emf $-L(\Delta i/\Delta t)$ is established in opposition to the battery voltage V_B. The net emf must equal the iR drop through the resistor. Thus

$$V_B - L\,\frac{\Delta i}{\Delta t} = iR \tag{40-15}$$

A mathematical analysis of Eq. (40-15) will show that the rise in current as a function of time is given by

$$i = \frac{V_B}{R} (1 - e^{-(R/L)t}) \tag{40-16}$$

This equation shows that the current i is zero when $t = 0$ and has a maximum of V_B/R when $t = \infty$. The effect of inductance in a circuit is to delay the establishment of this maximum current. The rise and decay of current in an inductive circuit are shown in Fig. 40-5.

Fig. 40-5 Rise and decay of current in an inductor.

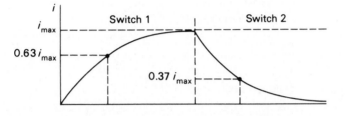

The time constant for an inductive circuit is

$$\boxed{\tau = \frac{L}{R}} \tag{40-17}$$

τ is in *seconds* when L is in *henrys* and R is in *ohms*. Insertion of this value into Eq. (40-16) shows that:

> *In an inductive circuit, the current will rise to 63 percent of its final value in one time constant (L/R).*

After the current in Fig. 40-4 has attained a steady value, if the switch is moved to position S_2, the current will decay exponentially, as shown in Fig. 40-5. The equation for the decay is

$$\boxed{i = \frac{V_B}{R} e^{-(R/L)t}} \tag{40-18}$$

Substitution of L/R into Eq. (40-18) shows that:

> *In an inductive circuit, the current decays to 37 percent of its initial value in one time constant (L/R).*

Once again, for practical reasons the rise or decay time for an inductor is considered to be five time constants $(5L/R)$.

40-3 ALTER- NATING CURRENTS

Now that we are familiar with the basic elements in an ac circuit, it is necessary to understand more about alternating currents. The quantitative description of an alternating current is much more complicated than that for direct currents, whose magnitude and direction are constant. An alternating current flows back and forth in a circuit and has no "direction" in the sense direct current has. Additionally, the magnitude varies sinusoidally with time, as we learned in our discussions of the ac generator.

The variation in emf or current for an ac circuit can be represented by a rotating vector or by a sine wave. These representations are compared in Fig. 40-6. The vertical component of the rotating vector at any instant is the instantaneous magnitude of the voltage or the current. One complete revolution of the rotating vector or one complete sine wave on the curve represents one *cycle*.

Fig. 40-6 Rotating vector and its corresponding sine wave can be used to represent ac current or voltage.

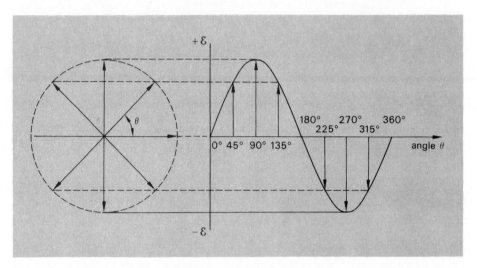

The number of complete cycles per second experienced by an alternating current is called its *frequency* and provides an important description of the current. The relationship between the instantaneous emf $\mathcal{E}$ or the instantaneous current i and the frequency was established in Chap. 39:

$$\mathcal{E} = \mathcal{E}_{max} \sin 2\pi ft \qquad (40\text{-}19)$$

$$i = i_{max} \sin 2\pi ft \qquad (40\text{-}20)$$

Note that the average value for the current in an ac circuit is zero since the magnitude alternates between i_{max} and $-i_{max}$. However, even though there is no *net* current, charge is in motion, and electric energy can be released in the form of heat or useful work. The best method of measuring the effective strength of alternating currents is to find the dc value which will produce the same *heating* effect or develop the same *power* as the alternating current. This current value, called the *effective current* i_{eff}, is found to be 0.707 times the maximum current. A similar relation holds for the effective emf or voltage in an ac circuit. Thus

$$i_{eff} = 0.707 i_{max} \qquad (40\text{-}21)$$

$$\mathcal{E}_{eff} = 0.707 \mathcal{E}_{max} \qquad (40\text{-}22)$$

One effective ampere is that alternating current which will develop the same power as one ampere of direct current.

One effective volt is that alternating voltage which will produce an effective current of one ampere through a resistance of one ohm.

Ac meters are calibrated to show effective values. For example, if an ac meter measures household voltage to be 120 V at 10 A, Eqs. (40-21) and (40-22) will show that the maximum values of current and voltage are

$$i_{max} = \frac{10 \text{ A}}{0.707} = 14.14 \text{ A}$$

$$V_{max} = \frac{120 \text{ V}}{0.707} = 170 \text{ V}$$

Therefore, the house voltage actually varies between $+170$ and -170 V while the current ranges from $+14.14$ to -14.14 A. The usual frequency of voltage variation is 60 Hz.

40-4 PHASE RELATION IN AC CIRCUITS

In all dc circuits, the voltage and the current reach maximum and zero values at the same time and are said to be *in phase*. The effects of inductance and capacitance in ac circuits prevent the voltage and current from reaching maxima and minima at the same time. In other words, the current and voltage in most ac circuits are *out of phase*.

To understand phase relations in an ac circuit, suppose we first consider a circuit containing a *pure* resistor in series with an ac generator, as in Fig. 40-7. This is an idealized circuit in which the inductive and capacitive effects are negligible. Many household devices, such as lights, heaters, and toasters, approximate a condition of pure resistance. In such devices, the instantaneous voltage V and current i are in phase. That is, variations in voltage will

Fig. 40-7 In a circuit containing pure resistance, the voltage and current are in phase.

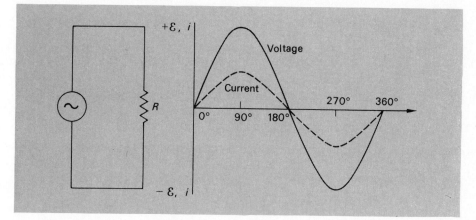

result in simultaneous variations of current. When the voltage is a maximum, the current is also a maximum. When the voltage is zero, the current is zero.

Next, we consider the phase relation between current and voltage across a *pure inductor*. The circuit illustrated in Fig. 40-8 contains only an inductor in series with the ac generator. We have seen that the presence of inductance in a circuit whose current is changing at the rate $\Delta i/\Delta t$ results in a back emf

$$\mathscr{E} = -L \frac{\Delta i}{\Delta t}$$

which delays the current in reaching its maximum. The voltage reaches a maximum while the current is still at zero. When the voltage reaches a minimum, the current is at a maximum. In a circuit containing only inductance, the voltage is said to lead (occur before) the current by one-fourth of a cycle (or 90°). See the curve in Fig. 40-8.

In a circuit containing pure inductance, the voltage leads the current by 90°.

Fig. 40-8 In a pure inductive circuit, the voltage leads the current by 90°.

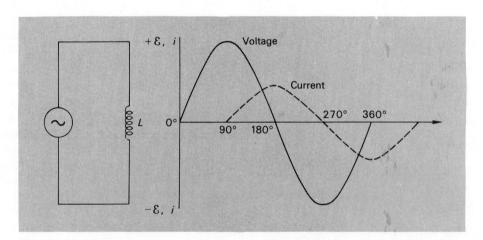

The effect of capacitance in an ac circuit is opposite to that of inductance. For the circuit shown in Fig. 40-9, the voltage must *lag behind* the current since the flow of charge to the capacitor is necessary to build up an opposing emf. When the applied voltage is decreasing, charge flows from the capacitor. The rate of flow of this charge reaches a maximum when the applied voltage is zero.

In a circuit containing pure capacitance, the voltage lags the current by 90°.

This means that the variations in voltage occur one-fourth of a cycle later than the corresponding variations in current.

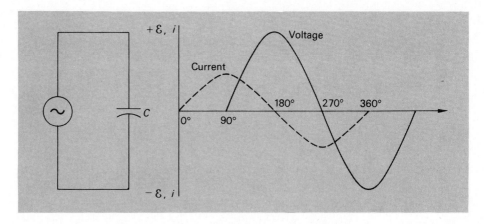

Fig. 40-9 In a circuit containing only capacitance, the voltage lags the current by 90°.

**40-5
REACTANCE**

In a dc circuit, the only opposition to current results from the material through which it passes. Resistive heat losses, which obey Ohm's law, also occur in ac circuits. However, in addition to normal resistance, one must contend with inductance and capacitance. Both inductors and capacitors impede the flow of an alternating current, and their effects must be considered along with the opposition of resistance.

The **reactance** of an ac circuit may be defined as its nonresistive opposition to the flow of alternating current.

We first consider the opposition to the flow of an alternating current through an inductor. Such opposition, called *inductive reactance*, arises from the self-induced back emf produced by a changing current. The magnitude of the inductive reactance X_L is determined by the inductance L of the inductor and by the frequency f of the alternating current and can be found from the formula

$$\boxed{X_L = 2\pi f L} \tag{40-23}$$

The inductive reactance is measured in *ohms* when the inductance is in *henrys* and the frequency is in *hertz*.

The effective current i in an inductor is determined from its inductive reactance X_L and the effective voltage V by an equation analogous to Ohm's law:

$$V = iX_L \tag{40-24}$$

EXAMPLE 40-2

A coil having an inductance of 0.5 H is connected to a 120-V 60-Hz power source. If the resistance of the coil is neglected, what is the effective current through the coil?

Solution

The inductive reactance is

$$X_L = 2\pi f L = (2\pi)(60 \text{ Hz})(0.5 \text{ H})$$

$$= 188.4 \ \Omega$$

The current is found from Eq. (40-24):

$$i = \frac{V}{X_L} = \frac{120 \text{ V}}{188.4 \ \Omega} = 0.637 \text{ A}$$

Opposition to alternating current is also experienced because of the capacitance in a circuit. The *capacitive reactance* X_C is found from

$$X_C = \frac{1}{2\pi f C} \tag{40-25}$$

where C = capacitance
f = frequency of alternating current

Capacitive reactance is expressed in *ohms* when C is in *farads* and f is in *hertz*.

Once the capacitance reactance X_C of a capacitor is known, the effective current i can be found from

$$V = iX_C \tag{40-26}$$

where V is the applied voltage.

40-6 THE SERIES AC CIRCUIT

In general, an ac circuit contains resistance, capacitance, and inductance in varying amounts. A series combination of these parameters is illustrated in Fig. 40-10. The total voltage drop in a dc circuit is the simple sum of the drop across each element in the circuit. However, in the ac circuit, the voltage and current are not in phase with each other. Recall that V_R is always in phase with the current but V_L leads the current by $90°$ and V_C lags the current by $90°$. Clearly, if we are to determine the effective voltage V of the entire circuit, we must develop a means of treating phase differences.

Fig. 40-10 Series ac circuit containing resistance, inductance, and capacitance.

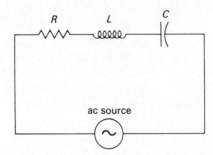

This can best be accomplished by using a vector diagram, called the *phase diagram.* (See Fig. 40-11.) In this method, the effective values of V_R, V_L, and V_C are plotted as rotating vectors. The phase relationship is expressed in terms of the phase angle ϕ, which is a measure of how much the voltage leads the current in a particular circuit element. For example, in a pure resistor, the voltage and the current are in phase and $\phi = 0$. For an inductor, $\phi = +90°$,

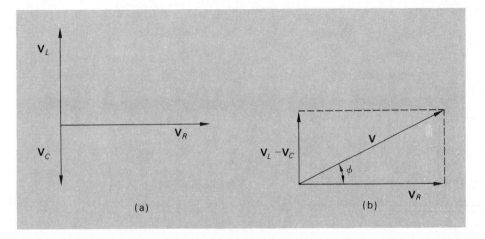

Fig. 40-11 Phase diagram.

(a)

(b)

and in a capacitor $\phi = -90°$. The negative phase angle occurs when the voltage lags behind the current. Following this scheme, V_R appears as a vector along the x axis, V_L is represented by a vector pointing vertically upward, and V_C is directed downward.

The effective voltage **V** in an ac circuit can be defined as the vector sum of $\mathbf{V}_R$, $\mathbf{V}_L$, and $\mathbf{V}_C$ as they exist on the phase diagram. It can be seen from the figure that the magnitude of **V** is

$$V = \sqrt{V_R^2 + (V_L - V_C)^2} \tag{40-27}$$

You should verify this equation by applying Pythagoras' theorem to the vector diagram.

Note from the phase diagram that a value of V_L which is greater than V_C results in a positive phase angle. In other words, if the circuit is inductive, the voltage leads the current. In a capacitive circuit, $X_C > X_L$, and a negative phase angle will result, indicating that the voltage lags the current. In any case, the magnitude of the phase angle can be found from

$$\tan \phi = \frac{V_L - V_C}{V_R} \tag{40-28}$$

A more useful form for Eq. (40-27) can be found by recalling that

$$V_R = iR \qquad V_L = iX_L \qquad V_C = iX_C$$

Upon substitution, we find that

$$V = i\sqrt{R^2 + (X_L - X_C)^2} \tag{40-29}$$

The quantity multiplied by the current in Eq. (40-29) is a measure of the combined opposition that the circuit offers to alternating current. It is called the *impedance* and is denoted by the symbol Z.

$$Z = \sqrt{R^2 + (X_L - X_C)^2} \tag{40-30}$$

The higher the impedance in a circuit, the lower the current for a given voltage. Since R, L_L, and X_C are measured in *ohms*, the impedance is also expressed in *ohms*.

Therefore the effective current i in an ac circuit is given by

$$i = \frac{V}{Z} \qquad (40\text{-}31)$$

where V = applied voltage
$\qquad$ Z = impedance in circuit

It must be remembered that Z depends on the frequency of the alternating current as well as on the resistance, inductance, and capacitance.

Since the voltage across each element depends directly upon resistance or reactance, an alternative phase diagram can be constructed by treating R, X_L, and X_C as vector quantities. Such a diagram can be used to compute the impedance, as indicated in Fig. 40-12. The phase angle ϕ in this representation can be found from

$$\tan \phi = \frac{X_L - X_C}{R} \qquad (40\text{-}32)$$

Of course, this angle is the same as that given by Eq. (40-28).

Fig. 40-12 Impedance diagram.

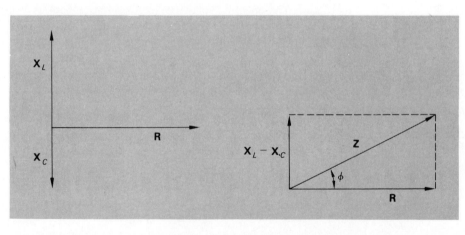

EXAMPLE 40-3 A 40-Ω resistor, a 0.4-H inductor, and a 10-μF capacitor are connected in series with an ac source which generates 120-V 60-Hz alternating current. (*a*) Find the impedance of the circuit. (*b*) What is the phase angle? (*c*) Determine the effective current in the circuit.

Solution (a) We must first compute X_L and X_C as follows:

$$X_L = 2\pi f L = (2\pi)(60 \text{ Hz})(0.4 \text{ H})$$

$$= 151 \ \Omega$$

$$X_C = \frac{1}{2\pi f C} = \frac{1}{(2\pi)(60 \text{ Hz})(10 \times 10^{-6} \text{ F})}$$

$$= 265 \ \Omega$$

The impedance of the circuit is

$$Z = \sqrt{R^2 + (X_L - X_C)^2}$$
$$= \sqrt{(40\ \Omega)^2 + (151\ \Omega - 265\ \Omega)^2} = 121\ \Omega$$

Solution (b)   From Eq. (40-32), the phase angle is

$$\tan \phi = \frac{151\ \Omega - 265\ \Omega}{40\ \Omega} = -2.85$$

$$\phi = -71°$$

The negative sign is used to indicate that the phase angle is in the fourth quadrant.

Solution (c)   Finally, we can determine the effective current from the known impedance.

$$i = \frac{V}{Z} = \frac{120\ \text{V}}{121\ \Omega} = 0.992\ \text{A}$$

The negative phase angle indicates that the voltage will lag behind this effective current. The circuit is more capacitive than it is inductive.

**40-7
RESONANCE**   Since inductance causes the current to lag behind the voltage and capacitance causes the current to lead the voltage, their combined effect is to cancel each other. The total reactance is given by $X_L - X_C$, and the impedance in a circuit is a minimum when $X_L = X_C$. When this is true, only the resistance R remains and the current will be a maximum. Setting $X_L = X_C$, we can write

$$2\pi f_r L = \frac{1}{2\pi f_r C}$$

and

$$\boxed{f_r = \frac{1}{2\pi\sqrt{LC}}} \qquad\qquad (40\text{-}33)$$

When the applied voltage has this frequency, called the *resonant frequency*, the current in the circuit will be a maximum. Additionally, it should be pointed out that since the current is limited only by resistance, it will be in phase with the voltage.

The antenna circuit in a radio receiver contains a variable capacitor which acts as a tuner. The capacitance is varied until the resonant frequency is equal to a particular signal frequency. The current peaks when this happens, and the receiver responds to the incoming signal.

**40-8
THE POWER
FACTOR**   In ac circuits, no power is consumed because of capacitance or inductance. Energy is merely stored at one instant and released at another, causing the current and voltage to be out of phase. Whenever the current and voltage are in

phase, the power P delivered is a maximum given by

$$P = iV$$

where i = effective current
V = effective voltage

This condition is satisfied when the ac circuit contains only resistance R or when the circuit is in resonance ($X_L = X_C$).

Normally, however, an ac circuit contains sufficient reactance to limit the effective power. In any case, the power delivered to the circuit is a function only of the component of the voltage V which is in phase with the current. From Fig. 40-11, this component is V_R, and we can write

$$V_R = V \cos \phi$$

where ϕ is the phase angle. Thus the effective power consumed in an ac circuit is

$$\boxed{P = iV \cos \phi} \tag{40-34}$$

The quantity $\cos \phi$ is called the *power factor* of the circuit. Note that $\cos \phi$ can vary from zero in a circuit containing pure reactance ($\phi = 90°$) to unity in a circuit containing only resistance ($\phi = 0°$).

Equation (40-21) and Fig. 40-12 show that the power factor can also be found from

$$\boxed{\cos \phi = \frac{R}{Z} = \frac{R}{\sqrt{R^2 + (X_L - X_C)^2}}} \tag{40-35}$$

EXAMPLE 40-4   (*a*) What is the power factor for the circuit described in Example 40-3? (*b*) What power is absorbed in the circuit?

Solution (*a*)   The power factor is found from Eq. (40-35):

$$\cos \phi = \frac{R}{Z} = \frac{40 \ \Omega}{121 \ \Omega} = 0.33$$

Solution (*b*)   The power absorbed in the circuit is

$$P = iV \cos \phi = (0.992 \text{ A})(120 \text{ V})(0.33)$$

$$= 39.3 \text{ W}$$

The power factor is sometimes expressed as a percentage instead of as a decimal. For example, the power factor of 0.33 in the above example could be expressed as 33 percent. Most commercial ac circuits have power factors from 80 to 90 percent because they usually contain more inductance than capacitance. Since this requires the electric power companies to furnish more current for a given power, the power companies extend a lower rate to users with power factors above 90 percent. Commercial users can improve their inductive power factors by adding capacitors, for instance.

SUMMARY

There are three principal elements in ac circuits: the *resistor*, the *capacitor*, and the *inductor*. A resistor is affected by ac current in the same manner as for dc circuits, and the current is determined by Ohm's law. The capacitor regulates and controls the flow of charge in an ac circuit; its opposition to the flow of electrons is called *capacitive reactance*. The inductor experiences a self-induced emf which adds *inductive reactance* to the circuit. The combined effect of all three elements in opposing electric current is called *impedance*. The major points to remember are summarized below:

- When a capacitor is being charged, the instantaneous values of the charge Q and the current i are found from

$$Q = CV_B(1 - e^{-t/RC})$$
$$i = \frac{V_B}{R} e^{-t/RC}$$

- *The charge on the capacitor will rise to 63 percent of its maximum value as the current delivered to the capacitor decreases to 37 percent of its initial value during a period of one time constant* τ.

$$\tau = RC$$
Time Constant

- When a capacitor is discharging, the instantaneous values of the charge and current are given by

$$Q = CV_B e^{-t/RC}$$
$$i = \frac{-V_B}{R} e^{-t/RC}$$

Both the charge and the current decay to 37 percent of their initial values after discharging for one time constant.

- When alternating current passes through a coil of wire, an inductor, a self-induced emf arises to oppose the change. This emf is given by

$$\mathcal{E} = -L \frac{\Delta i}{\Delta t}$$
$$L = -\frac{\mathcal{E}}{\Delta i/\Delta t}$$

This constant L is called the inductance. An inductance of one henry (H) exists if an emf of 1 V is induced by a current changing at the rate of 1 A/s.

- The rise and decay of current in an inductor are found from

$$i = \frac{V_B}{R}(1 - e^{-(R/L)t})$$
Current Rise

$$i = \frac{V_B}{R} e^{-(R/L)t}$$
Current Decay

- In an inductive circuit, the current will rise to 63 percent of its maximum value or decay to 37 percent of its maximum in a period of one time constant. For an inductor, the time constant is

$$\tau = \frac{L}{R}$$ *Time Constant*

- Since alternating currents and voltages vary continuously, we speak of an effective ampere and an effective volt that are defined in terms of their maximum values as follows:

$$i_{\text{eff}} = 0.707 i_{\text{max}}$$ $$\mathscr{E}_{\text{eff}} = 0.707 \mathscr{E}_{\text{max}}$$

- Both capacitors and inductors offer resistance to the flow of alternating current (called reactance), calculated from

$$X_L = 2\pi f L \quad \Omega$$ *Inductive Reactance* X_L

$$X_C = \frac{1}{2\pi f C} \quad \Omega$$ *Capacitive Reactance* X_C

The symbol f refers to the frequency of the alternating current in hertz. One hertz is one cycle per second.

- The voltage, current, and resistance in a series ac circuit are studied with the use of phasor diagrams. Figure 40-12 illustrates such a diagram for X_C, X_L, and R. The resultant of these vectors is the effective resistance of the entire circuit called the *impedance Z*.

$$Z = \sqrt{R^2 + (X_L - X_C)^2} \quad \Omega$$ *Impedance*

- If we apply Ohm's law to each part of the circuit and then to the entire circuit, we obtain the following useful equations. First, the total voltage is given by

$$V = \sqrt{V_R^2 + (V_L - V_C)^2}$$ *Voltage*

$$V_R = iR$$ $$V_L = iX_L$$ $$V_C = iX_C$$ $$V = iZ$$

$$V = i\sqrt{R^2 + (X_L - X_C)^2}$$ *Ohm's Law*

- Because the voltage leads the current in an inductive circuit and lags the current in a capacitive circuit, the voltage and current maxima and minima usually do not coincide. The phase angle ϕ is given by

$$\tan \phi = \frac{V_L - V_C}{V_B}$$ or $$\tan \phi = \frac{X_L - X_C}{R}$$

- The resonant frequency occurs when the net reactance is zero ($X_L = X_C$):

$$f_r = \frac{1}{2\pi\sqrt{LC}}$$ *Resonant Frequency*

- No power is consumed because of capacitance or inductance. Since power is a function of the component of the impedance along the resistance axis, we can write

$$P = iV \cos \phi$$ *Power Factor* $= \cos \phi$

$$\cos \phi = \frac{R}{Z}$$ $$\cos \phi = \frac{R}{\sqrt{R^2 + (X_L - X_C)^2}}$$

QUESTIONS

40-1. Define the following terms:
  a. Capacitance
  b. Inductor
  c. Inductance
  d. Henry
  e. Frequency
  f. Impedance
  g. Resonance
  h. Phase angle
  i. Effective current
  j. Effective voltage
  k. Phase diagram
  l. Capacitance reactance
  m. Inductive reactance
  n. Power factor
  o. Resonant frequency

40-2. Inductance in a circuit depends upon its geometry and upon the proximity of magnetic materials. Which of the following coils have higher inductances and why?
  a. Closely or widely spaced turns
  b. Long coil or short coil
  c. Large cross section or small cross section
  d. Iron core or air core

40-3. Recalling that the magnetic flux density B within a solenoid is

$$B = \frac{\phi}{A} = \frac{\mu N I}{l}$$

show that the self-inductance of a solenoid is given by

$$L = \frac{N\phi}{I}$$

40-4. Show that the unit for the time constant L/R and RC for inductive and capacitive circuits is the second.

40-5. Sketch a curve of current vs. time for **(a)** a circuit of high inductance and **(b)** a circuit of low inductance.

40-6. Plot a curve of voltage vs. time for **(a)** a charging capacitor and **(b)** a discharging capacitor. Compare these curves with those in the text for the current.

40-7. By plotting a curve of voltage as a function of time, show how the voltage changes in an inductive circuit. Compare these curves with those in the text for the current.

40-8. Should someone interested in establishing the breakdown voltage of a capacitor in an ac circuit be concerned with the average voltage, maximum voltage, or effective voltage?

40-9. A coil of wire is connected across the terminals of a 110-V dc battery. An ammeter connected in series with the coil indicates a current of 5 A. What happens to the current if an iron core is inserted into the coil? Now, disconnect the dc source, remove the iron core, and reconnect the system to a 110-V ac generator. The ammeter is adjusted to read ac effective amperes. Has the current decreased, increased, or stayed unchanged? What happens to the current if the iron core is inserted? How do you account for your observations?

40-10. An incandescent lamp is connected in series with a 110-V ac generator and a variable capacitor. If the capacitance is increased, will the lamp glow more brightly or will it be dimmed? Explain. What would happen if the generator is replaced by a battery?

40-11. As the capacitance of a circuit increases, what happens to the resonant frequency of the circuit?

40-12. As the frequency is increased in an inductive circuit, what happens to the current in the circuit?

40-13. Inductive reactance depends *directly* on the frequency of the alternating current whereas capacitive reactance varies *inversely* with the frequency. Both oppose the flow of charge in an ac circuit. Explain why their relationship to the frequency differs.

40-14. When a circuit is tuned to its resonant frequency, what is the power factor?

40-15. What is the power factor of a circuit containing **(a)** pure resistance; **(b)** pure inductance; **(c)** pure capacitance?

PROBLEMS

40-1. A series circuit consists of a 4-μF capacitor, a 5-Ω resistor, and a 12-V battery. **(a)** What is the time constant for charging the capacitor? **(b)** How long is required to charge the capacitor fully?

Ans. **(a)** 20 ms **(b)** 100 ms.

40-2. A series circuit contains a 6-μF capacitor and a 400-Ω resistor. **(a)** What is the maximum charge on the capacitor if the source of emf is 20 V? **(b)** Calculate the discharge time.

40-3. A 100-V battery is connected in series with a 0.06-H inductor and a 50-Ω resistor. Calculate the maximum current in the circuit and the time constant.

Ans. 2 A, 1.2 ms.

40-4. A series circuit contains a 0.05-H inductor and a 40-Ω resistor. If the source of emf is 90 V, what is the maximum current in the circuit and the time constant.

40-5. An *LR* circuit has a time constant of 2 ms. What is the inductance if the resistance is 2000 Ω?

Ans. 4 H.

40-6. A series circuit contains a capacitor and a 20-Ω resistor. The emf supplied is 12 V and the time constant is 40 ms. What is the capacitance? What is the maximum charge on the capacitor?

40-7. A 2-H inductor having a resistance of 120 Ω is connected to a 30-V battery of negligible internal resistance. **(a)** How much time is required for the current to reach 63 percent of its maximum value? **(b)** What is the initial rate of current increase in amperes per second? **(c)** What is the final current?

Ans. 16.7 ms, 15 A/s, 250 mA.

40-8. An ac voltmeter when placed across a 12-Ω resistor reads 117 V. What are the *maximum* values of current and voltage drop for this resistor?

40-9. A capacitor has a maximum voltage rating of 500-V. What is the highest effective ac voltage that can be supplied to it without breakdown?

Ans. 354 V.

40-10. A certain appliance is supplied with an effective voltage of 220 V under an effective current of 20 A. What are the maximum values for the voltage and current?

40-11. A 0.05-H inductor of negligible resistance is connected to a 120-V 60-Hz power line. **(a)** What is the inductive reactance? **(b)** What is the current in the coil?

Ans. **(a)** 18.8 Ω **(b)** 6.37 A

40-12. A 2-H inductor of negligible resistance is connected to a 50-V 50-Hz line. **(a)** What is the reactance? **(b)** What is the current in the circuit?

40-13. The frequency of an alternating current is 200 Hz and the inductive reactance for a single inductor is 100 Ω. What is the inductance?

Ans. 79.6 mH.

40-14. Find the reactance of a 60-μF capacitor in a 600-Hz ac circuit. What is the reactance if the frequency is reduced to 200 Hz?

40-15. A 3-μF capacitor when connected to a 120-V ac line draws a current of 0.5 A. What is the frequency of the source?

Ans. 221 Hz.

40-16. A 6-μF capacitor is connected to a 24-V 50-Hz line. What is the current in the circuit?

40-17. A series ac circuit consists of a 100-Ω resistor, a 0.2-H inductor, and a 3-μF capacitor connected to a 110-V 60-Hz line. **(a)** What is the inductive reactance? **(b)** What is the capacitive reactance? **(c)** What is the impedance of the circuit? **(d)** What is the phase angle? **(e)** What is the current in the circuit? **(f)** What is the power factor.

Ans. **(a)** 75.4 Ω **(b)** 884 Ω **(c)** 815 Ω **(d)** $-83°$
(e) 135 mA **(f)** 0.123.

40-18. Answer the questions of Prob. 40-17 for a circuit containing a 12-mH inductor, an 8-μF capacitor, and a 40-Ω resistor connected to a 110-V 200-Hz line.

40-19. When a 6-Ω resistor and an inductor are connected to a 110-V 60-Hz ac line, the current is 10 A. What is the inductance of the coil?

Ans. 24.5 mH.

40-20. A capacitor is in series with a resistance of 35 Ω and connected to a 220-V ac line. The reactance of the capacitor is 45 Ω. **(a)** What is the current in the circuit? **(b)** What is the phase angle? **(c)** What is the power factor?

40-21. A coil having an inductance of 0.15 H and a resistance of 12 Ω is connected across a 110-V 25-Hz line. **(a)** What is the current in the coil? **(b)** What is the phase angle? **(c)** What is the power factor? **(d)** What power is absorbed by the coil?

Ans. **(a)** 4.16 A **(b)** 63° **(c)** 0.454 **(d)** 208 W.

40-22. An 8-μF capacitor is in series with a 40-Ω resistor and connected to a 117-V 60-Hz ac line. **(a)** What is the capacitive reactance? **(b)** What is the impedance of the circuit? **(c)** What is the current? **(d)** What is the phase angle? **(e)** What is the power loss in the circuit?

40-23. An inductor, resistor, and capacitor are connected in series with a 60-Hz ac line. A voltmeter connected to each element in the circuit gives the following readings: $V_R = 60$ V, $V_L = 100$ V, and $V_C = 160$ V. **(a)** What is the total voltage drop in the circuit? **(b)** What is the phase difference between the voltage and current?

Ans. **(a)** 84.9 V **(b)** $-45°$

40-24. It is desired to construct a circuit whose resonant frequency is 950 kHz. If a coil in the circuit has an inductance of 3 mH, what capacitance should be added to the circuit?

40-25. A 50-μF capacitor and a 70-Ω resistor are connected in series across a 120-V 60-Hz ac line. **(a)** Determine the current in the circuit. **(b)** What is the phase difference between the voltage and current? **(c)** What is the power loss in the circuit?

Ans. **(a)** 1.36 A **(b)** $-37.3°$ **(c)** 131 W.

40-26. Refer to the circuit of Prob. 40-25. **(a)** What is the voltage across the resistor? **(b)** What is the voltage across the capacitor? **(c)** What inductance should be added to the circuit in order to reach resonance?

40-27. The antenna circuit in a radio receiver consists of a variable capacitor and a 9-mH coil. The resistance of the circuit is 40 Ω. A 980-kHz radio wave produces a potential difference of 0.2 mV across the circuit. **(a)** Determine the capacitance required for resonance. **(b)** What is the current at resonance?

Ans. **(a)** 2.93 pF **(b)** 5 μA.

40-28. A resonant circuit has an inductance of 400 μH and a capacitance of 100 pF. What is the resonant frequency?

Modern Physics

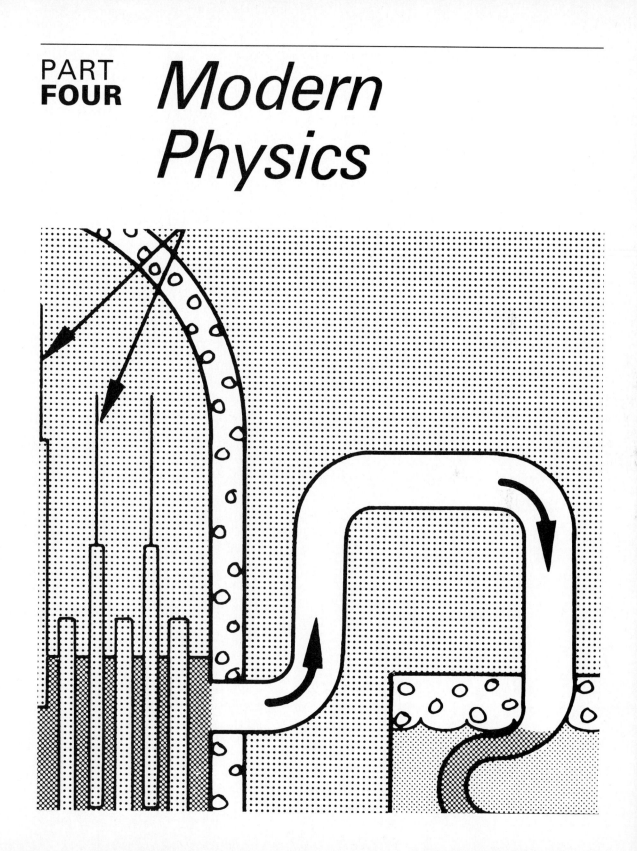

41 *Modern Physics and the Atom*

OBJECTIVES: After completing this chapter, you should be able to:

1. Discuss Einstein's postulates and determine the relativistic changes in length, mass, and time.

2. Demonstrate your understanding of the photoelectric effect, the equivalence of mass and energy, the de Broglie wavelength, and the Bohr model of the atom.

3. Demonstrate your understanding of emission and absorption spectra and discuss with drawings the Balmer, Lyman, and Paschen spectral series.

4. Calculate the energy emitted or absorbed by the hydrogen atom when the electron moves to a higher or lower energy level.

By 1900, physical events had been observed which could not be explained satisfactorily by the laws of classical physics. Light, which was thought to be a wave phenomenon, was found to exhibit properties of particles as well. Newton's concepts of absolute mass, length, and time were found inadequate to describe certain physical events. The light produced by an electric spark in gases did not produce a continuous spectrum on passing through a prism or diffraction grating. These and other unexplained phenomena signaled the beginning of entirely new ways of viewing the world around us.

In 1905, Einstein's first paper on relativity was published, followed in 1916 by a second paper. They put classical physics into a new perspective. Einstein's relativity laid the basis for a universal physics which limited classical newtonian physics to situations involving speeds considerably less than the speed of light.

The work of Einstein stimulated a rash of work by others, which has had immense ramifications; it establishes parameters for maximum energy use, space travel, modern electronics, chemical analysis, x-rays, nuclear weaponry, and many other applications.

41-1 RELATIVITY

Einstein's two papers on relativity dramatically altered physics, but they are not generally understood by many people outside the scientific community. To understand relativity, you must put aside all your preconceived ideas and be willing to view physical events from a new perspective.

The special theory of relativity, published in 1905, is based on two postulates. The first states that every object is in motion compared with something else, that *there is no such thing as absolute rest.*

For example, picture a freight car moving along a railroad track at 40 mi/h. The cargo in relation to the freight car is stationary, but in relation to the earth it is moving at 40 mi/h. According to the first postulate, it is impossible to name anything which is at absolute rest; an object is only at rest (or moving) in relation to some specified reference point.

Einstein's first postulate also tells us that if we see something changing its position with respect to us, we have no way of knowing whether *it* is moving or *we* are moving. If you walk to a neighbor's house, it is just as correct according to this postulate to say that the house came to you. This sounds absurd to us because we are accustomed to using the earth as a frame of reference. Einstein's laws were designed to be completely independent of such a preferred reference frame. From the standpoint of physics, the first postulate is often restated as follows:

> *The laws of physics are the same for all frames of reference moving at a constant velocity with respect to one another.*

Nineteenth-century physicists had suggested that there was a preferred frame of reference, the so-called luminiferous ether. This was the medium through which they thought electromagnetic waves propagated. However, experiments like the famous Michelson–Morley experiment of 1887 (discussed in Chap. 24) and others were unable to detect the existence of the ether. These experiments are the basis for Einstein's second revolutionary postulate:

> *The free-space velocity of light c is constant for all observers, independent of their state of motion.*

To see why this second postulate was so revolutionary, let us consider a bus traveling at 50 km/h, as in Fig. 41-1. A person riding in the bus first throws a baseball with a speed (relative to the person) of 20 km/h toward the front of the bus. Then a second ball is thrown with the same speed toward the rear of the bus. To the person who threw the balls, each ball traveled at 20 km/h, one toward the front of the bus and one toward the rear of the bus. But to an observer on the ground, the velocity of the bus adds to the velocity of the first ball, which appears to be traveling at 70 km/h in the same direction as the bus.

Fig. 41-1 The velocity of the bus is 50 km/h to the north (right). Two balls thrown with the same speed (20 km/h) in opposite directions have different speeds relative to the ground. However, the speed of light is independent of a frame of reference.

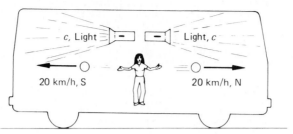

(a) Velocities relative to bus

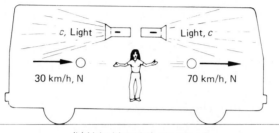

(b) Velocities relative to ground

And when the velocity of the bus is added to the second ball, the observer on the ground sees it traveling at 30 km/h *in the same direction as the bus.* But the speed of light does not change and will appear the same to the person on the bus and the observer on the ground. Light always travels at the same constant speed.

$$c = 3 \times 10^8 \text{ m/s}$$

whether it is traveling with the source or away from the source.

41-2 RELATIVISTIC LENGTH, MASS, AND TIME

Utilizing the above postulates, Einstein was able to predict a host of remarkable effects. Perhaps the most remarkable of these were the conclusions that measurements made by an observer on lengths and events are affected by relative motion. The effect becomes more and more pronounced as the velocity of objects v approaches the limiting velocity of light c. If we find that the length of the rocket ship in Fig. 41-2 is L_0 at rest, its length L when it is moving with a speed v relative to us will be given by

$$L = L_0 \sqrt{1 - \frac{v^2}{c^2}} \qquad \begin{array}{l} \textit{Relativistic} \\ \textit{Contraction} \end{array} \quad (41\text{-}1)$$

Such foreshortening of length in the direction of motion is referred to as *relativistic contraction.*

This means that the length of a moving object is observed to be shorter by a factor of $\sqrt{1 - v^2/c^2}$ than its length at rest. A study of the formula will reveal that the observed length will be equal to L_0 when $v = 0$ (the object is at rest). It will begin to shorten as the velocity v approaches c.

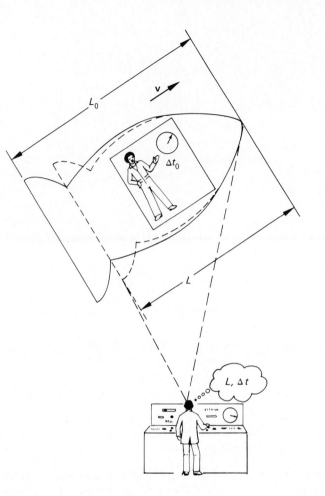

Fig. 41-2 The length of objects and the duration of events are affected by relative motion. The person aboard the rocket measures the length L_0 and the time interval t_0; the person in the laboratory observes a shorter length L and records a longer time interval t.

EXAMPLE 41-1

When a rocket ship is at rest with respect to us, its length is 100 m. How long do we measure it to be when it moves by us at a speed of 2.4×10^8 m/s, or $0.8c$?

Solution

Substitution into Eq. (41-1) gives

$$L = L_0 \sqrt{1 - \frac{v^2}{c^2}} = (100 \text{ m}) \sqrt{1 - \frac{(0.8c)^2}{c^2}}$$

$$= (100 \text{ m}) \sqrt{1 - \frac{0.64c^2}{c^2}} = (100 \text{ m}) \sqrt{1 - 0.64}$$

$$= (100 \text{ m}) \sqrt{0.36} = (100 \text{ m})(0.6) = 60 \text{ m}$$

Time intervals are also affected by relative motion. This fact is perhaps one of the most astounding ideas to come from the special theory of relativity, for it strikes at a measurement that has always been considered an absolute quantity. Nonetheless, a clock moving with respect to an observer ticks more slowly (to the observer) than it did at rest. If t_0 is the time interval measured by a clock on our moving rocket, then the time interval t we measure on earth is longer by an amount given by

$$t = \frac{t_0}{\sqrt{1 - v^2/c^2}} \qquad \textit{Time Dilation} \quad (41\text{-}2)$$

The increase of time intervals as a function of velocity is referred to as *time dilation*.

To be sure that you understand this equation you should recognize that t and t_0 represent time *intervals*, or the time elapsed from the beginning until the end of an event. Consequently, a clock that is running more slowly will record longer time intervals. We can say that time has stopped when it becomes impossible to measure an event; i.e., the time interval is infinite. This is exactly what is predicted by the time-dilation equation in the limit where $v = c$.

$$t = \frac{t_0}{\sqrt{1 - c^2/c^2}} = \frac{t_0}{\sqrt{1 - 1}} = \frac{t_0}{0} = \infty$$

EXAMPLE 41-2   Suppose we observe a rocket ship moving past us at $0.8c$, as in the previous example. We measure the time between ticks on the rocket-ship clock to be 1.67 s. What time between ticks is measured by the captain of the rocket ship?

Solution   In this case, $t = 1.67$ s, and we are to find t_0 from Eq. (41-2). It will be helpful to recall from the previous example that $\sqrt{1 - v^2/c^2} = 0.6$ when $v = 0.8c$. Solving Eq. (41-2) for t_0, we have

$$t_0 = t\sqrt{1 - v^2/c^2} = (1.67 \text{ s})(0.6) = 1.00 \text{ s}$$

The interval measured by the captain is shorter than that measured by us.

Let us now consider yet another physical quantity which varies with relative velocity. In order for momentum to be conserved independent of a frame of reference, the mass of a body must vary in the same proportion as length and time. If the rest mass of an object is m_0, the mass m of a body moving with a speed v will be measured by

$$m = \frac{m_0}{\sqrt{1 - v^2/c^2}} \qquad \textit{Relativistic Mass} \quad (41\text{-}3)$$

The mass m in this instance is referred to as the *relativistic mass*.

EXAMPLE 41-3   The rest mass of an electron is 9.1×10^{-31} kg. What is its relativistic mass if its velocity is $0.8c$?

Solution   In previous examples we found that $\sqrt{1 - v^2/c^2} = 0.6$ when $v = 0.8c$. Using this computation and substituting in Eq. (41-3), we obtain

$$m = \frac{m_0}{\sqrt{1 - v^2/c^2}} = \frac{9.1 \times 10^{-31} \text{ kg}}{0.6} = 1.52 \times 10^{-30} \text{ kg}$$

This represents a 67 percent increase in mass.

It should be clear from Eq. (41-3) that if m_0 is not equal to zero, the value for the relativistic mass m approaches infinity as v approaches c. This would mean that an infinite force would be needed to accelerate a nonzero mass to the velocity of light. Apparently, the free-space velocity of light represents an upper limit for the speed of such masses. However, if the rest mass *is* zero, as for photons of light, the relativistic-mass equation *does* allow for $v = c$.

Startling as the predictions of Einstein's equations are, they are experimentally verified daily in the laboratory. Their conclusions are amazing to us only because we do not have direct experience with such fantastic speeds. The giant atom smashers, the betatrons, and many other devices for accelerating particles are in use all over the country to accelerate atomic and nuclear particles at speeds very close to the speed of light. Protons in the big Brookhaven accelerator have been accelerated to within 99.948 percent of the speed of light. Their mass is shown to be increased precisely as relativity predicts. Electrons can now be accelerated to $0.99999999+$ the speed of light, causing their mass to increase by more than 40,000 times the rest value.

41-3 MASS AND ENERGY

Before Einstein, physicists had always considered mass and energy as separate quantities which must be *conserved* separately. Now mass and energy must be considered as different ways of expressing the same quantity. If we say that mass can be converted to energy and energy to mass, we must recognize that mass and energy are the same thing expressed in different units. Einstein found the conversion factor to be equal to the square of the velocity of light.

$$E_0 = m_0 c^2 \qquad (41\text{-}4)$$

From the way the equation is written, it is easy to see that a tiny bit of mass corresponds to an enormous amount of energy. For example, an object whose rest mass m_0 is 1 kg has a rest energy E_0 of 9×10^{16} J.

A more general discussion of energy must take the effects of relativity into account. The expression for the total energy of a particle of rest mass m_0 and momentum $p = mv$ can be written

$$E = \sqrt{(m_0 c^2)^2 + p^2 c^2} \qquad (41\text{-}5)$$

Now if we substitute for m_0 from the relativistic-mass relationship, Eq. (41-3), the total energy reduces to

$$\boxed{E = mc^2} \qquad (41\text{-}6)$$

where m represents the relativistic mass. This is the most general form for the total energy of a particle.

Note that Eq. (41-5) reduces to $E_0 = m_0 c^2$ when the velocity is zero and hence $p = 0$. Furthermore, if we consider velocities considerably less than c, the equation simplifies to

$$E = \tfrac{1}{2}m_0 v^2 + m_0 c^2 \qquad (41\text{-}7)$$

Here we have the usual expression for kinetic energy with a new term added for the *rest energy*.

The more general expression for the kinetic energy of a particle must consider the effects of relativity. Recall that the kinetic energy E_κ at speed v is defined as the work that must be done to accelerate a particle from rest to speed v. By the methods of calculus it can be shown that the relativistic kinetic energy of a particle is given by

$$E_\kappa = (m - m_0)c^2 \qquad (41\text{-}8)$$

This represents the difference between the total energy of a particle and its rest-mass energy.

EXAMPLE 41-4 An electron is accelerated to a speed of $0.8c$. Compare its relativistic kinetic energy with the value based on Newton's mechanics.

Solution In the previous example we found the relativistic mass of an electron at this speed to be 1.52×10^{-30} kg. Since its rest mass is 9.1×10^{-31} kg, we can determine its kinetic energy by substitution into Eq. (41-8).

$$E_\kappa = (m - m_0)c^2$$

$$= (15.2 \times 10^{-31} \text{ kg} - 9.1 \times 10^{-31} \text{ kg})(3 \times 10^8)^2$$

$$= (6.1 \times 10^{-31} \text{ kg})(9 \times 10^{16})$$

$$= 5.49 \times 10^{-14} \text{ J}$$

The newtonian value is based on $\frac{1}{2}m_0 v^2$, where $v = 0.8c$.

$$\frac{1}{2}m_0 v^2 = \frac{1}{2}(9.1 \times 10^{-31} \text{ kg})(0.8c)^2$$

$$= (4.55 \times 10^{-31} \text{ kg})(0.64c^2)$$

$$= (4.55 \times 10^{-31} \text{ kg})(0.64)(3 \times 10^8 \text{ m/s})^2$$

$$= 2.62 \times 10^{-14} \text{ J}$$

The relativistic kinetic energy is more than twice its newtonian value.

**41-4
QUANTUM
THEORY
AND THE
PHOTO-
ELECTRIC
EFFECT**

Recall from Chap. 24 that the photoelectric effect led to the establishment of a dualistic theory of light. (See Fig. 41-3.) The ejection of electrons as a result of incident light could not be accounted for in terms of the existing electromagnetic theory.

In an attempt to bring experiment into agreement with theory, Maxwell Planck postulated that electromagnetic energy is absorbed or emitted in discrete packets, or *quanta*. The energy of such quanta, or *photons*, is proportional to the frequency of the radiation. Planck's equation can be written

$$E = hf \qquad (41\text{-}9)$$

where h is the proportionality constant known as *Planck's constant*. Its value is

$$h = 6.63 \times 10^{-34} \text{ J/Hz}$$

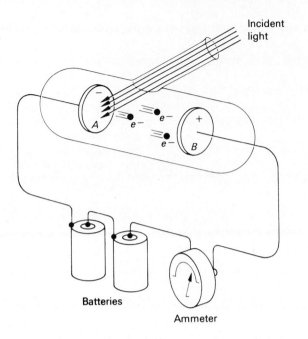

Fig. 41-3 The photoelectric effect.

Incident light

Batteries

Ammeter

Einstein used Planck's equation to explain the photoelectric effect. He reasoned that if light is emitted in photons of energy hf, it must also travel as photons. When a quantum of light strikes a metallic surface, it has an energy equal to hf. If all this energy is transferred to a single electron, the electron might be expected to leave the metal with energy hf. However, at least an amount of energy W is needed to remove the electron from the metal. The term W is called the *work function* of the surface. Thus, the ejected electron leaves with a maximum kinetic energy given by

$$E_\kappa = \tfrac{1}{2}mv_{max}^2 = hf - W \qquad (41\text{-}10)$$

This is *Einstein's photoelectric equation*.

As the frequency of incident light is varied, the maximum energy of the ejected electron varies. The lowest frequency f_0 at which an electron is emitted occurs when $E_\kappa = 0$. In this case,

$$f_0 = \frac{W}{h} \qquad (4\text{-}11)$$

The quantity f_0 is often called the *threshold frequency*.

EXAMPLE 41-5   Light of wavelength 650 nm is required to cause electrons to be ejected from the surface of a metal. What is the kinetic energy of the ejected electrons if the surface is bombarded with light of wavelength 450 nm?

Solution

The work function W of the surface is equal to the energy of the 650-nm light. Hence,

$$W = hf_0 = h\frac{c}{\lambda_0}$$

$$= 6.63 \times 10^{-34} \text{ J} \cdot \text{s}\left(\frac{3 \times 10^8 \text{ m/s}}{650 \times 10^{-9} \text{ m}}\right)$$

$$= 3.06 \times 10^{-19} \text{ J}$$

The energy of the 450-nm light is

$$hf = \frac{hc}{\lambda} = \frac{(6.63 \times 10^{-34} \text{ J} \cdot \text{s})(3 \times 10^8 \text{ m/s})}{450 \times 10^{-9} \text{ m}}$$

$$= 4.42 \times 10^{-19} \text{ J}$$

From Einstein's photoelectric equation,

$$E_\kappa = hf - W$$

$$= 4.42 \times 10^{-19} \text{ J} - 3.06 \times 10^{-19} \text{ J} = 1.36 \times 10^{-19} \text{ J}$$

41-5
WAVES AND
PARTICLES

Electromagnetic radiation has a dual character in its interaction with matter. Sometimes it exhibits wave properties, as demonstrated by interference and diffraction. At other times, as in the photoelectric effect, it behaves like particles, which we have called photons. In 1924, Louis de Broglie was able to demonstrate this duality of matter by deriving a relationship for the wavelength of a particle.

This relationship can be seen by looking at two expressions for the energy of a photon. We have already seen from Planck's work that the energy of a photon can be expressed as a function of its wavelength λ.

$$E = hf = \frac{hc}{\lambda}$$

Another expression for the energy of a photon was given earlier in the section on relativity:

$$E = \sqrt{(m_0 c^2)^2 + p^2 c^2} \tag{41-5}$$

This equation shows that photons have momentum $p = mv$ due to their relativistic mass. However, the rest mass m_0 of a photon is zero, so that Eq. (41-5) becomes

$$E = \sqrt{p^2 c^2} = pc \tag{41-12}$$

Since we also know that $E = hc/\lambda$, we can write

$$\frac{hc}{\lambda} = pc$$

from which the wavelength of a photon is given by

$$\lambda = \frac{h}{p} \tag{41-13}$$

De Broglie proposed that all objects have wavelengths related to their momentum—whether the objects are wavelike or particlelike. For example, the wavelength of an electron or any other particle is given by de Broglie's equation, which can be rewritten

$$\lambda = \frac{h}{mv} \qquad \text{de Broglie Wavelength} \quad (41\text{-}14)$$

EXAMPLE 41-6   What is the de Broglie wavelength of an electron which has a kinetic energy of 100 eV?

Solution   Recalling that 1 eV = 1.6×10^{-19} J, we see that 100 eV is equivalent to 1.6×10^{-17} J, which must be equal to $\frac{1}{2}mv^2$. Thus,

$$\tfrac{1}{2}mv^2 = 1.6 \times 10^{-17} \text{ J}$$

from which

$$v^2 = \frac{2(1.6 \times 10^{-17} \text{ J})}{m} = \frac{3.2 \times 10^{-17} \text{ J}}{9.1 \times 10^{-31} \text{ kg}} = 3.52 \times 10^{13} \text{ m}^2/\text{s}^2$$

The velocity of the electron is therefore

$$v = \sqrt{3.52 \times 10^{13} \text{ m}^2/\text{s}^2} = 5.93 \times 10^6 \text{ m/s}$$

Now the wavelength can be found from Eq. (41-14).

$$\lambda = \frac{h}{mv} = \frac{6.63 \times 10^{-34} \text{ J} \cdot \text{s}}{(9.1 \times 10^{-31} \text{ kg})(5.93 \times 10^6 \text{ m/s})}$$

$$= 1.23 \times 10^{-10} \text{ m} = 0.123 \text{ nm}$$

Note from de Broglie's equation that the higher the velocity of the particle, the shorter its wavelength. Remember that the relativistic mass must be used if the velocity of a given particle is large enough to warrant it.

**41-6
THE
RUTHER-
FORD ATOM**

Early attempts to explain the structure of an atom were based on a model attributed to J. J. Thomson, the discoveror of the electron. In this model the electrons are implanted in a spherical space of positive charge, as illustrated in Fig. 41-4. Such a model explained the observed neutrality of atoms by postulating equal amounts of positive and negative charge.

Fig. 41-4 The Thomson model of the atom consisted of electrons stuck in a sphere of positive charge.

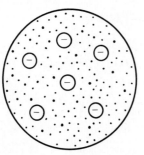

Thomson's model was short-lived, however, because of the work of Ernest Rutherford in 1911. He bombarded a thin metal foil with a stream of alpha particles, as illustrated in Fig. 41-5. An alpha particle is a tiny positively charged particle emitted by a radioactive substance such as radium. Most of the positively charged particles penetrated the foil easily, as indicated by a flash of light when they struck the zinc sulfide screen, and a few were deflected slightly.

Fig. 41-5 Rutherford scattering of alpha particles provided the first evidence for the atomic nucleus.

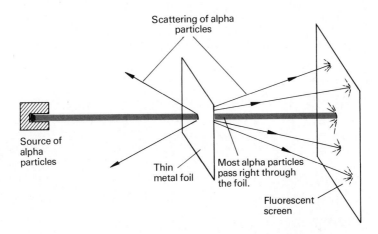

Much to Rutherford's surprise, however, others were deflected at extreme angles. Some were even deflected backward. (Rutherford himself said it was like firing a cannon-ball through tissue paper and having it come back and hit you in the face.) These extreme deflections could not be explained in terms of the Thomson model for the atom. If charge really was scattered through the atom, the electrical forces would be far too weak to repulse the alpha particles at the large angles actually observed.

Rutherford explained these results by assuming that all the positive charge of an atom is concentrated into a very small region, called the *nucleus* of the atom. The electrons were assumed to be distributed in the space around this positive charge. With the atom consisting largely of empty space, the fact that most of the alpha particles passed right through the foil is easily explained. Furthermore, Rutherford found the large-angle scattering to be a consequence of electrostatic repulsion. Once the alpha particle has penetrated the electrons surrounding the positive charge, it is close to a large positive charge of great mass. Large electrostatic forces are therefore expected.

Rutherford has been credited with the discovery of the *nucleus* because he was able to develop formulas to predict the observed scattering of alpha particles. On the basis of his calculations, the diameter of the nucleus was estimated to be approximately one ten-thousandth of the diameter of the atom itself. The positive part of the atom was seen to be concentrated in the nucleus, approximately 10^{-5} nm in diameter. Rutherford believed the electrons to be grouped around the nucleus so that the diameter of the whole atom is about 0.1 nm.

An immediate difficulty accompanying the Rutherford atom was related to the stability of the atomic electrons. We know from Coulomb's law that the electrons should be attracted to the nucleus. One possible explanation is that the electrons are moving in circles around the nucleus much as planets revolve around the sun. The necessary centripetal force would be provided by coulomb attraction.

Consider, for example, the hydrogen atom, which consists of a single proton and a single electron. We might expect the electron to remain in a constant orbit about the nucleus, as illustrated in Fig. 41-6a. The charge of the

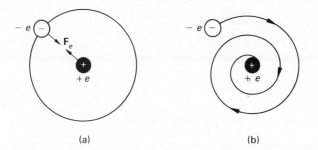

(a)   (b)

Fig. 41-6 (a) A stable electron orbit in which the centripetal force is provided by the electrostatic force F_e. (b) Instability due to electromagnetic radiation which would cause the electron to lose energy and spiral into the nucleus.

electron is labeled $-e$, and the equal but opposite charge of the proton is labeled $+e$. At a distance r from the nucleus, the electrostatic force of attraction on the electron is given by Coulomb's law,

$$F_e = \frac{e^2}{4\pi\epsilon_0 r^2} \tag{41-15}$$

where each charge has the magnitude e. For a stable orbit, this force must exactly equal the centripetal force, given by

$$F_c = \frac{mv^2}{r} \tag{41-16}$$

where m is the mass of the electron traveling with a velocity v. Setting $F_e = F_c$, we have

$$\frac{e^2}{4\pi\epsilon_0 r^2} = \frac{mv^2}{r} \tag{41-17}$$

Solving for the radius r, we obtain

$$r = \frac{e^2}{4\pi\epsilon_0 mv^2} \tag{41-18}$$

According to classical theory, Eq. (41-18) should predict the orbital radius r of the electron as a function of its speed v.

The problem with this approach is that the electron must be continually accelerated under the influence of the electrostatic force. According to classical theory, an accelerated electron must radiate energy. The total energy of the electron would therefore gradually decrease, reducing the speed of the electron. As can be seen from Eq. (41-18), gradual reduction in electron speed v results in smaller and smaller orbits. Thus, the electron should spiral into the nucleus, as shown in Fig. 41-6b. The fact that it does not compels us to acknowledge a fundamental inconsistency in Rutherford's atom.

41-8 ATOMIC SPECTRA

All substances radiate electromagnetic waves when they are heated. Since each element is different, such emitted radiation can be expected to provide clues to atomic structure. These electromagnetic waves are analyzed by a *spectrometer*, which uses a prism or a diffraction grating to organize the radiation into a pattern called a *spectrum*. For an incandescent source of light, the spectrum is *continuous*; i.e., it contains all wavelengths and is similar to a rainbow. If, however, the source of light is a very hot gas under low pressure, the spectrum of the emitted light consists of a series of bright lines separated by dark regions. Such spectra are called *line emission spectra*. The chemical composition of a vaporized material can be determined by comparing its spectrum with known spectra.

A line emission spectrum for hydrogen is shown in Fig. 41-7. The sequence of lines, called a *spectral series*, has a definite order, the lines becoming more and more crowded as the limit of the series is approached. Each line corresponds to a characteristic frequency or wavelength (color). The line of

Fig. 41-7 Line spectra for the Balmer series of the hydrogen atom.

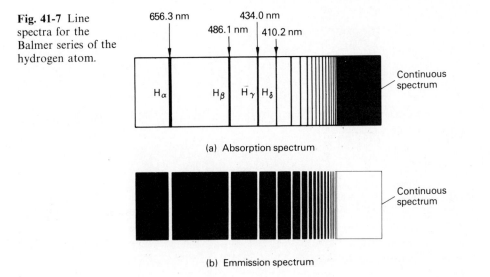

(a) Absorption spectrum

(b) Emmission spectrum

longest wavelength, 656.3 nm, is in the red and is labeled H_α. The others are labeled, in order, as H_β, H_γ, and so on.

It is also possible to obtain similar information from a gas or vapor in an unexcited state. When light is passed through a gas, certain discrete wavelengths are *absorbed*. These *absorption spectra* are like those produced by emission except that the characteristic wavelengths appear as *dark* lines on a light background. The absorption spectrum for hydrogen is compared with the emission spectrum in Fig. 41-7.

As early as 1884, Johann Jakob Balmer found a simple mathematical relationship for predicting the characteristic wavelengths of some of the lines in the hydrogen spectrum. His formula is

$$\frac{1}{\lambda} = R\left(\frac{1}{2^2} - \frac{1}{n^2}\right) \tag{41-19}$$

where λ = wavelength
R = Rydberg constant
n = 3, 4, 5, ...

If λ is measured in meters, the value for R is

$$R = 1.097 \times 10^7 \text{ m}^{-1}$$

The series of wavelengths predicted by Eq. (41-19) is called the *Balmer series*.

EXAMPLE 41-7 Using Balmer's equation, determine the wavelength of the H_α line in the hydrogen spectrum. (This first line occurs when $n = 3$.)

Solution Direct substitution yields

$$\frac{1}{\lambda} = 1.097 \times 10^7 \text{ m}^{-1}\left(\frac{1}{2^2} - \frac{1}{3^2}\right) = 1.524 \times 10^6 \text{ m}^{-1}$$

from which

$$\lambda = 656.3 \text{ nm}$$

Other characteristic wavelengths are found by setting $n = 4$, 5, 6, and so on. The limit of the series is found by setting $n = \infty$ in Eq. (41-19).

Since the discovery of Balmer's equation, several other series spectra have been discovered for hydrogen. In general, all these discoveries can be summarized by the single equation

$$\frac{1}{\lambda} = R\left(\frac{1}{l^2} - \frac{1}{n^2}\right) \tag{41-20}$$

where l and n are integers with $n > l$. The series predicted by Balmer corresponds to $l = 2$ and $n = 3$, 4, 5, ... The *Lyman series* is in the ultraviolet region and corresponds to $l = 1$, $n = 2$, 3, 4 ...; the *Paschen series* is in the infrared and corresponds to $l = 3$, $n = 4$, 5, 6, ...; and the *Brackett series*, also in the infrared, corresponds to $l = 4$, $n = 5$, 6, 7, ...

Observation of atomic spectra have indicated that atoms emit only a few rather definite frequencies. This fact does not agree with the Rutherford model, which predicts an unstable atom emitting radiant energy of all frequencies. Any theory of atomic structure must account for the regularities observed in atomic spectra.

The first theory to explain the line spectrum of the hydrogen atom satisfactorily was offered by Niels Bohr in 1913. He assumed, like Rutherford, that the electrons were in circular orbits about a dense positively charged nucleus, but he decided that electromagnetic theory cannot be strictly applied on the atomic level. Thus, he avoided the problem of orbital instability due to emitted radiation. Bohr's first postulate is as follows:

> *An electron may exist only in those orbits where its angular momentum is an integral multiple of h/2π.*

Thus, contrary to classical prediction, electrons may be in certain specified orbits without the emission of radiant energy.

The basis for Bohr's first postulate can be seen in terms of de Broglie wavelengths. The stable orbits are those in which an integral number of electron wavelengths can be fitted into the circumference of the Bohr orbit. Such orbits would allow for standing waves, as illustrated in Fig. 41-8 for four wavelengths. The conditions for such standing waves would be given by

$$n\lambda = 2\pi r \qquad n = 1, 2, 3, \ldots \qquad (41\text{-}21)$$

where r is the radius of an electron orbit which contains n wavelengths.

Since $\lambda = h/mv$, we can rewrite Eq. (41-21) as

$$n\frac{h}{mv} = 2\pi r$$

Fig. 41-8 A stable electron orbit, showing a circumference equal to four de Broglie wavelengths.

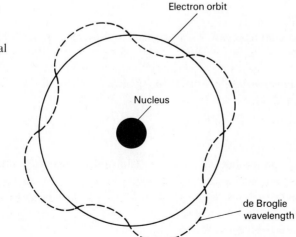

Electron orbit

Nucleus

de Broglie wavelength

from which it can be shown that the angular momentum mvr is given by

$$mvr = \frac{nh}{2\pi} \qquad (41\text{-}22)$$

The number n, called the *principal quantum number*, may take on the values $n = 1, 2, 3, \ldots$.

A *second postulate* given by Bohr places even further restrictions on atomic theory by incorporating the quantum theory.

> *If an electron changes from one stable orbit to any other, it loses or gains energy in discrete quanta equal to the difference in energy between the initial and final states.*

In equation form, Bohr's second postulate can be written

$$hf = E_i - E_f$$

where hf = energy of emitted or absorbed photon
E_i = initial energy
E_f = final energy.

Let us return to our discussion of the hydrogen atom to see whether Bohr's postulates will help to bring theory into harmony with observed spectra. Recall that application of Coulomb's law and Newton's law resulted in Eq. (41-18) for the radius r of the orbiting electron.

$$r = \frac{1}{4\pi\epsilon_0} \frac{e^2}{mv^2}$$

According to Bohr's theory,

$$mvr = \frac{nh}{2\pi}$$

Solving these two equations simultaneously for the radius r and for the velocity v, we obtain

$$r = n^2 \frac{\epsilon_0 h^2}{\pi m e^2} \qquad (41\text{-}23)$$

$$v = \frac{e^2}{2\epsilon_0 nh} \qquad (41\text{-}24)$$

These equations predict the possible radii and velocities for the electron, where $n = 1, 2, 3, \ldots$.

We now derive an expression for the total energy of a hydrogen atom for any electron orbit.

$$E_T = E_k + E_p$$

The kinetic energy is found by substituting from Eq. (41-24),

$$E_k = \tfrac{1}{2}mv^2 = \frac{me^4}{8\epsilon_0 n^2 h^2} \tag{41-25}$$

The potential energy of the atom for any orbit is

$$E_p = \frac{1}{4\pi\epsilon_0} \frac{e^2}{r} = -\frac{me^4}{4\epsilon_0^2 n^2 h^2} \tag{41-26}$$

after substitution of r from Eq. (41-23). The potential energy is negative because outside work is necessary to remove the electron from the atom. Adding Eq. (41-25) to Eq. (41-26), we find the total energy to be

$$E_T = -\frac{me^4}{8\epsilon_0^2 n^2 h^2} \tag{41-27}$$

Returning to Bohr's second postulate, we are now in a position to predict the energy of an emitted or absorbed photon. Normally, the electron is in its ground state corresponding to $n = 1$. If the atom *absorbs* a photon, the electron may jump to one of the outer orbits. From an *exited* state, it will soon fall back to a lower orbit, *emitting* a photon in the process.

Suppose an electron is in an outer orbit of quantum number n_i and then returns to a lower orbit of quantum number n_f. The decrease in energy must be equal to the energy of the emitted photon.

$$E_i - E_f = hf$$

Substituting the total energy for each state from Eq. (41-27), we obtain

$$hf = E_i - E_f$$

$$= -\frac{me^4}{8\epsilon_0^2 n_i^2 h^2} + \frac{me^4}{8\epsilon_0^2 n_f^2 h^2}$$

$$= \frac{me^4}{8\epsilon^2 h^2} \left(\frac{1}{n_f^2} - \frac{1}{n_i^2} \right)$$

Dividing both sides of this relation by h and remembering that $f = c/\lambda$, we can write

$$\frac{1}{\lambda} = \frac{me^4}{8\epsilon^2 h^3 c} \left(\frac{1}{n_f^2} - \frac{1}{n_i^2} \right) \tag{41-28}$$

Substituting in the values, we obtain

$$\frac{me^4}{8\epsilon_0^2 h^3 c} = 1.097 \times 10^7 \text{ m}^{-1}$$

which is equal to Rydberg's constant R. Therefore Eq. (41-28) is simplified to

$$\boxed{\frac{1}{\lambda} = R\left(\frac{1}{n_f^2} - \frac{1}{n_i^2}\right)} \tag{41-29}$$

The above relationship is exactly the same in form as Eq. (41-20), which was established by Balmer and others from experimental data. Thus, the Bohr atom brings theory into harmony with observation.

EXAMPLE 41-8 Determine the wavelength of the photon emitted from a hydrogen atom when the electron jumps from the first excited state to the ground state.

Solution In this case, $n_f = 1$ and $n_i = 2$. Thus

$$\frac{1}{\lambda} = R\left(\frac{1}{n_f^2} - \frac{1}{n_i^2}\right)$$

$$= (1.097 \times 10^7 \text{ m}^{-1})\left(\frac{1}{1^2} - \frac{1}{2^2}\right) = 8.23 \times 10^6 \text{ m}^{-1}$$

from which

$$\lambda = 1.22 \times 10^{-7} \text{ m} = 122 \text{ nm}$$

41-10 ENERGY LEVELS

From Bohr's work we now have a picture of an atom in which orbital electrons can occupy a number of energy levels. The total energy at the nth level is given by Eq. (41-27).

$$\boxed{E_n = -\frac{me^4}{8\epsilon_0^2 n^2 h^2}} \tag{41-30}$$

When the hydrogen atom is in its stable *ground* state, the quantum number n is equal to 1. The possible *excited* states are given for $n = 2, 3, 4, \ldots$.

EXAMPLE 41-9 Determine the energy of an electron in the ground state for a hydrogen atom.

Solution The following constants are needed:

$$\epsilon_0 = 8.85 \times 10^{-12} \text{ } c^2/\text{N} \cdot \text{m}^2 \qquad h = 6.63 \times 10^{-34} \text{ J} \cdot \text{s}$$

$$m = 9.1 \times 10^{-31} \text{ kg} \qquad e = 1.6 \times 10^{-19} c$$

Direct substitution into Eq. (42-30), with $n = 1$, yields

$$E_1 = -\frac{(9.1 \times 10^{-31} \text{ kg})(1.6 \times 10^{-19})^4}{8[8.85 \times 10^{-12}(\text{C}^2/\text{N} \cdot \text{m}^2)]^2(1)^2(6.63 \times 10^{-34} \text{ J} \cdot \text{s})^2}$$

$$= -2.17 \times 10^{-18} \text{ J}$$

A more convenient unit for measuring energy at the atomic level is the electronvolt (eV). Recall from Chap. 30 that an electronvolt is the energy acquired by an electron accelerated through a potential difference of 1 V. Consequently

$$1 \text{ eV} = 1.6 \times 10^{-19} \text{ J}$$

In applications where a larger unit of energy is required the megaelectron volt (MeV) is more appropriate.

$$1 \text{ MeV} = 10^6 \text{ eV}$$

From the previous example, the energy of the ground-state electron can be expressed in electronvolts as follows:

$$E_1 = -2.17 \times 10^{-18} \text{ J} \frac{1 \text{ eV}}{1.6 \times 10^{-19} \text{ J}}$$

$$= -13.6 \text{ eV}$$

This fact can be used to write Eq. (42-30) in a simpler form:

$$E_n = -\frac{13.6 \text{ eV}}{n^2} \tag{41-31}$$

Similar calculations will yield smaller negative values for the outer orbits. If the electron were to be entirely removed from the atom, a case where $n = \infty$, 13.6 eV of energy would be required. ($E_\infty = 0$.) Similarly, a photon of energy 13.6 eV could be emitted if an electron were to be captured by an ionized hydrogen atom and wind up in the ground state.

The atomic spectra observed for hydrogen is now understood in terms of energy levels. The Lyman series results from electrons returning from some excited state to the ground state, as seen in Fig. 41-9. The Balmer, Paschen, and Brackett series occur when the final states are orbits for which $n = 2$, $n = 3$, and $n = 4$, respectively.

An energy-level diagram for hydrogen is shown in Fig. 41-10. Such diagrams are often used to describe the various energy states of atoms.

Fig. 41-9 The Bohr atom and a description of the origin of the Lyman, Balmer, Paschen, and Brackett spectral series.

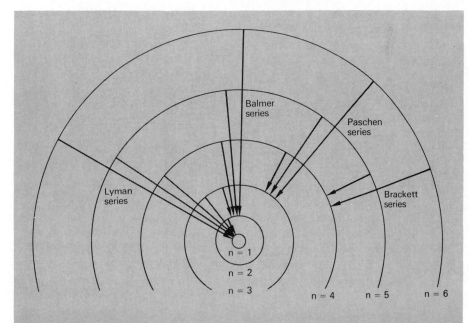

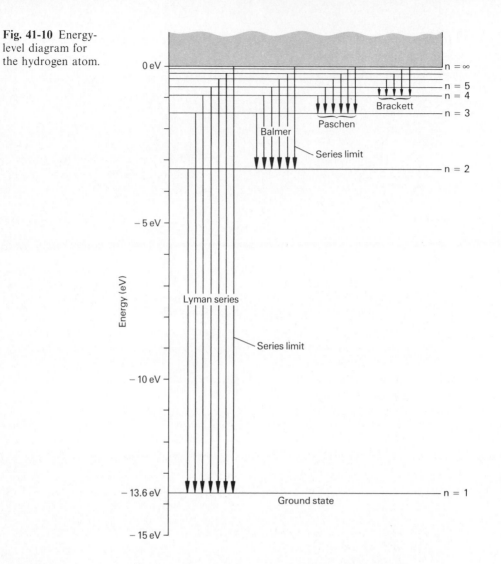

Fig. 41-10 Energy-level diagram for the hydrogen atom.

41-11
MODERN ATOMIC THEORY

Although the Bohr atom remains a convenient way to describe the atom, a much more refined theory has been found necessary. The model of the electron as a point particle moving in a perfectly circular orbit does not explain many atomic phenomena. Additional quantum numbers have been established to describe the shape and orientation of the electron cloud about the nucleus, as well as the spin motion of the electrons. It has also been established that no two electrons of the same atom can exist in exactly the same state, even though they may exist at the same Bohr energy level. A more complete description of modern atomic theory can be found in textbooks in the field of atomic physics.

SUMMARY

The works of Einstein, Bohr, de Broglie, Balmer, and many others have led to a much clearer understanding of nature. We no longer view the world as though all phenomena can be seen, touched, and observed in traditional ways. Greater understanding of the atom has lead to many industrial applications based on the principles discussed in this chapter. A summary of the major topics is given below:

- According to Einstein's equations of relativity, length, mass, and time are affected by relativistic speeds. The changes become more significant as the ratio of an object's velocity v to the free space velocity of light c becomes larger.

$$L = L_0 \sqrt{1 - \frac{v^2}{c^2}}$$ *Relativistic Contraction*

$$m = \frac{m_0}{\sqrt{1 - v^2/c^2}}$$ *Relativistic Mass*

$$t = \frac{t_0}{\sqrt{1 - v^2/c^2}}$$ *Time Dilation*

In the above equations, $c = 3 \times 10^8$ m/s.

- The total energy of a particle of rest mass m_0 and speed v can be written in either of the following forms:

$$E = mc^2 \qquad E = \sqrt{m_0^2 c^4 + p^2 c^2}$$ *Total Energy*

In these equations m is the relativistic mass as determined by the speed v, and p is the momentum mv.

- The *relativistic kinetic energy* is found from

$$E_\kappa = (m - m_0)c^2$$ *Relativistic Kinetic Energy*

- The quantum theory of electromagnetic radiation relates the energy of such radiation to its frequency f or wavelength λ.

$$E = hf \qquad E = \frac{hc}{\lambda} \qquad h = 6.63 \times 10^{-34} \text{ J/Hz}$$

- In the photoelectric effect, the kinetic energy of the ejected electrons is the energy of the incident radiation hf less the work function of the surface W.

$$E_\kappa = \tfrac{1}{2}mv^2 = hf - W$$ *Photoelectric Equation*

- The lowest frequency f_0 at which a photoelectron is ejected is the threshold frequency. It corresponds to the work-function energy W.

$$f_0 = \frac{W}{h} \qquad W = hf_0$$ *Threshold Frequency*

- By combining wave theory with particle theory, de Broglie was able to give the following equation for the wavelength of any particle whose mass and velocity are known:

$$\lambda = \frac{h}{mv} \qquad h = 6.63 \times 10^{-34} \text{ J/Hz}$$

de Broglie Wavelength

- Bohr's first postulate states that the angular momentum of an electron in any orbit must be a multiple of $h/2\pi$. His second postulate states that the energy absorbed or emitted by an atom is in discrete amounts equal to the difference in energy levels of an electron. These concepts are given as equations below:

$$mvr = \frac{nh}{2\pi} \qquad hf = E_f - E_i$$

Bohr's postulates

- Absorption and emission spectra for gases verify the discrete nature of radiation. The wavelength λ or frequency f which corresponds to a change in electron energy levels is given by

$$\frac{1}{\lambda} = R\left(\frac{1}{nf^2} - \frac{1}{n_i^2}\right) \qquad f = Rc\left(\frac{1}{nf^2} - \frac{1}{n_0^2}\right)$$

$$R = \frac{me^4}{8\epsilon_0^2 hc} = 1.097 \times 10^7 \text{ m}^{-1} \qquad \textit{Rydberg's Constant}$$

- The total energy of a particular quantum state n for the hydrogen atom is given by:

$$E_n = -\frac{me^4}{8\epsilon_0^2 n^2 h^2} \qquad \text{or} \qquad E_n = -\frac{13.6 \text{ eV}}{n^2}$$

where $\epsilon_0 = 8.85 \times 10^{-12} \text{ C}^2/\text{N} \cdot \text{m}^2$
$e = 1.6 \times 10^{-19} \text{ C}$
$m_e = 9.1 \times 10^{-31} \text{ kg}$
$h = 6.63 \times 10^{-34} \text{ J/Hz}$

QUESTIONS

41-1. Define the following terms:
  a. Relativistic mass
  b. Relativistic contraction
  c. Time dilation
  d. Einstein's postulates
  e. Planck's postulate
  f. Work function
  g. Photoelectric effect
  h. Spectrometer
  i. Line emission spectra
  j. Absorption spectra
  k. Spectral series
  l. Bohr atom
  m. Principal quantum number
  n. Energy level
  o. Excited atom

41-2. If it were possible for a material object to travel past you at the speed of light, describe the mass, length, and time interval you would observe.

41-3. An astronaut holds a clock of mass m and length L. Assume that the astronaut passes you at relativistic speed. Compare your measurements of m, L, and Δt with those made by the astronaut for the same clock.

41-4. Recalling Newton's second law of motion, what happens to the thrust requirements for propelling rockets to higher and higher relativistic speeds? Theoretically, what force would be required to achieve the velocity of light?

41-5. You are enclosed in a box with six opaque walls. Are there any experiments you can perform inside the box to prove that you are **(a)** moving with constant linear velocity, **(b)** accelerating, or **(c)** rotating with constant angular velocity?

41-6. Combine Eqs. (41-5) and (41-3) to obtain Einstein's equation for the total relativistic energy, $E = mc^2$.

41-7. Suppose you want photoelectrons to have a kinetic energy E_k and you know the work function W of the surface; how would you determine the required wavelength λ of the incident light?

41-8. Describe an experiment you might perform to determine the work function of a surface assuming you have a light source of varying wavelength.

41-9. Sketch on a single diagram the Balmer series and the Lyman series for the hydrogen emission spectrum. What is meant by the *series limit*?

41-10. Explain clearly what is meant when we say that the energy of the ground state is -13.6 eV for the hydrogen atom. What is the significance of the minus sign?

41-11. Describe an experiment which will demonstrate **(a)** a line emission spectrum, **(b)** a line absorption spectrum, and **(c)** a continuous spectrum.

41-12. Hydrogen atoms in their ground state are bombarded by electrons which have been accelerated through a potential difference of 12.8 V. Which lines of the Lyman series will be emitted by the hydrogen atoms?

PROBLEMS

41-1. Three metersticks travel past an observer at speeds of $0.1c$, $0.6c$, and $0.9c$. What lengths would be recorded by the observer according to Einstein's relativistic contraction equation?

Ans. 99.5, 80.0, and 43.6 cm.

41-2. Space ships A and B pass each other in space with a relative velocity of 6×10^7 m/s. The length of each ship is 23.6 m. A person aboard ship A will measure what length for ship B? Will an observer aboard B observe the same length for ship A? How will the person on ship A record his own ship's length?

41-3. A space ship A travels past an observer B with a relative velocity of two-tenths of the speed of light. The observer B determines that it takes a person on space ship A exactly 3.96 s to perform a given task? What time will the person on ship A measure for this same event?

Ans. 3.88 s.

41-4. Elementary particles called mumesons rain down through the atmosphere at 2.994×10^6 m/s. At rest the mumeson would decay, on average, 2 μs after it came into existence. What is the lifetime of the atmospheric mumeson from the viewpoint of an observer on the earth?

41-5. What is the mass of an electron traveling at a speed of 2×10^8 m/s? The rest mass of an electron is 9.1×10^{-31} kg. What is the total energy of the electron? What is its relativistic kinetic energy?

Ans. 12.2×10^{-31} kg, 1.10×10^{-13} J, 0.280×10^{-13} J.

41-6. Compute the mass and the speed of electrons having a relativistic kinetic energy of 1.2 MeV.

41-7. What mass is required to run about 1 million 100-W electric light bulbs for 1 year?

Ans. 35 g.

41-8. Assume that the price of energy is 8 cents per kilowatthour. What would be the cost of the rest energy of 1 kg of matter if it could be totally utilized?

41-9. Compute the mass and the speed of protons having a relativistic kinetic energy of 235 MeV. The mass of a proton at rest is 1.673×10^{-27} kg.

Ans. 2.09×10^{-27} kg, 1.8×10^8 m/s.

41-10. The rest mass of a proton is 1.673×10^{-27} kg. What is the total energy of a proton which has been accelerated to a velocity of 2.5×10^8 m/s? What is its relativistic kinetic energy?

41-11. A payload of 4000 kg is to be given a constant acceleration of 1 g (9.8 m/s^2) as it travels through space. What resultant force (thrust) is required at non-relativistic speeds? If the payload eventually reaches a speed of 1.5×10^8 m/s, what thrust is required to maintain the same acceleration?

Ans. 39.2 kN, 45.3 kN.

41-12. If the photoelectric work function of a material is 4.0 eV, what is the minimum frequency of light required to eject photoelectrons? What wavelength corresponds to this frequency?

41-13. The first photoelectrons are emitted from a copper surface when the wavelength of incident radiation is 282 nm. What is the threshold frequency for copper? What is the work function for a copper surface?

Ans. 1.06×10^{15} Hz, 4.4 eV.

41-14. The work function of a nickel surface is 5.01 eV. If a nickel surface is illuminated by light of wavelength 200 nm, what is the energy of an emitted electron?

41-15. When light of frequency 1.6×10^{15} Hz strikes a material surface, electrons just begin to leave the surface. This is the threshold frequency. What is the maximum kinetic energy of photoelectrons emitted from this surface when light of frequency 2.0×10^{15} Hz falls on the material?

Ans. 1.66 eV.

41-16. When monochromatic light of wavelength 450 nm strikes a cathode, photoelectrons are emitted with a maximum velocity of 4.8×10^5 m/s. Determine the work function W?

41-17. In a photoelectric process, the retarding electric potential difference just sufficient to stop the most energetic photoelectrons is called the *stopping potential*. Assume that photoelectrons are emitted from a surface irradiated with light of wavelength 450 nm and leave the surface at a maximum speed of 6×10^5 m/s. **(a)** What is the work function? **(b)** What is the stopping potential?

Ans. **(a)** 2.78×10^{-19} J **(b)** 1.74 V.

41-18. Determine the kinetic energy of an electron if its de Broglie wavelength is 2×10^{-11} m.

41-19. The rest mass of a proton is 1.673×10^{-27} kg and its charge is the same magnitude as for an electron. What is the de Broglie wavelength of a proton if it is accelerated through a potential difference of 500 V.

Ans. 1.28 pm.

41-20. What is the de Broglie wavelength of the waves associated with an electron which has been accelerated from rest through a potential difference of 160 V?

41-21. Determine the wavelength of the first three spectral lines of atomic hydrogen in the Balmer series.

Ans. 656, 486, and 434 nm.

41-22. Determine the wavelengths of the first three spectral lines of atomic hydrogen in the Paschen series.

41-23. Determine the radius of the $n = 4$ Bohr level of the classical Bohr hydrogen atom.

Ans. 850.5 pm.

41-24. What is the classical radius of the first Bohr orbit in the hydrogen atom?

41-25. Determine the wavelength of the photon emitted from a hydrogen atom when the electron jumps from the $n = 3$ Bohr level to the ground level.

Ans. 103 nm.

41-26. What is the maximum wavelength of an incident photon if it can ionize a hydrogen atom originally in its second exited state ($n = 3$)?

41-27. Calculate the frequency and the wavelength of the H_β line of the Balmer series. The transition is from the fourth Bohr level to the second Bohr level.

Ans. 6.16×10^{14} Hz, 486 nm.

42 *Nuclear Physics and the Nucleus*

OBJECTIVES: After completing this chapter, you should be able to:

1. Define the *mass number* and the *atomic number*, and demonstrate your understanding of the nature of fundamental nuclear particles.

2. Define *isotopes* and discuss the use of a mass spectrometer to separate isotopes.

3. Calculate the mass defect and the binding energy per nucleon for a particular isotope.

4. Demonstrate your understanding of radioactive decay and nuclear reactions; describe alpha particles, beta particles, and gamma rays, listing their properties.

5. Calculate the activity and the quantity of radioactive isotope remaining after a period of time if the half-lives and the initial values are given.

6. State the various conservation laws, and discuss their application to nuclear reactions.

7. Draw a rough sketch of a nuclear reactor describing the various components and their function in the production of nuclear power.

The work of Rutherford and Bohr left us with a picture of the atom as a dense, positively charged nucleus surrounded by a cloud of electrons at distinct energy levels. From this point of view, the nucleus is the center of an atom, containing most of the atom's mass. The behavior of the atom is also affected by the nucleus because in the neutral atom the total number of positive charges in the nucleus must equal the number of electrons.

In this chapter, we look at the basic internal structure of the nucleus. We shall find that classical physics is not adequate to describe interactions at this level. Topics to be discussed include nuclear binding energy, radioactivity, and nuclear energy. The emphasis will be on providing a broad understanding of the atomic nucleus and its behavior.

Nuclear technology has grown enormously since its beginning in the early 1940s. The study of the atomic nucleus once was a subject reserved mainly for physicists, but today there are few people whose lives are not touched by some aspect of nuclear science. As patients we see the doctor use radioactive materials to diagnose a condition or treat it. As citizens, we are concerned with the promises and dangers of large-scale nuclear power production. More than ever before, technicians and engineers need a better understanding of the atomic nucleus and its potential.

42-1 THE ATOMIC NUCLEUS

All matter is composed of different combinations of *at least* three fundamental particles: protons, neutrons, and electrons. For example, a beryllium atom (Fig. 42-1) consists of a nucleus which contains four protons and five neutrons. The fact that beryllium is electrically neutral requires that four electrons surround the nucleus. The two inner electrons are at a different energy level ($n = 1$) than the outer two electrons ($n = 2$).

Fig. 42-1 A model of a beryllium atom. The nucleus consists of four protons and five neutrons surrounded by four electrons. The positive charge of the protons is exactly balanced by the negatively charged electrons in the neutral atom.

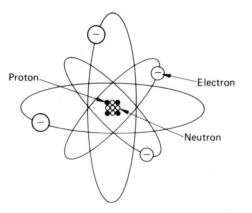

Rutherford's scattering experiments demonstrated that the nucleus contains most of the mass of an atom and that the nucleus is only about one ten-thousandth of the diameter of the atom. Thus, a typical atom with a diameter of 10^{-10} m (100 pm) would have a nucleus about 10^{-14} m (10 fm) in diameter. The prefixes *pico* (10^{-12}) and *femto* (10^{-15}) are useful for nuclear dimensions. Since the diameter of the atom is 10,000 times that of its nucleus, the atom, and therefore matter, consists largely of space that is almost empty.

Let us review what is known about the fundamental particles. The electron has a mass of 9.1×10^{-31} kg and a charge of $e = -1.6 \times 10^{-19}$ C. The proton is the nucleus of a hydrogen atom. It has a mass of 1.673×10^{-27} kg and a positive charge equal in magnitude to the charge of an electron ($+e$). Since the mass of an electron is extremely small, the mass of a proton is approximately the same as the mass of a hydrogen atom, which consists of one proton and one electron. The proton has a diameter of approximately 3 fm.

The other nuclear particle, the neutron, is present in the nuclei of all elements except hydrogen. It has a mass of 1.675×10^{-27} kg, which is slightly greater than that of the proton, but it has no charge. Thus, while neutrons contribute to the mass of a nucleus, they do not affect the net positive charge of the nucleus, which is due only to protons. The neutron also has a diameter of approximately 3 fm. Table 42-1 summarizes the data we have discussed for three fundamental particles.

Table 42-1 Fundamental Particles

Particle	Symbol	Mass, kg	Charge, C
Electron	e	9.1×10^{-31}	-1.6×10^{-19}
Proton	p	1.673×10^{-27}	$+1.6 \times 10^{-19}$
Neutron	n	1.675×10^{-27}	0

From what we now know about the fundamental particles, it is clear that diagrams like Fig. 42-1 cannot be taken too seriously. Distances are not normally presented to scale in such schematic representations. Moreover, classical laws of physics often do not apply for the microworld of the nucleus.

A true understanding of atomic and nuclear events will require a new way of thinking. For example, one might ask what holds the nucleus together. Clearly if Coulomb's electrostatic repulsion applies in the nucleus, it must be overcome by a much larger force. Both this much larger force and the electrostatic force are immense compared with the gravitational force. This third force is called the *nuclear force.*

The nuclear force is a very strong, short-range force. If two nucleons (which are protons or neutrons) are separated by approximately 1 fm, a strong attractive force occurs which quickly drops to zero as their separation becomes larger. The force appears to be the same, or nearly the same, between two protons or two neutrons or between a neutron and a proton. It is an attractive force until the nucleons get too close, when it becomes strongly repulsive, so that the nucleons cannot occupy the same space at the same time. If one nucleon is completely surrounded by other nucleons, its nuclear force field will be saturated, and it cannot exert any force on nucleons outside those surrounding it.

42-2 THE ELEMENTS

For many centuries, scientists have been studying the various elements found on the earth. A number of attempts have been made to organize the different elements according to their chemical and/or physical properties. The modern grouping of elements is the periodic table. One form of the periodic table is printed in Table 42-2.

Table 42-2 The Periodic Table (*Adapted from General Chemistry by Frederick Longo. Copyright 1974 by McGraw-Hill, Inc. Used with permission of McGraw-Hill Book Company.*)

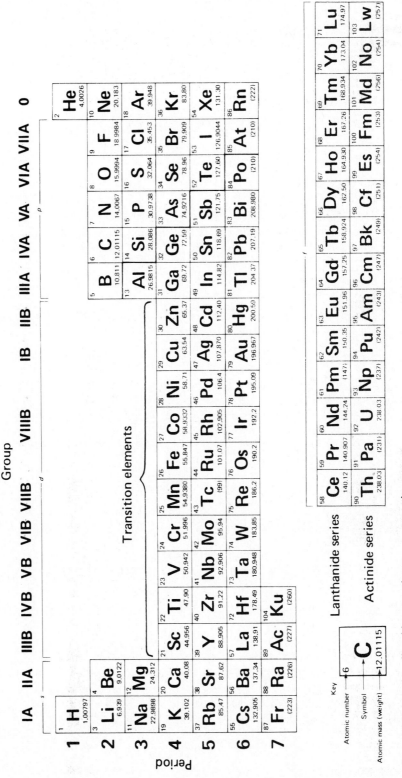

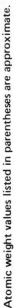

Atomic weight values listed in parentheses are approximate.

Table 42-3 International Atomic Weights (Based on Carbon 12)†

Element	Symbol	Atomic number	Atomic weight
Actinium	Ac	89	(227)
Aluminum	Al	13	26.9815
Americium	Am	95	(243)
Antimony	Sb	51	121.75
Argon	Ar	18	39.948
Arsenic	As	33	74.9216
Astatine	At	85	(210)
Barium	Ba	56	137.34
Berkelium	Bk	97	(247)
Beryllium	Be	4	9.0122
Bismuth	Bi	83	208.980
Boron	B	5	10.811
Bromine	Br	35	79.904
Cadmium	Cd	48	112.40
Calcium	Ca	20	40.08
Californium	Cf	98	(251)
Carbon	C	6	12.01115
Cerium	Ce	58	140.12
Cesium	Cs	55	132.905
Chlorine	Cl	17	35.453
Chromium	Cr	24	51.996
Cobalt	Co	27	58.9332
Columbium (see Niobium)			
Copper	Cu	29	63.546
Curium	Cm	96	(247)
Dysprosium	Dy	66	162.50
Einsteinium	Es	99	(254)
Erbium	Er	68	167.26
Europium	Eu	63	151.96
Fermium	Fm	100	(257)
Fluorine	F	9	18.9984
Francium	Fr	87	(223)
Gadolinium	Gd	64	157.25
Gallium	Ga	31	69.72
Germanium	Ge	32	72.59
Gold	Au	79	196.967
Hafnium	Hf	72	178.49
Helium	He	2	4.0026
Holmium	Ho	67	164.930
Hydrogen	H	1	1.00797
Indium	In	49	114.82
Iodine	I	53	126.9044
Iridium	Ir	77	192.2
Iron	Fe	26	55.847
Krypton	Kr	36	83.80
Lanthanum	La	57	138.91
Lawrencium	Lw	103	(257)
Lead	Pb	82	207.19
Lithium	Li	3	6.939
Lutetium	Lu	71	174.97
Magnesium	Mg	12	24.312
Manganese	Mn	25	54.9380
Mendelevium	Md	101	(256)
Mercury	Hg	80	200.59
Molybdenum	Mo	42	95.94
Neodymium	Nd	60	144.24
Neon	Ne	10	20.183
Neptunium	Np	93	(237)
Nickel	Ni	28	58.71
Niobium (Columbium)	Nb	41	92.906
Nitrogen	N	7	14.0067
Nobelium	No	102	(254)
Osmium	Os	76	190.2
Oxygen	O	8	15.9994
Palladium	Pd	46	106.4
Phosphorus	P	15	30.9738
Platinum	Pt	78	195.09
Plutonium	Pu	94	(244)
Polonium	Po	84	(209)
Potassium	K	19	39.102
Praseodymium	Pr	59	140.907
Promethium	Pm	61	(145)
Protactinium	Pa	91	(231)
Radium	Ra	88	(226)
Radon	Rn	86	(222)
Rhenium	Re	75	186.22
Rhodium	Rh	45	102.91
Rubidium	Rb	37	85.47
Ruthenium	Ru	44	101.07
Samarium	Sm	62	150.35
Scandium	Sc	21	44.956
Selenium	Se	34	78.96
Silicon	Si	14	28.086
Silver	Ag	47	107.868
Sodium	Na	11	22.9898
Strontium	Sr	38	87.62
Sulfur	S	16	32.064
Tantalum	Ta	73	180.948
Technetium	Tc	43	(97)
Tellurium	Te	52	127.60
Terbium	Tb	65	158.924
Thallium	Tl	81	204.37
Thorium	Th	90	232.038
Thulium	Tm	69	168.934
Tin	Sn	50	118.69
Titanium	Ti	22	47.90
Tungsten (Wolfram)	W	74	183.85
Uranium	U	92	238.03
Vanadium	V	23	50.942
Wolfram (Tungsten)	W	74	183.85
Xenon	Xe	54	131.30
Ytterbium	Yb	70	173.04
Yttrium	Y	39	88.905
Zinc	Zn	30	65.37
Zirconium	Zr	40	91.22

† Values in parentheses are mass numbers of longest-lived or best-known isotopes

Each element is assigned a number that distinguishes it from any other element. For example, the number for hydrogen is 1, the number for helium is 4, and the number for oxygen is 8. These numbers equal the number of protons in the nucleus of that element. The number is given the symbol Z and is called the *atomic number*.

> The **atomic number** Z of an element is equal to the number of protons in the nucleus of an atom of that element.

The atomic number indirectly determines the chemical properties of an element because Z determines the number of electrons needed to balance the positive charge of the nucleus. The chemical nature of an atom depends on the number of electrons, in particular the outermost, or valence, electrons.

As the number of protons in a nucleus increases, so does the number of neutrons. In lighter elements, the increase is approximately one to one, but heavier elements may have more than $1\frac{1}{2}$ times more neutrons than protons. For example, oxygen has 8 protons and 8 neutrons, whereas uranium has 92 protons and 146 neutrons. The total number of nucleons in a nucleus is called the *mass number A*.

> The **mass number** A of an element is equal to the total number of protons and neutrons in its nucleus.

If we represent the number of neutrons by N, we can write the mass number A in terms of the atomic number Z and the number of neutrons.

$$\boxed{A = Z + N} \tag{42-1}$$

Thus, the mass number for uranium is 92 + 146 or 238.

A general way of describing the nucleus of a particular atom is to write the symbol for the element with its mass number and atomic number shown as follows:

$$_{\text{atomic number}}^{\text{mass number}}[\text{symbol}] = {}_{Z}^{A}\text{X} \tag{42-2}$$

For example, the uranium atom has the symbol ${}_{92}^{238}\text{U}$.

The structures and symbols for the first four elements are shown in Fig. 42-2. An alphabetical listing of all the elements is given in Table 42-3.

EXAMPLE 42-1   How many neutrons are in the nucleus of an atom of mercury ${}_{80}^{201}\text{Hg}$?

Solution   The symbol shows that the atomic number is 80 and the mass number is 201. Thus, from Eq. (42-1), the number of neutrons is

$$N = A - Z = 201 - 80 = 121$$

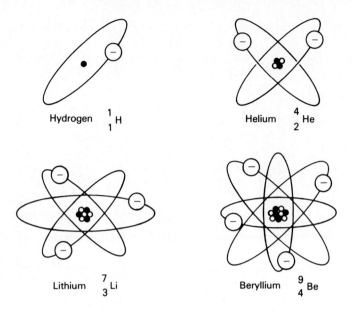

Fig. 42-2 The structure and symbols of the first four elements.

Hydrogen $^1_1$H

Helium $^4_2$He

Lithium $^7_3$Li

Beryllium $^9_4$Be

**42-3
THE
ATOMIC
MASS UNIT**

The very small masses of nuclear particles call for an extremely small unit of mass. Scientists normally express atomic and nuclear masses in atomic mass units/(u).

> One **atomic mass unit** (1 u) is exactly equal to one-twelfth of the mass of the most abundant form of the carbon atom.

In terms of the kilogram, the atomic mass unit is

$$1 \text{ u} = 1.6606 \times 10^{-27} \text{ kg} \qquad (42\text{-}3)$$

The mass of a proton is 1.007276 u, and that of a neutron is 1.008665 u.

EXAMPLE 42-2

The periodic table shows the average atomic mass of barium to be 137.34 u. What is the average mass of the barium nucleus?

Solution

The mass of the nucleus is the atomic mass less the mass of the surrounding cloud of electrons. Thus, we must first determine the mass of an electron in atomic mass units.

$$m_e = 9.1 \times 10^{-31} \text{ kg} \, \frac{1 \text{ u}}{1.6606 \times 10^{-27} \text{ kg}}$$

$$= 5.5 \times 10^{-4} \text{ u}$$

Since the atomic number Z of barium is 56, there must be the same number of electrons. This total mass is

$$m_T = 56(5.5 \times 10^{-4} \text{ u}) = 3.08 \times 10^{-2} \text{ u}$$

792   MODERN PHYSICS

The average atomic mass was given as 137.34 u. Thus, the nuclear mass is

$$137.34 \text{ u} - 0.0308 \text{ u}$$

or

$$137.31 \text{ u}.$$

The masses given for atoms in the periodic table include the electron masses.

It should be remembered that mass can be equated to units of energy from Einstein's relation

$$E = mc^2$$

Consequently, a mass of 1 u corresponds to an energy given by

$$(1 \text{ u})c^2 = (1.66 \times 10^{-27} \text{ kg})(3 \times 10^8 \text{ m/s})^2 = 1.49 \times 10^{-10} \text{ J}$$

In the more convenient units of electronvolts, we can write

$$(1 \text{ u})c^2 = 1.49 \times 10^{-10} \text{ J} \frac{1 \text{ eV}}{1.6 \times 10^{-19} \text{ J}}$$

$$= 9.31 \times 10^8 \text{ eV} = 931 \text{ MeV}$$

The conversion factor from mass units (u) to energy units (MeV) is therefore

$$\boxed{c^2 = 931 \text{ MeV/u}} \tag{42-3}$$

As an exercise you might verify that the electron and the proton have rest-mass energies of 0.511 and 938 MeV, respectively.

42-4 ISOTOPES

It is possible for two atoms of the same element to have nuclei containing different numbers of neutrons. Such atoms are called *isotopes*.

Isotopes are atoms which have the same atomic number Z but different mass numbers A.

For example, naturally occurring carbon is a mixture of two isotopes. The most abundant form, $^{12}_{6}\text{C}$, has six protons and six neutrons in its nucleus. Another form, $^{13}_{6}\text{C}$, has an extra neutron. Some elements have as many as 10 different isotopic forms.

Experimental verification of the existence of isotopes is accomplished with a mass spectrometer. This device, illustrated in Fig. 42-3, is used to separate the isotopes of an element. A source of singly ionized atoms of a particular element is positioned above the velocity selector. These ions are missing one electron and therefore have a charge of $+e$. They are propelled at varying speeds into the crossed **E** and **B** fields of the velocity selector. Ions with velocities sufficient to make the magnetic force $\mathbf{F}_m$ equal and opposite to the

Fig. 42-3 The mass spectrometer is used to separate isotopes of different mass, the crosses indicate that the direction of the magnetic field is into the paper.

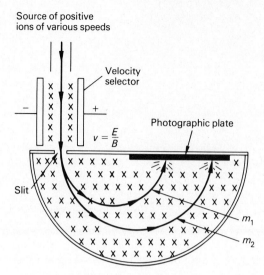

electric force F_e will pass through the bottom slit undeflected. Recalling that $F_e = eE$ and $F_m = evB$, we write

$$evB = eE$$

from which

$$\boxed{v = \frac{E}{B}} \qquad (42\text{-}4)$$

Only ions with this velocity will pass through the slit at the bottom of the selector.

The fast-moving positive ions next pass into the lower region, where another **B** field causes them to experience a perpendicular magnetic force. The magnitude of this force will be constant and equal to evB, but its direction will always be at right angles to the velocity of the ion. The result is a circular path of radius R. The magnetic force provides the necessary centripetal force. In this case, we have

$$F_{\text{magnetic}} = F_{\text{centripetal}}$$

or

$$evB = \frac{mv^2}{R}$$

where m is the mass of the ion of charge e. Solving for R, we find that the radius of the semicircular path is given by

$$\boxed{R = \frac{mv}{eB}} \qquad (42\text{-}5)$$

Since v, e, and B are constant, Eq. (42-5) gives the radius as a function of the mass of given ions. Ions of different mass will strike the photographic plate at different positions because their semicircular paths are different. Wherever a beam of ions strikes the plate, a darkened line will be produced. The distance of a particular line from the slit is twice the radius in which that beam of ions moves. In this manner the mass can be determined from Eq. (42-5).

The mass spectrometer is used to separate and study isotopes. Most elements are mixtures of atoms with different mass numbers. For example, if an ion beam of pure lithium is injected into the mass spectrometer, two types of atoms are observed. The darker band occurs because around 92 percent of the atoms have a mass of 7.016 u. The remaining 8 percent, producing a lighter band, are atoms with mass 6.015 u. These two isotopes of lithium are written $^{7}_{3}\text{Li}$ and $^{6}_{3}\text{Li}$.

Since some elements, e.g., tin, have many different isotopic forms, it is not surprising that the average atomic mass for elements is often not very close to an integer. Average atomic mass is affected by the mass numbers and relative abundance of each isotopic form. For example, chlorine has an average atomic mass of 35.453 u, which results from a mixture of the two isotopes $^{35}_{17}\text{Cl}$ and $^{37}_{17}\text{C}$. The lighter chlorine isotope occurs about 3 times as often as the heavier one.

EXAMPLE 42-3   While studying chlorine with the mass spectrometer, it is noted that a very intense line occurs 24 cm from the entrance slit. Another lighter line appears at a distance of 25.37 cm. If the mass of the ions which form the first line is 34.980 u, what is the mass of the other isotope?

Solution   Since the given distances represent diameters, the radii of the two paths are

$$R_1 = 12 \text{ cm} \quad \text{and} \quad R_2 = 12.685 \text{ cm}$$

Now from Eq. (42-5),

$$R_1 = \frac{m_1 v}{eB} \quad \text{and} \quad R_2 = \frac{m_2 v}{eB}$$

Since e, v, and B are constant, we have

$$\frac{m_1}{m_2} = \frac{R_1}{R_2}$$

from which the mass m_2 is found to be

$$m_2 = \frac{m_1 R_2}{R_1} = \frac{(34.980 \text{ u})(12.685 \text{ cm})}{(12 \text{ cm})}$$

$$= 36.977 \text{ u}$$

42-5
**THE MASS
DEFECT
AND
BINDING
ENERGY**

One of the startling results which can be demonstrated with the mass spectrometer is that the mass of a nucleus is not exactly equal to the sum of the masses of its nucleons. Let us consider, for example, the helium atom, $^4_2$He, which has two electrons about a nucleus containing two protons and two neutrons. The atomic mass is found from the periodic table to be 4.0026 u.

Now let us compare this value with the mass of all the individual particles which make up the atom:

$$2\ p = 2(1.0007276\ u) = 2.014552\ u$$

$$2\ n = 2(1.008665\ u) = 2.017330\ u$$

$$2\ e = 2(0.00055\ u) = 0.001100\ u$$

$$\text{Total mass} = \overline{4.032982\ u}$$

The mass of the parts (4.0331 u) is apparently greater than the mass of the atom (4.0026 u).

$$m_{\text{parts}} - m_{\text{atom}} = 4.0330\ u - 4.0026\ u$$

$$= 0.0304\ u$$

When protons and neutrons join to form a helium nucleus, the mass is decreased in the process. This difference is called the *mass defect*. A mass defect can be shown to exist for atoms of all elements.

> The **mass defect** is defined as the difference between the rest mass of a nucleus and the sum of the rest masses of its constituent nucleons.

We have seen from Einstein's work that mass and energy are equivalent. We might suppose, then, that the mass decrease in joining nucleons together will result in an energy decrease. Since energy is conserved, a decrease in the energy of the system means that energy must be released in joining the system together. In the case of helium, this energy would come from a mass of 0.0304 u and would be equal to

$$E = mc^2 = (0.0304\ u)\ \frac{931\ \text{MeV}}{1\ u} = 28.3\ \text{MeV}$$

The total energy which would be released if we could build a nucleus from protons and neutrons is called the *binding energy* of the nucleus. As we have just seen, the binding energy of $^4_2$He is 28.3 MeV, as illustrated in Fig. 42-4*a*.

We can also reverse the above process and state that the binding energy is the energy required to break a nucleus apart into its constituent particles.

> The **binding energy** of a nucleus is defined as the energy required to separate a nucleus into its constituent nucleons.

Fig. 42-4 (a) When two protons and two neutrons are fused together to form a helium nucleus, energy is released. (b) The same amount of energy is required to break the nucleus apart into its constituent nucleons.

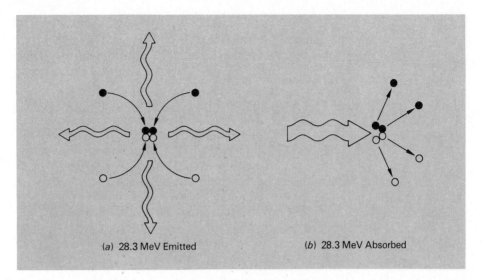

(a) 28.3 MeV Emitted   (b) 28.3 MeV Absorbed

In our example, an energy of 28.3 MeV must be supplied to $^4_2$He in order to separate the nucleus into two protons and two neutrons (Fig. 42-4b).

An isotope of atomic number Z and mass number A consists of Z protons, Z electrons, and $N = (A - Z)$ neutrons. If we neglect the binding energy of the electrons, a neutral isotope would have the same mass as Z neutral hydrogen atoms plus the mass of the neutrons. The masses of $^1_1$H and m_n are

$$m_H = 1.007825 \text{ u} \qquad m_n = 1.008665 \text{ u} \tag{42-6}$$

If we represent the atomic mass by M, the binding energy E_B can be approximated by

$$E_B = [(Zm_H + Nm_n) - M]c^2 \qquad \begin{array}{c} Binding \\ Energy \end{array} \tag{42-7}$$

In applying this equation, we should remember that $N = A - Z$ and that $c^2 = 931$ MeV/u.

EXAMPLE 42-4

Determine the total binding energy and the binding energy per nucleon for the $^{14}_7$N nucleus.

Solution

For nitrogen, $Z = 7$, $N = 7$, and $M = 14.003074$ u.

$$E_B = [(Zm_H + Nm_n) - M]c^2$$

$$= \{[7(1.007825 \text{ u}) + 7(1.008665 \text{ u})] - 14.003074 \text{ u}\}(931 \text{ MeV/u})$$

$$= (0.112356 \text{ u})(931 \text{ MeV/u}) = 104.6 \text{ MeV}$$

Since $^{14}_7$N contains 14 nucleons, the binding energy per nucleon is

$$\frac{E_B}{A} = \frac{104.6 \text{ MeV}}{14 \text{ nucleons}} = 7.47 \text{ MeV/nucleon}$$

The atomic mass M used in Eq. (42-7) must be the mass for the particular isotope of the element, not the mass taken from Table 42-2 or Table 42-3. These tables give the atomic masses of the naturally occurring mixture of isotopes for each element. The atomic mass of $^{12}_{7}C$, for example, is exactly 12.00 u by definition. The periodic table gives a value of 12.01115 u because naturally occurring carbon contains very small amounts of $^{13}_{7}C$ in addition of $^{12}_{7}C$ atoms.

The binding energy per nucleon, as computed in Example 42-4, is an important way of comparing the nuclei of various elements. A plot of the binding energy per nucleon as a function of increasing mass number is shown in Fig. 42-5 for many stable nuclei. Note that the mass numbers toward the center (50 to 80) yield the highest binding energy per nucleon. Elements ranging from $A = 50$ to $A = 80$ are the most stable.

Fig. 42-5 The average binding energy per nucleon for the most stable nucleus at each mass number.

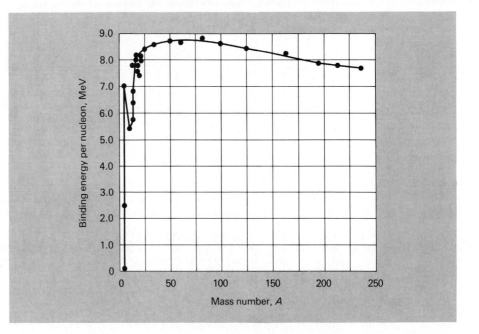

42-6 RADIO-ACTIVITY

The strong nuclear force holds the nucleons tight in the nucleus, overcoming the coulomb repulsion of protons. However, the balance of forces is not always maintained, and sometimes particles or photons are emitted from the nuclei of atoms. Such unstable nuclei are said to be *radioactive* and have the property of *radioactivity*.

All naturally occurring elements with atomic numbers greater than 83 are radioactive. They are slowly decaying and disappearing from the earth. Uranium and radium are two of the better-known examples of naturally radioactive elements. A few other naturally occurring, lighter, and less active elements have also been discovered.

Unstable nuclei are also produced artificially as by-products of nuclear reactors, for study in laboratories, or for other purposes. Additionally, some elements are made radioactive naturally by bombardment with high-energy photons.

There are three major forms of radioactive emission from atomic nuclei:

1. *Alpha particles* (α)

An alpha particle is the nucleus of a helium atom and consists of two protons and two neutrons. It has a charge of $+2e$ and a mass of 4,001506 u. Because of their positive charges and relatively low speeds ($\approx 0.1c$), alpha particles do not have great penetrating power.

2. *Beta particles* (β)

There are two kinds of beta particles, a beta minus particle (β^-) and a beta plus particle (β^+). The beta minus particle is simply an electron of charge $-e$ and mass equal to 0.00055 u. A beta plus particle, also called a *positron*, has the same mass as an electron but the opposite charge ($+e$). These particles are generally emitted at speeds near the velocity of light. The beta minus particles are much more penetrating than alpha particles, but beta plus particles easily combine with electrons; then rapid annihilation of both the positrons and electrons occurs, with the emission of gamma rays.

3. *Gamma rays* (γ)

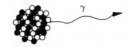

A gamma ray is a high-energy electromagnetic wave similar to heat and light but of much higher frequency. These rays have no charge or rest mass and are the most penetrating radiation emitted by radioactive elements.

To understand why these forms of radiation are emitted, it is helpful to look at nuclei which are relatively stable. Plotting the number of neutrons N vs. the number of protons Z for these stable nuclei gives a rough graph like that shown in Fig. 42-6. Note that the light elements are stable when the ratio of Z to N is close to 1. More neutrons are required for stability in the heavier elements. The additional nuclear forces of the extra neutrons are needed to balance the higher electric forces which result as more protons are collected together. Whenever a nucleus occurs which deviates very much from the line, it is unstable and will emit some form of radiation, thereby achieving stability.

42-7 RADIO-ACTIVE DECAY

Let us look at radioactive decay by alpha, beta, and gamma radiation and see what occurs during each process. The emission of an alpha particle $^4_2\alpha$ reduces the number of protons in the parent nucleus by 2 and the number of nucleons by 4. Symbolically, we write

$$^A_Z X \rightarrow {}^{A-4}_{Z-2}Y + {}^4_2\alpha + \text{energy} \qquad (42\text{-}8)$$

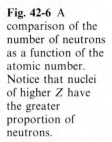

Fig. 42-6 A comparison of the number of neutrons as a function of the atomic number. Notice that nuclei of higher Z have the greater proportion of neutrons.

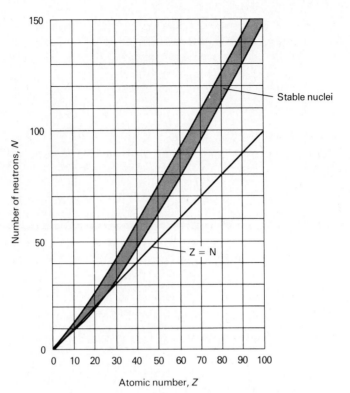

Number of neutrons, N

Stable nuclei

$Z = N$

Atomic number, Z

The energy term results from the fact that the rest energy of the products is less than that of the parent atom. The difference in energy is carried away primarily by the kinetic energy imparted to the alpha particle. The recoil kinetic energy of the much more massive daughter atom is small by comparison.

EXAMPLE 42-5   Write the reaction which occurs when $^{226}_{88}$Ra decays by alpha emission.

Solution   Applying Eq. (42-8), we write

$$^{226}_{88}\text{Ra} \rightarrow {}^{222}_{86}\text{Rn} + {}^{4}_{2}\alpha + \text{energy}$$

Notice that the unstable element radium has been transformed into a new element, radon, which is closer to the stability line.

Next consider the emission of beta-minus particles from the nucleus. If beta-minus particles are electrons, how can an electron come from a nucleus containing only protons and neutrons? This can be answered, at least in part, by analogy to the Bohr atom. We have seen that photons, which do not exist in the atom, are emitted by atoms when they change from one state to another.

Similarly, electrons, which do not exist in nuclei, can be emitted as a form of radiation when the nucleus changes from one state to another. When such a change does occur, the total charge must be conserved. This requires the conversion of a neutron into a proton and an electron.

$$^1_0n \rightarrow \, ^1_1p + \, ^{\,0}_{-1}e$$

Thus, in beta-minus emission a neutron is replaced by a proton. The atomic number Z increases by 1, and the mass number is unchanged. Symbolically.

$$\boxed{^A_ZX \rightarrow \, ^{\,A}_{Z+1}Y + \, ^{\,0}_{-1}\beta + \text{energy}} \qquad (42\text{-}9)$$

An example of beta emission is the decay of an isotope of neon into sodium:

$$^{23}_{10}Ne \rightarrow \, ^{23}_{11}Na + \, ^{\,0}_{-1}\beta + \text{energy}$$

The increase in Z is necessary to conserve charge.

Similarly, in positron (beta-plus) emission, a proton in the nucleus decays to a neutron and a positron.

$$^1_1p \rightarrow \, ^1_0n + \, ^{\,0}_{+1}e$$

The atomic number Z decreases by 1, and the mass number A is unchanged. Symbolically,

$$\boxed{^A_ZX \rightarrow \, ^{\,A}_{Z-1}Y + \, ^{\,0}_{+1}\beta + \text{energy}} \qquad (42\text{-}10)$$

An example of positron emission is the decay of an isotope of nitrogen into an isotope of carbon:

$$^{13}_7N \rightarrow \, ^{13}_6C + \, ^{\,0}_{+1}\beta - \text{energy}$$

In both types of beta emission, the kinetic energy is shared mostly by the beta particle and another particle called a *neutrino*. The neutrino has no rest mass and no electric charge, but it can have both energy and momentum.

In gamma emission, the parent nucleus maintains the same atomic number Z and the same mass number A. The gamma photon simply carries away energy from an unstable nucleus. Frequently, a succession of alpha and beta decays is accompanied by gamma decays, which carry off excess energy.

The radioactive disintegration of $^{238}_{92}U$ is shown in Fig. 42-7 as a series of decays through a number of elements until it becomes a stable $^{206}_{82}Pb$ nucleus.

Fig. 42-7 The uranium series of disintegration. Uranium decays, through a series of alpha- and beta-minus emissions, from $^{238}_{92}$U to $^{206}_{82}$Pb.

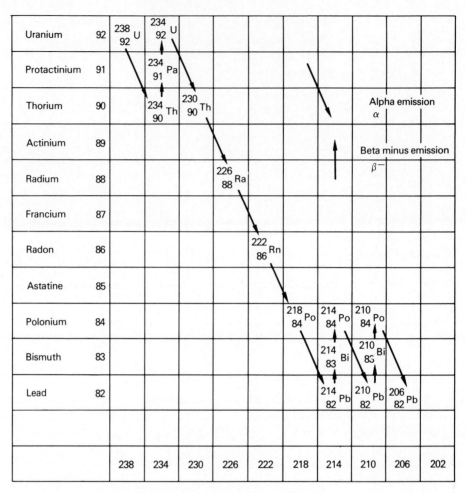

Mass number, A

42-8 HALF-LIFE

A radioactive material continues to emit radiation until all the unstable atoms have decayed. The number of unstable nuclei decaying or disintegrating every second for a given isotope can be predicted on the basis of probability. This number is referred to as the *activity R*, given by

$$R = \frac{-\Delta N}{\Delta l} \tag{42-11}$$

where N is the number of undecayed nuclei. The negative sign is included because N is decreasing with time. The units for R are inverse seconds (s^{-1}).

In practice, the activity in disintegrations per second is so large that a more convenient unit, the *curie* (Ci), is defined as follows.

One **curie** (Ci) is the activity of a radioactive material which decays at the rate of 3.7×10^{10} disintegrations per second.

$$1 \text{ Ci} = 3.7 \times 10^{10} \text{ s}^{-1} \qquad (42\text{-}12)$$

The activity of 1 g of radium is slightly less than 1 Ci.

The random nature of nuclear decay means that the activity R at any time is directly proportional to the number of nuclei remaining; i.e., as the number of remaining nuclei decreases with time, the activity must also decrease with time. Therefore, if we plot the number of remaining nuclei as a function of time, as illustrated in Fig. 42-8, we see that radioactive decay is not linear. The

Fig. 42-8 The radioactive decay curve illustrating the half-life as the time $T_{1/2}$ required for one-half of the unstable nuclei present at time $t = 0$ to decay.

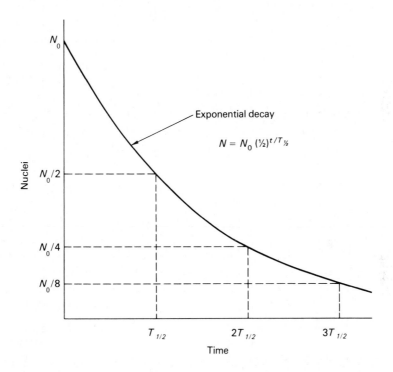

Exponential decay

$$N = N_0 \left(\tfrac{1}{2}\right)^{t/T_{1/2}}$$

time it takes for this curve to drop to one-half its original value is different for each radioactive isotope, and it is called the *half-life*.

The **half-life** $T_{1/2}$ of a radioactive isotope is the length of time in which one-half of its unstable nuclei will decay.

For example, the half-life of radium 226 is 1620 yr; 1 g of this isotope will decay to 0.5 g in 1620 yr, to 0.25 g in 2(1620 yr), to 0.125 g in 3(1620 yr), and so on.

We can use this definition of the half-life to determine how many nuclei are present at a time t. If we start out at time $t = 0$ with a number N_0 of unstable nuclei, then after n half-lives have passed, there will be left a number of nuclei N given by

$$N = N_0(\tfrac{1}{2})^n \qquad (42\text{-}13)$$

The number n of half-lives in the period of time t is, of course, $t/T_{1/2}$. Thus, a more applicable form of the above relation is

$$\boxed{N = N_0(\tfrac{1}{2})^{t/T_{1/2}}}$$

Since the amount of radioactive material is determined by the number of nuclei present, an equation similar to Eq. (42-13) can be used to compute the mass of remaining radioactive material after a number of half-lives.

The same idea applied to the activity R of a radioactive sample yields the relation

$$\boxed{R = R_0(\tfrac{1}{2})^{t/T_{1/2}}} \qquad (42\text{-}14)$$

EXAMPLE 42-6

The worst by-product of ordinary nuclear reactors is the radioactive isotope plutonium 239, which has a half-life of 24,400 yr. Suppose the initial activity of a sample containing 1.64×10^{20} $^{239}_{94}\text{Pu}$ nuclei is 4 mCi. (a) How many of these nuclei remain after 73,200 yr? (b) What will be the activity at that time?

Solution (a)

Substitution into Eq. (42-12) yields

$$N = N_0\left(\frac{1}{2}\right)^{t/T_{1/2}} = 1.64 \times 10^{20}\left(\frac{1}{2}\right)^{73,200 \text{ yr}/24,400 \text{ yr}}$$

$$= 1.64 \times 10^{20}(\tfrac{1}{2})^3 = 1.64 \times 10^{20}(\tfrac{1}{8})$$

$$= 2.05 \times 10^{19} \text{ nuclei}$$

Solution (b)

We obtain the remaining activity from Eq. (42-14).

$$R = R_0(\tfrac{1}{2})^{t/T_{1/2}} = 4 \text{ mCi}(\tfrac{1}{8}) = 0.5 \text{ mCi}$$

Both these calculations assume that no new $^{239}_{94}\text{Pu}$ nuclei are being created by other processes. It is easy to see from this example why disposal of some radioactive materials is such a difficult problem.

42-9 NUCLEAR REACTIONS

In a chemical reaction the atoms of two molecules react to form different molecules. In a *nuclear reaction*, nuclei, radiation, and/or nucleons collide to form different nuclei, radiation, and nucleons. If the colliding objects are charged, at least one of the colliding masses must be accelerated to a relatively high velocity. Normally the bombarding particle is very light, e.g., a proton ^1_1p or an alpha particle $^4_2\alpha$. These nuclear projectiles are accelerated with many different devices, e.g., Van de Graaff generators, cyclotrons, and linear accelerators.

In the nuclear reactions we shall study, several conservation laws must be observed, primarily *conservation of charge, conservation of nucleons,* and *conservation of mass-energy.*

Conservation of charge requires that the total charge of a system neither increase nor decrease in a nuclear reaction.

Conservation of nucleons requires that the total number of nucleons in the interaction remain unchanged.

Conservation of mass-energy requires that the total mass-energy of a system remain unchanged in a nuclear reaction.

Now let us observe what happens when an alpha particle $_2^4\alpha$ strikes a nucleus in a sample of nitrogen gas $_7^{14}N$. (Refer to Fig. 42-9.) The first step is the entry of the alpha particle, which adds 2 protons and 2 neutrons to the nucleus. The atomic number Z is increased by 2, and the mass number A is increased by 4. The resulting nucleus is an *unstable* compound nucleus of fluorine $_9^{18}F$. This unstable nucleus quickly disintegrates into the final products, oxygen $_8^{17}O$ and hydrogen $_1^1H$. The overall reaction can be written

$$_2^4\alpha + {}_7^{14}N \rightarrow {}_1^1H + {}_8^7O \qquad (42\text{-}15)$$

Note how charge and nucleons are conserved in these reactions. There was a net charge of $+9e$ before the reaction and a net charge of $+9e$ after the reaction, and there are 18 nucleons before and after the reaction.

Fig. 42-9 Striking a nitrogen-14 nucleus with an alpha particle.

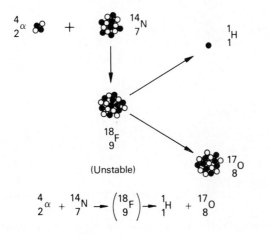

$$_2^4\alpha + {}_7^{14}N \longrightarrow \left({}_9^{18}F\right) \longrightarrow {}_1^1H + {}_8^{17}O$$

42-10 NUCLEAR FISSION

Before the discovery of the neutron in 1932, alpha particles and protons were the primary particles used to bombard atomic nuclei, but as charged particles they have the disadvantage of being repelled electrostatically by the nucleus. Consequently, very large energies are required before nuclear reactions occur.

Since neutrons have zero electric charge, they can easily penetrate the nucleus of an atom with no coulomb repulsion. Very fast neutrons may pass completely through a nucleus or may cause it to disintegrate. Slow neutrons may be captured by a nucleus, creating an unstable isotope, which may disintegrate.

Whenever the absorption of an incoming neutron causes a nucleus to split into two smaller nuclei, the reaction is called *fission* and the product nuclei are called *fission fragments*.

Nuclear fission is the process by which heavy nuclei are split into two or more nuclei of intermediate mass numbers.

Whenever a slow neutron is captured by a uranium nucleus $^{235}_{92}U$, an unstable nucleus ($^{236}_{92}U$) is produced which may decay in several ways into smaller product nuclei (Fig. 42-10). Such fission reactions may produce fast neutrons, beta particles, and gamma rays in addition to the product nuclei. For this

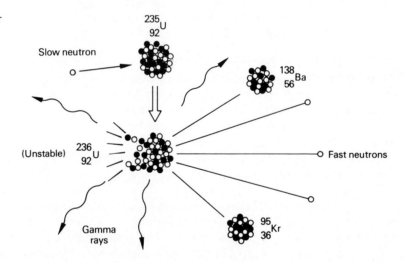

Fig. 42-10 Nuclear fission of $^{235}_{92}U$ by capture of a slow neutron.

reason the products of a fission process, including fallout from a nuclear explosion, are highly radioactive.

The fission fragments have a smaller mass number and therefore about 1 MeV more binding energy per nucleon (see 42-5). As a result, fission releases a large amount of energy. In the above example approximately 200 MeV per fission is produced.

Because each nuclear fission releases more neutrons, which may lead to additional fission, a *chain reaction* is possible. As seen in Fig. 42-11, the three neutrons released from the fission of $^{235}_{92}U$ produce three additional fissions. Thus, starting with one neutron, we have liberated nine after only two steps. If such a chain reaction is not controlled, it can lead to an explosion of enormous magnitude.

Fig. 42-11 Nuclear chain reaction.

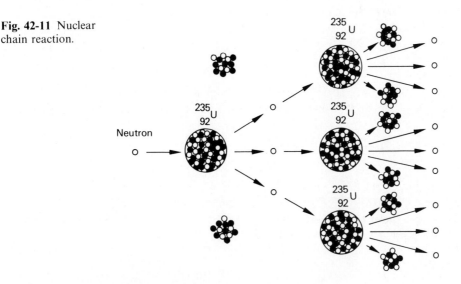

42-11 NUCLEAR REACTORS

A *nuclear reactor* is a device which controls the nuclear fission of radioactive material, producing new radioactive substances and large amounts of energy. These devices are used to furnish heat for electric power generation, propulsion, and industrial processes; they are used to produce new elements or radioactive materials for a multitude of applications; and they are used as a supply of neutrons for scientific experimentation.

A schematic diagram of a typical reactor is given in Fig. 42-12. The basic components are; (1) a *core* of nuclear fuel, (2) a *moderator* for slowing down fast neutrons, (3) *control rods* or other means for regulating the fission process, (4) a heat exchanger for removing heat generated in the core, and (5) radiation shielding. Steam produced by the reactor is used to drive a turbine, which generates electricity. The spent steam is changed to water in the condenser and pumped back to the heat exchanger for another cycle.

The essential ingredient in the reactor is the fissionable material, or nuclear fuel. About the only naturally occurring fissionable material is $^{235}_{92}U$, which constitutes about 0.7 percent of naturally available uranium. The remaining 99.3 percent is $^{238}_{92}U$. Fortunately, $^{238}_{92}U$ is a *fertile* material, i.e., it changes to a fissionable material when struck by neutrons. Plutonium $^{239}_{94}Pu$ produced in this manner can provide new fuel for the reactor.

The production of additional fuel as a part of the reactor's operation has led to the design of *breeder* reactors, in which there is a net increase in fissionable material. In other words, the reactor produces more fuel than it consumes. This does not violate the law of conservation of energy. It only provides for the production of fissionable material from fertile materials.

The fissionable fuel in most reactors depends on the availability of slow neutrons, which are more likely to produce fission. Fast neutrons liberated by the fission of nuclei must therefore be slowed down. For this reason reactor fuel

Fig. 42-12 Sche-
matic diagram of
a nuclear
reactor. Water
heated under
pressure in the
reactor core is
pumped into a heat
exchanger, where it
produces steam to
operate a turbine.

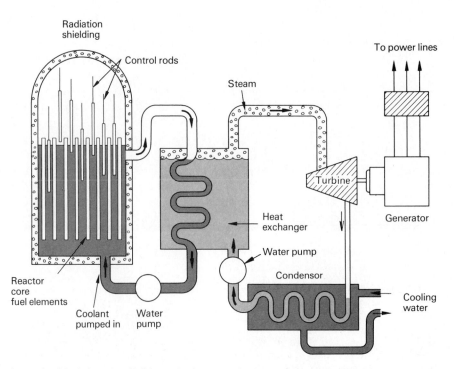

is embedded in a suitable substance called a *moderator*. The function of this substance is to slow neutrons without capturing them.

Neutrons have a mass about the same as that of a hydrogen atom. It might be expected, then, that substances containing hydrogen atoms would be effective as moderators of neutrons. The neutron is analogous to a marble, which can be stopped by a collision with another marble but will merely bounce off a cannonball because of the great mass difference. Water (H_2O) and heavy water, containing ^2_1H instead of ^1_1H, are often used as moderators. Other suitable materials are graphite and beryllium.

In order to control the nuclear furnace, it is necessary to regulate the number of neutrons which initiate the fission process. Substances like boron and cadmium capture neutrons efficiently and are excellent control materials. A typical reactor has control rods which can be inserted into the reactor at variable distances. By adjusting the position of these rods, the activity of the nuclear furnace is controlled. A supplementary set of rods is available to allow the reactor to be shut down completely in an emergency.

42-12 NUCLEAR FUSION

In our earlier discussions on mass defect we calculated that 28.3 MeV of energy is released in the formation of ^4_2He from its component nucleons. This joining together of light nuclei into a single heavier nucleus is called *nuclear fusion*. This process provides the fuel for stars like our own sun, and it is also the principle behind the hydrogen bomb. Many consider the fusion of hydrogen into helium as the ultimate fuel.

The use of nuclear fusion as a controlled source of energy is not without problems. For one thing, it requires that the fusing nuclei be given millions of electronvolts of kinetic energy to overcome their coulomb repulsion. In the hydrogen bomb, this enormous energy is supplied by an atomic explosion, which then triggers the fusion process. However, for peaceful production of energy, it poses a serious problem of containment. The nuclear fuel would have to be so hot that it would instantly disintegrate any known substance. Present research methods involve containment by magnetic fields or rapid heating by powerful lasers.

If and when the problems of heat generation and containment are solved, fusion could provide a solution to our formidable problem of dwindling resources. The deuterium commonly found in seawater could provide us with a virtually inexhaustible supply of fuel. It would represent more than a billion times the energy available in all our coal and oil reserves. In addition, it appears that fusion reactors would have much less of a problem with radioactive residue than fission reactors.

SUMMARY

In this chapter we have studied the fundamental particles which make up the nuclei of atoms. Protons and neutrons are held together in the nucleus by very strong nuclear forces which are active only within the nucleus. It was seen that when such particles are joined together, the resulting mass is less that of the constituent parts. For very massive nuclei it was also pointed out that energy results from tearing these nuclei apart. In either case, there is an enormous potential for useful energy. The major concepts which must be remembered in this chapter are as follows:

- The fundamental nuclear particles discussed in this chapter are summarized in the following table. The masses are given in atomic mass units (u) and the charge is in terms of the electronic charge $+e$ or $-e$, which is 1.6×10^{-19} C.

Fundamental Particles

Particle	Symbol	Mass, u	Charge
Electron	$-{}_{1}^{0}e$, $-{}_{1}^{0}\beta$	0.00055	$-e$
Proton	${}_{1}^{1}p$, ${}_{1}^{1}\text{H}$	1.007276	$+e$
Neutron	${}_{0}^{1}n$	1.008665	0
Positron	$+{}_{1}^{0}e$, $+{}_{1}^{0}\beta$	0.00055	$+e$
Alpha particle	${}_{2}^{4}\alpha$, ${}_{2}^{4}\text{He}$	4.001506	$+2e$

The atomic masses of the various elements are given in the text.
- The atomic number Z of an element is the number of protons in its nucleus. The mass number A is the sum of the atomic number and the number of neutrons N. These numbers are used to write the nuclear symbol:

$$A = Z + N$$

Symbol: ${}_{Z}^{A}X$

- One *atomic mass unit* (1 u) is equal to one-twelfth the mass of the most abundant carbon atom. Its value in kilograms is given below. Also, since $E = mc^2$, we can write the conversion factor from mass to energy as c^2.

$$\boxed{1 \text{ u} = 1.6606 \times 10^{-27} \text{ kg}} \qquad \boxed{c^2 = 931 \text{ MeV/u}}$$

$$1 \text{ MeV} = 10^6 \text{ eV} = 1.6 \times 10^{-13} \text{ J}$$

In the mass spectrometer, the velocity v and the radius R of the singly ionized particles are

$$\boxed{v = \frac{E}{B}} \qquad \boxed{R = \frac{mv}{e\text{B}}} \qquad \textit{Mass Spectrometer}$$

- The *mass defect* is the difference between the rest mass of a nucleus and the sum of the rest masses of its nucleons. The *binding energy* is obtained by multiplying the mass defect by c^2.

$$\boxed{E_B = [(Zm_H + Nm_n) - M]c^2} \qquad \textit{Binding Energy}$$

where $m_H = 1.007825$ u
$\quad m_n = 1.008665$ u
$\quad c^2 = 931$ MeV/u
$\quad M = $ atomic mass
$\quad N = A - Z$
$\quad Z = $ atomic number

- Several general equations for radioactive decay are

$$\boxed{{}_Z^A X \rightarrow {}_{Z-2}^{A-4} Y + {}_2^4 \alpha + \text{energy}} \qquad \textit{Alpha Decay}$$

$$\boxed{{}_Z^A X \rightarrow {}_{Z-1}^{A} Y + {}_{-1}^{0} \beta + \text{energy}} \qquad \textit{Beta-Minus Decay}$$

$$\boxed{{}_Z^A X \rightarrow {}_{Z-1}^{A} Y + {}_{+1}^{0} \beta + \text{energy}} \qquad \textit{Beta-Plus Decay}$$

- The *activity R* of a sample is the rate at which the radioactive nuclei decay. It is generally expressed in curies (Ci).

$$\text{One } \textit{curie } (1 \text{ Ci}) = 3.7 \times 10^{10} \text{ disintegrations per second (s}^{-1}\text{)}$$

- The *half-life* of a sample is the time $T_{1/2}$ in which one-half the unstable nuclei will decay.
- The number of unstable nuclei remaining after a time t depends on the number n of half-lives that have passed. If N_0 nuclei exist at time $t = 0$, then a number N exists at time t. We have

$$\boxed{N = N_0 \left(\tfrac{1}{2}\right)^n} \qquad \text{where } n = \frac{t}{T_{1/2}}$$

- The activity R and mass m of the radioactive portion of a sample are found from similar relations:

$$R = R_0 (\tfrac{1}{2})^n \qquad m = m_i (\tfrac{1}{2})^n$$

- In any nuclear equation, the number of nucleons on the left side must equal the number of nucleons on the right side. Similarly, the net charge must be the same on each side.

QUESTIONS

42-1. Define the following terms:
  a. Nuclear force
  b. Nucleon
  c. Atomic number
  d. Mass number
  e. Atomic mass unit
  f. Isotopes
  g. Mass spectrometer
  h. Mass defect
  i. Binding energy
  j. Radioactivity
  k. Alpha particles
  l. Beta particles
  m. Gamma particles
  n. Half-life
  o. Activity
  p. Curie
  q. Nuclear fission
  r. Chain reaction
  s. Nuclear reactor
  t. Nuclear fusion
  u. Moderator

42-2. Write the symbol $_Z^A X$ for the most abundant isotopes of **(a)** cadmium, **(b)** silver, **(c)** gold, **(d)** polonium, **(e)** magnesium, and **(f)** radon.

42-3. From the curve describing the binding energy per nucleon (Fig. 42-5) would you expect the mass defect to be greater for chromium $_{24}^{52}Cr$ or uranium $_{92}^{238}U$? Why?

42-4. The binding energy is greater for the mass numbers in the central part of the periodic table. Discuss the significance of this in relation to nuclear fission and nuclear fusion. How do you explain the release of energy in both fusion and fission in view of the fact that one process brings nuclei together and the other tears them apart?

42-5. How is the stability of an isotope affected by the ratio of the mass number A to the atomic number Z? Does the element whose ratio is closest to 1 always appear to be the more stable?

42-6. Define and compare alpha particles, beta particles, and gamma rays. Which are likely to do the most damage to human tissue?

42-7. Given a source which emits alpha, beta, and gamma radiation, draw a diagram showing how you could demonstrate the charge and penetrating power of each type of radiation. Assume you have at your disposal a source of a magnetic field and several thin sheets of aluminum.

42-8. Describe and explain, step by step, the decay of $_{92}^{238}U$ to the stable isotope of lead, $_{82}^{206}Pb$. (Refer to Fig. 42-7.)

42-9. Write in the missing symbol, in the form $_Z^A X$, for the following nuclear disintegrations:

  a. $_{90}^{234}Th \rightarrow\ _{91}^{234}Pa\ +\ \underline{\quad}$ **b.** $_{94}^{239}Pu \rightarrow\ _{90}^{234}Th\ +\ \underline{\quad}$
  c. $_{15}^{32}P \rightarrow\ \underline{\quad} +\ _{+1}^{0}e$ **d.** $_{92}^{238}U \rightarrow\ \underline{\quad} +\ _2^4\alpha$

42-10. Write the missing symbol for the following nuclear reactions:

a. $_1^2H + _1^3H \rightarrow _2^4He + \underline{\quad}$ **b.** $_4^9Be + _2^4\alpha \rightarrow _6^{12}C + \underline{\quad}$

c. $_{12}^{25}Mg + \underline{\quad} \rightarrow _{13}^{28}Al + _1^1H$ **d.** $_1^1H + \underline{\quad} \rightarrow _6^{12}C + _2^4He$

42-11. Explain the function of the following components of a nuclear reactor: **(a)** uranium, **(b)** radiation shielding, **(c)** moderator, **(d)** control rods, **(e)** heat exchanger, and **(f)** condenser.

42-12. Give examples to show how beta decay and alpha decay tend to bring unstable nuclei closer to the stability curve of Fig. 42-6.

42-13. Radon has a half-life of 3.8 days. Consider a sample of radon having a mass m and an activity R. What mass of radioactive radon remains after 3.8 days? Does this mean that the activity is reduced to one-half in the time of one half-life?

42-14. Radioactive carbon $_7^{14}C$ has a half-life of 5570 yr. In a living organism, the relative concentration of this isotope is the same as it is in the atmosphere because of the interchange of materials between the organism and the air. When an organism dies, this interchange stops and radioactive decay begins without replacement from the living organism. Explain how this principle can be used to determine the age of fossil remains.

PROBLEMS

42-1. How many neutrons are in the nucleus of $_{82}^{208}Pb$? How many protons? What is the ratio N/Z?

Ans. 126, 82, 1.54.

42-2. From a stability curve it is determined that the ratio of neutrons to protons for a cesium nucleus is 1.49. What is the mass number for this isotope of cesium ($Z = 55$)?

42-3. Calculate the binding energy of tritium $_1^3H$. What are the total binding energy and the binding energy per nucleon? How much energy in joules is required to tear the nucleus apart into its constituent nucleons? (The atomic mass of tritium is 3.016049 u.)

Ans. 8.48 MeV, 2.83 MeV, 1.36×10^{-18} J.

42-4. Calculate the mass defect of $_3^7Li$. What is the binding energy per nucleon? (The atomic mass of $_3^7Li$ is 7.0160 u).

42-5. Determine the binding energy per nucleon for **(a)** $_6^{12}C$ and **(b)** tin, $_{50}^{120}Sn$ (atomic mass = 119.90220 u).

Ans. **(a)** 7.68 MeV/nucleon **(b)** 8.5 MeV/nucleon.

42-6. Calculate the energy required to separate the nucleons in $_{89}^{204}Hg$ if the atomic mass is 203.9735 u.

42-7. The $_{27}^{60}Co$ nucleus emits gamma rays of approximately 1.2 MeV of energy. How much mass is lost by the nucleus when it emits a gamma ray of this energy?

Ans. 0.00129 u.

42-8. The half-life of the radioactive isotope indium 109 is 4.3 h. If the activity of a sample is 1 mCi at the start, how much activity remains after 4.3, 8.6, and 12.9 h?

42-9. The initial activity of a sample containing 7.7×10^{11} bismuth 212 nuclei is 4.0 mCi. The half-life of this isotope is 6.0 min. **(a)** How many bismuth 212 nuclei remain after $\frac{1}{2}$h? **(b)** What is the activity then?

Ans. **(a)** 2.41×10^{10} **(b)** 0.125 mCi.

42-10. Strontium 90 is produced in appreciable quantities in the atmosphere during the test of an atom bomb. If this isotope has a half-life of 28 yr, how long will it take for the initial radioactivity to drop to one-fourth its original activity?

42-11. The velocity selector in a mass spectrometer has a magnetic field of 0.2 T perpendicular to an electric field of 50 kV/m. The same magnetic field is across the lower region. **(a)** What is the velocity of singly charged $^7_3$Li ions as they enter the slit? **(b)** If the mass of the ion is 7.018 u, what is the radius of the path in the spectrometer?

Ans. **(a)** 2.5×10^5 m/s **(b)** 9.1 cm.

42-12. The electric field of 120 kV/m is perpendicular to a magnetic field of 0.6 T in a velocity selector of a mass spectrometer. If the distance from the slit to the photographic impression is 14.6 cm for a stream of ionized neon atoms, what is the mass number of the neon isotope?

42-13. Consider a sample of 24 mg of radioactive bismuth $^{210}_{83}$Bi. If its half-life is 5 days, how much of the sample will remain after 15 days?

Ans. 3 mg.

42-14. How long will it take for 40 mg of the unstable isotope $^{206}_{81}$Tl to decay to only 10 mg if the half-life is 9.0 min?

42-15. Determine the minimum energy released in the nuclear reaction $^{19}_9$F $+ {}^1_1$H $\rightarrow {}^{16}_8$O $+ {}^4_2\alpha$.

Ans. 5.09 MeV.

42-16. Determine the approximate kinetic energy imparted to the alpha particle when $^{226}_{88}$Ra decays to form $^{222}_{86}$Rn. Neglect the energy imparted to the radon nucleus. The nuclidic masses of $^{226}_{88}$Ra and $^{222}_{86}$Rn are 226.02536 u and 222.01753 u, respectively.

42-17. Find the energy evolved in the production of two alpha particles in the reaction

$$^7_3\text{Li} + {}^1_1\text{H} \rightarrow {}^4_2\text{He} + {}^4_2\text{He}.$$

Assume the atomic mass of $^7_3$Li to be 7.01600.

Ans. 17.5 MeV.

42-18. Compute the kinetic energy released in the beta minus decay of $^{233}_{90}$Th. The nuclidic masses of $^{233}_{90}$Th and $^{233}_{91}$Pa are 233.04147 u and 233.04013 u, respectively.

42-19. A nuclear reactor operates at a power level of 2 MW. Assuming that approximately 200 MeV of energy is released for a single fission of $^{235}_{92}$U, how many fission processes are occurring each second in the reactor?

Ans. 6.25×10^{16}.

43 *Electronics*

We are surrounded by electronics, ranging from stereos to wristwatches to automobile ignitions. The number of devices which are in some way electronic is constantly increasing. In fact, many of them would have been considered miracles 20 years ago. We now discuss some of the basic principles underlying this growing field of technology.

**43-1
THERM-
IONIC
EMISSION**

The roots of the electronic revolution go back to the late nineteenth century, when, in 1883, Thomas Edison noticed that black deposits were forming inside the glass light bulbs he was experimenting with. Further experiment showed that if a metal plate was also sealed inside the evacuated bulb and connected as shown in Fig. 43-1, the gavanometer would indicate a current between the filament and the plate. This current only flowed when the positive terminal of the battery was connected to the plate. Several years later this current was found to be the result of emission of electrons from the hot filament. The negatively charged electrons were attracted to the positive charge of the plate, generating an electric current between the plate and the filament.

Fig. 43-1 The Edison effect.

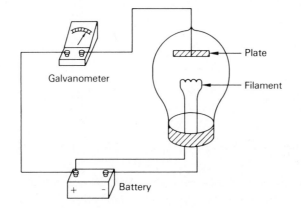

Plate

Filament

Galvanometer

Battery

The phenomenon which causes the emission of electrons from a heated filament is known as *thermionic emission*. It can only be observed in the absence of oxygen. A filament hot enough to cause thermionic emission will burn up in air.

43-2 VACUUM TUBES

The current flow observed by Edison occurred only when the plate (anode) was positive with respect to the filament (cathode). If the battery was reversed in the circuit, the current ceased. The negatively charged plate repelled the negatively charged electrons instead of attracting them, and the electrons which did escape the filament were attracted back to it by its positive charge.

Thermionic emission led to the development of the vacuum tube, which was the heart of all electronic devices until the 1950s. What made vacuum tubes so useful was the singular property that current could flow through them only in one direction.

A typical vacuum tube had a cathode heated by a separate heater filament and a plate anode. Tubes of this type, known as *diodes*, were the simplest form of the vacuum tube. A more sophisticated version, the *triode*, is shown in Fig. 43-2. The third element in the triode, the *grid*, was an electrode made up of a mesh of very thin wires; electrons could easily pass through the many holes in it. When the tube was in operation, if a small negative voltage was applied to the grid, the electrons emitted by the cathode were repelled by the grid and did not pass through it. The result was that no current flowed to the anode. However, if no voltage or a positive voltage was applied to the grid, the electrons from the cathode passed through the grid and current flowed between the

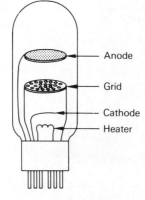

Fig. 43-2 Vacuum-tube triode.

Anode

Grid

Cathode

Heater

cathode and the anode. Small voltages applied to the grid were able to control the flow of current in the tube completely.

These and similar tubes made possible the development of radio, television, computers, and numerous other modern devices. Now, the development and spread of *solid-state* technology utilizing *semiconductors* has made them virtually extinct. Two vacuum tubes, however, are still very widely used, the cathode-ray tube (CRT) and the x-ray tube.

43-3 THE CATHODE-RAY TUBE

The cathode-ray tube is the key to electronically produced visual displays in oscilloscopes (Fig. 43-3), computers, and television sets. The tube consists of an *electron gun*, *deflection plates*, and the *screen*. These three parts are encased in a heavy-duty, evacuated, glass case. The electron gun is in the long, thin part of the tube, as shown in Fig. 43-4. It is made up of a cathode and two grids and anodes. The anodes are shaped to allow a stream of electrons to pass through them into the larger section of the tube.

This beam of electrons passes a set of flat metal deflection plates, which can be charged like a capacitor, creating an electric field between them. Depending on the direction of the electric field, the electrons are deflected toward one plate or the other. In this way the beam can be deflected up or down or from side to side and aimed at any point on the screen at the front of the tube.

In a television set, the horizontal and vertical deflections are produced by magnetic fields rather than by electric fields. By sending high-frequency alternating current through coils, it is possible to make the electron beam sweep back and forth across the tube. The screen itself is coated with *phosphor*, a substance that emits light when it is struck by high-energy electrons. Wherever the electron beam hits the screen, a bright spot appears. Wherever the picture should be light, the grid voltage is positive and the beam is strong, resulting in a bright spot. Wherever the picture should be dark, the beam is retarded by the grid and fewer electrons (or none) strike the screen, resulting in a dark spot. By covering the screen with very closely spaced lines varying in brightness the

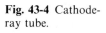

Fig. 43-3 A general purpose oscilloscope (*Thornton Associates, Inc.*)

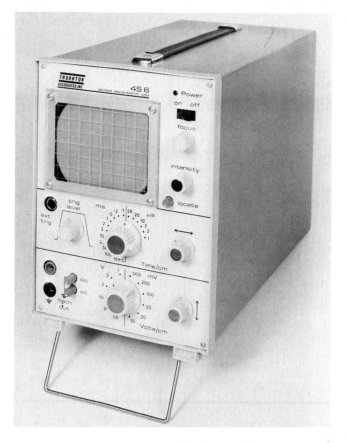

Fig. 43-4 Cathode-ray tube.

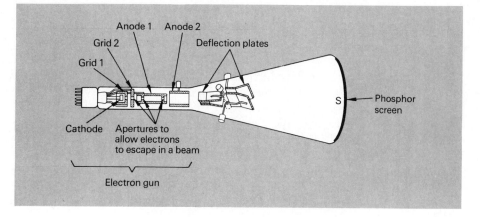

picture is produced on the screen. The lines are drawn at a rate of about 16,000 per second, and the entire screen is redrawn 60 times per second. Since both these speeds are much too great for the human eye to perceive, we see what appears to be a continuous, moving image.

43-4 THE X-RAY TUBE

Virtually all modern x-ray tubes (Fig. 43-5) are refinements of a tube designed in 1913 by William Coolidge, of the General Electric Company. As in other vacuum tubes, electrons are thermionically emitted by a hot cathode. In these tubes the cathode is cup-shaped to produce a narrow electron beam. The anode in the x-ray tube is held at a very high voltage (20 to 100 kV), and the electrons reach it with a great deal of kinetic energy. The highly energetic electrons strike a metal target embedded in the anode. When the electrons collide with the metal atoms, many of the bombarding electrons knock inner electrons out of the metal atoms leaving holes in the inner shells. As outer electrons fall into these holes, they emit x-ray photons with wavelengths characteristic of the target metal.

Fig. 43-5 Commercial x-ray tube.

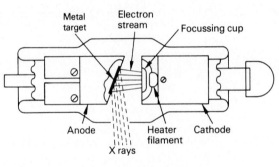

43-5 SEMICON-DUCTORS

Solid-state technology has completely replaced vacuum tubes in all but a few highly specialized applications. This has been possible because of the unique characteristics of *semiconductors*. These materials consist of a few elements and compounds which are not electrical insulators but do not exhibit the extremely high conductivity of true conductors either.

What makes something a conductor? The outer electrons of an atom, known as the *valence electrons*, are bound to the atom less tightly than the electrons which are closer to the nucleus. In a conductor they are really held very loosely, and in the solid state many of them break away from the atoms and roam freely throughout the solid. Thus they are called *free electrons*. When a battery or other means is used to place a potential difference across the solid, these free electrons are attracted to the positive potential and a current flows, as shown in Fig. 43-6.

Insulators, like rubber and glass, behave just oppositely. The outer valence electrons are held very tightly to the atoms, and they do not move freely about the solid. Unless an extremely high voltage is applied to an insulator, no current flows through it.

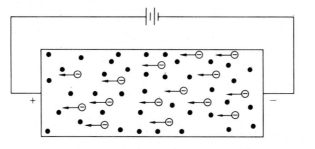

Fig. 43-6 Flow of free electrons in a conductor.

Semiconductors fall midway between conductors and insulators. Their valence electrons are neither as free as those in a conductor nor as tightly bound as those in an insulator. The valence electrons are actually shared by the atoms in the semiconductor. This process is known as *covalent bonding* and accounts for many of the properties of the semiconductors. Figure 43-7 shows how the electrons are shared by the hydrogen atoms in the H_2 molecule. Covalent bonding permits electrons to move from atom to atom without being entirely free. The process is much like moving from person to person around your set in a square dance. You are always with a partner, yet you are traveling completely around the set.

Fig. 43-7 Two covalently bonded hydrogen atoms.

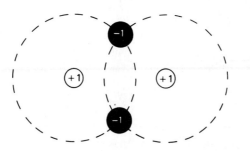

Another way to look at the difference between conductors, insulators, and semiconductors is the *energy-band theory*. Since electrons can occupy a discrete number of energy levels, they can have only those energies which fall into *allowed bands*. The energy band in which the valence electrons normally move is called the *valence band*. Electrons which are free to move and conductor current are in the *conduction band*. As can be seen in Fig. 43-8 the conduction and valence bands overlap in conductors, are very far apart in insulators, and are separated by a narrow energy gap in semiconductors. The overlap makes it very easy for electrons to move into the conduction band in conductors. The large gap makes it almost impossible for them to do so in insulators, and the small gap makes it fairly easy in semiconductors.

Let us look at a real semiconductor. Because of its availability, silicon is the most commonly used semiconductor, although germanium is also used. In its natural state silicon is a *crystal*. This means that in a piece of silicon the

Fig. 43-8 The band theory of conduction.

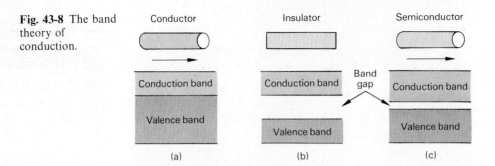

Conductor

Insulator

Semiconductor

| (a) | (b) | (c) |

atoms are located at specific points in an ordered *lattice*. Figure 43-9 shows a diagram of the silicon lattice. There are four valence electrons surrounding each atom. In a perfect crystal each of these electrons would be shared with a neighboring atom. The crystal would be an insulator because no electrons would be available for current flow. However, any imperfection will cause the silicon to conduct some current.

The most common impurity occurs when an atom of another substance is placed at a point in the crystal lattice that would normally be occupied by a silicon atom. Two important types of impurities are *N-type donors* and *P-type acceptors*.

Fig. 43-9 The atomic structure and shared electrons in pure silicon.

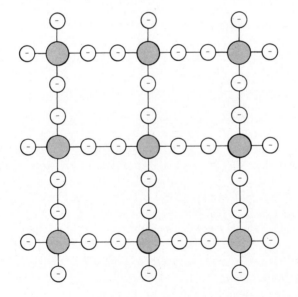

43-6
N-TYPE AND P-TYPE SEMICON-DUCTORS

When an impurity atom has more than the four valence electrons needed to pair with the neighboring silicon atom, the extra unpaired electrons are not covalently bonded and can move freely. Thus the impurity donates extra negatively charged electrons to the crystal. This explains the names donor and N-type (for negative). A typical N-type impurity can be seen in Fig. 43-10.

Fig. 43-10 In an N-type semiconductor, an impurity atom joins the silicon structure donating an extra electron.

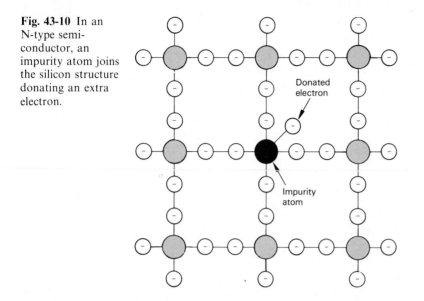

Commercial N-type semiconductor material is made by adding very small controlled quantities of a selected impurity to the silicon crystal. The intentional impurities are known as *dopants*. Phosphorus, arsenic, and antimony are common N-type dopants. Each has five valence electrons and therefore adds one free electron to the crystal. The P-type silicon is also commercially produced by doping. In this case the dopant has one less valence electron than silicon. Thus P-type dopants have three valence electrons, and common P-type dopants are aluminum, boron, gallium, and indium. Any of these dopants yields a semiconductor like the one in Fig. 43-11.

Fig. 43-11 In a P-type semiconductor, the absence of a valence electron produces an electronic hole.

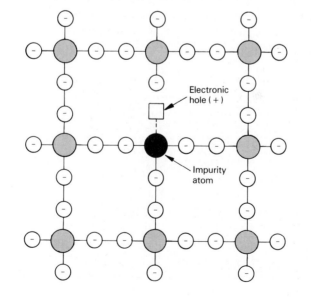

The *hole* marked in the figure is where the fourth valence electron would be if the spot were occupied by a silicon atom and not an impurity atom. When attracted by a positive potential, electrons near neighboring holes can jump over and fill the holes. Each time an electron moves in one direction, the hole moves in the opposite direction, to the atom from which the electron came. In this way a movement of electrons one way causes a movement of holes the other way. Since negative and positive charges always behave oppositely, it is just as if the holes were positive charges and the current can be treated as if it were a movement of positive charges (the holes).

43-7
PN
JUNCTION

Some interesting effects result from the combination of P-type and N-type materials. The most basic of these is formation of a *PN junction* by placing a slice of P-type material in contact with a slice of N-type material. When the two semiconductors are first joined, some of the free electrons from the N-type material jump past the junction and fill some of the holes in the P-type material. This leaves a thin layer of positively charged ions along the junction on the N side. These positive ions are the atoms which have lost an electron. Similarly, the atoms on the P side which have acquired electrons form a layer of negative ions. Once these layers are formed, the negative ions repel other electrons, preventing any more electrons from jumping over, and the positive ions prevent any holes from jumping over.

In this state the PN junction is rather stable. But things change when a battery is connected across the junction. We first look at what happens when the battery is connected with its negative terminal on the P side of the junction and its positive terminal on the N side, as in Fig. 43-12. The positive holes in the P-type material move toward the negative potential of the battery, and the negative electrons move toward the positive potential of the battery. The result is that both holes and electrons move *away* from the junction and there is no current flow across the junction. When connected in this manner, the junction is said to be *reverse-biased*.

Fig. 43-12 Reverse-biased PN junction.

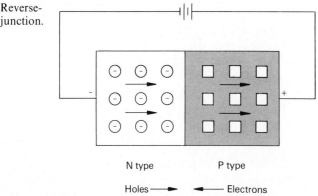

N type   P type

Holes ——▶   ◀—— Electrons

If the battery is connected across the junction in the opposite direction, positive to the P side and negative to the N side, the behavior is quite different. The electrons from the donor atoms in the N-type material are attracted to the positive potential and flow toward the junction. The holes flow toward the junction in the opposite direction toward the negative potential. In short, there is a current flow. This type of connection, shown in Fig. 43-13, is called *forward biasing* of the junction. The semiconductor device we have been discussing behaves just like the simplest vacuum tube discussed in Sec. 43-2; it allows current flow in only one direction. Because of this similarity it is also known as a *diode*.

Fig. 43-13 Forward-biased PN junction.

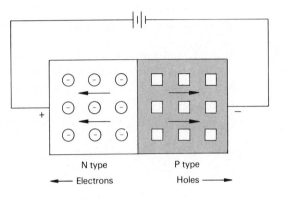

N type   P type

◄— Electrons   Holes —►

The significant advantages of the semiconductor diode over its vacuum-tube predecessor are shared by all other semiconductor devices. It is very small; it does not require high voltage to operate; and it is more durable.

The semiconductor diode also exhibits another very interesting characteristic. It does not obey Ohm's law. Figure 43-14 shows a graph of current vs. voltage for an ordinary conductor and the same information for a forward-biased semiconductor diode. The conductor shows the straight line that results

Fig. 43-14 The relationship between voltage and current for a conductor and for a semiconductor.

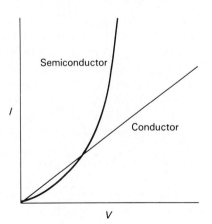

from the relation $V = IR$. The diode does not. Instead, the current rises very slowly at the start and then rises very rapidly. The slow rise at the beginning occurs because the forces resulting from the ion layers at the junction must be overcome. Once they are overcome, however, there is very little resistance to current flow. Diodes do not follow a simple rule like Ohm's law. Each diode has its own characteristic curve, which depends on the material used to make it and the dopants used in it.

43-8 DIODE APPLICATIONS

We have already seen that a PN junction diode passes current only when forward-biased. This immediately makes it an excellent choice to convert alternating current to direct current (rectifying). Figure 43-15 shows a diode inserted in a circuit as a *half-wave rectifier*. (Notice the symbol representing the diode. The triangle can be seen as an arrow pointing in the direction of allowed current flow.) The output of this circuit is not a true, constant direct current but a current which flows in pulses, only half of the time. The remainder of the current, which would normally flow the other way, is blocked.

Fig. 43-15 The semiconductor diode used as a half-wave rectifier.

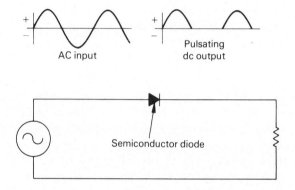

Often the pulsed output of the half-wave rectifier is not sufficient to meet the needs of a particular application. When this is the case, it is possible to *filter* the output of the rectifier to smooth out the pulses and make it look more like the continuous output of a battery. A possible circuit for such filtering is shown in Fig. 43-16. The filter consists of two capacitors and an inductor. The inductor opposes changes in current; thus it opposes the pulsed current passing through the diode. Excess current is diverted by the inductor during periods of high current flow from the diode and charges capacitor C_1. When the current flow between pulses is zero, C_1 discharges through the inductor, maintaining current flow through the inductor at a fairly constant level. Capacitor C_2, at the output end of the inductor, similarly smooths out any variations in the current output from the inductor.

The half-wave rectifier is not the only means of accomplishing that purpose. More common is a *bridge rectifier*, which uses four diodes arranged as

Fig. 43-16 An electronic filtering circuit.

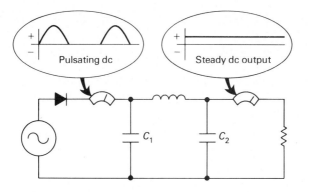

in Fig. 43-17. The ac input is connected to the bridge at points 1 and 3, and the output load is connected to points 2 and 4. When point 1 is positive and point 2 negative, the current flows as in Fig. 41-17a. Current entering the bridge at point 1 cannot pass through diode D_4, which is reverse-biased, but it can, and does, pass through diode D_2. It then leaves the bridge at point 2 and goes through the load R_L. It reenters the bridge at point 4, again facing two possible paths. D_4 remains reverse-biased and nonconducting, and so the current goes through D_3 and leaves at point 3. During the other half of the cycle, when the input polarity is reversed, the current flows the path shown in Fig. 43-17b using

Fig. 43-17 Bridge rectifier.

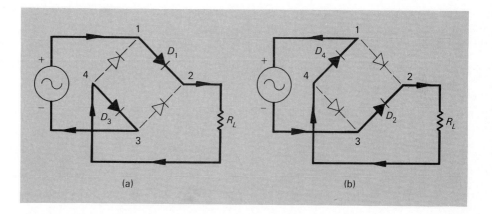

(a)   (b)

the other pair of diodes, D_2 and D_4, in a similar manner. In this way the diode pairs which are conducting alternate according to the alternations in the input polarity. Such a rectifier is called a *full-wave rectifier* since all of the input signal is transmitted.

A major advantage of the full-wave rectifier is its output form, shown in Fig. 43-18 in comparison with the ac input and the output of a half-wave rectifier. The figure shows that the full-wave rectifier leaves no gaps where the current output is zero. Instead, the current continuously varies between zero

Fig. 43-18 A comparison of waveforms.

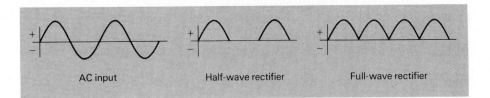

AC input Half-wave rectifier Full-wave rectifier

and its peak value in the forward direction. Thus the output requires much less smoothing to make it look like the constant output of a battery, and the device does not in effect ignore half the source current.

43-9
THE ZENER DIODE

So far we have been discussing diodes as purely one-direction devices; when forward-biased, they conduct, and when reverse-biased, they do not. A look at a complete characteristic curve for a typical semiconductor diode (Fig. 43-19) shows that this is not quite the case. When the diode is reverse-biased, the current remains virtually zero as the reverse voltage is increased until a critical voltage known as the *zener voltage* is reached. At that point the resistance of the diode abruptly drops, and the diode becomes an excellent conductor in the reverse direction.

Fig. 43-19 Diode characteristic curve.

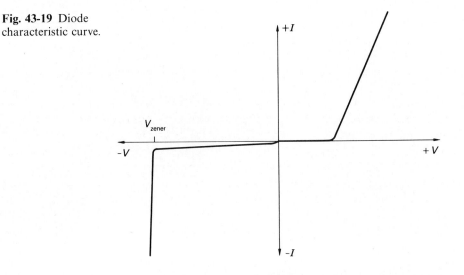

This apparently strange effect is easily explained by examining the behavior of the electrons and holes at the junction in the diode. When the diode is reverse-biased, the electrons and holes all move away from the junction, leaving it virtually free of charges of either type. There are, however, always a few electrons and holes created by random thermal motions in the crystal. These few created free holes and electrons flow away from the junction and constitute a nonzero *reverse current*. This reverse current, of a few microamperes, is always present when the diode is reverse-biased but can usually be ignored.

If the reverse-bias voltage is increased sufficiently, a point is reached where the electrons accelerated by this voltage have enough energy to knock more electrons loose from atoms with which they collide. These freed electrons knock more electrons loose, creating a large flow of electrons, known as the *avalanche*, or *zener effect*. Once the zener voltage is reached, the voltage across the diode does not increase to any extent, even though the current increases dramatically. This is another clear violation of Ohm's law.

We might expect that a diode operated at such comparatively high current in its reverse direction would burn itself up, as vacuum-tube rectifiers do. (If enough voltage is connected across them for current to flow in the reverse direction, they destroy themselves.) Special zener diodes are made for just this purpose, and as long as their specifications are not exceeded, they can be run perfectly well for long times. Figure 43-20 shows the circuit symbol for a zener diode.

Fig. 43-20 Zener diode symbol.

The tendency for a diode operating in the zener region of its characteristic curve to maintain a constant voltage regardless of current flow through it makes the zener diode especially useful in applications where a constant voltage at a particular point is critical, particularly in regulated power supplies. A regulated power supply is a voltage-current source whose output voltage remains constant at a specified value regardless of the output current.

Figure 43-21 shows a way of using two identical zener diodes connected back to back to limit the output of an ac source. When the two diodes are connected in this way, one of them is reverse-biased and voltage-limiting, while the other is forward-biased and conducting. When the ac source reverses its polarity, the diodes exchange roles and the conducting diode becomes the limiter and the limiter becomes the conductor. The peak output of this *voltage regulator* remains less than or equal to the zener voltage of the two diodes.

Fig. 43-21 Zener voltage regulator.

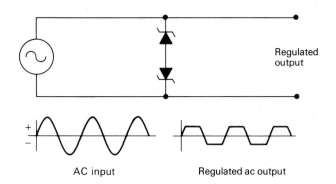

AC input   Regulated ac output

A single PN junction device is a diode. The next step is the *transistor*, which consists of a slice of N-type semiconductor sandwiched between two slices of P-type semiconductor (called a PNP transistor) or a slice of P-type semiconductor sandwiched between two slices of N-type semiconductor (called an NPN transistor). This transistor was invented in 1948 by Shockley, Bardeen, and Brattain at Bell Laboratories, and in the years since then has completely revolutionized the field of electronics and many associated fields.

Let us consider a typical NPN junction transistor biased as shown in Fig. 43-22. The left section is made of heavily doped N-type semiconducting material and is called the *emitter*. The center section is made of a very thin and lightly doped P-type semiconducting slice. It is called the *base*. The right section is made of a medium doped N-type semiconducting material and is called the *collector*. Note that the emitter and base form an NP junction, and the base and collector form a PN junction.

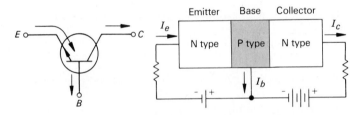

Fig. 43-22 An NPN transistor and its symbol. Arrows indicate the directions of electron currents. (Note that electron flow is opposite to conventional current.)

The emitter-base NP junction in Fig. 43-22 is forward biased allowing electrons to flow easily from the N side to the P side. The base region is very thin and has relatively few holes, allowing most of the electrons to diffuse right across it to the collector. But some of the electrons are trapped in the holes of the base region. If they are not removed from the base, the negative charge of the trapped electrons will repel the electrons from the emitter and rapidly shut off the electron current from the emitter to the collector. By removing or not removing this buildup of electrons from the base region, the transistor can be used as a switch.

When the electrons are removed from the base, there is an electron current from the base. The emitter current I_e is divided into base current I_b and a collector current I_c. That is,

$$I_e = I_b + I_c \tag{43-1}$$

The ratio of the collector current to the emitter current is called α (alpha).

$$\alpha = \frac{I_c}{I_e} \tag{43-2}$$

This number is a specification given by the manufacturer with each transistor. Since 95 to 99 percent of the electrons from the emitter travel through the base into the collector without being trapped, α typically ranges from 0.95 to 0.99.

If we know α, we can calculate the relation of the very small base current to the emitter current. Using Eq. (41-1), we can solve for I_b in terms of I_e and I_c.

$$I_b = I_e - I_c$$

But $I_c = \alpha I_e$, as computed from Eq. (41-2). Substitution gives

$$I_b = I_e - \alpha I_e$$

Finally, an expression for the base current of a transistor is

$$\boxed{I_b = I_e(1 - \alpha)} \qquad (43\text{-}3)$$

EXAMPLE 43-1   Given a transistor with $\alpha = 0.97$, calculate I_b and I_c when $I_e = 50$ mA and the transistor is connected as in Fig. 43-22.

Solution   Substitution into Eq. (41-3) gives

$$I_b = I_e(1 - \alpha) = (50 \text{ mA})(1 - 0.97)$$

$$= (50 \text{ mA})(0.03)$$

$$= 1.5 \text{ mA}$$

Now the collector current is found from Eq. (41-1).

$$I_c = I_e - I_b = 50 \text{ mA} - 1.5 \text{ mA}$$

$$= 48.5 \text{ mA}$$

The PNP transistor is constructed just like the NPN transistor, except that the N-type material is sandwiched between two slices of P-type material. Because of this reversal of the positions of the two material types, the primary current carriers in the transistor are holes instead of electrons. Since holes are effectively positive charges, the biases are necessarily reversed. For the emitter junction to be forward-biased the emitter voltage must be negative with respect to the base, and for the collector junction to be reverse-biased, the collector must be positive with respect to the base.

The biasing for a PNP transistor is shown in Fig. 43-23. The change in

Fig. 43-23 A PNP transistor and its symbol. Arrows indicate electron flow.

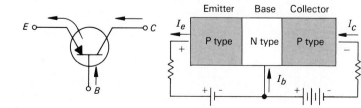

biasing does not affect the way the junctions operate. It merely accommodates the rearrangement of materials and their properties. In operation, most holes flow from the emitter junction to the base and then into the collector.

43-11 TRANSISTOR AMPLIFI-CATION

In an amplification device we want to be able to input a varying signal with low-magnitude voltage or current characteristics and output a similarly varying signal with much higher voltage or current. A vacuum-tube triode is controlled by voltage. A very small voltage on the grid of the triode controls a similar but much higher voltage in the plate circuit. The transistor, on the other hand, depends on the currents in it to control the amplification of the voltage or power in the output circuit.

Figure 43-24 shows a simple amplifier circuit utilizing the transistor. Normally ac circuits have two terminals for input and two for output. Because the transistor is a three-terminal device, one of its terminals must be common to both the input and output circuits. Any of the three terminals may be selected as the common terminal. In Fig. 43-24 the base is the common terminal.

Fig. 43-24 Common-base amplifier circuit.

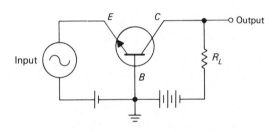

As we discussed in Sec. 43-10, the emitter curent and the collector current are almost equal. For this reason the ratio of output current to input current, called the *current gain*, is approximately 0.95 to 0.99 when the transistor is used in this configuration and is equal to α. In this case, collector current is considered as output and emitter current is considered as input.

Normally the voltage across the forward-biased region is small. This region represents a very low resistance, and little voltage is needed to send a relatively high current through it. The second diode region, which is reverse-biased, represents a much higher resistance to the passage of current. Since voltage is the product of current and resistance, the resulting voltage must be high.

The ratio of output resistance to input resistance in a typical transistor is usually quite high. A typical input resistance might be 500 Ω, and a typical output resistance might be as much as 500 kΩ. This results in a ratio R_{out}/R_{in} equal to 1000.

EXAMPLE 43-2

Assume a transistor to have an input resistance of 500 Ω and an output resistance of 400 kΩ. Determine the input and output voltages if the emitter current is 3 mA and $\alpha = 0.98$.

Solution

The input voltage is found from Ohm's law.

$$V_{in} = I_e R_{in} = (10 \times 10^{-6} \text{ A})(500 \text{ }\Omega)$$

$$= 5 \times 10^{-3} \text{ V} = 5 \text{ mV}$$

To determine the output voltage, we must first determine the collector current from α. Recalling that $\alpha = I_c / I_e$, we can solve for I_c as follows:

$$I_c = \alpha I_e = 0.98(3 \times 10^{-3} \text{ A}) = 2.94 \times 10^{-3} \text{ A}$$

Thus, the output voltage is

$$V_{out} = I_c R_{out} = (2.94 \times 10^{-3} \text{ A})(400 \times 10^3 \text{ }\Omega)$$

$$= 1176 \text{ V}$$

The *voltage amplification factor* A_v for a transistor is defined as the ratio of output voltage to input voltage.

$$\boxed{A_v = \frac{V_{out}}{V_{in}}} \qquad \begin{array}{c} \textit{Voltage} \\ \textit{Amplification Factor} \end{array} \quad (43\text{-}4)$$

This ratio is also referred to as the *voltage gain.*

Along with an increase in voltage comes an increase in power. Recall that the power dissipated by a circuit component is equal to the voltage across it times the current through it. In any case, the power gain G is given by

$$G = \frac{\text{power out}}{\text{power in}} = \frac{V_{out} I_c}{V_{in} I_e} \qquad (43\text{-}5)$$

But since $\alpha = I_c / I_e$, we can write

$$\boxed{G = \alpha \frac{V_{out}}{V_{in}} = \alpha A_v} \qquad \textit{Power Gain} \quad (43\text{-}6)$$

EXAMPLE 43-3   Determine the voltage amplification factor and the power gain for the transistor of Example 43-2.

Solution   In the previous example the input voltage was 1.5 V, and the output voltage was 1176 V. This gives an amplification factor of

$$A_v = \frac{V_{out}}{V_{in}} = \frac{1176 \text{ V}}{1.5 \text{ V}} = 784$$

Now the power gain can be found from Eq. (43-6),

$$G = \alpha A_v = (0.98)(784) = 768$$

where we used $\alpha = 0.98$ from the previous example

Transistors can also be connected with the emitter as the common terminal, i.e., connected to input and output circuits. A simple *common emitter* amplifier circuit is shown in Fig. 43-25. As before, the input is across the emitter and base contacts, but the output in this case is from the emitter and collector terminals. The emitter junction is forward-biased, and the collector junction is

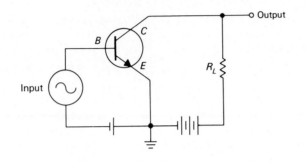

Fig. 43-25 Common-emitter amplifier circuit.

reverse-biased. If the bias on the emitter junction is increased, the current flowing through the collector junction will increase as a result of the increase in current through the emitter junction. However, the base current will retain its usual low value. This low base current is also the current flowing in the input circuit. Thus in this configuration we get a considerable current gain in the output circuit (collector circuit) over the current in the input circuit (base). We already know that the base current is given by

$$I_b = I_e(1 - \alpha)$$

and that the output, or collector, current is

$$I_c = \alpha I_e$$

These relations allow us to compute an expression for the current gain, or current amplification factor, A_i

$$A_i = \frac{I_{\text{out}}}{I_{\text{in}}} = \frac{\alpha I_e}{(1 - \alpha)I_e} = \frac{\alpha}{1 - \alpha} \tag{43-7}$$

A special symbol β is used to represent the current gain in the above form. Thus, for a transistor having a known α the current gain can be found from

$$\beta = \frac{\alpha}{1 - \alpha} \tag{43-8}$$

This is also known as the *base-collector current gain.*

EXAMPLE 43-4   In a common-emitter amplifier the value of α is 0.96. What is the current gain?

Solution   Substitution into Eq. (43-8) yields

$$\beta = \frac{\alpha}{1 - \alpha} = \frac{0.96}{1 - 0.96} = 24$$

Typically, the values for β range from 20 to several hundred.

To determine the voltage gain we must again look at the effective input and output resistances. As in the common-base circuit, the input resistance is across the forward-biased emitter junction and is very low. The output resistance is high but not quite as high as in the common-base circuit. The result is a voltage gain nearly as high as in the common-base circuit.

The power gain depends on the products of the current gain and voltage gain. While the voltage gain is slightly lower, the current gain β is much, much higher, and the power gain is also much higher.

The common-emitter circuit has one other very interesting feature. When the incoming signal causes the base potential to become more negative, increasing the forward bias of the emitter junction, the collector potential moves in the opposite direction and becomes more positive. As a result, the common-emitter circuit has the property of changing the phase angle of the signal by 180° and acting as a *signal inverter*.

The final method of connecting a transistor is illustrated in Fig. 43-26. This is the common-collector arrangement. Looking at the same parameters as

Fig. 43-26 Common-collector amplifier circuit.

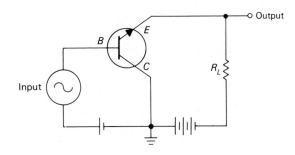

for the other two circuits, we get the following results. The input current is the base current, and the output current is the emitter current. The current gain is consequently

$$A_i = \frac{I_{\text{out}}}{I_{\text{in}}} = \frac{I_e}{I_e(1 - \alpha)}$$

from which

$$A_i = \frac{1}{1 - \alpha} \tag{43-9}$$

In this case the base voltage is greater than the output voltage, and the net gain is less than 1, the lowest of the three arrangements. Related to this, the input resistance is high and the output resistance is low. Finally, because of the very low voltage gain, the power gain is also the lowest of the three configurations. Table 43-1 compares the various gain characteristics of the three circuits.

Table 43-1 A Comparison of the Three Possible Transistor Amplifier Arrangements

	Common base	Common emitter	Common collector
Current gain	α (low)	β (high)	$\dfrac{1}{1 - \alpha}$ (highest)
Voltage gain	Highest	High	Low
Power gain	Moderate	Highest	Lowest

There are two points to remember when using transistors in circuits: (1) Transistors require a dc voltage source for biasing before an ac signal can be applied to them for amplification or other modification. This dc voltage is often supplied by a regulated power supply using a diode bridge and zener diodes. (2) Since transistors are easily damaged by high temperature, the current must be rather low.

Transistor manufacturers publish data sheets and graphs of transistor characteristics. These documents are useful for circuit design and for verifying that none of the relevant parameters will be exceeded, destroying the transistor or other sensitive semiconductor circuit elements.

43-12 OTHER SEMICON-DUCTOR DEVICES

Since the invention of the transistor, many other semiconductor devices have been developed. Some of them have interesting and unusual attributes which make possible many of the small electronic devices we enjoy today. One of the newest devices is the light-emitting diode (LED), used to provide visual displays in electronic devices. When arranged as shown in Fig. 43-27, a set of seven LEDs can be used to form numbers or letters. They are common in pocket-calculator and wristwatch displays. They are simply junction diodes which emit

Fig. 43-27 LED display.
(*a*) Arrangement of LEDs. (*b*) Pattern of lighting to form number 234.

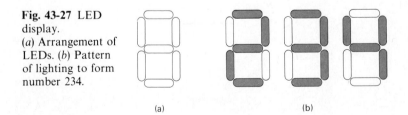

(a)   (b)

light due to the current flowing through them. The diodes are operated with a forward bias, allowing current to flow across the PN junction. At the junction, however, some of the electrons and holes combine to form electron-hole pairs. The electrons fill the holes, and the two are canceled out as current carriers. The energy of the recombined electrons and holes is released in the form of photons. Materials which behave this way are used to make LEDs, e.g., gallium arsenide, gallium arsenide phosphide, and gallium phosphide. The first two emit visible light, and the last emits infrared light.

Most visible-light LEDs emit red light, although some emit green and yellow light. They are not powerful light sources like incandescent light bulbs and cannot be used for general illumination, but they are bright enough to be visible under most conditions and ideal for indicator lights and digital displays. Their advantages are that they are very small and rugged; they use little current and require low voltages; and their useful lifetimes are extremely long. Some LEDs may last as long as 100 years.

Similar to the LED but functioning in an inverse manner are photosensitive semiconductor devices. One of these is the photodiode. These diodes are run reverse-biased. When struck by light, the photons are absorbed by the atoms. This raises the energy level of the valence electrons sufficiently to cause then to jump into the conduction band. Thus, an electron-hole pair is created for each absorbed photon, and the electrons and holes are both swept away by the bias voltage, producing a current flow. Just as the light output of the LED is related to the current flow in the diode, the current flow in the photodiode is related to the intensity of the light striking the diode. The circuit symbols for the LED and the photodiode and a set of characteristic curves for a photodiode are shown in Fig. 43-28.

An interesting application of LEDs and light-sensitive diodes is in the construction of a type of semiconductor *relay*. A relay is a device for indirectly switching an electric current by using another current. Before the advent of semiconductor technology relays were all electromechanical devices of various

Fig. 43-28 (*a*) Circuit symbols for the LED and photodiode. (*b*) Characteristic curves for a photodiode.

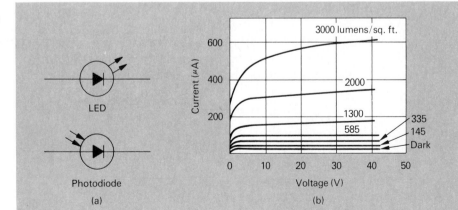

designs. One of the great advantages of a relay is that very high, and consequently dangerous, currents can be switched without handling them directly. A relay for this purpose is found in the starting circuit of a car. A small current in the starting switch activates the solenoid switch; it actually turns on the very high current which goes to the starting motor.

The optical semiconductor relay, which cannot be used for very high-current applications, is shown in Fig. 43-29. In operation, when a current is passed through the LED, it emits light. The light from the LED strikes the photodiode, which then conducts as long as the LED remains activated. In this way the photodiode acts as a switch turned on and off by the LED.

Fig. 43-29 Simple LED-photodiode relay.

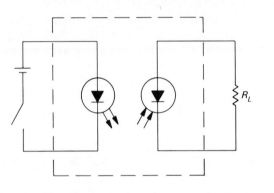

Another semiconductor device which may serve as a type of switch is the *silicon-controlled rectifier* (SCR) (Fig. 43-30). It is similar to a transistor with an extra layer of semiconductor material added to the stack. Just as a transistor can be viewed as two diodes in series, the SCR can be viewed as three diodes in series. For the SCR in the figure they are, from left to right, an NP junction, a PN junction, and another NP junction. In addition, the electrodes are renamed. The end electrodes are the *anode* and *cathode*, and the center electrode is called the *gate*.

Fig. 43-30 Silicon-controlled rectifier.

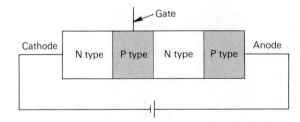

When a low bias voltage is applied between the anode and cathode, the center diode is reverse-biased and there is no current flow. In this state the device is said to be switched *off*. As the bias voltage is increased, a point is reached where the reverse-biased diode breaks down and the device begins to conduct. At this point the device has switched *on*. The point at which the SCR switches on, called the *breakover voltage*, is controlled by the positive bias applied to the gate. Once this point is reached, the gate loses control and the SCR must be disconnected in some way to restore control to the gate. The circuit symbol for the SCR and a set of characteristic curves for a typical SCR are shown in Fig. 43-31.

Fig. 43-31 SCR symbol and characteristic curves.

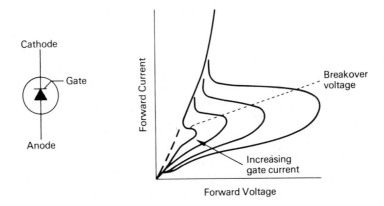

Two other simple semiconductor devices exhibit properties different from any others discussed up to this point, the *photoresistor* and the *thermistor*. The photoresistor is the key component of all modern light meters. In fact almost all cameras which use batteries use a photoresistor to measure light intensity. Most photoresistors in use today are made of cadmium sulfide (CdS). Unlike the other semiconductor devices we have discussed the photoresistor has no junction. It is a uniform crystal of CdS. When a voltage is applied across it, a current flows in proportion to the intensity of the light striking it. Conduction is not by free electrons but by electron-hole pairs, which are created when photons knock electrons loose from atoms in the crystal and into the conduction band. The more intense the light, the greater the number of photons hitting the crystal and the greater the conductance.

The last device to be discussed in this section is the thermistor. It takes advantage of the fact that the resistance of a semiconductor decreases as the temperature increases. The effect is opposite to, and much greater than, the change in the resistance of a conductor with temperature. This can be seen clearly in Fig. 43-32. The *y* axis, showing the resistance, is logarithmic to accommodate the large changes in resistance. When a thermistor is maintained with a constant voltage across it, there will be large changes in the current which flows through the device as a result of changes in the temperature of the device. This means that a thermistor can be used to measure the temperature of its environment.

It also may be used as a safety device in complex solid-state components. The thermistor is placed in the parts of such components where high temperatures may be experienced. The circuit is then designed so that when the

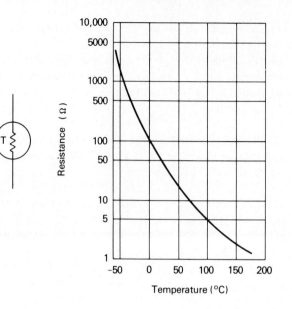

Fig. 43-32 Structure symbol and characteristic of a typical thermistor.

current through the thermistor rises to a critical value, the component shuts off, protecting the semiconductor devices within it from being destroyed by overheating. In this way the thermistor acts as a temperature-controlled fuse.

43-13 INTEGRATED CIRCUITS

As great as the electronic revolution the transistor caused in the 1950s and 1960s is a new revolution due to the *integrated circuit* (IC). These devices combine numerous circuit elements (resistors, capacitors, transistors, diodes, and others) on tiny slices of ultrapure silicon. Each IC represents a complete circuit of a particular type, and ICs can be combined with each other and with other semiconductor devices to make large-scale components. They have also made possible certain devices like electronic wristwatches, which depend on the IC to pack all the necessary electronics in a case small enough to wear on the wrist.

The most obvious attribute of the IC is its incredibly small size. A typical IC is 0.05 in. square and about 0.01 in. thick. This wafer may contain thousands of separate devices, enough to serve numerous complex purposes. It is protected by a container which usually measures only a small fraction of an inch in any direction.

Although the size of the IC is remarkable, it is not its only advantage over conventional devices. Because the entire circuit is fabricated at the same time, it is a highly reliable device, more so than any of its predecessors. This characteristic is invaluable in such things as spaceship guidance systems and pacemakers.

The individual devices which make up the IC function on the same principles as the semiconductor devices already discussed. They depend on the

PN junction and the action of both electrons and holes for their various properties.

The silicon wafer which makes up the IC is known as the *substrate*, and the two processes of fabrication are *diffusion* and *etching*. Diffusion, as in the manufacture of junction-dependent devices, is the controlled injection of appropriate dopants into the silicon. Etching is the use of hydrofluoric acid to remove materials from the surface of the substrate to expose a region for further processing. These steps are combined with several steps which deposit materials on the substrate to make the necessary P-type and N-type regions forming diodes, transistors, and related devices.

Let us outline the steps needed to create an area of P-type silicon in the substrate. The first step is the oxidation of the top surface of the silicon to form a thin layer of silicon oxide. This oxide layer is impervious to most contaminants and serves to isolate and protect the substrate.

After the oxide layer comes the *photoresist* layer. The photoresist is a material which becomes acid-resistant when it is exposed to ultraviolet light. Exposure to ultraviolet light changes its chemical properties so that the areas which are exposed cannot be dissolved by acids.

The exposure to ultraviolet light is made after the coated substrate has been covered with a *mask*. This is a pattern which is opaque in the areas into which the dopants are eventually to be diffused. Masks are produced photographically by taking a picture of the appropriate pattern and then reducing it to the microminiature size needed for the IC.

After the placement of the mask and the exposure, the exposed photoresist is washed away with a solvent. This leaves a layer of exposed silicon oxide covering the area which will become the P-type region. Etching with hydrofluoric acid removes the oxide and leaves bare silicon substrate. The various steps in this process, in order, are shown in Fig. 43-33.

The bare silicon can now be doped with the desired dopant to produce a P-type region in the substrate. If the same process is repeated on an immediately adjacent area with an N-type dopant, a P-type region will border on an N-type region and create a PN junction. The addition of metal contacts on top of these regions gives a usable semiconductor diode like the one in Fig. 43-34.

Similar processes can be used to form all other necessary components in the IC. A P-type resistor on a P-type substrate is illustrated in Fig. 43-35. The upper N-type region is formed by diffusing enough N-type dopant into the already formed P-type region to convert it to an N-type region in that area. The plus sign indicates a high concentration of the N-type dopant. The purpose of the two N-type regions is to isolate the resistor from the substrate and the rest of the IC. The resistance is controlled by adjusting the length and cross-sectional area of the P-type conductor region and the amount of dopant diffused into the region.

A capacitor is formed similarly to a resistor. A diffused conducting layer acts as one of the plates of the capacitor, a metal contact acts as the other

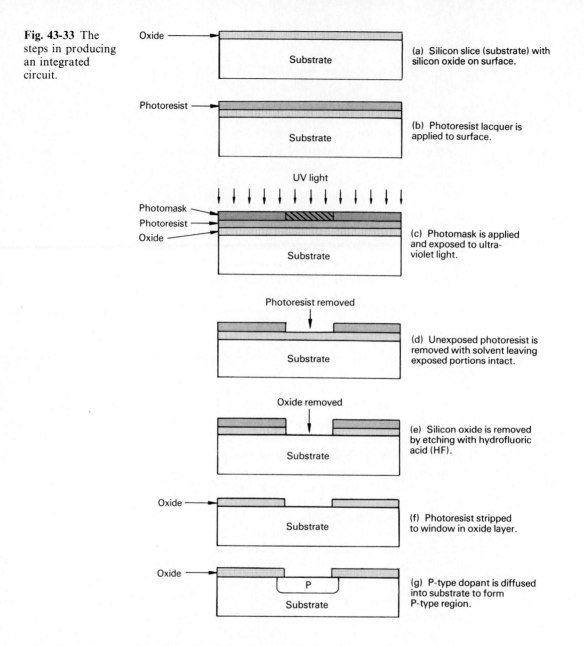

Fig. 43-33 The steps in producing an integrated circuit.

Oxide

Substrate

(a) Silicon slice (substrate) with silicon oxide on surface.

Photoresist

Substrate

(b) Photoresist lacquer is applied to surface.

UV light

Photomask
Photoresist
Oxide

Substrate

(c) Photomask is applied and exposed to ultraviolet light.

Photoresist removed

Substrate

(d) Unexposed photoresist is removed with solvent leaving exposed portions intact.

Oxide removed

Substrate

(e) Silicon oxide is removed by etching with hydrofluoric acid (HF).

Oxide

Substrate

(f) Photoresist stripped to window in oxide layer.

Oxide

P

Substrate

(g) P-type dopant is diffused into substrate to form P-type region.

plate, and the oxide layer between them acts as the dielectric. A possible arrangement is shown in Fig. 43-36.

Of course ICs could not be the highly sophisticated circuits they are without the ability to contain transistors. Several types of transistors can be formed in ICs, and they can be formed in several ways. The basic and the preferred structures for IC transistors are shown in Fig. 43-37.

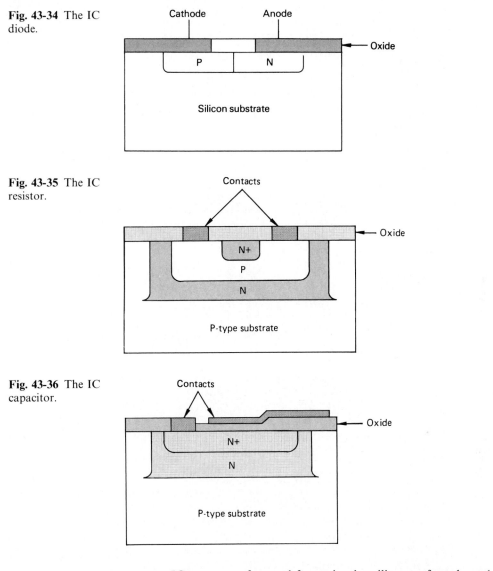

Fig. 43-34 The IC diode.

Cathode
Anode
Oxide
P
N
Silicon substrate

Fig. 43-35 The IC resistor.

Contacts
Oxide
N+
P
N
P-type substrate

Fig. 43-36 The IC capacitor.

Contacts
Oxide
N+
N
P-type substrate

ICs are manufactured from circular silicon wafers about 1.5 in. in diameter. Each wafer is large enough to produce about 500 ICs. After fabrication they are individually tested, and defective circuits are marked. The wafer is then cut apart and the defective circuits are discarded. The yield of good circuits is only about 10 to 40 percent, but since so many circuits are made at one time, the IC is one of the cheapest, smallest, and most reliable electronic devices produced. This fact has made pocket calculators, small computers, and similar high-quality electronic products as common and inexpensive as they are today, and it is hard even to imagine where the next step in the advance of electronics technology may lead is.

Fig. 43-37 The IC transistor.

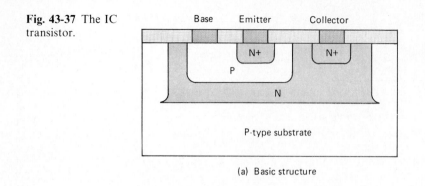

Base　　Emitter　　Collector

N+　　N+

P

N

P-type substrate

(a) Basic structure

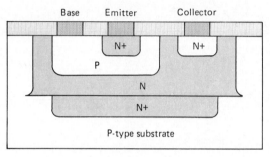

Base　　Emitter　　Collector

N+　　N+

P

N

N+

P-type substrate

(b) Preferred structure

SUMMARY

Electronics is much too broad a subject to give extensive preparation in one chapter. The intent of this unit of study was merely to cover in a descriptive way many of the concepts important for today's industrial workers. The major ideas are summarized below:

- A *diode* is an electronic device consisting of two elements. In a vacuum tube these elements are the plate and the filament; in the semiconductor diode, the two elements are formed by a PN junction.
- A *semiconductor* is a solid or liquid material with a resistivity between that of a conductor and an insulator. An N-type semiconductor contains *donor* impurities and free electrons. A P-type semiconductor consists of *acceptor* atoms and electron holes. A *PN junction* is the union of a P-type crystal with an N-type crystal in such a way that current is conducted in only one direction.
- A *transistor* is a semiconductor device consisting of three or more electrodes; usually the emitter, the collector, and the base.
- For a common-base transistor amplifier

Emitter current = base current + collector current

$$I_e = I_b + I_c \qquad a = \frac{I_c}{I_e}$$　　　　*Current Gain*

- The *current gain* for other connections is

$$\beta = \frac{\alpha}{1 - \alpha}$$ *Common-Emitter Amplifier*

$$A_i = \frac{1}{1 - \alpha}$$ *Common-Collector Amplifier*

- The voltage gain A_v and the power gain G are given by

$$A_v = \frac{V_{out}}{V_{in}}$$ *Voltage Gain*

$$G = \frac{power\ in}{power\ out} = \frac{V_{out} I_c}{V_{in} I_e}$$

$$G = \alpha \frac{V_{out}}{V_{in}} = \alpha A_v$$ *Power Gain*

QUESTIONS

43-1. In which case is there a larger current between anode and cathode in a vacuum-tube triode: when the grid is positive or negative?

43-2. Why is it necessary for vacuum tubes to be evacuated?

43-3. In terms of band theory, under what circumstances might an insulator be made to conduct? How can this be done?

43-4. In a semiconductor, why is the movement of a hole like that of a positive charge?

43-5. Why is doping necessary to make semiconductors conduct?

43-6. Explain the difference between P-type and N-type doping.

43-7. Discuss how a missing atom at a lattice site contributes to the conductivity of a semiconductor.

43-8. Which semiconductor device operates most like a check valve in a fluid system?

43-9. How could a change in the base bias be used to turn off a transistor so that no current would flow through it?

43-10. Transistors are sometimes mounted on finned metal heat sinks. Why is this necessary?

43-11. Which light source would be hotter, an LED or an incandescent light bulb? Why?

43-12. Which semiconductor device is best suited to ensuring that a specific point in a circuit is maintained at a specified voltage?

43-13. How does a photoresistor differ from a photodiode? Explain.

PROBLEMS

43-1. Given an NPN transistor with a common-base connection and $\alpha = 0.98$, determine the base current and the collector current when the emitter current is 40 mA.

Ans. $I_b = 0.8$ mA, $I_c = 39.2$ mA.

43-2. If the base current of a transistor with a common-base connection is 1.6 mA and the emitter current is 60 mA, what is α?

43-3. For a common-base amplifier, the input resistance is 800 Ω and an output resistance is 600 kΩ. **(a)** Determine the voltage gain if the emitter current is 12 mA and $\alpha = 0.97$. **(b)** What is the power gain?

Ans. **(a)** 727 **(b)** 706.

43-4. The power gain is 800 for a common-base amplifier, and the voltage amplification factor is 840. Determine the collector current when the base current is 1.2 mA.

43-5. Determine the current gain in a common-emitter amplifier circuit when α is known to be 0.98.

Ans. 49.

43-6. In the previous problem, what is the collector current if the emitter current is 20 μA? What is the base current?

43-7. A transistor with an effective input resistance of 400 Ω, an effective output resistance of 900 kΩ, and $\alpha = 0.96$ is connected in a common-base circuit. **(a)** What is the voltage gain when the input current I_e is 8 μA? **(b)** What is the power gain?

Ans. **(a)** 2160 **(b)** 2074.

43-8. Calculate I_c and I_b for the conditions described in Prob. 43-7.

43-9. For a transistor with $I_e = 8$ μA and $\alpha = 0.97$ connected with a common emitter calculate β, I_{in} and I_{out}.

Ans. 32.3, 0.24 μA, 7.76 μA.

43-10. For a transistor with $\alpha = 0.99$ connected with a common collector calculate I_{in}, I_{out}, and current gain A_i.

43-11. A transistor has $\beta = 99$; what is the value of α?

Ans. 0.99.

43-12. For the transistor of Prob. 43-11, if $I_b = 0.1$ mA, what are the values of I_e and I_c?

Appendix A *Mathematics Review*

The brief review of mathematics presented in this appendix is not intended to be rigorous. It is assumed that you have already gained experience in high school algebra and have a passing acquaintance with right-triangle trigonometry. The topics discussed below will provide a review or reference for the mathematics necessary for the solution of physical problems.

A-1 EXPONENTS AND RADICALS

If is often necessary to multiply a quantity by itself a number of times. A shorthand method of indicating the number of times a quantity is taken as a product is through the use of a superscript number called the *exponent*. This notation works according to the following scheme:

For any number a:

$$a = a^1$$
$$a \times a = a^2$$
$$a \times a \times a = a^3$$
$$a \times a \times a \times a = a^4$$

For the number 2:

$$2 = 2^1 = 2$$
$$2 \times 2 = 2^2 = 4$$
$$2 \times 2 \times 2 = 2^3 = 8$$
$$2 \times 2 \times 2 \times 2 = 2^4 = 16$$

The powers of the number a are read as follows: a^2 is read "a squared;" a^3 is read "a cubed;" a^4 is read "the fourth power of a," or "a to the fourth power." More generally, we speak of a^n as "a to the nth power." In these examples, the letter a is referred to as the *base*, and the superscripts 1, 2, 3, 4, and n are called the *exponents*.

If $a^n = b$, then not only is b equal to the nth power of a, but, by definition, a is said to be the nth *root of b*. For example, $2^2 = 4$ means that 2 is the square root of 4. Similarly, $2^3 = 8$ means that 2 is the cube root of 8, and $2^5 = 32$ means that 2 is the fifth root of 32.

In general, the nth root of the quantity b is written

$$\sqrt[n]{b} \qquad \text{the } n\text{th root of } b$$

In the case of the square root, we simply write the radical, omitting the number 2:

$$\sqrt{b} \qquad \text{the square root of } b$$

It can be shown that a radical may be expressed differently by using a fractional exponent such that

$$\sqrt[n]{b} = b^{1/n}$$

For example, $\sqrt[3]{4} = 4^{1/3}$, and $\sqrt{10} = 10^{1/2}$.

Six important rules regarding exponents and radicals are given below, with examples following each rule:

$$\boxed{\text{Rule 1} \quad a^m \times a^n = a^{m+n}}$$

Example: $\quad 4^3 \times 4^2 = 4^{3+2} = 4^5$

$$\boxed{\text{Rule 2} \quad a^{-n} = \frac{1}{a^n}}$$

Examples: $\quad 2^{-3} = \dfrac{1}{2^{+3}}; \qquad 10^2 = \dfrac{1}{10^{-2}}$

$$\boxed{\text{Rule 3} \quad (a^m)^n = a^{mn}}$$

Examples: $\quad (10^2)^3 = 10^6; \qquad (10^{-3})^4 = 10^{-12}$

$$\boxed{\text{Rule 4} \quad (ab)^n = a^n b^n}$$

Examples: $\quad (2 \times 3)^2 = 2^2 \times 3^2 = 4 \times 9 = 36$

$\qquad\qquad\quad (2 \times 10^2)^3 = 2^3 \times 10^6 = 8 \times 10^6$

$$\boxed{\text{Rule 5} \quad \sqrt[n]{a^m} = a^{m/n}}$$

Examples: $\quad \sqrt[3]{2^9} = 2^{9/3} = 2^3 = 8$

$\qquad\qquad\quad \sqrt{10^{-4}} = 10^{-4/2} = 10^{-2} = \dfrac{1}{100}$

$$\boxed{\text{Rule 6} \quad \sqrt[n]{ab} = \sqrt[n]{a} \times \sqrt[n]{b}}$$

Examples: $\quad \sqrt{4 \times 10^4} = \sqrt{4} \times \sqrt{10^4} = 2 \times 10^2$

$\qquad\qquad\quad \sqrt[3]{8 \times 10^{-6}} = \sqrt[3]{8} \times \sqrt[3]{10^{-6}} = 2 \times 10^{-2}$

Frequently in scientific work you may encounter very large or very small numbers. A convenient shorthand notation allows you to express any number as a number between 1 and 10 times an integral power of 10. Some multiples of 10 are:

$$
\begin{array}{lll}
0.0001 = 10^{-4} & 2.34 \times 10^{-4} = & 0.000234 \\
0.001 = 10^{-3} & 2.34 \times 10^{-3} = & 0.00234 \\
0.01 = 10^{-2} & 2.34 \times 10^{-2} = & 0.0234 \\
0.1 = 10^{-1} & 2.34 \times 10^{-1} = & 0.234 \\
1 = 10^{0} & 2.34 \times 10^{0} = & 2.34 \\
10 = 10^{1} & 2.34 \times 10^{1} = & 23.4 \\
100 = 10^{2} & 2.34 \times 10^{2} = & 234.0 \\
1,000 = 10^{3} & 2.34 \times 10^{3} = & 2,340.0 \\
10,000 = 10^{4} & 2.34 \times 10^{4} = & 23,400.0
\end{array}
$$

Thus the number 456,000 may be written in scientific notation by determining the number of times the decimal point must be moved to the left in order to arrive at the shorthand notation. Examples are:

$$467 = (4\ 6\ 7.) = 4.67 \times 10^2$$

$$30 = (3\ 0.) = 3.0 \times 10^1$$

$$35,700 = (3\ 5\ 7\ 0\ 0.) = 3.57 \times 10^4$$

Similarly, any small decimal number can be written as a number between 1 and 10 times a *negative* power of 10. The negative exponent in this case will be the number of times the decimal point is moved to the right. This will always be one more than the number of zeros that separate the first digit from the decimal. Examples are:

$$0.24 = (0.2\ 4) = 2.4 \times 10^{-1}$$

$$0.0032 = (0.0\ 0\ 3\ 2) = 3.2 \times 10^{-3}$$

$$0.0000469 = (0.0\ 0\ 0\ 0\ 4\ 6\ 9) = 4.69 \times 10^{-5}$$

To transfer from scientific notation back to decimal notation, the procedure is simply reversed.

Recalling the laws of exponents, scientific notation can be used for multiplication, division, and addition of very large or very small numbers. When two numbers are multiplied, the exponents of 10 are added. For example, 200×4000 may be written $200 \times 4000 = (2.0 \times 10^2) \times (4.0 \times 10^3) = 8.0 \times 10^5$. Other examples are:

$$2200 \times 40 = (2.2 \times 10^3) \times (4.0 \times 10^1) = 8.8 \times 10^4$$

$$0.0002 \times 900 = (2 \times 10^{-4}) \times (9 \times 10^2) = 18 \times 10^{-2}$$

$$1002 \times 3 = (1.002 \times 10^3) \times 3 = 3.006 \times 10^3$$

Similarly, when one number is divided by another, the exponent of the latter is subtracted from the exponent of the former. Examples are:

$$\frac{7000}{350} = \frac{7 \times 10^3}{3.5 \times 10^2} = 2 \times 10^{3-2} = 2 \times 10^1$$

$$\frac{1200}{0.003} = \frac{1.2 \times 10^3}{3 \times 10^{-3}} = 0.4 \times 10^{3-(-3)} = 0.4 \times 10^6$$

$$\frac{0.008}{400} = \frac{8 \times 10^{-3}}{4 \times 10^2} = 2 \times 10^{-3-2} = 2 \times 10^{-5}$$

When adding two numbers in powers of 10, care must be taken to convert all numbers to be added so that they have identical exponents. Then addition is performed as usual. Examples are:

$$100 + 300 = (1 \times 10^2) + (3 \times 10^2) = 4 \times 10^2$$

$$2000 + 400 = (2 \times 10^3) + (0.4 \times 10^3) = 2.4 \times 10^3$$

Of course, in the above examples, the scientific notation is not very useful. However, in the following examples, the longhand method would be very cumbersome:

$$(4.75 \times 10^{18}) + (6 \times 10^{19}) = (4.75 \times 10^{18}) + (60 \times 10^{18})$$

$$= 64.75 \times 10^{18}$$

$$(1.4 \times 10^{-19}) + (4 \times 10^{-21}) = (140 \times 10^{-21}) + (4 \times 10^{-21})$$

$$= 144 \times 10^{-21}$$

It should be noticed that, when two numbers differ by more than three powers of 10, the smaller can usually be ignored in the process of addition. For example,

$$(1.6 \times 10^{24}) + (2 \times 10^{21}) = (1600 \times 10^{21}) + (2 \times 10^{21})$$

$$= 1602 \times 10^{21}$$

The number 1602 does not differ from the number 1600 by sufficient margin to be significant.

A-3 LITERAL EQUATIONS AND FORMULAS

A literal equation is an equation in which some or all of the known quantities, usually constants, are represented by letters instead of numbers. Therefore, the roots of a literal equation are also expressed in terms of letters. For instance, the equation

$$ax - 5b = c$$

must be solved for x in terms of a, b, and c. Transposing, we have

$$ax = 5b + c$$

Dividing by a,

$$x = \frac{5b + c}{a}$$

Perhaps the most common occurrence of the literal equation is the formula. A *formula* is a mathematical statement of equality in which letter symbols are combined with numbers to express a physical relationship. For example, the volume of a cone is expressed by the formula

$$V = \frac{\pi r^2 h}{3} \tag{A-1}$$

in which it is assumed that the radius r and the height h are known and the volume V is to be found.

In formulas, the various letters and symbols can be thought of as variables, the value of any one depending on the values assigned to the others. For example, in Eq. (A-1), the volume V varies in accordance with values assigned for h and r. Should r and V be given and the value of h desired, the formula can be solved explicitly for h in accordance with the axioms of the preceding section. For instance, clearing Eq. (A-1) of fractions yields

$$3V = \pi r^2 h$$

Dividing by the literal coefficient of h, πr^2,

$$\frac{3V}{\pi r^2} = \frac{h\pi r^2}{\pi r^2} \qquad \text{or} \qquad h = \frac{3V}{\pi r^2}$$

A-4 TRIGO-NOMETRY

Often it is necessary to determine the components of forces or a resultant of two or more concurrent forces more accurately than graphs will allow. The graphical approaches are also time-consuming. By learning a few principles that apply to all right triangles, you can significantly improve your ability to work with vectors. Moreover, hand-held calculators make many of the calculations relatively simple.

First, let's review some of the things we already know about right triangles. We will follow the convention that uses Greek letters for angles and Roman letters for sides. Commonly used Greek symbols are

α alpha	β beta	γ gamma
θ theta	ϕ phi	δ delta

In the right triangle drawn as Fig. A-1, the symbols R, x, and y refer to the side dimensions, and θ, ϕ, and $90°$ are the angles. You should recall that the sum of the smaller angles in a right triangle is $90°$:

$$\phi + \theta = 90° \qquad\qquad \textit{Right Triangle}$$

Fig. A-1 The right triangle and the pythagorean theorem.

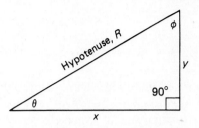

The Pythagorean theorem

$$R^2 = x^2 + y^2$$

There is also a relationship between the sides, which is known as the pythagorean theorem:

The pythagorean theorem: *The square of the hypotenuse is equal to the sum of the squares of the other two sides.*

$$\boxed{R^2 = x^2 + y^2}$$ *The Pythagorean Theorem* (A-2)

The *hypotenuse* is defined as the longest side. It is conveniently located as that side directly opposite the right angle—the line joining the two perpendicular sides.

EXAMPLE A-1

What length of guy wire is needed to stretch from the top of a 40-ft telephone pole to a ground stake located 60 ft from the foot of the pole?

Solution

Draw a rough sketch, such as Fig. A-2. Identify the length R as the hypotenuse of a right triangle, then from the pythagorean theorem

$$R^2 = (60 \text{ ft})^2 + (40 \text{ ft})^2$$

$$= 3600 \text{ ft}^2 + 1600 \text{ ft}^2 = 5200 \text{ ft}^2$$

Taking the square root of both sides gives

$$R = \sqrt{5200 \text{ ft}^2} = 72.1 \text{ ft}$$

In general, to find the hypotenuse we could express the pythagorean theorem as

$$R = \sqrt{x^2 + y^2}$$ *Hypoteneuse* (A-3)

On some electronic calculators, the sequence of entries might be as follows:

x $\boxed{x^2}$ $\boxed{+}$ y $\boxed{x^2}$ $\boxed{=}$ $\boxed{\sqrt{x}}$

Fig. A-2

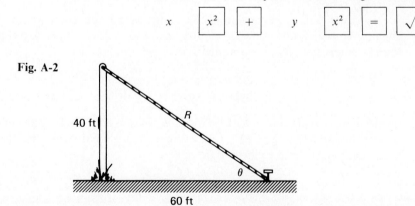

In this instance, x and y are the values of the shorter sides, and the boxed symbols are operation keys on the calculator. You should verify the solution to the previous problem using $x = 40$ and $y = 60$. (The input procedure varies depending on the make of calculator.)

Of course, the pythagorean theorem can also be used to find either of the shorter sides if the remaining sides are known. Solution for x or for y yields

$$x = \sqrt{R^2 - y^2} \qquad y = \sqrt{R^2 - x^2} \qquad \text{(A-4)}$$

Trigonometry is the branch of mathematics which takes advantage of the fact that similar triangles are proportional in size. For example, in two similar right triangles, the ratio of any two sides will be the same numerical value regardless of the dimensions of either triangle.

Once an angle is identified in a right triangle, the sides *opposite* and *adjacent* to that angle may be labeled. The meanings of opposite, adjacent, and hypotenuse are given in Fig. A-3. You should study this figure until you understand fully the meaning of these terms. Verify that the side opposite to θ is y and that the side adjacent to θ is x. Also notice that the sides described by "opposite" and "adjacent" change if we refer to angle ϕ.

Fig. A-3 Identification of the sides in a right triangle.

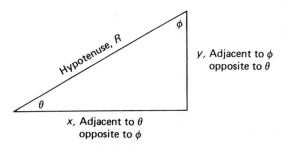

In a right triangle, there are three side ratios that are very important. They are the *sine*, the *cosine*, and the *tangent*, defined as follows for angle θ:

$$\sin \theta = \frac{\text{opp } \theta}{\text{hyp}}$$

$$\cos \theta = \frac{\text{adj } \theta}{\text{hyp}} \qquad \text{(A-5)}$$

$$\tan \theta = \frac{\text{opp } \theta}{\text{adj}}$$

To make sure that you understand these definitions, you should verify the following for the triangles in Fig. A-4:

$$\sin \theta = \frac{9}{15} \qquad \cos \gamma = \frac{m}{H} \qquad \tan \alpha = \frac{y}{x}$$

$$\sin \alpha = \frac{y}{R} \qquad \cos \beta = \frac{n}{H} \qquad \tan \phi = \frac{12}{9}$$

Fig. A-4

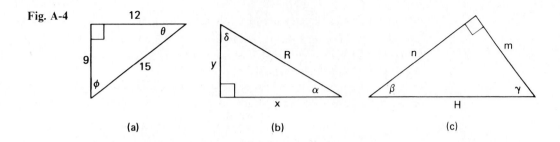

(a)   (b)   (c)

You should first identify the right angle, then label the longest side (opposite to the 90° angle) as the hypotenuse. Then, for a particular angle, the sides opposite and adjacent may be identified.

The constant values for the trigonometric functions of all angles between 0 and 90° have been calculated. They may be found from tables or, more conveniently, with a small calculator. Suppose we wish to know the cosine of 47°, for example. In a table of cosines we would see the number 0.682 adjacent to the angle 47°, and we would write

$$\cos 47° = 0.682$$

With some calculators, we would enter the angle 47, then strike the $\boxed{\cos}$ key to obtain the same result. From either a table or from your calculator, you should verify the following:

$$\tan 38° = 0.781 \qquad \cos 31° = 0.857$$
$$\sin 22° = 0.375 \qquad \tan 65° = 2.14$$

To find the angle whose tangent is 1.34 or to find the angle whose sine is 0.45, we would reverse the above process. On a calculator, for example, we would enter the number 1.34, then we would look for one of the following sequences, depending on the calculator. $\boxed{\text{INV}}$ $\boxed{\tan}$, $\boxed{\text{ARC}}$ $\boxed{\tan}$, or $\boxed{\tan^{-1}}$. Any of these will give the angle whose tangent is the entered value. In the above examples, we find that

$$\tan \theta = 1.34 \qquad \theta = 53.3°$$
$$\sin \theta = 0.45 \qquad \theta = 26.7°$$

You should now be able to apply trigonometry to find unknown angles or sides in a right triangle. The following procedure will be helpful:

Application of Trigonometry

1. Draw the right triangle from the stated conditions of the problem. (Label all sides and angles with either their known values or a symbol for an unknown value.)
2. Isolate an angle for study; if an angle is known, choose that one.

3. Label each side according to whether its relation to the chosen angle is opp, adj, or hyp.
4. Decide which side or angle is to be found.
5. Recall the definitions of the trigonometric functions:

$$\sin = \frac{\text{opp}}{\text{hyp}} \qquad \cos = \frac{\text{adj}}{\text{hyp}} \qquad \tan = \frac{\text{opp}}{\text{adj}}$$

6. Choose that trigonometric function which involves (*a*) the unknown quantity, and (*b*) no other unknown quantity.
7. Write the trigonometric equation and solve for the unknown.

EXAMPLE A-2   What is the length of the rope segment *x* in Fig. A-5?

Fig. A-5

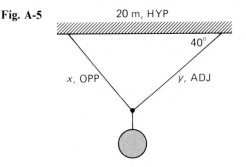

Solution   The sketch is already drawn, so we proceed with step 2. The 40° angle is selected for reference, and opp, adj, and hyp are labeled on the figure. The decision is made to solve for *x* (opp). Since the sine function involves opp and hyp, we choose that function and write the equation.

$$\sin 40° = \frac{x}{20 \text{ m}}$$

Solving for *x* by multiplying both sides by 20 m, we obtain

$$x = (20 \text{ m}) \sin 40°$$

If we use tables, we determine that sin 40° = 0.643, and then

$$x = (20 \text{ m})(0.643) = 12.9 \text{ m}$$

On some calculators, we would calculate *x* as follows:

20 $\boxed{\times}$ 40 $\boxed{\sin}$ $\boxed{=}$

It is easy to see what an advantage the calculator is in the application of trigonometry. As an additional exercise, you might show that *y* = 15.3 m.

EXAMPLE A-3   Refer back to Fig. A-2. What is the angle θ that the guy wire makes with the ground?

Solution   Note the location of the angle θ, then label opp, adj, and hyp. For the angle θ, we may write

$$\tan \theta = \frac{\text{opp}}{\text{adj}} = \frac{40 \text{ ft}}{60 \text{ ft}}$$

The tangent function was the only one that involved the two *known* sides. If tables are to be used, then θ is the angle whose tangent is $\frac{40}{60}$ or 0.667. In this case, we find that

$$\tan \theta = 0.667 \qquad \text{and} \qquad \theta = 33.7°$$

The sequence on some calculators might be as follows:

$$40 \quad \boxed{\div} \quad 60 \quad \boxed{=} \quad \boxed{\text{INV}} \quad \boxed{\text{tan}}$$

Of course, the procedure varies. Study your manual and work with your calculator until you understand the process thoroughly.

Appendix B Conversion Equivalents

LENGTH

1 meter (m) = 39.37 in. = 3.281 ft = 6.214×10^{-4} mi = 10^{10} Å = 10^{15} fermis
1 in. = 0.02540000 m; 1 ft = 0.3048 m; 1 mi = 1609 m
1 nautical mi = 1852 m = 1.1508 mi = 6076.10 ft
1 angstrom (Å) = 10^{-10} m; 1 mil = 10^{-3} in.; 1 rod = 16.5 ft; 1 fathom = 6 ft

AREA

1 m^2 = 10.76 ft^2 = 1550 in.; 1 hectare = 10^4 m^2 = 2.471 acres
1 ft^2 = 929 cm^2; 1 in.^{2} = 6.452 cm^2 = 1.273×10^6 circular mils; 1 acre = 43,560 ft^2

VOLUME

1 m^3 = 35.31 ft^3 = 6.102×10^4 in.^{3}
1 ft^3 = 0.02832 m^3; 1 U.S. gallon = 231 in.^{3}; 1 liter = 1.000028×10^{-3} m^3 = 61.02 in.^{3}

TIME AND FREQUENCY

1 year = 365.2422 days = 8.766×10^3 h = 5.259×10^5 min = 3.156×10^7 s
1 sidereal day (period of earth's revolution) = 86,164 s
1 hertz (Hz) = 1 cycle/s

SPEED

1 m/s = 3.281 ft/s = 3.6 km/h = 2.237 mi/h = 1.944 knots
1 km/h = 0.2778 m/s = 0.9113 ft/s = 0.6214 mi/h
1 mi/h = 1.467 ft/s = 1.609 km/h = 0.8689 knot

MASS

1 kg = 2.205 lb_m = 0.06852 slug
1 lb_m = 0.4536 kg = 0.03108 slug; 1 slug = 32.17 lb_m = 14.59 kg

DENSITY

1 g/cm^3 = 1000 kg/m^3 = 62.43 lb_m/ft^3 = 1.940 $slug/ft^3$
1 lb_m/ft^3 = 0.03108 $slug/ft^3$ = 16.02 kg/m^3 = 0.01602 g/cm^3

FORCE

1 newton (N) = 10^5 dynes = 0.1020 kg wt = 0.2248 lb
1 lb (force) = 4.448 N = 0.4536 kg wt = 32.17 poundals

PRESSURE

1 N/m^2 = 9.869 × 10^{-6} atm = 1.450 × 10^{-4} lb/in.^{2} = 0.02089 lb/ft^2
$\quad\quad$ = 7.501 × 10^{-4} cmHg = 4.015 × 10^{-3} in. of water = 10^{-5} bar
1 lb/in.^{2} = 144 lb/ft^2 = 6895 N/m^2 = 5.171 cmHg = 27.68 in. of water
1 atm = 406.8 in. of water = 76 cmHg = 1.013 × 10^5 N/m^2
$\quad\quad$ = 10,330 kg wt/m^2 = 2116 lb/ft^2 = 14.70 lb/in.^{2} = 760 torr

WORK, ENERGY, HEAT

1 joule (J) = 0.2389 cal = 0.481 × 10^{-4} Btu = 0.7376 ft · lb = 10^7 ergs = 6.242 × 10^{18} eV
1 kcal = 4.186 joules = 3.968 Btu = 3087 ft · lb
1 eV = 1.602 × 10^{-19} joule; 1 unified amu = 931.48 MeV
1 kW · h = 3.6 × 10^6 joules = 3413 Btu = 860.1 kcal = 1.341 hp · h

POWER

1 hp = 2545 Btu/h = 550 ft · lb/s = 745.7 watts = 0.1782 kcal/s
1 watt (W) = 2.389 × 10^{-4} kcal/s = 1.341 × 10^{-3} hp = 0.7376 ft · lb/s

ELECTRIC CHARGE

1 faraday = 96,487 coulombs; 1 electron charge = 1.602 × 10^{-19} coulomb

MAGNETIC FLUX

1 weber (Wb) = 10^8 maxwells = 10^8 lines

MAGNETIC INTENSITY

1 tesla (T) = 1 newton/amp · m = 1 weber/m^2 = 10,000 gauss = 10° gamma

Index